# Hungary

## THE BRADT TRAVEL GUIDE

## Adrian Phillips
## Jo Scotchmer

Bradt Travel Guides Ltd, UK
The Globe Pequot Press Inc, USA

**First published September 2005**

Bradt Travel Guides Ltd
23 High Street, Chalfont St Peter, Bucks SL9 9QE, England
www.bradtguides.com
Published in the USA by The Globe Pequot Press Inc, 246 Goose Lane,
PO Box 480, Guilford, Connecticut 06437-0480

Text copyright © 2005 Adrian Phillips and Jo Scotchmer
Maps copyright © 2005 Bradt Travel Guides Ltd
Illustrations copyright © 2005 individual photographers and artists

A catalogue record for this book is available from the British Library

ISBN-10: 1 84162 091 2
ISBN-13: 978 1 84162 091 6

**Photographs**
*Front cover:* Luciano Lepre/Tips Images (Men playing chess in thermal bath, Budapest)
*Text*: William Courage (WC), Karen Balazs/Novak László (KB/NL),
Rob Flemming/Swift Imagery (RF), Neil Setchfield (NS), Nigel Shuttleworth/Life File (NSh),
Jonathan Smith (JS), Tom Schulze/Still Pictures (TS), Balazs Szigeti/Ecotours (BS),
Gunter Ziesler/Still Pictures (GZ)

**Illustrations** Carole Vincer
**Maps** Matt Honour. Regional maps based on ITM *Hungary*.

Typeset from the authors' disc by Wakewing, High Wycombe
Printed and bound in Italy by Legoprint SpA, Trento

# Authors

**Adrian Phillips** and **Jo Scotchmer** spent six months travelling around Hungary, pestering museum curators and losing themselves (literally!) among its highways and byways. Adrian is a member of the British Guild of Travel Writers, senior editor at Bradt – which he joined in 2001 after completing a PhD in English literature – and co-author of *Singapore: The Bradt Travel Guide*. Jo is a public-relations director whose portfolio includes travel resorts, hotels and spas; she also dabbles in freelance journalism. Hungary is a pleasure they indulge at every opportunity, dragging friends and family in tow. They are also authors of *Budapest: The Bradt City Guide*.

## CONTRIBUTORS

We are grateful to the following for their invaluable assistance: Lucy Mallows (various), Carolyn Chapman (various), Kim Lyon (Danube Bend), Marti Andrews (spas, food), József Hunyady, Gábor Orbán, Balázs Szigeti, Shena Maskell, Martin Catt (all wildlife), Stuart Candy (music), Janet Phillips (various) and Bianca Otero (wine).

### PUBLISHER'S FOREWORD

At Frankfurt Book Fair last year I was showing our just-published Budapest guide to our new representative for eastern Europe. 'But this is amazing!' said Csaba. 'It describes restaurants that I thought only I knew about.' Adrian and Jo have gone one big step further – revealed insider secrets for all of Hungary. Dip into the guidebook at any point and I bet you find something you didn't know: Hungary is home to the furioso horse, for instance, and the 'frizzle' pig (I long to meet the latter). Ice cream is *fagylalt*, which seems to come straight from the pages of the *Hitchhiker's Guide to the Galaxy*, and Hungarians choose a name for their child from an approved list. I even found myself engrossed in a description of a car (that's definitely a first) – although I suppose the Trabant is only just a car. I learned that 52% of storks' nesting sites are on telegraph poles and that there are awards for outstanding service in stork protection. I learned... but why not read it for yourself?

*Hilary Bradt*

23 High Street, Chalfont St Peter, Bucks SL9 9QE, England
Tel: 01753 893444   Fax: 01753 892333
Email: info@bradtguides.com   www.bradtguides.com

# Contents

## LIST OF MAPS

For key to standard symbols, see page 2.

# Acknowledgements

Never has so much been owed by so few to so many – we salute you all. Thank you to Tsvia Vorley, Ildikó Balogh and Melinda Stein for smoothing the initial path; to Sally Brock, Matt Honour and all at Bradt for making sense of endless scribbles; to Kate Lyons and Janet Mears for casting a careful eye over the manuscript; to Dr Alex Vida for his information on national parks; to Carole Vincer for her lovely sketches; to Annalisa Rellie, Tim Burford, Adrian Courage and Neil Taylor for brochures, corrections and notes scrawled on airline sick bags; to Lucy Mallows, Carolyn Chapman, Kim Lyon, Bianca Otero, Erzsébet Courage and Marti Andrews for their tireless and expert assistance; to Jószef Hunyady, Gábor Orbán, Balázs Szigeti, Shena Maskell and Martin Catt for contributions to the wildlife sections, and János Malina for his information on music; to those readers who offered feedback on *Budapest: The Bradt City Guide*, most notably Anthony Stern and Henry Long; to our families (particularly Janet/mum!) and friends for their long-suffering support; and to Tricia Hayne and Hilary Bradt for the faith to entrust us with the project. Above all, thank you to Erzsébet and William Courage, and Péter and Zsanett Koltai, who were selfless in their help and guidance, and proved that friendships can grow in spite of endless impositions.

## FEEDBACK REQUEST

We've strived to tramp and nag and eat our way to accuracy. However, a guidebook is a snapshot in time, and as the world turns and things change we writers feel like painters on the Forth Bridge – once the last page is done the first needs re-checking. Would you lend us your ears and eyes to ensure that subsequent editions keep pace? What was new or different during your visit? What did you like or dislike about the book? Please drop us a line at hungarytravelguide@yahoo.co.uk, or write to us c/o Bradt Travel Guides, 23 High St, Chalfont St Peter, Bucks SL9 9QE. We'd love to hear from you, and will be sure to reply personally.

Happy travels!

Adrian and Jo

# Introduction

It has been said that Hungary 'grows on you and seems to squirt a divine soda water into your blood'. During our first encounter with Budapest we would have gladly swapped the squirt for a healthy splash of brandy. Nerves needed soothing in the back of an airport taxi driven by a man resolute in his commitment to overtaking on blind corners; stomachs needed settling after plates of cockerels' testicles unwittingly ordered from an impenetrable menu; tempers needed calming in the face of an ear-picking manager denying all knowledge of our hotel booking. But romantics know that love can blossom from unpromising first meetings. These initial snapshots were not uncharacteristic – Hungary's language can seem a closed book, its service industry is generally tardy, and its cockerels are an anxious breed – but they lacked the context of the rest of the album. In the days that followed, the capital offered up its rumbling trams, its faded mansions, its walls pocked with conflict's bullet holes. We wallowed in the thermal baths and watched night's lights play upon the Danube. And, yes, we had that brandy – not in trembling glasses but in those raised to a city with bite, elegance and romance.

Budapest's charms are no longer a secret; it is a name high on the tick-lists of self-respecting travellers in Europe. However, if our hearts were caught there the grip only tightened as we ventured beyond. We discovered a country with the diversity both to indulge established passions and spark new ones. There was wine, plenty of it, in Eger's Valley of the Beautiful Woman. And in the villages of the Tokaj region. And in Szekszárd and Villány. There were lush walking trails in the Northern Uplands, creamy-orange stalactites in Aggtelek and spring-time storms that flashed and crashed above the hilltops. The Great Plain came thick with legends of derring-do, with hairy pigs and 'horny' sheep, and with modern-day cowboys cracking their whips and galloping astride five horses at once. Pécs proudly showed off its Ottoman and Roman legacy, and elsewhere we found Transdanubian forts and thatched dwellings and the prettiest medieval towns you could wish to see. When we fancied a dip, we headed to central Europe's largest lake for windsurfing and wakeboarding, and further bouts of tasting among the vineyards. We could go on, but we're wasting valuable time – you should get cracking and experience all this for yourself.

After the publication of *Budapest: The Bradt City Guide*, we received a letter from a reader commenting on just how staid seem the statues and buildings of other countries when compared with those to be found in Hungary. He was spot on. For much of their history, Hungary's people lived under the shadow of foreign powers. Their monuments are not – could not be – the formal portraits of victory. Rather they are free-wheeling expressions of freedom desired, be that a slashing independence fighter, a herder struggling to control a rearing steed or a church smothered with vivid majolica roof tiles. To our minds, these monuments are symbolic of the complexities at the heart of the country as a whole. For all the much-remarked reserve and 'realism' of the national character, there is an underlying urge towards the carnivalesque. It makes for an exhilarating experience, and one of which we'll never tire.

# Part One

# General Information

## HUNGARY AT A GLANCE

**Country name** The Republic of Hungary (Magyarország)
**Language** Hungarian
**Population** 10,006,835
**People** Hungarian (Magyar) 89.9%, Roma 4%, German 2.6%, Serb 2%, Slovak 0.8%, Romanian 0.7%
**Religion** Two-thirds of the population are Roman Catholic; other faiths/denominations include Calvinist, Lutheran, Jewish and Greek Orthodox
**President** László Sólyom (elected June 2005)
**Prime Minister** Ferenc Gyurcsány (elected September 2004)
**Neighbouring countries** Austria, Croatia, Romania, Serbia and Montenegro, Slovakia, Slovenia and Ukraine
**Area** 93,000km²
**Time** Central European Time. Winter: GMT +1; summer: GMT +2 (clocks adjusted on last Sunday in March and last Sunday in October)
**Currency** Forint (Ft)
**Flag** Three equal horizontal bands: red (top), white (middle) and green (bottom)
**Telephone codes** Country code 0036, Budapest code 1

## KEY TO STANDARD SYMBOLS

**Bradt**

| | | | |
|---|---|---|---|
| —·—· International boundary | | Castle |
| Chapter content boundary | | Church, cathedral |
| National park boundary | | Synagogue |
| ✈ Airport (international) | | Archaeological or historic site |
| Ferry | | Old city wall |
| Railway | | Statue, monument |
| Tram, metro | | Zoo |
| Ⓜ Metro station | | Historical buiding |
| Bus station | ▲ | Summit |
| Hotel, panzió | | Tourist information |
| Hostel, college with accommodation | | Theatre, cultural centre |
| ✚ Hospital | | Museum, art gallery |
| ✚ Pharmacy | $ | Bank, ATM |
| Ⴟ Campsite | e | Internet café |
| Coffee house, café, café bar | ✉ | Post office |
| Wine bar, pub | | Cave |
| ✗ Restaurant | | Beach |
| ☆ Nightclub | | Swimming |

# Background Information

## GEOGRAPHY

The Republic of Hungary (Magyarország) lies in the Carpathian Basin in central eastern Europe. It occupies 93,030km², is landlocked and bordered by seven others: Austria, Slovakia, Romania, Serbia and Montenegro, Croatia, Slovenia and Ukraine. Budapest – occupying a central-northern position – is the capital and by a distance the largest city (525km²). The Danube runs through the country for 417km, dividing it roughly in half from north to south. The other major river is the Tisza, entering the country from Ukraine, flowing through the plains and exiting into Serbia. As for standing bodies of water, Balaton is comfortably the biggest of the lakes, followed by Tisza (a significant wildlife spot).

A broad-brushed description of the country's landscape can divide it into three main types. Mountain ranges (the Northern Uplands) stretch towards the Ukrainian border to the northeast of the country, with the highest point Mount Kékes (1,008m); the vast area to the east of the Danube (the Great Plain) is characterised by even plains, grasslands and agricultural land; the west (Transdanubia) is the most varied, comprising small mountains, rolling foothills and open plains, punctured by Lake Balaton. Budapest is sliced in two by the Danube; Buda on the western bank is green and hilly, while on the other side Pest is flat and built-up. (See also *Vegetation*, page 4.)

## CLIMATE

Three climate systems collide in Hungary, with cold Siberian influences meeting the hot weather cycles from the Mediterraean and mixing with more temperate weather from the Atlantic. With protection from surrounding mountains, the result is a temperate continental climate, with significant, distinct and quickly changing seasonal variations. Winter (*Dec–Feb*) is icy cold, with temperatures often dropping below freezing and some snowfall possible. Small streams and lakes – even Balaton – can freeze over. Spring arrives and the temperatures begin to perk up properly in April, although showers are also common. You should expect ten daily hours of sunshine during the summer months (*Jun–Aug*), which are at least warm and can be very hot – the August average is 22°C, but temperatures often break the 30°C barrier. It is also noticeable that temperatures do not peak at midday, but appear to continue rising well into the afternoon, and humidity can be high. Autumn can bring a warm and dry Indian summer, described in Hungarian as 'old women's summer'. The country's moderate rainfall, averaging 600mm per year, falls principally in spring and autumn. March and November are the wettest months, and are neither warm nor bitingly cold. The most extreme weather patterns are found on the Great Plain, where hot, dry summers are followed by bitterly cold and windy winters. Rainfall is highest in the country's southwestern hills. Although average monthly temperatures generally vary in a range of only three or four degrees between such places as Budapest, Miskolc to the north and Szeged to the south, if you're a real heat-seeker you should head for Gyula in the Southern Great Plain; just 4km from the Romanian border, it is Hungary's hottest place and boasts over 2,000 hours of sunshine each year.

For detailed **weather reports**, log on to the Hungarian Meteorological Service website at www.met.hu (which has information in English).

## NATURAL HISTORY AND CONSERVATION

With a temperate climate and a lack of topographical extremes like high-altitude mountain ranges or scorching deserts, Hungary has – at least since the end of the 18th century – been largely settled, tilled and grazed. Arable land now covers 50% of its area. Even so, thanks to a relatively low population density and extensive agriculture, the country is surprisingly rich in rare species of plant and animal. It is a particular favourite with the twitching fraternity.

### Vegetation

Many of the most important conservation areas in Hungary support **grasslands**, which occupy 12% of the land surface, are predominantly semi-natural in origin and usually comprise swathes of steppe (the so-called Hungarian *puszta*) or wet grassland flood plains. The steppe is found mainly in the lowlands, on saline, sandy or peaty soils. The *puszta* – prime examples of which are found in Hortobágy, Kiskunság and Körös-Maros national parks – is characterised by *Fescues*, *Festuca rupicola* and *Festuca pseudovina*, the latter being prevalent in degraded or overgrazed grasslands. Steppe grasslands also grow to a lesser degree in the west (on hilly parts like the Bakony and the Vertés) and northwest (on the Kisalföld, or 'Little Plain', in the Fertő-Hanság National Park). Steppic habitats are often associated with non-intensive methods of arable farming and widespread grazing, and have become fragmented as a consequence of intensified agricultural practices. They are vital for birds like the great bustard, the red-footed falcon, the short-toed buzzard, the stone curlew, the roller and the lesser grey shrike; the success of steppe-restoration programmes on the Moson plain (in the Fertő-Hanság National Park) is evident in the substantial increase in great bustard numbers.

Wet meadows are found in flood plains throughout the country, but the Ormánság in Baranya, the Bodrog flood plain in Borsod and the Ipoly river valley in Nógrád have the best examples. Upland meadows lie in the hill ranges to the north, while the Kali basin and Tapolca (in the Balaton National Park) are also well regarded. Meadows – which depend on regular mowing – contain the most varied vegetation in Hungary. Some meadows have been found to contain over 50 species of grass, and virtually all orchids are confined to such habitats; globally threatened birds including the corn crake and white stork depend upon them.

**Forests** blanket 19% of the country, a proportion that the government and the EU would like to increase to 25% within a decade. The woodlands are mainly of oak, hornbeam and beech, with plantations of non-native locust tree, poplar and coniferous species making up half of the total. Low mountains are covered by broad-leaved deciduous forests, while flood plains feature both soft-wood and hard-wood alluvial forest (willow, alder, ash, etc). Dendrologists should make for the pine forests of the Őrség National Park in the west, which was planted at the end of the 19th century, or the beech trees that flourish in the cooler climate of the Zala and Bükk hills. Mixed oak forests are the predominant indigenous vegetation type, with oak-hornbeam and oak-lime in the damper, higher areas; good examples are in the Börzsöny and Zselic ranges. Turkey oak and Hungarian oak thrive in the warmer, south-facing slopes of the Bakony, Vertés and Mecsek hills. The Great Plain is significantly less forested than the northern and westerly regions; nevertheless, there are areas of flood-plain forest (characterised by willow, poplar and English oak) in Hortobágy National Park, the Gemenc Forest of the Danube-Dráva National Park and along the upper reaches of the Tisza. Alder swamp forests are typical of southwest Hungary. Scrub forest usually appears in the form of scrub encroaching on meadows, but also includes karst rock forests like that in Aggtelek National Park.

Around 14% of the country remains uncultivated, and includes lakes, rivers and wetlands (as well as urban areas, infrastructure and military zones). Apart from Lake Balaton, Lake Velence and the major rivers, Hungarian **wetlands** are for the most part artificial. Kis Balaton (in the Balaton Uplands National Park) was created as a retaining basin to try to filter the Zala River water entering the Balaton; eight species of heron now nest among its vast reed beds. The Hortobágy fishponds, Hungary's leading nesting habitat for terns, was formed in the 1970s.

## Flora

Hungary has a very diverse flora. Its geographic situation means it harbours plants that originate from Russia, western Europe and the Adriatic and Mediterranean regions. There are over 3,000 flowering plant species, including many endemics which are not found outside Hungary or its immediate neighbours. Although much of the countryside has been used for agriculture, this is less intensive than western Europe; as a consequence, wild flowers are attractive and plentiful, particularly on roadside verges and along the edges of arable fields. The casual visitor cannot fail to notice the spectacular displays of flowers that thrive on disturbed ground. Roadside crop fields take on the glorious hues of plants like the red **poppy**, blue **cornflower**, pink/mauve **corn cockle**, white **mayweed**, yellow **corn marigold** and purple **larkspur**, a canvas of colour visible even from the major highways. If you stop by such a field you might find over 30 different wild flowers growing amongst the edge of the crop. The botanical richness of the country means that even service and picnic areas can be rewarding places for a spot of wild-flower-watching.

For the greatest variety of wild flowers it is worth exploring areas of rocky limestone hillsides. Aggtelek in the northeast is particularly good. The woodlands contain several species of orchid, among them the very rare **ghost orchid**, as well as **red helleborine**, **violet helleborine** and **greater butterfly orchid**. The limestone grasslands have an impressive range of colourful flowers, many of which are endemic to Hungary. Some of the showiest are the blue/purple **knapweeds**, **scabious** and **thistles**, which tower above the lower-growing herbs. Several tall yellow-flowered **mulleins** are widespread within this habitat, and the **purple mullein** is particularly noticeable.

The more acidic rock of the Bükk Hills attracts a contrasting group of flora. Distinctive plants of this habitat include the pink/mauve **martagon lily** and several orchid species including **white helleborine, butterfly orchid** and **bug orchid. Wolfsbane** is a very obvious, buxom daisy occurring at the woodland edges. **Crested cow-wheat** is another summer plant that stands out, with a vivid yellow-and-red spiky flower head.

Open areas of uncultivated hillside and low mountains are the richest areas for flowers. Many are small and hard to identify individually but include attractive **clovers, vetches** and **mints**. The latter produce wonderful aromatic scents as the visitor walks through grassland.

The flowering season runs from April to October, with the range of plants changing through the months. It is possible to see **primroses, Narcissi, snowdrops** and **crocus** on visits in the spring, with most of the **orchids** occurring in early to mid summer, and later the conspicuous grassland plants of **scabious** and **knapweed**. The flowering season draws to a close with **autumn crocus** and further **Narcissi.**

In the lowland and wetland areas there are many interesting plants but few with obvious and colourful flowers. Two notable exceptions are the bright yellow flowers of **yellow iris** and the pink/mauve umbrella-like flowers of **flowering rush**. One distinctive tree of the lowlands is the **black poplar**. Its massive form dominates the landscape and produces millions of fluffy seeds during mid summer.

Many species of **fungi** can be found even during the summer months. Local people collect them for personal consumption and for export to the West. Visitors may find

## HUNGARY FOR BIRDS

Hungary has lots to satisfy the 'avifaunatics'! Its birdlife is special because many eastern species reach their westernmost breeding range here. The rolling hills, broad grasslands, alkaline lakes, riverine forests, fishponds and wetlands conserve wildlife that remains both diverse and unique within Europe. A wide biodiversity is supported in areas of unspoiled countryside that is rarely found in industrialised Europe. In the interest of preserving this heritage, it is important to use licensed guides who are committed to conservation as well as tourism; for contact details, see page 38.

**Hortobágy National Park** (see page 298) is where the birdwatchers flock, the best-known of the country's twitching haunts. It consists of open plain dominated by saline grasses and arable land, its vast steppe area offering unbroken skyline and the space to walk for hours without meeting another soul. The park also holds an extensive 'fishpond system' of large lakes, and provides important feeding and breeding spots for many protected and migrating species. At some of these lakes, the habitat is now managed according to the needs of the bird populations rather than in the name of fish cultivation. Another measure taken in the park is the resurrection of original habitat through artificial flooding, which is crucial for the migrating and threatened lesser white-fronted goose. The *puszta* also provides the only known continental stop-over point for dotterels on their way from northern climes to their wintering range. The wet grasslands are home to the aquatic warbler, which has a stronghold here. The great bustard population is stable thanks to the careful management of arable lands; this magnificent bird's springtime courtship display – when the otherwise well-camouflaged male inverts his feathers to resemble a ship in full sail – attracts enchanted professionals and amateurs alike.

From October to December, many – many! – cranes stop to feed in the neighbouring fields, spending the nights in the fishponds and on the *puszta*. In recent years their numbers have reached 100,000, making crane migration the biggest single natural draw for bird lovers. Sturdy look-out towers allow people to watch the evening in-flight of tens of thousands of birds cruising low overhead, the cranes' cry creating a symphony of sound.

The period between autumn and winter has other highlights too. Stone curlews group before migration, while there might be 200 red-footed falcons gathered in one spot. By the beginning of November, hen harriers, rough-legged buzzards and Lapland buntings have normally arrived to spend the winter. After the cranes, the most numerous visitors are geese of various types – bean, white-fronted, lesser-white fronted and the keenly sought-after red-breasted. You should be able to see these by visiting some of the fishponds or by ascending the lookout towers.

While a significant portion of **Lake Fertő** (Neusiedler See; see page 497), on the country's western border, lies in Austria, the Hungarian part includes some of the 'Important Bird Area' (IBA) (an area of 75km$^2$); 88% is covered by reed beds (*Phragmites*), and adjacent mesophile and wet saline grasslands. The Fertő-Hanság National Park covers this area, and there are many cultural and tourist attractions. The lake holds central Europe's biggest reed bed, and is therefore home to many songbirds, herons and wildfowl. Visitors can either take a boat trip on the lake or delve by canoe into its most-hidden regions among the huge reeds – where they'll encounter its birds (and mosquitoes!). The star species are the penduline tit, bearded reedling, moustached warbler, bittern and little bittern, great white egret, and purple, squacco, grey and night herons. In the wetlands and habitat-reconstruction areas are shorebirds such as the black-winged stilt, avocet and Kentish plover. This is one of the best places to see the red-crested pochard, and you may even glimpse the endangered ferruginous duck. White-tailed eagles are resident too, and often flush out the feeding birds in a flurry of action. And the close proximity of the Austrian Alps provides a wonderful contrast; don't be surprised if snowy peaks hove into view as you train binoculars on an egret's flight.

The **Börzsöny Hills, Mátra, Bükk, Zemplén Hills** and **Aggtelek** stretch along the northern border with Slovakia, and these ranges yield up different habitats and species. Here the country's birds of prey live in greatest concentration; raptor species use the hills as a breeding site and the surrounding grazing land for hunting. Professional guides can often eke out saker falcons, and eagles of the imperial, lesser-spotted and short-toed varieties. Black storks also breed, and are slowly growing in number. The extensive beech and oak forests are occupied by the majority of Europe's woodpecker species. The black woodpecker and the elusive white-backed woodpecker prefer beech, the middle-spotted woodpecker breeds in old oak woods, while the Syrian woodpecker chooses areas of human habitation such as gardens filled with fruit trees. Wrynecks call loudly from the edges of little villages, among the mountain meadows with many trees and bushes. Green and grey-headed woodpeckers are found here too, often identified by their brash and piercing calls.

This is the stomping ground of another eastern species, the enigmatic Ural owl. Only the very fortunate witness this enormous bird while it roosts because its plumage precisely matches the beech bark of its perch; however, head for its hunting areas and there is a chance of seeing it in action. The huge eagle owl also inhabits these mountains, laying its eggs in the nooks and crannies of steep rock faces at the end of winter.

Those on short trips might make an outing to the **Börzsöny Hills** near Budapest, which belong to the Danube-Ipoly National Park, the country's newest. Renowned for its castles and the hundreds of natural springs, the area also harbours diverse flora and fauna; there are several glacial plant relicts among the 70 protected species that occur here and over 90 species of breeding bird. The Ipoly Valley is one of the most intact areas of the national park, with wet meadows, alder wood, special flowers, almost all the species of Hungarian amphibian – and innumerable birds. The collared flycatcher and wood warbler are typical woodland species, reproducing in good numbers, but there are a few pairs of red-breasted flycatchers too. There are nine woodpecker species, and you should come across the attractively marked rock bunting. Wet meadows aren't the quietest of places, with the calls of the river warbler by day and the corncrake by night, especially along the River Ipoly. Red-backed shrikes are very common and there are plenty of barred warblers.

**Kiskunság National Park** is a fascinating part of the Great Plain, nicknamed 'Little Hortobágy' because of the similarity of habitats and species over a more compact area that is much closer to the capital. The landscape is largely a perfect plain covered by loess or sand, dotted with reeds, wet marshes, bogs, pastures, forests and steppes. As it has saline vegetation and alkaline lakes, there are unique species for botanists and birders to search out. Kiskunság boasts the largest great bustard population in Hungary – during winter and spring there can be as many as 150 birds visible from the same place. However, there's more beside the bustard, and it is not unusual to see 100 bird species in a day. In fact, close to the full spectrum of Hungarian specialities are here – the pygmy cormorant, squacco heron, ferruginous duck, saker and red-footed falcon, white-tailed eagle, black-winged stilt, stone curlew, collared pratincole, Kentish plover, white-winged black tern, whiskered tern, hoopoe, roller, bee-eater, Syrian woodpecker, moustached warbler, penduline tit, golden oriole and tawny pipit.

purveyors in country villages or at the roadside but – although there are many good edible species – don't be tempted to try any specimens unless you are very sure what you'll be eating. The main markets of large towns have stalls where you can take your mushrooms to be checked by an expert (*gomba vizsgáló*).

## Fauna

### Mammals

The beaver, the bear, the wolf and the lynx – all until recently thought to be extinct in Hungary – are making comebacks. The **beaver** was deliberately reintroduced in the Gemenc Forest (in the Danube-Drava National Park), but the large carnivores are re-colonising by crossing from neighbouring countries. They are being encountered with increasing frequency along the borders: the **jackal** close to Croatia in southern Somogy and southern Baranya, and the **bear**, the **wolf** and the **lynx** in the northeast (in the Tatra Mountains bordering Slovakia and Ukraine). Of course, the chance of actually meeting any of these secretive mammals remains very small – which disappoints naturalists and rather cheers the average lay hiker.

Hungary's **deer** are more famous than they probably wish they were among the hunting fraternity, and world records are regularly shot in the country. Zala, Somogy, and the area of Tamási and the Gemenc in Tolna – the largest areas of lowland forest – are the places where deer thrive. **Fallow deer** are concentrated in a few hunting areas such as Lábod (in Somogy), Gyulaj and Tamási (in Tolna) and Pusztavacsi (on the border of Pest and Bács-Kiskun).

**Mufflon**, introduced in relatively recent times, can be found in the rocky wooden terrain of the Zemplén Hills in the northeast and of the Bakony range in the west. The **wild boar** is common throughout the country but especially so in the west and the north where the forest cover is at its densest. As elsewhere in Europe, its numbers have grown in recent years. The **hare** is most numerous in the east, on the flat and open terrain of the Great Plain.

### Birds

Hungary is a twitcher's delight – it is quite possible to witness over 200 species of wild bird during a week's visit. The most productive times to come are during spring (April/May) and autumn (August/October) migrations.

The **cormorant** is very common and you'll see it on most bodies of water where fish are present (even on the Budapest stretch of the Danube). The largest nesting colonies are in Kisbalaton (in the Balaton Uplands National Park), on the Danube Bend, in the Biharugra fishponds and in the Pusztaszer Landscape Protection Area. The **pygmy cormorant**, however, is much rarer; while it breeds only in the Hortobágy, it might occasionally be seen making its way through other areas (especially in the Danube Plain in Bács-Kiskun, Pest).

All species of **heron** nest in Hungary. The rare **bittern** is found in the vast reed-beds of the Hortobágy, the Kis Balaton and the Fertő-Hanság national parks. The more common **little bittern** nests in the reeds along smaller surfaces of water (like fishponds) throughout the country. The **great white egret** can often be seen foraging in fields, either on its own or alongside the **grey heron**. You'll increase your chances of sightings by heading for the west of the country, though, near Kis Balaton, Lake Fertő, Lake Velence and the Sárvíz in Fehér County.

The more bashful **squacco heron** and **night heron** are concentrated in colonies in the Hanság, Kis Balaton, the Pacsmag fishponds in Tolna, the Béda-Karapancsa in Baranya, the Pusztaszer Landscape Protection Area, the Hortobágy and the Bodrog Flood Plain. Some of these areas are also strongholds of the **purple heron**, although lesser populations can be found in reed-beds throughout the country.

The **white stork** remains an enchanting and regular presence in most of Hungary. It prefers to concentrate in lowlands rich in meadows and pastures, and is particularly fond of nesting on electricity poles (rather than chimneys, as was the case in centuries past). Most of the poles have been fitted with special platforms to ensure their safety, and a recent census recorded over 4,000 pairs. The **black stork** lives in forests with abundant watercourses, such as those of the southwest (in Inner Somogy and Gemenc) and the northeast (in the Bodrog Flood Plain, the Upper Tisza and Zemplén Hills).

Large numbers of **geese** winter in Hungary; in the west we find predominantly the **bean-goose,** while the east harbours the **white-fronted** variety. The **ferruginous duck** is a very rare waterfowl globally but still relatively common in Hungary. It lives even in the smaller fishponds throughout the country.

The **white-tailed eagle** is found in wet lowland regions – favourites are Inner Somogy, the Gemenc, the Ormánság, Pusztaszer, Biharugra and the Hortobágy. Hungary's population of the **imperial eagle** – one of Europe's scarcest birds – amounts to 50 breeding pairs. These couples circle above mountains along the northern border with Slovakia and the Ukraine (the Gerecse, Börzsöny, Mátra and Zemplén ranges in particular). The **red-footed falcon** is a diminutive raptor that nests in colonies in old rook nests, usually in the *puszta* of the east (and especially in Hortobágy).

The **crane** doesn't nest in Hungary but can be seen in remarkable numbers – over 100,000 – during migration in October. It is a treat for wildlife lovers; Hortobágy sees the majority of the birds, although lesser numbers rest on other grassland areas of the east (Pitvaros, Pusztaszer and the Bodrog Flood Plain).

The most renowned bird of the puszta, and the best-protected animal in Hungary, is the **great bustard** (see box, page 381). If you're eager for a glimpse, try the Moson, Danube, Dévaványa, Bihar or Heves plains, or the Hortobágy.

Adding a splash of real colour, the **roller** is widespread among the scattered trees and open landscape of the east. An interesting programme is underway to boost the numbers of this beautiful bird in Hungary, involving the construction of special nest boxes in areas of open countryside. You will notice that they are very large boxes when compared to those erected for smaller birds. The bee-eater also shakes a vibrant tail feather, nesting in sandbanks and found throughout the country.

### Reptiles and amphibians

Over 40 species of reptile and amphibian may be encountered within Hungary. Those most likely to make their presence felt are some of the 'vocal' amphibians, which have loud and distinctive calls and can be heard from some distance. The smallest of these – at less that 4cm long – is the **European tree** frog; like some children we've sat next to on planes, it produces an incredible volume of sound relative to its size. It has a piping call, and can occur several kilometres from water bodies where it breeds and will often be found some metres above the ground in trees and shrubs.

**March frogs** are present in most areas of open water and can be very distinctive with their territorial croaking, disappearing with a loud splash if disturbed. The **fire-bellied toad** is found primarily in the lowlands, while the **yellow-bellied toad** is an upland species. These little toads measure under 4cm in length, and are dark (almost black) on the back with a glaring patterned colouration on their undersides. Once seen, never forgotten! Both their calls are familiar sounds in wetlands throughout Hungary during May and June.

The yellow and black **fire salamander** is widespread in Hungary, especially in wooded areas. Normally secretive and nocturnal, it will surprise the visitor by appearing during the day after showers of rain and can often be seen crossing busy roads in wet conditions. While in wetland areas, particularly in the lowlands, the visitor may also encounter the **European pond terrapin** or the introduced **Mexican red-eared terrapin**. Both are very shy, diving into the water when disturbed, but they do like to sunbathe on floating logs or muddy banks during the heat of the day.

The commonest snakes are probably **grass** and **dice snakes**. Both species are comfortably aquatic, swimming quite happily on the surface as well as hunting for prey in shallow water. They regularly bask to warm their bodies, and this practice means they can often be found in the lowlands at the edges of minor roads. Unfortunately tourists will usually only spot them as squished casualties of the road or as dangling prey in the talons of a **short-toed eagle**. **Orsini's viper** is at the northern edge of its distribution, and is limited to the Hanság and Kiskunság. The **adder**, also a viper, is much more prevalent and enjoys warm, sandy and rocky areas with sparse vegetation.

Hungary has several lizard species, most of which make their presence known when scurrying for cover. The **European green lizard** occurs throughout the country, often climbing into bushes to sunbathe in the morning. Its overall colour of emerald green with a blue throat and yellow undercarriage makes it a very distinctive and attractive creature. In areas that see high numbers of tourists (like archaeological sites), the lizard can be pretty tame – and in reaching a respectable length of up to 40cm, it is the species that people are most likely to eyeball.

**Sand lizards**, with a broad green stripe down their backs, are fairly common in lowland areas; they can grow up to 25cm. Smaller **wall** and **common lizards** can also be very widespread, but their dull brown colouration means they are generally overlooked unless sunbathing on light-coloured rock. The **snake-eyed skink** lives on south-facing hillsides that catch the sun rays, such as the Mecsek, the Börzsöny and the Bakony.

## Fish

The **European mudminnow**, which lives in small lakes, ponds and swamps, is among the rarest and most protected fish in Europe. It can be found in the Kiskunság National Park and in a few other sites between the Danube and the Tisza. The **pikeperch**, the Hungarian 'fogas', is the country's best-known fish – although most people witness it on its journey from plate to mouth aboard fork. Prior to that, it swims in Balaton and Velence lakes and the Danube. **Carp** is bred in fishponds and fish farms all over. **Catfish** of over 3m in length and 50kg in weight can be found patrolling the waters of the Tisza and the Danube.

## Insects

The majority of the creepy-crawlies in Hungary are fairly small and dull-coloured, but there are several distinctive and brightly coloured species.

Over 40 species of **dragonfly** and **damselfly** occur here. They all breed in water but the flying adults can be seen in many locations between April and October. Although identifying the species can be difficult, the sheer beauty of their colours makes it worthwhile watching for them. They range from the stunningly vivid red of the scarlet darter through the blues of black-tailed skimmers, the yellow-and-black hoops of the golden-ringed dragonfly, to the delicate blues and greens of the emerald and beautiful damselflies.

It is possible to see over 100 different **butterfly** species within the diverse habitats of Hungary. Many are difficult to identify and also fairly widespread in the rest of mainland Europe. The more distinctive ones include the bright yellow-and-orange Cleopatra, the yellow-and-black swallowtail, and the white-and-orange orange-tip. Two of the most striking families of butterflies are the coppers (which are mainly orange/red) and the blues (which are various shades of pastel and metallic blue).

Hungary of course has its own special butterfly – the Hungarian glider, which is a beautiful black-and-white creature that can be found flying and basking along sheltered woodland edges, particularly in the northeastern regions.

Most of the several-thousand **moth** species are nocturnal, although in rural parts these will often be attracted to the lights around accommodation like moths to the . . . er, you know. The largest and most spectacular commonly encountered is the peacock moth, with distinctive eye patterns on the upper surface of its wings and a wingspan of about 10cm. There are many types of hawk moth, big and pretty creatures with delicate (often pastel-coloured) upper wings that contrast with the striking hues of the hind wings (which they show when disturbed). You might watch seven or more species of these gathering around honey-suckle flowers or outdoor lights during June and July.

During summer evenings visitors cannot fail to notice the magical delights of glow worms and fireflies as they produce their bio-luminescence to attract a partner. Their eerie glow will be seen just after dusk, with the fireflies causing the most spectacular display as they flash their lights on and off while flying around sheltered woodland edges. Despite their names, both of these are **beetles**. Other notable members of this group are the imposing **stag beetle**, the male with antler-like projections on its head. These can be almost 7cm long and are often found near woodland in June and July; to see them in flight on a sunny day still captivates us.

**Long-horned beetles** also inhabit landscape near woodlands. These big, narrow beetles, with antennae longer than their bodies, live within dead and dying timber. Their exit holes, often over a centimetre in diameter, can be visible on old tree stumps. The beetles themselves feed on the nectar of woodland flora.

Several species of **preying mantis** occur in Hungary, fascinating creatures that are generally seen sitting on flowers awaiting an unsuspecting insect on which to feast. In late spring and early summer, millions of **long-tailed mayflies** swarm on the Tisza for a few hours while mating and laying their eggs before falling exhausted (and dead) on the water. This is a quite astonishing spectacle of the natural world.

## National parks and conservation areas

There are ten **national parks** in Hungary, covering over 175,000ha. Hortobágy, on the Northern Great Plain, is the oldest, largest and best-known of these, a Unesco World Heritage Site and home to the biggest area of *puszta* grassland in central Europe. There are two other parks on the Great Plain (Kiskunság and Körös-Maros), two in the Northern Uplands (Bükk and Aggtelek), one around the Danube Bend (Duna-Ipoly), three in Transdanubia (Duna-Dráva, Őrség, and Fertő-Hanság) and one at Lake Balaton (Balaton Uplands). (See the relevant regional chapter for detailed information on each.) In addition, a total of 26,200ha have been declared **nature conservation areas**, which are smaller (usually under 1,000ha) zones of important natural value; bird sanctuaries generally fall under this category. **Landscape protected areas** (467,000ha in all) fall between the two, providing protection for medium-sized landscapes (over 1,000ha) like Lake Balaton. As such almost 8% of Hungary is nationally protected, and when wetlands, alkaline lakes and areas of local significance are considered we can say that 10% of the territory is under some form of nature protection.

## Ecotourism

Hungary has a respectable enough history of nature conservation; laws designed to protect its birds and forests were passed well over a century ago, the first landscape-protection area was established in 1952, and the first national parks in the 1970s. Since then, thousands of protected areas have been created at local, county, national and international levels. While there is a danger to wildlife from EU-sponsored 'development', the government is aware of the importance of its habitats for ecotourism; the Ministry of the Environment and the national-park directorates have funded the erection of information centres, hides and nature trails, and the tourist board has produced a series of *Ecotourism* brochures in several languages. Pollution from industry and agriculture has declined significantly in the recent past, in good part due to the drive to meet EU environmental standards. Ecotourism is a relatively new and exciting sector of the tourist market. Hungary is ripe for such tourism: there are close to 400 recorded species of bird, nearly 200 of butterfly, over 3,400 types of moth, and thousands of plant species. Sensitive ecotourism can help to protect this abundant range.

## Natural highlights and activities

There are several – often spectacular – **seasonal highlights** that those interested in wildlife should pen into their diaries. Some of these are breathtaking for the sheer numbers involved. The flowering of the River Tisza in spring involves the emerging, mating and dying of huge quantities of the ephemeral mayfly; during summer, there are clouds of butterflies in the untouched natural meadows of the Balaton Uplands, Bükk and Aggtelek; the autumn migration of cranes in the Hortobágy, when tens of thousands of the birds fly low overhead at sunset, is stunning (see page 297); snowy winters are equally blessed by the massing together of red-breasted, white-fronted and lesser white-fronted geese at the Hortobágy, the Danube Bend and Lake Tata. During the second half of September and the beginning of October, you can witness red deer in rut. Spring, summer and autumn all offer botanical treats too, with the flowering of a great variety of protected plants and wildflowers, including over 50 orchid species and many other endemics. Tours incorporating these can be arranged through nature tour operators (see pages 38–9).

Hungary also holds thousands of limestone **caves**. In Aggtelek National Park alone there are 700, some of which remain to be explored. The Baradla-Domica system (*www.showcaves.com/english/hu/showcaves/Baradla.html*; see pages 265–9) is one of Europe's largest stalactite caves; it is a World Heritage site and ranks among the world's most beautiful and intriguing geographical phenomena. The underworld offers another, rather warmer pleasure – **thermal water**, which bubbles up through rock fissures and forms the raw material for the country's many natural spas. Some of these – such as those at Egerszalok, Hévíz and Budapest's City Park – allow you to don your swimming costume in mid winter as snow falls on the water. And where the water is medicinal, you may be tempted to drink an eggy concoction in the hope of relieving respiratory or gastric complaints – or a hangover headache.

For **horse-riding** and **hiking**, see page 74.

## Some ecotourism projects, centres and events

Sustained protection efforts have resulted in stable and growing populations of some globally threatened bird species – notably the **eastern imperial eagle** (*conservation project in the Carpathian Basin, www.imperialeagle.hu/indexa.html*), **saker falcon** (*nest-site-protection project,* ↘ *70 339 5903*) and **great bustard**. One of the most exciting rehabilitation schemes is taking place in the Körös-Maros National Park at Dévaványa, where they are protecting the great bustard. At the visitor centre, you can get close to the birds and enjoy their spectacular springtime display rituals (see page 380).

After thousands of years, the aurochs, wild horses and other grazing animals of the Hortobágy grasslands were gradually replaced by domesticated stock. In Hortobágy village, part of Hortobágy National Park, the Puszta Animal Park (see page 300) has an excellent range of **protected breeds** – Hungarian grey cattle, equine species like the Lipizzaner, shagya, nonius, gidran, furioso, kisbér halfbreed, murinsulaner and hucul, sheep including the racka, tsigai and cikta, poultry such as the Hungarian yellow, white, speckled and Transylvanian naked-necked hens, the bronze turkey, and the mangalica pig (sometimes referred to as a 'frizzle' on account of its hairy hide). There are also several intriguing types of **sheep dog** – the long-haired komondor, with a thick fringe covering its eyes, the kuvasz and the puli (see page 185). Thatched farms, or *tanya*, dot the *puszta* landscape, and beside them tall wooden structures called 'heron wells' (*gémeskút*) that are reminiscent of Arab *shadoofs*; equestrian shows, riding tours and goulash parties are other highlights (and can be arranged through tour operators like Ecotours; see page 39).

Some **bird-ringing** stations allow visitors to assist with the work. That at Lake Tata hosts summer camps for tourists, and school parties can participate in tented 'ringing camps'. For further details contact Peter Csonka (✆ *06 70 339 5903*), nature conservationist at Duna-Ipoly National Park who also runs the saker falcon nest-site-protection project (see above) and the winter bird race (see below). There is another ringing site to the south of Budapest, at Ócsa (✆ *1 275 6247;* e *ringers@mme.hu*; see also page 190). **International bird races** welcome participants too, at the Hortobágy fishponds (Halastó) (usually first weekend in Sep) and Lake Tata (in Nov). The races take place over 24 hours, and have in recent years included entrants from the UK and USA; they are announced by email in Hungarian (contact Ecotours at the time for English translations of the details).

As for **butterfly conservation**, volunteers can participate in an international monitoring programme operated by Ecotours Hungary Ltd (*contact Gábor Orbán;* ✆ *06 30 645 9318;* e *natours@axelero.hu*; see page 39) and the British Butterfly Conservation Society. **Hungarian Moth Nights** are run by the Szalkay József Hungarian Lepidopterological Society (*Magyar Lepkészeti Egyesület; Debrecen, Zoványi utca 19/B/9;* e *kadar.mihaly@mail.vpop.hu*), when volunteers join professional lepidopterologists in searching for and identifying moth species in different regions of the country and submitting their data to provide a snapshot of local moth populations. Over the next couple of years the event is scheduled to take place Apr 28–30 2006 and Oct 12–14 2007; information can be obtained from the vice-president of the society, Sáfián Szabolcs (✆ *06 20 346 1883;* e *lepkeved@yahoo.co.uk; www.lepidoptera.freeweb.hu/program/emn/emn1.htm*).

---

### WHAT'S IN YOUR ECO-KIT?

If you're going to Hungary for the wildlife – on an organised or independent tour – the following are some of the items to be found in the pack of any self-respecting eco-tripper:

#### Essentials

- Small rucksack
- Torch
- Water bottle (and hip flask, for those long hours in the hide!?)
- Notebook and pencil
- Sunhat, sunglasses, towel, swimwear, lipsalve, handcream, sunscreen and insect repellent
- Field guides. You can purchase the *Collins Bird Guide* (by Mullarney, Svensson et al) from UK bookshops; *Butterflies of Europe* (by Tristan Lafranchis) is available by contacting lafranch@otenet.gr.
- Maps of the Hungarian national parks (try the websites www.omnimap.com or www.stanfords.co.uk)

#### Technical clobber

- Pair of binoculars (8.5 x 42 a personal favourite)
- Telescope (optional) – carry on the plane as hand luggage, with the tripod in your suitcase
- Camera (with lenses, film or memory cards and spare batteries)
- Hand-lens and specimen inspection pot for espying insects

For further details of operators running **eco tours**, see pages 38–40; the *Giving something back* section (pages 81–2) lists other worthy conservation projects.

# HISTORY
## Time's mists

In 1965 the 400,000-year-old bones of a man – nicknamed Samuel by archaeologists – were found at Vértesszőlős (near Tata); he crafted flint tools, bathed in thermal springs and ate (or perhaps was eaten!) in this ancient camp. Several caves show signs of **Stone Age** man, of Neanderthals who picked berries and stalked mammoth, bear and ibex 40,000 years ago. With the thawing of the Ice Age, the Palaeolithic hunter-gatherers moved out and in 5000BC were replaced by migrants from the Near East via the Balkans. These **Neolithic** clans were producers rather than crude predators, and imported knowledge of agriculture, animal husbandry and pot-making, and belief systems based around goddess worship; their 'Körös culture' is named after the southeastern river valley in which their settlements were based, making use of the fertile soil. The advanced Neolithic culture slowly spread through the Danube Basin to the rest of Europe, but the Southern Great Plain is the westernmost region where *tell* can be found – artificial mounds formed by the accumulated remains of long-term habitation, and a feature more typical of the eastern Mediterranean.

From 3000BC fresh tribes arrived from the Balkans, Indo-European herders taking advantage of drier climatic conditions to supplant the agriculturalists. These shepherds stamped their authority with revolutionary technology – notably copper weapons and the four-wheeled cart. (A drinking vessel unearthed at Budakalász, near Budapest, is the earliest known representation of the cart in Europe.) During the early **Bronze Age** there were influxes from the south, and between 1700 and 1300BC a clutch of ethnically different lowland tribes were governed by horsemen living in a system of hillside forts. While the subsequent ebb and flow of migrating peoples was frequently bloody, it also ensured invention's spread; Iranian-speakers from the East introduced iron in 800BC and the Scythians brought with them the potter's wheel in 500BC. By the 4th century BC the **Celts** controlled the Carpathian Basin, their dominance based on the advanced use of iron. However, it was not until the arrival of Roman legions in the 1st century BC that a true, sandal-footed leap was made towards a sophisticated and civilised society.

## The Romans and the Great Migrations

The **Romans** were determined to put proper distance between themselves and the Germanic barbarians to the east, and by 35BC they had extended their imperial boundary as far as the Danube. They protected this border with a line of forts known as the *limes*, and behind it established the province of Pannonia (subsequently divided into lower and upper administrative zones). Between AD106 and 271 they also controlled the province of Dacia further east in today's Transylvania. The strategic importance of Pannonia is evident in the fact that four of the empire's 25 legions were permanently based there. The Latin impact was immense. Remnants of the urban infrastructure – roads, baths, villas, temples and amphitheatres – can still be seen in Óbuda, Szombathely, Sopron, Győr and Pécs; cultural and spiritual influences (in the form of viniculture and Christianity)were no less important. During the 4th century the empire came under mounting pressure from waves of attack, and in the early 5th century they finally abandoned Pannonia.

This triggered the **second age of migrations** as Asiatic peoples from the east moved into the Carpathian Basin. Initially the Huns filled the vacuum under the notorious Attila. After murdering his brother in AD445, Attila commanded unswerving loyalty from his people. Such was the force of his personality that many later claimed blood ties with him, including Magyar rulers. After his death in AD453, however, the Huns' short-lived empire crumbled. Several nomadic tribes rose and fell over the next 400 years, the Avars most successful in grasping the nettle and holding it until the 8th century. By the 9th century, though, no group was in overall control, and the region was ripe for the plucking.

## The Magyar Conquest

The question of true Hungarian ancestry has caused much squabbling and head scratching. The erroneous belief in a blood tie with the Huns continued well into the 18th century, and Attila was a heroic figure in the cultural consciousness during the period of national awakening – indeed Hungarians retain a soft spot for the 'Scourge of God' still. More recently there have been claims of kinship with groups including the Etruscans, Sumers and even the Incas, but scholars usually accept that the Magyars were a Finno-Ugric group hailing from lands between the River Volga and the Urals. In 500BC, a branch of this group splintered off and travelled southwest to Bashkiria in central Asia (north of the Caspian Sea); they called themselves Magyars, a name formed of the Finno-Ugric words *mon* ('to speak') and *er* ('man'). At some point after AD500, some members moved further southwest to the Don River and joined other tribes in a collective known as the Onogur (from which the Western name 'Hungary' stems). Their final journey prior to the conquest took them around the top of the Black Sea to an area called Etelköz, between the Danube and the Dnieper rivers.

The position there was a precarious one, and after an attack by nomads from the Asian steppe the decision was taken to make the short hop west for greater security beyond the Carpathian Mountains. Divided between seven tribes under the overall leadership of a chieftain called Árpád and joined by three smaller groups of Kuns – making a combined invasion force of around 600,000 – the Magyars are said to have crossed the mountains via the Verecke Pass (in Ukraine). The ancestors of today's Hungarians had arrived. Resistance was negligible, and no match for a breed acutely skilled in both horsemanship and archery. In the early years they aspired to even greater things, and their armies travelled light in forging westward with devastating effect (reaching as far as France). However, after a string of losses culminated in a real spanking in Augsburg they elected to cut their losses and consolidate their new homeland.

## The Árpád kings and the Hungarian State

In the following years, **Prince Géza** (great-grandson of Árpád) invited missionaries from the West to introduce the Magyars to Christianity – although he himself never converted, claiming he was 'powerful enough to worship as many gods as he pleased'. Born around AD975, Géza's son Vajk was christened **István** (Stephen), and it was he who pushed on with centralising control – until then, the clans were effectively just a confederation that co-operated in times of war – and establishing a single, powerful state under the banner of Christianity (and, of course, the rule of his own fair hand). Lauded in Hungary as the prince among all their kings, it is forgotten that István was ruthless in his purpose. In snuffing out an alternative challenge to his primogeniture from his older cousin Koppány, István hung pieces of his body from four separate castles as a warning to others.

After his coronation in AD1000 with a crown sent by Pope Sylvester II, István set about bedding in his position, carefully dividing the land into counties governed by royal-appointed officials (not hereditary feudal rulers), fortifying the country borders and founding eight episcopal sees and two archbishoprics (at Esztergom and Kalocsa). Marriage to Gizella (niece of the German King Otto I 'the Great', the victor at Augsburg) and a friendship alliance with the Byzantine empire ensured István could get on with all this undistracted by international struggles. His success was rewarded with the title of 'Apostolic King', bestowed by the pope, and the right to use the double cross (still visible in the country's coat of arms). By the time of his death in 1038, István had transformed the country into a Christian monarchy with legal and administrative structures. When he was canonised 45 years later, his right hand was found still to be preserved and it is now held in Budapest's basilica, Hungary's most holy relic.

As he grew up, István's only son **Imre** had been carefully groomed to continue his father's work. It was therefore a tragic blow when Imre died in a hunting accident in 1031, an event that famously led István to offer the protection of his kingdom to the Virgin Mary. The death of the now-heirless István triggered **four decades of fighting** between a succession of weak kings and the nobility, and a final anti-Christian uprising under the pagan clan-chief Vata (during which Imre's former spiritual tutor, the Venetian Bishop Gellért, was stuffed into a spiked barrel and tossed down a hill into the Danube).

Stability returned with the reign of **László I** (1077–95), a shrewd monarch who governed with an iron fist, made careful alliances, reinforced the authority of the Church and even extended Hungary's influence by adding the crowns of Croatia and Dalmatia to his own (after the death of his brother-in-law and previous ruler of those territories). (The gold bust of László, containing his skull, is on display in Győr Cathedral.) The bookish **'Könyves' Kálmán I** (1095–1116) therefore took over a peaceful place, and was able to indulge and encourage love for the arts. During the 12th century Hungary flourished further, particularly under **King Béla III** (1172–96). Educated in Constantinople, Béla III based himself at Esztergom, quietened threatening rumbles from Byzantium, and went about overhauling the country's administrative framework; one of his enlightened moves was to declare it compulsory that legal and Crown dealings be documented in writing. In the same spirit, this was the era of the unknown scribe **Anonymus**, whose *Gesta Ungarorum* chronicled the events of Hungary's early history and remains a rare source for students today.

**András II** (1205–35) was feeble by comparison. After attempting to impose a tax to fund his participation in the Crusades, he provoked a rebellion and was forced in 1222 to sign a charter of rights called the **'Golden Bull'**, a sort of Magna Carta that decreed a yearly meeting (Diet) of nobles in Pest and curtailed the powers of the king. His son **Béla IV** (1235–70) was of a very different mould, but his rule was destined to overlap the devastating **Mongol invasion** of 1241–42, when the country was razed and vast swathes of the population massacred. He returned from exile determined to protect Hungary from future hostility – the country's first properly fortified castles, including that on Buda's Castle Hill, dated from the aftermath of the invasion – but the Mongols had wiped out a third of the population and he had to rely on the influx of German immigrants and the assistance of regional magnates. Civil war was almost inevitable in such raw circumstances, and Béla was forced to hand over half the country to his son; the barons capitalised, increasing their power by switching their support from one ruler to the other. The kingdom remained a turbulent one right up until the curtain was finally drawn on the Árpád line with the death of **András III** (1290–1301).

## The Golden Age

A series of foreign dynasties put forward claims to the vacant throne, but the struggle was eventually won by **Károly Robert** (1308–42), an Angevin (or Anjou) king from Naples with the backing of the pope. He settled things down, moving the court to a new palace at Visegrád to negate the threat of disgruntled nobles in Buda and stabilising the economy with proceeds from gold mines in the north. **Lajos the Great** (1342–82) continued the expansion and captured the Polish throne in 1370. When he died without a male heir, **Zsigmond of Luxembourg** (1387–1437) – later King of Bohemia and Holy Roman Emperor – took over; his reign coincided with Turkish expansionist ambitions in Europe which Zsigmond (continually flitting about his territories abroad) did very little to counter. The defeat of his armies at Nicopolis in 1396 signalled the beginning of the Ottoman charge into central Europe.

The Ottoman advance was halted at the **Battle of Nándorfehérvár** (now Belgrade) in 1456 when Hungary's greatest general, the Transylvanian Prince János Hunyadi, achieved a famous victory for which he was lauded as the saviour of Christendom. Pope Callixtus III declared that the noon Angelus should be prayed, and church bells rung across Catholic Europe in grateful remembrance. Hunyadi succumbed to the plague shortly afterwards, but in 1458 his teenage son **Mátyás** (1458–90) took the throne after victory in the baronial struggle that followed the death of Zsigmond's son László V. His reign proved something of a purple patch. The economy prospered, and Mátyás – known as 'Corvinus' after the raven in his coat of arms – and his Italian wife Beatrice made the court at Buda one of the centres of Renaissance art and learning. For men of letters, he put together a stunning library in one wing of the palace; for men of action, he set up the Black Army, one of Europe's first professional units. An able statesman and a famously fair man, he was deeply respected and even liked by his subjects – on his death, it was said truth had died with him. Hungary's political and cultural influence never again blossomed so fulsomely.

There was the familiar feudal infighting following Mátyás's demise, climaxing in the **Peasant Revolt** of 1514. This was provoked by increasing pressures put upon the peasantry by the noble landlords, and was enacted by a peasant army under György Dózsa that had originally been assembled by the Franciscans to embark on a crusade against the Turks. The rebellion made the ruling classes put aside their differences, and they united to crush the peasants ruthlessly – Dózsa was burnt to death on a metal throne – and enforced a Tripartitum law that reduced the peasants to a state of '**serfdom in perpetuity**' whereby they were tied to the estates of their landowning masters. It was a division that remained for several hundred years. Such turbulence, though, was as nothing compared with that to come.

## Turkish occupation

For Hungarians, August 29 1526 is the most tragic date in a past littered with them. On that day the Turks – who were on the march once more and had taken castles in Serbia before crossing the Drava – obliterated the Magyar army under Lajos II at **Mohács** in southern Hungary. Fifteen years later the Ottomans had conquered much of eastern and central Hungary. Lajos II had drowned while fleeing the battlefield, and in the urgent need to prevent the Turks mustering their forces and pressing on to Vienna, **Ferdinand I of Habsburg** (1526–64) – with a claim to the throne through the Habsburg brother-in-law of Zsigmond, who'd briefly ruled Hungary – moved into Transdanubia. Over subsequent years the Turks made further incursions into the north and across into Southern Transdanubia. Instances of bold, last-gasp resistance at the fortresses of Szigetvár and Eger are the stuff of folklore; it is equally true that Habsburg armies often sat back and watched blood spill from a distance, unwilling to risk their troops and ready to sacrifice Magyar fighters as long as the Turks were stalled. This naturally engendered a burning sense of betrayal in the towns that were captured, whose people had accepted Ferdinand's kingship in the expectation he would protect his territories. At the **Treaty of Adrianople** in 1568 the division of land was agreed: the Turks held the Great Plain, areas to the north of it and Transdanubia below Balaton; the west and north of Transdanubia and the remaining parts of the uplands in the north and northeast were subsumed into the Habsburg empire (with Royal Hungary's capital in Pozsony, or Bratislava); and Transylvania – much to the annoyance of the Habsburgs – retained its status as a semi-autonomous principality, permitted its own rulers on the condition of allegiance to the Turks.

Come the dawn of the 17th century, it seemed that Hungary was destined to remain divided in three for ever more. The **Fifteen Years War** (1593–1606) represented the only concerted early effort to boot out the Turks and integrate Transylvania into Royal

Hungary. It petered out having wreaked further damage and depopulation and achieved little beyond local successes. For their part, the Protestant **Transylvanian princes** – István Bocskai (1605–06) and Gábor Bethlen (1614–29) – were keen to shift the Catholic Habsburgs and reunite non-Turkish Hungary with Transylvania once more, often calling on mercenary Hajdúk (Heyduck) peasants soldiers to help in the effort. Imre Thököly led a failed revolt in 1682, but it was Ferenc Rákóczi whose name became synonymous with the anti-Habsburg fight in the early years of the next century. Meanwhile Turkish powers were fading. In 1686 a pan-European army evicted the Turks from Buda after a siege that lasted months, and in 1697 **Eugene of Savoy** secured the conclusive victory at Zenta (now in Serbia).

## Habsburg rule

The Habsburgs were in charge, but they certainly hadn't won over hearts and minds. The blunt policies of **Leopold I** (1657–1705) had made many enemies. Resentment had been heightened by the **Treaty of Vasvár** in 1664, when he handed back to the Turks areas that Hungarian General Miklós Zrínyi had only just recaptured. Like the Romans before, he was using Hungary to put distance between his empire and the threat (now Turkish rather than Germanic) to the east, and the impression he gave was that the bodies in between were dispensable in this cause. In response a **Hungarian plot** had been hatched in 1670; when uncovered, leaders including Péter Zrínyi were executed and the noble privileges dating to the 'Golden Bull' revoked. Counter-Reformatory measures (half the population was Protestant) became violent and land taken back from the Turks was given to favoured courtiers with no concern for legal claims of prior ownership. Against such a backdrop, resistance was gathered around the romantic figure of **Ferenc Rákóczi II**, a member of the Zrínyi plot spared because of his Catholic mother. Nobles and peasants joined the *kuruc* (independence fighters) forces and waged an eight-year rebellion partly financed by Louis XIV of France. The struggle eventually failed, but Rákóczi had been the first to muster Hungarians across the social spectrum in opposition to Habsburg rule.

After the wars, Hungary was but a province of the Habsburg empire, but under the enlightened absolutism of **Maria Theresa** (1740–80) it actually enjoyed a period of sustained growth. **József II** steeped himself in the ideas of the Enlightenment – he even refused to be crowned as he didn't believe in being tied by the Coronation Oath – and his rule divided attitudes. While he ruffled the feathers of feudal nobles by abolishing perpetual serfdom and insisting that German (rather than Latin) was the official language, he garnered support from progressive Hungarians like Ferenc Széchenyi. In part he was let down by tactlessness rather than malevolent intent. **Ferenc I** (1792–1835) was far more conservative; plagued by fear of the revolutionary fire that was raging in France, he came down heavily on a Jacobin plot of 1995 led by the priest Ignác Martinovics (who had ironically acted as a Crown informant in the past).

Despite this imperial conservatism, the first decades of the 19th century witnessed the **Age of Reform**, in large part spurred by aristocrats like Count **István Széchenyi** – 'the greatest Hungarian'. His progressive bourgeois vision was influenced by visits to England, and he inspired the founding of the Hungarian Academy of Sciences, the laying of the first railway line and the regulation of the Danube and Tisza rivers. While Széchenyi was radical in a practical sense, politically he was a believer in evolution rather than revolution; however, a group emerged that lacked his patience – its leading beacons Baron Miklós Wesselényi, poet Ferenc Kölcsey, Ferenc Deák and the eloquent lawyer Lajos Kossuth. Their desire to drag Hungary away from its feudal roots was coupled with resentment of absolutist rule by foreign monarchs who neither spoke their language (Ferenc József was the first to do so) nor spent much time on Magyar soil. While only 5% of adult males had the franchise, and Vienna ensured that the incumbent government had plenty of money to wine and dine come election time, there was nevertheless a groundswell of support for progressive reform both in the chambers of Parliament (or Diet) and beyond. Things were beginning to bubble.

## The 1848–49 War of Independence and the 1867 Compromise

The catalyst for change came during the revolutions that erupted in Europe in March 1848. The liberals grabbed their chance and the Diet passed a raft of Acts that became known as the **April Laws**. These extended the franchise, made the ministry responsible to Parliament alone, reunited Transylvania with the rest of Hungary and abolished the legal distinctions between citizens (including tax exemptions and the right of nobles to peasant services) – in effect laying the foundations for a constitutional monarchy and the consequent curtailment of royal power. The weak **Ferdinand V** (1835–48) wavered but eventually gave his royal assent and **Count Lajos Batthyány** was appointed as prime minister. However, the poet **Sándor Petőfi** and other young radicals gathered on the streets of Pest to demand that reforms go further, urging Hungarians to rise up in revolution.

In September the Habsburg forces responded by attacking Hungary, and a national defence committee was organised with **Kossuth** – 'the Moses of the Hungarians' – at its head. Initially the independence government – which in April 1849 declared the country free from the rule of Habsburg monarchy – was successful in pushing back the imperial armies. However, the new **Emperor Ferenc József** (1848–1916) enlisted reinforcements from the Russian Tsar Nicholas I, and the revolution was over by August. Petőfi had died in battle and Kossuth went into exile. The notorious Austrian Field Marshall Haynau – the 'Hyena of Brescia' – was tasked with putting on a show of Habsburg might. Batthyány was executed, together with 13 generals in Transylvania (the 'Martyrs of Arad'); thousands were imprisoned and thousands more fled abroad to escape reprisals.

However, renewed hope came more swiftly than expected. The Austrians suffered several defeats to Italian, French and Prussian armies, and – anxious to shore up the Habsburg empire – acceded to an agreement drawn up by the liberal politician **Ferenc Deák**. The **Compromise** (*Ausgleich* or *Kiegyezés*) of 1867 established a dual monarchy, whereby Hungary had its own government, parliament and even small army, but operated jointly with Austria in matters of foreign policy and defence. Hungarians were buoyant, the economy boomed and there was a flurry of cultural and creative activity most evident during the **millennial celebrations** of 1896 commemorating the Magyar conquest. A mighty exhibition showcased Hungarian technology and achievement in Budapest's City Park, and ambitious building programmes were undertaken in the capital and beyond. Not all was rosy though. Minorities in particular felt oppressed by nationalist domestic policies of '**Magyarisation**'; these stemmed from the urge to re-establish a firm sense of national identity, for so long suppressed under the occupation of foreign powers, and demanded full cultural assimilation from non-Magyars. By the early 20th century, there were also discontented stirrings from society's disenfranchised lower echelons.

## The World Wars

Hungary was tied to Austria through thick and thin – and in the early years of the Compromise few could see past the current thick to the possible thin, dangerous times ahead. Those came with a bang in 1914. In June a Serbian youth assassinated Archduke Ferenc Ferdinand, the heir to the thrones of Austria and Hungary. Despite the initial objections of Hungarian Prime Minister István Tisza, war was declared on Serbia in July. The Austro-Hungarian empire was decisively defeated in **World War I**, and the Habsburg monarchy collapsed. In the aftermath, a short-lived communist regime known as the **Republic of Councils** was established for 133 days under Béla Kun – using 'Red Terror' to impose nationalisation of land. On June 4 1920 Hungary was forced by the victorious powers to sign the uncompromising **Treaty of Trianon**, which handed two-thirds of its territory to neighbouring countries that even included Austria. Three million Magyars found themselves sudden exiles in foreign states. This division of countryman from countryman had a lasting impact on Hungarian culture and sense of self, and the memory of 'Greater Hungary' – and the treatment of ethnic Hungarians in Romania and elsewhere – remains a hot topic to this day. The exiled Magyars frequently met with little sympathy from those of the Successor States of which they were now members – memories of the punitive measures imposed on minorities who resisted 19th-century 'Magyarisation' remained fresh.

A counter-revolutionary army had begun to form at Szeged; it was headed by **Admiral Miklós Horthy** – the last commander of the Austro-Hungarian fleet that had been bottled up in the Adriatic during the war – who targeted 'Reds' in a regime of 'White Terror' at the other end of the political spectrum and displayed ruthless elements of anti-semitism. When Horthy rode into Budapest with his troops in November 1919, Kun fled abroad (ultimately to be executed by Stalin during 'purges' of the 1930s) and on March 1 1920 Horthy was elected Regent (as the self-declared representative of exiled Habsburg Emperor Karl IV). Horthy led a **right-wing dictatorship** whose policies were conservative, anti-semitic and nationalistic. Its primary aim was to retrieve the lands stripped from Hungary at Trianon, an ambition supported universally by Hungarians. Prime Minister **István Bethlen** (1921–31) was an able administrator well-regarded by the Allied powers, and a few concessions were secured (such as the return of Sopron and Kőszeg after referendums); on the home front, Count Bethlen helped to develop industry and education, stabilise the economy and tone down some of the anti-semitic extremes. However, he leant towards the Catholic Church and the landowners, and the agricultural workers in particular were subject to restrictive controls designed to protect the interests of the gentry. The urge to find a way of reclaiming land confiscated at Trianon, together with the right-wing bent of the governing class, inevitably pushed Hungary towards alliance with fascist Germany.

In 1941 – against the advice of Prime Minister Teleki, who subsequently committed suicide – Horthy supported Germany in the **unprovoked attack** upon Yugoslavia. Hungary was rewarded with the return of some lost lands, but it was now inextricably and actively involved in **World War II**, and its army suffered very heavily on the eastern front. When Horthy secretly entered into negotiation with the Allies, the Germans learned of the betrayal and **occupied** the country in March 1944. They installed the leader of the Hungarian Nazis (the **Arrow-Cross Party**) at the head of the government, ushering in the horrors of the **Holocaust**. Ghettos were established and Adolf Eichmann oversaw a programme of deportation of Jews to death camps that started in the countryside and moved in towards Budapest. Only the intervention of Horthy and the actions of Raoul Wallenberg (the Swedish diplomat), Carl Lutz (the Swiss consul) and the Catholic Church saved those in the capital from the wholesale deportation that was carried out in the rest of the country. The end was nigh for the Germans, however, as the Russians advanced from the east and, after a viciously contested siege at Buda, the Germans finally fled in April 1945.

## The communist years

The communists came to power in 1947 on the back of a campaign of intimidation and a rigged election. **Mátyás Rákosi** – acting in total subservience to Moscow – imposed a **Stalinist dictatorship** between 1947 and 1953, emulating his mentor in the brutal use of spies, torture and murder. Private businesses were nationalised without compensation, peasants were forced into state farms and the feared ÁVO – the secret police – conducted their dark operations from headquarters at Andrássy út 60 in Budapest. Over 500,000 people were executed or jailed in labour camps at home (there was one at Recsk) or in the Soviet Union. Rákosi's position was undermined by Stalin's death in 1953, and **Imre Nagy** – a reformist in the Communist Party – took over as prime minister. He was expelled for introducing mild reforms, but the spectre of a kindly, humane communism had been raised.

On October 23 1956 a student demonstration in Budapest demanded democracy, neutrality in foreign policy and the reinstatement of Nagy. After gathering for a tentative speech by Nagy outside Parliament, some split off to the radio station on Bródy utca with the intention of voicing their feelings more widely. As they attempted to enter, they were fired upon by members of the ÁVO and peaceful protest flared into **revolution**. The statue of Stalin that stood to the south of City Park was broken to pieces. Nagy set up an administration, declared the country's withdrawal from the Warsaw Pact, and looked hopefully to the West for recognition and assistance. However, Western powers were focused upon the Suez crisis, and – after bloody street fighting – Soviet tanks brutally suppressed the revolution. The Russian military placed **János Kádár** in charge of the 'Revolutionary Worker-Peasant' government; pacification and stabilisation of the country featured the execution of 2,000, the arrest of 20,000, and the shipping off of many more to Soviet labour camps. Around 200,000 people – two per cent of the population – fled to the West, a serious leak of enterprising young talent (the average age was just 20). Nagy was imprisoned and quietly exterminated in 1958; his body, along with many others, was laid in a distant corner of Budapest's Újköztemető (New Public Cemetery), in overgrown 'Plot 301'.

Initially repressive in consolidating his position, and hated for being the Soviets' man, once Kádár was entrenched he managed a delicate balancing act, both appeasing Soviets and introducing liberal policies that gradually thawed the frost between the governing and the governed. Where Rákosi had declared 'Those who are not with us are against us', Kádár's appeasing mantra was 'Those who are not against us are with us'. He instituted a platform of national reconciliation, and from 1968 implemented a programme of radical economic reforms. This 'market socialism' was nicknamed **'Goulash Communism'** abroad, and led to strengthened relations with the West. It also further relieved domestic tensions and gradually improved living standards; Hungary was known as the 'happiest barracks in the Bloc'.

## The fall of communism

By 1988 Kádár was struggling to control a spiralling economic crisis and was finally dismissed after a remarkable 32 years of cautiously responsive rule that had successfully prevented a return to tyranny and revolution. The MSZMP (Hungarian Socialist Workers' Party) recognised the shape of things to come and permitted a series of 'round table' discussions with 'non-official' new 'opposition' parties – the first move positively towards democracy proper. The sign that the worm had turned irrevocably in the modern history of Hungarian politics came during the **reburial of Imre Nagy** in 1989. In a reconciliatory act on the anniversary of the executions, Nagy (and other victims of the revolution) were reburied in a spruced-up Plot 301. During the ceremony a young hippie of a student, Viktor Orbán, gave voice to what many were thinking in demanding that Soviet troops leave his country. The last soldier did so on June 19 1991.

As the Iron Curtain began to draw back, Hungary played a significant role in pulling the cord. Gyula Horn (the foreign minister) allowed East Germans to climb into their Trabants and sputter through the country to reach the West. A picnic was held on the border with Austria, after which East Germans crossed a field where the dividing barbed wire had been symbolically cut. In 1989, the reform communists declared the advent of **party-political democracy**; the first free elections in March 1990 resulted in a coalition led by the Hungarian Democratic Forum (Magyar Demokrata Forum – MDF), who campaigned on a blend of conservative and nationalist policies. The first president of the new democracy was the enduringly popular Árpád Göncz, a Free Democrat (SzDSz) translator and author who had been imprisoned after 1956. With a quiet simplicity wholly alien to significant events in Hungary's history, the communists had been voted out. The People's Republic of Hungary became the Republic of Hungary, and the contemporary era of parliamentary democracy had begun. (For details of the landscape since, see *Politics* and *Economy* below.)

## POLITICS
### Democratic Hungary

In the 15 years since the *rendszerváltás* (change of political system), Hungarian politics has been consistent only in its swinging backwards and forwards between left and right (or, more accurately, centre-left and centre-right). In 1994, the **Socialist Party** (Magyar Szocialista Párt – MSzP) returned to power on the back of a feeling of nostalgia for past stability. The MSzP and its liberal Free Democrat (Szabad Demokraták Szövetsége – SzDSz) coalition partner were led by Gyula Horn, the man who had waved through the soap dishes on their journey to the West five years earlier. The government introduced an 'austerity package' to set the country back on course towards EU membership.

A policy with 'austerity' as its mantra – however well meant – is rarely a vote winner, and in 1998 (when the four-year tenure came to an end) the country inevitably looked rightwards once more in electing a third party, **Fidesz** (Fiatal Demokraták Szövetsége). This Alliance of Young Democrats was originally formed in the late 1980s by Viktor Orbán, who had spoken with such passion and charisma at Nagy's funeral. In the early days the party was characterised by youthful liberalism, but it became increasingly conservative in the ensuing decade. Orbán began to promote staunchly conservative, Christian family values – 'God, Homeland, Family' ('*Isten, Haza, Család*'). In a move rich with political, religious and social meaning, Orbán shifted the iconic symbol of Hungary – the crown of St István – from the National Museum to the Parliament building.

As for international ties, Hungary joined **NATO** in 1999, and for many years there was a US military base at Taszár. Opened in 1995, it attracted its share of controversy. Although built to provide backup for peacekeepers serving in Bosnia, in 1999 it was used as a launch pad for NATO air strikes against Serbia during the Kosovo crisis. The action was unpopular in Hungary, where there was much sympathy for the Hungarian minority living in the Vojvodina region. The US air force withdrew in June 2004.

In 2002, the country elected the socialist **MSzP** once more (again with coalition partners SzDSz). The elections were savage and the socialists' victory tiny (a majority of just ten seats). So narrow was the margin that Fidesz refused to accept the result, and established local action groups, Civic Circles (Polgári Kör), to drum up support in the countryside (where conservative values still predominate). Despite being slender, however, the majority of the centre-left coalition – similar in many respects to a Western European social-democratic government – initially proved stable. There are signs though that things are getting rocky, with polls showing the government losing ground rapidly to Fidesz. The current prime minister (elected in September 2004), Ferenc Gyurcsány, is one of the richest men in Hungary – for which he is regarded with deep suspicion by older Hungarians who find it difficult to believe that such a fortune could be earned legally. He is a protégé of his predecessor, Péter Medgyessy, who steered Hungary into the **EU** on May 1 2004 (see page 24) but who quit after a poor showing by the MSzP in the European election the following summer (when the socialists won just nine of Hungary's 24 seats – to Fidesz's 12). Gyurcsány models himself on Tony Blair, and has made it his mission to revitalise the Socialist Party.

The climate remains discouraging for him. The 2005 presidential election (characterised by particularly vociferous bickering all round) was won narrowly by the nominee of the centre-right opposition, former chief justice of the Constitution Court

## A CAR FOR THE PEOPLE

**Q** 'How do you double the value of a Trabant?'
**A** 'Fill it with petrol.'

The Berlin Wall fell in 1989, but the blue-smoke-belching Trabant – symbol of the old communist era – is still a visible presence. City governments have tried to run it off the road, but people love their 'soap dishes'. Owners were offered a BKV transport pass worth 30,000Ft in 1995 as an incentive to trade in their Trabis; of 300,000 on the road, just 200 were handed in. The Budapest city government recently increased the reward to 200,000Ft.

During the 1960s and '70s, the waiting list for a Trabi was 15 years long. It cost a year's wages for an average Hungarian worker, and came in beige, light blue or olive green. On delivery, new owners were advised to tighten visible screws and grease all working parts. In actual fact it was never meant to be a car, but a rainproof motorcycle with a boot, and thus cheap transport for all the family. It was an innovation in the 1950s, the engine so light it could be lifted out by one man – rally-racing Trabants often carried a spare in the boot. In a 'reindeer test' – which simulates the ability of a car to avoid an obstacle (such as an animal) at speed – the Trabant apparently bettered a Mercedes. It was handmade of Duroplast – a mixture of compressed resin and polyester – and is light, rust-proof and cheap. However, it is also totally non-recyclable, has the acceleration of an overweight slug and gets reduced to smithereens in a collision.

In the last days of the Berlin Wall, rickety East German Trabants escaping to the West through Hungarian territory became symbols of freedom. Consumerism, however, and the competing claims of shiny Audis and Fiats, meant it quickly reverted to a sad symbol of socialism: inefficient and dull. There were even small ads in local papers offering to swap cars for packets of cigarettes. The Trabi gained cult status in the West, though; in the early 1990s, U2 took a fleet of them on tour as part of their *Achtung Baby* set.

The last Trabant was made in 1992, but Zwickau in the former East Germany (where it was manufactured) remains a place of pilgrimage for the annual rally, attended by enthusiasts from all over Europe. The proudly ugly Trabi has outlived the demise of the system and the factory, and remains the most communist car of all – a true car for the people.

László Sólyom. The president (whose official residence is the Sándor Palace) serves for five years, and has relatively little executive power under the constitution, but does provide a check on the constitutionality of government legislation. Perhaps of greater significance is the prevailing political mood that the result represents; it is undoubtedly a boost for Viktor Orbán's future election hopes. We shall wait and see.

While smooth and unbloody, the transition from the rule of state to democratic government was nevertheless a significant social, ideological and political change that took place just 15 years ago. The swing-ball nature of the country's elections is an understandable feature of a system still bedding in. If we are looking for regional voting trends, then as a rule the SzDSz only has support among city liberals, while people in the countryside tend to be more conservative and Fidesz-leaning. Parliament is a more exciting place, and a centre of lively argument; it is also a place where debate is often confrontational, and focused upon political points-scoring rather than genuine policy differences. Where consensus comes in the parliamentary chamber is over Euro-Atlantic integration and the development of a free-market economy. And always hovering in the background is the cultural issue of the territory Hungary lost after World War I and the millions of ethnic Hungarians living beyond the re-defined borders.

### The process and the parties

Parliamentary elections are held every four years (the last in 2002) on the basis of a complicated, 'mixed' system. The country is broken down into constituencies, in each of which citizens vote for their preferred candidate; in a first-past-the-post system, the one with the majority is elected to parliament. At the same time, however, voters also indicate their choice of party. For this the system is proportionate, and parties receive their mandates according to the percentage of votes they win. At least 5% is required for parliamentary representation. There are 386 MPs in the Hungarian Parliament; 176 MPs are elected from the constituencies, while the rest of the MPs are appointed from the list of parties.

The **main political parties** are the Hungarian Socialist Party (MSzP), Alliance of Free Democrats (SzDSz), Hungarian Civic Alliance (Fidesz-MPP), Hungarian Democratic Forum (MDF), Hungarian Workers' Party (MMP), Hungarian Justice and Life Party (MIEP), Christian Democratic People's Party (KDNP), and Hungarian Democratic People's Party (MDNP).

## ECONOMY

Hungary has made the most successful transition of all the new EC member states from a centrally planned to a **market economy**, and continues to demonstrate strong growth. The economy is helped by a lower level of the corruption that is prevalent in other new member states. It has brought under control the high inflation that characterised the early years after its change of political system – from 14% as late as 1998 to 4% in 2005 – and its reward was admittance to the EU in May 2004. The **private sector** accounts for over 80% of GDP, and foreign investment in (and ownership of) Hungarian firms has been a primary force in this economic success. Since 1989, direct foreign investment has amounted to around US$25 billion, attracted by relatively low working costs and wages, and an educated workforce. The national unemployment rate is now under 6%, although there are wide regional variations. Western Europe is Hungary's principal export market, and Germany her most significant economic partner. GDP has increased by almost 4% each year since joining the EU.

Standing at its crossroads, **Budapest** has emerged as the financial and commercial hub of central Europe. It is inevitably at the forefront of Hungary's economy, and consequently of its economic growth. It is here that the country's important transport arteries are gathered and it is here that 60% of foreign capital investment is funnelled. The unemployment rate is just 2.4%, the GDP per capita is a staggering 90% higher than the average, and the capital generates 35% of the national income. Reform of cumbersome welfare provisions will be a necessary future part of strengthening Hungary's economy.

### EU Membership

On May 1 2004, ten acceding eastern European and Mediterranean countries joined the European Union. Hungary was among them, and the economic effect of this membership is likely to be profound. On accession, Hungary's 10.1 million population had a per capita GDP of £6,975/US$12,515. Average earnings were €5,870. And of all the joining countries, Hungary's Northern Great Plain enjoys (or doesn't!) the lowest per capita GDP at only 34% of the existing EU states' average. Compared with the £16,192/US$29,052 per capita GDP of the existing 15 member states at date of entry,

Hungary clearly has some catching up to do. Its prospects are encouraging; annual industrial production output has risen by nearly 10% since EU entry. As the EU expands eastwards, we are seeing inward investment and a rise in manufacturing. Investors are taking advantage of the freedom of movement of goods inherent in the principle of single-market free trade, combined with the benefits of Hungary's stable political and economic climate and its cheaper and energetic young workforce.

Having said that, the transition isn't an easy one, either economically or politically. After experiencing a crisis with the forint in April 2003, exchange-rate stability has returned. Proper management of the currency will be key to Hungary's success when entering the EU's Exchange Rate Mechanism before the eventual planned adoption of the euro. Hungary's lingering Soviet-era state bureaucracy still finds itself unprepared to enforce the EU's legally binding regulations and directives. EU rules on food, water control and pollution challenge Hungary's current political administration and business culture – and these have applied from day one, while the advantages of Common Agricultural Policy food subsidies and generous state benefits will not equal that of the existing states for another nine years. It is to be hoped that the dynamism of Hungary's educated youth will rapidly overcome the current gap in living standards, as happened when Spain and Portugal joined the EU in the mid-1980s.

## PEOPLE

> When a Hungarian enjoys himself, he will cast himself on to a bench, lean
> his arms on the table amidst the bottles and glasses, put his head down on
> them and sob audibly… But this is only when he is having a good time
> and thoroughly enjoying himself.
>
> H Ellen Browning, *A Girl's Wandering in Hungary* (1897)

Pick up a guidebook – any guide to any destination – and you'll invariably read of a country whose people are unrivalled in toothy bonhomie. Well, the Hungarians don't fit this global community of Cheshire cats. They are a rare and intriguing breed that looks on the gloomier side of life, who notice the cloud from afar but develop myopia when it comes to its lining. They acknowledge this trait, although typically describing it as 'realism'. They are more Eeyore than Tigger, and hooray for that.

We can look to history to make sense of this tendency towards pessimism. Foreign nations (Ottomans, Habsburgs, Germans and Soviets) have conspired to subject the people and destroy their precious monuments. The Treaty of Trianon stripped the country of two-thirds of its territory. Borders have buckled through the ages, and five million ethnic Hungarians are now 'exiles', dividing families and isolating pockets of the populace. The upshot is a social psyche that expects to be dealt the rough cards in any hand. On an individual level, this melancholy can manifest itself in tragic ways. It is estimated that alcoholism is a problem for 10%, and Hungary used to top the 'suicide league table'.

It is therefore surprising that Hungarians are neither lethargic nor submissive; on the contrary, they are fiercely patriotic and take deep pride in their past heroic struggles against oppression. Countless towns and villages are pieces of standing proof of a willingness to rebuild – repeatedly – from conflict's rubble. They have been resourceful, energetic and inventive, claiming a clutch of Nobel prizes and making a bigger splash in the spheres of science, music and medicine than their population size entitles them. As the proverb states, 'only a Hungarian can enter a revolving door behind you and come out in front'. Such nationhood and high achievement stem from a desperate urge to resist forces that might snuff them out.

The issue of where the country stands in relation to its past divides Hungarians. Some

## THE NAME GAME

What's in a name? Nothing, it seems, as long as it's not that of Belgian movie star Jean-Claude van Damme or former communist leader János Kádár. These were among those submitted to – and rejected by – the Interior Ministry last year. Hungarians are obliged to choose names from an official list, a practice introduced under the communists; while Rózsa would no doubt smell as sweet by any other name, that other name had better be in the approved 'Ládó' book.

Those wishing to deviate from the list must apply for permission, and unusual or foreign-sounding names are often turned down. There are exceptions; 'Jennifer', for instance – very possibly popularised by singer Jennifer Lopez – has made it into the 1,900 permitted first names as 'Dzsenifer'. Historical names are also protected, and applicants would usually have to prove a familial link. Typical requests for name changes come from married women starting in business who want to free themselves of 'né' (see below), or from Roma looking to disguise their roots after marrying non-Roma.

Registered forenames are assigned a calendar 'name day' (névnap), which is celebrated with cards and gifts. (The name-day calendar can be found at www.behindthename.com/namedays/hungarian.) A married woman may either retain her maiden name or adopt her husband's with the appendage 'né' ('belonging to'). As such, if Szabó Anna married Kovács János, she could call herself one of four versions: Kovács Jánosné, Kovácsné Szabó Anna, Kovács Jánosné Szabó Anna or just Szabó Anna. Confused? Well you'll be dismayed to hear that, in addition to all this, in Hungary surnames appear in front of forenames...

– more usually city folk – are westward-facing Europeans. Others are fervent nationalists who believe in a Greater Hungary. They stress the importance of ancient tradition, of their Asiatic roots, and are frequently suspicious of the liberal cosmopolitanism (by which they usually mean 'Jewish-ness') of Budapest. Some right-wing politicians have played upon geographical insecurities, positioning Hungary as an island in a sea of Slav, surrounded by neighbours they cannot trust. This fear of anything that isn't 'pure Magyar' can seem strange when common surnames like Németh (meaning 'German'), Tóth (Slovak), Horváth (Croatian) and Orosz (Russian) are indicative of a more mixed heritage. Nevertheless, such isolationist views make prejudice common; while there is growing public discussion about the shame of the Hungarian Holocaust, anti-Semitism is not unusual and dislike of the Roma minority is often openly expressed. Hungary also lags behind some Western countries in their ready acceptance of feminist views and alternative lifestyles (such as homosexuality).

If it seems paradoxical (even oxymoronic) to talk of people as proud pessimists or suicidal self-improvers, there are other ways in which the coin of the Hungarian national character has two apposite sides. As we've said, Hungarians – even urbanists and the young – are inherently conservative and home loving, preferring the Magyar way of life. Yet they can also be wholly lacking in prudery. The pornography business is strong in Budapest, and porn stars like Michelle Wild and Monique Covet household names who appear regularly on breakfast television. And while the people are reserved, their social codes based on formality and politeness, you may find this difficult to credit in some restaurants, where it is quickly clear that the service industry has yet to recover fully from 40 years of communism.

The Hungarian character evades simple stereotypes. This is a race of people made tough by repeated slaps from history's hand; it is also one with stamina, with resourceful answers to difficult questions, and with a little less of the commercial superficiality so familiar in the West. Tourists will find that the Budapest boulevard is a purposeful place where people hurry about their business. There are few exchanged smiles on the metro. However, there is never any sense in which this is intimidating or uncomfortable, and it masks a genuine and earnest helpfulness that lurks close beneath the surface. A terse face can be transformed by 'köszönöm' from a foreign tongue, and more sustained interaction reveals an openness, an engaging and sophisticated humour, and a commitment to friendship that is all the more valuable because not casually offered.

The **ethnic make up** of Hungary is 89.9% Hungarian, 4% Roma, 2.6% German, 2% Serb, 0.8% Slovak, 0.7% Romanian.

## RELIGION

Those who regularly attend church are in a minority in Hungary, especially in the cities. **Roman Catholicism** (*Katolikus*) is the main religious denomination (67.5% of Hungarians). István, Hungary's first king, introduced Christianity as the religion of state over a thousand years ago, and it survived in spite of sustained Turkish occupation (when many Hungarians converted temporarily to Islam) and the secularity of communist rule. The largest **Protestant** denomination is the Calvinist or Reformed Church (*Református*; 20% of the population), followed by the Lutherans/Evangelicals (*Evangélikus*; 5%).

Seven per cent are listed as affiliated to other religious orders that include **Serb** and **Greek Orthodox** (*Szerb/Görög ortodox*) and **Judaism** (*zsidó vallás*). Before World War II, Budapest had one of the most significant Jewish communities in the world, estimated at 200,000. However, over half perished during the Holocaust, and after the war only 90,000 Jews remained in the city; populations beyond the capital were all but wiped out during the programme of deportation to Nazi concentration camps. Numbers dwindled further still under communist rule, particularly following the 1956 revolution. The demise of communism saw a revival of sorts, and today 80,000 Jews live in Budapest (the biggest community in central Europe), a number that continues to grow. In addition, as in most post-communist countries, Hungary is seen as fertile ground for the 'new' **religions**; Mormons, Hari Krishna, Faith Congregation and Scientologists are all commonly found on the streets and subways.

## CULTURE
### Literature and art

Hungary has a proud cultural history, but much of its output remains closed to a world that can't speak the tongue. Some of the finest **literature** is set in regions now beyond the country's borders, and represents the constant prick of loss. An early narrative of roaming Magyars fleeing hostile foes in their own land has a strong hold, while there's a tradition of rebellion, isolation and despair among the popular songbooks. The most renowned writers hark from the Romantic age, kings among them being the young revolutionary poet Sándor Petőfi (see page 342) and his friend János Arany. Others you'll come across – often through the names of streets or squares – are the Romanticists Ferenc Kölcsey (author of the national anthem) and Mihály Vörösmarty, the late-19th-century Realists József Eötvös and Mór Jókai, the anguished Endre Ady and the Expressionistic, avant-garde and ultimately suicidal Attila József. In October 2002, Imre Kertész – author of *Sorstalanság* (*Fateless*), a shocking Holocaust novel – won the Nobel Prize for Literature.

Your best bet for getting a flavour of the nation's **art** is to take a spin around the Hungarian National Gallery (see page 166), which encompasses ecclesiastical works – medieval panel paintings and 18th-century masterpieces by F A Maulbertsch (responsible for the wondrous 'Rococo Sistine Chapel' at Sümeg) – as well as late-Renaissance and Baroque courtly portraits. The emergence of recognisably 'Hungarian' art came during the 19th-century creative explosion that went hand in hand with a thriving economy and a new national self-confidence. The Romantic Historicist works of Bertalan Székely (1835–1910) and Gyula Benczúr (1844–1920) were accompanied by pieces of Impressionism by László Paál (1846–79) and Realism by Mihály Munkácsy (1844–1900). The turn of the 20th century saw the establishment of deeply influential artists' colonies at Nagybánya and Gödöllő, each turning away from rigid formalism, the latter by seeking inspiration from folk art. Also of this period were the Post-Impressionist paintings of József Rippl-Rónai (1861–1927) and the vast and visionary canvases of Tivadar Csontváry Kosztka (1853–1919). The Expressionists Gyula Derkovits and József Egry produced inter-war works, while the best-known painter after that, Victor Vasarely (1908–97), created most of his ground-breaking Op-Art in Paris after emigrating in 1930. As for sculptors, 20th-century favourites include Zsigmond Kisfaludi Strobl (1884–1975), notorious for his 'pragmatism' in adapting his output to suit the prevailing political climate, the ceramicist Margit Kovács (1902–77), and Imre Varga, whose polished-metal creations are fabulous (and whom you might bump into during a visit to his collection in Óbuda; see page 168).

While **folk art** is still alive and kicking in areas of Transylvania, within Hungary's borders it's largely the stuff of museums and the odd decorated interior of a Calvinist church. It represents the untutored work of peasant families jazzing up their immediate surroundings with painted domestic items like headboards and chests, patterned or grooved pottery and clothes or bedspreads embroidered with vivid thread. The clearest attempt to preserve (and market) folk heritage can be seen from the Palóc people of Hollókő in the Northern Uplands, but the Mátyó group from Mezőkövesd also has a strong tradition, and the women of Kalocsa are famous for painting the living spaces of their houses. During the search for a Hungarian sense of nationhood in the late 19th and early 20th centuries, these vernacular forms had a significant impact upon 'high art'.

## Music

If Hungary needs a cultural ambassador, it surely has one in its exotic music. The famous big hitters were of course Ferenc Liszt, Béla Bartók and Zoltán Kodály, each an established name in the canon of European composers. To try to isolate and define Hungarian music would be to overlook the fact that its *diversity* is intrinsic to understanding this corner of the world. The musical landscape in central Europe reflects a tangled web of historical relationships and influences. The base layer is closely related to the folk music of Turkic and Finno-Ugric peoples from the Urals and Siberia (as uncovered by Kodály and his colleagues in the early 20th century). There has also been mutual borrowing from regional traditions – Slavonic, Romany, Jewish and more. It's certainly rich territory for the ethno-musicologist.

That with greatest popular resonance is gypsy music, performed by the dazzling dynasties that have enchanted visitors for centuries. Haydn, who was in the service of the Esterházy family for most of his life, drew extensively upon the gypsy strains around him; Beethoven and Schubert were frequent visitors and Hungarian music informed their work; two of Brahms' major influences were Hungarian concert violinists, and his series of Hungarian dances came as no surprise. The first Hungarian-born composer to achieve fame in Europe was Liszt; although he only lived in Budapest for a few years, he left a lasting legacy by founding the Academy of Music (see page 172). Bartók and Kodály studied and taught at the academy, and it has since produced many other students who have spread Hungarian traditions across the world.

These days, the minimalist textures of modern composer György Ligeti are helping to carry on the Hungarian claim to musical pre-eminence – his compositions featured in *2001 A Space Odyssey*, and his was the eerie piano music in Stanley Kubrick's *Eyes Wide Shut* – while the haunting vocals of folk singer Márta Sebestyén can be heard at the beginning of *The English Patient*. The contemporary Hungarian music scene is one of the most intriguing faces of cultural change underway in the country.

## STRINGY MASTERS

We can attribute the current abundance of distinguished Hungarian string players to one man: Jenő Hubay. A pupil of Brahms' Hungarian-born friend Ede Reményi, he was the Academy of Music's Professor of Violin between 1886 and 1934 and his chair one of the foremost centres of its kind in Europe. A skilled composer and conductor, he was also a breathtaking virtuoso. However, his greatest achievement was to mould two generations of talented violin and viola players. The individual characteristics of the 'Hubay school' have roots both in the Paris and Brussels traditions and in the virtuoso Hungarian gypsy violinists whom, like Liszt, he much admired. Chamber music was an organic part of his teaching creed. With the Austrian cellist David Popper, he formed the Hubay-Popper quartet – the outstanding Hungarian quartet of the 20th century. Other quartets taught by Hubay and Popper followed throughout the century, and eminent soloists (like today's internationally renowned Barnabás Kelemen) achieved fame after serving apprenticeships under students of those two.

In the 1980s the first chamber orchestra playing period instruments was created in Hungary. Since then orchestras like the Capella Savaria and Concerto Armonico have gained international recognition. Hungary has no fewer than three excellent period-instrument string quartets; the first of them, the Festetics Quartet, is well known outside Hungary, while the violinists István Kertész, László Paulik and Zsolt Kalló and the cellist Balázs Máté travel the globe as soloists, quartet players, leaders of orchestras or teachers.

Within Hungary, there is no shortage of music companies or venues. Budapest has five symphony orchestras, two opera houses, the Art-Nouveau Great Hall of the Academy of Music (with its perfect acoustics) and the newly opened Palace of Arts (see page 122). All the large cities have their own opera companies and orchestras, and in addition to the standard music arenas you'll be tripping over tickets for concerts hosted in churches and former synagogues around the country. As for annual events, the capital hosts two major arts festivals (the Spring and Autumn festivals), while regional highlights include Miskolc's Bartók Plus opera festival in June, the Sopron Festival (especially the Sopron Early Music Weeks), also in June, the Zemplén Art Days in August (with events in castles, churches and villages halls) and 'Haydn at Esterháza' at Fertőd in August/September.

### Folk music

Stifled under communism because nationalistic songs were out of keeping with the professed internationalist ethic, folk music now thrives again. The early 1970s saw the emergence of the *táncház* ('dance house') movement, a custom imported from Transylvania in which young villagers would hold a dance in a rented house. The roots of its appearance can be traced to a reaction against sanitised State ensembles, a sense of national pride, a concern for the Magyar minority in Transylvania (where the best music was concentrated), and the influence of research into folk culture by Béla Bartók, Zoltán Kodály, Zoltán Kallós and others. Young urbanites travelled to rural communities to learn and preserve dying traditional music and dances. They then played and taught these to those in cities. Béla Halmos is an outstanding name in this folk-music renaissance. Such dance houses continue. They are usually held in cultural centres, where traditional dance is accompanied by folk music played on traditional instruments by groups like Muzsikás. Visitors take an active part in the dance, or sit around with glasses of *pálinka* and watch as musicians play and dancers dance. Dance houses take place less often in summer. (For *táncház* venues in Budapest, see page 125.)

For other folk music experiences, try listening to Kaláka, or Muzsikás with Márta Sebestyén. Other notable groups exemplifying distinctive regional music styles include the renowned ambassadors of *klezmer* (a Jewish folk tradition originating in central and eastern Europe) the Budapest Klezmer Band and purveyors of Croatian dance Vujicsics. (There are regular performances by such groups at cultural centres like Fonó in Budapest; see page 125.)

## Gypsy music

The distinctive and passionate violin-playing of the gypsy bands epitomises the rich and individual identity of Hungarian music. With flamboyance and impromptu innovation, the Roma performers bring an interpretation of the indigenous folk music of Hungary, helping to close the divide between two oft-clashing cultures. It is important to recognise, however, that this is not the traditional music of the Roma – their songs, sung in the Romany language, are for private consumption. Instead gypsy bands perform centuries-old Hungarian popular songs (known as *Magyar nóta*), the themes rooted in sentimentally romanticised versions of the gypsy way of life; the agony of love lost or unrequited and the turbulent history of Hungary's oppression also find outlet in the gypsy tradition. Go to any traditional Hungarian restaurant and you will be serenaded at your table by a violinist of virtuosity (if you are lucky), supported by a strange and characteristically Magyar dulcimer known as the *cimbalom*. (To hear the instrument's capabilities explored in full, look out for Balogh Kálmán and the Gipsy Cimbalom Band.) Be aware that if the musicians approach your table, and you accept their invitation to play, they will expect to be tipped at the end of the performance. If you are interested in hearing true gypsy music – or modern renditions of it – then Parno Graszt, Romano Drom, Kalyi Jag and Ternipe are all bands that work in the Romany strand. Beyond this true gypsy music and the *Magyar nóta*, there is also the peasant music discovered by the Bartók-Kodály generation that has almost nothing to do with the popular song tradition. The *táncház* movement mainly resurrected the instrumental part of this; the vocal repertoire has often been arranged in the compositions of Bartók and Kodály (and their successors), and was part of the musical curriculum in schools from the 1930s.

## Jazz

Jazz fans might try the Dresch Mihály Quartet or the Balázs Elemér Group, while the upcoming group The Next Generation is made up of highly talented young musicians in their teens and 20s. Admirers of instrumental virtuosity should make a note of pianist Béla Szakcsi Lakatos and his son Robi, the latter a rising star in his own right. Dynamic young violinist Lajkó Félix – imagine a kind of Balkan Nigel Kennedy – from northern Serbia now lives and regularly performs in Budapest. The very young and very alternative jazz group Punch boasts a fantastic female player called Luca Kézdy, an artist with a crystal-clear tone and endless musical fantasy.

## Popular music

In the second half of last century, while rock and roll boomed in the West, Hungarians only had access to it via Radio Luxembourg and Radio Free Europe (which were illegal). Communism prohibited commercial radio, and the musical diet was officially limited. During this era underground radio played a crucial counter-establishment role, both cultural and political (indeed, some people partly attribute the bloody 1956 Hungarian uprising to its subversive influence). As a consequence, Hungarians are even now 'catching up' with some of the music that passed them by – and it hardly needs stating that Hungarian classic rock is unknown in the West. Although local rock bands required a permit to play for live audiences, there were some very successful home-grown artists in the 1960s and '70s (such as Bikini, LGT, Illés, Metró and Omega).

## CHEESY CHAT-UP LINES

Your eyes meet over a crowded bar and only language is the barrier to romance. Here are some cheesy chat-up lines to smooth love's path.

| | |
|---|---|
| Do you come here often? | *Gyakran jársz ide?* |
| Can I buy you a drink? | *Meghívhatlak egy italra?* |
| What are you drinking, girls? (to more than one, keeping options open…) | *Mit isztok, lányok?* |
| Hungarian women are the most beautiful in the world! | *A magyar lányok a legszebbek a világon!* |
| Are you coming back to my place? | *Feljössz hozzám?* |

Popular music underwent a rapid change in the late 1980s. The cultural influx that came with the political shift has continued unabated since. Young Hungarians are generally fashion-conscious and up to date. Nevertheless, seismic cultural change has inevitably resulted in generational differences. Those in their 30s and 40s tend to go out less frequently as family and work commitments take precedence; older Hungarians arguably hold a limited definition of 'culture', partly due to the entrenched Soviet practice of 'cultural houses', which served for the staging of everything from poetry readings to chess games. The established view in Hungary is that pop is a subculture belonging to the commercial – not the cultural – domain, and full acceptance will take time.

### DJs

Among well-regarded **DJs** active in Budapest, and at the cutting edge of Hungarian sounds, are turntable veteran Palotai and the talented young Yonderboi. Electronic and dance artists you can pursue in record shops (or perhaps catch live) include Anima Sound System, Korai Öröm, Zagar, Másfél and Yonderboi (again). These acts are notable for fusing global and local elements in a way that is original and eclectic, but avoids seeming contrived. The fusion of new and old is emblematic of the meeting of world and local cultures occurring in this part of Europe. Contemporary Hungarian music is especially interesting for the way many of the artists disregard, and so transcend, boundaries between musical genres and traditions.

### Architecture

Where some cultural output can be inspired and concentrated by conflict – just ask Petőfi – architecture is the physical body destined to suffer in the front line. For much of its history, Hungary was forced to pick up the pieces; the country's structural heritage is one of a canvas repeatedly re-painted. The earliest significant remains are those left from the Roman province of Pannonia, evident at Aquincum and in Transdanubian centres like Pécs. Romanesque ecclesiastical architecture of the 11th–13th centuries – including the first reaching cathedrals of István's Christian kingdom – was obliterated by the Mongols in 1240–41, and generally survives as recycled features in later churches or as subterranean crypts. Both the Romanesque and the Gothic buildings that followed them were generally westward-looking (in the cultural sense), frequently showing the hands of immigrant craftsmen from Italy and Germany.

The flowering of the Renaissance occurred during the golden age of Mátyás in the 15th century, and his palaces at Visegrád and Buda were among the very cream of the European crop. Unfortunately a healthy imagination is required to conjure their former splendour from the fragments that remain. While some medieval and Renaissance works still stand in the northwest and northeast, regions that didn't fall to the Turks, the Ottoman

## THE ELECTRIC BIRD

A huge, scruffy nest is a familiar sight in many villages, belonging to the fondly loved white stork (*Ciconia ciconia*). Hungary has one of southern Europe's largest nesting populations of this migrating marvel, which has a wingspan of 2.5m and helps to keep pest numbers down in fields and pastures. Before post-war socialist 'reorganisation', the wide chimneys of peasant houses provided natural nesting perches but industrialisation and state-run collectivised farming methods decimated these traditional homes and the stork population in Hungary halved between the late '50s and mid '70s. It was then that some brainy birds discovered they could build their nests on the tops of the telegraph poles and transmission lines that were rapidly appearing over the Hungarian countryside. In 1968, 91 such nests were spotted; by the late 1980s, it had become common practice among stork home-makers and telegraph poles accounted for an astonishing 52% of nesting sites. Aware of the potential danger inherent in combining feathers and high-voltage electricity – and keen to avoid telegraph-top scrambled eggs – a programme of stork protection was implemented. The most precarious nests are carefully relocated, support platforms are added to the poles, special insulation and warning equipment is mounted on lines, and prizes are awarded in recognition of outstanding service in the name of stork protection.

occupation wiped out those everywhere else. Nor is there much to show for those 150 years (the odd Turkish bath in Buda, a minaret in Eger, a square mosque in Pécs), which added up to a period of creative stagnation. Instead the towns bear the stamp of the Baroque, Neoclassical and other styles that came during re-building afterwards. Many of the richest 18th-century mansions were those of families who'd profited by cosying up to the Habsburgs when others were fighting alongside Rákóczi in the doomed struggle for independence. Another architectural feature of the 18th century is the divide between the whitewashed Calvinist churches of the Great Plain and Southern Transdanubia, their interiors decorated with the folk art of peasant artisans, versus the grand onion-domed edifices of the Catholic tradition evident in the centre and west of the country.

A growing national self-confidence – manifested architecturally in the monumental Neoclassical designs of men like József Hild and Mihály Pollack – was temporarily dented by the failed revolution of 1848–49, but it bounced back during the reformatory and creative zeal of the century's second half. After the Compromise of 1867, a desire to assert and consolidate Hungarian nationhood took hold. The millennial celebrations in particular spurred an intensive programme of building, and threw up grandiose pieces of Historicist architecture like the Parliament building and Mátyás Church. A separate strand of this impulse expressed itself in a return to rural roots, to the forms of the earthy vernacular, and in striving for a specifically 'Hungarian style' Ödön Lechner employed folkloric and oriental motifs to give Art Nouveau a uniquely Magyar face. The bulk of the 20th century has, of course, been shaped by war and its consequences. The bombardments of World War II had a devastating effect on many cities, Budapest chief among them, and ushered in the functional and drab architecture of communism. You can see the Bauhaus and Socialist-Realist 'aesthetic' – an oxymoron to our ears – at Dunaújváros, but you're probably better looking out for the softer, organic forms of the leading Postmodernist Imre Makovecz, whose wooden creations can take the forms of owls or open books. The definitions below encompass the styles you'll encounter during your travels.

**Art Nouveau (Secessionist or Jugendstil)** Art Nouveau hit Hungary in the late 1800s and early 1900s, a style characterised by flowing lines and the organic forms of nature. As elsewhere in

Europe, it represented a rebellion against imitative forms, but in Hungary it was also something more – an architectural expression of independent national identity. Ödön Lechner was the leader in developing this specifically Hungarian form of Art Nouveau; the Museum of Applied Arts (see page 175) is a prime example.

**Baroque** This is the most common historical style you'll find in Hungary, the fashion during the 17th and 18th centuries when there was widespread building – both because of the necessary reconstruction following 150 years of Turkish occupation, and because the Catholic Church erected a wave of new temples as part of the Counter-Reformation. It is characterised by blowzy, barley-sugar twisted columns, sweeping *trompe-l'oeil* deceits, arching domes and complex ornamentation.

**Gothic** The Gothic style, prevalent in western Europe between the 12th and 16th centuries, came to Hungary after the 13th-century Mongol invasion. The characteristic pointed arches, flying buttresses and soaring, star-vaulted ceilings are beautifully illustrated in the Calvinist church at Nyírbátor. You will more usually come across earlier Gothic fragments incorporated into reconstructed churches and houses.

**Eclectic** See *Historicism*

**Historicism** Historicism drew upon the architectural styles of earlier historical epochs during the building boom of the 19th century. It is evident in structures like Steindl's Neo-Gothic parliament, Schulek's Mátyás Church and the mansions lining the avenues of Pest. It is also referred to as Eclectic.

**Louis XVI** Emerging during the late 1700s, the Louis XVI style was a departure from the Baroque and the precursor to the Neoclassical. It is characterised by straight lines, reflecting the Enlightenment philosophy of order and reason. It is often known by its German label, Zopf – which means 'plait', a reference to the laurel-leaf motifs that adorn the façades and look like pigtails.

**Neoclassical** This reflects the revival of the Greek classical style of architecture that first arose at the end of the 18th century in a movement away from the extravagance of the Baroque. It is typified by plain, straight (often massive) columns – as seen in the cathedrals at Eger and Esztergom.

**Postmodernist** The late-20th-century reaction against the functional forms of the Bauhaus and Socialist-Realist schools. Its best exponent is Imre Makovecz, whose designs represent an organic return to nature, and often employ softer materials like wood – he once said 'trees are the most complete representation of life, their branches supernatural aspirations and their roots representative of the mysterious unconscious' – or even turf. Makovecz's buildings were a conscious rebuttal to the anti-aestheticism of the communist regime. Examples of 'organic architecture' can be seen in the community centres at Sárospatak and Kakasd, the forest buildings near the campsite at Visegrád, and the Roman Catholic church at Paks.

**Renaissance** Italy took the lead in Renaissance architecture – a revival of earlier classical models – but under King Mátyás (and his Italian queen) 15th-century Hungary wasn't far behind, and boasted some breathtaking palaces. Unfortunately most of it was later trampled during history's skirmishes and only fragments remain (such as the Hercules Fountain at the Visegrád Royal Palace and the funerary Bakócz Chapel at Esztergom).

**Rococo** The Esterházy Palace at Fertőd is one of the few Hungarian examples of this style, a variation of late-Baroque ornamented with swirling, asymmetrical shell and rock (*rocaille*) motifs.

**Romanesque** The Romanesque style of architecture – typified by rounded arches and vaulting and galleries supported on columns – can be seen in the country's earliest extant ecclesiastical buildings, constructed between the 11th and 13th centuries. The stand-out model is Ják's Benedictine abbey.

**Romantic** The Neoclassical concern with form and uncluttered line gave way in the 19th century to a style that preferred the grand and picturesque, and featured fantastical medieval ornamentation (with castellations and crenellations galore). It is evident in the highblown Pesti Vigadó of 1865.

**Zopf** See Louis XVI.

# Practical Information

2

## WHEN TO VISIT

Hungary has somewhere offering something all year round, although in winter it is difficult to look beyond the biggest cities or the ski slopes of the Mátra Hills (which are, in fairness, rather feeble by comparison with alpine resorts elsewhere). The cold settles in from the end of October until the middle of March, and bites in December and January when the sun pushes off early at 16.00. However, don't discount the winter period entirely for it's a frosty heart that turns from the romance of Budapest with snow under foot and Christmas markets selling piping mulled wine. Just bring your scarf and gloves. Come in spring or autumn if you want to avoid traipsing in the wake of beetroot-red gaggles of tourists, and to enjoy cultural festivals in Budapest and other towns and cities. These are the seasons to watch nature by, when the climate is warm enough for strolling (although it can be wet between April and mid May and in November) and the play of light beautiful. Autumn is when the grape is harvested and when countless cranes fill the skies at Hortobágy. Furthermore, hotels have not yet hiked their prices for the peak season. That of course comes in summer, which is long and hot (with temperatures hitting up to 32°C). Landlocked they may be, but Magyars adore their water, and you can choose from thousands of outdoor lido-style bathing complexes and swimming areas (strands). Locals traditionally ship out of Budapest and other large cities in the sticky months of July and August, many heading to Lake Balaton (whose southern shore in particular heaves with bodies).

## HIGHLIGHTS

Diversity and accessibility come together in Hungary; there's something here for everyone and it's never far away. A highlights list is something of a pick-and-mix, as arbitrary as it is subjective. It also can't allow for that riverside goulash on a canoe trip down the Tisza, that peek into courtyard gardens from a church tower or that winter soak in a thermal bath with the snow falling on the water. Treat the following with caution – and please drop us a line to tell us about the particular places and moments that made your trip special.

Most first steps beyond the capital (for Budapest's best bits, see box, page 91) are to the towns of the **Danube Bend**. The river view here is as good as any in Europe, and the favourable light has traditionally attracted artistic types to Szentendre in particular. Further up is Visegrád and its castle (see page 201) – be sure to stop for a dip among the 'onion skins' of the wonderful Visegrád-Lepence baths (page 204) – and the one-time royal capital of Esztergom (page 204). For Baroque beauty and fewer crowds, Vác (page 210) should be your target on the outside of the bend. The region has hiking trails in the Pilis, Visegrád and Börzsöny hills, while the orchids at Ócsa (page 190) and the butterflies at Fót (page 194) are wildlife treats known to few.

The **Northern Uplands** to the northeast of the capital have the greatest concentration of high ground. Hungary's tallest peak lies in the Mátra Hills, which are dotted with resorts in which to base yourself for local treks. Hollókő (page 225) preserves

Palóc peasant houses and traditions, and is a Unesco World Heritage Site (although it feels a little forced to us), while there are fossilised trees and animal prints at Ipolytarnóc (page 228). Eger (page 242) is renowned as one of the country's prettiest towns and has its own valley crammed with wine cellars. Take a narrow-gauge railway from Szilvásvárad into the Szalajka Valley (page 255), with its waterfalls and trout ponds, and explore the stalactite caves at the Unesco World Heritage Site of Aggtelek (page 265). It's in Tokaj (page 271) you'll find what Louis XIV called 'the king of wines, the wine of kings'.

The **Great Plain** covering the bulk of the country's eastern side is the place of the '*puszta*', the grasslands where outlaws and herders roamed in centuries past. Equestrianism is strongest in this region, both in the form of dare-devil horse shows and riding tours and schools. In Lajosmizse (page 339) you can stay in a rustic villa or an all-inclusive hotel, and indulge in horsey pursuits until your bum goes numb. Hortobágy National Park (page 297) is the biggest in Hungary, and is particularly popular with twitchers drawn by over a million migratory waterbirds and raptors. The spectacular autumn arrival of 100,000 cranes is a sight that will impress even the staunchest of urbanites. Lake Tisza (page 291) is another wildlife hotspot, harbouring 150 nesting bird species. Heading right into the northeastern corner you'll reach the most isolated places, many of which retain strong rural traditions; be sure to pop into Szatmárcseke's cemetery (page 322) with its wooden boat-shaped grave markers. Kalocsa (page 344) is the capital of paprika production, while it's salami in Szeged (page 361), a city that also shines a cultural light in the southern part of the plain. Ópusztaszer (page 358) is where the Magyar chieftains are said to have gathered in the aftermath of conquest, and the memorial park contains a quite breathtaking cyclorama.

**Transdanubia** lies to the west of the Danube, and was the easternmost frontier of the Roman empire. Pécs (page 412) contains early-Christian tombs from that period, as well as rare surviving Ottoman architecture from 150 years of occupation. Villány and Villánykövesd (page 405) are tiny villages lined from top to toe with wine cellars. The Gemenc Forest (see page 398) is Hungary's broadest expanse of flood plain, which you can explore on a narrow-gauge train or in a boat with a guide. Mohács (page 400) occupies a dark place in the nation's heart for the Turkish victory here in 1526 broke the back of Hungarian resistance. Today its citizens don hairy costumes and scary masks to celebrate Shrove Tuesday. Dunaújváros (page 435) is notable for its surviving Socialist-Realist monuments, so many of which were torn down elsewhere after the fall of communism. Veszprém and Székesfehérvár (pages 445 and 440) were early royal centres, the latter the scene for coronations and burials for 500 years. Don't miss the 'Rococo Sistine Chapel' – a masterclass in painting at the Sümeg parish church (page 451). There are further outstanding ecclesiastical trappings to be sniffed out – the painting that shed bloody tears in Győr Cathedral (page 465), the gorgeous 13th-century Romanesque abbey at Ják (page 483), and the Pannonhalma Monastery (yet another Unesco World Heritage Site; page 469) looming at the edge of the Kisalföld. The medieval squares of Sopron and Kőszeg (pages 487 and 484) are as lovely as they come, while the high-blown Esterházy Palace at Fertőd (page 496) and the restrained Széchenyi Mansion at Nagycenk (page 495) are as different in style as they are close in kilometres.

**Lake Balaton**, the biggest lake in central Europe, is where Magyars come to play – to sunbathe, paddle and windsurf. Its southern shore is more developed, studded with brash resorts like Siófok (page 502) with its bars and nightclubs. The reeds and deeper water on the other side offer more serene pleasures. Kis-Balaton (page 518) at the western tip is another bird-watching haunt, and also has a bison reserve. Near by, the university town of Keszthely (page 506) has a Neo-Baroque Palace with a fountain that radiates changing coloured lights after dark, and Hévíz (page 510) holds the second-largest thermal lake in the world. Set back a little from the shore, Tapolca (page 514) has an 18th-century watermill and a narrow cave lake that you can boat along. The Tihany peninsula (page 517) is a lovely tongue of land licking into the lake with an abbey church and some interesting geology. You can ride a jeep taxi up to the vineyards above Badacsony (page 511) and enjoy some fabulous views while sipping your wine.

## TOURIST OFFICES
### Abroad
**UK** 46 Eaton Place, London SW1X 8AL; ℄ +44 (0)20 7823 1032/1055;
e info@gotohungary.co.uk; www.gotohungary.co.uk
**Czech Republic** Rumunska 22, 25537 Prague 2; ℄ +42 (0)2 2109 0135;
e htprague@hungarytourism.hu
**France** 140 Av Victor Hugo, 75116 Paris; ℄ +33 (0)1 53 70 67 17; e htparis@hungarytourism.hu;
www.hongrietourisme.com
**Germany** Karl-Liebknecht Str 34, D-10178 Berlin; ℄ +49 (0)30 243 1460;
e htberlin@hungarytourism.hu
**Italy** Via Alberto Da Giussano1, 20145 Milano; ℄ +39 (0)2 4819 5434;
e htmilan@hungarytourism.hu
**USA** 150 East 58th St, 33rd Floor, New York, NY 10155; ℄ +1 212 355 0240;
e htnewyork@hungarytourism.hu

### In Hungary
Tourist information (*turista információ*) is best sought from a branch of the Hungarian National Tourist Office. These offices are known as **Tourinform**; there are around 140 in the country, manned by (usually) multilingual staff who can offer advice and help on accommodation, restaurants, transport, events and attractions. They also distribute free brochures, leaflets and listings magazines, and sell tourist discount cards, local transport tickets, phonecards and the like. They are open during normal office hours, and often at weekends too in high season. For further details, contact the information centre (*H-1548 Budapest; 24-hr* ℄ *1 438 8080;* e *hungary@tourinform.hu; www.tourinform.hu or www.hungary.com*); in addition you can ring a hotline on 06 80 63 0800 (from Hungary) or 0800 36 000000 (from the UK).

## TOUR OPERATORS
Package holidays, city breaks, and tailor-made tours and flights are readily available through UK- and US-based tour operators specialising in eastern Europe. In addition to the companies below, local guides and tour operators are included under the relevant regional sections.

### General
#### In UK
**CME Travel** 39 Spencer Rd, Rendlesham, Woodbridge IP12 2TJ; ℄ 0870 128 0636;
e mike.silford@cmefortravel.co.uk; www.cmefortravel.co.uk. City breaks to Budapest and excursions to the Hungarian countryside.
**Fregata Travel** 177 Shaftesbury Ave, London WC2H 8JR; ℄ 020 7375 3187;
e fregata@commodore.co.uk; www.fregatatravel.co.uk. Concise tour of Budapest includes all the city's main attractions.
**Great Rail Journeys** Saviour House, 9 St Saviourgate, York YO1 8NL; ℄ 01904 521900;
e grj@greatrail.com; www.greatrail.com. Runs several rail tours departing from Waterloo to European cities including Budapest.
**Jules Verne Tours** 21 Dorset Sq, London NW1 6QG; ℄ 020 7616 1000; e sales@vjv.co.uk;
www.vjv.com. Tours include a 4-night programme taking in all the main city sights, as well as longer tours that feature Budapest, Vienna and Prague.

**Interchange (The Spirit of Travel)** Interchange House, 27 Stafford Rd, Croydon, Surrey CR0 4NG; ☎ 020 8681 3612; e interchange@interchange.uk.com; www.interchange.uk.com. Can arrange flights, transfer, car hire, accommodation and excursions. Spa, golf and horse-riding programmes are available, as is a 6-day steam-engine-driving course in Budapest!

**Kirker Holidays** 4 Waterloo Court, Theed St, London SE1 8ST; ☎ 0870 112 3333. Specialises in short/city breaks.

**Martin Randall Travel** Voysey House, Barley Mow Passage, London W4 4GF; ☎ 020 8742 3355; e info@martinrandall.co.uk; www.martinrandall.com. Culture vultures can join a musical or historical tour of Budapest.

**Operas Abroad** The Tower, Mill Lane, Rainhill, Prescot, Merseyside L35 6NE; ☎ 0151 493 0382; e info@operasabroad.com; www.operasabroad.com. Specialist packages including operas, ballets and concerts.

**Our Hungary** 17 Sutton Sq, Middx TW5 0JB; ☎ 020 8230 7162; e info@ourhungary.co.uk; www.ourhungary.co.uk. Hungary specialists offering a variety of tours and tailored packages.

**Page & Moy** 136–140 London Rd, Leicester LE2 1EN; ☎ 08708 334012; e holiday@page-moy.co.uk; www.page-moy.com. Tours to Budapest and river cruises on the Danube.

**Regent Holidays** 15 John St, Bristol BS1 2HR; ☎ 0117 921 1711; e regent@regent-holidays.co.uk; www.regent-holidays.co.uk. Respected independent operator specialising in eastern European destinations.

**Trailfinders** 194 Kensington High St, London W8; ☎ 020 7937 1234; www.trailfinders.com. A one-stop shop for advice, flights and tailor-made packages to Budapest.

## In USA

**Abercrombie & Kent** 1520 Kensington Rd, Suite 212 Oak Brook, Illinois 60523-2156; ☎ +1 630 954 2944; www.abercrombiekent.com. High-end tailor-made private tours for individuals and small groups.

**General Tours** 53 Summer St, Keene, New Hampshire; ☎ +1 800 221 2216; e info@generaltours.com; www.generaltours.com. All-inclusive 3–6-day tours of Budapest, or longer ones featuring Budapest, Krakow and Prague.

**Grand Circle Travel** ☎ +1 800 959 0405; e reservations@gct.com; www.grandcircletravel.com. Offers a variety of all-inclusive tours to Budapest and other eastern European cities.

## Active, nature and eco tours
### In UK

**Avian Adventures** 49 Sandy Road, Norton, Stourbridge DY8 3AJ; ☎ 01384 372013; e aviantours@argonet.co.uk; www.avianadventures.co.uk. Fully inclusive escorted birdwatching holidays.

**British Trust Conservation Volunteers** www.btcv.org. The BTCV is a charity involved in 3 conservation areas in Hungary, including an otter park near Balaton and the Aggtelek region. The charity organises week-long trips in summer – half hard work, half conservation and nature-related fun. Accommodation is of the simple kind.

**Cycle Riders** Victoria Works, Lambridge Mews, Bath BA1 6QE; ☎ 01225 428452; www.cyclerides.co.uk. Group tours to Budapest (and beyond) on 2 wheels.

**Earthwatch Institute** 267 Banbury Rd, Oxford OX2 7HT; ☎ 01865 318838; e (general enquiries): info@earthwatch.org.uk; (project enquiries): projects@earthwatch.org.uk; web: www.earthwatch.org/europe. Non-profit-making organisation assisting with research into the decline of songbirds migrating from Europe to sub-Saharan Africa. At the research centre in the Ócsa wetland (see page 190) volunteers learn to set up and patrol mist nets, assess birds' health, and conduct vegetation surveys. Be aware that while such projects are rewarding they are aimed at proper research, and are not guided tours.

**Ecotours** ☎ 07980 606502; e ecotours@tiscali.co.uk. British-based representative of the Hungarian ecotour company (see opposite).

**Greentours** Leigh Cottage, Gauledge Lane, Longnor, Buxton, Derbyshire SK17 0PA; ☎ 01298 83563; e enquiries@greentours.co.uk; www.greentours.co.uk. Small natural-history tour operator running gentle wildlife trips to countries including Hungary. Committed to conservation.

**Limosa Holidays** Suffield House, Northrepps, Norfolk NR27 0LZ; ☎ 01263 578143; e enquiries@limosaholidays.co.uk. Year-round birdwatching and wildlife tours, including a weekend expedition to witness the spectacular crane migration in autumn.

**Naturetrek** Cheriton Mill, Alresford, Hants SO24 0NG; ☎ 01962 733051; e info@naturetrek.co.uk. Bird-watching and natural-history tours to the hills, plains and wetlands of Hungary led by leading British ornithologists and botanists.

**Quest for Nature** 29 Straight Mile, Romsey, Hants SO51 9BB; ☎ 01794 523500; e info@questfornature.co.uk; www.questfornature.co.uk. Inclusive butterfly-watching trips.

**Sherpa Expeditions** 131A Heston Rd, Hounslow, Middx TW5 0RF; ☎ 020 8577 2717; e sales@sherpa-walking-holidays.co.uk; www.sherpa-walking-holidays.co.uk. Arranges self-guided cycling tours that take in the Northern Uplands and Danube Bend.

**Sunbird** PO Box 76, Sandy, Beds SG19 1DF; ☎ 01767 262522; e sunbird@sunbirdtours.co.uk; www.sunbirdtours.co.uk. Well-regarded bird-watching tour company that runs programmes in the Hortobágy National Park (where it has its own sponsored observation tower) and bird-watching combined with the Zemplén Festival.

**Wildlife Worldwide** Chameleon House, 162 Selsdon Rd, South Croydon, Surrey CR2 6PJ; ☎ 020 8667 9158; e sales@wildlifeworld.com; ww.wildlifeworld.com. Tailor-made wildlife tours for individuals, couples and groups.

## In USA

**Earthwatch Institute** 3 Clock Tower Place, Suite 100, PO Box 75, Maynard, MA 01754; ☎ +1 (978) 461 0081 or +1 (800) 776 0188; e info@earthwatch.org. For description, see under *UK*.

**Forum Travel International** 91 Gregory Lane, Suite 21, Pleasant Hill, Calfornia 94523; ☎ +1 (800) 252 4475; e fti@foruminternational.com; www.foruminternational.com. Offers a biking tour from Vienna to Budapest, tracing the course of the Danube.

**Wilderness Travel** 1102 Ninth St, Berkeley, CA94710; ☎ +1 800 368 2794; www.wildernesstravel.com. 13-day hiking tour taking in Budapest, Eger and Tokaj, en route to Slovakia and Poland.

## In Australia

**Earthwatch Institute** 126 Bank Street, South Melbourne, VIC 3205; ☎ +61 (0) 3 9682 6828; e earth@earthwatch.org. For description see under *UK*.

## In Hungary

Ecotours and Aquila are the only fully licensed tour companies in Hungary concentrating solely on ecotourism (birding, botany, butterflies, etc).

**Aquila** Debrecen, Peterfia utca 46, 2nd floor; ☎ 52 456744; e aquila@elender.hu. Company situated in Debrecen that offers birdwatching programmes in eastern Hungary. The leader is János Világosi.

**Ecotours** XI Budapest, Villányi út 62; ☎ 1 361 0438; e natours@axelero.hu (butterfly/general nature tours), ecotours@hu.inter.net (birding/photography tours), ecotours@tiscali.co.uk (general enquiries from the UK); www.ecotours.hu. Budapest-based specialised company (with a representative in Britain) offering tailor-made (birdwatching, butterfly, botanical, canoe, horse-riding, hiking and biking) tours and general nature and culture tours to Hungary's national parks and other eastern European destinations. The leaders and principal guides are Balázs Szigeti (professional birder; ☎ 30 606 1651) and Gábor Orbán (zoologist; ☎ 30 645 9318), with Shena Maskell a UK volunteer (☎ 07980 606502).

**Hubertus Ltd** I Budapest, Ady Endre utca 1; ↘ 1 316 0469; e andrea@hubertus.com; www.hubertus.com. Offers small-game hunting, fishing on Lake Velence and Lake Tisza (and fishing camps for children at Rétimajor and Örspuszta), birdwatching in the Rétszilas fishponds and themed riding holidays in the Kiskunság and Hortobágy national parks.

**MME/Bird Life Hungary** ↘ 1 275 6247; www.mne.hu. Budapest-based company that can organise birdwatching tours with an English-speaking guide.

**Pegazus Tours** V Budapest, Ferenciek tere 5; ↘ 1 317 1644; pegazus@pegazus.hu; www.pegazus.hu. Arranges all-inclusive riding tours for those of any level, as well as adventure holidays and tours to sports events (including the Hungarian Grand Prix).

**Somogy Provincial Association for Nature Conservation (SPANC)** H-8714 Keleviz, Lehner Major; ↘ 85 708142 or 06 30 226 9553; e info@hunyady.hu or j.hunyady@t-online.hu; www.hunyady.hu. Friendly and eco-sensitive riding company offering 6-day tours from Lake Balaton to the River Dráva. Can also organise shorter tours on request. Recommended.

**Vista Visitor Centre** VI Budapest, Paulay Ede utca 7; ↘ 1 429 9950; e incoming@vista.hu; www.vista.hu. Can organise canoe and kajak trips on the Danube, Rába and Tisza rivers. Ask to speak to Victoria Rajnics.

**Vizitura** IX Budapest, Hurok utca 1; ↘ 1 280 8182; e info@vizitura.hu; www.vizitura.hu. Organises 'water' tours, including river canoeing and kayaking trips.

**www.jegmadarviziturak.hu** Website offering canoe trips on the Moson arm of the Danube in the Szigetköz region, with its beautiful flood forests.

**www.vidamdelfin.hu** Hungarian website through which you can book canoe and cycling trips or arrange equipment hire and boat delivery; the site is in Hungarian, but the company welcomes English enquiries. They have set annual tour dates into which tourists can slot; a British party of 16 recently went on one, and their feedback was very positive.

# RED TAPE
## Entry requirements

European Union (EU) nationals, including those from Britain, may visit Hungary as indefinite tourists providing they have valid passports; visitors from France, Germany, Italy and Spain require only a national ID card. EU nationals need a European Economic Area resident-citizen permit if staying longer than three months. Apply at the local regional agency of the Hungarian Immigration and Nationality Office before the last two weeks of your stay.

Tourists from all other European countries (excluding Albania, Turkey, Macedonia and Bosnia and Herzegovina), the USA, Canada, Australia and New Zealand can visit without a visa for up to 90 days. Travellers wishing to exceed a 90-day stay should apply for a visa from their country's consulate and allow at least four weeks for it to be processed. More information is available on the website of the Hungarian Immigration and Nationality Office (www.bm-bah.hu).

Although in exceptional cases visas can be issued at Hungarian border crossings, the authorities strongly urge you to apply for visas at the embassy. In order to apply for a visa you'll need your passport (valid for at least six months from the time of exit from Hungary), a signed application form, two recent passport-sized photos, return travel tickets and proof of accommodation. A single-entry tourist visa currently costs US$40, double-entry US$75 and multiple-entry US$180. Transit visas are valid for up to 48 hours and are compulsory for visa-requiring travellers who pass through Hungarian borders. A single-entry transit visa costs US$38, double-entry US$65 and multiple-entry US$150. For additional visa information, log on to Hungary's foreign ministry website at www.mfa.gov.hu. In England the Hungarian embassy's website is www.huemblon.org.uk.

## Customs regulations

Visitors aged 16 or over may take 250 cigarettes, 50 cigars or 250g of tobacco, two litres of wine, one litre of spirits and five litres of beer, 250ml of cologne and 100ml of perfume out

*Above* Hill view over Visegrád, with the Danube curving away (TS)
*Below* Night time at Vajdahunyad Castle in Budapest's City Park (TS)

*Above left* Budapest trams (RF)

*Above right* A coned turret of the Fishermen's Bastion (JS)

*Below* Parliament across the Danube, Budapest (JS)

of the country. Export of museum pieces or antiques requires an export permit, registered in your name; such permits can usually be obtained from the shop of purchase (see www.muemlekvedelem.hu for more details). If you buy an antique at auction, the organisers will give you an invoice and, for a charge of 2–4% of its selling price, a relevant museum issues the *kiviteli engedély* (export permit). Different museums issue permits for different items; specialist companies can arrange this paperwork for you, if you're willing to pay – try Jeff Taylor of First European Shipping (\ *06 20 958 2545; www.firsteuropeanshipping.com*), who speaks English. The special *bírálati csoport* (appraisal team) evaluates the art work if you do not have an invoice. Importation of any currency worth more than 1,000,000Ft must be declared, and raw meat or milk products and potted or rooted plants cannot be taken in or out of Hungary. Unsurprisingly, it is prohibited to import pornography, drugs and unlicensed weapons. Now that Hungary has joined the EU, you can only claim back VAT (ÁFA) on goods over a certain value if you are a non-EU citizen. Hand the refund form (available from shops) to customs on leaving the country.

## HUNGARIAN EMBASSIES AND CONSULATES
### Abroad
**Australia** 17 Beale Crescent, Deakin, ACT 2600; \ +61 (0)2 6282 2555;
e hungcbr@ozemail.com.au; www.matra.com.au/~hungemb
**Canada** 299 Waverley St, Ottawa, Ontario, K2P 0V9; \ +1 613 230 2717; www.docuweb.ca/hungary
**Germany** Unter den Linden 76, 10117 Berlin; \ +49 (0)30 203 100; e info@ungarische-botschaft.de; www.ungarische-botschaft.de
**Ireland** 2 Fitzwilliam Place, Dublin 2; \ +353 (0)1 661 2902; e hungarian.embassy@eircom.net; www.kum.hu/dublin
**Italy** Via dei Villini 12–16, 00161 Roma; \ +39 (0)6 4423 0598; e titkarsag2@huembrom.it; www.huembit.it
**UK** 35 Eaton Place, London SW1X 8BY; tel +44 (0)20 7235 5218; e office@huemblon.org.uk; www.huemblon.org.uk/index.htm
**USA** 3910 Shoemakers St NW, Washington DC 20008; \ +1 202 362 6730;
e office@huembwas.org; www.hungaryemb.org

### In Hungary
**Australia** XII Budapest, Királyhágó tér 8–9; \ 1 457 9777; www.ausembbp.hu. *Open Mon–Fri 09.00–12.00.*
**Canada** XII Budapest, Budakeszi út 32; \ 1 392 3360; www.kanada.hu. *Open Mon–Thu 08.30–10.30, 14.00–15.30.*
**France** VI Budapest, Lendvay utca 27; \ 1 374 1100. *Open Mon–Fri 09.00–12.00.*
**Germany** I Budapest, Úri utca 64; \ 1 488 3500. *Open Mon–Fri 09.00–12.00.*
**Ireland** V Budapest, Szabadság tér 7; \ 1 302 9600. *Open Mon–Fri 09.30–12.30, 14.30–16.00.*
**UK** V Budapest, Harmincad utca 6; \ 1 266 2888; www.britishembassy.hu. *Open Mon–Fri 09.30–12.30, 14.30–16.30.*
**USA** V, Szabadság tér 12; \ 1 475 4400; emergency out of hours \ 1 475 4703; www.usis.hu. *Open Mon–Fri 08.15–17.00.*

## GETTING THERE AND AWAY
There are 56 road crossings, and 26 rail, five water and 17 air-entry points into Hungary. Ensure all your documentation is at hand when crossing borders as guards have the right otherwise to refuse entry.

### By air
As with air travel to most European destinations, ticket prices to Hungary are at their highest during the summer period (*Jun–Aug*), and at Christmas and New Year. Costs may

also rise during city festivals, and especially during the Hungarian Grand Prix (see page 73). The cheapest season is winter (*Nov–Mar*). Shop around for cut-price flights and last-minute bargains on the internet (try www.expedia.com, www.travelocity.co.uk, www.lastminute.co.uk and www.cheapflights.co.uk). Flight schedules, prices and routes listed below were correct at the time of going to press, but be aware that these are constantly subject to change and you should always check directly with travel agents or airlines.

Until recently, Budapest's Ferihegy International Airport was Hungary's only entry point for foreign travellers. It remains by far the largest carrier of traffic, but a second international airport of sorts has opened in a former Soviet airbase 15km from Keszthely. Owned by a consortium of Irish-Hungarians, Fly Balaton ('Hungary's Friendly Airport'; *8391 Sármellék, Repülőtér Pf 4;* \ *+36 83 355 500;* e *info@fly-balaton.com; www.fly-balaton.com*) schedules budget flights from Germany and Switzerland, and rumour has it that Ryanair is also sniffing about. Keep an eye on their website.

## From the UK and Ireland

The no-frills airline revolution has made deep in-roads into eastern Europe. Before Hungary's admission to the EU, only British Airways and the Hungarian carrier Malév offered direct flights to Budapest from London; now a host of budget airlines are getting in on the act, including easyJet, Sky Europe and Wizz Air. Incredibly, there are now (in 2005) three times more seats available between London and Hungary than there were in 2003, and prices are increasingly competitive.

While in the very recent past, direct flights from the UK were only available from London airports (taking around 2½ hours) – necessitating a connecting flight from another European city or a trip to London for those outside the capital – since the end of 2004 some alternative budget routes have opened up. In addition to its London services, easyJet now operates daily flights from Newcastle and Bristol, and Jet2 also flies from Manchester. As such, it should be less of a difficulty for those living north of the Watford gap to get to their departure point. If you do intend to fly from London, connecting flights on one of the budget airlines start from around £40 (standard return), while British Airways also do 'add-on' fares from £70. Aer Lingus now offers a service from Dublin, as does Malév.

**Aer Lingus** \ +353 1886 8844; www.aerlingus.com. Daily flights from Dublin for around €210–260 return.

**Air Berlin** \ 0870 738 8880; www.airberlin.com. Germany's second-largest air carrier operates a daily direct connection between London Stansted and Budapest, costing from £65 return.

**British Airways** \ 0870 850 9850; www.ba.com. Operates two flights a day from London's Heathrow to Budapest (Terminal 2B) for £100 return. You can get a discount on your flight if you book online and use BA's excellent 'e-ticketing' system, which also allows a speedier check-in.

**easyJet** \ 0870 600 0000; www.easyjet.com. The popular low-cost airline celebrated Hungary's accession to the EU by opening a daily service between London Luton and Budapest (which has now risen to two daily), with return tickets from £35.00. A second service from Gatwick costs about the same. The airline also runs a daily service in summer (four-times weekly in winter) from both Newcastle and Bristol from £30 return.

**Jet2** www.jet2.com. Flights from Manchester starting at around £50.

**Malév Airlines** \ 0870 909 0577 (customer reservations); www.flymalev.co.uk. Flies twice-daily direct from London Stansted and London Heathrow to Budapest (Terminal 2A). You can expect to pay around £79 for a return ticket from Stansted, and a return from Heathrow costs £100–250. Malév flies direct from Dublin at least once daily, and twice daily on Mondays, Wednesdays and Saturdays. Costs start from around £200 return.

**Sky Europe** \ 020 7365 0365; www.skyeurope.com. The Slovakian carrier runs a once-a-day service between London Stansted and Budapest, with return flights costing from as little as £51. Flights land at Ferihegy Terminal 1.

**Wizz Air** ✎ 0048 22 500 9499; www.wizzair.com. New budget European airline with flights between London Luton and Budapest (Terminal 2B). A return flight costs from £60, but there is currently only one evening flight per day. Wizz Air doesn't distribute paper tickets; you'll be issued with a registration number provided at the time of booking, which must be presented at check-in along with your passport.

## From the US

Only Malév runs direct flights between New York's JFK Airport and Budapest. There are seven flights a week, taking just over nine hours, and you can expect to pay roughly US$725 return. KLM operates non-direct flights from the US via Amsterdam.

## From the rest of the world

There are no direct flights from **Australia**; the cheapest way to reach Budapest is to fly to London from Sydney or Melbourne and transfer to a budget airline from there. Qantas offers daily flights direct to London for around US$2,500.

Malév operates five direct flights a week between **Canada** (Toronto) and Budapest costing around US$750 standard return. You could also try Air Canada and Lufthansa for indirect flights from Vancouver and Montreal. No direct flights are available from **New Zealand**; you'll need to take a flight to London or Paris (with Air New Zealand), and get a connection from there.

In addition to the above, you can catch direct Malév flights to Budapest from **Lyons** (seven flights a week), **Ljubljana** (12 a week), **Vienna** (twice daily) and **Dubrovnik** (three a week). Other international airlines that operate in and out of Ferihegy include Turkish Airlines, Alitalia, Finnair, Czech Airlines and Aeroflot.

## Airline/airport contact numbers

**Aeroflot** +36 1 318 5955
**Air France** +36 1 318 0411
**British Airways** +36 1 411 5555
**Central airport info** +36 1 296 9696
**Finnair** +36 1 317 4296
**Flight information** +36 1 296 7000
**KLM** +36 1 373 7737
**Lost luggage Terminal 2A** +36 1 296 8108
**Lost luggage Terminal 2B** +36 1 296 7948
**Lufthansa** +36 1 266 4511
**Malév** +36 1 235 3222/3888

## Budapest Airport

Ferihegy International is Hungary's main commercial airport, located 25km southeast of Budapest. There are two adjacent terminals: Terminal 2A services Malév flights, while Terminal 2B looks after most other airlines. The airport is compact and clean, and contains a handful of souvenir and duty-free shops, a bar, coffee shop and restaurant, and currency-exchange bureaux (that in Terminal A charges no commission, whereas that in Terminal B charges around 250Ft). The old Terminal 1 (✎ *+36 1 296 0427/8/9 or +36 1 296 0424/5*), located on the same road as Ferihegy 2 but closer to town, is used primarily by private aircraft and budget airlines (eg: Sky Europe).

For details on **transfers** from the airport into Budapest itself, see Budapest's *Getting there and away* section, page 90.

## By train

Travelling from the UK to Hungary by train is only worth the time and effort if you're planning a round-Europe trip, would like to stop off along the way, or are afraid of flying.

With the rise of the low-cost airline, flights are now considerably cheaper than return rail tickets; for example, a 2nd-class return ticket from London Waterloo (via the Eurostar) to Budapest Keleti costs approximately £300. The journey from London takes 22 hours (including the three-hour journey on the Eurostar), and you can travel via Cologne and Munich, Frankfurt and Nürenberg or Paris and Vienna. Tickets are usually valid for around three months, allowing you to get off to explore along the way (although you can't depart from your booked route). For information on crossing the Channel from London, contact **Eurostar** (↘ *08705 186186;* e *info@eurostar.com; www.eurostar.com*). Rail tickets to Budapest can be booked through the **Rail Europe Travel Centre** (*178 Piccadilly, London W1;* ↘ *0870 830 2000;* e *reservations@raileurope.co.uk; www.raileurope.co.uk*), who can also help to plan your trip.

As Budapest has direct rail connections with 25 European cities, it can be a great platform from which to delve around in central Europe. All international trains through Budapest are equipped with sleepers in 1st- and 2nd-class carriages, and most (though not all) have dining cars. If you're planning to travel with a bicycle, you'll pay an additional charge of about a quarter of the price of your main ticket. See www.mav.hu or www.elvira.hu for details of international rail timetables and ticket costs, or call 1 322 9035. Keep your passport and tickets to hand as they are likely to be regularly inspected, and you will need to produce them when crossing borders. Snoring soundly in your cabin will not exempt you from this – staff will shake you awake if they need to.

International trains to Budapest arrive at/leave from one of the three main railway stations. The **Eastern Railway Station** (*Keleti pályaudvar; VIII, Baross tér*) handles the bulk of them, including those to/from Belgrade, Bratislava, Bucharest, Kiev, Krakow, Ljubljana, Moscow, Munich, Prague, Sofia, Venice, Vienna and Zagreb. The **Western Railway Station** (*Nyugati pályaudvar; VI, Nyugati tér*) was the city's first main station, built in 1877 by Eiffel, and serves international destinations such as Warsaw, Bratislava, Berlin and Prague. The **Southern Railway Station** (*Déli pályaudvar; I, Krisztina körút*) handles international journeys to and from Cologne, Ljubljana, Munich, Sarajevo, Venice, Vienna and Zagreb. Each of these has a connection to the underground system.

If you're travelling from Budapest, you should aim to buy your ticket (*jegy*) at least a day or two in advance as services can get booked up. Seat reservations (up to 60 days in advance) are essential for those marked with a circled R on the timetable. Tickets can be bought from each of the three main Budapest stations, but it might be easier to head for the MÁV central ticket office. Contact details for this office, and other information on train travel, are included under *Getting around* (page 92). There is a 24-hour helpline for international passengers (↘ *1 461 5500*).

### Some international services

Rail connections between Hungary, its neighbouring countries and beyond are good. This paragraph provides a brief overview of some of the main routes. It's a three-hour journey from **Vienna** to Budapest Déli passing through the Hegyeshalom border and on via Győr and Tatabánya. It can take as little as 2½ hours to reach Budapest from **Bratislava** either over the Szob border and directly on to Budapest Keleti or via the Rajka border, through Győr to Déli. A full day's travelling is required to reach the Hungarian capital from **Kiev** and usually one change or more is necessary at the border. Trains then continue their journey through the Hungarian entry point at Záhony, to Debrecen, Szolnok and Keleti. From **Bucharest** the train enters Hungarian soil at Lőkösháza before heading to Békéscsaba, Szolnok and Keleti, taking around 13 hours. Trains from **Belgrade** run via Novi Sad and Subotica, with some services crossing the border at Kelebia (travelling via Kiskunhalas to Budapest Keleti) and others at Röszke (going on to Szeged). It's possible to travel from **Zagreb** to Budapest in as little as five hours. The journey cuts the Croatian border at Koprivnica before heading through Nagykanizsa, around the southern side of Balaton and on to Budapest Keleti. Alternatively you can cross the border further east, near Villány, and travel on to Pécs. The quickest route from **Ljubljana** to Budapest is via Zagreb (as above), which takes around 7½ hours. There are also two crossings further north at Hodoš (travelling on to to Zalalövő, Veszprém and terminating at Budapest Déli) and Szentgotthárd at the Austrian border (offering a less direct journey to Budapest via Szombathely). The quickest way from **Prague** is via Bratislava, through the Szob border and on to Keleti, taking from seven hours. The fastest and most direct route from **Warsaw** again goes through Bratislava and Szob before stopping along the way to Keleti at Tata and Tatabánya. It's an epic 35-hour journey from **Moscow** through Poland, with at least one change (and often more), before heading on to Slovakia, the Rajka border, Győr and Tatabánya to reach Keleti. You can also go via Kiev.

### Rail passes

The **InterRail Pass** (*see www.interrail.com*) gives European rail travellers the freedom to enjoy unlimited travel across the continent. The pass has a three-tiered pricing structure that divides the participating European countries into eight zones (*see www.raileurope.co.uk/inter-rail for details*), with the cost of the passes varying according to the number of zones you wish it to cover. Hungary resides in zone D alongside the Czech Republic, Poland, Slovakia, Bosnia-Herzegovina and Croatia. InterRail passes can be bought from Rail Europe (see opposite), international rail stations and STA Travel Centres. A ticket for a single-zone pass (valid for 16 days) costs £215 for adults, £145 for under 26s and £108 for kids; a two-zone pass (valid for 22 days) costs £295/205/148; an all-zone pass (valid for a month) costs £405/285/203.

A classic **Eurail Pass** (*see www.eurailnet.com;* e *info@eurailnet.com*) allows limitless travel across 17 European countries, including Hungary. Prices range from £323 to £900, depending on the duration of the pass's validity (from 15 days to three months). If you're under 26 then you are eligible for a Eurail Youthpass, which dramatically cuts the cost. Holders of both the above passes are entitled to discounts on Eurostar travel.

## By coach

Travel to Hungary from afar by coach is an exhausting proposition. It used to be the cheapest option, but is now under severe pressure from the budget airlines. As long as you're not overly tall, and can sit still for extended periods, the coaches are comfy enough with reclining seats, TV and video, and washroom facilities. **Eurolines** (☎ *0870 5143219; www.eurolines.co.uk or www.nationalexpress.co.uk*) operates in over 30 other countries, and under the National Express banner in the UK and Volánbusz in Hungary. In England, direct and indirect coaches depart from London Victoria Coach Station and Dover Eastern Docks to Budapest Népliget – the capital's main coach station – via France, Belgium, Germany, Austria and Győr in northwest Hungary. The journey takes a mind-numbing 27½ hours. Coaches depart daily from both coach stations in peak season (Jun 26–Sep 11), and every day except Wednesday and Saturday the rest of the year. Standard fares are single £79 (£75 for under 26s) and return £109 (£99).

If you are planning a European tour, it could be worth investing in a **Eurolines Pass**, which gives holders unlimited deluxe coach travel for between 30 and 60 days to 18 major European cities (including Budapest). Passes range from £149 to £355. For more information, visit the Eurolines website, the Eurolines ticket office at Népliget (*open Mon–Fri 06.00–18.00, Sat–Sun 06.00–16.00*), the Volánbusz Travel Office (*V, Erzsébet tér 1;* ☎ *1 318 2122 or the central office at Népliget Bus Station*) or any National Express agent in the UK.

In Budapest, Népliget Bus Station (for contact details see page 91) deals with all international services, which include Naples via Rome, Toulouse via Vienna and Lyons,

Berlin via Prague, Paris via Strasbourg and Amsterdam via Frankfurt. International services also run to and from other towns and cities, including Debrecen, Baja, Szeged, Miskolc, Győr, Szombathely and Siófok.

## By car

The overland drive from the UK to Budapest would certainly make an epic of a road movie – all 1,684km (1,047 miles) of it – but there's a certain romanticism and some wonderful scenery. Once on mainland Europe the easiest route to Budapest is via Ostend, Belgium, Cologne, Frankfurt and Vienna. On a good day the journey should take around 17 hours but, obviously, this doesn't take into account food (and ablution) stops, sleep breaks, traffic problems, border queues, etc. See www.michelin.com for a detailed route planner. It's important to keep to hand your driving licence, vehicle insurance and registration documents (as well as your passport), and to display your country-identification letter on your vehicle. It is vital to take out adequate breakdown cover in case the unthinkable happens. The AA (↘ *0800 085 2840/0870 600 0371; www.theaa.com*) operates a European Breakdown Cover policy that will protect you on your trip. Finally, be aware that tolls and high fuel prices in mainland Europe can considerably inflate your anticipated expenses.

To drive in Hungary (on the right-hand side, remember!), you must hold a full driving licence that is valid for at least 12 months upon your return home. UK citizens with the old fold-out green licence will need to travel with an International Driving Permit (IDP) too – see your local post office for details. Third-party insurance is also a necessity but cars with licence plates and national-identification letter for A, B, CH, D, DK, E, F, FL, GB, HR, I, IRL, IS, L, NL, P, S, SK, SLO countries will already be covered. If your country is not listed above then you'll have to produce a Green Card and may be asked to buy the insurance at the border if you don't already have it. For further details on driving in Hungary, see page 56.

There are 80-odd road border crossings into Hungary, 37 of which are international stations and open around the clock. The remaining smaller border crossings are for locals only (prohibited to foreigners). Some of the main border crossings (open 24 hours to all travellers) are:

**Ukraine** Záhony/Csop (Road E573 from Nyíregyháza); Beregsurány/Berehove (Road 41 from Nyíregyháza)

**Romania** Csengersima/Petea (Road 49 from Mátészalka); Nyírábrány/Valea lui Mihai (Road 48 from Debrecen); Ártánd/Borş (Road E60 from Berettyóújfalu); Gyula/Vărşand (Road 44 from Gyula); Nagylak/Nădlac (Road E68 from Makó)

**Serbia and Montenegro** Röszke/Horgoš (Road E75 from Szeged); Tompa/Kelebija (Road 53 from Kiskunhalas); Hercegszántó/Bački Breg (Road 51 from Baja)

**Croatia** Udvar/Kneževo (Road 56 from Mohács); Barcs/Terezino Polje (Road 6 from Szigetvár); Letenye/Goričan (Road 7 from Nagykanizsa)

**Slovenia** Rédics/Dolga Vas (Road 86 from Körmend)

**Austria** Bucsu/Schachendorf (Road 89 from Szombathely); Sopron/Klingenbach (Road 84 from Sopron); Hegyeshalom/Nickelsdorf (Road E60 from Mosonmagyaróvár)

**Slovakia** Vámosszabadi/Medvedov (Road 14 from Győr); Komárom/Komárno (Road 13 from Komárom); Esztergom/Štúrovo (Road 111 from Esztergom); Somoskőújfalu/Siatorská Bukavinka; Bánréve/Kráľ (Road 26 Miskolc); Tornyosnémeti/Seňa (Road E71 Miskolc)

## By hydrofoil

A hydrofoil service (*daily Apr 8–Oct 30, two-daily in Aug*) operated by **Mahart PassNave** (*V Budapest, Belgrád rakpart;* ↘ *1 484 4013/4010;* e *hydrofoil@mahartpassnave.hu; www.mahartpassnave.hu*) floats between Vienna and Budapest via Bratislava, and takes 5¹/₂ hours. Tickets from Vienna to Bratislava cost adult/concessions single €69/59 (return €89/76), and from Vienna to Budapest adult/concessions single €79/67 (return €99/84). Children aged 6–15 are entitled to a 50% discount, while those under 6 go free. Bicycle carriage costs an additional €18. In Budapest, the ferry departs from Pest (between the Szabadság and Erzsébet bridges), in Vienna from the Reichsbrücke pier.

# HEALTH
*with Dr Felicity Nicholson*

Generally the standard of public health in Hungary is good, the tap water safe to drink and no vaccinations are legally required. However, it is wise to be up to date with routine vaccinations such as diphtheria, tetanus and polio. Hepatitis A should also be considered.

If you are planning to visit deep-forested areas outside the capital, consult your doctor about getting immunisation against encephalitis, which is carried by forest ticks (*kullancs*). Take precautions by using tick repellents, wearing long-sleeved clothing and a hat, and tucking trousers into boots. After a day in the forest it is important to check yourself for ticks, or get someone else to do it for you. For those travelling with children, concentrate particularly on checking their hair. (See the website www.masta.org/tickalert for more details.) The other primary irritant is the mosquito, which whines around the riverside on summer evenings, and is particularly tiresome when you're trying to enjoy a nice piece of fish at the Római part. Cover exposed skin with a DEET-based insect repellent (*rovarirtó*) and they'll feast on some other suckee.

For those who are going to be working in hospitals or in close contact with children, hepatitis B vaccination is recommended. Pre-exposure rabies vaccine (ideally three doses given over a minimum of 21 days) should also be considered for anyone who is specifically going to be working with animals. For **emergency telephone numbers**, see page 76.

## The European Health Insurance Card

EU nationals who are taken ill or have an accident when visiting Hungary are entitled to healthcare. In June 2004, a European Health Insurance Card was introduced to improve access to healthcare in the EU and to speed up the reimbursement of costs. It replaces the E111 form, which remains valid only until the end of 2005. Some countries incorporate this health-insurance card into their national cards while others issue separate ones. UK citizens should ask for this card at their local social security or sickness insurance offices.

Only publicly funded health treatment is included in this scheme for the moment. In Hungary, while emergency treatment is free for visiting EU citizens, you have to pay the full cost of drugs and non-emergency treatment and then claim a refund. It is important to keep all your bills, prescriptions and receipts.

Further information about the European Health Insurance Card is available at http://europa.eu.int.

## Travel clinics and health information

A full list of current travel clinic websites worldwide is available on www.istm.org. For other journey preparation information, consult www.tripprep.com. Information about various medications may be found on www.emedicine.com/wild/topiclist.htm.

## In Hungary

Free emergency health care is available to foreigners, but any required medication or follow-up treatment will have to be paid for. It is therefore important to ensure that your travel insurance covers medical costs. Take a copy of your policy certificate with you and keep the policy number to hand in case you are obliged to quote it. Hungarians swear by the curative properties of thermal baths (*gyógyfürdő*), and doctors will frequently prescribe dips for conditions ranging from skin problems to arthritic pains.

For those minor ailments, you'll find Budapest has a rash of pharmacies (*gyógyszertár* or *patika*); all towns and most villages will boast at least one pharmacy. It is nevertheless worth bearing in mind that some medicines available over the counter in the UK and US –¬ like antihistamine – require a prescription in Hungary. If you suffer from allergies, take relevant medication with you. Normal pharmacy opening hours are 09.00–18.00 on weekdays; they often close at lunchtime on Saturday, and don't usually open at all on Sunday. Local listing magazines, Tourinform or signs in pharmacy windows should indicate the nearest all-night pharmacy.

Hungary has a first-rate and highly affordable dental service, of which many Austrians make use during trips here. The *Budapest Sun* and *Budapest Times* often contain advertisements for private dental practices.

## SAFETY

Happily Hungary is a safe country with a low rate of violent crime, particularly by Western standards. However, like many other European countries, incidents of pick-pocketing, mugging, car theft and overcharging with threats are sadly on the increase. The bulging tourist wallet is inevitably at greatest risk, so it is wise to stay vigilant when travelling on public transport, strolling in busy and built-up areas, shopping in markets and malls, and relaxing in restaurants and bars. As a general rule, don't let your belongings out of your sight, try not to flash around valuable items and make use of your hotel safe. Never walk the streets with large sums of cash, or – as we learnt to our cost – leave your cellphone in an unzipped shoulder bag as you peer at the bus timetable.

It is not unknown for criminals to go to more extreme lengths to extort money from tourists. There have, for example, been instances of conmen posing as policemen and demanding cash. If in any doubt, ask for the 'officer's' credentials and insist on being taken to a police station with access to a translator. Theft of cars and the possessions inside them is not uncommon, so don't tempt opportunists by leaving things of value on the seats. Drivers should be cautious about stopping to help apparent breakdowns; there has been a recent upsurge in thieves posing as motorists in distress, flagging down fellow drivers for assistance, before stealing from them and driving away in their cars.

Gentlemen, if an attractive young woman approaches and asks you to join her for a drink, consider the possibility that she is drawn by more than your irresistible masculine charms. Unwary, strutting men have lost both their swagger and their swag when, after tripping over their tongues into a seedy joint with a 'consume girl', they have been forced by burly bouncers to pay an extortionate price for the drinks.

On a more mundane level, check your bills in restaurants and bars carefully for 'mistakes' in the maths. Never order from a menu that does not display prices alongside its fare. Always use a recognised taxi firm, and agree a price or check the meter is cleared before climbing in (see page 94). And resist dealing with unlicensed moneychangers in the street.

We must stress again that by Western standards Budapest is extremely safe, and you are unlikely to feel threatened. Please don't have nightmares, do sleep tight. For up-to-date security information, check the Foreign and Commonwealth Office website at www.fco.gov.uk.

### Women travellers

There is a typical central European machismo to Hungarian men, and they can hold attitudes that many in the West would consider sexist. Such thinking tends to manifest itself in high-blown compliments rather than anything more sinister. Women will find men unafraid to 'check them out' as they pass in the street and perhaps less inhibited in approaching them in bars than in more reserved cultures such as Britain; however, provided women take sensible precautions they should encounter no harassment.

> **MY ONLINE SAFE.COM**
> This innovative new service allows customers to upload scanned images of important documents (such as passport/insurance/medical details, serial numbers, etc) into a personal online 'safe'. These are stored on remote secure servers and encrypted; they can be accessed and printed with a password should you need to refer to documentation that you either didn't wish to carry with you or lost on your travels. For further details, contact info@myonlinesafe.com.

## Terrorism

The threat of terrorist activity is a current danger in Hungary as elsewhere in the world. Obvious targets such as the British and American embassies are presently protected with concrete barriers and armed guards. Tourists are advised to behave as they would at home and be alert to any suspect behaviour, especially in busy public places. The FCO website (see above) offers up-to-the-minute advice.

## The law

It is now legal for prostitutes to stand in a 'tolerant zone' (*türelmi zóna*), wait for customers to stop their cars, and then 'conduct their business' in the cars or nearby bushes. You may see scantily clad women beside some of the main roads leading out from Budapest. Other more solid trappings of the trade – pimps and madams, brothels etc – remain illegal (although some strip joints are rather feeble covers for prostitution rackets). Recreational drug use is prohibited. Tourists are most likely to brush with the law as a result of motoring offences. Random road blocks are extremely common – during a four-month period we were pulled over on seven occasions in a Hungarian car. You will be asked to show your passport, driving licence and car registration papers. Minor offences can be punished with on-the-spot fines, while fines for speeding (usually 10,000Ft) must be settled at a post office. It is illegal to drink any alcohol at all prior to driving.

## The police

While the police force (*rendőrség*) has enjoyed a better reputation than counterparts in other eastern European nations, it has nevertheless been regarded with suspicion by Hungarians. Accusations of corruption have plagued the constabulary for years. In 2003 the director of police in Budapest went so far as to offer his officers cash rewards in return for their blowing the whistle on instances of bribery in an attempted clean up. On the whole, though, the situation is improving and tourists are unlikely to encounter any problems in their dealings with officers, which will primarily come in being stopped at road blocks (see page 57) or very occasionally during passport inspections. There is a good police presence on the streets of Budapest during high season, when patrols aim at deterring thieves. Officers usually speak little or no English, but in July, August and September such patrols are often accompanied by translators.

Lost passports should be reported immediately to the Office for Immigration and Citizenship (*XI Budapest, Budafoki út 60;* ✆ *1 463 9165*), which is open 24 hours a day. If your passport has been stolen you'll need to report it to the police either by calling one of the emergency numbers or via the tourist police office (*in the Tourinform at V Budapest, Sütő utca 2; 24-hour* ✆ *1 438 8080*).

For emergency telephone numbers, see page 76.

## WHAT TO TAKE

There is little that isn't readily available in Budapest and the other main cities. Pack your swimsuit for a spa visit, your driving licence if you are looking to hire a car, and a jacket and tie if you're a gentleman who wants to dine at the Gundel (see page 114). Young women in Budapest like to make an effort when go nightclubbing, so a set of trendy threads might deserve a place in your suitcase. Some medication that can be bought over the counter in the West requires a prescription in Hungary, so ensure you've got your relevant tablets. Choose your clothes remembering that it can be very cold in winter, wet in early spring and very hot in summer; there are winds and occasional storms in summer, and a jumper is worthwhile for those cave or cellar visits. Take out comprehensive travel insurance before your trip to cover lost baggage, theft and medical emergencies, and bring copies of the documentation with you (or use a computer safe; see box, page 49). A plug adaptor (two-prong, round-pin) will allow you to use your own electrical devices. Beyond that, bring some comfortable shoes, a patient frame of mind and a packet of indigestion tablets. Oh, and *Hungary: The Bradt Travel Guide*!

## ELECTRICITY

Hungary's **electrical current** is 220 Volts/50Hz, accessible via the European two-pin plug. Plug adaptors for use with three-pronged plugs are generally available from large supermarkets and chemists in cities.

## MONEY, BANKING AND BUDGETING
### Money

The forint (Ft or HUF) is Hungary's official unit of currency and is issued in banknote denominations of 200, 500, 1,000, 2,000, 5,000, 10,000 and 20,000 and coins of 1, 2, 5, 10, 20, 50 and 100. Small shops, cafés or taxis may have difficulty with notes worth more than 5,000Ft, and you'll be treated with incredulity in most places if you present a 20,000Ft note. With this in mind, request notes of no higher value than 10,000Ft when changing money, and ask your hotel to break down larger denominations before going out for the day.

While Hungary joined the EU on May 1 2004, the country will not be embracing the euro in the immediate future. However, some businesses have been accepting the euro for some time, and hotels at the upper end of the price range will often list their prices in euros because of the changing value of the forint. Any goods purchased in Hungary require the payment of a value-added tax levy known as ÁFA (between 11 and 25%). Most quoted prices in shops include this tax but it's worth checking in case. Non-EU country members can claim this tax back if purchasing goods worth over 50,000Ft within six months of purchase. See page 59 for hotel tax rates and page 80 for a guide to tipping.

The current **exchange rate** (September 2005) is £1 = 355Ft, US$1 = 202Ft, €1 = 245Ft.

### Exchanging currency and travellers' cheques

Banks, post offices, hotels, *bureaux de change*, tourist offices and travel agencies usually exchange **currency**. The commission charged by *bureaux de change* (which you'll find in railway stations, shopping centres and on the shopping streets of main cities) can be high (at times extortionate) and their rates of exchange vary considerably so be sure to shop around. Always ask how much it will cost to change £1 or US$1 – some places mislead customers by quoting a rate that only applies if you change over a certain amount of money. The safest place to exchange cash is at a bank, where you should get an acceptable rate and should not be charged commission.

The profusion of ATMs means that **travellers' cheques** are increasingly rare things, and we have found that many *bureaux de change* do not deal with them. You should, in any case, avoid such booths as the rates on offer are likely to be very low. Banks will exchange travellers' cheques (American Express are the most widely used) at decent rates without fuss; travel agencies like Ibusz may be able to exchange them, though usually for a commission. You can also try the post office. Remember to take your passport as a means of identification.

## BUDGETING

So how hard is Hungary going to hit your bank balance? It's certainly true that this is considerably less of a bargain-bucket destination than it once was, but in general you'll get far more for your money in shops, restaurants, hotels and on public transport than you will in the West. Costs are highest in Budapest and Balaton, and (as you'd expect) things are cheapest in those areas that see fewest tourists (such as the eastern reaches of the Great Plain). For the sake of giving you the 'worst-case' scenario, the budget below is based on staying in Budapest. Be aware that there is actually a very real spectrum of costs within the city itself, and that a beer in a prime spot by the river will cost over double that of a beer elsewhere. The following estimate provides for pockets shallow, medium and deep, and the figures are for a daily spend per person; the calculation assumes two people sharing accommodation (and therefore paying half each of the room cost) – a single traveller may find the accommodation cost slightly higher. Costs beyond Budapest and Balaton should be between one-third and two-fifths lower.

**Strapped** Church mice can scrape by on around 5,500Ft (£15.00/US$28) per day by staying in a hostel dorm, eating in a basic büfé and getting around on foot. There might even be change for a decilitre of wine in a backstreet *borozó*.

**Modest** If you can't splash out but can afford a minor ripple, you'll get along comfortably with 13,000Ft (£35/US$64) a day by seeking out a cheap panzió (10,000Ft for a double). This will allow you to have a light snack for lunch, visit the odd museum and gallery, travel around by public transport, and eat a two-course meal with wine at an inexpensive restaurant.

**Comfortable** A daily allowance of 30,000Ft (£80.00/US$148) will permit a stay in a four-star hotel, ample sightseeing, cake stops, a meal in a decent restaurant, some late-night drinks in a bar, and a taxi back to your room.

**Indulgent** For 50,000Ft (£133/US$246) you can kick off your shoes and live the city high life. Stay in a luxury hotel, drink cocktails, eat well and make merry, travel where you want to go and see most of what you want to see. You'll rarely need to check the restaurant prices before taking a table, and you should still have a bit of loose change at the end of the day.

**Hey, big spender** If money is no object, book a plush room at the Four Seasons, dine at the Gundel, drink top Tokaji Aszú until it's coming out of your ears, take in a performance at the State Opera House, bet bravely at the Várkert Casino and set about the shops of Váci utca. If you want to spend a fortune in Budapest it is quite possible to do so – it will simply take a little longer than in London or Paris.

### Visa TravelMoney

A safe and convenient alternative to carrying cash or travellers' cheques is the Visa TravelMoney scheme (offered through Travelex; ✆ 020 7837 9580; e *customerservices@travelex.com*). The system is based on a pre-paid travel card that allows holders 24-hour access to their money in any local currency. You simply load the card up with funds before your trip and draw the cash out as you go along from ATM machines. Once you've exhausted your funds you throw the card away.

## Credit cards

Although locals tend to pay for goods and services in cash, major credit cards are accepted in Hungary, particularly in tourist-heavy shops, hotels and restaurants. However, smaller outlets – including some supermarkets, museums and transport ticket offices – may not take them. If your card is lost or stolen, notify your credit-card company immediately to prevent the possibility of fraud.

**American Express** ✆ 1 235 4330
**Visa** ✆ 0800 963833 (UK 24-hour hotline)
**Mastercard (Hungary)** VI Budapest, WestEnd City Center, Tower C, Floor 6, Vaci út 1–3; ✆ 1 238 7500

## Banks

Hungary has both state-run and privately owned banks that operate entirely separately from each other. In general, banks are open from 08.00–16.00/17.30 on weekdays and 08.00–12.00 on Saturdays – however, some close as early as 15.00 during the week and don't open at all at the weekend. All are shut on Sundays. Twenty-four-hour automated teller machines (ATMs) are fairly commonplace (you'll find them even in small towns) with most accepting American Express, Visa, Mastercard, as well as debit cards from Cirrus and Maestro. Check with your bank before you travel whether you'll be charged a commission fee.

## Discount cards

The International Student Card (ISIC) or International Youth Travel Card (for non-students under 26) will entitle you to reductions on entry to many museums, galleries and other attractions, and on journeys on some public transport networks. Concessionary rates for pensioners usually only apply to Hungarian nationals, although it is a little-publicised fact that over-65s can travel free on all forms of public transport in Budapest and that elderly EU residents can enter the Parliament building without charge by showing their passports. If you are travelling extensively beyond Budapest, the Hungary Card might be worth investing in. Accepted at participating outlets around the country, it allows discounts on accommodation, restaurants, museums, public transport and certain cultural events – it will even get you 20% off the price of the Budapest Card (see page 98). You'll also receive reductions on highway tolls, the hydrofoil, and car rental. The card is valid for 13 months, is transferable, and can be bought from Tourinform offices for 7,935Ft. For more information, see www.hungarycard.hu or call 1 266 3741.

## GETTING AROUND

Public transport within Hungary is efficient, reliable and cheap; most villages and towns are accessible by either train or bus (although certain very remote areas – such as the extreme northeast – are most readily navigated by car). Many settlements can be explored by foot but public transport within larger towns is also excellent. Buses, trolleybuses and trams run throughout the day until around 23.00; tickets can be purchased from newsagents, street stands and some hotels, and should be stamped in the punching machines aboard the vehicles. There are no scheduled internal flights.

### By train

Trains operated by the Hungarian state railway company MÁV (Magyar Államvasutak) certainly can't be described as modern, but – like a favourite pair of slippers (or Jimmy Choo-choos?!) – they are plain, roomy and comfortable. There are first- and second-class carriages, and often a buffet car; you must buy a separate ticket for your bike (costing an additional 25%), and place it in the front or back carriage (if there isn't a specified area set aside for cycles). Budapest is the central hub for all the major rail routes that link the main cities and towns, and in some cases it is quicker to travel via the capital – even if it adds distance to the journey – than taking secondary branch lines where services are slower. InterCity trains (IC) are the quickest and most comfortable services, offering direct routes that stop only at major towns and cities. The InterCity Express (EX) also only halts at main settlements, but doesn't get up the same speed on the way. The 'fast trains' (*sebesvonat* and *gyorsvonat*) cost around 10% less than Express trains, and stop more frequently. Avoid the 'slow trains' (*személyvonat*) unless you only have a short distance to go – they don't miss a station, calling in at even the piddliest little places, and the fares are no cheaper than for the fast trains.

There are three main railway stations in Budapest serving domestic destinations: the Eastern Railway Station (*Keleti pályaudvar*; see page 92) is the point of arrival and departure for trains from the Northern Uplands and northeast (Gyöngyös, Szécsény, Eger, Miskolc, Tokaj, etc), the Western Railway Station (*Nyugati pályaudvar*; see page 92) serves the Great Plain (Szeged, Kecskemét, Szolnok, Debrecen, Nyíregyháza, etc) and the Danube Bend (Esztergom, Visegrád, Vác, etc), and the Southern Railway Station (*Déli pályaudvar*; see page 92) caters for journeys to and from the remainding chunk – Balaton (Keszthely, Siófok, Tapolca, etc) and Transdanubia (Győr, Tata, Pécs, Kaposvár, etc). While these are loosely the rules, there are a few wild cards – Sopron, Szombathely and Herend trains, for example, use Keleti – so be sure to check before travelling. Each of these stations is also on the Budapest underground system.

In addition to the standard trains, MÁV Nosztalgia operates a number of steam trains in summer months; for details see *Local tours*, page 97. MÁV also runs four narrow-gauge railways (Budapest Children's Railway, Balaton, Kecskemét and Nyíregyháza), and there are 12 maintained by United Forest Railways (ÁEV), some of them leading through national-park areas. For details of all these, check out the website www.narrowrail.com/hungary.

## Tickets and timetables

Train timetables can be confusing for the uninitiated (see box, page 55, for help with some of the abbreviations you might encounter). Those indicating arrivals (*érkezés*) are in yellow and those for departures (*indulás*) in white; faster trains are highlighted in red. Where there is automated information, the platform (*vágány*) number/letter will appear when the train is ready for boarding.

Tickets (*jegy*) – single (*egy útra*) or return (*retur* or *oda-vissza*) – can be purchased from the departure station or (in Budapest) from the main **MÁV Ticket Office** (*VI, Andrássy út 35;* \ *1 461 5400;* e *informacio@mav.hu; open Mon–Fri 09.00–17.00; for 24-hr international information,* \ *1 461 5500*), which accepts credit cards. Unfortunately station staff may speak little English; if you want to take the hassle out of booking, deal instead with a travel agent like Vista (see page 97). First-class tickets cost 50% more than second-class. Where possible reserve your seat in advance, particularly for faster trains and when travelling to popular destinations in the summer period. Reservation is compulsory for intercity express services – look for the letter R in a circle or square on the timetable – and can be made up to 60 days in advance at MÁV offices. If you are caught without a ticket you can expect to be fined up to 6,000Ft. You can check your train route, timings and prices on www.elvira.hu; as yet there is no ticket-purchase facility available on the site, but apparently there are tentative plans for one.

## Euro Domino Rail Pass

The Euro Domino pass allows 'free' travel (for European residents only) on the Hungarian network for between three and eight days within a one-month period. The

RAIL NETWORK

BUDAPEST

## TIMETABLES

Hungarian bus and train timetables seem designed to bewilder even the most rabid Magyar nationalist with their labyrinthine linguistics. *Szabadnap* translates literally as 'free day', usually meaning a Saturday when people beyond the service industry don't work but shops are open. *Munkaszüneti nap* – 'a break-from-work day' – is a Sunday or bank-holiday Monday when everything is closed. Here goes with a few explanations of the abbreviations you'll encounter:

### Train

V     *közlekedik: keddtől–szombatig; de nem közlekedik IV.22-én és VI. 10-én*
train runs Tue–Sat, but not on Apr 22 and Jun 10

m     *munkanap* working day

z     *szombat, vasárnap és ünnepnap* Sat, Sun and special hols/bank hols (ie: festival days like Mar 15, Aug 20, Nov 1)

x     *hétköznap* weekday

w     *közlekedik: szombaton és XII. 24-én de nem közlekedik: XII. 28, IV. 26, V.3, X.18, X.25*
train runs on Sat and on Dec 24, but not on Dec 28, Apr 26, May 3, Oct 18 or Oct 25

u     *közlekedik: vasárnap és IV 21-én, VI. 9-én, de nem közlekedik: IV.20, VI.8*
train runs on Sun and on Apr 21 and Jun 9, but not Apr 20 and Jun 8

### Bus

+     *munkaszüneti napokon* on non-working day (Sun and hols)

D     *naponta, kivéve szabadnapokon* daily except for Sat (literally 'free day')

E     *a hetek első munkanapján* on the first working day of these weeks

I     *iskolai előadások napján* on school days

M     *munkanapokon* on working days

O     *szabadnapokon* on free days (usually this means Sat)

U     *a hetek utolsó munkanapján* on last working day of these weeks

V     *a hetek első munkanapját megelöző napon*
on day prior to first working day of these weeks

X     *naponta, kivéve munkaszüneti napokon* daily except non-working days (Sun and hols)

Z     *szabad és munkaszüneti napokon* on free days and non-working days

HF     *hétfői napokon* on Mon

V+     *hetek első munkanapját megelöző napok kivételével munkaszüneti napokon*
on non-working days except the day prior to the first working day of these weeks

W     *hetek első iskolai előadási napját megelöző napon*
on the day prior to the first school day of the week

VV     *V. hó 25-tol IX. hó 14-ig vasárnapi napokon* on Sun May 25–Sep 14

For V, m, z, x, w and u, see entries under *Train* above. And if you are still confused, don't worry – when it comes to the details of Hungarian transport timetables, so's everybody else...

price (*adult €41–92, under 26 €32–68*) depends upon how many days you want the pass to cover; passes are available from www.raileurope.co.uk/railpasses/eurodomino.

## By bus

Buses reach the nooks and crannies that trains cannot, and can be a quicker alternative to the railway branch lines (although they are a touch pricier than 2nd-class train fares); they are often the only viable option in remoter regions of the Great Plain and Southern Transdanubia. They are generally comfortable, with adequate legroom, and on long journeys the driver will stop every few hours to allow passengers to stretch their legs. In towns and cities, there are usually separate stations for local and inter-city services; for details of those in Budapest (and the regions they serve), see page 91. The timetables posted in the bus stations are inevitably confusing; for help with the various symbols, see box, page 55. Volánbusz operates most of the domestic buses to and from Budapest as well as the majority of the regional lines (see www.volanbusz.hu for up-to-date timetables).

### Tickets

You can buy tickets aboard the buses or guarantee a seat by pre-booking from the relevant bus station (the latter is not possible in rural areas with bus stops only). Some routes can be busy, and it's worth turning up at least 30 minutes before departure. Bus fares are based upon the length of road travelled. The following is a guide to Volánbusz charges:

| Distance | Cost | Distance | Cost |
|----------|------|----------|------|
| 0–5km | 97Ft | 30km | 423Ft |
| 10km | 133Ft | 50km | 665Ft |
| 20km | 302Ft | 100km | 1,330Ft |

## By car

Hungary is in some ways a walk in the park when you can drive in a car; the country's furthest reaches are within five or six hours of Budapest. The government has recently spent considerably on improving major roads and extending motorways. It's not all dreamy, though. Beyond the main routes, single-lane carriages can prove frustrating when stuck behind a choking Trabant held together with sticking tape and, at the other end of the spectrum, impatient boy racers can be a pain in the rear bumper. Hungarians tend to treat blind bends as overtaking opportunities too, and this can seem hairy at times. If you are involved in an accident, report to the police immediately before contacting Hungária Biztosító (*V Budapest, Bajcsy-Zsilinszky út 52;* ✆ *1 301 6060*), a company that helps foreigners with insurance claims. Most petrol stations accept credit cards and sell unleaded fuel, and some are open 24 hours. There are often pump attendants on hand, and it's polite practice to give them a small tip. For information on the required driving licences etc, see page 46.

### Roads

Hungarian motorways are prefixed with the letter M (see below), international roads with 'E' and smaller roads have two- or three-digit numbers (the first of which reflects the highway it joins). In Hungary there are nine dual carriageways, Roads 1–7 and 10 radiating from Budapest like a wagon wheel and Road 8 beginning at Székesfehérvár (and going westwards). (With typical Magyar perversity, the planners omitted a road numbered 9.) There are currently five motorways. The M0 ringroad half circles Budapest; the M1 connects Budapest with Vienna via Győr; the M7 runs to the southern Balaton shore and currently stops short of Balatonföldvár (but is being extended); the M3 ties the capital with the eastern part of the country, leading into

Miskolc and going almost as far as Hajdúbőszőrmény (construction is underway to stretch it to the Ukrainian border via Nyíregyháza); the M5 leads in a southerly direction from Budapest to Kecskemét (and is being lengthened to reach the border town of Rözske via Szeged, providing access to Serbia and Montenegro and a direct connection to southern Europe).

The M1, M3, M5 and M7 motorways require the purchase of a motorway toll sticker, which must be displayed on your vehicle's windscreen. These stickers (*vignette* or *matrica*) should be purchased before you set wheel on the motorway and can be bought from petrol stations and post offices. For a car or motorbike whose weight does not exceed 3.5 tonnes, tolls stickers cost 1,120Ft for four days (1,460Ft between May 1 and Sep 30), 2,300Ft for ten days, 3,900Ft for a month and 35,000Ft for a year. When you buy your toll sticker ensure you hold on to the sales receipt and silver counterfoil as if you are stopped by traffic patrol you will be asked to produce these as well. Without all three you will be subject to an on-the-spot fine. For more information see www.motorways.hu.

Emergency telephones (24-hour) are situated every few kilometres along the M1, M5, M7 and M5. The Magyar Autóklub (❱ *1 345 1800*) provides a 24-hour breakdown service but if you are a member of the AA or AAA the Yellow Angels (❱ *1 345 1744*) will provide roadside assistance and repair minor faults free of charge.

### Driving laws

You can't drink a drop of alcohol if you choose to drive as drinking and driving is strictly prohibited and the law fiercely enforced. Outside built-up areas, you should have dipped headlights switched on at all times (even during daylight hours). Seat belts are compulsory for front-seat passengers, and those in the back should buckle up outside cities and towns. Vehicles drive on the right. Overtaking on the right is illegal, as is using a hand-held mobile phone while driving and tooting your horn in urban areas unless in an emergency. Speed limits are 130km/h on motorways, 110km/h on dual carriageways and 90km/h on all other roads (except in built-up areas, where the restriction is 50km/h). The police are hot on traffic violations and will indiscriminately pull over vehicles to check the credentials of both the cars and the drivers. On-the-spot fines of up to 10,000Ft can be issued by the police, with much heavier penalties by the authorities in the event of a more serious infringement. Pedestrians should note that Hungarian motorists rarely notice pedestrian crossings. For information on taxis, see Budapest's *Getting around*, page 94.

### Car hire

To rent a car in Hungary you must be aged 21 or over, and in possession of a driving licence (valid for at least a year) and passport. You will need to leave a deposit – usually a temporary debit from your credit card. Some companies will deliver the car to your hotel (and pick it up again); the car will have a full petrol tank on delivery and you must ensure it is full when returned.

The following companies have good reputations:

**Avis** V Budapest, Szervita tér 8; ❱ 1 318 4240; international reservations ❱ +36 1 318 4685; e info@avis.hu; www.avis.hu. Reliable company whose office is located in the underground car park of Szervita tér. *Cars from €231/week.*

**Fox Autorent** XXII Budapest, Nagytétényi út 48–50; ❱ 1 3829000; e fox@fox-autorent.com; www.fox-autorent.com or Fly Balaton Airport, 8391 Sármellék, Repülőtér; ❱ 06 70 455 4020. Full range of cars, most with A/C. There is the option of airport/home/hotel delivery, and 24-hour road assistance. *Cars from €223/week. Open 08.00–20.00 daily.*

**Worldwide Rent A Car** V Budapest, Sas utca 10–12; ❱ 1 302 0431. Situated in front of the Basilica, on the corner of Sas Utca and Zrínyi utca. This is the place to try if you want to pay very little and don't mind an older, unflashy car with a high mileage.

## By boat

**Mahart PassNave** (*V Budapest, Belgrád rakpart;* ✆ *1 484 4013/4010;* e *hydrofoil@ mahartpassnave.hu; www.mahartpassnave.hu*) operates a daily hydrofoil service between Budapest and destinations on the Danube Bend every Saturday, Sunday and bank holiday from May 21 to September 18. The ferry departs daily at 09.30 from Vigadó tér landing stage and travels to Esztergom via Visegrád and Nagymaros (the total journey taking two hours). Tickets to Visegrád and Nagymaros cost sgl/rtn 1,990/3,490Ft, and to Esztergom sgl/rtn 2,490/3,990Ft; tickets from Visegrád to Esztergom cost sgl/rtn 990/1,490Ft. There are discounts available for children while infants (under 6) travel free on a parental lap. Mahart is constantly amending its tour schedules so you may find additional services that we haven't listed – see the website for the most up-to-date information. The **Balaton Shipping Company** (*Balatoni Hajózás; Siófok, Krúdy sétány 2;* ✆ *84 310050;* e *infor@balatonihajozas.hu; www.balatonihajozas.hu*) operates a ferry service across 22 ports around Lake Balaton. Ferries cost adult/concessions 360/300Ft; motorcycle 500Ft, car 1,040Ft.

## By bike

There are 2,000km of cycling paths in Hungary, and this network is being extended all the time. It's illegal to cycle on motorways or major roads (those marked with a one-digit number) and a white front headlight, and a red tail-light, yellow light reflectors on the spokes of both wheels, a bell (or similar) and working breaks are compulsory. Pedestrians may also use cycle lanes (although cyclists have right of way), so keep your eyes peeled. You may take bikes on trains for an additional 25% of the ticket price. However some intercity trains don't carry bikes – look out for a bicycle symbol on the timetable or check when purchasing your ticket. Before you set off, speak to the **Hungarian Bikers Association** (*VI Budapest, Bajcsy-Zsilinszky út 31;* ✆ *1 311 2467*); in Budapest, the **Friends of the City Cycling Association** (*VBB; V, Curia utca 3, 2nd floor, Room 1; tel: 06 30 922 7064; www.vbb.hu*) is also a good contact point, and arranges tours.

## Hitchhiking

Hitchhiking is prohibited on motorways, but is legal on all other roads, and is a popular way for students to get about. Hitching is as safe as it can be, but there is always an inherent risk in climbing into the vehicle of a stranger. If you must hitchhike, travel in daylight and preferably with someone you know (particularly if you are female); if you are alone, keep a mobile phone to hand and notify someone beforehand of your intended destination and estimated route.

## ACCOMMODATION

There is no shortage of places to stay in Hungary, suiting all budgets and most whims. Once the state monopoly was undone in the 1980s, a wave of visitor accommodation rolled in that shows no signs of breaking (particularly now the country has joined the EU). The gamut of hotels runs from exclusive converted 19th-century mansions, luxury spa centres and upper-end conference hotels based on Western models, through comfortable mid-range affairs that have good facilities without every trimming, and on to basic joints that might be clean and well-kept or downright depressing and tatty. Overlapping them from the mid-range downwards are pensions, an imprecise label that is used equally by private guesthouses (often family-run) and smallish hotels that undercut (or hope the name gives the impression of undercutting) the prices of other hotels in the area. The very cheapest options of all are private rooms, campsites and beds in hostels or university digs. With the exception of campsites, hostels and the very top hotels (generally rooted in big cities or major tourist haunts), you can expect to find examples of each of the above in even little towns.

Deciding whether or not to **book ahead** depends on where you're going and when – and, in all honesty, your character. We've rarely had problems finding somewhere to lay our heads when we've turned up in a town, but we're a fairly happy-go-lucky and unfussy pair; if the day's end is something you'll worry about or you're after something specific, you should certainly make a reservation. Booking during festivals and events is strongly advised; remember too that summer (*Jun–Sep*) is high season, and crowds gather in Budapest, the Danube Bend, Lake Balaton, resorts in the Northern Uplands, and ever-popular pockets like Pécs and Sopron. At this time, spa towns in particular can reach capacity. Large hotels will invariably have English-speaking staff answering their telephones, as well as email and website booking services. It can be more complicated making arrangements with smaller hotels and pensions, who may or may not have English speakers manning the phone – they'll almost always understand some German – and may or may not have websites. In these cases you will usually make yourself understood in the end with a few basic words in Hungarian (see *Appendix 1*). An alternative is to use a local travel agency, and the Hungarian travel agent Ibusz can usually book private rooms; you'll pay a small fee for the service. Tourinform offices can offer advice on all types of accommodation, but do not themselves arrange bookings.

High-season accommodation **rates** – generally a 15–30% hike – can start as early as April and run as late as mid October; however, some city hotels exclude the hottest months of July and August (when many customers look elsewhere for cool air). The higher rates are also imposed at Christmas and New Year, and during festivals and events. The prices quoted in this book are walk-in high-season rates for a single night's stay; while these are inevitably subject to change, they were all researched during a four-month period and can therefore be used as a comparative guide. You can get reductions for advance and group bookings, and stays of more than one night. VAT (12%) and a variable local tourist tax (3% in Budapest) are usually included in the quoted price, but it is worth checking before accepting your room.

## Hotels

While hotels (*szálló* or *szálloda*) are categorised according to a star system, this is a less reliable guide to facilities than in the West; you may find, for instance, that a four-star establishment has a swimming pool where a five-star does not. Nor can a star rating account for character, and some of the historic hotels fall outside the top bands. You can expect as a minimum that rooms in hotels above two-star category will have en-suite bathroom, TV and telephone; where bathrooms are shared, we say so. Top hotels offer satellite TV, fitness suite, sauna, restaurant, bar and sometimes boutiques and a swimming pool; those in the mid range will generally have a restaurant and fitness facilities of some sort, but beyond that are difficult to predict (they can surprise you with luxuries like saunas and swimming pools). 'Wellness' tourism – tapping into Hungary's rich resources of thermal water – is big business, and there are many spa hotels catering both to guests with specific medical complaints and those after a simple pampering.

Breakfast is a buffet spread; a peculiar (irritating!) quirk is that while it is generally included in the price of budget and mid-range accommodation, you may be charged extra in the higher-cost places. Many hotels can arrange bike hire, theatre trips and excursions. Most of the better hotels offer discounted deals on weekend breaks. (Keep an eye on websites like www.lastminute.com and www.expedia.com.) If you are travelling alone, be aware that there are few single rooms; while some hotels will charge a lower rate for a single occupant, others may insist on the full double-room price.

## Pensions and inns

At their finest, pensions (*panzió*) or inns (*fogadó*) represent better value than hotels in the same star bracket. Some are simply hotels by another name (and can have facilities including a restaurant, sauna and even, rarely, a small swimming pool). Others are the equivalent of guesthouses or bed and breakfasts – rooms in a family house – and are wholly fashioned by the tastes and energies of the owners. If you find a good 'un, a place run by warm and welcoming people who take pride and care in what they do, the stay can knock spots off that in any luxury hotel.

## Private rooms and apartments

Bagging a bed in someone else's house is usually a far cheaper alternative to hotels and most pensions, and also allows you a peek behind domestic curtains. **Private rooms** can be arranged through an agency like Ibusz. In doing so, you accept a room unseen and clearly take a gamble of sorts; you can cut the odds by specifying a location in the very centre (Belváros), where buildings are likely to be better (and more convenient) than those in the suburbs (which can be tatty high-rise blocks). Alternatively you can knock at houses with *szoba kiadó* or *Zimmer frei* signs. Your hostess is likely to be a retired lady with but a smattering of English, so don't bank on any meaningful chitchat. Rooms usually have TV, bedding and towels. Expect to pay 3,000–6,000Ft for a single room and 4,000–9,000Ft for a double. Rates should include heating and electricity (but not food), and are dependent upon the season and duration (there may be a minimum length of stay to qualify for the quoted rate). Self-contained **apartments** are an alternative for families and small groups. Most come with a fully equipped kitchen, bed linen and towels, TV and radio. Rates include all utility costs.

## Hostels and college accommodation

Beyond Budapest, **youth hostels** (*ifjúsági szálló*) can seem thin on the ground and are generally open in summer only. You rarely need a Hostelling International (IYHF) card, although this might get you a small reduction in price. Beds are available from around 2,500Ft. For further information or reservations, contact the Travel Section of the Hungarian Youth Hostel Association (*V Budapest, Molnár utca 3;* ❧ *1 411 2390;* e *info@youthhostels.hu; www.youthhostels.hu or www.reservation.hu*).

During student vacations (and sometimes all year round), many **colleges** rent out vacant student rooms or dormitories. These can be offered for as little as 1,500Ft per person, and are the cheapest option of any available. Regional Tourinform offices can usually provide a list of colleges and contact numbers.

## Campsites

It is illegal to camp rough. Camping grounds range from swish sites with restaurants, sports facilities and even swimming pools to lonely fields with little more than pitching space. In addition to a nightly charge for the ground rent for your tent or caravan, and for any other vehicle, you will usually also pay a charge per person per night on top of local tax. The charges vary (and are particularly high around Lake Balaton), but you can expect to pay from 600Ft/person, 600Ft/tent and 900Ft/caravan. Most campsites are open between April/May and September/October, although a few open all year. Some have wooden bungalows for those without tents (which may or may not have en-suite facilities), and others pensions and motels within their grounds. Tourinform produces a brochure showing all the country's campsites.

# EATING AND DRINKING

*I am not a glutton – I am an explorer of food.*

Erma Bombeck (1927–1996)

## Food

**Hungarian cuisine** (*Magyar konyha*) has been influenced by the kitchens of Serbia, France and Turkey; the Renaissance court of King Mátyás introduced Italian ingredients like garlic, onion and dried pasta; the Germans and Austrians muscled in during the Austro-Hungarian period with their cream-filled desserts, sauerkraut and dumplings. All these tastes add nuances to a no-nonsense, homely tradition of peasant cookery.

Pork became a staple of the Hungarian diet after the Turkish invasion, when the Muslim occupiers left pigs wholly to the natives. 'Be not afraid of scooping in the piquant sour cream' one of the Gundels once cried, and his advice was not ignored; it is handsomely applied to soups and sauces, as well as dishes of meat, cabbage and sweet pasta. Vegetable accompaniments are pickled or from the freezer, and salads plate-edge afterthoughts. The vegetarian diner may feel put upon in traditional restaurants, where the choice is often restricted to fruit soups and cheese or mushrooms in breadcrumbs. A one-time Hungarian peasant phrase for 'add spices' (*trágyázd meg*) – no longer much in use, unfortunately – literally translated as 'fertilise with manure'; cumin, caraway, black pepper and marjoram are frequent fertilisers, but when you think Hungary it's red (*piros*) paprika that sets the tastebuds tingling. Probably introduced from Spain in the 16th century (although not widely used until the 19th), it imparts vivid culinary colour, and ranges in taste from sweet and fruity (*édes*) to fiery (*erős*), the latter proffering a kick like a hussar's horse. And woe betide he who gets between a Magyar and a piece of fresh bread (*kenyér*); it is regarded as the greatest of feasts.

While many busy Hungarians may just grab a roll on the run, if they greet the day properly then it is early and with a **breakfast** (*reggeli*) of open sandwiches. Salami (*szalámi*) or dried, chorizo-like sausage (*száraz kolbász*), ham, cheese, yellow pepper and tomato are eaten with white bread. The weekend may see omelettes on the table, while at Easter there is gammon-like ham with boiled eggs and horseradish. The reviving morning brew is hot (often black) coffee or tea with lemon (not milk).

**Lunch** is the main event, and comprises two courses. The first is likely to be soup (*leves*). Freshwater lakes like Balaton provide the specimens for fish soup (*halászlé*) – a customary dish on Christmas Eve. Chicken soup (*tyúk húsleves*) is packed with vegetables and light pasta (similar to Italian *vermicelli*), while fruit soup (*hideg gyümölcsleves*) is a refreshing summer slurp, flavoured with cherry or strawberry, topped with cream and served cold. The meaty Hortobágy pancake (*Hortobágyi húsos palacsinta*) is a speciality of the Great Plain; seasoned minced pork or poultry is folded into thin pancakes and baked in a sauce of paprika and sour cream. Please don't miss this one – it shades the number-one spot on our Hungarian-dish wish list.

The second course is invariably a meat-based rib sticker. The international superstar is, of course, goulash (actually *gulyás*, and pronounced 'gooyash'), strictly a soup rather than a stew, and containing beef or pork, pinched dumplings, vegetables and the ubiquitous paprika. Cooked in a cauldron (*bogrács*), its roots can be traced to the country's nomadic ancestors. While today's Hungarians at home tend to treat it as a main course, in restaurants you'll find it among the starting line up. The same applies to the smoky, meaty and gorgeous kidney-bean soup (*jókai bableves*). Each of the above should be mopped up with a hunk of dunking bread, but other specialities are served with weighty side dishes including egg dumplings (*galuska* or *nokedli*), couscous-type pasta (*tarhonya*), potato croquettes (*krokett*) and rice. A traditional stew (*pörkölt*) might be concocted from any of the main meats, but our vote goes to that with chicken (*csirkepaprikás*) – creamy, golden as toffee, and occasionally with the coxcomb thrown in! Other popular choices are stuffed cabbage (*töltött káposzta*) or pepper (*töltött paprika*) filled with minced meat, a piece of the earthy-tasting pike perch (*fogas*), and a plate-sized slab of Wiener schnitzel (*bécsi szelet*). The latter is often eaten for Sunday lunch.

**Pudding** (*édességek* or *desszertek*) requires a healthy appetite and a sweet tooth. Any room for a cake, an ice cream, a strudel or a crêpe? At times savoury becomes sweet; *túróscsusza* is a hot pastry with ricotta, sour cream and – believe it or not – pork crackling.

Pastas, too, are familiar dessert dishes. *Rétes* is an Austrian strudel filled with either fruit, walnut, peppery cabbage or poppy seeds and ricotta, while walnut cream and chocolate sauce is the heavenly mix in a Gundel pancake (*Gundel palacsinta*). For other sweet options, see box, page 64.

## Drink

Thirsty? Big-name fizzy **soft drinks** are available everywhere, as are bottled mineral waters (*ásványvíz*) and fruit juices. Hungarians satisfy regular coffee cravings (see opposite); although they are less enamoured with tea, which is sipped straight or with lemon, teahouses are popping up with growing frequency in Budapest. For something stronger, fruit **brandy** (*pálinka*) is a popular tipple – even at breakfast time for rural diehards. It's distilled from apricots (*barack*), plums (*szilva*), pears (*körte*), cherries (*cseresznye*) or peaches (*őszibarack*), although if you try a home brew – a common hobby of the older generation – you'll get some fire with your fruit. Another *apéritif* is the herbal and distinctive Unicum, said to have been invented by the court physician to József II, and distilled by the Zwack family for 200 years. Many claims have been made for this bitter liquid – that it is an aid to digestion, a restorative and even an aphrodisiac; the only undeniable truth is that it is an acquired taste. Drink it straight, with cola or even as a hot toddy. And give it as many second chances as you feel able. (There is a small museum at the Budapest Zwack plant at Soroksári út 26. Contact them on 1 476 2308 to arrange a visit.)

Much **beer** (*sör*) is imported from the Czech Republic or brewed under the licence of foreign companies like Tuborg and HB, but Hungarian beers are deserving of attention. They might be bottled or on tap, and fall into two types – lager (*világos*) and brown (*barna*), the latter similar in colour to English bitter but with a sweet flavour. The leading breweries are Dreher and Borsodi, the first marginally our preferred choice, while other regional brands can be found in the supermarkets. The word for 'cheers!' – *egészségedre* – is a mouthful at the best of times, but becomes a particular trial after a drink or two. Remember not to clink together those beer glasses (see page 80).

It is said that Hungarians can be divided into the few who produce **wine** and the many who would dearly love to. For much of the 20th century, you'd be forgiven for thinking the amateurish majority had been let loose on the vineyards. There was a massive decline in quality behind the Iron Curtain; vineyards were neglected, fine sites abandoned, and state co-operatives devoted themselves to mass production. During the 1980s, Hungary's main export, Bull's Blood, became a byword for vinegar; the Soviets were the sole bulk buyers. However, change has been rapid since the advent of privatisation. Joint ventures with foreign vintners and investment in technology have resulted in some fine wineries, many of them family-owned.

Some facts. There are 22 wine regions and around 20 Hungarian grape varieties. Seventy-five per cent of wines are white (*fehér bor*), although recently it is the reds (*vörös bor*) that have attracted attention. In very rough terms – there are exceptions – white is produced in the north and red in the south. Grapes include Hungarian and imported varieties. Good-to-fine white wines are made from Furmint (the base wine of Tokaji Aszú), Királyleányka, Hárslevelű, Irsai Olivér and Olaszrizling, along with Sauvignon, Chardonnay and Tramini. Quality home-grown reds include Kékfrankos (the most widely planted) and Kadarka, while Cabernet, Merlot and Pinot Noir have all been produced at very respectable levels. Reds are characteristically light because of the country's cold winters, and they are often served at a lower temperature than you might usually expect. There is a Hungarian equivalent of the French *appellation controlée*, so before buying check for *minőségi* (quality) or *különleges minőségi* (special quality) on the bottle. During the day and in bars, wine is sometimes mixed with soda or sparkling water to make a spritzer (*fröccs*).

## Where to eat and drink

Light bites of pickles, cold meats and sandwiches are available to take away from delicatessens in towns, while those who want to take the weight off their feet for a short while seek out a *bisztró* or *büfé*, which offer small selections of hot food alongside filled rolls. Burger and sandwich (*szendvics*) stands are burgeoning in cities, together with global fast-food giants that vie with cheaper kebab shops and Chinese buffets. Otherwise seek out a place selling *főzelék*, dishes of puréed vegetables (not unlike baby food) that are cooked in the home but generally overlooked by restaurants. They can be made from whatever vegetables are in season and make great bar food. The pumpkin version is very tasty, if you like gloop. One popular snack on the move is a *perec*, a large and salty piece of pretzel-shaped bread (try to avoid stands where they are uncovered and therefore likely to be stale), and another a *lángos*, something of a bulky hybrid of the Yorkshire pudding and the doughnut. A *lángos* is often topped with ladlefuls of runny garlic sauce, sour cream and cheese, and is enough to give your heart an attack just looking at it. Fresh produce is available in supermarkets, but head instead for outdoor markets or market halls, which have an excellent array of meat, fish, vegetables and fruit.

### Restaurants

There are several words for different types of restaurant, although in reality some are used interchangeably. *Étterem* or *vendéglő* indicate a restaurant, the latter supposedly a cheaper establishment than the former (although this is by no means always true), while you can usually expect traditional Hungarian specialities in a *csárda* (inn). Lunch is customarily the main meal of the day, but restaurants in cities cater equally for the evening crowd; despite this, you risk bed without supper if you arrive much later than 22.00 (and aim for 21.00 or earlier in the provinces). What, then, can you expect from the dining experience? How long's a piece of string? There are courtyard gardens and river terraces, brick cellar restaurants and dining rooms, modern lounges and rustic spaces strung with dried paprika. Traditional restaurants range from classy and intimate to cavernous coach-party traps. You might be treated to the lively strains of a gypsy violinist, or suffer the tinny torture of a cheap synthesiser. While Budapesters no longer double-take on seeing a vegetarian restaurant, in the main those averse to meat are poorly catered for; even the obligatory fried vegetables are sometimes cooked in animal fat. Beyond the top restaurants, the biggest unknown is likely to be the quality of service. While many owners are waking up to tourist expectations, it remains far from unusual for a waiter to don the proverbial blinkers. If this is the case, don't tip.

What else to bear in mind? You shouldn't have difficulty securing a table in the majority of restaurants, although it is worth booking at the best. Dress codes are generally relaxed; Gundel (see page 114) is the exception rather than the rule in requiring diners to wear jacket and tie. Don't order if food or drink menus are missing prices, and always check your bill carefully. Despite the brilliance of the Hungarian mind, errors of calculation are common and curiously tend to fall above the line rather than below it. Ask whether a service charge is included – it usually isn't – and tip ten–15 per cent if you're satisfied. (For tipping etiquette, see page 80.) Major credit cards are usually accepted in cities, but always ask in advance if you haven't got cash in reserve.

### Pâtisseries and coffee houses

Hungarians love sugar and caffeine in equal measure. By rights, they should spend their days bouncing off the walls and their nights in wide-eyed insomnia. **Pâtisseries** (*cukrászda*) display a tempting selection of cakes, pastries and ice creams. Some are shops selling sticky things to take away, while others allow you to have your cake and eat it amid chandeliers and marble, and with a coffee at your elbow. You'll find cakes in **coffee houses** (*kávéház*), too. At the turn of the 20th century, there were nearly

## SWEET STUFF

You'll have no problem sating that craving for sweetness. Hungary's restaurants, cafés and (especially) pâtisseries promise things naughty but nice. If you can forget the scales, the doctor's orders and your conscience's wagging finger, below are some of the treats that await you.

### Cake

**Dobos torta** (cake) Dobos József, a master chef, prepared his cake for the Hungarian National Exhibition of 1885, and it worked gourmets and confectioners into a drooling frenzy. Competitors were desperate to learn the recipe, and orders flooded in from home and abroad. It became Hungary's most famous cake. Five layers of white sponge filled with chocolate cream and glazed caramel on top.

**Sacher torta** Rich chocolate cake with jam running through the middle. Originated in Vienna.

**Gyümölcs torta** Sponge cake with fruits and whipped cream.

**Rigó Jancsi** A two-inch-square sponge cake with chocolate cream and chocolate glaze atop.

**Somlói galuska** Layers of sponge cake, rich chocolate sauce, walnuts, raisins and a whirl of whipped cream served in a bowl.

### Pancakes, pastries and strudels

**Palacsinta** Crêpes with a choice of fillings, such as sweet cottage cheese, nuts, fruit, chocolate cream or jam. The classic dish of this family is the Gundel palacsinta, a folded pancake containing walnut and rum filling and drenched in chocolate sauce and more rum. It may be served flaming. Flaming good.

**Krémes** Square flaky pastries with French pâtisserie and whipped creams.

**Rétes** Strudels are available with a range of fillings, including sour (or Morello) cherry (*meggyes*), sweet cottage cheese (*túrós*), and poppy seeds (*mákos*).

### Ice creams

**Fagylalt** There can be no nation more committed in its devotion to ice cream. Roadside vendors, pâtisseries and ice-cream parlours (*fagylaltozó* or *fagyizó*) really are hubs of the community in summer, and they'll do a very respectable trade in winter too. *Fagyi* (the slang term) is served in cones and you pay by the scoop (*gombóc*). The range of flavours can be daunting – anything from vanilla to poppy seed.

1,000 coffee houses in the Hungarian capital, with a staggering 64 places along the Nagy körút alone to drink the 'black soup' (*fekete leves*). As in many continental countries, these places were traditionally kaleidoscopes of social colour where newspapers were read, politics discussed, poems composed and rebellions plotted (see page 115). Penniless poets would famously settle bills with sonnets written on napkins. Coffee still very much matters. The standard cup is a small and strong espresso (*eszpresszó* or *kávé*). You can order it with milk (*tejeskávé*), but beyond that the standard varies. A cappuccino may be little more than a filter coffee with whipped cream, and isn't worth a scribbled couplet.

## Bars etc

The various categories of watering hole might confuse the raw Western recruit. Far from upmarket, a wine bar (*borozó*) often equates to a den of men drinking rough vintages ladled from metal drums for 30Ft a decilitre. You might find spit and sawdust in a beer hall (*söröző*), too, but you are just as likely to find a well-turned-out pub. The word *pince* indicates a cellar, be that a brick beer tavern with wooden benches or a place for tasting wine (*borospince*) from regional vineyards. Some wineshops (*italbolt*) also offer tastings. Modern bars often bear the name 'café', and are contemporary reinterpretations of an earlier coffee-house culture that declined in the mid-20th century; they may serve food and coffee, and have music and dancing, but they are more bar than traditional café or club. When wetting your whistle, you can order draught beer by the half-litre (*korsó*) or smaller (*pohár*) glass, while wine is served by the bottle (*üveg*), by the glass (*pohár*) or – usually in wine bars – by the decilitre.

## PUBLIC HOLIDAYS AND FESTIVALS

Hungary's promotional literature justifiably makes much of its status as a country of festivals. This is a cultured place with a proud musical heritage, a place of wine production and regional variants in cuisine, and one keen to preserve folk traditions (at least for a few days a year). You'll find the staples are performances of music, song, dance and theatre, wine and food galore, processions and floats, and demonstrations of folk art or equestrian pageantry. However, there are some weird and wonderful ones among the line-up – the world's biggest celebration of fish soup in Baja, *gulyás* cooks fighting for the coveted 'golden stirring spoon' in Gyöngyös, celebrants prancing about in hairy suits and sinister masks on Shrove Tuesday in Mohács. And of course on the patron saint's day a 1,000-year-old mummified hand is paraded through the streets. Top that!

Festivals are celebrated throughout the country throughout the year, although the greatest concentration is between June and August, and the real biggies are in Budapest (particularly the Spring and Autumn festivals). Information on regional festivals and events are included under the relevant city, town or village sections. The following public holidays are celebrated annually (note that most businesses and shops close on these days).

### EASTER

The week leading up to Easter is a busy one for the women of Hungarian households, who perform a thorough spring clean and go into baking overdrive. In addition, they paint hard-boiled eggs with folksy motifs and patterns, and present them to visitors as Easter gifts. The celebrations themselves begin on Good Friday, with mass services held at 15.00 in churches all over the city. On Easter Sunday, following morning services, children are treated with chocolate eggs and small presents from the Easter Bunny. The real fun, though, comes on Easter Monday, when the traditional 'sprinkling' (*locsolkodás*) takes place. Men customarily 'sprinkle' their female relatives and friends with cheap perfume, in return for which they receive a reward – a painted egg, some chocolate coins or a shot of *pálinka* (potent fruit brandy). The latter reward means that by mid-afternoon there can be some rather giddy sprinklers! Originally this ritual was a fertility rite, when men visited the single women of the village and sprinkled their friends and relatives along the way. Even today it is used as a form of courtship. It is less sodden than it was in the past, however – when buckets of water were used in the villages rather than cologne.

| January 1 | New Year's Day |
| March 15 | Independence Day |
| March/April | Easter Monday |
| May 1 | Labour Day |
| May/June | Whit Monday |
| August 20 | St Stephen's Day (founding of the state) |
| October 23 | Republic Day (anniversary of the 1956 revolution and the 1989 proclamation of the republic) |
| November 1 | All Saints' Day |
| December 25–26 | Christmas (*Karácsony*) (usually December 24 too) |

## SHOPPING

**Popular gifts or souvenirs** include wine, foods and spices (see box opposite), and folk art (embroidered tablecloths and napkins, decorated boxes, hand-made dolls and wooden toys, and painted vases, jugs and mugs) – for the latter you're best to head for the regional sources (like Kalocsa, Hollókő and Mezőkövesd for embroidery, and Hódmezővásárhely, Tiszafüred and Hajdúszoboszló for pottery) rather than tourist-tat shops in Budapest. You won't have difficulty finding a piece of porcelain either, contemporary or antique. There are delicate Hollóháza ceramics and chunky Sárospatak pots. However, Herend and Zsolnay are the premier manufacturers, each established for over 150 years, and producing hand-moulded dishes, bowls, figurines and, in the latter's case, vivid majolica roof tiles. Herend is classy and conservative, while Zsolnay is distinctive for the dark iridescence of some of its pieces, like the feathers of a cormorant. These two are the dinner-service favourites of quality restaurants; discreetly check the maker's mark under your next *gulyás* bowl. Ajkas produces quality leaded crystal.

The run-away winners in the shopping stakes, both in terms of value for money and all-round atmosphere, are bustling market halls (*vásárcsarnok*) and flea markets (*bolha piac* or *ócskapiac*). In most cases – and particularly if buying fresh food – it is best to get there early. It's strictly cash only; your flexible friend will be laughed all the way to the nearest bank ATM. You should not try to haggle in market halls, but you can do so in flea markets – although Hungarians are not very enthusiastic traders, and tend to seem a bit fed up with the process.

Everyday items are widely available in towns and cities. **Non-food shops** are usually open 10.00–18.00 on weekdays and 09.00–13.00 on Saturdays, while **those selling foodstuffs** are open 07.00–19.00 during the week and 07.00–14.00 on Saturdays. **Malls** will often keep longer hours (that include Sundays), and **markets** shorter ones that vary from site to site. International stores and malls in cities accept credit cards, but you're best to carry cash to be guaranteed of closing deals elsewhere. See *Money*, page 50, for details of tax that non-Europeans can reclaim on goods.

## ARTS AND ENTERTAINMENT

Since the 19th century, culture has been an important touchstone of Hungarian self-identity – initially as a means of tacit resistance to occupation. It is celebrated in regular festivals, and there are plenty of places in Budapest and other main cities to let dinner settle over performances of folk music, opera, dance or Hungarian takes on jazz, blues and rock. Alternatively you could let good digestion wait on some energetic clubbing.

Hungary has good reason to be proud of its **classical** heritage. Concert performances are two-a-penny, offering home-grown and international talent, although in the hot months these are more likely to be outdoor. **Operas** in Budapest are full-blown affairs, with elaborate sets and luxuriant costume. They are also often performed in Hungarian, which is considerably less romantic than Italian but probably no worse than English. Opera buff or not, you should take advantage of the ridiculously cheap tickets for performances at the stunning State Opera House. Attending performances of

## FOOD GIFTS

If you seek a tasty gift or a flavoursome reminiscence of your trip, there are a variety of specialities available in the shops, market halls and supermarkets. How about:

**Sausage/salami** (*kolbász/szalámi*) You'll find a wide selection behind the supermarket's meat counter or hanging from market stalls, ranging from mild to spicy (*csípős*). The best-known brand is Pick salami, manufactured in Szeged. Some *kolbász* needs to be cooked, rather like standard English sausages. Be aware that meats brought into the UK must be vacuum packed – you can be fined for having a bare *kolbász* in your suitcase.

**Red paprika** (*piros paprika*) The crimson spice of Hungarian life can be bought as a dried whole or in finely ground form. There are seven strengths: mild (*különleges*), also mild (*csípősségmentes*), mildish (*csemege* – the most commonly used in Hungarian dishes), medium (*édes-nemes*), slightly hot (*félédes*), hot (*rózsa*) and very hot (*erős* or *csípős*). You'll pay more for a fancy presentation bag. One of the main centres of production is Kalocsa.

**Goose liver** Available in black-and-gold tins, liver is produced by the Merian Orosháza Rt of Orosháza (in the heart of goose-gagging country), who have a monopoly on the goose-liver market. A 200g tin costs 4,400Ft.

**Caviar** A popular offering among the tins of goose liver and the Tokaji in market halls. It's not Hungarian, but it is cheap by Western standards – ranging from 3,800Ft to 19,800Ft (and small tins of Russian Astrakhan caviar for 3,500Ft). Tins are usually marked '*malosol*' (meaning 'little salt').

**Wine** (*bor*) 'Wine is sunlight, held together by water', Galileo once observed. He very probably hadn't been to Kecskemét. However, there are some among the country's 22 regional wines that are very worth drinking; those particularly favoured by connoisseurs internationally are the sweet, white Tokaji Aszú (in its distinctive long-necked bottle) and Bull's Blood (Bikavér) from Eger or Szekszárd.

**Spirits** Brandy or grappa (*pálinka*) is a popular digestif. Kecskemét redeems itself with an apricot brandy (*barack pálinka*), and there are other fruity flavours that'll take the skin off your tongue (see page 62). Alternatively, take back some Unicum, a 'healthy' spirit concocted from a secret recipe of herbs. The branding is striking, with its dark orb of a bottle and a disconcerting poster of a man emerging from water that has become an advertising classic, but the taste is of the 'acquired' variety.

Shakespeare in Hungarian probably doesn't sound much fun (and isn't), but you'll find the odd English-language **theatre** and performance (particularly in Budapest).

Most venues have their own box offices, but you can also secure seats for performances at ticket agencies (*jegyiroda*) and cultural centres. Even small towns have **cultural centres**, which are often the first ports of call for information on what's on while you're there. Cultural centres frequently host events and exhibitions themselves, and are also the places for *táncház* evenings (see page 29). Alternatively, pick up a copy of *Programme in Ungarn/in Hungary* (from Tourinform), a bilingual monthly publication listing performances scheduled around the country; *Pesti Est* and its regional equivalents also have such listings, although they are in Hungarian only.

## AN IMPORTANT NOTE ON MUSEUM PRICES

In 2004 a government decree made admission to permanent exhibitions at museums free. The Culture Ministry subsidises the museums and the number of visitors has grown significantly. Many museums – like the Hungarian National Gallery – separate their permanent exhibitions (that are now free to enter) from their temporary exhibitions (for which there is a charge). However, this is not universally applied, and the majority of museums were still charging entrance fees during the period of our research. As such, please treat the listed admission prices throughout this guidebook with caution – you may find that some institutions have dropped their charges by the time you visit.

If you want to watch a Hollywood blockbuster in a mainstream **cinema**, head for an American-style shopping mall, which often holds multiplexes. Many are in the original English with Hungarian subtitles, although comedies are frequently dubbed. If a film is advertised with its English title, you can assume it will be subtitled; alternatively look for *feliratos* (or *fel*) in the listings. Dubbed films are indicated by *magyarul beszélő* (or *mb*). Be wary of the peculiar Hungarian way of displaying times (see *Time*, page 80). It is a source of great shame that some of Budapest's art-house cinemas have been forced to close. Nevertheless, investment by the Budapest Film Company has meant that many others have been renovated, and they showcase art films from Hungary and other countries, often in intimate and ambient screening rooms.

## HINTS ON PHOTOGRAPHY

*Nick Garbutt and John Jones*

From flamboyant Secessionist architecture to simple peasant dwellings, from the sweeping Danube Bend to the streams of the Northern Uplands, from a great bustard's mating display to the machismo daring of a Magyar *csikós* – you'll find plenty of reasons to reach for your camera. For the best results, give some thought to the following tips.

As a general rule, if it doesn't look good through the viewfinder, it will never look good as a picture. Don't take photographs for the sake of taking them; be patient and wait until the image looks right.

Photographing **people** is never easy and more often than not it requires a fair share of luck. If you want to take a portrait shot of a stranger, it is always best to ask first. Focus on the eyes of your subject since they are the most powerful ingredient of any portrait, and be prepared for the unexpected.

There is no mystery about good **wildlife** photography. The secret is getting into the right place at the right time and then knowing what to do when you are there. Look for striking poses, aspects of behaviour and distinctive features. Try not only to take pictures of the species itself, but also to illustrate it within the context of its environment. Alternatively, focus in close on a characteristic which can be emphasised.

Photographically, the eyes are the most important part of an animal – focus on these, make sure they are sharp and try to ensure they contain a highlight.

Look at the surroundings – there is nothing worse than a distracting twig or highlighted leaf lurking in the background. Getting this right is often the difference between a mediocre and a memorable image.

The popularity of **museums** came with the emergence of the middle classes, the growth of an urban population and the 19th-century urge to reassert – and display – Hungarian nationhood and heritage. There was a particular boom between 1867 and 1914, prosperous years, and the period of the Millennial Exhibition. The legacies of these enlightened patrons among the upper-middle or noble classes remain in Budapest, often framed by magnificent works of architecture. There is no shortage of museums and galleries beyond the capital either – Pécs has a specific street devoted to them. Museums are generally closed on Mondays, and open between 10.00 and 18.00 on other days during high season (although ticket offices often shut up to an hour before closing time). Hours are usually shorter in winter. You may be charged an admission fee (see box opposite), and permission to take photos or videos inside costs a significant amount extra. Guided tours may or may not be in English; museum attendants, often elderly ladies, may or may not speak English. We list prices for adults and concessions (always children, and often students and pensioners).

**Nightlife** is best in the capital, which has the choicest clubs (including outdoor beach-style ones in summer). Beyond that it varies, although you'll be sure to find lively places to dance away the early hours in student cities and towns. As you'd expect, DJs and drum 'n' base are thin on the ground in rural areas.

For further information on arts in Hungary, see the *Culture* section.

## THERMAL BATHS

A British novel was once much derided for its all-too-descriptive description of love's 'liquid noises'. Well, there may be no shoreline, but the sounds of Hungarian passion are those of splashing and soaking and dripping and gulping, all liquid noises with bells on.

A powerful flashgun adds the option of punching in extra light to transform an otherwise dreary picture. Artificial light is no substitute for natural light, though, so use it judiciously.

Getting close to the subject correspondingly reduces the depth of field. At camera-to-subject distances of less than a metre, apertures between f16 and f32 are necessary to ensure adequate depth of field. This means using flash to provide enough light. If possible, use one or two small flashguns to illuminate the subject from the side.

**Landscapes** are forever changing, even on a daily basis. Landscape photography is all about good light and capturing mood. Generally the first and last two hours of daylight are best, or when peculiar climatic conditions add drama or emphasise distinctive features. Never place the horizon in the centre – in your mind's eye divide the frame into thirds and either exaggerate the land or the sky.

### Film

You'll have no difficulty purchasing major brands of film in Hungary, nor in processing it in cities and larger towns. If you're using conventional film (as against a digital camera), select the right film for your needs. Film speed (ISO number) indicates the sensitivity of the film to light. The lower the number, the less sensitive the film, but the better quality the final image. For general print film, ISO 100 or 200 fit the bill perfectly. If you are using transparencies for home use or for lectures, then again ISO 100 or 200 film is fine. However, if you want to get your work published, the superior quality of ISO 25 to 100 film is best.

- Try to keep your film cool. Never leave it in direct sunlight.
- Don't allow fast film (ISO 800 and above) to pass through X-ray machines.
- Under weak light conditions use a faster film (ISO 200 or 400).

Hungary is afloat on a hot reservoir of water that breaks the surface through natural springs and drilled wells. There are almost 400 registered thermal springs in 85 different locations. The thermal water absorbs minerals from the earth's crust, and the Ministry of Health has recognised the medicinal properties of 50 of the country's baths. Budapest is unique among the world's capitals in offering such a plethora of places to bathe; beyond it, some previously obscure towns now purr under the attention of tourists drawn by the prospect of a warming wallow.

## History

The **Romans** were the first to take advantage of Hungary's hot springs in any sophisticated sense. There were 14 baths in Budapest alone. Aquincum holds stretches of an aqueduct that channelled spring waters from the hills, and the central military complex at Florian tér is the largest of the country's 21 Roman baths. Many centuries later, Buda became Hungary's courtly centre and a bathing culture bloomed once more. Zsigmond built the Imre Bath (today called Rác fürdő) in the 15th century, and Matyás even added a corridor linking them to the palace. However, it was the Turks who constructed a baths network. They blended Roman bathing traditions with their own, and remains of these bathhouses – with main halls and pools – are the period's noticeable surviving monuments in the capital. Eight were recorded by a 17th-century English traveller, and of these the Rác, Császár, Király and Rudas still stand.

Advances in engineering and the development of '**balneology**' (the science of medicinal waters) provided fresh impetus in the 19th century. Baths were built or renovated by some of the country's greatest architects. In 1937 Budapest received the official title 'Bath Town/Spa City' from the first International Balneological Congress. In the aftermath of World War II, many were subsumed into the social-security system and rendered dull by socialist-style renovation. However, Hungary embarked on a huge programme in the '60s and '70s to develop hotels offering facilities focused around medicinal water. In the past ten years, therapies have come to include gymnastics, massage and electrotherapy, but healing waters remain the mainstay in this natural approach to treatment. In addition, there are numerous (usually seasonal) outdoor pools (*strand*), which are particularly popular on steamy summer days. While some of these have medicinal waters, and are occasionally linked to hotels or day-time hospitals, they are more properly areas for relaxation and recreation.

## Therapy

The medicinal spring waters of Hungary are usually over 30°C (although there are a few outdoor medicinal baths that are cooler), and contain a range of minerals. **Spa treatments** are recommended for those suffering from arthritic and rheumatic pain (muscle tension, aches), blood-circulation or breathing difficulties, for those requiring injury rehabilitation, and those with chronic gynaecological problems or certain skin conditions. And some baths have drinking halls where you can swallow as well as wallow (see box, page 135).

Visitors can choose how they approach these soups of minerals. Some just enjoy spending a few hours sitting in the regenerative waters and enjoying their warmth. Others take advantage of the packages available at thermal hotels. Treatments beyond general dips in the pools or tubs, or refreshing massages (such as mud or weight baths, healing massages, etc) require a medical referral. Hungarians receive prescriptions from specialised physicians, and they pay a small fee to the cashier (subsidised under the country's social-security system). However, professional bath physicians on site provide consultations for other visitors (for a charge).

Besides the public bathing complexes, there are also **hotels** offering treatment packages. These divide into two types – thermal hotels (*gyógyszálló*) and 'wellness' hotels, which cater for the modern interest in health tourism. Thermal hotels are based at the sites of thermal springs, and have spa therapy centres. They provide traditional Hungarian remedies, and have tended to cater to the older market; however, most offer fitness centres and other 'luxuries', and are increasingly attracting a younger crowd. While wellness hotels are generally located in spa cities, they have neither on-site medicinal waters nor medical centres. Instead they represent non-medical health retreats, where the focus is upon the promotion of well-being through pampering and exercise.

## Baths and the bathing experience

A decade or so ago, **thermal baths** were primarily frequented by the mature lady or gent; however, these days you'll find wrinkled palms among younger Magyars too. Indeed, the pools in some ways fulfil the same function as coffee houses, allowing people to gather, chat and relax.

Thermal baths are very different from recreational swimming pools. Some have the forbidding aspect of a sanatorium, with white tiles and staff in starched uniforms, while others have fabulous ornamentation, such as mosaics and fluted columns. Complexes usually comprise several pools or bathtubs, together with saunas or steam rooms. Bathing is often mixed, although some establishments offer same-sex bathing on different days of the week (and Budapest's Gellért Baths have separate pools). You will be provided with a **changing cabin or a locker** (for extra security, the locker number differs from the tag you are issued with – the tag number is chalked on the inside of the locker door – so be sure to memorise the locker number itself), and sometimes a bathrobe on getting changed. **Swimming costumes** are usually worn (you can hire a costume or towel if you have come without) – although same-sex pools may allow nude bathing, and men are issued with aprons at baths like the Rudas and Rác in Budapest. You will on occasions be required to don a **swimming cap**. The medicinal pools are peaceful places for sitting and soaking. There is usually a **swimming pool** on the same site, however, for those of a more energetic disposition.

It is generally recommended that you spend 20–30 minutes in the **medicinal pools**, depending upon the concentration of the minerals. For the purposes of healing, regular visits are important. Doctors provide patients with prescriptions, and Hungarians receive state-subsidised discounts for up to two courses of 15 visits. Without a doctor's prescription, visitors cannot receive specialised treatments beyond healing massages and bathing; as a tourist, you'll need to join the queue of those with prescriptions to arrange a consultation with the **on-site physicians**. Those who receive treatment will often be expected to **tip** 'gate keepers'. If you are simply taking a dip in the baths, tip the locker *néni* about 50Ft; masseurs make little in wages, and should be tipped 200Ft or so. Beware, though, that queues to buy tickets can be long because patients with social-security referrals often use the same entrance as 'temporary' visitors. Cashiers rarely speak English.

Where the entrance price to the baths exceeds 1,000Ft, there may be a graded system of **refund** whereby a certain portion of money is returned if the visitor leaves within four hours. Note that children can only use recreational facilities, such as swimming pools, and are prohibited from the medicinal pools.

## SPORT AND ACTIVITIES

Hungary has no preening, globally recognised sporting icon in the David Beckham mould, but the country actually punches above its weight on the sporting stage. At the 2004 Athens Olympics, the country finished in 13th place overall, with a highly respectable haul of 18 medals. Hungarians could actually argue that in a historical context this was a below-par performance; they have won over 150 gold medals in all Olympics, positioning them at eighth in the games' world rankings. They placed third in 1952 and 1968, and were fourth in 1956 (a year that is remembered for other things). The country enjoys an enviable reputation in fencing, the pentathlon and water polo. Among more cerebral celebrated successes was that at chess in 1988, when a quartet of child prodigies – including the three Polgár sisters, the youngest just ten years old – won the women's team event at the Chess Olympics in Athens, defeating the seasoned Russian champions.

For Budapest offices selling **tickets** to sporting events, see page 121.

## ERNŐ RUBIK

*Kate Lyons*

With 43,252,003,274,489,856,000 possible moves, it isn't surprising that many of us have been driven to breaking open the infamous Rubik's cube with a screwdriver to rearrange the pieces or, more often than not, peeling off the stickers and putting them back one by one (guilty as charged!). What is perhaps more surprising is that the creation of Rubik's 'Bűvös kocka' ('Magic Cube' in Hungarian) was very much an accident.

Born in a bomb shelter during World War II, Ernő Rubik started out as an architect and teacher, initially interested in investigating the geometry of 3-D forms. His source of inspiration for the cube actually came one summer's day on the banks of the Danube while remarking on the shape of rounded river pebbles. Keen to help his students appreciate the dynamics of three-dimensionality, and fascinated by the possibility of moving the individual blocks of a cube independently without the whole thing falling apart, Rubik began creating the rounded architecture for the interior of the famous cube.

Each coloured face was composed of three rows and three columns; the central cube of each was attached to an internal mechanism that allowed it to rotate through 360°. Rubik began to twist, intrigued to see how 'after only a few turns, the colours become mixed, apparently in random fashion', which brought him face to face with the 'Big Challenge' – how to return the colours to their original positions. He hypothesised that through randomly twisting it could take more than a lifetime. So he began working on a solution, aligning the eight corner 'cubies' and following sequences of moves in an attempt to get back to the start.

Realising what he had hit on, Rubik quickly applied for a patent. The cube became an icon of the 1980s, enchanting people of all ages and nationalities. 'Cubic Rubes' appeared (fans eager to solve the puzzle in the fastest possible time) and formed clubs. Winning the Toy of the Year award in 1980, the Rubik's Cube even got its own entry in the *Oxford English Dictionary*. 'Rubik's wrist' became a medical condition, where cube fanatics developed what we now know as Repetitive Strain Injury. Rubik was perhaps right when he claimed that 'we turn the cube and it, in turn, twists us'.

The mind-bending puzzle can in fact be solved in just 52 moves – an amazing feat when there is only one correct answer and 43 trillion wrong ones! It was at the first World Championships in Budapest in 1982 that a 16-year-old Vietnamese student from the US became champion by unscrambling a cube in less than 23 seconds. This world record has since been beaten by Denmark's Jess Bonde, who solved the puzzle in 16.53 seconds in 2003. Since its appearance 30 years ago, Rubik's brain child has become the best-selling toy in history. As the first self-made millionaire from the communist block, Rubik has also set up a foundation for promising inventors and is still, to this day, creating games and puzzles to continue and develop his theories on geometrics.

## Football

Football is the country's favourite game, and Hungary was once a round-ball heavyweight. Between 1950 and 1954, under the leadership of Ferenc Puskás, the national team went unbeaten; its most heralded victory came when pummelling England 6–3 during a friendly at Wembley in 1953. This is now but a distant 1950s memory, a sepia-tinted time of pig-skin balls and long shorts. Poor funding and financial problems have crippled the sport to such an extent that Hungary hasn't qualified for the World Cup for over 20 years. The most-successful club side is Budapest's Ferencváros, who play at the FTC Stadium (*IX, Üllői út 129; see www.ftc.hu for information on fixtures*).

## Hungarian Grand Prix

Undoubtedly the biggest event in the sporting calendar, the annual Hungarian Grand Prix is held at the Hungaroring racetrack 20km northeast of the capital in Mogyoród (see page 193). There have been ominous threats in the past to remove Hungary from the racing map by Formula 1 organisers – the track has been repeatedly criticised as dull (with a dearth of overtaking opportunities) and dangerously slippery; however modifications in 2003 pacified officials. Late July/early August sees an invasion of F1-lovers and an astronomic hike in hotel and restaurant prices. If the latter doesn't put you off, log on to www.hungaroring.hu for ticket and visiting details.

## Budapest Marathon

The annual marathon (*Oct 3*) starts and finishes in Heroes' Square; if you don't mind the blisters and dehydration, it actually provides an excellent sightseeing circuit of the city. Alternatively you can relax among the spectators lining the streets and enjoy the sight of dehydrated people with blisters. See www.budapestmarathon.com for information.

## Swimming, watersports and fishing

Hungary has made quite a splash in the international pool. The country's most-successful individual athlete of all time is swimmer Krisztina Egerszegi, who won gold and silver medals in Seoul, becoming the youngest-ever Olympic champion at just 14 years of age (and a delicate 41kg in weight). She added three further golds to her display case at the 1992 Barcelona Games. The water-polo team has dominated the world, winning gold in every one of the last eight Olympics. The most famous victory came in Melbourne in 1956, when Hungary met the Soviet Union. Unsurprisingly in the context of that infamous year, the sporting battle was a brutal one that frothed the water and turned it red; the 5–2 win created global Mexican waves (metaphorically speaking). (Incidentally, did you know that water-polo players throw the ball at 80km/h?)

If you're looking for a proper **swim** rather than a thermal soak, most towns have open-air and covered pools. Changing facilities include lockers for your clothes; the attendant will shut the door and give you a numbered band or tag. As a security precaution, the locker and tag numbers are different, so be sure to remember your locker number to avoid being caught cold later. In addition to man-made pools, rivers often have grassed sunbathing and swimming areas (*strand*); some are free to use, others charge entrance and might feature *bufé* stands and places to hire boats.

Lake Balaton is the mecca for those seriously committed to **windsurfing** and **sailing**, and Siófok even has **wake-boarding** mechanisms (a popular, cheaper and more practical offshoot of waterskiing); you'll find places to rent equipment around the shoreline. Canoeing and kayaking holidays are growing in popularity, particularly on the Tisza and Danube rivers. Guided visits to protected wetland habitats like Lake Fertő may also feature canoe trips into the reed channels. For company's arranging canoeing trips or equipment, see *Tour operators*, pages 38–40. There are countless places to go **fishing**; you'll need a permit, available from tackle shops and some post offices. The National

Federation of Hungarian Anglers (*XII Budapest, Korompai utca 17;* ℩ *1 www.mohosz.hu mohosz@axelero.hu*) can provide fuller information on regulations and the best places to cast a line. There is English-language text on the helpful website.

## Horse-riding, hiking and cycling

Hungarians arrived in the Carpathian Basin on horseback from Asian steppes in the 9th century AD, and equestrian pursuits remain strong. During the last decade **horse-riding** and related ancient traditions have emerged once more. There are many opportunities for riding in areas all over the country, and horse-riding holidays are popular. A number of 'horse inns' offer quality rooms and horse-riding at hourly rates. Lipizzaner horses of the famous Viennese Spanish Riding School are bred at Szilvásvárad (see page 254) and Csipkéskút in the Bükk Hills, and can often be seen in the verdant meadows of the Bükk plateau. Asiatic hucul horses graze in Aggtelek National Park. There are horse-riding centres all over the country, although they are particularly prevalent on the Great Plain in places like Lajosmizse. See under *Tour operators*, pages 38–40, for some companies running riding trips. Otherwise, log on to the website of the Hungarian Equestrian Tourism Association (*V Budapest, Ferenciek tere 4;* ℩ *1 266 8697; www.equi.hu*), which can send out brochures on equestrianism and recommended horse-riding schools. The Hungarian tourist board also produces a couple of weighty booklets covering Hungary on horseback including *Equestrian Centres and Riding Schools*, which lists a selection of reliable riding centres in every region.

If you prefer to stand on your own two feet, the hilly western and northern regions are criss-crossed with excellent and well-marked **hiking** trails, and there are also routes through the Great Plain and other lowland areas. The National Blue Trail is a long, circular hiking path that connects almost all the famous spots. Further information can be found at MTSZ, the Hungarian Ramblers' Association 'Friends of Nature' website (*www.fsz.bme.hu/mtsz/bemutata.htm*). An extensive selection of maps are available from Cartographia, showing educational tracks, cycling, hiking and riding routes; you can buy copies either from their shop in Budapest (see page 132) or through their website (*www.cartographia.hu*). The tourist board also publishes brochures showing regional trails. The country is particularly well suited to **cycling**; the terrain is often gentle, and there are picturesque and well-marked trails. There is an abundance of literature available – start with the tourist board's *Cycling in Hungary* – and bike hire is offered in many resorts and hotels. For further details see page 58, and for tours on two wheels see pages 38–40.

## Hunting

While it's not our bag, hunting is popular in Hungary where game is rich among the hills of the Northern Uplands and the woods of Transdanubia. Contact Hubertus Ltd (see page 40) for information or to arrange tours.

## MEDIA
### Print

The Hungarian press is independent (foreign and locally owned), but journalism is not very daring, critical or investigative. Budapest is – relatively speaking – a small town, and tends to be nepotistic and incestuous. Everyone knows everyone and there is a reluctance to give (as well as receive) criticism, however constructive. Items such as restaurant reviews tend to be bought off in advance and lack objectivity. Of the Hungarian-language press, **Pesti Est** and its equivalents produced for other towns around the country are probably the only publications of any practical use to the foreign tourist. This is the weekly pocket-sized listings guide to the best bars, clubs and events in town, and can sometimes help with addresses and opening hours; it's also a good prop for affecting an air of Magyar cool in bars. There are some English translations on the website (*www.est.hu*). Among the mainstream nationals, **Blikk** is now the most widely read daily – full of gossip, naked women, film stars, and no obvious news. It has supplanted the perennial favourite **Népszabadság** (*People's Freedom*), the serious broadsheet and former organ of the one-party ruling MSzP.

## English-language press

There are a number of English-language publications, several of which are available free of charge from hotels, tourist offices and coffee houses in Budapest. Major international newspapers and lifestyle magazines can be picked up from larger newsagents and bookshops, although you should expect to pay considerably above the cover price and foreign newspapers are usually at least a day out of date. For details of shops in the capital that sell dailies on their date of publication, see page 131.

**Budapest Business Journal** The weekly *BBJ* concentrates on business with some news and lifestyle features. Founded in 1992 by an American-owned company. The online edition can be found at www.bbj.hu.

**Budapest Sun** A weekly, running since 1993; traditionally popular with ex-pats, many feel it has lost its way in the last few years, and it has come under pressure from the *Budapest Times*. It contains local news – at times a little late – as well as restaurant reviews, arts and entertainment listings, business and sport. Associated Newspapers owned. There is also an online edition (*www.budapestsun.com*). The cover price is 359Ft, but complimentary copies are available in most hotels of three stars or more.

**Budapest Times** A newish weekly (since September 2003) with good news and business and a growing culture section. Formed independently as a sister paper to the *Budapester Zeitung*. Retails at 360Ft.

**Where Budapest** A glossy monthly distributed free through hotels, tourist offices, embassies and restaurants. Information on shopping, dining, entertainment, nightlife and cultural events, together with regularly updated listings and a sprinkling of well-informed features.

## Television

On the whole, the fare on the Hungarian goggle box makes for pretty depressing viewing. The state owns two television channels: **MTV1** (Magyar Televízió 1 – not to be confused with the American music channel!) and **MTV2** (Magyar Televízió 2). During the communist period, these were used as tools for political propaganda, and even today parliament has a strong influence over their content. They air very conservative programmes that have changed little since the '80s, often featuring serious-looking men with droopy moustaches who pontificate on political or literary topics. Occasionally, the schedule is jazzed up with a variety show, invariably wheeling out the same old performers.

The state-run stations come off very badly in competition with two newer and fresher commercial stations. **Duna TV** is run by a foundation (very conservative in nature) that places emphasis on the 'larger Hungary' of times pre-Trianon Treaty. The channel concentrates on more artistic programmes, and has reasonable European art films (but only shown after 23.00). **RTL Klub** is run by RTL in Germany and shows the same low-brow chat shows, reality shows, shock shows, daytime drivel and Hollywood action movies. A third commercial station is **TV2** (the country's first national commercial channel), which has similar programming. When TV2 ran a Hungarian Big Brother, RTL Klub hit back with its own version – 'Való Világ' ('Real World') – with slightly different rules. It proved considerably more popular, and is now in its fourth season.

There are many more local independent stations: **Bp TV** (run by local celebrity Anettka, who often appears naked during live phone-ins), **Hír TV** (a right-wing news channel), **Film Múzeum** (showing old Hungarian films) and **Spektrum TV** (a kind of

'National Geographic' channel). Almost everyone in Budapest has either cable or satellite, offering dozens of foreign channels (usually German) and dubbed channels such as National Geographic, Hallmark, Club TV, and the Discovery Channel. At 23.00, the Travel Channel suddenly changes to hardcore porn with local 'stars' performing in tourist spots such as the Gellért Hotel or Fishermen's Bastion – a novel way of showcasing the capital's sights...

## Radio

Since the fall of communism, the airwaves have been flooded with commercial stations. **Rádió 1** (103.9fm), **Danubius** (103.3fm), **Est FM** (98.6fm) and **Juventus** (89.5fm) offer a mix of local and international popular music. **Bridge FM** (102.1fm) plays rock. **Tilos Rádió** (90.3fm) started off as a pirate radio station (*tilos* means 'forbidden') and is liberal in style. It was once taken off the air for several weeks after a drunken radio-show host said something derogatory about Christianity during a Christmas broadcast. **Rádió C** (88.8fm) is a new station for the Roma minority, and popular with younger listeners seeking an alternative to the tired old rotation lists of Juventus and Danubius. There are three state radio channels: **Kossuth Rádió** (107.8fm) broadcasts mainly news and politics, **Petőfi Rádió** (94.8fm) is more mixed, with culture, entertainment and news, and **Bartók Rádió** (105.3fm) is devoted to classical music. **Info Rádió** (95.8fm) is a news channel, seemingly conservative in influence (and Fidesz-biased).

You can listen to BBC World Service at certain times on **BBC-RFI Budapest** (92.1fm), a non-profit-making station launched in 2003 in collaboration with Radio France Internationale. For programme schedules, log on to www.bbc.co.uk/worldservice.

## COMMUNICATIONS
### Telephone and fax

Most public telephones in Hungary are operated by **phone cards** (*telefonkártya*), which can be purchased from newsagents, hotels, tourist offices and post offices (800Ft/50 units and 1,800Ft/120 units). The fewer coin-operated public phones take 20Ft, 50Ft and 100Ft pieces. Main post offices offer a **fax** service, as do hotels with business centres and some internet cafés.

Local areas in Hungary each have a two-digit prefix code – except Budapest, whose **area code** is '1'. Budapest telephone numbers are seven digits long (excluding the area prefix), those of other areas six. Local calls can be made by directly dialling the required telephone number. For those beyond Budapest, dial '06' (the inter-area code), wait for a slightly different-sounding dialling tone, and then enter the specific area code and telephone number. (For cellphones, see below.) For calls out of the country, dial the international access code '00', listen for the second tone, and proceed with the relevant country code and number. Some country codes are listed below:

| | | | | | |
|---|---|---|---|---|---|
| **Australia** | 61 | **Hungary** | 36 | **UK** | 44 |
| **France** | 33 | **Ireland** | 353 | **USA/Canada** | 1 |
| **Germany** | 49 | | | | |

### Useful/emergency telephone numbers

**Ambulance** 104
**Domestic operator and directory inquiries** 198
**Fire brigade** 105
**General emergency** (for English, German and French speakers) 112
**International operator and international directory inquiries** (English spoken) 199
**Police** 107
**Tourinform 24-hour hotline** (info and reporting crimes; English speakers) 1 438 8080

## Cellphones/mobiles

The three cellphone providers are Westel, Pannon and Vodaphone. To call a cellphone from a landline, you must prefix both the standard intercity code (06) and the provider's regional code – 30 or 60 (Westel), 20 (Pannon) or 70 (Vodaphone). Calls between same-network cellphones do not require either of these codes, while a call to a mobile on a different network only requires the regional prefix. If you are taking your cellphone with you, check with your own provider first about call charges. Essentially, though, if you are making outbound calls the Hungarian network you are on will simply bill your carrier at home (adding a small premium). However, you have to pay to receive calls. Text messages are only marginally more expensive than in your provider country, and so can be particularly useful.

## Post offices

Post offices (*posta*) are usually open Monday–Friday 08.00–18.00, Saturday 08.00–12.00. You can post letters and parcels, buy stamps (*bélyeg*) – although you'll save queue time by getting these at newsagents – pay parking and speeding fines, send faxes (main branches only), and exchange Eurocheques, American Express travellers' cheques and postal orders. If you're **sending a letter**, head for the desk marked with an envelope symbol. Letters or postcards to other European destinations will take around five or six days, while those to the US take eight to ten. Letters/postcards within Hungary cost 33/30Ft, to Europe 170/120Ft, to the US 180/130Ft. Be aware that it's far from unusual for 'interesting-looking' packages to go walkabout in the Magyar postal system – a postman somewhere, for instance, is doing his rounds in a fetching pair of pastel M&S knickers. Always send anything of value to or from Hungary by registered post. To do this in Hungary, ask for an *ajánlott levél* form; its instructions are in Hungarian, but it's fairly straightforward to fill out (name, address, weight, value, etc) – the clerk can usually help, especially in larger post offices. You keep the form, which is stamped and numbered, while the letter or parcel is marked with an identification number.

## Addresses

Hungarian addresses are written with the postcode first, followed by the street and building number. Each digit of the postal code provides a piece of information – the regional area (first digit), the district (second and third) and the precise neighbourhood (fourth). The second and third digits can be particularly useful navigational tools in big cities. In the case of Budapest, for example, you can establish that the address 'H-1014 Budapest, Fő utca 4' falls in district (*kerület*) 1 (the Castle Hill area of Buda). Floors of buildings (*emelet*) are numbered from the level above ground upwards (as in Britain), written as III emelet (third floor), IV emelet (fourth floor), etc.

## Internet

Internet cafés are commonplace across all main cities and towns; they are less readily found in villages. Most places charge for access by the minute. If you're struggling, head to a hotel as many permit internet use by guests and non-guests, although the charge is generally higher than in the cafés.

## MAPS

The Hungarian National Tourist Office is a particularly rich resource for information, and it publishes many maps that might meet your needs – showing campsites, hiking and cycling trails, equestrian centres, etc. These can be picked up (often free of charge) from regional Tourinform offices, which should also be able to provide a tourist map of the town or city you're visiting. Tourist maps are frequently available from hotel receptions too. More detailed or professional maps can be bought from bookshops or, again, from Tourinform offices.

## THE GREAT AND THE GOOD

Think you haven't been touched by the brilliance of the Hungarian mind? Consider some of the following contributors to the worlds of science, culture, art and entertainment. And think again.

**Ede Teller** (1908–2003) Born in Budapest, Teller was a physicist who co-developed the atomic bomb and invented the hydrogen bomb.

**Albert Szent-Györgyi** (1893–1986) Awarded a Nobel Prize in 1937 for discovering vitamin C.

**Oszkár Asbóth** (1891–1960) A flight-obsessed engineer who invented the propellor helicopter.

**Ernő Rubik** (1944–) Mathematician and creator of the irritating '80s cubic puzzle the Rubik Cube, which baffled and frustrated millions around the world.

**László József Bíró** (1899–1985) Not content with inventing the ball-point pen (or Biro), he also fashioned the automatic gearbox.

**Imre Kertész** (1929–) Acclaimed Jewish writer, deported from Budapest during World War II (aged 11). His novel *Sorstalanság* (*Fateless*) documented his experiences in Nazi concentration camps, and won him the Nobel Prize for Literature in 2002.

**Harry Houdini** (1874–1926) Real name Ehrich Weisz. Perhaps the most-accomplished escapologist the world has known.

**Ferenc Liszt** (1811–86) Renowned 19th-century composer and pianist who founded his own music academy in Pest.

**Béla Bartók** (1881–1945) Discovered by Liszt, Bartók was one of Hungary's greatest composers of classical and folk music.

**Zoltán Kodály** (1882–1967) A popular composer and teacher who, with Bartók, collected Hungarian folk music. Kodály also devised his own method of music study to encourage the less talented to learn and play.

Hungarians were also responsible for inventing colour television, the hologram, the phosphorus match and the horse-drawn coach. Actors Tony Curtis, Drew Barrymore, Freddie Prinze Junior and Zsa Zsa Gabor have Hungarian ancestry, as do fashion designer Calvin Klein, singer Paul Simon and comedian Jerry Seinfield.

The leading Hungarian map producer is Cartographia, which produces country, city, regional and hiking maps, as well as a couple of road atlases (*Magyarország autóatlasza*) that show both the country's road network and street plans of individual towns. Cartographia has two shops in Budapest (see page 132), and you can also order through the website (*www.cartographia.hu*). For travel bookshops in Budapest, see page 131. If you want to buy your maps before you go, Stanfords (*12–14 Long Acre, London WC2E 9LP;* e *sales@stanfords.co.uk; www.stanfords.co.uk*) is an excellent UK specialist in travel books and maps; it also has branches in Manchester and Bristol. ITMB publishes a full-country *Hungary* map.

## BUSINESS

Business etiquette is similar to that in western Europe and the US. The suit is the standard uniform, the handshake is used for greeting (it is customary to wait until the woman offers her hand), business cards (*névjegy kártya*) are exchanged (although Hungarian cards will list the holder's surname before his/her forename), and it is common to give a token gift. The principal language of business is English, although on occasion a translator may be required; it is prudent to ask about this beforehand, and the British embassy can advise on interpretation services. While the usual hours of business are 08.00–16.30 during the week, companies (and especially government offices) often close early in the afternoon on Friday, and spring and autumn are the main business seasons. Budapest's location makes it a popular place for international business conferences, and there are plenty of hotels that cater for these. Many four- and five-star hotels have business centres and even individual internet access in their rooms. The capital's financial district is in Pest.

## Useful contacts

**American Chamber of Commerce** Budapest V, Deák Ferenc utca 10; ℩ 1 266 9880; e info@amcham.hu; www.amcham.hu

**British Chamber of Commerce** Budapest V, Bank utca 6; ℩ 1 302 5200; e bcch@bcch.com; www.bcch.com

**Hungarian Chamber of Commerce and Industry** Budapest V, Kossuth tér 6–8; ℩ 1 474 5100; e mkik@mail.mkik.hu; www.mkik.hu

### BUYING PROPERTY IN BUDAPEST

If you fancy becoming a property mogul abroad, you could do worse than think about investing in a flat in one of the handsome apartment blocks on the Danube banks of Budapest. While demand is rising, it remains the case that there is a current over-supply of such accommodation. An outlay of £75,000 would get you a one-bedroom apartment in a listed renovated building. A more modest £50,000 would buy you 46m$^2$ of sunny space on Wesselényi utca (district VII) with panoramic views to the synagogue. And if you have £230,000 to spare, you could boast one of the most pukka addresses in Budapest, with 186m$^2$ of beautifully renovated and spacious flat on Bajcsy-Zsilinszky utca (district VI).

The opportunity to rent out such apartments looks rosy, with tourism being Hungary's primary foreign currency generator. A one-bedroom flat costing £60,000 with views of the Danube would generate rental income of £550–600 per month. If you need to borrow, the normal mortgage in Hungary is 50% payable over 20 years, so UK buyers usually raise the additional funds from equity in property at home.

As Hungary enthusiastically takes on its EU identity, the bureaucratic legacy of its recent communist past is fading rapidly. You would be wise, however, to avoid some of the monstrous buildings that were thrown up in that era, and you will need a good lawyer to protect you against problems that can arise because of outdated land records or dubious evidence of title. There are other potential pitfalls. Foreign nationals need a permit to purchase property in Hungary. It usually takes a few weeks but a local lawyer will organise this for you. You would have to pay tax at 20% and there may be stamp duty of up to 6%. Other costs to swallow would be the estate agent's commission and transfer tax, together adding about 4% to your outlay. Serious property investors set up as a company in Hungary. This brings advantages of paying a reduced rate of tax, as well as the possibility of multiple purchases in any one district – a right denied to individuals.

Useful websites to browse are www.centralhomehungary.com, www.primelocation.com and www.hungaryproperty.net.

**ITD Hungary** Budapest VI, Andrássy út 12; ⤷ 1 472 8100; e info@itd.hu; www.business2hungary.com. The headquarters of the Hungarian government's investment and trade-development agency, which offers consulting, business match-making services, trade directories, conference facilities and a business library. *Open Mon–Fri 09.00–16.30.*

## TIME

Hungarian time is one hour ahead of Greenwich Mean Time, six hours ahead of Eastern Standard Time and nine hours ahead of Pacific Standard Time. Bear in mind when checking cinema or theatre listings that when expressing the time Hungarians refer to the full hour *to come* rather than that passed. Thus 6.30 is expressed as 'half to seven' (*fél hét óra*); in shorthand/24-hour forms, it may therefore appear as 'f7', 'f19', '¹/₂7' or '¹/₂19'. The same applies to ¹/₄- and ³/₄-hour intervals. In this book, time is given using the 24-hour clock in the usual way.

## PUBLIC TOILETS

Hungary isn't dripping with public facilities in which to spend a penny; when you do find somewhere, you'll more frequently spend between 20Ft and 100Ft, and pay it to an elderly attendant. In summer months, cafés and fast-food restaurants (like McDonald's) in tourist-heavy areas occasionally charge even customers a fee for the use of their public conveniences. Doors are marked with *nők* or *női* (women) and *férfiak* or *férfi* (men).

## CULTURAL DOS AND DON'TS

**Tipping** It is customary to give a tip (*borravaló*, meaning 'something to buy wine with'...!) to waiters, hotel porters, bath attendants, bar staff, taxi drivers, hairdressers and tour guides. As in most countries, the amount to tip is something of a grey area. Ten–15% is generally acceptable, although with bar and café bills and taxi fares it is common simply to round up to the nearest 'convenient' amount. Give porters 300–500Ft, masseurs 200Ft and locker attendants 50Ft. When paying the bill in a restaurant, do not leave your tip on the table. Instead tell the waiter precisely how much you would like to pay (including the tip); if you say 'thank you' as you pass over payment, the waiter will assume that you don't want any change. Check whether service is included before paying – the staff are unlikely to point out your error if you tip twice – and shelve any embarrassment about refusing to tip if the service is poor. Service in Hungary is variable to say the least, and will not change while disinterested staff know they'll get paid regardless.

**'Cheers!'** The convivial toast when drinking is *'egészségedre'* – a twister for the foreign tongue thickened with wine. However, the clinking of beer glasses is something of a social *nem-nem*. Why? After crushing the rebellion against Habsburg rule in 1849, the Austrian military leader Haynau – known as the 'Hyena of Brescia' – toasted the execution of 13 Hungarian generals by clinking his beer glass. Angry Hungarians swore that for the next 150 years they would refrain from clinking their own glasses out of disgust for what they had seen. The period has passed but the custom continues.

**Bars** Most bars in Hungary offer table service. Open a tab and settle the bill with the waiter or waitress before you leave.

**Smoking** Smoking is popular in Hungary, and you'll see many a local drawing on a thin, white-tipped cigarette and lingering over a coffee. A law was passed in 1999 stipulating that restaurants must provide a non-smoking section; hunt out the sign reading *'tilos a dohányzás'* (no smoking) – it usually marks the tiny area shoved away at the back.

**Thanks Doc** Hungarian doctors were paid meagre salaries by the state during the communist period, and it became customary for grateful patients to offer physicians a tip (*hálapénz*, or 'gratitude money'), given discreetly in a plain envelope, for their help and advice. Doctors are much better off today, but many Hungarians still adhere to this tradition – a friend recently gave 50,000Ft, for example, after a small operation.

**What's the point?** As a rule of thumb, Hungarians consider it rude to point at other people with the index finger – it is OK, however, to point at an object. When counting on their hands, Hungarians start with the thumb. As such, if a shop assistant wants to check that you really only want one banana, she will give what looks like a thumbs-up sign. Two bananas would be thumb and index finger, and so on.

**Train escalators** Unlike escalator etiquette in the UK, Hungarians do not stand to the right to allow others to pass on the left. If you're in a hurry and fear dawdlers ahead, you'll have to grin and stair it.

**House visits** If invited to a Hungarian's home for a meal, take a bottle of good Hungarian wine with you – a fine Tokaji is always well received – and perhaps some flowers or chocolates. You may be expected to remove your shoes before entering. Few topics of conversation are off limits, but remember that the average Hungarian salary is considerably lower than those of many other Europeans, so be sensitive that discussions of your earnings might cause discomfort.

**Shopping** When entering a chemist or food shop, you must pick up a basket – even if you plan to buy just one item or simply to browse. Large electrical stores often ask customers to leave their bags in secure lockers before they shop to make theft more difficult.

# GIVING SOMETHING BACK

Hungary ain't Africa, and while it is a poor country by Western standards you are unlikely to find yourself experiencing your pleasures guiltily or having your heartstrings tugged around every corner. You are in any case contributing to an economy that relies heavily on tourism simply by visiting the place, travelling responsibly, spending your dollars and extolling Hungary's charms to others on your return home. However, if you do want to give something more there are plenty of charities and projects that would receive your help very gratefully. Which you choose will depend entirely on your personal interests and cares.

The Roma remain a deeply hard-pressed minority, and the bulk of the charity work undertaken by the **Foundation for School Meals** (*Gyermekétkeztetési Alapítvány; XX Budapest, Mária utca 3;* ☎ 1 283 2510; *www.gyea.hu*) is directed towards Roma children. Children are also the priority for the **Education for Blind Children** (*Vakok Szolgáltató Központja; XIV Budapest, Ajtósi sor 39;* ☎ 1 363 3343; e *latasserultek@vakisk.hu; www.vakisk.hu*) and the **Károlyi István Children's Centre** (*Gyermekközpont; web in English: www.gyermekkozpont.hu*). The **Foundation for the Women of Hungary** (*Magyarországi Női Alapítvány; 1537Bp, PO Box 453/277;* ☎ 1 350 1311; e *mona.fwh@matavnet.hu; www.mona-hungary.org*) provides support to women in violent relationships, while the **White Cross** (*tel in English: 06 20 958 2545; www.feherkeresztliga.hu*) does excellent work rounding up the absurdly high number (two million) of domestic moggies and pooches that go astray annually in Hungary.

If you're a naturalist, you could consider assisting **WWF Hungary** (*XII Budapest, Németvölgyi út 78/B;* ☎ 1 214 5554; e *panda@wwf.hu*), which has operated here for a decade. Its activities are focused towards the conservation of forests, rivers and endangered fauna, and on helping the country meet the environmental challenges of EU membership. Field projects involve species like the wolf, beaver, lynx and European pond turtle, but equally significant are the attempts to revive the traditional agriculture of floodplains in the Middle Tisza region and the southernmost reaches of the Danube. Volunteer groups are vital to such work, and have so far assisted in constructing nature trails, surveying hiking resorts in the Buda Hills and studying European pond turtles. Another worthy long-term conservation programme (scheduled to run until 2008) is the **LIFE-Nature Project**, which aims to restore grasslands, create woodlands and nesting sites, and open up reedbeds in Egyek-Pusztakócs. For details, contact the Hortobágy National Park Directorate (*Debrecen, Sumen utca 2*; \ *52 529920*; e *hnp@www.hnp.hu*). **Hungary Conservation Volunteers** organises an excellent programme for those who wish to get actively involved in the monitoring of key European butterfly species (including the large copper and anomalus blue) and in the management of their habitat. The next project is due to take place in summer 2006 (*Jul 23–Aug 5*) at sites in Aggtelek and Örség national parks; those in England can contact the Butterfly Conservation Head Office (*Manor Yard, East Lulworth, Wareham, Dorset BH20 5QP*; \ *0870 774 4309*; e *info@butterfly-conservation.org*). For further information on wildlife conservation, see pages 12–14.

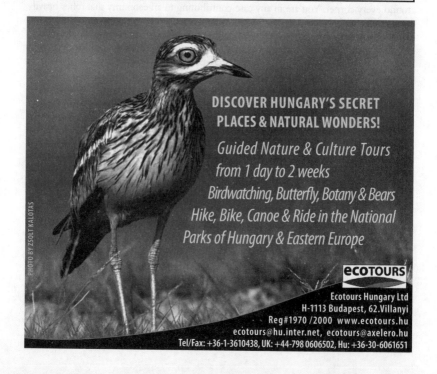

# Part Two

# The Guide

## HOW TO USE THIS CHAPTER

Symbols are used where appropriate to indicate transport routes:

$\overline{\underline{\text{B}}}$ bus
$\overline{\underline{\text{M1}}}$/$\overline{\underline{\text{M2}}}$/$\overline{\underline{\text{M3}}}$ metro (number indicates line)
$\overline{\underline{\text{T}}}$ tram
$\overline{\underline{\text{TB}}}$ trolleybus
$\overline{\underline{\text{HEV}}}$ suburban railway

**Hotels** are divided initially by price, and then subdivided between Buda and Pest.

**Restaurants** are divided between Buda and Pest, and then further subdivided between districts or convenient areas. All prices were verified within a period of four months, so use them as a comparative guide.

**Maps** There are maps for Castle Hill and the Belváros, with sights beyond them plotted on the main overview map.

The sections *Discovering Buda* and *Discovering Pest and the Islands* guide you to the sights as you walk the streets of Buda and Pest. They include cross-references to the *Museums and More* section, containing full entries for museums, galleries and major sights.

BUDAPEST

where

# Budapest

Great cities are forged from moments of tragedy as well as triumph, but Budapest has seen more than its fair share of blood and bullets. During the many times that Hungary dropped its toast, the capital invariably got much of the jam on its trousers. It has witnessed several revolts and some ding-dong street battles in the struggles to throw off the shackles of foreign powers. As we write, however, Hungarians are in charge, and the only gangs of foreigners are coach parties. It's immediately evident that tourism is thriving in the capital; entry to the EU and the sudden interest from low-cost airlines suggests the boom will get boomier still. Budapest is big enough to take it. Areas like Váci utca and the Castle District already cater for tourists, and can look after themselves. Elsewhere, one of the city's strengths is the elbowroom around its sights. While there are quaint narrow streets on Castle Hill, Budapest is characterised more typically by the broad and the bold. These are features of nature, such as Buda's craggy hills and caves, and the sweeping river; they are also features of architecture, such as Pest's Historicist and Art-Nouveau mansions and Parisian boulevards, which replaced the medieval and Baroque during 19th-century expansion. Another strength is the diversity of attractions. The city is significant both for its museums and its nightclubs, for its opera house and its contemporary music festivals; it suits both the flâneur and the hill walker. For all the exoticism of its Turkish baths and the impact of its communist past, this is a cosmopolitan capital that has always looked longingly westward. However, with the odd smoking Trabant, rumbling tram, and flower-selling *néni* comes destinational bite, and a flavour quite unique.

## History

Peering through history's early mists, excavations suggest that the site of the capital was inhabited as long ago as the **fourth millennium** BC. There were communities here during the Bronze and Iron ages, including Celts who arrived in the 4th century BC and constructed a citadel on Gellért Hill. In around 35BC the area's strategic advantages were properly exploited for the first time when the **Romans** extended their imperial boundary eastward to the Danube, occupying the Celtic settlement of Ak-Ink (adopting the Latinised form of Aquincum). A legionary camp was established in today's Óbuda and a civilian town to its north; the river formed a natural barrier to attacks from Asiatic tribes, and a couple of advanced fortified positions were constructed on the other bank – including Contra-Aquincum, remains of which still stand in Március 15 tér. Aquincum flourished and became the capital of Pannonia Inferior, one half of the Roman province of Pannonia; as provincial governor, Hadrian built himself a palace on Shipyard Island.

During the 4th century the empire declined, and the Romans finally abandoned Buda at the beginning of the 5th century. When the **Magyars** arrived, Buda and Pest (they

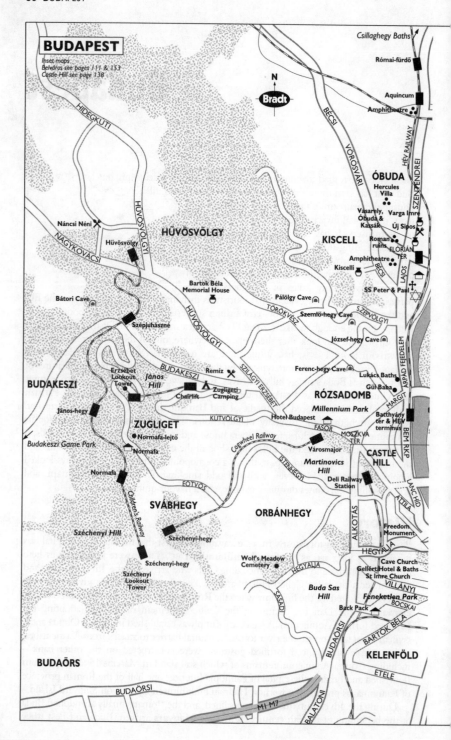

# BUDAPEST

*Inset maps*
*Belváros see pages 111 & 153*
*Castle Hill see page 138*

N

Bradt

Csillaghegy Baths

Római-fürdő

Aquincum

Amphitheatre

HÉV RAILWAY

BÉCSI

VÖRÖSVÁRI

SZENTENDREI

ÓBUDA

Hercules Villa

Vasarely, Óbuda & Kassák

Varga Imre

Új Sipos

Roman ruins

KISCELL

FLÓRIÁN TÉR

Amphitheatre

Kiscelli

SS Peter & Paul

LAJOS

BÉCSI

HIDEGKÚTI

HŰVÖSVÖLGYI

Náncsi Néni

Hűvösvölgy

NAGYKOVÁCSI

HŰVÖSVÖLGY

Bartok Béla Memorial House

Pálölgy Cave

Szemlő-hegy Cave

TÖRÖKVÉSZ

SZÉPVÖLGYI

Bátori Cave

Szépjuhászné

HŰVÖSVÖLGYI

József-hegy Cave

ÁRPÁD FEJEDELEM

Erzsébet Lookout Tower

BUDAKESZI

János Hill

Remíz

BUDAKESZI

SZILÁGYI ERZSÉBET

Ferenc-hegy Cave

Lukács Baths

Gül Baba

MARGIT

János-hegy

Chairlift

Zugligeti Camping

ZUGLIGET

KÚTVÖLGYI

RÓZSADOMB

Millennium Park

Hotel Budapest

Batthyány tér & HÉV terminus

BEM RKP

Budakeszi Game Park

Normafa-lejtő

Normafa

Cogwheel Railway

FASOR

MOSZKVA TÉR

Városmajor

CASTLE HILL

Normafa

EÖTVÖS

ISTENHEGYI

Martinovics Hill

Déli Railway Station

ATTILA

LÁNCHÍD

Children's Railway

SVÁBHEGY

ORBÁNHEGY

ALKOTÁS

Freedom Monument

Széchenyi Hill

Széchenyi-hegy

HEGYALJA

Cave Church

Gellért Hotel & Baths

St Imre Church

VILLÁNYI

Wolf's Meadow Cemetery

HEGYALJA

Széchenyi-hegy

Széchenyi Lookout Tower

Buda Sas Hill

Feneketlen Park

Back Pack

BOCSKAI

SASAD

BUDAÖRSI

BARTÓK BÉLA

KELENFÖLD

BUDAÖRS

BUDAÖRSI

BALATONI

M1 M7

ETELE

weren't joined officially until the 19th century) were still just villages. It wasn't that they lacked for excitement – it was, after all, from Gellért Hill that the spiritual tutor of King István's son was launched in a barrel full of spikes by miffed pagans – but the royal and religious centres were elsewhere. After the Mongol invasion, **Béla IV** fortified Castle Hill, moved the populations of Buda and Pest behind the safety of its walls, and in doing so was lauded as the second state founder. Castle Hill was subsequently ranked a city and named Buda (the area to its north relegated to Óbuda – 'Old Buda'), while Pest developed as a commercial centre and attracted immigrant craftsmen from other corners of Europe.

The 14th-century **Angevin kings** shifted the royal court from Visegrád to Buda. Subsequent monarchs enlarged upon the regal residence on Castle Hill, in particular Zsigmond of Luxembourg who constructed the beautiful Gothic Friss Palace. King Mátyás extended it further, and the court became a hotspot of European Renaissance art and learning.

In 1541 the **Turks** came, and many of the townspeople cleared out. There were several attempts to re-take Buda before a European army eventually vanquished the Turks in 1686 after a siege that lasted months. Buda was reduced to rubble by the fighting, and Pest was by now a virtual ghost town; their combined population was just 1,000. There was a massive process of rebuilding and re-population ahead (the latter with German, Slovak and Serbian settlers, as well as Hungarians from other parts of the country).

During the 18th century Pest became an important trading centre and a wealthy town, attracting fresh groups of immigrants including Serbs and Jews. The 19th-century **Age of Reform** saw the construction of the first permanent bridge crossing the Danube here and the founding of the Hungarian Academy of Sciences. It was also during this period that Pest took on its current face. The **Great Flood** of 1838 had an effect as dramatic as London's fire of 1666, flattening the Neoclassical and Baroque dwellings and making way for the broad Parisian boulevards that replaced them. Some surviving churches bear markers recording the height reached by the waters.

On March 15 1848 **revolution** broke out on Pest's streets, its spokesmen the poet Sándor Petőfi and his fellow radicals. Once they'd crushed it, the Habsburgs built a citadel looking down from the Buda bank. The Compromise of 1867 provided new hope, and in 1873 Buda, Óbuda and Pest were **unified** to form Budapest, a union that had been inevitable since the erection of the Chain Bridge linking both banks. The city developed a capitalist infrastructure, the population grew rapidly, Pest became a place of great municipal construction and the hub of the empire's rail system, and cultural output rivalled that of Vienna. This spirit of energy and independence was evident during the **millennial celebrations** of 1896; an exhibition featured 220 halls showcasing Hungarian achievements, while lasting monuments like City Park, Heroes' Square, the first underground railway line, Mátyás Church and the Museum of Applied Arts were also born of this staggeringly ambitious and productive moment.

**World War II** hit the city like a hammer blow. A ghetto was established in the area around the Great Synagogue and troopers executed Jews on the Danube banks. Twenty per cent of the capital's inhabitants were Jews, and only the intervention of a precious few souls saved them from the wholesale deportation that occurred in the rest of the country. Allied aerial bombardment took a serious toll on the city, and this was worsened when the Germans made a desperate last stand against the advancing Russians, destroying all the bridges and holing up on Castle Hill. Budapest was surrounded on December 24 1944, and Hitler ordered the 22,000 mainly SS troops to defend it to the last soldier; on February 12 1945, down to just 1,800, they finally succumbed. Three-quarters of Budapest's buildings bore the scars of battle, over a third were destroyed and 38,000 civilians had been killed by hunger, illness or the violence itself.

*Above* Esterházy Palace in Fertőd (WC)
*Below left* Lion guarding the Chain Bridge, Budapest (NS)
*Below right* Sculpture in Budapest's Statue Park – *Proletarians of the World Unite* (WC)

*Above left* Red-roofed church in Palkonya, near Villány (WC)

*Above right* Windmill in Ópusztaszer National Memorial Park, Southern Great Plain (WC)

*Right* Mátyás Church in Budapest's Castle District (NS)

*Below* Boat-shaped gravemarkers in Szatmárcseke in the Upper Tisza region (WC)

Afterwards the daunting process of reconstruction began; historic buildings were restored, and drab, utilitarian residential blocks raised on the outer city limits. However, the buildings bore fresh bullet wounds when blood spilt on the streets once more during the **revolution of 1956**, which started with a student demonstration against the communist government and ended with Soviet tanks in the boulevards.

In recent years conflicts have thankfully been restricted to wars of words, at the centre of which has invariably been the combative Mayor Gábor Demszky (now in his fourth term). During the four years that Fidesz ruled (1998–2002), the relationship between the government and the capital scraped rock bottom. Demszky, a former dissident, and Fidesz fought a series of bitter battles over the cost of large projects in the city (such as the National Theatre; see page 121). At the heart of this were contrasting views of the very capital itself, which Demszky promotes as a 'world city' and Fidesz sees as the embodiment of dangerous, non-Magyar forces of cosmopolitanism and liberalism. Demszky provided his opponents with further ammunition in August 2004 when it was revealed he owns a luxury seaside villa in Croatia that he hadn't included on his asset declaration form. Public outrage over his apparent power-hungry behaviour forced him to resign his position as a member of the European Parliament shortly afterwards. The next Budapest mayoral elections in 2006 should be interesting.

# Practical Information

## A PRACTICAL OVERVIEW

The first thing to ask yourself is 'On which side of the river am I?' The 525km² city is divided in two by the blue Danube, which runs through here for 28km and is spanned by seven road and two rail bridges. If you're among narrow streets or leafy hills to the west, you are in Buda, which makes up a third of the city; if you're in the more built-up area to the east, you're in Pest. If you're wet and treading water, you've fallen between the two.

Administratively, Budapest is carved into 23 districts (I–III, XI–XII and XXII in Buda, IV–X, XIII–XXI and XXIII in Pest; see Budapest districts map, page 89). The tourist is most likely to spend time in districts V (the downtown), I (where you'll find the Castle District), VI (Terézváros, which holds Andrássy út), XIV (home of City Park), VII and VIII (Erzsébetváros and Józsefváros respectively), III (where the Roman ruins of Aquincum lie) and II and XII (the Buda Hills). Districts or areas within them often also bear historic names (such as Erzsébetváros – or Elizabeth Town).

The city's street plan is well laid out. In essence, the centre of Pest is defined by two ring roads – the Kiskörút (the Small Boulevard), a semicircular thoroughfare that links the Chain and Liberty bridges and hems in the Belváros (city centre), and the Nagykörút (Great Boulevard), which runs outside it between Petőfi and Margaret bridges. Radiating outward from the Kiskörút are several broad avenues that cut through the Nagykörút and beyond. The result is an easily navigable spider web of tarmac. Buda is characterised more by its features than its roads, with Castle and Gellért hills dominating the immediate riverscape. On a map, Margit körút makes a teasing play of continuing the natural line of the ringroad, before leading off towards Lake Balaton. Attila út, Hegyalja út, Bartók Béla út and Fő utca are Buda's main roads – the first three busy and noisy – while Moszkva tér and Móricz Zsigmond körtér are the transport hubs. In addition to all this, there are three metro lines (all serving Pest, one of which crosses the river to the north of Castle Hill), suburban railways, and three main railway stations (Déli in Buda, and Keleti and Nyugati in Pest) that run trains to national and international destinations.

# GETTING THERE AND AWAY
## By air
For details of international flights to and from Budapest, see page 42. There are no scheduled flights to destinations within Hungary itself. On landing at Budapest Ferihegy International, passengers have the following options for travelling to the city centre. There is no public-transport representation at the airport itself, but the newsagent sells bus tickets.

**Airport Minibus Service** ✆ 1 296 8555. Those travelling in ones or twos should consider the minibus shuttle. The counter is open daily (05.00–01.00) and the bus will drop you off at any address in Budapest. Book your seat at the minibus desk (there is one in the arrivals hall of each terminal); you may have to wait up to 30 mins before being collected. A one-way ticket costs 2,300Ft, and a return 3,900Ft. For your return journey, call the office 24 hours in advance, and quote your flight number and hotel location. (Note that while we have never encountered difficulties, we recently spoke to tourists stranded at their hotel when the return minibus failed to turn up. As well as booking 24 hours ahead, you are advised to telephone on the day to check your booking has been logged.)

**Airport bus and metro** The public bus is the cheapest transfer (170Ft from the airport newsagent, or 200Ft if you pay the driver – you'll need the exact change for the latter). It leaves every 10–15 mins (between 05.00–23.00 daily) from the stop marked 'BKV Plusz Reptér busz' outside Terminal 2. Disembark at the very last stop, Kőbánya Kispest metro, and from there take the underground blue metro line 3 into the heart of Pest (Deák Ferenc tér station) and beyond. Buses back from KK run between 04.30 and 23.45, and the trip takes around 20 mins. Bus 94 leaves for KK every half-hour from Terminal 1. KK is rather a rough-and-ready station, with a fair few drunks hanging about. Be sure to head for the underground (and not the mainline) section of the station. KK is an ideal place to stock up on food and drink for your return journey home – the airport prices for such things are frightening.

## HIGHLIGHTS/SUGGESTED ITINERARIES
### If you're staying a weekend

- Make an early-morning trip to the bustling Big Market Hall, with its salamis and lace and glass and caviar.
- Ride the funicular railway up Castle Hill, trawl a leisurely course around the Castle District, and scoff a cake at the Ruszwurm.
- Pick a museum and gallery or two – choose from extensive holdings at the Museum of Fine Arts, the Hungarian National Museum and the Hungarian National Gallery, or more specialised exhibitions like the polished Varga Imre Collection or the sombre, compelling and stylised House of Terror.
- Soak away your aches in a thermal spa – and admire the proud Art-Nouveau architecture and wide-girthed men of the Gellért or Széchenyi baths.
- Wrap yourself around a pastry in a fin-de-siècle coffee house.
- Take in the sights and shops of the city centre, including the St István Basilica and the Parliament building.
- Join the metro to Heroes' Square and City Park, with its ducks, zoo and Eclectic castle.
- Eat gulyás soup, Hortobágy pancakes, and paprika chicken with dumplings.
- Try a shot of fruit brandy, and a glass or three of sweet Tokaji Aszú.
- Watch the day draw to a close in a café-bar on Liszt Ferenc tér.

### And longer...

- Hire a bike and pedal around Margaret Island.
- Take the cogwheel and children's railways into the Buda Hills, and return by chairlift from János hegy.
- Visit the Cave Church dug into the side of Gellért hegy, and then push on up to the Freedom Monument and Citadella on top.
- Take in a performance at the stunning State Opera House, or an outdoor concert in front of the St István Basilica.
- Book an evening river trip.
- Travel to Statue Park, the dumping ground for communist statues.
- Eke out the Roman amphitheatres and mosaics of Óbuda.

**Taxi** For three passengers or more, a taxi should work out a cheaper option per person than the Airport Minibus. Be wary, though, of hailing a cab outside the airport – there is a real danger of being stung. Either telephone a taxi firm from the airport, or agree a price before getting into the vehicle (see page 94). A realistic fare for a journey into the centre of the city is around 4,000–5,000Ft. Many taxi companies offer a flat-rate airport fare if you order by telephone. Taxis can be pre-booked by email (*http://programs.ohb.hu/transfer/index.en.html*); the driver will meet you at the gate with a name board, and the journey costs around €20.

## By bus

The three primary **bus stations** for domestic services are all on the Pest side of the city. Each station has its own connecting metro station. For details of international services to/from Budapest, see *Chapter 2*, page 45.

**Népliget Bus Station** IX, Üllői út 131; ☎ 1 219 8080. For destinations in northern and north-central Hungary. Ticket office open 06.00–21.00 daily. The blue M3 metro line runs to Népliget station.

**Stadion Bus Station** XIV, Népstadion; ☎ 1 252 2995 *(domestic)*, 1 252 1896 *(international)*. Daily services run from 06.00–21.00 to areas in eastern Hungary. Stadionok (meaning 'stadia') is on the red M2 metro line.

**Árpád híd Bus Station** XIII, Forgách utca; ☎ 1 329 1450. Operates services to the Danube Bend. Ticket office open 06.00–20.00 daily. On the blue M3 metro line.

## By train

Budapest has three main railway stations that serve both international and domestic destinations, and all have metro stations attached. In addition, there are four suburban rail lines (known as the **HÉV**) that run a shortish distance beyond the city to Szentendre, Gödöllő, Csepel and Ráckeve. For international services to/from Budapest, see *Chapter 2*, page 44. The destinations served by the main stations are:

**Eastern Railway Station** (*Keleti pályaudvar*) VIII, Baross tér. Trains to/from the Northern Uplands and northeast (Győngyős, Szécsény, Eger, Miskolc, Tokaj, etc).

**Western Railway Station** (*Nyugati pályaudvar*) VI, Nyugati tér. Trains to/from the Great Plain (Szeged, Kecskémet, Szolnok, Debrecen, Nyíregyháza, etc) and the Danube Bend (Esztergom, Visegrád, Vác, etc).

**Southern Railway Station** (*Déli pályaudvar*) I, Krisztina körút. Trains to/from Balaton (Keszthely, Siófok, Tapolca, etc) and Transdanubia (Győr, Tata, Pécs, Kaposvár, etc).

While this division of station to region usually holds true, always check before travelling because there can be some differences – Sopron, Szombathely and Herend trains, for example, use Keleti. You can purchase tickets from each of the stations; alternatively try the **MÁV Ticket Office** (*VI, Andrássy út 35;* ☎ *1 461 5400;* e *informacio@mav.hu; open Mon–Fri 09.00–17.00; for 24-hr international information,* ☎ *1 461 5500*) or a travel agency like Vista (see page 97).

## By boat

There is a hydrofoil service operated by Mahart PassNave and running between Budapest, Bratislava and Vienna. For full details, see *Chapter 2*, page 46. The same company runs hydrofoils and ferries connecting Budapest with Esztergom, Visegrád, Szentendre and Vác between May and October. The services leave from Pest's Vigadó tér and usually stop five minutes later at Batthyány tér before continuing up the river. Details are included under the *Getting there and away* sections of each of the Danube Bend towns.

## GETTING AROUND

Here are the statistics: 180 buses (*autóbusz*), 14 trolleybuses (*trolibusz*), 29 trams (*villamos*), three underground metro lines, and a suburban railway (HÉV) – in addition to the Hungarian State Railway (MÁV), which takes passengers to national and international destinations beyond the city. Oh, and there are taxis, and funicular, children's and cogwheel railways. Of course, 89% of statistics mean absolutely nothing, but Budapest is genuinely blessed with an efficient and punctual public-transport network, both easy to navigate and cheap to travel on. Getting around is a doddle.

If you wish to **report an incident** that occurs on the transport system, contact the Traffic Security Department of Budapest Transport Limited (*VIII, Baross utca 132;* ☎ *1 461 6500*). If an **item goes astray**, contact the Budapest Public Transport Company's (BKV) lost-and-found office (*VII, Akácfa utca 18;* ☎ *1 267 5299; open Mon–Thu 07.00–15.00, Fri 07.00–14.00*). Up-to-date **public transport information** is available in English from the BKV website at www.bkv.hu/angol.

## Tickets

Public transport in Budapest is primarily based on good faith. Passengers purchase their tickets (*jegy*) before boarding the metro, bus, tram or trolleybus – tickets are not available on the vehicles – and are trusted to validate them by inserting them into 'punching' machines. On the underground, these machines are automated and are usually found at the top of the escalators, while buses and trams have them on board (where you have to pull down on the slot to operate the puncher). Inspectors (with red armbands) sometimes patrol to check tickets, and may also wait at the metro station exits; they will issue fines for fare dodgers (2,000Ft if paid on the spot, 6,500Ft if paid within 30 days). A few of the newer transport vehicles have ticket-issuing machines on board, but these are far between.

Tickets are available individually or in books, and can be purchased from hotels, newsagents and train stations. The same type of ticket can be used on the underground, trams, buses and trolleybuses; one ticket allows one journey on one transport system (without changing). If you're travelling on the underground and intend to change lines then you'll require a transfer ticket that needs to be validated. A Budapest Card allows free use of public transport. The standard single ticket is valid on the HÉV up to the city limits, but you'll need to buy a separate ticket for travel onward. Ferry tickets can be purchased from ticket machines at the docking points. While BKV do not publicise it widely, pensioners over 65 can travel free on all modes of public transport within the city limits (you'll pay a surcharge on the HÉV beyond that) – it helps to have your passport as proof of age, but according to one reader you can simply point to your grey hair if confronted by the ticket inspector!

## Ticket prices
**Single** 170Ft
**Book of 10/20** 1,450/2,800Ft
**One-day ticket** 1,350Ft
**Tourist ticket** 2,700Ft (3-day); 3,100Ft (7-day)

**Metro section ticket** (valid for up to 3 stops only) 120Ft
**Metro section transfer ticket** (up to 5 stops with one line change) 185Ft
**Metro transfer ticket** (as many stops as you like with one line change) 270Ft

## By metro

Budapest's metro was the first underground transport network in continental Europe – the second in the world after London's – and consists of three lines: yellow (M1), red (M2) and blue (M3). The yellow line, which travels the entire length of Andrássy út to City Park and beyond, is the oldest and was built to celebrate the country's millennium in 1896. It is affectionately known as the *'kisföldalatti'* (or 'little underground'), and its stations are decorated with patterned tiles. All three lines are reliable and safe, and the trains arrive at frequent intervals of a few minutes. The metro runs from 04.30 until around 23.00 every day. The three lines intersect at Deák Ferenc tér station in the heart of Pest. Plans are afoot to add a fourth metro line that will run between Kelenföld and Keleti railway stations (and possibly as far east as Bosnyák tér). You can visit a small museum dedicated to the metro (see page 172).

## By bus, tram and trolleybus

The blue single-decker **bus** service is frequent and dependable. Busier bus routes have express services – indicated by a red (rather than black) number – that only stop at major bus stops, while those with an 'E' suffix run direct from terminal to terminal. Day buses operate between 05.00 and 23.00, and can get very crowded during the rush hour. They are particularly useful for getting into the Buda Hills; Buda's main terminals are at Moszkva tér and Móricz Zsigmond körtér. **Night buses** (*éjszakai járatok*) run between 23.30 and 04.30, following the routes of the red and blue underground lines and the main tram paths. Night buses bear the accented letter 'É' after the bus number (eg: 52É). Budapest has three bus stations for national and international services (see page 91).

There's something slightly special about riding a **tram**; Budapest's enjoy some of the city's choice cuts, running over four of the bridges, along both riverbanks and around the Great Boulevard. It's a great, unsung, yellow rumble of a way to see the city's various aspects. The transport brainchild of the '40s, the **trolleybus** is still surging onward along its overhead cables. It was introduced to commemorate Stalin's 70th birthday in 1949, which is why the first working bus was numbered '70'; each succeeding route was numbered upwards. Trams and trolleybuses run from around 05.00 to 23.00 daily. Most stops have a printed **timetable** (*menetrend*).

## By HÉV

The suburban railway, known as the HÉV, consists of four lines that run to the outer reaches of the capital and nearby towns of Szentendre, Gödöllő, Csepel and Ráckeve. The green trains are used predominantly by commuters, although the 45-minute journey between Batthyány tér and Szentendre is very popular with day trippers, and also passes through Óbuda and Aquincum on the way. In daylight hours trains for Szentendre leave every 20–30 minutes.

## By taxi

Taxis are everywhere in Budapest, but tourists are vulnerable to unscrupulous drivers who charge significantly over the odds. The best way to avoid this is to order a taxi by telephone from a reputable firm. If you call from a public telephone, you can usually quote the number in the booth and the taxi will know precisely where to collect you. If you must hail a cab in the street, always ensure it is a marked car (with a company name on the side), ask for an approximate cost from the driver, and ensure the meter is visible and re-set. Remember that the driver is unlikely to be able to change large currency bills, and that you should give a tip (either 10% or round the fare up to the nearest convenient amount). Legally, taxis are allowed to charge up to the following rates: (*06.00–22.00*) 200Ft basic fee, 200Ft/km, 60Ft/min for waiting; (*22.00–06.00*) 280Ft basic fee, 280Ft/km, 70Ft/min for waiting. Firms will usually have a standard charge for the journey to the airport from Pest or Buda.

**Reputable taxi firms** include Fő (✆ *1 222 2222*), Buda (✆ *1 233 3333*), City (✆ *1 211 1111*), Rádió (✆ *1 377 7777*), 6x6 (✆ *1 266 6666*), Tele5 (✆ *1 355 5555*) and Taxi 2000 (✆ *1 200 0000*).

## By ferry

A pleasant way to enjoy the riverbank sights is to board a ferry. These operate between Boráros tér on the Pest side to the Római part in Buda via Batthyány tér; don't expect to get there in a hurry – the full journey takes an hour. Ferries depart from Boráros tér May 1–Sep 3 Thu–Sun at 09.00, 11.40, 12.40, 15.20 and 16.20 (the last of these only as far as Batthyány tér). The final boat from the Római part leaves at 17.20, and goes to Jászai Mari tér (by Margit híd) via Hajógyári-sziget (Shipyard Island) and Margit-sziget (Margaret Island).

## By car

There's little joy for the driver in the centre of Budapest, with the congestion and maze of one-way streets that you expect from major capitals. The system of public transport is by far the better option. However, a car can be useful for trips into the hills, and you may anyway have a car for pressing on into the rest of Hungary after your Budapest stay. If you do have a car, good luck finding somewhere to park it – a Herculean task, particularly in Pest. You pay for a space at coin-operated meters or through pay-and-display machines. Time restrictions on parking in the downtown area are enforced by wheel clampers. Multi-storey car parks can be found at V, Szervita tér 8; V, Aranykéz utca 4; VIII, Futó utca 52; and VII, Osvát utca 5. For car rental firms, see *Practical Information*, page 57.

## By bicycle

While cycling is fraught with danger in the city centre, and bikes are prohibited on most major roads, Budapest does have 140km of marked cycle paths. There are pleasant rides along the Danube, around Margaret Island and into the Buda Hills – grab a copy of the excellent *Biking in Budapest* (1:60,000) map, available free from Tourinform offices. For an additional charge, bikes can be taken aboard the HÉV, state, cogwheel and children's railways (but not on buses, trolleybuses, trams or the metro). Hotels sometimes offer bikes for rent; alternatively, try:

**Charles Rent a Bike** I, Hegyalja út 23; ✆ 1 202 3414
**Palatinus Strand** XIII, Margaret Island; ✆ 1 966 6453. From 800Ft/hour.
**Yellow Zebra** V, Sütő utca 2; ✆ 1 266 8777; e yellowzebrabikes@yahoo.com. *Costs 3,000Ft/1 day and 5,000Ft/2 days, plus 20,000Ft deposit.*

The **X-Factor** in MOM Park (*XIII, Alkotás utca 53;* ✆ *1 487 5606;* e *x-factormom@hu.inter.net*) is a bicycle-repair shop.

# TOURIST INFORMATION, LOCAL TOURS AND TRAVEL AGENTS
## Tourist information

All four of the Tourinform offices in the capital offer excellent (multi-lingual) advice and free tourist literature to help you make the most of your visit. Be sure to pick up the English-language publications *Where Budapest* and the pocket-sized *Budapest Guide* if you can. Tourinform offices can be found at:

I, Szentháromság tér; ☎ 1 488 0475; e var@budapestinfo.hu. Known as 'Várinfó'; stands adjacent to the Mátyás Church. *Open daily 09.00–21.00 (Jun–Sep), 09.00–19.00 (Oct–May).*
V, Sütő utca 2 (just off Deák tér); ☎ 1 317 1248/438 8080 (24-hour). *Open daily 24 hrs.*
VI, Liszt Ferenc tér 11; ☎ 1 322 4098. *Open daily 09.00–19.00 (Apr–Oct), 10.00–18.00 (Nov–Mar).*
VI, Nyugati pályaudvar (Western Railway Station); ☎ 1 302 8580. *Open daily 09.00–19.00 (Mar–Oct), 09.00–18.00 (Nov–Feb).*

Computerised **information touch points** are found at Blaha Lujza tér, the upper terminus of the funicular railway, Déli Railway Station, both terminals of Ferihegy Airport, the Big Market Hall, Tourinform (*Sütő utca 2*), Moszkva tér and Keleti Railway Station.

## Local tours
There's no shortage of organised tours of the city and beyond, both for those who pre-book and for impulsive types. As well as the buses, boats and balloons, there are cycling, nature, walking and horse-riding tours.

**Absolute Walking Tours** V, Sütő utca 2; ☎ 1 266 8777; www.absolutetours.com. A variety of alternative tours (*costing 3,500–5,500Ft*) depart from outside the Lutheran church on Deák Ferenc tér, including a whizz around some communist sites (*Mon, Wed, Fri–Sat 10.30; Jan–Feb Sat only*) and a stagger around Budapest's bars (*Mon, Wed, Fri–Sat 20.00; Jan–Feb Sat only*). Conventional sightseeing walks leave daily from outside the Exhibition Hall on Hősök tere, as well as from the Lutheran church. No need to book. *Office open daily 09.00–20.00 (high season), 10.00–19.30 (other times).*
**Budapest Eye** VI, West End Shopping Centre Roof Garden, Váci út 1–3; ☎ 1 238 7623; info ☎ 06 20 589 7907; e budapestballon@muber.hu; www.budapestkilato.hu. A tethered hot-air balloon that takes passengers 150m above the city. You'll pay extra for permission to take a camera with you, which will be strapped to your wrist; we learnt it's best if the nominated cameraman is not the trembling one with his eyes tight shut. Flights subject to weather. *Adult/concessions 3,000/2,000Ft, child (under 6) 1,000Ft, discount with Budapest Card; open daily Nov–Apr 10.00–20.00, May–Oct 10.00–24.00 daily.*
**Budatours** VI, Andrássy út 2; ☎ 1 374 7070; e btours@budatours.hu; www.budatours.hu. Standard sightseeing buses (open-topped or covered) with recorded commentaries in various languages (inc English). Depart from outside Andrássy út 3. *Adult/concessions 4,800/2,400Ft; depart daily 10.30, 11.30, 13.30, 14.30 & 15.30.*
**Cityrama Sightseeing Tours** V, Báthori utca 22; ☎ 1 331 0043; e cityrama@cityrama.hu. Sightseeing by bus or boat. The 10-hour Danube Tour visits the Danube Bend, and includes a 3-course lunch and guided walk (*adult/concessions 16,000/8,000Ft*). Private tours by minibus are also available for small groups. *Open Mon–Fri 08.00–18.00, Sat–Sun 09.00–15.00.*
**EUrama Sightseeing Tours** V, Apáczai Csere János utca 12–14; ☎ 1 327 6690; www.eurama.hu. Half- and full-day tours by bus and on foot. The kids' tour (*8,000Ft/pp*) visits the Tropicarium (see page 171) and the summer bobsleigh run (see page 136). Also folklore events, horse shows and Jewish-theme tours (from 6,000Ft), and trips to the Danube Bend, Gödöllő, Herend and Lake Balaton.
**Koltour Bt** XI, Rákó utca 3; mobile: +36 20 935 9511; e koltour@koltour.hu; www.koltour.hu. Péter was our tour guide on an early visit to Budapest. He is knowledgeable, helpful and abundantly energetic. He and his family offer English- and German-language sightseeing trips in Budapest and beyond, and can arrange restaurants, hotels, airport transfers and personalised tours ranging from city walks and boat rides to searches for the graves of relatives.
**Legenda Travel Agency** V, Vigadó tér, Pier No 7; ☎ 1 266 4190; www.legenda.hu. Two hour-long boat trips along the Danube with recorded commentaries (in a choice of 30 languages). The daytime tour on the *Duna Bella* costs 3,600Ft, while the evening excursion on the *Duna Legenda* costs 4,200Ft (inc glasses of wine).

**Mahart Passnave** V, Belgrád rakpart; 1 484 4000; e passnave@mahartpassnave.hu; www.mahartpassnave.hu. Offers boat-trip programmes up and down the Danube, and organised tours for individuals and groups to international destinations. Local programmes include a 2-hour sightseeing folklore evening (*May 1–Sep 29, every Wed & Sat at 20.00*) at a pricey 9,500Ft/pp, and a 1-hour city cruise (*10/day in summer*) for a more affordable 2,400Ft/pp. Also operates scheduled hydrofoils from Budapest to Vienna via Bratislava (see page 46). *Ticket and information office open Mon–Fri 08.00–16.00.*

**MÁV Nosztalgia** V, Belgrád rakpart 26; 1 302 3580; e nostalgia_trains@mail.matav.hu; www.mavnosztalgia.hu. Nostalgic railway excursions (to destinations in Hungary and beyond, inc Serbia and Slovakia) on 50 restored vintage trains. Trains to the Danube Bend leave from Nyugati station at 09.40 (*May 6–Sep 30*) and arrive at the final destination of Szob at 11.48.

**Paul Street Tours** 06 20 958 2545; e faurestk@mail.datanet.hu. American Kristin Faurest runs personally tailored neighbourhood tours of Budapest, focusing upon the architecture and culture, as well as taking tourists on antiques-shopping trips in the capital and other cities. For a specialised tour, call a few days in advance.

**Program Centrum City Tours** Le Meridien Hotel, Erzsébet tér 9–10; 1 327 0055; e agency.programcentrum@axelero.hu; www.cityrama.at. Sightseeing, wine-tasting, Parliament and folklore tours, as well as excursions to the Danube Bend, Lake Balaton and even Vienna. 3-hour city tour costs 6,000Ft/pp (half price with Budapest Card).*Open Mon–Fri 09.00–14.00, Sat (Apr–Oct only) 09.00–15.00.*

**TGV Tours** VI, Hajós utca 23; 1 354 0755; e info@tgvtours.hu; www.tgvtours.hu. Reasonably priced tours, including Danube trips and day visits to the Hungarian wine regions of Eger and Tokaj (*adult/concessions 22,000/11,000Ft*).

**To-Ma Tour** V, Budapest, Október 6 utca 22; 1 353 0819; e tomatour@axelero.hu; www.tomatour.hu. Friendly company specialising in tailor-made and group tours of the city, as well as offering a range of private apartments (see page 106).

**Yellow Zebra** V, Sütő utca 2; 1 266 8777; e yellowzebrabikes@yahoo.com. Night and day, rain or shine, the Yellow Zebra 4-hour bike tours cover the city's main sights. *Adult/concessions 4,000/3,500Ft; bike hire from 3,000Ft (excl deposit); office open daily 09.00–20.00 (high season), 10.00–19.30 (other times).*

## Local travel agents

Travel agents can offer assistance with accommodation, programmes and excursions, car rental, and with tickets for shows and international and domestic travel; they can also often provide information, brochures and tourist maps, while some offices exchange travellers' cheques.

**Express** V, Semmelweis utca 4; 1 266 3277; e expresstravel@mailbox.hu; www.expresstravel.hu. *Open Mon–Fri 08.00–18.00, Sat 09.00–13.00.*

**Ibusz** Main office: V, Ferenciek tere 10; 1 485 2700; www.ibusz.hu; other offices: VII, Dob utca 1 and V, Vörösmarty tér 6. Largest travel-bureau network in Hungary. *Open Mon–Fri 08.30–16.30.*

**Kata Tourist** V, Régi Posta utca 12; 1 486 0147. Small but helpful office that's great for those on a budget. *Open daily 10.00–20.00.*

**Koltour Bt** See opposite

**Vista Travel Club** VI, Paulay Ede utca 2; 1 429 9766. Bilingual staff assist with outbound travel. There is also internet access, and travel bits and bobs for sale. At the junction with Andrássy út. *Open Mon–Fri 09.00–18.30, Sat 09.00–14.30.*

**Vista Visitor Centre** VI, Paulay Ede utca 7; 1 429 9950; e incoming@vista.hu; www.vista.hu. Located in a modern coffee house, the second Vista centre (on the same road) handles incoming travel and is the place to head for excellent travel help and advice about Hungary. *Open Mon–Fri 09.00–23.00, Sat 10.00–23.00, Sun 11.00–20.00.*

## OTHER PRACTICALITIES
### Health
In an emergency, contact **Főnix SOS Ambulance** (*II, Kapy utca 49;* ☏ *1 200 0100*), which provides round-the-clock health care and has its own ambulance service. The private **Rózsakert Medical Center** (*II, 2nd Floor, Gábor Áron utca 74-78;* ☏ *1 391 5905*) is housed in the shopping mall of the same name and has helpful, American-trained doctors in residence; it is closed at weekends.

Most **pharmacies** close between 18.00 and 20.00, but at least one in every district is open 24 hours a day. If it's very late you may have to ring the bell for admittance (and you may also be charged a small fee). Some pharmacies running non-stop services can be found at the following addresses:

VIII, Rákóczi út 39; ☏ 1 314 3695/3694
VI, Teréz körút 41; ☏ 1 311 4439
XII, Alkotás utca 1B; ☏ 1 355 4691/4727
II, Frankel Leó út 22; ☏ 1 212 4406/4311
IX, Üllői út 121; ☏ 1 215 8947/3900

If you're in need of urgent dental care, contact **SOS Dental Service** (*VI, Király utca 14;* ☏ *1 267 9602*), which operates 24 hours a day. For general health information, see page 47.

### Banks and money
The greatest concentration of banks is in downtown Pest – if in doubt, head to the busy shopping areas of Váci utca or the Great Boulevard. Banks to look out for are Budapest Bank, OTP, K&H and Postabank and most have 24-hour ATM facilities. For general information, see pages 50–2.

### *Exchanging currency*
Numerous bureaux de change booths can be found on Váci utca and the Great Boulevard, as well as in hotels, railway stations and shopping centres. The Interchange counters offer poor rates, and should be avoided. There are also foreign-currency exchange machines at several points around the city (including at *II, Margit körút 43–45*, *V, Károly körút 20*, and *VI, Andrássy út 49*). We'd recommend sticking to banks when exchanging cash and travellers' cheques. Dealing with black-market money-changers is illegal, and you run a high risk of being ripped off. The **American Express Exchange** (*V, Deák Ferenc utca 10;* ☏ *1 235 4330; open Mon–Fri 07.00–17.30, Sat 09.00–14.00*) changes AmEx travellers' cheques commission-free and also dispenses cash to its cardholders. A smaller branch in the Castle District at the Sisi Restaurant has a currency exchange that operates daily from March to mid January.

### Discount card
If you're exploring the city to the full, the **Budapest Card** is an option to mull over, although tourists are finding that it's considerably less of a bargain since the introduction of free entry to some of the permanent exhibitions of the city's museums and galleries (see page 68). It might prove cheaper to purchase the tourist travel tickets (see page 93) and pay for entry to those museums that still charge. The Budapest Card offers free admission to some of the sights, half-price sightseeing tours, discounts in some restaurants, shops and thermal baths, plus free and unlimited use of public transport. Cards are valid for 48 hours (*4,700Ft*) or 72 hours (*5,900Ft*), cover one adult and one child (up to the age of 14), and can be purchased from tourist offices, the airport, travel agencies, hotels and main metro ticket offices. Sign the card and fill in the date from the moment you want to start using it (you can choose when the period begins). A brochure

listing the places where the card is accepted can be picked up from Tourinform offices. See www.budapestinfo.hu/card for more information.

## Post offices

A few main post office in Budapest keep late hours. For general information, see page 77.

**Posta** V, Petőfi Sandor utca 19. *Open Mon–Fri 08.00–20.00, Sat 08.00–14.00.*
**Posta** V, Városház utca 18. *Open Mon–Fri 08.00–20.00, Sat 08.00–14.00.*
**Keleti Pályaudvar Posta** VIII, Baross tér 11/C. *Open Mon–Sat 07.00–21.00.*
**Nyugati Pályaudvar Posta** VI, Teréz körút 61. *Open Mon–Sat 07.00–21.00, Sun 08.00–20.00.*

## Internet

Most hotels offer internet access, but there are plenty of cheaper internet cafés all over Budapest.

**City Press Café** V, Petőfi Sándor utca 17–19. *Open daily 07.00–22.00.*
**Hotel Charles** See page 103. Has a small internet café, with 3 terminals. Very reasonably priced for a hotel. *Open 24 hrs daily.*
**Internet Café** VI, Andrássy út 46; ↘ 1 331 9102. *Open 24 hrs daily.*
**Kiber@Buda** XI, Budafoki út 22; ↘ 1 209 9257. *Open 24 hrs daily.*
**Szakkönyváruház** VI, Nagymező utca 43; tel/fax: 1 373 0500. Large Hungarian bookshop with 12 stations. Other internet shops forming part of this chain can be found at VIII, József korut 52; VII, Rákoczi utca 14 (in the Fokusz bookstore); and VI, Liszt Ferenc tér 9. *Open Mon–Sat 10.00–18.00, Sun 09.00–13.00.*
**VideoMania & Internet Kávézó** VI, Andrássy út 29. *Open Mon–Thu 10.00–22.00, Fri–Sat 10.00–24.00.*
**Vista kávéház** VI, Paulay Ede utca 7; ↘ 1 429 9999. *Open Mon–Fri 09.00–18.30, Sat 09.00–16.30.*
**Yellow Zebra** V, Sütő utca 2; ↘ 1 266 8777. *Open daily 09.00–20.00 (high season), 10.00–19.30 (other times).*

# WHERE TO STAY

During excavations of Aquincum, several cubicles were unearthed just outside what was then the south gate. Together they represented the city's earliest known 'hotel', a resting place for weary travellers who arrived too late to pass through the walls and had to hunker down until sunrise. Thankfully you get more for your money now – although you'll need a bit of it, for there's certainly no surplus of truly budget accommodation anymore. The best bet is to head for one of the few hostels, stay in an empty college dorm or arrange a private room (see pages 105–6).

## Hotels, pensions and hostels

So, where do you lay your hat? If it's velvet-lined with a feather on top, you'll have no trouble putting it down in a top-end hotel targeting the business and affluent-tourist dollar. The desirable locations are along the river, in the Castle District, in or around the Belváros and near City Park. These might be elegant turn-of-the-century edifices or modern hotels based on Western models – and priced as such. (For the vagaries of Hungary's star system, see page 59.) Because Budapest sits on hot spring water, several hotels offer thermal treatments. There are also a good number of mid-range hotels. Pensions flourish in the Buda Hills; unfortunately there are fewer in the city centre, and those there are tend to be considerably more expensive than their counterparts beyond the capital. At the lower end of the budget range are hostels and basic hotels or pensions, usually located either in shabbier neighbourhoods or in suburbs beyond the tourist centre. We've sorted our listings by price (with sub-categories of Buda and Pest). Be aware that hotels fill up during festival periods, and that prices soar during days around the Formula 1 Hungarian Grand Prix (*Aug*).

## Luxury (£125/US$224 and upwards)
### Buda
**Art'otel** (164 rooms) I, Bem rakpart 16–19; ☎ 1 487 9487; e budapest@artotel.hu; www.artotel.hu. When a hotel gets someone in to add a lick of paint, you don't usually expect a contemporary American artist to turn up. The walls of the Art'otel display 600 works by Donald Sultan, creating a modern, sophisticated and clean-lined interior. The rooms are jazzy and spacious; request one with a river view. The Chelsea Restaurant is well worth a look (see page 108). *Superior €198, executive €225, suite €318.*

**Corinthia Aquincum Hotel** (310 rooms) III, Árpád fejedelem útja 94; ☎ 1 436 4100; e info@aqu.hu; www.corinthiahotels.com [**B̄** 86; **HEV** *Árpád híd*] It's not as plush as its sister hotel, the Corinthia Grand, but its trump card is its spa. Thermal pools are filled with water pumped from Margaret Island, and are free for guests to use (although wellness treatments are extra). Non-guests may access the spa for 3,500Ft. Swimming pool. Stands at the foot of Árpád Bridge. *Sgl €210, dbl €228, executive €248, apt €380 (excl City Tax).*

**Hilton Budapest** (322 rooms) I, Budapest, Hess András tér 1–3; ☎ 1 889 6600; e sales.budapest@hilton.com; www.budapest.hilton.com. Location, location, location; the Hilton is the property gurus' mantra made flesh. Nestled next to the Mátyás Church, with eastern-facing rooms offering unrivalled views over the Danube, it is the envy of every other hotel in the city. Its design incorporates rows of metallic-tinted windows with the Baroque façade of a 17th-century Jesuits' college, and the ruins of a 13th-century Dominican monastery. While it lacks the grandeur of some 5-stars, and the position doesn't allow for a swimming pool, it remains one of Budapest's best-known hotels. In summer, the Dominican courtyard hosts exhibitions, concerts and plays, while the fabulous Dominican Restaurant offers the cream of views to go with its goose-liver specialities. Guests can park in the Castle District for no charge – get your ticket stamped at reception before exiting. Rooms are not enormous, but are elegant and suitably well equipped. *Deluxe €130–220, executive €180–270, suites €450–2,000 (all excl VAT and City Tax); excellent buffet b/fast €20.*

## Pest
**Andrássy Hotel** (70 rooms) VI, Andrássy út 111; ☎ 1 462 2100; e reservation@andrassyhotel.com; www.andrassyhotel.com [**M̄** *Bajza utca*; **B̄** 4] Once a state-owned hotel putting up communist delegates (including Gorbachev), the Bauhaus building was designed by architect Alfréd Hajós (an Olympic swimmer). It's now a charming sophisticate, with a limousine service and tinkling fountains in the lobby. There's a Mediterranean-café feel about the place, and it's well situated for City Park and the State Opera House. The new Zebrano restaurant is very good, serving a kind of international fusion. Ask for a room with balcony. *Sgl €134–147, dbl €218–240, suites €161–393.*

**Corinthia Grand Hotel Royal** (414 rooms) VII, Erzsébet körút 43–49; ☎ 1 479 4000; e royal@corinthia.hu; www.corinthiahotels.com [**T̄** 4, 6] The building is over a century old, and once contained the Café Royal – a beacon for Bohemians and the literati. After grey days as an office block it emerged in 2003 as the brightest of butterflies. There's yesteryear dignity about the lobby and ballroom, but any stuffiness is tempered by an airy layout that pits rooms around atrium courtyards. The main restaurant has continental and Hungarian cuisine (including reasonably priced set lunches), and there's a luxurious oriental restaurant and sushi bar. Guests can use the spa of the sister Hotel Aquincum (see above). Executive rooms have views over the inner atrium or boulevard rather than the rear of the hotel. All rooms have bath and separate shower. *Sgl €240, dbl €280, executive sgl €300–340, suites €400–3,000 (all excl VAT); b/fast €20.*

**Four Seasons Hotel** (179 rooms) V, Roosevelt tér 5–6; ☎ 1 268 6000; www.fourseasons.com/budapest. Utterly stunning; this hotel will smack the gobs of the most difficult to please. The Gresham Palace started life as a temple to capitalism, created in 1907 for the London Gresham Life Assurance Society. Fashioned during Hungary's Golden Age, this was one of the finest examples of Art-Nouveau architecture in the world. During the winter of 1944–45 Soviet soldiers occupied the palace, burning furniture to keep warm while the residents huddled in the cellar. Half a century later – and after restoration costing US$110 million – the country's most luxurious hotel was opened in 2004. It is 5-star-plus, with rooms furnished in Secessionist style, and a spa with swimming pool. The Páva (Peacock) Restaurant serves Mediterranean and contemporary Hungarian cuisine. *Sgl €280–800, dbl €310–830, suites €975–4,500.*

**Hotel Helia** (262 rooms) XIII, Kárpát utca 62–64; ↘ 1 889 5800; e helia@danubiusgroup.com; www.danubiushotels.com/helia [**B** *133;* **TB** *76;* **M3** *Dózsa György út*] This conference, wellness and thermal hotel is located slightly to the north of the centre, on the riverbank overlooking Margit-sziget. Rooms lack trappings of luxury but your money gives access to some serious liquid therapy – there's a swimming-pool complex, a brace of thermal baths, a sauna and steam baths, a 2-level fitness centre, and treatments that include a Cleopatra bath of milk and honey. Some rooms have balconies (€11 supplement for a river view), and a couple of the suites have their own private saunas. *Sgl €135–163, dbl €154–176, suite €266–378 (inc use of spa).*

**Hotel Taverna** (227 rooms) V, Váci utca 20; ↘ 1 485 3100; e hotel@hoteltaverna.hu; www.taverna.hu. Smack in the heart of the pedestrian quarter, this is the height of tourist convenience. There's a restaurant, brasserie and bowling bar. *Sgl/dbl €126/170.*

**Intercontinental Budapest** (398 rooms) V, Apáczai Csere János utca 12–14; ↘ 1 327 6333; e budapest@interconti.com; www.interconti.com. When voted the best view of Budapest, the judges were clearly inside looking out. It's less of an eyesore than the Budapest Marriott next door (V, Apáczai Csere János utca 4; *www.marriotthotels.com/budhu*), but it still does the Pesti riverscape near the Chain Bridge few favours. Both hotels are nevertheless superbly equipped and located precisely where you want to be. The Marriott has an all-you-can-eat cake buffet in its lobby lounge (which raises it considerably in our estimations), and we have had feedback from readers that the Intercontinental's restaurant is first-class. Swimming pool. *Dbl €280–360, business room €310–390, suites €580–610 (excl VAT & City Tax); b/fast €20.*

**Kempinski Hotel Corvinus** (365 rooms) V, Erzsébet tér 7–8; ↘ 1 429 3777; e hotel.corvinus@kempinski.com; www.kempinski-budapest.com. Madonna hid here when filming *Evita* and Michael Jackson fans camped outside during his stay. Perhaps the pretty-headed A-listers come for the breakfast, which includes over 150 items on a sumptuous buffet menu; perhaps they drink the night away in the brick Bavarian beerhouse or enjoy a meal in the Bistro Jardin (see page 112). The standard rooms are tastefully kitted out, while each suite is unique in style and has a music system. Immaculate, with a 5-star-plus rating. Swimming pool and wellness centre. *Sgl €260–410, dbl €300–450, suites €570–2,600 (excl VAT & City Tax). B/fast (Mon–Fri 06.00–10.30, Sat–Sun 06.00–11.00) €27; you don't have to be a guest to join the gorging fest.*

**Le Méridien Budapest** (218 rooms) V, Erzsébet tér 9–10; ↘ 1 429 5500; e reservations@le-meridien.hu; www.lemeridien-budapest.com. Housed in the protected Adria Palace, this is a classically furnished hotel with genuine star quality. There are chandeliers in the lobby, brown marble in the rooms, and an Art-Deco glass-domed glory of a Parisian brasserie-restaurant. Small pool with a glass roof. *Sgl €245–395, dbl €285–435, suites €370–1,700 (excl VAT and City Tax); b/fast €20.*

## Margaret Island

**Grand Hotel Margitsziget** (164 rooms) XIII, Margit-sziget; ↘ 1 889 4700; e resind@margitsziget.danubiusgroup.com; www.danubiushotels.com/grandhotel [**B** *26*] The stocky, mansion-like Grand was designed by Miklós Ybl in 1873, attracting literary greats like Arany János and Bródy Sándor. Guests may use the spa and medical facilities of the adjacent hotel (see next entry), which is linked to the Grand via an underground corridor. (Rooms in the Grand are smaller, but also 10% cheaper.) Each room has period features, while some of those on the 2nd and 3rd floors have terraces. Bus 26 runs between the hotel and Nyugati station every 15 mins. Ferry operates between the island and downtown in summer. Car access via Árpád Bridge. *Sgl €135–168, dbl €154–190, suite €194–244 (inc use of spa).*

**Thermal Hotel Margitsziget** (267 rooms) XIII, Margit-sziget; ✎ 1 889 4700;
e resind@margitsziget.danubiusgroup.com; www.danubiushotels.com/thermalhotel. The Thermal Hotel was once a hospital and is less noble of aspect than its neighbour, but it is here that guests get down to the serious business of health and beauty. The spa complex makes use of 3 hot springs, and there are indoor and outdoor swimming pools. If you want to know just how much of you is fat, they'll tell you the percentage with no holds barred; if you dream of a healthier spine, this is the place to come; the 'drinking cure' is warmer, eggier and altogether less alcoholic than you might have hoped. *Sgl €148–178, dbl €168–200, studio €184–204, suite €244 (inc use of spa). Spa use for non-guests 4,500–5,500Ft/day.*

## Expensive (£75–124/US$135–222)
### Buda
**Congress Park Hotel Flamenco** (358 rooms) XI, Tas vezér utca 7; ✎ 1 889 5600;
e flamenco.reservation@danubiusgroup.com; www.danubiushotels.com/flamenco [T̄ *61 from Moszkva tér,* T̄ *49 from Deák Ferenc tér or* T̄ *19 from Batthyány tér to Kosztolányi Dezső tér;* B̄ *7, 7A, 27, 12, 86*] On the western side of Feneketlen-tó (see page 148), the Flamenco has conferences in mind, allowing guests to take a stroll around the reedy (and somewhat whiffy) lake in between seminar dozes. The facilities are excellent, including a swimming pool and access to nearby tennis courts. *Sgl/dbl €95–140, suite €220.*

**Hotel Gellért** (234 rooms) I, Gellért tér 1; ✎ 1 889 5500;
e gellert.reservation@danubiusgroup.com; www.danubiushotels.com/gellert. If a turn-of-the-20th-century dandy were to meet Medusa's eye, the Hotel Gellért might be the result. This is an old-money aristocrat in stone. Ironically it was completed in 1918, and its first guests were political officials of the Hungarian Republic of Soviets. With a grand history comes a disdain for homogeneity; this is a hotel for lovers of faded noble charm rather than wall-to-wall comforts. Rooms (in 3 categories) vary considerably in size and shape. Those facing the river offer wonderful views (although light sleepers should note that trams rumble along the road below) while others overlook an inner courtyard. Some rooms are yet to be renovated. The hotel's café and terrace serves great cakes and snacks, and the recently renovated Gellért söröző operates as a beer garden and sun trap. Most rooms without A/C. *Sgl €75–190, dbl €170–210, suite €250–270 (inc use of adjacent Gellért Baths).*

**Hotel Gold Buda** (24 rooms) I, Hegyalja út 14; ✎ 1 209 4775; e goldbuda@goldhotel.hu; www.goldhotel.hu [B̄ *8, 112 stop outside*] With its distinctive conical turret, this is an appealingly quirky and asymmetrical little hotel. It's fairly well located near Erzsébet Bridge, at the western foot of Gellért Hill, although a busy road runs past the doorstep. *Sgl €89, dbl €99, triple €115, room for 2 in tower €125 (excl City Tax).*

**Hotel Lido** (54 rooms) III, Nánási út 67; ✎ 1 436 0980; e lidohotel@elender.hu; www.bestwestern-ce.com/lido [B̄ *106 from Árpád Bridge;* HEV *Rómaifürdő*] This is one for sporty types, with squash and tennis courts, a swimming pool, fitness centre and bowling alley. Stands near the river, just behind the Római part. *Sgl € 90, dbl €130, apt €230.*

### Pest
**Astoria** (131 rooms) V, Kossuth Lajos utca 19–21; ✎ 1 889 6000;
e astoria.reservation@danubiusgroup.com; www.danubiushotels.com/astoria. The Astoria retains much of its *fin-de-siècle* elegance – indeed, it is often used by film-makers producing period pieces. Its walls could tell a tale or two; in 1944 the basement was used as a detention centre for prisoners of the Gestapo, and ironically it formed the Soviet HQ during the 1956 revolution. Today the rooms vary in size, but are recently renovated and classically furnished. *Sgl €83–166, dbl €94–180, suite €175; b/fast €14.*

**Grand Hotel Hungaria** (499 rooms) VII, Rákóczi út 90; ☎ 1 889 4400;
e grandhungaria.reservation@danubiusgroup.com; www.danubiushotels.com/grandhotel-hungaria [M2 *Keleti*; B *7 and 78 stop outside*] This Goliath of a hotel – the country's biggest – stands a 5-min walk from Keleti station, and it's a good bet for larger tourist parties. The ongoing renovation programme is something of a labour of Hercules, but refurbished rooms are neutral and understated; those at the front of the building have terraces. Solarium, A/C, underground parking (€15/day). *Sgl €110, dbl €130, apt €200, suites €130–150.*

**Hotel Erzsébet** (123 rooms) V, Károlyi Mihály utca 11–15; ☎ 1 889 3700;
e erzsebet.reservation@danubiusgroup.com; www.danubiushotels.com/erzsebet. This fabulously central hotel was originally built in 1872, and was named after the queen. The cellars were transformed into a beer hall in 1927, the walls decorated with murals illustrating an epic poem – 'János Vitéz' ('John the Valiant') by Sándor Petőfi. The hall features live gypsy music from 19.00. Rooms basic but comfortable. A/C. *Sgl €75–97, dbl €85–105.*

**NH Budapest** (160 rooms) XIII, Vígszínház utca 3; ☎ 1 814 0000; e nhbudapest@nh-hotels.com; www.nh-hotels.com [T *4, 6;* B *26, 91, 191*] This hotel keeps the downtown within easy grasp, and is newly out of its wrapper – it only opened at the end of 2003. The furnishings have not had time to get tatty, and remain sharp, clean and contemporary. Solarium, A/C, underground parking. The smart rooms look either outwards or over an inner courtyard atrium; some have balconies. Located directly behind the Vígszínház (Comedy Theatre) on the Great Boulevard. *Rooms €93–145; b/fast €17.*

**Radisson SAS Béke Hotel Budapest** (247 rooms) VI, Teréz körút 43; ☎ 1 889 3900;
e sales.budapest@radissonsas.com; www.radissonsas.com [T *4 & 6 stop almost outside*] The novelist Ferenc Móra considered the Britannia – the Radisson in its previous incarnation – his second home. During the mid 1900s, the fashionable flocked to the hotel's vaunted nightclub for live jazz and dancing. The façade remains, and the Zsolnay Café is turn-of-the-century elegant, but otherwise this is a modern hotel with swimming pool, sauna, solarium and massage treatments. You're right in the thick of the city here, on the busy Nagykörút, and well placed for both the Belváros and City Park. Rooms comfortable, without knocking any socks off. A/C. *Sgl/dbl €140–170, suite €340 (excl all taxes); b/fast €17.*

## Mid-range (£35–74/US$63–133)
### Buda

**Ábel Panzió** (10 rooms) XII, Ábel Jenő utca 9; ☎ 1 381 0553/372 0289 [T *61 from Moszkva tér or Móricz Zsigmond körtér stops near top of road*] A pretty villa with creeper-covered walls and a veranda overlooking a well-kept garden. It's a very high-class guesthouse and is ideal for those after some last-century peace and relaxation. On a quiet backstreet off Villányi út. No TV, but radio. *Sgl €68, dbl €74.*

**Burg Hotel** (26 rooms) I, Szentháromság tér 7-8; ☎ 1 212 0269; e hotel.burg@mail.datanet.hu; www.burghotelbudapest.com. Lacking the river views of its illustrious neighbour the Hilton Budapest (see page 100), this hotel is nevertheless very reasonably priced considering the desirability of its location. Most of its rooms overlook the square and are as you would expect from a 3-star establishment – functional and lacking in trimmings. A/C. *Sgl €105, dbl €115, apt €134.*

**Hotel Budapest** (289 rooms) II, Szilágyi Erzsébet fasor 47; ☎ 1 889 4200;
e budapest.reservation@danubiusgroup.com; www.danubiushotels.com/budapest [T *18 and 56 from Moszkva tér;* B *5 from Erzsébet Bridge*] This satisfying cylinder of a hotel is a striking landmark at the point where grey meets green in Buda. Opposite is the lower terminus of the Cogwheel Railway (see page 182). There are no inconvenient pillars or square corners, and on a clear day the views from rooms near the top of the 15 storeys will set your heart doing the quickstep. There is no extra cost for rooms on upper levels – so aim high when booking. Sauna. A/C. *Sgl €70, dbl €95, suite €90–120.*

**Hotel Charles** (70 rooms) I, Hegyalja út 23; ☎ 1 212 9169; e reservation@charleshotel.hu; www.charleshotel.hu [B *112 & 8 stop outside*] The Charles was built for visiting businessmen who wanted to burn their own dinner after a hard day at the office. Each of the studio rooms and apts has a little kitchen. The location isn't the prettiest, but it's fairly convenient for the main tourist areas, the staff are courteous and helpful and the value is excellent. Bike hire (see page 95). *Sgl €53, dbl €70, triple €95, apt (for 1–4) €75–120.*

**Hotel Normafa** (61 rooms) XII, Eötvös út 52–54; ☎ 1 395 6505;

e registration@normafahotel.com; www.normafahotel.com [Ḃ *21 from Moszkva tér stops outside*] Just a few metres from the southern entrance to Normafa lejtő (see page 183) on Sváb hegy, and 2km from János hegy with its biking and walking routes, this alpine-style hotel is a great base for families exploring the Buda Hills. Fitness centre, sauna, outdoor swimming pool (with a children's pool and play area). Bike hire available. The adjacent Normafa Café and Grill (☎ *1 395 1771*) serves international cuisine of good repute. *Sgl €70–85, dbl €85–105, apt €105–135.*

**Hotel Kalmar** XI, Kelenhegyi út 7–9; ☎ 1 372 7530; e kalmar@ohb.hu. An excellent location up the road behind the Hotel Gellért, although more faded in its nobility. *Dbl €77.*

**Kulturinnov Hotel** (16 rooms) I, Szentháromság tér 6; ☎ 1 355 0122/375 1651;

e mka3hotel@dbassoc.hu. The interior of this Neo-Gothic palace on the northern side of the square has a faded splendour, but don't expect royal luxury from the small hotel in its wings. Owned by the Hungarian Culture Foundation, the hotel's rooms are very basic. Nevertheless, these are relatively affordable rooms within fly-casting distance of the Fishermen's Bastion. Parking 2,500Ft/day (accessed via the barrier at the northern end of Dísz tér or via Bécsi kapu). Most look inward over the building's central courtyard; no TV. *Sgl 14,500Ft, dbl 23,000Ft, triple 26,000Ft.*

**Vadvirág Panzió** (18 rooms) II, Nagybányai út 18; ☎ 1 275 0200/394 4292;

e vadvirag.panzio@axelero.hu [Ḃ *5 from Március 15 tér to Pasaréti tér, then 8-min walk in direction of Bartók Memorial House*] Much care has gone into this super *panzió*, divided between two buildings and tucked into Buda's green belt. All rooms have period elegance and some have balconies offering hill views. The beautifully tended garden is a pleasure in summer months, and there's also a terrace for sunbathing and a sauna. It's a touch pricier than some pensions, but it's plusher too. *Sgl €52, dbl €75, apt €75–85.*

## Pest

**Domina Inn Fiesta** (112 rooms) VI, Király utca 20; ☎ 1 328 3000; www.ahotelfiesta.com [M̄1, M̄2, M̄3 *Deák Ferenc tér;* T̄ *47, 49*] Stylish, modern hotel; spacious rooms are unfussy, colourful and clean, the superior larger than the standard. A/C. Located 400m from Deák Ferenc tér. *Sgl €95, dbl €105, suite €125.*

**Hotel Gold Panzió** (22 rooms) XIV, Pándorfalu utca 15 (near Ungvár utca); ☎ 1 252 0470;

e panzio@goldhotel.hu; www.goldhotel.hu. [T̄B *74 stops a few mins' walk away;* M̄1 *Mexikói út; near* M̄3 *motorway*] On a quiet suburban backstreet 1km northeast of City Park, this *panzió* is friendly, cosy and competitively priced. Tasteful rooms with small balconies. *Sgl €54, dbl €59, triple €74 (excl Tourist Tax).*

**Hotel Liget** (139 rooms) VI, Dózsa György út 106; ☎ 1 269 5300; e hotel@liget.hu; www.liget.hu [T̄B *75, 79 or* Ḃ *20, 30 stop close by*] Well positioned for City Park and Heroes' Square, less so for the downtown. The rooms are muted and uninspiring, but large and comfortable enough. Sauna, solarium, bike rental. *Sgl €105, dbl €120.*

**Hotel Queen Mary** (26 rooms) VII, Kertész utca 34; ☎ 1 413 3510; e info@hotelqueenmary.hu; www.hotelqueenmary.hu [T̄B *70, 78 to top of Kertész utca;* M̄1 *Oktogon,* M̄2 *Blaha Lujza tér, then* T̄ *4, 6 a short way to junction with Király utca, and walk*] Opened in 2003, the Queen Mary remains as eager as a puppy. There are few decorous frills, but all is unsullied and as yet un-dog-eared. Just off the Nagykörút, it's a short elope to the café-bars of Liszt Ferenc tér. A/C. *Sgl €69, dbl €75, triple €94, room for 4 €112.*

**Hotel Stadion** (379 rooms) XIV, Ifjúság útja 1–3; ☎ 1 889 5200;

e stadion.reservation@danubiusgroup.com; www.danubiushotels.com/stadion [M̄2 *Népstadion*] Near the Puskás Stadium on the outskirts of town, the Stadion inevitably receives its fair share of athletes, spectators and school touring teams. High-tech fitness room, swimming pool, sauna, solarium. Rooms are a good size, newly refurbished, many with balconies. *Sgl/dbl €90–110*.

**Leó Panzió** (14 rooms) V, Kossuth Lajos utca 2/A; ↘ 1 266 9041; e panzioleo@mail.datanet.hu. With Váci utca a mere 30m away and the Franciscan church at Ferenciek tere opposite, she can go shopping while he prays the credit card can take it. You couldn't ask for a more central location; it's on the second floor of a shabby-looking building with a cage lift, but the rooms are spacious and well-furnished. A/C. *Sgl €71, dbl €87*.

## Budget (£34/US$61 and under)

Youth hostels (*ifjúsági szálló*) may be open during the summer only, although this is unusual in Budapest. The Hungarian Youth Hostels Association (*VII, Almássy tér 6;* ↘ *1 413 2065 or 1 343 5167; www.youthhostels.hu*) can provide further information, and make reservations. A final bargain-basement option is to stay in college accommodation during the summer recess (*Jul & Aug*). Tourinform should be able to provide a list of these, although local tourist agencies (see under *Private rooms*, page 106) can also make bookings for you.

### Buda

**Back Pack Guesthouse** (8 rooms) XI, Takács Menyhért utca 33; ↘ 1 209 8406; e backpackguest@hotmail.com; www.backpackbudapest.hu [B̄ 7, 7A; T̄ 19, 49. *Alight at Tétényi út and then short walk*] Jungle murals, rainbow colours, a decked 'chillout' garden and a room called the 'love shack'. This is a fun-time commune of a guesthouse, with clean, comfortable and cheerful rooms. Dbls have TV, basin. Shared toilets, showers, kitchen, laundry facilities. 15 mins by bus from centre. *Private dbl €28, dorm bed €10–12/pp*.

**Büro Panzió** (10 rooms) II, Dékán utca 3; ↘ 1 212 2929; e buro-panzio@axelero.hu [M̄2̄ *Moszkva tér;* T̄ 4, 6] Fairly basic and a touch bleak, the Büro is just off Moszkva tér (less than 10 mins on foot from Castle District). Considering this, it's cheap as chips, but don't expect modern furnishings. Some rooms with TV. *Sgl 6,500Ft, dbl 12,000Ft, triple 18,000Ft*.

**Hotel Citadella** (12 rooms) I, Citadella sétány; ↘ 1 466 5794; e citadella@citadella.hu; www.citadella.hu [B̄ 27 *as far as Búsuló Juhász Étterem, then 300m walk*] Those who fancy doing a bit of holiday porridge should head for the chunky ramparts of the former Habsburg fortress. There are few home comforts here, but can prison have been all that bad with views like these from the walls? Most rooms sleep 2–4, and there is a dorm for 14. Shower and basin, but shared toilets. No TV. *Rooms €46–51, dorm €10/pp*.

**Hotel Korona** (24 rooms) XII, Sasadi út 123; ↘ 1 319 1255; e korona.pension@axelero.hu; www.koronapension.hu [B̄ 53 *from Karinthy Frigyes út stops outside;* T̄ 59 *from Moszkva tér runs to Farkasréti tér, at northern end of Sasadi út*] A well-equipped villa-style hotel on the cusp of the Buda Hills, with beautifully maintained gardens and modern, clean rooms (some with balcony, some with A/C). Excellent value. Sauna. *Sgl €50, dbl €60, triple €70, apt €60–100*.

**Hotel Papillon** (20 rooms) II, Rózsahegy utca 3/B; ↘ 1 212 7450; e rozsahegy@axelero.hu; www.hotelpapillon.hu [B̄ 11 *from Batthyány tér*] More family guesthouse than hotel, with homely rooms and a welcoming owner. There's room to dip little more than a toe in the tiny swimming pool at the back, but the garden allows you to relax after the sapping climb up Rose Hill. *Sgl €51, €71, triple €82 (excl Tourist Tax)*.

### Pest

**Best Hostel** VII, Podmaniczky utca 27; ↘ 1 332 4934; e bestyh@mail.datanet.hu; www.besthostel.hu [T̄ 4, 6 *from Moszkva tér;* B̄ 72; T̄B̄ 73; M̄3̄ *Nyugati tér*] A calm and comfortable hostel near Nyugati station. Ring doorbell 33 for access to the inner courtyard of the block, and the hostel is on the 1st level. Communal kitchen, common room (with TV), internet access, shared showers and toilets. *Dorm bed 3,000–3,600Ft/pp, private dbl 4,200Ft/pp*.

**Marco Polo Hostel** VII, Nyár utca 6; ℡ 1 413 2555; e info@marcopolohostel.com; www.marcopolohostel.com [TB *74 stops close by;* M2 *Blaha Lujza tér is 3 streets away*] Upper-end hostel in the business district, with cheerful rooms, a washer and dryer, and a disco bar open into the wee hours. Rooms (not dorms) are en-suite and have TV and telephone. Free minibus from Keleti station. *Sgl 12,500Ft/pp, dbl 8,500Ft/pp, triple 6,300Ft/pp, room for 4 5,800Ft/pp, dorms (for 12) 4,500Ft/pp. 10% discount with student or IYHF card.*

**Medosz Hotel** (70 rooms) VI, Jókai Mór tér 9; ℡ 1 374 3000 [B̄ *4 along Andrássy út;* T̄ *4, 6;* M̄1 *Oktogon*] Drab but affordable option right on top of the bars and restaurants of Liszt and Jókai squares. Rooms are spartan but well enough equipped, and there's a decent b/fast. Credit cards not accepted. *Sgl 11,500Ft, dbl 15,000Ft, triple 18,000Ft, suite 23,000Ft.*

**Red Bus Hostel** V, Semmelweis utca 14; ℡ 1 266 0136; www.redbusbudapest.hu [M2 *Astoria,* M3 *Ferenciek tere, then few mins' walk*] No-nonsense hostel owned by a friendly South London geezer. On 1st floor of residential block; climb the stairs around the inner courtyard. Standard dorms, as well as sgl, dbl and triple rooms, communal kitchen and laundry facilities, internet access, and shared toilets and showers. Centrally located just inside Károly körút, on the corner of Gerlóczy utca and Semmelweis utca. *Dorms (for 4, 6 and 8) 3,000Ft/pp, twin 8,000Ft/room.* The owners run a second hostel in summer (*VII, Szövetség utca 35;* ℡ *1 321 7100*), offering dorm beds only.

## Private rooms

(For general information, see page 60.) Rooms are available in most districts, although beyond the downtown or surroundings of the Castle District there's the risk of a run-down neighbourhood or a high-rise block. Double-check with the agency concerned. Expect to pay 4,000–6,000Ft for a sgl and 5,000–9,000Ft for a dbl. The following places can organise a private room on your behalf:

**Ibusz** V, Ferenciek tere 10; ℡ 1 485 2767; e accommodation@ibusz.hu; www.ibusz.hu. *Rooms 4,000–6,500Ft/pp; office open Mon–Fri 09.00–17.00.*

**Kata Tourist** V, Régi Posta utca 12; ℡ 1 486 0147. Helpful tourist office that can organise cheap accommodation in hostels and dorm rooms in universities. *Open 10.00–20.00 daily.*

**To-Ma Tour** V, Október 6 utca 22; ℡ 1 353 0819; e tomatour@axelero.hu; www.tomatour.hu. *Sgls 4,500–6,000Ft, dbls 5,500–8,000Ft; open Mon–Fri 09.00–12.00, 13.00–20.00, Sat–Sun 09.00–17.00.*

**Tribus Hotel Service** V, Apáczai Csere János utca 1; ℡ 1 944 2455; e tribus.hotel.service@mail.datanet.hu. *Rooms 5,000–9,000Ft; office open 24 hours daily.*

## Private apartments

(For general information, see page 60.) The following companies organise bookings:

**Boulevard City Apartments** XII, Virányos utca 10/A; ℡ 1 214 6262; www.aktivtours.hu. Superior 2- and 3-room accommodation in a modern building just beyond the Nagykörút. *Apts €66–88 (min 2 nights, excl Tourist Tax).*

**To-Ma Tour** See above. Although the 1-, 2- and 3-bedroom apts are not luxurious, they are centrally located, clean and well-equipped. There's wiggle room over prices. *Apts €45–85.*

**Tribus Hotel Service** See above. Pleasant apts for 1–6 people, mainly in downtown Pest. *Apts 10,000–20,000Ft.*

**www.budapestrooms.com** ℡ 30 454 3017; e info@budapestrooms.com. Website with apt details and online booking form. *Apts €40–70 (1–2 people), €50–80 (3–4), €80–100 (5–6).*

## Camping

The best places to pitch up are on the Buda side of the river. Sites are well equipped without giving Eurocamp undue cause for worry, and can be crowded in high season.

**Csillebérci Camping** XII, Konkoly Thege Miklós út 21; ℡ 1 275 4033 [B*21 from Moszkva tér, or Children's Railway to Csillebérc terminus*] Not the most modern campsite, but it has excellent sports

**COMMIE LOVE**
Durex, the condom manufacturer, conducted a survey in 2003 to find the nation that most enjoyed sex. The French? The Italians? Oh, *nem nem*. Hungarians topped the poll as the Buda-best lovers, followed by citizens from Serbia and Montenegro, Croatia, Bulgaria and the Czech Republic. Perhaps a communist past is the Viagra of central Europe…

facilities (outdoor pool, tennis courts etc), and is beautifully situated on Széchenyi hegy. Tent and caravan camping, bungalows (bathroom, fridge, radio) and youth hostel (shared bathrooms); showers, cooking appliances, on-site café and restaurant. *Tent €5, caravan €11, plus €4/pp; bungalow €38/48 (for 2/3); youth hostel rooms (shared bathrooms) dbl €16–20, triple €21–27; apt (for 4) €36–45. Camping open May 1–Sep 30; bungalow/youth hostel open all yr.*

**Római Camping** III, Szentendrei út 189; ☎ 1 368 6260; www.hotels.hu/romai_camping [HÉV *Rómaifürdő*] Large campsite with swimming pool, decent showers, restaurant and shop. Opposite the Római Strand, on the road running north to Szentendre. 15-min train journey to Buda centre, 30-min to Pest. *Tent 1,950Ft, caravan 2,970Ft, plus 990Ft/pp; bungalows 1,690–15,000Ft. Open all yr; reception Mon–Fri 08.00–15.00 (call at site restaurant 15.00–22.00).*

**Zugligeti 'Niche' Camping** XII, Zugligeti út 101; ☎ 1 200 8346; www.campingniche.hu [B *158 from Moszkva tér stops by entrance*] The campers' favourite, and understandably so. Small but inviting, well kept and attractively located. Very good restaurant. 9km from city centre. *Open Mar–Nov.*

## WHERE TO EAT

You can't properly enjoy rooting around a city without the anticipation of good food and drink to come. Budapest doesn't disappoint. Coffee and cake is the cement between sights in a day spent wandering, and you'll reflect fondly on that evening passed people-watching on a terrace with a glass of beer and a bowl of bean soup. Hungarian food fuelled shepherds, hunters and fishermen, and it more than fills the legs of today's tourists. Prepare to loosen the belt and lose a few buttons.

### Restaurants

Greek, Italian, French, Chinese, Japanese, Indian, Mexican, Russian – the whole gamut of global fare is represented in Budapest. You'll even find Hungarian. Such culinary internationalism is relatively recent and, as such, the range and sophistication of some menus are slightly limited. Prices at the bottom and top ends are higher than elsewhere in the country, considerably so where *haute cuisine* is concerned, and eateries in Váci utca and the Castle District will charge what they know they can get. Nevertheless, the average cost of a meal in any of the brackets remains significantly lower than in Western capitals. Eat-all-you-like brunches and fixed two- or three-course tourist menus offer added value. We've chosen to divide restaurants by area; entries include the average cost of a main course, together with the upper and lower limits.

### Buda
#### Castle District

**Arany Kaviár** I, Ostrom utca 19; ☎ 1 201 6737/225 7370; www.aranykaviar.hu. This intimate restaurant specialises in Russian, Armenian, Ukrainian and Georgian cuisine; its rich decoration emulates the dining-rooms of the 19th-century Russian bourgeoisie. Have your tastebuds tickled by fine caviar and your head befuddled with frozen glasses of syrupy vodka, thick enough to spread on toast. By comparison with the West, caviar remains relatively inexpensive here. It is worth bearing in mind that the sturgeon is endangered; if you want to do your bit to ensure its survival, choose red caviar, which is from the salmon. Just outside Bécsi kapu. *Caviar specialities 4,500–8,990Ft, other mains 2,250–4,500Ft, avg 3,200Ft; open 12.00–24.00 daily.*

**Budavári Fortuna** I, Hess András tér 4; ↘ 1 375 6857; www.miwo.hu/fortunarest. A 14th-century building and a choice of three sumptuous main dining-rooms, each with its own regal castle 'theme'. Before wolfing down some traditional Hungarian food, you can turn vintner and bottle your own sparkling wine. The process takes just a few mins, costs 8,000Ft, and has encouraged some rather glamorous figures to stain their manicured fingers with the grape. ABBA, Antonio Banderas, Roger Moore and Gloria Gaynor all have autographed bottles in the cellar waiting to accompany their next meals. *Mains 1,800–4,500Ft, avg 3,200Ft; open 12.00–16.00 & 19.00–24.00 daily.*

**Rivalda** I, Színház utca 5–9; ↘ 1 489 0236; www.rivalda.net. The Rivalda is highly rated by luvvies and foodies alike. A colourful interior pays homage to those who have trodden the boards, and there is also a very pretty dining area in the Carmelite courtyard. Outdoor theatrical productions are held here in Aug, and for an additional charge you can eat while enjoying a performance. Contemporary Mediterranean and international cuisine, and a distinguished wine list. Prices lean towards the expensive, but the food is good. Just off Dísz tér, next to the National Dance Theatre. *Mains 1,600–3,800Ft, avg 2,800Ft; open daily 11.30–23.30.*

## Gellért Hill, the Tabán and surrounds

**Hemingway** XI, Kosztolányi Dezső tér 2, Feneketlen-tó; ↘ 1 381 0522; www.miwo.hu/hemingway [B *12;* T *19, 49*] The owner's a Hemingway nut; Latin, Mediterranean and African motifs evoke the writer's world, and photos and furniture his epoch. This large and popular open restaurant has a decked terrace overlooking the reedy 'Bottomless Lake'. Its international menu specialises in grilled dishes, and fishy dishies in particular. There are good selections of teas, coffees and cigars too. *Mains 1,350–3,200Ft, avg 2,400Ft; open daily 12.00–24.00.*

**Tabáni Terasz** I, Apród utca 10; ↘ 1 201 1086; www.tabaniterasz.hu. There's a Parisian-style restaurant and café, a decked terrace at the front, a quieter courtyard garden complete with walnut tree, and a wine cellar for tastings. It's popular both with the coffee crowd and the pre-dinner cocktailers, while a diverse international spread makes room for cajun steaks, venison, paella, lasagne and shrimps. *Mains 1,200–3,800Ft, avg 2,000Ft; open 12.00–24.00 daily.*

**Villa Doria** I, Döbrentei utca 9; ↘ 1 225 3233; www.villadoria.hu. Few 18th-century buildings remain in the Tabán; this Neoclassical house of 1700 is where the Pauline poet Benedek Virág (1754–1830) – who is buried in the Cave Church (see page 177) – spent the last years of his life. It is now home to the Villa Doria, with its polished floors you could skate on and cobbled courtyard bar. The Italian chef prepares a large selection of excellent dishes from his native land. Some more expensive choices were planned – inc langoustine for 2 at a wallet-weeping 29,000Ft. Set buffet lunch available at weekends *(12.00–17.00; 3,000Ft)*. Also accessible from Apród utca (through Tabáni Terasz). *Mains 1,100–4,500Ft, avg 2,300Ft; open 12.00–23.00 daily.*

## Víziváros

**Chelsea Restaurant** I, Bem rakpart 16–19; ↘ 1 487 9487; www.artotel.de. Chic and fashionably understated, the Chelsea has something of a gallery feel to it – unsurprising since it is part of the Art'otel (page 100), itself a paean to American painter Donald Sultan. The menu is refreshingly brief, featuring delicate international dishes that bend towards Mediterranean and Asian flavours. Entrance on Fő utca or through the hotel lobby. A weekly menu offers discount dishes. *Mains 1,600–3,350Ft, avg 2,200Ft; open daily 12.00–15.00 & 18.00–23.00.*

**Kacsa Vendéglő** II, Fő utca 75; ↘ 1 201 9992; www.kacsavendeglo.hu. [B *11;* T *4, 6*] Well, pluck a duck! Move over Disney, with your Daffy and your Donald, for there are higher artists at work in the kitchen of 'Duck Restaurant'. The chef has over 60 duck dishes in his portfolio; on request, he'll put together a plate featuring a 'taste' of several. Let the attentive waiters guide you. This is exclusive, expensive dining, and very much all it's quacked up to be. Opposite the Király Baths. *Mains 2,700–5,900Ft, avg 3,500Ft; open Mon–Fri 12.00–15.00 & daily 18.00–01.00.*

**Le Jardin de Paris** I, Fő utca 20; ℄ 1 201 0047. Make your meal here an evening one, for the garden is at its most atmospheric after dark. There are fairy lights in the trees, oil lamps on the tables, an al-fresco kitchen and an open-fronted cellar bar. Among the French offerings are snails, calamari, sweet breads, truffles and lobster. Near the French Institute. *Mains 1,650–3,500Ft, avg 2,700Ft; open daily 12.00–24.00.*

**Margitkert** II, Margit utca 15; ℄ 1 326 0860; www.margitkert.com [T̄ *4, 6*] The Margitkert tempts diners with a big cheese. The bald-headed Lajos Boross is the 'Gypsy King' – the chief violin soloist (*primás*) – of the Budapest Gypsy Symphony Orchestra (*www.100violins.com*), the largest of its type in the world. The food is traditional and well-priced, the speciality of the rather kitsch house a wooden platter of grilled meats (for 2 or more). Make some room for all this by walking to the restaurant, which is up a steep hill opposite Margaret Bridge. Gypsy music daily from 18.00 (Boross usually from 19.30). *Mains 840–2,680Ft, avg 1,600–1,800Ft; open 12.00–24.00 daily.*

**Seoul House Korean Restaurant** I, Fő utca 8; ℄ 1 201 7452. OK, Budapest isn't overflowing with Korean restaurants, but this is where smartly dressed Asian diners come for their *kimchi*. It's upmarket and a touch pricey. At the corner with Apor Péter utca. *Mains 2,000–4,500Ft, avg 2,200Ft; open Mon–Sat 12.00–15.00 & 18.00–23.00.*

**Új Lan Zhou** II, Fő utca 71; ℄ 1 201 9247. Chinese restaurant rightly lauded by Budapest's foodies. In addition to the usual dishes, the speciality is eastern Chinese cuisine with adventurous choices like jelly fish, pig's tongue and various animal innards. North end of Fő utca. *Mains 1,190–2,990Ft, avg 1,290Ft; open 11.00–23.00 daily.*

## Moszkva tér

**Marxim** II, Kis Rókus utca 23; ℄ 1 316 0231; www.extra.hu/marxim [M2 *Moszkva tér;* T̄ *4, 6*] This communist-themed pizzeria near Moszkva tér throws up the usual paradoxes, revelling in a certain nostalgia for agitprop murals while dividing booths with barbed wire. There's a mixed bag of clientele too: young-buck students, bearded 'thinkers' smoking roll-ups, and middle-class 40-somethings gorging on pieces of Gorbi Gorbi or Pizza à la Kremlin. Loud and lively. Pittas and pastas alongside good-value pizzas. *Mains 540–1,190Ft; open Mon–Thu 12.00–01.00, Fri–Sat 12.00–02.00, Sun 18.00–01.00.*

**Szt Jupát** II, Dékán utca 3; ℄ 1 225 0339; www.stjupat.hu [M2 *Moszkva tér;* T*4, 6*] When the sensible of Budapest are long abed, the Szt Jupát is a beacon for those more committed to an active nightlife. Duvets await, but first some steps towards dulling hangovers to come. Cast a bleary eye over the never-ending story that is the menu, and line the stomach with daunting wooden platters of Hungarian specials. Quantity lords it slightly over quality here, and our starters had barely started before the main courses crashed the party, but it's busy, buzzy and the prices please the tightest of wallets. A litre of beer costs just 740Ft. Just behind Moszkva tér. *Mains 890–3,800Ft, avg 1,300Ft; open 12.00–06.00 daily.*

## Óbuda

**Új Sipos Halászkert** III, Fő tér 6; ℄ 1 388 8745 [HEV *Árpád híd;* B̄ *18, 37, 42*] Slap in the middle of the peaceful Fő tér, this grand fish restaurant serves Hungarian and international dishes. Be tempted by grilled prawns in honey and cognac or trout fillets with red wine and prunes. *Mains 1,450–2,950Ft (avg 2,300Ft); open daily 12.00–24.00.*

## The Buda Hills

**Fuji Japan** II Csatárka utca; ℄ 1 325 7870; www.fujirestaurant.hu. Hidden high in the hills, this upmarket Asian restaurant is worth its weight in *sushi*. Sip a *sake* while you watch the chef create delicious Japanese food. Not cheap and reservations recommended. *Open 12.00–24.00 daily.*

**Náncsi Néni** II, Ördögárok út 80; ℄ 1 398 7127; www.nancsineni.hu [T̄ *56 or* B̄ *56 from Moszkva tér to Hűvösvölgyi terminus, then* B̄ *157, which stops outside*] The restaurant strives to feel like a 'grandmother's kitchen'. The owner asks that if you enjoy the food you recommend it to your friends, and if not that you recommend it to your mother-in-law. Friends, it's worth the trip. The dishes are Hungarian and international (inc seafood), and the extensive menu is not for the indecisive. It's good to see *főzelék* included (*only on Mon, Wed & Fri*). Booking advised. *Mains 1,250–6,666Ft, avg 2,600Ft; open Mon–Fri 12.00–23.00, Sat–Sun 09.00–23.00.*

**Remíz** II, Budakeszi út 5; ↘ 1 275 1396; www.remiz.hu [B̄ *22;* T̄ *56 from Moszkva tér*] You'll yearn to hug the chef tightly to your breast, and listen to whispered secrets of aubergine mousse, of crispy catfish and truffles, of venison and blueberries. The Remíz (Tram Depot) blends past and present; tram paraphernalia and tinkling ivories evoke an era of silent movies and full moustaches, while traditional dishes are infused with modern international influences on the monthly menu. One of the city's best; if only it were more central. *Mains 1,620–3,280Ft, avg 2,500Ft; open 09.00–24.00 daily.*

**Serpenyos Vendéglő** II, Szépvőlgyi út 62; ↘ 1 335 5361; www.reziserpenyos.hu. [B̄ *65 stops almost outside*] Take along a hearty hunger and an elasticated waistband. If your appetite is daintier, the restaurant offers its dishes in smaller sizes too. Among the homely Hungarian choices during our visit was a plate of crispy goose leg, roasted goose liver, mashed potato and onion. Smack those lips. *Mains 900–2,480Ft, avg 1,700Ft; open 12.00–24.00 daily.*

## Pest
### Downtown and beyond
**Bangkok House** V, Só utca 3; ↘ 1 266 0584. We feel guilty faulting a restaurant for an excess of enthusiasm, but any self-respecting Bangkok homeowner would start and run screaming from the clichéd Asiana. If you can lever yourself into a seat among the intense clutter of rattan work, you'll find some decent enough Thai food on a heaving menu. *Mains 1,350–4,550Ft, avg 1,750Ft; open 12.00–23.00 daily.*

**Baraka Restaurant** V, Magyar utca 12–14; ↘ 1 483 1355. The Baraka is tucked away on a back street, with a polished but cosy setting of dark-wood furnishings. Its food can be excellent, influenced by French and Asian flavours, but there are reports that it has become a victim of its own success recently, and is struggling to maintain its consistently high standard in the face of the increasing customer numbers. Large selection of plonk. *Mains 1,900–4,000Ft, avg 3,000Ft; open Mon–Sat 18.00–23.00.*

**Biarritz Restaurant and Café** V, Balassi Bálint utca 2; ↘ 1 311 4413. The interior is rustic and uncomplicated, the modern European cuisine first class, and the service correct. It's not cheap, however; you'd think mashed potato was a delicacy at 1,500Ft for three dollops. Near the Parliament building. *Mains 1,250–3,150Ft; open 09.00–24.00 daily.*

**Fakanál Étterem** V, Vámház körút 1–3; ↘ 1 217 7860. Take a break from browsing at the Big Market Hall, and fill up on typical Hungarian food at very cheap prices. On the 1st-floor gallery. *Open Mon–Fri 10.00–17.00, Sat 10.00–14.00.*

**Fatál** V, Váci utca 67; ↘ 1 266 2607/2608. There have been discontented rumbles of late at the 'Wooden Plate'. Not from stomachs, you understand – food mountains on wooden boards and brim-filled bubbling pans leave no room for those. Instead it is said that the cellar restaurant has become a production line. There's some truth in the complaint. It's a cacophonous brick cauldron of chatter and whirring fans, where you'll fight for elbowroom on wooden benches and suffer waiters who ignore and lean across you by turns. The silence rings when you exit. Cheap, super-sized dishes ooze Hungarian rusticity and manliness, the fare of tough-skinned farmers with big hands: liver sausage, black pudding, deep-fried brains, red cabbage. You'll love every minute. Entrance on Pintér utca. *Mains 900–1,500Ft; open 11.30–02.00 daily.*

**Firkász** XIII, Tátra utca 18; ↘ 1 450 1118 [T̄ *4, 6*] The Firkász (Scribbler) is something of a modern variation on the literary theme of early 20th-century coffee houses. There's even the odd jobbing journo. Filling Hungarian specialities (of variable quality) at a fair price, and twice-monthly wine tastings. Just north of the downtown. *Mains 1,500–2,800Ft, avg 2,000Ft; open 12.00–24.00 daily.*

**BUDAPEST BELVÁROS**
**Hotels, Restaurants & Bars**

Marquis de Salade

ÖKTOGON

Médosz

JÓKAI TÉR

Bombay Palace

LISZT FERENC TÉR

Corinthia Grand/ Royal Casino

SZABADSÁG TÉR

John Bull

Articsóka

Vörös és Feher

Box utca

Két Szerecsen

Művész

Queen Mary

Morrisons Music Club

ARANY JÁNOS

Lou Lou

Govinda

Leroy Café

SZÉNT ISTVÁN TÉR

KLAUZÁL TÉR

Old Man's Pub

Club Seven

Mokka

Shakespeare

JÓZSEF ATTILA

Four Seasons

Művészinas   Fiesta

Foccacia & Las Vegas Casino

ERZSÉBET TÉR

KIRÁLY

Marco Polo Hostel

Inter Continental Hotel

Gerbeaud

Kempinski

DEÁK FERENC TÉR

Le Meridien

Tropicana Casino

VÖRÖSMARTY TÉR

Green's

Longford

Champs

Columbus, Spoon

Étno

Taverna

Portside Pub

Red Bus Hostel

Faustos

Ócean

Leó Panzió

Astoria

Baraka

Múzeum

Karpatia

FERENCIEK TÉRE

Centrál

Erzsébet

Irish Cat

Darshan

Darshan

Capella

Fat Mo's Music Club

Janis Pub

KÁLVIN TÉR

BAROSS

Taverna Dionysos

Fatál

Trattoria Toscana

Fregatt

Bangkok House

Café Intenzo

ÜLLŐI

Soul Café

Danube

Big Market Hall

N

Bradt

Time

0          200m
0          200yds

**Focaccia** Pest V, Apáczai Csere János utca 19; ℄ 1 266 1234. We'll spare blushes by naming no names, but the restaurant of the Sofitel Atrium was a whispered recommendation from the manager of a rival hotel. Thank heaven for treacherous staff; Focaccia brings the Mediterranean sun and *joie de vivre* to the banks of the Danube. Fresh sea fish, vegetables and olive oil. Near the Chain Bridge. *Open Mon–Sat 12.00-23.30, Sun 18.00–23.30.*

**Govinda Vegetarian Restaurant & Salad Bar** V, Vigyázó Ferenc utca 4; ℄ 1 473 1309. Hare Krishna Indian restaurant serving a large selection of vegetarian and vegan options. Dishes for around 400Ft, a big plate selection for 1,500Ft. Just off Roosevelt tér. *Open 12.00–21.00 Mon–Sat, closed Sun.*

**Kárpátia** V, Ferenciek tere 7–8; ℄ 1 317 3596; www.karpatia.hu. A Pest institution. With hand-painted vaulted ceilings and a smattering of stained glass, this is the closest you'll get to dining in the Mátyás Church. The only regret is that the décor far outshines the food. The brasserie at the front has a cheaper menu (*2-course meal for 2, with wine, 8,500Ft*). *Mains 2,800–6,900Ft, avg 3,000–4,000Ft; open 11.00–23.00 daily.*

**Kempinski Restaurants** V, Erzsébet tér 7–8; ℄ 1 429 3777. The Kempinski's glass conservatory becomes something of a goldfish bowl in the evening; wave a cheery fin at the ogling masses on Deák Ferenc utca and get your gills around some delectable food. There are two restaurants (Ristorante Giardino and Bistro Jardin), offering Italian or international and Hungarian. Quite delicious, if expensively so. There's an outdoor summer terrace. Booking essential. *Mains 3,200–5,600Ft, avg 4,000–4,500Ft; open 06.30–23.00 daily.*

**Lou Lou** V, Vigyázó Ferenc utca 4; ℄ 1 312 4505; www.lou-lou.hu. Pest's answer to Buda's Le Jardin de Paris (see page 109), Lou Lou attracts the city crowd with its refined bistro styling. There are French, Italian and Spanish wines alongside the Hungarian bottles. Excellent pan-fried foie gras. *Mains 1,950–4,500Ft, avg 3,500Ft; open Mon–Fri 12.00–15.00, 19.00–23.00, Sat 19.00–23.00.*

**Mokka Café and Restaurant** V, Sas utca 4; ℄ 1 328 0081. Hookahs and woven throws convey Moroccan funkiness, but the menu is international with a Mediterranean flavour. A set lunch for around 1,000Ft gives added value on weekdays. We've had good additional feedback on this from readers who visited after it appeared in our Budapest guidebook. *Mains 1,450–4,950Ft, avg 2,600Ft; open daily 12.00–24.00.*

**Óceán bár & grill** V, Petőfi tér 3; ℄ 1 266 1826; www.oceanbargrill.com. Mussel chowder, tiger prawns, monkfish? New England cod and chips? The capital's only dedicated seafood restaurant. While the interior mimics the deck of a ship, and there must have been mutiny in the air when staff were introduced to their sailor suits, it avoids being overly camp. The seafood is imported from all over the world, but the focus (like the owner) is Scandinavian – Nordic delicacies are sold in the adjacent delicatessen. A gem – and one of the few places you can turn up at 23.00 and not raise waiterly eyebrows. *Mains 1,690–7,490Ft, avg 2,700Ft; restaurant open 12.00–24.00 daily; deli open Mon–Sat 10.00–21.00.*

**Okay Italia** XIII, Szent István körút; ℄ 1 349 2991 [T 4, 6] A popular spot among young Hungarians and ex-pats, who chow down on decent pizza and pasta at reasonable prices. On the Great Boulevard. *Mains 1,200–2,730Ft, avg 1,300Ft; open Mon–Fri 11.00–24.00, Sat–Sun 12.00–24.00.*

**Papageno** V, Semmelweis utca 19; ℄ 1 485 0161. Intimate restaurant serving tasty continental dishes with a changing daily specials menu. Reasonably priced to boot. *Open Mon–Fri 12.00–24.00, Sat 18.00–24.00.*

**Shakespeare Theatre Pub** V, Sas utca 4; ℄ 1 266 8758; www.shakespeare.hu. 'To eat or not to eat, this is not a question!' Thus does the restaurant open its tribute to the bard by murdering him. Suppress the urge to brain the owner with his lady's fan, and make your choice from a playbill menu offering good-quality and imaginative international vittles. Let good digestion wait on a spicy goulash starter and duck pepper steak in rosemary sauce. *Mains 1,200–2,600Ft, avg 1,700Ft; open 11.30-24.00 daily.*

**Spoon Café and Lounge – The Boat** V, by the Chain Bridge; ℄ 1 411 0933; www.spooncafe.hu. Very much a new kid on the dock, the gleaming Spoon is moored next to the

Columbus (see page 118). In contrast to its neighbour, this is sophisticated dining for captain rather than crew, with candlelight and international choices like garlic octopus and goose liver. In front of the InterContinental Hotel. *Mains 1,690–4,950Ft; avg 3,500Ft; open daily 12.00–02.00.*

**Taverna Dionysos** V, Belgrád rakpart 16; ꔷ 1 318 1222. Popular faux taverna serving all the Grecian specialities. There are misses to balance the hits – beware Greeks bearing dayglo wallpaper paste masquerading as taramasalata – but the moussaka and dolmades with tzatziki were delicious, the staff spirited and the music cheerful. *Mains 1,250–2,740Ft, avg 1,700Ft; open 12.00–24.00 daily.*

**Trattoria Toscana** V, Belgrád rakpart 15; ꔷ 1 327 0045; www.toscana.hu. Tuscan cooking by an Italian chef in a cosy villa facing the Danube. The food wasn't piping hot when we sat down here for lunch, but the restaurant's reputation is strong and so we'll assume an off-day in the open kitchen. Between Erzsébet and Szabadság bridges. The adjacent wine shop (L'Enoteca) serves Tuscan-speciality food and wine. *Mains 1,190–3,900Ft, avg 1,800–2,000Ft); pizzas 1,290–1,950Ft; restaurant open 12.00–24.00 daily, wineshop Mon–Sat 12.00–21.00.*

## Terézváros

**Articsóka** VI, Zichy Jenő utca 17; ꔷ 1 302 7757; www.articsoka.hu [M3 *Arany János utca;* TB *70, 78*] With its creepers, potted palms and skylight, you'll be forgiven for thinking you've intruded upon a biosphere project. Fortunately we don't suffer from hayfever, and love the foliage and airy feel. The cuisine is primarily Mediterranean, with emphasis on fish, and is inventive, good looking and fine tasting. *Mains 1,390–3,990Ft, avg 2,700Ft; open 12.00–24.00 daily.*

**Bombay Palace** VI, Andrássy út 44; ꔷ 1 332 8363 [M *Oktogon;* B *4*] Indian eateries are few and far between in Hungary; this one is part of an international chain, and serves Budapest's Bombay best. On corner of Jókai Mór tér. *Mains 800–4,500Ft, lunch/supper set menus 2,000/3,000Ft; open 12.00–14.45 & 18.00–23.00 daily.*

**Chez Daniel** VI, Szív utca 32; ꔷ 1 302 4039 [M *Kodály Körönd;* TB *72*] Pay no heed to the tatty homes around it; Daniel's house is very much in order. The staple of the French food is fresh produce from local markets, and there's a sunny courtyard with open-fronted bar. In addition to exclusive à-la-carte options, there are exclusive set menus for 2,900–8,400Ft (the latter 6 courses). If you feel inspired, the restaurant has a bookstore devoted to the gastronomical arts. *Restaurant open daily 12.00–15.00 & 19.00–23.00.*

**Dzsungel Étterem** VI, Jókai utca 30; ꔷ 1 302 4003; www.dzsungelcafe.hu [T *4, 6*] Unique, riotously over the top, this one's for the child or the chest-beating Tarzan in your party. Swing into a jungle of vines, plastic animals and pools, of taped squawks and chirrups and a real-life parrot. The adjoining bar and café is deforested, and positively peaceful by comparison. *Mains 1,190–2,590Ft, avg 2,000Ft; open 12.00–01.00 daily.*

**Két Szerecsen** VI, Nagymező utca 14; ꔷ 1 343 1984; www.ketszerecsen.com [TB *70, 78*] The 'Two Saracens' was a coffee shop in the 18th century. Today it blushes terracotta from head to toe, and provides a popular glass-fronted spot for theatregoers. Tapas, black spaghetti with cockles and other Mediterranean selections are very reasonably priced. Try to snag a window table in the raised section. *Mains 1,270–2,470Ft, avg 1,400–1,500Ft; open Mon–Fri 08.00–01.00, Sat–Sun 09.00–01.00.*

**Mare Croaticum** VI, Nagymező utca 49; ꔷ 1 311 7345 [TB *70, 78*] Tiled basement restaurant offering specialities from Croatia. Gorge on the 'all-you-can-eat' menu, which includes drinks, or go more à-la-carte easy. Entrance on Weiner Leó utca. *Fixed menu 2,000Ft (Mon–Fri 12.00–17.00) or 3,000Ft (Mon–Fri 18.00–24.00, Sat–Sun throughout); à-la-carte mains 950–5,890Ft, avg 2,200Ft; open 12.00–24.00 daily.*

**Marquis de Salade** VI, Hajós utca 43; ꔷ 1 302 4086 [TB *70, 78*] This cellar restaurant serves an extensive range of well-prepared and sizeable specialities from Azerbaijan, Russia and Hungary. Alongside the lamb and fish is a fair vegetarian selection, and above the restaurant is a bar and coffee house. *Mains 1,100–2,800Ft, avg 1,800Ft; open 11.00–01.00 daily.*

**Művészinas** VI, Bajcsy-Zsilinsky út 9; ꔷ 1 268 1439; www.directinfo.hu/muveszinas [M1, M2, M3 *Deák Ferenc tér*] If you're a city slicker with a high-maintenance lady to impress, Művészinas is high on your list. It radiates turn-of-the-20th-century romance, while among the international dishes are uppercrust classics like Russian caviar, goose liver and chateaubriand. Blue-blooded chic. *Mains 1,800–6,900Ft, avg 3,200Ft; open 12.00–24.00 daily.*

**Premier** VI, Andrássy út 101; ✆ 1 342 1768; www.premier-restaurant.hu [**Mi** *Bajza utca*] Premier's Art-Nouveau mansion is also home to the Association of Hungarian Journalists, so expect to find the odd hack lurking among the velvet curtains. There is piano music in the theatre-inspired dining room during winter months, while the terrace is the popular spot once spring has sprung. Stop here for a coffee, or order something more substantial from a menu featuring international food – including a weekly changing seafood selection – and Hungarian specialities. *Mains 1,900–3,500Ft, avg 2,800Ft; restaurant open 12.00–23.00 daily; coffee house open 08.00–23.00 daily.*

**Sir Lancelot** VI, Podmaniczky utca 14; ✆ 1 302 4456; www.sirlancelot.hu [**TB** *72, 70, 78*] There are no forks here, so ditch your inhibitions, grab a bib and prepare to get greasy, medieval style. Busty wenches, wooden platters of meat and goblets of wine, with jousting displays in the evening. Sophisticated? Erm…no. There's a sister restaurant on the Buda side – King Arthur's *(III, Bécsi út 38–44;* ✆ *1 437 8243). Open daily 12.00–01.00.*

**Vörös és Fehér** VI, Andrássy út 41; ✆ 1 413 1545; www.vorosesfeher.com [**Mi** *Oktogon;* **B** *4*] We couldn't decide between the *vörös* or the *fehér*, so we raised several glasses of each to the chef and a dish of meaty butterfish. The portions tend towards the moderate in size, but the quality is unquestionable. Bustling atmosphere; we recommend it highly. Some tapas choices on an international menu. *Mains 1,780–5,140Ft, avg 2,300Ft; tapas avg 1,200Ft; open 12.00–24.00 daily.*

## Heroes' Square and City Park

**Bagolyvár** XIV, Állatkérti út 2; ✆ 1 468 3110; www.bagolyvar.com [**Mi** *Hősök tere;* **TB** *75, 79*] 'Owl's Castle' was established by Hungarian-American restaurateur George Lang, who also revived Gundel after communism. While the Baroque and Biedermeier furnishings radiate 19th-rather than 21st-century charm, Bagolyvár is consciously less formal in atmosphere than its neighbour, as well as less imposing on the pocket. The canopied terrace is a joy in summer months, and the all-female staff are at the heart of the restaurant's lightness of touch. Mild, but traditional, Hungarian flavours dominate; the strudel desserts are a particular pleasure. *Mains 1,170–4,000Ft, avg 2,500Ft; open 12.00–23.00 daily.*

**Gundel** XIV, Állatkerti út 2; ✆ 1 321 3550; www.gundel.hu [**Mi** *Hősök tere;* **TB** *75, 79*] It's fashionable to decry Gundel. 'You'll get more for your money at the sister restaurant next door,' they drawl. For all the merits of Bagolyvár, it's like comparing a strawberry gateau with a chocolate sponge. Eating at Gundel is the city's culinary rite of passage. Ask Budapesters to name 3 restaurants and Gundel will be one of them. Guaranteed. The main dining room evokes high *fin-de-siècle* grace and there's also a beautiful garden. The menu offers refined creations based upon Hungarian classics, as well as dishes from France and elsewhere. The gypsy musical ensemble is as accomplished as any you will find. What about the cost? Well, all this comes at a very high price by Hungarian standards, but it remains low when compared with fine dining in western Europe. Enjoy a 5-course set menu with wine for 15,500Ft, 6 courses for 18,900Ft or a Sun brunch buffet *(11.30–15.00)* for around 5,000Ft. Gents require a jacket. *Mains 2,980–8,890Ft, avg 5,000Ft; open 12.00–16.00 & 18.30–24.00 daily.*

**Robinson** XIV, Városligeti-tó; ✆ 1 422 0222 [**Mi** *Hősök tere;* **TB** *75, 79*] On a sun-drenched day, life seems tickety-boo from under a pagoda on Robinson's decked jetty. An expensive menu that makes a good stab at being truly international – Hungarian broth, Thai prawn soup, French onion soup, New Zealand beef. In fact, it's an appealing place during winter too, toasty warm next to the fire in the pavilion's hearth. The Caffé Vergnano above the restaurant offers a lofty view of the park. *Mains 2,000–5,800Ft, avg 3,600Ft; restaurant open 12.00–16.00 & 18.00–24.00 daily; café 12.00–24.00 daily.*

## Erzsébetváros

**Fausto's** VII, Dohány utca 5; ✆ 1 269 6806 [**T** *47, 49;* **TB** *74*] Established by an ex-pat restaurateur, Fausto's is the city's Italian stallion. The décor is immaculate, the chef concocts delicate regional dishes, and the bill is on the steep side. *Mains 3,000–6,000Ft, avg 4,000Ft; open Mon–Sat 12.00–15.00 & 19.00–23.00.*

**Green's Söröző és Főzelékbár** VII, Dob utca 3; ℡ 1 352 8515 [T 47, 49] There's something refreshingly uncomplicated about *főzelék*, food that's pulped into submission (see page 63). This cellar bar also includes some cheap international choices and several Bavarian meals. *Mains 699–1,999Ft, avg 1,300Ft; főzelék 300–400Ft; open 10.00–24.00 daily.*

**M** VII, Kertész utca 48; ℡ 1 342 8991 [TB 70, 78] The owner was economical with the alphabet when naming this place, and he saved a few forints when decorating it too. The walls are covered with brown parcel wrap – it's like joining your picnic in its paper bag. Unfortunately, during our visit there was also some economising in the kitchen. A limited selection of international and Transylvanian-influenced dishes changes regularly on the menu. It's quirky and cucumber cool, but don't go there hungry. *Mains 1,100–1,700Ft, avg 1,200Ft; open 18.00–24.00 daily.*

## Pâtisseries and coffee houses

Coffee houses were traditionally meeting places where views were discussed and grievances grumbled about. The young revolutionaries of 1848 are said to have penned their demands for reform in the Pilvax kávéház, while two decades later Ferenc Deák negotiated the terms of the 1867 Compromise in the coffee house of the Queen of England Hotel. Some establishments even had their own notepaper for artists to use; where they didn't, an impoverished poet would scrawl a sonnet on a napkin in lieu of payment for his drink. The importance of the coffee house as a forum for social discussion and expression diminished in the 1940s, and the more staunchly working-class and socialist coffee bar took hold (see page 117), but many of the classics of the era remain. Furthermore, a hundred years on there's been a renaissance, with a crop of new venues. Some – like the Centrál, which re-opened in 2000 – fall within the grand Pesti tradition, while others are modern, trendy interpretations that are more properly café-bars.

### Buda

**Angelika kávéház** I, Batthyány tér 7; ℡ 1 212 3784. Housed in the former crypt of the adjacent St Anna Church, the Angelika has a sprawling terrace outside that combines cobbles with elevated platforms. At night, the candlelit tables are particularly inviting. *Open 8.00–21.00 daily.*

**Auguszt cukrászda** II, Fény utca 8; ℡ 1 316 3817; XI, Farkasréti tér, XI Sasadi utca; ℡ 1 249 0134; www.augusztcukraszda.hu. The name Auguszt is synonymous with fine pastry in Budapest. Since 1870, 5 generations have strived to maintain the family reputation. The dynasty operates from 3 locations, each managed by a family member and each selling fine sweets, ice-creams and pastries made on the premises. (To get to the Farkasréti tér outlet, take tram 59 from Moszkva tér.) *Open Tue–Sat 10.00–18.00.*

**Coffee-Inn** I, Apor Péter utca 2; ℡ 1 201 2935. A peaceful little find, where people enjoy relaxing over a game of backgammon or cards. *Open 11.00–23.00 daily.*

**Corona Café** I, Dísz tér. The first café reached on walking north from the upper station of Castle Hill's funicular. Excellent hot chocolate and reasonable-value cakes (despite its touristy position). *Open 10.00–19.00 daily.*

**Daubner cukrászda** II, Szépvölgyi út 50. It ain't much to look at, but this is the city's sugar daddy. Devotees queue down the road to have flasks filled with creamy ices. Recollections of banoffee-pie ice cream make us dribble. *Open daily 09.00–19.00.*

**Nagyi palacsintázója** I, Batthyányi tér 5; ℡ 1 212 4866. Delicious savoury or sweet pancakes at any time of day or night. *Open 24 hrs daily.*

**Ruszwurm cukrászda** I, Szentharomság utca 7; ℡ 1 375 5284; www.ruszwurm.hu. The oldest café in Budapest, operating since 1827; the simple elegance of its interior presents a fine example of the Biedermeier style popular during the period. The cakes are traditional and homemade, and in the past graced the tables of palatines and duchesses; 'Sisi' (Empress Erzsébet) came here for hot chocolate. Look out for the lion with a bridle in its paw on the arch of the building's gate; a former trader here boasted that the leather belts he made were strong enough to hold a lion. It is not recorded how he met his end… *Open 10.00–19.00 daily.*

## Pest

**Auguszt cukrászda** V, Kossuth Lajos utca 14–16; ☎ 1 337 6379; www.augusztcukraszda.hu. Pesti branch of the family chain (see page 115). *Open Tue–Sat 10.00–18.00.*

**Café intenzo** IX, Kálvin tér 9; ☎ 1 219 5243; www.cafeintenzo.hu. This building housed the Two Lions Inn until 1881, but it is now a popular pavement café. Avoid the noise of traffic by sitting in the garden courtyard.

**Centrál kávéház** V, Károlyi Mihály utca 9; ☎ 1 266 4572. In 2000, the Centrál reopened after half a century. In its pomp during the late 1800s and early 1900s, this was a hub of artistic life. Men of letters were seated on a special gallery (now part of the no-smoking section) so that ordinary mortals could watch them as they worked, like so many specimens in a cerebral zoo. The artist József Rippl-Rónai scrawled 'I drew this in the Centrál Coffee House' on one of his paintings. Today you'll find high ceilings, polite service and snacks for the modest purse (*zóna ételek*, at the 700Ft mark) alongside more expensive Hungarian and international dishes. Located on the corner of Ferenciek tere. *Open 08.00–24.00 daily.*

**Cukrászda kávézó** VI, Andrássy út 14; ☎ 1 332 4559. An Italian parlour serving whacking portions of ice-cream, including a spaghetti ice dressed up to look like a dish of bolognese. *Open 09.00–24.00 daily.*

**Európa kávéház** V, Szent István körút; ☎ 1 312 2362. Upmarket, Austrian-style café with a takeaway bakery and ice-cream shop next door. *Café open 09.00–23.00 daily; shop Mon–Fri 07.00–20.00, Sat 09.00–20.00, Sun 10.00–20.00.*

**Gerbeaud** V, Vörösmarty tér 7–8; ☎ 1 429 9000. Hungary's most famous café, Gerbeaud is a refined behemoth in marble, walnut and wicker. Emile Gerbeaud – the Swiss pâtissier who managed the place from 1884 – brought the Parisian taste to Budapest. He gave birth to the cognac cherry (*konyákos meggy*), and was the first to use chocolate boxes for bonbon treats to take away. Foreign princes were drawn by his artistry. Service can be slow. In the café's cellar, accessed via Dorottya utca, is a beer hall serving home-brewed drinks. *Café open 09.00–21.00 daily; Gerbeaud Sörház Sun, Tue–Thu 11.00–24.00, Fri-Sat 11.00–02.00.*

**Lukács cukrászda** VI, Andrássy út 70; ☎ 1 302 8747. It's changed much since being refurbished during the 1990s, but this used to be where secret policemen ate pastries in between interrogations at their headquarters (Andrássy út 60). *Open Mon–Fri 9.00–20.00, Sat–Sun 10.00–20.00.*

**Művész** VI, Andrássy út 29; ☎ 1 352 1337. 'The Artist' was a favourite of the upper middle classes during the communist era. It exudes old-world grandeur, and the terrace on a warm evening is great for a pastry before watching the fat lady sing at the State Opera House opposite. *Open 09.00–23.45 daily.*

**New York kávéház** VII, Erzsébet körút 9–11. Designed by Alajos Hauszmann in 1894, the New York kávéház could justly claim to be at the birth of modern Hungarian literature. Ferenc Molnár is said to have tossed the café's key into the Danube in protest at its closing at night; he went on to write his great work *Liliom* here. Regulars were provided with paper and unlimited coffee, while impoverished authors lingered over the 'writers' dish' – a bargain plate of bread, cheese and salami. The café declined after World War I and was rammed by a Russian tank in 1956. It has now been restored and is set to re-open as a luxury hotel and coffee house shortly. Near Blaha Lujza tér.

**Palacsinta Porta** VI, Liszt Ferenc tér 3; ☎ 1 343 1263. The place to go if you're dying for a crêpe. Have a savoury main with mushroom and corn, and then a sweet one with cinnamon and plum. *Open Mon–Fri 12.00–22.00.*

## WHERE TO DRINK

You'll have no trouble finding a place for a proper drink in Budapest; the primary clusters of café-bars are on the Pest side of the river, and on Liszt Ferenc tér and Ráday utca in particular. During summer such areas make a very Parisian use of public space as tables

## COFFEE BARS

The *presszó* or *eszpresszó* is less traditionally highbrow than the *cukrászda* or *kávéház*. The author Sándor Márai complained in 1940 that in *eszpresszó* bars 'one can only chat – one cannot write a great work as there is no space on the table'. It is instead a communal place for the local working class, where groups of ladies enjoy cakes and gangs of workmen play dominoes and eat *somlói galuska* with their beer. Its floor is stone or covered with beige linoleum, and there are net curtains, tiled walls and little gnome stools. Surly waitresses wear long, lace-up boots that give support during endless hours of standing. A proper old-style *presszó* has a neon sign proclaiming a socialist name such as 'Terv' (Five-Year Plan), 'Béke' (Peace), 'Haladás' (Progress) or even 'Májas' (Liver Sausage). But the *eszpresszó* is an endangered species. One by one, they have closed as rent soars and the fast-food chains and banks move in.

Budapest was once the city of *eszpresszó* bars, where elderly couples would drink brandy and have sing-songs on Friday nights, where old *bácsis* danced with little girls and *nénis* danced together, where workers spent their wages on beer, and the air was thick with the fog of Munkás (Worker) cigarettes. In 1937, the Quick in Vigadó utca was the first coffee bar to open (it is an office now), and was followed by many more. After 1956, Socialist-Realist architecture began to wane. Shops destroyed during the uprising were rebuilt in the modern style. There was a craze for neon, and for radical slogans like 'Prosperity' and 'Spartacus'. While some of the 1950s *eszpresszós* still exist, the original style is harder to find. The neon lights are fading, the Traubi (grape) and Márka (cherry) soft drinks are hard to find, the Bambi pop has disappeared, the wheels of progress grind on. However, the following are hanging on in there:

**Bambi** II, Frankel Leó út 2/4. One of the few untouched interiors dating back to the 1960s. Red leatherette seats and old men playing dominoes on a Sunday afternoon.
**Ibolya** V, Ferenciek tere 5. Very popular with students, enjoying a quick *eszpresszó* before heading into the main library opposite. Smoky.
**Mester** IX, Mester utca 45. A real *eszpresszó* announced by wonderful tableau signs and a massive ceramic stove. Waitresses take no nonsense from behind the '60s counter. On a street of craftsmen.
**Terv** V, Nádor utca 19. Smartened up, but *cukrászda* pretensions are undermined by working men drinking beer and spirits in the morning.
**Tik-Tak** XII, Böszörményi út 17/C. Neon cuckoo clock above the doorway. Refined, silver-haired gentlefolk of the vicinity used to drop in for coffee and cognac.
**Tulipán** V, Nádor utca 32. Belongs to the group of *presszós* in District V bearing the names of flowers – the Ibolya (Violet) and the Muskátli (Geranium) tourist trap on Váci utca. Back room of high stools, mushroom tables and walls turned beige by cigarette smoke – at least until its recent gentrification, when everything was spruced up.

spill on to pavements, squares and courtyards. All are generally open daily from 11.00 or 12.00 until 24.00, although closing times often extend into the early hours on Fridays and Saturdays. (See also *Pâtisseries and coffee houses*, page 115.)

## Bars and pubs
### Buda
**Café Miró** I, Úri utca 30; ☎ 1 375 5458. A self-consciously contemporary wine-bar-cum-café in the Castle District. Inspired by the work of Catalan artist Joan Miró, its bold splashes of colour

and wiry metal furnishings draw the fashionable and young like moths to its flame. The waitresses appear to feel that cheerful and attentive service is very last season, however, and could do with a slap from the smile fairy. Good view of Mátyás Church. *Open 09.00–24.00 daily.*

**Club Casanova Bar** I, Batthyány tér 4; tel; 1 212 9717. Academics may debate the authenticity of the disco mirror ball, but there's historical justification for the sequinned masks. In the 18th century, this hostelry was the venue for grand masque balls attended – it is said – by Casanova himself. Happy 'hour' *(12.00–21.00)* offers 50% off a range of drinks. Just below street level at the western side of Batthyány tér. *Open Mon–Sat 12.00–06.00.*

**Dokk Café** II, Mammut II, 2nd Floor, Lövőház utca 2–6; ➧ 1 345 8531; www.dokkcafe.com. The main event is later at the Dokk Club (page 126), but this is the swanky starting point for the élite and beautiful of Budapest. If you want to avoid the judgemental eye of the self-appointed fashion police, steer well clear. Sells the inevitable cocktails, together with international snacks. In the Mammut shopping mall. *Open Sun–Thu 11.00–01.00, Fri–Sat 11.00–02.00.*

**Oscar Bar** I, Ostrom utca 14; ➧ 1 212 8017. Dingy, below-street drinking-hole devoted to the world of American film. A favoured haunt of ex-pats. Just below the Castle District and a short walk from Moszkva tér. *Open Sun–Thu 17.00–02.00, Fri–Sat 17.00–04.00.*

## Pest

**Becketts** V, Bajcsy-Zsilinsky út 72; ➧ 1 311 1033; www.becketts.hu. It's named after Samuel Beckett, there is passable Guinness in the taps and a *Commitments* poster on the wall, which all adds up to about as authentic an Irish pub as Hungary has to offer. Ex-pats love the place. Live music and half-price whiskies from 20.00 on Thu. The pub grub is also excellent. *Open Sun–Thu 12.00–01.00, Fri–Sat 12.00–03.00.*

**Box utca** VI, Bajcsy Zsilinsky út 21; ➧ 1 354 1444; www.box-utca.hu. You may or may not have heard of him, but the Hungarian boxer István 'Ko-Ko' Kovács was an Olympic gold-medal winner in 1996 and a world champ in 2001, and he's since made a pretty good fist of this upmarket sports bar and restaurant. During his visit, David Coulthard carelessly left behind his racing car in the restaurant. Very child-friendly. Opposite the Arany János metro. *Open Mon–Fri 08.00–24.00, Sat–Sun 10.00–24.00.*

**Champs Sports Pub** VII, Dohány utca 20; ➧ 1 413 1655; www.champs.hu. Massive cellar bar swaddled in sporting paraphernalia and with raised television screens for sporting nuts. Decent portions of grub at reasonable prices. *Open 12.00–02.00 daily.*

**Columbus Pub** V, Vigadó tér 4; ➧ 1 266 7514. We're not sure what Columbus would have made of the neon drinks adverts, nor what the Celts make of its claim to Irishness. By contrast, we are very sure what the staff make of their sailors' neckerchiefs, which must shiver their timbers. Beyond that, however, this moored theme pub scrubs up well as the deck of a 15th-century galleon, and makes a surprisingly relaxed place for a yo-ho-ho and a bottle of rum. There's also international pub fare. *Open 12.00–late daily.*

**Darshan Café** VIII, Krúdy Gyula utca 8; ➧ 1 266 7797. A young and hippyish crowd sprawl among the stone-chip mosaics of this small café. The exotic Darshan Udvar, a colourful, Asian-inspired bar, club and concert venue, is set back in the parade opposite. Just off Lőrinc pap tér. *Café open Mon–Sat 07.00–24.00, Sun 16.00–24.00; bar Mon–Wed 10.00–01.00, Thu–Fri 10.30–02.00, Sat 18.00–02.00, Sun 18.00–24.00.*

**Etno Coffe & Lounge** V, Fehérhajó utca 5; ➧ 1 411 0643; www.etno.hu. Don a pair of shades and a cool expression, and relax in the knowledge that you're among the trendy set. Sip cocktails, coffees, milkshakes or flavoured teas. Fits the bill for an afternoon break, an informal meal (food with an Asian bent) or an evening drink. *Open 11.00–23.00 daily.*

**Irish Cat** V, Múzeum körút 41; ➧ 1 266 4085. One of the city's good-time meat markets. There's flat Guinness and thumping chart music, but also a surprisingly diverse crowd and an unthreatening atmosphere. Opposite the National Museum. *Open Mon–Thu 11.00–02.00, Fri–Sat 11.00–04.00, Sun 17.00–02.00.*

**Janis's Pub** V, Királyi Pál utca 8; ☎ 1 266 2619. A blessed refuge from the teeny-boppers, Janis's (Joplin, obviously) emanates creaky-kneed maturity. Perfect for an inoffensive sup of Kilkenny or a 15-year-old malt. *Open Mon–Thu 16.00–02.00, Fri–Sat 16.00–03.00, Sun 18.00–24.00.*

**John Bull Pub** V, Podmaniczky tér 4; ☎ 1 269 3116. With gold-patterned wallpaper and cream drapes, English visitors may find this rather smarter than the typical boozer back home. It's also quieter and less smoky. Unfortunately, the inflated prices are depressingly familiar. *Open 12.00–24.00 daily.*

**Leroy Café** VI, Westend City Center, 1st Floor, Váci út 1–3; VI, Sas utca 11; ☎ 1 266 5248. Two in a chain of bar-restaurants popular with 20- and 30-somethings; that on Sas utca is a very recent link, and is well located overlooking Szent István tér. *Sushi* is supplied by the posher parent establishment, the Tom-George Restaurant (*V, Október 6 utca 8;* ☎ *1 266 3525; www.tomgeorge.hu*). *Open 12.00–24.00 daily.*

**Longford Irish Pub** V, Fehérhajó utca 5; ☎ 1 267 2766. Longford is one of several bars and cafés that have sprung up around Szomory Dezső tér, offering a diluted version of Liszt Ferenc tér for those who can't face the trip out of the centre. To call it 'Irish' is a load of blarney, but it's modern, smart and a favourite for those who enjoy people watching. *Open 11.00–02.00 daily.*

**Szimpla kert** VII, Kazinczy utca 14; ☎ 1 32 15880. Locals immediately kicked up a stink and petitioned for its closure when this al-fresco, buzzy bar was relocated to this residential courtyard. Thankfully it's still hanging in there, although the opening hours have been curbed. *Open 12.00–24.00 daily.*

## Liszt Ferenc tér and Jókai Mór tér

Liszt tér is the established scratching post for the city's young and trendy. It is here that they gather in real concentrations around the café-bars that line either side of the square, perched at the tables and chairs that litter it in summer months. (For further history etc, see page 159.)

**Buena Vista** VI, Liszt Ferenc tér 4–5; ☎ 1 344 6303; www.buena-vista.hu. This is an elegant club sandwich of a place, with a tavern at the bottom, a café in the middle and a restaurant (serving Hungarian, French and Italian) in the gallery atop. Wine lovers can choose from an extensive selection that runs from 1,800Ft to 35,000Ft a bottle; those with simpler tastes slouch at wooden tables in the cellar and draw their own pints of beer from individual taps. *Open 10.00–01.00 daily.*

**Cactus Juice** VI, Jókai Mór tér 5; ☎ 1 302 2116. A western-themed bar that is loud and popular with stag parties. *Open Mon–Thu 12.00–02.00, Fri–Sat 12.00–04.00, Sun 16.00–02.00.*

**Café Vian** VI, Liszt Ferenc tér 9; ☎ 1 268 1154. Café Vian hogs the sun's first rays. Head here early for a hearty b/fast, with English, American, Hungarian and continental on the menu. The place is named after the 20th-century French author and poet, Boris Vian, and has a small stage for regular art exhibitions and theatrical evenings. *Open 09.00–24.00 daily.*

**Karma Café** VI, Liszt Ferenc tér 11; ☎ 1 413 6764. If karma is the result of the actions of a life, you'll need to sacrifice a few merit points in jostling for a seat at the square's most popular café-bar. The Buddhist-inspired interior is calm and intimate. If you're peckish, plump for some Asian and Mediterranean cuisine. Live music at weekends. There's a sister bar in the WestEnd City Centre (see page 133). *Open 11.00–02.00 daily.*

**Pesti Est Café** VI, Liszt Ferenc tér 5; ☎ 1 344 4381. There's a downstairs nightclub where parties are hosted every few weeks (check *Pesti Est* magazine for forthcoming events). Otherwise the café-bar serves a range of cocktails and snacks. *Open 11.00–02.00 daily.*

**Winston's Bar** VI, Jókai Mór tér 3; ☎ 1 331 1955; www.winstons.hu. Comfortable English-pub atmosphere, with dark wooden tables, groaning bookshelves and shepherd's pie. *Open 12.00–24.00 daily.*

## Ráday utca

Linking Kálvin tér and the lower reaches of the Nagykörút, the regenerated Ráday utca is the upstart challenger to the hegemony of Liszt Ferenc tér, sustained by the custom of

## WINNING WINES

What should you plump for with dinner? Aged in networks of mould-clad cellars, Tokaji Aszú (see box, page 272) is long-lived and nectar sweet, with a volcanic mineral edge. It was favoured by Europe's royal houses, and Louis XIV declared it 'the king of wines, the wine of kings' – which must have had the marketing people gleefully rubbing their hands. It suffered under the state economy, but is heralded as back to its freshest and fruitiest. Aszú is created from grapes affected by noble rot, and the number of hods (*puttonyos*) of such grapes added to a dry base wine determines the wine's sweetness. Most is produced at levels of between three and six *puttonyos*, with Aszú Esszencia sweeter still. Top recent vintages were 1996 and 2000, while those of 1993 and 1999 are judged to be classics. Dry Tokaji wines are also available – look out for those of 2000 and 2002 – but more readily acclaimed are the light and young-drinking whites from Lake Balaton (especially the Olaszrizling of Badacsony). If you fancy something bubbly, the country's main sparkling wine (*pezsgő*) is the relatively inexpensive Törley champagne. It's produced by Hungary's largest wine company, Hungarovin, and compares favourably with versions from New World countries.

Bull's Blood (Bikavér) derives its name from the period of Turkish occupation; the sober Ottomans thought that their opponents were made brave by consuming flagons of animal blood, when the Hungarians were actually more sensibly seeking Dutch courage in flagons of red wine. Moves are underway to protect Bull's Blood, which became synonymous with a Hungarian product ruined by commercialism, but its definition remains loose – simply encompassing 'quality' blended red wine from Szekszárd or Eger. One problem is that large companies continue to cling to its potential as a brand, looking enviously at the success of Australian Rosemount or Jacob's Creek. A leading firm even attempted to spark success by replacing its bull's head logo with a rather Spanish-looking matador. Stick to bottles from small producers who take time over the product rather than the branding and you'll find some excellent wines. Alternatively, reds from Villány are expressive, full-bodied and rightly rated.

students from the three universities near by. Look elsewhere for picture-postcard prettiness – there's a gritty edge about the place, and an absence of pavement posing – but the number of restaurants and bars has doubled in the last few years and the road is consolidating its new status as a leading nightspot. We've plucked a couple of bars from the group, but there are many more.

**Soul Café** IX, Ráday utca 11–13; ☏ 1 217 6986; www.miwo.hu/soulcafe. One of the leading lights on the busy strip, Soul has an open fireplace and a terrace, which makes it popular in winter and summer alike. Media types enjoy weekend lunches of fresh fish and chocolate cake from the international menu. *Open 12.00–01.00 daily.*

**Time Café and Lounge** IX, Ráday utca 23; ☏ 1 476 0433; www.timecafe.hu. Despite arriving 30 mins late, our colleagues insisted they were 'on time' as they stood on the clock face sunk into the floor of the café-bar. How they chuckled! We found it less amusing, but were quickly calmed by Mediterranean colours, soothing jazz and cool beers.

## ENTERTAINMENT AND NIGHTLIFE

There's no excuse for calling it a day when the sun sets over Budapest. No city wears night's cloak with more elegance. The castle turns on its illuminations, bridges follow suit, lights ride the river's ripples and romance's stage is set. Choose a bar for that post-dinner digestif, and decide upon where next. There are few people whose darkness hours Budapest can't find a way to fill. Several publications list what's on, available (often free) from Tourinforms, hotels, pubs and bars. *Pesti Est* and *Pesti Műsor* give information on arts and entertainment, but are mainly in Hungarian. Grab a free copy of *Súgó* for theatre listings that are translated into English in July and August. In general, the best bet for English speakers are titles like *Where Budapest*, the *Budapest Sun* or the *Budapest Times* (with its 11-day calendar detailing upcoming events at bars, cultural houses etc).

## Ticket offices

Most venues have their own box offices, but the following agencies (*jegyiroda*) sell tickets to sporting events, opera and ballet, concerts (including pop, jazz, classical), theatre performances, and folklore programmes.

**Jegyiroda** VI, Nagymező utca 19; ℣ 1 302 3841; www.ticket.matavnet.hu

**Mérleg Jegyiroda** V, Mérleg utca 10; ℣ 1 485 0473. *Open Mon–Wed 10.00–18.00, Thu 10.00–14.00, Fri 10.00–18.00*

**Music Mix 33** V, Váci utca 33; ℣ 1 266 1651. *Open Mon–Fri 10.00–18.00, Sat 10.00–13.00*

**Ticket Centrum** V, Vigadó utca 6; ℣ 1 318 3862. *Open Mon–Fri 10.00–16.00*

**Ticket Express** VI, Andrássy út 18; ℣ 1 312 0000; www.tex.hu. Also a branch in the Ibusz office at Ferenciek tere 10 (℣ 06 3030 30999; *open Mon–Fri 09.00–17.00*). *Open Mon–Fri 09.30–18.30*

**Vigadó Jegyiroda** V, Vigadó tér 5; ℣ 318 9903. Specialises in concerts at the nearby Vigadó theatre. *Open Mon–Fri 10.00–18.00*

**www.online.jegymester.hu/index_eng.html** Purchase tickets online for the State Opera House, Erkel Theatre, National Theatre and Budapest Festival Orchestra.

## Theatre

Budapest has a strong relationship with the theatre, and while it would benefit from greater financial support, there is a varied selection of plays, musicals and comedies to be found on over 40 stages around the city. The main cluster of these is just off Andrássy út, on Nagymező utca, which is known as the Pest Broadway. Alongside productions by domestic playwrights such as Mihály Babits and Ferenc Molnár, there is international drama including Shakespeare. However, the Anglo-Saxon visitor yearning to see *The Tempest* in Hungarian is a breed we've yet to meet, and only the Merlin is a safe bet for English-language drama. Curtains usually rise at 19.00.

**Buda Park Theatre** (*Budai Parkszínpad*) XI, Kosztolányi Dezső tér; ℣ 1 466 9849 [T̄ *19, 49;* **B**7, 7A] Open-air arena next to the 'Bottomless Lake' (see page 148), staging drama and concerts. The programme is listed outside the gates. *Ticket office open Wed–Sun 15.00–18.00.*

**Merlin Szinház** V, Gerlóczy utca 4; ℣ 1 317 9338; www.szinhaz.hu/merlin [T̄ *47, 49;* B̄ *9*] Contemporary dance, classical, modern and alternative English-language productions. You can purchase tickets via the website (in English). 15% discount with Budapest Card. Popular with ex-pats and foreigners. Tickets 1,000–2,000Ft. *Box office open 10.00–18.00 daily.*

**National Theatre** (*Nemzeti Színház*) XI, Bajor Gizi Park 1; ℣ 1 476 6800; www.nemzetiszinhaz.hu [M̄3 *Kálvin tér;* T̄ *47, 49*] The National Theatre was for some time a subject of drama. Thirty years after the communists demolished the splendid original in Blaha Lujza tér, an almighty slanging match erupted over its replacement. As the Fidesz government bickered with the Budapest mayor over costs (see page 89), the enormous foundation hole at Erzsébet tér was tagged the 'National Pit' by city wags. Eventually a new site was chosen near Petőfi híd and the theatre – a bold, self-consciously modern building, resembling a ship's prow – opened in 2002. It is a showcase for Hungarian drama – and very Magyar – but Sándor Román's ExperiDance (a famous local company) also performs dance here. *Ticket office open Mon–Fri 10.00–18.00, Sat–Sun 14.00–17.30.*

**Palace of Arts** (*Művészetek Palotája*) IX, Komor Marcell utca 1; ☎ 1 555 3444 [T̄ *2, 24;* HEV *Lágymányosi híd*] A concrete cube has sprung up between Lágymányosi híd and the National Theatre (some say to make the latter shine by comparison), opened in 2005 as the city arts centre. It contains a massive National Concert Hall and the Festival Theatre, as well as the Ludwig Museum (see page 175).

**Puppet Theatre** (*Bábszínház*) VI, Andrássy út 69; ☎ 1 342 2702; www.budapest-babszinhaz.hu [M̄ *Vörösmarty utca;* B̄ *4*] Puppets to some extent transcend the language barrier, and perform in a dirty black building next to the Liszt Museum. There are shows for children in the mornings and afternoons, and for adults on some evenings; starting times vary. Tickets around 350–600Ft. *Ticket office open 09.00–18.00.*

**Thália Színház** VI, Nagymező utca 22–24; ☎ 1 312 1280; www.thalia.hu [M̄ *Opera*] Links up with the Operetta Theatre for musicals and operettas (see opposite). *Ticket office open Mon–Fri 10.00–18.00, Sat–Sun 14.00–18.00.*

**Vígszínház** XIII, Szent István körút 14; ☎ 1 329 2340; web: www.vigszinhaz.hu [T*4, 6;* B̄ *26, 91, 191*] Budapest's oldest and biggest (seating 1,000) stands on the Great Boulevard, its pale lemon façade bursting from the surrounding browns and greys. For Hungarians, a visit to the Comedy Theatre is a time to polish shoes and consider with more care than usual whether shirt matches trousers. The Neo-Renaissance building was constructed in just one year, opening in 1896, and now shows a diverse range of Hungarian and foreign productions, all in Hungarian. *Ticket office at side (on Ditrói Mór utca) open 11.00–19.00 daily, or at Pannonia utca 8 open Mon–Thu 10.00–18.00, Fri 10.00–17.00.*

# Music
## Opera and classical

**Operas** in Budapest are extravagant affairs usually performed in Magyar (rather than Italian); aficianado or not, you should take advantage of some of the cheapest ticket prices in the world (from as low as 300Ft, but around 3,000–4,500Ft for a good view), and a sumptuous setting at the State Opera House. You don't need to wear top hat and tails, but jeans distress the usherettes. The 'father of Hungarian opera' was Ferenc Erkel, who conducted his own *Hunyadi László* and *Bánk Bán* at the opening of the State Opera House. Both operas remain popular today; there are also performances throughout the year by foreign masters like Mozart and Wagner.

Hungary has good reason to be proud of its **classical** heritage. Concert performances are two-a-penny, offering home-grown and international talent, although in the hot months these are more likely to be outdoor. The **Budapest Philharmonic Orchestra** was founded by Erkel in the mid 19th century; when it is not touring, its home is at the State Opera House. (There are, however, fears that cuts in funding could force the orchestra to disband; in May 2005, members played a funeral march outside the Ministry of Culture in protest.) **Buda Castle Summer Nights** – opera, classical and jazz concerts in the Hotel Hilton's Dominican Courtyard (see page 100) – run every other evening for much of July (book tickets through the hotel or on the website below), while there are concerts every five days or so in July in Szent István tér, the Basilica providing a stunning backdrop. In addition, regular organ recitals, choral performances and classical concerts are hosted in the city's churches – including the Lutheran Church (*V, Deák tér*), Mátyás Church (*Castle District*), and St Anna Church (*I, Batthyány tér 7*) – as well as at the Vajdahunyad Castle in City Park and the Dome Hall of the Parliament building. Information is available from Tourinforms, ticket offices or listings magazines; alternatively, details are given at www.viparts.hu, where you can also reserve tickets online, and in the Hungarian-language *Koncert Kalendárium* (*www.koncertkalendarium.hu*).

**Béla Bartók Memorial House** (*Bartók Béla Emlékház*) II, Csalán út 29; ☎ 1 394 2100. See page 170.

**Budapest Operetta Theatre** (*Budapesti Operettszínház*) VI, Nagymező utca 17; ℄ 1 269 3870; www.operettszinhaz.hu [**M** *Opera*] Along with Vienna, Budapest is a capital of operetta (light musicals); this is the best place to watch one, in glamorous Art-Nouveau surroundings. Classic Magyar operettas (usually subtitled in German) and modern musicals (usually subtitled in English). (See also Thália, opposite.) Tours available at weekends – call in advance. *Ticket office (next door) open Mon–Fri 10.00–19.00, Sat–Sun 13.00–19.00.*

**Duna Palace** (*Duna Palota*) V, Zrínyi utca 5; ℄ 1 317 2754 [B̄ *15*] Neo-Baroque palace and base for the distinguished Duna Symphony Orchestra. Classical performances are held every Sat at 20.00 May–Oct and once/twice monthly the rest of the year. There is also folk dancing by the Duna Folk Ensemble.

**Erkel Theatre** VIII Köztársaság tér 30; ℄ 1 333 0540 [B̄ *7, 7A*; T̄ *37A, 37, 28*] The city's leading ballet company play here, and there are also operas and musicals. *Ticket office open Tue–Sat 11.00–17.00 (or show start), Sun11.00–13.00, 16.00 to show start.*

**Hungarian State Opera House** VI, Andrássy út 22; ℄ 1 332 8197; info ℄ 06 60 594594; www.opera.hu [M̄ī *Opera*] It is said that Ferenc József only allowed the construction of Budapest's opera house on the condition that it was smaller than that in Vienna. When completed in 1884, it was certainly relatively small in size; however, the emperor lamented that he hadn't stipulated it be less pretty too. Designed by Miklós Ybl, it's a breathtaking Neo-Renaissance building. The entrance hall has a winding staircase, swirling blue pillars and an opulent ceiling that undulates like a choppy ocean, while the horseshoe-shaped auditorium glows golden-red. The Historicist artists Károly Lotz, Bertalan Székely and Mór Than painted the frescoes, influenced by those of Paris and Vienna in illustrating music's power, while Alajos Stróbl created the sculptures of Erkel and Liszt in alcoves at the entrance. As well as looking great, it sounds pretty good too, the acoustics reputedly second only to La Scala. And it's cheap. Box office inside main entrance (also selling tickets to Erkel and Thália theatres); guided tours at 15.00 and 16.00 daily. *Open Mon–Sat 11.00–19.00, Sun 16.00–19.00.*

**Liszt Music Academy** (*Liszt Zeneakadémia*) VI, Liszt Ferenc tér 8; ℄ 1 462 4600; www.musicacademy.hu [M̄ī *Oktogon;* B̄ *4*] Situated on Liszt Ferenc tér, this turn-of-the-20th-century Art-Nouveau music academy has two auditoriums – the huge Nagyterem (*closed Jul–Aug*), seating 1,200 people, and the smaller Kisterem. The acoustics are fabulous, like the décor; pop your head into the entrance hall, with its greens and golds, mosaics and marble columns. A seated bronze of Ferenc Liszt is positioned above the entrance, and gargoyles leer at passers-by. The academy's central library contains the country's most extensive music-related collection.

**Pesti Vigadó** V, Vigadó tér 2; ℄ 1 317 5067 [T̄ *2, 2A*] The 'place of merriment' – one of Pest's foremost 19th-century historic buildings – was erected in 1865 on the site of Mihály Pollock's Redoute, which was destroyed during the Independence War. The architect made a self-conscious attempt at a 'Hungarian' style, and it is consequently ornamental and highblown. The acoustics are notoriously average, but that didn't deter composers like Liszt, Bartók, Kodály, Wagner, Strauss and Brahms from holding concerts inside. It's the city's second-largest. The Hungarian State Folk Ensemble also dances here, and there's a gallery hosting temporary exhibitions by contemporary artists (℄ *1 318 7070; open Tue–Sun 10.00–18.00*).

## Jazz and easy listening

There are several excellent jazz clubs in which to tap your toes, representing Hungarian and foreign talent. The Budapest Jazz Orchestra travels the country, and usually performs in the capital during the Autumn and Spring festivals.

**Cotton Club** VI, Jókai utca 26; ℄ 1 354 0886/1341; www.cottonclub.hu. Old-fashioned speak-easy club, bar and café with a determined whiff of 1920s America. There are varied live performances of music and dance at the weekends and on some week nights, featuring jazz, blues and revue-style shows. *Open daily 12.00–01.00.*

**Fat Mo's Music Club** V, Nyáry Pál utca 11; ℄ 1 267 3199; www.fatmo.hu. Early 20th-century-themed club whose Saturday disco is popular with prowling meat marketeers. However, there are live jazz, blues and country performances on other evenings (*Sun–Wed*). *Open Sun–Fri 12.00–02.00, Sat 12.00–04.00.*

**Jazz Garden Music Club** V, Veres Pálné utca 44/A; �‎ 1 266 7364; ww.jazzgarden.hu. The outside's in at this romantic little club, decorated to feel like a pavement café under a starry night sky. A firm favourite among jazz lovers, it attracts top Hungarian and international musicians who perform live in the evenings between 21.00 and 24.00. *Open 12.00–24.00 daily.*

**New Orleans Jazz Club** VI, Lovag utca 5; �‎ 1 451 7525; www.neworleans.hu. A classy modern club that features big international jazz names, who perform at 21.00 every evening except Sun and Mon. The website (in Hungarian) lists the monthly programme. *Open 18.00–02.00 daily.*

## Contemporary

The electronic music scene is strong. As in western Europe, some musical events are managed by the same company at different locations, while other venues run consistently interesting programmes. For electronica and dance-music fans, **Cinetrip**, a regular party whose venue varies, is just as remarkable for its large screens and VJs (improvisational video-based DJs) as its music. It has been staged at the Railway Museum and at Turkish baths, where fans take along a towel and a swimsuit to change into. You might also try **Trafó** (opposite) or **A38**. The municipal government-owned **Petőfi csarnok** is a large 'youth leisure centre' in City Park, which aims for more mainstream appeal. Large international acts appear at the Puskás Stadion or at the smaller arenas in the vicinity (such as the Kisstadion).

In warmer weather, the **Sziget Festival** is an August staple of the partying calendar (page 128), while the day-long **Budapest Parade** is a huge rave similar to the Berlin Love Parade (page 128). In addition, outdoor clubs like **Zöld Pardon**, **Rio**, and the roof of the **A38** boat take advantage of the summer months. The music scene is inevitably in a perpetual state of flux. For up-to-date information, see www.port.hu, www.index.hu or www.est.hu. Tickets for performances are available from the city-centre ticket offices (see page 121).

**Almássy téri Szabadidő Központ** VII, Almássy tér 6; �‎ 1 342 0387; www.almassy.hu. Just north of Blaha Lujza tér, this cultural centre offers a varied selection of live music.
**A38 Club** XI, Állóhajó, near Petőfi híd; www.a38.hu. A beautifully renovated Ukrainian stone-carrier ship moored near Petőfi Bridge that serves as an innovative live-music venue, restaurant and nightclub. The website lists a monthly programme including jazz, rock, drum 'n' bass, hip hop and classical. Recent acts have included Anima Sound System, Erik Marchand and the Holmes Brothers.
**Millenáris Park** II, Fény utca 20–22; www.millenaris.hu. Two concert halls, one a vast brick hangar (the Teátrum) and the other a more informal space, that host world music and folk. Always a diverse programme of music, dance and entertainment.
**Morrisons Music Club** VI, Révay utca 25; �‎ 1 269 4060. A smoky old pub off Dalszínház utca that's inexpensive and popular with students. There's a dance floor and a chill-out room, and karaoke on Wed nights. *Admission from 500Ft; open Wed–Sat 21.00–04.00.*
**Old Man's Music Pub** VII, Akácfa utca 13; �‎ 1 322 7645; www.oldmans.hu. A lively basement bar in the Jewish quarter, with friendly staff and live jazz, blues, Latino, swing or rock acts 21.00–23.00 most nights. *Open Mon–Thu 15.00–04.00, Fri–Sat 15.00–04.30.*
**Petőfi Csarnok** XIV, Zichy Mihály út 14; www.petoficsarnok.hu. Concert venue in City Park. Also has an open-air stage and arena, with folk-music performances in summer and bands like Massive Attack, Placebo, and Earth, Wind and Fire.

## Dance
### Folk

The *táncház* movement (see page 29) began 30 years ago as a reaction against sanitised state ensembles, and dance houses continue (although they are less frequent in summer). Entertainment listings magazines will show what's on, or log on to www.tanchaz.hu. If you want a polished performance rather than a workshop, it's worth checking the programmes at the National Dance Theatre, the Vigadó or the Duna Palota.

**Aranytíz Youth Centre** V, Arany János utca 10; ⟍ 1 311 2248. Every Sat evening, the Kalamajka táncház is found here, with Béla Halmos (the founder of the dance-house movement) and his band playing. Listen while enjoying *pálinka* from the makeshift bar.

**City Cultural House** XI, Fehérvári út 47. A concrete block with regular dance houses, featuring Balkan and Moldavian troupes.

**Fonó Buda Music House** XI, Sztregova utca 3; ⟍ 1 206 5300; www.fono.hu [T̄ *41, 47, 18;* B̄ *14, 103, 114 stop near by*] Slightly out of the centre, Fonó is a cultural centre and live-music venue. There are regular performances by Hungarian and eastern European folk bands and dance troupes – including Muszikás – as well as modern concerts. Dance-house events take place on Wed, and there's an excellent CD shop. Closed in high summer *(Jul 1–Aug 31).*

**Marcibányi tér Cultural Centre** II, Marcibányi tér 5/A; ⟍ 1 212 0803/4885. Performances of Csángó music (the ethnic Hungarians from Moldavia), as well as informal sessions by Muzsikás on some Thu from 20.00 and a weekly dance house every Wed evening.

## Other

Ballet has been popular in Hungary for 200 years; the most prestigious of today's companies is the National Ballet Company, the country's first ensemble, which is based at the State Opera House. The National Dance Theatre also includes ballet among its repertoire. There are several venues offering contemporary dance.

**Central Europe Dance Theatre** *(Közép Európa)* VII, Bethlen Gábor tér 3; ⟍ 1 342 7163; www.cedt.hu [B̄ *78, 7;* M̄2̄ *Keleti, then short walk along Bethlen Gábor utca*] Quality contemporary dance, with frequent workshops. Alongside the modern dance, there is a strong folkloric heritage with traditional dances deriving from the Carpathian Basin.

**National Dance Theatre** I, Színház utca 1–3; ⟍ 1 356 4085 *(theatre),* 1 201 4407 *(ticket office),* 1 375 8649 *(box office);* www.nemzetitancszinhaz.hu. The country's only 18th-century theatre still functioning as such. Previously a Carmelite monastery, it became a place of drama when József II dissolved the religious order in 1784. The first professional Hungarian-language theatrical production (of *Igazházi* by Simai Kristóf) was staged here in 1790; Haydn attended a performance of his own 'Creation' oratory in 1800, and Beethoven played a concert in the same year. Since 2001, the theatre has specialised in dance and related performing arts – from folklore to classical ballet and contemporary dance. There are two auditoriums, and during Aug performances (usually folkloric) are held outside in the Carmelite courtyard. Stands next to the Sándor Palace. *Ticket office (at front) open Mon–Fri 10.00–17.00, box office (behind theatre) Mon–Fri 13.00–18.00.*

**Trafó House of Contemporary Arts** IX, Liliom utca 41; ⟍ 1 456 2040; www.trafo.hu [M̄3̄ *Ferenc körút;* T̄ *4, 6 Üllői út*] A contemporary cultural centre and nightclub with a diverse programme. It hosts international-standard contemporary dance, theatre and music, as well as temporary exhibitions of graphic art. *Ticket office open daily 17.00–20.00 (gallery 16.00–19.00); tickets also available from Ticket Express (see page 121).*

## Nightclubs

While Budapest isn't a clubbing mecca in world terms, and you'll come across the odd trashy Euro-pop track, there are some excellent nightclubs to be sought out – both indoor and out – and some talented Hungarian DJs (see page 31). Clubbing is popular and nightclubs crowded, particularly after midnight. There is sometimes (although not always) an admission charge, which varies between about 500Ft and 5,000Ft depending on the event and venue. It is unjust, but not uncommon, for clubs to make just the men dip into their pockets at the entrance. Jeans are usually acceptable, although trainers may not be. When it comes to the clubbing uniform, Hungarian women seem to believe that 'less is more' when dressing and 'more is more' when applying make-up! Many clubs are connected to a bar, and so open for most of the day; the remainder open between 18.00 and 21.00, and usually continue until 03.00 or 04.00. If you like a club to have warmed up by the time you arrive, don't bother getting there until at least 22.30. Clubs can appear and disappear very quickly – criminal gangs have their fingers in the pie of nightclub ownership, and as a consequence the scene can be unstable.

## Buda

**Bed and Bed Beach** III, Szentendrei út 89–93 and Római part 7; ☎ 06 70 208 8389. A cross between a warehouse and a basketball court, with bleachers stacked around the main dance floor. The atmosphere is heady but friendly, the music a contemporary fusion of funky house and dance played by DJs who know how to work a crowd and attract more serious clubbers than those at the Dokk. During the summer, the club moves outside to a man-made beach on the Római part. *Bed open Sat 21.00–06.00 (end of Dec–May 2 only); Bed Beach Sat 21.00–06.00 (May 3–Sep/Oct).*

**Dokk and Dokk Beach** III, Hajógyári-sziget 122; ☎ 1 457 1023; www.dokkbistro.com. An uber-cool club that drags Budapest's young élite to its breast, Dokk is *the* party destination for the beautiful people. Follow the trail of parked sports cars lined outside, don your top togs and be prepared to be the view. Come Jul and Aug, the action is al-fresco (Dokk Beach), with a bridge leading to a timber platform on the water, and a venue that rivals the Ibiza beach clubs. *Terrace bar & restaurant open Mon–Wed 12.00–24.00; dance club Thu–Sat 12.00–05.00.*

## Pest

**Bahnhof** VI, Váci út 1; ☎ 1 302 4751; www.bahnhofmusic.hu. A thumping train-themed dance club, located behind McDonalds in Nyugati station (just off Teréz körút). *Open Thu–Sat 21.00–04.00.*

**Bank Dance Hall** V, Terez körút 55; www.bankdancehall.hu. Banging bass lines in a huge and sweaty dance hall. There's a range of dance genres, including rap, R&B, funk, house and trance, played over 3 levels and across 4 separate rooms. Popular with teens and early 20s. Situated within the Nyugati train station building. *Open Fri–Sat, with smaller theme nights on some week nights.*

**Buddha Beach** IX Fővám tér 11–12, ☎ 1 476 0433. Sitting on the riverbank behind Big Market Hall, Buddha Beach features 3 cocktail bars, Thai 'sungalows' to chill out on and a giant golden statue of Buddha. *Open daily 11.00–05.00 (in summer).*

**Club Seven** VII, Budapest, Akácfa utca 7; ☎ 1 478 9030. Doesn't come to the boil until at least midnight; there are occasionally live jazz acts. Stands on the other side of Dohány utca from the Old Man's Music Pub. *Café open Sun–Thu 10.00–04.00, Fri–Sat 10.00–05.00; disco 20.00–04.00/05.00 daily.*

**E-Klub** X, Népligeti út 2; ☎ 1 263 1614; www.e-klub.hu. Large club in the wooded Népliget park. DJs spin the usual Euro-trashy dance, trance and house music, but there's also a floor that features more retrospective tunes from the '80s and '90s. *Open Fri–Sat 20.00–05.00.*

**Szóda udvar** V, József Nádor tér 1; ☎ 1 461 0007; www.szoda.com. Bar housed in a delightfully crumbling old building and packed with a hip crowd. The perfectly dressed shake their booties on the tiny dancefloor to some good dance music. A few mins from the Chain Bridge. *Open summer only 12.00–late.*

**Zöld Pardon** XI, Goldmann György tér; www.zp.hu. [Ⓣ 4, 6] Outdoor club in the shadow of Petőfi Bridge. This is a rock-fest venue – be prepared for some moshing. *Admission 100Ft; open 20.00–06.00 daily (May–Sep).*

# Gay Budapest

After a slow start the gay scene has perked up somewhat in the capital, and several bars and clubs have opened. Most clubs either charge an entrance fee or require a minimum drinks spend (running a tab that you settle on leaving). Some of the baths are established gay meeting points. For information on forthcoming events, log on to www.gay.hu or www.gayguide.net.

**Angyal Privát Club** VII, Szövetség utca 33; ☎ 1 351 6490. Budapest's best-known gay club has an inconspicuous exterior but a decidedly harder core. There are 3 bars, a downstairs dancefloor and a restaurant with cross-dressing staff. Sat nights are male-only, but women are welcome at other times, and Sun is popular with heterosexuals. Located halfway between Erzsébet körút and Rákóczi út. *Open Thu–Sun 22.00–05.00.*

**Capella** V, Belgrád rakpart 23; ☏ 1 318 6231. A dark and dingy spot that doesn't take itself seriously, revelling in drag acts and occasional foam parties. The crowd is mixed – in age, gender and sexual preference (many straight people enjoy the atmosphere). Live acts start at around midnight on Fri and Sat; there is an entrance fee after 23.00. It is also a good place for picking up information about other gay events taking place in the city. *Open Tue–Fri 21.00–04.00, Sat–Sun 21.00–05.00.*

## Cinema

For general details, see page 68. As well as multiplexes in American-style shopping malls, renovated art-house cinemas provide intimate and atmospheric venues for art films. The *Budapest Sun* has a listings page containing all English-language movies; *Pesti Est* and *Pesti Msor* have information in Hungarian. The art-cinema website is www.artmozi.hu. Tickets cost from 600Ft (for fading art-house cinemas) to 1,150Ft (for multiplexes).

**Corvin Film Palace** VIII, Corvin köz 1; ☏ 1 459 5050; www.corvin.hu. Revolutionaries of '56 scored a strategic victory here when the Russians were unable to pass down the narrow Corvin köz. A tram conductor held a tank up with a handgun; there's a statue of a boy martyred during the uprising outside.

**Mammut Budai Moziközpont** II, Mammut II, Third Floor, Lövőház utca 2–6; ☏ 1 345 8140; www.mammutmozik.hu

**Művész Mozi** VI, Terez körút 30; ☏ 1 332 6726. There's an 'ethnic' ambience here; stalls in the lobby sell beaded jewellery, as well as books and CDs. Five screens show popular and less-mainstream productions.

**Palace MOM Park** XII, Alkotás út 53; ☏ 1 487 5670

**Palace WestEnd** VI, Váci út 1–3; ☏ 1 238 7222

**Puskin Mozi** V, Kossuth Lajos utca 18; ☏ 1 429 6080. Restored Neoclassical-style cinema. Shows Hollywood films alongside art-house releases in its cosy screening rooms. There's also a video club (*open 10.00–22.00 daily*).

**Uránia National Film Theatre** VIII, Rákóczi út 21; tel 1 486 3400; www.urania-nf.hu. Henrik Schmal's Art-Nouveau design and Venetian-Moorish interior are stunning. The seats lack padding, but – numb bum aside – this makes a film an experience.

## Casinos

The demise of communism has seen a surge in casinos and gaming arcades. You'll usually need to present photo identification (like a passport) and pay a joining fee of 2,000–3,000Ft, for which you'll be given some complimentary playing chips.

**Las Vegas Casino** V, Roosevelt tér 2; ☏ 1 317 6022; www.lasvegascasino.hu. Inside the Sofitel Atrium Hotel. *Open 14.00–05.00 daily.*

**Royal Revue and Casino** VII, Erzsébet kórút 43–49; ☏ 1 413 1413. Inside the Corinthia Grand Hotel Royal. Also stages cheesy variety shows. *Open daily 22.00–05.00.*

**Tropicana Casino** V, Vigadó utca 2. ☏ 1 266 3062 www.tropicana.hu. *Open daily 11.00–05.00.*

**Várkert Casino** I, Ybl Miklós tér 9; ☏ 1 202 4244; www.varkert.com. Most elegant gambling den, in a building designed by Miklós Ybl. Avoid trainers, shorts or jeans. A complimentary taxi will return you to your hotel. On the Buda bank between the Chain and Elizabeth bridges. *Open 24 hours daily.*

## FESTIVALS AND EVENTS

Budapest celebrates a range of festivals devoted to sport and the arts. The country's two biggest cultural events are the Spring (Tavaszi) and Autumn (Ászi) festivals. Tickets are available from the Budapest Spring-Autumn Festival Office (*V, Egyetem tér 5;* ☎ *1 486 3300;* e *info@festivalvaros.hu; www.festivalcity.hu*). Tourinforms and listings magazines will offer precise details of the attractions on offer and their venues.

**New Year's Day Concert (Jan 1)** The Dohnányi Orchestra Budafok and the Danube Folk Ensemble perform classical pieces during an extravaganza of music and dance at the State Opera House. *See www.hungariakoncert.hu.*

**Independence Day (Mar 15)** Commemorates the anniversary of the 1848 revolution. The date is often marked by political gatherings and soap-box rants by the far-right around Heroes' Square.

**Budapest Spring Festival (around Mar 19–Apr 4)** A 17-day national arts festival. The capital hosts 200 events, including orchestral recitals, and opera, ballet and folk-dancing performances. *See www.festivalcity.hu.*

**National Dance House Gathering and Crafts Fair (around Mar 27–28)** A celebration of traditional dancing and art, with performances from folk artists, musicians and dancers, plus an arts-and-crafts sale. *See www.tanchaz.hu.*

**Labour Day (May 1)** During the communist era, Labour Day was commemorated with great street parades; today there are parties in City Park and on Margaret Island. The country joined the EU on May 1 2004, so celebrations now have added significance.

**Danube Carnival International Cultural Festival (around Jun 11–20)** The capital jigs to a ten-day festival of music and dance, held at various locations. *See www.dunaart.hu/carnival.*

**Ferencváros Festival (around Jun 18–Jul 12)** Lively summer music and arts, with various concerts and a grand opera première. Held at Bakáts tér open-air stage, at the southern end of Ráday utca, or in Bakáts tér church. *See www.szinhaz.hu/fesztival.*

**Budapest Equestrian Summer Festival (Jun 26–27)** Thousands flock to Shipyard Island for thrilling displays of equestrian martial arts, show-jumping, dressage, stunt shows and carriage driving. *See www.karneval.hu.*

**Budapest Farewell (Búcsú) (last weekend of Jun)** A series of outdoor concerts that commemorate the day the last Soviet troops left Hungarian soil in 1991.

**Chain Bridge Festival (end of Jun)** A recent addition to the events calendar, this 2-day festival closes the Chain Bridge to traffic and enrages motorists. However, it's short in duration and small in scale, with stalls selling food and items of folk art, and performances of traditional music and dance.

**Sziget Festival (end Jul/start Aug)** Budapest's very own Glastonbury is held on Shipyard Island, with music from some of Europe's best bands. *See www.sziget.hu.*

**St Stephen's Day (Aug 20)** A public holiday in honour of Hungary's patron saint and first king, Szent István. His mummified right hand is paraded through the streets, and church services are held across the capital, along with plays, shows, dances and a craft fair in the Castle District (*see www.nesz.hu*). The day climaxes with a spectacular river procession and fireworks on Gellért Hill.

**Budapest Parade (around Aug 28)** A thumping carnival and street party modelled on Berlin's Love Parade. *See www.sziget.hu/budapestparade and www.sziget.hu/afterparty.*

**Jewish Summer Festival (around Aug 29–Sep 5)** A celebration of Jewish culture, music, dance, cuisine and film. *See www.jewishfestival.hu.*

**Budapest International Wine Festival (around Sep 5–15)** A merry festival concentrated on the Castle District (with smaller events in Budafok and Szentendre), and featuring a wine auction and a harvest procession. *See www.winefestival.hu.*

**Autumn Festival (around Oct 15–31)** Contemporary arts festival that has been running for 20 years.

**Republic Day (Oct 23)** A national holiday marking the anniversary of the outbreak of the 1956 uprising. It also commemorates the 1989 proclamation of the Hungarian republic.

**Budapest Antiques Fair (last weekend of Nov)** Held in the Exhibition Hall on Heroes' Square. *See www.antik-enterior.hu.*

**New Year's Eve Gala Ball (Dec 31)** The capital's glitterati dig out their penguin suits and ball gowns, and step out to the State Opera House for a wonderful gala concert, a banquet prepared by the Gundel chefs and dancing until dawn. Tickets are sought after and very expensive. *See www.viparts.hu.*

## SHOPPING

Budapest is no Rome or Paris. Nevertheless, the variety of shops has grown significantly in the last decade, and elegant boutiques are now as much a part of the scene as the noisy market halls. The city is a fun-time place to browse and buy. Pest is where the retail action's at. The touristy Váci utca, Vörösmarty tér, Petőfi Sándor utca and the streets branching from them are lined with glamorous international designer outlets, and stores selling antiques, paintings, folksy items and cosmetics. Products here are pricier than elsewhere (and beyond the means of many Hungarians), but what stroll isn't enhanced by a spot of leisurely window shopping? Get your nose up to the windows, work yourself into the narrow aisles, and cast a curious eye over coloured glass, quirky antiques and hanging lace.

Budapesters target the **Great Boulevard** and streets stemming from or out towards it, such as **Rákóczi út** and **Kossuth Lajos utca**. Shops here are lower key, generally a touch shabbier, and more affordable. In addition, **American-style shopping malls** have sprung up like mushrooms; they are not particularly cheap, but they open late, have everything under one roof and have inevitably placed pressure on small independent retailers. For information on opening hours and popular gifts, see *Shopping*, page 66.

### Antiques, art and furniture

Just off Szent István körút, Falk Miksa utca is the first stop for those in quest of antiques. The street is lined with commanding six-storey residences, and a rash of shops selling collectibles. Elsewhere there are a number of antiques shops in both the Castle District and on Váci utca, but these tend to be significantly overpriced. Instead look out for BÁV stores and auction houses, outlets of a well-respected Hungarian chain that are dotted all around the city. These usually have a range of period furniture, porcelain, fine art and glassware, and also stage auctions throughout the year. For more information, log on to their website www.bav.hu (with English language). Superior modern furniture and furnishings can be found on VI, Király utca.

Some BÁV stores and others are listed below. Remember when making purchases, however, that antiques require a permit for export (*kiviteli engedély*), so be sure to pick up the necessary paperwork at the shop. The form requires a special stamp of permission if antiques are over 70 years old. (See page 41 for further details.)

V, Kossuth Lajos utca 1–3; ℡ 1 317 3718; e info@bav.hu; www.bav.hu. *Open Mon–Fri 10.00–18.00, Sat 09.00–13.00.*

V, Falk Miksa utca 21; ℡ 1 353 1975. A small gallery. *Open Mon–Fri 10.00–18.00, Sat 09.00–13.00.*

VI, Andrássy út 43; ℡ 1 342 9143. Good for antique jewellery. *Open Mon–Fri 10.00–18.00, Sat 09.00–13.00.*

**Nagyházi Galéria** V, Balaton utca 8; ℡ 1 475 6000; www.nagyhazi.hu. Collectible works of art. *Open Mon–Fri 10.00–18.00, Sat 10.00–13.00.*

**Polgár Galéria & Aukciósház** V, Kossuth Lajos utca 3; ℡ 1 318 6954; www.polgar-galeria.hu. Specialises in fine art and furniture. *Open Mon–Fri 10.00–18.00, Sat 10.00–13.00.*

### Folk art, porcelain, pottery and glass

The centres of folk art lean very heavily towards the kitsch, and they are marketed firmly at the tourist; nevertheless, the craftsmanship is often good, and folk items make super souvenirs. The leading porcelain and glass producers have outlets in Budapest.

**Ajka Kristály** XIII, Szent István körút 18; ☎ 1 340 5083 & V, József Attila út 7; ☎ 1 317 8133. Hand-crafted lead crystal. *Open Mon–Fri 10.00–18.00, Sat 10.00–13.00.*
**Art-Agora** I, Országház utca 15; ☎ 06 20 365 4413. Small glass shop in the Castle District. *Open 09.00–19.00 daily.*
**Folkart Kézművesház** V, Régiposta utca 12; ☎ 1 318 5143; www.folkartkezmuveshaz. Busy folk-craft house, with quality traditional products from regional artisans. *Open Mon–Fri 10.00–19.00, Sat 10.00–16.00.*
**Handmade Studio** I, Tárnok utca 1; ☎ 1 212 7050. Traditional costumes and jewellery in the Castle District. *Open daily 10.00–18.00.*
**Herend Porcelain** V, József nádor tér 11; ☎ 1 317 2622. Over-priced Herend pieces. *Open Mon–Fri 10.00–18.00, Sat 10.00–13.00.*
**Herend Village Pottery**; II, Bem rakpart 37; ☎ 1 356 7899. Squashed beneath a block of flats between Bem rakpart and Fő utca. Sells the more 'rustic' – rather than refined – pieces. *Open Tue–Fri 09.00–17.00, Sat 09.00–12.00.*
**Zsolnay** V, Kígyó utca 4; ☎ 318 3712. Hand-made Zsolnay pieces, with their unique reflective design. *Open Mon–Fri 10.00–18.00, Sat 10.00–13.00.*

## Food and drink
(See also *Markets*, below.)

**A Magyar Pálinka Háza** VIII, Rákóczi út 17; ☎ 1 338 4219. Traditional brandy and other spirits. *Open Mon–Sat 09.00–19.00*
**Aureum Vinum Pincészet** V, Belgrád rakpart 19; ☎ 1 483 1456; www.aureumtokaji.hu. Wine shop specialising in Tokaji from a family-owned winery. Organises wine tasting (phone a week in advance). *Open Mon–Fri 10.00–18.00, Sat 10.00–14.00*
**Bortársaság** I, Batthyány utca 59; ☎ 1 212 2569; www.bortarsasag.hu. Wine Society shop; offers free tastings on Sat. There are 4 other outlets: IX, Ráday utca 7; XII, MOM Park, Alkotás út 53; II, Budagyöngye shopping centre, Szilágyi Erzsébet fasor; II, Rózsakert shopping centre, Gábor Áron utca 74–78. *Open Mon–Fri 10.00–20.00, Sat 10.00–18.00.*
**House of Hungarian Wines** (*Magyar Borok Háza*) I, Szentháromság tér 6; ☎ 1 212 1030; www.magyarborokhaza.hu or www.winehouse.hu. Claims to be the 6th-largest wine-tasting establishment in the world. Showcases 600 regional wines, with 60 bottles open at any one time. Bring a sweater (the cellar gets chilly). Opposite the Hilton. *2-hr tasting 3,500Ft, with or without a guide (book ahead for the former); open daily 12.00–20.00.*
**La Boutique des Vins** V, József Attila utca 12; ☎ 1 317 5919; www.malatinzky.hu. Wines from Villány (plus some French vintages). *Open Mon–Fri 10.00–18.00, Sat 10.00–15.00.*
**Librairie Gourmande** VI, Budapest, Szív utca 32; ☎ 1 302 4039. Fresh deli stuffs alongside books on Hungarian cooking. *Open 11.00–21.00 daily.*
**Portéka Hungaria** V, Magyarok Háza, Semmelweis utca 1–3; ☎ 1 486 0336. Where locals shop for traditional foodstuffs. *Open Mon–Fri 10.00–18.00, Sat 10.00–14.00.*
**Szeged Pick Salami Shop** V, Kossuth Lajos tér; ☎ 1 331 7783. *Open Mon–Thu 06.00–19.00, Fri 06.00–18.00.*

## Markets
For general details on markets see *Shopping*, page 66. During December, festive markets pop up in many of the city's squares, the biggest in Vörösmarty tér.

### Market halls
When the Nagycsarnok opened in 1897 (see below), four smaller roofed markets were also opened on the same day. Each was given a number (the Nagycsarnok was No I); look up for the numeral carved in stone or forged in metalwork above the *csarnok* sign and the entrance/exit. The other four markets can be found at: Rákóczi tér (No II),

Klauzál tér (No III), Hunyadi tér (No IV) and Hold utca (No V). There is also one on Batthyány tér.

**Fény utcai piac** II, Lövőház utca 12, ☏ 1 345 4100. Buzzy food and flowers market next to Mammut (page 133). *Open Mon–Fri 06.00–18.00, Sat 06.00–14.00.*
**Lehel-csarnok** XIII, Váci út 15. [T̄ *14 terminus directly outside;* M3 *Lehel tér*] A garish-toy-ship of a building selling super-cheap fresh produce. *Open Mon–Fri 06.00–18.00, Sat 06.00–14.00, Sun 06.00–13.00.*
**Nagycsarnok** IX, Vámház körút 1–3 [T̄ *2, 47 & 49 stop directly outside*] The Big Market's Art-Nouveau styling was the work of architect Samu Pecz in 1897. It was designed as a sheltered area for traders, who previously sold their wares from beneath umbrellas on the Danube bank. When first constructed, the hall had an indoor canal running through it along which goods were delivered to the stalls. It's a privilege to shop beneath its girders. On the ground and lower-ground floors are fresh produce (vegetables, meats, chickens' feet, river fish mouthing furiously in cramped tanks), pickles, wines and spices, while upstairs are stalls selling Hungarian handicrafts. Prices are good by Hungarian standards and cheap by those of western Europe, and there is usually a little room for negotiation (a 10% reduction the limit). There are also some cheap and hearty *büfés*. One of the ground-floor stalls proudly displays a photo of Margaret Thatcher haggling over some paprika in 1984; the Iron Lady was the first foreign dignitary to visit the hall. Southern end of Váci utca. *Open Mon–Fri 06.00–18.00, Sat 06.00–14.00.*

## Flea markets
**Hasznalt cikk piac (Ecseri Flea Market)** XIX, Nagykőrösi út 156 [B̄ *54 from Boráros tér to Autópiac stop;* M3 *Határ út, then* B̄ *154*] Treasure hunters usually try the Ecseri Market, in a southeastern suburb (40 mins by bus from centre). The place comes alive on Sat, when serious collectors mingle with tourists. Jeans and leather jackets starting at 6,000Ft fight for space with heaps of machine parts. There's a huge selection of furniture and you'll still find oddities like communist badges. *Open Mon–Fri 08.00–16.00, Sat 07.00–15.00.*
**Józsefvárosi piac** VIII, Kőbányai út 16 [T̄ *28 from Blaha tér;* B̄ *9 from Deák tér*] The city's largest marketplace, known as the 'Chinese market' because of its Far Eastern vendors. Sportswear is the primary focus. Every sign shows two prices – *'egy'* (one) and *'sok'* (many), the latter for bulk buying. You'll find rock-bottom prices, but also some strange spellings – stereos by 'Panasoanic' and trainers by 'Adiads'. Prick a keen ear for cries of *'Vigyázz!'* ('Look out!') from traders pushing sharp-edged trolleys. Situated close to Kerepesi Cemetery, behind the yard of Józsefvárosi railway station. *Open Mon–Fri 06.00–18.00, Sat–Sun 06.00–16.00.*
**Kőbánya bazár** X, Maglódi út 18 [T̄ *37, 28 from Blaha Lujza on Népszínház út to Sibrik Miklós út*] Used to be known as the 'Russian market'. Many traders still travel here daily by bus from Slovakia, Ukraine, Romania and Croatia. Electrical goods, training shoes and tools. Take tram 28 almost to the end stop. *Open Mon–Fri 07.00–17.00, Sat–Sun 07.00–16.00.*
**Novák piac** VIII/XIV (district border), Dózsa György út [M2 *Keleti, then 5-min walk up Verseny utca, behind the station*] Probably the best place for bargain tat. Go at the weekend for the best atmosphere. In the shade of the Puskás Stadion. *Open Mon–Fri 07.00–18.00, Sat–Sun 06.00–18.00.*
**Petőfi Csarnok** XIV, Zichy Mihály út 14, Városliget [M *to Széchenyi fürdő*] Little flea market in City Park. *Open Sat–Sun 07.00–14.00.*

## Newspapers, books and maps
**Bestsellers** V, Október 6 utca 11; ☏ 1 312 1295; www.bestsellers.hu. One of the city's best English-language bookshops. International newspapers and lifestyle magazines too. *Open Mon–Fri 09.00–18.30.*
**Bono Travel Centre & Bookshop** V, Nádor utca 8; ☏ 1 235 8010; e info@bonoutazas.hu; www.bonoutazas. New travel bookshop inside the Bono Travel Centre. *Open Mon–Fri 09.00–18.00, & Sat 09.00–13.00 (Jun–Aug only).*

## THE DEATH OF CRAFT

Budapest's artisans – workers taking pride in using their hands to make beautiful things or fix what's broken – are representatives of a declining species. Shoe menders, boot makers, zip and watch repairers, goldsmiths, engravers, milliners and ladies who stitch up ladders in stockings once crowded the backstreets of Budapest. No longer.

Traditional shoemaking was a thriving industry, but there are just a few exponents of the craft now. Lajos Pető is in his 60s, and makes fashion shoes for women with extra-small feet. His signboard on Wesselényi utca was first used by his father in the early 20th century, and still reads 'czipész' (the old word for 'shoemaker'). His clients come from far and wide – he claims that no other shoemaker in Europe specialises in such teeny sizes (of 30 to 35).

Magdolna Szabó followed her father into the engraving profession, gaining her master's qualification in 1971. She too now works on Wesselényi utca. 'I make everything with my hands; I do not use machines, although more and more people in our trade do. It is a profession that follows the whole life circle – I make plaques for births, marriages and cremation urns,' she explained. Sadly, unless there is an increase in the appreciation of, and demand for, such traditional skills, the economic epitaph of artisans like Szabó will be etched into the ledger of the capital's history. If you've lost a lens from your specs or your fly gets stuck, consider visiting the artisans below:

**Spectacle repairs** (*látszerész*) V, Veres Pálné utca 7 (Libál Lajosné)
**Master goldsmith** (*ötvös mester*) VII, Wesselényi utca 11 (György Falk)
**Engraver master** (*vésnök mester*) VII, Wesselényi utca 11 (Magdolna Szabó)
**Stocking repairs** (*szemfelszedő*) V, Kamermayer Károly tér (with huge plants in the window)
**Umbrella maker** (*ernyős*), V, Vitkovics Mihály utca 10
**Shoemaker** (*czipész*) VII, Károly körút 3 (István Priska)
**Watch and clock repairs** (*órás*) V, Ferenciek tere 5 (the sign on the door reads 'We do not repair quartz watches! We don't stock batteries either!') or VIII, Bródy Sándor utca 22 (Tibor Feig)
**Zipper, shoe, lock repairs** (*cipzár csere, cipő javító, lakatos* ) XIII, Pozsonyi út 35
**Locksmith** (*lakatos*) XIII, Csanády utca 16 (József Horváth and son) Also mend window blinds and mosquito nets!
**Piano repairers** (*zongora javító mester*) IX, Mester utca 5 (János Heigli and son)
**Baba Klinika** (doll and teddy-bear repairs) V, Múzeum körút 5. Also does leather working.
**Furrier** (*szűcs*) XIII, Pozsonyi út 13 (Ica Nagy) Cleaning, dying and repairing of leather and fur. (Fur is very popular among elderly women in Hungary in winter.)

**Cartographia Map & Globe Shop (I & II)** VI, Bajcsy-Zsilinszky út 37; ℡ 1 312 6001 & XIV, Bosnyák tér 5; ℡ 1 221 4407; www.cartographia.hu. Two stores stocking national and international maps by Hungary's leading cartographic company. *Open Mon–Thu 09.00–18.00, Fri 09.00–17.00.*
**Famulus** XIII, Új Pesti Rakpart. Stocks Oxford University Press and a good range of other books.
**Freytag & Berndt** V, Kálvin tér 5; ℡ 1 318 5844; e bolt@freytagbrendt.hu. Travel bookshop. *Open Mon–Fri 10.00–18.30, Sat 10.00–13.00.*
**Hungaro Press** V, Városház utca 3–5. Magazine and newspaper shop with an excellent choice of international daily, weekly and monthly publications. *Open Mon–Fri 07.00–19.00, Sat 07.00–16.00, Sun 07.00–14.00.*

**Központi Antikvárium** V, Múzeum körút 13; ☏ 1 317 3514. One of the largest antique bookshops. *Mon–Fri 10.00–18.00, Sat 10.00–13.00.*

**Libri Studium** V, Váci utca. Recently re-opened as a foreign-language bookshop (mainly English).

**Oxford University Press Könyvesbolt** V, Gerlóczy utca 7; ☏ 1 318 8633. OUP publications, including academic and fiction. *Open Mon–Fri 09.00–17.00.*

**Parisi Udvar Bookshop** V, Petőfi Sándor utca 2; ☏ 1 235 0380. Great range of travel guides and maps.

**Pendragon** XIII, Pozsony út 21–23; ☏ 1 340 4436. Perhaps the largest range of English-language books at good prices.

## Shopping malls

**Mammut** II, Lövőház utca 2–6; ☏ 1 345 8020; www.mammut.hu. Just off Moskva tér, Mammut is a beast, comprising two buildings (I and II) that straddle Lövőház utca and are connected by a walkway. Alongside the shops, you'll find a cinema, bowling alley, tonnes of trendy bars and a nightclub. *Shops open 10.00–19.00 daily; bars often open until 04.00 at weekends.*

**MOM Park** XII, Alkotás út 53; ☏ 1 487 5501; www.mompark.hu. The city's newest complex. There is a fitness centre, as well as Budapest's first Virgin megastore. *Open Mon–Sat 07.00–24.00, Sun 08.00–24.00.*

**Rózsakert** II, Gábor Áron utca 74–78; ☏ 1 391 5998. Smart, glass-fronted shopping mall in a residential area of Buda. Restaurants, post office and medical centre (see page 98). *Open Mon–Fri 10.00–20.00, Sat 10.00–19.00, Sun 10.00–16.00 (restaurants until 22.00 daily).*

**Westend City Center** VI, Váci út 1–3; www.westend.hu. Central Europe's biggest mall, with 400 shops, 40 cafés and restaurants, a cinema, a hotel and a 3ha roof garden. *Shops open Mon–Sat 10.00–20.00, Sun 10.00–18.00.*

## THERMAL BATHS

Budapest stands on a fault line dividing the Buda Hills from the Great Plain; three million litres emerge daily, feeding around 40 baths and seasonal pools, 15 with medicinal ranking. For information on the history and etiquette of bathing, see page 69.

### Buda

**Csillaghegy** III, Pusztakúti út 3; ☏ 1 250 1533 [HÉV *Csillaghegy*] 'Star Hill' is the oldest open-air lido complex in Budapest, fed by a karst-water spring and situated on the side of a hill in northern Buda. The swimming (24°C) and lido (22°C) pools are found on the first terraced level near all the *büfé* stalls, while the children's paddling pool (28°C) and the grassy sun terrace are situated on the upper level. The main pool remains open in winter, covered by a tented roof. *Adult/concessions 1,000/800Ft; swimming pool open May 1–Sep 15 07.00–19.00 daily, Sep 16–Apr 30 Mon–Fri 06.00–19.00, Sat 06.00–16.00, Sun 06.00–12.00; lido pool open May 1–Sep 15 07.00–19.00.*

**Gellért Baths** XI, Kelenhegyi út 4–6; ☏ 1 466 6166 [T̄ *18, 19, 47, 49*] Here, one feels, a decadent of ancient Rome could draw contented breath, cast off toga and sandals, and plunge in with a hearty '*Carpe diem!*' The domed entrance hall, frescoed ceilings, Neo-Romanesque columns and spouting gargoyles ooze opulence; a visit here is as much about gawping as soaking. There is a pool for mixed bathing, as well as separate areas for men and women – where you can choose between your moon and your costume. Outside is a summer terrace and pool replete with vigorous wave machine. Guests of the adjacent Gellért Hotel may use the baths gratis. A sliding refund is paid on stays of under 4 hours (except on already discounted afternoon tickets) – retain the coupon issued as you enter and collect your refund from the cash desk on leaving (ensure you ask for this – the notoriously unhelpful staff here tend to 'forget'). *Entrance locker/cabin 2,500/3,000Ft; reduced rates after 17.00; discount with Budapest Card; open May 1–Sep 30 indoor & outdoor pools 06.00–19.00 daily, Fri–Sat 20.00–24.00 (Jun 13–Aug 16), Oct 1–Apr 30 Mon–Fri 06.00–19.00, Sat–Sun 06.00–17.00.*

**Király Baths** II, Fő utca 82–86; ☎ 1 201 4392 [**B** *60, 86*] Set back slightly from the road, the Király (King) Baths date to the 16th century. The baths are the most atmospheric of any in the country, with lowly shafts of daylight from the original Turkish dome casting a murky, steamy haze. Open to men or women only on alternate days, visitors may go 'full monty' if they wish. Be aware that the baths are popular with gays and lesbians, and some readers have reported witnessing some very 'intimate' canoodling. There are just 2 warm indoor pools, with a dry and wet steam room and saunas (under the smaller dome). The main pool is on the cosy side, so it is best visited on weekdays to avoid the crowds. Tickets are sold in 1½-hour slots. On purchasing your ticket, go upstairs and take a bath towel from one of the uniformed staff members. Choose a cabin along one of the long corridors; ensure that you return within 90 mins or you'll be charged extra. The shower facilities are next to the pool, under the 2nd dome, and so it is probably worth taking your shampoo with you on heading down to the baths. *Adult 1,100Ft, children prohibited; open Mon, Wed & Fri 07.00–18.00 (for women), Tue, Thu & Sat 09.00–20.00 (for men).*

**Lukács Baths** II, Frankel Leó út 25–29; ☎ 1 326 1695 [**T** *4, 6, 17;* **B** *6, 60, 86*] The elegant watering hole of the Buda literati. Facilities include 8 pools – among them a fancy whirlpool and weight baths – a roof-top sunbathing terrace and mineral drinking cures. There is separate bathing for men and women. Close to the bridgehead of Margit híd. *Thermal steam baths adult 1,500–1,700Ft; swimming pool adult 1,500–1,700Ft (sliding discounts & cheaper entrance in the later afternoon); open 06.00–19.00 daily (some facilities shorter hours at weekends). Mud & weight baths open Tue, Thu & Sat (for men), Mon, Wed & Fri (for women).*

**Rác Baths** I, Hadnagy utca 8–10; ☎ 1 356 1322. Named after the Tabán's 18th-century Serbian population, the building was reconstructed in 1869 by Miklós Ybl, and only a stone pool remains of the original complex established here by the Turks. The baths have been closed for sometime now for extensive renovation and will (as before) receive men and women on alternate days when it reopens. A popular meeting place for homosexuals. *Entrance costs not yet published; due to open (women) Mon, Wed, Fri 06.30–19.00, (men) Tue, Thu, Sat 06.30–19.00.*

**Római Strandfürdő** III, Rozgonyi Piroska utca 2; ☎ 1 388 9740 [**HEV** *Római fürdő*] There used to be a Roman bath here. The water is 22°C – chilly compared with many of the other baths in town. The long-haired must wear swimming caps. There are saunas, slides and outdoor pools. Modern and well-equipped. *Adult/concessions 1,200/1,000Ft; adult with changing cabin 1,600Ft; open 09.00–20.00 daily (summer only).*

**Rudas Baths** XI, Döbrentei tér 9; ☎ 1 375 8373. Constructed by the Turks in the mid 16th century, the Rudas has an octagonal thermal pool and turquoise cupola, and is open only to men (who are issued with aprons to spare blushes). It is the favourite of many of the city's male bathers; it is also a forthright gay cruising zone. The indoor swimming pool is open to members of both sexes. Immediately to the south of Erzsébet Bridge. *Thermal baths 1,000Ft; swimming pool adult/concessions 900Ft/700Ft; massages from 1,900Ft; open Mon–Fri 06.00–20.00 (swimming pool 06.00–18.00), Sat–Sun 06.00–13.00.*

## Pest

**Dagály Baths & Strand** XIII, Népfürdő utca 36; ☎ 1 452 4500 [**T** *1 to Árpád híd;* **M3** *Árpád híd, then short walk up Váci út & left along Dagály utca*] A marvellous *strand*-lido complex in the working-class district of Angyalföld (Angel Land) in northern Pest. Open all year, the smaller swimming pool is covered in winter, but the outdoor Olympic-length pool is heated and you can do lengths in Dec with the snow falling gently on your bathing cap. The thermal pool also stays open in all seasons; sit in the eggy water at dusk on a cold autumn evening and watch the steam rise through the surrounding pine trees. There's also a curling fun slide and massive communal saunas. A real Magyar experience. *Adult/concessions 1,500Ft/1,300Ft; open 06.00–19.00 daily.*

**Széchenyi Baths** XIV, Állatkerti körút 11; ☎ 1 363 3210; www.szechenyifurdo.hu. Opposite the circus in City Park is the Neo-Baroque edifice housing one of Europe's largest spa complexes. Built in 1913, the sitting-pools are based in enormous halls, suggestive of the Roman bathing culture, while steam rooms and cold-water tubs draw on Turkish and Nordic traditions.

## THE MINERAL WATER STORY
### A bit of bottle

Hungarians do not just sit in the life-enhancing mineral springs that bubble beneath them – they also sometimes drink them. Twenty-one are bottled nationwide, and four in Budapest itself (Apenta, Óbudai Gyémánt, Margitszigeti Kristályvíz and Gellérthegyi Kristályvíz). Of course, Magyars generally prefer beer and wine, but they still get through an average of 50 litres of mineral water a year. There are strict rules governing the sale of mineral water; it must be bottled at source, cannot be treated (beyond removing excess iron), and must have a minimum mineral content of 1000mg/litre. Check the label – if a bottle reads 'asványi anyaggal dúsított? (enhanced with minerals), you'll be paying good money for purified tap water.

### At smelly source

Mineral-water aficionados or those with health problems should head for drinking halls (ivócsarnok), where they can taste the water at its warm and sulphurous source. It's an acquired taste, like drinking a stink bomb; pinch your nose and toss it quickly down your throat. Some find that chilling the water makes it more bearable.

The **Rudas ivócsarnok** (beneath Erzsébet híd, on the Buda side) sells glasses for 25Ft; the marble-lined hall is filled with pensioners supping korsós (half-litre mugs) and chatting as if they were down at the pub. The Rudas offers three of the mildly radioactive waters: Hungária is good for stomach and kidney problems, water from the Attila spring helps those with bronchial, stomach, intestinal, gall-bladder and liver ailments, while Juventus is good for high blood pressure, rheumatism and even premature ageing! The **Lukács Baths** have a drinking market set in a stylish stone structure near the entrance. The water is effective for treating stomach and kidney problems. At the southern side of the **Széchenyi Baths** you'll find an ivócsarnok in an elegant pavilion (built in 2003). A korsó costs just 18Ft, and reputedly assists with nervous stomach problems, chronic gall-bladder disorders and inflammation of the kidneys. A new addition to the family of curative waters gushes outside the **Dagály Baths** from the mouth of a gargoyle named 'Well of Peace'. A group of elderly men surrounds the fountain, one by one filling plastic bottles from the steaming pipe. 'My wife drinks this water every day,' says one, 'and the best thing is it's free.'

There are 9 pools in total, all of which (inc those outside) are open all year. Prepare for hot, hot water, and bathers playing chess. The daytime hospital at the back of the complex offers treatments, including drinking cures and Finnish saunas. Head for the entrance facing the circus – it doesn't accept those with medical referrals, and you are less likely to become caught up in queues. Cheaper and less intimidating than the Gellért Baths. *Entrance 2,000–2,300Ft, sliding refunds & reduced entry from 15.00; open May–Sep 06.00–19.00 daily, Oct–Apr Mon–Fri 06.00–19.00, Sat–Sun 06.00–17.00.*

## Margaret Island

**Palatínus Strand** XIII, Margit-sziget; ✆ 1 966 6453. Biggest open-air lido in the capital, with numerous pools, waterslides and bathing areas, as well as fountains and snack shacks. *Adult/concessions 1,500–1,900F/1,300–1,700Ft; discount after 17.00 or with Budapest Card; open daily May 1–Aug 20 Mon–Sun 08.00–19.00, Aug 21–end of season 10.00–18.00 daily.*

# SPORT

For general information, see page 71; for offices selling **tickets** to sporting events, see page 121.

## Swimming and watersports

If you're looking for a proper swim rather than a thermal soak, try one of the following. In addition, several sports centres have swimming pools.

**Császár Komjádi Swimming Pool** II, Árpád fejedelem útja 8; ↘ 1 326 1478 [T̄ *17*; B̄ *6, 60, 86*] Complex of 3 swimming pools favoured by professional competitors. It famously hosted the first European swimming, diving and water-polo championships in 1926. *Adult/concessions 900/600Ft; open Mon–Sat 06.00–21.00, Sun 06.00–19.00.*

**Hajós Alfréd National Sports Swimming Pool** XIII, Margit-sziget; ↘ 1 340 4946. A belly flop from Margit híd, this specialist pool is named after Hungary's first swimming Olympic gold medallist and respected architect, and hosted the European Water-Polo Champs in 2001. 1 indoor and 2 outdoor pools (*the latter May–Sep only*). *Admission from 700Ft; open daily 06.00–19.00.*

## Sport centres, squash and tennis

**Lido Sports Centre** III, Nánási út 67; ↘ 1 242 4479. Modern fitness centre on the Római part on the Buda bank. Facilities include an indoor swimming pool, whirlpool, sauna, 5 squash courts, 2 tennis courts, a fitness suite and a gym. *Open 07.00–23.00 daily.*

**MOM Wellness Center** XII, Alkotás út 53; ↘ 1487 5600; www.mom-wellness.hu. Massive fitness emporium with 2 aerobics studios, an indoor swimming pool and state-of-the-art gym. *Open Mon–Fri 06.00–22.00, Sat–Sun 09.00–20.00.*

**City Squash & Fitness** II, Marcibányi tér 13; ↘ 1 325 0082; www.squashtec.hu. 8 squash courts, a fitness centre and gym. *Squash courts 2,200–4,000Ft/hour, fitness centre 1,400Ft/daily ticket; open Mon–Fri 07.00–22.00, Sat–Sun 09.00–21.00.*

**Margaret Island Tennis Club** ↘ 1 340 4484. 8 outdoor clay courts on the southeastern side of Margaret Island. *Courts 600–2,000Ft/hour; open 07.00–22.00 daily.*

**Match-point Tennis Club** II, Marcibányi tér 13; ↘ 1 214 5433; www.matchpoint.hu. Numerous covered courts, next to City Squash (see above). *Courts from 1,600Ft/hour; open 08.00–21.00 daily.*

**Park Teniszklub** I, Bartók Béla út 63–65; tel:1 209 1595; e info@parktenisz.hu; www.parktenisz.hu. Near Feneketlen-tó; 13 clay tennis courts. *Costs 1,000–1,600Ft/hour in summer, double that in winter (heating expenses); open all yr 06.00–22.00 daily.*

## Horse-riding, racing and fishing

**Kincsem Park Galopp-pálya** X, Albertirsai út 2, ↘ 1 263 7818 [M2 *Pillangó utca*] If you'd rather watch than participate – a horse, after all, is dangerous at both ends and uncomfortable in the middle – there is horse racing and trotting (where riders sit in 2-wheeled buggies) at Kincsem Park, near the big Hungexpo site east of Kerepesi Cemetery. Of course, your wallet may end up frayed at both ends and empty in the middle, but you'll be able to sit down without wincing.

**Petneházy Horse Centre and Hussar Inn** II, Feketefej utca 2–4; ↘ 1 397 5048; e petnehazy-lovascentrum@matavnet.hu; www.mediaguide.hu/petnehazy. A horse centre and guesthouse in hilly District II. The summer horse shows are also worth catching – check the website for details. *Lessons for beginners from 1,400Ft/25 min; cross-country programmes for advanced riders from 3,300Ft/hr; pony rides for kids from 800Ft/15 mins.*

**Anglers' Union Budapest Association** (*Horgászegyesületek Budapest Szövetsége*) V, Galamb utca 3; tel 1 318 5472 or 1 486 1602. You'll see many anglers on the Danube banks. For information, contact this association; the portal http://horgasz.lap.hu is a starting page with links to many fishing sites.

## Other sports

**Bobpálya** XI, Balatoni út 7; ↘ 1 310 4122 [*Take Road 7 leading towards Balaton, & the course is on the left*] Dry bobsleighing course for the kids. *Open Apr–Sep 11.00–16.00 daily.*

**Buda-Ring GoKarting** XI, Floracoop, Budaörsi út; ↘ 06 30 311 9856. Go-karting track next to the main highway to Vienna. *8 mins on the track adult/concessions 2,200Ft/1,600Ft; open Mon–Fri 14.00–22.00, Sat–Sun 10.00–22.00.*

**Canoe & Kayak hire** III, Római-Part 29; ↘ 06 20 943 6521/06 30 257 7457

**Lido Bowling Club** III, Nánási út 67; ↘ 1 242 1937. New 6-lane 10-pin bowling alley and bar just off the Római-part. *Open 12.00–24.00 daily.*

**Wakeboarding** XIII, Hajógyári-sziget; ↘ 06 20 9228 328. Similar to waterskiing, you ride the wake as you're tugged around a ropeway circuit. For more information, log on to www.wakeboarder.hu/center_eng.htm.

# Discovering Buda
## CASTLE HILL

Castle Hill (Várhegy) rises 60m above the Danube, bears aloft the former royal palace, and is the master of the western bank. It is overpriced and often overcrowded. However, visit at the right time of day (earlyish morning or lateish afternoon) and in a patient frame of mind, and this World Heritage Site's cobbled streets and Baroque dwellings provide the backdrop for some of the city's most pleasant strolls and river views. The museums and galleries of Buda Castle Palace, the wonderfully extravagant Mátyás Church, and the natural caves running beneath also make this a short-break must-see.

It was not until after the **Mongol invasion** of 1241–42 that Castle Hill was considered as a potential stronghold. King **Béla IV** (1235–70) constructed a fort to the south of Castle Hill and a royal residence to the north, near Bécsi kapu. Citizens from the Víziváros and other vulnerable areas were moved to residences in a new burghers' town (the Castle District or Várnegyed) that occupied the remaining two-thirds of the hilltop, and which was surrounded by fortified walls.

A diverse community of Hungarians, Germans and other European traders grew up around the hill's castle and churches, and flourished until the arrival of the **Turks**. Castle Hill's fortifications did not deter conflict. There were over 30 sieges during subsequent centuries, and the district had to be rebuilt on numerous occasions. Following the **1686 siege** that drove the Turks from Buda, most of the houses were reconstructed over two (rather than the original three) storeys in Baroque and Louis XVI styles by successive Habsburg rulers. Similarly, few buildings escaped unscathed after the last gasp of the German army here in 1945.

### Getting up there

The **funicular railway** (*Budavári sikló; open 07.30–22.00 daily, closed 1st and 3rd Mond each month for maintenance; adult 600/500Ft uphill/downhill, concession 400Ft either direction*) offers the most direct and sedate journey, while also providing stunning views of Budapest. (Join the lowest of the carriage's compartments for the best of these.) It is accessed at the western side of Clark Ádám tér. There is a **lift** running from Dózsa tér up to the palace complex, next to the Lions' Courtyard (same hours as Széchényi Library; see page 169). The '**Várbusz**' – a dinky little chap that bears a castle symbol rather than a number – runs from Moszkva tér to Dísz tér every six or seven minutes. Alternatively, bus 16 travels between Déak Ferenc tér on the Pest side and Dísz tér throughout most of the day.

Much of the Castle District is pedestrianised, and most **cars** can only drive as far as Dísz tér – via Palota út or the one-way Hunyadi János út – where you must park and disembark. Only authorised vehicles and hotel residents may enter via Bécsi kapu (Vienna Gate). Another option is to drive up below the Fishermen's Bastion and park on the street there. Drivers collect a ticket on entering the district and pay on leaving (*400Ft/hr*). If you are staying in one of the hotels, the receptionist will stamp your card to

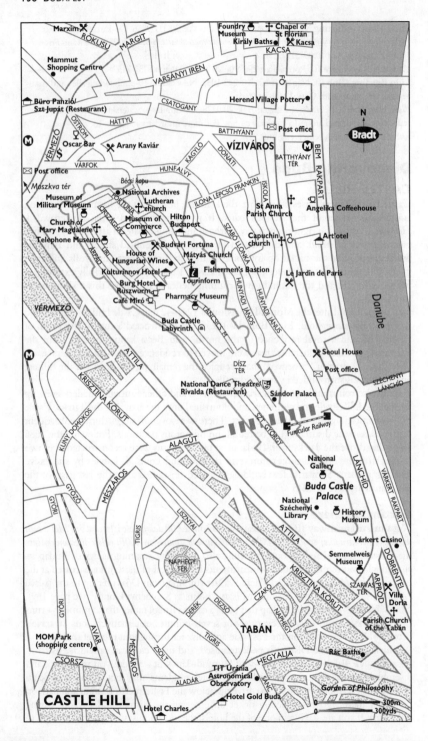

Marxim
RÓKUSI
MARGIT
Mammut
Shopping Centre
VARSÁNYI IRÉN
Büro Panzió/
Szt Jupát (Restaurant)
CSATOGÁNY
HÁTTYÚ
OSTROM
VÉRMEZŐ
Oscar Bar
Arany Kaviár
Post office
VÁRFOK
HUNFALVY
Moszkva tér
Bécsi kapu
National Archives
Museum of
Military Museum
FORTUNA
Lutheran
church
Church of
Mary Magdalene
ORSZÁGHÁZ
Museum of
Commerce
Telephone Museum
ÁRPÁD ÚRI
Budvári Fortuna
House of
Hungarian Wines
Mátyás Church
Kulturinnov Hotel
Burg Hotel
Ruszwurm
Café Miró
Pharmacy Museum
VÉRMEZŐ
Buda Castle
Labyrinth
TÁNCSICS M
ATTILA
KRISZTINA KÖRÚT
KUNY DOMOKOS
GYŐZŐ
MÉSZÁROS
GYŐRI
LISZNYAI
TIGRIS
ALAGÚT
DEREK
DEZSŐ
NAPHEGY
TÉR
CZAKÓ
NAPHEGY
ATTILA
MOM Park
(shopping centre)
AVAR
CSÖRSZ
MÉSZÁROS
ZSOLT
TIGRIS
ALADÁR
SÁNC
TABÁN
HEGYALJA
TIT Uránia
Astronomical
Observatory
Hotel Gold Buda
Hotel Charles
CASTLE HILL

Foundry
Museum
Chapel of
St Florián
Király Baths
Kacsa
KACSA
Herend Village Pottery
Ő
Post office
BATTHYÁNY
VÍZIVÁROS
BATTHYÁNY
TÉR
BEM
RAKPART
DONÁTI
KAGYLÓ
ILONA LÉPCSŐ FRANKIN
ISKOLA
St Anna
Parish Church
Angelika Coffeehouse
Hilton
Budapest
SZABÓ ILONKA
Capuchin
church
Ő
Art'otel
Fishermen's Bastion
Tourinform
Le Jardin de Paris
HUNYADI JÁNOS
HUNYADI JÁNOS
Danube
Seoul House
DÍSZ
TÉR
Post office
SZÉCHENYI
LÁNCHÍD
National Dance Theatre/
Rivalda (Restaurant)
Sándor Palace
SZT GYÖRGY
Funicular Railway
National
Gallery
LÁNCHÍD
VÁRKERT RAKPART
Buda Castle
Palace
National
Széchenyi
Library
History
Museum
Várkert Casino
Semmelweis
Museum
DOBRENTEI
KRISZTINA KÖRÚT
SZARVAS
TÉR
ÁPRÓD
Villa
Doria
Parish Church
of the Tabán
Rác Baths
Garden of Philosophy

N
Bradt

Moszkva tér
M

Post office

VÁRFOK

Dísz tér

0       300m
0       300yds

allow you to exit through the barrier. Parking is free for guests at the Hilton, while the Kulturinnov charges a daily fee for the use of its car park (see page 104).

There are approaches from most sides for those with the energy to puff and pant up **on foot**. Several roads lead up to Bécsi kapu. Steeper flights of stone steps (*lépcső*) snake up the hill's eastern side and provide more taxing but ultimately rewarding routes to the top. One set finishes next to the upper station of the funicular railway, another at the Fishermen's Bastion; these can be picked up at various points on and around Hunyadi János út, including from Clark Ádám tér. Alternatively you can take a route up from Szarvas tér to the southern end of the hill, and there are further flights leading up the western slope.

## Walking around Castle Hill
### The castle complex
(For details of the palace itself, see page 176; for museums and galleries, see pages 168–9.)

There are two points of access to the **Buda Castle Palace** complex (*open 06.00–22.00 daily*) in Szent György tér, near the upper terminal of the funicular railway. The ornamental arch immediately to the left is most striking for its fierce neighbour, a huge bronze *turul* (Gyula Donáth, 1905). As it glares grumpily over the city from its prime perch, you'd be forgiven for thinking that it finds the view a little irksome. If so, it's feathered of brain; on passing through the gate and down to the cobbled terrace, you can look unhindered over the river as it cuts forcefully between Buda and Pest, and sweeps away around the bend.

Once you've enjoyed the views, turn to the statues. In the first portion of the yard is a fountain (**Fishing Children**, Károly Senyei, 1912) of three children wrestling with an over-sized fish. Beyond it is the vast Neo-Baroque equestrian statue of **Prince Eugene of Savoy** (1663–1736), who led the armies that liberated Hungary from Ottoman rule, forcing the Turks to sign the Treaty of Karlowitz in 1699. The citizens of the town of Zenta (now part of Serbia), scene of the seminal battle in 1697, commissioned this statue by József Róna 200 years later. After they ran out of cash, Ferenc József stepped in to help pay for the work. A relief on the plinth shows the fighting at its thickest. Prince Eugene had attacked Sultan Mustafa II's forces as they crossed the Tisza River, overcoming an army twice the size of his own.

An archway behind the statue leads to another courtyard at the palace's rear. On the left is the bronze **Mátyás Well** (*Mátyás-kút*) created by Alajos Stróbl in 1904. The popular and just Mátyás was fond of donning the clothes of commoners and mingling among his people. As such, he made the ideal subject for a legendary tale of romantic love, recorded originally by his chronicler and then woven into a 19th-century ballad by Mihály Vörösmarty. Here Mátyás is shown with his hunting hounds – all ears and tongues – slaking their thirst in the waterfall below. To the left sits his falcon-bearing chronicler, while to the right is the beautiful peasant girl, Ilonka Szép (Helen the Fair). The poem describes her seeing this handsome huntsman and falling deeply in love; on learning his

## THE TURUL
This mythical bird, resembling an eagle, is said to have sired Árpád's father, Álmos, and thus brought forth the Árpád dynasty. It became a symbol of national identity during the millennial celebrations of 1896. The weapon in its talons is the sword of Attila. While elsewhere in the world he was about as popular as a garlic mouthwash, Attila became a heroic figure in Hungarian cultural consciousness during the 18th century because of theories of an ancestral link between the Huns and the Magyars.

identity, and the impossibility of a match, she dies of a broken heart.

The 'Fresh' (*Friss*) Palace of Zsigmond of Luxembourg probably stood in this courtyard. The area in front was also the scene of medieval tournaments, as well as the execution of László Hunyadi. The theme of the *The Horseherd* (*Csikós*), a 1901 statue by György Vastagh of a Hortobágy herdsman struggling to control his excitable steed, was popular among Neo-Baroque sculptors of the 19th century. To the right of the Mátyás Well is the entrance to the **Lion Courtyard** (*Oroszlános udvar*), guarded by a pair of kingly beasts looking faintly aloof. On the other side of the arch, which is topped by two angels and the Hungarian coat of arms, they roar violently at the temerity of those who have passed between them. A corridor to the right as you pass beneath the arch leads to a small exhibition of artefacts from the castle, together with a written history in English. (Opening hours same as the library; see page 169.) At the courtyard's southern end is the **Budapest History Museum** (Wing E; page 168), accessed via the Telegraph Gate, either side of which are sculptures of war and peace (Károly Senyei, 1900). On the eastern side is Wing D of the **National Gallery** (page 166), and opposite that the **National Széchényi Library** (Wing F; page 169).

Beyond the History Museum are the restored **medieval southern fortifications**, including the Mace Tower (*Buzogánytorony*) and the Great Bastion, as well as the palace gardens. You can descend to the Tabán (page 147) via Ferdinánd Gate, next to the Mace Tower. However, if you wish to explore the rest of the Castle District, retrace your steps and brave the lions, continue northward past the herdsman and his horse – stopping briefly to look down upon the continuing excavations taking place below the courtyard's western side – and exit the complex via the **Corvinus Gate**. On the top of the web-like gate is perched a raven with a ring in its beak – the raven (*corvus* in Latin) was the heraldic symbol of King Mátyás.

## The old town

If the palace is the noble head of the hill, and the prime target of any knockout punch during the epic fights that have taken place here, the **Castle District** (*Várnegyed*) or burghers' town has inevitably suffered the sapping body blows. It has undergone the same cycle of destruction and reconstruction. Little of its medieval Gothic apparel remained after the siege of 1686; the town had to be pulled to its feet and given a fresh Baroque set of clothes. It gained in strength, and during the late 19th century even boasted splendid mansions like Sándor Palace (see opposite), the bowers of preening aristocrats jostling for position beside the newly grandiose main palace. However, the Russian bombardment at the end of World War II brought it to its knees once more. A quarter of the buildings were flattened, and a measly group of just four escaped unscathed.

Nevertheless, the streets still follow their original medieval routes, and the recycling of building materials means that the eagle-eyed will recognise pieces of earlier architectural features – sections of wall, Gothic arches, stone niches, and window and door frames. Furthermore, during the clear-up operation after World War II, many medieval remnants were uncovered, shedding fresh light on the appearance of the district's original buildings, which were elaborately painted in a range of striking colours. Excavation of such early constructions and their foundations are ongoing; for all the pretty restoration, it is in such historical flotsam that the area's violent past is revealed, together with the resilience of the people who kept on piecing it back together.

### Szent György tér

Szent György tér represents a broad breathing space, a place to toss a coin and tilt your cap at the palace to the south or the body of the old town to the north. Spare a thought for the square's prouder past as the site of noble mansions, tucked snug in the shadow of the palace. The stony rubble of some of these buildings can be seen towards the back of the square. The Neoclassical **Sándor Palace** (*nos 1–2*) still stands, immediately to the right of the funicular railway and now the president's official residence. Built in 1806 for Vince Sándor, it even had marble mangers in the stables. It was the scene of Pál Teleki's suicide in 1941. Just months after signing a friendship treaty with Yugoslavia, Admiral Horthy committed Hungary to the Nazi attack on its new 'ally'; his prime minister felt unable to live with the dishonour.

The square once held the **Heinrich Hentzi monument**, erected by Ferenc József I in 1852 as a memorial to the Austrian general who died defending the castle from the Hungarians in 1849. The column struck deep at Hungarian pride and was finally removed in 1899. Oral tradition speaks of a second former landmark here – a tree that once grew at the square's southern end, and was used by the Turks as a gallows from which to hang a captain of the hussars, **Ramocsaházy**. The tree bent under his weight and his toes reached the floor, allowing him to support himself until rescuers arrived. In time he was made Castellan by Emperor Leopold I, and was always careful to look after the failed 'hanging' tree.

The yellow **National Dance Theatre** (page 125) – graced by performers including Haydn and Beethoven – is next to the Sándor Palace. The promenade at the back of Szent György tér is popular with buskers, who entertain strollers heading towards or away from the palace. At the northern end, near the start of Tóth Árpád sétány and the Fehévár Bastion, are the sculptures of a **medieval knight and his herald** by Károly Antal and that of **Artúr Görgey** by László Márton. The latter depicts the young commander of the Hungarian forces that took Buda Castle during the 1848–49 War of Independence.

## Dísz tér

Walking up one of either Szent György utca or Színház utca you will reach Dísz tér and the southern extent of the burghers' town proper. Here it was that market sellers plied their trades during the Middle Ages, and where parades by the palace guards took place in the years after the expulsion of the Turks. Today much of the square is given over to **parking**, and it is the main point of traffic access to the Castle District. At the centre of the square is the **Honvéd statue** by György Zala, cast from cannon metal and erected in 1893 as a memorial to those 'defenders of the homeland' who fought in the 1848–49 War of Independence. Cardinal Angelo Rotta, the Vatican's ambassador, was resident in the building at **numbers 4–5** during World War II, and was credited with saving the lives of many Jews at this sickening time. On the eastern side is a handicrafts market (*open daily 10.00–18.00*) whose inflated prices make it worth avoiding.

Two roads forge away from the top of the square – Úri utca, which hugs the remaining length of the district's western side as far as Kapisztrán tér, and **Tárnok utca**. Take the latter for the moment, with its collection of little shops to keep you interested as you head towards Mátyás Church. Keep an eye out for (but don't bother stopping at) the **Tárnok Café** – difficult to miss, with its swirling red and orange *sgraffitoed* walls – and **Arany Hordó Vendéglő** at numbers 14 and 16 respectively. Their Renaissance exteriors were exposed following damage during World War II.

The **Golden Eagle Pharmacy Museum** (page 168) originally housed the district's first apothecary. In an upper-storey niche of the Neoclassical façade stands a curious painted statuette of the Madonna and child. Its elongated form is reminiscent of the fantastical illustrations of *Alice's Adventures in Wonderland*. Welcome to the glorious, unmistakable world of Margit Kovács. Kovács died in 1977, and is considered Hungary's greatest ceramicist. Moving just beyond the museum, you pass the tiny side street of **Balta köz**. Claustrophobic and darkly romantic, 'Axe Alley' is said to be where the brothers Hunyadi (László and Mátyás) were captured by László V, and where they defended themselves with axes during the violent struggle. Shortly before Tárnok utca emerges into Szentháromság tér you will find a **Tourinform**. Here too is a pick-up point for horse-drawn-carriage rides (*fiáker állomás*).

## Szentháromság tér

We have now reached the highest point of Castle Hill and one of the pouting cover girls of Budapest's picture postcards – the bustling and asymmetrical Szentháromság (Holy Trinity) tér. The Council of Buda erected the Baroque **Trinity Column** (1711–14) on behalf of plague survivors. It was funded in part through a system of fines imposed on naughty citizens found guilty of offences like adultery. Around the column are carved saints who stand as guardians of the city; these are actually replicas – the original sandstone protectors are themselves protected from the elements in the Kiscelli Museum (page 171).

At the northern side of the square stands a **Neo-Gothic palace** (*no 6*) originally constructed in the early 20th century. It served as accommodation for students at the Technical University between 1954 and 1981, many of whom were heavily involved in the 1956 uprising. The Hungarian Culture Foundation owns most of the building, and hosts free arts and technical exhibitions here throughout the year (*open 10.00–16.00 daily*).

The two-storey building with the diminutive green clock tower across from the Burg Hotel is the **former town hall** (*no 2*), constructed by the Italian architect Venerio Ceresola in the late 1600s. A chapel was later added specifically to hold a holy relic – one of the feet of St János the Charitable. Originally a gift to King Mátyás from the Turks, the foot now 'stands' in the church of his name (see page 177). The statue in a niche at the building's corner is Pallas Athene, the 'Protector of Buda'. Above it is a corner balcony, examples of which are most famously found in Györ, with a carved face at its bottom edge that is an eerie mix of lion and man.

A few metres to the west along Szentháromság utca is a horsy **statue by György Vastagh** (1936). The noble animal's green-and-black colouring is broken by its golden 'crown jewels' (ahem!), polished by generations of students who give them a rub for luck. Such superstition is, of course, a load of balls, but at exam time those with imagination may notice a faint smile playing around the stallion's lips. The figure atop is the popular András Hadik (1710–90), a man who rose through the ranks to become a hussar general – and later chairman of the Vienna Military Council, the only Hungarian to reach such dizzy heights under the Habsburgs – and was a favourite of Maria Theresa. The original of the sabre at his side can be seen in the Museum of Military History (page 169). A document bearing the name of every soldier to fall during the life of the Third Royal and Imperial Hussars (1702–1918) lies in a glass case entombed in the statue's pediment.

The square's show stealer, of course, is **Mátyás Church** (page 177). Next to this is the **Fishermen's Bastion** (*Halászbástya*); you might think that its stones are too brightly white and its medieval silhouette too sharp and unworn to have weathered the storms of several centuries – and you'd be correct. It was erected by Frigyes Schulek in 1902 as a purely decorative companion for his church, and stands at the section of the hill supposedly defended in the past by the guild of fishermen. The coned turrets symbolise the tents of the nomadic Magyar tribes.

In front of the bastion is an equestrian **statue of St István**. It was commissioned of Alajos Stróbl at the time of the millenary celebrations, although the great Historicist sculptor took ten years over his masterpiece – he even researched the history of the 11th-century stirrup. The statue is hung with intricately crafted riding regalia, in particular a loose-hanging saddle cloth whose fringes sway when the wind picks up. The altar-like pedestal was designed by Schulek, a man whose fingers were in so many of the square's pies; it is inset with carved reliefs depicting defining moments in the king's reign, including his coronation and his founding of Székesfehérvár Church.

Steps behind the bastion lead down to Hunyadi János út and the Víziváros. Shrouded by trees at the base of these steps is a **statue of Hunyadi** himself (István Tóth, 1903), the Turkish flag at his feet marking his famous victory of 1456 (see page 17).

## Hess András tér

The funnel-shaped square immediately to the north of Szentharomság tér is named after the first printer of Buda who lived here in the 15th century. The Hess press printed the earliest Hungarian book in 1473, the only remaining complete copy of which is in the Széchényi Library (page 169). At the square's centre is a **statue of Pope Innocent XI**, who is known as the 'saviour of Hungary' because of his endeavours in funding the European forces that freed Hungary from Turkish rule. The house behind the statue once held the **Red Hedgehog Inn** (*no 3*) – splendidly christened after the nobleman's coat of arms above its gate. The inn actually hosted the first theatrical performances of Buda in 1760, while the building itself is one of the oldest of the district, dating back to 1390.

The **Budapest Hilton** (*no 1*) is a heady mix of Baroque, Gothic and 20th-century tinted chic. Opened in 1977, it was built on the site of a Dominican church and monastery of 1252 and incorporates the remains of its walls, together with a 15th-century tower and the reconstructed Baroque façade of a 1688 Jesuit college. The tower is topped with a very modern interpretation of a turret; the relief of Mátyás – a copy of one on a gatehouse in Bautzen (Silesia) – is a true likeness of the king. The Dominican courtyard, together with a Renaissance well and monks' gravestones, can be visited by non-guests; concerts are held here (see page 100). Opposite is the **House of Hungarian Wines** (page 130).

## Táncsics Mihály utca and Fortuna utca

From Hess András tér, streets strike out northwards in a two-pronged attack on Bécsi kapu tér. In taking that on the right, **Táncsics Mihály utca**, you follow a curving road of two-storey houses painted from a pretty pallet of fading pastel shades. From the 15th century, this street was the hill's **Jewish quarter**. The Castle District had traditionally been a haven for religious groups. Béla IV granted legal privileges to Hungarian Jews in the 13th century, attracting those suffering from persecution in western European countries.They eventually settled along Táncsics Mihály utca, remaining here throughout the period of Ottoman occupation – indeed, at that time the road was called Zsidó (Jew) utca. There is a **16-century prayer house** at number 26 (page 169).

The arched corridor at **number 7** leads to a beautiful courtyard, with pigmented cobblestones and iron lanterns. The **Baroque mansion** surrounding it was built for Count Erdődy between 1750 and 1769, among whose guests here was Beethoven. Such peaceful areas – to be found nestling behind the house fronts of many of the city's avenues and boulevards, though rarely as stately as this – are simple pleasures that are worth hunting out. Number 9 next door is believed to have been the site of the original royal residence before the monarch's quarters were relocated to the hill's southern end. Much later it was transformed into a barracks whose armoury was used as a **prison** from the early 19th century. Behind the huge gates, still visible today, several prominent anti-Habsburg 'subversives' were confined, including Lajos Kossuth (1837–40) and Mihály Táncsics (1847–48 and 1860). The prison was stormed during the uprising of March 15 1848, and Táncsics was freed and carried through the streets. Jókai, the writer, was also held here in 1863 for a libellous article. There are literary connections at **number 13** too, where the poet Árpád Tóth lived from 1918 and died ten years later. Look out for the carved Turkish head – replete with turban and plump moustache – on the gateway of **number 24**.

The parallel left-hand road from Hess András tér is **Fortuna utca**, which features a sprinkling of shops and galleries selling prints, antique collectibles and curiosities. The street is named after the goddess of fortune, and breaking the duck-blue façade at **number 9** is a white relief of her made by Ferenc Medgyessy in 1921. The goddess

## IGNÁC MARTINOVICS

In the 18th century, Ignác Martinovics juggled life as a monk with shadowy work as a secret agent for Emperor Leopold II, before becoming deeply affected by the revolutionary wave breaking in France. He gathered like-minded Hungarian intellectuals and radicals around him, discussed dark plots of republican uprising and swore a freemasons' oath against the king. Unfortunately for them, the conspiracy was uncovered, and the prime movers executed in 1795 on the Vérmező – 'Field of Blood' – an area of park at the western lower slope of Castle Hill.

certainly appears to have favoured a previous inhabitant of **number 6**, where a large number of 16th-century coins emerged during excavations in the 1930s. Cupid lies lazily above the door, so maybe the householder had love to match. Number 4 holds the **Museum of Commerce and Catering** (page 168). Originally, however, it was the site of the Fortuna Inn, and possibly the late-18th-century meeting place for Martinovics's Jacobin schemers (see box above).

### Bécsi kapu tér

**Bécsi kapu** (Vienna Gate) is the northern entrance to the old town. It has stood in its present incarnation since 1936; its medieval ancestor was reduced to gravel during the 1686 siege. Margit Kovács's **glazed relief** outside depicts a violent assault upon Buda's walls. It is a fitting companion for Ostrom utca – or 'Siege Street' – and for the square it introduces, once site of the medieval Saturday market but later marked as a place of remembrance for those who fell for freedom in 1686.

The bulging side walls and staggered tower of the square's **Lutheran church** were built in 1895 by Mór Kallina. The southern façade has a plaque dedicated to Sztehlo Gábor, a clergyman who saved the lives of thousands of children during World War II. An olive tree grows in his honour in Jerusalem's Grove of the Faithful. Next to the gate is a drab academic in harlequin's headgear – the **National Archives** (*Országos Levéltár; nos 2–4*) building, its sombre stone blocks topped with a majolica-tiled celebration of colour. Raised between 1913 and 1920, its roof betrays its designer – Samu Pecz – who was also responsible for the Big Market Hall (page 131). Outside it is a **bronze statue** by János Pásztor dedicated to Ferenc Kazinczy (1759–1831), leader of the 19th-century language reform movement and later participant in Martinovics's conspiracy. For the latter he was given seven years to mull things over. The olive-green house at **number 7** hosted literary soirées in the 1930s; Thomas Mann is believed to have stayed here.

The fortified **outer walls** were primarily the work of the Turks, who incorporated medieval walls wherever possible. One way of joining these is from Bécsi kapu tér, with access next to the archives building on to a promenade leading around the northern tip of the district. After 100m you will pass the **memorial to Abdurrahman** on the Anjou bástya, a symbolic grave dedicated to the last Turkish governor (pasha) of Buda. He was 70 years old when he was killed in battle, and with this monument the Hungarians honour a heroic adversary. From this point onwards, as you walk beside the chestnut trees that line the path, the Buda Hills are presented in all their splendour, with clutches of houses thinning out in the distance. It is a peaceful and reflective place to watch a day begin or end. Immediately below is the Vérmező, where on May 20 1795 Martinovics and his comrades faced the day's end knowing they would never see another begin.

The entrance to the **Museum of Military History** (page 169) can be found on Tóth Arpád sétány. Also along this western stretch is the **monument of the Second**

**Transylvanian Hussars**, an inter-war interpretation of Leonardo da Vinci's Renaissance horse and rider (as seen in the Museum of Fine Arts; page 167). The promenade leads eventually into Dísz tér.

## Kapisztrán tér

Petermann Biró utca – named after a medieval magistrate (not a ballpoint pen), but for a time following the 1686 siege bearing the pithy title Vér (Blood) utca – carries you westwards from Vienna Gate into Kapisztrán tér. The square is striking for the lonely Gothic tower of the **Church of Mary Magdalene** (page 177). Near the church's skeletal window is one of the enchanting details so typical of this district. A **ghostly blue-robed nun** passes through the walls of the building at Petermann Biró utca 4, her upper body on one side and her feet the other. The figure is a reminder of the 18th-century convent that once stood at Országház utca 28. Next to the **town hall** (*no 1*) at the northern side of the square stands a Neoclassical palace, built as a barracks in 1847. At its entrance are two formidable cannon, one pointing poignantly towards the shell of the church, and signalling that the **Institute and Museum of Military History** (page 169) are now housed inside. Cannon balls are embedded in the façade, signs of the Hungarian army's liberation of the Castle District in 1849. Also here is a **statue of János Kapisztrán** (1386–1456) stepping over the body of a slain Turk. The Italian Franciscan monk fought with his private peasant army alongside János Hunyadi in the famous victory at Nándorfehérvár in 1456, succumbing to the plague shortly afterwards. A fresco in the Mátyás Church (opposite the Loréto Chapel) also commemorates this battle; Kapisztrán actually used the church for a troop-recruitment speech in 1455.

## Országház utca

Országház (Parliament) utca runs between Kapisztrán tér and Szentháromság tér, and is so named because several parliamentary sessions were held in **number 28** at the turn of the 19th century. Before that the building had been the convent of the Order of the Poor Clares, the female arm of the Franciscans. It is now occupied by the Hungarian Academy of Sciences, and joins Úri utca 49 at its rear (home of the Telephone Museum; page 169). There are several Gothic features to be seen on buildings along the street, most obviously extant alcoves or '*sedilia*' set within the openings of gates. Such intriguing architectural characteristics – unique to Hungary – came to light all over the district during post-war excavations and have perplexed boffins ever since. The educated assumption is that they were covered niches for nightwatchmen or for citizens and servants to duck into for rest or shelter. Whatever their purpose, they became canvases for carved decoration and display, as neighbourly peacocks strove to out-strut each other. Among other nuggets to root out is the piece of bread carved on the keystone of **number 17**, which was once the residence of a master baker. The great 19th-century sculptor István Ferenczy lived for a decade at **number 14**. Our favourite house, however, is that in pea green at **number 22**, with its jutting closed balcony and sturdy entrance arch. It once belonged to a master chimney sweep. The present façade dates to 1770.

## Úri utca

Úri utca is the final piece in the district's jigsaw, the only street to last the course through the whole length of the town. Religious devotees once shut themselves away from earthly pleasures in the Franciscan monastery at **number 53**, while the followers of Martinovics were more reluctant detainees here in the 1790s (see box opposite). **Number 49** is linked to number 28 on the parallel Országház utca, and was donated to the Order of the Poor Clares following Buda's liberation from Turkish rule. After József II suppressed the order, the Diet and royal court moved into the buildings. The present wings – bordering a beautiful courtyard – were designed by Franz Anton Hillebrand, who rebuilt the cloister at the end of the 18th century. A century later it served as the Ministry of Interior and the castle exchange.

The 15th-century house at **number 31**, looking down upon its neighbours, provides the only standing evidence that there were once three-floor houses on the hill. There are medieval *sedilia* sunk into the gateway walls at **number 32**. The massive lucky charm that is the Hadik statue (page 142) is at the junction with Szentháromság utca, while further on at **number 19** József Eötvös, the novelist and minister, drew his first breaths in 1813. If you're hoping the district will throw up one last ornamental quirk, you won't be disappointed with the two lions at the corner of **number 13**, resting their shared head on a heraldic shield like a pair of watchful Siamese twins. Finish off with a visit to the dank **cave system** (page 184), and then on to the creamy offerings at **Ruszwurm** (page 115) – the café that has been serving buns to burghers since 1827.

## GELLÉRT HILL, THE TABÁN AND SURROUNDS
### Walking around Gellért Hill
Gellért Hill (*Gellért-hegy*) raised its granite head over 200 million years ago, a craggy henchman to the south of Castle Hill. Water from its bowels feeds the three thermal baths (pages 133–4), while at the top the fortress and monument to freedom represent rather unlikely bedfellows. Inhabited since Neolithic times, transcripts of witch trials during the 17th and 18th centuries reveal that the rock was a favoured gathering place for exponents of the dark arts, and this is also supposedly where the Venetian monk Gellért (see page 16) was martyred.

You are less likely now to encounter witches' spells or falling bishops, but it still takes a certain commitment to brave the 140m on foot. The panoramic views, however, reward any effort. A series of stone steps and sloping paths lead up the southeastern side of the hill (from opposite the Gellért Baths), while there are walkways from the north too. If you'd prefer to have some breath left for the views to take there is a **car park** on Citadella sétány, while **bus 27** (from Móricz Zsigmond körtér) stops 300m below the Citadella (outside the Búsuló Juhász restaurant).

At the Buda foot of **Freedom Bridge** (*Szabadság híd*), **Gellért tér** is a beacon for those hankering after some stylish soaking or a turn-of-the-20th-century flourish to their hotel stay (pages 133 and 102). Freedom Bridge, topped with *turul* birds (see box, page 139), was built for the millennial celebrations and initially bore the name of Ferenc József. While it would be an exaggeration to say that the latter was a key construction worker, he did push a button that activated a hammer that drove the final rivet into the bridge. The rivet was silver and bore his initials; unsurprisingly it was later stolen. A little to the south of the square is the mammoth **Budapest University of Technology and Economics** (*Műegyetem rakpart 1–5*), designed by Alajos Hauszmann. The atrium inside contains a pantheon of the university's famous alumni.

Across the road from the Gellért Baths is the romantic **Cave Church** (page 177) after which you can begin the ascent to the summit. With its 14m poker-straight woman thrusting high above the hill's peak, the **Freedom Monument** is visible from miles around. Finally erected in 1947, it was commissioned originally by Admiral Horthy as a memorial to his son, who had died during a wartime test flight. In an ironic twist, the Russians arrived before the sculpture was complete, and Zsigmond Kisfaludy Stróbl adapted the design to suit his new patrons. A palm frond (instead of the intended propellor) was placed in the hands of the woman, transforming the piece from a personal – if very public – tribute into a political symbol of Russia's role in liberating the city. After the demise of communism, the bronze soldier was moved to Statue Park (page 167), leaving the muscle-bound beast slayer and striding torchbearer to convey an allegorical message shorn of specific historical associations. The plinth's inscription now reads 'In memory of all of those who sacrificed their lives for Hungary's independence, freedom and prosperity'. Next to the monument is the imposing **Citadella** (page 177).

A little further down the hill's northern end, Gellért (or 'Gerard') flourishes a cross above the traffic passing back and forth over Elizabeth Bridge. A waterfall flows beneath **Gyula Jankovics's statue** of 1904, and a walkway – guarded by a pair of *turul* birds – begins directly below it. It is said that at this point in 1046 the bishop took a more direct and less leisurely trip down the hill in a barrel full of spikes. The Italian missionary had been appointed Bishop of Csanád by King István, before becoming the country's first Christian martyr during the power struggle and pagan backlash that followed the monarch's death.

A short walk to the northwest of the Citadella, near the junction of Orom utca and Sánc utca, is a grassed area. In the **Garden of Philosophy**, bronze statues of history's great religious figures form a circle of spiritual unity around a marble-floored fountain. Fifty metres away is one of our favourite public sculptures, a chunky **landscape of Budapest**. Symbolic of the marriage of the city's two sides, the kingly Buda reaches across to his bride on the other side of the Danube.

## The Tabán

Plugging the gap between the two hills on the river's bank is the Tabán, an area of grass, a large traffic junction and two of the city's thermal spas. In summer it is the site of al-fresco concerts, while sledding and snowballs are popular during the snowy season. In Turkish times, foreign artisans set up shop here, and in the 18th century a village was built by Serbian (Rác) settlers. It became a lively place, with many restaurants and bars, but in 1933 the bulk of the single-storey houses were demolished for hygiene reasons (open sewers and diseased grape vines). Just outside it, on the lower southeastern slope of Castle Hill, is the zigzagging ceremonial pathway of the **Várkert-bazár**. It's in a sorry state now but in its heyday this was a splendid pleasure garden designed by Miklós Ybl in 1872. A **statue of Ybl** (1814–91) stands near the **Várkert Casino** (page 127), which was originally constructed as an engine house to power the palace's water-supply system, and was also Ybl's work. Near by too is the **birthplace of Ignác Semmelweis** (see page 170).

The provincial-looking **Parish Church of the Tabán** presents its lopsided self in Szarvas tér. Built in the 18th century, it was preceded by a Turkish mosque; the western tower was added by the architect Máté Nepauer. Immediately to the north of Elizabeth Bridge is the pedestrianised Döbrentei tér, its paths leading away underneath the busy flyover that circles overhead. Here sits a **youthful Erzsébet** (1837–98), fondly sculpted in a flowing gown with roses lying beside her. She was a popular queen who made determined efforts to engage with the Hungarian people, and her assassination by an Italian anarchist was met with genuine sadness. A statue of the ultra-right-wing politician **Gyula Gömbös** (1886–1936), who allied Hungary to the Nazi cause, once occupied this spot; it was destroyed by communist resistance fighters during the war. (There's still a small plaque to him in the grass, usually defaced with black paint.) Underneath the bridge is a **drinking market** (page 135), while on the southern side are the **Rudas Baths** (page 134). The **Rác Baths** (page 134) are a short distance to the west of Döbrentei tér.

**Nine statues** – grim-faced toughs with axes in hand – stand with Dózsa György tér at their backs and the rear of Buda Palace looming above. They represent participants in the peasant uprising of 1514 (see page 17), and were sculpted in 1961 by István Kiss.

## The surrounds

From Gellért tér, Bartók Béla út strikes out through Móricz Zsigmond körtér, the primary traffic junction of southern Buda. When Bartók died in New York in 1945, his will decreed that no place in Budapest should be named after him so long as there were still places like Hitler tér (now Kodály körönd) and Mussolini tér (now Oktogon). As a result, with the demise of Nazism at the end of World War II, the city decided to rename Horthy Miklós út (this one) after their famous Hungarian composer, together with eight other streets around Budapest. On its way towards the city's southwestern suburbs, Bartók Béla út passes **Feneketlen-tó** ('Bottomless Lake'), something of a leafy respite from the traffic arteries around it. The pretty lake is bordered with rushes and gravelled walkways, as well as an open-air theatre (page 121). The sandy, twin-towered **Cistercian church** (*Villányi út 23–25*) stands just outside the park's northern boundary, built in 1938 for the growing population of Lágymányos district. Outside is a large **statue of Count Klebelsberg Kuno** (1875–1932), a prominent interwar minister of religion and education. As well as several buses, trams run from Deák Ferenc tér (49), Batthyány tér (19) and Moszkva tér (61) to the nearby Kosztolányi Dezső tér.

## MOSZKVA TÉR

Moscow Square, a short distance to the north of the Castle District, is Buda's main transport junction, and as such a portal for getting elsewhere rather than a place of interest in itself. It's gritty and fume-filled, and an early-morning congregation point for black-market workers after labour. The turreted building to the west is a **post office** (its entrance at Krisztina körut 6), while **Mammut** shopping mall is a few short steps away (page 133). Also near by is the **Millennium Park** (*Millenáris Park; II, Lövőház utca 37; www.millenaris.hu*), a sterile modern recreation area based around an artificial lake. Among the entertainments for children are a plastic 'ice-skating' rink and a wooden fort, while two industrial buildings have been converted into spaces for exhibitions, concerts and dance performances (*Tánc és Színház a Millenáris; Fény utca 20–22;* ❧ 1 438 5335). For further information, see page 124.

## WALKING THE VÍZIVÁROS

The Víziváros (Water Town) squeezes between Castle Hill and the Danube, before breathing out and filling the space northward to Margit híd and westward to Moszkva tér. The main street (Fő utca) follows the route of a Roman road that linked the hill and Aquincum, and retains a healthy dash of old-world romance. In the years prior to the Turkish occupation, fishermen and artisans dwelt here; today it offers a straight-lined, uncomplicated walk between the Chain and Margit bridges. If you do it one way, choose Fő utca; if you have the stamina for a return journey, walk back along the parallel Bem rakpart next to the river.

Start at **Clark Ádám tér**, named after the 19th-century Scottish engineer who constructed both Széchenyi Lánchíd (the Chain Bridge) and the **tunnel** through the hill that connects the city centre with the western parts of Buda. The tunnel is 350m long, large enough, it is said, to accommodate the beautiful bridge in bad weather. The **Chain Bridge** itself was designed by Englishman William Tierney Clark (think Hammersmith Bridge), replacing a pontoon that had to be dismantled with the arrival of winter's ice. In December 1820, István Széchenyi was called to Buda on learning of the death of his father; however, the bridge was down, he could find no ferryman willing to navigate the drifting chunks of ice, and he very nearly missed the funeral. He campaigned thereafter for a permanent structure; it was finally opened in 1849, although Széchenyi himself was by then incarcerated in a mental asylum.

Another member of the Széchenyi clan, István's son Ödön, suggested the construction of the **funicular railway** (page 137) that trundles a 45° course up Castle Hill. It was built in 1870, and reconstructed after being smashed during World War II. Near the lower terminus is an oval-shaped monument – the **zero-kilometre stone** – from which distance markers along Hungary's main roads are measured. The sculptor intended to represent 'the birth of distance', which is why it resembles a woman's birth-giving parts.

---

**BEASTLY MOUTHS**

Take note of the four lions guarding the abutments of the Chain Bridge. Sculptor János Marschalkó was so proud of them that he challenged anybody to find fault; at the inauguration ceremony, an apprentice is reputed to have loudly criticised the fact that the lions appeared to be tongueless; Marschalkó threw himself into the river in frustration. He later wrote several articles defending his animals, pointing out that lions do not loll their tongues like dogs. He also responded to one critic by sniping 'Would that your wife had such a tongue as my lions!'

---

**Fő utca** straddles districts I and II, carrying you north of Clark Ádám tér as far as Bem József tér. Some buildings appear sunk into the surface – at the end of the 19th century the street level was raised by over a metre to reduce its vulnerability to flooding. Immediately on the right, at **number 1**, is a central court building designed by Miklós Ybl in 1867–69. The building of the District I **cultural centre** (*Fő utca 11–13*) was built in 1880 for Count Gyula Andrássy; a team of Polish doctors was killed here during fighting on March 19 1944. The **French Institute** is at Fő utca 17, while György Békesy (1899–1972), the Nobel Prize-winning scientist, lived and worked at **number 19** until 1946.

The **church** at the south side of **Corvin tér** (*Fő utca 30–32*) was originally constructed in the medieval period, used as a mosque during the Ottoman occupation (note the Turkish *ogee*-arched door in the southern wall) and then as a Capuchin monastery in the 18th century. A statue of St Erzsébet gazes down from high above the entrance. At the square's north is the faded but splendid **Buda Vigadó** (*Corvin tér 8*), built in 1900 and home of the Hungarian State Folk Ensemble and Civil Rádió.

You'll emerge for a few paces before disappearing into **Szilágyi Dezső tér**. The Hungarian-Indian artist Amrita Sher-Gil (1913–1941) was born at **number 4**, a house that Béla Bartók called home in the 1920s. Opposite stands the red-brick Neo-Gothic **Calvinist church**, with a slender steeple – the tallest in Buda – and a roof adorned with ceramic Zsolnay tiles. A pint-sized statue of Samu Pecz, who clearly enjoyed playing with geometry in constructing the church in 1893–96, stands outside dressed in the garb of a medieval master builder. On the river bank is a memorial to the March 15 1848 revolution, bearing the message 'Steadfastly for your homeland'. It was at this place that the Arrow Cross murdered hundreds of Jews in 1945, dumping their bodies in the water.

**Batthyány tér** contains the Baroque **St Anna Parish Church** (1740–62), twin clock-towered, dressed in gold and white and adorned with God's all-seeing eye. The church wasn't actually consecrated until 1805 because the finishing touches were hampered by an earthquake. Organ concerts are held inside (*ticket info* ✆ 1 317 2754). On the northern side of the square is a **former hospital** run by Elizabethan nuns; a statue in front depicts Ferenc Kölcsey (1790–1838), the bald-headed Romantic poet who composed the Hungarian national anthem 'Hymn' ('*Himnusz*'). The adjacent pastel-blue **Church of the Elizabethan Nuns** (*Fő utca 41–43*) was built on the site of a Turkish mosque in 1731–57 by Jakab Hans, and has a rich Baroque interior. Two centuries ago, the **Casanova Bar** (page 118) was the White Cross Inn, where the serial seducer Giovanni Jacopo Casanova is meant to have stayed while taking the Buda water cure. The high-pitched pop singer Jimmy Zámbó (who accidentally shot himself at a New Year's party in Csepel in 2001) began his musical career at the Casanova. Batthyány tér is served by both the metro (M2) and the HÉV, while tram 19 terminates here.

Cross Csalogány utca, spare a glance for the **Socialist-Constructivist relief** at Fő utca 68 – depicting three masons struggling with a block of stone – and join **Nagy Imre tér**. Nagy was leader of the government during the 1956 revolution; it was in the midst of the intimidating symmetry of the **military court and prison** building (*Fő utca 70–78*) to the square's north and northwest that he was sentenced to death two years later. Luckier was Attila Ambrus, the 'Whisky Robber', who in 1999 escaped from an upper storey with a rope he'd fashioned from bed sheets.

Just beyond the junction with Kacsa utca are the **Király Baths** (page 134), while on the other side of Ganz utca is the **Chapel of St Flórián** (*Fő utca 88*). This tiny church – as yellow as egg yolk, and with just eight pews either side of a golden altar – was built in 1759–60 and later given to the Greek Catholics. After the raising of Fő utca, the church's portico slipped over a metre below street level; in the 1930s the church was itself lifted by 1.4m to minimise future flood damage.

Fő utca culminates at **Bem József tér**. The Polish General Bem József, known as 'Papa' (Apó), fought with the Hungarians in the 1848 revolution, scoring victories over Austrian and Russian armies in Transylvania. Bem fled to Turkey after the collapse of the uprising, and died in 1854 bearing the name Amarut Pasha after converting to Islam. The statue in the centre commemorates the 1849 Battle of Piski – 'I will take this bridge or I will die. Go Hungarians!' – and was a rallying point for students during the 1956 revolution, when the Russian hammer and sickle was cut from the Hungarian flag (creating a gaping touchstone of the revolutionary cause).

From here you can visit the **Foundry Museum** (page 171) on Bem József utca, which leads away from the square's southwestern corner, while the Rózsadomb and **tomb of Gül Baba** (page 178) are a short but steep walk away. Alternatively make your way back along the river on **Bem rakpart**, running the gauntlet of speeding cyclists and enjoying the views of Parliament on the opposite bank.

## ÓBUDA, AQUINCUM AND THE RÓMAI-PART

The primary concentration of ancient history is to be found in Óbuda (Old Buda), which became 'old' in the 13th century when Béla IV shifted the centre of the region's power to Castle Hill. Two millennia ago the area was occupied by Celts and then Romans. The Danube represented the eastern boundary of the Roman empire; Flórián tér was the site of a camp supporting 6,000 legionnaires, while to its north was a civilian settlement called Aquincum. The sites of interest are scattered between – and even sheltered beneath – highways and 1960s residential blocks, and as such it is best to move about by **public transport** if you want to avoid long treks through concrete jungle. You can travel here on bus 86 or tram 1 (over Árpád híd), but the HÉV suburban railway provides the simplest route; pick it up from Batthyány tér or Margit híd.

Alight at Timár út and walk eastwards to the corner of Nagyszombat utca and Pacsirtamező utca where you'll find a 2nd-century **military amphitheatre**. Holding 15,000 spectators, this was the largest of its type north of the Mediterranean; here gladiators fought with beasts or took part in naval battles in the flooded arena. North up Pacsirtamező utca is **Flórián tér**, straddling the western bridgehead of Árpád híd, and for the most part a monument to bleak 20th-century modernity with its roaring road and pre-fab buildings. There's a slight respite to the square's southeastern side, where stands the **Parish Church of SS Peter Paul** (*Lajos utca 168*), erected by the Zichy family (that owned much of Óbuda) in 1744–49. A stone's throw away is a **Neoclassical synagogue** (*Lajos utca 163*) designed by András Landherr in 1820–21, and boasting imposing pillars beneath its portico. There was a ghetto here during the war; it now houses a Hungarian television studio.

Duck under the Szentendrei út flyover and you'll enter a subway like no other, an unexpected trove of Roman ruins. These were the **legionary baths**, excavated in 1778, and the tiled heating courses are still evident. A few hundred metres east along Kórház utca is the former market place and present-day haven of **Fő tér** (behind Árpád híd station in Szentlélek tér). This pretty cobbled square contains a daffodil-yellow **town**

**hall** (*Fő tér 3*) at its northern side, with a little balcony and acorn finials, while on the eastern edge is the 18th-century **Zichy Palace**. Inside its Baroque wings, and those of an adjacent Trinitarian monastery, are the **Óbuda History Museum**, and collections of works by **Lajos Kassák** and **Victor Vasarely** (page 170). Pass out of the square's northeastern corner (*Laktanya utca*) and take a photo with the four ladies strolling towards you beneath their umbrellas. Imre Varga's intriguing sculpture is a taster for the fabulous exhibition of his layered and polished metal works near by (page 168).

There are mosaics a short walk north of Flórián tér at **Hercules Villa** (page 170), but head for **Aquincum** for the real orgy of Roman ruins. Take the HÉV to the Aquincum stop and you'll be at the heart of what became the principal town of the province of Pannonia Inferior until the soldiers (and consequently the civilians too) pulled out in AD404. It was established as the base for those civilians associated with the military camp 3km to the south, but quickly became a major administrative and commercial centre in its own right, with an amphitheatre, law courts, baths and temples. Walk across the road to the Neoclassical **museum** (page 170), which makes sense of the stone lines and piles, and displays other archaeological finds.

Go 1km north – or board the HÉV once more – to **Római-fürdő**, where you'll see the remains of the civilian amphitheatre and an aqueduct (which carried water through Aquincum and on as far as the military amphitheatre), and where there is an eponymous strand (page 134) on the site of original Roman baths. There is another swimming pool set in park land at **Csillaghegy** (page 133), one stop further on. Alternatively, walk east towards the river and the **Római-part** (Roman bank). This stretch of river is popular for cycling, canoeing and fishing, and has a resort feel to it in summer months. The small shacks and al-fresco tables are lively places in the evenings; take a pew and relish some of the tastiest fish you'll find in Hungary. The woody riverside is popular with mosquitoes too, so bring repellent. In summer, a ferry (*Mar 1–Sep 1;* ☎ *1 369 1359; www.ship-bp.hu*) runs between the Római-part, Boráros tér and Jászai tér.

## BUDA HILLS AND BEYOND

With the exception of Pest's downtown, districts II and XII in the Buda Hills hold the city's most desirable residences. There are some stunning detached houses, and these leafy suburbs are where the rich and famous choose to settle. Even the president and prime minister have homes here. For tourists and workers sweating away in the streets of the Belváros, the hills – running in a semi-circle around the western edge of Buda – promise a little space and a cooling breeze. There are walking trails, cycling routes and viewing towers, conservation areas and a wildlife park, caves and quarries and birds and boars. This is where nature lives. The main mode of public transport is the bus, but there are also cogwheel and children's railways, and even a chairlift. For details of all these, see *Natural Budapest*, page 182. In addition, there are a few interesting museums to visit, both among the hills themselves (the **Bártók Béla Memorial House** and the **Kiscelli Museum**; pages 170–1) and a little further out (**Statue Park** and the **Nagytétény Castle Museum**; pages 167 and 171). And don't miss **Wolf's Meadow Cemetery** (page 179).

# Discovering Pest and the islands
## WALKING THE DOWNTOWN

The downtown (District V) is Pest's beating heart, a gathering point for the city's shopping, commercial, banking and tourist centres. The bulk of the Belváros (inner city) portion is hemmed in by the Kiskörút (Small Boulevard), a near semi-circle of road running from Freedom Bridge along the original lines of the medieval walls (dismantled during 19th-century expansion) before becoming a little ragged on its way to the Chain Bridge. It is lanced by Kossuth Lajos utca, running from Erzsébet híd out to Keleti station.

The Lipótváros (Leopold Town) north of József Attila utca holds two of the country's most significant buildings in the Parliament and St István Basilica. The tracks of tram 2 run alongside the Danube and circle the Parliament, offering views to rival those from public transport anywhere in Europe. Moving in from the tracks, though, the downtown is a compact area of one-way or pedestrianised roads that's best explored on foot.

## Belváros

There's no simple way of tackling the inner city – the chances are that you will start somewhere in the vicinity of Váci utca and dive off into those squares and side streets that take your fancy. No single linear walk properly covers the sights of interest; we've divided it into two chunks, south and north of Erzsébet híd. Pick and mix your way around.

### The southern half

At the southern end of the inner city is **Szabadság híd** (page 146), spanning the river to Gellért Hill. The grimy-bricked building near the bridgehead – actually falling on the Ferencváros side of the road (page 163) – was originally a customs house designed by Miklós Ybl, but has served as the **Budapest University of Economic Sciences** (*Fővám tér 8*) since the mid 20th century. Next to it is the cleaner, magnificent **Big Market Hall** (page 131).

Vámház körút leads in an easterly direction around to **Kálvin tér**, a busy square rather dominated by the glass building of the Erste Bank. The white Neoclassical **Calvinist Church** was built by József Hofrichter and József Hild (1813–51), while the sandy building (*Kálvin tér 9*) next to it – now holding a café and flower shop – was once the **Two Lions Inn** (see the weather-worn beasts above the doorway). Hector Berlioz first heard the 'Rákóczi March' while staying here – originally used to recruit freedom fighters to the anti-Habsburg cause in the early 1700s. Berlioz drew from the song in composing his own version over a century later. One of the **medieval gates** through the city walls stood at Kálvin tér; you can see a surviving piece of the wall itself on nearby Bástya utca, embedded in the northern side of the Jazz Garden (page 124). Branching southeast from the square (further into Ferencváros) is **Ráday utca** (page 119), a rising star on the city's drinking circuit.

If you follow the Small Boulevard northwards you'll join **Múzeum körút**, with a cluster of shops hawking antique books, maps and coins. Addresses on the opposite side of the road actually have a District VIII postcode (page 161), and these include the **Hungarian National Museum** (pages 167–8). The museum is difficult to miss – it's the largest in the country – and you certainly shouldn't because it holds the Hungarian coronation mantle and some breathtaking ceiling frescoes. It was from the museum steps that Petőfi's 'National Song' was recited at the outset of the 1848 revolution, and from the **Radio station** on the adjacent Bródy Sándor utca that secret police fired the opening salvos at student demonstrators during the revolution of 1956. A little further on, just before the Astoria junction where Kossuth Lajos utca meets the boulevard, is the faculty of arts of the prestigious **ELTE University** (*Eötvös Loránd Tudományos-egyetem; Múzeum körút 4–8*); designed by Imre Steindl, this was once the department of natural sciences and *alma mater* of Ede Teller, inventor of the hydrogen bomb.

Cross the road and head back towards the depths of the inner city along Ferenczy István utca to **Károlyi kert**. This was a private garden belonging to the palace behind it, once home of Mihály Károlyi, the president of the 1918–19 Hungarian Republic. During the mid 19th century, the notorious Baron Haynau (see page 19) took the place as his headquarters after crushing the 1848 revolution, and from here dictated those vengeful measures designed to dampen future thoughts of rebellion. It is now the headquarters of the **Petőfi Literary Museum** (page 172). (There's a further tribute to literature past at the **Ady Endre Memorial Museum** – page 171 – on the parallel Veres Pálné utca.)

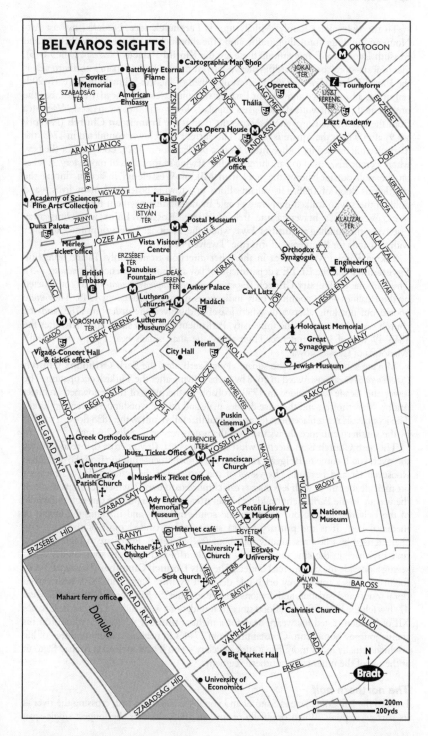

# BELVÁROS SIGHTS

Cartographia Map Shop

Soviet Memorial

Batthyány Eternal Flame

SZABADSÁG TÉR

American Embassy

JÓKAI TÉR

OKTOGON

Operetta

Tourinform

Thália

LISZT FERENC TÉR

Liszt Academy

ZICHY JENŐ

HAJÓS

NAGYMEZŐ

ANDRÁSSY

KIRÁLY

ERZSÉBET

DOB

State Opera House

LÁZÁR

RÉVAY

ARANY JÁNOS

OKTÓBER 6

SAS

Ticket office

KERTÉSZ

VIGYÁZÓ F

Basilica

Academy of Sciences, Fine Arts Collection

SZÉNT ISTVÁN TÉR

Postal Museum

PAULAY E

AKÁCFA

KLAUZÁL TÉR

ZRINYI

Duna Palota

Mérleg ticket office

JÓZEF ATTILA

Vista Visitor Centre

KIRÁLY

KAZINCZY

Orthodox Synagogue

Engineering Museum

NYÁR

KLAUZÁL

British Embassy

VÁCI

ERZSÉBET TÉR

Danubius Fountain

DEÁK FERENC TÉR

Anker Palace

Carl Lutz

DOB

WESSELÉNYI

Lutheran church

Lutheran Museum

Madách

VÖRÖSMARTY TÉR

DEÁK FERENC

SÜTŐ

City Hall

Merlin

KÁROLY

Holocaust Memorial

Great Synagogue

DOHÁNY

Vigadó Concert Hall & ticket office

VIGADÓ

JÁNOS

RÉGI POSTA

PETŐFI

GERLÓCZY

SEMMELWEIS

RÁKÓCZI

Jewish Museum

Puskin (cinema)

Greek Orthodox Church

FERENCIEK TERE

KOSSUTH LAJOS

MAGYAR

Ibusz, Ticket Office

Franciscan Church

Contra Aquincum

Inner City Parish Church

Music Mix Ticket Office

SZABAD SAJTÓ

Ady Endre Memorial Museum

KÁROLYI M

Petőfi Literary Museum

MÚZEUM

BRÓDY S

National Museum

IRÁNYI

Internet café

EGYETEM TÉR

St Michael's Church

NYÁRY PÁL

University Church

Eötvös University

ERZSÉBET HÍD

Serb church

VERES PÁLNÉ

SZERB

KÁLVIN TÉR

BAROSS

Mahart ferry office

BELGRÁD RKP

Danube

BASTYA

VÁCI

Calvinist Church

ÚLLŐI

RADAY

VÁMHÁZ

Big Market Hall

ERKEL

University of Economics

SZABADSÁG HÍD

N

Bradt

0 ————— 200m
0 ————— 200yds

To the right along Károlyi Mihály utca is **Ferenciek tere**, bordered by vast Art-Nouveau buildings funnelling traffic along the thoroughfare between Erszébet híd and Kossuth Lajos utca. Prime among these are the **Klotild Palaces** (*Szabadsajtó út 5 & 6*), identical six-storey twins guarding the western entrance. On the square's northern side is the **Párisi Udvar** (*Ferenciek tere 5*), commissioned of Henrik Schmahl in the early 20th century as a bank office and elegant Parisian shopping arcade. Its heyday is past, but the ornamented interior with stained-glass cupola is lovely still. (You can access Váci utca from the arcade, via Kigyó utca.) Across the road is the **Franciscan Church** (*Ferenciek tere 9*) after which the square is named. The current church was completed in 1743, the Turks having trashed its 13th-century Gothic predecessor in 1526. Look out for the pew where Ferenc Liszt used to park himself while staying in the adjacent monastery. A relief on the wall outside shows the nobleman **Miklós Wesselényi** in action during the murderous flood of 1838. His valiant efforts in a rowing boat saved many lives – and unlike others who milked desperate people by demanding payment for access to their boats, Wesselényi's bravery came free of charge. **Kossuth Lajos utca** runs away eastwards; the building at **number 3** was where the 'National Song' was printed, together with demands for bourgeois reform (the 'Twelve Points').

Taking Károlyi Mihaly utca in the other direction from Károlyi Palace brings up **Egyetem tér** and the **ELTE**'s departments of law and political science (*Egyetem tér 1–3*). The Baroque **University Church** (*Egyetemi templom; Papnövelde utca 9*) was constructed by the Paulines – the country's only indigenous monastic order – in 1748. They were booted out not long afterwards when József II dissolved the orders in 1782, and the church was taken over by the university. Parliament met for a short time here after the 1848–49 War of Independence. High above the altar, angels bear a copy of Poland's 'Madonna of Czestochowa'.

Moving southwest from the square along Szerb utca, the **Serb Orthodox Church** (*Szerb utca 6*) was constructed in 1698 by Serbs arriving after the Turkish occupation. The tower and façade were added in 1750, probably to the plans of the renowned architect András Mayerhoffer, and the nave divides male and female worshippers over two levels. The iconostasis is a replacement for an original that fell victim to the 1838 flood; a marker by the southern entrance shows the level the waters reached – fully 2m high.

The Serb Church is an incense whiff from Váci utca. (If you cross that road towards the river, you'll come to **Belgrád rakpart**, the embankment running from Fővám tér to Roosevelt tér and beyond. The views of the castle over the water make it a pleasant promenade, but those with less energy can climb aboard tram 2, which accompanies it all the way up to the Parliament building.) **Váci utca** is the vein pulsing through the whole of the Belváros, linking our northern and southern halves and marking the length of medieval Pest. It is the primary tourist street, pedestrianised most of the way, and characterised by cafés, restaurants and shops (see *Shopping*). Prices are as high as you'll find anywhere in the city, but it's busy and colourful and there are some sights worth seeing alongside the commercial outlets. The **City Council Chamber** (*Váci utca 62–64*), for instance, is a four-storey brick pile designed by Imre Steindl in 1870, with carved floral motifs and garlands, and dragons on its upper tier. **St Michael's Church** (*Váci utca 47*) has felt the lick of fire and flood since its foundations were laid in 1703, while Charles XII of Sweden rested his weary head for a night at **number 43** (now a school) on his frantic journey home from Constantinople in 1714. On meeting a sculptural tree of life – which actually looks more like a stick of celery – you'll have arrived at Szabad Sajtó út at the top of the inner city's southern segment.

## The northern half

Look to the left along Szabad Sajtó út and you'll see **Erzsébet híd**, crossing the river at its narrowest point. When originally opened in 1903, this was the longest single-span chain bridge in the world (at 380m). Destroyed by the retreating Germans in 1945, it was the last of Budapest's bridges to be replaced and – with its new cable design – the only one not restored to its former shape. A significant slice of medieval architecture was sacrificed to make way for the bridge, and the wrecking ball whistled past the left cheek of the **Inner City Parish Church** (page 179). In front of the church in **Március 15 tér** are remains of **Contra-Aquincum**, a 3rd-century fort built by the Romans to protect their settlement on the other side of the river.

Duck under the subway to continue on Váci utca, which leads uninterrupted to Vörösmarty tér. If you take the direct route, keep your eyes peeled for the intricate blue façade of **Thonet House** at number 11, designed in 1888 by Ödön Lechner ('the father of Hungarian Art Nouveau'); the former **Inn of the Seven Electors** (*Váci utca 9*; now the Pesti Színház), where Liszt gave a performance in 1823 at the tender age of just 11; the well in Kristóf tér bearing a statue of the *Fisher Girl*; and the jagged line of marble cobblestones just a little further on, which traces the position of the northern medieval **Vác Gate** before it was removed in 1789.

Alternatively, take a slight detour left into Régi posta utca, looking up to the painted relief of a stagecoach by ceramicist Margit Kovács on the building at **number 13**. When the McDonalds opposite opened in 1989, it was the first in the country and attracted a lengthy queue of locals; it's now just one of 13 in Budapest alone. At the end of the street you'll emerge into **Petőfi tér**, a favoured rallying point for both protest and celebration. The cloaked and goateed statue at the centre is Sándor Petőfi (see box in *Kiskőrös* section, page 342), around which students gathered to denounce the Rákosi regime on October 23 1956. The **Greek Orthodox Church** was built by 18th-century Greek and Macedonian merchants; one of its two towers was destroyed in World War II and never replaced.

Move northwards along the Duna-korzó to **Vigadó tér**, a riverside eating and drinking spot. On the railings next to the tram track sits the harlequinesque *Little Princess* (Marton László, 1989). The square takes its name, however, from the flamboyant **concert hall** (see page 123) at the eastern side. The promenade continues on to the Chain Bridge and Roosevelt tér, but we'll take a right down Vigadó utca to the side of the concert hall and on to **Vörösmarty tér**. It is broad and elegant, filled with portraitists and plane trees, with seasonal markets and performances of folk music. At its centre the poet **Mihály Vörösmarty** rests his pins; the opening line of 'Szózat' ('Admonition'), an appeal in 1836 for Hungarian unity, is inscribed on the statue's plinth – 'Be steadfastly faithful to your homeland, oh Magyars'. During winter the lucky chap surveys the world from inside a heated plastic bubble, designed to prevent his marble cracking. At the square's northern side is the celebrated **Gerbeaud** (page 116), while next to that is the western terminus of the city's **oldest metro** line. To the south is the Bank Palace of 1915, now holding the **Budapest Stock Exchange**.

Southeast of Vörösmarty tér is **Szervita tér**, which used to belong to the Order of Servites whose Baroque church was consecrated in 1748. The relief above the portal's pediment depicts the order's founding saints – Julianna on the right and Peregrin (the patron saint of leg-pain sufferers) on the left. The square's three **Art-Nouveau façades** are wonderful, particularly Miksa Róth's allegorical mosaic of Hungary at number 3. **Petőfi Sándor utca**, a shopping street, leads south from the square, as does **Városház utca**. The latter is dominated by the salmon-pink and custard-yellow **City Hall** at 9–11, originally built in the 18th century to house disabled soldiers, Budapest's biggest Baroque building and thought by Maria Theresa to better her own palace in Vienna.

North of Vörösmarty tér, **József nádor tér** is bordered by heavy Neoclassical residences and the magnificent **Postabank Headquarters** (1860–61), which fills the entire western side. At the square's centre is a statue of Archduke József, the Habsburg palatine for 50 years from 1797. As palatines went, he was relatively popular in Pest; he loved the city, and made determined efforts to improve it – he was, for instance, the instigator for the planting of its greatest parks (at Margaret Island and City Park). **Erzsébet tér** was originally earmarked for the National Theatre before monumental squabbles put a halt to proceedings (see page 121). A modern park, with a glass-bottomed pool, has opened in its stead, with a car park and cultural and conference centre beneath. The square's bus terminal has now moved to Népliget, but some coach tours still depart from here. The **Danubius Fountain** is a replacement for a 19th-century original (Miklós Ybl and Leó Feszler, 1880–83) destroyed in World War II; its broad bowls are topped by an allegory of the Danube, with its half-naked tributaries seated around the base. Look out too for the statue of the shepherd piping to his sheep at the square's northern edge.

**Deák Ferenc tér** meets at the east, but feels more properly a part of bustling Pest. The simple **Lutheran church** was designed at the turn of the 19th century by Mihály Pollock; the sons of Lajos Kossuth were baptised inside, and Sándor Petőfi was schooled here. The **Lutheran Museum** (page 171) is next door, while the **Underground Railway Museum** (page 172) in the station underpass tells the story of the continent's oldest metro line, one of several ambitious constructions built as part of the millennial celebrations. The beige and fading **Anker Palace** (*Deák Ferenc tér 6*), with its helmet turrets, was an insurance building that many felt a blight on the cityscape when it first appeared. It now contains a series of shops.

## Lipótváros and beyond

The area north of József Attila utca is known as Leopold Town, which developed following the construction of the Chain Bridge. It is still part of District V but a world away from the Belváros; colourful side streets make way for straight roads and broad squares, and shops and cafés for offices and 19th-century residential blocks. It feels a more serious place, one of industrious commerce and government, and holds pockets that resonate strongly with some of the city's tragic moments.

Start with the elliptical **Roosevelt tér** at the foot of the Chain Bridge. The grassed island in the centre was the site of **Coronation Hill**, a mound of soil gathered from points all over Hungary. Following the 1867 Compromise and the crowning of Ferenc József in Mátyás Church, Hungary's new king clambered the hillock, pointed to the four compass points with St István's sword, and pledged to be the country's defender – a symbolic act that harked back to pagan clan ceremonies. There was significant controversy when the **Four Seasons Hotel** (page 100) constructed its car park underneath. The hotel itself has finally opened in the renovated Art-Nouveau Gresham Palace, originally built for an English insurance company. There are statues to Ferenc Deák, the architect of the Compromise, and István Széchenyi, who made possible the **Hungarian Academy of Sciences** (*Roosevelt tér 9*) at the square's northern side. In 1825 the count donated a year's income to the founding of the society in this Neo-Renaissance palace. When asked how he'd live for a year with no money, Széchenyi replied 'My friends will help me'.

Zrínyi utca leads eastwards as far as **Szent István tér**, a pedestrianised space that seems rather undersized in the presence of the looming **Basilica** (page 181). Behind it is Bajcsy-Zsilinszky út – named after a politician who stood up to the Nazis and was executed for it in 1944 – which links Deák tér to Nyugati tér; the latter holds the iron-and-glass **Western Railway Station** (*Nyugati pályaudvar*), built by Gustave Eiffel's firm (1874–77). Adjacent is 'the world's most beautiful McDonald's', and to the rear the WestEnd City Center shopping mall (page 133).

If, instead of going east, you follow Széchenyi rakpart north from Roosevelt tér, you'll arrive at **Kossuth Lajos tér**. Imre Steindl was victorious in the competition to build **Parliament**, and his vision stands overlooking the river on the western side (page 181). Remarkably, however, the second- and third-placed entries were also constructed, becoming the Palace of Justice (*no 12*, now the **Museum of Ethnography**; page 171)

## KOSSUTH LAJOS

You know you've made it when streets in more than one continent are named after you and your face smiles out from your nation's banknotes. Hungary's great bourgeois nationalist Lajos Kossuth, born in 1802 and dying in exile in Turin almost a century later, claims such fame. A man of fine intellect, and trained as a lawyer, his early career was temporarily halted by a spell in prison, accused of sedition. On his release he established the *Pesti Hirlap*, and became one of the chief advocates of the revolutionary drive towards liberty. By 1847 he was the most prominent opposition leader, and when the revolution came he took up the post of Chairman of the National Defence Commission in the Independence government. When that government declared the country a republic, Kossuth was the putative Head of State. The press of the day hailed him as the 'Moses of the Hungarians'. But the Promised Land failed to materialise – crushed by the Habsburgs, Kossuth fled to Turkey, and from there to England, America and Turin. While his political clout fell after the Compromise of 1867, over the 50 years following his departure from Hungary his radical ideas excited and influenced thinkers in diverse political movements from hard-line republicans to communists (although Karl Marx condemned him as bourgeois).

and **Ministry of Agriculture** (*no 11*) respectively. As well as statues to those figureheads of independence Lajos Kossuth and Ferenc Rákóczi II, the lawn has memorials – a **symbolic grave** and an **eternal flame** – to victims of October 25 1956 when ÁVO shooters fired on a peaceful crowd. Each metal 'bullet' set into the walls of the Ministry of Agriculture represents one of the dead. Two days before, revolutionaries had torn the Soviet emblem from the Hungarian flag during the uprising, and the gravestone bears a relief of this symbol of freedom.

Madonna sang 'Don't Cry for me, Argentina' from one of the balconies of **Alkotmány utca** – running east from the square – during filming of the Hollywood movie *Evita*. Leaving via the southeast corner, however, you'll pass through the tiny **Vértanúk (Martyrs') tere**; standing on a bronze bridge and looking westward for American support is a **statue of Imre Nagy** (1896–1958), the communist reformer and prime minister during the '56 revolution who the Soviets executed two years later (see page 21).

Beyond it, at the end of Vécsey utca, is the lengthy **Szabadság tér**. Until the late 1800s, this was the site of a barracks, where significant participants in the 1848–49 War of Independence were incarcerated and then executed by Baron Haynau. Among them was Lajos Batthyány, prime minister of the 1848 independent government, and close by on Aulich utca an **Eternal Light** in a greening casket glows perpetually in remembrance. The square's four corners once held allegorical representations of land stripped from Hungary by the Trianon Treaty, together with a central *Monument to Grief*. This was replaced in 1945 by the **Soviet monument**. After the fall of communism, the Russian government was allowed to nominate one public piece to remain in situ (rather than being carted off to Statue Park) and this was its choice. The hulking Eclectic palace housing the Hungarian Television offices (*Szabadság utca 17*) is the **former Stock Exchange**, built by Ignác Alpár in 1905. Facing it across the square is another of Alpár's designs, the **Hungarian National Bank** (*Szabadság tér 8*), with reliefs showing personifications of art, industry and commerce. (Among these is Alpár himself, in the clothes of a medieval master builder.) The outstanding **Post Office Savings Bank** (1901) backs on to it (on Hold utca); Ödön Lechner fused Art-Nouveau and Magyar folk motifs into the façade, and ceramic bees – symbolic of saving – climb towards shiny honey pots. Near the **American embassy** (*Szabadság tér 12*) is a **statue of US General**

**Harry Hill Bandholtz**, who prevented Romanian soldiers from looting the National Museum while serving with the peacekeeping force in 1919.

**Szent István körút** is the northernmost stretch of the Great Boulevard, joining Margit híd and marking the border with District XIII (Újlipótváros, or New Leopold Town). The beautiful **Vígszínház** (page 122) stands out among the otherwise grey eclectic buildings along its length. Prior to World War II, a high number of Jews lived in this district, and many of Wallenberg's safe houses were established here (one was at Pozsonyi út 14; see box, page 180). A tribute to the Swedish saviour by Pál Pátzay – comprising a half-naked man clubbing a hissing serpent – stands in **Szent István Park**, parallel with the southern tip of Margaret Island. The Jewish community is actually returning, and the area has been nicknamed 'Kis (Little) Tel Aviv'. Head up **Váci út** for the WestEnd City Center (page 133) and the Palace of Wonders (page 172). Look out too for the concrete, Neo-Romanesque **Parish Church of St Margaret** (*Lehel tér*); its construction was funded by Lord Rothermere, whose family coat of arms are shown in one of the stained-glass windows.

## TERÉZVÁROS

Falling on the eastern side of Bajcsy-Zsilinszky út, and locked between Király utca, Dózsa György út and the tracks of Nyugati Railway Station, much of Theresa Town (District VI) is a touch shabby. **Király utca** (named after the King of England in 1860) was a major thoroughfare at the end of the 19th century, and has a thriving collection of shops selling second-hand clothes and electrical goods, some swanky interior-design showrooms at its western end, the Liszt Ferenc Academy of Music (page 123) at numbers 64–66, and the district's 19th-century parish church (where it meets Nagymező utca), with chapels by Mihály Pollock and spire by Miklós Ybl. **Liszt Ferenc tér** and **Jókai Mór tér** are popular drinking spots, and **Nagymező utca** contains the city's main clutch of theatres. However, the splendid big boy of the district is Andrássy út, the main avenue flying arrow straight from the Small Boulevard to Heroes' Square, and rated by many as the city's prettiest.

### A walk along Andrássy út

In the 1860s, politician and nobleman Count Gyula Andrássy returned to Hungary after a period in France with his head full of ideas. He was determined that Budapest should have its own Champs Elysées to complement the city's boom in building, transport and culture. The elegant avenue – declared a Unesco World Heritage Site in 2002 – went some way towards fulfilling the dream; when the underground railway was constructed underneath in 1896 (three years before the Parisian metro), it could justifiably claim to have gone one better. The street is a showcase for turn-of-the-century star talent (including Alajos Strobl, Károly Lotz and Miklós Ybl). Writer and gourmand Gyula Krúdy noted the street 'lay in the body of Budapest like the Danube within Hungary. [I]t was the hope of the city.' The avenue stretches for over 2km; if you don't fancy strolling the whole length, break your walk by joining the metro for a stop or two, or hopping on bus number 4.

First called Sugár (Radial) út – and re-named variously Sztálin út, Magyar Ifjúság útja (Hungarian Avenue of Youth) and Népköztársaság útja (People's Republic Avenue) under communism – it was always popularly referred to as Andrássy út. Its buildings are Neoclassical and strong-lined, with heavy doors and wide windows. The western portion features grand offices and apartments before it broadens after Oktogon into a tree-lined sweep of villas and gardens. Be sure to cast eyes into gloomy courtyards, and watch for portals supported by muscle-bound Atlases and graceful caryatids. To walk here is to peer into the life of the city and its history.

The **Postal Museum** (*no 3*; page 173) is your first stop, if only to see the frescoed stairwell. The breathtaking **State Opera House** (*no 22*; page 123) is a little further on.

Strobl was just 26 when he carved the marble sphinxes outside; poet Endre Ady, who was fond of a drink, slipped off the back of one and cracked his head on the pavement. The Eclectic **Dreschler Palace** (*no 25*) was designed by Ödön Lechner (who famously explained that he decorated the roofs of his buildings to give the birds pleasure), and used to house the Ballet Institute. Just north of the opera house is **Nagymező utca**, the 'Hungarian Broadway', which also has a proliferation of hairdressing salons and sun-bed shops. The **Parisian Grand Department Store** (*Párizsi Nagyáruház; no 39*), with its bold Art-Nouveau façade, opened in 1911 as the city's most exclusive store; you could even ice-skate on the roof terrace in winter. Take a break at a café-bar on **Jókai Mór tér** or **Liszt Ferenc tér** (page 119), which straddle the avenue shortly afterwards. The **Liszt Music Academy** (page 123) is at the southeastern end of the latter; László Márton's statue near by shows the great composer in mid, manic flow.

In the eight-sided **Oktogon**, you may wonder why the **mayor's office** (*Teréz körút 13*) is adorned with six iron mooring rings. This is a hangover from the early 1800s, when a deep stream ran the length of the Great Boulevard – indeed, as the city developed, there was talk of transforming it into a canal with gondolas. Rather than Little Venice, however, Oktogon is today known as 'American Square' because of its fast-food restaurants (including the world's largest Burger King). Moving onward, the building at number 60 chilled hearts during much of the 20th century; it now holds a **museum to the terror regimes** (page 165). Ferenc Liszt lived in an apartment of the Music Academy at number 67 (the academy moved to its current location in 1907), and a **memorial museum** there allows you to have a snoop (page 172). The **Puppet Theatre** (page 122) and **Hungarian College of Applied Art** occupy the building at number 69, into which Adolf Láng crammed as many features of Italian Renaissance as he could in 1877.

**Kodály Körönd** is the most atmospheric circus in Pest, and the one in the worst state of repair. Its flaking buildings have dark turrets, rounded towers and Transylvanian-style boxed roofs. The statues gracing its four corners are fighters for freedom – the lyrical poet Bálint Balassi (who died in battle against the Turks), Miklós Zrínyi and György Szondi (16th-century heroes), and Vak Bottyán (a leader of the 18th-century anti-Habsburg independence war) – while the composer Zoltán Kodály lived at number 89, where there's now a **museum** (page 173). From here onward the spacious villas have fenced gardens, originally the homes of 19th-century industrial magnates but now belonging to embassies and law firms. Two collections of Asian art can be found at the **Hopp Ferenc** (*no 103*; page 172) and **Ráth György** (*Városligeti fasor 12*; page 173) museums, before the avenue reaches its dramatic climax in the vastness of Heroes' Square.

## HEROES' SQUARE, CITY PARK AND THE SPORTS DISTRICT

**Heroes' Square** (*Hősök tere*) was one of the millennial projects, constructed to celebrate the anniversary of the supposed date of the Magyar arrival in the Carpathian Basin. It is a monumental, triumphalist expression of Hungarian patriotism and confidence at a time when the Compromise had restored a nation's self-respect and the economy was buoyant; aside from the odd glaring omission (see below), its statues represent a chronological catalogue of the nation's first 1,000 years. In 1896, it also formed the gateway to the celebratory exhibition, whose 200 pavilions attracted visitors from all over the world.

At the square's centre is the 36m-high fluted column of the **Millennium Monument** (which wasn't completed until 1929), with the Archangel Gabriel atop bearing the Holy Crown that he is said to have offered to István in a dream. Around the base are the menacing Magyar tribal chieftains, their horses tossing and snorting, and the leader Árpád to the fore. A marble tablet in front covers an **empty coffin**, laid in 1989 to honour those killed during the 1956 revolution, and inscribed with 'In memory of our heroes'. All this is framed by a pair of colonnades bearing statues of the country's major leaders, starting with István and culminating in Lajos Kossuth, who headed the 1848 revolution before going into exile in America (and becoming a successful statesmen over there). One dynasty is noticeable by its absence; originally the last five statues in the sequence depicted the Habsburgs (Lipót II, Károly VI, Maria Theresa, József II and Ferenc József). The latter was an unpopular figure whose statue was quickly torn down when the monarchy fell at the end of World War I, and the others were later removed by the communists. The replacements are all heroes of the independence struggle against Turks, Habsburgs or both, with Ferenc Rákóczi II among the Transylvanian princes alongside Kossuth. The chariots charging above are allegories of work and welfare, war, peace, and art and science.

Splendid examples of Neoclassical architecture, the **Museum of Fine Arts** (page 167) and the **Exhibition Hall** (page 173) stand to the north and south. A cross marks the point on **Dózsa György út** – which runs across the square – where a church once stood before it was dismantled by the communists in 1951 to make way for a parade ground. Here was placed a massive statue of Stalin that insurgents subsequently bashed to bits during the '56 revolution. The statue of Lenin that succeeded it is in Statue Park (page 167).

**City Park** (*Városliget*) is grassed and wooded, accessed from the back of Heroes' Square via a bridge (designed by Gustave Eiffel) over an artificial lake. The water is ideal for a summery splash around in a pedalo, or for a spot of ice-skating during winter when the southern portion is transformed into a rink (*cost 300/600Ft/hr weekdays/weekends; open Mon–Fri 09.00–13.00 & 16.00–20.00, Sat 09.00–13.00 & 14.00–18.00, Sun 10.00–14.00 & 16.00–20.00*). Standing on an island, the **Vajdahunyad Castle** is as fantastical as any construction you are ever likely to see. Ignác Alpár used 21 buildings as the models for a design that incorporated all the styles of Hungary's architectural heritage. Its most striking sections were based upon the former castle of the Hunyadi clan in Transylvania, after which the creative mishmash is named. Originally fashioned from wood, the fairy-tale castle so enchanted those who saw it that it was rebuilt in stone as a permanent fixture. Just outside is a **statue of Alpár** surveying his masterpiece, and in the courtyard of the Baroque wing (which holds the **Museum of Agriculture**; page 173) sits the hooded '**Anonymus**' (Miklós Ligeti, 1903). While his true identity is lost to us, the 12th- or 13th-century 'Anonymous' chronicled the country's early history in his *Gesta Hungarorum*, which is now held by the Széchényi Library (page 169). Touch his pen – it's considered good luck.

In summer, there are outdoor concerts at the castle, while at the park's eastern edge are the **Petőfi Csarnok** (page 131) and the **Transport Museum** (page 174). On the pathway leading from the rear of the castle is a **statue of US President George Washington**, donated in 1906 by Hungarian emigrants. America is home to a large number of Hungarian exiles, that in Cleveland representing the biggest population outside Europe. To the north of Kós Károly sétány are delights zoological, gastronomical and balneological; within a few hundred yards of each other are the country's biggest zoo (page 174), most famous restaurant (page 114) and largest spa (page 134), together with a circus (page 174) and an amusement park (page 174). It is difficult to find nothing to do.

To the southeast of City Park, on the other side of Thököly út, is the city's **sports district** (still part of District XIV). The main stadium among a sprinkling of sports halls and arenas is the **Puskás Ferenc Stadion** (or Népstadion), named after Hungary's iconic footballer (see page 73). It seats 80,000, and is where big football matches and concerts are held. Socialist-Realist statues that once lined the avenue leading to its entrance are now in its garden (see box opposite), and there's a **Sport Museum** (page 173) near by, but in truth there is little else to draw you to what is otherwise a rather bleak area of the capital.

Hősök tere and Széchenyi fürdő stations are on the M1 underground line, while buses 4 and 30 and trolleybus 72 also serve City Park et al. Puskás Stadion is reached via Stadionok on the M2 metro line.

## THE COMMIE TOUR

The last Soviet soldier left in 1991, but there are communist reminders to be found in places other than Statue Park. Pest contains the odd shop with swirling neon sign, typical of the communist era. The former state-owned bookshops are still marked by a blue neon owl. A *közért* (literally 'for the public') is a local corner shop stocking traditional items. Try District VIII, which hasn't changed much, and you'll find unusual products in tins and jars – Traubisoda and Márka (fizzy drinks), Túró Rudi (a tube of cottage cheese with a hint of vanilla and covered in plain chocolate, found in the chiller cabinet), and Munkás (Worker) cigarettes.

In the garden at Puskás Ferenc Stadion are 16 Socialist-Realist statues, depictions of health and sport that lined the avenue leading to the stadium (built in 1953). On the corner of Dózsa György út and Városligeti fasor, near City Park, is a massive mural showing labourers on the wall of a former trade-union office. The Workers' Pantheon of Kerepesi Cemetery (page 180) is inscribed with 'They lived for communism and the people'; despite the law banning 'images of oppression', a nearby plot for fallen Soviet soldiers displays a hammer and sickle. This also features on the World War II monument in Szabadság tér (page 157). The island of Csepel in southern Budapest was always a stronghold of the workers' movement, and a statue called *Olvasó Munkás (Reading Worker)* by András Beck adorns Béke tér. The Young Pioneers built what is now the Children's Railway (pages 182–3) in 1950. A museum at Hűvösvölgy station has a charming collection of memorabilia, while Virágvölgy displays a plaque with three pioneers pointing towards a brighter socialist future.

Several **restaurants** preserve flavours of the socialist era. Resti kocsma (V, Deák Ferenc utca 2; tel: 1 266 6210; open Mon–Sat 12.00–05.00) takes its name from the railway-station buffets where you can buy lukewarm coffee and stale pastries. Communist signs urge the workers on, and everything in the cellar restaurant is red – down to the pioneer's tie draped over the beer pump. The food is too edible to represent a real *resti*, and the prices too high (mains around 1,500Ft). For details of Marxim, see page 109. Menza (VI, Liszt Ferenc tér 2; tel: 1 413 1482; open daily 10.00–24.00) – or 'Canteen' – opened in 2003, and evokes the Socialist-Realist dining-hall aesthetic of the 'Goulash Communism' period, with brown colours, polyester tablecloths and boarding to protect the walls from splashes of soup. The 'best-of' menu even includes socialist favourites like *lángos*. Paprika gyorsétterem (V, Pilváx köz 1) was the Hungarian version of a fast-food restaurant, with goulash in plastic dishes and red wine sold in little paper cups. The restaurants gradually disappeared during the 1990s, but this last hanger-on is enjoying a renaissance.

# ERZSÉBETVÁROS

District VII – Elizabeth Town – runs from the Small Boulevard's outer rim as far as Dózsa György út, and is bordered by Király utca to the north and **Rákóczi út** to the south. The latter is one of the city's main shopping streets, the route linking the Eastern (Keleti) Railway Station to the city centre a natural magnet for traders. It used to be a seedy area frequented by prostitutes, but it's cleaner now and the popular choice for well-priced clothes. While you're browsing the blouses and shirts, keep an eye out for the wonderful Art-Nouveau **Uránia film theatre** (*no 21*; page 127). At the corner with Gyulai Pál utca, the Baroque **Szent Rókus Chapel** (*no 31*) was built in 1711 in the hope that it would secure saintly protection for the citizens of Pest during a period when the plague was hitting hard. The 1838 flood is commemorated in a relief on the façade; the street level was raised in 1846, which is why the church now sinks below the tarmac's tide. Next to the chapel, is the **capital's oldest hospital** (*Gyulai Pál utca 2*), constructed in 1796 – at that time well outside the city walls – to treat infectious diseases. It is named after the 19th-century head doctor **Ignác Semmelweis**, who was christened the 'saviour of mothers' after discovering that scrubbed staff reduced incidents of child-birth fever (see page 170). Further on, **Blaha Lujza tér** on the Great Boulevard is named after a 19th-century actress (who sang like a nightingale) and used to be the site of the National Theatre; a memorial stone marks where it stood before making way in the 1970s for the metro station.

The city's **Jewish quarter** falls in the area between the Small and Great boulevards. The first major influx of Jews to Budapest came during the tolerant reign of Béla IV in the 13th century, and they assisted with the process of rebuilding following the Mongol invasion. There were periods of repression in centuries to come, but Hungary more usually represented a haven from harsher persecution elsewhere. The community's contribution has been valuable; during the 20th century, seven of Hungary's 12 Nobel Prize winners were of Jewish descent. By 1939 there were 200,000 Jews living in Budapest. Then came Adolf Eichmann and the **Holocaust** in 1944; 600,000 were murdered or deported nationwide, the population in the countryside obliterated. In Budapest, the Nazis established a ghetto between Dohány utca, Király utca and Erzsébet körút; 70,000 were crammed in here under brutal conditions, the majority around Klauzál tér. Bodies of the dead were kept in fridges at Klauzál tér market before burial in the square. Fortunately, however, annihilation was averted by the arrival of the Soviets. Today there are 80,000 Jews, less than half the pre-war number but still the largest community in central Europe.

## A walk along Dob utca

The district's prime sight is the **Great Synagogue** (*Dohány utca 2*; page 179), one of the city's foremost architectural works; the silver willow in its memorial park is both a striking sculpture and a touching tribute. The **Rumbach Sebestyén utca synagogue** (*nos 11–13*) – established in 1872 as a moderately conservative ('status quo' Jewry) alternative to the more reformist Great Synagogue – can be found on the road opposite the rear of the complex. However, if you fancy a walk through the district your best bet is **Dob (Drum) utca** (named after a former pub called the Three Drums), which traverses the very heart. Along its length a dying breed of craftsmen (see box, page 132) ply their trades, and the cuisine available in its restaurants ranges from kosher to curry.

Keep an eye out early on for the **memorial to Swiss consul Carl Lutz** who, like Wallenberg after him (see box, page 180), saved many Jews from deportation. Placed at the one-time entrance to the ghetto, and looking like something out of the Cirque de Soleil, a gold angel stands perpendicular to a wall and offers a cloth lifeline to a figure lying prone below. An inscription from the Talmud reads 'He who saves one single person could also save the world.'

At number 16 is the gateway to the **Gozsdu udvar**, whose string of courtyards once represented a thriving centre for artisans' workshops, and which formed a wall of the ghetto. A modest sign at Dob utca 22 heralds one of the street's treasures; the **Fröhlich cukrászda** offers delicious cakes, and claims to be the only genuine kosher café in Hungary. At the corner of Kazinczy utca, look right to see Pest's **Orthodox Synagogue** (*Kazinczy utca 29–31*), designed by the Löffler brothers (Béla and Sándor) in 1913, and serving the city's small community of just over 3,000 Orthodox Jews. It looks dark and forlorn, but the Hebrew lettering at the top of the façade – 'This is the House of God and the Gate of Heaven' – remains in good condition. It isn't open to visitors, but you can get a closer look around the corner at Dob utca 35; through the courtyard by the kosher butchers (*no 41*) and the strictly kosher Hanna restaurant is the former **Orthodox**

**school**. Further down Kazinczy utca is the **Museum of Electrical Engineering** (*Kazinczy utca 21*; page 174), while further up Dob utca is **Klauzál tér**, which was at the centre of the ghetto. Today, Roma people make up a high proportion of the residents in the single-room flats with outdoor toilets that are common in the area. There are some workshops immediately beyond the Great Boulevard, but thereafter the character of the street changes. Statues of István and others guard the giant post office on the corner of Hársfa utca, while next door is the **Stamp Museum** (*Hársfa utca 47*; page 175). Before leaving the district, be sure to run the gauntlet of a *néni*'s wrath by peering through the odd doorway to the leafy courtyards within; in these nooks you'll find children playing football, housewives beating carpets and grandmothers watching from balconies above. We're especially fond of that at Dob utca 82.

## JÓZSEFVÁROS, FERENCVÁROS AND BEYOND

The segment south of Rákóczi út to Üllői út is **Józsefváros** (Joseph Town, District VIII). East of the Great Boulevard has traditionally been the haunt of scoundrels and ne'er-do-wells, but as long as you keep your purse safe from wayward fingers, there are some real gems here. Appropriately enough, the **Crime Museum** (page 175) is in the vicinity. The **Eastern (Keleti) Railway Station** is surely one of the most beautiful and romantic in the world, a monumental Eclectic structure in iron and glass. It was constructed in 1882 by Gyula Rochlitz, and outside are statues of the great English rail pioneers George Stephenson and James Watt. A short distance away is **Kerepesi Cemetery** (page 180), its paths the city's most peaceful, while there's nature to be had at the district's southern edge in the **Budapest Botanical Garden** (page 185) and **Natural History Museum** (pages 175–6).

Several university buildings are located inside the sweep of the Great Boulevard, and this was a hot spot during the '56 uprising. **Bródy Sándor utca** was where it all erupted on October 23 after students were fired on outside the **Hungarian Radio headquarters** (*no 7*); there is a famous black-and-white photograph showing a Hungarian flag fluttering from an upper window of the building, the Soviet crest ripped from its centre. Opposite, a marble tablet commemorates 18-year-old János Vizi, who was the first to die that day. Sándor Bródy was a turn-of-the-20th-century writer, and while he didn't live here, many others of the literary world did. The street has an appropriately bookish culmination point at **Gutenberg tér**, named after the 15th-century printing-press pioneer; he is portrayed with wide-brimmed hat and open book on the house at number 4. Those who scurry between the square and Múzeum körút often miss the painted wooden **relief of the Last Supper** at Bródy Sándor utca 19, which can apparently be illuminated by an electric lamp above it on the wall. Múzeum körút, with its **National Museum** (pages 166–7) and **antiquarian bookshops** is dealt with under the Belváros section.

**Ferencváros** (Francis Town, District IX), framed by Üllői út and the river, was flattened by the Great Flood in 1838; it is now an area dominated by blue collars and green-and-white flags, the latter the colours of the local football team Ferencvárosi Torna Club (FTC; see page 73). 'Fradi' has the best stadium in town and the most passionate (and at times thuggish) fans. The **Big Market Hall** (page 131) near Szabadság híd is an absolute must, and next to it is the **University of Economics**; we've dealt with these and **Kálvin tér** (page 152) during our walk around the downtown. **Ráday utca**, forging southeast from Kálvin tér, is a trendy night spot (pages 119–20). You'll generally witness the grubby Üllői út on your way to or from Ferihegy Airport (although if you're unlucky you'll discover that it also holds several clinics and hospitals). At the junction with Ferenc körút is the **Museum of Applied Arts** (page 175), a veritable Art-Nouveau free-for-all. A new **Holocaust Memorial Centre** (*Páva utca 39*; page 175) is a short distance east in a former synagogue.

Around 3km further out is **Népliget**, founded in the 1860s and Budapest's biggest public park. It can be accessed via Népliget metro station (M3), but as a landscaped space it offers nothing that isn't available more centrally at City Park or Margaret Island. However, there is a Planetarium and laser show (page 176). The FTC stadium is opposite the bus and metro station. Another 20km away in District X is the **New Municipal Cemetery** (*Új köztemető*; X, Kozma utca), where Imre Nagy and other martyrs of the 1956 revolution were dumped by the communists in plots 300 and 301. Nagy was reburied in 1989 with great ceremony and political significance (see page 21). The grave is in the far northeast of the cemetery, a half-hour walk from the entrance; a microbus (marked *temető járat*) also runs visitors there at peak periods. A Jewish cemetery stands next to it. Take tram 28 or 37 from near Blaha Lujza tér or bus 95 from Keleti station.

# THE ISLANDS
## Walking Margaret Island
Margit-sziget is the city centre's prime piece of park. Ecclesiastical buildings, royal residences and aristocratic hunting grounds are now largely lost in history's mists, as are memories of the Turkish period, when the pashas' horses and 'women of ill repute' were kept here. Today shady chestnut trees, quiet walkways and open pieces of grass make it the playground of sunbathers, joggers and strollers without time to head for the hills. Formed from three islets that were artificially fused in the late 19th and early 20th centuries, the island now measures 2½km long by 500m wide, and settles between Margit and Árpád bridges. Before World War II, 'undesirables' were deterred from the gardens and medicinal baths by an entrance fee, but you may now visit freely however undesirable you are.

Motorists can access the island via Árpád híd, and must pay to leave their vehicles in a car park at the northern tip. Bus 26 traverses the island on its journey between Nyugati station and Árpád híd; alternatively, alight from tram 4 or 6 on Margit híd. If you fancy sparing some shoe leather once there, you can hire a variety of bicycles, pedal cars or electronic buggies from near the southern end.

Approaching from **Margit híd**, you'll be using the city's second permanent river crossing, built 1872–76. It was designed in Parisian style by a colleague of Eiffel, and predictably became nicknamed the 'French Bridge'. Scores of pedestrians were killed when the retreating Germans blew up the structure during World War II. Follow the pedestrian bridge that runs from here down to the island, and ahead will be the **Centenary Monument**, erected on the 100th anniversary of the union of Buda, Pest and Óbuda. A short distance beyond that is the country's largest **fountain**, a spectacular affair with shooting jets that rise to 25m; it is illuminated at night, and if you're lucky you'll catch its water spurts dancing to snatches of music.

To the right of the path, between the **Hajós Alfréd Swimming Pool** (page 136) and the **Palatinus Strand** (a few hundred metres further up; page 135), lie the remains of a 13th- to 14th-century **Franciscan church** with a Gothic tracery window. Leave the track and aim towards the centre ground, walk between the blooms of an **elliptical garden**, and then bear northeast a short while to the island's main archaeological site – the **cloister and church of the Dominican nuns**. When the Mongols sacked the country in 1241, Béla IV swore an oath that his future daughter would devote her life to God if his people were delivered from the hordes. Margit was born the following year, and the king had the complex built in honour of the Blessed Virgin. Margit lived a life of utmost piety here, and was famed for performing curing miracles; she was also known never to wash above the feet, so perhaps her greatest achievement was in persuading people to let her near enough to heal them. The cult of Margit began soon after her death at 28, although she wasn't finally canonised until 1943. The foundations – and the marble coffin of Margit's brother, István V, complete with golden funeral crown (now in the Budapest History Museum) – were discovered during the clear up after the Great Flood of 1838.

Look westward above the treeline to the 57m-tall **water tower** (*víztorony*), constructed in 1911 and a protected industrial monument. Beneath it is an open-air theatre. Directly northward is the reconstructed medieval **Premonstratensian chapel**, originally erected in the 12th century. In its tower hangs the oldest bell in Hungary, dating back to the 15th century; the bell lay hidden – probably from the Turks – until 1914, when a storm brought down a tree and revealed it among the roots. Near here too is the **Artists' Promenade**, a series of busts depicting greats of Hungarian literature, music and art.

The northern portion of the island contains the hotels **Grand** and **Thermal** (pages 101–2), which make use of the thermal medicinal waters that have been tapped here since the 1860s. The excellent spa is open to non-residents. From 1869, Miklós Ybl's magnificent neo-Renaissance **bathing hall** stood on the site, and it became a favourite retreat for aristocrats and poets; the writer János Arany (1817–82) spent his last summers on the island, and penned a host of poems from beneath the oak trees. It is a crying shame that, unlike the Grand Hotel, the hall was not reconstructed after the war. Beyond the hotels, on the western bank, is a **Japanese garden** whose plashing waterfall is a rare extant feature of the doomed bathing complex. Near by is a domed, music-playing **Neoclassical well**, a replica of an 1820 original.

## Shipyard (or Óbuda) Island

The island to the north of Margit-sziget suffers something of an identity crisis, referred to variously as Hajógyári- (Shipyard) and Óbudai-sziget. Either way, this is where **palaces of the Roman proconsuls** stood when Aquincum was at its height, and much later where an industrial **shipyard** was sited. Today tourists will be less interested by the warehouses than by the wakeboarding lake, tennis courts, assault course, horse-riding opportunities and the achingly trendy Dokk nightclub (page 126). The island is invaded by music lovers during the Sziget Festival and by horsy types for the Budapest Equestrian Summer Festival in June (see page 128), while the Ladik Csárda puts on traditional banquets accompanied by performances of gypsy music and dancing. (The main banquets in its huge barn are primarily aimed at tour groups – telephone in advance to find out when the next one is taking place. Tickets can be purchased from hotels, and the entertainment usually kicks off at 20.00. A ferry will take guests from Vigadó tér to the island in summer.) While cars can drive on to the island, buses 34, 42 and 106 only run as far as Szentendrei út, from where you'll need to walk on along Mozaik utca.

# Museums and more

There are some fine museums in Budapest. The Hungarian National Museum, the Hungarian National Gallery and the Museum of Fine Arts rank among the best of European cultural houses, while individual attractions like the Varga Imre Collection are real treats. For details of exhibitions during your stay, grab a copy of *Pesti Műsor PM Tárlat*, an A5-sized guide that is published quarterly, has English translations and is available free from tourist and ticket offices, coffee houses, museums and exhibition centres. See *Arts and entertainment*, pages 68–9, for information on opening hours and a caveat on listed prices.

## THE UNMISSABLES

**House of Terror** (*Terrorháza*) VI, Andrássy út 60; ☏ 1 374 2600; www.houseofterror.hu [Ⓜ *Vörösmarty utca;* Ⓑ 4] This stately apartment in powder blue bore witness to some of the blackest acts of the blackest years of the 20th century. In 1944 the Hungarian Nazis set up their party headquarters inside, torturing and murdering Jews in the former coal cellars; the communist political police (the PRO, ÁVO and ÁVH) succeeded them until 1956, burning, electrocuting and executing those resistant to the Party. Closer to a piece of installation art than a traditional museum, this exhibition represents a sensual assault more about atmosphere than artefacts. The displays include video footage of communist propaganda, photographs of political leaders and prisoners, screen prints and props. There are explanatory sheets (in English) in each room. *Adult/concessions 1,200/600Ft; open Tue–Fri 10.00–18.00 (last admission 16.30), Sat–Sun 10.00–19.30 (last admission 18.00).*

**Hungarian National Gallery** (*Magyar Nemzeti Galéria*) I, Budavári Palota, Épület B, C, D, Szent György tér 2; ⊠ 1 224 3700 or 1 375 7533; www.mng.hu. The National Gallery is daunting in size, sprawling across three wings of the Buda Castle Palace, and is one of the country's most significant museums. There are 100,000 works in the gallery. On the ground floor of Wing D is a **lapidarium** containing medieval and Renaissance stone carvings, including fragments of 11th- to 15th-century architecture and marble carvings from King Mátyás's palace. In vaulted rooms facing the Danube are **medieval panel paintings** and **wooden sculptures**, such as the *Madonna and Child from Toporc* of around 1420, with its milky-faced Mary and curly-haired Christ. In the first-floor throne room is an array of dazzling late-Gothic winged altars that adorned churches in northern Hungary.

Next door is the collection of **late-Renaissance** and **Baroque art**, including a 1712 portrait of Ferenc Rákóczi II by the court painter Ádám Mányoki and 18th-century religious works by F A Maulbertsch. Towards the end of the period more secular genres emerged that embraced allegory and scenes of country life, thus anticipating the full flowering of Romanticism.

The same floor of Wings C and B holds the **19th-century collections**, which display the main parallel strains of Romanticism - the portraiture typical of the Neoclassical form and the landscapes of Biedermeier (or middle-class Romanticism). Historical painting, another related branch of the Romantic tradition, is represented by Bálint Kiss and Mihály Kovács; the infusion of realism in the latter half of the century is embodied in works such as the *Condemned Cell I* (1870) by Mihály Munkácsy. Among the sculptors, Miklós Izsó was a true exponent of National Romanticism in tackling both rural working life and portrait sculpture. National self-confidence after 1867 manifested itself in competitions to shape the city's buildings and public spaces. Many of the models on display by sculptors like Izsó, Alajos Stróbl, János Fadrusz and György Zala are the results of such competitions.

**Art of the first half of the 20th century** occupies the second floor of Wing C. Here you'll find works by Károly Ferenczy, the leading artist of the supremely influential Nagybánya artists' colony (an area now part of Romania); some vast canvases by Tivadar Csontváry Kosztka, visionary and drenched in colour; a range of Post-Impressionist paintings by József Rippl-Rónai, including the beautiful *Woman with Bird Cage* (1892), painted during the artist's 'black period'; and inter-war Expressionist pieces by Gyula Derkovits and József Egry. Picasso was a fan of Csontváry, apparently requesting that he be left alone to admire the paintings during an exhibition of 1949. He was lucky to be able to see them at all; on Csontváry's death, his family had arranged to sell some of the pieces as tarpaulin before someone fortunately intervened to buy the canvases – to hang on walls rather than tent poles. On the third floor is a collection of **post-1945 art**. The **Habsburg Crypt** (*Nádor kripta*), the remaining part of the Chapel of St Zsigmond, can also be accessed from the museum. It is here that Archduke József was buried, the palatine (or *nádor*) between 1796 and 1847.

The museum's main entrance is near the statue of Eugene of Savoy on the eastern side of the palace, although there is also access from the western side. *Free entrance to permanent exhibitions; special shows adult/concessions from 800/400Ft; open Tue–Sun 10.00–18.00.*

**Hungarian National Museum** (*Magyar Nemzeti Múzeum*) VIII, Múzeum körút 14–16; ⊠ 1 338 2122; www.hnm.hu [T̲ 47, 49 from Deák tér 2 stops to Kálvin tér; M3 Kálvin tér] The largest museum in Hungary, and regal with it. Among its garden statues is that of Ferenc Széchényi (1754–1820), the enlightened rock on whose collection the museum was founded. The Neoclassical palace was built in 1847 by Mihály Pollack and became a symbol of the Independence War a short time later. On March 15 1848 radical intellectuals gathered outside and demanded reform, and copies of Petőfi's 'National Song' were distributed.

Your entrance fee is justified immediately by the **rich frescoes** that adorn the main stairwell. The work of Mór Than (1828–99) and Károly Lotz (1833–1904), those on the ceiling show allegories of virtues and learning, while the wall friezes depict a broad sweep of Hungarian history, from the Huns leaving Asia up to the birth of the museum. The collection at the top of the stairs charts the **period 1000–1990**, from the Árpád dynasty (including goods buried with Béla III, the era's only royal grave to survive intact) to the collapse of communism. Descend from the foyer to a **lapidarium** and a 3rd-century mosaic excavated from a villa in Balácpuszta. To the right of the entrance hall is an exhibition with artefacts dating from the prehistoric **Palaeolithic Age to the Age of the Avars** (AD567–804). To the left is the museum's star attraction. You can take your Holy Crown and sceptre – the more lauded items of the coronation regalia that were moved from here in 2000 to the Parliament building; for us, the **cloak** is the true crowning piece. This semi-circular stretch of purple silk, shimmering with gold embroidery, is a textile masterpiece, and the sole item among the regalia that actually belonged to St István. He gave it to the church in Székesfehérvár in 1031, and he is included with his wife Gizella among the angels at the bottom of the cloth. *Free entry; open Tue–Sun 10.00–18.00.*

**Museum of Fine Arts** (*Szépművészeti Múzeum*) XIV, Dózsa György út 41; ✆ 1 363 2675; www.szepmuveszeti.hu/index.htm [**M̄1** *Hősök tere;* **B̄** *4;* **T̄B̄** *79*] Indisputably Hungary's premier collection of international art, and very arguably one of central Europe's. The building has the look of a classical temple and the interior is a shrine to past masters. The place to head in a hurry is the renowned **Old Picture Gallery**; there are paintings by Raphael and Titian in the Italian collection, works by Breughel and Rubens in the Dutch one, and – featuring El Greco, Murillo and Goya – the richest group of Spanish pieces outside Spain itself. You'll find Monet, Manet, Renoir, Delacroix, Gauguin, Cézanne and Hungary's very own Op-Artist Vasarely popping their heads up in the modern department, while Pisano's marble *Madonna and Child* is one of the darlings among the sculpture. If that isn't enough, the **Egyptian section** has mummies and painted sarcophagi, and there are statues and pottery in the display of **Greek and Roman finds**. The cream of the exhibition was gathered between the 17th and 19th centuries by the aristocratic Esterházy family; keep these princes fondly in your thoughts, for they left a wonderful, inspiring, sense-stirring hoard of art. *Free entry to permanent exhibitions; guided tours 4,000–5,000Ft, free (in English) on Tue & Fri at 11.00; open Tue–Sun 10.00–17.30.*

**Statue Park** (*Szoborpark*) XXII, corner of Balatoni út and Szabadkai utca; ✆ 1 424 7500; www.szoborpark.hu [**B̄** *from Deák Ferenc tér near the Volánbusz terminus – the Statue Park timetable faces away from the square – leaving at 10.00, 11.00, 15.00 & 16.00 in high season or red 7 from Ferenciek tere to Etele tér, then yellow Volán bus from stall 7–8 to Diósd-Érd*] 'Heroic' monuments to communism were not only symbols of ideology, but vast instruments of repression that bullied public spaces. The undersized Statue Park divests them of such registers. Of course, the setting is as much a product of its historical moment as the statues are products of theirs. When communism fell, this wasn't intended as a memorial; by contrast it was a dumping ground (15km from the centre) for beacons of the socialist period, a country's act of closure. And it feels like it. But don't be unimpressed; try to imagine the statues in their original political and historical context, as they stood on hills, on squares, on boulevards. And remember that, because so many other nations destroyed such monuments as the Iron Curtain fell, these 42 bulky relics are rare extant markers of one of the significant periods of 20th-century European history.

To the right as you enter is the figure of the **Soviet soldier** by Zsigmond Kisfaludy Strobl that used to stand beneath the Freedom Monument. You'll find statues of **communist martyrs**, memorials to Lenin, Marx, Engels, and **Hungarian communist leaders** like Béla Kun and Árpád Münnich. What you won't find is an image of Stalin; the city's only statue was cut off at the knees during the 1956 revolution, and many Budapesters still own fragments of the metal torso. The souvenir shop sells model Trabants, Soviet medals, CDs containing songs of the Movement, and T-shirts. *Adult/concessions 600/400Ft; free with Budapest Card; return bus ticket (inc entrance to park) 1,950Ft (1,350Ft with Budapest Card); open daily 10.00–dusk.*

**Varga Imre Collection** III, Laktanya utca 7 [HEV *Árpád híd*] All that glisters is not gold; polished sheet metal glisters too, and in the hands of Varga is moulded, bent and folded into layered and textured works of art that delight those with eyes for shiny things. Varga came to major prominence in the 1960s and – despite being a favoured sculptor under János Kádár, crafting statues that were subsequently banished to Statue Park – sustained his popularity after the political changes. This concentrated collection shows why, a rich feast of statues, busts and sculptures that includes the gaunt figure of St István (the original of which is in St Peter's Basilica in Rome), the hatted Béla Bartók, and, leaning against a wooden gate, the tormented Jewish poet Miklós Radnóti, who was killed on a forced march from a labour camp in 1944. You can sit at the museum café while admiring the collection. Varga often holds court here on Saturdays between 10.00 and 12.00, and speaks English. Greatly admiring his works, we try to forget that he is supposedly a rather unlikeable chap... *Adult/concessions 500/250Ft; free with Budapest Card; open Tue–Sun 10.00–18.00.*

# MUSEUMS, GALLERIES ETC
## Buda
### Castle Hill

**Budapest History Museum** (*Budapesti Történeti Múzeum*) I, Budavári Palota, Épület E, Szent György tér 2; ☎ 1 224 3700. The popularly known 'Castle Museum' can be found at the southern side of Lion Court. Reached from the basement below the museum itself are **remains of the medieval palace** at various stages and under various rulers. The greater share belongs to the Gothic **palace of Zsigmond of Luxembourg** (1387–1437), including the elaborately restored **Knights' Hall**, which now contains a series of Gothic statues (of contemporary courtiers and biblical apostles) that were unearthed from a ditch in 1974. Evidence of Mátyás's pad is largely restricted to stove tiles and fragments of red-marble balustrades, which can be viewed in the **Renaissance Hall**. The lower portion of the **Royal Chapel**, constructed by Lajos Nagy in the 1360s, also survives. Among the museum's other permanent displays are finds dating from prehistory to the end of the Avar period (2nd floor), and exhibits charting those moments that have caressed or buffeted the capital over the years since 1686, from transient domestic fashions to the devastating flood of 1838 and the tragic consequences of 20th-century war (1st floor). *Adult/concessions 900/450Ft; free with Budapest card; open May 16–Sep 15 daily 10.00–18.00, Nov 1–Feb 28 Wed–Mon 10.00–16.00, Mar 1–May 15 & Sep 16–Oct 31 Wed–Mon 10.00–18.00.*

**Golden Eagle Pharmacy Museum** (*Arany Sas Patika Múzeum*) I, Tárnok utca 18; ☎ 1 375 9772. Prior to the late 17th century, if you were struck by a jippy tummy in the Castle District you had little option than to adopt a steely grin, clench those glutes and run like the (proverbial) wind. In 1687, Ferenc Bösinger resolved to clear up this messy state of affairs by opening the district's first pharmacy at his home in Dísz tér. It was later moved to this 15th-century merchant's house. The museum includes original furnishings and instruments from the apothecary's shop, together with a reconstruction of an 'alchemist's workshop'. Look out for the figurative wall and ceiling paintings, some of which survive from as early as 1500. *Free entry; open Tue–Sun Nov 1–Feb 28 10.30–15.30, Mar 1–Oct 31 10.30–17.30.*

**Hungarian Museum of Commerce and Catering** (*Magyar Kereskedelmi & Vendéglátóipari Múzeum*) I, Fortuna utca 4; ☎ 1 375 6249. We can almost hear the excited squeals from catering students. The focus is the period from the Compromise of 1867 until World War II, when modern forms of trade emerged. It captures a snapshot of the period's atmosphere, lifestyle and fashions. Here are histories of two of Hungary's great foodies – Gerbeaud (see page 116) and Gundel. Károly Gundel was just 27 years old when he bought his renowned restaurant in 1911. Among exhibits in the 2nd room is a mock-up of a 1938 general store (which served as a social hub in the way that the pub does today). The final item in the exhibition is a drawn blind marked 'Closed for Nationalisation' – an emphatic sign of the very different political and economic climate from 1948. *Free entry; temporary exhibitions from 500Ft; open Wed–Fri 10.00–17.00, Sat–Sun 10.00–18.00.*

**Institute and Museum of Military History** (*Hadtörténeti Intézet & Múzeum*) I, Tóth Árpád sétány 40; ☏ 1 356 9522/9370. There are enough boys' toys in here to satisfy the most macho of holidaying males. You'll find weapons dating from the Turkish period and before, as well as more modern machinery, medals and uniforms worn by the Hungarian Hussar regiment. The royal army of Regent Horthy is represented, together with an excellent exhibition devoted to the national army (*Honvéd*) of the 1848–49 War of Independence. The display related to the 1956 uprising will move even the stoniest of hearts. Admission to the museum is just behind the square's western side, on Tóth Árpád sétány. *Free entry; open Tue–Sun Oct 1–Mar 31 10.00–15.45, Apr 1–Sep 30 10.00–17.45.*

**Medieval House of Prayer** (*középkori zsidó imaház*) I, Tancsics Mihály utca 26. The exhibition in this 16th-century Jewish prayer house includes early gravemarkers and the late-Gothic keystone from a much larger synagogue of 1461, found in the garden of number 23 and yet to be properly excavated. Pictures and Hebrew inscriptions on the interior walls attempted to buoy up worshippers in the face of fears of persecution by Christians as power shifted during the 17th century. *Adult/concessions 400/150Ft; open May 1–Oct 31 Tue–Sun 10.00–18.00.*

**National Széchényi Library** (*Országos Széchényi Könyvtár*) Budavári Palota, Épület F; ☏ 1 224 3742; e pr@oszk.hu. Some people collect stamps or beer mats; during the 18th century, Count Széchenyi Ferenc, father of István, set himself the modest task of collecting every available example of 'Hungarica'. His obsession stemmed from a desire to reinforce Hungarian nationhood and establish the country's place as an 'intellectual' centre of Europe. Based on his hoardings, the national library opened in 1803 in Pest.

The library now occupies 8 floors of the palace (the entrance in the Lion Courtyard is on the library's 5th floor). There are currently 10,000,000 items. Among the holdings are the only complete copy of the first book published in Hungary (the *Chronica Hungarorum* of 1473) and the *Gesta Hungarorum*, the early-13th-century work of an unknown chronicler (labelled Anonymus by the history books) charting the early centuries of Hungarian history. There are also 33 surviving 'corvina' codices from the acclaimed 15th-century library of King Mátyás (see page 176). A museum on the 8th floor includes a filing cabinet damaged by gunfire in 1956. *Foreign-lang tours (by appointment only; ☏ 1 224 3745) 300Ft; day reader pass adult/concessions 500/250Ft; reading rooms open Mon 13.00–21.00, Tue–Fri 09.00–21.00, Sat 09.00–17.00; closed Aug.*

**Telephone Museum** (*Telefónia Múzeum*) I, Úri utca 49; ☏ 1 201 8188. OK, OK, so you think you'd have to be an oxy*moron* to place 'interesting' and 'telecommunications' in a sentence free of the word 'not'. Well, a Hungarian, Tivadar Puskás, built the first telephone exchange in 1879, and this museum deserves a chance. In the 19th and early 20th centuries, the castle exchange (*várközpont*) was housed in this former convent. Between 1928 and 1985, here operated – stay with us – the first mechanically switched automatic telephone exchange. This immense whirring and dinging piece of kit is preserved in its original splendour, and is the museum's *pièce de résistance*. Other exhibits include phones belonging to Hungary's last two kings, and that of János Kádár. Entry at weekends and holidays is via Országház utca 30. *Adult/concessions 100/50Ft; open Tue–Sun 10.00–16.00.*

## HALLO EVERYONE!
The name Puskás Tivadar may not ring any bells, but this ex-student of the University of Technology invented the telephone exchange in 1877 and was a colleague of the rather better-remembered Thomas Edison. He also brought us the world's most familiar greeting. On testing his invention, and hearing a voice at the other end of the telephone line for the first time, he cried out 'Hallom!' meaning 'I hear you!' in Hungarian. A slight mishearing and a dropped consonant later, and the word 'hallo' was born.

## Gellért Hill, the Tabán and surrounds

**Semmelweis Museum of Medical History** (*Orvostörténeti Múzeum*) I, Apród utca 1–3; ℡ 1 201 1577; www.semmelweis.museum.hu. Ignác Semmelweis (1818–65) solved one of medicine's tragic mysteries by discovering that grime was the primary cause of puerperal (childbirth) fever. In pioneering hospital cleanliness and antiseptics, the surgical scrubber slashed mortality rates in his Viennese maternity hospital by 80%, and was labelled the 'saviour of mothers'. Fate and irony colluded to ensure that Semmelweis died of septicaemia in a mental asylum. The house in which he was both born and buried (the urn containing his ashes was placed in a wall of the building) stands to the south of Castle Hill, and charts the history of medicine from the Stone Age through to the 19th century. *Free entry; temporary exhibitions adult/concessions 300/150Ft; open Tue–Sun Oct 15– Mar 15 10.30–16.00, rest of yr 10.30–18.00.*

## Óbuda and Aquincum

**Aquincum Museum** III, Szentendrei út 139; ℡ 1 250 1650 [M2 *Batthyány tér, then* HEV *to Aquincum stop; turn right & museum is 200m away, on opposite side of road*] The civilian Roman town of Aquincum was an important place, situated as it was at the eastern frontier of the empire. The artisans, tradesmen and vintners left over a million artefacts for archaeologists to unearth, including early-Christian religious items, an altar dedicated to Mithras, and even a portable organ. The grounds surrounding the museum encompass one-third of the town, and there are remains of the courthouse, the great shrine, the public baths and the market, as well as evidence of a sophisticated sewage system (featuring flush toilets). The lapidarium has stone finds, while the civilian amphitheatre, which could hold 6,000 spectators, is near Aquincum station. *Adult/concessions 700/300Ft; free with Budapest Card; open Tue–Sun Apr 15–May 1 & Oct 1–31 ruins garden/exhibition 09.00–17.00/10.00–17.00, Jun 1–Sep 30 09.00–18.00/10.00–18.00.*

**Hercules Villa** III, Meggyfa utca 19–21; ℡ 1 250 1650 [B *6, 86, 118, 106*] Roman 3rd-century villa belonging to an imperial official, with Italian-stone mosaics. On the corner of Meggyfa utca and Vihar utca, to the north of Flórián tér. *Free entry; open Tue–Sun Apr 15–31 & Oct 1–31 10.00–17.00, May 1–Sep 30 10.00–18.00.*

**Kassák Museum** III, Fő tér 1; ℡ 1 368 7021 [HEV *Árpád híd*] On the 1st floor of the pink Baroque mansion – the 18th-century abode of the Zichy family, which owned Óbuda – is an exhibition of the works of Lajos Kassák (1887–1967), poet, author and leading artist of the Hungarian avant-garde. A working-class socialist, and of uncompromising artistic integrity, he was persecuted successively by Béla Kun in 1919, by the Horthy regime and by the Stalinists after 1945. *Free entry; temporary exhibitions from 150Ft; open Tue–Sun Mar 17–Oct 31 10.00–18.00, Nov 1–Mar 15 10.00–17.00.*

**Óbuda Museum** III, Fő tér 1; ℡ 1 388 2534. [HEV *Árpád híd*] Adjacent to the Kassák Múzeum, this is an eclectic collection of items relating to the local history of Óbuda. *Adult/concessions 300/200Ft; open Tue–Sun 10.00–17.00.*

**Varga Imre Collection** See page 168.

**Vasarely Museum** III, Szentlélek tér; ℡ 1 388 7551. [HEV *Árpád híd*] Yet another museum in a pocket of the Zichy Mansion, this one devoted to 20th-century Hungarian Op-Artist Victor Vasarely. The extensive collection includes early Matisse-like sketches and distorted Picasso-like still-life paintings. Of most interest, however, are the stylised later pieces of the 1960s and '70s that make kaleidoscopic use of coloured geometrical shapes, playing with expectations of dimension and space. The effect can be giddying, almost psychedelic, as squares and dots swim before your eyes; take an anti-nausea pill before you visit. *Free entry; temporary exhibitions adult/concessions 600/300Ft; open Tue–Sun 10.00–17.00.*

## Buda Hills and beyond

**Bartók Béla Memorial House** II, Csalán út 29; ℡ 1 394 2100; www.bartokmuseum.hu [B *5 from Ferenciek tere to Pasaréti tér, then short walk*] This villa was Bartók's home during the 1930s (prior to his emigration to America). Inside is the study where the composer composed, complete with writing desk and Bösendorfer piano, while rustic furniture and earthenware reflect his fascination with folk culture. A circular theatre in the wooded garden hosts open-air concerts, and the indoor concert hall has an 18th-century cofferwork ceiling that originally graced a church in Tök. Concert tickets can be bought here or at Ticket Express offices (see page 121). (Note: The house is closed for refurbishment until Mar 2006.) *Adult/concessions 400/200Ft; open Tue–Sun 10.00–17.00.*

**Foundry Museum** (*Öntödei Múzeum*) II, Bem József utca 20; ☏ 1 201 4370 [M̄2̄ *Batthyány tér;* B̄ *11, 60, 86;* T̄ *4, 6*] The Swiss industrialist and man of steel Ábrahám Ganz founded this chill-casting foundry in 1858. *Free entry; open Tue–Sun 10.00–18.00.*

**Kiscelli Museum** III, Kiscelli utca 108; ☏ 1 388 7817; www.btm.hu [T̄ *17;* B̄ *60, 165*] This crumbling Baroque edifice once housed monks of the Trinitarian order; it's now filled with Hungarian art of the 19th and 20th centuries, featuring Cubist works by János Kmetty, the puppet-themed paintings of Margit Anna and avant-garde art of the 1960s, 1970s and 1980s. There is also an exhibition of antique printing presses, among them that on which Petőfi's 'National Song' was illegally published, and there are Biedermeier furnishings from the Golden Lion Pharmacy, which stood in the Belváros between 1794 and 1945. Some of Hungary's foremost chamber orchestras perform concerts here in summer. *Adult/concessions 600/300Ft; free for over-65s; open Tue–Sun Apr 1–Oct 31 10.00–18.00, Nov 1–Mar 31 10.00–16.00.*

**Nagytétény Castle Museum** (*Nagytétényi Kastélymúzeum*) XXII, Kastélypark utca 9–11; ☏ 1 207 5462; www.museum.hu/budapest/nagytetenyi [B̄ *3 from Móricz Zsigmond körtér to Petőfi utca, cross road & follow Pohár utca*] Fluted legs and well-turned feet aplenty in an exhibition of 15th–19th-century European furniture. *Free entry; temporary exhibitions adult/concessions 500/250Ft; open Tue–Sun 10.00–18.00.*

**Statue Park** See page 167.

**Tropicarium-Óceanárium** XXII, Nagytétényi út 37–45; ☏ 1 424 3053; www.tropicarium.hu [B̄ *3 from Móricz Zsigmond tér*] Flora and fauna of rivers, lakes and seas, together with a rainforest habitat containing alligators and iguanas. The sharks take luncheon on Wed and Sun. *Adult/concessions 1,700/1,000Ft; discount with Budapest Card; open 10.00–20.00 daily.*

# Pest
## Downtown and beyond

**Ady Endre Memorial Museum** V, Veres Pálné utca 4-6; ☏ 1 337 8563. Documents and furnishings belonging to Ady (1877–1919), Hungary's premier *fin-de-siècle* poet whose collection of 1906 – *New Poems* – is said to have kick-started the country's 20th-century literary output. This apartment was his last residence. *Free entry; open Wed–Sun Mar 1–Oct 31 10.00–18.00, Nov 1–Feb 28 10.00–16.00.*

**Fine Arts Collection of the Hungarian Academy of Sciences** (*Magyar Tudományos Akadémia*) V, Roosevelt tér 9; ☏ 1 411 6100. They keep themselves tucked away, but the fine arts in the august Academy of Sciences are spoken of with reverence by those in the know. Spare a glance for the bas-relief of Empress Erzsébet grieving over the corpse of Ferenc Deák in the hallway before climbing the marble staircase. Alongside the portraits and sculptures on the uppermost floor, the 17th-century Flemish and Dutch landscapes are especially striking. *Free entry; open Mon–Fri 10.00–16.00.*

**Lutheran Museum** (*Evangélikus Országos*) V, Deák tér 4; ☏ 1 483 2150. Adjacent to the Lutheran church, the prize pupil of this collection is Martin Luther's last will and testament of 1542, a facsimile copy of which is on display (the original is in the archives). *Adult/concessions 300/150Ft; free with Budapest Card; open Tue–Sun 10.00–18.00 (10.00–16.00 in winter).*

**Museum of Ethnography** (*Néprajzi Múzeum*) V, Kossuth Lajos tér 12; ☏ 1 473 2440; www.hem.hu. Like the Ministry of Agriculture next door, this building (by Alajos Hauszmann) was a losing entry in the fierce 19th-century contest to design Parliament. It was constructed nevertheless, destined to look greenly upon Steindl's victorious vision across the square, and until 1949 served as the Supreme Court. Its interior includes a gorgeous fresco by Károly Lotz depicting *The Triumph of Justice*. The present museum collection is founded on the late-19th- and early-20th-century interest in national folklore. The exhibition displays costumes, craftwork and photos of the peoples of historical Hungary, as well as artefacts gathered during expeditions further afield. There are frequent temporary displays too. *Free entry; temporary exhibitions adult/concessions 500/250Ft; open Tue–Sun 10.00–18.00 (winter 10.00–17.00).*

**Palace of Wonders** (*Csodák Palotája*) XIII, Váci út 19; ℄ 1 350 6131; www.csodapalota.hu [M3 *Lehel tér, then walk north up Váci út*] An interactive science centre (in Újlipótváros) where children can bang, press buttons, ride a high-wire tricycle, and generally have a jolly good mess around while weary parents reassure themselves it's all in the name of learning. Young children revel in the energy and din; adults should take a cool flannel and a headache pill. *Adult/concessions 650/600Ft, family 2,000Ft; free with Budapest Card; open Mon–Fri 09.00–17.00, Sat–Sun 10.00–18.00.*

**Petőfi Literary Museum** (*Petőfi Irodalmi Múzeum*) V, Károlyi Mihály utca 16; ℄ 1 317 3611; www.pim.hu. The national museum of modern literature is housed in the renovated Károlyi Palace, itself offering more than a sniff of historical interest. Queen Maria Theresa visited in 1791, Lajos Batthyány (the first Hungarian prime minister) was arrested here in 1849, and it was the birthplace of Mihály Károlyi (the first president of Hungary, in 1919). Bookworms will find some of Petőfi's personal items among the museum's exhibits. Note the wooden cobbles as you pass through the archway leading from Egyetem tér; these were common features of aristocratic mansions, dulling the din of horses' hooves. *Adult/concessions 280/140Ft; free with Budapest Card; open Tue–Sun 10.00–18.00.*

**Underground Railway Museum** (*Földalatti Vasúti Múzeum*) V, Deák tér underpass; ℄ 1 461 6500. Hungary can claim the first underground railway on mainland Europe and the second in the world (pipped by London's Metropolitan line), opened in 1896 to coincide with the millennial celebrations and running from Deák tér to City Park. In the subway (at the top of the escalators), this little museum displays original carriages and fixtures in telling the tale of the metro's history. On the walls are majolica tiles, manufactured in Pécs by the Zsolnay factory and a dainty feature of the stations on the oldest line. *Free entry; open Tue–Sun 10.00–17.00.*

## Terézváros

**Hopp Ferenc Museum of Eastern Asiatic Arts** (*Kelet-Ázsiai Művészeti*) VI, Andrássy út 103; ℄ 1 322 8476 [M Bajza utca] Much of the Oriental collection squirreled away by Hopp – whose villa this was – is in the Ráth György Museum (opposite). What remains here is Indian art inspired by the cult of Vishnu and Shiva, *wayang* puppets from Indonesia, and other works from Nepal, Tibet and Mongolia. *Adult/concessions 400/200Ft; free with Budapest Card; open same as Ráth György Museum.*

**House of Terror** See page 165.

**Liszt Ferenc Memorial Museum** (*Liszt Ferenc Emlékmúzeum*) VI, Vörösmarty utca 35; ℄ 1 322 9804; www.lisztmuseum.hu [M *Vörösmarty utca metro station;* B 4] One of music's masters, the silver-haired Liszt (1811–1886) was a symbol of Hungarian nationhood, his very concerts bold statements of opposition to the absolutism that followed the 1848–49 Independence War. He was elected president of the Academy of Music on its inauguration in 1875, and lived out his final years on the 1st floor of the academy's Neo-Renaissance building. The man behind the music played whist (there's a card table and a card box); he smoked cigars (there's a case and a few coronas); he took snuff from a silver box. He needed a cognac snifter before a composing session. And his fingers! A bronze replica of his elderly hand shows a thumb that reached to the knuckle of the forefinger! These lengthy digits cascaded over the keyboard; as one observer remarked, 'We had never been confronted by such passionate, demonic genius.' The building also holds a research library, and a small concert hall. On the corner where Andrássy út meets Vörösmarty utca. *Adult/concessions 400/200Ft; open Mon–Fri 10.00–18.00, Sat 09.00–17.00.*

**Postal Museum** VI, Andrássy út 3; ✆ 1 268 1997 [Ⓜ *Bajcsy-Zsilinszky út*] You'll have to buzz for entry; as you climb the stairwell to the first floor be sure to admire the ceiling frescoes by Károly Lotz, which give an insight into the splendour of a wealthy 19th-century townhouse (owned by the merchant Andreas Saxlehner, whose family fled to America in 1938). The museum holds the trappings of postal history, and items relating to telecommunications and broadcasting. King Mátyás established the very first mail coach in 1458, which delivered missives between Buda and Vienna. *Adult/concessions 100/50Ft; free for under 7s, over 65s, and with Budapest Card; open Tue–Sun 10.00–18.00 (Nov 1–Mar 31 10.00–16.00).*

**Ráth György Museum** VI, Városligeti fasor 12; ✆ 1 342 3916 [Ⓣ🅑 *70, 78*] The country's prime collection of Oriental art, based upon items accumulated by Ferenc Hopp during his travels (1882–1913). There are additional temporary exhibitions at the nearby Hopp Ferenc Museum (see opposite). *Free entry; temporary exhibitions adult/concessions 300/150Ft; open Tue–Sun 10.00–18.00 (Jan 1–Mar 31 10.00–16.00).*

**Zoltán Kodály Memorial Museum** VI, Andrássy út 87-89; ✆ 1 352 7106 [Ⓜ *Kodály körönd*] Kodály (1882–1967) was one of the 20th century's most-influential composers, and a music teacher who devised the revolutionary 'Kodály Method'. This was his apartment for much of his life. Among his possessions are pieces of earthenware decorated with folk motifs; like Bartók, Kodály embarked on a journeyman's crusade to collect folk music, and he picked up such ceramics on his travels. Press the buzzer in the courtyard for entry. *Adult/concessions 300/150Ft; free with Budapest Card; open Wed 10.00–16.00, Thu–Sat 10.00–18.00, Sun 10.00–14.00.*

## Heroes' Square, City Park and around

**Exhibition Hall/Kusthalle** XIV, Dózsa György út 37; ✆ 1 460 7000/7014; 3-D film info: 1 460 7033 [Ⓜ *Hősök tere*] One half of the exquisite Neoclassical brace of buildings on Hősök tere, the Exhibition Hall (formerly known as the Palace of Arts) represents the country's largest gallery space and hosts temporary lashings of contemporary art. There are regular screenings of a 3-dimensional film about Hungary's highlights. *Adult/concessions 600/300Ft; combined (gallery & film) ticket adult/concessions 990/490Ft; free with Budapest Card; open Tue–Wed, Fri–Sun 10.00–18.00, Thu 12.00–20.00.*

**Hungarian Agricultural Museum** (*Magyar Mezőgazdasági Múzeum*) XIV, Vajdahunyadvár, Városliget; ✆ 1 363 1971; www.mezogazdasagimuzeum.hu [Ⓜ *Hősök tere*] Europe's largest agricultural museum is held in the intriguing Vajdahunyad Castle, conceived in 1896 as a temporary flex of Hungary's architectural muscles (see page 160). The museum's collection is planted in the Baroque and Gothic wings, and is devoted to animal husbandry (István Széchenyi imported English methods of horse-breeding during the 19th century), hunting and wine production. *Adult/concessions 500/200Ft; free with Budapest Card; open Tue–Fri 10.00–17.00 (10.00–16.00 in winter), Sat 10.00–18.00 (10.00–17.00 in winter), Sun 10.00–17.00.*

**Hungarian Railway History Park** (*Magyar Vasúttörténeti Park*) XIV, Tatai út 95; ✆ 1 450 1497/238 0558; www.vasuttortenetipark.hu and www.mavnosztalgia.hu [🅑 *30 from Keleti Station to Rokolya utca; Ⓣ 14 from Lehel tér to Dolmány utca. Vintage diesel shuttle runs between Nyugati Station and museum Apr 1–Oct 31, departing 09.45, 10.45, 13.45 and 15.45*] Central Europe's largest outdoor railway museum is a real heavyweight. The bays of the former North Depot's 1911 roundhouse are crammed with carriages and engines dating back to the late 19th century. Among them are the Árpád rail car, which ran between Budapest and Vienna from 1937, and an *Orient Express* dining carriage. Many are used for tourist trips by MÁV Nosztalgia. You can drive a steam engine or a horse tram, and there's a model railway. *Adult/concessions 900/300–400Ft; interactive rides 100–1,000Ft; open Tue–Sun Mar 13–Apr 2 & Oct 25–Dec 19 10.00–15.00, Apr 3–Oct 24 10.00–18.00; interactive rides only open Apr 3–Oct 24 10.00–16.00.*

**Hungarian Sports Museum** XIV, Dozsa Gyorgy út 3; ✆ 1 252 1696 [🅑 *95, 130;* Ⓣ *1, 1A;* Ⓣ🅑 *75, 77*] Utilitarian block profiling Hungarian sporting gods of the past. One room is dedicated to the winner of the country's first Olympic gold medal, Alfréd Hajós, who took up swimming after his father drowned in the Danube. *Free entry; open Sat–Thu 10.00–16.00.*

**Municipal Grand Circus** (*Fővárosi Nagycirkusz*) XIV, Állatkerti körút 12; ℩ 1 343 8300/344 6008 [M̄ *Széchenyi fürdő*; T̄B̄ 72; B̄ 4, 30] Flanked by a pair of inflatable clowns in City Park, Pest's circus has a provenance dating to the 18th century. *Adult/concessions 900–1,400Ft/700–1,200Ft; summer performances (mid Apr–Aug) on Wed, Fri, Sun 15.00 & 19.00, Thu 15.00, Sat 10.00, 15.00, 19.00.*

**Municipal Zoo and Botanical Garden** (*Fővárosi Állat-és Növénykerty*) XIV, Állatkerti körút 6–12; ℩ 1 363 3797/3710. Few elephants around the world trumpet away beneath a turquoise domed roof. The Moorish enclosure – whose tower you can climb – was inspired by the remains of a Turkish mosque, but there is early-20th-century architectural adventure elsewhere, not least in the garish Secessionist entrance gate. At the western side of City Park (next to the circus), the zoo is also home to Hungary's only gorillas, and holds a good children's playground and a botanical garden. *Adult/concessions/family 1,300/900/4,100Ft; open Nov–Feb 09.00–16.00 daily, Mar–Apr & Sep–Oct 09.00–17.00 daily, May–Aug Mon–Thu 09.00–18.00, Fri–Sun 09.00–19.00; cash desk closes 1hr earlier.*

**Museum of Fine Arts** See page 167.

**Transport Museum** (*Közlekedési Múzeum*) XIV, Városligeti körút 11; ℩ 1 363 2658; www.km.iif.hu [T̄ 1; T̄B̄ 70, 72, 74] This is no 'tram, bam, thank-you ma'am' museum; the collection of trains, boats, motorcycles and vintage cars – both replicas and the real things – is vast. The model train engines, intricate and precise copies, are magnificent. In front of the museum are pieces of the Chain Bridge that was destroyed by the Germans during World War II. On the edge of City Park. *Free entry; open Tue–Fri 10.00–17.00, Sat–Sun 10.00–18.00.*

**Vidámpark** XIV, Városligeti körút 14–16; ℩ 1 363 3825; www.vidampark.hu/english/indexe.html [M̄ *Hősök tere*] The 1906 merry-go-round (immortalised in the Rogers and Hammerstein musical *Carousel*) is a protected national monument encased in a glass building, and the roller-coaster terrifies not because of the dips and lurches, but because it is made of wood and feels a bit overly rickety... Generally quite deserted, this is a fun place on a dreary Sunday afternoon. *Adult 300Ft, child under 120cm free; free with Budapest Card; rides cost 300–600Ft; open daily 11.00–sunset (winter), 10.00–20.00 (summer).*

## Erzsébetváros

**Hungarian Electrical Engineering Museum** (*Magyar Elektrotechnikai Múzeum*) VII, Kazinczy utca 21; ℩ 1 322 0472 [M̄2 *Blaha Lujza tér*; T̄B̄ 74] Magyars have been to the fore in the highly charged field of electrical engineering. Ányos Jedlik – a monk at Pannonhalma – devised the commutator DC motor and Imre Bródy filled bulbs with krypton gas to create lights as we know them. As all this whizzed in one ear and out the other, we spent a happy hour in the former transformer station winding handles to light glass tubes and creating static thunder claps that made our hearts flop over. In fairness, there are some human stories to be dug out too. Jedlik constructed the first dynamo (the original is here) but failed to patent it; 7 years later someone else's version appeared, and Jedlik's achievement was forgotten to history. *Free entry; open Tue–Sat 11.00–17.00.*

**Jewish Museum** (*Zsidó Múzeum*) VII, Dohány utca 2; ℩ 1 342 8942 [T̄ 47, 49; B̄ 7, 7A] The first of the two exhibitions focuses upon religious objects associated with Jewish holidays. As well as silver menorahs and chalices, borrow someone's reading glasses and take a careful look at the tapestry on the left as you enter. The words of the Torah are embroidered in tiny script; it was made in 1828, and used for covert worship during World War II. Contemporary photographs in the Holocaust exhibition bring up close the chilling plight of Hungarian Jews in 1944, many of whom perished in labour camps. There is also a more uplifting tribute to those who strove to help them, among them Raoul Wallenberg (see box, page 180). Next to the Great Synagogue (page

179). *Adult/concessions 1,000/400Ft; open Mon–Thu 10.00–17.00 (Nov 1–Apr 14 10.00–15.00), Fri & Sun 10.00–14.00.*

**Stamp Museum** (*Bélyegmúzeum*) VII, Hársfa utca 47; ❧ 1 341 5526 [$\overline{T}$ 4, 6; $\overline{TB}$ 74] Join the stampede of philatelists to view a collection of 12 million stamps. On the corner of Dob utca and Hársfa utca. *Adult/concessions 150/75Ft; free with Budapest Card; open Tue–Sun 10.00–18.00 (Nov 1–Mar 31 10.00–16.00).*

## Józsefváros, Ferencváros and beyond

**Crime and Police History Museum** (*Bűnügyi és Rendőrség Történeti Múzeum*) VIII, Mosonyi utca 7; ❧ 1 477 2183; www.policehistorymus.com [$\overline{M2}$ *Keleti;* $\overline{T}$ *23, 24;* $\overline{B}$ *7, 7A*] The history of the Hungarian police force, with gruesome details of real 20th-century criminal cases. *Free entry; open 10.00–17.00.*

**Dreher Beer Museum** (*Dreher Sörmúzeum*) X, Jászberényi út 7–11; ❧ 1 432 9700; www.dreherrt.hu. A fun exhibition of the history of Hungarian brewing in which you're transported on a little train. You'll need to book to tour the factory (❧ *1 432 9850*). *Adult 200Ft; open Mon–Fri 09.00–18.00, Sat–Sun 10.00–16.00.*

**Holocaust Memorial Centre** IX, Páva utca 39; ❧ 1 455 3333; www.hdke.hu [$\overline{M3}$ *Ferenc körút*] The exhibition halls and archive rooms are built around a restored synagogue that served as an internment camp, and form a deliberately angular and uncomfortable space. In just 56 days, 437,000 Jews were deported from Hungary, all but 15,000 to Auschwitz – the fastest and largest deportation of the Holocaust. In the courtyard is a wall bearing the names of 60,000 victims. Those behind the centre strive for a fuller acceptance of the Holocaust as a part of Hungarian, as well as German, history. They invite discussion of the lack of resistance, the looting of property and the assistance provided by the authorities. They remind visitors of the nightly massacres by Arrow Cross troopers on the Danube's banks during the winter of 1944, and they pay tribute to the Roma people, who also suffered murderous persecution. By promoting a fuller understanding of, and accountability for, the past, the exhibition hopes to foster better relations in the present. *Free entry; open Tue–Sun 10.00–18.00.*

**Hungarian National Museum** See pages 166–7.

**Ludwig Museum – Museum of Contemporary Art** XI, Komor Marcell utca 1; ❧ 1 555 3444; www.ludwigmuseum.hu [$\overline{T}$ *2, 24;* $\overline{HEV}$ *Lágymányosi híd*] Recently moved from the Buda Palace to the new Palace of Arts, this museum of international contemporary art is spread over 3 floors, and represents a bite-sized romp through works by some of the 20th century's most flamboyant artists. There are 3 late Picassos here, examples of American pop art by Andy Warhol and Roy Lichtenstein, and European trans-avantgarde works, as well as material by artists from the Soviet Union, Bulgaria, East Germany and Hungary. *Free admission to permanent exhibitions; open Tue, Fri & Sun 10.00–18.00, Wed 12.00–18.00, Thu 12.00–20, Sat 10.00–20.00.*

**Museum of Applied Arts** (*Iparművészeti Múzeum*) IX, Üllői út 33–37; ❧ 1 456 5100; www.imm.hu [$\overline{T}$ *4, 6*] Blissfully over the top, the Art-Nouveau building was designed for the 1896 millennial celebrations by Ödön Lechner and Gyula Pártos. The pair clearly had some fun. Lechner – whose hunched statue sits outside – determined to create a uniquely Hungarian style, and there are folksy and oriental elements, as well as Indian influences deriving from the contemporary belief that the Magyar tribes arrived from the subcontinent. The white interior contains arts and crafts, 17th-century costume, a selection of oriental rugs and examples of the Art-Nouveau movement. *Free entry; temporary exhibitions adult/concessions 600/300Ft; open Tue–Sun 10.00–18.00 (10.00–16.00 Nov–Mar).*

**Natural History Museum** (*Magyar Természettudományi*) VIII, Ludovika tér 6; ❧ 1 210 1085; www.nhmus.hu [$\overline{M3}$ *Klinikák*] A permanent exhibition details man's often disharmonious relationship with nature, while alongside the usual stuffed monkeys are reconstructions of ancient faces, a giant clam donated by the Hungarian storyteller Mór Jókai, a piece of moon rock from the Apollo expedition, and an extensive palaeontological display that includes dinosaur eggs and footprints. *Free entry; open Wed–Mon 10.00–18.00.*

**Planetarium** X, Népliget Park; ☎ 1 263 0871; www.lezerszinhaz.hu [**M3** *Népliget;* **B** *103;* **TB** *75*] The paths of the planets are on show during the day, while in the evening there's a laser display in tune to music by galacticos of the pop world. 'The Wall' was the score to which the Berlin Wall fell, and Pink Floyd remains one of the laser theatre's best-loved shows. Tickets available from 18.30 or from city ticket offices; alternatively book by telephone (☎ 1 263 0871). At the intersection of Könyves Kálmán körút and Üllői út. *Planetarium adult/concessions 1,190/790Ft; laser show adult 2,090Ft, student 1,590Ft, child 600Ft; discount with Budapest Card; Planetarium open Tue–Sun 09.00–16.00; laser shows start at 19.30 (closed Jun).*

# MAJOR SIGHTS
## Buda

**Buda Castle Palace** (*Budavári Palota*) I, Vár hegy. The vast pile that commands the southern end of Castle Hill is the last in a line of palaces built since the early-medieval period. **Béla IV** first chose to construct a town here in the 13th century, and the **Angevin kings** also established strongholds. However, the golden age of the royal complex came during the **15th century**. First Zsigmond of Luxembourg (1387–1437) established a considerably larger Gothic palace (featuring the renowned Knights' Hall). After that the cultured and progressive Mátyás (1443–90) expanded upon it with a Renaissance flourish. His second wife, Beatrice, was from Naples, and she brought with her a gaggle of Italian artists and a legendarily hospitable nature. Scholars and gentlemen from all over Europe flocked to the majestic palace, with its fine art and marble details. The king's library – the *Bibliotheca Corviniana* – was among the world's richest, holding 2,000 books and manuscripts. Scattered by the Turks, today only 200 remain worldwide (33 of them in the current National Széchényi Library; page 169).

The palace fell into decline under **Ottoman occupation**. It was finally put out of its misery in 1686, when Buda was liberated but its greatest building reduced to rubble. The country's **Habsburg rulers** began anew. Maria Theresa (1740–80) enlarged upon her father's Baroque palace; it became the residence of the palatines, and from 1776 also held the Holy Right Hand of St István – the country's most prized and revered relic.

The palace's feathers were ruffled again during the 1848–49 War of Independence, when it was occupied by Hungarian forces struggling against imperial rule. Restoration came on a grand scale following the Austro-Hungarian Compromise of 1867, first to the designs of Miklós Ybl and then, after his death, to those of Alajos Hauszmann. The expansion was an expression of a fresh sense of independence, and it was hoped that the splendacious palace would shift the dual monarchy's beating heart from Vienna to Budapest. Hauszmann doubled the length of the palace's façade (to over 300m) and added its outstanding feature, the central dome. Ferenc József, who had been crowned in Buda, laid one of the foundation stones during the millenary celebrations of 1896. Once completed, it formed the impressive backdrop to the coronation procession in 1916 of Károly IV, the last Habsburg king.

In the **aftermath of World War I**, Admiral Miklós Horthy moved into the palace and lived the right royal high life. Shortly after his removal in a German coup of 1944, the Buda Castle Palace was brought down for the 31st and final time. The German army's centre of operations was based here, and as the soldiers holed up in a doomed final stand the palace was battered by Russian bombardment. The **post-war reconstruction** incorporated those walls that were still standing, and included Gothic and Baroque elements, but paid little regard to many aspects of the original design. However, archaeological excavations went hand in hand with the reconstruction and revealed previously hidden medieval sections that can be viewed on the lower levels of the **Budapest History Museum** (page 168). A series of Gothic statues of saints, knights and bishops found in 1974 probably date to Zsigmond's time. In 1959 the decision was made to devote the building to Hungarian culture, and, as well as the history museum, it now houses the **Hungarian National Gallery** and the **National Széchényi Library**.

**Cave Church** (*Sziklatemplom*) I, Gellért tér. A jagged-walled cavern and rugged place of worship. Its hill was originally called Mount 'Pest', the Slavic word for 'cavity', while the cave itself was named St Iván after a medieval healing hermit who lived inside. In 1926 the grotto church was built, inspired by a pilgrimage to Lourdes. During World War II, Pauline monks disguised Jews in their robes and hid them in the adjacent turreted cloister. In 1950, however, the saviours turned victims when communists seized monasteries all over Hungary. In total, over 10,000 of the country's monks and nuns were forced out, and many executed or imprisoned. The cave entrance was blocked with concrete, the cloister became a dormitory for students of the state ballet school and the Paulines had to wait almost 40 years for the political climate to permit their return. To the right of the cave entrance, a piece of the concrete wall remains as a reminder of the enforced period of exile. Masses are held daily at 11.00, 17.00 and 20.00, and on Sundays and holidays at 09.30 and 10.30. Non-observants may not visit at these times. *Open 09.00–21.00 daily.*

**Church of Mary Magdalene** I, Kapisztrán tér. The first church was erected in Romanesque style in the 13th century, and traditionally served the Hungarian population of the burghers' town. During the Turkish occupation, for some time it was the only church in the Castle District where Christian services were permitted; making the best in difficult times, Protestants used the nave and Catholics the chancel. The Habsburg Ferenc I was crowned here in 1792, adorned in ceremonial Hungarian garb, and the Neoclassical porch facing on to Úri utca was commissioned at the same time. Shortly afterwards Martinovics was stripped of his priesthood in the church, a further humiliation prior to his execution (see box, page 144). Massive World-War-II damage led to the demolition of most of the walls in 1952 and only the tower was preserved. The pathetic ruins of what was the church's main body lie behind it, culminating in an unsupported and fragile arched window, assembled from gathered fragments. It is said that if you look through the window your wishes will come true. This sounds laced with irony; in the face of this phantom of a church we're reminded of a dog with one ear and one eye called 'Lucky'.

**Citadella** I, Gellért hegy. Like the Freedom Monument (see page 146), the stronghold next to it had significant symbolic overtones when constructed by the Habsburgs following the 1848–49 War of Independence. Built with Hungarian forced labour, its forbidding presence against the skyline was designed to quash further rebellious impulses. However, tempers had cooled by the time the Austrian garrison took up residence, and the grey fortress began to look something of a white elephant. In 1894 it was handed over to the city, and parts of it demolished as a token of the country's unshackled self. It subsequently served, among other things, as a prison and a hostel for the homeless, but its walls now contain an **open-air exhibition** devoted to Gellért Hill, covering its history from ancient times up until the 20th century. There is a section on the martyrdom and cult of Gellért himself that challenges the traditional legend of the bishop's death (see page 16), arguing instead that the pagan insurgents of Vata tied him to a chariot, stoned him to death and pierced his heart with a lance. Infinitely preferable! Sellers of items irresistible to coach parties cluster outside the walls of the fort. *Adult 300Ft; exhibition and panoramic views open 12.00–24.00 daily.*

**Mátyás Church** I, Szentháromság tér 2. Different brushstrokes for different folks. Some deplore the old town's centrepiece as a tattooed millionaire of a church, all chunky jewellery and no class; others see a triumphant marriage of 13th-century Gothic design and late-19th-century national pride. It is something of a miracle that there is anything left to argue about. During World War II, tanks rammed through its main gates, the roof was burned out, and it was used alternately as a German field kitchen and a stable for Soviet horses. Mátyás was twice married here, and the walls – or parts of them – witnessed the coronations of Károly Róbert (the first Angevin king, in 1309), Ferenc József (for which Liszt's 'Coronation Mass' was composed, in 1867) and Károly IV (the country's last, in 1916).

The church was first raised on this site by Buda's **German population** in the reign of Béla IV. It was reconstructed by **King Lajos** in the 14th century (when the Maria portal was added) and **Mátyás** in the 15th (who oversaw the construction of the bell tower), and subsequently appropriated by the **Turks** as their main mosque during the 150 years of occupation. As part of the 1896 millennial celebrations, the architect **Frigyes Schulek** stripped away many of the later architectural layers in his quest to remain faithful to the spirit of the Gothic original. The result is a hall church characterised by its elegant Mátyás Tower, complete with lace-like stonework and bobbly spire, a fabulous Zsolnay-majolica-tiled roof, and interior decoration that thumps the eyeballs.

The **14th-century relief** above the southern Maria portal depicts the death and assumption of the Virgin Mary (after whom the church is properly named); the **raven** perched on the easternmost turret recognises the mighty impact of Mátyás Hunyadi's patronage. Inside, candy-sweet paints adorn every pillar of the nave and vaulted undulation of the ceiling. The geometric and floral designs were supposedly based upon Middle Age fragments, although the influence of Hungarian Art Nouveau is also clear. Other frescoes and stained-glass windows depict events of Hungarian history, and make the church as much a shrine to national consciousness as religious worship. These are the work of the renowned Romantic Historicist artists Károly Lotz and Bertalan Székely, who were responsible for other paintings in the opera house and Parliament.

There are subtler details to be winkled out inside. Our favourites can be found near the Mátyás coat of arms, within the arch of the organ loft to the left after you pass through the Maria portal. Look carefully and among the leafy motifs adorning two 15th-century capitals you will spot **four carved heads** – the wispy-bearded face of János Hunyadi, the curtain-haired Mátyás, the lopped-off noggin of László and, gazing towards the chancel, what is presumed to be a representation of the tower's builder. Next to the Hunyadi capital is the **Loréto Chapel**, the first of several side chapels. There's a legend attached to its statue. When the Turks converted the church into a mosque, they walled up a Madonna statue rather than taking the trouble to remove it. During the siege of Buda 145 years later, an explosion caused the wall to fall away, revealing the long-forgotten figure to startled Muslim worshippers. This was regarded as a sign, and a contributing factor in accelerating the Christian victory – although the current statue was sculpted later than 1686, and could not itself be the Madonna of the legend.

The **St Imre Chapel** is dedicated to the son of István, who died in a hunting accident in 1031. Without an heir, the monarch symbolically offered the crown to Mary. Next to it is the **Béla Chapel**, containing the remains of Béla III (1173–96) and his wife, moved here in the 19th century. The sarcophagus was paid for by Ferenc József, an act more political than benevolent: Béla's daughter had married a Habsburg, thus establishing a historic link between the dynasties, and justification for Habsburg claims to the throne.

The **St László Chapel**, to the left of the altar, contains a replica of the reliquary – a stunning gold bust of László (reigned 1077–95) – held in Győr Cathedral (see page 465). One fresco shows the famously tall king saving a Hungarian maiden from a pagan Cuman chief, while in another he summons water from a stone to quench the thirst of his soldiers. The **crypt** and **royal oratory** hold stonework remains, a collection of ecclesiastical art (none medieval, as József II auctioned most of this in 1785) and copies of the Hungarian crown and coronation regalia. In **St István Chapel** is the right foot of St János (see page 142). There are regular organ recitals and concerts; tickets can be purchased at the entrance. *Adult/concessions 600/300Ft; free with Budapest Card. Holy Mass Mon–Fri 07.00, 08.30 & 18.00, Sun & public hols 07.00, 08.30, 10.00 (choral, & in Latin), 12.00 & 18.00. Open Mon–Fri 09.00-17.00, Sat 09.00–12.00, Sun 13.00–17.00.*

**Tomb of Gül Baba** (*Gül Baba türbéje*) II, Mecset utca 14 [B 91, 191] The cobbled stairway of Gül Baba utca leads you up the peaceful Rózsadomb (Rose Hill). In an octagonal mausoleum at the top lies the Turkish dervish Gül Baba, who took part in the capture of Buda but dropped dead during the thanksgiving service afterwards in Mátyás Church; Süleiman the Magnificent attended his funeral prayer. The dervish later became known as the 'Father of Roses', reputedly because he grew flowers on the hillside but more probably a reference to tributes left at his tomb. The shrine was erected in 1548, the tablet pointing towards Mecca, and is a place of Muslim pilgrimage. Remove your shoes before entering. *Adult/concessions 400/200Ft; open Tue–Sun May 1–Sep 30 10.00–18.00, Oct 1–31 10.00–16.00.*

**Wolf's Meadow Cemetery** (*Farkasréti temető*) XI, Németvölgyi út 99 [⊤ *59 from Moszkva tér to the terminus*] Draw a line west from Gellért hegy, pass the queue of mourners at the flower stalls outside, and you're among the chestnut and ash trees of a sprawling cemetery. This is the resting place of many former dissidents and refugees, among them Béla Bártók and the conductor Sir Georg Solti. Here too lies Mátyás Rákosi, the squat dictator – 'Stalin's best Hungarian disciple' – whose name is synonymous with mid-20th-century suffering; before being removed in 1956, he executed around 2,000 of his fellow citizens and incarcerated at least 100,000 more. The cemetery's focal point is the unprecedented mortuary chapel by Imre Makovecz, its winged doors opening on to a timber chamber fashioned like a torso. Caskets are placed where the heart would be. Makovecz was himself imprisoned at the time of the 1956 uprising, and went on to develop an organic, spiritual form of architecture that deliberately flouted the communist preference for regular, pre-fab blocks. *Mon–Fri 07.00–21.00, Sat–Sun 09.00–17.00.*

# Pest
**Great Synagogue** (*Nagy Zsinagóga*) VII, Dohány utca. The 'Tobacco Street' synagogue (named after a factory here) was raised in 1859, its Moorish minarets the work of Austrian architect Ludwig Förster. It is the world's second-largest (after that in New York) and seats 3,000. The magnificent interior – which caters for the Neolog community (a Hungarian denomination) – is unusual in several ways. As well as containing an organ and 25 copies of the Torah (rather than the usual 12), it also has two pulpits from which the words of the rabbi are repeated so that all can hear (there are no microphones). Neglected under communism, renovation came in the 1990s, funded partly by the Emanuel foundation (established by actor Tony Curtis and named after his father, who emigrated in the 1920s). Festivals attract worshippers from all over Europe, and at other times there are concerts.

There was a ghetto here at the end of World War II, and a portion of the wall can be found in the **central courtyard**. The wall was demolished by the Soviets on January 18 1945, but a mass grave contains those who perished in the months before. Towards the back is **Heroes' Temple**, built in 1931 to commemorate Jews who died fighting at the front in World War I, often so poorly equipped that they didn't even have uniforms. The **Raoul Wallenberg Memorial Park** behind the complex is dedicated to the Swedish saviour (see box, page 180); its silver willow tree remembers the 600,000 Jews who died and the heroes of all faiths who risked their lives to save others. Relatives pay to have the names of victims inscribed upon the leaves. Next to the synagogue's main entrance is the **Jewish Museum** (see page 174); Tivadar (Theodor) Herzl (1860–1904) was born on this site, the journalist who founded the modern Zionist movement after witnessing anti-Semitism in Paris. *Adult 500Ft; open Mon–Thu 10.00–17.00, Fri 10.00–15.00, Sun 10.00–14.00.*

**Inner City Parish Church** (*Belvárosi plébániatemplom*) V, Március 15 tér 2. Nestling tight against Erzsébet híd, the Inner City Parish Church is Pest's oldest building. It was first constructed in the 12th century over the southern wall of the Roman fort at Contra-Aquincum, and actually recycled some of the stones; the south tower contains remnants of this original. (There had been an even earlier church on the site, where the martyred Bishop Gellért was buried in 1046.) The current Gothic sanctuary was raised in the 15th century, although there was a Baroque overhaul in 1739 and 19th-century renovation by Imre Steindl (at which time little shops operated from the spaces between the exterior buttresses). Work in the 1930s and 1940s uncovered *sedilia* in the sanctuary, together with a prayer niche (*mihrab*) that proves Turkish worship here during the occupation. The fragments of a medieval tabernacle were also found in the clear up after World War II; pieced together, it sits to the left of the high altar.

## RAOUL WALLENBERG AND ELIZABETH WISKEMANN

Raoul Wallenberg is cherished as foremost among the 'righteous gentiles'. In 1944, SS officer Adolf Eichmann was arranging the annihilation of Hungary's Jewish population, and mass deportations were taking place daily. By summer, 400,000 had been carried away to concentration camps, the majority to Auschwitz. Wallenberg – a 32-year-old Swedish businessman – was sent to Budapest as secretary of the Swedish legation in the hope that he could stem the tide. He had no diplomatic experience, but was a tough man, ready to use bribery and extortion as necessary. He distributed protective passes to Jews that granted them protection as Swedish (neutral) citizens, and set up 30 safe houses in Pest under the Swedish flag. As deportations intensified, he even ran alongside the wagons, handing out passes and offering aid; German soldiers were so impressed with his bravery that they aimed high when ordered to shoot. It is estimated that Wallenberg saved the lives of 100,000. When the Russians arrived, however, he was taken to their military headquarters – and never seen again. It seems that he was arrested on suspicion of spying for the Americans, but his fate thereafter is unknown. The Russians claimed he had died of a heart attack, while many others claimed he was still alive in a Soviet prison. The likelihood, however, is that he was executed.

A less-celebrated figure is the British agent in Switzerland, Elizabeth Wiskemann. In May 1944 – just as deportations from Hungary were beginning – the location of the 'unknown destination' to which European Jews were being taken was revealed by two escapees to be Auschwitz. A request was sent for the allies to bomb the railway lines. However, resources were stretched and the request was denied. As a cunning ploy, Wiskemann therefore sent a deliberately uncyphered message providing the addresses of individuals and government offices involved in the deportation plans and asking for target bombing of these should deportations continue. As expected, it was intercepted and passed to Regent Horthy. Six days later, entirely coincidentally, American raids on Budapest's marshalling yards accidentally hit some of the government buildings listed in the telegram. This caused panic in Budapest, and Horthy demanded an immediate end to deportations; without the assistance of Hungarian police and rail workers, the last major removal of Jews to Auschwitz had come to an end on July 6.

**Kerepesi Cemetery** VIII, Fiumei út [M2 *Keleti, walk down Festetics György utca & left into Fiumei út*] In our view, this is the city's prime haven – 54ha of parkland criss-crossed with paths and chestnut avenues, and history's movers all around. It's peaceful and fascinating. It's also one of the few places you'll see the red star and the hammer and sickle (officially outlawed as symbols of oppression). In one corner is the 1958 **Workers' Pantheon**, a white-stone piazza with Socialist-Realist statues and the words 'They lived for communism and the people'. The red-marble gravestone of **János Kádár** (see page 21) stands near by. Fallen revolutionary heroes of 1956 are buried in a plot behind the pantheon; secret policemen who died 'upholding the system' lie on the opposite side of the cemetery to prevent fights during memorial services. There are **magnificent mausoleums** for Ferenc Deák, Lajos Kossuth and Lajos Batthyány – the latter raided by robbers in 1993, who stole a sword but overlooked the earrings of Batthyány's wife (now safe in the National Museum). József Antall – the first post-communist leader – is also here. Teenager Mária Csizmarovits is buried close to the Russian memorial; she died during the 1849 revolution, having disguised herself as a man to gain admission to the army. In the **artists' plot**, look out for sculptor János Pásztor, whose round-buttocked wife was the model for the statue on his grave; a widow was later so affronted to hear her husband was to be buried in the face of this peachy backside that she ordered the newly deceased be interred in another cemetery altogether! *Open daily Jan–Feb & Nov–Dec 07.30–17.00, Mar & Oct 07.00–17.30, Apr & Aug 07.00–19.00, May–Jul 07.00–20.00, Sep 07.00–18.00.*

**Parliament** (*Országház*) V, Kossuth Lajos tér 1–3. The symmetrical Parliament is a grandiose counterweight to the palace across the river, the symbol of democratic rather than aristocratic governance. (With this in mind, it is a typical irony of Hungarian history that for much of the 20th century, this 'democratic' institution simply rubber-stamped authoritarian decisions taken elsewhere.) It was the winning entry in a competition of 1882, its Neo-Gothic aspect influenced by London's Parliament. However, Imre Steindl brought Eclectic elements such as the central dome to the medieval-style buttresses, spires and archways. The statistics are staggering. The building took 17 years to construct, with 1,000 (often convict) labourers working at any one time; it is 268m long, its dome 96m high (a measured reference to the Magyar arrival in AD896), and contains 40 million bricks and 40kg of gold gilding. It is said that the cost of the project was equal to that of building a town for 60,000 people.

The true splendour of the place is evident as soon as you enter (via the south side, facing Kossuth tér). A **vaulted hall** is supported by 8 columns carved from a single block of Swedish marble, a gift from the Swedish king (there are 4 of these in the English Parliament too); the imposing staircase carries you up to the **Dome Hall**, beneath frescoes by Károly Lotz and an allegorical portrait of Hungary with István Széchenyi and Sándor Petőfi at her feet. The Dome Hall itself is surrounded by Zsolnay ceramic statues of the country's rulers (Árpád, the original Magyar, casting dagger eyes towards the Habsburgs to his right). The glass-cased centrepiece is the **coronation insignia**, with the Sacred Crown (Hungary's national symbol), sceptre, orb and sword, which were placed here in 2000 (the mantle remains in the National Museum). While the legend goes that the crown was presented to István in 1000 as a sign of papal support for his rule, it was actually bashed together from two different pieces in the 12th century. Its skew-whiff cross is evidence of a turbulent history that saw it lost, dropped, buried in a bog and transported to various safehouses over the centuries, eventually ending up in America's Fort Knox before being returned in 1978. Since 1944, the legislature has been monocameral, and members sit in the **Chamber of Representatives** in the southern wing; the Upper House to the north is now used for international conferences. The **Hunter Hall** opposite the main staircase is the official dining area. *Adult/concessions 2,000/1,000Ft. Tourists may only visit on a guided tour; tickets are available from Gate X from 08.00 (ask the guard for permission to pass), & tours (in English) start at 10.00, 12.00, 14.00 & 18.00 daily. EU residents may enter as far as the Dome Hall free of charge; you must show your passport at the ticket gate.*

**Szent István Basilica** (*Bazilika*) V, Szent István tér. The Basilica got off to something of an inauspicious start. The first version of the capital's largest church, designed in 1845 by József Hild and constructed with inferior materials, had to be demolished after the dome collapsed. Miklós Ybl began anew, basing his Renaissance-inspired plan around a dome of 96m (like Parliament) flanked by stocky towers. During World War II, the dome was hit by a bomb that mercifully failed to detonate, but a fire in 1946 brought it down once more. After restoration, Pope John Paul II took Mass here in 1991. As you move up the steps and through the entrance's triumphal arch, you'll pass beneath a tympanum of carved Hungarian saints worshipping Mary and Christ, a statue of St István in Italian marble, and a gilded mosaic of Christ by Mór Than. The **interior** – laid out in the shape of a Greek cross – strikes you with contrasts, of light and dark, black and white, sturdy architecture and delicate art. Like the Mátyás Church (page 177), the artists present the Christian story very much in the context of Hungary's history, using St István as the focus. His statue (by Alajos Stróbl) graces the high altar, while major events in his significant life are played out in bronze reliefs on the walls behind. It is interesting to note that, for all the iconography portraying István's saintliness, he was actually a brutal and brooding king (see *History*, page 15), merciless in suppressing challenges to his authority. Look up to the dome, and mosaics by Károly Lotz, and to the Altar of the Virgin Mary at the southern end of the transept where Gyula Benczúr records the moment that István offered his crown to Mary on the death of his only son. There is a tiny **treasury** to the right of the entrance, and you can climb 300 steps (or take the lift most of the way) up to a **gallery** running around the outside of the Basilica's drum. However, the primary draw is the gnarled **right hand of István** himself, mounted in a casket in the Chapel of the Sacred Right. It is paraded through the streets during celebrations of the saint's day on Aug 20. Check listings magazines for details of concerts in the church or on the square outside. *The church is free to enter (it has been known for conmen to try to charge tourists at the entrance); treasury 100Ft, Panorama Tower adult/concessions 500/400Ft; open daily Apr 1–May 31 10.00–16.30, Jun 1–Aug 31 09.30–18.00, Sep 1–Oct 31 10.00–17.30.*

# Natural Budapest

There are few large cities where natural greenery is so readily accessible. The Buda Hills are known as the 'lungs' of the capital, and – clichéd as it sounds – the woodlands and clearings really do promise kisses of life on stifling days. In winter, they are places to sledge, or even ski. The Buda Landscape Protection Area (*Budai Tájvédelmi Körzet*) covers 10,000ha in total, and is characterised by outcrops of white dolomite and limestone rock, by forested areas and grasslands, and by over 150 caves (themselves cool retreats). It contains the strictly protected meadows of Kis-Szénás hegy and Nagy-Szénás hegy, the only spots in the world that the yellow-flowered *Linum dolomiticum* calls home.

Some of the most fragile habitats are barred to the casual tourist boot, but Hármashatár, Kis- and Nagy-Hárs, Remete, János and Széchenyi hills are all within easy reach and feature trails for ramblers, families and cyclists. Over 100 species of bird breed up here, wild boar and deer (fallow and red) inhabit the forests, scarce reptiles like the Armenian whipsnake (*Coluber jugularis*) bask in the sun, and edible funghi are to be found such as the brown-capped common mushroom (*Agaricus sp*) – although check before guzzling a handful as there are also poisonous varieties. Furthermore, to the north of Budapest are the Pilis, Visegrád and Börzöny hills (see *Chapter 4*). We've merely scratched a muddy surface with the following, and green fingers will find value in probing deeper. If you're going walking, Cartographia's *A Budai-hegység* (1:30,000) **map** shows the network of marked trails running through the Buda Hills. For operators running **nature-related tours**, see pages 38–40.

## THE RAIL TRAIL

Several buses run to points along the edge of the Buda Landscape Protection Area, but the train is an enjoyable way to ignore these limits and plunge straight on in. It also affords an easy introduction to a decent chunk of nature. The **Cogwheel Railway** (*Fogaskerekű vasút; XII, Szilágyi Erzsébet fasor 14–16*) is the first stage of your two-track journey. Its lower end station is Városmajor, best reached by tram (18 or 56) from Moszkva tér. Trains run every 15–20 minutes to Széchenyi hegy (*05.00–22.20 daily; last train back leaves around 23.30*) and you can travel using an ordinary bus/train ticket. (You can also take your bike aboard, although it requires a ticket too.) Don't expect a quaint or relaxing ride; teethed cogs pull the carriages uphill, and it's something of a brain-sloshing 20 minutes.

On disembarking, signposts offer several options. You can walk a short distance along Rege út to the **Széchenyi kilátó** (a TV tower at the top of the hill), you can follow Golfpálya út on the considerably longer route on foot to János hegy (see opposite), or you can take a few steps to the second stage of the railway trail 200m away.

The **Children's Railway** (*Gyermekvasút; Hegyhát út; ⑆ 1 397 5394/395 5420; www.gyermekvasut.com; sgl/rtn adult 200/400Ft, child 65/130Ft; on the hr Oct 25–Mar 12 Tue–Sun 10.00–16.00, Mar 13–Oct 24 Tue–Sun 10.00–18.00, May 1–Aug 31 daily 10.00–18.00*) is a narrow-gauge line that preserves the tradition – established by the communist youth movement and the Hungarian State Railway in 1948 – of giving work experience to children aspiring to a career on the railways. The kids collect and sell tickets conscientiously, but are not yet trusted with driving the engine. The carriages are wooden-benched and open-sided; they snake their way into the landscape protection area, and proceed northwards for 11km as far as Hűvösvölgy. The whole journey takes 45 minutes, but you may wish to alight at one of the eight stations along the way. The track passes Normafa lejtő, János hegy and Hárs hegy, while the Budakeszi Game Park (*Vadaspark*; see page 184) is accessible from Szépjuhászné. A nostalgia train also runs on the Children's Railway (*one-way supplement adult/concessions 100/50Ft*).

## NORMAFA LEJTŐ AND JÁNOS HEGY

**Normafa** – Róza Klein once sang an aria from Bellini's *Norma* under a tree (*fa*) here – is a very popular walking, biking, jogging and picnicking spot, particularly at weekends. At 479m above sea level it is one of the highest points in town, and offers some snow sports in winter; in truth, though, the views are more thrilling than the skiing. Bus 21 runs here from Moszkva tér at regular intervals; alternatively, you can take the Children's Railway to Normafa station (and follow Eötvös út north). If you want to escape the crowds, and enjoy a gentle downward lope, follow the route marked with a green cross next to the final bus stop (on the other side from the Danube view). Cross the Children's Railway line, and head down the valley, through Budakeszi forest towards Makkosmária Church in its lovely clearing. After the church, continue down Makkosmária út towards the centre of Budakeszi. From here you can take bus 22 back to Moszkva tér, passing the wildlife park on the way (see page 184).

A more strenuous walk from 184 is northwards to **János hegy**, the capital's highest peak (527m), along the blue-circle route. Up here you'll find the Erzsébet-kilátó, a viewing tower designed by Frigyes Schulek that takes you even higher for superb views, and further sign-posted walking routes (including a nature trail). Best of all, however, is the **chairlift** (*libegő; open daily summer 09.00–19.00, autumn/winter 09.30–16.00, spring 09.00–17.00; adult 900/450Ft, student/pensioner 600/300Ft, child 400/200Ft*), which offers peaceful carriage down the hill to Zugligeti út (from where you can take bus 158 to Moszkva tér). It can get chilly up there, so take a sweater. There's a walking/cycling route running beneath the lift, but it's very steep.

## CAVES

Budapest is unique as a world capital in being riddled with caves (*barlang*). There are over 60 thermal springs in Buda, welling up in groups at Gellért hegy, Hármashatár hegy and in the Csillaghegy-Rómaifürdő area; over thousands of years, the corrosive, toasty water broadened rock faults into chambers. The Bátori Cave on top of Hárs hegy was mined for iron ore during the Middle Ages, and the caves under the Castle District were used variously as cellars, burial vaults and air-raid shelters. Lime material deposited by the water as spring travertines at the surface was used in building the city, while the very name 'Pest' probably derives from the slavic word for cave.

Many other caves were only discovered during the urban expansion of the last hundred years (including most among the cluster of 80 in the Rózsadomb area). The five largest cave systems – Pál-völgy, Mátyás-hegy (a popular cavers' training site), Ferenchegy (a maze of narrow passages), Szemlő-hegy and József-hegy (only discovered in 1984) – are all located within an area of a couple of square kilometres, and are strictly protected. Despite this, there is limited access to a few of them for non-specialists. In addition to those below, some companies offer more active tours with qualified cavers, usually of the Mátyás-hegy system. For **further information** on caves, contact the Budapest Nature Conservation Directorate (*Budapesti Természetvédelmi Igazgatóság; II, Szépvölgyi út 162;* ✆ *1 325 5722/7833*).

**Buda Castle Labyrinth** I, Úri utca 9; ☏ 1 212 0207; e labirint@mail.elender.hu. The labyrinth has seen its share of wine, women and war. Once there were cellars, while during Turkish times, ladies past their prime from the pashas' harems were drowned in the pools. Corpses were brought down here following the 1686 siege; later it held first a World-War-II shelter and then a secret Cold-War military installation. Now organisers have tried to invest the complex with metaphysical meaning, adding stone-carved figures and taped heartbeats, and rather washy evocations of Hungarian history. Nevertheless, stumbling about with your oil lamp is dank and thoroughly enjoyable. There is a 2nd entrance outside the walls of the Castle District, at Lovas út. *Cost (with or without guide) adult/concessions 1,200/1,000Ft; free with Budapest Card; open daily 09.30–19.30.*

**Pálvölgy Stalactite Cave** II, Szépvölgyi út 162; ☏ 1 325 9505 [B̄ 65 *from Kolosy tér – alight at 5th stop*] You'll need to scale a ladder and 417 steps in your tour of the stalactite cave (*cseppkőbarlang*), with formations that are crocodiles to the imaginative eye, and fossils of 40-million-year-old sea urchins in the limestone. At over 13km, this is the 2nd-longest cave in Hungary; the public may see 500m of it. Guided tours (*50 mins*) leave 15 mins past every hour. (If you purchase a combined ticket for both Pálvölgy and Szemlő-hegy caves, the tour times suit a visit to the latter first.) *Adult/concessions 700/500Ft, combined ticket adult/concessions 900/600Ft, free with Budapest Card. No admission for children under 5. Open Tue–Sun 10.00-16.00.*

**Szemlő-hegy Cave** II, Pusztaszeri út 35; ☏ 1 325 6001 [B̄ 29 *from Kolosy tér – alight at 5th stop, on Felsőzöldmáli út*] The 2.2km-long cave is nicknamed 'the underground garden of Budapest' because of its popcorn-coralloid and other speleothems – in English, pretty mineral and crystal formations. The cave's glories were revealed in 1930, when a slim lady was passed through a narrow slit (later named the 'Needle's Eye'). Fat ladies (opera singers) now visit the 'Giant Corridor' to benefit from the curative effects of the cave's humid air. A 300m stretch is open to the public; tours (35 mins) start on the hour. *Adult/concessions 600/400Ft, free with Budapest Card, combined ticket (see above); open Mon & Wed–Fri 10.00–15.00, Sat–Sun 10.00–16.00.*

## OTHER SITES OF NATURAL INTEREST
### Buda

**Buda Arboretum** XI, Villányi út 35–43 & Ménesi út 41 [T̄ 61 *from Móricz Zsigmond körtér to 2nd stop;* B̄ 27 *from Móricz Zsigmond körtér to 1st stop*] Two sites around the buildings of the University of Horticulture and Food, straddling Ménesi út. There's an artificial pond and over 1,400 ligneous species, including several rare and exotic plants. Access may not be possible out of university term.

**Buda Sas hegy** XI Tájék utca 26; ☏ 1 319 6789 [B̄ 8 *from Március 15 tér to Meredek utca stop, then walk left up Meredek utca & right into Tájék utca*] Much of Sas hegy is residential, but there are 30ha of protected landscape at the top of the 266m white block of rock. The reserve contains dolomite flora such as Hungarian meadow saxifrage, Buda knapweed and St Stephen wild pink; this is also the habitat of the Pannonian lizard and many species of spider and insect. A lovely, elevated spot for a walk. You can only visit with a guide, by prior arrangement. Mr Siklósi Engelbert (☏ 06 70 330 3813) and Mr Halász Antal (☏ 06 70 330 3801) are the guides who facilitate entry; they live on site, but do not speak English. *Open Mar 15–Jun 15 & Sep 1–Oct 15 Sat–Sun 10.00–16.00.*

**Budakeszi Game Park** (*Budakeszi Vadaspark*) XII, Budakeszi; ☏ 1 2345 1783 [B̄ 22 *from Moszkva tér to Szanatórium utca, turn right at hospital, a short distance from bus stop, & take forest path for 1km; Children's Railway to Szépjuhászné, then* B̄ 22 *from Budakeszi út to Szanatórium utca; by car along Budakeszi út, then Szanatórium utca to car park*] The wildlife park spreads over 327ha on the border of Budapest and Budakeszi, and contains game species (like wild boar and fallow deer), indigenous livestock and an exhibition of small predators and birds. Several nature trails begin from the main entrance, taking walkers through woodland areas of beech, oak, spruce and pine. Pack some bread and sausage, and stop at one of the picnic spots. *Adult 400Ft, student/pensioner 250Ft, child 200Ft; open Mar 1–Oct 31 Mon–Fri 09.00–17.00, Sat–Sun 09.00–18.00, Nov 1–Feb 28 Mon–Fri 09.00–15.00, Sat–Sun 09.00–16.00.*

## ONE MAN AND HIS MOP

When we first saw a *puli* running down the street in Budapest, we looked around with some chagrin for the joker who was throwing mop heads around. It is one of the oddest dogs you'll see, a compact canine whose shaggy coat forms a series of natural cords – often mistaken for dreadlocks – that reach to the ground, covering its whole body. If the dog is standing still, it can be difficult to tell whether it is wagging a tail or shaking a head. When lying flat, you'd be forgiven for thinking it was a bath mat – although it would be a poor performer in this respect, for the *puli* can take three days to air dry, and will walk carefully around a small puddle.

Despite appearances, the *puli* is highly agile. It looks more sheep than shepherd, but was brought to Hungary by Magyar tribesmen over 1,000 years ago as a herder of livestock on the plains. The dogs gathered the stock from the villages, and drove them between grazing areas or to market. *Pulik* differed from other working dogs, such as border collies, in having to move huge numbers of sheep – often upwards of 400, many with foot rot – in tall grass. As a result, theirs was a vigorous and less-refined method than other breeds – bouncing to see over the grass and yelping to spur the flock into motion. They are usually black in colour (originally to distinguish them from the sheep), highly intelligent, extremely active, and expressive watchdogs. Bred to be the sole companion of the shepherd during months of isolation, they are also affectionate and loyal.

Indeed the bond was so strong between man and dog, that shepherds would only ever sell *pulik* between themselves (at prices as high as a year's salary), believing that others could never properly understand the dogs' unique temperament. Practicality supplanted sentiment when the *pulik* became old – once unable to work, they were killed.

The *puli* was aided in his sheep-guarding duties by two other indiginous Hungarian breeds – the shaggy-coated *komondor*, that has been likened to an Old English sheepdog, and the fluffier, white *kuvasz*.

## Pest

**Eötvös Loránd University Botanical Garden** (*Botanikus kert*) VIII, Illés utca 25 [M3 *Klinikák or Nagyvárad tér*] The Budapest Botanical Garden will be familiar to Hungarians for its place in *The Boys of Pál Street* (*Pál utcai fiúk*), a book by Ferenc Molnár about rival gangs of children fighting over this patch of land. There are 7,000 species of plant and tree in the 2.5ha, including tropical varieties in the greenhouse. Among the collection are orchids, the herbal remedy *Ginkgo biloba*, and the Chinese mammoth pine (*Metasequoia glyptostroboides*), found in 1950 after it was thought to have died out. *Adult/concessions 300/150Ft (tickets from the porter's lodge, just inside the entrance); garden open Mon–Thu & Sat–Sun 09.00–16.00, Fri 09.00–12.00, greenhouse Mon–Thu & Sat–Sun 11.00–12.00 & 14.00–15.00.*

186

AROUND BUDAPEST

0       20km
0       20 miles

N

Bradt

SLOVAKIA

Ipoly

Balassagyarmat

Ipoly

Šahy

Börzsöny Hills

Danube-Ipoly
NP

Diósjenő

Romhány

Cserhát Hills

Nagybörzsöny

Nógrád

Királyrét

Nagyirtás puszta

Kóspallag

Szob

Zebegény

Kismaros

Basaharc

Pilismarot

Nagymaros

Vác

Esztergom

Viségrád

Dömös

Visegrád Hills

Tahitótfalu

Szentendre
Island

Dobogó-kő
△ 699

Danube-Ipoly
NP

Pilisszentkereszt

Göd

Vácrátót

Pilis Hills

Szentendre

Pilisszántó

Aszód

Csobánka

Pomáz

Dunakeszi

Pilisvörösvár

Budakalász

Fót

Pilisszentiván

Mogyoród

Gödöllő

Solymár

Nagykovácsi

Budakesz

BUDAPEST

Szigetszentmiklós

Halásztelek

Szigethalom

Monor

Tököl

Danube

Ócsa

Ráckevei (Soroksári) Danube

Gárdony

Kiskunlacháza

Dabas

Pusztaszabolcs

Danube

Ráckeve

Dömsöd

# Around Budapest and the Danube Bend

While we've included a few places of interest running around Budapest's nether regions, the main concentration of sights hover above. The Danube Bend (Dunakanyar) is just what it says it is – the point at which Europe's second-longest river (after the Volga) alters its west–east course to slice Budapest and surge southwards through the rest of the country. There's beauty here – the river views match those you'll find anywhere in Europe; there's nature, with rich birdlife and striking rock formations among the peaks and valleys of the Pilis, Visegrád and Börzsöny hill ranges; and there's history, with the remains of Roman forts and watchtowers – this area represented the northern boundary of the Roman empire – and the palatial and ecclesiastical trappings that signal its importance as a medieval royal and episcopal centre. Szentendre in particular is close enough to the capital to allow a day trip, but that is to do the Danube Bend an injustice by attempting to bolt down a rich meal in a few high-piled spoonfuls; instead linger awhile, allow yourself time to taste and digest, for the bend both deserves and rewards a few days of your time.

A rail line from Budapest passes through Vác and follows the outside of the Danube Bend, but the inside is less well served by train; there are services to Szentendre and Esztergom, but not to Visegrád (which requires a ferry crossing from Nagymaros on the opposite bank). Fortunately there are frequent buses both direct from Budapest and running between the towns, while the ferry from Vigadó tér is a more leisurely option and particularly pleasant in summer.

## AROUND BUDAPEST
### Ráckeve

A little under 50km south of Budapest, towards the lower end of Csepel Island, Ráckeve reveals a Serb (Rác) heritage in its name. Refugees arrived in the 15th century, fleeing Turkish advances in the south, and in 1487 hoisted what is now the country's oldest **Serb Orthodox church** (*Viola utca 1*). The 16th-century freestanding tower had a Baroque extension plonked on top in the 18th century, but otherwise the exterior of the Gothic church is largely unaltered. Inside the walls are thick with Byzantine frescoes that were added in 1771 but are thought to have traced and revived the fading 15th-century ones already there; the iconostasis was painted at the same time. There are still services on Orthodox festival days, but the villagers themselves can no longer fill the pews and the congregation has to be reinforced with people from other local communities.

During the 17th century, Ráckeve was bought by Prince Eugene of Savoy, hailed victor over the Turks at the Battle of Zenta in 1697 and subject of the equestrian statue outside Buda Castle Palace (see page 139). Basking in the glory, he had a young Johann Lucas Hildebrandt – later responsible for Vienna's Belvedere Palace – design him a **mansion**; built between 1702 and 1720, this is the second of the town's country 'firsts', being the oldest Baroque palace in Hungary. As a campaigning soldier, the prince actually never stayed here; however, you can for it is now the **Savoyai Kastély Hotel** (*Kossuth Lajos utca 95;* ＼ *24 485253; info@savoyai.hu; www.savoyai.hu; 30 rooms; sgl/dbl €35/54*), and has a decent restaurant.

Also on Kossuth Lajos utca, which runs level with the Danube, is the **Árpád Museum** (*Kossuth Lajos utca 34;* ＼ *24 385364; adult/concessions 200/100Ft; open Tue–Sun Mar 16–Oct 31 10.00–18.00, Nov 1–Mar 15 10.00–16.00*), with a collection of local history and folk art. A statue of the leader of the Magyar tribes stands in Árpád tér, sculpted for the millennial celebrations and showing the festivities held on Csepel Island at the birth of Árpád's son.

Ráckeve is within easy reach of the capital. By **car**, take Road 51 south from Budapest and turn right after passing Kiskunlacháza; by **train**, board the HÉV at Budapest's Közvágóhíd, and buses carry you the final stretch to town from the station; there are **buses** from Budapest's Népliget (three on weekdays, but none direct at weekends), which take about an hour.

## Ócsa

Thirty kilometres to the southeast of Budapest, Ócsa's 13th-century Romanesque **Calvinist church** (*Bercsényi utca 2*) was originally built by Premonstratensians, and has medieval wall paintings and a Turkish prayer niche (*mihrab*) from the period of occupation. Moving outside, the **Ócsa Landscape Protection Reserve** covers 3,576ha, the most valuable habitat being wet meadow. The depressions hold bogs and alder trees, while there are broad buckler ferns beneath ash trees and European mud minnows, pond tortoises and moor frogs (with their blueish breeding colours) in the marshes. The reserve also has a cemetery with wooden grave markers, which vary in size according to the sex and age of the deceased; opinion is divided as to whether these are shaped like boats or human profiles. The reserve's **visitor centre** (*Bercsényi utca 4–6;* ＼ *06 30 948 9150; open May 1–Oct 30 Fri–Sun 09.00–17.00*) next to the church has an ethnographical exhibition, while twitchers make a beeline for the bird hide (＼ *28 454443*). If you contact the hide in advance, you may also be able to participate in bird ringing. Ócsa's real treasures, however, are its spectacular orchids in the peat bog meadows. Enjoy them on two walking trails, one of which (Selyemrét) is freely accessible. You'll need a guide for the second; contact Ágnes Pap (＼ *06 30 948 9150;* e *tarnics@vipmail.hu*), who can arrange one for 2,500Ft/hour (as well as offering bikes for hire). Earthwatch organises summer bird-ringing camps in Ócsa (including accommodation etc; see page 38), and Ecotours Hungary also runs excursions to the area (see page 39).

There are branches to Ócsa off both Road 5 and the M5 from Budapest, as well as a **railway station** reached from Budapest's Kőbánya-Kispest (at the end of metro line 3) and less frequently from Nyugati. Otherwise catch one of the half-hourly **buses** from Népliget bus station and alight at Községháza; from there, go downhill and right, and look for the church.

## Gödöllő

Gödöllő town is the centre of the Gödöllő hill region 30km east of Budapest. It was but a prettily situated village until the 18th-century noble Antal Grassalkovich I got his hands on it. He built up his estate near the then town of Pest and went about constructing the largest Baroque palace in Hungary (and supposedly the second-largest in Europe, after Versailles). The village grew into market town, attracting craftsmen and shopkeepers; baths and pleasure grounds were added, and it became a favourite summer resort of the Habsburgs. In 1901 the little town's significance was cemented further by the establishment of the hugely influential Gödöllő Artists' Colony. In the town's coat of arms, a pelican feeds her chicks with her own blood, a symbol of a town proud of its repeated investment in its own.

## Getting there and away

Gödöllő can be reached from Budapest on both the **MÁV** network (regular services from Keleti) and the bone-rattling **HÉV** (half-hourly from Örs vézer tere, with the last return at 22.44; alight at Szabadság tér). If you're going by **car**, take either the M3 or Road 3 towards Miskolc, which can be picked up from the top of Rákóczi út; the motorway is quicker, but there's no toll to use Road 3. There are numerous daily **buses** from Stadion, taking between 35 minutes and an hour.

## Information and other practicalities

**Cultural centre** Szabadság út 6; \ 28 514130. Concerts, plays and exhibitions, together with information on what's on. *Ticket office open Mon–Tue 08.30–13.00, 08.30–12.00, Fri 08.30–13.00.*
**Tourinform** Gödöllő Royal Palace; \ 28 415402; e godollo@tourinform.hu. Located inside the palace, and offering information on the town and broader region. *Open Tue–Sun Apr 1–Oct 31 10.00–18.00, Nov 1–Mar 31 10.00–17.00.*

## Where to stay and eat

You're unlikely to need to stay overnight in Gödöllő when the capital is within spitting distance.

**Galéria** (5 rooms) Szabadság tér 8; \ 28 418691. Gets the thumbs up for colourful, light and comfortable rooms in the main square. Its restaurant (*mains 600–2,000Ft; open 11.00–23.00 daily*) is superb, with an intriguing and extensive menu that features choice dishes such as wild boar, shark and fried brains. *Rooms 5,500/4,800Ft/pp en-suite/not en-suite.*
**Kastélykert** Szabadság út 4; \ 28 527020. On the opposite side of the road from the Town Museum, this restaurant is cheap and has choices including pike perch and venison. The outdoor area is a good place for a drink. *Mains 990–1,690Ft, avg 1,200Ft; open daily 12.00–23.00.*
**Pizza Max** Dózsa György utca 36; \ 28 416207. A modern, fashionably turned-out steakhouse and pizzeria. *Open 09.00–24.00 daily.*
**Sunshine Hotel** (20 rooms) Szabadság út 199; \ 28 420602; e sunshinehotel@vnet.hu; www.hotels.hu/sunshine. The Sunshine is 1.5km east along the road towards Aszód; its restaurant (*open 07.00–22.00 daily*) serves Chinese, Hungarian and international food. *Rooms €40–68 (depending on size).*

## What to see and do

The 136-room **Gödöllő Royal Palace** (*Gödöllői Királyi Kastély;* \ *28 415402;* e *informacio@kiralyikastely.hu; www.kiralyikastely.hu; adult/concessions 1,400/700Ft; open Tue–Sun Apr 1–Oct 31 10.00–18.00, Nov 1–Mar 31 10.00–17.00*) was commissioned by Grassalkovich in 1741, designed by Antal Mayerhoffer in a style that became tagged 'Gödöllő Baroque'. It very quickly became a Habsburg playground and, as all palaces should, has more than a few tales of mystery and eccentricity. In the summer of 1751, the notoriously spoilt Empress Maria Theresa is said to have insisted on going sledging; a year's yield of salt from the Felvidék mine was laid down to humour her, while lackeys sweated in winter coats. Rumours abounded about secret tunnels leading from the palace to the town, and in recent years they were found, big enough to accommodate a coach and horses; they were possibly dug by the Habsburgs, who used the palace as a headquarters during the Napoleonic Wars, but nobody knows for sure. There is a deep irony in the fact that in 1849 Lajos Kossuth drafted the motion demanding the overthrow of the Habsburg monarchy from within the palace, for after the Compromise in 1867 it was bought by the State and converted by Miklós Ybl into a residence for Ferenc József; Queen Erzsébet (the popular 'Sissi') loved it here – particularly when hubby wasn't, for she apparently loathed him and preferred the company of the dashing Count Andrássy.

When the Romanians invaded to remove the short-lived communist regime in 1919, they allegedly stripped the palace of many of its artworks. Between the wars Admiral Horthy used it as a summer residence, while after World War II the edifice entered its worst period of neglect. The Soviet army stored petrol in the stables, painting everything a dull grey and stencilling the red marble arches and watering troughs with 'no-smoking' signs; some of the magnificent rooms were used as an old people's home, and the park was chopped up into smaller plots. Conservation and restoration couldn't begin in earnest until the final troops had left their 'barracks' in 1990.

Inside there are banqueting rooms to be seen, as well as an exhibition covering the first century of the palace's existence on the first floor. You can visit the suites of Ferenc József and his queen, including Erzsébet's dressing room, decorated in violet (her favourite colour) and with portraits of her on horseback (she was a mad-keen rider). From there you move through into her bedroom, which before that had been a room set aside by Grassalkovich for Maria Theresa and adorned with marble and gilding. Next are memorial rooms to Erzsébet, one of which was formerly used by her during quiet moments; among the Biedermeier furnishings are the settee on which she read, and paintings of her ladies in waiting. The final room in the set records the outpouring of grief following the queen's assassination, and her subsequent immortalisation – the newspaper article announcing her death, the tribute coins issued afterwards, and 20th-century postcards of sites that came to bear her name. In 2003, the renovation of the Baroque theatre in the southern wing – which hadn't been used for over two centuries – was finally completed at a cost of over US$5 million, and was unveiled with a performance by the Hungarian State Opera House. (There are also open-air concerts in the courtyard in summer.) The palace chapel, to the far right of the main entrance, was built in 1749 in place of an earlier Calvinist church on the spot. There's a mosaic of Grassalkovich on the back wall.

In the main square northwest of the palace, the **Town Museum** (*Gödöllői Városi Múzeum; Szabadság tér 5;* \ *28 422003; adult/concessions 500/250Ft; open Tue–Sun 10.00–18.00*) shows works by the massively influential Gödöllő School, a collection of artists brought together by Sándor Nagy and Aladár Kőrösfői Kriesch whose colony operated in town between 1901 and 1920. Inspired by the Pre-Raphaelites, Tolstoy and the idealistic Englishmen artist William Morris and essayist John Ruskin, the group developed an Arts-and-Crafts movement that was anti-capitalist in thrust and that aimed to nurture a uniquely Hungarian brand of earthy, folkloristic Art Nouveau. As well as paintings, they produced book illustrations, stained glass and textiles (employing local girls to operate looms brought from a bankrupt weaver's factory), and were among the pathfinders of Hungarian Secessionism. In addition, the museum has an exhibition of local history documenting the golden years first under Grassalkovich and then under the royals, a natural-history display, and a collection gathered by the 20th-century priest Mihály Zoltán that includes Ferenc Deák's pipe, Prime Minister Gyula Andrássy's inkwell and a dress worn by Erzsébet's sister to the 1867 coronation. An **applied arts workshop** (*Iparművészeti Műhely Alkotóháza; Körösfői utca 15–17*) and a walking tour taking in the various artists' houses are open at weekends only.

## Other
The village of Máriabesnyő, 3km to the east of Gödöllő on the way to Aszód (Road 30), was part of the Grassalkovich estate. The great landowner arranged for a church to be built here by Antal Mayerhoffer (designer of the palace) in the 1760s. Nothing unusual about that, of course, except that during the laying of the foundations a 13th-century *Madonna and Child* statuette came to light. Word of the find got around, as did tales of miracles in connection with it, and the so-called **Pilgrimage Church** (*Kapucinusok tere 1;* \ *28 510025; open Mon–Fri 09.00–12.00, 15.00–17.00*) became a site of … well,

pilgrimage. Grassalkovich had a precious container made for the relic, and the family vault was sunk into the crypt. In the 20th century, Pál Teleki (see pages 20 and 141) was also buried at the church, which is at the top of a 200m dust track off the main road, lined with stations of the cross. The interior is breathtaking in its opulence; behind it is a former Capuchin monastery, with a statue of Pope Pius XI in the courtyard. If you're in the area, it would be criminal not to make a brief visit; you can catch the bus from Gödöllő, alighting at the Máriabesnyő templom stop outside.

In August, thousands of petrol heads make a pilgrimage of a different sort to Mogyoród, 8km northwest of Gödöllő on Road E71. Just outside the village is the **Hungaroring**, the Formula 1 racetrack built in 1986 and central European stage for the Hungarian Grand Prix (see page 73).

## Aszód

Situated in the Galga valley 12km east of Gödöllő, Aszód – from *aszó*, meaning 'dry valley' – was once a Stone-Age 'metropolis', its hill settled by Neolithic man 5,000 years ago. Kurszán, one of the 9th-century conquering Magyar chieftains rooted his clan here, making use of the fertile land. However, the arrival of the Turks emptied the town; the revival came after the occupation, when János Podmaniczky – a Protestant noble who acquired the territory through a marriage tie – repopulated it with Slovaks, Germans and Jewish traders. Thanks to Podmaniczky's enlightened farming methods, the town (and its vegetables) grew quickly. In 1914, it was home to the country's largest munitions factory, producing biplanes and automobiles.

The 18th-century former **Podmaniczky Palace and residence** (*Szabadság tér 7–8*), a sandy-yellow Baroque structure whose neglect during the communist period is very evident, provides the backdrop to the main square. Despite its broken windows and flaky plaster, you can get a sense of past grandeur as you walk the grounds and courtyard. In the square outside is a white war memorial bearing both a Christian cross and a menorah, the latter a tribute to the Aszód Jewish victims of the Holocaust.

Follow Petőfi utca for 100m and turn left into an uneven cobbled street holding the **Petőfi Museum** (*Szontágh lépcső 2;* ✆ *28 500650; adult/concessions 400/200Ft; open Tue–Sun Apr 1–Oct 31 09.00–17.00, Nov 1–Mar 31 09.00–16.00*), housed in a Neoclassical former Lutheran grammar school completed in 1771. The Hungarian poet Sándor Petőfi – whose name then was Alexander Petrovics – was dispatched here in 1835 at the age of 13 after his parents became concerned at his slack attitude to scholarship (he was more interested in loitering around theatres, apparently). He spent three years under the direction of István Koren, who kindled in him a love for verse. A room displays items relating to those days, including Petőfi's school reports written by his tutor, while other collections showcase Neolithic finds from the hill above (look out for the pottery bird walking on human pegs, reckoned to represent early beliefs about life and the afterlife), agricultural and industrial life in the Galga valley between the 18th and 20th centuries, and various village folk costumes (which conveyed subtle messages about the wearers, from marital status to wealth).

In the garden outside are three gravestones representing the religions of the town's settlers (Roman Catholic, Lutheran and Jewish). The adjacent **Lutheran church**, originally built in the 15th century and re-vamped in the 18th, witnessed both the marriage of Petőfi's parents and later their young son's first poetic effort (*Búcsúzás*, or 'Farewell').

There are very regular **buses** from Budapest's Stadion, as well as from Gödöllő. The **railway station** is to the east of the centre (follow the road in front of the station and turn left at the top), and lies on the line to Budapest Keleti (that passes through Gödöllő). You can also travel northeast on the route towards Miskolc (some direct, others with a change at Hatvan) and northwest to Balassagyarmat.

## Fót

To the northwest of Gödöllő (and 25km northeast of Budapest), the village of Fót on the edge of the Gödöllő hills has a **palace** (*Vörösmarty tér*) in its main square commissioned by the Károlyi landowners – the family of politician Mihály Károlyi, president of the first republic in 1919 – and rebuilt by Miklós Ybl in 1847; today a children's care home (with a memorial plaque to Mihály on its wall) fills part of the mansion, together with other buildings in the surrounding park. Ybl was also behind the four-towered **Roman Catholic church** (*Vörösmarty utca 2; open 08.00–12.00, 14.00–18.00 daily*), completed in 1855 and comprising eastern, Arabic and Moorish features. The crypt holds the Károlyi family vault, and a side chapel contains the relics of St Lucentius donated to the church by Pope Pius IX. However, naturalists rate Fót's Somlyó Hill as the place to see **butterflies**. The path starts at the **Fáy Présház**, the 19th-century winery built by the writer András Fáy, which is signposted in the village. You can get here via turn-offs from both the M3 and M2 motorways; alternatively, there are regular **buses** from Árpád híd bus station or the Újpest Városkapu terminus. Up to 25 **trains** run daily to Fót from Budapest Nyugati (taking 30 minutes) on the line that loops eastward before heading back towards Vác and the Danube Bend.

## Nagy-szénás

Standing 25km northwest of Budapest, in the outer parts of the Buda Hills between Nagykovácsi and Pilisszentiván, the 550m Nagy-szénás is a beautiful place, and one with a botanical rarity – the *Pilis flax*. Contact Pál Kézdy (✆ *06 70 330 3812*) for an English-speaking guide. Note that it is a strictly protected area, and if you come by bus or car you will have to alight and walk from the village. Follow the path marked with a yellow stripe heading south from the edge of the village for about 2km. To get to the village from Budapest, drive north towards Szentendre, fork left on Road 10 towards Pilisvörösvár, and turn left after 10km to Pilisszentiván. There are buses regularly from Árpád híd bus station. Alternatively, you can follow the marked (green line) path from Solymár, which has a railway station on the line passing through Aquincum and Óbuda and is near the British Military Cemetery where RAF pilots downed over Hungary are buried. From Nagy-szénás, you can pick up red trails to Pilisszentkereszt (see page 200) around 15km to the north.

## SZENTENDRE

Szentendre (St Andrew), bustling and touristy, is the first town of the Danube Bend, 19km north of Budapest. There was an influx of Serb refugees fleeing the Turks in the 14th century and, after depopulation during the occupation, another surge during the 17th century when Hungary was freed of Ottoman shackles but fighting still raged in the Balkans. Wooden buildings were replaced with stone ones, and Szentendre became the ecclesiastical centre for the diaspora Serb Orthodox Church; four remain of the several temples they built during their time here, each named after the region from which their congregation originated. The citizens were farmers and vintners, but many left after phylloxera and floods hit the area in the 19th century, and those who stayed replaced the vines with fruit orchards. Only a dozen or so Serbian families remain now, but the cosmopolitan legacy is reinforced by the modern flood of visitors from the capital.

The sun smiles on Szentendre, and artists are attracted like moths to its favourable light. In the 1920s an artists' colony was established, and many continue to paint the town red. You can admire their handiwork in the seeming myriad of galleries, many ensconced in beautiful old town houses. Szentendere's virtues give rise to its faults: you'll barely scratch the rich surface of the art on a day trip, you'll need to jostle with many others in the museums during summer months, and the cheerfully coloured buildings are too often occupied by fleecers, whose tat laminates rather than celebrates

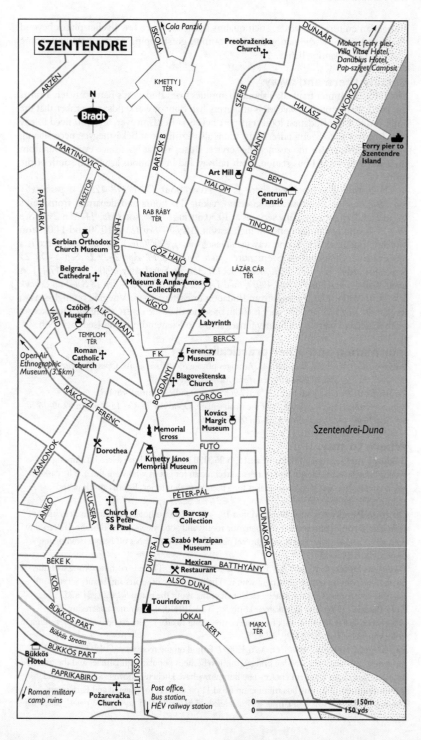

SZENTENDRE

N
Bradt

Cola Panzió

ISKOLA

Preobraženska
Church

DUNA AR

Mahart ferry pier,
Villa Vitae Hotel,
Danubius Hotel,
Pap-sziget Campsit

KMETTY J
TÉR

ARZÉN

BARTÓK B

SZERB

BOGDÁNYI

HALÁSZ

DUNAKORZÓ

MARTINOVICS

PÁSZTOR

Art Mill

MALOM

BEM

Centrum
Panzió

Ferry pier to
Szentendre
Island

PATRIÁRKA

HUNYADI

RAB RÁBY
TÉR

GŐZ HAJÓ

TINÓDI

Serbian Orthodox
Church Museum

Belgrade
Cathedral

National Wine
Museum & Anna-Amos
Collection

LÁZÁR CÁR
TÉR

VÁRDI

Czóbel
Museum

ALKOTMÁNY

KIGYÓ

Labyrinth

BERCS

Open-Air
Ethnographic
Museum (3.5km)

TEMPLOM
TÉR

Roman
Catholic
church

F K

Ferenczy
Museum

BOGDÁNYI

Blagoveštenska
Church

GÖRÖG

RÁKÓCZI FERENC

KANONOK

Memorial
cross

Kovács
Margit
Museum

Dorothea

Kmetty János
Memorial Museum

FUTÓ

Szentendrei-Duna

JÁNKÓ

KUCSERA

Church of
SS Peter
& Paul

PÉTER-PÁL

Barcsay
Collection

DUNAKORZÓ

BÉKE K

KŐR

DUMTSAI

Szabó Marzipan
Museum

Mexican
Restaurant

BATTHYÁNY

ALSÓ DUNA

BÜKKÖS PART

Bükkös Stream

Tourinform

JÓKAI

KERT

MARX
TÉR

Bükkös
Hotel

BÜKKÖS PART

PAPRIKABÍRÓ

KOSSUTH L

Roman military
camp ruins

Požarevačka
Church

Post office,
Bus station,
HÉV railway station

0          150m
0          150 yds

Hungarian culture. However, such qualms aside, there are few livelier places beyond the capital to enjoy the national artistic output, go shopping or stroll along winding alleys and the Danube banks.

## Getting there and away

The HÉV commuter train takes about 40 minutes from Budapest's Batthyány tér. **Trains** run every 20 minutes on weekdays and every half hour at weekends; remember that the outer limit of the Budapest local transport tickets is Békásmegyer, and you need to pay extra to travel on to Szentendre. Many trains also terminate at Békásmegyer, necessitating a platform change for the connecting service. **Buses** run at least once every hour from Budapest's Árpád híd bus station. Both railway and bus stations are 800m south of the centre.

The romantic way to get there is by **river boat** (↘ *1 318 1233;* e *passnave@ mahartpassnave.hu; www.mahartpassnave.hu*), taking 1½ hours and departing from Pest's Vigadó tér. Mahart runs daily services at 10.30 during low season (*May 14–May 29 & Sep 19–Oct 9*), and twice-daily ones in high season (*May 30–Sep 18*) at 10.30 and 14.00. You can only purchase tickets one way (*adult/concessions 1,400/700Ft*). In addition, there is a service from Budapest via Szentendre (*adult 990/1,485Ft; Apr 2–29 & Sep 5–Oct 23 Sat–Sun & bank hols only 09.00, return 17.15; Apr 30–Sep 4 daily 09.00, return 17.45*). A **hydrofoil** (*adult sgl/rtn 1,990/3,490Ft, child 1,490/2,590Ft; May 21–Sep 18 Sat–Sun & bank hols 09.30 , return 17.15*) travels from Budapest to Esztergom via Visegrád on high-season weekends. The Mahart ferry pier is 600m or so north of the centre along the Dunakorzó; a closer, second pier serves hourly ferries across to Szentendre Island (see page 199).

## Information and other practicalities

**Ibusz** Bogdányi utca 11; ↘ 26 310181. Arranges private rooms and tours. *Open May–Sep Mon–Fri 09.00–17.00, Sat–Sun 10.00–14.00, rest of year Mon–Fri 10.00–16.00.*
**Tourinform** Dumtsa Jenő utca 22; ↘ 317 965; e szentendre@tourinform.hu; www.szentendre.hu. To the south of the main square. *Open Mar 15–Oct 15 Mon–Fri 09.30–16.30, Sat–Sun 10.00–14.00, rest of year Mon–Fri 09.30–16.30.*

## Where to stay

**Bükkös Hotel** (16 rooms) Bükkös part 16; ↘ 26 312021; e bukkosh@axelero.hu. Among extensive facilities are the services of a dental technician for guests who want them. The dark-green faux marble and gold décor makes for a pseudo-posh interior. Rooms are clean and comfortable, and the staff are welcoming. *Sgl €21, dbl €25.*
**Centrum Panzió** (6 rooms) Bogdányi utca 15; ↘ 26 302500; e hotel.centrum@axelero.hu. As central as its name suggests, and with fantastic rooms and good views of the Danube. It's recently been given a make-over, and you might feel obliged to take your shoes off before treading the carpets. *Sgl €50, dbl €52.*
**Danubius Hotel** (48 rooms) Ady Endre út 28; ↘ 26 312511. There is nothing wrong with this hotel, nor anything oustandingly right with it. The wide range of sports and beauty services available compensates for the general lack of charisma about the place. *Sgl €20, dbl €25.*
**Cola Panzió** (12 rooms) Dunakanyar körút 50; ↘ 26 310410; e colairen@axelero.hu. This homely pension is 10 mins' walk from the centre, along Road 11. The owner will do everything to make you feel at home. *Sgl €20, dbl €25.*
**Pap-sziget Campsite** Pap-sziget; ↘ 26 310697. Found on the recreational island 2km north of the centre (accessed via a wooden bridge), this lovely site is popular with families and the riverside location makes it an excellent choice. The bungalows have kitchens, showers and toilets, and there's a pension. Take any bus running up Road 11 on the way to Visegrád and Esztergom. *Camping 1,200Ft/pp, tent 700Ft, c/van €17; bungalows €40 (for 2), €45 (for 3), €48 (for 4); panzió dbl €25. Open May–Oct.*

**Villa Vitae Wellness Hotel** Ady Endre út 26; ☎ 26 311 882; e immobill@axelero.hu; www.immo-bill.hu/villavitae. This calming, comfortable and healthful place to stay is set in lush wooded grounds. The restaurant serves organic food, there's a pool, sauna and aroma steam bath, and the unfashionable can make use of the hotel's stylist consultancy. *Sgl 12,900Ft, dbl 16,700Ft.*

## Where to eat and drink
There are plenty of pleasant cafés and restaurants in which to take refreshment, although – as with everything – they can be crowded in high season.

**Corner** Dunakorzó 4; ☎ 26 300027; e milenko@vipmail.hu. The choice of Serbian, in addition to Hungarian, dishes makes this an interesting choice. There's a montage of old money above the bar, but with the efficiency of service here you might not have much time to look at it. *Serbian mixed dish 2,200Ft; open daily 10.00–23.00.*
**Dorothea** Jankó János utca; ☎ 06 20 579 3800. A dream of a café. Homely and cosy, with comfy cushioned seating, games to play and plenty of magazines to read. Popular with locals and tourists. There are many home-made cakes, dips, and fancy coffees available; you'll probably stay longer than you intended. *Open daily 07.00–23.00.*
**Labyrinth** Bogdányi utca 10; ☎ 26 317054; e bormuzeum@bor-kor.hu; www.bor-kor.hu. The restaurant is divided into various rooms, each uniquely styled and given names like 'Hunting Hall', 'Cup Hall' and 'Cellar'. The 'big fish dish of Szentendre' is exactly that – they aren't shy with portions here. As part of the National Wine Museum (see page 198), there is the perfect glass for every dish. Good range for vegetarians. Dishy waiters too. *Szentendre style rolled pork 1,450Ft; open daily 10.00–23.00.*
**Mexican Restaurant** Dumtsa Jenő 14/A; ☎ 26 302418; www.palap.hu. You can base an evening around this lively, colourful garden eatery. The quirky menu (featuring a dessert called 'Very Hot Love') can make a welcome change from typically lardy Hungarian norms. Great cocktails. *Enchiladas 1,480Ft; open Mon–Fri 17.00–24.00, Sat–Sun 12.00–24.00.*
**Szabó Marzipan Museum** Dumtsa Jenő utca 12; ☎ 06 30 330 6044; e info@elender.hu. When you visit a café whose tables are reserved on a sleepy Sunday morning, you can be sure the cakes taste as good as they look. The display really is a feast for the eyes, and you'll barely notice the attractive tiles and comfy seating. *Open daily 10.00–19.00.*

## What to see and do
It's nice just ambling around the cobbled streets of Szentendre, but there are lots of museums, galleries and churches to structure a day, most of which are close to Fő tér. Before digging in to these, though, you might want to have a peek at the lapidarium containing the stone remains of a **Roman military camp** (*Dunakanyar körút*), on the southern side of the Bükkös Stream; Ulcisia Castra was built in the 2nd century, and was an important station on the Danube. To get there, follow Római sánc köz away from Kossuth Lajos utca. On the same side of the stream is the **Požarevačka Church** (*Kossuth Lajos utca 1*), one of the permanent stone Serb Orthodox churches built in the 18th century, and holding a Byzantine-style iconostasis.
Crossing the water and taking the right-hand fork, the first exhibition you'll reach is the lightweight **Szabó Marzipan Museum** (*Dumtsa Jenő utca 12; ☎ 26 311931; adult 350Ft; open daily May–Sep 10.00–19.00, Oct–Apr 10.00–18.00*). The self-proclaimed 'world's only marzipan museum' – ignoring the fact that there's at least one other in Hungary alone (see under *Keszthely*) – has a workshop devoted to marzipan handicraft, together with some marzipan masterpieces including edible models of the Hungarian parliament building and national and international celebrities. (It made us dream of a better world in which you could lick some celebrities and bite the heads off others.) Further along, the **Barcsay Collection** (*Dumtsa Jenő utca 10; ☎ 26 310244; adult/concessions 400/200Ft; open Tue–Sun Mar 15–Sep 15 10.00–18.00, rest of year*

*10.00–16.00*) shows the art of Jenő Barcsay (1900–88), an influential 20th-century artist and one of the founders of Szentendre's colony. His early pieces were dark – *The Madman of the Village*, painted when he was 23, a good example – while his later works fall into the abstract genre of Constructivism. His anatomical drawings were used for training medical students.

On the other side of the Péter-Pál Gallery (*Péter-Pál utca 1*), which sells lace and pottery, is the **Church of SS Peter and Paul** (*Péter-Pál utca 6*). This was formerly owned by the Dalmatians, who arrived from the shores of the Adriatic, and is one of the town's two Roman Catholic churches. From there it's a short hop north into **Fő tér**, lined with 18th- and 19th-century trade houses; those on the eastern side (*Fő tér 2–5*) were built in the 1720s after a fire, and share a common gabled roof. The Merchant Cross in the middle of the square was erected in the aftermath of a plague outbreak in 1763; it is said that there are bodies buried upside down beneath it. On the square's southern side is the **Kmetty János Memorial Museum** (*Fő tér 21;* ❧ *26 310244; adult/concessions 400/200Ft; open Tue–Sun Mar 15–Sep 15 10.00–18.00, rest of year 10.00–16.00*), devoted to an artist who belonged to the Szentendre colony in the 1940s, and who brought the influence of French Cubism into the sphere of Hungarian fine art.

The little Baroque **Blagoveštenska Church** (*admission 100Ft; open Tue–Sun 10.00–17.00*) across the way was built in 1752 on the site of a previous 17th-century wooden version, and is thought to be the work of Antal Mayerhoffer. It is known as the 'Greek Church' – a headstone near the gate suggesting that the church was actually founded by Greek merchants – and has a Rococo iconostasis (whose subjects' eyes follow you all about). Next door is the **Ferenczy Museum** (*Fő ter 6;* ❧ *26 310790; adult/child 200/100Ft; open Wed–Sun 09.00–17.00*), showcasing the output of a whole family blessed with creative genes. Károly Ferenczy (1862–1917) specialised in Impressionist *plein air* art, his canvases full of brightness and grace, and he went on to lead the Nagybánya Colony. His eldest son became an Expressionist painter and the younger twins a sculptor and a weaver of Gobelin tapestries; Mrs Ferenczy was one of no mean talent too, although she made far less of it.

The **Kovács Margit Museum** (*Vastagh György utca 1;* ❧ *26 310244; adult/concessions 600/300Ft; open 09.00–17.00 daily*): you'll either love it or hate it, but you have to see it. The ceramics of Margit Kovács (1902–1977) are often poo-pooed in elevated art circles but they are widely adored by down-to-earth bods. Geometric forms and folkloric effects come together in statuettes and reliefs tackling themes of religion and family. Several of her distinctive pieces adorn Budapest's Castle District, fantastical and cartoon-like, her later works increasingly simplified to cone or column shapes. We're in the love camp.

Heading north from the square, a tasty way to end a cultured day is in the **National Wine Museum** (*Nemzeti Bormúzeum; Bogdányi utca 10;* ❧ *26 317054;* e *bormuzeum@bor-kor.hu; www.bor-kor.hu; 1,700Ft/pp for a tasting tour that includes 10 wine samples and snacks*), which is linked to the Labirintus Restaurant and is well laid out and presented. Be sure not to dull the senses before a visit to the captivating **Anna-Ámos Collection** (*Bogdányi utca 10/B;* ❧ *26 310790; adult/concessions 400/200Ft; open Tue–Sun Mar 15–Sep 30 10.00–18.00, rest of year 10.00–16.00*), where quality prevails over quantity in the collection of husband and wife Margit Anna and Imre Ámos. Anna's post-war self-portraits reveal her profound despair in the aftermath of the Holocaust, when her Jewish husband died in a labour camp.

A short distance further, a square opens to the right with a **memorial cross** at its far corner. The cross marks the spot of a former wooden church where 17th-century Serbian refugees kept the bones of Tsar Lázár – the Serbian king executed by the Turks after the 1389 Battle of Kosovo – before the Treaty of Karlowitz allowed the coffin's return to their homeland in 1699. Continue to the **Art Mill** (*Művészet Malom; Bogdányi utca 32;* ❧ *26 319*

*128;* e *malom@mail.matav.hu; free admission; open daily 10.00–18.00*), a former 19th-century sawmill converted with government funding into an exhibition hall for 'serious' contemporary local artists. A sound collection has been established here already, but it continues to expand. Beyond that is the **Preobraženska Church** (*Bogdányi utca 40*), built in 1746 by the tanners' guild and containing a gilded iconostasis. The church is the focal point for the traditional Serbian festival on August 19.

A small hill rises above Fő tér, reached via steps leading up either from the northern end of the square or from Rákóczi Ferenc utca, and provides an ideal vantage point from which to peek into the town's gardens and courtyards below. It originally held a medieval castle, but that's gone; the **Roman Catholic church** (*Templom tér*) dates to the same period, and retains some Romanesque and Gothic features, although 18th-century reconstruction means that it is primarily Baroque in style. The Gothic sanctuary is decorated with inter-war frescoes by members of the Artists' Colony. Near the church is the **Czóbel Museum** (*Templom tér 1;* ❧ *26 312721; adult/concessions 400/200Ft; open Tue–Sun Mar 15–Sep 30 10.00–18.00, rest of year 10.00–16.00*), occupying the building of a former school. Béla Czóbel (1883–1976) – who studied under Matisse – lived and worked in Szentendre between 1940 and 1966, and his landscapes and portraits from this period are on display, together with nudes painted during the last decade of his life in Budapest.

To the north of Templom tér, the **Belgrade Cathedral** (*Belgrád Székesegyház; Alkotmány utca*) is the Hungarian Serbian Orthodox episcopal seat, completed in 1764. In addition to its dark red tower it has an altar of red marble; the Baroque iconostasis was painted by an artist from Novi Sad, and a Rococo doorway fashioned by a local craftsman. Its chancel has a fresco showing a rich man revelling in his wealth, ignorant that behind him stalks Death with his scythe. Near the courtyard at the back of the cathedral is the **Serbian Orthodox Church Museum** (*Pátriárka utca 5;* ❧ *26 314547/312399; adult/concessions 400/200Ft; open Tue–Sun May 1–Sep 30 10.00–18.00, rest of year 10.00–16.00*), an Aladdin's cave of ecclesiastical art and vestments from churches all over the country that gradually declined as Serb settlers returned to the Balkans.

### Other

A couple of kilometres north of the centre, **Pap Island** (*Pap-sziget*) is a recreational area where you can swim, play tennis, catch some rays or rent a boat; there's a strand and a swimming pool. You can get there by boarding any bus running northward along Dunakanyar körút (Road 11).

Szentendre's prize museum is 3km to the northwest of town on Sztaravodai út, reached by hourly buses from stop number 7 of the bus station. The **Open-Air Ethnographic Museum** (*Szabadtéri Néprajzi Múzeum; Sztaravodai út;* ❧ *26 312304/ 502500;* e *sznm@sznm.hu; www.skanzen.hu; adult/concessions 600/400Ft; open Apr 1–Oct 31 Tue–Sun 09.00-17.00*) is a massive, 50ha showcase of Hungarian regional architecture that gives urbanites a rich sense of what rural Hungary was and is about. The original structures from villages and small towns range in date from the 18th to the early 20th centuries, and represent the Upper Tisza, Western Transdanubia, the Kisalföld in Northwest Transdanubia, the Bakony and Balaton Uplands, and a market town from the Great Plain (with an animal farm). It has been a work in progress since its initiation in the 1960s, and ten areas are planned in total. There are regular interactive folk displays – usually, but not always, on Sundays – and the site also hosts events during festivals. Tourinform (see page 196) can furnish you with a current programme of events.

### Szentendre Island

Curving scimitar-like from below Szentendre up around Visegrád, the 31km-long Szentendre Island is the source for much of Budapest's drinking water. Standing at the divide between lowlands and hills, its wildlife includes hill-loving flora, rare floodplain snails on the riverbanks, foraging upland raptors and bee eaters nesting in the hollows of sand dunes at the northern end. **Kisoroszi** was named after the members of a Russian Basilite Order who settled here at the turn of the 11th and 12th centuries; there is a **campsite** (*open May–Sep*) among the willow trees to the west of the village, from where you can enjoy watching Visegrád across the water. (Hourly ferries cross between Kisoroszi and the bank to the southwest of it.) Moving down the island, you will pass a golf course and several riding schools on your way to the resort at Surány and Szigetmonostor, once owned by the Zichy family.

There is just one bridge spanning the Danube at Tahitótfalu (burial place of architect Mihály Pollack), further up Road 11 from Szentendre, and a single **vehicle ferry** running from the opposite side of the island across to Vác. Szentendre has a **ferry** taking foot passengers to the island (*hourly Mar–Oct 07.00–19.30 daily*), as do several villages to the north of it. The alternative is to **row across** (boat hire is available at Pap Island; see page 199).

## THE PILIS AND VISEGRÁD HILLS

The Pilis and Visegrád hill ranges, spanning more than 400km$^2$ and reaching 756m at Pilis-tető, are part of the Duna-Ipoly National Park (see box, page 217). The **Pilis Hills** – their once treeless peaks inspiring their name, which means 'tonsure' in old Hungarian – are formed of limestone and dolomite, their forests the hunting grounds for medieval aristocrats; as well as ravines and hot springs, the landscape is characterised by karstic features common when limestone and water come together. There are hundreds of caves, many of them showing evidence of ancient occupation; Stone-Age tools were found in Kőfülke in Pilisszántó and a 4,000-year-old drinking vessel in the shape of a clay wagon unearthed near Budakalász. This is a region of beautiful hikes, and mountain bikers, climbers, horse-riders and skiers will find an ample playground around Oszoly Rock, the River Dera Canyon, the Vaskapu Pass and the Holdvilág Ditch. The Vaskapu Pass represents a pair of natural portholes – formed after the collapse of a cave roof – jutting from the side of Vaskapu Hill.

Pomáz – 17km from Budapest, and once site of a medieval royal hunting lodge – is the gateway for walks into the Pilis, easily reached from Budapest by train (on the HÉV line running to Szentendre), and with several walking trails leading away from it. To the west, Csobánka is an ethnically mixed bag, founded by Serbs fleeing the Turks at the end of the 17th century, swelled by Germans and Slovaks during the 18th, and Romanians in the 20th. If you follow the red trail northwards, you will come to the Holdvilág Ditch (*Holdvilág-árok*); the limestone ravines can be tough walking terrain, and you'll need to climb an iron ladder to reach the Lajos Spring (*Lajosforrás*). A blue trail leads northwest along the Dera Valley to Pilisszentkereszt, which has the scant remains of a 12th-century Cistercian monastery. This was occupied by monks brought to Hungary by the French wife of Béla III, and the tomb of Gertrude of Andechs-Meran, András II's wife, was found here (now in the Hungarian National Gallery; see page 166); Gertrude was murdered in 1213, and the monastery was the scene for József Katona's drama *Bánk Bán*. From here you can take a trek through the Kovács Stream Canyon, in the shadow of Pilis-tető; the trail begins at the lime kiln. The Esztergom Education Centre (*Esztergom-Kertváros;* ↘ *33 435015*) is in the Pilis Hills southwest of Esztergom, and has a nature trail.

The bridge between the Pilis Hills and the **Visegrád Hills**, which follow the line of the Danube, is the resort of Dobogókő; it can be reached by bus from Pomáz, Esztergom, Budapest (Árpád híd), Visegrád or Dömös, or by walking north from Pilisszentkereszt. At 699m, it is the highest spot of the range and has a lookout tower with views towards the river that include the romantically named Sorrow Valley (*Búbánat völgy*), opening up from the end of Pilismarót, and the Shivering Cross (*Hideglelős Kereszt*) jutting above the Danube at Basaharc. The area is clearly blessed with some mystical force. A report on Magyar television named Dobogókő as the site of the natural heart chakra of all Europe, a powerful source of healing, while the Shivering Cross was erected in the 18th century to inspire religious feelings in those using the river and is said to cure those who walk around it of the shakes (very useful for those hangover mornings). The resort was popular with the communist élite in the 1950s. From here you can hike for 8km (aided by fixed chains) along the narrow gorge called the Rám Precipice (*Rám-szakadék*) down to Dömös (taking approximately 4hrs), which is on the river bank and has a beach. You can also pick up routes into the hills from Dömös; follow Duna utca (south of the village along the Malom Spring) for 2–3km to marked trails leading right to the Rám Precipice or left to the saw-edged formations of the Vadálló Rocks (*Vadálló-kövek*) and the lookout tower of Pulpit Seat (*Prédikáló-szék*) above, the latter a steep and potentially dangerous rock of 640m that should be attempted only by experienced climbers. Kő-hegy has mushroom-shaped stones and a crater lake on top, home to the protected spade-foot toad. If you're going to hike in the hills, buy a copy of Cartographia's *A Pilis és a Visegrádi-helység* (1:40,000), which shows the routes in full.

## VISEGRÁD

Above Szentendre, the eastward-flowing Danube changes its mind and decides to make a swan dive south. Just before it does, though, there's a moment of indecision as it makes a last-ditch attempt to chart a course through the Pilis and Börzsöny hills. This wiggle of uncertainty formed a commanding strategic position utilised first by the Romans and then by Slav immigrants, who built a fort called '*Vyšehrad*' ('high fortress'). A Hungarised version of the name stuck, and became synonymous with the settlement at one of the country's prettiest points.

In the 11th century András I built a monastery here, but construction began in earnest under the Angevin king Károly Robert. The king was intent on quashing challenges to his authority by Buda's German population, and moved the royal seat to Visegrád in 1326; he based his palace in the lower castle erected the century before (along with the hilltop citadel) by Béla IV after the Mongol invasion. Subsequent kings enlarged and improved, and after King Mátyás's Italian architects had provided a monumental Renaissance flourish in the 15th century, a papal legate declared it 'a paradise on earth'.

Things were less heavenly after a siege by the Turks in 1543, which destroyed much of the palace and overran the seemingly invincible upper fortress; the town was utterly unloved during occupation. Afterwards, the Habsburgs detonated the citadel to deny independence fighters a stronghold and German settlers raided the town's rubble for material to build their houses; Visegrád's status as a royal seat was downgraded to that of market town and what remained of the palace gradually disappeared beneath earth sliding from the hillside. The fall from grace was so complete that until excavations began in the early 20th century, many dismissed talk of a former riverside edifice as so much pie in the sky. However, restoration of the castle began in the 1870s, and doubting Thomases were put straight in 1935 when archaeologists located the site of the 600m-long palace.

### Getting there and away

**Trains** from Budapest's Nyugati station take 45 minutes on their way to Visegrád-Nagymaros (*ticket 1,024Ft*), on the line to Szob; from there you can board one of the hourly ferries (*ticket 280Ft*) across to Visegrád itself. There are yellow Volán **buses** at least every hour from Budapest's Árpád híd bus station, Esztergom and Szentendre. The pier for the Visegrád-Nagymaros ferry is 500m south of the palace, and there's one bus stop here and another by the Mahart pier.

Mahart (\ *1 318 1223; www.mahartpassnave.hu*) operates two **river-boat** services to Visegrád, one via Szentendre (*Apr 30–Sep 4 daily 09.00, rest of year Sat–Sun & bank hols 09.00*) and the other via Vác (*Apr 30–Sep 4 daily 07.30, Apr 2–29 & Sep 5–Oct 2 Sat–Sun & bank hols 07.30*). Ferries depart from Pest's Vigadó tér, stopping to pick up passengers five minutes later from Buda's Batthyány tér, and take around three hours; tickets cost the same for either service (*sgl/rtn 1,090/1,635Ft*). For a speedier journey, hop on the **hydrofoil** (*May 21–Sep 18 Sat–Sun & bank hols 09.30; adult sgl/rtn 1,990/3,490Ft, concessions sgl/rtn 1,490/2,590Ft*), which also departs from Vigadó tér, arriving at Visegrád in an hour and continuing on to Esztergom. The Mahart pier is next to Solomon's Tower.

## Information and other practicalities

**Video Café** Rév utca 13. Offers internet access, as well as coffee. *Open daily 09.00–22.00.*
**Visegrád Tours** Rév utca 15; ❧ 26 398160; www.visegradtours.hu. Organises tours and programmes in and around the Danube Bend, and owns the Hotel Visegrád. They should be able to provide information if you need it. *Open daily May–Sep 08.00–19.00, Oct–Apr 09.00–16.00.*

## Where to stay

It's unlikely you'll be stuck for accommodation in Visegrád, as '*Zimmer frei*' signs abound.

**Danubius Spa and Conference Hotel Visegrád** (174 rooms) Lepencevölgy; ❧ 26 802900; e info@thv.hu; www.danubiushotels.com/visegrad. If pampering is on your holiday agenda, stay at this plush hotel. There are two thermal pools, a jacuzzi, swimming pool, saunas, aroma cabin, steam bath and solarium – it has it all, living up to its blurb boasting luxurious accommodation. *Sgl €88, dbl €118.*
**Hotel Honti** (30 rooms) Fő utca 66; ❧ 26 398120; e hotelhon@axelero.hu. Set on the bank of the Apátkuti Stream in Visegrád's centre, the Honti is a hotel and panzió suiting those seeking a quiet and romantic stay. *Hotel sgl 12,000Ft, dbl 14,000Ft, triple 19,500Ft; panzió sgl 7,800Ft, dbl 9,300Ft.*
**Hotel Visegrád** (40 rooms) Rév utca 15; ❧ 26 397034; e hotelvisegrad@visegradtours.hu; www.visegradtours.hu. This centrally located hotel houses the pricey Sirály Restaurant and the Visegrád Tours travel agency. Its classy rooms have balconies, with splendid views of Visegrád Castle or the Danube. Guests have free use of a sauna and jacuzzi, but if it's a pampering you want, the Danubius down the road is better. *Sgl €47, dbl €60.*
**Mátyás Tanya Inn** (16 rooms) Fő utca 47; ❧ 26 398309 or 1 313 1420 (reservations). A traditional and cosy inn with old-fashioned, faintly austere-looking rooms. The friendly and welcoming owner will do his best to accommodate your needs. There are charming eating areas indoors and out, where you can enjoy authentic, freshly made meals from the restaurant. *Dbl 9,900Ft.*

## Where to eat and drink

There are few restaurants or cafés in Visegrád, and it's worth considering the restaurants of the hotels featured above to supplement those that follow. Nagymaros, across the river, has a wider and more inspired choice. With walls plastered in jazz memorabilia, a working juke box and piano in the corner, **Don Vito Pizzeria** (*Fő utca 83;* ❧ *26 397230; pizzas from 360Ft; open daily 12.00–24.00*) feels more like a music bar than a restaurant. There's a cosy leather-seated *salsa di cosa nostra* and a bright, sun-lit room if you prefer a quieter eating environment. Some pasta and meat dishes are offered, but the focus is definitely pizza, with interesting sweet pizzas to boot. Look out for jazz and karaoke nights at the weekends. Near the Mahart pier, **Reneszánsz** (*Fő utca 11;* ❧ *26 398081; mains avg 1,800Ft; open daily 12.00–23.00*) is targeted at tourist groups and is as tacky as hell with its medieval theme and wenchy waitresses. It's also not cheap, but in for a penny (or many pennies)…

## What to see and do

The main sights are all ranged along or above the river to the north of the central pocket. The **Royal Palace** (*Királyi palota; Fő utca 29; 26 398026; adult/concessions 400/200Ft; open Tue–Sun 09.00–17.00*) is the first of them, reached after a 500m stroll up Fő utca. This was a palace of European significance; in 1335, for instance, a two-month summit was hosted here by Károly Robert at which Polish, Czech, Saxon and Lower Bavarian heads met to resolve territorial disputes and forge a trade agreement that bypassed the increasingly powerful Habsburgs. The terraced complex – its Gothic styling complemented by the Renaissance additions made by King Mátyás – was reconstructed after 20th-century excavations, and was a hefty project given that the Court of Honour was buried beneath a layer of stones 15m deep.

Behind the ticket office is a field that hosts displays of medieval crafts, jousting and archery during the annual Visegrád Palace Games (*www.palotajatekok.hu*) on the second weekend in July. In front is a collection of stone finds dating from Roman times up to the medieval period, and beyond that the palace itself. Much of what you see dates to Mátyás's reign, when there were apparently 350 rooms, and a plethora of courtyards, fountains and hanging gardens. At its heart is the ornamental Court of Honour on the second tier, flanked by a Gothic arcade and holding a copy of the Hercules Fountain bearing Mátyás's crest. The third level holds the chapel and queen's apartments (where Beatrix held court); on the uppermost terrace at the palace's rear is a bathing area, and a courtyard holding a replica of the Lion Fountain with its beasts and basins (the original is in Solomon's Tower). The Mátyás Museum tells the palace's tale, and has red marble columns among its display.

Continue along Fő utca and keep right at the fork in the road on to Salamon-torony utca, where you'll find **Solomon's Tower** (*Salamon Torony utca; 26 398233; adult/concessions 400/200Ft; May 1–Sep 30 Tue-Sun 09.00–17.00*), the lower of the castle fortifications built by Béla IV in the 13th century. The tower is one of the best-preserved Romanesque keeps in central Europe, and formed part of a connected defensive system with walls running up to the citadel and down to a water bastion from where guards kept watch on the Danube. You can get a bird's eye view of these from the top of the tower; the structures were in part funded by the sale of jewellery brought from Byzantium by Béla's wife, Queen Maria Lascaris. Inside the keep – which is oddly named after the son of András I, whom King László imprisoned in Visegrád during a power struggle fully 200 years before the thing was built – are fragments from the Renaissance palace, including the original Hercules and Lion fountains.

Atop the rock directly above is the citadel or **Upper Castle** (*Fellegvár; adult/concessions 750/350Ft; open Mar 15–Oct 15 10.00–17.00 daily, Oct 16–Mar 14 09.30–16.00 Sat–Sun only*). It was constructed between 1245 and 1255 as a bolt hole for Dominican nuns from Hare (now Margaret) Island in case of further Mongol raids; among the nuns there was Princess Margit, whom Béla had pledged to God and who was famous for never washing above the ankle (see page 164). The precious Holy Crown was housed here for 200 years up until the Turkish invasion, save for a period during the 15th century when it went walkabout. During a vacuum in which several factions were claiming the right to succession of the throne, a lady-in-waiting to the widowed Elizabeth of Luxembourg (daughter of Zsigmond) stole it away in an attempt to settle things in favour of her mistress's unborn child. The baby was actually crowned with it when born, but it all came to nothing when the Hunyadis won through and the crown was returned to the fortress in 1464.

In the southern wing of the citadel's lower courtyard is a waxwork display of 18th-century instruments of torture. The wings of the innermost courtyard contain exhibitions on aristocratic hunting and on the less-leisured lives of foresters, stone carvers and fishermen in the Pilis Hills. A fourth collection charts the history of the castle and its restoration, using drawings and archive photographs; there are keystones carved with the coats of arms of Mátyás and his queen, window and door frames from the Angevin and Zsigmond years, and part of a 13th-century fireplace from Solomon's Tower. The ramparts were built in several rings, and you can clamber over them and admire views that include ruins of the 4th-century Roman military camp on Sibrik Hill.

There are two routes up the 350m hill to the citadel. The steeper of these runs from Solomon's Tower, but if you fancy taking it slightly easier follow Kálvária sétány from the centre, leading off Nagy Lajos Király utca from the back of the Roman Catholic church.

## Other

As you move away from the river you start to hit the Visegrád Hills, which form a belt running behind Visegrád around to Esztergom and are themselves buttressed by the Pilis Hills at their back. From Visegrád, the best starting point for proper bracing hikes into these ranges is Dömös (see page 201), around the lower western side of the river wiggle; buses run there along Road 11 *en route* to Esztergom. On the way, after 2km you'll pass a road leading left to Pilisszentlászló and Szentendre; at the junction lies Lepence and the **Visegrád-Lepence Baths** (*strandfürdő; Visegrád-Lepence;* ➘ *26 398208; www.castrumvisegrad.hu; day ticket adult/concessions 1,100/750Ft, morning/afternoon ticket 500Ft; open May 1– Sep 30 daily 06.00–08.00 morning swim, 09.00–15.30 day swim, 16.00–18.30 afternoon swim*). Set in woods, you'll search in vain for a more picturesque wallowing hole. Circular thermal pools on terraces cling to the hillside, decorated with an unusual concrete structure that is somewhat '60s *szocreál* in style. The pools, in concentric rings and nicknamed 'onion skins', are supplied by thermal waters gushing from springs below at 39°C. Jets of water burst from the walls and provide an excellent underwater massage. There is also a children's pool and a 33m swimming pool. Spectacular.

There are some gentle hikes in the immediate area of the citadel. The paths from Solomon's Tower and the centre become one to the north of the citadel, and this meanders up towards the **Nagy-Villám lookout tower**. (You can marginally shorten the trip by following the main road from the citadel car park for the first half, picking up the last section of the path at the second, higher car park.) Beyond a campsite to the north of the tower (take the left branch of the path as you ascend) are some **forest buildings** constructed by the nationalist architect Imre Makovecz, whose organic designs spoke loud in defiance of communist homogeneity during the Kádár years. The turf-roofed cultural centre has a woodland display. To the south of the tower is a **'bobsleigh' run** (*Nagy-Villám bob-pálya;* ➘ *26 397397;* e *visegradbob@dunainfo.net; adult/concessions 400/300Ft; open daily Mar–Apr & Oct–Nov 10.00–17.00, May & Sep 10.00–18.00, Jun–Aug 09.00–19.00, Sat–Sun Jan–Feb & Dec 11.00–16.00*), a 700m winding metal track down which riders can whizz in sled carts.

## ESZTERGOM

If Budapest is central Europe's definitive city of superlatives, Esztergom is the town. Facing Slovakia across the water, it boasts the first and largest church in Hungary, and the oldest synagogue; as a settlement with a heritage spanning over 1,000 years, Esztergom has plenty to offer history buffs. The site was originally a Roman outpost, part of the fortifications lining the Danube that represented the empire's eastern border, and one where the future emperor Marcus Aurelius wrote his *Meditations* while waging a campaign against Germanic tribes. A fortress was constructed on Castle Hill in AD972, and the town – the 'Cradle of Hungary' – was the place of birth and coronation for King István, founder of the State and Church. Esztergom remained the royal capital until Béla IV shifted to Buda after the Mongol invasion in the mid 13th century. The Treaty of Trianon reduced the town's secular importance by stripping away two-thirds of Esztergom County, and it wasn't until after the fall of communism that attempts were made to re-instate some political power by relocating the constitutional court here. However, as the seat of Roman Catholicism in Hungary its religious role has remained enormously significant for much of a millennium, interrupted only by the Turkish occupation when the clerics fled to safer havens. The Archbishop of Esztergom, who lives in the Primate's Palace, traditionally wielded great authority, and during medieval

## CARDINAL MINDSZENTY

The conservative cleric Cardinal József Mindszenty famously became a figure of resistance first to the Germans and subsequently to the communists, who subjected him to a show trial in 1949 before imprisoning him. There are transcripts recording his suffering at the hands of secret-police torturers on display in the House of Terror (see page 165). During the revolution of 1956 he was freed, and took haven in the US Embassy in Budapest – where he stayed for a full 15 years, becoming a focal point for communist opposition and rejecting State proposals such as the secularisation of Roman Catholic schools. It was only in 1971 that he was persuaded by the Vatican to leave the embassy and move to Austria, where he died four years later at the age of 83. In 1990, shortly after the change of political system, the cardinal's body was returned to Hungary and buried in Esztergom Basilica; Pope John Paul II knelt before his grave during his papal visit to Hungary the year after, and since then the crypt has become a place of pilgrimage for Roman Catholics. It is hoped – nay, expected – that Mindszenty will one day be canonised.

flashpoints over legitimate royal succession it was the archbishop who assumed control until the squabbles were resolved. Such privileges were enjoyed until World War II, when Cardinal Mindszenty – a reactionary who couldn't stomach even democratic socialism, and faced the considerable consequences of saying so – was relieved of them. Today Esztergom is a favourite tourist town, conveniently laid out, readily walked around and signalled from afar by the dominant form of the 'enormous snail'.

## Getting there and away

**Trains** from Budapest's Nyugati station take 90 minutes, departing up to 25 times a day. There is also a steam-hauled vintage train that runs in summer from Nyugati (*leaves Apr 24–Oct 2 at 09.40 on alternate Sats*); for further information on this, contact the MÁV Nosztalgia Kft office (*Budapest XIV, Tatai út 95;* ☎ *1 238 0558; www.mavnosztalgia.hu*). Esztergom's station (*Bem József tér*) is 2km south of the centre; you can pick up local buses 1 and 5 the rest of the way.

Yellow **buses** run twice an hour (*the last at 22.50*) from Budapest's Árpád híd bus station to Esztergom, via Visegrád or Dorog (the latter 45 mins quicker). There are regular services to Visegrád (taking 40 mins) and Szentendre (90 mins). The bus station is on Simor János utca, which leads south from Rákóczi tér.

If you have time to spare, the Mahart **river boat** (☎ *1 318 1223/484 4000;* e *passnave@mahartpassnave.hu; www.mahartpassnave.hu*) is the scenic way to travel from Budapest. Boats depart (*sgl/rtn 1,490/2,235Ft; Apr 30–Sep 4 07.30 daily, Apr 2–Apr 29 & Sep 5–Oct 2 07.30 Sat, Sun & bank hols only*) from Pest's Vigadó tér, picking up passengers at Buda's Batthyány tér at 07.35 and stopping again at Vác and Visegrád before arriving at Esztergom at 13.00. The return ferry departs at 16.00. In addition, there is a high-season boat from Esztergom travelling as far as Visegrád (*sgl/rtn 790/1,185Ft; Jun 4–Sep 4 09.00 daily*), with a return service at 16.00. There is also a two-hour **hydrofoil** service (*adult sgl/rtn 2,490/3,990Ft, child sgl/rtn 1,690/2,990Ft; May 21–Sep 18 09.30 Sat, Sun & bank hols only*) from Vigadó tér, which cuts the travel time by half but is a pricier option. The ferry pier is on Nagy-Duna sétány, to the south of Mária Valéria Bridge.

## Information and other practicalities

**Gran Tours** Széchenyi tér 25; ☎ 33 413756. Travel information and currency exchange bureau that can organise private accommodation. *Open Sep–May Mon–Fri 08.00–16.00, Jun–Aug Mon–Fri 08.00–18.00, Sat 09.00–12.00.*

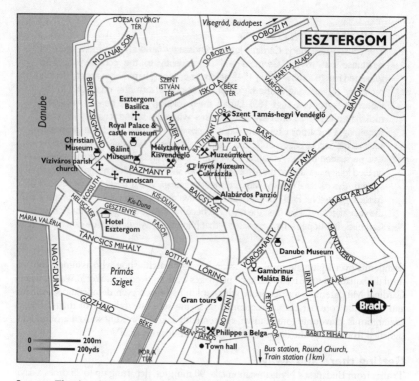

**Internet** There's an internet terminal at the Hotel Esztergom (see below).

**Listings magazine** *Komárom-Esztergomi Est*

## Where to stay

**Alabárdos Panzió** (22 rooms) Bajcsy-Zsilinszky utca 49; ⎝ 33 312640. Watch out for the huge dog when entering the gates! Although the rooms are small, this is a comfortable pension hung with historical paintings of the town and with great views of Castle Hill. You couldn't ask for friendlier or more welcoming staff. *Sgl 8,500Ft, dbl 10,500Ft.*

**Hotel Esztergom** (36 rooms) Prímás sziget, Nagy-Duna sétány; ⎝ 33 412555; e info@hotel-esztergom.hu. We're unsure what the interior designers were thinking when decking the reception hall in dull beige, yellow and pink but the effect is outmoded and drab. The rooms themselves are modern enough, although ours could have done with a hoovering. Guests receive a 20% discount at the hotel restaurant *(open daily 18.00–21.30)*, which serves Hungarian classics. *Sgl 10,000Ft, dbl 11,000Ft, studio 15,000Ft.*

**Panzió Ria** (15 rooms) Batthyány utca 11–13; ⎝ 33 401429; e riapanzio@invitel.hu; www.riapanzio.com. This is a pension with that little bit extra – spacious rooms facing a pleasant courtyard, an internet room, sauna, fitness room and bike hire. If exploring the basilica – standing virtually on the doorstep – isn't enough, the staff will help you arrange excursions beyond. *Rooms €54.*

Contact Gran Tours (see page 205) if you wish to book **college** or **private accommodation**. **Gran Camping** *(Prímás sziget;* ⎝ *33 402513; www.hotels.hu/gran_camping; open May 1–Oct 15)* is the best and most central of the campsites, and has bungalows.

## Where to eat and drink

**Ínyes Hidegkonyha Múzeum Cukrászda** Bajcsy-Zsilinszky utca 48; ⎝ 06 30 310 2507. Aesthetic variety of cakes, pancakes and other sins. The colour-clashing walls and dance music make the atmosphere more clubby than homely, but the sweetmeats are sumptuous. *Open daily 10.00–22.00.*

**Mélytanyér Kisvendéglő** Pázmány Péter utca 1; ＼ 33 412534; www.melytanyer.hu. This cheerful restaurant is a good choice for families, with gingham furnishings and a wall of football scarves. Service is quick and the atmosphere relaxed. *Mains avg 1,600Ft; open Mon–Thu & Sun 11.00–22.00, Fri–Sat 11.00–24.00.*

**Padlizsán** Pázmány Péter utca 21; ＼ 33 311212. An upmarket restaurant that teeters on being ostentatious. The clean, light and roomy interior, jaunty music and range of game and poultry dishes lends itself to an élite Hungarian dining experience. The set menu can be a saviour if deciding between noisette of venison and duck-liver risotto is too much like hard work. *Mains avg 2,250Ft; open 11.00–22.00 daily.*

**Philippe a Belga** Széchenyi tér 16. In a word, classy. Cerise walls and arty mosaics contribute to a vibrant, kitsch atmosphere. You can watch the chef as he prepares fine Belgian specialities; polite and friendly staff ensure a first-rate meal. *Mains avg 1,900Ft; open Wed–Sun 12.00–15.00, 18.00–23.00.*

**Pizzéria di Stefarta** Lörinc utca 5; ＼ 33 312952. Recommended by locals, this lively spot is the most popular eatery in town. The staff may not speak English, but they do know how to make a fantastic pizza and there's a magnificent list of toppings from which to select. *Avg pizza 1,200Ft; open daily 11.00–22.00.*

**Restaurant Muzeúmkert** Batthyány utca 1; ＼ 06 30 977 9384. Not for vegetarians. Animal skins adorn the seats and walls and a huge choice of pork, beef and poultry dishes should satisfy the most avid of meat eaters. Beware a snappy waitress. *Mains avg 2,000Ft; open daily 12.00–24.00.*

**Szent Tamás-hegyi Vendéglő** Táglaház utca 4; ＼ 33 401638. Fairy lights, numerous plants and *lángos* mania. There are sweet and savoury versions of the Hungarian snack – try the one with ewe cheese – as well as stock meat and potato fare. *Lángos 450–750Ft; open Mon–Sat 11.00-22.00.*

## Entertainment and nightlife

There are no nightclubs in Esztergom, but there are various drinking holes. The **Gambrinus Maláta Bár** (*Vörösmarty utca 5;* ＼ *33 402844; www.gastroport.hu; open Mon–Fri 11.00–02.00, Sat–Sun 15.00–02.00*) is one of them, with loud and funky beats, wood panelling and a collection of Hungarian ornaments. You can squander your spare coins in the **24-hour casino** on Széchenyi tér; there are **organ concerts** held in the basilica in summer months and drama and dance in the Rondella. You can buy tickets or get details from Grantours (see page 205) or from the ticket office (*Széchenyi tér 7; www.esztergominyarijatekok.hu; open Mon–Fri 09.00–16.00*).

## What to see and do
### Castle Hill
**Esztergom Basilica** (*Szent István tér 1;* ＼ *33 411895;* e *bazilika.esztergom@museum.hu; admission free; open Apr–Oct daily 07.00–18.00, rest of year Mon–Fri 07.00–16.00, Sat–Sun 07.00–17.00*) crowns the town; it is the country's biggest, erected on the spot where Prince Géza's 30-year-old son was anointed King István in AD1000 with a crown sent by Pope Sylvester. In replacing the 12th-century Gothic St Adalbert Cathedral that was maimed by the Turks, the 19th-century planners worked with the grandiose aim of producing a Magyar version of the Vatican's St Peter's Square. The behemoth is 100m high and 107m long, and took almost 50 years to build; it was completed by József Hild, who added the last piece of the monumental jigsaw – the dome – in 1869. Liszt had composed and conducted its consecration mass 13 years before. Regarded as a masterpiece of Neoclassical architecture, the basilica is actually formally rigid and rather stark; it doesn't float everybody's boat.

The main altar in the cavernous interior has an appropriately over-sized copy of Titian's *Assumption*, the largest single-canvas oil painting in the world. The highlight though is the **Bakócz Chapel** on the southern side of the nave, built by Archbishop Tamás Bakócz in 1507 as his future sepulchre. Carved of red marble from nearby Süttő, this wonderful piece of Renaissance work stood in St Adalbert's before its demolition; at that time, the chapel was carefully dismantled and later re-assembled to adorn the new basilica. It is unsurprising that Bakócz should have commissioned Italian craftsman of the highest order in constructing this tribute to himself in death; in life he was notorious as a brilliant but deeply conniving and greedy prelate, who used all means possible (including conning Queen Beatrice after the death of Mátyás) to accrue a massive personal fortune. He is also remembered as the man tasked with raising a peasant army to tackle the Turks in 1514 – an army whose appointed commander, György Dózsa, ended up leading his peasants in revolt (see page 17).

Through a door to the right of the main altar painting is the nation's most precious liturgical collection, a trove that looks to have been manhandled by Midas himself. The **cathedral treasury** (*adult/concession 400Ft/200Ft; open Tue–Sun Mar 1–Oct 31 09.00–16.30, Nov 1–Dec 31 11.00–15.30, closed Jan–Feb*) has been raided on several occasions over the centuries, but it still contains 400 items of ecclesiastical jewellery and textiles dating back as far as the Árpáds. Chief among the attractions are a 13th-century coronation cross on which Hungarian kings swore the oath of accession, the beautiful 16th-century Suki Chalice, and the Calvary of King Mátyás. The latter comprises two parts, the Gothic upper portion presented to Zsigmond by the French Queen Isabelle in 1424, and the lower Renaissance part made for Mátyás by Italian goldsmiths working in Buda. Beside the entrance to the basilica are two sets of stairs, one leading down to the **crypt** (*adult 50Ft; open daily 09.00–17.00*) – the resting place for archbishops and other clergy (including Cardinal Mindszenty; see box, page 205), and straight out of a Gothic novel – and the other up to the **cupola** (*adult 100Ft; open May–Oct daily 09.00–17.00*), equally chilling for those lacking heads for heights.

A short step south of the basilica is the former **Royal Palace**, whose partly reconstructed remains represent the earliest structure extant in Hungary. They were excavated during the 1930s, the palace having sunk beneath the earth after being destroyed during the Turkish occupation. At the southern end are walls dating to Prince Géza's 10th-century palace, including the St István Hall where his son (called Vajk before he received the baptismal name by which he was revered for ever more) was supposedly born. The bulk of the building though was added in the 12th century by Béla III, with subsequent decorative alterations by the archbishops who occupied the palace from the 13th century (after the royal capital was moved to Buda). The first-floor Hall of Virtues, which once hosted royal receptions, was used as a study by Archbishop János Vitéz in the 1470s; it gets its name from the painted allegories of Intellect, Temperance, Fortitude and Justice that were added shortly afterwards, perhaps by Ippolito d'Este (see box opposite). Just to the north is the 12th-century late-Romanesque/early-Gothic royal chapel with a splendid rose window; among the frescoes are a tree of life and a lion whose style reflect the Byzantine background of Béla III, and eight later half-length apostles from the 14th century. All these remains are part of the **Castle Museum** (*Szent István tér 1;* ❧ *33 311821; adult/child 400/200Ft; open Tue–Sun mid Mar–Oct 31 09.00–17.00, Nov 1–mid Mar 11.00–15.30*), which also contains finds from the local area (including stonework from St Adalbert Cathedral). There are summer arts performances hosted in the **Rondella**, one of the bastions that made up the fortifications surrounding Castle Hill.

### The rest of town

If you descend the steps leading down the hill's southeastern side, and then pick up Pázmány utca bearing westwards around the bottom, you'll enter the Baroque **Vízíváros** (Watertown) district. At the eastern end of Pázmány utca is the **Archdiocesan Library**

## GOD'S YOUNG GUN

There was more than a whiff of nepotism involved in the appointment of Ippolito d'Este as archbishop in 1477. At just eight years old, it could have been argued that he lacked for something in experience; however, he was the nephew of Mátyás's wife and this put him at something of an advantage over the other candidates. He took over after the death of János Vitéz, and held the post for a decade. Queen Beatrice certainly lacked such sway after the death of Mátyás; instead it was the scheming Archbishop Bakócz who was able to manipulate things, and Beatrice lived unhappy in a tower of the palace before eventually returning to her native Italy.

(*Bibliotéka*), which is among the country's oldest collections of books, while further on you'll find temporary exhibitions of archaeology and local history at the **Balassi Bálint Museum** (*Mindszenty hercegprímás tere 5;* ❧ *33 412185; adult/concessions 100/50Ft; open Nov 1–Apr 30 Wed–Sun 11.00–15.00, May 1–Oct 31 Tue–Sun 09.00–17.00*). Opposite is the two-steepled Baroque **Franciscan church** and adjoining monastery (*Pázmány utca 18*).

A short distance further west is the early-18th-century **Víziváros Parish Church**, and the **Christian Museum** (*Keresztény Múzeum; Mindszenty hercegprímás tere 2;* ❧ *33 413880; adult/concessions 500/250Ft; open Tue–Sun Mar 1–27 10.00–17.00, Mar 29–Oct 30 10.00–18.00, Nov 2–Dec 31 11.00–15.00*) in the Neo-Renaissance former Primate's Palace. Founded in 1875 by Archbishop János Simor, it represents Hungary's stand-out display of medieval and Renaissance religious art. As well as native works (from 15th-century painted panels to a 17th-century portrait of the poet Balassi, who turned to religion at the end of a far from virtuous life), there is a particularly rich collection of Trecento and Quattrocento paintings (Italian art of the 14th and 15th centuries), as well as Austrian, German, Flemish and French pieces. Be sure not to miss the two works most commonly mentioned in association with this museum – Tamás of Kolozsvár's *Calvary* altarpiece (1427), where Christ's suffering is emphasised in his hollow face and distorted toe joints, and the wooden *Coffin of Our Lord* (c 1480), a symbolic sepulchre on wheels that was used in liturgies at Easter and whose carved figures were modelled on actors in passion plays of the time. Both came from the Benedictine monastery of Garamszentbenedek in Slovakia.

A bridge at the southern side of Mindszenty hercegprímás tere crosses over to **Prímás sziget** (Primate's Island), and Nagy Duna sétány leads around the island's outer edge. After 100m you'll reach a second bridge, this time spanning the water to the Slovakian town of átúrovo ('Párkány' in Hungarian). For nearly 60 years the **Mária Valéria**

## A LOVER AND A FIGHTER

Bálint Balassi (1554–94) was one of the great Renaissance poets, innovative in experimenting with form, writing in the vernacular and producing a significant body of love poetry. But he was a maverick who broke moulds beyond the sphere of art, and was a man of his 'sword' (metaphorically and literally) as much as his pen. He embroiled himself in a series of notorious sexual relationships that resulted – among other things – in a prosecution for incest (after he married his first cousin, the daughter of István Dobó; see pages 242–3). His fondness for battling the Turks brought about his final downfall at the age of just 40; during the attempt to recapture Esztergom in 1594 he was injured in the legs, dying of blood poisoning a short while later. There is a statue of him in Szent István tér.

**Bridge** meant a forlorn pair of twisted stubs protruding from the water after the retreating Germans detonated it during World War II. During those years the opposite bank could only be reached by ferry. However, after protracted discussions the 500m-long 19th-century structure was finally resurrected, and opened at a ceremony attended by the Hungarian and Slovakian prime ministers in 2002.

Moving back off the island, the river-hugging Kis-Duna sétány is a pretty promenade and a pleasant way of moving towards the heart of town to the south of Castle Hill. On the way, it passes the invigorating **thermal baths** (*Bajcsy-Zsilinsky utca 14;* \ *33 312249; adult/concessions 350/150Ft; open outdoor pools May–Sep daily 09.00–18.00, indoor pool Mon & Sat 06.00–18.00, Tue–Fri 06.00–19.00*). The second road on the left takes you to Széchenyi tér and its Baroque, Rococo and Neoclassical architecture. The **town hall** (*Széchenyi tér 1*) was originally built in the 17th century, and was home to János Bottyán, the one-eyed general known as 'Bottyán the Blind' who served under Rákóczi II; there used to be a sword suspended outside reminding those with crime on their minds that murderers could be sentenced to death. Kossuth Lajos utca passes to the square's eastern side and continues south to Hősök tere where stands the **Round Church**, inspired by Rome's Pantheon, intended as a practice run for the basilica, and completed in 1835.

To the northeast of Rákóczi tér, at the top of Vörösmarty utca, the **Danube Museum** (*Kölcsey Ferenc utca 2;* \ *33 500250; www.dunamuzeum.org.hu; admission free; open Wed–Mon Nov 1–Dec 31 & Feb 1–Apr 30 10.00–16.00, May 1–Oct 31 10.00–18.00*) is devoted to water administration and environmental protection, and has exhibitions showing the solutions and equipment used in regulating Hungary's main river during the 19th century.

### Festivals and events

The town is at its liveliest in summer, with an annual drama festival in the open-air Castle Theatre (*Vörösmarty utca 2;* \ *33 400945/501175;* e *tender@holop.hu*), which runs from the middle of June until the end of August (*performances Fri, Sat and Sun 20.30*). There is an International Guitar Festival in August (contact Gran Tours above for more information) and a Gizella Festival in May.

### VÁC

On the eastern bank 35km north of Pest, Vác is a walkable town less tourist-infested than elsewhere on the Danube Bend and seems laid back by comparison. This atmosphere belies a very active and frequently influential past, however; the town basked in the immortal glow of Ptolemy's *Geographia* (in which it was recorded as an ancient river crossing called Uvcencum), and in the 11th century it was one of the ten episcopal sees founded by King István. One theory regarding its current name posits that before their battle to decide the Hungarian succession in 1074, the princes Géza and László met a hermit called Vác while riding in a nearby forest. After the Mongols had ripped out its early-medieval heart – including Géza's Romanesque cathedral, where he was buried in 1077 – Béla IV gathered his noblemen here to decide the way forward in protecting the country from future attack. During the 14th century, it benefitted from close proximity to the royal capital at Visegrád and for a time Vác's silver coinage served as the national currency. However, a position of strategic importance meant it featured heavily in the struggles when the Turks came on the scene, and changed hands 40 times before finally succumbing to Ottoman occupation – and a second episode of heart ripping.

Fate conspired against the town's revival when a fire in 1731 razed 90% of the buildings. The Baroque town you see now is the result of successive bishops' efforts during the rest of the 18th century to haul it back up by its bootstraps, a period that also saw repopulation with Germans, Czechs, Slovaks, Croatians and Serbs. Confirmation that things were back on track came literally in 1846 with the construction of the rail link with Budapest, the first in the country. A memorial at the town's southern gate commemorates two battles during the 1849 War of Independence, but during the 20th century the town was linked inexorably with its fearsome prison, a place used first by Miklós Horthy and then by Rákosi to incarcerate their political opponents.

## Getting there and away

Vác is on Road 2, which runs parallel to the river from Budapest. The **bus station** (*Szent István tér*) is 300m northeast of the centre; there are loads of daily buses from Budapest's Árpád híd, as well as services between Vác and Vácrátót (24), Balassagyarmat (18), Salgótarján (four), Gödöllő (eight) and many other towns. The **railway station** is 500m from the centre, at the northeastern end of Széchenyi utca. There are very regular train services from Budapest Nyugati to Vác, which continue around the Danube Bend to Szob (and a few on over the Slovakian border to Štúrovo). You can also take the train a 12-minute journey southeast to Vácrátót (up to three of which continue on to Aszód), and to Balassagyarmat (up to ten). A **steam train** (*www.mavnosztalgia.hu; Apr 23–Oct 8 09.40 Sat only*) chuffs from Budapest Nyugati through Vác and Visegrád on its way to Szob; you'll need to pay a supplement (*adult/child 400/250Ft*) on top of the standard second-class MÁV ticket.

A **ferry** going across to Szentendre Island (see pages 199–200) leaves fairly regularly from the pier at the junction of Ady Endre sétány and Eszterházy utca, and can take both foot passengers and cars. Further north along the bank is the Mahart ferry pier (*Liszt Ferenc sétány*). Mahart operates a **river boat** between Budapest and Esztergom, which stops at Vác (*arriving at 09.50; sgl/rtn 490/735Ft*) and Visegrád on the way, returning from Vác at 18.10; for full details of the days and seasons, see under Esztergom (page 205).

## Information and other practicalities

**Duna Tours** Széchenyi utca 14; ☎ 27 310950. This office can arrange local, domestic and international tours, and private rooms; it stands on the road running from the eastern side of the main square. *Open Mon–Fri 08.00–16.00, Sat 08.00–12.00.*

**Tourinform** Március 15 tér 16–18; ☎ 27 316160; e vac@tourinform.hu. At the eastern side of the square. *Open Jun 1–Sep 30 Mon–Fri 09.00–18.00, Sat–Sun 09.00–17.00, rest of year Mon–Fri 09.00–17.00.*

## Where to stay

**Fónagy & Walter** (3 rooms) Budapesti főút 36; ☎ 27 310682; e walter@fonagy.hu; www.fonagy.hu. The 'antique' furnishings of this pension 400m southeast of the cathedral could have been pinched from your grandmother's, but the rooms are large and have sofas. *All rooms €38.*

**Teréz Karacs College** Budapesti főút 8; ☎ 27 315480. Just beyond the southern corner of Konstantin tér, the college has dorm rooms available during vacation periods. *Beds from 1,500Ft/pp.*

**Vörössipka Hotel** (16 rooms) Honvéd utca 14; ☎ 27 501055; e okktart@netelek.hu; www.szallasjegyzek.hu. To the east of the centre, this fire-engine-red hotel has spotless rooms with gleaming floors, although the service was poor during our stay and the rooms lack telephones. *Sgl 7,700–11,200Ft, dbl 9,000–13,500Ft.*

## Where to eat and drink

**Barlang Restaurant** Március 15 tér. At the heart of the square – indeed running beneath it – this cool cellar bar brims with Gothic character, with torch light and a hanging iron candelabra. Pizza is the order of the day. *Mains 800–1,600Ft, avg 1,200Ft; open Mon–Thu 11.00–23.00, Fri–Sat 12.00–01.00, Sun 12.00–22.00.*

**Duna Espresso** Március 15 tér 13; ☎ 27 310569. Enjoy the square in this coffee house and bar next to the town hall. *Open Mon–Thu 08.00–23.00, Fri 08.00–13.00, Sat 08.00–24.00, Sun 08.00–22.00.*

**Halászkert** Liszt Ferenc sétány 9; ☎ 27 315985. On the old-fashioned side, the Halászkert serves up traditional fare – featuring a good number of fish specialities – that is decent and cheap. There's a river terrace and cheesy music. *Mains 1,200–1,950Ft, avg 1,400Ft; open 11.00–22.00 daily.*

**Margaréta Coffee House** Széchenyi utca 19. This buzzing bar and café is a good people-watching spot, and sells ice cream by the bucket load in summer. *Open Mon 06.00–16.00, Tue–Fri 05.00–16.00, Sat 05.00–13.00, Sun 06.00–12.00.*

**Momo** Timáru utca 9; ☎ 27 306777. Overlooked by the spire of the Franciscan church and fronting on to the Danube, this is the town's best restaurant and a decent place for a beer too. Outside it spreads over a three-tiered terrace, while the modern interior has wicker chairs and lots of space. The menu includes Hungarian and international dishes such as Hungarian stews, steak, veal and spaghetti. *Mains 980–3,890Ft, avg 2,000Ft; open daily 11.00–24.00.*

**Streets of Dublin Irish Pub** Zrínyi utca 3; ☎ 27 306785. Up some steps opposite the bus station, the Streets of Dublin is the favourite drinking hole for the locals. It's 'Irishness' is debatable – there's no Guinness and the staff speak no English – but there's dependable (if unadventurous) food like pizza, pasta and steak to soak up the not-so-black stuff, and live music. *Mains 780–3,150Ft, avg 1,500Ft; open Mon–Sun 12.00–24.00.*

**Vincellér** Dr Csányi Lászlo körút 85; ☎ 27 301521. International food in a cosy enough restaurant with a small terrace. *Mains 1,500–2,500Ft; open Mon–Sat 12.00–22.00, Sun 12.00–17.00.*

## What to see and do
### Március 15 tér and around

Március 15 tér looks like a Neapolitan ice cream, lined with civic buildings and town houses in shades of pink, yellow and brown. It gained its triangular shape in 1761 when a church at the southeastern end was demolished, bringing into view the newly completed **Dominican church** (*Március 15 tér 22*). Known as the Church of the Whites (after the habit worn by the monks), the Baroque exterior hides rich Rococo furnishings inside, while next door is the monastery. In 1994, a forgotten, sealed crypt was found in the church that had served as a burial chamber during the 18th century. The conditions had led to mummification of the corpses, many of which were interred in formal costume – the women in bonnets, the men in jackets or cloaks – and the children in coffins of blue or green. In the cellars to the right of the church, the **Memento Mori** (*Március 15 tér 19;* \ *27 315064; adult/concessions 400/200Ft; open Mar 1–Nov 31 Tue–Sun 10.00–18.00*) displays some of the discoveries – jewellery, rosaries and children's shoes – as well as three of the mummies themselves, lying with their arms folded. It's fascinating stuff, and sombre rather than creepy.

On the other side of Eszterházy utca is the custard-yellow Baroque **town hall** (*Március 15 tér 11*), built in 1764 in time for the visit of Maria Theresa to the town. On the gable is an allegory of Justice, with reclining figures either side bearing the coats of arms of Hungary and Bishop Kristóf Migazzi. Migazzi was incumbent during Vác's golden age, and presided over the building of the cathedral, the Triumphal Arch and the town hall itself; he went on to become Archbishop of Vienna and a cardinal. Next to the town hall is the 18th-century former **monastery of the Order of Mercy** (*Március 15 tér 7–9*), while the **Institute for the Deaf and Dumb** (*Március 15 tér 6*) has functioned in the building opposite since 1802, although in the aftermath of Turkish occupation it served for a while as the Bishop's Palace and was where Maria Theresa stayed. The former **Grand Provost's Palace** (*Március 15 tér 4*) stands adjacent to it.

There is a lovely promenade running along the river bank, and you might wish to enjoy a short stretch of it before rejoining Köztársaság utca and its notorious **prison** (*Köztársaság utca 64–66*) 600m north of Március tér. (You'll pass the **Pointed Tower** at Liszt Ferenc sétány 12 on the way, which was a corner turret of the medieval town walls and is now incorporated into the structure of a residential building.) The jail was originally a school, one of Maria Theresa's institutes for the education of noble children (known as Theresianums), but since 1855 its watchtowers and gridded windows have restrained prisoners rather than pupils. Its hulking form stands at a particularly pretty point, and inmates no doubt request a river-facing room. Just beyond it is the Neoclassical **Triumphal Arch** (commonly called Kőkapu, or Stone Gate), another of Bishop Migazzi's monuments erected specifically for Maria Theresa's visit in 1764. It is said that the bishop actually placed theatrical scenery props along her route through the town to screen any unappealing architecture.

### Konstantin tér and around

Moving out through the southeast corner of Március 15 tér, behind the Dominican church is an **outdoor market** (*open Mon 06.00–16.00, Tue–Fri 05.00–16.00, Sat 05.00–13.00, Sun 06.00–10.00*) selling clothes, flowers and vegetables, and further down on the other side of the road is the **Hincz Collection** (*Káptalan utca 16;* \ *27 313463; adult/concessions 400/200Ft; open Tue–Sun Mar 1–Oct 31 10.00–18.00, Nov 1–Feb 28 10.00–16.00*). The museum has two permanent exhibitions showcasing the history of Vác and the work of avant-garde painter and graphic artist Gyula Hincz (1904–86).

Konstantin tér was the ecclesiastical engine room of the town, and is bullied by the vast and boxy **Vác Cathedral**. It was built between 1763 and 1767, originally to the plans of the Austrian architect Franz Anton Pilgram before Bishop Migazzi brought in the Frenchman Isidore Canevale to finish the job. Many regard the cathedral as a supreme example of Hungarian Neoclassical architecture, but to us the proportions feel uncomfortable, both in the building itself and its surroundings, like the first pupil in class to hit his growth spurt. Enormous Corinthian columns dominate the façade, with six enormous statues by József Bechert peering down from above them; the green cupola is hardly visible. The interior is considerably lighter in touch, with cream walls and a fresco of the triumphant Holy Trinity by Franz Anton Maulbertsch giving a splash of colour to the dome; the main altar painting (*The Meeting of Mary and Elizabeth*) by the same artist was only discovered during restoration in the 1940s – it was not to Migazzi's taste, and had been covered over. Pieces of the sanctuary rail are taken from the earlier Renaissance cathedral built by Bishop Miklós Báthori – a bishop whom King Mátyás threatened to chuck in the Danube if he continued to torture his tenants – and there are other stone fragments in the crypt.

On the western side of the square, paved with stones of grey, blue and terracotta, and dotted with ornate lamp posts, is one side of the late-Baroque **Provost's Palace** (*Migazzi Kristóf tér*), which faces on to Migazzi tér and was built between 1782 and 1784 by Viennese architect József Meissl. Múzeum utca runs northwards to Szentháromság tér and the flaking **Piarist Church**, finished in 1741; inside is as spartan as outside, with the notable exception of its carved and gilded Venetian mirror altar. Keep a look out too for the graceful statue of a timid Mary in a red dress. The sandstone **Trinity Column** was erected by Bishop Althann in 1755.

To the south of Konstantin tér is a **Franciscan church** (*Géza Király tér 18*), built in the 18th century with stone from the old fortress destroyed by the Turks; the pulpit bears exuberant allegories of the Virtues, while the church's centrepiece is the elaborate, two-storey Rococo altar. Continue further southwards on Budapesti főút and you'll reach a **stone bridge** that has spanned the Gombás Stream since 1757, and is adorned with seven statues of saints by József Bechert. It is the country's only surviving Baroque bridge of its type. Beyond that is a monument to those who died in the battles at Vác during the 1849 War of Independence, topped with a cannonball, and the early-18th-century **Chapel of the Seven** (*Hétkápolna; Derecske dűlő 2*) named after the seven sorrows of the Virgin Mary.

### Other

Vácrátót, 11km to the southeast of town, has a super **arboretum** (*Alkotmány utca 4; adult/concessions 200/130Ft; open daily May 1–Sep 30 08.00–18.00, Oct 1–Apr 30 08.00–16.00; greenhouses closed Mon*), complete with waterfalls, a water mill and exotic plant species. There are trains and buses there from Vác (see page 211); if you're driving, follow Road 2 south for a short distance, turn left on towards Aszód and then right towards Gödöllő. There is also a 500m-long **nature trail** managed by the Göncöl Foundation (*Ilona utca 3; ☏ 26 304484*) on the flood plains near Vác. It can be reached from the stone bridge over the Gombás Stream; the wooden path takes you through forest containing aquatic flora including the rare broad-leaved helleborine orchid, and there are two bird-observation towers.

### NAGYMAROS, ZEBEGÉNY AND SZOB

Road 12 follows the line of the upper bank of the Danube and there are a few riverside towns and villages that serve as starting points for an exploration of the Börzsöny Hills behind them. **Nagymaros** stands directly opposite Visegrád (see page 201), and provides the rail and ferry link for visiting the former royal capital. You'll need an active imagination to envisage the town that prospered here during the Middle Ages, bolstered by the significant status of its neighbour across the water and lined with the mansions of nobles. The Turkish occupation resulted in destruction and depopulation, and plague swept through in 1709; German immigrants started again in 1715, and many among today's raspberry-growing population of 5,000 are their descendants. The main point of historical interest is the Gothic-Baroque Roman Catholic church (*Szent Imre tér*), standing on the upper side of the rail track from the ferry pier. Its 14th-century nave was reconstructed after the Turks left, but the tower of 1509 is as originally constructed. You

## TOO DAM MUCH

During the 1950s, negotiations began between the Czechoslovakian and Hungarian governments to construct a dam at Gabčikovo (now in Slovakia). Originally envisaged as a way of altering the shallow Danube to allow navigable access for transport ships, in the 1970s the focus changed to hydroelectric energy production with two dams and plants planned at Gabčikovo and Nagymaros. In Hungary there was widespread concern at the prospect of the Czechs having control of the river upstream, but the Soviets pushed the idea forward. Increasingly the project became a target for anti-communist demonstration; those supporting it were labelled Stalinist traitors, and in the 1980s there were protest marches in Budapest. In 1990, the newly elected right-wing coalition unilaterally cancelled the agreement.

However, the dam at Gabčikovo was almost completed, and the project became a symbol of strength for the newly independent Slovakians. They pushed forward and diverted water through the turbines of the Slovakian plant; but the second plant had been intrinsic to the design, and little energy was squeezed at the cost of significant environmental damage to the river at Győr. Both sides turned to the International Court of Justice in 1993. A year later the socialists were back in power in Hungary, and when the court decreed the governments should negotiate a way out, they returned to the table. With eyes on European Union membership, the neighbours were anxious to show they could resolve their squabbles and it was agreed that the project should proceed and that ecological concerns would be addressed. But the swings and roundabouts of Hungarian politics intervened; the right-wing opposition joined forces with the Greens, anti-dam rallies were held and the issue helped lever the socialists out in the elections of 1998. The new right-wing government had promised to put an end to the idea once and for all, and spent millions of dollars dismantling the half-built Nagymaros dam. The matter is no longer in the political limelight, and ecologists on both sides agree that the environmental damage has already been done. The Slovaks remain quite proud of their dam – which is fully operational (extra water is allowed into other arms of the Danube at Szigetköz to limit the eco impact) – and you can take a boat trip to see it from Bratislava. On the Hungarian side, there remain some apartments in Nagymaros built to house the dam workers, but there are no dam workers to live in them.

can follow a path leading to the Julianus Lookout Tower on Hegyestető (Pointed Peak), which gets the better of 480m and offers a spectacular view of the river's curve.

There are several hiking trails running around and through **Zebegény**, which sits at the point where the Danube makes its first charge south. This is another fruit-growing town, the good times of wine production brought to a halt by the phylloxera epidemic. If you're interested in architecture, its Roman Catholic church (*Petőfi tér*) is an absolute unmissable, an invigorating piece of late-Secessionist design by the Transylvanian Károly Kós and Béla Jánszky in 1908. A ten-minute walk or so behind the church along Szőnyi utca brings up the István Szőnyi Memorial Museum (*Bartóky utca 7;* ✆ *27 370104; adult/concessions 400/200Ft; open Mar 16–Oct 31 Tue–Sun 10.00–18.00, Nov 1–Mar 15 Fri–Sun 10.00–16.00*); this was the house of Szőnyi himself, a 20th-century artist who spent his life in Zebegény making use of the beautiful location to create warm and gentle canvases. A school for fine arts is hosted in its gardens during the summer.

Five kilometres further west, **Szob** lies where the Danube and the Ipoly meet, and is the railway crossing point into Slovakia – indeed, Zoltán Kodály's father was once the

### SISKA THE HIGHWAYMAN

Betyár (Highwayman) Spring takes its name from the notorious outlaw Pista Siska, who lay low in nearby rocky hollows. It is said that he once joined an unsuspecting girl as she walked along the brook and asked her whether she feared walking here alone. She replied that her only concern was meeting the evil Siska; to punish her for these words the highwaymen nailed horseshoes to her feet.

station master. (You cannot cross here by car, though – for that you must head 25km north to Parassapuszta.) The **Börzsöny Museum** (*Hámán utca 14; free admission; open Mar–Oct Tue–Sun 10.00–18.00, Nov–Feb Fri–Sun 10.00–16.00*) has carved tombstones and ethnographic costumes, while (like Zebegény) the town offers a variety of summer programmes during the Danube Bend Art Days.

## BÖRZSÖNY HILLS

The Börzsöny Hills lie on the northern side of the Danube, and are part of the Danube-Ipoly National Park. There were once over 20 fortresses in the range, including the formidable Nógrád Castle. Lightning hit this castle in 1685, igniting the gunpowder store, and leading to the surrender of the Turkish occupiers. The best known, however, is that on top of the **Drégelypalánk peak** close to the northern border with Slovakia; here in 1552 a force of 150 under the command of György Szondi held out valiantly for three days before being overrun and killed by a far superior Turkish force. (You can get there along Road 2, or by train from Budapest, Vác or Balassagyarmat.) Numerous springs feed the local habitat, creating a damp and mild microclimate in the valleys. Among the fauna, the spotted salamander is found only in the Börzsöny, while a significant population of the strictly protected white-backed woodpecker can be found in the beech woods at the centre. The hills are characterised by volcanic cones with sharp ridges and steep sides; some of the lava trails are still visible and there are areas of boulders deposited during the Ice Age. The highest peak (and most testing to climb) is that of Csóványos at over 900m, while the most beautiful meadows are the Királyrét, around the Foltánkereszt, and the Ispán Meadow. Buy a copy of Cartographia's *Börzsöny-hegység* (1:40,000) before setting out, which shows the trails and accommodation options.

**Királyrét**, named after Mátyás who used to hunt in the region, is a popular weekend destination because it is served by a narrow-gauge railway (*Apr 1–Oct 31 Mon–Fri twice daily, Sat–Sun five daily, rest of year Sat–Sun three daily*) running 10km through the Valley of the Morgó from **Kismaros**; the Kismaros main station (across the road) is on the line running through Vác from Budapest Nyugati. Királyrét has an education centre (*Szokolya, Királyrét;* ✆ *27 385432*) that organises programmes for schools or nature enthusiasts. In addition, there are several hiking trails; you can strike east to **Nógrád**, southwest to **Kóspallag** or northwest to the peaks of **Magas-Tax**, **Nagy Hideg** and finally **Csóványos**. The latter route continues around to the village of **Diósjenő** (to the north of Nógrád). Diósjenő is the alternative departure point for hikes, particularly for those climbing Csóványos; its railway station is on a branch that breaks north shortly before Kismaros, and can be reached from Vác and Budapest. Kóspallag is worth mentioning because 6km northwest of it is the second of the hills' narrow-gauge railways running from Nagyirtás to Nagybörzsöny (*Fri & Sat only, with extra services on Fri in mid Jul–end Aug*). The Szent Orbán Fogadó is an upmarket campsite and hotel 200m from the Nagyirtás station.

## DANUBE-IPOLY NATIONAL PARK

Probably the most varied of Hungary's national parks – with hill ranges, river valleys and flood plains – the Danube-Ipoly National Park was founded in 1997. Over 63,000ha, it covers the Pilis and Börzsöny hills, Szentendre Island, the valley of the River Ipoly (which runs along the Slovakian border), and the Danube valley between Vác and Pest. Its renowned feature is the Danube Bend close to Esztergom, with stunning views of the terraced valleys and the majestic river below. The hill ranges vary in composition, the Pilis Hills formed from marine sediment and the Börzsöny and Visegrád hills from volcanic stone. On the steep slopes of the Börzsöny Hills are karst bush forests, and rare dolomite grasslands and slope steppes; in the flatter parts are *puszta* oak forests. Over half of the country's bird species twitter in these peaks, and there are several glacial plant relicts among the 70 protected types. The River Ipoly on the border with Slovakia, which used to meander profusely, has undergone a process of artificial straightening; as well as the resulting dead channels and ox-bows, 12km have been left unaltered, resulting in one of the last relatively undamaged river-catchment basins in the Carpathian Basin. The river here is allowed to flood, and the valley holds wet meadows, alder wood, marshes, more birds and representatives of virtually every one of Hungary's amphibian species. The park harbours the endemic butterfly *Dioszeghyana schmidtii*, and vulnerable species including the European mudminnow and striped ruffe, the lesser white-fronted goose, the lesser horseshoe bat and the otter. Among the species you might spot springing about in the Pilis and Visegrád hills is the saw-legged grasshopper, one of the country's longest insects. It's a blinder of an area for nature walks, and there are also narrow-gauge railways into the Börzsöny Hills from Kismaros to Királyrét and Nagyirtás to Nagybörzsöny (see opposite). For more information, contact the Danube-Ipoly National Park Directorate (*Main office: Budapest II, Hűvösvölgy út 52;* ⟍ *1 200 4066;* e *tka@mailcity.com. Pilis office: Visegrád, Mátyás király utca 4;* ⟍ *26 397440. Börzsöny office: Diósjenő, Öreghegy-dűlő;* ⟍ *35 364358*).

# Northern Uplands

Castles and caves, wildlife, wine and a valley of beautiful women – what more could you wish for? The Northern Uplands fill an area between the Great Plain and the border with Slovakia, extending in a west–east direction from the Danube Bend to Sátoraljaújhely. This is hill country, the Bükk and Mátra holding the highest peaks, and a place of forests and valleys, clear springs, startling rock formations and caves dripping with creamy stones. Some areas were once the hub of the iron industry, thriving on ore mined from the hills, while others – notably Eger and the Tokaj-Hegyalja region – represent vinicultural strongholds. A fierce national pride burns among the towns and villages of the region; it was a centre of resistance to Turks and Habsburgs, and the grasp on folk tradition is firmer here than elsewhere in Hungary. For all the passion, though, this is a spot to relax – to quaff a glass of wine after a day spent cycling, hiking or riding a narrow-gauge railway.

## THE CSERHÁT HILLS REGION

While the Cserhát Hills were formed at the same time as the Mátra (see page 232), fashioned from the same material (andesite) and by the same violent volcanic forces, they are a poor relation when it comes to hiking opportunities. They are stunted in height by comparison, and much of their original forest cover has been cleared for ploughing or housing. As they look over the 2,500km² of Nógrád County, they instead promise cultural highlights – notably the colourful peasant traditions of the Palóc people from the Cserhátalja, most famously preserved in the Unesco-protected village of Hollókő.

### Balassagyarmat

At the border with Slovakia, 80km from Budapest, Balassagyarmat's unwieldy eponym is the result of the coming together of the names 'Gyarmat' (one of the seven tribes that conquered the Carpathian Basin in the 9th century) and 'Balassa', the family who later owned the area. There are scanty remains on Bástya utca of the fortress they built following the devastating Mongol rampage of 1241. The castle was eventually destroyed by the Turks in 1663; in the aftermath of the Turkish occupation, an ethnically diverse population of merchants and manufacturers filled the vacuum, and in 1790 the town was made the capital of Nógrád County. Harder times were to come. The Treaty of Trianon divided the place, with the portion north of the River Ipoly absorbed into Czechoslovakia, while in 1950 the town's status as main county seat was lost to Salgótarján.

Nevertheless, Balassagyarmat retains its claim to being the capital of the Palóc region in the Cserhát Hills. The Palóc people are noted for their strong folk traditions and for their dialect – the latter unusual (and essentially unexplained) in Hungary, where speech and accents are remarkably consistent from region to region. The origins of the Palóc Hungarians remain something of a mystery; some believe that they are of ancient

Hungarian ancestry, while others argue a Mongol link. Whichever is true, cultural expression burned strong in generations past, who produced decorative furniture and donned distinctive colourful costume. It is rare now to see such dress worn in everyday life – the inhabitants of Hollókő (see page 225) are the exceptions that prove the rule in doing so, and attract the tourist pound as a consequence – but you can see examples of it in Balassagyarmat's Palóc Museum.

## Getting there and away
The **railway station** is located 500m from Köztársaság tér, at the southern end of Bajcsy-Zsilinszky utca, while the **bus station** is centrally located behind the town hall. Trains run to Balassagyarmat from Vác (14 daily) and Aszód (nine daily), the former journey taking a little over two hours with the latter around half an hour quicker. (From the capital, trains to Aszód depart from Budapest Keleti.) From Balassagyarmat, you can catch trains further northeast to Szécsény and Ipolytarnóc. There are up to 15 buses a day from Budapest's Árpád híd, travelling via Vác; the total journey takes about two hours, which makes it a quicker proposition than the train (once changes are factored in). Frequent services run to/from Szécsény and Salgótarján.

## Information and other practicalities
**Tourinform** Köztársaság tér 6; ➦ 35 500640; e balassagyarmat@tourinform.hu; www.balassagyarmat.hu. Relatively new information office, housed in the former County Hall.

Rákóczi fejedelem útja contains the main **shops**, a couple of **banks** and a **post office**.

## Where to stay, eat and drink
**Balassa** Rákóczi fejedelem útja 34–36; ➦ 35 500321. Fairly spartan restaurant serving low-priced East European dishes. *Open Mon–Thu 10.00–2.00, Fri–Sat 10.00–24.00.*

**Campsite** Kóvári út 12; ➦ 35 301168. As well as pitching space, there are 3 cabins for 12 guests, and tennis courts and a lido next door. *Open Jun 15–Aug 31.*

**Club Panzió** (18 rooms) Teleki út 14; ➦ 35 301824. Central and simple, with nicely appointed rooms, and a bar and moderately priced restaurant to wet whistles and silence stomach rumbles. *Dbl 8,000Ft, apt 20,000Ft.*

**Dolce Vita** Thököly utca 20; ➦ 35 300810. Has a family feel, and cooks pizzas to eat in or take away. *Pizza 320–650Ft; open Mon–Thu 11.00–22.00, Fri–Sat 11.00–23.00, Sun 17.00–22.00.*

**Inkognitó** Tihanyi utca 1. A suitably understated and dark little bar near the market on Thököly utca. *Open Mon–Thu 08.00–22.00, Fri–Sat 08.00–24.00.*

**Pool Café** Rákóczi fejedelem útja 28; ➦ 35 302898. Café with games machines and pool tables; in a courtyard at the end of an alleyway leading from the main high street. *Open Mon–Thu 09.00–23.00, Fri–Sat 09.00–02.00, Sun 14.00–22.00.*

**Svejk** Szabó Lőrinc utca 16; ➦ 35 300999. Specialises in food Magyar and Czech from its position behind the bus station. *Open daily 11.00–22.30.*

**Sztár Motel** (8 rooms) Kóvári út 12; ➦ 35 301152. En-suite dbl rooms and a cheap restaurant open 24hrs; to the west of the centre. *Dbl 5,000Ft.*

**Zorda Háza** Rákóczi fejedelem útja 28. Pizza joint in the same courtyard as Pool Café. *Open Mon–Thu 11.00–22.00, Fri–Sat 17.00–23.00, Sun 17.00–22.00.*

## What to see and do
Located in an early-20th-century building in a green park to the southwest of Köztársaság tér, the **Palóc Museum** (*Palóc liget 1;* ➦ *35 300168; adult/concessions 280/140Ft; open Tue–Sun 10.00–16.00*) is the town's prime attraction. Devoted to the lives lived by the Palóc peasants of Nógrád County – from the chores of the house to festival feasts – it features folk art, traditional costumes and everyday utensils. Among the early crafted

furniture is a *szuszék* – an etched chest used for storing grain – together with corner benches bearing paintings of noble hussars. Next to it is an **outdoor exhibition** (*closed Oct 1–Apr 30*) of outhouses and white thatched buildings typical of the Palóc architectural style, and including a reconstruction of the church at Szanda and a 200-year-old home dismantled and transported here from Karancslapujtő.

Köztársasag tér runs across the northern end of Bajcsy-Zsilinszky utca. The **Town Gallery** (*Városi Képtár; Köztársaság tér 5;* ☎ *35 300186; adult/concessions 100/50Ft; open Tue–Sun 10.00–12.00, 13.00–17.00*) is painted in gaudy turquoise and displays the works of Vladimir Szabó (the painter and graphic artist born in Balassagyarmat in 1905) and other modern artists of Nógrád County. Opposite stands the Neoclassical former **County Hall** (*Köztársaság tér 6*), completed in 1835, and now housing the Tourinform. Either side of its entrance are plaques devoted to two of Hungary's great 19th-century writers. A carving of a man wreathed in a serpent's coils reminds us that Imre Madách (1823–64) – responsible for the universal drama *The Tragedy of Man* – once worked here as a notary, judge and county chief assessor. This was also the workplace of the outstanding novelist Kálmán Mikszáth (1847–1910), who garnered material for his humorous satires on the Hungarian nobility. There are more substantial statues of each near by, and the names of the lettered men are linked once more in the **Imre Madách Town Library** and **Kálmán Mikszáth Cultural Centre**, both behind the arching brick façade at Rákóczi fejedelem útja 50 (☎ *35 300622; open Mon–Fri 08.00–20.00, Sat 13.00–20.00*). The latter contains a gallery named after the graphic artist Endre Horváth, whose work included coins and stamps depicting the scenery of the Palóc region and who lived in the town. On the other side of Madách utca is the immaculately painted **Town Hall**, Eclectic in style and constructed in 1914, while facing that is a monument of a smiling, bare-breasted female warrior spearing a snarling mythical beast – honouring

Balassagyarmat's title as the bravest town (**'Civitas Fortissima'**), earned after citizens helped to drive Slovak forces from the region in 1919.

The **Roman Catholic church** (*Rákóczi fejedelem útja*) was built between 1741 and 1746; it holds a barrel-like oak pulpit, along with the relics of Szent Felícián in a glass sarcophagus, donated by Pope Clement XIII in the 18th century. The **Serb Orthodox church** (*Szerb utca 5;* ⍐ *35 300622; free admission; open Tue–Sun 14.00–18.00*) on Óváros tér culminates in an onion spire and now serves as a small gallery space. For the **Collection of Local History** (*Helytörténeti Gyűtemény; Csillag-ház, Rákóczi fejedelem útja 107;* ⍐ *35 300663; adult/concessions 300/150Ft; open Tue–Sun 08.00–12.00, 13.00–16.30*), head further eastward along the town's main road to an *L*-shaped 18th-century mansion, set back on the right-hand side and once home of Horváth (see page 221).

## Szécsény

Move a little under 20km eastwards along the Ipoly Valley and you'll reach Szécsény, a town whose diminutive size belies its historical importance. The town is first mentioned in written records of the 13th century, when a villager sued his neighbours to the value of ten oxen. A touch more significant, however, is the fact that in 1705 a Diet was held here in Borjúpást Meadow (just north of the centre) at which the Transylvanian Ferenc Rákóczi II was declared the country's ruling prince (and leader of the independence struggle against the Habsburgs). It's a peaceful spot with several sights deserving of attention – notably a Baroque mansion, a Gothic monastery and a leaning fire tower.

### Getting there and away

The **train station** lies on Vasút utca, 1,500m north of the centre along Rákóczi út, and is on the line connecting Balassagyarmat and Ipolytarnóc (up to seven trains a day); you

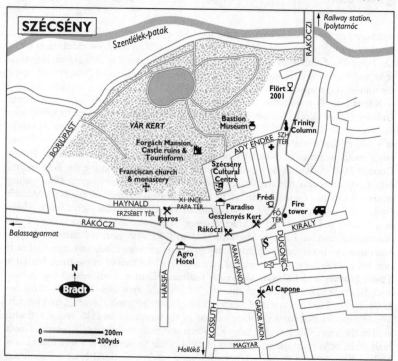

will need to change at Balassagyarmat for trains to/from Vác or Aszód. The **bus station** is on Király utca, immediately to the east of Fő tér. There are nine direct buses on weekdays from Budapest's Árpád híd (taking a little under 2½ hours), as well as indirect services (with a change at Balassagyarmat); buses from Budapest Stadion require a change at Salgótarján. There are regular buses to Balassagyarmat and Salgótarján, and a handful to Hollókő (taking half an hour).

## Information and other practicalities
**Tourinform** Ady Endre utca 12; ℺ 32 370777; e szecseny@tourinform.hu; www.szécsény.hu. In a wing of the Forgách Mansion (see below). *Open Mon–Fri 08.00–18.00, Sat–Sun 10.00–18.00.*

A **bank** and a **post office** sit either side of the town hall, just to the south of Fő tér.

## Where to stay
Szécsény certainly does not spoil you for accommodation choices.

**Agro Hotel** (12 rooms) Rákóczi út 90/B; ℺ 32 370 382. Connected to a school building on the corner with Hársfa utca, Agro is as basic and boxy as they come. The reception is open Mon–Fri 08.00–16.00, and you may need to telephone to make bookings outside these hours. *Sgl 2,500Ft, dbl 4,200Ft, rooms for 3–4 1,800Ft/pp.*

**Paradiso Panzió** (17 rooms) Ady Endre utca 14; ℺ 32 372427; www.paradiso.gyaloglo.hu. The Paradiso's building dates to 1664, and was where the servants of Forgách Mansion curled up for the night. It took on its current form in 1991, and is comfortable enough without being anything to shout about. The restaurant (*open daily 12.00–22.00*) serves fair regional fare, and there's a disco and bar (see below). *Sgl 5,000Ft, dbl 8,000Ft, triple 11,500Ft, room for 4 15,000Ft.* Varying discounts for children, according to age.

## Where to eat and drink
**Al Capone** Gábor Áron út 1; ℺ 32 372606. Around 60 types of pizza to choose from (*420–780Ft*). *Open Sun–Thu 11.00–23.00, Fri–Sat 11.00–24.00.*

**Flört 2000** Rákóczi út 61. A short distance from the Trinity Column (see page 224), this is a shabby little bar with table football and other attractions to distract youths or procrastinating travel writers. *Open Mon–Fri 16.00–01.00, Sat 16.00–02.00.*

**Frédi Cukrászda** Rákóczi út 85; ℺ 32 370372. Cakes and ice creams, and a few pavement tables. *Open Mon–Sun 09.00–18.00.*

**Gesztenyés Kert** Rákóczi út 87; ℺ 32 372600. The interior is pink and vibrant, but head instead for its large chestnut-shaded garden. There's a barbecue and live music out here in summer months. Mainly Hungarian food, with some international dishes. *Mains 500–1,590Ft, avg 700Ft; open Sun–Thu 08.00–21.00, Fri–Sat 08.00–22.00.*

**Iparos** Erzsébet tér 3; ℺ 32 370091. Like the rest of the town's restaurants, there's nothing decadent or luxurious here. The Iparos stands near the Franciscan church, and serves Palóc specialities in understated surroundings. *Mains 650–2,600Ft, avg 900Ft; open Tue–Sat 11.30–22.00.*

**Paradiso Disco Bar** Ady Endre utca 14; ℺ 06 20 912 6422; http://paradiso.gyaloglo.hu. The disco (affiliated to the Paradiso Panzió) offers Saturday-night cheesiness and seediness aplenty, with theme nights and dance shows that feature much female skin. *Disco open Sat 21.00–05.00.*

**Rákóczi** Rákóczi út 95; ℺ 32 370277. No-frills bar and canteen restaurant selling cheap Hungarian cuisine (*mains all under 1,000Ft*). There's something of a youth-centre atmosphere, and if you're intolerant of listening to kids playing table football while you eat, it's probably best avoided. On corner of Rákóczi út and Ady Entre utca. *Restaurant open Mon–Thu 11.00–20.00, Fri–Sat 11.00–16.00; bar open 11.00–22.00 daily.*

## What to see and do
The bright-yellow, Baroque **Forgách Mansion** (*Forgách-kastély; Ady Endre utca 7;* ℺ *32 370 143; www.nograd.hungary.net/museum/kubinyi.html*) was erected in 1770 from the stones

of the medieval castle that previously filled the site (see below). Inside now is the **Kubinyi Ferenc Museum** (*adult/concessions 280/140Ft, concessions free on Sun; open Tue–Sun 10.00–16.00*), named after a palaeontologist of the Reform era from Ipolytarnóc. Among the exhibits are items detailing the archaeology of Nógrád County, including a reconstruction of a Neolithic house, Bronze Age tools and jewellery, and Turkish swords and stirrups dating to the Ottoman occupation. Taxidermy is to the fore in the upper rooms, where – from ducks to bears – you'll find the animal kingdom stuffed. There are also carved horns and long guns, paraphernalia relating to three famous Hungarian hunters.

There can be few Europeans whom Buddhists revere as saints, but the collection (*adult 140Ft*) contained in the gatehouse (where the Tourinform is also found) is dedicated to one of them. The Transylvanian **Sándor Csoma Kőrösi** (1784–1842) travelled on foot to Tibet, where he was convinced there were monastic chronicles that might unravel the mysteries of Hungarian ancestry. He spent nearly a decade in the country, sleeping in unheated monks' cells in temperatures as low as –16°C, and compiled both the first Tibetan–English dictionary and a book of Tibetan grammar with explanatory notes in 16 languages. He eventually died of malaria, and was buried in the Himalayas. Some of his original artefacts are here, displayed in a cell that would have been typical of his humble and chilly quarters.

The entrance ticket to the Kőrösi exhibition also allows access to the two extant bastions of the medieval **Szécsény Castle**. Foundations for the original fortress were probably sunk in the 14th century; the structures that remain date to the 16th century, though, when the castle was an important link in a fortified border chain designed to resist expansion of the Turkish empire. It fell several times to the Turks, and was later a place of struggle during the 17th-century independence wars led first by Bocskai and then (against the Habsburgs) by Gábor Bethlen. Most of the castle was eventually destroyed by the Habsburgs, but two northern **corner bastions** survived. That within the grounds of the mansion can be climbed for views over the surrounding fields – where the famous Diet took place (see page 222). The northeastern one stands 100m down the road, and holds the **Bastion Museum** – comprising a set of stocks and some other chains used to incarcerate prisoners in the dungeon at the bastion base.

A short distance to the southwest of Forgách Mansion is a **Franciscan church and monastery** (*Ferences templom és kolostor; Haynald Lajos út 9;* ☏ *32 370076; requested donation adult/concessions 100/50Ft; open Tue–Sat 10.00–16.00*), constructed in 1332 to house 12 mendicant monks. The current Baroque façade is the result of early-modern face-lifts, but inside there are significant original Gothic features, including carved animals, rosettes and an octagonal pillar in the sacristy. Ferenc Rákóczi is said to have prayed in the oratory above the sacristy. Looking around, you will see that some of the statues are faceless, their visages cut away by the Turks when they used the church for worship; there is a further reminder of Ottoman occupation in the *mihrab* (prayer niche), set into the south wall and the northernmost remnant of Turkish architecture in the country. During the communist era, the Franciscan order was disbanded and a single parish priest was charged with caring for the buildings; since 1990, novice Franciscan monks have come here to undertake a year's quiet contemplation. A smartly dressed guide will lead you around the complex, but he speaks no English. (You may be lucky enough – as we were – to pass a monk prepared to break his silent vow, and answer a few whispered questions in English before he hurries guiltily on his way.)

During the 19th century, a lookout would keep watch from the town's two-storey **fire tower** (*Rákóczi út 86;* ☏ *32 370199*); a further storey was later added after the new town hall blocked the view. However, it would take a dedicated sentry to take up position now in this tilting tower, whose foundations have subsided in the clay beneath. To the north is a crumbling 18th-century **Trinity Column**, placed in grateful thanks for the passing of plague, while behind that is the oldest serving **pharmacy** (*gyógyszertár; Rákóczi út 67*) in Nógrád County, snuffing out sniffles since 1741.

## Hollókő

Hungarians are proud of Hollókő; as they watch the fading ways of bygone days – and sense a cultural heritage being lost – this little village 15km southeast of Szécsény serves as a defiant last hurrah in the face of historical pressures and the march of modern progress. Here the 400 villagers – who average over 50 years old – speak with the Palóc dialect, they celebrate the Palóc Easter Festival, they live in traditional vernacular houses, and some still wear Palóc costumes that they've made themselves. It is undoubtedly a beautiful place, snug in a valley and protected by the forested Cserhát Hills. When it was added to the Unesco World Heritage List in 1987, it was the first village in the world to receive such an accolade.

And yet from the moment you pay 250Ft to leave your vehicle in the large car park at the village entrance, something doesn't quite ring true. The peasant rusticity feels contrived, as though the village is forever competing in a 'Hungary in Bloom' contest, and there is an inevitable tension in adhering to a sleepy, past-century existence while basking under the attention of coach loads of 21st-century tourists. Of course, the collective attempt to guard folk traditions is laudable, deeply valuable and inherently fascinating; however, the village is equally a testament to a shrewd understanding of modern wants, and the truth of a life lived apart from that world is as illusory as the truth purveyed by the makers of reality television programmes.

Settlement of the village dates back to the 13th century, when the castle was built on Szár-hegy (Stalk Hill) in the aftermath of the Mongol invasion. As with all castles worth the name, there is a legend that goes with it. A maiden was supposedly abducted by András Kacsics, the main landowner of the area; her nurse – whom happened to be a witch – arranged for the devil to secure the maiden's release. The devil sent ravens to rescue her and demolish the warlord's fort; with the stones, the birds constructed the castle here – hence Hollókő, or 'Raven Stone'. The ravens subsequently kept watch over the damsel as she ruled from her new castle. It is said that the women of the village are her descendants, and that the ravens continue to protect them from the unwanted advances of men. Gents, you have been warned!

## PALÓC COSTUME

The Palóc people form an ethnic group that – in pockets such as Bugac, Rimóc and Hollókő – serves as one of the last examples of living folk tradition. The most visible aspect of such tradition is in costume; while it is rare now to see folk dress worn in everyday life, it is brought out during festivals. The rich Palóc garments probably originate from the mid-19th century (in contrast to the medieval-style garb of the Matyó people of Mezőkövesd). Women don several layers of embroidered short underskirts – young girls as many as 20 – over which are added decorated aprons. Unmarried girls wear ribbons and braid their hair, while wives cover their heads with scarves. Strings of pearls are hung around their necks, and the ensemble is completed with a pair of high-heeled boots. The costume of the menfolk is a touch less extravagant (though impressive still), with black trousers, embroidered shirts, colourful belts, felt jackets, black boots and upturned hats.

Until the 20th century, the houses of the village were thatched, and fire ravaged them on several occasions. After the last of these infernos in 1909, the buildings were restored with tiled roofs. Beyond that, however, the 58 protected structures in the Old Village (Ófalu) remain faithful to the layout of 17th-century Palóc peasant homes, with wooden verandas, protruding roofs and three distinct rooms. The Old Village consists of two streets running either side of the church, and makes a romantic ramble; there are also easy marked trails snaking around the village and leading up to the castle. Be mindful that the day closes early here, and it is generally as dead as a doornail after 20.00.

### Getting there and away
The **bus** stop is at the southeastern end of Kossuth Lajos utca. There is a solitary 08.30 service direct from Budapest Stadion via Pásztó (taking 2 hours), as well as three others with changes at Salgótarján or Pásztó (be aware you'll wait an hour for the connection at the latter). Alternatively, there are five buses from Árpád híd via Szécsény (with a 20-minute connection delay). Buses run regularly between Hollókő and Szécsény (note the last bus back leaves at about 20.00), although there are just five on Sunday; there are up to four a day to Pásztó, and a sprinkling direct between Hollókő and Salgótarján (although otherwise you'll need to change at Szécsény or Pásztó).

If you are **driving**, take the M3 motorway from Budapest as far as Hatvan, where you pick up Road 21; the route branches off towards Hollókő just before Pásztó.

### Information
**Tourinform** Kossuth Lajos utca 68; ℡ 32 579 011; e holloko@tourinform.hu; www.holloko.hu. *Open daily 09.00–17.00.*

### Where to stay, eat and drink
Most people staying overnight do so to sleep in one of ten **traditional Palóc houses** lining Petőfi utca that can be booked through the Foundation for Hollókő (*Hollókőért Közalapítvány;* ℡ *32 579011;* e *kozalapitvany@holloko.hu; rooms from 7,500Ft, houses from 14,000Ft*), which shares the Tourinform office. The Tourinform can provide a list of private houses offering rooms. There are only two restaurants in Hollókő, and we wouldn't hurry back to either. Considering the village is so popular with tourists, however, the prices are as cheap as chips (which, judging by our meals here, would be greasy). Note their early closing times.

**Muskátli** Kossuth Lajos utca 61; ❧ 32 379262. As you'd expect, the waitresses are wrapped in folk dress, and there's traditional Palóc food on the menu. The colourful terrace – rather than any great wizardry in the kitchen – gives it the edge over Vár. *Mains 990–1,650Ft, avg 1,250Ft; 2-course set meals (inc wine, beer or coffee) 2,400Ft; open Wed–Fri 11.00–17.00, Sat 11.00–18.00, Sun 11.00–17.00.*
**Panorama Panzió and Campsite** Orgona út 31; ❧ 32 379 048. Perched on a hill just to the south of the village. As well as pitches for caravans or tents, Panorama offers 9 rooms (sleeping 2–4) and 5 bungalows (for 4), all with bathrooms. There's an on-site restaurant. *Panzió dbl 4,000Ft, room for 4 6,000Ft; bungalow 5,000Ft; camping 400Ft/pp, tent/caravan 400/450Ft.*
**Teaház** Petőfi utca 4. Booth-like tea house adjacent to the church. *Open Tue–Sun 11.00–17.00.*
**Vár** Kossuth Lajos utca 93–95; ❧ 32 379029. Choose the brick-floored restaurant or its shady garden to sample fatty and rather uninspiring plates of traditional Palóc cuisine. *Mains avg 1,300Ft; open 11.00–19.00 daily.*
**Szabó Kocsma** The spartan, unloved 'Tailor Inn' is the only pub in the village. *Open daily 07.00–13.00, 14.00–20.00.*

## What to see and do
### The church, shops and museums
There are several small museums and craftshops in the Palóc houses ranged along Kossuth Lajos utca and Petőfi utca. We list them in the order they appear on a stroll starting from the lower (eastern) end of the village. Opposite the Tourinform, **Portéka** (*Kossuth Lajos utca 75*) sells examples of folk arts and crafts. Two houses further on is the **Irén Ács Photo Exhibition** (*Ács Irén Fotóművész; Kossuth Lajos utca 79; open Apr 1–Oct 31 10.00–17.00 daily; adult/concessions 120/60Ft*); as well as showcasing the superb photos of Palóc villages by Ács, the exhibition also displays wood carvings by local master Ferenc Kelemen (who lives next door). For further information, contact the village hall (*Kossuth Lajos utca 74; ❧ 32 379255*).

Just north of here Kossuth Lajos utca passes to the left of the **village church**. A medieval predecessor was razed by the Turks, and the current building dates to 1889. It is elegant in its plainness, a lime-washed lower portion capped with a brown wooden spire. Inside are a flag and a crucifix from the 18th century, donated by the Museum of Christianity in Esztergom.

The **Postal Museum** (*Kossuth Lajos utca 80; ❧ 32 379288; adult/concessions 100/50Ft; open Apr 1–Oct 31 Tue–Sun 10.00–17.00*) is devoted to the postmen of Nógrád County, who had more to contend with than dogs barking at letter boxes – among the exhibits are weapons they had to carry to deter attacks from highwaymen. Next door is the **Village Museum** (*Falumúzeum; Kossuth Lajos utca 82; ❧ 32 379258; adult/concessions 100/50Ft; open Apr 1–Oct 31 Tue–Sun 10.00–16.00, Nov 1–Mar 31 Thu 10.00–14.00, Fri 12.00–14.00, Sat–Sun 10.00–16.00*), which allows you to look around the typical layout of a peasant house: three rooms, including a 'Sunday room' at the front (where beds were stored and guests entertained), a living area (where the family slept and spent the majority of their time), and a kitchen. There is a 19th-century oak winepress in the yard.

**Kosaras** (*Kossuth Lajos utca 86; open 10.00–17.00 daily*) sells charming handmade goods, including children's prams, rocking chairs and baskets; next to it is **Csuhé Csodák** (*open Tue–Sun 10.00–18.00*), where you can shop for crafted lamp shades, wine-bottle holders and bags. The **Loom House** (*Szövőház; Kossuth Lajos utca 94; adult/concessions 150/100Ft; open daily 10.00–17.00*) is a workshop containing two weaving machines – one of which harks back to old methods of textile production, while the other has a flying shuttle. There is a small shop.

Maybe we've watched too many horror movies, but **doll museums** give us the heeby-jeebies; hopefully the multi-layered Palóc dresses worn by the china-faced specimens here (*Babamúzeum; Kossuth Lajos utca 96; ❧ 32 379088; adult/concessions 150/100Ft; open Apr 1–Sep 30 daily 10.00–17.00*) would slow them down if they sprang to life and gave us chase. The Tájház contains a **Landscape and People Exhibition** (*Táj és a Nép; Kossuth Lajos utca 99–100; adult/concessions 160/120Ft; open Apr 1–Oct 30 Tue, Thu–Sun 09.00–17.00, Nov 1–Mar 31 Tue, Thu–Sun 10.00–15.00*) featuring the natural history of the 141ha Eastern Cserhát Landscape Protection Reserve – the country's smallest – that surrounds the village.

A little shop at Kossuth Lajos utca 105 (*open Wed–Sun 10.00–17.00*) peddles local crafts (pottery, candles and dolls), while **Mívesház** (*Petőfi utca 4;* ❧ *32 379257; open Tue–Sun 11.00–17.00*) offers a broader selection including tablecloths, wine, peasant costumes and pop-up puppets.

### Hollókő Castle and some walking trails

The **fortress** (*adult/concessions 250/100Ft, family 700Ft; open Apr 1–Oct 31 10.00–17.30 daily*) on the volcanic-rock hilltop above the village was constructed in the 13th century by the local landowner, András Kacsics. During the period of Turkish occupation, it fell alternately into the hands of Turks and Hungarians before the Polish King Jan Sobieski finally banished the Ottomans in 1683. When the Habsburg Leopold I decreed that Hungarian fortifications should be demolished two decades later, Hollókő Castle had already fallen into disrepair and was consequently left alone. After a programme of reconstruction in 1996, it is the best surviving example of 13th-century defences in Nógrád County; there is now an exhibition showing some of the finds made during excavation.

Aside from the castle itself, the hill is worth visiting for its views over the surrounding landscape – narrow agricultural plots and forested areas that are steadily reclaiming land formerly cleared for pasture. You can follow **trails** leading up there either from the car park or from opposite the Tájház on the western section of Kossuth Lajos utca. The walks take around 15 minutes, but are fairly steep in places. If you'd like a closer view of the local habitat of the Cserhát region, a longer green 'study trail' – with information boards – follows a loop into the nature conservation area and around the northern side of Stalk Hill. It can be picked up a few hundred metres along the castle trail (from either starting point), and is around 5km in length. For more information, contact the **Bükk National Park Directorate** in Eger (❧ *36 411581*).

### Festivals and events

The best time to visit is during one of the festivals, when the villagers are dressed to the nines in traditional costumes. During the Easter Festival (*late Mar/Apr*), there is song, dance, folk crafts and food aplenty. In addition, the Raspberry Festival and Nógrád Folklore Festival take place in July, the Castle Tournament – with medieval jousting – in August, and the Grape Harvest Parade in September.

## Ludányhalászi and Ipolytarnóc

If you fancy your history more natural than human, there are a couple of convenient excursions within a relatively short distance north of Szécsény. The nearer of these is **Ludányhalászi**, which stakes a claim to being central Europe's longest village; on its western side lies a series of lakes fed by the River Ipoly. The wildcat prowls the area, while in the waters anglers can try for pike, catfish and pike perch (*contact the Öreg Potyka Fishing Association for further information;* ❧ *32 556011*). Or you can simply enjoy the sight of sand-martins careering above the surface at dusk. You won't have to wait long for a bus to take you the 4km from Szécsény; alternatively, it will take under ten minutes by train.

Follow the Ipoly for another 18km as it wriggles north, and you'll reach the village of **Ipolytarnóc**. There are up to 11 trains daily, running from Balassagyarmat via Szécsény; there are buses from Szécsény, most of them requiring a connection change, and regular direct services from Salgótarján (taking about an hour). You'll need to walk 2km up to the

## THE CASTLE AT SZIRÁK

If you're after a little aristocratic, old-world luxury during your stay in Hungary, you could do worse than check yourself into the Baroque **Hotel Kastély** (*Szirák;* \ *60 353053/485300;* e *kastelyszirak@matavnet.hu; 25 rooms; dbls* €*79–105, apt* €*125*) for a night or two. Sitting on the southern slopes of the Cserhát Hills, it's 90km from Budapest and 26km from Pásztó, and was originally built in 1748 by Tamás Királyfalvi Róth. His daughter married the cultured Count József Teleki – a man no stranger to the Parisian court of Louis XV, and one who numbered Voltaire and Rousseau among his acquaintances – and the pile became the Róth-Teleki Castle. The village itself offers little for those after excitement; this is a place to come to be peaceful. The surrounding parkland is well tended and there are 18th-century paintings on the walls of the opulent banqueting hall; the rooms themselves are immaculate, and the suites have period features. In addition, there's a library, sauna, solarium, pub, international restaurant (*mains 1,100–3,250Ft, avg 1,800Ft*), and opportunities for tennis and horse-riding (*2,000Ft/hour*).

To get there, take the bus from Budapest Stadion; there are up to 15 daily, five of these direct, and the journey takes between 1½ and two hours. Indirect services require changes at Aszód or Hatvan, among others. There are also buses from Pásztó. The bus stops outside the church in the village (300m away).

visitor centre on alighting at the village. Twenty million years ago, a massive volcanic eruption buried the area in hot, fine ash, and – like Pompeii – in doing so entombed a prehistoric time capsule. In the Csapás Valley, 2km from the village, are petrified the delicate marks of that prehistoric period, including leaf impressions and the footprints of birds and rhinoceros, as well as the trunks of massive pine trees and the teeth of sharks that had patrolled the waters of an earlier tropical sea. There are trails on which to explore this protected geological site (*Ipolytarnóc, ´smaradványok TT;* \ *32 454113;* e *tarnoc@freemail.hu; www.nograd.net/ipolytarnoc*). The **biological study paths** (*Tue–Sun 09.00–14.30*) – of either 2km or 4km in length – can be followed unaccompanied, and take in some of the native species that are returning after deforestation during the 18th century. However, it's on the 800m-long geological study trail that you'll see the fossilised imprints; this can only be visited with a guide, and takes just under an hour. Tours are available in English, and depart Tue–Sun 09.30, 10.30, 11.30, 12.30, 13.30, 14.30, 15.30, 16.00 (*Apr 1–Oct 31*) and 09.30, 10.30, 11.30, 12.30, 13.30, 14.30 (*Nov 1–Mar 31*); adult/concessions 400/250Ft.

## Salgótarján

J B Priestley once described a certain town as having been planned by an enemy of the human race; the phrase sprung to mind when we first saw the capital of Nógrád County. It seems astonishing today that Salgótarján's 1960s facelift – when the existing houses and streets were levelled to make room for a modern city centre – won a prominent architectural award. It's a place of industrial constructions and sterile residential blocks 2km from the Slovakian border. The limited colour brought by Fő tér is drained by stark buildings and the unforgiving Rákóczi út that runs it through; there's little to see for a town of its size. Thank goodness for the forest and hills either side, which – while making the man-made scar glare angrier still by contrast – nevertheless offer respite and peaceful walks. This was where the Tarján tribe settled after the Magyar conquest, and the Salgó fortress protected the area from the 13th century. However, it was with the discovery of coal that expansion came; mining began in 1845, and related industries – iron, glass and power – soon followed. The miners have gone, but the town preserves its past with the country's first underground mining museum. A reminder of a grimmer period in the town's history is found in December 8 tér, to the south of Nógrád History Museum, where a monument of an agonised, modern-day martyr pays respect to demonstrators killed by secret police in 1956. There are 53 names in the black marble, although these probably reflect fewer than half the actual death toll.

## Getting there, away and around

The **bus** station is just to the west of Erzsébet tér; take the subway beneath the railway track to reach the square. The **train** station is even more central. There are three daily direct trains from Budapest Keleti; the 12 other services require a change at Hatvan to join the line branching northwards to Somoskőújfalu (and over the border to Luāenec in Slovakia). The train also passes through Pásztó. There are buses every 30–40 minutes from Budapest's Árpád híd and Stadion bus stations, the majority of them direct. Among the many other destinations are frequent services to Szécsény and Balassagyarmat, and to Ipolytarnóc (up to ten direct), Eger (nine), Gyöngyös (five), Hatvan (four), Hollókő (three), Miskolc (two), Parádfürdő (one). If you need a **taxi**, try 6x6 Taxis (⟩ 32 666666).

## Information and other practicalities

**Ibusz** Fő tér 6; ⟩ 32 511634; e 078@ibusz.hu. Located at the back of the Karancs Hotel, on the eastern side of the square; can exchange money, book private accommodation and arrange tours to the castles (see opposite). *Open Mon–Thu 08.00–16.00, Fri 08.00–15.00.*

**József Attila Cultural Centre** Fő tér 5; ⟩ 32 310503. In the same building as the Tourinform, the cultural centre hosts performances of theatre and music, as well as exhibitions of art and photography. The poet Attila József is honoured in a Pál Kő relief in the foyer; look out too for Imre Varga's statue of another poet, Miklós Radnóti, in Fő tér outside. This stringy Jewish figure, shown swamped in a long coat and leaning against a gate, died during a march from a labour camp in 1944. *Open Mon–Fri 10.00–18.00 (ticket office 14.00–18.00 daily).*

**Listings magazine** *Nógrádi Est*

**Nógrád Tourist** Erzsébet tér 5; ⟩ 32 310660. Can offer information and exchange money. Situated on first-floor walkway of the shopping arcade. *Open Mon–Fri 08.30–16.00, Sat 09.00–12.00.*

**Tourinform** Fő tér 5; ⟩ 32 512 315; e tourinform@nmkti.hu. *Open Mon–Fri 09.00–17.00, Sat 10.00–13.30.*

## Where to stay

**Karancs Hotel** Fő tér 6; ⟩ 32 410088. The exterior is 1960s bleak, and the rooms depressingly drab. The view over the town from its roof garden is apparently beautiful. *Sgl 7,500Ft, dbl 9,300Ft, apt (for 2) 11,600Ft.*

**Kulacs Szálloda** Bartók Béla út 14; ⟩ 32 310993; e kulacs@hu.inter.net. A good class of hotel, with a restaurant serving Palóc and international dishes (*open daily 11.00–23.00; mains 900–2,800Ft, avg 1,500Ft*). *Sgl 9,500Ft, dbl 12,500Ft.*

**Galcsik Panzió** (32 rooms) Alkotmány út 2; ⟩ 32 316524. Located 200m from the city centre, the pension rooms are clean without being special. The lively restaurant (*open Mon–Sat 07.00–22.30, Sun 07.00–21.00; mains 790–1,990Ft, avg 1,000Ft*) is probably the best in town, with an elevated terrace, welcoming staff and a Hungarian and international menu that includes beef steak à la England and spag bol. *Sgl 4,980Ft, dbl 7,480Ft, triple 9,980Ft, room for 4 12,480Ft.*

**Tó Strand** Füleki út; ⟩ 32 432400. The open-air lido – itself something of an oasis from the industrial heart – has a pension (25 rooms), motel and campsite. 3km north of the centre. *Pension dbls 3,500Ft, apts 8,000Ft; motel 1,200Ft/pp.*

## Where to eat and drink

Galcsik and Kulacs have their own restaurants (see opposite).

**CZZ Kisvendéglő** Fő tér 1; ⏴ 32 311384. Opposite the Karancs Hotel, this is no-frills dining – the most expensive main course a trifling 1,000Ft. *Open Mon–Sat 07.30–21.00.*
**Godó Cukrászda** Rákóczi út 12; ⏴ 32 416068. An elegant terrace, good cakes, ice creams, cocktails and frothy cappuccinos with whipped cream and cinnamon. *Open Mon–Fri 10.00–19.00, Sat–Sun 09.00–17.00.*
**Old Timers Pub** Rákóczi út 13; ⏴ 32 422509. A fat chef bears a gargantuan tankard of beer at the entrance and invites you into a comfortable, informal interior. A place to eat as well as drink, the menu includes pastas, salads and Hungarian cuisine. *Mains 750–1,800Ft; open Sun–Thu 10.00–22.00, Fri–Sat 10.00–23.00.*
**Svejk Söröző** Erzsébet tér 6; ⏴ 32 423191. Low-priced brews and snacks beside the railway track. *Open Mon–Wed 09.00–23.00, Thu–Sat 09.00–24.00, Sun 10.00–23.00.*
**Yellow** Rákóczi út 11; ⏴ 32 310480. It's certainly cheap, if not particularly cheerful – the service was terse to say the least during our visit. Predominantly a bar, you can also eat decent-sized portions of pizza or pasta. *Pizzas 490–1,000Ft, avg 800Ft; open daily 09.00–24.00.*

## What to see and do

Constructed in the aftermath of World War II, the building housing the **Nógrád History Museum** (*Nógrádi Történeti Múzeum; Múzeum tér 2;* ⏴ *32 310140; adult/concessions 200/100Ft; open Wed–Fri 09.00–16.00, Sat 09.00–13.00*) has soft corners and a space-age feel. Inside is an exhibition devoted to the history of Nógrád County, and including the mining heritage of the area. A sculpture of Count István Széchenyi – whose progressive reforms earned him the tag 'the greatest Hungarian' – stands in front, a sleepy-eyed pelican perched above his head.

A few minutes' walk away to the west of the railway track (behind the Spar supermarket), the **Underground Mining Museum** (*Földalatti Bányamúzeum; Zemlinszky Rezső utca 1;* ⏴ *32 420258; adult/concessions 280/140Ft; open Tue–Sun Oct 1– Mar 31 10.00–14.00, Apr 1–Sep 30 09.00–15.00*) preserves the memory of the town's mining past. Outdoor are the little grey coal trains and carriages, while there is further paraphernalia in the shaft itself and in a former official's flat.

The 18th-century Baroque **Roman Catholic church** (*Rákóczi út 24*) elevated above Rákóczi út has something of the fantastical castle about it, with turreted towers either side of the main gun-blue spire. It is believed that a church has stood at this site since the Árpád era. Further north on Acélgyári út, **Szent József Church** is also Roman Catholic, but forbidding and jail like. Outside it is the **Millennium Monument**, a pole bearing a Holy Crown and carved representations of significant events over Hungary's 1,000-year history.

You can take a tour of the **Glass Factory** (*Huta utca 1;* ⏴ *32 410433*), a working, industrial complex to the south of December 8th tér; contact Tourinform for details. Keep an eye out for Viktor Kálló's sculpture of glass blowers outside one of the gates – a surreal depiction of faceless figures puffing coloured balloons of glass. There is a small **Jewish cemetery and Auschwitz Memorial** (*Füleki út 57*) opposite the hospital.

### Festivals and events

The annual celebration of jazz – the International Dixieland Festival – takes place at the beginning of May, concentrating on the cultural centre and the square outside.

## Salgó and Somoskő castles

The crow would need to fly 7km northeast from the centre of Salgótarján to the ruins of **Salgó Castle**; *you* can take the 11B bus on its slightly longer route to the nearby village of Salgóbánya, alighting at the end stop, and following Vár út and the path it leads in to.

If you fancy a longer walk, pick up a wriggling path from near the Strandfürdő campsite. The castle – on which Sándor Petőfi based his poem 'Salgó' in the mid 19th century – looks down precariously from a 625m basalt cone and affords good views of the surrounds. The castle was originally constructed by a member of the Kacsics clan in the 13th century. In 1554 it fell to the Turks, the defenders fleeing after seeing their attackers carrying wooden logs up the hill and mistaking them for cannon. You can visit at any time for no charge. There is a nature trail among the rock flora of Boszorkány-kő, a few hundred metres to the south of the castle.

Three kilometres further north is the village of **Somoskő**, which boasts a second, better-preserved castle *(adult 150Ft/20 Slovak crowns, concessions 75Ft/10Slovak crowns; open daily autumn/winter 08.00–16.00, spring/summer 08.00–20.00)*. This one stands on top of a 526m hill, on the cusp of the Medves Plateau – the largest basalt plateau in central Europe (and presenting fascinating 'organ-pipe' geological formations). The hill is actually bisected by the Hungarian-Slovakian border, and the 14th-century fortress lies on the wrong side. The border crossing can be made at Somoskőújfalu (you'll need your passport or ID card), a couple of kilometres to the west – bus 11 runs here. Alternatively you can hop on bus 11A to Somoskő village, from where the castle is visible if not visitable.

# THE MÁTRA HILLS REGION
The Mátra Hills stretch for around 50km and are divided between five regions – the western Mátra, central Mátra (containing the country's highest peak – that of Kékes, at 1,015m), eastern Mátra, Mátralába and Mátraalja. The villages of the area have little in the way of varied attractions, but then the thousands who come here each year are after life's simple pleasures – to hike among the forested hills and enjoy some of the country's most beautiful scenery. There is also some rather tame skiing in the winter, and opportunities for hunting if that's your bag. A network of trails connects the major villages, with lookout points along the way. To make the best use of them, pick up a copy of the *Mátra és a Mátraalja* map (1:30,000) by Imre Faragó, which is available from Tourinform and some local hotels. The snaking Road 24 also provides a gorgeous drive through the oak and beech trees for those making their way between Gyöngyös and Eger.

## Pásztó
Tucked next to the River Zagyva as it runs between the Cserhát and the Mátra hills, Pásztó is a good starting point for those trekking into the western Mátra. However, the town itself has some historical buildings to look at before you don your hiking boots. An 11th-century Benedictine monastery stood on the site of the current Cistercian one, and Pásztó represented an important religious centre in the Middle Ages. The citizens packed up and shipped out during the period of Turkish occupation, and for a century this was a virtual ghost town; things didn't pick up again until the mid 1600s.

### Getting there and away
Pásztó is near Route 21, 30km from Hatvan. The **railway station** is a short distance west of the centre; it is on the line running north between Hatvan and Somoskőújfalu. There are three direct trains from Budapest Keleti; all others require a change at Hatvan (regular trains from there). There are regular **buses** from Salgótarján, as well as services from Balassagyarmat (two daily), Gyöngyös (eight), Hatvan (nine), Mátrafüred (two).

### Where to stay and eat
The sleeping and scoffing options are limited here.

**Bence** Fő út 92; ☏ 32 460687. Decent enough pizzas. *Mains 550–900Ft; open Mon–Sat 11.00–22.00.*

**Hotel Zsigmond** (26 rooms) Nagymező út 4; ↘ 32 460442. An uninspiring little place to crash for the night, although desperately cheap. The rooms are big but barren, and have fridges; the café-style restaurant serves Hungarian food and snacks (*mains 600–1,150Ft*). *Twin 2,500Ft.*
**Ózon** Deák Ferenc utca 3; ↘ 32 461 713; Pizzas, soups, salads, pastas, burgers, cakes and ice creams. *Mains 660–1,500Ft; open Mon–Sat 11.00–22.00.*

## What to see and do

**St Lawrence Parish Church** (*Szent Lőrinc plébániatemplom; Múzeum tér 1*) is something of an architectural mishmash, its Baroque and Gothic elements the result of reconstructions to the original church, which was built in the 15th century over 13th-century Romanesque foundations. We particularly like a pair of chubby angels inside that spread their arms towards a painting on a side altar, and rather cheekily display an oversized rump. The eastern windows were only discovered in 1959; one of these bears a rose-like detail that is unique in Hungary. The Baroque **parsonage** (*Múzeum tér 2*) was constructed in the 18th century. Outside the church railings is Sándor Kiss's **statue of King Zsigmond** – who bestowed town status on Pásztó in 1407 – standing on top of a resting lion.

The garden of medieval ruins is at the ancient centre of the town. At its heart is the whitewashed **schoolmaster's house**, first mentioned in a will of 1428, and the country's last 15th-century market town house. During excavations in 1978, a hoard of 16th-century domestic items was found buried in containers beneath the floor – doubtless hidden by the occupant before he fled from the advancing Turks. These are now exhibited inside, together with instruments used for medieval wine production in the cellar. At its southern side the **remains of a workshop** were uncovered, used by the monks to make glass during the 11th and 12th centuries before burning down in 1230.

At the western side of the square is the Baroque **former Cistercian monastery**, completed in 1720. There was a monastery here much earlier, though – mentioned in town charters of 1138, and belonging initially to the Benedictine order before passing to the Cistercians in 1190. It lay dilapidated following the Turkish invasion (the stones of its base walls still litter the ground about), before the Cistercians returned and rebuilt. Today it houses the **Local History Museum** (*Helytörténeti Múzeum; Múzeum tér 1;* ↘ *32 460194; open Apr 1–Sep 30 Mon–Sat 09.00–15.00, Oct 1–Mar 31 Mon–Fri 08.00–16.00, Sat 10.00–14.00*), with an exhibition of prehistoric finds, a memorial room to Benjámin Rajeczky, the musicologist and last prior of the town, and details of the history of the Cistercian order. The nearby bronze **statue of Szent István** was sculpted by Sándor Kiss as part of the 2000 millennium celebrations.

The **Csohány Kálmán Gallery** (*Múzeum tér 4;* ↘ *32 460194; Mon–Fri 08.00–16.00, Sat 10.00–14.00 in winter, 09.00–15.00 in summer*) shows 150 of the works of 20th-century graphic artist Csohány, who was born and buried in Pásztó. There is an open-air **strand** (*Kossuth Lajos út 116;* ↘ *32 460750; open Jun 1–Aug 31 daily 06.00–19.00*) at the northern end of the town; its water is 33°C and registered as medicinal. For some final ruins, visit **Hasznos** a short distance to the northeast. In the past, a series of castles defended the route through the Mátra Hills, and this settlement (belonging to Pásztó) bears the remnants of one of them. The hill on which the tower foundations lie also offers splendid views of not only the Mátra Hills, but the Cserhát and Karancs hills to the west and north respectively.

## Gyöngyös

The 'gateway to the Mátra' stands 80km from the capital, at the meeting point of the forested hills and the northern cusp of the Great Plain. The second-largest town in Heves County, Gyöngyös has traditionally been noted for its textiles and handicrafts, and as the centre of wine production in the northern hill ranges (see box, page 237). It was declared a market town by the Anjou king Károly Róbert in 1334, and continued to flourish throughout the period of Turkish occupation when it was granted protected status by the sultan. It didn't have all its own way, however. In the 1880s its vineyards were blighted by the phylloxera plague, and in 1917 a fire sparked in the hospital and wiped out 549 houses, leaving 8,000 homeless. As the inferno raged, the citizens even used their stores of wine in their desperate attempts to douse the flames. The long process of construction began in the years following World War I.

## Getting there, away and around

The main **railway station** stands to the east of the centre, on Vasút utca – follow Kossuth Lajos utca into the centre. The **bus station** is 600m closer in on Koháry út. Gyöngyös is at the end of a short spur off the main Budapest–Miskolc line. The spur comes at Vámosgyörk, and you'll have to change there for the final push. There are up to nine trains daily from Budapest Keleti and Kelenföld stations to Vámosgyörk. There is also a **narrow-gauge railway** departing from Előre station (*Mátravasút;* ☏ 37 312447) close to the Mátra Museum. It started a century ago as a forest railway, but today transports tourists rather than dead wood; there are services to Mátrafüred (*daily between about 07.00 and 18.00; sgl/rtn adult 200/380Ft, concessions 100/200Ft*) and Lajosháza (*May–Sep Sat–Sun between 08.00 and 16.00, with additional trains in high season on Wed and Fri; adult 240/450Ft, concessions 120/240Ft*). There are two buses an hour from Budapest Stadion, and regular runs between Mátrafüred, Mátraháza, Hatvan and Eger; you can also reach Salgótarján (five), Miskolc (two) and Debrecen (two). If you need a **taxi**, call Mátra Taxi (☏ 37 313033).

## Information and other practicalities

**Franko Tourist** Kossuth Lajos utca 13; ☏ 37 311339; e franko@mail.datanet.hu. Offers various sightseeing programmes around the Mátra region, including trips by coach and narrow-gauge railway to Eger and Mátrafüred (where it has its own guesthouse). A 6-day tour costs around €340/pp.

**Ibusz** Kossuth Lajos utca 6; ❧ 37 311861; e gyongyos@iroda.ibusz.hu

**Panorama Tours** Fő tér 5; ❧ 37 500885. *Open Mon–Fri 08.00–17.00, Sat 08.00–12.00.*

**Post office** Mátyás Király utca (in Bugát Pál tér). *Open Mon–Fri 08.00–20.00, Sat 08.00–12.00.*

**Tourinform** Fő tér 10; ❧ 37 311155; e gyongyos@tourinform.hu. Housed in the 3-storey avocado-coloured Baroque Grassalkovich Mansion, which also holds the town's library and an exhibition of 20th-century paintings by Herman Lipót. *Open Jun 15–Sep 15 daily 09.00–18.00, rest of year Mon–Thu 07.30–16.00, Fri 07.30–13.30.*

There is an **open-air market** (*Termelői piac*) on Köztársaság tér (*open Fri 05.00–13.00, Sat 06.00–13.00, Sun 06.00–12.00*).

## Where to stay

Ask at Tourinform for their *Gyöngyös Mátra Accommodation* booklet, which gives a list of **private rooms**; these can also be booked through Ibusz.

**Hotel Mátra** (40 rooms) Mátyás király út 2; ❧ 37 313063; e inn-side@mail.matav.hu; www.hotels.hu/matra. Uninspiring hotel on the main square; its restaurant has a small terrace. *Sgl 6,250Ft, dbl 9,000Ft.*

**Hotel Opál** (16 rooms) Könyves Kálmán tér 13; ❧ 37 300455; e hotelopal@mail.gyfk.hu. An unostentatious little hotel, located 600m east of the centre in between the bus and train stations. Convenient for the Mátra Museum and its gardens. *Sgl 6,250Ft, dbl 9,000Ft, suite (for 4) 19,500Ft.*

**Vincellér Panzió** (16 rooms) Erzsébet királyné utca 22; ❧ 37 311691; www.hotels.hu/vincellerpanzio. Apart from the dawn squawks of an inconsiderate cockerel outside our window, we were satisfied with compact and clean rooms. The pension's popular restaurant has a good ambience, friendly staff, a garden patio lit with candles, and a varied selection of dishes (*mains 980–2,400Ft, avg 1,400Ft*). *Sgl 6,500Ft, dbl 8,000Ft, apts 9,250–13,500Ft; b/fast 600Ft.*

## Where to eat and drink

The Vincellér has a decent restaurant (see above).

**House of Mátra Wines** (*Mátraaljai Borok Háza*) Fő tér 10; ❧ 37 302226; e matraiborokhaza@tvnetwork.hu. The most convenient place to have a glug of the region's bottles. The house showcases 100 of the wines produced in the 22 villages of the Mátraalja – the region at the 'foot of the Mátra Hills'. With advance notice, the cellar can accommodate up to 50 tasters. *Wine shop open Mon–Thu 09.00–19.00, Fri 09.00–22.00, Sun 10.00–14.00; wine tasting Fri 19.00–22.00, Sat 16.00–22.00.*

**Kékes** Fő tér 7; ❧ 37 311915. Specialising in Hungarian food, this is the town's most expensive restaurant. It boasts an elegant interior, with a wooden upper seating section and low-hanging lights, and an outdoor area sheltered by a canopy. *Mains 1,400–3,000Ft, avg 2,000Ft; open 11.00–22.00 daily.*

**König** Arány János utca 13; ❧ 37 315809. Spartan restaurant serving good Hungarian fare. *Mains 850–1,700Ft, avg 1,000Ft; open Mon–Thu 12.00–22.00, Fri–Sat 12.00–23.00, Sun 12.00–22.00.*

**Korzó kávézó** Fő tér 10; ❧ 06 30 275 9125. Airy little coffee house down an alleyway next to the Tourinform office. *Open 09.00–19.00 daily.*

**Pizza Il Caminetto** Kossuth Lajos utca 19; ❧ 37 312652. Watch pizzas being freshly prepared in the restaurant's open kitchen; eat them while enjoying the atmosphere on the al-fresco terrace. There are also pastas to choose from. *Pizzas 210–1,020Ft, avg 700Ft; open Sun–Thu 12.00–22.00, Fri–Sat 12.00–23.00.*

**Viktória** Török Ignác utca 24/2; ❧ 06 30 504 3626. Hungarian and international dishes, and courtyard seating. Situated in the narrow side-street linking Török Ignác utca and Kossuth Lajos utca. *Mains 800–1,600Ft; open daily 12.00–22.00.*

## Entertainment and nightlife

The ticket and information centre of the **Mátra Cultural Centre** (*Barátok tere 3;* ❧ *37 312281/2/3*) is open Mon–Fri 14.00–18.00. Just off the main square, **City Disco Club** (*Fő tér 9;* ❧ *37 312281*) – with a pizzeria and three dancefloors – was being refurbished during our last visit, but should have re-opened by the time you read this. There are several bars to the south of Fő tér.

## What to see and do

**Fő tér** is the pedestrianised main square containing **St Bertalan Parish Church** (*Szent Bertalan út 1*) at its northern end. The twin-towered 'Big Church' is appropriately nicknamed – it is the country's largest Gothic temple, although its face became more properly Baroque during rebuilding in the 18th century. Original features of the 15th-century hall church (built on the site of a church that had stood here since 1301) remain in the form of Gothic twin windows on either side of the apse, and in a bronze Gothic baptism font at the southern side of the shrine. Look out too for the frescoes of Hungarian freedom fighters (*kuruc*). Near the church is a skinny **statue of Károly Róbert**, commissioned to mark the 650th anniversary of the settlement's accession to town status. The **town hall** (*Fő tér 13*) bears the town's coat of arms – depicting a howling wolf beneath a golden sun and moon – and these images are replicated in three of the square's corner fountains. The fourth shows the vine, a nod towards the strong tradition of wine production in the region.

The **Holy Crown House** (*Szent Korona Ház; Szent Bertalan út 3;* ❧ *37 311143; open Tue–Sun 10.00–12.00 & 14.00–17.00*) is to the south of the church, so-named because the Hungarian crown was three times hidden in an upper room during the Napoleonic Wars. This is commemorated in the painted ceiling of the ceremonial hall. The building now holds the **treasury** (*kincstár*) of the St Bertalan Church, said to be the third-richest ecclesiastical collection in the country. Here are works by medieval and Renaissance goldsmiths, as well as vestments and statues. To the east of the church is a music school that was once a **secondary school** for Jesuits and then Franciscans. Its niches hold Baroque wooden statues of St Ignatius and St Francis; the original stone versions are in the Mátra Museum.

Two former synagogues stand southwest of the main square, testament to the strength of the town's Jewish population prior to the horrors of World War II. Opposite the County Hall is the classicist **Memorial Synagogue** (*Vármegye utca*), built between 1816 and 1820 by Károly Rábl, a local of the town. Next to it is the domed **New Synagogue** (*Kőrösi Csoma Sándor utca*), a Moorish edifice designed by Lipót Baumhorn in 1930.

Franciscan monks arrived during the 14th century, and their **church and monastery** (*Ferences templom és rendház; Barátok tere 1–2*) were founded in 1370 (although the 18th century saw a Baroque overhaul). Gyöngyös was in the thick of the struggle for independence led by Ferenc Rákóczi II between 1703 and 1711, and the prince held negotiations with the Habsburg ambassador here. One of the insurrection's best-known generals – János Vak (Blind) Bottyán – is buried in the crypt. The monastery houses the **Memorial Library of the Hungarian Franciscan Friars** (*Magyar Ferencesek Műemlék Könyvtára;* ❧ *37 311361; open Tue–Fri & Sun 14.00–18.00, Sat 10.00–18.00*), a collection of 16,000 volumes (including antique decorative works by various European printing houses, five codices and 210 incunabula) preserved by the religious order since the Middle Ages and uniquely surviving the Turkish period unharmed. There is a permanent exhibition covering the history of the Franciscan order in the entrance hall.

The **Mátra Museum and Mikroárium** (*Kossuth Lajos utca 40;* ❧ *37 311447; adult/concessions 460/230Ft; mikroárium adult/concessions 100/80Ft; open Tue–Sun Mar 1– Oct 31 09.00–17.00, Nov 1–Feb 28 09.00–14.00*) can be found in the Neoclassical and tatty 18th-century Orczy Mansion. There are carved lions guarding the entrance, while another (sculpted by István Ferenczy in 1840) sleeps in the lovely gardens. The iron fence

## WINES OF THE MÁTRAALJA WINE REGION

Formerly known as Gyöngyös-Visonta – the name was altered in the 1960s – the region at the foot of the Mátra Hills is the second-largest of the country's 22 regions. It occupies a 20km strip of land on the southern slopes of the Mátra Hills, bordered by the Tarna River to the east and the Zagyva River to the west. There is an ancient tradition of viniculture here, its climate and soil types most suited to flowery, fruity whites – today including Italian riesling and Ottonel muskotály, Szürkebarát or Leányka, as well as global varieties of Chardonnay. There was wine-making here even prior to Hungarian settlement, but the golden age came during the period of the Napoleonic Wars, sustained during Habsburg rule. The phylloxera plague of 1880 was devastating, and the region relied on significant government assistance in its rejuvenation. Today the region's big-boy wineries are Szőlőskert and Danubiana, but there are also many small, family-run ones. An increasing number of these offer tastings for visitors – particularly since the founding of the Wine Route Association in 1998 – but the simplest way of sampling what is on offer is at the Mátraalja House of Wine (see page 235).

is said to have been fashioned from gun barrels of the Napoleonic Wars. In the museum is the second-largest natural-scientific collection in Hungary. The ground floor holds an exhibition about the history of the town and surrounding region, from 13th-century Kisnána tombstones discovered at Benevár, Mátrafüred, through Turkish weapons to items melted by the devastating fire of 1917. Upstairs is a selection of the geology of the Mátra Hills, as well as a mammoth skeleton and hunting items.

There are open-air **thermal baths** (*Pesti út;* ✆ *37 311561; adult/concessions 400/190Ft; open Jan 1–May 15 Tue–Fri 06.00–18.00, Sat–Sun 08.00–17.00, May 16–Sep 14 Mon–Fri 09.00–19.00, Sep 15–Dec 31 Tue–Fri 06.00–18.00, Sat–Sun 08.00–17.00*) a kilometre or two to the south of the centre. Follow Jókai Mór utca to Pesti út.

### Gyöngyöspata
Twelve kilometres west of Gyöngyös (and accessible by bus), Gyöngyöspata is worth a trip for its **15th-century Gothic church** (✆ *37 364250; telephone in advance*). Inside is an 8m-tall high altar – probably the work of Polish artists of the 17th century – bearing the carved and painted **family tree of Jesus Christ**. This 'Tree of Jesse' is a Baroque masterpiece, although late-Gothic in look.

### Villages of the Mátra Hills
#### Mátrafüred
Although Mátrafüred is a small and pretty resort, it is nevertheless a lively place – particularly at weekends, when several of the restaurants and pensions put on music (inevitably of the cheesy, synthesiser brand). A dainty **Baroque church** opposite the narrow-gauge railway station was built in 1767, and is now almost swallowed by horsechestnut trees. At the **Palóc Private Ethnographic and Doll Exhibition** (*Palóc Néprajzi Magángyűjtemény, Palóc Babák; Pálosvörösmarti út 2;* ✆ *37 320137; open Mon–Fri 09.30–17.00*) there are dolls dressed in the traditional costumes of Nógrád and Heves counties, from feasting outfits to casual clothes. The former primary school also contains woven textiles and other works of folkloric art. However, most people come here to **walk**. To get started, head for Tornyos Panzió (see page 238), from where eight marked trails (of varying lengths) depart to other villages to the north and northeast, including Mátraháza (5km), Sástó (3km) and Kékestető (8km). There are **cycling** routes too; pick them up from near the ethnographic museum.

## Getting there and away

Mátrafüred – like the other villages of this region – can be accessed by **car** on Route 24, which runs through here on its way between Gyöngyös and Eger. There are up to eight **buses** daily from Budapest Stadion; of these, all also go to Mátraháza and Sástó, three of them to Kékestető and two to Parád, Parádfürdő, Recsk and Sirok. There are regular buses from Gyöngyös, and less-frequent services from Eger and Miskolc. Far more enjoyable, though, is the **narrow-gauge railway** to Mátrafüred from Gyöngyös; the trip takes around 20 minutes, and there are as many as ten departures a day (although fewer outside peak season). Tickets cost 200/380Ft sgl/rtn; there is a discount with the Hungary Card.

## Where to stay and eat

You'll be tripping over **private rooms** here – try along Béke út – and there are **stalls** aplenty on Parádi út selling pancakes, pizzas and alcohol, and opening late.

**Benevár** Parádi utca 10. The most popular place to eat Hungarian food; the restaurant is divided inside between three simple rooms and has hanging baskets in the garden. *Mains 550–1,350Ft, avg 750Ft; open daily 11.00–23.00.*

**Diana Hotel** Turista út 1; ◗ 37 320136. Basic accommodation. *Dbl 7,000Ft, triple 9,000Ft, apt 15,000Ft.*

**Feketerigó** Avar út 2; ◗ 37 320052. Serves cheap if unexceptional food like deer goulash and turkey breast stuffed with goose liver. Its accommodation lacks the modern touch – and rooms don't have bathrooms – but they are comfy enough, and similarly lowly in price. *Sgl 2,000Ft, dbl 3,200Ft, triple 4,200Ft, suites 7,400–8,600Ft; open Tue–Sun 12.00–21.00.*

**Füredi Terasz** Parádi utca 3; ◗ 37 320240. A wide selection of well-priced pizzas and pastas. *Pizza/pasta avg 680Ft, Hungarian dishes 780–1,680Ft; open daily 12.00–23.00.*

**Hegyalja-Fenyveskert** (16 rooms) Béke út 7; ◗ 37 320027; e hegyalja@matavnet.hu. A handsome guesthouse and restaurant (serving Hungarian grills and stews; open daily 12.00–22.00) with a well-maintained interior and log furniture shaded by pine trees outside. *Sgl 8,250Ft, dbl 10,500Ft, triple 14,000Ft.*

**Hotel Avar** Parádi út 24; ◗ 37 320400; e avarhotel@mail.datanet.hu; www.hotels.hu/avarhotel_matrafured. Standard 3-star hotel. Its rooms are light and airy, and have balconies, while there is also an indoor pool. You can hire bikes here for 300Ft. *Sgl 10,850Ft, dbl 13,300Ft, apt (for 2) 16,000Ft.*

**Hotel Füred** (10 rooms) Kékesi utca 1–3; ◗ 37 520030. Around 500m from the village centre, this hotel is tucked among blue-green fir trees. Its rooms are clean, and its facilities include a sun terrace, a football field and an area for clay-pigeon shooting. *Sgl 6,500Ft, dbl 7,500Ft.*

**Hotel Gyöngyvirág** (25 rooms) Béke út 8; ◗ 37 520001; e info@gyongyvirag.hu; www.gyongyvirag.hu. Has a beer garden and grill buffet during the summer months, and an outdoor swimming pool. *Sgl 5,000–6,000Ft, dbl 6,000–7,000Ft, apt 7,000–8,000Ft.*

**Tornyos** (8 rooms) Parádi utca 25; ◗ 37 320236; www.hotels.hu/tornyospanzioetterem. Restaurant with good fish and friendly staff; it also has a small attached pension. *Dbl 8,000Ft, apt (for 4) 15,000Ft; mains 550–1,100Ft, avg 900Ft; restaurant open Sun–Fri 08.00–22.00, Sat 08.00–23.00.*

## Sástó

Located bang in between Mátrafüred and Mátraháza on the winding Road 24 that leads from Gyöngyös, Sástó is one of the highest lakes in the country (500m above sea level) and is a popular spot for fishing or messing about in boats. There are numerous stalls selling refreshments around the water's edge, and you can cross wooden bridges that straddle the lake to access a 50m-high **lookout tower** (*Sástói Kilátó; adult 45Ft*).

Sástó is a pleasant 30-minute walk uphill from Mátrafüred (follow the yellow-circle trail from Tornyos Panzió), although there are also buses running here from Budapest,

Eger, Gyöngyös and Miskolc. The bus stops directly outside **Mátra Camping** (*Farkas utca 4;* ❧ *37 574 002;* e *sasto@elpak.hu; www.sasta.elpak.hu*), a large and pretty site that offers accommodation of some sort all year round, and has a snackbar, pub, restaurant and supermarket. There's space for 200 tents (*available Apr–Oct*), while there are also welcoming bungalows (*with TV and refrigerator; dbl 6,200Ft, triple 7,400Ft*), less-comfortable huts (*dbl 3,100Ft, triple 4,300Ft*) and a motel (*shared bathrooms; dbl 4,100Ft, triple 5,000Ft*). The **Tourinform** in Gyöngyös can provide any further information you might need.

## Mátraháza

A little further north of Sástó, Mátraháza is like an understudy for Mátrafüred – slightly less pleasing on the eye and with fewer amenities, but with a good spread of choice walks. Join the marked trails from close to the bus stop – to Sirok (blue horizontal line; 24km), Kékestető (red plus sign; 3km), Sástó (yellow plus sign; 3km), Lajosháza (yellow plus sign; 4km), Galyatető (the country's second-highest peak at 965m; blue horizontal line; 10km) or Párádsasvár (red horizontal line; 6km). The village stands in the shadow of Mount Kékes, and is consequently also a base for skiers in winter.

### Where to stay and eat

**Bérc Hotel Mátra** (128 rooms) ❧ 37 374102; e berchotel@matavnet.hu. One of a brace of big hotels on the Panorama Road (No 24) that you'll pass on your way from Sástó to Mátraháza. Among the facilities are a swimming pool, bowling lane and crumbling tennis courts, and each of the rooms has a balcony. *Sgl 6,500–7,300Ft, dbl 9,500–10,500Ft, apts 12,000–13,000Ft; b/fast 1,300Ft.*

**Borostyán** ❧ 37 374090. Next to the Pagoda Hotel (and belonging to the same owner), Borostyán serves fair traditional cuisine with game specialities. It is elevated from the road, with animal skins on the walls and seating outside in individual wooden pavilions. *Mains 920–1,750ft, avg 1,100Ft; open daily 09.00–22.00.*

**Hotel Edzőtábor** ❧ 37 374016. An ex-trade-union hostel, with a canteen-style restaurant and a preponderance of school parties among its guests. *Rooms 2,500Ft/pp; b/fast 700Ft.*

**Ózon Hotel** (59 rooms) ❧ 37 374004; e reserve@hotelozon.hunguesthotels.hu; www.hunguesthotels.hu. On the same road as the Bérc (and a slightly more upmarket proposition), the Ózon is divided between 2 buildings. Some of its rooms are a touch old fashioned, but pleasant nonetheless, with balconies attached to those on the 1st and 2nd floors. (Request a room at the back for hill views.) The hotel can organise horse-riding trips, wine tasting and forest walks, bikes can be hired for 400Ft/hr, and there are tennis courts, a fitness room and sauna. *Sgl 6,900–13.500Ft, dbl 7,900–14,800Ft.*

**Pagoda Hotel** (26 rooms) ❧ 37 320028; e hegyalja@axelero.hu. The name refers to the multi-tiered roof of its main building. Indeed, this 19th-century structure in the middle of the village was once the only house in the area, and gave its name to Mátraháza itself – 'the house of Mátra'. There are several wings spread over the hotel's grounds; among the facilities are tennis courts and free bike hire. *Sgl 5,800Ft, dbl 9,500Ft, triple 13,300Ft, room for 4 18,000Ft.*

### Kékestető

At 1,015m, 'Blue Peak' is Hungary's highest point; it also enjoys more autumn and winter sunshine than anywhere else, and is thus regarded as a therapeutic spot. It is a short distance up a steep, winding road from Mátraháza; you can take one of the marked walking trails or a bus. In snowy months, there are two **ski slopes** available, one of them running down to Mátraháza (*open Sun–Thu 09.00–16.00, Fri–Sat 09.00–20.00*). The upper section has a ski lift (*10 rides 1,500Ft, day pass 2,500Ft*), but those continuing further down need to jump on a bus for the re-ascent. You can rent skis here during the season, and there is a ski school for children. Alternatively you can climb 38m to the lookout gallery of the 187m **TV tower** (*adult/concessions 400/250Ft; open daily May–Sep 09.00–18.00, Oct–Apr 09.00–16.00*).

Next to the tower is the forbidding-looking **Hotel Hegycsúcs** (❧ *37 567004; www.hotels.hu/hegycsucs; dbl 8,300Ft, triple 10,800Ft, suite 14,900Ft*), on whose upper floors you can rest satisfied that you are above every other tourist in any other hotel in the country. More fusty and basic – verging on the time-warped – is the **Kányai Uram Fogadó** (*Üdülőtelep 1;* ❧ *37 367064; 15 rooms; 2,000Ft/pp*). Its rooms have shared bathrooms, and there's a Hungarian restaurant (*mains 720–2,900Ft, avg 1,000Ft; open 07.00–21.00 daily*).

## Parádsasvár

Just to the east of Galyatető (at 965m, the country's runner-up in the highest-hill stakes), in a valley at the northern foot of the Mátra, Parádsasvár is significant for glassworks – established by the Orczy family in 1767, and still going strong – and sulphurous medicinal water from the Csevice Spring. The latter is reputedly effective in treating not only respiratory and stomach complaints, but hangovers. The **Parád Crystal Factory** (*Kristály Manufaktura; Rákóczi utca 46–48;* ❧ *36 364353; open Tue–Sat 10.00–15.00*) produces crystal and glass as fine as you'll find anywhere. You can buy pieces from its shop (*open Mon–Fri 09.00–15.00, Sat–Sun 09.00–13.00*), and there are further examples in the **Sasvár Galéria** (*open Mon–Fri 09.45–12.30, 13.45–14.30, Sat 08.00–09.00, 09.50–11.30*) opposite. Several residential houses also have small glass workshops that can be visited, and which offer decanters, drinking vessels and novelty bits and bobs – try **László Ólankristály Üzlet és Műhely** (*Arany János utca 13;* ❧ *36 373574*).

If you fancy a **walk**, there are a couple of trails signposted as you enter the village. Alternatively you can head for the **Fényes Major Equestrian Farmstead** (*Fényes Major Lovastanya;* ❧ *36 444444; e sasvar@sasvar.hu; www.sasvar.hu; entrance adult 500Ft, child under 12 free; riding lesson 3,000Ft/hr, cross-country riding with guide 4,000Ft/hr, carriage ride 8,000Ft/hr; open Wed–Sun 08.00–18.00*), 30 minutes' walk east of the centre or a short bus ride (alight at the Fényespusztai Elág stop). Follow the track adjacent to Túra Camping for 1km. The 32ha ranch holds Lipizzaners and Hungarian half-breds, as well as donkeys, buffalo, goats and sheep. Lessons and excursions are available for riders of all levels, as well as carriage trips.

One hundred kilometres from Budapest, take the Gyöngyös exit off the M3 motorway, and follow Road 24 for 24km. **Buses** run to and from Eger, Párad, Páradfürdő, Recsk and Sirok; alight just outside the St Hubertus Panzió.

### Where to stay and eat
The former mansion of Mihály Károlyi (1875–1955) – Hungarian prime minister of the republic in 1918 – was designed in the late 19th century by Miklós Ybl and was refurbished in the 1990s to become the **Kastély Hotel Sasvár** (*Kossuth Lajos utca 1;* ❧ *36 444444; e sasvar@sasvar.hu; www.sasvar.hu; 57 rooms; sgl 30,000–50,000Ft, dbl 40,000–60,000Ft, suites 70,000–270,000Ft*). 'Eagle Castle Hotel' is an impressive, turreted affair, with super facilities – bowling alley, squash courts, pools indoor and out. Each of its suites has its own sauna and Jacuzzi, and there are separate wings for honeymooners and families. For all its splendour, however, we felt there was something slightly soulless about the place, as though the restoration had been done by a team from Disney World. Non guests can pay 10,000Ft for a day ticket, which gives them access to the facilities and restaurant (*for an extra 5,000Ft*).

More rustic and less pressing on the pocket is the nearby **St Hubertus Panzió** (*Rákóczi út 2;* ❧ *36 544060; 10 rooms; dbl 8,800–11,800Ft, triple 12,500–17,600Ft, room for 4 16,000–23,000Ft, b/fast 600Ft*), a renovated 19th-century 'Bailiff House'. Its restaurant specialises in game dishes (*mains 580–1,700Ft, avg 1,100Ft; open Sun–Fri 12.00–21.00, Sat 12.00–22.00*).

**Túra Camping** (❧ *36 364079; camping adult/concessions 600/300Ft, tent 600Ft, c/van 900Ft, dorm room 1,100Ft/pp, dbl 3,300Ft*) is located just off Road 24 on the way out of

## THE BIRTH OF THE COACH

The word *kocsi* derives from the Hungarian village of Kocs in Komárom County, a stage on the road from Buda to Vienna during the reign of King Mátyás when nimbler, light-weight carriages replaced clumsier wagons in use up until then. They were quickly adopted elsewhere around the world; the Hungarian *kocsi* is evident in the word *coach* – one of the few to leap the linguistic divide from Hungarian to English – and the German *Kutsche*.

Parádsasvár towards Eger, next to a small go-kart track. The facilities are basic, and include an on-site restaurant more reminiscent of a school canteen and some plain rooms.

### Parád and Parádfürdő

Parád and Parádfürdő stand shoulder to shoulder, and – like Parádsasvár – have traditionally drawn those seeking therapy from the area's odoriferous medicinal water. Behind Parád's church, in the northwest of the village on the bank of the Tarna Brook, is a traditional, thatched **Palóc Cottage** (*Palócház; Sziget utca 10; open Tue–Sun Mar 1– Oct 31 09.00–17.00, Nov 1–Feb 28 10.00–14.00*). Built at the end of the 18th century, it serves as a museum of folk art and peasant architecture, with hand-woven embroidery and painted wooden furniture. Another exhibition displays the masterful **wood carvings** of Joachim Asztalos (*Fafaragó kiállítás; Hársfa utca 6; open daily 09.00–18.00*).

The State Hospital of Parádfürdő holds a collection of bottles of mineral water from countries around the world in its **Medicinal Water Museum** (*Gyógyvíz Múzeum; Kossuth Lajos út 221;* \ *36 364233; adult/concessions 100/50Ft*). You'll need to ask at the hospital reception for access, and it isn't really worth the effort. Far better is the **Coach Museum** (*Kocsi Múzeum; Kossuth Lajos út 217;* \ *36 544073; adult/concessions 350/220Ft; open Apr–Oct daily 09.00–16.50, Nov–Mar Tue–Sun 10.00–16.00*), housed on the site of the Cifra Istálló (Decorated Stable) that Count György Károlyi commissioned in 1880. He was determined to own a splendid stable that would shade all others, and put the job into the hands of Miklós Ybl, who made use of red marble in his design. Today you'll find an array of coaches and horsey paraphernalia dating to the 19th and early 20th centuries. Lipizzaners are still bred in two wings.

### Where to stay and eat

On the main street running through Parád, **Parádi Kisvendéglő** (*Kossuth Lajos utca 234;* \ *36 364831*) serves traditional Hungarian dishes and Palóc specialities (*mains 500–1,200Ft, avg 1,000Ft; open Apr–Sep Wed–Mon 12.00–21.00, Oct–Mar Wed–Sun 12.00–21.00*) and has a few rooms (*dbl 5,200Ft*).

Parádfürdő has a greater choice of accommodation. A few minutes east, the **Erzsébet Királyné Park Hotel** (Kossuth Lajos utca 372; \ 36 444044; e erzsebethotel@axelero.hu; www.erzsebetparkhotel.hu; 42 rooms; sgl €70–92, dbl €84–106, suites €132–156) is another of Ybl's creations, a beautiful building and a sprawling, comfortable hotel. Among the amenities are a swimming pool, sauna and fitness room.

**Hotel Freskó** (*Kossuth Lajos utca 221;* \ *36 544083; 38 rooms; sgl without bathroom 4,400Ft, dbl with/without bathroom 5,800/7,000Ft, apt with kitchenette 12,000Ft; b/fast 1,400Ft*) stands next to the medicinal hospital and has a vast dining hall decorated with painted panels of battle and hunting scenes, and a limited Hungarian menu (*mains 800–1,500Ft, avg 1,000Ft; open daily 08.00–22.00*). Its rooms are basic but cheap.

There are several pensions on Peres út (just off the main thoroughfare); **Muflon Panzió** (*Peres út 8;* \ *36 544086;* e *muflon.panzio@netquick.hu; rooms from 3,000Ft/pp*) is slightly tatty but has neat rooms sleeping two–eight guests; not all of these are en suite, and most don't have TV. Other recommended guesthouses are **Valentin Panzió** (*Peres út 16;* ↘ *36 364295*) and **Boróka Mini Hotel** (*Peres út 18;* ↘ *36 364527*).

## Recsk

Many Hungarians make the trip a couple of kilometres further east along Road 24 to pay their respects to the memory of countrymen who toiled here in the early 1950s. Mátyás Rákosi established a secret labour camp in Recsk in 1950, where opponents of the communist regime were transported after being sentenced (without trial) to forced labour. They mined the quarries close by, and hundreds died under appalling conditions. Imre Nagy shut the place down in 1953, but it was the recollections of the only prisoner to successfully flee the camp that revealed its existence to the West. In the book *My Jolly Days in Hell*, György Faludy describes how he memorised the names of fellow prisoners to ensure that justice would eventually prevail, and in doing so kick-started the process that led to the dismantling of the gulag camps. A memorial to the **labour camp** (*Recski Kényszermunka Haláltábor; adult/concessions 100/50Ft; open May–Sep Mon–Fri 09.00–17.00, Sat–Sun 09.00–14.00, Oct–Apr Sat–Sun 09.00–15.00*) is 4km south of the village.

## Sirok

Continuing yet still eastward along Road 24, the ruins of the **Castle of Sirok** provide great views over the eastern and western sides of the Mátra and Bükk hills respectively, as well as ranges on the Slovakian side of the border. The 13th-century castle was constructed of rocks chiselled from the 296m-high hill on which it sits; it was blown up by the Habsburgs in 1713 in the aftermath of the War of Independence.

## THE BÜKK HILLS REGION

The Bükk Hills protect Eger from the bullyingly industrial Miskolc, and derive their name from the beech (*bükk*) trees that carpet them. King of the hills in this range is the Istállóskő, which is 958m tall and can be accessed from Szilvásvárad; the average height of the hills tops that of any in the uplands. The hills were formed of calciferous sediment left by an ocean that covered the region for 70 million years. The area is awash with springs and streams, and there are caves aplenty in the limestone surface. Although from the 19th century the region was plundered for the iron ore and timber that fed the iron-working towns in the Sajó Valley (running around the hills' eastern side), much of it remains strikingly beautiful. A large portion has been declared a national park (see box opposite), and the combination of interesting geology and rich wildlife makes it excellent territory for hiking. Be sure to purchase a decent map – look for those produced by Cartographia.

## Eger

Resting in the valley of the River Eger, between the Mátra and Bükk ranges, Eger – from the Latin word *ager* (earth) – is one of the country's charmers, an enchanting town of cobbled streets, Baroque buildings and Bull's Blood (*Egri Bikavér*). It is easy to see why visitors flock here and coo. But Eger is not just a pretty face; its defiance of Turkish force in 1552 was immortalised in the 1901 novel *Egri Csillagok* (*Eclipse of the Crescent Moon*) by Géza Gárdonyi (1863–1922), and its citizens became linked in the Hungarian mind with the most spirited of patriots.

Settled by the Magyar tribes, Eger was made a bishopric by King István in the 11th century. Its rise as a significant centre of Renaissance culture was curtailed by the Turks. The womenfolk of the town famously fought shoulder to shoulder with István Dobó's 2,000 soldiers in repelling the first siege in 1552. The victory over a far superior force was acclaimed around Europe, and effectively stalled (temporarily) the spread of the Ottoman

## BÜKK NATIONAL PARK

Established in 1976, no less than 90% of the 43,200ha that make up Bükk National Park – encompassing Eger, Lillafüred, Bükkszentkereszt, Bélapátfalva, Felsőtárkány, Szarvaskő, Szilvásvárad, Répáshuta and their surroundings – is covered by forest (predominantly beech, *Fagus sylvatica*). But in addition to towering trees, there are open limestone meadows displaying various karst forms produced by erosion – fissures, sinkholes, underground streams and caverns. Indeed the surface is riddled with caves – around 850 at the last count, with a total length of 35km – and many have yielded rich collections of Stone Age tools. The region's communities tap into the huge quantities of pure karst water, which doesn't need filtering or chlorinating. Crags and cliffs afford excellent vantage points, while water has fashioned weird and wonderful rock formations, the best-known of which are Három-kő, Tar-kő, Vörös-kő, Őr-kő and Bél-kő in the 'rock parade' (Kövek Vonulata); this can be reached on hiking trails to the north of Répáshuta village and east of Szilvásvárad.

Among the highlights of the park is the stepped waterfall on the Szalajka Stream (see page 256); another notable place is the Őserdő (Ancient Forest; head for the Olaszkapu car park from Szilvásvárad, and hike the rest of the way) where there has been no felling for over a century. Lillafüred is home to the Szent István and Anna caves (see page 258), with their stalactites, stalagmites and fossilised trees. The central part of the hills comprises the Bükk Plateau, 20km in length, surrounded by ridges, pocked with sink holes, and very popular with hikers. Nagymező contains some of the Bükk's rarest plants.

There are over 22,000 species of animal living in the Bükk. With its many cliffs, the park offers ideal nesting conditions for rare raptors, and most valued among the 90 types of bird are the imperial eagle, the lesser-spotted eagle, the short-toed eagle and the saker, while Ural and eagle owls are the largest of the nocturnal hunters. Dense deciduous forest harbours numerous warblers and woodpeckers; warm limestone rocks and flowering meadows are ideal for butterfly spotting. The long-eared bat breeds and hibernates in some of the caves, and the wolf and lynx – up until 30 years ago declared extinct in Hungary – have recently made a comeback.

The Orbán House Exhibition (see page 256) examines the natural features of the Bükk. For further information, contact the Bükk National Park Central Office (*Eger, Sánc utca 6;* ⟍ *36 411581;* e *buknpi@ktm.x400gw.itb.hu*).

empire. It was also during this struggle that Dobó's troops are said to have been issued with wine – which the attackers mistook for bull's blood – to assist them in screwing their courage to the sticking place. There was considerably less backbone on display when the Turks returned in 1596, however, and a defending garrison of mercenaries surrendered with barely a whimper (excepting, it is hoped, the trumpeter, who was apparently a deep-chested Englishman). Despite a promise of safe passage, the Walloons (who had re-populated the town after the Mongol invasion in 1241) among the many foreign fighters were slaughtered mercilessly in revenge for their part in an earlier massacre of Ottomans living in nearby villages. Today a solitary minaret and a few bath stones are the only reminders of the occupation that lasted until 1687.

Eger was heavily involved in the War of Independence led by Rákóczi, and the Habsburg Emperor Leopold crippled some of the castle fortifications to ensure it couldn't be used by freedom fighters. There was swift development of the town during the rest of the 18th century, with the construction of private houses and ecclesiastical

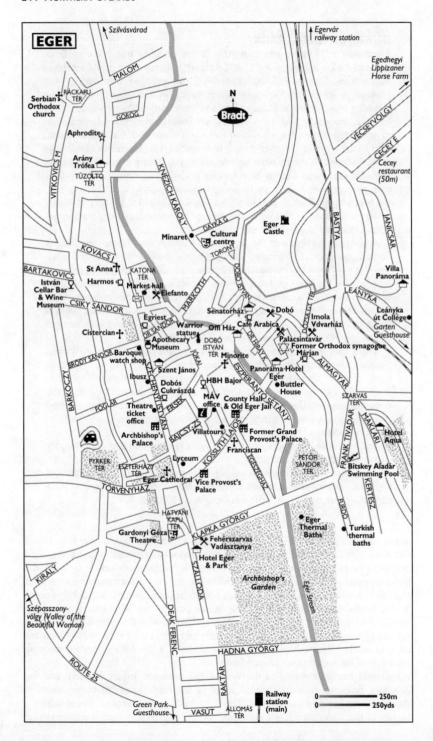

buildings. Look down from the fortress at the many church steeples spiking the skyline and you'll understand why it earned the nickname 'the Hungarian Rome'.

## Getting there and away

The **bus** station is in Pyrker János tér, around 500m southwest of Dobó István tér. There are 21 direct buses from Budapest Stadion, taking three hours; Eger is well served by buses to/from many other destinations, including Miskolc (12), Mezőkövesd (25), Aggtelek (one direct, leaving Eger at 08.45), Gyöngyös (46), Mátrafüred (four), Tiszafüred (up to 12), Szilvásvárad (31) and Salgótarján (nine). There is an information bureau at the bus station.

The main **railway station** is to the south, on Vasút utca; follow Deák Ferenc utca northwards for a kilometre to reach the centre. There are five direct trains a day to Eger from Budapest Keleti, the journey taking about two hours; the indirect route requires a change at Füzesabony on to the line running northwards to Putnok. There is a single daily direct train from Debrecen (two on Sun), but all others require a connection at Füzesabony, as do all trains to and from Miskolc. The Füzesabony–Putnok line includes Szilvásvárad (six daily). Egervár – a very small station near the castle on Vécseyvölgy utca – is on the same line. You can book train tickets at the **MÁV Office** *(Jókai utca 5; ↘ 36 314264; open Mon–Thu 09.00–17.00, Fri 09.00–13.30)*.

## Getting around

**Bus** numbers 10, 11 and 12 run along Deák Ferenc utca (close to the main train station) into the middle of town. Two motorised **sightseeing trains** trundle around the town, and one goes out to Szépasszony-völgy; they leave from Dobó István tér on the hour from 09.00, and tickets *(300Ft)* are purchased on board. **Taxi** firms include City Taxi (↘ 36 555555) and Egér Taxi (↘ 36 411111).

## Information and other practicalities

**Bükk National Park Directorate** Sánc utca 6; ↘ 36 411581. Information on the region's nature.
**Express** Széchenyi utca 28; ↘ 36 427757. Bookings for tours and private accommodation. *Open Mon–Thu 08.00–16.30, Fri 08.00–16.00.*
**Ibusz** Széchenyi utca 9; ↘ 36 312652; e eger@iroda.ibusz.hu. Can exchange currency, as well as arranging tours and private rooms.
**Internet** There are terminals at Broadway Palace and Egriest Café (see pages 247–8)
**Listings magazine** *Egri Est*
**Tourinform** Bajcsy-Zsilinszky utca 9; ↘ 36 517715; e eger@tourinform.hu. The usual first port of call for local information, including recommendations for English-speaking tour guides. *Open Jun–Aug Mon–Fri 09.00–19.00, Sat–Sun 10.00–18.00, Sep–May Mon–Fri 09.00–17.00, Sat 09.00–13.00.*
**Villatours** Jókai utca 1; ↘ 36 410215. *Open Mon–Fri 08.00–16.00.*

## Where to stay

**Bacchus Panzió** (24 rooms) Szépasszony-völgy utca 29; ↘ 36 428950; e bacchuspanzio@axelero.hu; www.bacchuspanzio.hu. With a name like Bacchus, it could only be in the valley of wine cellars – and the old soak would enjoy sleeping off his excesses in one of the spacious, comfortable and modern rooms at this welcoming guesthouse. He may not be the type to appreciate them, but the grounds are lovely too. Rooms with balconies are slightly more expensive. *Sgl €34, dbls €40–48, apt (for 2) €64.*
**Garten Guesthouse** (11 rooms)Legányi Ferenc utca 6; ↘ 36 320371. If you prefer to be ensconced away from the thick of things, the Garten is a 15-min walk east of the centre – and it's pretty, with a shady garden and a light conservatory in which to breakfast. The lady owner is a dear. *Dbl 9,000Ft, apt 18,000Ft.*

**Hotel Arany Trófea** (14 rooms) Széchenyi utca 41/b; ✆ 36 510 840; e aranytrofea@agria.hu; www.aranytrofea.hu. It looks rather like a doll's house from the outside, and some of the rooms are also on the diminutive side, but the Arany Trófea is central, bright and furnished with mod cons. *Dbl 16,000Ft, apt (for 4) 26,000Ft.*

**Hotel Eger and Park** (165 rooms) Szálloda utca 1–3; ✆ 36 522222; e hotelegerpark@axelero.hu. Located in the northwestern corner of the Archbishop's Garden, the Eger and Park are two hotels in one. The former is a blocky '70s affair, the latter kinder on the eye. Neither is modern, but the location is pleasant, and there's a sports centre with swimming pool, tennis courts and fitness room. *Sgl €57, dbl €77, triple €99.*

**Hotel Senator Ház** (11 rooms) Dobó István tér 11; ✆ 36 320466; e hotelsen@axelero.hu; www.hotels.hu/senatorhaz. Right in the historical heartland, the Senator Ház is a charming 250-year-old town house with a café and restaurant at the front, and green-shuttered windows peeping from among the roof tiles. Half its rooms overlook the square. *Sgl €54, dbl €76.*

**Imola Udvarház** (6 apts) Dózsa György tér 4; ✆ 36 516180; e udvarhaz@imolanet.hu; www.imolanet.hu. Adjacent to the castle entrance, the Imola has well-equipped apts (choose rooms 1 or 2 for the best views) and an excellent restaurant (see opposite). *Dbl 16,500Ft.*

**Panoráma Hotel Eger** (38 rooms) Dr Hibay Károly utca 2; ✆ 36 412886; e panhotel@elender.hu; www.hotels.hu/panorama_hotel. This modern hotel is the only 4-star in town; its 'thermarium' has a sauna, jacuzzis and a fitness room, and there's a funky restaurant. The rooms have lightwood furnishings and are of the inoffensive (but unexciting) ilk common in chain hotels. *Sgl €69, dbl €81, triple €98, apts from €104.*

**Tulipán Camping** Szépasszony-völgy 71; ✆ 36 410580; e tulipancamping@tulipankert.axelero.net; www.eurocampings.net. The ideal site for campers who've sampled the cellars until they're several sticks short of a teepee. Well equipped with a swimming pool, laundry, shop and restaurant; there's a 30-room panzió and 6 bungalows. (It should be noted that the location makes access for caravans and motorhomes tricky.) *Tent/caravan 400/1,750Ft, plus 850Ft/pp; panzió dbl 8,000Ft, apt (for 2) 12,000Ft; bungalow 10,000Ft. Open Feb 15–Oct 31.*

**Villa Panoráma** Bálint pap utca 3; ✆ 36 410121; e villapanorama@agria.hu; www.hotels.hu/villapanorama. It's a bit of a schlep from the centre, but there are superb views over the town from this contemporary villa. It is also very well equipped, with a sauna, solarium and swimming pool. *Sgl 6,000Ft, dbl 9,000Ft.*

The **Leányka úti Kollégium** (*Leányka utca 2; from 1,500Ft/pp*) is an ugly concrete college that rents out basic dormitory accommodation; Tourinform can provide details. In the same area – for example, on Joo János utca or Cecey Éva utca – there are several pensions and houses offering **private rooms**. There are good views of the city from here, but it's a steep walk up to these roads from the castle's eastern side; if you catch a bus along Bástya utca for a short distance, it will bring you closer and take much of the strain for you. Ibusz and Express (see page 245) can also arrange private lodgings.

## Where to eat and drink

While there is no shortage of cafés, restaurants are perhaps Eger's blindspot – great places to eat are thin on the ground in the centre.

**Arany Oroszlán** Dobó István tér 5; tel 36 311005. The restaurant of the Offi Ház Hotel stands next to the little bridge leading into the larger portion of the square, and serves international cuisine. There are pew-like benches inside and further seating outdoors. *Mains 550–1,200Ft; open daily 11.00–24.00.*

**Arany Trófea** See above. This intimate and chintzy hotel restaurant specialises in game. If you'd prefer, there's less frilly clutter on the grill and beer terrace. *Mains 990Ft–3,200Ft, avg 1,600Ft; open 10.00–22.00 daily.*

**Café Arabica** Dr Hibáy Károly utca 22. Quaint café on a corner just outside Dobó István tér; you can choose from vast arrays of teas and coffees – the friendly staff will let you sniff the leaves or beans before making your selection – and either drink your brew among the doilies and bean barrels or buy a packet to take away. *Open daily 10.00–19.00.*

**Dobós Cukrászda** Széchenyi utca 6; ✆ 36 413335. The best cakes are probably to be had here, near the Archbishop's Palace, among the wood panelling, chandeliers and stained glass. Such upmarket ambience is reflected in the price. There are also ice creams, coffees and cocktails. *Open daily 09.30–21.00.*

**Egriest Café and Internet** Széchenyi utca 16; ✆ 36 411105. A relaxed place for a coffee that also offers internet access. Opposite St Bernard's Church. *Open Mon–Sat 11.00–24.00.*

**Elefanto** Katona István tér 2; ✆ 36 411031; e elefanto@freemail.hu. A wooden terrace wraps itself around the elevated restaurant; we love it here at night, when its lanterns and fairy lights in the surrounding trees are at their best. Game is the speciality, but there is also a wide range of pizzas. There is a determined anti-smoking policy inside. *Mains 960–3,050Ft, avg 2,000Ft; open daily 12.00–24.00.*

**Fehérszarvas Vadásztanya** Klapka út 8; tel.: 36 411129; www.feherszarvasetterem.hu. The 'Farm of the White Stag Hunter' looks like a theme restaurant gone mad, with hunting paraphernalia stuffed (literally!) in every cranny. Naturally game is the order of the day, and the quality is as good as anywhere in town. The spicy stews are recommended. Next to the Park Hotel. *Mains 880–3,500Ft, avg 1,800Ft; open daily 12.00–24.00.*

**Harmos Cukrászda** Széchenyi utca 25; ✆ 36 517608. Dreamy and creamy ices are popular with the locals, who often queue at the street-level hatch. *Open daily 09.00–19.30.*

**HBH Bajor Sörház** Bajcsy-Zsilinsky utca 19; ✆ 36 515516. Beer house with Hungarian and Bavarian brews – including home-made tipples – and food specialities. *Mains 1,000–3,000Ft, avg 1,500Ft; open daily 10.00–22.00.*

**Imola Udvarház** Dózsa György tér 4; ✆ 36 414825; e udvarhaz@imolanet.hu; www.imolanet.hu. Situated near the entrance to the castle, this is one of Eger's best. It has an ivy-clad courtyard and serves well-presented nouvelle-Hungarian cuisine.

**Ködmön Csárda** Szépasszony-völgy; ✆ 36 413172; e csarda@axelero.hu. The valley's restaurants almost inevitably cater for tourist parties attracted by the wine-sampling opportunities. The Ködmön nevertheless serves tasty Hungarian fare. *Mains 850–3,000Ft, avg 1,800Ft; open daily 12.00–23.00.*

**Kulacs Csárda** Szépasszony-völgy; ✆ 36 311375. Kulacs is cut from Ködmön's cloth, trapping tourists with local dishes, gypsy music, vines and lanterns. The dish of cockerel testicles wrapped in onion and egg was something to crow about. *Mains 1,200–1,700Ft, avg 1,400Ft; open daily 12.00–23.00.*

**Marján Cukrászda** Kossuth Lajos utca 28; ✆ 36 312784. An elegant interior with high-backed seating and a daunting selection of cakes piled with cream, cherries, chocolate, walnuts... There's a terrace outside. *Open daily May 1–Sep 30 09.00–22.00, Oct 1–Apr 30 09.00–19.00.*

**Palacsintavár** Dobó utca 9; ✆ 36 413980. There's a bustling atmosphere at Palacsintavár, set deep below street level near the castle, and a serious commitment to calorie counting – think of a number and multiply it many, many times! Among a staggering choice of pancakes is 'Lucifer's palascinta' – featuring pork, turkey, chicken, potato and cream. Fabulous. *Pancakes 550–1,070Ft; open daily 12.00–23.00.*

The main **market hall** (*Katona tér; open Mon–Fri 06.00–18.00, Sat 06.00–13.00, Sun 06.00–10.00*) sells fresh fruit, vegetables and cakes.

## Entertainment and nightlife

The Tourinform or main **ticket office** (*Széchenyi utca 5;* ✆ *36 518347*) have details of drama and concerts. The **Gárdonyi Géza Theatre** (*Hatvani kapu tér 4;* ✆ *36 310026; www.gardonyiszinhaz.hu; ticket office open Tue–Sat 14.00–19.00*) stands near the basilica, and is named after the literary son the town clutches tight to its bosom (see page 251); unfortunately the drama, musicals and children's productions are in Hungarian.

Perhaps more likely to leap the linguistic gap is the **Harlekin Puppet Theatre** (*Harlekin Bábszínház; Bartók Béla tér 6;* ✆ *36 413073*), its auditorium hosting shows for adults and children. Alternatively, in summer there are **organ recitals** in the basilica (*May 15–Oct 15 Mon–Sat 11.30, Sun 12.45*), and plays at the **Lyceum** (see below). The **cultural centre** (*Knérich Károly utca 5*) also hosts concerts and local productions.

**Broadway Palace** (*Pyrker tér 1–3;* ☎ *36 517220; café open daily 09.00–23.00, club Thu–Sat 22.00–06.00*) is sequestered beneath the basilica steps, operating as a bar and internet café by day and a club by night. **Aphrodite Nightclub** (*Széchenyi utca 3*) is a rather cheesy, Euro-pop-tune club at the end of Széchenyi utca. The **Hippolit Club** (*Katona István tér 2;* ☎ *36 412452;* e *hippolit@agria.hu; open Fri–Sat 21.00–04.00*) is a disco at the Elefanto (see page 247), while **Champ's Pub** (*Maklári út 9;* ☎ *36 512512*) in the Hotel Aqua has draught beer and a summer grill terrace.

### What to see and do
#### Eszterházy tér, Széchenyi István utca and around
There were no horses spared in building the Neoclassical **Eger Cathedral** (*Eszterházy tér*); József Hild's design – the country's second-largest church (after Esztergom) – was finished in 1836 after just six years' work. The cupola is 40m in height, while two broad flights of steps lead up to the colonnade's six monumental Corinthian pillars at the basilica's entrance. Statues of kings Laszló and István and apostles Peter and Paul either side of the steps are the work of Venetian sculptor Marco Casagrande, who had a hand in many of the church's artistic adornments. Inside are clusters of chocolate- and caramel-coloured marble columns, an altar painting (*The Martyrdom of St John*) of 1835 by Viennese artist Joseph Danhauser, and the biggest organ in Hungary. (For details of recital times, see above.) The cathedral was raised to 'basilica' rank by the pope in 1970.

Just to the north of the basilica is the **Archbishop's Palace** (*Érseki Palota; Széchenyi István utca 5*), the Baroque residence of the town's bishops for over 250 years. Its **Ecclesiastical Collection** (*Egyházi Gyűtemény;* ☎ *36 421332; adult/concessions 250/150Ft; open Apr 1–Oct 31 Tue–Sat 09.00–17.00, Nov 1–Mar 31 Mon–Fri 08.00–16.00*) charts the history of Eger's top ministers between 1699 and 1943, featuring canonical treasures of the 18th and 19th centuries. Some of the items were gifts to Bishop Gábor Erdődy from Empress Maria Theresa, including the cloak she wore at her coronation.

The rectangular **Lyceum** (*Eszterházy tér 1;* ☎ *36 520400; adult/concessions 350/200Ft; open Apr 1–Sep 30 Tue–Sun 09.30–15.30, Oct 1–Mar 31 Sat–Sun 09.30–13.30*) faces the basilica across Széchenyi István utca. It was built in late-Baroque style during the mid-18th century as a school. Bishop Károly Eszterházy (1725–99) subsequently expanded the building with the intention of developing it into a Hungarian-language university, establishing an extensive library and an astronomical tower. However, Maria Theresa scuppered these plans by decreeing that there should be no further higher-education institutions under church control, and denying Eger the right to university rank.

While it now operates as a teacher-training college, the Lyceum also houses the splendid **Archdiocesan Library** on its first floor, the Hungarian Church's only public holdings. Presiding over Louis-XVI-style oak furnishings and creaking floorboards, the ceiling is decorated with a 1778 fresco by János Kracker and József Zach depicting the Council of Trent (held between 1543 and 1563). Among the important decisions taken during the synod debates was the censorship and destruction of heretical writings, symbolised in the painting by a flash of lightning. Comprising 20,000 volumes when opened in 1793, the library now has 130,000, among them medieval codices, the first book printed in Hungarian (the *Buda Chronicle* of 1473) and a letter in Mozart's hand (the only one in Hungary).

A big trek up to a small collection, the **Astronomical Museum** is on the sixth floor of the east wing, and displays refracting and reflecting telescopes and quadrants from the 18th century, together with a horizontal sundial found in the small village of Mezőnyárád. Climb higher for a reconstruction of an astronomer's room, and a viewing gallery running around the outside of the tower. A final push brings you to the **camera obscura**, the 'eye of Eger'; a twiddle of the periscope's mirrors and lenses projects an image of the town outside on to a table inside the pitch-black Dark Chamber. Constructed in 1776 by the Viennese astronomer Miksa Hell – purely to amuse himself and his pals – the device is the second-oldest of its type in the world (pipped by Edinburgh).

**Széchenyi utca** is the strollers' street of choice, with its atmospheric restaurants, bars and terraced patisseries. There's plenty to keep you interested as you move northwards from the Lyceum. Look out for the Baroque **clock shop** (*no 13*) at the corner with Bródy Sándor utca, designed by Italian architect Giovanni Carlone in 1725; there's a statue of a lady ruffling a cherub's hair in a niche above the entrance. Next door is the **Cistercian Church** (*Széchenyi utca 15*), constructed on the site of an earlier Turkish mosque. Originally a Jesuit church, the foundation stone was laid by Bishop István Telekessy in 1700, but the Rákóczi Uprising put a halt to work and the church wasn't completed until 1743. It was taken over by the Cistercians at the end of the 18th century. While the frescoed ceilings and walls are not as sharply colourful as they once were, they remain impressive; the statue on the Rococo high altar depicts the kneeling Jesuit St Francis Borgia, and dates to 1770.

Opposite is an **Apothecary Museum** (*Apothekemúzeum Telekessy Patikamúzeum; Széchenyi utca 14; ❨ 36 312744; adult 40Ft; open Apr 1–Oct 31 Tue–Sun 09.00–17.00*), its Baroque and florid Rococo furnishings crafted in the Jesuit monastery during the mid 1700s. The pharmacy was established in the monastery on the back of a donation from Bishop Telekessy, and moved to its current location in 1900. Further up, the stones of a mosque were recycled in the construction of **St Anna Church** (*Széchenyi utca 29*) in 1731; a plaque records the height reached by a flood that wrought havoc in 1878. You can access the **Serbian Orthodox Church** (*Szent Miklós Görögkeleti; Széchenyi utca 55; adult 200Ft; open Tue–Sun 10.00–16.00*), with its magnificently gilded Louis-XVI-style iconostasis (1789–91), via some covered steps at no 55. Alternatively you can go around the corner to a door at Vitkovics utca 30. It was established in 1789 by Serbs and Greeks who settled here after fleeing the Turks; in a deliberate snub to the intolerant archbishop, who had previously forbidden any non-Roman-Catholic churches in Eger, József II personally granted permission for its construction. In the former parsonage – the **Vitkovics Ház** (❨ 36 412023; adult/concessions 300/150Ft; open Mon–Sat 10.00–16.00*) – is the memorial room of the Serbian poet Mihály Vitkovics and an exhibition of the work of 20th-century Hungarian artist György Kepes.

## Kossuth Lajos utca

Kossuth utca is studded with fine 18th-century Baroque buildings, many adorned with intricate wrought-iron work. The heavy-metal master was Henrik Fazola, hailing originally from Germany, whose hand was in the balcony and billowing window covers of the peach-coloured **Vice-Provost's Palace** (*Kispréposti Palota; Kossuth Lajos utca 4*). Your eyes will need some time to adjust on entering the dimly lit **Franciscan church** (*Kossuth Lajos utca 14*), famed for its altar by painter Pál Kronewetter and sculptor Antal Steinhauser, with branching vines like tinsel on a tree. The church's foundation stone was laid in 1736, and many of the monastery's doors and fittings are original.

The genius of the ironwright Fazola is evident again in the gates and door of **County Hall** (*Kossuth utca 9*), where metal twists and turns and blooms into flowerbuds, where branches form a bower of justice, and the golden figures of Faith, Hope and Justice sit among dark stems. We also love the cuddly lions that hold the door knockers. The building itself was finished in 1756, based on the designs of Mátyás Gerl. Moving through to the courtyard, you'll reach the former Eger prison; today it houses the **Local History Museum** (covering Heves County and Eger between the 18th century and now) and the **Watersports Museum** (showing trophies won by the county's star swimmers and waterpolo players; *both museums adult/concessions 120/60Ft; open Apr 1– Oct 31 Tue–Sun 09.00–17.00*).

The former **Grand Provost's Palace** (*Kossuth Lajos utca 16*) now contains the county library; doubtless among its books is Kálmán Mikszáth's *A Strange Marriage*, which featured **Buttler House** (*Kossuth Lajos utca 26*) – now a decrepit building just beyond the bridge over the Eger Stream. A smidgen further, set back on the left, is a former 19th-century **Orthodox synagogue** now serving as a furniture outlet.

### Dobó István tér and the minaret

Bisected by a stream, the pleasingly asymmetrical Dobó István tér was the town's market square from the Middle Ages; in summer, bursting window boxes adorn the houses, and there's an unbroken murmur from customers seated at the cafés. The eponymous commander and defiant Eger hero (see pages 242–3) is remembered in **Alajos Stróbl's statue**, flanked by one of the local women who pitched in to assist in repulsing the attack. A second monument – *Soldiers of the Border Fortress* – is all movement and wild-eyed, gaping-mouthed stallions in its depiction of a fearless Hungarian assault on a pair of Turks.

The prime sight, though, is the twin-towered **Minorite church** (*Dobó István tér 4*), rated among the most handsome pieces of Baroque ecclesiastical architecture in Europe. It was designed by the Prague master Kilián Ignaz Dientzenhofer, and finished in 1767; the altarpiece showing St Anthony and the Virgin Mary is a cracker of a painting by the painter János Kracker. Look up also to the piggy-faced gargoyles running around the outside, with their double chins and sausagey lips. Near by is the **Palóc Folk Art Exhibition** (*Dobó István utca 12:* ❧ *36 312744; adult/concessions 140/70Ft; open Apr 1– Oct 31 Tue–Sun 09.00–17.00*), an ethnographic collection of Palóc ceramics and costumes.

A shortish distance to the north of Dobó tér is one of the lonely reminders of Turkish occupation in Eger – and Europe's northernmost remnant – a spindly sandstone finger in the middle of Knézich Károly utca. You can take a vertiginous and cramped climb up the 40m **minaret**'s 97 steps to a narrow viewing ledge (*adult 100Ft; open Apr 1–Oct 31 Tue–Sun 10.00–18.00*) – pity the 17th-century Muslim crier who had to do this five times a day in calling the faithful to prayer.

### The castle and around

From Dobó István tér, a steep cobbled lane brings you to **Eger Castle** (*Egri Vár; Vár 1;* ❧ *36 312744; grounds only adult/concessions 260/130Ft, grounds and Castle Museum adult/concessions 800/400Ft; grounds open daily Apr 1–Aug 31 08.00–20.00, Sep 1–30 08.00–19.00, Oct 1–31 08.00–18.00, Nov 1–Feb 28 08.00–17.00, Mar 1–31 08.00–18.00*), which is virtually synonymous in national consciousness with the heroic stand made against the Turks in 1552. It means István Dobó, it means 2,000 men seeing off a force of 80,000, it means women hurling boiling pitch from the ramparts, it means red wine or bull's blood to fortify wilting spirits (see page 243). The 13th-century castle – built in the aftermath of the Mongol invasion – had actually fallen into disrepair in the years leading up to this first siege, and it wasn't until after 1552 that Dobó properly set about strengthening and updating its fortifications. However, the Turks were unwilling to give up on a castle that they saw as strategically vital to the northern portion of the country, and successfully captured it 44 years later. In 1702, 15 years after the departure of the Ottomans, the castle was blown up by the Habsburgs.

The majority of the buildings now inside the walls are the result of modern reconstruction – the exception being the ruined foundations of the 11th-century **Romanesque cathedral** in the eastern section. The restored **Bishop's Palace** was originally built in Gothic style during the 1470s. The occupying Turks later used the ground floor as a prison, but the palace is now home to the **Dobó István Castle Museum** (*open Tue–Sun Nov 1–Feb 28 09.00–15.00, Mar 1–Oct 31 09.00–17.00; Heroes'*

*Hall open Mon only*), whose exhibitions include a history of the complex (complete with Turkish items), artefacts from villages of the region, the 'Heroes' Hall' (resting place of Dobó himself) and a collection of instruments of torture and execution. An **art gallery** near by in the courtyard displays works by Italian, Dutch and Austrian artists, as well as pieces by Mihály Munkácsy, while other attractions for which you'll need to pay extra are a **coinage** and a **waxworks** (featuring characters from Gárdonyi's *Eclipse of the Crescent Moon*; *adult/concessions 250/175Ft*) in the northwestern Föld Bastion.

The soft stone beneath Eger allowed the digging of a series of **underground passages** (*kazamaták*) that connected various parts of the castle and were used as storage rooms. Subterranean battles were intrinsic to the struggle for the castle. In 1552, Hungarian defenders watched peas on drums to detect the vibrations of Turkish picks as they attempted to tunnel beneath the walls. The Hungarians would then dig towards the sounds and detonate explosives to snuff out the invaders. You can visit a section of the system with a guide (*leaving from information desk within outer castle walls; open Mon only*).

On top of the southeastern Várkoch Bastion is the **grave of Géza Gárdonyi**, marked as he wished with the simple words 'Only his body lies here'. The writer lived in the town for his last 25 years; his house lies 50m to the north of the castle and now contains a **memorial museum** (*Gárdonyi utca 28;* \ *36 312744; adult/concessions 200/100Ft; open Tue–Sun Mar 1–Oct 31 09.00–17.00, Nov 1–Feb 28 09.00–15.00*). The 'hermit of Eger', as he became known, took two years to compose *Eclipse of the Crescent Moon* and did so with his windows boarded up and his doors stuffed with pillows to guarantee privacy and focus. His library, desk and a few writings (some in code) are on display. To the south of the castle complex in Dózsa György tér are the ruins of a **Turkish bath** (*Valide Szultána fürdő*), currently under a corrugated covering; it is hoped that this will eventually be reconstructed.

### Valley of the Beautiful Woman

At the end of an afternoon's sightseeing, take a 20-minute walk west along Király utca to Szépasszony-völgy – where there are 200 numbered wine cellars carved into the valley sides, looking like a series of dungeon cells. The name is intriguing. Some say it harks back to a goddess of love named Szépasszony to whom sacrifices were made in the valley; some say it refers to a particularly lovely lady who once ran a cellar here. We're not sure, but it could be because everybody looks beautiful after a few glasses of wine!

The mould-clad cellars were dug from the tufa centuries ago, and they remain at a constant temperature of 10–15°C. Cellars have variable hours, but generally there are some open at 10.00 and some still going at 20.00 or 21.00. Wine by the glass costs as little as 50Ft; it is also common to purchase by the refillable plastic bottle. There's an area for picnics or barbecues, and a couple of restaurants (see page 247). Dip into those caverns that take your fancy – but remember to dedicate your last drink to St John, protector of the vines.

If you don't want to walk to the valley, one of the motorised tourist trains runs there (see page 245); alternatively, a taxi should cost approximately 800Ft.

### Other

There is a cluster of places to take a dip. The pleasant **Eger Thermal Baths** (*Petőfi tér 2;* \ *36 412202; adult/concessions 700/500Ft; open May 1–Sep 30 Mon–Fri 06.00–19.30, Sat–Sun 08.00–19.00, Oct 1–Apr 31 daily 09.00–18.30*) is an area of open-air and adventure pools in the Archbishop's Garden; the mildly radioactive thermal water is said to ease rheumatic and locomotor disorders. Close by is a **Turkish Bath** (*Fürdő utca 1–3;* \ *36 413356; adult/concessions 700/500Ft; open Sat 14.00–18.00, Sun 08.00–18.00*), originally completed in 1617, and now a therapy centre based around its curative waters. It is only open to the public at weekends. (While few Turkish traces remain now, the bathing culture remained popular after their departure. In 1791, the mayor decreed that 'any persons found in the bath after ten o'clock by the city guards shall be given 24 lashes

## THE WINES OF EGER

Eager for some Eger plonk? Sniff and gargle your way around some of the following in the Valley of the Beautiful Woman:

**Egri Olasz Rizling** Light and dry white, with a fresh bouquet and sharp aftertaste

**Egri Leányka** Mild white – dry, semi-dry or semi-sweet – with a surprisingly rich aroma

**Egri Muskotály** Semi-sweet white

**Egri Chardonnay** Full-bodied, fruity and crisp white

**Egri Kéfrankos** A bright red that's subtle on the nose

**Egri Cabernet Sauvignon** Deep and dry red, with a strong, long-lasting aroma

**Egri Bikavér** The famous 'Bull's Blood', a dry, ruby red made from at least three grape types

with a stick in the market place.' We're assured the current authorities are more lenient...) The **Bitskey Aladár Indoor Swimming Pool** (*Frank Tivadar utca;* ☏ *36 511810; adult/concessions 550/330Ft; open Mon, Wed, Fri 06.00–21.00, Tue, Thu 06.00–22.00, Sat 08.00–20.00, Sun 08.00–18.00*) is an impressive modern structure containing an Olympic-sized pool.

The **Egedhegyi Lippizaner Horse Farm** (*Lipicai Lovastanya; Noszvaji út mellett;* ☏ *36 517937; www.matyusudvarhaz.hu; riding from 2,500Ft/hr, with trainer 4,500Ft/hr*) is 2km from Eger on the way towards Noszvaj (the bus from the centre stops outside). Its stables can cater for riders of all levels, and the farm also offers hunting, wine and cross-country programmes, as well as carriage driving. Board is available in the Mátyus Udvarház (*sgl €19, dbl €32*), which also has a restaurant.

### Festivals and events

Among the town's annual events are the Eger Spring Festival (featuring performances of contemporary art, folklore, theatre and ballet; *Mar 18–Apr 3*), Army Bands' Festival (brass and woodwind bands; *Jun*), Agria Summer Games (theatrical events; *Jun–Jul*), the Eger Wine Festival (a celebration of Bull's Blood, with food to accompany it, in Dobó István tér; *Jul 8–10*), the Castle Festival (medieval tournaments, battle re-enactments and processions, together with puppetry and other street performances; *Jul 15–24*), the Baroque Festival (three weeks of dance music and street activities; *late Jul/early Aug*), the Musical August Festival (concerts of jazz, popular and classical music; *Aug*), the Szépasszony-völgy Festival Mátra (wine, wine-songs competition and food; *Aug 20–22*), the Agria International Folk Festival (a convention of international folk-dance groups, who put on shows in the streets and squares; *Aug 25–28*) and the lively Eger Harvest Days (folkdancing, parades of floats and various wine-related events; *Sep*). The dates given are for 2005, and will change slightly from year to year.

### Egerszalók and Bogács

You'd be forgiven for double-taking on first seeing **Egerszalók's hot spring** (*Vörösmarty utca 14;* ☏ *36 515300; adult 350/400Ft before/after 18.00, concessions 200Ft; open daily 07.00–04.00*), and people lounging around icebergs in their bathing suits in the dead of a winter's night. The water emerges at 70°C (and is 20,000 years old), and contains calcium, sulphur, sulphide – and the salt whose deposits form the 'icebergs'. The minerals are certified as therapeutic, and useful in treating a range of ailments such as joint and bone disorders. A little beyond the spring is a nude bathing area. Apparently a new spa complex and bottling plant has opened around the spring.

It's just a 13-minute bus ride southeast from Eger to Egerszalók; buses leave regularly, passing through Egerszalók on their way to Kerecsend via Demjén. The spring itself is on the main road between Egerszalók and Demjén – follow the wooden signposts for the short walk from the road.

Southeast of Eger (and 10km north of Mezőkövesd), the village of **Bogács** is also popular for its **thermal baths** (*Dózsa György utca 16;* \ *49 534410;* e *bogacs-strand@axelero.hu; open daily Jun 1–Aug 31 09.00–20.00, May & Sep 09.00–19.00, Oct 1–Apr 30 09.00–17.00, closed Mon in winter*). There are seven outdoor thermal pools. Regular buses run from Mezőkövesd station on the Budapest–Miskolc railway line.

## Mezőkövesd
South of Bogács, Mezőkövesd is the capital of the 'Matyóföld' – where the Matyó people are responsible for Hungary's brightest and most vivid folk art. The settlement is defined by the floral-patterned needlework that its people have developed over the last 150 years, and which is renowned even beyond the national borders, while the protruding roofs of its houses – reminiscent of the Palóc style (see page 226) – also mark it out. It is thought that the ethnic group derived its name from that of Mátyás, the Renaissance monarch who conferred market status on the town. There's no point in staying here overnight when Eger is under 20km away.

### Getting there and away
Mezőkövesd is on the line from Miskolc to Budapest, and there are up to nine direct **trains** a day from Budapest Keleti or Kelenföld. Hatvan is also on this line; you'll need to change at Füzesabony if you're travelling from Debrecen or Eger. There are three direct **buses** a day from Budapest Stadion, the rest requiring a change at Eger. There are regular buses to Eger and Miskolc, and services to Debrecen (two), Gyöngyös (four) and Tiszafüred (five).

### Information
**Tourinform** Szent László tér 23; \ 49 500285; e mezokovesd@tourinform.hu; www.mezokovesd.hu. *Open Mon–Fri 10.00–16.00.*

### What to see and do
The **Matyó Museum** (*Szent László tér 20;* \ *49 311824; adult/concessions 250/175Ft; open Apr 15–Oct 15 Tue–Sun 09.00–16.00, Oct 16–Apr 14 by prior notice through Tourinform*) reveals the life, times and culture of the Matyó people. There are displays of coloured furniture, crockery, rich head gear and bell-shaped skirts. At the entrance is a bust of Bori Kis Jankó, the 'woman of a hundred roses' who founded a Matyó folkart school. The

### LIPIZZANERS
Contrary to popular belief, you can find the world-famous Lipizzaner horses (which were originally trained as nimble battle steeds) outside Vienna – indeed, they are bred at the Slovenian karst village of Lipica (meaning 'small linden tree' in Slovenian, and from where the horse's name derives), as well as in Hungary. The dazzling white coat comes with time; Lipizzaners are actually grey or black at birth, and gradually whiten with age – if you see a pure white, it is at least six years old. Aside from the beautiful colour, Lipizzaners are distinctive for their broad and muscular frame, reaching a height of over 2m, and for their graceful movement and thick manes. The

**Bori Kis Jankó Memorial House** (*Kis Jankó Bori Emlékház; Kis Jankó Bori utca 22;* ℄ *49 411873; adult/concessions 200/100Ft; open May 1–Oct 31 Tue–Sun 09.00–16.00*) shows some of her rosy embroidery in the 19th-century cottage in which she lived, and also provides an insight into the lifestyle of the area's peasant workers.

The **Agricultural Machine Museum** (*Eötvös utca 32;* ℄ *49 312820*) is an exhibition (indoor and out) of threshing equipment, tractors and other tools used by the farmers here, and focuses too on the work of local blacksmiths. **St László Church** (*Szent László tér 28; open daily Mar 21–Sep 21 08.00–16.30, Sep 22–Mar 20 08.00–15.30*), near the Matyó Museum, has a 15th-century Gothic sanctuary inside its primarily Baroque body. The frescoes were by István Takács, whose art adorns many churches around the country. In 1806, the Holy Crown spent a night in the parsonage, one among the numerous places it was hidden during its fugitive history.

## Bélapátfalva

Moving north from Eger – three-quarters of the way to Szilvásvárad – Bélapátfalva was named after the Bél clan. Its cement factory would usually make it a place to scurry past, but the **abbey church** was part of a monastery constructed by Cistercian monks in 1232 and, as such, is a rare surviving Romanesque building (with later Gothic additions). Most buses and trains running between Eger and Szilvásvárad stop at Bélapátfalva. The church is 2km east of the centre along Apátság utca; you may need to ask for the key (*kulcs*) at Rozsa Ferenc utca 42.

## Szilvásvárad

At the northwestern edge of the Bükk Hills, 30km from Eger, the area around Szilvásvárad has been inhabited since the Palaeolithic Age – evidence of ancient occupation was found in the cave at the foot of Istállóskő (itself the highest Bükk peak, at 958m). The village is now a focal point for the breeding of Lipizzaners, those snowy equine aristocrats. There are excellent indoor and outdoor equestrian arenas – where Prince Philip once competed in the '80s – and September sees the Lipizzaner Horse Festival, while each summer the national coach-riding championships are held here. The primary attraction, however, is the Szalajka Valley, one of the country's most captivating corners. Waterfalls and trout ponds dot its length, and you can visit them on foot or by boarding a wooden carriage of the narrow-gauge railway.

### Getting there and away

There are **bus** stops in the middle of the village, with between two and four daily buses going to Budapest and regular services to Eger (up until around 18.30 at weekends and 20.00 on weekdays). Among other destinations on the bus route are Gyöngyös (five a day), Parádfürdő and Mátrahaza (one), and the pretty village of Szarvaskő (regular). The village has two **train** stations (on the Füzesabony–Putnok line, which includes Eger and Egervár); the main one is 3km to the north but you are better to alight at Szilvásvárad-Szalkavölgy just under a kilometre to the southeast along Egri út. If coming from Budapest, you'll need to change at Füzesabony.

### Where to stay and eat

There's oodles of accommodation in Szilvásvárad – the only times you might struggle are during the horse festival or carriage championships.

**Fenyő** Szalajka-völgy út; ℄ 36 564015; www.restaurantguide.hu/fenyovendeglo. Like Lovas, this is a good 'un with friendly staff and local specialities. You can rent a private apt here too (from 1,600Ft/pp), and book a variety of programmes. *Mains 660–1,370Ft, avg 1,100Ft; open daily Apr 1–Oct 31 08.00–22.00, Nov 1–Mar 31 10.00–20.00.*

**Gasthaus Szilvásvárad** (9 rooms) Egri út; ☎ 36 355185. A modern guesthouse just outside the barrier marking the entrance to Szalajka Valley. The owner is a surly chap, but the rooms are tidy enough and the restaurant (*mains 1,000–1,500Ft, avg 1,000Ft; open Tue–Sun 07.00–22.00*) specialises in local game and trout. *Dbl 8,000Ft.*

**Hegyi Camping** Egri utca 36A; ☎ 36 355207; www.hegyicamping.com. This large site at the base of Kalapat Hill has log cabins, dorm rooms and tent-pitching space. You can also hire horses (*2,000Ft/hr*). *Cabin dbl 4,800Ft, triple 6,100Ft, room for 4 7,200Ft; tent/caravan 950/1,350Ft/pp; open Apr 15–Oct 15.*

**Lipicai Tourist House** (29 rooms) Egri út 12–14; ☎ 36 564036; e lipicaihotel@axelero.hu; www.szilvasvarad-lipicaihotel.hu. A hostel popular with student groups and consequently both lively and lacking in luxury. The rooms (sleeping 2–5), however, do have showers and TVs. There's a small restaurant attached, and the hotel can arrange excursions on foot, by horse or by jeep. *Rooms 3,900Ft/pp.*

**SZILVÁSVÁRAD**

**Lovas** Szalajka-völgy út; ☎ 36 355593; e gals@enternet.hu. We really enjoyed eating at Lovas, next to the open equestrian arena. It's deliberately quirky and atmospheric, with tables made from sewing machines, chairs topped with saddles and menus like newspapers. The restaurant organises tourist excursions – including truffle hunting and trout barbecuing in the valley, horse-riding and wine tasting. *Mains 790–2,680Ft, avg 1,500Ft.*

**Szalajka Fogadó** Egri út 2; ☎ 36 564020; e szalajka.fogado@axelero.hu. Shaded by trees at the bank of a little stream (300m north of the Lipicai), the recently renovated inn has a fountain bubbling at its entrance and contemporary rooms. Its restaurant is rather good; game and trout again feature prominently on the menu (*mains 1,000–2,400Ft, avg 1,500Ft*). *Sgl 9,000Ft, dbl 12,500Ft, triple 15,900Ft, apt (for two) 19,800Ft.*

**Szilvás Hotel** (40 rooms) Park utca 6; ☎ 36 355159; e reserve@hotelszilvas.hunguesthotels.hu; www.hunguesthotels.hu. Housed in the former Neo-Baroque Pallavicini Castle (designed by the prolific Miklós Ybl), the hotel's grand façade is let down by an interior that feels like a boarding school. Nevertheless, there are 40ha of beautiful grounds (containing further accommodation in bungalows). *Sgl €26–31, dbl €39–45.*

**Villanegra** (9 rooms) e villanegravendeghaz@axelero.hu. Real romance in the heart of the Szalajka Valley. The panzió is tastefully furnished and squeakily clean, and its rooms are of a reasonable size. It also has its own little restaurant (*mains 1,500–2,000Ft, avg 1,800Ft*). You'll find it well signposted along the walking trail once you've alighted from the narrow-gauge railway. *Dbl 14,500Ft.*

## What to see and do
### Szalajka Valley
The 5km valley itself is presaged by a road buzzing with places to eat and huts selling pottery and faux animal skins. The main walking trail can be picked up 300m south of

the entrance barrier. A path branching immediately to the left leads to the **Millennium Lookout Tower** (*adult/ concessions 200/150Ft; open Tue–Sun 09.00– 18.00*). There is also an **Adventure Forest** (*kalanderdő; adult/concessions 800/700Ft; open Jun 15–Aug 31 11.00–19.00 daily, Sep 1–Oct 15 11.00–19.00 weekends only*), a playground in the trees with rope bridges and high walkways, and a place to hire **bicycles** (*kerékpár; ⓑ 06 30 335 2695; 800Ft/hr, 2,000Ft/day*). Opposite that, however, is the Szalajka-völgy 6 station for the **narrow-gauge railway**, which operates between April 1 and October 31 and during the summer runs six daily trains on weekdays and nine at weekends and holidays. A ticket on the regular train costs 180/90Ft adult/concessions, while the nostalgia steam train is pricier at 360/270Ft. The journey in the open carriages is a real treat, weaving through leafy glades pierced by beams of sunlight and past trickling streams and still ponds. Alight at Szalajka Fátyolvízesés, from where it is a few minutes' walk further south to **Mount Istállóskő** and the **cave** at its base.

If you can, make the return trip under your own steam; the main trail back to Szilvásvárad takes you to a treasure of the Bükk – the **Fátyol Waterfall**, where the Szalajka stream cascades over 17m of staggered limestone shelves, throwing a veil (*fátyol*) of fine droplets into the air. The steps grow by a couple of millimetres a year as further lime is deposited. Further along (at the juncture with the start of the Horotna Valley) is the **Open-Air Forestry Museum** (*Szabadtéri Erdei Múzeum; open all year*), erected in the 1970s as a monument to the men who have lived and worked in the forests, and featuring wood carts, the slatted huts of lumbermen and shinglers, and lime and charcoal kilns. A wonderful cameo is a warning sign of 1834 that reads 'Do not fish, you villain!' Continue following the stream, with its eddying pools and quaint wooden bridges – past the Rock Spring (*Szikla-forrás*), a waterfall that emerges from underground caves (but can dry up in summer) – and after 20 minutes you will reach the indoor **Forestry Museum** (*Erdészeti Múzeum; for info, contact Egri út 16; ⓑ 36 355197; adult/concessions 170/100Ft; open Tue–Sun Jan 1–Apr 15 08.30–14.00, Apr 16–Apr 30 08.30–16.00, May 1–Sep 30 08.30–16.30, Oct 1–Oct 31 08.30–15.00, Nov 1–Dec 31 08.30–14.00*). Held in a 19th-century manor house that was once the headquarters of the mining authorities, the museum includes hunting knives and horns, a massive wild-boar pelt, forestry tools and documents (some dating back to the 18th century), and flora and fauna of the Mátra and the Bükk.

## Other sights

Staying with the nature theme for a while, in the village itself the **Orbán House** (*Miskolci út 58–60; ⓑ 36 355133; adult/concessions 200/150Ft; open Apr 1–Oct 31 Tue–Sun 09.00–17.00*) covers the creation and natural history of the Bükk. You can learn about Lipizzaners at the **Horse Museum** (*Lovas Múzeum; Park utca 8; open Apr–Oct Tue–Sun 09.00–12.00, 13.00–17.00, Nov–Dec weekends only*) – which also has coaches and a blacksmith's workshop – and ride them at the **Lippizaner Stud Farm** (*Lipicai Ménesgazdaság; Fenyves utca: ⓑ 36 355155; riding from 2,500Ft/hr*).

The **Prison Waxwork Museum** (*Panoptikum Börtön Múzeum; ⓑ 06 20 969 3017*), near the barrier entrance to the valley, is rather lightweight but entertaining nevertheless. Among its exhibits are shame masks (used to ridicule prisoners) and stocks. There is also a record of the fees earned by 17th-century executioners – 1Ft for torture, 18Ft for the burial of hanging victims and 24Ft for impalement or quartering. Criminals paid a high price, it seems.

Fatelep station

Halastó station · Forestry Museum

Fátyol vízesés station

Open-Air Forestry Museum · Fátyol waterfall · Szalajka stream

Mount Istállóskő Cave

## SOME WILDLIFE OF THE SZALAJKA VALLEY

The **common alder** (*Alnetum glutinosae-incanae*), which thrives in the alluvial deposits at the edges of streams, is the valley's dominant tree species; its cones grow in bunched groups, while in spring catkins appear. The shallower valley sides also harbour willows, particularly the **white willow** (*Salix alba*). Spring sees the valley's damper areas blanketed with the **common marsh marigold** (*Caltha palustris*), also known as the 'kingcup', its five petals flowering between March and August. There are many species of **fern** among the alder groves, along with the **butterbur** (*Petasites hybridus*), which flowers between March and May and whose roots were once used to treat the plague.

The fauna is typified by wet-loving species. The **common brown trout** (*Salmo trutta fario*) is as wet as you can get in the streams, and is also reared in artificial ponds. The creeks – fed by karstic springs – shelter species that are sensitive to environmental change. Here are **snails** (like the endemic *Sadleriana pannonica*), **sand-hoppers** (which are found under pebbles and leap about when disturbed), **bloodworms** (larvae of the midge family *Chironomidae*, which degrade organic material in the water), **may flies** (*Ephemeroptera*, fans of fresh flowing water during their notoriously short lives), **beetles** (like rhynchites, plant beetles), **dragon flies, caddis flies, caperers** and **lace wings**. Amphibians such as **salamander, common brown frog** (*Rana temporaria*) and **brown toad** (*Bufo bufo*) enjoy the ponds and creek overflows in spring. **Water rats** hunt the waterside butterbur meadows.

The **wood warbler** (*Phylloscopus sibilatrix*) is common to deciduous forests; it has a yellow throat and eye stripe, but is small and difficult to see – listen out for its hissing song. The **robin** (*Erithacus rubecula*), a red-breasted and sparrow-sized bird found all over Europe, nests in scrubby forest. The **grey wagtail** (*Motacilla cinerea*) is never found far from water, and favours brooks and mountain streams. It is unfortunately decreasing in number. The distinctive **dipper** (*Cinclus cinclus*) – dark, dark brown, with a bright-white belly – is common in much of Europe. In Hungary, however, its population fell to under ten pairs, and a couple of these nest in the Szalajka Valley. Dippers have an unusual feeding method – they run along the bed of the brook, catching snails, crayfish and insect larve. The **blue tit** (*Parus caeruleus*) nests in hollow trees.

The **Calvinist Church** (*Aradi utca 30*), dominating the northern end of the village, was built in 1840 by József Hild; it is Neoclassical, with a domed roof and Doric columns. One of the bells in the 17th-century belfry dates to 1488.

### Lillafüred

Pack your Toblerones and fondue forks, for Sándor Petőfi wrote in his *Travel Letters* of 1847 that Lillafüred was as 'nice a place as Switzerland'. When Count András Bethlen, the agriculture minister, stumbled across it while hunting in 1892, he was so enchanted that he dedicated it to his wife, Lilla Vay. It's certainly romantic; mist hangs in the early morning, and flashing thunderstorms illuminate the hills on May evenings. The diminutive resort lies on the eastern edge of the Bükk Hills (and is an excellent base for hiking), at the meeting point of the Szinva and Garadna valleys on the shore of Hámori-tó. It is said that when they were forbidden from marrying, a mill-owner's daughter and her mill-hand lover threw themselves from the white limestone Molnár-szikla – a couple of kilometres east of the lake – into the Szinva ravine. Miskolc is 10km – and a world – away.

## Getting there and away

You can take the **bus** (numbers 5 or 15) to Lillafüred from Diósgyőr Villamos in the western portion of Miskolc; get to Diósgyőr by taking bus or tram 1 from Tiszai railway station. More enjoyable though is the **narrow-gauge railway**, which stops at Lillafüred on its journey between Kilián-Észak (in western Miskolc) and Garadna stations; on the way you'll cross the country's highest narrow-gauge viaduct. There are at least four a day between May and September (fewer during other months; *adult/concessions 200/170Ft*). Be wary not to board one of the infrequent weekend services that branch north at Papírgyár to Taksalápa.

## Information

**Lillafüred Foundation** Erzsébet sétány 69; ↘ 46 403 387; e foldshe@gold.uni-miskolc.hu. A small organisation that helps to promote tourism in the area, and can provide information. Alternatively head for the Tourinform in Miskolc.

## Where to stay and eat

**Lillafüred Camping** Erzsébet sétány 39; ↘ 46 333146; e kovatt@freemail.hu; www.extra.webzona.hu. Further south from the Ózon along the same road to Eger. The amenities are not top class, but the setting is perfect. Tents and caravans only. *Adult/concessions 800/500Ft, tent/caravan/motorhome 500/700/1,200Ft.*

**Ózon Panzió** (19 rooms) Erzsébet sétány 19; ↘ 46 532594; e ozon_panzio@axelero.hu; www.hotels.hu/ozon_lillafured. Large pension a short distance further up the hill from the railway station. Set in pleasant grounds, it is comfortable but unexciting. *Sgl 5,200Ft, dbl from 11,000Ft, triple from 13,500Ft (rooms with balcony are more).*

**Palota Hotel** (129 rooms) Erzsébet sétány 1; ↘ 46 331411; e reserve@hotelpalota.hunguesthotels.hu; www.hunguesthotels.hu. This former Neo-Renaissance castle of the 1920s is the resort's focal point, and undoubtedly rules the roost. Surrounded by a hanging garden and a large park, the best of the rooms offer views of the Szinva Stream and Hámori-to. Among the facilities are a fitness centre, swimming pool and bowling lanes. Of the three restaurants, the Mátyás (*open daily 08.00–24.00*) is the swankiest, with its stained lead-glass windows; however, we felt it was over-priced and its international fare no better-tasting than the cheaper Tókert. *Sgl 16,800–19,500Ft, dbl 19,400–24,000Ft, suites 27,000–31,000Ft.*

**Tókert Panzió** (8 rooms) Erzsébet sétány 3; ↘ 46 533560; e tokert@tokert.hu; www.tokert.hu. Next to the Palota, and with good-sized rooms. The restaurant's elevated eating area outside is bedecked with fairy lights, and provides a pretty space from which to watch the resort below; inside it is too brightly lit and its staff unsmiling (*mains avg 1,500Ft; open daily 07.00–23.00*). *Sgl 10,100Ft, dbl 11,900Ft.*

Stalls near the narrow-gauge station sell fast and fatty **snacks**.

## What to see and do

The area's prime attraction is the limestone stalactite cave system. A large number of Ice-Age flint tools and laurel-shaped spearheads were discovered in **Szeleta Cave**, but this isn't open to the public. Head instead for **Anna Cave** (↘ 46 370239; open Apr 15–Oct 15 daily 10.00–15.00), whose entrance can be found near the **Szinva Stream waterfall** in the park surrounding the same hotel. Follow the rumbling sound of the water as it tumbles from a height of 20m. The travertine formations show the imprints of mosses, pine needles, roots and grasses that became covered with deposits of freshwater limestone 40,000 years ago.

Around 400m south of the station, **Szent István Dripstone Cave** (↘ 46 334130; open daily Apr 15–Oct 15 09.00–16.00, rest of year 09.00–15.00; adult/concessions 500/300Ft) is one of the biggest and deepest in the region – its passages reach for 700m, of which 170m are accessible. The cave came to light when an unfortunate dog fell through an opening. The chambers hold a variety of stalactite formations. Both caves are managed by the Bükk National Park Directorate; guides run tours of each on the hour.

The **Herman Ottó Memorial House** (*Erzsébet sétány 33;* ℘ *46 370703; adult 250Ft; open Tue–Sun 10.00–16.00*) was the villa of the naturalist who revealed in the late 19th century that the caves around Miskolc had been inhabited by prehistoric man. His collections of Bükk flora and fauna are on display.

The 1.5km-long **Hámori-to** (Foundry Lake) came to be when Henrik Fazola built a sluice dam at the juncture of the Garadna and Szinva streams in the early 19th century to power the ironworks of Hámor. In summer you can hire rowing boats (*350Ft/30 mins*) or pedalos (*300Ft/30 mins*).

There are several marked **hiking trails**, a couple following the Szinva and Garadna valleys, others snaking through the surrounding hills; plan any walk carefully (and take a good map), however, because the forest can be dense and there are few alternative settlements in which to seek refuge should the weather turn or the night fall. One possible excursion is to the **ancient foundry** (*őskohó*), 4km west at Újmassa. Henrik Fazola originally established a furnace in the 1770s to produce crude iron for processing at the Hámor ironworks; his son Frigyes later expanded it, and there's now an adjacent museum (℘ *46 370864; open Apr 15–Oct 15 Tue–Sun 09.00–16.30*). Follow the blue-cross trail from the Palota Hotel around Hámori-to and then along the Garadna Valley.

Further west, Bánkút holds a **ski centre** with seven pistes running down the Borovnyák and Bálvány peaks, the longest of which is 1,500m. There is accommodation and ski hire; for further information, contact the Bánkút Ski Centre on 46 390135. If you don't have a car, follow the S+ (yellow cross) trail markings for 4.6km from Ómassa (bus 15 runs from Miskolc to the latter).

## Miskolc

Miskolc has nearly 200,000 residents, and is Hungary's third-largest city. There are 14,000 students at the country's biggest university, and the city also claims the nation's earliest stone-built theatre (of 1823) and the first public tramline (of 1897). However vigorously it wags such statistics, though, this is a practical rather than a pretty city. Rising, green tower blocks and defunct factory buildings – hulking relics of the heavy industry that thrived here until its collapse in the 1990s – offer a drab welcome. There are some good restaurants, coffee shops and bars, together with a sprinkling of Eclectic, Neo-Renaissance and Baroque architecture, but generally it will struggle to capture your heart. Rather it is a functional gateway to Lillafüred and the hills of the Bükk National Park, and the caves at Aggtelek.

The Miskóc tribe settled here in the 11th century, but the industrialisation began in 1770 with the arrival of Henrik Fazola and the iron furnace he constructed in Ómassa (see above). Flame and then flood devastated the city in the 19th century, after which it all had to be put back together again.

### Getting there, away and around

The main, renovated **railway station** (Miskolc Tiszai) is to the southeast on Kandó Kálmán tér; outside is the terminus for trams 1 and 2, which run into the centre and on as far as Diósgyőr. There is a second, smaller station (named Gömöri) – board a bus to the centre from nearby Zsolcai kapu. There are up to 19 daily trains direct from Budapest Keleti to Miskolc Tiszai. Miskolc is also on a line running to Nyíregyháza (16) that passes through Tokaj and Szerencs on its way, and less frequently continues to Debrecen (three; if there's no direct train, pick up a connection at Nyíregyháza). Change at Nyíregyháza for services to Nyírbátor. A fork at Mezőzombor leads up to Sárospatak and Sátoraljaújhely (12). There are up to eight trains a day to Aggtelek on a line branching

MISKOLC

Népkert, Vigadó, Café du Boucher, Lévay Villa Panzió, City Hotel Miskolc, Toscana Art Café

northeast. As for international services, some trains on the line to Hidasnémeti continue over the border to Kosice (three direct) in Slovakia, and there's a daily train to Kraków. Change at Nyíregyháza for Kiev and Moscow. There are two trains a day to Oradea in Romania, with a change at Püspökladány.

The intercity **bus station** is on Búza tér, within walking distance to the east of the centre. There are no direct buses to/from Budapest, and instead you must travel via Eger or Ózd. There are up to 19 a day to Eger (taking about 1½ hours), Debrecen (23), Mezőkövesd (half-hourly), Nyíregyháza (two on weekdays, one on Sat), Szerencs (up to 11) and Sátoraljaújhely (one daily, except Sun).

You can catch a **narrow-gauge railway** (*Dorottya utca 1;* ✆ *46 379086*) to Lillafüred from Kilián-Észak to the west of the city, near Diósgyőr (accessible by bus or tram 1); for further information, see page 258. For **taxis**, try DH Taxi (✆ *46 323323*) or Klima (✆ *46 333444*).

## Information and other practicalities
**Bükk National Park Directorate** Árpád utca 90; ✆ 46 334104
**Co-op Tourist** Széchenyi út 14; ✆ 46 328812; e outgoing@cooptourist.hu. Can provide assistance with tours, accommodation and train tickets. *Open Mon–Fri 09.00–17.00, Sat 10.00–12.30.*
**Forestry Directorate Building** Deák tér 1; ✆ 46 501526; e info@eszakerdo.hu. Information on the nature of the surrounding area, based in a lovely Neo-Renaissance building that is worth a look in its own right.
**Ibusz** Széchenyi út 15; ✆ 46 508211. Accessed via a courtyard; help with private accommodation and tours, and can exchange travellers' cheques. *Open Mon–Thu 08.00–16.30, Fri 08.00–14.00.*
**Listings magazine** *Miskolci Est*

**Netgate Internet Café** Déryne utca 18; ↘ 46 505832. It's well disguised from the outside – walk through the wooden doors and to the back to gain access. Internet is available for 150Ft/30 mins. *Open Mon–Fri 09.00–17.00.*

**Tourinform** Városház tér 13; ↘ 46 350425; e miskolc@tourinform.hu. A friendly and helpful office; there's a touch-screen information machine inside offering details of transport timetables etc. *Open Jun 15–Sep 15 Mon–Fri 09.00–19.00, Sat–Sun 09.00–18.00, rest of year Mon–Fri 09.00–17.00, Sat 09.00–13.00.* There is also a Borsod County Tourinform office (*Széchenyi utca 35;* ↘ *46 508773*).

Beyond the smaller **shops** on Széchenyi út, the swanky **Miskolc Plaza** (*Szentpáli utca 2–6;* ↘ *46 504002; open Mon–Sat 09.00–21.00, Sun 09.00–19.00*) is a modern precinct within easy reach. Alternatively there is an indoor and outdoor **market** behind Búza tér, selling snacks, fruit and veg among the diesel fumes from the bus station.

## Where to stay
There is but a limited choice of accommodation, much of it at the budget end of the spectrum. It is worth throwing the pensions at Miskolc-Tapolca (see page 265) into the mix before making your decision.

**City Hotel Miskolc** (23 rooms) Csabai kapu 6; ↘ 46 555100; e hotelmiskolc@chello.hu. An ugly outer shell masks spacious and pleasant rooms, together with a bubbling, glass-roofed jacuzzi. *Sgl 15,200Ft, dbl 20,300Ft, suite 24,400Ft.*

**Hámor Holiday Hotel and Camping** Miskolc-Alsóhámor, Szeleta utca 12–14; ↘ 46 531130; www.harmorholiday.hu. The village of Alsóhámor is 15km from the centre, overlooking the Szinva Stream a short distance north of Lillafüred, and as such is a convenient and picturesque base both for the city and for Bükk walks. The site is superb, with a hotel and apts alongside the camping options; among the facilities are a restaurant, sauna, gym, open-air swimming pool, solarium, snooker room and bar. The hotel has 21 comfortable but kitsch rooms, while there are 15 apts. *Hotel sgl/dbl 13,000/16,500Ft, apt (for 3) 24,000Ft; tent/caravan 1,400/2,500Ft, plus 700Ft/pp.*

**Hotel Pannonia** (34 rooms) Kossuth Lajos utca 2; ↘ 46 504980. Slap in the city centre, the Pannonia has compact rooms (with bath or shower) painted in burgundy, 2 restaurants and a set of 7 apts (each with kitchen) in a separate building 100m away. *Sgl 16,100Ft, dbl 18,000Ft, apt (for 2) 21,600Ft; b/fast 1,300Ft.*

**Központi Leány College** Palóczy László utca 1; ↘ 46 341871. College dormitories, holding 6 to a room; limited capacity outside summer. *Beds 300–1,600Ft (discounts with student card).*

**Lévay Villa Panzió** (21 rooms) Lévay József utca 13; ↘ 46 500890; e levayvilla@axelero.hu; www.hotels.hu/levayvilla. In a greenish suburb just south of the Népkert public garden (bus 31 stops outside), the Lévay combines the looks of an early-20th-century villa with freshly furnished rooms. Among the facilities are a sauna, fitness room and cold plunge pool, while 2 Finnish saunas were in the pipeline when we visited. Recommended. *Sgl 12,900Ft, dbl 19,900Ft, suite (for 2) 24,900Ft.*

**MÁV Hotel** Kandó Kálmán tér 1–2; ↘ 46 356559. Spartan hostel for workers or tourists with light wallets – the latter are actually charged slightly more than their Hungarian counterparts. As you'd expect, there are no en-suite facilities, but the place is clean. In the same square as the Miskolc Tiszai railway station. *Costs 1,300–1,800Ft/pp (excl tourist tax).*

• **Petőfi Sándor College** Bajcsy-Zsilinsky út 33; ↘ 46 381042. Rock-bottom prices for basic student rooms holding up to 6 people. There is only limited availability outside summer months. The college is a fair distance from the centre – trams 1 and 2 run along its road. *Beds 800–1,500Ft.*

**Székelykert Panzió** Földes Ferenc út 4; ↘ 46 411222. This guesthouse is a short walk from the main area, and as such the prices are reasonable; expect the rooms to be on the old-fashioned and fusty side. Perhaps more notable for its restaurant (see page 262) than its accommodation. *Dbl 7,000Ft, triple 9,000Ft.*

## Where to eat and drink

**Alabárdos** Kisavas, Első sor 15; ☎ 46 412215. On the road leading up to Avas Hill, Alabárdos has both a brick-floored beer hall and a wine cellar. The décor in the medieval-theme restaurant is pleasingly understated, and there's an open fireplace in the centre of the room. One of the city's oldest restaurants, it is also one of the better places to chow down; good-quality traditional food is served on Herend crockery, and the final preparatory flourishes to the dishes are made at the table. Commendable wine list. *Mains 1,200–2,600Ft, avg 2,000Ft; restaurant open 18.00–24.00 daily, beer hall 16.00–24.00 daily.*

**Café & Bar Vian** Széchenyi út 38; ☎ 46 413934. There's a lively, if smoky, atmosphere in this modern bar. You'll find it through a courtyard and at the top of some winding concrete steps. *Open 11.00–23.00 daily.*

**Café Big Ben** Kossuth Lajos utca 8 ☎ 46 351311. Just to the north of Hotel Pannonia, Café Big Ben is reminiscent of a homely dining room; there's also a pretty covered area outside, with hanging plants. International menu, including 'English-themed' dishes like King Henry VIII's favourite (which apparently was turkey with broccoli, ham and cheese). Excellent atmosphere and value, and also a good bar. *Mains 600–1,500Ft, avg 1,000Ft; open 11.00–23.00 daily.*

**Café du Boucher** Görgey Artúr utca 42; ☎ 46 432320. The first in the international 'Belgian Beer Café' chain to open in Hungary has Belgian beer and Flemish, Walloon and Hungarian delicacies. The food is pricey, but high quality. *Mains 1,750–4,330Ft, avg 2,500Ft; open Mon–Thu 11.00–24.00, Fri–Sat 11.00–01.00.*

**Gösser** Déryné utca 7; ☎ 46 505045. Southwest of Hősök tere, Gösser's pizzeria looks like a playschool, with its bright-yellow booths. Tasty pizzas are the order of the day, available to eat in or take away. There's also a duller-looking restaurant, and rooms in the panzió. *Pizzas 480–1,000Ft, avg 700Ft; open 12.00–22.00 daily.*

**Rákóczi Pince** Rákóczi utca 23; ☎ 46 343916. Like a familiar pair of slippers, this cellar-style restaurant is comfy and reliable without courting excitement. Specialities on a menu of Hungarian and Bavarian dishes include catfish and carp. There's a bar at its top end. *Mains 990–1,800Ft, avg 1,400Ft; open 11.00–22.00 daily.*

**Székelykert** See page 261. A classy little restaurant – attached to the panzió – that successfully blends relaxed, peasant styling with a hint of luxury. The varied menu features very good Székely and Borsod dishes; the management are justly proud of their jaunty gypsy players. *Mains 880–2,200Ft, avg 1,400Ft; open 11.00–23.00 daily.*

**Toscana Art Café** Csabai kapu 26; ☎ 46 432232. Toscana is a nice little find, and worth a trot south of the centre. Its inviting interior is decorated with sketched paintings of the hilly countryside and odd plaster mouldings representing rocky outcrops. Outside are thatched booths. A daunting selection of food includes pizzas, pastas and steaks. Buses 2, 22, 12, 39 and 33 run along this road. *Mains 490–3,000Ft, avg 1,400Ft; open Mon–Thu 10.00–23.00, Fri 10.00–24.00, Sat 11.00–24.00, Sun 11.00–22.00.*

**Vigadó** Görgey Artúr utca 23; ☎ 46 358845; www.miwo.hu/vigado. Standing in Népkert, Vigadó is big but graceful, with Biedermeier furnishings and a late-19th-century building. One of the city's premier restaurants. There's also a beer cellar. *Open 11.00–23.00 daily.*

## Entertainment and nightlife

**Miskolc National Theatre** (*Miskolci Nemzeti Színház; Déryné utca 1;* ☎ *46 344711; www.olh.hu/szinhaz*) was Hungary's first permanent playhouse – erected in 1823 – and the first to perform drama in the Hungarian language. Unfortunately it was destroyed by fire in 1843 (learn more in the Theatre Museum; see opposite); parts of the theatre that replaced it in 1857 are incorporated into the current Neoclassical structure that was resurrected in the 1990s. Today there are plays, musicals and concerts by ensembles such as the Miskolc Symphonic Orchestra and the National Philharmonic. The ticket office is next door (*Széchenyi utca 23;* ☎ *46 344864; open Mon–Fri 10.00–19.00, Sat–Sun 15.00–19.00*).

The **Rónai Cultural Centre** (*Mindszent tér 3;* ✆ *46 342408*) hosts concerts and other productions, while you can catch a blockbuster at the **Hollywood Multiplex Szinvapark** (*Bajcsy-Zsilinszky út 2–4;* ✆ *46 502700; www.hmpix.hu*).

**John Bull Pub** (*Hunyadi utca 3;* ✆ *46 350524; open Sun–Thu 11.00–24.00, Fri–Sat 11.00–03.00*) has an English theme and is popular with the city's youth. If you prefer Ireland, **Shannon Pub** (*Széchenyi István út 54;* ✆ *46 413904; open Mon–Sat 10.00–22.00*) has flat Guinness, fiddle music and a 'fresco' of the emerald isle. Pots of crayons allow you to doodle on the paper table cloths. There are hearty plates of stew, fish and sandwiches for the peckish (*mains 1,300–2,000Ft, avg 1,500Ft*).

The super **Liky Pera** (*Széchenyi út 94;* ✆ *30 2061244; open Mon–Thu 10.00–22.00, Fri–Sat 11.00–01.00, Sun 16.00–22.00*) is trendy and chilled, spreading itself over three floors, and serving coffee and alcohol among ferns, wicker and sofa chairs. Located opposite the Szinva Park Shopping Centre. **Club Havana** (*Városház tér 3;* ✆ *46 344872; open Mon–Sat 08.00–22.00, Sun 12.00–21.00*) is a relaxed and intimate bar; funk, jazz and blues fill the air, and a younger crowd lounge under the low lighting. There is an enticing selection of cocktails to get your night rolling at **Rock Café** (*Papszer út 48;* ✆ *46 348264*), together with a dance floor and pool tables.

Sister bar of the Havana, the basement-based **Manana Club** (*Hunyadi utca 5;* ✆ *46 411190; open Tue–Sat 06.00–02.00*) scorns music of the techno variety, preferring the more sophisticated sounds of club, funk, Latino and jazz. There is a plethora of cocktails, and a trendy, contemporary crowd. You'll need to pay a small fee to sit in the courtyard, where there are parties in summer. To access the club, pass through an archway and descend some steps at the rear of the building.

## What to see and do

Széchenyi út is the city's main thoroughfare, running horizontally through its belly and hoarding several pretty residences in Baroque and Neoclassical styles. The National Theatre (see opposite) stands at the junction with Déryné utca, while beside it is the **Museum of Theatre and Acting** (*Színháztörténeti és Színészmúzeum; Déryné utca 3;* ✆ *46 327900; adult/concessions 120/60Ft; open Tue–Sat 09.00–17.00*). As well as an exhibition of costumes and playbills, there are drawings of the original theatre and photographs of Róza Déryné, the popular actress who performed many times in Miskolc during the early 19th century. There's also a stage lighting machine from England, used between 1959 and 1990. The explanatory notes are in Hungarian.

Further west along Széchenyi út is an 18th-century passage known as the **Dark Gate** (*Sötét kapu*) that leads to Rákóczi utca. Since 1996, Rákóczi-ház has held the **Miskolc Gallery of Fine Arts** (*Városi Művészeti Múzeum; Rákóczi utca 2;* ✆ *46 500680;* e *galeria@mail.olh.hu; open Tue–Sun Jun 1–Sep 30 10.00–18.00, Oct 1–May 31 09.00–17.00*) – with its permanent and temporary collections of modern fine, applied and photographic art – but much earlier the 17th-century Baroque mansion was home to Prince Rákóczi. There are further art exhibitions in the **Feledy-ház** (*Deák Ferenc tér 3;* ✆ *46 355472; adult/concessions 112/56Ft; open Tue–Sat 09.00–16.30*), presenting the life work of Hungarian graphic artist Gyula Feledy, and the **Petró-ház** (*Hunyadi utca 12;* ✆ *46 355472; adult/concessions 120/60Ft; open Tue–Sat 09.00–17.00*), former abode of the doctor Sándor Petró where you'll find photos, reliefs and other pieces by painter Lajos Szalay (1909–95)

A short distance to the west of the Dark Gate is **Erzsébet tér**, with its bathhouse and assured statue of Lajos Kossuth. It opens into **Városház tér**; the 18th-century County Hall (*no 1*) is dressed in yellow, while the peach-coloured town hall (*no 8*) is a favourite venue for musical concerts.

The **Herman Ottó Museum** (*Papszer utca 1;* ✆ *46 346875; www.hermuz.hu; adult/concessions 400/200Ft, discount on Sat; open Tue–Sun 10.00–16.00*) occupies a former school building dating to the 15th century. There's a statue of Herman Ottó the scientist outside, with his short calves and slight paunchiness, while inside is an exhibition of rocks and minerals, archaeological finds dating as far back as the Magyar arrival, and a display of some masterpieces from the Petró collection (see page 263). A second building (*Görgey Artúr utca 28;* \ *46 560170*) stages temporary exhibitions.

From Papszer utca, some steps lead up to the late-Gothic **Avas Calvinist Church** (*Papszer utca 14;* \ *46 358677 to arrange visit; open Mon–Sun 14.00–17.00*), built after the Turks levelled a 13th-century church on the site in 1544. There is a beautiful painted and coffered ceiling that was added in the 1700s, and outside is an elegant 16th-century **belfry**, constructed from wood and stone and topped with a steep-tiled 'wizard's hat' of a roof. Gravestones crowd in upon the church and add to a sense of Gothic mystery. Push on up Avas Hill along a zig-zagging cobbled path to a **TV tower** and glass-enclosed viewing gallery; its coffee shop (*open 10.00–22.00 daily*) can slake parched throats. The hill is also notable for the many **wine cellars** lining its narrow streets.

In the area north of Széchenyi út are several houses of worship that testify to the Jewish and Greek communities that once thrived here. The **Orthodox synagogue** (*Kazinczy utca 7*) is a sparrow-brown lump of a building that has seen better days; its Neo-Romanesque and Moorish design was the work of Ludwig Förster, but the Jewish population can no longer fill its three-aisled interior after being decimated during the deportations of World War II. Overlooking it is the Baroque **Minorite church and monastery** (*Hősök tere 5*) of 1740, with two towers, vast frescoed ceilings, a Rococo pulpit and attractive iron doors added in 2000.

To the west in Deák Ferenc tér is the Calvinist '**Cockerel Church**' (*Kakas templom*), so-named after the bird perched on its steeple. The 18th-century **Hungarian Orthodox church** (*Deák Ferenc tér 7*) behind the Minorite church was built by the offspring of Greek merchants who set up home here after fleeing the Turks. The gem-studded Mount Athos Cross was brought by the original settlers. Also inside is one of central Europe's biggest iconostases; its 88 painted panels were crafted in 1793, and make up a whole that measures 16m in height. The icon known as the 'Black Mary of Kazan' was a gift from the Russian Tsarina Catherine II ('the Great'). In front of the church is the **Hungarian Orthodox Ecclesiastical Museum** (*Magyar Orthodox Egyházi Múzeum;* \ *46 415441; adult/concessions 100/80Ft; open Tue–Sun Nov 1–Mar 31 10.00–16.00, Apr 1– Oct 31 10.00–18.00*), whose books and manuscripts chart both the assimilation of the Greeks into Miskolc society and the Byzantine traditions they brought from the Balkans. The highlight is the 'Good-Friday grave pall', embroidered in Vienna in 1760.

The **Church of Planks** (*Deska templom;* \ *46 506613 to visit*) looks over Petőfi tér, an asymmetrical and angular wooden Calvinist church that dates to 1938 but had to be reconstructed following a fire in 1997. It emulates the Transylvanian style, and has floral, swirling patterns cut and painted into its wood.

## Further out
### Diósgyőr Castle
Eight kilometres west of the centre, Diósgyőr Castle (*Miskolc-Diósgyőr, Vár utca 24;* \ *46 533355; www.diosgyorivar.com; adult/concessions 600/250Ft; open daily May 1–Sep 30 09.00–19.00, Oct 1–Apr 30 10.00–16.00*) stands on a hill by the Szinva Stream. The scribe Anonymus – writing during the reign of Béla III in the late 12th and early 13th centuries – documented a structure here, but the current castle came into being between 1342 and 1382 under Lajos I. It was used as a residence by several kings and queens before stagnating after damage in the early 18th century. Restoration during the 20th century lacked finesse. Today there are several permanent exhibitions here, including a selection of medieval weaponry, a minting press and some waxworks. The northeast tower offers grand views, while in summer there are a series of open-air concerts, theatre productions and games (programme of events on the website). The nearby **lido** (*Vár utca 1;* \ *46*

*379146; open May–Sep 09.00–18.00 daily*) has a hot sauna and a cold rock plunge-pool. Buses 1, 101 and 101B and tram 1 run out here from Miskolc. If you need a bite, the terrace of the nearby **Talizmán** (*Vár utca 14;* \ *46 378627; open 12.00–22.00 daily*) is very pleasant, and the local cuisine good; it also offers accommodation.

## Miskolc-Tapolca

Bus 2 from Miskolc journeys 7km southward to the quaint resort of Miskolc-Tapolca, whose waters have been used in cures since the 16th century. The **Cave Bath** (*Barlangfürdő; Miskolc-Tapolca, Pazár István sétány;* \ *46 304128; www.barlangfurdo.hu; day pass adult/concessions 1,600/900Ft; open daily summer 09.00–19.00, winter 09.00–18.00, closed Jan*) consists of a series of pools in a natural cave system. The water temperature ranges between 27 and 31°C, there's a waterfall or 'thrashing shower', and the humid air is reputedly good for bronchial complaints. Massages and other treatments are available, and there are cooler pools and sun terraces outside. In addition, the town's park holds a lively **lido** (*Miskolctapolcai utca 1;* \ *46 368127; open May 1–Sep 30 daily 09.00–18.00*), complete with separate pools for the kiddies, and a lake on which you can go **boating** (*boat hire May 1–Sep 30 daily 10.00–16.00; 800Ft/30 mins*). If you fancy a decent stretch, there is a walking trail (marked by a yellow square with a blue diagonal line) from the Cave Bath entrance to Diósgyőr Castle; it will take a little over two hours.

There is no shortage of accommodation in Miskolc-Tapolca. **Hotel Kolibri** (*Fecske út 15–17;* \ *46 555010;* e *hotelkolibri@hu.inter.net; www.hotelkolibri.hu; 9 rooms*) is well kept, and has a swimming pool and pleasing views. There's wood galore at the quirky-looking **Tapolca** (*Csabai út 36;* \ *46 562215;* e *tapolcafogado@chello.hu; www.tapolca-fogado.freeweb.hu; dbl 8,000Ft, apt 12,000Ft*). **Park Hotel** (*Csabai út 35;* \ *46 360811; 70 rooms*) is less characterful but quite adequate. **Bástya** (*Miskolctapolcai út 2;* \ *46 369154;* e *bastyahotel@axelero.hu; www.bokik.hu/bastya; 16 rooms*) is a decent pension 100m from the lido. Campers should head for **Éden** (*Károlyi Mihály utca 1;* \ *46 561510;* e *botour@elender.hu; www.kemping.hu/eden*), which also has 28 bungalows.

## Festivals and events

The main programme of events takes place during Miskolc Summer (Miskolci Nyár). Among these are the Bartók and International Opera Festival (*mid Jun*; top European performers, inc soloists from the Scala and Bolshoi); the Borsodi Fonó International Folk Festival (*end Jun*); Kaláka International Festival of Folk Music (*start Jul*; folk performances at the Diósgyőr Castle); and the Diósgyőr Revels (*mid Aug*; a range of events culminating in a feast for 5,000 in the castle moat). In addition, there are concerts and fireworks on May 11 to commemorate the day in 1909 that Ferenc József made the town an independent municipality, while at the end of the same month there is medieval jousting and archery during the Castle Games.

# THE AGGTELEK RANGE

Established in 1985, Aggtelek National Park lies on the border with Slovakia, its limestone bed formed almost 250 million years ago by a shallow sea. Divided in two by the Bódva River valley, its densely forested 20,000ha present oodles of opportunity for hiking and cycling, enhanced by diverse species of flora and fauna (see box, page 267; Cartographia's *Az Aggtelekeki Karszt* map, 1:40,000, shows walking and cycling trails in the region). Its real prizes, though, are the karst cave systems – most notably that of Baradla-Domica, whose chambers spread over 25km (a quarter of the length on Slovak territory) and are filled with gorgeous dripstones of orange and cream. These caves rank as high as any in Europe; they have enjoyed international protection since 1979 and were added to the Unesco World Heritage List in 1995. The Baradla is flanked by the villages of Aggtelek and Jósvafő; there are entrances at each of these, and a third at Vörös-tó (Red

Lake), close to Jósvafő. You can cross overground into Slovakia to the western Domica entrance, but you cannot pass between the two sections via the caves themselves.

## Getting there, away and around

There are two daily direct **buses** from Budapest Stadion (taking four hours), stopping at both Aggtelek and Jósvafő; there are also buses from Miskolc (one) and Eger (one). Up to ten **local buses** link Jósvafő and Aggtelek.

Jósvafő-Aggtelek **railway station** is around 15km from Jósvafő and 20km from Aggtelek – a coach will take you from the station the rest of the way. There are no direct trains from Budapest (change at Miskolc); six services run to/from Miskolc.

For **bicycle rental**, try Zsolt Bacsó in Jósvafő (*Fenyves utca 11;* ❧ *48 350128 or 06 30 408 4099; open Sat–Sun Sep 1–Jun 30 09.00–18.00, Jul 1–Aug 31 09.00–19.00*), on a residential street off Petőfi Sándor utca.

## Information and other practicalities

**Aggtelek National Park Directorate** Tengerszem oldal 1; ❧ 48 350006. In the middle of Jósvafő. An educational centre, offering study tours for schoolchildren (and on-site dorm rooms), as well as grown-up information on the region's nature.

**Post office** Kossuth Lajos utca 39

**Tourinform** Baradla oldal l; ❧ 48 503003; e aggtelek@tourinform.hu. Opposite the Baradla Restaurant. Contains useful information on the caves and trails in the area, and walking and cycling maps. *Open Apr 1–Sep 30 daily 08.00–18.00, Oct 1–Mar 31 08.00–16.00.*

## Where to stay and eat

Both Aggtelek and Jósvafő (6km to the east) have numerous private rooms and guesthouses, with prices starting at around 1,500Ft/pp. Tourinform can provide a list, although you'd need to be as blind as a European horseshoe bat to miss the signs advertising rooms; we took a chance on a spartan but quite sufficient little house in Aggtelek (*Ady Endre út 40;* ❧ *48 343180; 2,500Ft/pp*), complete with kitchen.

**Baradla Hostel and Campsite** Aggtelek, Baradla oldal 1; ❧ 48 503005. Near the cave entrance. There are 9 hostel rooms with shared bathrooms; 25 huts (a few with kitchens and bathrooms) and camping pitches (*available Apr 15–Oct 15*). Prepare for squealing school parties. *Hostel room 1,600Ft/pp, huts 4,800–10,000Ft.*

**Baradla Restaurant** Aggtelek, Baradla oldal 1. Next to the cave entrance, and offers Hungarian dishes.

**Berecz-szőke** Jósvafő, Dózsa György utca 5; ❧ 48 350053. A better choice than the Tengerszem for accommodation in Jósvafő, this is an atmospheric cottage for 4 by the village's babbling brook. It nestles a few yards up a track, between the museum and the bell tower (see pages 268–9). *2,500Ft/pp.*

**Cseppkő Hotel** (70 rooms) Aggtelek, Baradla oldal; ❧ 48 343075; e hcseppko@axelero.hu. This hotel has a good vantage point 200m from the cave entrance, but its rooms are drab. The hotel also serves grub. *Sgl 5,200Ft dbl 8,400Ft.*

**Tengerszem Hotel** (18 rooms) Jósvafő, Tengerszem oldal 2; ❧ 48 506005. A pretty outside – in a scenic and peaceful spot – and a basic centre. Few animals are safe from its restaurant (*mains 1,000–2,300Ft, avg 1,600Ft*), whose meat-heavy menu includes venison, boar and veal. It's a relaxed, student-tuck-shop of a place, and the staff aren't precious about muddy boots; the food is unexceptional but filling. *Dbl 9,500–11,500Ft.*

## What to see and do
### Caves

**Baradla Cave** (*open daily Apr 1–Sep 30 08.00–18.00, Oct 1–Mar 31 08.00–16.00*) was first mentioned in literature of 1549, although prehistoric finds (including pottery and bears'

## WILDLIFE OF AGGTELEK NATIONAL PARK

This relatively small area is home to species of flora and fauna whose ecological demands are often very different. Typically northern Carpathian montane species grow in the beech forests on the northern slopes and in the cool ravines. Dog's tooth violet (*Erythronium dens-canis*) is a beautiful early-spring bloomer in the linden-ash woods of steep escarpments. The grasslands and oak parklands harbour steppe-woodland species, while in the rocky karst of drier slopes you'll find even sub-Mediterranean and Balkan elements. Juniper-heath tracts and plants similar to those that thrive on western European heaths inhabit covered karst areas, and enrich the natural scene further; the most renowned native plant of the Aggtelek karst is the Tornaian yellowdrop, with its drooping, bell-like flower.

The diverse geological, relief, climatic and phytogeographical conditions of the Aggtelek National Park (as well as its geographical situation) ensure that the area's fauna is also wide ranging. The insect world is very rich. Hungary's largest species, the sparsely distributed matriarchal katydid (*Saga pedo*) is here, as well as several unusual butterflies – the clouded Apollo (*Parnassius mnemosyne*), the purple-edged copper (*Palaeochrysophanus hippothoe*) and the poplar admiral (*Limenitis populi*). The longest watered caves – such as the Baradla Cave – are inhabited by some intriguing arthropods like blind carabid beetles, blind crayfish and micro-whip scorpions (*Palpigradi*). Indeed there are around 500 animal species in the cave system, most of them microscopic, with 40 species of plants (mainly white algae and moss).

The springs and brooks represent another special habitat. In addition to certain invertebrates, some protected fish species – like the bait minnow (*Phoxinus phoxinus*), the Mediterranean barbel (*Barbus meridionalis*) and the Danubian lamprey (*Petromyzonidae*), a brook-trout parasite – also occur in the waters. The most valuable reptile species of the Aggtelek karst is a little lizard called the snake-eyed skink (*Ablepharus kitaibelii*).

The imperial eagle (*Aquila heliaca*), lesser-spotted eagle (*A pomarina*), short-toed eagle (*Circaetus gallicus*) and honey buzzard (*Pernis apivorus*) are among the feathered fliers that nest here, as are the hazel grouse and the dipper. The dipper nests at mountain streams (sometimes in Jósvafő village), while the hazel grouse frequents denser woodland and is very rare, very shy and very hard to spot. Other birdie highlights are the Ural and eagle owls, and – during spring – the rock bunting and rock thrush. As for furry fliers, the park numbers 21 of the 28 European bat types, including the Mediterranean horseshoe (*Rhinolophus uryale*) variety. And the region is notable for its big game; the wolf and the lynx, for example – two animals that had died out in Hungary – have reappeared over the last two decades, and there are also deer, boar and wild cat.

bones) show it was inhabited much earlier, and ancient torches have left their sooty marks in places. This is the country's longest and richest, packed full of nobbly stalactites and stalagmites in which you're invited to see the shape of a dragon's head, a Chinese pagoda or a mother-in-law's tongue. The main branch runs between Aggtelek and Jósvafő. You can listen to classical music in the domed 'Concert Hall' chamber as lights play over its otherworldly dripstones, and – if the water is high enough – float in a boat on the subterranean Styx Stream. It's damp and cold, so wear an extra layer.

There are three entrances to the cave on the Hungarian side – at Aggtelek, Jósvafő and Vörös-tó – and tours of varying lengths (*one, two, five and seven hrs*) to choose from. The

Aggtelek end of the cave has more wonder in a concentrated space, and is a better option for the shortest tours; the very longest generally leave from the artificial entrance at Vörös-tó, and should be booked in advance. The regular one-hour tours are not strenuous, but be sure you are up to it before booking the more extended options. There are reductions for those who wish to do more than one of the tours on consecutive days – retain your ticket from the first tour, and receive a discount on a subsequent purchase at the other ticket office.

**Aggtelek entrance** Baradla oldal 1; ↘ 48 503003; www.aggtelek.hu. The 1-hr tour is 1km long, and includes music in the 'Concert Hall'. Tours depart at 10.00, 13.00, 15.00 and 17.00 (last of these in high season only). *Adult 1,400/1,200Ft (high/low season), concessions 650/550Ft.*

**Jósvafő entrance** Tengerszem oldal 3; ↘ 48 506009. The entrance is just to the west of the village, next to the Tengerszem Hotel. The 1-hour tour is 1.5km long, and includes the 'Giants' Hall' (the largest chamber in the system). Tours depart at 09.00 and 17.00 (high season) and 10.00 and 15.00 (low season). *Adult 900/800Ft (high/low season), concessions 450/400Ft.*

**Vörös-tó entrance** In between Aggtelek and Jósvafő. The Red Lake – now largely overrun with rushes – was so-named after a herd of wallowing pigs stirred up ferric oxide in its bed and turned the water crimson. A 2-hour, 2.3km tour leaves from here; it follows the course of the Styx Stream, and takes in the 'Astronomical Telescope' (Hungary's tallest stalagmite) and 'Giants' Hall' on the way to its finish at the Jósvafő end. Tickets should be bought from the Jósvafő ticket office. Tours depart at 10.00, 12.00, 13.30 and 15.00 (high season) and at 12.00 only in low season. *Adult 1,500/1,300Ft (high/low season), concessions 750/650Ft.*

If you're still hankering for things speleological, there are several other caves that can be visited. Tickets for the **Vass Imre Cave**, to the north of Jósvafő and with its 'Orange Cascade' formation, can be purchased from Jósvafő (*tours depart at 15.00 in high season, and by advance booking only in low season; adult 2,500Ft*); the price includes a 2km guided nature walk from the ticket office to the cave itself. There are longer visits to a 1,200m stretch of **Béke (Peace) Cave**, and its gravel terraces and rimstone dams. The tour lasts three hours and comes on top of a two-hour hike to get there; while torches are provided, waterproofs and sturdy footwear are essential as you'll need to negotiate an underground stream. (Overalls can be hired for 800Ft.) Book at least two weeks in advance from Aggtelek (*adult 6,000Ft, no children under 14*). The humid air in both the Vass Imre and Beké caves is thought to be beneficial to those with respiratory disorders. Trips into **Rákóczi Cave**, near the village of Bódvarákó, can be arranged (*with two weeks' notice; adult 2,500Ft*) at either Jósvafő or Aggtelek.

## Nature tours

Those who prefer to feel soil underfoot and sky overhead can take one of several eco tours or nature trails available. Guided tours eke out the region's wildlife and geology; there are advanced as well as more general tours. Prices start at 600Ft, and should be booked ahead at Jósvafő and Aggtelek. Alternatively, you can contact Litkei Krisztina (*Gömörszőlős, Kassai utca 37;* ↘ 48 434181) who organises three-hour tours in the company of a local qualified biologist (*5,000Ft/pp*), as well as 'herbal' walks that feature stops for herbal tea (*3,000Ft/pp*). If you're happy to go it alone, follow one of the park's educational trails. Among these are the **Baradla Trail** (a 7km route running between the Aggtelek and Jósvafő caves, over open and covered karst areas; yellow waymarking) and the **Tohonya-Kuriszlán Trail** (a 9km geological path in Jósvafő; yellow waymarking). Tourinform can provide fuller details of these and others.

## Other sights

A **Village Museum** (*Tájház; Dózsa György utca 3;* ↘ 48 350072; *adult/concessions 150/75Ft; open daily Apr 1–Sep 30 10.00–16.00; for visits during rest of year,* ↘ 48 350084) in Jósvafő is held in a traditional group of buildings from the late 19th century, and has exhibitions on local industry, agriculture, domestic life and cave exploration. The ticket office can provide an English-language leaflet, but it wants for much in detail. Behind the museum is the 13th-century **Calvinist church** (*Faluséta 11*), a white-washed villa-like building with a coffered ceiling and a detached belfry.

The **Hucul Stud** (*Táncsics Mihály út 1;* ↘ *48 350052 for info; open daily 08.00–15.00, by advance booking only*) is the only one of its kind in the country; the *hucul* is a small-bodied horse that is indigenous to the Carpathian region, and the purpose here is to preserve the breed. Horse and carriage riding is available (*from 2,500Ft/hr*). To the north of Petőfi Sándor út (up Ady Endre utca), you can reach the stud via the National Blue Trail from Jósvafő or the yellow-marked Tohonya-Kuriszlán Trail.

### Festivals and events
The **Gömör-Torna Festival** in the latter part of July features pop, classical and percussion concerts in Baradla Cave and the local churches, as well as 'village days' of folk events, fireworks and sport. Other performances of chamber music in the cave take place during the summer and at the end of December; contact Tourinform for details. Cycling, climbing and nature events are held between March and October.

### Excursions
There are many pretty villages in the surrounding area that are worth a visit if you have a bicycle or car. In the southern portion of the national park (3km from Martonyi) are the ruins of the medieval **Háromhegyi Pálos church and monastery**, built by the only monastic order founded in Hungary. The monastery was erected in 1341 and the church in 1411, and functioned up until the Turkish occupation; today the nave, gable and side-walls remain, and there is talk of reconstruction. Close by is **Szalonna**, notable for its 11th-century frescoed church with an odd-shaped 13th-century nave. Southwest of that (and 20km from Aggtelek) is **Rudabánya**, where iron ore was once mined; in 1967, an ancient monkey jaw – ten million years old – was found in one of the shafts, and is now on display.

## THE ZEMPLÉN HILLS AND AROUND
The region of the Zemplén Hills is something of a split personality; divided by the River Bodrog, the territory falling to the north and reaching to the Slovakian border is proper tough highland stuff of significant natural beauty, while that below is more plain-like in character. The tallest peak in the volcanic range is Nagy-Milic, a touch short of 900m. The bulk of visitors make the pilgrimage here in the name of wine – specifically the Tokaj-Hegyalja wines that are produced from vines on the warm slopes at the south and southeastern edges. The communities of historical significance are Sárospatak, Sátoraljaújhely, Szerencs and Tokaj; the region was a hotbed of Rákóczi-fuelled anti-Habsburg sentiment and action, but there was brain here as well as brawn, and some of its sons were prominent in the 19th-century literary and linguistic reform movements.

### Szerencs
Standing at the meeting point of the Great Plain and the Zemplén Hills, Szerencs is the gateway to the Hegyalja. It is frequently overlooked by tourists, but the whiff of history hangs strong and one of its churches hides a fascinating relic that adds real bones to tales of the past.

Szerencs has been inhabited since the Neolithic age, and developed into an important trade route – the Transylvanian salt road, for example, ran through here on its way from Tokaj to Buda and Pest. Devastated by the Mongol invasion in 1241, Szerencs's purple patch was to come between the 16th and 18th centuries. A castle was built in the 1550s, incorporating an earlier Benedictine monastery; the area and its fort quickly came into the possession of the Rákóczi family, leading participants in the independence struggles against the Habsburgs. In 1605, a parliament here elected the Transylvanian István Bocskai reigning prince, and he subsequently bestowed royal rank upon the town. On his death, Zsigmond Rákóczi was voted to succeed him, and the town remained at the forefront of resistance up until the suppression of the War of Independence led by Zsigmond's famous great-grandson, Ferenc Rákóczi II. In the aftermath, the fort declined in significance, and was gifted to more loyal nobles by the victorious Habsburgs. Economic revival came with the building of a sugar plant in 1889 and a chocolate factory in 1923 – sweet success once more.

## Getting there and away

The **bus** and **train** stations are situated next to each other. On alighting, turn right to the end of the road, turn left on to Rákóczi út at the top, past the Nestlé factory on the left, move over the crossroads and continue straight to the centre – it's around a 15-minute walk. The train station is on the line running between Miskolc and Nyíregyháza (that also includes Tokaj), and there are frequent services to each of these. There are 11 direct daily trains from Budapest Keleti, as well as several indirect (change at Miskolc). Buses run to Tokaj (up to nine), Miskolc (12) and Monok (12).

## Information and other practicalities

**Cultural centre** \ 47 362290. In summer months, the centre organises folklore events, wine exhibitions, art days and outdoor concerts. Opposite the library in the castle.
**Zemplén Tourist** Rákóczi út 67; \ 47 560059; e zemplen.tourist@axelero.hu
Tourist information, accommodation and Tokaj wine tours. Currency exchange available. *Open Mon–Fri 07.30–16.00.*

There's a **bank** at Kossuth Lajos tér 3A, and a **post office** at Rákóczi út 74–80.

## Where to stay and eat

You're unlikely to stay in town with Miskolc and Tokaj so relatively close, but if you do the **Hotel Huszárvár** (*Huszárvár út 11*; \ 47 362518; e *szerburghotel@elender.hu; 20 rooms; sgl 4,500–6,000Ft, dbl 5,500–8,000Ft*) occupies an outer wing of the castle. It's lacking in mod-cons, and rooms on the second floor have shared toilets, but both the location and price defy whining. Its restaurant (*mains 1,090–2,190Ft, avg 1,500Ft; open daily 10.00–22.00*) is kitted out medieval-banquet style. Snacks are available at **Sörház Za-nor** (*Petőfi út 5;* \ 47 364029; open Mon–Fri 08.00–21.00, Sat 08.00–14.00 & 18.00–22.00*), pizzas and other fast food at **Pizzeria Étterem & Pub** (*Rákóczi út 60; open Mon–Thu 09.00–21.00, Fri–Sat 11.00–23.00*), and sweet things at **Kovács Cukrászda** (*Rákóczi út 25;* \ 47 362693; open daily 08.00–20.00*).

## What to see and do

**Rákóczi Castle** (\ 47 362121; open Tue–Fri 09.00–17.00, Sat 08.00–14.00) is the hub of town. Zsigmond Rákóczi – whose barrel-chested statue stands in the castle grounds – acquired the estate in 1586, and after reinforcing the fortress and adding outer bastions, the family lived within its thick walls until 1616. It is said that Ferenc Rákóczi II spent time here on his 18th birthday. The castle witnessed several battles against the Turks during the 1600s; after the War of Independence, the new occupiers restructured things to make it more palatial than military.

Today the **Zemplén Museum** (\ 47 362842; adult/concessions 400/200Ft; open Tue–Sun May 1–Oct 31 10.00–16.00, Nov 1–Apr 30 10.00–17.00) fills the eastern wing. Its exhibitions include the world's third-largest collection of postcards (some dating back to

1860), period furniture and costumes from the Rákóczi era, and the work of Fery Antal (a local graphic artist). The castle also holds a library and cultural centre, and hosts several events during the year (see below).

The **Sugar Museum** (*Cukor Múzeum; Gyár utca 1;* ✆ *47 565100; 3-day advance booking required; open Tue–Fri 09.00–13.00, Sat–Sun 09.00–13.00*) stands to the east of the castle, at the junction of Rákóczi út and Road 37; it was unwrapped on the centenary of the town's sugar plant, and tells its history.

For us, though, the town's jewel is its 13th-century Gothic **Calvinist church** (*Kossuth tér 3;* ✆ *47 362090*), a short distance northwest of the castle up a sloping track where Kossuth Lajos utca and Rákóczi út touch. You may need to get the key from the vicarage at the bottom of the pathway up to the church itself. Thick metal doors protected the church from Turkish attack. In 1605 parliament was held inside, and István Bocskai declared Prince of Hungary. His successor was Zsigmond Rákóczi II. A red marble sarcophagus stands to the right, while a trapdoor beneath the carpet leads into a dank chamber and to a casket bearing the bones of Zsigmond and his second wife. The prince died peacefully, but two slashes across his skull testify to a life spent battling Turks and Habsburgs. The bones had to be re-gathered after they were scattered by the Habsburgs during the Revolution of 1849.

### Festivals and events
A wine exhibition and folklore events are held in June, while August sees both the Zemplén Art Days (open-air concerts and drama at the castle) and the International Folk Dance Festival.

## Excursions from Szerencs
The western side of the Zemplén Hills is relatively free of the tourist boot, and is consequently light on accommodation and other facilities, but there is some beautiful landscape and some villages with merit. It's most easily accessed by car, although there are buses from Szerencs, as well as stops on the railway as it travels up the Hernád Valley from Szerencs to Hidasnémeti at the border with Slovakia.

Around 15km north of Szerencs, **Monok** was the birthplace of Lajos Kossuth, and there is a memorial museum (*Kossuth Lajos utca 18*) in his residence. **Boldogkőváralja** has a 13th-century castle (*adult/concessions 500/250Ft; open mid-Apr–mid-Oct Tue–Sun 09.00–17.00*), which declined after the suppression of Imre Thököly's revolt in the late 1600s. At the peak of a commanding hill, the vistas are lovely; the castle is a couple of kilometres east of the railway station.

At the end of the 16th century, the first Hungarian translation of the Bible was printed in **Vizsoly**, the work of Gáspár Károlyi who was a priest at Gönc. The Calvinist church has a copy of the original, together with some beautiful medieval frescoes. Twelve kilometres further on, **Gönc** gives its name to the Tokaji wine barrels that were produced here in the past. **Telkibánya**, to the east, was once a centre of gold mining, while **Abaújvár**, to the north, has some faded frescoes in its 14th-century Gothic church.

## Tokaj
The statue of a naked Bacchanalian reveller in the centre is a prominent clue; a registered 'International Town of Vine and Wine', Tokaj is all about grapes and glasses. It is 'capital' of the Tokaj-Hegyalja (Tokaj Foothills) region, where the country's most-lauded wine is produced. The quality nose-dived with the mass production typical of the socialist market economy, but since 1991 private estates have re-emerged in place of the massive state-owned factories. Tokaj is just one of almost 30 wine towns in the area; it's pretty enough, but wine is the religion here, and teetotallers will find little else to occupy their time.

## THE WINE OF KINGS, THE KING OF WINES

Tokaji is an amber-hued white wine from the Zemplén Hills or the Tokaj-Hegyalja, a location considered a sacred part of Hungary; its rich colour, texture and taste are unique, and earn it a distinct place in the world of plonk. During the 16th century, Italian writers documented that it contained gold. In 1703, Ferenc Rákóczi II – who used it to secure political favours – presented Louis XIV of France with bottles from his own vineyards. Louis pronounced it the 'wine of kings, king of wines', and since then it has been considered one of the world's noblest. It is claimed that Peter the Great of Russia insisted on Tokaji for special occasions (and that he regarded it as a tonic for the troops), and that it was the favoured tipple of Catherine the Great, Frederic II of Prussia, Voltaire, Goethe and Schubert. And many thought it had medicinal properties; George V of England was one of those who drank it to speed recovery from illness, and early-18th-century European physicians swore by the healing power of the soil itself. One bevvie legend was that if a man drank Tokaji on his wedding night, his wife would give birth to a son. (Interestingly, it is thought that Tokaji may have been a dry wine until the 17th century. The significance of aszú – botrytis-affected berries – was only discovered when the threat of Turkish invasion pushed harvests back in the region, and 'noble rot' set in; the consequent deeper and sweeter flavour was revealed when the wine was later tasted.)

The paradox is that, despite dripping with pride in its past, Tokaji is in some ways just 15 years old. For over 40 years the wines lost their lustre as state farms and wineries (imposed under the state monopoly) modified them with sugar and alcohol to serve the masses back in the Soviet Union. It is only since communism's fall that the age-old traditions have been resurrected (often after foreign investment), and that the wine has made its mark once more.

Only four white-grape types are allowed to be grown in the region: Furmint, Hárslevelű (both original Hungarian varieties), Muscat Lunel and Oremus. Seven wines can be made from them. Furmint is the most famous, a light, dry white, produced by a reductive procedure. Szamorodni can be sweet or dry, its Polish name translating as 'as it was born'. Aszú – produced only in Tokaj according to traditional methods – is divided into wines of three, four, five and six puttyonyos (tub or butt), referring to the number of 30-litre tubs of Aszú paste added to the fermenting must. Aszúesszencia is prepared in the same way, but a greater amount of paste is used – equivalent to a seven- or eight-puttyonos Aszú wine. The other wines are Hárslevelű (as in Linden leaf), Muscat Lunel (different from the Italian Muscat, and with a wonderful bouquet and tart flavour) and Oremus (both the name of a grape and a major vineyard in the Tokaj region). Tokaji wines are usually very sweet, and drunk as an aperitif or with dessert. However, you can also now get good dry whites like the Degenfeld 2003 Tokaji Muscat Lunel from the vineyards belonging to the German-Hungarian Count Degenfeld in Tarcal (see box, page 274).

### Getting there and away

The main **bus stop** is south of the town's synagogue on Serház utca. There are no direct buses from Budapest – the single daily indirect service involves a change at Nyíregyháza. There are two a day to Debrecen, two to Nyíregyháza, nine to Szerencs (four at weekends) and two to Sárospatak. The **railway station** is a kilometre to the south of the town (buses run from outside to the centre approximately hourly until early evening). Tokaj is on the line running between Miskolc and Nyíregyháza, and there are regular services to these destinations (as well as Szerencs), and a few continue to Debrecen. Change at Mezőzombor for Sárospatak and Sátoraljaújhely.

## Information and other practicalities

**Tourinform** Serház utca 1; ☎ 47 352259; e tokaj@tourinform.hu. *Open Jun–Sep daily 09.00–18.00, Oct–May Mon–Fri 09.00–16.00.*

There's a **post office** (*Rákóczi út 24*) opposite Makk Marci Pizzeria, and a **bank** opposite the town hall on Rákóczi út.

## Where to stay

**Degenfeld Panzió** (5 rooms) Kossuth tér 1; ☎ 47 553050; e contact@tokajtc.com; www.tokajtc.com. Linked to the central Degenfeld Restaurant, the rooms here are excellent – spacious, contemporary and with small kitchens. Highly recommended. *Sgl 6,700–8,200Ft, dbl 8,200–10,200Ft.*

**Luz Panzió** Serház utca 14; ☎ 47 352145. You'll search in vain for a cheaper pension, but rooms are rather archaic. The staff fall over themselves to be helpful; they also play origami with the bath towels. *Dbl 4,900Ft (excl b/fast).*

**Makk Marci Panzió** (7 rooms) Liget köz 1; ☎ 47 352336; e makkmarci@axelero.hu. Spotless rooms in a pension attached to the pizza parlour. *Sgl 5,040Ft, dbl 8,400Ft, triple 10,640Ft, room for 4 13,440Ft.*

**Millennium Hotel** (18 rooms) Bajcsy-Zsilinszky út 34; ☎ 47 352247; e millennium@alexero.hu; www.hotels.hu/millennium_tokaj. Built in – you guessed it – the year 2000, the Millennium has something of a Travel-Inn feel, but the rooms are roomy and the staff friendly. *Dbl 12,000Ft, triple 15,000Ft, apt (for 4) 20,000Ft.*

**Tisza Camping** 4465 Rakamaz, Szent István út 116; ☎ 47 352012. At the foot of the Tokaj Bridge, this campsite (1 of 3 in close proximity) has its own hostel with 24 simple but clean rooms (only 6 have en-suite facilities). You can make use of the riverside location by renting kayaks or canoes (*500Ft/day*), or splash out on a motorboat for a fishing excursion (*5,000Ft/day*). There's also bike hire (*1,000Ft/day*). *Hostel room 1,500Ft/pp; tent/caravan 600/700Ft, plus 700Ft/pp; open Apr 15–Oct 31.*

**Vasko Panzió** Rákóczi utca 12; ☎ 47 352107. Comfortable boarding house with a cellar bar next door – not far to stagger after a night on the local vino. *Dbl 6,000Ft.*

## Where to eat and drink

Also see *Wine cellars and shops*, pages 276–7.

**Billiard Bar & Amusement Arcade** Kossuth tér. If you don't mind bass-heavy music and posturing youngsters, this spartan hall above a supermarket is the place for a late-night drink. There are 10 pool tables.

**Degenfeld Restaurant & Wine Pub** Kossuth tér 1; ☎ 47 553050; e contact@tokajtc.com. Fresh international and Hungarian fare in highly polished surroundings. They take pride here – this is

## A WINE TOUR OF TOKAJ-HEGYALJA

The Tokaj-Hegyalja (Tokaj Foothills) make up the southernmost part of the volcanic mountains that branch from the Carpathian chain, the region filling a triangle between the slopes of Sátorhegy-Sátoraljaújhely, the Sátorhegy-Abaújszántó and the Kopasz mountains. Fifty-five kilometres long and 15km wide, the mountains fill the horizon; tucked away here are 28 diverse villages. German, Slovakian and Jewish communities settled in the past, and linguistic variations persist. Spring and autumn are the seasons to visit, particularly during the Tokaj Spring Festival (last weekend of May) and the Harvest Festival (last week of October).

**Getting around** Tokaj-Hegyalja is simple. Road 37 from Szerencs runs through the centre to its end at Sátoraljaújhely. Every village is within 8km of turn-offs from the highway. There are buses from Szerencs and Tokaj to most villages, but it's easiest with a car.

Starting at the southwestern end of Tokaj-Hegyalja and passing eastward through Szerencs, the last town before entering the region, you'll reach a sign indicating **Mád** to the left. Hills full of the distinctive cellar doors embedded in their rocky sides surround this little village and its single main road, Rákóczi út. Mád is currently the home of the premier wine maker in the whole area. István Szepsy (*Szepsy Mád-Királyi Szőlészet; Táncsics utca 57;* ❧ *47 348349*) has been producing wines since communist times; although Szepsy does host tastings in his cellar, his workload means that such opportunities are rare, and it is better instead to head for the Királyudvar winery in Tarcal (see below), where he joins forces with another celebrated winemaker, Zoltán Demeter. The other big name is Tokaj Classic (*Rákóczi út 45, opposite the town hall*), owned by a Hungarian-American couple, András and Phyllis Bruhács. There are also many smaller winemakers scattered in Mád, offering full cellars and visitor tastings.

Joining Road 37 once more, and going due southeast towards Tokaj, the renowned **Disznókő (Rock Boar) winery** (*Mezőzombor, Disznókő dűlő;* ❧ *47 569410;* e *disznoko@disznoko.hu; www.disznoko.hu*), a dome-shaped building perched on a hill, stands just before the turn off for Tarcal. What makes Disznókő particularly unusual is its white pavilion atop a jetting boulder; the boulder is said to look like a wild boar, and the structure was designed by the organic architect Imre Makovecz. **Tarcal** is a town located on the western side of Bald Mountain (see page 276), and has several wineries worth seeing: the Dorogi Vineyard (*Arany János utca 7;* ❧ *47 380003;* e *dorogi@freemail.hu*), Tokaj Nobilis, Királyudvar (*Fő utca 92;* ❧ *47 380111;* e *kiralyudvar@elender.hu; www.kiralyudvar.com*), Kikelet and Degenfeld (*Terézia kert 9;* ❧ *47 380173;* e *degenfeld@axelero.hu; www.grofdegenfeld.com*). The last of these recently unveiled the Gróf Degenfeld Castle Hotel (❧ *47 580400;* e *hotel@degenfeld.hu; www.hotelgrofdegenfeld.hu; 21 rooms; sgl 27,600–30,000Ft, dbl 30,000–32,400Ft, suite 36,000–38,400Ft*) in its grounds, an elegant place with 19th-century ambience but modern facilities.

Continue southwards and around the bottom of Bald Mountain, you'll reach **Tokaj** itself. One of the gurus of this area is János Árvay, the top vintner after Mád's Szepsy.

The Bodrog River courses through **Bodrogkeresztúr**, which stands beside Route 38 on the way back to Road 37. The Dereszla Estate (*Felső utca 2;* ❧ *47 396004;* e *dereszla@dereszla.com; www.dereszla.com*) here is half-owned by French Wine Makers, the D'Aulan family from Champagne. In the immediate aftermath of the political changes of 1989, several French investors and wine makers arrived to work with the locals in harnessing traditional regional techniques with contemporary machinery. The result is spectacular. The Dereszla wines are full-flavoured and wonderful; the Dereszla cellars are a favourite of the region, winding deep underground. Supping direct from the barrels is a frequent pleasure during tours of this winery, but there is also a recently refurbished tasting room. Choosing the best of their wines is a tough task, but special mention should go to the Muskotály 2000; free of the acidic taste that usually characterises Tokaji Muscat, this one yields a soft, slightly sweet wine with a swift and sharp finish. Füleky (*Iskola köz 15;* \ *47 396478;* e *fulekypince@freemail.hu; www.fuleky-tokaj.com*), one of the leading smaller wineries, is also in Bodgrogkeresztúr. Judit Bott is the wine maker and in recent years she has received rave reviews. The Furmint 'Pallas' is the most popular of the wines. Judit speaks excellent English and is a super wine guide.

Back on Road 37, vineyards envelope the landscape. The majority are owned by Hétszőlő, Dereszla and private landowners. The turn for **Erdőbénye** is further northeast along the highway. Tiny in size but beautiful in look, it is known for its makers of traditional Tokaji barrels (*gönci*), which hold 136 litres. Attila Homonna came to Tokaj six years ago, and has been making his name during the past two of them with his fantastic Szamorodni and Furmint wines.

**Olaszliszka** is the next stop, 5km further along our route, where just one maker plies his trade. Samuel Tinon is a Frenchman who moved to Tokaj 14 years ago to revamp many of the larger wineries, introducing up-to-date processes and techniques. Eight kilometres on is **Tolcsva**, home of the Spanish/Hungarian Tokaj Oremus winery (*Bajcsy-Zsilinszky utca 45;* \ *47 384505;* e *oremus93@axelero.hu; www.tokajoremus.com*). Oremus is internationally known, and boasts one of the most advanced wine-making systems (with a 'gravity-flow' process, considered to provide the 'clearest' extract from the grapes). The estate is huge. Of all the cellars of the wineries, this is the one to go to. Mouldy, low-ceilinged corridors are lined with backlit bottles that project shafts of amber-coloured light all around. Oremus also holds the 'Wine of the Century' – voted the best dessert wine in the world – from the 1972 vintage. Keep an eye out for the 1999 Hárslevelű late harvest and Szamorodni dry and sweet wines.

At the heart of the town is the Ős Kaján (*Kossuth utca 14–16;* \ *47 384195;* e *oskajan.restaurant@axelero.hu; www.oskajan.hu; open Feb 20–Dec 20 Tue–Sat 12.00–22.00, Sun 12.00–20.00*), a restaurant owned by a French couple, Anne and Pascal, who have contributed greatly to the process of resurrecting Tokaji's place in the tradition of Hungarian cuisine. They have studied old Hungarian recipes, and reinvented the art of the true Hungarian kitchen; their restaurant is rustic, antiquated and intimate. A garden holds plum, apple and peach trees, and is the venue for summer concerts on Fridays and Saturdays, while inside are regular exhibitions of Hungarian and foreign artists. As for food, ingredients are home grown and dishes carefully matched with the right Tokaji wine.

**Sárospatak** (see page 277) is 20km on, while another 10km of tarmac brings up **Sátoraljaújhely**, right on the Slovakian border. This town is home to the Tokaj Pendits (MWB) winery (*Abaújszántó, Béke út 111, Pf 27;* \ *47 330567;* e *pendits@axelero.hu; www.pendits.de*), owned by the Wille-Baumkauff family, who have just renovated and restored their estate; the views from the hill here are top-notch, and make this winery the perfect place to take a final draught, draw a deep sigh and complete your tour of Hungary's prime wine region.

Wine tasting on the estates usually **costs** between 500Ft and 1,500Ft, although occasionally it is free. For **further information**, contact Tokaj Renaissance (*Tokaji Nagy Borok Egyesülete; Tokaj, Pf 17;* \ *47 353612;* e *tokaji@tokaji.hu; www.tokaji.hu*). The headquarters of the state-run wine company **Tokaj Kereskedő Ház** – whose wines are considered good but not the best – are in Sátoraljaújhely (*Mártírok utca 17;* \ *47 321526;* e *tokajvin@axelero.hu*).

one of the region's best. There's wine-tasting available in the wine pub. *Mains 900–2,500Ft, avg 1,800Ft; restaurant open 12.00–22.00 daily, pub 13.00–23.00.*

**Makk Marci Pizzéria** Liget köz 1; ` 47 352336. Cheap and cheerful pizza and pasta joint – the ravenous can tuck in to a 40cm pizza for 1,800Ft. *Open daily 10.00–20.00.*

**Murphy's Bar** Rákóczi út 42; ` 47 353013. A typical pub without a wine-tasting programme in sight. *Open daily 14.00–22.00.*

**Rona Restaurant** Bethlen Gábor utca 19; ` 47 352116. Basic restaurant selling unadventurous Hungarian cuisine including pork, carp and pancakes. *Mains 800–2,000Ft, avg 1,600Ft.; open daily 11.00–21.00.*

**Tokaji Borbár** Rákóczi út 34; ` 47 352320. An elevated bar with minimal furnishings; wine available by the glass or bottle. *Open daily 12.00–22.00.*

**Toldi Fogado** Hajdú köz 2; ` 47 353403. Inviting interior with high wooden benches and stained glass, as well as an outdoor area at the back. The menu features fish and game dishes; there are also 6 en-suite rooms. *Mains 890–2,500Ft, avg 1,600Ft; open daily 11.00–23.00.*

## What to see and do

The **Tokaj Museum** (*Bethlen Gábor utca 7;* ` *47 352636; adult/concessions 400/200Ft; open Tue–Sun 10.00–16.00*) stands at the northern end of the main square, its building constructed by a Greek merchant in 1790. It holds a collection of religious art representative of northern Hungary's churches, including icons, Baroque statues and Russian and Ukrainian woodcuts, as well as Jewish artefacts from the former synagogue. Here too is an exhibition devoted to life along the Tisza and Bodrog rivers, and another displaying the tools of winemaking (from transportation carts to bottle labels). The cellars – that 'world under the ground where the world above is forgotten', as Kálmán Mikszáth once wrote – contain casks and bottles from the best of the region's producers. Further up the same street, the late-Baroque **Greek Orthodox Church** (*Bethlen Gábor utca 17;* ` *47 352003; free entry; open May–Oct daily 10.00–16.00*) was built in the 1780s, and now has a gallery showcasing local artists. The key is available at the Billiard Bar/youth centre (see page 273).

The **former synagogue** (*Serház utca 55*) is east of the gallery, a sad and broken reminder of the significant Jewish presence in the town (and in the town's wine trade) prior to World War II. It has been earmarked for conversion into a conference hall, and there's a Jewish cemetery (with Classicist tombstones) a few kilometres north in Bodrogkeresztúr. By contrast, the **Roman Catholic church** on Kossuth tér is spick and span, its interior a beautiful example of understated decoration. We particularly like the juxtaposition of the church and the half-naked figure of the Bacchanalian reveller outside – which inevitably highlights wine's contrasting roles as symbol of sacrifice and practical means to excess.

To the west, **Kopasz-hegy** (Bald Mountain) has a TV tower and splendid views. There are several **hiking trails** in the hills, whose flora includes the woolly Michaelmas daisy, footgrass, fringe flower, desert bloodgrass and red lednek. Alternatively you can stroll the Széchenyi Trail, which starts at the confluence of the Bodrog and Tisza. On the opposite bank there is a **beach** and camping, from where you can hire canoes (see page 273). Between spring and autumn, **ferry tours** leave from the Mahart pier (` *47 352937*) at Hősök tere, running between Tokaj and Sárospatak.

## Wine cellars and shops

Wine is Tokaj's *raison d'être*. The **Rákóczi Cellars** (*Kossuth tér 15;* ` *47 352009;* e *rakoczip@axelero.hu; open mid Mar–mid Oct daily 10.00–19.00 or 20.00 in summer*) are the town's most renowned. Pouting staff were enough to turn the wine sour during our last visit, but the history of the cellars is fortunately more impressive. The 24 tunnels, branching from a central hall, were built in the 15th century, and in 1526 formed the backdrop to the Hungarian Diet that elected János Szapolyai king. Oak barrels line the chambers as Tokaji Aszú and Szamorodni mature inside. Tours and tastings (*from 1,900Ft/pp*) begin on the hour.

The **Hímesudvar Pincészet** (*Bem út 2;* \ *47 352416;* e *tokaji@himesudvar.hu; www.himesudvar.hu; open daily 09.00–21.00*) is a short walk northwest of Kossuth tér; the building was constructed by Szapolyai in the 16th century as a hunting lodge and cellar. The Várhelyi family restored it in the 1980s, and now offers its own wines and others from the region (*tastings from 1,200Ft/5 wines*). **Tokaji Hétszőlő** (*Bajcsy-Zsilinszky út 19–21;* \ *47 352009;* e *hetszolo@axelero.hu*) has an impressive cellar burrowing through the ground with corridor after corridor of rooms with barrels and traditional tasting areas.

**Borostyán** (*Ráckózi út 11;* \ *47 353381; open Mon–Fri 10.00–22.00, Sat–Sun 11.00–22.00*) is a specialist wine shop and drinking hole, where you can choose from an extensive list of wines by the glass or bottle. **Furmint Vinotéka** (*Bethlen Gábor utca 12/A;* \ *47 353340;* e *tokajwac@enternet.hu; open daily 09.00–17.00*) has a wide range of wines from over 30 of the region's wineries. You can also book tours or tastings, and purchase gifts such as personalised bottles.

**János Árvay** makes just about every kind of Tokaji and is one of the region's top vintners. His new winery is in the former town hall (*József Attila utca 2;* \ *47 552155;* e *tokaj.hetfurtos@axelero.hu*), its renovation completed in 2004. Inside are a coffee shop, a wine-tasting room, cellars below and a pressing room on the top floor.

### Festivals and events

Inevitably the main events are wine soaked – there are festivals in May, August and October.

## Sárospatak

The 'Hungarian Cambridge' or 'Athens on the Bodrog' – so named because of the formidable reputation of its Calvinist college – lies 20km north of Tokaj; the actual meaning of Sárospatak is rather less salubrious – 'muddy stream'. The college was founded in 1531, and numbers some greats among its alumni: the Czech humanist and teacher J A Comenius studied here in the 1650s, and other past pupils include the Enlightenment poet Mihály Csokonai Vitéz, the language reformer Ferenc Kazinczy, the statesman and 'Hungarian Moses' Kossuth Lajos, and the 20th-century author Géza Gárdonyi. The town is also inextricably linked with the Rákóczis, who acquired it in 1616 and ensured that it was at the forefront of the revolutionary struggles. In 1708 it hosted the last Diet during the War of Independence, and Sárospatak was also the town from which Rákóczi II was exiled after the dream had died. There's plenty in its compact centre to fill an enjoyable day, and a couple of spanking pensions for overnight stays.

### Getting there and away

The **bus** and **train** stations are next to each other, a short distance to the north. On alighting from either station, follow Tánsics Mihály utca for a short distance to the Calvinist college; turn right to reach the centre. Sárospatak railway station lies on an offshoot northeast from the main line running between Miskolc and Nyíregyháza. There are six daily trains from Budapest Keleti. Alternatively there are nine from Miskolc; from Debrecen or other towns to the east, change at Szerencs or Mezőzombor. There is a single service daily across the Slovakian border to Slovenské Nové Mesto. There are no direct buses from Budapest; there are services to Debrecen (two), Miskolc (once, excluding Sun), Nyíregyháza (two), Tokaj (two) and Sátoraljaújhely (frequent).

## Information and other practicalities

**Bank** Eötvös út 2

**Listings magazine** *Miskolci Est*

**Tourinform** Eötvös utca 6; ⟍ 47 315316; e sarospatak@tourinform.hu; www.sarospatak.hu. In the cultural centre. *Open Jun 16–Sep 15 Mon–Fri 09.00–18.00, Sat–Sun 09.00–17.00, rest of year Mon–Thu 07.30–16.00, Fri 07.30–13.30.*

## Where to stay

**Dezső Lajos College** Eötvös utca 7; ⟍ 47 312211/206. Cheap dorm beds during student vacation periods. *Beds from 1,500Ft/pp.*

**Hotel Bodrog** (50 rooms) Rákóczi út 58; ⟍ 47 311744; e bodrog@matavnet.hu; www.matavnet.hu/bodrog. The building is stale and dated, but the rooms themselves are spacious and light, and there's a sauna and fitness room. More costly rooms on the 1st and 2nd floors are bigger and have balconies. *Sgl 8,500–12,000Ft, dbl 10,000–13,000Ft (excl tax); b/fast 1,100Ft.*

**Kert Panzó** Rákóczi út 31; ⟍ 47 311559. Sparkling, wood-floored rooms with everything you need – inc use of a communal kitchen and pretty garden. It's centrally positioned, but quiet. And crumbs it's cheap. *Sgl 3,500Ft, dbl 4,600Ft.*

**Liget Panzió** Arany János út 28; ⟍ 47 314507; e ligetvendeghaz@mail.matav.hu. A lot of love has gone into the well-presented and contemporary rooms of the Liget, and you can take advantage of a great garden. Top marks. *Dbl 6,000Ft, triple 7,500Ft, quadruple 9,000Ft; b/fast 500Ft.*

**Tengerszem Camping** Herczeg Ferenc utca 2; ⟍ 47 312744. Just 2km northeast of the centre (close to the thermal baths), this manicured campsite has an outdoor pool, restaurant, tennis courts and 45 cute bungalows (all with bathrooms and most with small kitchens and TVs). Hedges provide privacy between camping pitches. *Bungalow 5,000Ft (for 2), 8,500Ft (for 4); tent/caravan 800/1,200Ft, plus 700Ft/pp; b/fast 1,500Ft. Open Apr–Oct.*

## Where to eat and drink

**Vár Vendéglő** Árpád út 35; ☎ 47 311370. Top of the food tree – a rustic restaurant with upbeat staff across the water from the castle. Fish is the dish of the house, and there's a good wine selection. If you choose to sit outside of an evening, bring some insect repellent – mosquitoes enjoy dining by the Bodrog River too. *Open Mon–Sat 12.00–22.00, Sun 12.00–20.00.*

**Rákóczi Restaurant** Rákóczi út 30; ☎ 47 511423. Specialises in game, as well as a dish of pork and chicken for the carnivorous to share. The English-speaking manager was very welcoming during our visit. *Mains 800–2,000Ft, avg 1,400Ft; open daily 07.00–22.00.* **Ristorante Pizza Collegno** Szent Erzsébet utca 10; ☎ 47 314494. Atmospheric cellar and a good selection of pizzas. *Pizzas 500–1,500Ft; open Mon–Sat 11.00–24.00, Sun 16.00–23.00.*

**V András Restaurant and Coffee House** Béla Király tér 3; ☎ 47 312415. Standard Hungarian cuisine; there's a tourist menu (read 'bland-but-cheap') for around 1,000Ft. *Mains 500–2,500Ft, avg 1,200Ft; open daily 10.00–22.00.*

**McIntosch Fagyizó** Szent Erzsébet utca 22; ☎ 47 312929. Ice-cream parlour that also serves burgers, pizzas and pancakes. *Open Mon–Thu 10.00–22.00, Fri–Sat 10.00–22.00, Sun 10.00–20.00.*

**Rákóczi Cellar** Szent Erzsébet utca 26; ☎ 47 311902; e pajzosmegyer@axelero.hu. Dug deep beneath the castle grounds and snaking to around 1km in length, the cellar has changed little in the centuries since it was constructed in 1530 – dim corridors, mould-clad walls and oak barrels. The humidity is 96% and the temperature a constant 12°C. The Szamorodni, Tokaji Aszú and Esszencia of Chateau Megyer (the current owners) mature inside. The entrance is just to the right of the castle complex. *Wine tastings (starting on the hour) 400–1,200Ft; open Jan 1–Apr 30 & Oct 1– Dec 31 Mon–Fri 10.00–14.00, Mar 1–Sep 30 Mon–Fri 10.00–17.00, Sat–Sun 10.00–18.00.*

## Entertainment and nightlife

**Club Win** (*Szent Erzsébet utca 22; open Mon–Tue 19.00–23.00, Wed 19.00–24.00, Thu 19.00–23.00, Fri–Sat 19.00–02.00*), on the road leading to the castle, is a student favourite and is packed to the rafters at the weekends. Next to the Tourinform, the **Sárospatak Cultural House** (*Eötvös utca 6;* ☎ *47 311811; www.sarospatak.hu/muvhaz; open Mon–Fri 08.00–20.00, Sat–Sun 10.00–18.00*) hosts theatrical productions, concerts, dance classes and discos; its adventurous, exhilarating building was designed in the 1970s by Imre Makovecz, and is intended to resemble a human face or an open book. Makovecz was something of an outcast of the establishment during the communist period, when his organic, natural designs ran visibly counter to the rigidity of the prevalent architectural style and its associations with the party.

## What to see and do

Slightly south of the town centre, **Rákóczi Castle** (*Szent Erszébet utca 19–21; adult/concessions 340/170Ft; tour 2,500Ft; open Tue–Sun Mar–Oct 10.00–18.00, Nov–Feb 10.00–17.00*) stands in an area that was a royal estate from the 11th century, positioned at the crossing point of the River Bodrog. It is an eclectic patchwork in stone, the product of several centuries of architectural tinkering – but tinkering of the very finest. The oldest portion is the late-15th-century Red Tower – 'red' because of coloured plaster that originally covered its walls – while Renaissance wings were constructed in the next century. The complex came into the possession of the Rákóczis on the marriage in 1616 of its owner, Zsuzsanna Lorántffy, to György I (later elected Prince of Transylvania). It stayed in the family until the failure of Ferenc Rákóczi II and his *kuruc* armies, after which the Habsburgs demolished its fortifications and handed it over to foreign aristos.

The **Rákóczi Museum**, which is housed in the Renaissance building, holds permanent exhibitions devoted to the castle, the Rákóczi family, the history of the Independence War, and period furniture and weaponry. Carved door and window frames in the Perényi wing and a beautiful open-sided arcade of 1646 that leads from the courtyard to the Red Tower are first-class examples of Renaissance artistry. In the corner of the northeast bastion, the Knights' Hall was the site of a Diet during the War of Independence; there had been anti-Habsburg plans afoot in 1670 too when plotters met in the adjacent balcony room, congregating beneath the stone rose in its ceiling. The leaders subsequently got the chop, but the conspiratorial connotations of the Latin term '*sub rosa*' lived on in the room. (The rose as a symbol of silence dates back to antiquity; it came to be a popular decoration in banqueting halls, reminding diners to guard against wine's power to loosen their tongues!)

Moving away from the castle, north along Szent Erzsébet utca, the **Sárospatak Gallery** (*Szent Erzsébet utca 14;* ❧ *47 511012; adult/concessions 250/125Ft; open Tue–Sun 10.00–16.00*) sits in an 18th-century Baroque building just inside the outer fortified wall. It hosts temporary exhibitions, and is presaged by a statue of a boy riding a distinctly giraffe-like horse outside. Close by is the 14th-century **Castle Church** (*Szent Erzsébet utca 7; adult/concessions 150/80Ft; open Tue–Sat 09.00–16.00, Sun 11.30–16.00*), every part of which shouts 'big'. This is one of the largest Gothic hall churches in the country, its enormous interior supported by enormous columns and punched with enormous arched windows. The wooden altar – inevitably Hungary's biggest – originally stood in Buda Castle's Carmelite church until the monastic order was outlawed in the late 1700s. Regular concerts are played on the Baroque organ.

The main building of the **Calvinist college** (*Sárospataki Református Kollégium; Rákóczi út 1; adult/concessions 200/100Ft; open Mon–Sat 09.00–17.00, Sun 09.00–13.00*) – imposing, Neoclassical and based around a central courtyard – was completed in 1834, although there had been a college on the site since 1531. Between 1650 and 1654, the Czech humanist Johannes Amos Comenius taught here, and wrote the pioneering educational work *Orbis Sensualium Pictus* (*The Visible World*). Other significant alumni are commemorated by statues in the college garden. The stock of the library – in a stunning oval hall designed by Mihály Pollack – includes 2,000 volumes remaining from the original 16th-century holdings. (Another 15,000 were taken by Russian troops in 1945, and have not yet been returned.) There are hourly tours. An 18th-century Baroque side wing has scientific collections, an exhibition of religious art and details of the college's history.

The town's outdoor **thermal baths** (*Végardó;* ❧ *47 311639; adult/concessions 500/300Ft; open daily 08.00–18.00 in summer*) are around a kilometre north of the centre, just beyond the Tengerzem campsite.

### Festivals and events

The primary festival takes place in mid August, when a series of classical-music concerts are staged in conjunction with other towns and villages as part of the region's Zemplén Arts Days. There's a two-day festival in commemoration of Szent Erzsébet (who was born here in 1207) at the start of June, while the Dixieland and Blues Festival comes to town at the latter end of July.

### Sátoraljaújhely

What's in a name? Well, in Sátoraljaújhely's case, many syllables – *Sha-tor-a-ya-ooi-hay*. There's little else of significant interest in a one-street town bereft of decent restaurants, dead as a doornail by mid evening, and blighted by surrounding residential blocks. From the 18th century, this was actually a prosperous wine-trading town and capital of Zemplén County until the Treaty of Trianon broke the country and shifted power to Sárospatak, 12km to the south. Like Sárospatak, the town stands on its history. In 1697 a peasant rebellion broke out here that spread throughout the Hegyalja region, and it was at the heart of the 17th-century struggles led by the Rákóczis, the landowners of the period. It was later to witness the first flowerings of Lajos Kossuth's political career. Today, though, it functions primarily as a board for springing elsewhere – be it into the hills, to nearby villages or over the border at the crossing into Slovakia.

## Getting there and away

The **bus** and **railway** stations both stand to the south. On exiting the stations, walk straight ahead up Fasor utca (past the Temple of Wine), and at the top of the road turn right on to Kossuth Lajos utca to the centre. It is about a 15-minute walk. The railway station is on the same line as Sárospatak (the next stop northwards). There are five trains direct from Budapest Keleti; otherwise you can access the town from Miskolc (up to 11) or Szerencs (14). Destinations further east require a change at Mezőzombor. You can also take occasional daily services across the border into Slovakia.

There are frequent buses to Sárospatak (5km away). You can pick up services to other places in the northern Zemplén too, including Hollóháza (up to ten), Füzér (four) and Hidasnémeti (one); the latter offers trains over the border.

## Information and other practicalities

**Bank** Széchenyi tér 13. *Open Mon–Fri 08.00–16.00.*

**Internet Café** Rákóczi utca 30a; ℄ 47 325150. A shop rather than café, with 4 computer terminals (*350Ft/hr*). *Open Mon–Fri 08.00–17.00, Sat 09.00–12.00.*

**Kossuth Cultural Centre** Táncsics Mihály tér 3; ℄ 47 321727. Regular theatre productions and other events.

**Listings magazine** *Miskolci Est*

**Tiszi BT** Kossuth tér 22; ℄ 47 322563. Super-helpful office that can arrange tours and accommodation, and provide information on Zemplén County. *Open Mon–Thu 09.00–17.00, Fri 09.00–15.00.*

**Tiszi is Újhelyi Írisz** Kossuth Lajos tér 26; ℄ 47 321757. Private accommodation, transport and money exchange. *Open Mon–Fri 08.00–16.00, Sat 08.00–14.00.*

**Tourinform** Táncsics Mihály tér 3; ℄ 47 321458. Housed in the cultural centre. *Open mid Jun–mid Sep Mon–Fri 09.00–18.00, Sat–Sun 09.00–17.00, rest of year Mon–Thu 07.30–16.00, Fri 07.30–13.30.*

## Where to stay

**Csillagfény Panzió** (10 rooms) Mártírok utca 29; ℄ 47 322619; e csillagfenypanzio@axelero.hu. Comfortable and characterful guesthouse close to the Greek Orthodox church; ski-hire available. *Dbl 7,000Ft, triple 8,500Ft, room for 4 10,000Ft, apt (for 2) 12,000Ft.*

**Hotel Henriette** Vasvári Pál utca 16; ℄ 47 323118. If you've packed one, there's plenty of room to swing a cat in the rooms of the Henriette, a short distance east of the Ferenc Kazinczy Museum. The furnishings are more than adequate too. *Dbl 7,000Ft, triple 8,500Ft; b/fast 1,000Ft.*

**Hotel Hunor** (26 rooms) Torzsás utca 1; ℄ 47 521521. Situated at the foot of Magas-hegy, next to the lower station of the chairlift (see page 283), the Hunor is a sparkling new hotel with well-appointed rooms and excellent facilities (including a fitness centre, bowling alley, tennis court and small swimming pool). A little out of the centre, it is on the bus route towards the village of Rudabányácska. Bike and ski hire available. *Dbl 12,500Ft, apt 17,000Ft.*

**Hotel Konig** (24 rooms) Széchenyi tér 5; ℄ 47 321696; e konighotel@axelero.hu. A gleaming-floored, Holiday-Inn-type hotel right in the centre, with a fitness room and sauna. The standard rooms are compact, while the 3 larger suites have the luxury of baths. *Sgl 11,700Ft, dbl 12,900Ft, suite 17,500Ft (excl b/fast).*

## Where to eat and drink

**Black Coffee** Széchenyi tér 2; ℄ 06 30 981 3817. Standing next to the Roman Catholic church (accessed via an archway), Black Coffee has an elegant but cheerful restaurant, serving international food, and a coffee house with some outside seating. *Mains 550–2,000Ft, avg 1,200Ft; café open 10.00–22.00 daily, restaurant 12.00–22.00 daily.* **Bodnár Wine House** Balassi Bálint utca 31; ℄ 47 321579; e bodnarpinceszet@freemail.hu. To the north of the centre up a steep track running off Kazsincy Ferenc utca. The friendly owner – whose family runs 6ha of vineyards – will show you around the computer-regulated pressing room, mouldy cellar and collection of 5,000 *ex libris* wines, before plying you with glasses in a rustic tasting room. Telephone in advance of a visit. *Tasting 2,500Ft/7 wines.*

**Csillagfény Restaurant** See page 281. The panzió restaurant offers Hungarian fare in a dated dining area decorated with kitsch mountain scenes and faux-candle chandeliers. *Mains 700–1,600Ft, avg 1,200Ft; open daily 11.00–22.00.*

**Henriette Café House** Dózsa György utca. The pavement corner outside the café is a popular place for the 20- and 30-somethings to pass time. *Open daily 10.00–22.00.*

**Spaten** Kossuth Lajos utca 10; ⟍ 47 321527. Rather dingy pub serving pasta, pancakes and other Hungarian dishes. *Mains 440–1,450Ft, avg 900Ft; open Mon–Sat 09.00–22.00, Sun 10.00–22.00.*

**Zempléni Casinó** Kazincsy utca 1–3; ⟍ 47 321470. Airy pizzeria. *Pizzas 570–2,160Ft; open daily 11.00–21.00.*

### What to see and do

The **Kazinczy Ferenc Museum** (*Dózsa György út 11;* ⟍ *47 322351; adult/concessions 400/200Ft; open Tue–Sun May 1–Sep 30 09.00–17.00, Oct 1–Apr 30 08.00–16.00*) is housed in a Neoclassical building that between 1835 and 1850 was the site of the Zemplén Casino, where the progressive movers and shakers met to chew the cud. An exhibition charting the town's history between 1261 and 1848 includes a reconstruction of the casino and a room devoted to Kazinczy, the leader of the language-reform movement (which established Hungarian as the literary lingo rather than German) during the Enlightenment period. Kazinczy had a colourful life during which he was imprisoned for six years – narrowly avoiding the death penalty – after implication in Martinovics's Jacobin conspiracy (see box, page 144). He was superintendent of the Sátoraljaújhely Calvinist Church (to the west of the museum) and the county archivist from 1820 in the current town hall. (He lived and was buried in nearby Széphalom, where there is an Ybl-designed literary memorial.) There is also a natural-history display, heavy on stuffed and pinned fauna from around Zemplén County.

Towards the northern end of Kossuth Lajos tér, the Baroque **town hall** (*Kossuth Lajos tér 5*) was erected in 1768, and is special for its rather unspectacular balcony; it was from here that Lajos Kossuth, the soul of the 1848–49 Revolution and War of Independence, delivered his first public speech in 1830. There is a **statue** of the man in the centre of the square, with a sword at his hip.

To the south of the statue is the broad and understated **Roman Catholic church** (*Széchneyi tér 10*), completed in 1792. More elaborate is the former **Piarist church** (*Deák utca 14*) to the northeast of the centre, with its extravagant altarpiece. A succession of churches rose and fell on this site – succumbing to the Turks, *kuruc* insurrections and fire – and the current late-17th-century incarnation only narrowly survived after Ferenc Rákóczi's instruction to level it was overlooked. Several earlier portions remain, such as the Gothic tower and northern wall of the Anjou-funded 14th-century church. The adjoining Pauline monastery became defunct after József II disbanded the order in 1786. A **Greek Orthodox church** (*Benczur Gyula utca*), slightly northwest of here on the other side of Kazinczy Ferenc utca, is also worth a peek for its peacock-iridescent iconostasis of 1759.

Before World War II, a significant proportion of the population was Jewish, and the town has two cemeteries. Among the stunted, sorry-looking gravestones of that to the south, in the fork between Kossuth Lajos utca and Esze Tamás utca (*to gain access,* ⟍ *47 312029*), is a restored memorial to rabbi Mózes Teitelbaum – who expounded an 18th-century form of Jewish mysticism, and purportedly performed miracles. A short distance further south, opposite the train and bus stations, is the early-20th-century turreted **Temple of Wine** (*Bortemplom; Fasor utca*), with colourful reliefs depicting towns of the region; the cellars of its decaying interior can store up to 12,000 hectolitres of wine.

The **Town Swimming Pool** (*Városi uszoda; Balassi Bálint utca 6;* \ *47 321116; adult/concessions 400/300Ft*) is just beyond the eastern end of Dózsa György utca, but those after exercise would do better to head for **Magas-hegy** (Tall Hill). There are walking trails and ski and sledge runs in winter. The **chairlift** (*libegő; Torzsás út 5;* \ *47 322346; adult/concessions 550/350Ft; open Tue–Wed 14.00–18.00, Fri 12.00–18.00, Sat–Sun 10.00–19.00*) is a real treat, the country's longest and cutting a 1,333m-long gash through the trees. Buses to Rudabányácska can drop you here; specify your destination to the driver. There are great views from the narrow-stepped (be careful if you're larger of foot) lookout tower (*kilátó*) at the top.

### Excursions from Sátoraljaújhely

There are a couple of villages worth sniffing out beyond the Zemplén Hills, tucked into the very northernmost tip of the country. **Széphalom** – with the Kazinczy mausoleum (see opposite) – falls on the way there, 6km north of Sátoraljaújhely. **Füzér** is 10km from Pálháza (with its narrow-gauge railway running to Rostalló), and has some wonderful and romantic peasant houses. On a hill above it (and giving spectacular views) are the remains of a 13th-century fortress razed by the Habsburgs in the aftermath of the Rákóczi-led War of Independence; its claim to fame is that the Holy Crown was kept within its walls following the devastating defeat by the Turks at Mohács. East of that, **Hollóháza** is renowned for its porcelain factory, producing pieces characterised by bright floral decoration. The modern church contains religious works by the renowned Margit Kovács. Buses run to these villages from Sátoraljaújhely, but you'll be less restricted if you visit by car.

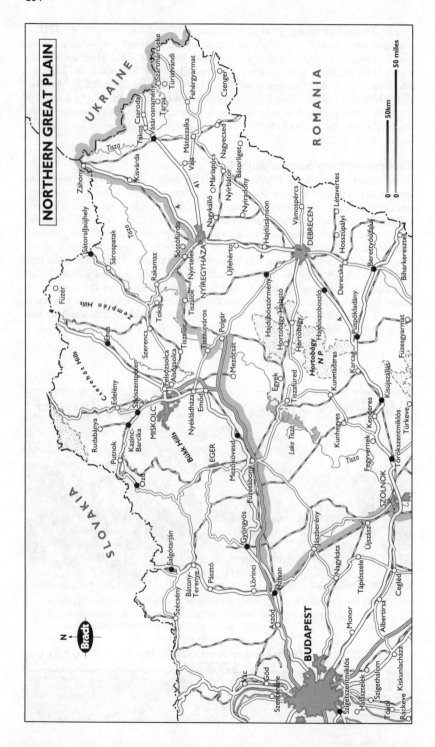

# Northern Great Plain

The Great Plain (Nagyalföld) is the heartland of Hungarian romanticism. It is a profoundly enigmatic place, a landscape occupied by the minds of poets and storytellers, by legends and folklore, a territory where the imagined and the actual blend like ink in water. Mirages deceive the weary traveller through the summer heat, and Petőfi observed that 'the earth and sky flow together'; it has been said that if your eyesight is good, gaze across the flat expanse and a week later you will see the back of your own head. Here the real can be unreal.

The Great Plain covers half of Hungary, filling a tract of lowland framed by the Danube in the west, the upland foothills in the north and the borders with Ukraine, Romania and Serbia. Perhaps appropriately, it has proved to be of shifting appearance. Originally it was forested and fertile, watered by regular floods from the Danube and Tisza. However, the Turks raped the land, stripping it of vegetation in their hunt for rebels and need for timber, and laying the topsoil bare to the wind. With no roots to bind the earth or suck up moisture, some portions turned to sandy wasteland and others to saturated marsh barely navigable in flat-bottomed boats. Fear of harsh Ottoman rulers drove country folk to the towns, particularly those towns under the direct protection of the sultan. A few brave toughs tilled in summer, living on isolated farmsteads (*tanyák*) – you'll come across them occasionally as you journey between settlements – but in essence this was inhospitable, bleak land. It became known as '*puszta*' – or 'abandoned'.

With the land uncultivated for such an extended period, and travel tricky, when life picked up again it was livestock and lawlessness that held sway. Domestic animals included racka sheep, hairy pigs and ill-tempered white cattle; the hardy shepherd, with his fleece coat and odd-looking herding dogs (see box, page 185), is a perennial figure in the colourful folklore of the plains. However, it was the horse and its uniformed herdsmen (*csikós*) that fully fired the imagination. This was – at least retrospectively – the age of romance, the Hungarian variation on the American 'Wild West', a time of hard riding and hard drinking, of horsemen and highwaymen, and the flamboyant, unbending, whip-cracking human spirit unbowed by the bully-boy force of authority.

Of course, the *csikós* of today are simply strutting showmen for tourists, and the *puszta* a shadow of its former barren self. In the 19th century a massive programme of river regulation tamed the Danube and the Tisza, and reclaimed much of the marshland for planting. It didn't achieve its purpose everywhere, though; the soil in some parts became increasingly alkaline, and came to harbour swathes of grassland rather than vegetables. The livestock and herders frolicked, but the days of the cowboys were numbered. With advances in industrial agriculture and irrigation, landowners were able to cultivate crops and needed fewer hands to do so. Agrarian movements did their best to fight – often bloodily – for the evicted peasant small holders and herders, but the intensive agricultural economy had arrived; romance was no match for mechanisation.

All is not lost. Sand dunes, alkaline lakes, grasslands and bogs remain preserved in national parks like Hortobágy, as do some of the ancient livestock breeds, curious creatures of corkscrew horns and matted fur. Horse shows replay the tricks that were once the trade of the manly herdsmen. One can clutch at the will o' the wisp of past isolation while journeying between towns and villages, lonely farmsteads forming islands in a considerable landscape. With the exception of a few pockets, the region remains Hungary's least touched by tourism and least readily travelled.

The colour and richness to be found elsewhere can at first sight seem thinly spread in the Great Plain. This is a place of dogged Calvinism rather than ebullient Catholicism, a place with a scarcity of historic buildings, a place where big towns are few and far between. However, there are several globally significant national parks, strong folk traditions, some important ecclesiastical, cultural and academic centres, the River Tisza (increasingly popular for kayak trips) and a few lively and pretty towns.

★  ★  ★

The Northern Plain (Észak Alföld) is the wilder section, the northeastern pocket Hungary's remotest region. In the past, this was somewhere to fear, its marshes difficult to navigate and prowled by wolves in winter. After the Turkish occupation the pastures between the swamps were leased to herders and shepherds who would drive their livestock to markets in Turkey, Poland, Austria and Italy. Debrecen, second-biggest city in the country, is its main staging post, reached from Budapest either on Road 4 or by leaving the M3 and following Road 33 via Tiszafüred and Hortobágy. An extension of the M3 from Polgár is under construction, and will pass beneath Nyíregyháza before heading northeast to the Ukrainian border. To the west of Debrecen is the famous Hortobágy National Park, which is a Unesco World Heritage Site and maintains the grassy steppe that thrived after the regulation of the Tisza in the 1840s, and Lake Tisza, an excellent spot for birdwatching and watersports. Other highlights include painted churches, wooden water mills and boat-shaped grave markers.

## SZOLNOK

Lying at the confluence of the Tisza and Zagyva 100km east of Budapest, Szolnok has been an important river-crossing point for centuries. As such, its 11th-century fortress had a particular significance, which was why the Habsburgs decided to do away with it after the town supported Rákóczi's War of Independence. The great reformer István Széchenyi also saw the potential of the place for the control of steamboating on the Tisza and in the development of rail; the Pest–Szolnok line – the country's second – opened in 1847, just in time to help in moving troops of the Hungarian army during the 1848–49 Independence War. By the turn of the 20th century, industry was thriving on the excellent transport links and the good times rolled. Not for long, though. World War I brought growth to a juddering halt, particularly towards the latter stages when the town found itself at the front and taking some serious pummelling. More was to come in 1944, when many, many buildings were destroyed during air raids in the summer and in the final autumnal fights before capture by the Soviet army. Historic buildings are inevitably thin on the ground, but who needs them when there are spas, riverbank promenades and watersports?

### Getting there and away

Route 4 links Szolnok with Budapest and Debrecen. The **bus station** (*Ady Endre utca*) is northwest of the Tourinform, on a road parallel with the main Baross Gábor út. There are direct services to and from many towns, including Budapest (Népliget and Stadion, but those from the former take half the time), Cegléd (up to four), Hatvan (one on weekdays), Kecskemét (up to ten), Szeged (up to eight), Szentes (up to six), Kalocsa (one on weekdays) and Jászberény (16). Buses to Debrecen require a change, usually at Tiszafüred.

The modern **train station** (*Jubileum tér 1–3*) lies on 1,100 pillars sunk down to a depth of 11m, and is 2km west of the centre along Baross Gábor út; local bus numbers 6, 7, 8 and 15 run from there into the middle. Szolnok is the hub of a railway-line wagon wheel, with no changes required for Budapest (Nyugati and Keleti), Debrecen, Békéscaba, Cegléd, Jászberény and Nyíregyháza. There are around five trains direct to Kecskemét and two to Szeged, but otherwise you'll need to change at Cegléd; change at Hatvan for Miskolc. You can take international trains to destinations over the Romanian border like Arad, Baia Mare and Bucharest.

## Information and other practicalities

**Cultural centre** Hild János tér 1; ☏ 56 514569. Close to the Tourinform, the cultural centre can give details of what's happening entertainment-wise.

**Jász-Nagykun-Szolnok County Nature Lovers' Association** Kossuth Lajos utca 11; ☏ 56 513730. Information on nature and walks in the area. *Open Wed 16.00–18.00.*

**Listings magazine** *Szolnoki Est*

**Szolnok Plaza** Ady Endre utca 28; ☏ 56 506502. Large American-style shopping mall. As well as shops, there is a multi-screen cinema and casino. *Open Mon–Sat 09.00–21.00, Sun 10.00–19.00.*

**Tourinform** Ságvári Endre körút 4; ☏ 56 420704; e szolnok-m@tourinform.hu. Hidden in one corner of a block of offices, behind Baross Gábor út . *Open Jun 15–Sep 15 Mon–Fri 08.00–19.00, Sat–Sun 09.00–18.00, rest of yr Mon–Fri 08.00–16.00, Sat 08.00–12.00.*

## Where to stay

**Diaktanya Szálló** (20 rooms) Tiszaligeti sétány 10; ☏ 56 413588; e diaktanya@sziszaki.sulinet.hu. Cheap student digs ten mins outside town that are open all year around. *Sgl 2,400Ft, dbl 3,400Ft, room for 4 7,200Ft.*

**Garden Hotel** (46 rooms) Tiszaliget; ✆ 56 420763; e info@gardenhotel.hu; www.gardenhotel.hu. A new but rather expensive hotel in the recreational area over the bridge from the centre. *Sgl 12,000Ft, dbl 17,000Ft, apt 25,000Ft.*

**Hotel Student** Mártírok útja 12–14; ✆ 56 421688. In the low-price bracket, but with accommodation available Jul 1–Aug 31 only. Right on the river. *Rooms 2,000–2,500Ft/pp.*

**Hozam Hotel** (11 rooms) Mária utca 25; ✆ 56 510530; e hozam@chello.hu; www.hozamrt.hu. The first 4-star hotel and the best in town – although you'll pay heftily – located in a quiet area close to the centre. *Sgl 17,000Ft, dbl 23,000Ft.*

**Sóház Hotel** (12 rooms) Sóház út 4; ✆ 56 516560; e reserve@sohazhotel.hu; www.sohazhotel.hu. The Sóház has been perching near the river for just 3 years; its rooms come in 3 sizes, and have comfortable (if slightly flimsy) fixtures, including kitchenettes. There is a tennis court. *Small 10,500–12,500Ft, medium 11,500–13,500Ft, large (up to 4) 15,000Ft; b/fast 800Ft.*

**Tisza Hotel & Spa** (33 rooms) Verseghy park 2; ✆ 56 210850; www.hoteltisza.hu. Near by – indeed, a step even closer to the water – is the town's Neo-Baroque old duchess, with rooms that are correspondingly staid (although there was promise of renovation when we visited). Attached is a Turkish-style spa and rounded, vaulted swimming halls (entrance inc in room price). *Sgl 11,300–13,300Ft, dbl 15,700–17,800Ft.*

There is **camping** at the western end of Tiszaligeti sétány.

## Where to eat

With up to a quarter of the population students, you'll have no difficulty finding somewhere to pick up a pizza.

**Galéria** Szapány út 1; ✆ 56 513053. Has a park terrace, good food and a good atmosphere. There's an international and Hungarian menu, as well as the obligatory pizza choices. *Mains 750–2,800Ft, avg 2,200Ft; open 12.00–23.00 daily.*

**Hozam** Mária utca 25; ✆ 56 510530. High ceilings and a classy ambience. *Mains 850–3,200Ft, avg 1,700Ft; open 12.00–23.00 daily.*

**Ristorante da Michele** Petőfi Sándor utca 6; ✆ 56 421242. A semi-Italian to the northwest of the centre, serving Hungarian dishes alongside its pizzas and pastas. The courtyard garden is lined with conifers and trellised creepers, and an outdoor grill quietens growling tums in summer months. Rightly popular. There's a student discount of 30% (15.00–18.00 daily). *Mains 900–2,000Ft, avg 1,500Ft; open 11.00–24.00 daily, barbecue 18.00–24.00.*

**Tisza Hotel Restaurant** See above. Like the Hozam, this is an elegant place to eat. *Mains 1,500–2,500Ft, avg 1,800Ft; open 12.00–23.00 daily.*

## Entertainment and nightlife

In Tiszaliget, **Moment-Ibiza Music Klub** (*Tiszaligeti út 1;* ✆ *64 421205; open Thu–Sat 20.00–late*) draws the students for schmoozing, boozing and boogying. The **Irish Pub** (*Szapáry utca 24*) on the opposite side of the river is lively too, but the choice for those who like to enjoy their drinks sitting down. Some of the time.

The **Szigliget Theatre** (*Szigligeti színház; Tisza park 1*), opposite the Tisza Hotel, blends elements of the modern and the Art Nouveau in its handsome look, a reflection of amendments made in 1991 to its original 1912 form. Beside the theatre is a statue of the theatre's eponym, the Hungarian dramatist Ede Szigligeti. Buy tickets at the **box office** (*Kossuth tér 17–23;* ✆ *56 422902; open Mon–Fri 09.00–13.00, 14.00–17.00*).

## What to see and do

Across the River Zagyva just east of Szabadság tér, you could very easily miss the lone standing piece of wall that is the sum remaining total of the once-formidable **Szolnok Castle** (*Gutenberg tér*). It was built in the 11th century, renovated and reinforced in 1550 (with the help of the renowned warden and hero of Eger Castle, István Dobó; in an attempt to stave off the Turks, before finally being obliterated by the Habsburgs in 1710. On the site of the former castle, the **Artists' Colony** (*Gutenberg tér 4;* ✎ *56 425549*) was established in 1902 and is one of the leading of its kind in the country. It has been the hive for great 20th-century artists like Béla Iványi Grünwald, Vilmos Aba-Novák, János Vaszary and Adolf Fényes. View work produced in the colony at the **Szolnok Gallery** (*Templom utca 2;* ✎ *56 378023; open Tue–Sun 09.00–17.00*), housed in the Moorish former synagogue designed by Lipót Baumhorn in 1899; concerts are also held here. There are summer organ concerts in the nearby 18th-century Baroque **Franciscan church and cloister** (*Templom utca 8*) too; the church is one of the town's oldest extant buildings.

Just to the north of Kossuth Lajos út is Kossuth tér, home to the town hall of 1884 and the **Damjanich János Museum** (*Kossuth tér 4;* ✎ *56 421602; www.djm.hu; admission free; open Mon–Tue May 1–Oct 31 10.00–17.00, Nov 1–Apr 30 10.00–16.00*). The late-Classical museum is named after the celebrated general who led the victorious fight against the Habsburgs at the 1849 Battle of Szolnok; he was later among the 13 generals martyred in Arad (now Romania) at the conclusion of the war (see page 19), and there is a marble memorial to him in Gutenberg tér. Exhibitions of archaeology, folk art (primarily pottery and fur) and ethnography chart the history of the Jász-Nagykun-Szolnok County, and there are works by the artists of the local colony and caricatures by Tibor Pólya.

The **Tabáni Tájház** (*Tabán utca 24;* ✎ *46 421602; adult 100Ft; open Apr 1–Sep 30 Thu–Sun 13.00–17.00*) – a peasant house next to the River Zagyva, 15 minutes from the centre – preserves the domestic set up in the Tabán district during the 1930s. This was a neighbourhood of water people; the fishing equipment in the yard was used for fixing nets, the main trade for anglers in winter.

If you follow Road 442 south out of the city for a few kilometres to Szandaszőlős, you'll come to an **Aeronautical History Museum** (*Hadtörténeti Aero Múzeum; Kilián utca 1;* ✎ *56 371831; adult/concessions 300/150Ft; open Apr 1–Oct 31 Tue–Fri 10.00–15.00, Sat–Sun 10.00–14.00*), with MIGs and other aircraft on the grass outside. Buses 34B and 37A run here.

### Other

Other attractions inevitably feature water. **Tisza Park Thermal Baths** (*Tiszaligeti sétány; adult/concessions 500/200Ft; open daily May–Aug 08.00–18.00*) are outdoors in Tiszaliget, while the **Damjanich Swimming Pools** (*Damjanich utca 3; adult/concessions 450/300Ft; open daily May–Sep 07.00–21.00, rest of yr 06.00–18.00*) are situated near the bridge on the other side of the Tisza, and have been something of a bastion for champion waterpolo players. The 'Dami' has thermal water too. There's a Turkish-style spa attached to the Hotel Tisza (see opposite), and an international rowing course on a dead channel of the Tisza.

### Festivals and events

Szolnok certainly isn't short of celebrations. Among the excuses for a party are the Music Festival in March and April, the Etelköz Festival in August, the Tisza Water Parade (along the promenade by the Hotel Tisza) on August 20, and the Goulash Festival in September. During the Tisza Summer Festival, there's a re-enactment of the Battle of Szolnok.

# JÁSZBERÉNY

Fifty kilometres east of Budapest, near the northern edge of the Great Plain, Jászberény is the cultural centre and largest town of the area known as the Jászság region, which was originally settled by an ethnic group of Iranian origin. The Jász (Jazygians) are said to have arrived here in the 13th century, Orthodox Christians who had split from the Alan clan. The dozen or so surrounding towns whose names begin with 'Jász-' bear testimony to the extent to which this ethnic group once controlled the region; the prefix is equally, however, one of the few remaining traces of the Persian-speaking people, whose mark is invisible even in the folk art. The citizens nevertheless still proudly refer to themselves as 'Jász's'.

Jászberény is relatively spread out, but everything of interest lies in the compact town centre. The majority of the structures worth seeing can be found on Lehel vezér tér – the leafy central square – or within a block or two of it. Lehel vezér tér is lined with Baroque buildings, churches, and monuments and plaques to the town's heroes of war and revolution. A narrow portion of the River Zagyva flows through the middle of town (parallel to Lehel Vezér tér, and one block north of it), and there are walking paths along the river bank.

## Getting there and away

The railway station is on Vaspálya utca, almost 2km from the centre, and a 30-minute walk down Rákóczi út. The bus station is a five-minute walk, on Petőfi tér. Buses and trains run regularly between Jászberény and Budapest. There is one daily **bus** to Debrecen, 12 to Kecskemét, three to Miskolc and three to Szeged. Direct **train** connections are limited – you need to transfer at Szolnok for most destinations – but there are regular trains to Szolnok and Hatvan. There is a train to Budapest nearly every hour.

## Information and other practicalities

**Ibusz** Szövetkezet utca 7/A; ↘ 57/412 143; e i056@ibusz.hu. Can arrange stays in private rooms, which cost around 2,500Ft/pp. *Open Jun–Aug Mon–Fri 08.00–16.00, Sat 08.00–12.00, weekdays only rest of yr.*
**Tourinform** Lehel vezér tér 33; ↘ 57 406439; email jaszberenyi@tourinform.hu. Sells good town maps for 250Ft and small booklets describing the town's sights for 30Ft, and can provide contact numbers for private rooms. *Open Mon–Fri 08.00–17.00.*

## Where to stay and eat

**Private rooms** can be arranged through Ibusz (see above); however, if you'd like to book in advance, the house of the Sárközi family (Mályva utca 8; ↘ 57 410 301 or 06 30 258 8736; e megilinda@freemail.hu; www.extra.hu/sarkozivendeg) comes highly recommended. There are two small panziós in town.

**Arizona Steakhouse** Serház utca 1; ↘ 57 412 042. Offers a decent range of steaks and ribs with a Hungarian accent, as well as typical national specialities. *Mains 1,100–2,200Ft, avg 1,400Ft; open daily 11.00–24.00.*
**Jóbarát Panzió** Dózsa György utca 22; ↘ 57 412646. This is the cheaper of the town's pensions, although the drop in price is matched by a drop in quality. *Rooms 2,500Ft/pp.*
**Kőhídi Vendeglő** Serház utca 1; ↘ 57 411234. In the same building as the Arizona Steakhouse, Kőhídi opens for lunch only, serving simple and cheap Hungarian food. *Mains 340–600Ft, avg 450Ft; open Mon–Fri 10.00–15.00.*
**Krémes Mézes** Dózsa György út 1; ↘ 57 412207. Has the largest selection of pastries and cakes, if you fancy something sugary to finish. *Open daily 08.00–18.00.*
**Morik Caffe** Piac téri sor; ↘ 57 405235. Delicious coffee, and a few sweets. *Open Sun–Thu 08.00–21.00, Fri–Sat 08.00–23.00.*
**Sólyom Panzió** Sólyom utca 8; ↘ 57 401267. Simple, clean and comfortable. *Rooms 6,500Ft/pp.*
**Touring Hotel** (26 rooms) Serház utca 3; ↘ 57 412051; email hoteltouringjb@vnet.hu. Although outdated and uninspiring, Touring is quite friendly (and is, in any case, the only real hotel in town). It is located between the bus station and Lehel Vezér tér, and does much of its business with the electronic company across the street. *Sgl 8,400–12,000Ft, dbl 9,700–13,500Ft.*

**Viktorio Pizzeria** Lehel vezér tér 31–33; \ 57 406858. Sitting just behind the Tourinform office, the Viktorio's pizzas and Hungarian dishes are popular both with students and local business people. *Pizza 170–860Ft, mains 77–2,200Ft, avg 800Ft; open Mon–Thu 11.00–24.00, Fri–Sat 11.00–02.00.*

## What to see and do

If your time is limited, you won't miss much by skipping the town's two museums. The main attraction of the **Jász Múzeum** *(Táncsics Mihály utca 5;* \ *57 412753;* e *jaszmuseum@mail.datanet.hu; adult 200Ft; open May 1–Sep 30 Tue–Sun 09.00–17.00, Oct 1–Apr 30 Tue–Fri 09.00–16.00, Sat–Sun 09.00–13.00)* is the Lehel horn, which is the symbol of the town and the entire region. Legend states that the intricately carved ivory horn belonged to a Magyar general named Lehel, who helped to conquer the area. It was said that after defeat by the German emperor in 955AD Lehel requested that he be allowed to blow his horn for a final time; when permission was granted, he killed the emperor with it. Academics have spoilt the story, though, by proving that the horn actually dates back only to the 11th century, and was probably originally used as a circus prop. The rest of the museum has sections on the Jazygian region, but (like many small town museums) is slightly amateurish and has few explanations in English.

The **Hamza Collection and Jász Gallery** *(Gyöngyösi utca 7;* \ *57 503260;* e *hamza.jaszbereny@museum.hu; adult/concessions 200/100Ft; open Wed–Sat 14.00–18.00, Sun 10.00–12.00)* is held in the former home of local artist Ákos Hamza. The museum presents his paintings and sculptures, his library, and hundreds of intriguing sketches by his fashion designer wife, Mária, who began her career in Paris.

Jászberény's **thermal spa** *(Hatvani utca 5;* \ *57 412108; thermal baths open all year Tue–Sun 09.00–18.00, outdoor pool May 1–Aug 31 only)* has five pools, a sauna, a fitness room and offers various massages.

### Festivals and events

The most notable of Jászberény's annual festivals is the Csángó Festival *(end Jul/early Aug)* celebrating the tiny Csángó group from Moldavia and other ethnic minorities.

## LAKE TISZA

Lake Tisza was created in the 1960s and '70s, when the River Tisza was dammed as part of the development of an irrigation system on the Great Plain. A happy by-product, it was hoped, would be a lake to rival Balaton. Lake Tisza spans 127km², and is treasured for its pristine natural environment, water-chestnut fields, mass of lily pads, winding channels surrounded by lush flora, and thriving birdlife. Two-thirds of it comprises significant wetland areas best visited by small boats capable of navigating the dozens of narrow courses. Scores of small islands, dead river arms and marshes make the lake popular with anglers, the experienced among whom know the deep or shallow points, the portions where catfish lurk and where carp are abundant. Indeed, it's claimed that there are more than 50 types of fish in the Tisza river and lake, which are stocked to keep supplies plentiful. Because the river runs through the lake, there are also sections of choppy water that are ideal for water sports. The lake can be divided into three parts. That north of Highway 33 is a bird reserve and part of Hortobágy National Park, and can only be visited with a guide at certain times. The middle portion is also under the auspices of the national park, but its giant white water lilies and colonies of heron and cormorant can be visited by following established trails. Other parts of the lake are not protected (the Sarud and Tiszafüred basins and the southern Abádszalók section), and is where the splashing and sporting takes place.

Those who want to avoid the crowds of Balaton come here instead. Bird lovers delight in nearly 150 species of bird nesting around the lake, and generally visit during the months between April and October. Note that it is forbidden to approach nests during the hatching period in April and May. Besides bird watching, the lake's shores are popular with cyclists, horse riders, boaters, fishers and sunbathers.

## Tiszafüred

Archaeological artefacts have been found in Tiszafüred dating back to 4500BC, and the settlement was first mentioned in 13th-century documents. However, beyond being an army headquarters during the 1849 War of Independence, when Lajos Kossuth spent quite a bit of time in town, very little of note happened here until the lake came into being. Now Tiszafüred is the central town, and with 15,000 residents it's the largest. This is where you are likely to base yourself, for it has the lion's share of the accommodation and facilities; there's a big, grassy strand, with lots of eateries, rental companies, open-air showers and stores. While Lake Tisza generally attracts bird spotters rather than night owls, Tiszafüred is one of the few towns that doesn't shut down after dinner and where sunbathers are prevalent during the day. Nevertheless, Tisza isn't like Balaton, and even in the height of the tourist season it's more about wildlife than wild nights.

### Getting there and away

Tiszafüred is on the Füzesabony–Debrecen rail line, and is 1½ hours by **train** from Debrecen (seven to nine daily trains). There are frequent trains to Karcag, two trains to Eger, and one daily train to Egyek (except Saturdays). The railway station (*Vasút utca 29;* ↘ *59 352648*) is a few blocks north of the Tourinform.

The **bus** station (*Bartók Béla út 37;* ↘ *59 351044*) is just south of the train station. There are eight daily direct buses to Debrecen (taking about 1½ hours). There are four daily buses to Budapest, but it's also possible to reach the capital by transferring at Eger or Szolnok. There are over a dozen daily buses to Eger, eight to Szolnok and seven to Hortobágy village. There's one direct bus to Hajduszoboszló, but it's easy to transfer there from Debrecen.

### Information and other practicalities

**Central Tisza Conservation Area** Szolnok, Tabán 5; ↘ 56 376899. This office in Szolnok, to the southwest, can provide information on conservation efforts at the lake and river. Call in advance.

**Lake Tisza Tourism Project Office** Kossuth tér 1; ↘ 59 351753; **e** rmitiszato@hungarytourism.hu; www.tisza-to-info.hu. This organisation will mail information on the Tisza region to those who want it in advance of their trip.

**Tourinform** Fürdő utca 21; ↘ 59 511123; e tiszafured@tourinform.hu. On entering Tiszafüred from the direction of Hortobágy (to the southeast), the office stands at the point where Highway 33 meets Fürdő utca. *Open Jun–Aug Mon–Fri 08.00–19.00, Sat–Sun 08.00–16.00, Sep–May Mon–Fri 08.00–16.00.*

For **fishing information** (including regulations, varieties and seasonal differences), contact MOHOSZ (↘ *59 352113;* e *mohosz@axelero.hu*) or the Tisza Lake Sport Fishing Company (↘ *06 20 972 0840*). Water quality is measured regularly; details about current **water conditions** can be found on the website of the Ministry of Environment and Water (*www.ktm.hu*).

## Tours and rentals

For further companies offering nature tours in Hungary, most including Lake Tisza, see *Tour operators*, pages 38–40.

**Bike rental** Kiss Pál út 1; ↘ 06 20 477 6828. Costs 1,000Ft/day. *Open daily 08.00–13.00, 14.00–17.00.*

**Bird Watching Hungary** ↘ 06 30 490 9303; e info@birdwatching.hu; www.birdwatching.hu. Organise nature tours and sightseeing trips by four-wheel drive at Lake Tisza. These range from a few hours to several days in length, and cost 12,500–15,000Ft/day.

**Borsod-Abaúj-Zemplén County Nature Walks Society** Miskolc, Selyemrét utca 1; ↘ 46 380471; e hegyitura@eszaktura.ngo.hu. Miskolc-based company that organises kayaking trips on the lake, and walking tours along the banks (*Jul 1–Aug 25*).

**Fidibus Ship Hotel** See page 294. The hotel and Ferenc Kovács offer 4-hour tours of the lake on small ships (holding 40 people), and specialised fishing trips (*May–Oct 15*).

**Gábor Füstös** Tiszafüred-Örvény, Kossuth utca 7; ↘ 59 350963. A fishing guide who rents motor boats and provides private accommodation.

**Gulyás Tanya** Tiszafüred-Örvény, Esze Tamás utca 2/B; ↘ 59 351814. A farm run by Kálmán Gulyás that has a year-round riding school, carriage rides and equestrian shows. It can also arrange riding tours (except during the winter) of up to a week and 'goulash parties' to accompany the equestrian shows. There are boats for hire and boat trips can be mapped out. The farm, 1½km from the lake, operates a small pension (*rooms 7,500Ft*).

**Horgász Centrum** Fishing Centre; Kasfonó út 12; ↘ 59 353443 or 06 30 965 9824; www.horgaszcentrum.hu. The proprietor, Sándor Szövetes, has been fishing on the Tisza for decades, and has made this store near the lake shore an indispensable stop for all things fishing related. You'll find fishing supplies (for sale and hire), and boat rentals and instruction; you can also book fishing trips (of up to a week). *Open Apr 15–Oct 15, 24 hrs a day.*

**Imre Fatér** ↘ 06 30 445 6856. Imre works for the Hungarian Ornithological Society, and offers bird-watching tours at Lake Tisza for groups of no more than 8 (*Apr–Oct*). Guests are transported by Land Rovers, and binoculars, telescopes and field guidebooks are provided.

**Imre Szabics** ↘ 06 30 954 8620. Offers boats for rent and organises other activities.

**Kormorán Kft** Ady Endre utca 16; ↘ 59 350350. Fishing guides, canoe and motor-boat rentals, and 2-hour boat tours (*max 4 people/boat; Apr–Nov*).

**Tiszai Sporthajózási Egyesület** X, Budapest, Érsemlyéni út 10; ↘ 06 20 492 9821; e lostris@axelero.hu. Budapest-based company that organises excursions of up to ten days on Lake Tisza. These can be eco-tours or water-sports trips.

## Where to stay

There are no swish hotels in Tiszafüred, which instead has dozens of modest private pensions (some of which are only open in summer). Alternatively, keep an eye out for '*Zimmer frei*' signs (indicating private rooms) or, if you're travelling with others, consider renting an apartment (which can work out very cheap). There are also several campsites – most of the ports, for instance, have one alongside (see page 297); bungalows generally cost 2,000–3,000Ft/night, and tent space 500Ft (plus 500Ft/pp).

**Fidibus Ship Hotel** (10 rooms) Tiszafüred, Pf 95; ☎ 59 351818; e fidi@fidi.hu; www.fidi.hu. One for the most dedicated waterbabies, who can stay out on the lake over night. Anchored on a dead branch of the Tisza, this hotel on a boat unsurprisingly has the top lake views in town. Guests also get a range of discounted services (occasional boat trips, equipment usage) and the hotel owns another boat that can be chartered out to groups (*40,000Ft/day*). *Rooms 1,800Ft/pp.*

**Füzes Panzió** (10 rooms) Húszöles út 31/B; ☎ 59 351854. Near the lake, rooms here are comfortable and clean, although the décor is nothing to shout about. Breakfast isn't included, but there's a restaurant next door. *Sgl 2,900Ft, dbl 5,900Ft.*

**Gál Guest House** (5 rooms) Hársfa út 2; ☎ 59 352359. A family-run pension with a yard, terraces and a kitchen that guests are free to use. *Rooms €10/pp; b/fast €2.*

**Horgász & Családi Camping & Panzió** (29 apts, 39 bungalows) Kastély út; ☎ 59 351220; e horg.camp@dpg.hu. The owners reel in the anglers by offering special fishing packages, organising fishing trips, helping with fishing licences and serving as tour guides. If you're a fisherman out of water, the complex also has plenty of dry-land entertainment – including volleyball and tennis courts. *Accommodation 7,000Ft/pp, camping 500–600Ft/pp; open Apr 1– Nov 30.*

**Magdalena Guest House** (3 rooms) Gesztenyés utca 22; ☎ 06 30 349 8299. Pleasantly decorated pension with a yard, standing just 300m from the lake. *Rooms 3,000Ft/pp; open Mar 1–Oct 31.*

**Mani Resort** (10 apts) Szabadság utca 20–22; ☎ 59 350484. A small apartment-complex of a hotel about 1km from the lake, with traditional thatched roofs and a pool. The apts (for 4) have private bathrooms. *Apt 15,000Ft; open Mar 1–Oct 31.*

**Nádas Panzió** (9 apts) Kismuhi utca 2; ☎ 59 551401. This cosy little pension has a wine cellar, a pool, and beautifully furnished rooms with fully equipped kitchens. *Apts (2–6) €18–22/pp.*

**Service Plus Tourism** Húszöles út 78/D; 59 511167; e serviceplus@axelero.hu. This organisation arranges private, fully-equipped rental houses for 4–12 people. The houses are well stocked, and even come with a gardener to care for the lawn. A 2-hour boat trip on the lake is included in the weekly rental price. *Houses 85,000Ft/week (for 4), 255,000Ft/week (for 12).*

## Where to eat

This region is famous for its inns or saloons (*csárda*), old-style restaurants located on the highways. Originally built to provide resting places for shepherds or travellers, they are most often located outside towns and cities. Tiszafüred has few real, sit-down restaurants. In the warm months, open-air snack bars and food stands open along the strand and in the town.

**Molnár Vendéglő** Húszöles út 31/B; ⍦ 59 352705. The leading restaurant in Tiszafüred, serving typical Hungarian specialities, and a huge variety of fish (particularly pike perch and trout). It has fancier stuff too (like caviar), and a decent vegetarian selection. *Mains 950–2,000Ft, avg 1,800Ft; open daily 11.00–20.00.*

**Pánorama Restaurant** ⍦ 59 360109. On the lake shore, Pánorama serves the kind of cheap, satisfying food that caters to a post-swim hunger. The kitchen puts out simple Hungarian dishes, and lots of fish. *Mains 400–2,000Ft, avg 800Ft; open daily Sep 1–May 31 10.00–22.00, Jun 1–Aug 31 08.00–23.00.*

**Patkós Csárda** ⍦ 52 378605. A traditional-looking place between Tiszafüred and Hortobágy that cooks up regional specialities, and is one of the best inns. There is frequently live gypsy strumming, and if you're really lucky you'll pitch up during an ox roast. The Patkós also operates a pension and campsite. On Highway 33, by the turn off to Egyek. *Mains 700–2,300Ft, avg 1,400Ft; open daily 08.00–22.00.*

**357 Western Restaurant** Húszöles utca 163; ⍦ 59 351151. Looks Texan from the outside, but its menu is like many others in offering Hungarian choices and pizza. There is also Tisza fish and good game specials, and a pizza-delivery service if you're staying in town. *Pizza 900Ft, mains 700–2,300Ft, avg 1,200Ft; open daily 08.00–22.00.*

## What to see and do

The Lake Tisza region is rated highly for its **folk art**, particularly basket weaving, pottery and leather work, and the bulk of the non-wet attractions revolve around such cultural output. Many local artists throw open their workshops and homes to visitors, to show and sell their colourful creations; there are no fixed opening hours for these places.

**Imre Szűcs** (*Belsőkertsor utca 4/A;* ⍦ *59 351483; free admission*) is one of the best-known potters in the area, and holds the title 'Master of Folk Art'. In the 1970s when folk-style pottery was steadily going out of fashion, Szűcs endeavoured to revive the old traditions. His most popular creations revolve around animals – pigs, hens, roosters and other birds – but he uses a range of motifs and shades. Some of his pieces have found their way into museums. Imre often gives demonstrations at his workshop, and his wife and daughters are also potters; there is a 'house museum' in the basement where all of the items on view are for sale. **Zsóka Török Nagy** (*Szőlősi út 27;* ⍦ *59 353538*) once worked at Imre Szűcs's studio, but her style is quite different since she also studied under other potters. At Zsóka's studio, you can get your hands dirty and have a bash at making a pot yourself.

The **Nyúzó Gáspár Pottery Museum** (*Malom utca 12;* ⍦ *59 352106; adult 100Ft; open May 1–Sep 30 Tue–Sat 09.00–12.00, 14.00–17.00*) is located inside the former home of two of Tisza's most-famous potters (father and son). Nyúzó junior died in 1922. The house is still furnished as it was when inhabited by the Nyúzó family, and the museum shows how the old potters from the region lived and worked.

The **Kiss Pál Museum** (*Tariczky sétány 6;* ⍦ *59 352106; adult 100Ft; open Thu–Sat 09.00–12.00, 13.00–17.00*) displays further craftwork in the Neoclassical Lipcsey Hall, particularly the leather saddles produced by highly skilled artisans. You can learn how to create such masterpieces yourself at the **Leatherwork Production House** (*Ady Endre*

## THE BIRDS OF LAKE TISZA

The bird sanctuary at Lake Tisza, to the north of the Debrecen–Füzesabony railway line (and close to Tiszafüred), is technically part of the Hortobágy National Park and is one of the best places in the country for bird watching and observing the rest of the lake's largely unspoiled flora and fauna. The western half of the reserve is covered in water during summer (the floodgates open in spring, filling the reservoir, which reaches its peak level by June), while to the east the oxbow lakes, ponds, marshes and scrubland form a varied landscape. The most strictly protected areas can only be visited with a guide, but you can twitch from the edges of the reserve and the embankments, so unofficial visitors should head for these vantage points. A good way to see birdlife is with a walk on the dyke at Poroszló as far as Négyes, a stretch that offers decent views over the reserve. Lake Tisza's combination of two very different habitats – the river bed (with its currents attracting fish like the sturgeon) and the atmospheric dead channels and basins (most of which were cut off during the river regulation, and now home to bream, pike and carp) – is unique, and pulls in animals aplenty. Over 147 species of bird nest at the lake, and expert bird guides are easy to find (see page 293). In addition, there is a bird rescue centre at the Górés Tanya (❧ 06 30 515 3463), where you can mingle with recuperating storks; the Egyek-pusztakócs marshland bicycle track (at the Egyek exit of Highway 33) takes in the farm.

Hortobágy is said to be the largest bird migration congregation point in central Europe, and after Lake Tisza was created the same types of birds began to migrate there. It's estimated that 80,000–100,000 birds inhabit Lake Tisza during the spring migration, with over 250,000 passing through. Wild geese are visible in the open areas; shore birds like ruffs, black-tailed godwits, and lapwings are abundant; heron and cormorant colonies are plentiful; ducks, particularly mallards, are everywhere towards the end of the summer; and white-tailed eagles are regular winter visitors. Among the others you might encounter are the osprey, common gull, great reed warbler, kingfisher, common tern, whiskered tern, white-fronted goose, grey duck, golden-eye, tufted duck, little egret, great white egret, greylag goose, black stork, night heron and tufted heron. Don't forget your binoculars!

út 45; ❧ 59 353501; costs 500Ft/hr, plus materials); there is also a collection of leatherwork by a regional craftswoman.

### Other activities

The main attraction at Lake Tisza is **swimming** among water lilies in secluded channels, but there's also fishing, boating, hiking and horseback riding. The southern part of the lake is the place to head for **motor boating** and other **water sports**, and boats can be hired from most of the 'ports' around the lake; motor boats (3,500–4,800Ft/day, plus petrol, for 5 people) or canoes (1,500–2,000Ft/day) can be rented on the spot with no training necessary. A **canoe** is the ideal way to explore the lake; motor boats are banned beyond the southern section, and can't in any case reach the smaller, narrower channels and canals or many of the islands that are most worth experiencing. For **birdwatching**, see box above.

If you are unsure of how to get started, or want a more thorough tour of the lake, you should enlist the services of a guide. There are six specified tour routes on the lake; of these, one requires a guide and Tourinform recommends the use of a guide for four of the others. Tour guides can be booked at the ports, along with boat trips (4,000–5,700Ft/2 hours) and fishing trips (*3,000–5,700Ft/day, plus petrol*). Details of the ports in the vicinity of Tiszafüred are as follows; alternatively see page 293 for details of local tour and rental companies.

**Albatrosz Port** Tiszafüred, Bán Zsigmond utca 67; ⟍ 06 30 967 6037
**Kormorán Port** Tiszafüred-Örvény; ⟍ 06 20 939 1979
**Szabics Port** Tiszafüred-Örvény; ⟍ 06 30 954 8620
**Katamarán Port** Tiszafüred-Örvény; ⟍ 06 30 952 7039

There are **hiking** and **biking** trails around the lake, with no steep hills to spoil the fun; Tourinform can provide detailed maps. The **Tiszafüred Thermal and Medicinal Baths** (*Poroszlói utca 2;* ⟍ *59 352366; adult 450Ft; open daily May 1–Oct 31 07.30–19.00, Nov 1–Apr 30 08.30–17.00*) have four pools, and offer a range of massages and treatments.

# HORTOBÁGY

Hortobágy, 25 miles west of Debrecen, is a tiny village in the thick of the vast Hortobágy National Park. This area looms very large in Hungarian folklore and poetry, and the image of horsemen in traditional garb galloping across the wide plain is as much a part of the country's identity as goulash and Bull's Blood. The place drips with romance, the legends alive from the days when cattle herders, shepherds and cowboys were abundant on the *puszta*. There are homesteads, barns and long-handled *shadoof*-like wells (*gémeskút*); ancient burial mounds (*sírdomb*) are also conspicuous when they break the pancake-flat landscape. A recurrent phenomenon recorded in literature is the appearance of ghostly forms here, from broad cities to solitary human figures. These mirages (known as *délibáb*) are said to form during muggy summer days, when layers of humid air with different temperatures come together. The tourist industry has very much hitched its wagon to the Hortobágy's mystique; be prepared for the ubiquitous overblown horse shows and busloads of tourists ushered in for packaged versions of old-style Hungarian living.

Although Hortobágy includes the largest area of grassland in central Europe, it also has its marshy swampland. Hortobágy village is the place to start your exploration, and is where the majority of the restaurants, hotels and facilities are located (although most visitors come on day trips). Animal breeding and keeping is one of the prime occupations at Hortobágy, and it is famous for its animal park. The animals presumably keep a wary eye on the Hortobágy Csarda across the street, which dishes up some of the Hungarian special breeds for eating. Another classic Hortobágy site is the Nine-Arch Bridge, where the Bridge Festival is held each year.

This is horse country, and riding schools abound; for the less active, there are carriage tours too. Otherwise the national park is full of walking paths and bird-watching areas, and is best visited in the warmer months. Few come in winter, but if you do, be prepared for biting winds blowing across the flat landscape. An admission ticket is required to visit a few protected areas of the park (*800Ft from Tourinform*) and some others are only accessible with a guide (contact a specialist tour company; see pages 38–40 and 298).

## Getting there, away and around

Hortobágy is best explored by **car**, since trains and buses won't take you to the lesser-visited pockets. Highway 33 cuts through the park, and you can take in a traditional *csárda* along the way. There are, however, decent train and bus connections to the village itself. From Debrecen, **trains** in the direction of Tiszafüred and Füzesabony call at Hortobágy (over a dozen daily trains in the summer from Debrecen, and around seven the rest of the year). From Nyíregyháza, trains stop at Óhat-Pusztakócs (a few kilometres west of Hortobágy village), and you can pick up a connecting train from there. There are two daily trains to Eger. There are no direct trains from Budapest; instead you'll need to change at Füzesabony. The train station (Dékány köz) is a few blocks from the Hortobágy Csárda, via Kossuth utca.

## HORTOBÁGY NATIONAL PARK

Hortobágy is Hungary's biggest and oldest national park, founded in 1973 and now spreading over 81,000ha. Up until the drainage project undertaken in the middle of the 19th century, the area was regularly flooded by the Tisza; at that time, boats (not wagons) were the chosen means of transport. The engineering resulted in a landscape dominated by alkaline floodplains covered with grasslands – known as *puszta*. The park's flat expanse of *puszta* grassland is not only the largest in Hungary, but in the whole of central Europe. And on it graze traditional national livestock breeds – Hungarian grey cattle and racka sheep – just as they have done for hundreds of years. This is shepherd country.

Apart from the *puszta*, the national park is characterised by two other main habitats. The first is floodplain forest and oxbow lakes, lush left-overs from the days when the Tisza oozed free on the plain. The second is similarly sodden, comprising marshes and lakes. The park holds over 5,000ha of fishponds, together with 7,000ha of Lake Tisza; these bodies of water in part compensate for the surface water lost during the drainage programme. Such diverse habitats spawn unique species, including salt-tolerant types in the seasonal salt marshes, aquatic sedge and rush communities, loess deserts, grasslands and special woods. The entire wetland complex forms a very significant breeding, feeding, staging and wintering site for many species of migratory waterbirds and wetland-related raptors – indeed, the total number exceeds a million. Among these, Hortobágy regularly supports 60–80,000 European cranes, lesser white-fronted and red-breasted geese, dotterel and black-tailed godwit during migration periods; with a permit (from Tourinform), you can observe these from birdwatching towers at the fishpond system.

**Buses** leave from the Hortobágy Csárda. The bus service is less frequent into the park, but there are buses from Debrecen, Hajdúszoboszló, Eger and Tiszafüred. There are no direct buses between Budapest and Hortobágy; the most convenient route is to make a transfer at Eger. There are eight daily buses from Hortobágy to both Debrecen and Eger. Once there, Tourinform can advise of places to hire **bikes**.

## Information and other practicalities

**Hortobágy National Park Directorate** Debrecen, Súmen utca 2; ☎ 52 529920; e hnp@hnp.datanet.hu; www.hnp.hu. If you're coming from Debrecen, pop into the national-park office first for information.

**Tourinform (Pusztainform)** Petőfi tér 1; ☎ 52 589321; e hortobagy@tourinform.hu. Inside the Herdsmen's Museum at Hortobágy village. Pick up detailed park maps here, as well as admission tickets for those protected areas that require them. *Open Apr 15–Oct 15 daily 09.00–17.00, Oct 16–Apr 14 Mon–Fri 09.00–16.00.*

### Tour guides

**Bird Watching Hungary** ☎ 06 30 490 9303; e info@birdwatching.hu; www.birdwatching.hu. Organises nature tours and sightseeing trips by four-wheel drive in the Hortobágy. These range from a few hours to several days in length, and cost 12,500–15,000Ft/day.

**Imre Fatér** ☎ 06 30 4456856. Imre works for the Hungarian Ornithological Society, and offers bird-watching tours at Hortobágy for groups of no more than 8 (*Apr–Oct*). Guests are transported by Land Rovers, and binoculars, telescopes and field guidebooks are provided.

For further details of companies arranging nature tours of the region, see page 38.

## Where to stay and eat

Accommodation options are limited in Hortobágy, but the Tourinform does have a list of more than 40 families offering **private rooms**. Many people prefer to stay in Debrecen and take day trips to Hortobágy.

**Hortobágy Club Hotel** (54 rooms) Hortobágy-Máta Pf 11; ✆ 52 369020; e hortobagyhotel@axelero.hu; www.hortobagyhotel.hu. Just north of Hortobágy village (near the Epona Equestrian Village), this is one of the best-equipped (and most expensive) hotels in the area, with 2 pools, a sauna, a tennis court, spa facilities and 2 restaurants. There are great views of the plain from the grounds, and rooms are spacious and comfortable. *Rooms 12,000–29,000Ft.*

**Hortobágy Csárda** Petőfi tér 1; ✆ 52 589339. The area's most-renowned restaurant by a country mile. The 300-year-old building sits just across from the Nine-Arch Bridge, and specialises in dishes concocted from animals bred in the national park (including Hungarian grey cattle, buffalo, mangalica pig, racka lamb and guinea fowl). The grey-cattle steaks are among the tenderest you'll taste. *Mains 1,000–2,000Ft, avg 1,600Ft; open daily 08.00–22.00.*

**Hortobágy Fogadó** (11 rooms) Kossuth utca 1; ✆ 52 369137. Simple rooms and no fancy extras. The whole place is slightly run down, but it's one of the few places to stay in the centre of Hortobágy village. The restaurant downstairs (*mains 600–1,000Ft, avg 800Ft; open Mon–Sat 06.00–20.00*) has cheap tucker, but has little else to tempt you away from the superior Hortobágy Csárda. *Sgl 3,500Ft, dbl 6,000Ft, triple 8,000Ft, room for 4 10,000Ft.*

**Hortobágy Hotel & Camping** (20 rooms) Borsósi utca 12; ✆ 52 369071; e hortobagyhotel@freemail.hu. The hotel has slightly outdated en-suite rooms. The farm-like grounds are perfect for evening walks, and there is an attached restaurant. On Highway 33, near mile post 74. *Sgl 2,900Ft, dbl 5,800Ft, triple 7,800Ft, room for 4 9,800Ft; camping 750Ft.*

**Kadarcsi Csárda** ✆ 52 370101. The first restaurant on this site was built in 1761, although the current incarnation has stood since 1843 and is considered a historical monument. The whitewashed walls, period furnishings and old-style atmosphere is typical of the region's *csárda*; as you'd expect, there's traditional Hungarian food with occasional live gypsy music. The regional specialities are excellent. On Highway 33, at the 86km mark. *Mains 900–2,300Ft, avg 1,600Ft; open daily 10.00–22.00.*

**Pásztortanya Vendégfogadó** (5 rooms) Hortobágy Halastó; ✆ 52 369127; e pasztortanya@freemail.hu. Sparse rooms and a small restaurant with a limited Hungarian menu and a pleasant terrace. On Highway 33, near mile post 67. *Dbl 4,000Ft.* **Puszta Camping** ✆ 52 369300. Stands on the river bank, just past the Herdsmen's Museum. *Open May–Oct.*

## What to see and do

The **Nine-Arch Bridge** is the longest stone road bridge (167m) in Hungary, and is the symbol of Hortobágy village. Constructed in 1826, it replaced earlier wooden bridges at the same point that gave way during floods; considering it's the park's leading architectural monument, it is surprising that cars are still allowed to cross (it forms part of Highway 33).

The **Herdsmen's Museum** (*Pásztormúzeum; Petőfi tér 2;* ✆ *52 369119; adult/concessions 250/150Ft; open daily Mar 16–Apr 30 10.00–16.00, May 1–Sep 30 09.00–18.00, Oct 1– Dec 31 10.00–14.00, Jan 1–Mar 15 by prior arrangement*) commemorates the shepherds and herders of the Great Plain, showcasing the trappings of their everyday lives – embroidered leather cloaks, cooking utensils and equestrian clobber. There are also beautiful wildlife postcards on sale, together with national-park maps and CDs of ethnic shepherd music. The building, raised in 1785, was once the coach house for patrons of the Hortobágy Csárda across the street.

There are several other little collections to visit. Behind the museum, the **Hortobágy Gallery** (*Petőfi Sándor tér 1;* ✆ *52 369401; free admission; open Tue–Sun Apr 1–Oct 31 09.00–17.00, Nov 1–Mar 31 09.00–16.00*) shows works of art taking the *puszta* for their muse, and has an exhibition introducing the park's flora and fauna. The **Meggyes Csárda** (*Highway 33, 60km mark;* ✆ *06 70 231 4073; open by appointment only*) is a tavern museum with ethnographical pieces celebrating life in the Hortobágy and the *puszta* around the turn of the 19th century, when there were over 40 *csárda* touting for business. The three-room building was constructed in 1760, and contains tables, benches and shepherds' cloaks (*szűr*) hanging from the coat peg. The **Hortobágy Village House** (*Kossuth Lajos utca 8;* ✆ *52 369570*) hosts temporary art exhibitions and cultural events. There is a display covering the park and its birds of prey at the **Hortobágyi Körszín** (*Round Theatre; open Tue–Sun May 1–Jun 30 & Sep 1–Oct 15 10.00–16.00, Jul 1–Aug 30 09.00–17.00*).

The **Puszta Animal (or Rare Breed) Park** (✆ *52 701037; open daily Mar 1–Nov 1 09.00–17.00, Jun–Aug 09.00–18.00; adult 250Ft*) rears traditional Hungarian species, several of which are native to the Great Plain. Among the animals snuffling, trampling or fluttering around are curly haired mangalica pigs, Hungarian grey cattle, racka sheep (with horns like twists of ribbon), domestic water buffalo, Transylvanian bald-neck hens, several types of turkey, and Hungarian pigeons. The striking dreadlocked dogs that you'll see springing around here (and throughout the region) are sheep herders called *puli* (see box, page 185). An exhibition gives some background to the animals. This place makes meaty forkfuls at Hortobágy Csárda guilty ones. To get to the park, turn left after the Nine-Arch Bridge.

### Hortobágy-Halastó

Six kilometres west of Hortobágy village (and one stop on the train), the Hortobágy-Halastó (fishpond) is ideal for bird watching. The area covers approximately 2,000ha, and has a bundle of watch towers offering fantastic views of the storks, mallards and cranes. The fishponds also harbour the strictly protected spoonbills and great white egrets; even the retiring grey heron is found among its old reedbeds. Spring and autumn are ideal twitching times, with flocks of thousands of birds filling the sky in preparation for their migration. It is said that 342 bird species have been spotted in Hortobágy, and 152 of those nest in the park. An educational track embarks from between kilometre markers 64 and 65 on Highway 33. An admission pass is required to visit Halastó. For details of guides, see above, page 298.

## Horseriding

Two kilometres from the village, the **Hortobágy Máta Stud Farm** (*Hortobágy-Máta, Czinege János utca 1;* ☎ *52 589369*) is one of the country's major breeding centres, much of its effort directed towards the preservation of the *noniusz* – considered an ideal horse. There are over 250 horses at this 300-year-old farm, and some of these are available for hire. Cross-country and short-distance riding options are available, together with lessons, carriage tours, competitions and equestrian shows.

**Epona** (*Hortobágy-Máta;* ☎ *52 369020*), the Hortobágy equestrian village (1½km from the bridge), claims to be Hungary's largest riding centre. You can watch a touristy horse show, take riding lessons or carriage trips, or hire your own horse for gallops across the *puszta*.

## Festivals and events

The annual Bridge Fair is one of Hortobágy's big events, and takes place at the foot of the Nine-Arch Bridge on August 20 (and a weekend either before or afterwards). Originally a livestock market, you no longer need to work out how to fit a cow in your suitcase; the fair sells a range of goods, from local foods and wines to arts, crafts and folk items from all over Hungary. The highlight for many is the traditional ox roast, and the preparation of other specialities like *shlambuts* (a *puszta* potato-and-pasta dish). The music and dancing isn't bad either!

On Village Day (*May*), there are folklore programs, traditional games and food, equestrian events, and folk song and dance. International Hortobágy Equestrian Days (*first weekend in Jul*) has show jumping, carriage-driving competitions, a folk-art fair and horse-herding shows, while at the Herdsmen's Goulash Contest (*Jun*) you can learn how to cook goulash and other *puszta* shepherds' favourites. If cooking isn't your thing, sit back and taste all the expert efforts of the locals.

## DEBRECEN

Debrecen is the second-largest city in Hungary, a lively university town, and a significant centre for Hungarian Calvinism. Less than 50km from the Romanian border and 100km from Ukraine, it is off the beaten tourist track; nevertheless it is a good base for exploring eastern Hungary. In the 14th and 15th centuries, Debrecen was an important and wealthy market town – indeed, it still hosts several annual markets – and during the 15th century its citizens were granted rights and privileges only equalled by those of Buda. Trouble came in the 16th century when the country was split (see page 17), and Debrecen ended up on the border; residents were obliged to pay taxes both to Austria and Turkey, a financial burden that hit hard. Things improved with the introduction of Calvinism, which rapidly spread in the mid 16th century and proved a durable faith – today 20–30% of Hungarians are Calvinists.

The Calvinist Reformed College was founded in 1538, and students from all corners of the country gathered to participate in its rigorous programme. After the departure of the Turks, Debrecen was granted the title of 'free royal town' by the Habsburgs. It continued to grow, and when the Great Reformed Church was erected in 1821 (becoming the symbol of the city), Debrecen began to take its modern face. During the 1848 revolution, the nation's capital was transferred from the embattled Budapest and parliament met in the Great Reformed Church. Kossuth gave a famous speech there before the revolution was quashed. The suppression of the revolution didn't prevent Debrecen from expanding rapidly over subsequent decades; its population steadily increased and several universities were established. The city was severely hurt during World War II, and much of it was bombed and burned. Now, however, Debrecen is one of Hungary's great university cities and an important cultural centre of eastern Hungary. It attracts many international students, especially for its renowned, intensive Hungarian-language course (*www.nyariegyetem.hu*); it is said that after a month of lessons students leave speaking fluent Hungarian – an impressive (and questionable) boast when many English ex-pats still struggle after a decade's exposure to the lingo.

## Getting there, away and around

The **railway station** (*Petőfi tér 12;* ❧ *52 346777*) is a few blocks south of the end of Piac utca, which leads to the city centre. There are good train connections in and out of Debrecen, including almost a dozen daily services to Budapest, trains to Nyíregyháza every half an hour, and regular services to Hortobágy. The **bus station** is conveniently located too, near the meeting point of Széchenyi utca and Nyugati utca. To reach the centre, walk east on Széchenyi utca until you hit the pedestrian Piac utca. Hajdú Volán (*Külső Vásár tér 12;* ❧ *52 413999*) offers frequent connections to all the small towns of the region (including Hajdúböszörmény and Hajdúszoboszló), and tickets can be bought on board the buses. To get to Hortobágy National Park, however, the train is preferable since there are few daily buses. Getting to other regions of the country is more difficult from Debrecen via bus, although there are daily buses to Békéscsaba, Eger, Gyula, Jászberény, Nyíregyháza, Szeged and Tiszafüred.

Debrecen has reliable **tram** and **bus** networks, but unless you are heading out to the university area, the thermal baths or the Nagyerdei Park you will have little need to use them. For a good and cheap sightseeing tour of the city, take the number 1 tram (the only tram line) out to the leafy university area and Nagyerdei Park. You can pick up the tram from its terminus at the train station, or along Kossuth tér. It runs in a circle, and riding its length will allow you to get your bearings. For **taxis**, try Főnix Taxi (✆ *52 444444*), Főtaxi (✆ *52 444555*) or City Taxi (✆ *52 422222*).

## Information and other practicalities

**Hajdú-Bihar County and Debrecen Hiking Association** Simonffy utca 1/C; ✆ 52 342951. Information on walking, hiking and nature in the region. *Open Wed 15.00–17.00.*

**Hortobágy National Park Directorate** Sumen utca 2; ✆ 52 349922. The national park office, which can offer advice on where to go, what to see and which areas can only be accessed with a guide or pass.

**Ibusz** Révész tér 2; ✆ 52 415555. *Open Mon–Fri 08.00–17.00, Sat 09.00–13.00.*

**Tiszántúl Representation to the Hungarian Human Ecology Society** Jerikó utca 17–19; ✆ 80 200494. Organises bicycle tours, field trips and excursions to the national parks.

**Tourinform** Piac utca 20; ✆ 52 412250; e tourinform@ph.debrecen.hu. Centrally located next to Kossuth tér and the Great Reformed Church. *Open Jun–Aug daily 08.00–20.00, Sep–May Mon–Thu 09.00–17.00, Fri 09.00–16.00.*

## Where to stay

It's prudent to book in advance during main festivals, but at other times there's enough room space – from expensive spa hotels to budget options. Tourinform holds a list of families offering **private accommodation**; prices are 2,000–6,000Ft/pp.

**Aquaticum Termál & Wellness Hotel** (96 rooms) Nagyerdei Park 1; ✆ 52 514111; e hotel@aquaticum.hu; www.aquaticum.hu. With thermal water and a wellness centre attached, this is worth a splash if your budget allows. *Sgls 18,000–19,500Ft, dbls 20,500–21,500Ft, apts 21,900–32,900Ft.*

**Cívis Grand Hotel Aranybika** (205 rooms) Piac utca 11–15; ✆ 52 508600; e aranybika@civishotels.hu; www.civishotels.hu. Debrecen's most famous hotel, the Art-Nouveau 'Golden Bull' is utterly central and deserving of a splurge. The hotel, designed by Alfréd Hajós – Hungary's first Olympic champion before turning to architecture – was built in 1915 and is chock-full of amenities (including a wellness centre). *Sgls €43–79, dbls €52–167.*

**Hunguest Hotel Nagyerdő** (99 rooms) Pallagi út 5; ✆ 52 410588; e reserve@hotelnagyerdo.hunguesthotels.hu; www.hunguesthotels.hu. Anchored in the green university area, the rooms here are good value, and include use of the tennis court and sauna, indoor pool and thermal baths. *Sgl €45, dbls €61–74.*

**Itália Hotel** (40 rooms) Wesselényi utca 4; ✆ 52 420891. If price is paramount, the Itália – more youth hostel than hotel – is the top choice. All rooms have bathrooms. *Dbl 6,500Ft, room for 4 2,550Ft/pp.*

**Péterfia Panzió** (19 rooms) Péterfia utca 37/B; ✆ 52 418246; e peterfiapanzio@axelero.hu. There are simple and clean rooms, and a nicely manicured little backyard. *Sgl 7,200Ft, dbl 7,600Ft; b/fast 1,200Ft.*

**Play House Panzió** (12 rooms) Batthány utca 24–26; ✆ 52 411252. Despite being above an Irish bar, this pension has quiet, pleasant rooms with TVs and private bathrooms. *Rooms 5,200Ft/pp.*

**Stop Panzió** (14 rooms) Batthány utca 18; ✆ 52 420301; e stoppanzio@vnet.hu. A few doors down from Play House, Stop has a more retro, 1960s feel to it, with chunky brown furniture and red fittings. It has laundry facilities, and all rooms have bathrooms, TVs and fridges. *Dbl 7,100Ft, triple 9,100Ft; b/fast 800Ft.*

## Where to eat and drink

There are numerous eating options, from fine dining to simple, local cooking. This is also a prime place to sample some regional specialities, like the Hungarian grey cattle and Mangalica pigs that are raised on the Great Plain. Hotel Aranybika and the Aquaticum Wellness Hotel (see page 303) both have nice but pricey restaurants. You'll get better value elsewhere; Piac utca has many scoffing spots and watering holes.

**Csokonai** Kossuth utca 21; ℄ 52 410802; www.vendegvaro.hu/37-2514. Debrecen's most celebrated restaurant, based in a cellar with heavy wooden seats and tables. The food is Hungarian. *Open Mon–Sat 11.30–23.00, Sun 11.30–22.00.*

**Flaska Vendéglő** Miklós utca 4; ℄ 52 414582. A local favourite ensconced in a vaulted cellar; the décor is peasant-style, and the place has a super selection of local and regional specialities. Try the Debrecen stuffed cabbage or the Hortobágy stuffed pancakes. *Mains 800–2,500Ft, avg 1,500Ft; open Mon–Sat 11.30–23.00, Sun 11.30–22.00.*

**Kalóz Pub** Batthyány utca 24; ℄ 06 30 588 7575. Next door to the Play House, the Kalóz has occasional live music. *Open Tue–Thu 18.00–24.00, Fri–Sat 18.00–02.00.*

**Klub Barabás** Vár utca 11; ℄ 52 502231. One of Debrecen's fanciest – and purportedly 'English' in style – the Klub Barabás serves excellent food. It's more Hungarian than English, though, but not wholly Hungarian either. *Mains 850–3,000Ft, avg 1,800Ft; open Mon–Thu 11.00–23.00, Fri–Sat 11.00–24.00, Sun 11.00–17.00.*

**Luculus** Piac utca 41; ℄ 52 418513. Housed in an early-19th-century building, Luculus is a folksy restaurant with good, traditional food. *Mains 1,200–2,500Ft, avg 1,800Ft; open daily 11.30–23.00.*

**Morik Caffe** Miklós utca 1. The Debrecen branch of this café empire. There are delicious coffee and sweets, and the café even has its own special coffee blend on sale. *Open Sun–Fri 07.00–23.00, Sat 9.00–24.00.*

**Pizza Toro D'oro** Piac utca 15; ℄ 52 533408. This is a busy, centrally situated pizza place that also serves pasta and Hungarian choices. There are daily 3-course menus for 600Ft. *Mains 1,000–2,300Ft, avg 1,600Ft; open daily 11.30–24.00.*

**Play House Pub** Batthyány utca 24–26; ℄ 52 452738. Below the Play House Panzió, this popular Irish-themed pub has a cosy bar, comfy leather couches and occasional live music. It also serves full meals and lighter pub food. *Mains avg 1,200Ft; open Sun–Thu 07.00–24.00, Fri–Sat 07.00–02.00.*

## What to see and do

One block east of Piac utca, **Batthyány utca** represents a pleasing stroll; it has a couple of lively pubs, and vendors selling fruit, vegetables, clothing and other items.

Most of Debrecen's sights are concentrated around the central pedestrianised area leading from Piac utca through Kossuth tér to Kálvin tér. Your first port of call is likely to be the Neoclassical **Great Reformed Church** (*Nagy templom; Kossuth tér;* ℄ 52 412694; adult/concessions 200/100Ft; open Mon–Sat 10.00–13.00, Sun 12.00–13.00), which has been the city's symbol since it was constructed 1819–23 to the design of Mihály Péchy (who attended the adjacent school); it occupies the site of a medieval church destroyed by fire in 1802. The interior is stark white, with little embellishment. While the organ is among the largest in Hungary, the bricks and mortar go one better – this is the country's biggest Protestant church. The chair that Lajos Kossuth sat in when he read the Declaration of Independence (from the Habsburg empire) during the Diet of 1849 has been proudly preserved inside. Climb the tower for a panoramic view of the city.

North of the church, the **Calvinist Reformed College** (*Református Kollégium; Kálvin tér 16;* ℄ 52 414744; open Tue–Sat 09.00–17.00, Sun 09.00–13.00) was founded in 1538, although much of the current building was the 19th-century work of Péchy. Its library contains an important collection of more than 600,000 volumes. There's a small **museum** (*adult 100Ft*) telling the history of the college, and a courtyard in the middle.

The main attraction of the Neo-Baroque **Déri Múzeum** (*Déri tér 1;* ❧ *52 322207;* e *deri@derimuz.hu; www.derimuz.hu; adult/concessions 500/290Ft; open Tue–Sun Apr 1– Oct 31 10.00–18.00, Nov 1–Mar 31 10.00–16.00*) is its collection of enormous Mihály Munkácsy paintings – and particularly the so-called 'Jesus trilogy'. Munkácsy, who lived during the second half of the 19th century, spent half his life in Paris but is nevertheless one of Hungary's best-known artists, renowned particularly for religious and historical works. There is also an exhibition on the history of Debrecen, a selection of works by other well-known and minor Hungarian artists, and ethnographic exhibits including some beautifully embroidered leather clothing worn by shepherds. The recently renovated Déri tér is a good spot for a picnic.

**Szent Anna Catholic Church** (*Szent Anna utca*) was an important addition to the city in the 18th century for it wasn't until the predominantly Calvinist community also had a Catholic church and parish that it could be granted the title of 'royal free town'. The **Nagyerdei (Great Forest) Park** is a ten-minute tram ride (number 1) northwards, and spreads over 1,000ha. The forest contains university buildings, streets lined with splendid villas, a zoo and botanical garden, and the **Thermal Bath Centre** (*Gyógy & Fürdőközpont; Nagyerdei Park 1;* ❧ *52 514100; www.aquaticum.hu; open daily 07.00–21.00, strand and outdoor pools May–Sep daily 06.00–19.00, indoor pool Sep–May 06.00–19.00, water park all yr Mon–Thu 11.00–21.00, Fri–Sun 10.00–22.00*). The latter has both indoor and outdoor pools (complete with tropical plants), steam baths, saunas, an assortment of therapeutic treatments, and an expansive children's section with slides, cave pools and waterfalls. The medicinal waters are similar in mineral content to those of Hajdúszoboszló.

The **Great Forest Cultivated Park Zoological and Botanical Gardens** claim to hold 170 animal species and 700–800 varieties of plants. The spiky stars of the botanical garden (*Egyetem tér 1;* ❧ *52 316666; free admission; open 08.00–18.00 daily*) are its cacti – there are thousands of them. Although fully open to the public, the garden is also used by the university for research. The zoo (*Ady Endre utca 1;* ❧ *52 310065; adult/concessions 400/350Ft; open daily summer 09.00–18.00, rest of yr 09.00–16.00*) has 1,400 animals.

## Festivals and events

Debrecen's Spring Festival (Mar or Apr; national and international performers at over 50 concerts and exhibitions), Flower Carnival (Aug 20; flower-festooned floats, folklore programmes and a firework display in celebration of St Stephen's Day) and Jazz Days (Sep; the country's oldest jazz festival, attracting musicians from as far afield as America) are all worth checking out.

# THE HAJDÚ REGION

The Hajdúk people (Heyducks) were herders who also fought as mercenary soldiers, and had a ferocious reputation. They formed guerilla armies, and took up arms initially during the Peasant's Revolt of 1514 led by György Dózsa and in 1604–6 during war against the Habsburgs under István Bocskai. Bocskai, who owned vast estates in the region, had originally joined the Habsburgs in opposition to the Turks, but he found himself disgruntled with Habsburg policy towards his homeland. He masterminded a successful insurrection against his former allies (ironically with Turkish assistance), and secured concessions at the Treaty of Vienna – including the right of nobility to govern themselves and freedom of worship for Protestants. The Bockskai Uprising was the first Hungarian revolt against the Habsburgs, and an important chapter in Europe's Fifteen Years' War involving France, the Holy Roman Empire and the Turks. The Hajdúk were rewarded for their military support with land and privileges, and seven Hajdú towns were established. At the end of the 17th century they joined forces into a specific Hajdú district, with Hajdúböszörmény at the centre.

## Hajdúböszörmény

Hajdúböszörmény is 19km northwest of Debrecen, and represents an easy day trip from the city. With its 15th-century circular layout, this is one of the most interesting towns in the Hajdúság. Originally there was a fortress at the centre, and houses have been built in concentric circles around it ever since. In addition to the struggles against the Habsburgs under Bocskai (see above), the citizens played another important part in the Hungarian Revolution of 1848. Even prior to that, however, Hajdúböszörmény was the centre of the Nyírség Muslims; in old Hungarian, 'Böszörmény' meant Muslim, but little is known of this group of people and no traces of them remain.

### Getting there and away

The **train** station (*Baross Gábor tér 2;* ↘ *52 227960*) is a ten-minute walk from the centre, and is on the Debrecen–Tiszalök line, with trains to Debrecen roughly hourly. The **bus** station is on Kálvin tér, and is little more than a few covered bus stops where regional buses pick up and drop off. There are eight daily buses to Hajdúszoboszló, one to Békéscsaba, and to Gyula. Several local buses run each hour to Debrecen, up until 23.00. Unfortunately, the regional transportation system makes it difficult to travel direct to many other towns, and it is often necessary to return to Debrecen, and then catch another bus or train from there.

### Information

**Tourinform** Kálvin tér 6; ↘ 52 561851; e hajduboszormeny@tourinform.hu. Next to the bus station, and a 10-min walk from the train station (via Rákóczi Ferenc utca). *Open daily Mar 1–Oct 31 09.00–17.00, Nov 1–Feb 28 09.00–15.00.*

### Where to stay and eat

**Tourinform** can assist with arranging private accommodation, and there is one hotel, a campsite and three pensions.

**Hajdú Hotel** (10 rooms) Petőfi Sándor utca 2; ↘ 52 228307. The town's only hotel – a pleasant 3-star located just off Bocskai tér. Most of the rooms have sofas and desks, and are tastefully decorated with watercolour paintings of the region. *Sgl 6,900Ft, dbl 8,200Ft, apt 10,400Ft; b/fast 800Ft.*

**Erika Panzió** (3 rooms) Mester utca 3; ↘ 52 280684. No-frills accommodation inside a local family's home; guests share a common bathroom. *Rooms 4,500Ft/pp.*

**Káplár Kemping** Polgári utca 92–100; ↘ 52 227408; e alfred@privatzimmerdienst.hu. Although there's tent-pitching space, this is considerably more than a campsite; instead it is an ethnographic museum and *skanzen* (preserved folk village) of adobe and thatched-roof houses, replete with folk-style furnishings, which can be rented. If you don't object to the 1km walk to the centre, a night at the *skanzen* is preferable to the town's pensions. *Dbls 4,000Ft; triples 5,000Ft; tent space 400Ft.*

**Halász Csárda** Iskola utca; ↘ 52 229227. It is a curious fact that there is virtually no fish to be had at the Fisherman's Inn; choose instead from simple dishes of fried or stuffed meat, breaded vegetables or *gulyás*. *Mains 380–600Ft, avg 500Ft; open daily 08.00–22.00.*

**Petőfi 4** Petőfi Sándor utca 4; ↘ 52 228490. Offers a simple selection of Hungarian food (with 650Ft daily specials), and is one of the few late-night hangouts. *Mains 650–1,850Ft, avg 800Ft; open Sun–Thu 11.30–24.00, Fri–Sat 11.30–04.00.*

**Pizza Ház** Domb utca 11; ↘ 52 280498. Average pizzas. *Pizzas 600–2,000Ft; open Mon–Thu 11.00–22.00, Fri 11.00–02.00, Sat 16.00–02.00.*

**Old Man's Pub** Baltazár Dezső utca 83; ↘ 06 70 281 0718. The place to get a strong drink. *Open Sun–Thu 14.00–24.00, Fri–Sat 14.00–02.00.*

### What to see and do

Bocskai tér (where the town's four main avenues intersect), named after the town's hero, is at the centre of the settlement's circle; it is where you'll find City Hall, a big Protestant

**HAJDÚBÖSZÖRMÉNY**
(SKETCH MAP)

church, a monument to Bocskai, and the Bocskai Grammar School. Just off the square, the **Hajdúsági Múzeum** (*Kossuth utca 1;* ✆ *52 229038; free admission; open Apr 1–Sep 30 10.00–18.00, Oct 1–Mar 31 10.00–16.00*) is located inside the town's oldest public building. The museum spreads over more than a dozen rooms, and gives a thorough ethnographic, archaeological and local history of the town. In the museum's courtyard is a statue park filled with busts of famous artists and scientists connected to the town.

Even if you're not staying there (see opposite), the *skanzen* on Polgári utca is worth seeing for it's open-air presentation of folk-village life. The town hosts a community event of some sort almost every week; in August it celebrates **Hajdú Week**, with exhibitions about the region, fireworks, traditional music and dance, and other cultural programmes.

## Hajdúszoboszló

Hajdúszoboszló is famous for its thermal bath complex, which – occupying an area of 30ha – it claims is the biggest in Europe. It attracts over 1½ million visitors annually, mainly from Poland, Austria, and Germany, and the town is the self-proclaimed 'mecca of the rheumatics'. If you're not a mecca-seeking rheumatic or a lover of a warm soak, you'll miss little by skipping this town. Everything is geared to the business of bathing, and there are hotels everywhere you look.

### Getting there and away

The **train** service to Hajdúszoboszló is excellent, since it lies on the Budapest–Debrecen–Nyíregyháza–Záhony line; the station (✆ *52 362391*), however, is 4km from the town centre. Taxi rides (*Főnix Taxi;* ✆ *52 434343*) are a fixed 500Ft; alternatively local buses leave from the bus station. All fast trains and six daily inter-city trains call at Hajdúszoboszló, and there are services nearly every hour to Budapest, Debrecen, Nyíregyháza, Záhony and stops in between. During the summer there is also a direct connection to Lake Balaton. The **bus** station (✆ *52 361408*) is opposite the entrance to the baths, near the intersection of Fürdő utca and Sport utca. Local buses to Debrecen leave several times hourly. Like Hajdúböszörmény, regional bus services often require a trip back to Debrecen for the necessary connection.

## Information

**Tourinform** Szilfákalja út 2; ✆ 52 558928; e hajduszoboszlo@tourinform.hu. A 10-min walk southwest of the bath complex and bus station. *Open Mon–Fri 09.00–17.00, Sat 09.00–14.00.*

## Where to stay

The town has dozens of hotels and pensions to suit all tastes and budgets, and until the day Hajdúszoboszló hosts a global convention of rheumatics, you'll have no problem finding a room. Many of the hotels are concentrated along Mátyás Király sétány. **Tourinform** has a list of over 1,300 families providing private accommodation; you can also keep your eyes open for the '*Zimmer frei*' signs, which are everywhere. There are, however, few independent restaurants – although most of the hotels have their own restaurants and cafés. During the summer, fast-food-type places open along Mátyás Király sétány.

**Cívis Hotel Délibáb** (240 rooms) József Attila utca 4; ✆ 52 362059; www.civishotels.hu. Among the biggest hotels, and has spacious rooms to boot. The service is reliable, the restaurant has live gypsy music on most evenings and rooms are well priced. *Sgl €30–50, dbl €42–68.*
**Hajdúszoboszló Thermal Baths** Böszörményi utca 35/A; ✆ 52 558552. There is a camping ground adjacent to the spa, for which campers receive discounted day passes. The site also has a restaurant and a small supermarket. *Tent 770Ft.*

---

## THE HUNGARIAN ROMA

The largest ethnic minority in the country, the Hungarian Roma number an estimated 500,000–700,000 people (5–6% of the current population). The Roma arrived in Europe in waves starting in the 9th century, and were recorded in Hungary from the end of the 14th century. Their name derives from the Romany word for 'men', but European confusion surrounding the origins of the Roma peoples is evident in the alternative names used to describe them. The English 'gypsy' (and Spanish equivalent '*gitano*') stems from 'Egypt', reflecting a wide belief that the Roma were descendants of an Islamic sect. The Hungarian '*cigány*' has its roots in a corruption of the Greek term '*atsingani*', a heretical sect of Asia Minor. It wasn't until 1753 that a Hungarian student spotted linguistic ties between Romany vocabulary and a central group of Hindi tongues, tying the Roma to a homeland in northern India. In 1976, at the first Roma festival in Chandigarh, Mrs Indira Gandhi pledged her support for recognising the Roma as a national minority of India.

Only 25% of Hungarian Roma are now Romany speakers, these are divided into two clearly distinct groups, one speaking the *lovári* language, the other *beás*. Historically the *lovári* speakers were horse traders and metalworkers, while the *beás* Roma worked with their hands, making baskets and traditional wooden tubs used for washing clothes or storing meat. However, the itinerant Roma lifestyle militated against steady education and reduced employment prospects, and they gradually lost not only their traditional professions and language, but their social structure as they moved into cities. Although now largely settled, unemployment among Hungarian

**Hotel Aqua-Sol** (142 rooms) Gábor Áron utca 7–9; ✆ 52 273310;
e reserve@hotelaquasol.hunguesthotels.hu; www.hunguesthotels.hu. This is one of the fanciest –
indeed it even has an air-conditioned bridge linking it to the bath complex next door. *Sgl 14,000Ft,
dbl 20,000Ft.*
**Hotel Mátyás Király** (106 rooms) Mátyás Király sétány 17; ✆ 52 360200; e
matyashotel@axelero.hu; www.matyashotel.hu. A nice one close to the spa; all rooms have
balconies, and there are fitness and spa facilities, and a large restaurant. *Sgl €50–66, dbl €58–76.*
**Kemencés Csárda** Szilfákalja utca 40/1; ✆ 52 362221. One of the better restaurants, serving
traditional Hungarian food to the sound of Hungarian folk music. It has an attached pension with
20 rooms. *Mains 1,000–2,500Ft, avg 1,300Ft; open 08.00–24.00.*
**Nelson** Hősök tere 4; ✆ 52 270226. Has a nautical theme, and serves good food in hearty
portions. *Mains 1,300–2,400Ft; open daily 09.00–24.00.*
**Szilfa** József Attila utca 2–4; ✆ 52 273110. Szilfa is splayed out and touristy, and the food is fair
rather than fantastic. On the plus side, it is central, it offers regional specialities, and a plate for 2 is
piled high enough to feed 4. *Mains 950–2,800Ft, avg 1,300Ft; open 11.00–23.00.*

## What to see and do
The baths are considered to be the town's point of focus. Mátyás Király sétány – where
most of the hotels are concentrated – is a good place to start. Besides a few scattered
churches and monuments, there's little else to see in town, and the several large roads
don't make for the most enjoyable walking routes.

The **Hajdúszoboszló Thermal Baths** (*Szent István park 1–3;* ✆ *52 558558;
www.hajduszoboszlogyogyfurdo.hu; open thermal bath 07.00–19.00 daily; outdoor bath May 1–
May 31 08.00–18.00, Jun 1–Aug 22 08.00–20.00, Aug 23–Sep 30 08.00–18.00; aquapark May
& Sep Fri–Sun 12.00–16.00, Jun 1–Aug 31 10.00–18.00; indoor swimming pool Jun 16–Aug
31 09.00–19.00, Sep 1–Jun 15 Mon–Fri 15.00–19.00, Sat–Sun 09.00–19.00*) is a sprawling
complex. The thermal water – nicknamed 'hot gold' by residents – was discovered during

Roma currently runs at 60–70%; they live in greatest concentrations in the country's
poorer areas, such as the northeastern corner.

It is in gypsy music (*cigányzene*) that one might see a solitary surviving strain of cultural
identity. In its purest form, this has deep historical roots; Roma musicians were reported
on Csepel Island in Hungary in 1489, and Romany bands played in the Austro-Hungarian
court of Esterháza (at Fertőd) in 1714. However, the variant played by 'musical gypsy
families' in today's restaurants is as far removed from original gypsy folk songs as it is
from the tunes of Hungarian peasants (with which it is often confused abroad). Instead
the ensembles play mainly Magyar songs, and are dressed in Magyar-type costumes.

Historically and across Europe, the Roma have been persecuted; floggings, the
shaving of heads, beatings, deportations and hangings were once commonplace.
Such prejudice culminated in the extermination of 1½ million Roma during the
Holocaust. Interestingly, in 19th-century Hungarian literature the gypsy was treated
with a certain affection, as a comic figure or symbol of romantic freedom. However,
this was supplanted by images of crime and poverty, and hostility to the Roma
people is still very evident. While in politically correct circles the word *cigány* is
becoming taboo, this is counterbalanced by expressions like '*cigányútra ment*' ('gone
the gypsies' way') – to describe the moment when food goes down the wrong
channel – that is still heard beyond these circles. Roma feature little in Hungarian
cultural, commercial or political life (although Hungary has a Roma MEP), and
despite the country's progress since the fall of communism continue to feel an
isolated and persecuted minority.

a search for oil in 1925. The spa opened two years later, and in 2000 was expanded into what you see today. There are 13 thermal pools, an indoor lap pool, an outdoor aquapark with nine water slides, a wave pool, a sandy strand (complete with palm trees), and several enormous swimming pools. There's even a naturist island in one of the outdoor pools, and an open-air stage for summer performances; over 40 different kinds of medicinal and relaxation treatments are available. It's a humungous theme park of a place, and can feel overwhelming. Admission starts at 500Ft and varies depending on what type of ticket, and services you want.

The holdings of the **István Bocskai Museum** (*Bocskai utca 12;* ✆ *52 362165; adult 300Ft; open Tue–Sun Apr–Oct 09.00–13.00, 14.00–18.00, Nov–Mar 09.00–13.00, 14.00–17.00*) are divided between three different buildings. The permanent exhibitions represent an eclectic mix of folk art, town history, relics of the area's military past and the work of local artists.

## SZABOLCS-SZATMÁR-BEREG COUNTY

The northeastern chunk of Hungary – bordered by Slovakia, Ukraine and Romania – falls under the administrative blanket of the huge Szabolcs-Szatmár-Bereg County. Beneath this blanket live the poorest of the country's people – many of them Roma – a population that suffers from a paucity of employment opportunities and whose most easterly communities are decreasing as sons and daughters are drawn by brighter city lights elsewhere. With the exception of the county capital of Nyíregyháza, whose success was founded on an industry that has itself suffered significantly since the political changes of the 1990s, the way of life here is agricultural, the sandy, undulating landscape – formed by soil blown from the Tisza flood basin by northerly winds – peppered with orchards and crop fields. This is a corner with a history of isolation and sadness, imposed upon it by forces geographical and political. Prior to the 19th-century drainage project that regulated the River Tisza, boggy land made travel in or out difficult, while the 1920 Treaty of Trianon slashed away Transylvania and Ruthenia (in the far east of Slovakia) at a stroke and the deportations during World War II decimated the strong Jewish community. It is no surprise that fresh licks of paint are unusual in this pocket, that there is more than a hint of dilapidation and little in the way of sophisticated tourist infrastructure.

Yet these very pressures have created a rough diamond that will reward those who've the energy and spirit to seek it out. Isolation breeds preservation; here is rural life laid out, and tradition, culture and architecture less damaged or altered by hostile invasions of the past or progressive moves of the present. Painted medieval churches, wooden belfries, water mills and boat-shaped grave markers are among the region's human highlights, while fishing and canoeing is good on the Tisza (you can book canoe trips or arrange equipment hire and boat delivery through the website www.vidamdelfin.hu; it is in Hungarian, but the company welcomes English enquiries), and naturalists will not be disappointed by the varied habitats of the marshes, wooded pasture and grassland.

### The Nyírség region

The towns and villages of the Nyírség region – many of whose names are helpfully prefixed with 'Nyír' (meaning 'birch', after the forests that grew in the depressions) – lie north and northeast of Debrecen on Hungary's second-largest sand bed. Nyíregyháza is the focal point and the main town not just of the Nyírség but of the northeast as a whole; this is the place to stock up on tourist information before taking a deep breath and plunging into the remoter spots out towards the borders.

#### Nyíregyháza

A town of squares and statues, Nyíregyháza lacks thrills but its eclectic architecture, mixed bag of churches and wide-ranging museum provide enough to fill a pleasant day.

Owned by the Transylvanian Prince István Bocskai in the early 17th century, a series of violent squabbles between town and county factions caused many to up sticks and move out – the dawn of the 18th century was greeted by just 50 families still resident in Nyíregyháza. However, it was re-settled by Slovaks, and went on to become the easternmost market town of the Eastern Bloc during the communist period. (The Slovak descendants continue to speak an archaic form of Slovakian.) While its industry has died with the times in which it thrived, the town remains nevertheless the county seat of Szabolcs-Szatmár-Bereg and the main centre of the Nyírség. The resort of Sóstófürdő a few kilometres to the north, with its open-air village museum and baths, is a major bonus.

### Getting there, away and around

Both the bus and train stations are 1.5km from the action, at the ends of Széchenyi utca and Arany János utca respectively (as they run westwards out of the city). You can catch local buses 7 or 8 from here to the centre. The **train station** is a modern affair, and stands at the junction of two main lines running west–east and south–north. Twenty-one trains run daily from Budapest (either Keleti or Nyugati), taking between three and four hours; there are a good number to Miskolc (passing through Tokaj and Szerencs on the way) and Debrecen, and services to Nyírbátor (eight, with some also stopping at Máriapócs and Nagykálló) and Záhony (18). The latter also passes through Kisvárda, and up to two continue over the Ukrainian border to Csop. A smaller third line also links the town with Vásárosnamény.

The **bus station** is 150m north of the train station on Petőfi tér. One daily bus runs direct between Nyíregyháza and Budapest Stadion, except on Saturday when you have to change at Eger or Gyöngyös. There are services to Debrecen (five, taking between one and two hours), Eger (two), Sárospatak (two), Tokaj (two), Miskolc (up to two, but none on Sun), Gyöngyös (up to two) and Kisvárda (five on weekdays, one at weekends). In addition, there are regular services to Nagykálló, Máriapócs and Nyírbátor, and daily international buses to Košice, Satu Mare and Uzhgorod.

Taxis can be arranged through **Fő Taxi** (↘ 42 444444) or **Radio Gold FM Taxi** (↘ 42 414414).

### Information and other practicalities

**Bank** Kossuth Lajos tér 2. Worth a peek for its Neo-Baroque styling, neat balconies and decorative supporting pillars. Open Mon 07.45–18.00, Tue–Thu 07.45–17.00, Fri 07.45–16.00.
**Europa Net Café** Hunyadi utca 2; ↘ 42 508670. A two-floor café next to the Europa Hotel with comfy sofas and ten internet terminals.
**Ibusz** Országzászló tér 6; ↘ 42 312695. Can arrange private accommodation and local tours, and change travellers' cheques. Open Mon–Thu 08.00–16.00.
**Listings magazine** Nyíregyházi Est
**Tourinform** Országzászló tér 6; ↘ 42 505697. All the usual information; the theatre ticket office is also here. Open Jun 15–Oct 15 Mon–Fri 09.00–19.00, Sat–Sun 09.00–18.00, rest of year Mon–Fri 09.00–17.00.

### Where to stay

**Európa Hotel** (60 rooms) Hunyadi utca 2; ↘ 42 508670; www.europahotel.hu. Standing on Szabadságsag tér, the Európa looks like a hotel from Legoland, but its rooms are more ordinary. Sgl 7,000Ft, dbl 8,500Ft.
**Hotel Centrál** (33 rooms) Nyár utca 2–4; ↘ 42 411330; www.centralhotel.hu. Modern hotel with comfortable charm in a quiet spot just to the north of Hősök tér. Among the facilities are a pleasant little indoor pool and a jacuzzi. Sgl 12,000Ft, dbl 14,000Ft, apt 16,000Ft.
**Korona Hotel** (35 rooms) Dózsa György utca 1; ↘ 42 409300; http://members.chello.hu/korona. Grand, characterful, stunning inside and out, the century-old Korona is an excellent choice. It also

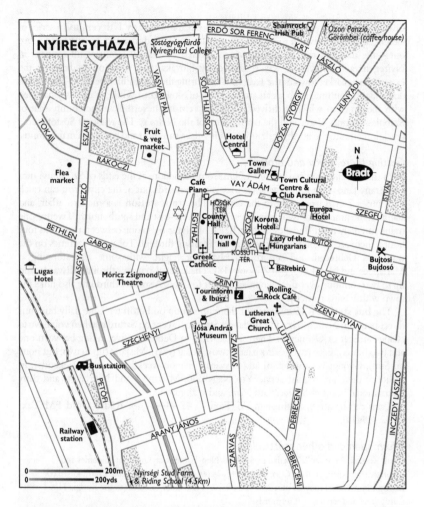

has its own pub, pizzeria, café, casino, solarium and sauna. *Sgl 10,800Ft, dbl 11,900Ft, apt 15,000Ft; b/fast 1,100Ft.*

**Lugas** (26 rooms) Prága utca 3; ☎ 42 342777; e lugashotel@chello.hu; www.lugashotel.hu. On the outskirts of town, the Lugas is worth the effort. As well as a landscaped garden area, it has a pool, bowling alley and a top-notch restaurant (see opposite). From the centre, travel westwards along Bethlen Gabor utca, cross the rail tracks, take the first left into Derkovits Gyula utca followed by the first right into Prágá utca. *Dbl 11,000Ft, triple 12,500Ft, apt (for 2) 15,500; b/fast 1,000Ft.*

**Nyíregyházi College** Sostoi utca 31/B; ☎ 42 599419. The college is located around 2km north of the centre, and has rooms available in Jul and Aug. To reserve one, you must call ahead or make arrangements through Tourinform. If you're walking it, follow Kossuth Lajos utca, cross Ferenc körút and the college is 800m or so up on the left; alternatively, buses 13, 20, 19, 8 and 8A stop near by. *Rooms 1,200Ft/pp.*

**Ózon Panzió** (19 rooms) Csaló köz 2; ☎ 42 402001; www.ozonpanzio.hu. The Ózon has a chalet feel to it, in a leafy (or pine-needly) suburb on the way out towards Sóstófürdő. The hotel operates as a training school for local catering students, who enjoy firing up barbecues in the summer. The dbl rooms are smallish, but comfortable; the apts are rather fusty. Bus 9 stops 200m away. *Dbl 9,200Ft, apt 12,200Ft, b/fast 850Ft.*

## Where to eat and drink

**Bujtosi Bujdosó Restaurant** Bujtos utca 34. Five minutes east of the centre, this café-style restaurant has staff as eager as puppies and a menu that's as cheap as the chips that accompany a number of its dishes. *Mains 500–1,800Ft, avg 1,000Ft; open Mon–Sat 11.00–22.00.*

**Café Piano** Hősök tere 8; ✆ 42 400377. There's a trombone and other brass instruments, together with an obligatory piano. Selling cocktails and cakes at the northern end of the square, this is a popular coffee house, although its high ceiling and tiled area at the front dilute the atmosphere somewhat. *Open Mon–Thu 09.00–22.00, Fri 09.00–23.00, Sun 15.00–20.00.*

**Centrál Restaurant** Nyár utca 2–4; ✆ 42 411330. We haven't tested the chef's expressed willingness to prepare any dish you desire, but we can vouch for the foie gras starter. The restaurant of the Hotel Centrál (see page 311) isn't bad at all, although we'd prefer the lighting a little less glaring. *Mains 1,500–3,600Ft, avg 2,000Ft; open 07.00–23.00 daily.*

**Görömbei Cukrászda** Korányi Frigyes utca 23/A; ✆ 42 500795. As nice as they are naughty, the cakes, biscuits and ice creams at Görömbei are the town's best. Burn off the guilt with the 2km walk there (northeast along Dózsa György utca and beyond the ring road) – or squeeze into buses 5, 7 or 12. *Open daily 10.00–20.00.*

**Lugas Restaurant** Prága utca 3; ✆ 42 342777. Hotel restaurant serving high-class international nosh in an airy, cheerful conservatory-style dining room. The line-up includes veal, crêpes, pastas and fish dishes. *Mains 1,500–3,700Ft, avg 2,000Ft; open 10.00–23.00 daily.*

**Rolling Rock Café** Geduly ház, Luther utca 5. One in the chain of America-theme bars, the Rolling Rock is a busy haunt serving American-sized portions of fajitas, steaks and burgers (alongside traditional Hungarian specialities). *Mains 750–3,400Ft, avg 1,500Ft; open Mon–Sat 11.00–02.00, Sun 11.00–24.00.*

There is a **fruit, meat and veg market** on Búzsa tér (*open Mon 06.00–13.00, Tue–Fri 06.00–17.00, Sat 06.00–14.00, Sun 07.00–11.00*), where you can also pick up a cheap snack.

## Entertainment and nightlife

Ferenc Bán's **Town Cultural Centre** (*Szabadság tér 9;* ✆ *42 411822*) was acclaimed when finished in 1981, but the concrete block with its cylindrical protrusions won't be to everybody's taste; this is, however, the place to head for details of listings and events. The palatial **Móricz Zsigmond Theatre** (*Bessenyei tér 13; ticket office* ✆ *42 507006; www.moriczszinhaz.hu*) is considerably easier on the eye, and can also offer help; the theatre hosts some acclaimed international orchestras and choirs, including the American Cantemus Chorus. The ticket office is in the Tourinform. Outside is a statue of the Hungarian socialist poet Mihály Váci, dressed in a shabby polo neck; the book in his hand had been graffitied with 'porno mag' when we last visited, but we suspect it's more likely to represent a collection of his verse. The **Hollywood Multiplex** (*Nyíregyháza Plaza, Szegfű utca 75;* ✆ *42 501660; www.hmplx.hu*) has big-screen blockbusters.

If you need to wet your whistle, you can try the seedy-looking **Békebíró Söröző** (*Bocskai utca 1;* ✆ *06 20 414 0411; open Mon–Thu 10.00–24.00, Fri–Sat 12.00–03.00, Sun 17.00–23.00*), the **Shamrock Irish Pub** (*Korányi Frigyes utca;* ✆ *42 403317*) just to the north of Ferenc körút, or the **John Bull** (*Dózsa György utca 1*), a cellar-like piece of Blighty at the Korona Hotel. Below that, the **X Café** doubles as a dance club; alternatively, you can cut some shapes to thumping base lines at the dark and smoky **Club Arsenal** (*Szabadság tér 9;* ✆ *06 20 967 2850; open Tue, Fri–Sat 21.30–05.00*), underneath the cultural centre.

## What to see and do

The town centre consists of a series of interlinked squares, prime among which is Kossuth tér, built in 1910 and paved with coloured stones. At its heart is a huge statue of a barrel-chested Kossuth (by Gyula Bethlen, 1912), while on the western side is the **town hall** (*Kossuth Lajos tér 1*) – Neoclassical when built in 1841, but later restyled – with its long balcony and iron fretwork. Facing it across the square is the Neo-Romanesque **Lady of the Hungarians Church** (*Kossuth Lajos tér 15*), a magnificent twin-steepled Roman Catholic temple built in 1904 by József Kommer and Virgil Nagy. A pastel rainbow of colours covers the grey stone inside, as though a class of innocents was given free rein to make the church its own, and the effect is completed by vivid stained glass adorning the nave and chancel.

If you're feeling particularly ecclesiological, there are other churches to see. Behind the town hall, the Art-Nouveau **Greek Catholic Church** (*Görög Katolikus Egyház; Bethlen Gábor utca 5*) has cheerful orange patterning; there's a collection of ecclesiastical art in the nearby episcopal palace and college. The **Lutheran Great Church** (*Evangélikus nagytemplom; Luther tér 14;* ` 42 508770*) was built in 1786 by Italian master Giuseppe Aprilis, and is sited at the town's highest point. (Keep an eye out for organ and choral concerts held here.) Changing religious tack, the pink **synagogue** (*Mártírok tere 6*) was designed by Lipót Baumhorn (1924–32), is adorned inside with animal motifs, and has a small Holocaust exhibition next door (where you also ring for access; *open Mon–Thu 09.00–12.00*).

Hősök tere is home to the Eclectic **County Hall**, an elegant brute of a building designed by Ignác Alpár in 1892. To the northeast, opposite the cultural centre, the **Town Gallery** (*Selyem utca 12;* ` 42 408720; free admission; open Tue–Sat 09.00–17.00*) displays the 20th-century work of Pál Gyula, which has something of the J S Lowry about it. There are also temporary exhibitions by contemporary artists.

To the south is Országzászló tér, with its late-20th-century **Hungarian Hussars Monument** (Sándor Győrfi, 1997) commemorating the role of the cavalry in the bloody battles of the Napoleonic Wars. Southwest of that (linked by Széchenyi utca), the narrow Benczúr Gyula tér holds the **Jósa András Museum** (*Benczúr Gyula tér 21;* ` 42 315722; adult/concessions 400/200Ft; open Tue–Sat 09.00–16.00, Sun 09.00–14.00*), guarded by a brace of pint-sized lions. Benczúr Gyula (1844–1920) – whose statue also stands outside – was born in the town and numbered among his works the altar painting and mosaic in Budapest's St István Basilica. András Jósa (1834–1918) was a famous archaeologist and doctor (turning to medicine after medical men failed to diagnose his own illness). He lived in the Neoclassical building, and founded the museum in 1868. The exhibitions include paraphernalia from the local regiment of the 4th Hussars and other fearsome weaponry, coins dating back to the Roman Age and a display of local history. Most valuable are the pieces relating to Nyíregyháza's two renowned Gyulas – the painter Benczúr and the writer Krúdy (1878–1933).

For some colourful bustle, head for the outdoor **flea market** (Tokaji út; open Mon–Sat 06.00–16.00, Sun 06.00–14.00), just beyond the train track at the meeting point of Rákóczi utca and Tokaji út, where you'll find traders hawking anything and everything. Buses 1 and 1A run there.

## Horse-riding

The **Nyírségi Stud Farm and Riding School** (*Bem József utca 22–23;* ` 42 728826; e *lovi@szabolcs.net; www.szabolcs.net/eng*) offers an extensive range of programmes, including a week-long Tokaj riding tour and three-day hunting tour. It also has an indoor arena for riding lessons (*from 1,750Ft/hr*). The on-site panzió has five cosy rooms (*dbl 6,000Ft*). Turn on to Simai utca (near the bus and train stations) and then left into Bem József utca.

## Festivals and events

Nyíregyháza Arts Week takes place in April, when there's also a regional ballet festival. The main annual event is the Autumn Festival (*Aug–Sep*), but there is also an International Bird Exhibition (*Oct*) and even a Father Christmas Beauty Contest (*Dec*). The mind boggles.

## Sóstófürdő

'Salt Lake Baths' is 6km north of Nyíregyháza, and derives its name from a 10ha saline lake upon which the resort has grown since the 1920s. The mineral-rich water is said to aid recovery from a range of ills, but the lake is also popular for boating. An even more worthy attraction is the excellent Village Museum, and the surrounding oak forest promises cooling walks.

Bus 8 (not 8A) runs here from Nyíregyháza, and there are regular trains to Sóstó station (on the southeastern side of the zoo). Alternatively, you can take the narrow-gauge train from Nyíregyháza NyK through the Sóstó Forest (*Sóstó-erdő*) on the Balsa/Dombrád line; trains leave every three hours or so. Buses and the narrow-gauge train stop near the Krúdy Hotel, a short distance southeast of the Village Museum and west of the lake.

## Information and other practicalities

**Szabolcs-Szatmár-Bereg County Nature Lovers' Association** Mártírok tere 9; ✆ 42 311577. Information on walks and other nature highlights of the region. *Open Thu 15.00–20.00.*

**Tourinform** Water Tower (*Víztorony*); ✆ 42 411193; e sostofurdo@tourinform. The town's distinctive octagonal monument was built in 1911 and originally functioned as a well, but is now home to the helpful seasonal tourist office. *Open May 21–Jun 14 Mon–Fri 08.30–16.30, Jun 15–Sep 15 Mon–Fri 08.30–17.30, Sat–Sun 08.30–15.30.*

## Where to stay

There are several campsites near both the Village Museum and the outdoor baths. Alternatively there are several decent guesthouses.

**Hotel Sóstó Turistaszálló & Camping** Sóstói út 76; ✆ 42 402011. A fairly new campsite in between the Village Museum and outdoor baths; it is well kept and well equipped (with swimming pool, tennis courts, a restaurant and horse-riding opportunities). It also has a no-frills hotel. *Hotel sgl 7,000Ft, dbl 8,900Ft, triple 11,900Ft, apt 12,800Ft; tent/caravan 800/3,000Ft, plus adult/child 800/500Ft.*

**Blaha Panzió** (12 rooms) Blaha Lujza sétány 7; ✆ 42 403342. Blends contemporary furnishings with a hint of simple rusticity, and is superbly located. It's also pretty cheap. *Dbl 6,900Ft.*

**Hotel Svájci-Lak** (10 rooms) Sóstói út; ✆ 42 411191; www.furdohaz.hu. Once frequented by Gyula Krúdy and Lujza Blaha, this is a tidy hotel linked to the adjacent Fürdőház Panzió and Bath House (see page 316). *Sgl 7,200Ft, dbl 10,800Ft, triple 15,300Ft, apts 14,800–19,200Ft.*

**Hotel Tara** (21 rooms) Fürdő utca 51; ✆ 42 475903; e bchu@axelero.hu. Offers plain accommodation 2 mins from the outdoor baths, and is run by an Irishman (whose son, Brian Carney, plays for the Great Britain rugby league team).

**Krúdy Hotel** (20 rooms) Sóstói út 75; ✆ 42 596 187; e info@krudyvigado.hu; www.krudyvigado.hu. An Eclectic, achingly romantic hotel overlooking the lake and next to the Irish Pub.

## Where to eat and drink

**Beatles Nosztalgia Club** Szódaház utca 14; ✆ 42 475731. This is a real gem, an outlandish bar filled with plush red seating and varnished tree trunks a short distance east of the northern section of the lake. It's a curious blend of indoor forest, cavern and beach bar, and like nothing else we've ever seen.

**Krúdy Hotel Restaurant** See page 315. A fabulous place to dine, with its canopied terrace illuminated with fairy lights. *Mains 870–1,980Ft, avg 1400Ft; open 12.00–23.00 daily.*

**424 Irish Restaurant & Pub** Blaha Lujza sétány 1; ＼ 42 726222. The Irish Pub has a rounded outdoor terrace set among the trees. Beyond the Murphy's and Guinness, and the green furnishings, there's little obviously Irish here but it bursts at the seams in summer. We found the food – Hungarian, with fish the speciality – fairly average. *Mains 670–2,700Ft, avg 1,600Ft; open 11.00–22.00 daily.*

## What to see and do

The **Open-Air Village Museum** (*Sóstói Múzeumfalu; Tölgyes utca 1;* ＼ *42 479704; adult/concessions 400/200Ft; Eng-speaking guide 4,000Ft; open Tue–Sun Apr 1–Jun 14 09.00–17.00, Jun 15–Aug 31 09.00–18.00, Sep 1–Oct 31 09.00–17.00*) is devoted to the architecture and lifestyles of people from five ethnographic regions in the county (Szatmár, Rétköz, Nyírség, Nyíri Mezőség and Bereg). Among its buildings are a school, church and belfry, grocery store, pub and fire station, together with a farmhouse typical of the Slovakian settlers (Tirpák) who repopulated Nyíregyháza in the 18th century. A cemetery contains distinctive Szatmár grave markers, while Roma huts nestle tellingly at the edge of the village – indicative of the social segregation that remains evident even today. Craft shows and demonstrations are often held here devoted to traditional trades, and on Wednesdays regional dishes are cooked up for visitors to sample. The 7½ha site has much to see; join Tölgyes utca from near the Krúdy Hotel.

The **Sóstó Lake** (*Blaha Lujza sétány 1;* ＼ *42 475736; open May 27–Aug 31 daily 09.00–19.00; adult/concessions 600/400Ft*) is on the other side of Sóstói út from the museum, its upper section given over to boating and its lower to a cold-pool beach. There are snackbars, a volley-ball court and waterslide, and ladies can go topless if so inclined. The **Park Baths** (*Berenát utca 3;* ＼ *42 475736; adult/concessions/family 600/400/2,500Ft; open May 27–Sep 10 daily 09.00–19.00*) were opened to the north when the lake began to suffer from overcrowding in the 1950s, and the water is equally mineral-rich. Alongside the various pools, there are go-karts, tennis courts, an inflatable trampoline and an area for nude sunbathing. If you're here out of season, the **Bath House** (*Fürdőház; Sóstói út;* ＼ *42 411191; adult 1,500Ft; open daily 10.00–20.00*) is open all year round (having been resurrected in 2000 after stagnating for 25 years), and has bathing tubs and opportunities for massages.

**Sóstó Zoo** (❨ *42 479 702;* e *sostozoo@szabinet.hu; www.sostozoo.hu; adult/concessions/family 800/600/2,300Ft; open daily Apr 1–Sep 30 09.00–19.00, Oct 1–Mar 31 09.00–16.00*) is southwest of the lake; it is Hungary's second-largest, and has nearly 300 species including rare snow leopards and Mexican macaws. Our feeling is that some of the cages holding the bigger beasts are on the small side, and some of the pacing cats looked pretty miserable. You can watch them being fed every second hour on Sat and Sun.

## Other excursions from Nyíregyháza

**Nagykálló**, 12km to the southeast, was the county capital until 1876 and former site of a Heyduck fort (levelled in 1769); today, however, the town is more popularly associated with the mental hospital in the old County Hall than for its past history. There are some handsome Neoclassical buildings and two 15th-century churches, but most visitors are either Hasidic Jews making a pilgrimage to the tomb of the mystical Rabbi Isaac Taub (in the Jewish cemetery) or those drawn by a folk-art festival at the end of June. Details can be obtained from the Tourinform in Nyíregyháza. The railway station is on the line between Nyíregyháza and Nyírbátor; change at Nyíregyháza or Nyíradony for Debrecen. There are very regular buses from Nyíregyháza, and on to Máriapócs.

Just off the road running between Nagykálló and Nyírbátor (another 8km on), **Máriapócs** is a settlement of just 2,000 that was first mentioned as 'Pócs' in records of 1280. 'Mária' was added when the village was declared a holy place; Pope John Paul II visited in 1991, and each year a million pilgrims make the trip. Why? Because of a special icon of the Virgin Mary at the northern end of the village's 18th-century Greek Catholic Basilica (*Görög katolikus bazilika; Kossuth tér 25*). In 1696, this votive picture – painted in 1676 by a travelling artist who had escaped the Turks – was seen to shed tears. When Lipót I heard of this, he moved it to Vienna (it is still there, in St Stephen's Cathedral), but a copy was made in Kosice and proved to be equally weepy – crying in 1715 and again for 18 days in 1905. The current twin-towered Baroque church was completed in 1756 after the number of worshippers outgrew the original wooden version; it was raised to 'basilica' status in 1946. The days that see the most traffic – thousands upon thousands of Greek Catholics – are August 15 (Feast of the Assumption) and the nearest Sunday to September 8 (Feast of the Blessed Virgin Mary). The **train station** is a couple of kilometres from the church, and there are daily services between Nyíregyháza (nine), Mátészalka (seven) and Fehérgyarmat (two). **Buses** stop near enough outside the church; there are regular buses to Nyírbátor, as well as to Nyíregyháza (nine) and Nagykálló (nine).

If you follow Route 41 northeast from Nyíregyháza for just under 40km, and turn right on to Road 49, you'll come to **Vaja**, notable for the 16th-century Vaj family mansion and grounds. Ádám Vaj was a supporter of the Rákóczi-led independence struggle against Habsburg rule; the building now houses a museum of local history (*open Tue–Sun 09.00–17.00; adult 150Ft*). There's also a Gothic Calvinist church nearby, originally built in the 15th century but reconstructed in the 19th. Buses run here from Nyíregyháza, Mátészalka and Vásárosnamény. **Mátészalka**, from where the parents of Hollywood star Tony Curtis herald, is a few kilometres further along Road 49. Its railway station is on the same line as Nyíregyháza, and also on that running north to Záhony (and on over the Ukrainian border) and south to Ágerdőmajor (and on over the Romanian border).

## Nyírbátor

Nyírbátor is undoubtedly the town of the Báthori family, a significant aristocratic clan whose most famous member was István, Prince of Transylvania and King of Poland. The Báthoris owned it for four medieval centuries and left their powerful stamp on its main monuments: the Calvinist church, which ranks among the country's best late-Gothic religious architecture, and the former Minorite church, containing some magnificent Baroque wood carvings.

### Getting there and away

Nyírbátor is on Road 471 leading northeast from Debrecen. The **railway** and **bus** stations (*Ady Endre utca*) are a few hundred metres north of the centre along Kossuth Lajos utca. Trains run west through Nagykálló on their way to Nyíregyháza (change there for Miskolc), and are also on the Apafa–Zajta line (including Mátészalka and Fehérgyarmat). There are 11 daily direct to Debrecen (or change at Apafa). Buses run very regularly to nearby Máriapócs, and to Nyíregyháza and Nagykálló; there are four daily services to Debrecen.

### Where to stay, eat and drink

**Bowling Club & Bar** Pócsi út; ☎ 42 284488. Has a lively reputation, and is where the young head to let off steam and knock over some pins. It is 2km outside the centre on the road to Máriapócs (just beyond the railtrack). *Open daily 16.00–24.00.*

**Café Code** Szabadság tér 7. One of the few places that opens late. The Ibiza Klub is next door. *Open Mon–Thu 08.00–22.00, Fri 08.00–02.00, Sat 08.00–14.00, 19.00–03.00, Sun 17.00–22.00.*

**Hotel Bástya** (20 rooms) Hunyadi utca 10; ☎ 42 281657; www.hotels.hu/bastya_nyirbator. You won't lose the Bástya in a crowd; its vivid colour and central bastion make it something of an attention seeker. A step inside is a step back to the '70s – the bathrooms in particular could do with an overhaul – but it's kitschly comfortable and there are moderately modern conveniences such as air conditioning. *Sgl 4,800Ft, dbl 6,800Ft (excl tourist tax).*

**Hotel Hódi** (17 rooms) Bátori utca 11; ☎ 42 281012. The top hotel by a long chalk is based in a former Báthori residence and has played host to some big guns. The Hungarian president stayed here in 2001, and if you want a right royal night's kip choose room 16 where the King of Spain laid his head in 2002. As you'd expect, the accommodation is of a high standard and full of character; there's also a wonderfully opulent indoor swimming pool, a friendly owner, and a reasonable price tag. Unless there's no room at the inn, there's no need to look elsewhere. *Sgl 11,700Ft, dbl 12,700Ft.*

**Kakinkk** Szabadság tér 21; ☎ 42 281050. The main eatery in the town's main square, serving Hungarian and international cuisine. *Mains 780–2,000Ft, avg 1,500Ft; open Mon–Thu 11.30–22.00, Fri–Sat 11.30–23.00.*

**Nyírbátor College** Kossuth utca 28; ☎ 42 281290. Call in advance for cheap dorm beds out of term times. *Beds 1,000Ft/pp.*

## What to see and do

The 15th-century **Calvinist church** (*Báthori utca 24*) is a Gothic masterpiece; its vast ceiling is adorned with geometric vaulting, and there are 12m lancet windows and Renaissance *sedilia*. This was originally a Roman Catholic church, before falling into Calvinist hands in the 16th century. A red-marble sarcophagus was fashioned in 1493 to cover the bones of the church founder, the Transylvanian Prince István Báthori, while an adjacent tomb holds a second István of the family, one who served as lord chief justice and sponsored German and Hungarian translations of the Bible before leaving this earthly sphere in 1605. (For details of the third István, see box, opposite.) There is a pair of organs; the Neo-Gothic one has stood in the centre for over a century, while the other is just a decade old, a pipsqueak in years but well endowed with pipes (over 2,000 of them). During the Nyírbátor Music Days in August, audiences enjoy the magnificent acoustics. Outside, the free-standing and oriental-looking wooden **belfry** has a shingled roof and reaches 35m skywards; it was built in 1640, and the bigger of its brace of bronze bells weighs 600kg and is engraved with images of the four evangelists. The tower is a beautiful example of craftsmanship, but is only made of wood because non-Roman-Catholic denominations were forbidden from erecting attached stone belfries during the Counter-Reformation. Be careful on the uneven stairs if you choose to climb it.

The **Minorite church** (*Károlyi Mihály utca 19; open Mon–Fri 09.00–17.00, Sat 09.00–19.00, Sun 08.00–16.00*) was also built by Báthori as a Roman Catholic church in 1480, in the aftermath of his victory at the Battle of Kenyérmező in 1479. In 1587, however, the marauding Turks claimed vengeance and went to work on the place, and it was members of the Franciscan Minorite order who resurrected it in its current Baroque form during the 18th century, adding the adjacent monastery. Among several splendid altars, that known as the Krucsay Altar of the Passion (first on the left) is most worthy of attention. János Krucsay suspected his first wife, Borbála Tolvay, of playing away from the marital home; she was found guilty of adultery at the county court and subsequently executed. Just three months later Krucsay was married again, and – perhaps in an effort to appease a troubled soul and dull conscience's prick – he commissioned this carved and painted altar in the 1730s. He is buried in the crypt. Ring at the side door to the left (with the tiny painted statuette above its porch) for admission if the church is locked.

The **Báthori István Museum** (☎ 42 283134/281885; *adult/concessions 200/100Ft; open Apr–Sep Tue–Sun 09.00–17.00, Oct–Mar Mon–Fri 08.00–16.00* ) is housed in the former monastery next door, and contains a rich collection of local artefacts dating from the Middle Ages to the middle of the 20th century. Among them are stones and glazed tiles

## THE BÁTHORI FAMILY

The Báthori dynasty was one of the most important in Transylvania between the 15th and 17th centuries. Born in Somlyó, István Báthori lived 1533–86 and was a *fejedelem* or Transylvanian prince (1571–86). He married a Jagello princess and became King of Poland (1575–86) after fighting off an attack in 1578 from Gáspár Bekes, a pretender to the throne supported by the Habsburgs. Báthori ascended to the Polish throne and moved to Krakow for a while, leaving the rule of Transylvania to his elder brother Kristóf. In 1579 he set off with a conscripted army to fight the Russian Tsar Ivan the Terrible, and in 1582 struck a ten-year ceasefire deal with Ivan. Towards the end of his life he created an alliance against the Turks, with the help of Pope Gregory III and comprising Transylvania, Hungary and Poland. He died in Grodno.

from the fortified castle that once stood near the Calvinist church, as well as a row of 15th-century choir stalls from the same church, produced in Florence in 1511 and the largest extant example of such Renaissance carving in Europe.

### Excursion from Nyírbátor

Let's get primeval. About 15km to the southeast, tucked beside a tributary of the River Kraszna, is a 53ha relict bog conservation area at **Bátorliget**. The special characteristics of this area, and the consequent importance of its wildlife, were recognised in 1913; the microclimate of the spot, in a depression sheltered from warm air currents by hills and oak groves, has helped to preserve glacial flora that has died out elsewhere. The sunnier southern slopes of the surrounding dunes harbour earlier-still heat-loving species that were able to cling on here during the Ice Age. In all, there are over 1,000 types of plant (such as the globe flower, Siberian iris, turban lily, flesh-coloured orchid and a plethora of fungi) and 7,000 of fauna (including the viviparous lizard, roller, black stork, 18 snail species and many of the insect kingdom). The Museum of the Primordial Marsh (*Bátorligeti Ősláp Múzeum; corner of Bajcsy-Zsilinsky utca and Botanikus utca;* \ *42 269708; adult 100Ft; open May 1–Sep 30 Tue–Sun 10.00–16.00*) can fill you in further; the marsh itself can only be visited on a guided tour (telephone the museum in advance). There are **buses** from Nyírbátor, Nyírvasvári, Terem and Vállay.

### The Rétköz region

Settled in a dip to the northeast of Nyíregyháza, with the Tisza above and its tributaries wrapping round below, the Rétköz (Meadow Land) used to be a particularly swampy and tough place to be. Things have eased considerably, but it doesn't clammer for your attention; you're more likely to pass through on the way to Záhony, the crossing point for the Ukrainian border. If you need to stop for any reason on the way, choose Kisvárda, 24km from the border, which is preferable to Záhony itself.

### Kisvárda

Kisvárda reached its zenith during the Ottoman occupation, when its castle cast an important defensive glow, but after that its status faded. The **fortress** (northwest of Flórián tér) was originally constructed in the 15th century, before corner towers were added in the 16th. Very nearly demolished in the 19th century, the ruins survived to serve as a venue for al-fresco summer-time **theatre** productions, while the grounds contain some **baths** (*Városmajor utca*). At the town centre, Flórián tér has a **Roman Catholic church** (*Flórián tér 11*) bearing a few Gothic features (such as traceried windows) of its original 15th-century self prior to a late-Baroque overhaul.

Just to the east of the square, the **Rétköz Museum** (*Csillag utca 5;* ✆ *45 405154; adult/concessions 200/100Ft; open Apr 1–Oct 31 Tue–Sun 09.00–12.00, 13.00–17.00*) is within a former synagogue built in the early 1900s. A Jewish community grew in the town from the 18th century. The descendants were to suffer desperately during World War II; those that hadn't already been sent to perish at forced labour camps in Ukraine were placed in a regional ghetto in April 1944 before being deported to Auschwitz. A stone at the entrance commemorates the 1,000 who died there. The museum itself contains several exhibitions of folk art and craft, as well as a local-history display.

If you're staying, your best bet is the central **Bástya Hotel** (*Krucsay Márton utca 2;* ✆ *45 421100; 18 rooms; dbl 5,000–5,500Ft*). For food, the **Opál Vendéglő** (*Halasy utca 34; mains 600–2,000Ft, avg 1,200Ft; open daily 10.00–22.00*) is 200m from the museum and has palatable enough fare, although during our visit the waitresses appeared to feel diners were an inconvenience best ignored. The **bus** and **train** stations are around 2km southwest of the centre (with local bus connections). There are between five and 11 daily trains to Budapest's Nyugati and Keleti (the latter the quicker journey), and very regular services from Nyíregyháza on the line running up to the Ukrainian border. There are direct buses from Nyíregyháza (up to four), Vásárosnamény (up to 13) and Sárospatak (one on weekdays).

## The Tiszahát and Erdőhát regions

The remotest areas of Szabolcs-Szatmár-Bereg County (and of Hungary as a whole) lie in the bump at the country's most easterly point, sandwiched between the border and the Tisza's banks – the Tiszahát on the northeastern side and the Erdőhát to the south. Navigating the swamps and water channels was traditionally tricky, and while things are drier now, transport remains far from a breeze; roads are rarely in tip-top nick, and, while there are local buses, they are not always regular or convenient. The main – in the loosest sense of the word – towns are Fehérgyarmat and Vásárosnamény. This region retains an unbroken link with its past, largely untouched by invaders that had such an impact elsewhere; even the Turks steered clear, judging that anyone willing to live in such inhospitable terrain was welcome to it.

### Vásárosnamény

The gateway to the Bereg stands at the meeting point of three rivers – the Tisza, Szamos and Kraszna – and was once a trading post on the 'Salt Route' between Transylvania and Debrecen. The inhabitants make their living the agricultural way – their main produce the red Namény apple – but this is nevertheless one of the significant town centres of the region (with seven churches, six schools and a cinema). Among some decent hotels are the **Marianna Center** (*Szabadság tér 19;* ✆ *45 470401; sgl 7,000Ft, dbl 8,000Ft*) and the **Fehér Hotel and Restaurant** (*Bereg köz 1–4;* ✆ *45 470854;* e *hotelfeher@axelero.hu; 16 rooms; €40/pp*), the latter a clean and modern place in front of the sport centre. The main square also holds **Tourinform** (*Szabadság tér 33;* ✆ *45 570206; vasarosnameny@tourinform.hu*). In 1969 the town was connected with the villages of Vitka and Gergelyiugornya, the latter having wooden huts on piles and a willow-strewn beach beside the bridge over the Tisza, making it a popular summer resort. There are two campsites – **Diófa Camping** (*Gulácsi út 71;* ✆ *45 712298*) and **Tiszavirág Camping** (*Tisza-part;* ✆ *45 570062*).

The **Bereg Museum** (*Rákóczi utca 13;* ✆ *45 470638; adult/concessions 300/150Ft; open Apr 1–Oct 31 Tue–Sun 08.00–16.00, Nov 1–Mar 31 Mon–Fri 08.00–16.00*) has permanent exhibitions of archaeological finds, cast-iron stoves and local folk art, including traditional Bereg embroidery. The varied patterns of the rich textiles were personalised to the wearer, indicating age and marital status. There are no direct **buses** to Vásárosnamény from Budapest (you'll need to change at Nyíregyháza); you can catch direct services from Nyíregyháza (ten), Kisvárda (up to 13), Fehérgyarmat (six most days, but just one on

Sunday) and Mátészalka (up to five, but none on Saturday). The **railway station** is the terminus for the line running from Nyíregyháza (eight daily), and on the line between Záhony and Ágerdőmajor that includes Mátészalka (seven).

### Tákos

Ten kilometres further along Route 41 (between four and 11 buses from Vásárosnamény), Tákos has a wattle-and-daub **Calvinist church** (*Bajczy-Zsilinszky utca 25; open daily 08.00–19.00; adult/concessions 100/75Ft*), known variously as the 'peasants' cathedral' or the 'barefoot Notre Dame'. Built in the 1760s, the white-washed exterior contrasts powerfully with folksy paintings inside, the ceiling adorned with 58 panels of floral patterns, the work of Ferenc Lándor in 1766. A wooden belfry stands in front. The village is a centre for the production of hand-made crossed embroidery, the women employing two colours in stitching images of deer, tulips and roses.

### Csaroda

Csaroda lies on a stream a short distance eastward on Route 41, just to the south of the Báb Lake bog-moss moor (with its trees of birch, willow and poplar). During renovation of its tiny 700-year-old Romanesque **Calvinist church** (*Kossuth utca 2*), some 14th-century frescoes were uncovered from beneath whitewash and floral

## THE RIVER TISZA

The Tisza is Hungary's second river, originating in the eastern Carpathian mountains where the 'White' and 'Black' branches come together. Running north to south through Hungary, via Tokaj in the Northern Uplands and on through the Great Plain past Szolnok and Szeged, its extravagant bends and curves slowed its flow and made it prone to regular flooding. As such, it was an ever-present force for both good and bad on the Great Plain, providing many with their livelihoods but equally – particularly after the deforestation of the Turkish period – transforming significant areas into unmanageable marshland. In the 1840s, on the initiative of Count István Széchenyi, a river regulation programme was begun, the architect Pál Vásárhelyi overseeing a straightening of the channel to allow the water to run more quickly. The result was that much boggy land became cultivable once more.

Things haven't been wholly rosy since then, however. The citizens of Szeged were victims of a fit of the river's pique in 1879 when it flooded and obliterated their city overnight (see page 364), and more recently the levels have risen dangerously again on several occasions in the late 1990s and early 2000s, possibly as a result of global warming. A disaster of a different sort hit the river in January 2000, when a cyanide leak had a devastating impact on its wildlife, poisoning the *poissons* and hitting tourist numbers hard. The eco disaster made itself felt even on the sporting stage. The leak allegedly emanated from a mine in Romania part-owned by Australians, and during a football match between the two countries a month later, Hungarian fans jeered their way through *Advance Australia Fair*, held up banners accusing the Socceroos of being 'fish murderers' and threw dead fish on to the pitch.

The river has in part recovered, although it is unlikely to be fully fighting fit for several years. It is increasingly popular for canoeing and kayaking tours (see pages 38–40), while many of its dead channels – those bends cut off from the main course during straightening – have become wildlife reserves, or haunts for anglers, sunbathers and watersports enthusiasts.

patterns added during the Reformation. Among the apostles in the Byzantine frescos are the so-called 'smiling saints' of Peter and Paul, an unusual detail in church paintings. The stylised red tulips and leafy decorations (many of which remain on the northern and southern walls) were evidently done by a Calvinist village craftsman; his inscription records that they were completed in 1642 – and suggests that his talents were rather unrefined, judging by the piling together of the final letters as the available space ran out. Nevertheless, the rich – if raw – artistic effort in such a diminutive church offers a glimpse of a heritage that was all but eradicated through war and occupation. The 14m-high turreted wooden belfry was built in the 18th century. Characteristic peasant houses can be found on Kossuth utca (*nos 13 and 21*), while you'll have to travel to the Village Museum at Sóstó (see page 316) to see the Calvinist vicarage that originally stood here from the 1870s. The same buses to Tákos from Vásárosnamény run on to Csaroda.

## Tarpa

Storks, grey herons and waterfowl live in the pastures and marshes along the riverside at Tarpa; the villagers themselves grow fruit (used in jams and brandies) and produce wine. Tarpa is known, though, for its 19th-century **dry mill** (*Árpád utca; open daily Apr 1–Oct 31 10.00–18.00, Nov 1–Mar 31 10.00–15.00*), the only one of its kind in the northeast. The mill has a conical roof covered with Tokaj wooden shingles, and was once powered by horses; you can only gain access if a worker is there. The **Calvinist church** (*Kossuth Lajos utca 13*) has a 15th-century oak door with original hinges, and Gothic frescoes on the northern wall. Near by, in the former granary, is a **Museum of Local History** (*Kossuth utca 25/A*), among its exhibitions a display dedicated to Endre Bajcsy-Zsilinszky. Bajcsy-Zsilinszky was a politician during the 1930s and 1940s, and took up arms against the Germans in spring 1944; he is buried in the village. There are **buses** from Vásárosnamény (up to 13) and Fehérgyarmat (up to six, but just one on Sunday).

## Fehérgyarmat

Fehérgyarmat is the main centre in the section south of the Tisza, located on Road 491 as it crosses the River Szamos. The reference to 'Gyarmat' in its name suggests that it was occupied by one of the conquering Hungarian tribes during the 10th century. It is said that Lajos Kossuth gave a recruiting speech here in 1848, and there is a memorial to this in the park. By the 19th century the town was making its money from the production of tobacco, but it smoked itself in 1872, 1895 and 1900, a series of fires that proved very bad for its health. In 1970 it was water that caused the damage during the Tisza-Szamos flood that destroyed many of the traditional peasant houses.

The 15th-century Gothic **Calvinist church** (*Kossuth utca 29*) has four pinnacles on its steeple and a bell presented by István Báthori (see page 319). The late-Baroque **Roman Catholic church** (*Kossuth utca 1*) originally dates to 1816, but was reconstructed in 1900. Telephone in advance if you'd like to visit the exhibition of **Szatmár-Bereg Nature Reserve** (*Vörösmarty utca 1;* ✆ *44 364060; adult 100Ft; open Tue–Sun 09.00–14.00*), which teaches about the region's wildlife and includes some mammoth bones that were unearthed near by.

There's precious little accommodation in town, and you're best looking elsewhere. The **railway station** is a couple of kilometres south of the centre, and is on the Mátészalka–Zajta line. There are up to ten trains to Mátészalka, where you can change for Vásárosnamény; you can also change for Nyíregyháza or Debrecen, although there are also a few daily direct services. The **bus station** is central, and has an information desk (✆ *44 361823; open Mon–Fri 05.30–20.00, Sat–Sun 05.30–17.30*). There are regular services to Mátészalka, Nyíregyháza, Debrecen and Budapest, as well as to the villages of the region (including Tarpa, Túristvándi, Szatmárcseke and Tivadar).

## Túristvándi

On the bank of the River Túr at the heart of Szatmári plain, Túristvándi's wooden **water mill** (*vízimalom; adult/concessions 200/100Ft; open daily Apr 1–Oct 31 09.00–18.00*) was originally built in 1800 (and reconstructed in the 1960s). Inside is a complex set of cogwheels and pulleys that clatter and ring and work the millstones when the sluice is opened. A small display explains how the mechanism works, and gives a bit of history. If there's nobody there, contact Madics Illés (*Zrínyi út 8;* ✆ *44 721073*). A memorial tablet on the corner house in the village, with its belltower, records that the writer Zsigmond Móricz spent childhood days here with his blacksmith uncle in 1885–87.

**Vízimalom Camping** (*Malom utca 3;* ✆ *42 437053; tent/caravan 900/2,000Ft, plus 900Ft/pp; panzió room 3,000Ft/pp; open all yr*) is a small grassy site in a charming spot on the river bank near the mill. There's a no-frills panzió and a restaurant (*mains 600–2,200Ft, avg 1,500Ft; open daily 09.00–21.00 in summer*), and little else to do beyond swim, canoe (*800Ft*), float on an inflatable ring and enjoy the surroundings. There are regular **buses** from Fehérgyarmat and Turistvándi; the bus stop is 100m from the mill.

## Szatmárcseke

Szatmárcseke is a plummy place, growing the fruit that is used for the firey national brandy (*pálinka*); it is said that the drink can raise the dead. This claim is rather undermined by the village's **cemetery** (*Tancsics Mihály utca*), its pride and joy. Its wooden gravemarkers are quite unique, shaped like vertical rowing boats; they have earned the site protected status since 1973. Various theories have been mooted as to the significance of the shape. Some say it harks back to a Finno-Ugric belief in death as a journey, others that it refers more simply to the time centuries ago when the cemetery was on a peninsula and bodies had to be rowed across the water. You may notice letters carved on the wood; 'ABFRA' stands for 'under the hope of happy resurrection' and 'BP' for 'peace to his ashes'. Breaking the trend in the centre of the plot is a tomb in white stone, that of Ferenc Kölcsey – poet, language reformer and the man who penned the Hungarian national anthem in 1823. Kölcsey lived

### WILDLIFE OF THE SZATMÁR-BEREG NATURE RESERVE

The Szatmár-Bereg Nature Reserve covers 22,246ha in the region of the Tisza, Szamos and Túr rivers, and features the volcanic peaks of Kaszonyi-hegy near Barabás and Tarpa Nagy-hegy, as well as former streams, oxbows and sediment-filled river beds. Fish species of the rivers include Danube trout, grayling, Tisza lamprey, gudgeon and loach, while several strictly protected peat bogs (such as those at the Nyíres, Báb, Zsig and Bence lakes) provide the habitat for marsh cinquefoil, cranberry, common sundew, cottongrass and eared willow. Half of the reserve has tree cover, comprising willow-poplar and ash-elm-oak gallery forests on the floodplain and hornbeam-oak forests further from the water.

Among the mammals of the region are the wild cat, otter, numerous bat species and a stable population of red deer. Reptiles are represented by the common viper and viviparous lizard, while birds of prey include the goshawk, buzzard, sparrow hawk and harrier (and more unusually the honey buzzard, black kite and saker falcon). The black stork lives in the mature forest, the kingfisher and bee eater dart among the river and sand banks, and there are around 100 species of passerines (most interestingly the thrush nightingale). Other rare birds are the corn bunting and the country's largest number of corncrake (over 100 pairs), breeding in freshly mown grasslands and wet meadows. For further information, visit the exhibition centre in Fehérgyarmat (see opposite).

in the village for over 20 years; the **cultural centre** (*Kölcsey utca 31*) stands on the site that once held his house, and has a room dedicated to him. The **Kölcsey Ferenc Memorial House** (*Kölcsey utca 46;* ✆ *44 432142; adult/concessions 100/50Ft; usually open daily 10.00–17.00, but telephone ahead*) has another exhibition about the poet, containing books, pictures and photos. Opposite the entrance to the cemetery is a **world map** with a plaque showing the number of Hungarians living abroad.

There is very simple accommodation (in summer only) at the **Kölcsey Hotel and Restaurant** (*Honvéd utca 6;* ✆ *44 377623; 13 rooms; dbl 4,000Ft*), with shared bathrooms; the cellar restaurant serves regional specialities. The **bus** stop is opposite the post office, just off the main street. There are services to Fehérgyarmat (up to 13), Kömörő (12), Turistvándi (eight) and Mateszalka (one).

## Csenger

On the border with Romania, Csenger has a Gothic 14th-century **Calvinist church** (*Hősök tere*) whose polygonal tower is topped with a parapet and shingled spire. The coffered ceiling was painted in the mid 18th century. Calvinist Protestantism was adopted at a synod convened in the church in 1576. A second, modern church – together with several other buildings in the village – are the work of renowned architect Imre Makovecz. The **Local History Museum** (*Hősök tere 3; adult 400Ft; open Tue–Sun 08.00–17.00*) has archaeological artefacts and pieces of folk art, as well as a reconstruction of a room in a peasant home.

The **Hotel Schuster** (*Ady Endre utca 12;* ✆ *44 520146; 14 rooms; dbl 16,000Ft*) is a charming hotel, housed in a 200-year-old building set in pretty grounds and with well-furnished rooms. There are **buses** between Csenger and Fehérgyarmat (up to five) and Mátészalka (16); the **railway station** is on the line from Mátészalka (four or five daily). There is a road border crossing into Romania at Csengersima, a short distance to the north.

# Southern Great Plain

*(For background to the whole Great Plain, see pages 285–6.)*

The Southern Plain (Dél-Alföld), covering the counties of Bács-Kiskun, Békés and Csongrád, is more cultivated than the north, with large areas of farmland and a greater number of towns. In the 19th century, acacias, poplars, fruit trees and vines were planted to bind the barren earth; the river courses were straightened in an effort to reclaim land saturated by floodwater, and the resulting dead channels – those bends cut off during the process – now form fishing lakes, reserves and bathing spots. There is still *puszta* to be found – notably at Bugac – and wildlife must-sees include the great bustard reserve at Dévaványa and Lake Fehér, a significant stopover site for migrating birds.

The south was hit hard during the Ottoman occupation; a lucky few like Kecskemét and Szeged came under the direct administration and protection of the sultan, but the regional architecture generally dates from the period afterwards. There is also a multi-ethnic feel, a result of Slovak, Serbian, Romanian and German immigrants who repopulated (and rebuilt) certain towns and villages in the 18th century. Both Kecskemét and Szeged are sophisticated and attractive towns, and others like Hódmezővásárhely and Gyula are equally deserving of attention. Horse-riding is widely offered in centres like Lajosmizse, and there are spas galore to the east of the Tisza, fed by thermal water discovered during surveys for oil in the mid 20th century. The memorial park at Ópusztaszer, the supposed meeting place for the Magyar chieftains after the 9th-century land taking, has become one of the most-visited attractions in the country; Árpád Feszty's breathtaking cyclorama alone makes the admission fee money worth spending. In addition, the region is the country's warmest, enjoying over 2,000 hours of sunshine a year.

## KECSKEMÉT

Equidistant from the Danube and the Tisza, Kecskemét is the principal town of Bács-Kiskun County. *Kecske* means 'goat' in Hungarian, and it is said this derives from the peculiar practice of the 13th-century bishop in presenting an animal to each convert to Christianity. History does not record how successful he was in appealing to them with the Father, the Son and a holy goat . . . Youthful in feel, architecturally adventurous in look, it isn't hard to see what people like about Kecskemét. Once you've accustomed yourself to what at first feels a confusing centre – a merging cluster of squares – it's worth putting aside a couple of days rather than hours to gape at some beautiful buildings, peruse a good selection of museums, shop from a decent range of boutiques and eat in some above-average restaurants. Kecskemét will keep you busy.

Kecskemét was a prosperous market town by the 15th century, and its layout – surrounded by a belt of farmsteads that give way to gardens and orchards – is typical of such settlements on the Great Plain. It suffered less than most during the Ottoman occupation, governed as it was directly by the sultan and enjoying his protection from the

Turkish officers that intimidated and exploited the unfortunate towns that fell under their administration. Turning in earnest to viniculture in the 19th century, the citizens were fortunate once more when the rampant phylloxera louse decided it disliked the area's sandy soil. The luck ran out in 1911 when an earthquake caused severe damage. 'Twas but a temporary set back; today the town rivals Szeged and Debrecen as the region's major educational and cultural player, and its apricot orchards yield renowned, throaty bottles of brandy (*barackpálinka*).

## Getting there, away and around

The composer Zoltán Kodály was born in the building now housing the **railway station** (*Kodály Zoltán tér 7*), just behind József Katona Park to the northwest. From the station it is a 500m walk through the park (where you should keep an eye out for the busts of some of the town's famous citizens) and along Nagykőrösi utca to the centre. Kecskemét is on the Szeged line; there are trains from Budapest Nyugati (ten daily) and Szeged (up to 13), as well as Kikunfélegyháza and Nagykőrös. There are a few direct trains to Szolnok (five) and Debrecen (two), but otherwise you'll need to change at Cegléd. In addition to the main station, the **narrow-gauge** Kecskemét KK station has two branches, one going to Kiskőrös and the other Kiskunmajsa. The latter passes through Bugac felső, and can thus be taken to get to Bugac and the Kiskunság National Park (see page 335); there are three a day, but it is a two-hour journey and there remains a 3km walk from Bugac felső to Bugac itself. (As such, you are probably better to take the bus.) Kecskemét KK is 1km southwest of the centre on Halasi út (which joins Batthyány utca); you can catch bus 2 there from the local bus station.

The **bus station** is near the train station, at the northern end of József Katona Park. There are services to a good number of towns around the country, including Budapest Népliget (regular), Szolnok (ten), Szeged (ten), Debrecen (one) and Pécs (two). The station for **local buses** is on Széchenyi tér, opposite the Otthon Cinema. If you need a **taxi**, try Hírös (✎ *76 484848*) or Zebra (✎ *76 444444*).

## Information and other practicalities

**Bugac Tours** See page 335.

**EuroNet Internet Café** Beniczky utca 1; ✎ 76 516221. There's no coffee at this café, but you can surf the net for 400Ft/hr. *Open Mon–Sat 10.00–22.00, Sun 16.00–22.00.*

**Ibusz** Kossuth tér 3; ✎ 76 486955. Located next to the Hotel Aranyhomok (enter through the same door). Book private accommodation, tours and exchange travellers' cheques and currency. *Open Mon–Fri 09.00–12.30, 13.00–17.45, Sat 09.00–12.45 (May–Oct only).*

**Listings magazine** *Kecskeméti Est*

**Market** Piac tér. North of the centre at the point where Budai utca and Erdosi Imre utca meet. Sells fresh produce, flowers and household goods. *open Sep 1–Apr 30 Tue–Fri 06.00–14.00, Sat 06.00–13.00, Sun 06.00–11.00, May 1–Aug 31 Tue–Fri 05.30–14.00, Sat 05.30–13.00, Sun 05.30–11.00.*

**Piramis Internet Café** Csányi utca 1–3; ✎ 76 418134. Next to the Hotel Udvarház, this cybercafé offers internet access for 480Ft/hr. *Open Mon–Fri 10.00–20.00, Sat–Sun 13.00–20.00.*

**Tourinform** Kossuth tér 1; ✎ 76 481065; e kecskemet@tourinform.hu. This office, in the northern corner of the town hall, can give details of cheap student digs and private accommodation. *Open Jun 1–Aug 31 Mon–Fri 08.00–17.00, Sat 08.00–18.00 (09.00–13.00 rest of year).*

## Where to stay

**Autós Camping** Csabay Géza körút 5; ✎ 76 329398. This campsite is adjacent to the water park, and therefore no stranger to excited squeals and splashes. As well as tent and caravan space, there are 25 bungalows (for 4) with showers. *Bungalow 5,800Ft, tent/caravan 550/1,600Ft (15% discount with student card); open Apr 15–Oct 15.*

# KECSKEMÉT

Háry Hotel

International bus station

Railway station

Rolling Rock Café

BETHLEN-VÁROS

BELSŐ

Cíoróka Puppet Theatre

BETHLEN-VÁROS

Caissa Panzió

Koppány verzér

Market

SZÉCHENYI VÁROS

GYENES MIHÁLY TÉR

Bank & ATM

FRÁTER GYÖRGY

Tanítókepző College

Fábián Panzió

HOMOKDOMB

Görög Udvar

Atrium

Bank & ATM

Leskowsky Musical Instrument Collection

Greek Orthodox Church

Otthon Cinema

House of Science & Technology

Bugac Tours

Bus station

Hotel Aranyhamok

Ornamental palace

RÁKÓCZI VÁROS

Caissa Panzió

Ibusz

BELVÁROS

Calvinist college

Liberté & Fodor

Piramis

Great Catholic Church

Ráday Museum

Kecskeméti Csárda

Calvinist Church

Post office

Erdei Ferenc Cultural Centre

Medical & Pharmaceutical Museum

Tourinform

Franciscan

Euronet

Mágnas Pince

Museum of the Hungarian Naive Artists

Town hall

Kodály Zoltán Institute of Music

Toy museum & workshop

River Pub

Hungarian Museum of Photography

Arboretum, (2km)
Skék-tó Leisure Park, (1km)

Katona József Theatre

LA TÁBÁR KÁLMÁN TÉR

Katona József Memorial House

Hotel Centrál

Nelson Pub & Xtreme Music Club

CZOLLNER TÉR

ÁRPÁD VÁROS

Béta Hotel Szauna (1.3km),
Aqua & waterslide park (1.3km),
Autós Camping (1.3km),
Fedett indoor swimming pool (400m),
Silver Mediterrán shopping centre (800m),
Sport Hotel (800m)

N

Bradt

FORRAS

KOSSUTH VÁROS

ERZSÉBET KÖRÚT

ERZSÉBET VÁROS

Zwack Exhibition (500m),
Kecskemét KK station (1km)

0    200m
0    200yds

**Béta Hotel Szauna** (38 rooms) Csabay Géza körút 2; ☎ 76 501190; e hotelszauna@axelero.hu; www.betahotels.hu. There's a fusty, 'college-dorm' feel to the Szauna, which is begging for a spruce up, but the rooms are huge and it's right on top of the water park. *Sgl 6,500Ft, dbl 8,500Ft, apt 11,000Ft.*

**Caissa Panzió** (6 rooms) Gyenes Mihály tér 18; ☎ 76 481685; e caissa@axelero.hu. Standing among flats on a quiet square shrouded by trees, Caissa has rooms that vary in size and facilities (with or without bathroom and TV), some of which are very cheap and therefore popular with students (who choose them rather than dorms). There are regular chess tournaments held here. *Sgl 4,000–6,000Ft, dbl 5,800–8,900Ft.*

**Fábián Panzió** (10 rooms) Kápolna utca 14; ☎ 76 477677; e panziofabian@freemail.hu; www.hotels.hu/fabian. A short walk from Széchenyi tér, this family-run guesthouse is blessed with good looks, a central garden and an owner as keen as mustard. It's been here for 15 years, but has clearly been loved and cared for. Well recommended. *Sgl 8,500Ft, dbl 9,500Ft.*

**Hotel Aranyhomok** (111 rooms) Kossuth tér 3: ☎ 76 503730; e aranyhomok@axelero.hu. It's unpretty from the outside, but it's what's inside that counts; the rooms are modern, and there's a fitness centre. It's worth paying the 2,000Ft extra to bag a room with a balcony overlooking the square. *Sgl 8,500–10,600Ft, dbl 13,600–15,600Ft, triple 22,000Ft, suite 18,000–23,100Ft.*

**Hotel Centrál** (26 rooms) Kisfaludy utca 10; ☎ 76 502710. This newish hotel to the southwest of Katona József tér has well-appointed but simple rooms. It has a similarly priced sister hotel – the Udvarház – just to the west of Kossuth tér. *Sgl €47, dbl €55.*

**Háry Hotel** (22 rooms) Kodály Zoltán tér 9; ☎ 76 480400; e hotel@hary.hu; www.hary.hu. Built in 2002, the Háry – named after a Falstaffian soldier of the Napoleonic Wars immortalised in a musical piece by Kodály in 1927 – has rooms that are on the 'cosy' side for 2, but are airy nevertheless. The location is handy for the bus station, but the surroundings are correspondingly drab. Sauna and fitness room. *Sgl €43, dbl €48, triple €60 (excl tourist tax).*

**Hotel Talizmán** (18 rooms) Kápolna utca 2; ☎ 76 504856; e talhot@axelero.hu; www.hotels.hu/talizmanhotel. On the same road as the Fábián, the Talizmán lacks for character by comparison, but its whitewashed rooms are contemporary. *Sgl 9,150Ft, dbl 11,300Ft, triple 13,450Ft.*

**Sport Hotel** (51 rooms) Izsáki út 15; ☎ 76 496822; e sporthotel@axelero.hu. Around 1km southwest of the centre (on Road 52), the Sport has a swimming pool and fitness room, and adequate rooms lacking in homely touches. Well situated for the leisure park and arboretum. *Sgl 7,600Ft, dbl 11,500Ft.*

**Tanítóképző Főiskola Kollégiuma** (100 rooms) Piaristák tere 4; ☎ 76 486977. Central college offering accommodation in summer (*Jul 1–Aug 30*). *Rooms 1,600Ft/pp.*

## Where to eat and drink

**Atrium Coffee House** Hornyik János körút 2; ☎ 76 486793. Busy and intimate backstreet bar with outdoor terrace. *Open Mon–Thu 08.00–22.00, Fri–Sat 08.00–23.00.*

**Fodor** Szabadság tér 2; ☎ 76 496545. Sit in the pink parlour or on the outdoor terrace, and enjoy excellent ice cream and cake. There is a second branch at Nagykörösi utca 15, although the views of the main road make it less enticing. *Open 09.00–18.30 daily.*

**Görög Udvar** Széchenyi tér 9; ☎ 76 492513. The name and music might suggest otherwise, but there are as many Hungarian as Greek dishes on the menu here. The outdoor courtyard, with its hanging baskets, is the place to dine; it's atmospheric, and the food is good. *Mains 950–2,500Ft, avg 1,500Ft; open 11.00–23.00 daily.*

**Kecskeméti Csárda** Kölcsey utca 7; ☎ 76 488686. Around the corner from the Pharmacy Museum, the Kecskeméti Csárda is the town's top restaurant. The menu features generously ladled Hungarian food with Mediterranean specials, and dishes like venison steak with roasted apple and walnut sauce are worth the extra few forints. The peasant-style décor is nevertheless sophisticated – rustic chic – and the al-fresco area is beautiful on a balmy night. The language on the English menu could do with some polishing – we avoided the 'fish food' option, and wished the 'obsessed goose liver' would lighten up. *Mains 1,390–3,490Ft, avg 2,000Ft; open daily 12.00–23.00.*

**Kisbugaci Csárda** Munkácsy utca 10. Unfussy and understated restaurant serving Hungarian grub. *Set menus 1,900–2,300Ft; mains 750–2,000Ft, avg 1,500Ft; open Mon–Sat 12.00–22.00, Sun 12.00–15.00.*

**Koppány Vezér** Erdősi Imre utca 6; ✆ 76 480779. Medieval-theme restaurant serving 'feasts' for up to 10. The menu is inevitably meat-heavy. Located next to the market. *Feasts 3,200–24,600Ft; mains 1,250–4,100Ft, avg 2,400Ft; open 12.00–23.00 daily.*

**Liberté** Szabadság tér 2; ✆ 76 328636. A tasteful jewel of a place for a coffee, a beer or a meal, with a lengthy terrace overlooking Szabadság tér. Hungarian cuisine with a few beef steaks thrown into the line-up. *Mains 690–2290Ft, avg 1,600Ft; open daily 09.00–23.00.*

**Mágnás Pince** Csongrádi utca 2; ✆ 76 417640. A refined and lengthy cellar restaurant, with high-backed chairs and an impressive selection of wines. Among the Hungarian fare during our visit – tasty, and in decent portions – were fillet of pike perch in pastry, and honeyed goose leg. *Mains 900–2,200Ft, avg 1,600Ft; open 11.30–23.00 daily.*

**Nelson Pub** Kisfaludy utca 4; ✆ 76 500922. Given the name, you won't be shocked to hear that the Nelson aspires to being a 'traditionally English' pub – nor that it's very different from your standard boozer in England. Admire the effort, though, and wrap yourself around a 'traditional' London toastie. *Mains 1,290–2,590Ft, avg 1,800Ft; open Mon–Fri 11.00–24.00, Fri 11.00–02.00, Sat 12.00–24.00, Sun 12.00–23.00.*

**River Pub** Lestár tér 1; ✆ 76 415405. A pubby pub serving Kilkenny and Guinness and with a mural of a paddle steamer dominating the back wall. International food is served in hearty platefuls, and there's also a wide winelist. *Mains 950–2,250Ft, avg 1,500Ft; open Mon–Sat 11.00–23.00, Sun 12.00–23.00.*

**Rolling Rock Café** Jókai utca 44; ✆ 76 506190. Plonked next to a garage to the north of the centre, the Rolling Rock has live music and DJs on Thu–Sat nights; soak up the alcohol with snacky food including burgers, fajitas and nachos. *Mains 390–2,850Ft, avg 1,400Ft; open Wed–Sat 18.00–01.00.*

## Entertainment and nightlife

A mischievous smile plays about the lips of the 19th-century Eclectic **Katona József Theatre** (*Katona József tér 5;* ✆ *76 483283; www.katonaj.hu*), with cherubs cavorting above its entrance and tooting on horns. Good humour was in short supply when the contract to design the theatre – part of the millennial celebrations – was awarded to foreign (Viennese) architects Fellner and Helmer (also responsible for Budapest's Vígszínház – see page 122 – and the resemblance is clear). The **ticket office** (✆ *76 501174;* e *jegyiroda@katonaj.hu; open Tue–Fri 10.00–13.00, 15.00–19.00, Sat 10.00–14.00*) can tell you what's on. The Holy Trinity Monument outside was erected in 1742 by survivors of the plague, which had claimed 5,000 lives two years before.

**Ciróka Puppet Theatre** (*Bábszínház; Budai utca 15;* ✆ *76 482217; www.ciroka.hu*) stages performances for kids of kindergarten age and upwards; shows run most days (except Mon), and usually start at 10.00–10.30 and 14.00 – although this can vary, so check beforehand at the ticket office (*open Tue–Sun 10.00–16.00*). **Otthon Cinema** (*Kossuth tér 4;* ✆ *76 481686; www.extra.hu/kio*) is the only traditional film house in town, open for 60 years and decorated with folk motifs. It screens children's, European and Hungarian classic movies, as well as Hollywood blockbusters. The **Erdei Ferenc Cultural Centre** (*Deák Ferenc tér 1;* ✆ *76 503880;* e *efmk@axelero.hu; open Mon–Sat 11.00–13.30, 16.00–19.00*) hosts temporary exhibitions and a variety of cultural programmes, and is the best place to go for information on other events in town.

A couple of kilometres southwest of the centre, the buzzing **Silver Mediterrán Club** (*Izsáki út 2;* ✆ *06 20 919 0392; www.clubsilver.hu; admission 700/1,000Ft before/after 24.00, but may vary; open Sat 22.00–05.00 & occasional Fri*) is in a shopping mall. Based over two levels, you can dance on the first and chill out on the second. Down an alley next to the Nelson Pub, **Xtreme Music Club** (*Kisfaludy utca 4;* �‌ *76 500926; open Wed, Fri–Sat 10.00–04.00*) plays rock, dance or disco, depending on the day of the week. Wednesday is student night, and Saturday usually rock night (when there may be an admission charge).

## What to see and do
### Kossuth tér and around
If you can unravel the tangle of squares, then Kossuth tér is just about the centremost of them; bustling and spacious, its monuments include a statue of Kossuth and a cone-shaped distance marker, a popular slippery playground with the town's kiddies.

In 1891, a competition was opened to design the **town hall** (*Kossuth tér 1*), with entrants asked to follow the theme of the town's motto – 'Neither height nor depth deter me'. Ödön Lechner and Gyula Pártos were the victors, and put together the salmon-pink building with its stained glass and majolica roof of yellow diamonds; the result was one of Lechner's early attempts at a distinctive national style, an influential masterpiece of Hungarian Art Nouveau (Secessionism). It is adorned with fire-glazed tiles of floral motifs, and contains a ceremonial hall bearing frescoes by Bertalan Székely (1897) in the pseudo-historical romantic style of the period and a bronze chandelier weighing in at a mammoth 1,200kg. (*To visit the hall,* �‌ *76 483683 in advance, and between 10.00 and 11.30; adult/concessions 300/150Ft, guide 700Ft.*) The glockenspiel above the entrance plays snatches of music on the hour – including Kodály and Erkel (*12.00*), Handel, Beethoven and Mozart (*18.00*) and Hungarian folk songs (*20.00*). A broken block of stone in one of the flower beds out front marks the spot where playwright József Katóna (see page 332) collapsed and died of a heart attack in 1830 at the age of just 39.

Adjacent to the town hall, the Piarist Gáspár Oszwald's late-Baroque **Great Catholic Church** (*Nagytemplom; Kossuth tér 2; open 09.00–12.00, 15.00–18.00 daily*) nudges 75m – the largest on the Great Plain – and was built 1774–1806. Somehow the very vastness of its interior presses the fragility of the human condition upon you, a feeling reinforced when looking down from the frightening height of the gallery running around the clock tower. Niches above the entrance hold statues of saints István and Lászlo; the dongs of the church's bell used to call the workers in from the fields at lunchtime.

At the square's eastern side, the **Franciscan church** (*Szent Miklós ferences templom; Kossuth tér 3*) is the town's oldest building, originally constructed in the 14th century before later Gothic and Baroque reconstruction. The modern frescoes inside – with a hieroglyphic feel to them – are striking, although they may not appeal to traditionalists. The **Kodály Zoltán Pedagogical Institute of Music** (*Zenepedagógiai Intézet;* �‌ *76 481518; adult/concessions 100/50Ft; open Mon–Fri 12.00–13.00, 16.00–18.00, Sat–Sun 10.00–18.00*) occupies the former early-18th-century monastery next door. The institute – whose staff follow Kodály's revolutionary teaching method – has a small museum devoted to the man himself. Kodály was born in Kecskemét in 1882; he was a composer, but is best remembered for his theory that music skills should be acquired through singing and the programme he devised based upon Hungarian folk songs.

### Szabadság tér
To the northeastern side of its bigger brother, Szabadság tér has trees and benches to enjoy their shade. The **Calvinist church** (*Szabadság tér 7*) was completed in 1684, the only stone church to be built during the era of Turkish rule. While religious tolerance – as evidenced by the churches of various denominations in close proximity – was a feature of the town, this church actually replaced a wooden version burnt by Catholics in 1678 during a spell of Counter-Reformatory pique. The Art-Nouveau **Calvinist college**

(*Szabadság tér 7*), with its terracotta roof and Transylvanian motifs, was built in 1912 and holds the parish library and the **Ráday Museum** (❧ *76 486226; adult/concessions 50/30Ft; open Tue–Sun Nov 1–Feb 28 09.00–17.00, Mar 1–Oct 31 10.00–18.00*). The latter has displays of Calvinist religious art from the region, as well as a translation of the New Testament by János Erdősi Sylvester in 1541 – the first work printed wholly in Hungarian. The promulgation of vernacular Christianity was a prime reason for the rise in Calvinism's popularity (in contrast to the Latin used by the Catholic clergy), and it became entrenched in many areas of the Great Plain during the 16th century. (Note that there were talks of closing the museum during our last visit.)

The **Ornamental Palace** (*Cifrapalota; Rákóczi út 1*), to the college's right, houses the town gallery (❧ *76 480776; adult/concessions 260/130Ft; open Tue–Sat 10.00–17.00, Sun 13.30–17.00*), with works by László Mednyánszky (1852–1919), Auschwitz-victim István Farkas (1887–1944) and Menyhért Tóth (1904–80). The building itself, though, is the outstanding work of art; constructed in 1902 by Géza Márkus – originally as a town house with ground-floor shops – its façade has floral decoration and its roof of green, orange and blue supports seven glazed chimneys. The Peacock Hall boasts several of the favoured motifs of the Hungarian Art Nouveau inspired by Lechner – flowers, lianas and peacocks.

Across Rákóczi út, the **House of Science and Technology** (*Tudomány & Technikaháza; Rákóczi út 2*; ❧ *76 487611; admission free; open Mon–Fri 08.00–16.00*) occupies the Moorish-Romantic former synagogue (built 1864–71), and is used as a conference centre. Winding stairs lead to a gallery of plaster-cast copies of Michelangelo sculptures; some of these look forlorn and faintly ridiculous in such a limited space, but the resplendent stained-glass windows are beautiful.

## Museums and galleries

The **Hungarian Museum of Photography** (*Magyar Fotográfiai Múzeum; Katona József tér 12*; ❧ *76 483221; www.fotomuseum.hu; adult/concessions 150/100Ft; open Wed–Sun 10.00–17.00*) has temporary exhibitions of work by Hungarian photographers old and new, as well as a library, shop and collection of technological bits and bobs. The 18th-century building has had a varied existence, serving over the years as a horse-changing station, restaurant, dance club and Orthodox synagogue.

The **Katona József Memorial House** (*Katona József utca 5*; ❧ *76 328420; adult/concessions 100/50Ft; open Feb 1–Dec 15 Tue–Sat 10.00–14.00*) pays tribute to one of the town's past leading lights. Katona wrote the classic drama *Bánk Bán* (on which Ferenc Erkel based his opera), which features the murder of a German-born queen by a servant, and addresses the inherent tension between an individual's duty to his own conscience and that due to a foreign-controlled government. Katona's talent was not properly recognised prior to his premature death in 1830 (see page 331), and the drama was not published until after it.

To the west of Deák Ferenc tér, the **Museum of the Hungarian Naive Artists** (*Gáspár András utca 11*; ❧ *76 324 767*; e *naivmuzeum.kecskemét@museum.hu; admission free; open Mar 15–Oct 31 Tue–Sun 10.00–17.00*) is inside an 18th-century nobleman's mansion. The 'naive' style originated in the early 20th century, practised by artisans with no formal artistic training who anchored their work in the themes of rural peasant life – the world of markets, harvest festivals and local celebrations. Among the leading early artists were Rezső Mokry-Mészáros and the 'peasant painter' Péter Benedek, and the pieces are raw, instinctive and refreshingly clumsy.

The adjacent **Toy Museum and Workshop** (*Szórakaténusz Játékmúzeum & Műhely; Gáspár András utca 11*; ❧ *76 481469; adult/concessions 300/150Ft; open museum Mar 15– Dec 31 Tue–Sun 10.00–12.30, 13.00–17.00, workshop Wed & Sat 10.00–12.00, 14.00–17.00, Sun 10.00–12.00*) is a child's paradise, with dolls, puppets, carved wooden wagons and a jigsaw puzzle made in the 1760s. The workshop organises programmes where children can have a go at making wooden toys.

Just 100m away, the **Medical and Pharmaceutical History Museum** (*Orvos & Gyógyszerészettörténeti Múzeum; Kölcsey utca 3;* ✆ *76 329964; adult/concessions 200/100Ft; open May 15–Sep 30 Tue–Sun 10.00–14.00*) has medical objects used in Bács-Kiskun county over the past 200 years. Follow Petőfi Sándor utca a block beyond the ring road and turn right to reach the **Museum of Hungarian Popular Arts and Crafts** (*A Magyar Népi Iparművészeti Múzeum; Serfőző utca 19;* ✆ *76 327203; adult/concessions 200/100Ft; open Jan 15–Dec 14 Tue–Sat 10.00–17.00*), which has a daunting collection of wood carvings, embroidery, pottery, basketwork and more in a 200-year-old former brewhouse.

The **Leskowsky Musical Instrument Collection** (*Zimay László utca 6/A;* ✆ *76 486616; adult/concessions 500/300Ft; visits by prior registration only*) has a private collection of 1,500 instruments from all over the globe, which the owner will play for you. The **Zwack Fruit Brandy Distillery and Exhibition** (*Gyümölcspálinka-főzde & Kiállítás; Matkói út 2;* ✆ *76 481005; adult 1,350Ft; visit on Fri at 13.00 or groups on weekdays by prior registration*) is a temple for lovers of fruit brandy, for which Kecskemét is renowned. The English King Edward VIII remarked that 'when mixed with sparkling water, this brandy is better than whisky; with tea, it is better than rum'. Zwack Unicum is the market leader, and you can look around the plant, learn a little about the Zwack family, and have a taste. You'll find it just over 1km to the south of the centre; follow Batthyány utca into Halasa út, and turn left immediately after the rail track.

### Other activities

There are several places to take a dip to the west of the centre. The **Szék-tó Leisure Park** (*Szabadisopark; entrance to lake 50Ft, fishing adult/concessions 990/590Ft; open in summer Mon–Fri 06.00–21.00, Sat–Sun 05.00–21.00, variable hours other seasons*), just beyond Csabay Géza körút, comprises a large artificial lake and swimming pools. The relatively new **Aqua and Waterslide Park** (*Élményfürdő & Csúszdapark; Csabay Géza körút 2;* ✆ *76 481724; www.hiros.index.hu/csuszdapark; adult/concessions 800/600Ft, reduced cost after 15.00, waterslide tickets 500–2,900Ft; open May 1–Aug/Sep 09.00–19.00 daily*) has pools, slides, whirlpools and wave machines. (Local buses 1, 11 and 22 run out here from Széchenyi tér.) The **Fedett Indoor Swimming Pool** (*Izsáki út 1;* ✆ *76 482152; adult/concessions 450/300Ft; open daily main pool 06.00–21.00, thermal pool 06.00–19.00*) has regular and thermal pools, as well as sauna, solarium and massage options.

A few kilometres northwest of the centre, the 62ha **arboretum** (*Nyíri út 48;* ✆ *76 492455; free admission*) operates not only as a nature haven but also as a natural wind shield for the town. There are species common to the Great Plain, as well as more exotic types. The wood-chipped paths, wooded picnic area and wooden viewing tower make this an excellent spot for walks or picnics. The main entrance and car park are at the southern end. The path here leads past a series of statues of Hungarian saints beyond which is the Mary Chapel (*Mária-kápolna; open daily summer 08.00–20.00, winter 08.00–16.00*). It is said that a man was chased by a bull here in 1718, and built the chapel to thank the Virgin Mary for his escape.

**Equestrian tourism** is strong in these parts, and Tourinform can provide details of farms in the vicinity offering horse-riding, horse shows and private accommodation.

### Festivals and events

There are concerts and exhibitions during the Kecskemét Spring Festival in March, while Summer in the Main Square (*end Jun–start Jul*) sees folk performances and an open-air folk-art fair. The Kodály Seminar and Festival takes place every other July, with educational programmes and concerts. The Hírös Week Festival (*end Aug*) showcases traditional crafts and food.

# KISKUNFÉLEGYHÁZA

The 'Kiskun-' ('Little Kun') prefix to this and other towns in the region refers to a nomadic Turkic people called the Cumans (or Kun), skilled horsemen who settled here during the 13th century and were gradually assimilated into Hungarian society. They arrived in Kiskunfélegyháza in 1239, but the town was deserted during the Turkish invasion and had to be repopulated all over again (this time by Jazygians) in the mid 18th century. It developed as a market town and rose to be administrative centre of the Kiskun district between 1753 and 1876. Its main claim to fame, though, is that it was the birthplace of Ferenc Móra, one of the country's most significant writers of the early 20th century.

## Getting there and away

The **bus station** is to the south of the parish church on Bajcsy-Zsilinszky Endre utca; there are services to Budapest Népliget (17), as well as to closer destinations like Kecskemét (regular), Szeged (11), Csongrád (20) and Bugac (11). The **railway station** is at the western end of Kossuth Lajos utca; there is a taxi rank outside, but it is a relatively easy walk to the centre (straight ahead from the station and up Kossuth Lajos utca). Kecskemét is at the meeting point of several lines, including those to Szeged and Kiskunhalas. There are services to Budapest Nyugati (ten), Szeged (17), Cegléd (ten), Kecskemét (17), Kiskunhalas (eight) and Szolnok (three); for trains to Kelebia (and onward journeys to Belgrade), change at Kiskunhalas.

## Information

**Kiskun Nova** Martirok utja 1; ↘ 76 4333243. Travel agency organising foreign and domestic travel, and able to provide limited information about the town. *Open Mon–Fri 09.00–17.00.*

## Where to stay

**Borostyán Panzió** Szőlő utca 1; ↘ 76 466785; e pepu@netquick.hu. Staying here is rather like staying in the spare room of someone's house; there's little luxury, but it's low in price. To get there, follow Szentesi út off the main high street, turn right into Nefelejcs utca and, after 500m, turn left into Szőlő utca. *Sgl/dbl €22, triple €32.*

**Hotel Óázis** (16 rooms) Szegedi út 13; ↘ 76 461913. To the south of the main square, this hotel is more central than the other options and marginally more appealing. *Sgl 6,700Ft, dbl 10,200Ft.*

**Mónika Panzió** (10 rooms) Szőlő utca 1; ↘ 76 455022. Next to Borostyán Panzió, Mónika could hardly be called modern and could certainly be called basic. Rooms are en suite, though. *Dbl 6,000Ft, room for 4 11,000Ft.*

## Where to eat and drink

There are several pizza and pasta places on Kossuth Lajos utca, and in terms of location and atmosphere they are probably the best eating bet.

**Csillag Vendéglő** Szegedi út 41; ↘ 76 462640. A minimalist affair serving goodly portions of average but cheap Hungarian food. *Mains 700–1,530Ft, avg 1,000Ft; open Mon–Sat 11.00–22.00, Sun 11.00–15.00.*

**Gyorsétkezde** Kossuth Lajos utca 76; ↘ 76 462273. The most popular of the pizzerias. It is also a pub and coffee house. *Pizzas 600–1,800Ft, avg 740Ft; open Mon–Thu, Sun 09.00–24.00, Fri–Sat 09.00–02.00.*

**Hotel Óázis** See above. This hotel restaurant is plasticky, overly bright and distinctly forgettable. *Mains 820–2,000Ft, avg 1,400Ft; open daily 06.00–10.00, 18.00–22.00.*

## What to see and do

The town consists of three main streets – Szegedi út, running through its centre, and Kossuth Lajos utca and Bajcsy-Zsilinsky Endre utca perpendicular to it – with the primary square, Petőfi tér, merging with Béke tér and Szent János tér. The citizens' pride and joy is their **town hall** (*Petőfi tér*), a beautiful monument to the vernacular Hungarian Art-Nouveau style of the early 20th century, and looking like a Zsolnay-majolica-studded princess's castle.

Opposite is the white **Swan House** (*Hattyúház; Szent János tér 9;* ⟍ *76 461429; open Mon–Tue 08.00–17.30, Wed–Thu 12.00–17.30, Fri 08.00–17.30, Sat 08.00–12.00*), built in 1819 in Neoclassical style; today it houses a library, but between 1824 and 1830 there were sausages – Sándor Petőfi's father ran a butcher's shop from here. A short distance to the east, behind the Roman Catholic church, the **Petőfi Memorial Museum** (*Petőfi Sándor utca 7;* ⟍ *76 461468; adult/concessions 240/120Ft; open Wed–Fri 09.00–12.00*) has various bits and pieces connected with the future poet in the house where he spent much of his childhood. Although he wasn't born in Kiskunfélegyháza, Petőfi was to say that 'This is the town where I first saw the light'.

The terracotta-coloured mid-18th-century **Roman Catholic church** dominates Béke tér, a Baroque building with colourful Rococo pulpit and side altars. Among the monuments to the right of the church is one to Károly Kertbeny, a Hungarian-German writer who devoted his life to popularising Hungarian literature abroad – and gave the world the terms 'homosexual' and 'heterosexual'.

Continue east along Bajcsy-Zsilinszky utca and turn right into Móra Ferenc utca for the **Móra Ferenc Memorial House** (*Móra Ferenc utca 19;* ⟍ *76 461468; adult/concessions 120/60Ft; open Wed–Fri 09.00–12.00*); this thatched cottage set back from the road was the birthplace and childhood home of the writer. The top collection in town, however, is at the **Kiskun Museum** (*Dr Holló Lajos út 9;* ⟍ *76 461468; adult/concessions 240/120Ft; open Mar 15–Oct 31 Wed–Sun 09.00–17.00*) in the former county prison house. There are paintings by László Holló, a local and prominent Expressionist artist who depicted the misery of peasants, and died in 1976; there are archaeological and ethnographic items relating to the region, including a reconstruction of a peasant living room; there is the butcher's block and cleaver used by István Petrovits (Petőfi senior) and Ferenc Móra's school desk; and there are torture tools used at the jail, as well as toys made by prisoners – chief among which is a fabulous wooden clock of 1918. In the courtyard is a windmill that operated on a nearby farm between 1860 and 1942; windmills were once plentiful in Kiskunság, with 62 in and around Kiskunfélegyháza alone in the 1850s. It is a shame that few remain.

The **swimming pool and lido** (*Blaha Lujza tér 1;* ⟍ *76 463201; adult/concessions 380/280Ft; open Mon–Fri 06.00–19.00, Sat–Sun 08.00–19.00*) is towards the western end of Kossuth Lajos utca, near the train station.

# KISKUNSÁG NATIONAL PARK
## Bugac

Bugac – the 'pearl of the Kiskunság', a few kilometres southwest of Kiskunfélegyháza – is the second-largest *puszta* in Hungary and a good introduction to the national park. **Bugac Tours** (*Kecskemét, Szabadság tér 5A;* ⟍ *76 482500;* e *bugac@mail.datanet.hu; open Mon–Fri 08.00–16.30*), with a small office (*Nagybugac 135;* ⟍ *76 372688*) at the gateway to the national park, have something of a monopoly here. As well as organising a variety of programmes featuring horse shows and horse-riding, they can arrange accommodation in thatched farmhouses (*from 8,000Ft/night*). Next to the office is the **Bugaci Karikás Csárda** (*Nagybugac 135;* ⟍ *76 575112;* e *bugac@mail.datanet.hu; www.bugacpuszta.hu; mains 900–1,850Ft, avg 1,400Ft; open 09.00–22.00 daily*), a traditional 'folksy' restaurant that makes the bulk of its cash from serving clients on programmes organised by Bugac Tours. There is also a basic **campsite** (*arrange through Bugac Tours; 700Ft/pp*) in a field behind the restaurant.

A track running into the *puszta* leads 1.5km to a farm and stables of 100 halfbreds. During **horse shows** (*daily at 13.15, with a second at 15.15 if there is sufficient demand*), the

## KISKUNSÁG NATIONAL PARK

The second-biggest national park in Hungary (covering 76,000ha), the Kiskunság was founded in 1975 and is, like the Hortobágy, a Unesco World Heritage Site. Comparisons with the Hortobágy don't stop there, for the landscapes and the species to be found in them are similar, and there are opportunities in both for enjoying horse shows and puszta parties. Located between the Danube and the Tisza, the Kiskunság is composed of nine separate areas covered with loess or sand, and dotted with reeds, wet marshes, bogs, pastures, forests and steppe; much of this is barred to the casual tourist boot.

**Lake Kolon** in Izsák is a typical example of a freshwater marshy area in a former river branch, and is characteristic of the Danube floodplain; the site hosts a strong population of the globally threatened European mudminnow, and all of Hungary's eight heron species breed here. During the Turkish occupation, locals often hid from the Ottoman armies among the lake's reeds. Head with your binoculars to the Bikatorok Hill, just west of the lake, to watch the birds without disturbing them.

The **Fülöpháza area** is known for its mobile sand dunes, which are blown in the direction of the prevailing wind (from northwest to southeast); there is a 1.5km study trail, departing from near kilometre marker 20 on Road 52. The **Bócsa-Bugac** is the most extensive and diverse area of the park; as well as dunes, you'll find alkaline grasslands, oak forests, ancient juniper stands, wet meadows, bogs, marshes, cultivated fields and exposed sandy soil.

The most frequently visited part of the park – the River Tisza oxbow at **Szikra** and the surrounding Tőserdő, 27km east of Kecskemét – is also the smallest. Many head for Szikra (the riverside part of Felső-Alpár puszta) to fish or bathe, but others follow the trails through the bog woods that flank the oxbow. The southernmost section holds the Alpár meadow, where it is said a great battle took place between the invading Hungarian tribes and the Bulgars, who inhabited the site in the 9th century; here the water violet blooms in spring and whiskered terns nest in the fens. The **Upper Kiskunság** in particular is notable for being a stronghold of the great bustard, as well as of the saker falcon, stone curlew, collared pratincole, roller and bee-eater. In addition, the national park actively preserves the natural and human features fashioned by the traditional rural way of life on the Great Plain, including isolated farmsteads (tanya), wells and wooded pastures. In keeping with this, significant herds of old Hungarian domestic animal breeds are reared here.

The national park's official HQ and visitor centre is the **House of Nature** (Liszt Ferenc utca 19; ⎞ 76 482611; adult/concessions 200/150Ft; open Tue–Fri 09.00–16.00, Sat 10.00–14.00), standing a few kilometres to the north of Kecskemét's centre. It features a display of the park's various habitats, together with photos and the obligatory stuffed fauna.

brightly waistcoated herders (csikós) perform the famous 'Puszta Five' (see page 341), as well as making their steeds go through a range of equestrian tricks; you can walk, drive or take a carriage ride from the entrance (1,000Ft/pp). In addition, there is **horse-riding** on offer (riding from €8/hr, instruction from €32/hr, full-day tour with picnic from €56/pp). Near by is the **Pastoral Museum** (Pásztormúzeum; adult/concessions 800/400Ft; open Apr 1– Oct 31 daily 10.00–16.00), housed in a circular hut and displaying shepherding memorabilia – musical instruments, sheep identification tags, tools, bells and the shepherd's ubiquitous sheepskin coat. Bugac Tours arrange a programme that includes the museum, a show and lunch at the csárda (*from 4,500Ft/pp, with optional carriage ride extra; May 1–Sep 30, departing from the entrance at around 12.00 daily*).

There are several marked **walking trails**; it might help to purchase a map of the national park from the House of Nature (see box opposite) or Bugac Tours (*Kiskunsági Nemzeti Park*, 1: 90,000).

If you have a car, you can park at the park entrance; otherwise the journey is a slightly awkward one, and you may not arrive to coincide with a programme. Bugac itself is 6km from the entrance, so if you take a **bus** from Kecskemét you'll need to ask the driver to drop you at the most convenient stop along the way – and you'll still have 1½km to walk. At the weekend, you can take the **narrow-gauge railway** from Kecskemét KK (south of the centre); alight at Bugac-felső (not Bugac Puszta or Bugac), which is 2km south of the entrance. Trains depart Kecskemét KK at 08.00, 14.00 and 19.50 for the 1½ hour journey; the last train back leaves Bugac-felső at 18.09.

## NAGYKŐRÖS

Like Cegléd 15km to its north (see below), Nagykőrös goes all gooey over Lajos Kossuth, who gave a speech from its **town hall** (*Szabadság tér*) balcony on September 25 1848 (the day after he addressed the citizens of Cegléd). However, another favourite also stamped his name on the town. The poet János Arany lived here in the 1860s (at what is now Arany János utca 28, south of the main square), teaching grammar and literature at the **high school** (now called the Arany János Gimnazium; *Szabadság tér 8*) for nine years. In the grounds of the **Calvinist church** (*Szabadság tér 6*) is Alajos Stróbl's statue of him, slumped in a chair with his dog by his side.

To the north of the centre, the **Arany János Museum** (*Ceglédi út 19;* ❧ *53 350810; adult/concessions 350/150Ft; open Tue–Sun summer 10.00–18.00, winter 09.00–16.00*) – once a hussars' barracks – tells the story of Nagykőrös, and displays the detritus of its history from 5000BC up to the period of socialist construction. Of particular interest are the years following the failed War of Independence, when the market town was nevertheless able to fall back on its relative wealth and retain a degree of autonomy. In an extraordinary act of patronage, seven distinguished scholars from the Hungarian Academy of Sciences were invited to teach at the secondary high school. One of these was the patriotic Arany, who had lost his job because of his support for the rebellion; he went on to write many of his poems here – inspired by English classical ballads and Hungarian folk songs – and to attract a steady stream of cultural lions to his door (such as Mór Jókai and Mihály Tompa). Among the extensive holdings (accompanied by notes in English – oh, were all museums so helpful!) are some of his personal belongings, while outside is a satisfyingly tactile statue of the *Great Teachers* by Imre Varga.

The hungry can head for the Wild-West-themed **Pizzeria Saloon** (*Szechényi tér 2; pizzas 500–800Ft; open Mon–Thu 10.00–22.00, Fri–Sat 10.00–24.00, Sun 10.00–23.00*) or the peasant-style **Cifra Csárda** (*Nagykőrös út 21;* ❧ *53 351212; www.extra.hu/cifracsarda; mains 750–1,700Ft, avg 1,400Ft; open Mon–Sat 09.00–23.00, Sun 09.00–22.00*), a few hundred metres north of the museum.

The **railway station** is 1km from the centre, along Kossuth utca; there are regular services to Kecskemét, as well as trains to Cegléd (up to 12 daily), Szeged (nine), Budapest Nyugati (six), Szolnok and Debrecen (two). Buses depart for Kecskemét every 30 minutes from the **bus station** (*Derkovits utca*), across the road from Szabadság tér; they also go to Szolnok and Jászberény (six), Eger (three) and Miskolc (one). For Budapest, Szeged and Gyula you'll need to travel via Kecskemét.

## CEGLÉD

Thirty kilometres north of Kecskemét, Cegléd's marketplace was where Lajos Kossuth first urged the people of the Great Plain to cast off the Habsburg shackles. On September

24 1848, he declared 'I have come to you, good Hungarians, hope, bastion and pillar of my betrayed homeland'. Agitated speechifiers were clearly fond of the spot for in 1514 György Dózsa, leader of the peasant revolt (see page 17), also spoke here (his second-in-command, Lőrinc Mészáros, heralded from Cegléd). The town makes much of its Kossuth connection, but it has also recently directed attention to its thermal baths in the hope of building a reputation for health tourism.

## Getting there and around

The **bus station** is at the northern end of Kossuth Ferenc utca (follow it into the centre); it serves destinations including Szolnok and Gyöngyös (four daily), Eger and Lajosmizse (three), Baja and Kalocsa (two), and offers regular services to Kecskemét and Nagykőrös. The **railway station** is 100m away, with trains to Kecskemét (12), Debrecen and Szeged (seven), and Nyíregyháza (six). It also has regular (every 30 mins) connections to Budapest Nyugati and Szolnok.

## Information and other practicalities

**Listings magazine** *Szegedi Est*

**Tourinform** Kossuth tér 1; ❧ 53 500285; e cegled@tourinform.hu. In the town hall building. *Open Mon–Tue & Thu 08.00–16.00, Wed 08.00–18.00, Fri 08.00–14.00.*

**Ibusz** Kossuth tér 8; ❧ 53 314716; e i044@ibusz.hu. Private accommodation and currency exchange. *Open Mon–Fri 08.00–16.00.*

**Kossuth Cultural Centre** Kossuth tér 5/A; ❧ 53 311004; e cegledi.muv.kozpont@axelero.hu. The town's main arts centre, site of concerts and plays and a gallery of temporary exhibitions. *Open Mon–Fri 10.00–18.00, Sat–Sun 08.00–20.00; gallery Mon–Fri 09.00–16.00, Sat–Sun variable times.*

## Where to stay, eat and drink

**Arizona Pizzeria and Burger Bar** Kossuth tér 8; ❧ 53 321480. An understated 'Wild-West' theme inside, with shady outdoor seating overlooking the square. Good fast food. *Mains 640–1,380Ft, avg 900Ft; open Mon–Tue, Sun 09.00–24.00, Fri–Sat 08.00–01.00.*

**Castrum Thermal Camping** Fürdő utca 27; ❧ 53 505009; e info@castrum-group.hu; www.castrum-group.hu. Campsite in the grounds of the super-duper aqua park and thermal baths. *Open Apr 15–Oct 15.*

**Kossuth Hotel** (11 rooms) Rákóczi út 1; ❧ 53 310990. An estate agent would describe the rooms as 'compact', but they are clean and welcoming nonetheless. Some are not en suite. The restaurant (*mains 750–2,500Ft, avg 1,400Ft; open Mon–Sat 07.00–15.00*) is open for lunch only, and has a patchy choice of Hungarian food and token pasta dishes. *Sgl/dbl (without bathroom) 6,000/6,500Ft, dbl/triple (with bathroom) 8,200/11,000Ft.*

## What to see and do

**Kossuth tér** is dotted with flowerbeds and trees; at its very heart is the Neoclassical **Church of the Holy Cross**, completed in 1825 on the site of a Gothic predecessor demolished in 1821. The Calvary scene on the main altar was painted by Pest artist József Schöfft in 1830, while the Trinity Column outside was sculpted by György Kiss – and marks the place of Kossuth's ne'er-forgotten recruitment speech. At the square's northern end is the imposing late-19th-century **town hall**, also Neoclassical in style.

Kossuth's son Ferenc assisted János Horvay with getting the likeness of his father just right in the statue standing in **Szabadság tér**; so fine was it that it became the template for the version erected in New York in 1928. The Neo-Gothic **Lutheran church** (*Bercsenyi uyca 2*) of 1896 represents an allusion in brick to the greeting 'A mighty fortress is our God'. However, it is the **Calvinist Great Church** (*Szabadság tér*) across from it that really holds court, designed by József Hild, finished in 1857 and successfully fusing sturdiness with elegance. It is the biggest Calvinist church in central Europe, seating over 2000; concerts are held beneath its turquoise dome. In the garden behind is a sculpture of a figure trapped in a tree trunk; the *Freedom Tree* was erected in 1989 to commemorate the 1956 revolution, the first such monument in Hungary. The millennium belfry above it was added in 2000, its bells etched with significant dates in the country's history. Remarkably, the garden also holds the balcony once belonging to the Zöldfa (Green Tree) Inn in Bratislava, from where Kossuth declared the March Decrees (later ratified by Ferenc József) and introduced the country's first prime minister, Lajos Batthyány (see page 19).

North of Szabadság tér, the **Kossuth Múseum** (*Múzeum utca 5;* ↘ *53 310637;* e *kossuth.cegled@museum.hu; adult/concessions 350/150Ft; open Tue–Sun Nov 1–Feb 28 09.00–17.00, Mar 1–Oct 31 10.00–18.00*) displays works by 'peasant painter' Péter Benedek, a leading exponent of the Naive School. The main draws, though, are items relating to Kossuth – including his curved pipe, a locket containing his hair and his death mask. There is a reconstruction of his study in Turin, where he went into exile after the failure of the War of Independence, and a letter to the *Manchester Guardian* in 1860 accusing the newspaper of infringing his copyright by printing a lecture he gave while visiting England. A fascinating collection, it is a crying shame that there are no explanations in English.

Follow Rákóczi út away from Szabadság tér, and turn right for the **thermal baths** (*Fürdő út 27;* ↘ *53 505000; adult/concessions 1,000/500Ft; open Mon–Sun 09.00–19.00, Thu–Sat also 20.00–24.00*), the centrepiece of the town's drive towards health and leisure tourism. It's a large complex, featuring ten pools altogether – pools indoor and outdoor, pools medicinal and swimming, pools for children and pools set with splashing fountains – and a range of 'wellness' treatments. There's also a park with boating lake, sports fields and al-fresco theatre; the intention is to expand it further in the coming years and establish a resort-style village.

## LAJOSMIZSE

If you thought that one-street and one-horse towns were one and the same, Lajosmizse (to the northwest of Kecskemét) will change your mind. There are few in the way of permanent sights here beyond **Szent Lajos Church** (*Cégledi út*), built in 1896 and with a carillon above its entrance, and the **Hungarian Farm Museum** (*Magyar Mezőgazdasági Múzeum Tanyamúzeum;* ↘ *1 341 2011; adult/concessions 150/70Ft; open Mar 15–Oct 14 Tue–Sat 10.00–17.00, Sun 10.00–18.00*), an outdoor ethnographic collection in 19th-century thatched cottages beside the Öreg Tanyacsárda (see page 340). No, this is an area of farmsteads and the venue for galloping horse shows, monthly horse markets and horse-riding tours. For **further information** on equestrian tourism here and elsewhere in the county, contact the Tourinform in Kecskemét (see page 327).

### Getting there and around

The **railway station** is 1km west of the centre at the far end of Rákóczi utca (follow dirt track on to Rákóczi utca, continue to the end, and turn right to the centre); there are up to 13 trains a day to Budapest, as well regular trains to Ócsa and Dabas and up to 3 a day to Kecskemét. The main **bus stop** (*Cégledi út*) in town is by St Lajos Church; there are two buses an hour to Kecskemét, up to 19 daily to Budapest Népliget, three to Cegléd and two to Szeged. There is a cycle track between Lajosmizse and Felsőlajos.

### Where to stay, eat, drink (and horse around)

The places offering accommodation and victuals are also often the places offering riding and horse shows. Some can be tough to get to, scattered not only outside the town centre but at times set well back from the roads.

**Gerébi Kúria** Alsólajos 224; ➤ 76 356555; e gerebi@gerebi.hu; www.gerebi.hu. Set in extensive grounds surrounding a 19th-century mansion, the Gerébi Kúria can cater for those who want rustic without the rough. There is little the site can't provide for – it boasts a whirlpool bath, Finnish sauna, solarium, gym, swimming pool, wine cellar, folklore shop, restaurant (*mains 990–2,690Ft, avg 1,500Ft; open daily 07.00–22.00*) and sports courts. The riding school runs lessons, cross-country gallops, carriage rides and much more, and there are horse shows every couple of days in high season. Accommodation is available in the 26-room mansion and 65-room hotel, while there are also more basic bungalow blocks (38 rooms). Guests can be collected from the bus or train stations in Lajosmisze; the site sits 2km back from Cégledi út, 5km east of the town centre. *Bungalow sgl 8,900Ft, dbl 10,900Ft; main house sgl 11,900Ft, dbl 13,900Ft; hotel sgl 13,900–15,900Ft, dbl 15,900–17,900Ft, suite 17,900–19,900Ft; f/bd and h/bd options.*

**Kobza Tanya Panzió** (15 rooms) Közös 168; ➤ 76 555173; e kobza@mail.datanet.hu. A kilometre northwest of the centre (along Route 5), and opposite the Új Tanyacsárda (see below), this pretty guesthouse has a swimming pool and wine cellar. The owners organise horse-riding for all levels – from lessons for beginners through 5-day cross-country treks to equestrian paintballing. Turn off the M5 between the 64km and 65km markers. *Sgl 5,000Ft, dbl 7,500Ft; f/bd and h/bd options.*

**Öreg Tanyacsárda** Bene 65 (Route 5); ➤ 76 356166; e tanyacsarda@tanyacsarda.hu; www.tanyacsarda.hu. The 'Old Inn' is a thatched peasant-style restaurant with a muscular statue by Imre Varga sewing seed at the front. Its menu, served by costumed staff, features classic Hungarian dishes. However, together with the Új Tanyacsárda (same company), it is as much a programme organiser as a restaurant. There are myriad folk events – the advertised line-up includes a horse show after dark, a camp fire with 'witches' dance', goulash parties, peasant wedding feast, *puszta* Olympics, ox roasts and assorted excursions. If you choose the trip aboard a nostalgia train from Budapest to Felsőlajos (and then on to the inn), the ladies in the party should be prepared to be 'abducted' from the train by a gang of horsemen. All good fun. Each of the taverns can accommodate up to 1,000 guests; if you're interested in participating in a programme, you'll need to gather a group of 30 or more and book at least a week ahead (*contact the sales manager;* ➤ *76 356166/356010; mob: 06 30 958 9460; email as above*). Horse shows start at 2,500Ft/pp and themed events go as high as 350,000Ft/group; riding lessons are 3,000Ft/hr. Located 3km southeast of the centre (on Route 5 in the direction of Szeged). *Mains 780–2,400Ft, avg 1,600Ft; open 11.00–22.00 daily.*

**Ricsováry Major** (30 rooms) Mizse hrsz 0505, off Cegléd út; ➤ 76 454112; Budapest office ➤ 1 349 8551; email: info@majortours.hu; www.majortours.hu. Set fully 3km back from the main road, this is a treat of a retreat, a family-run estate as secluded, idyllic and downright peaceful as you could wish. There are few distractions in the rustic chalets – no TV, telephone or minibar; rather you must relax in the gazebo outside the main house, lounge by the swimming pool or wine taste in the cellar. An unfancy 3-course meal is served each evening (*2,000Ft/pp; daily 19.00–22.00*), and the owner can arrange horse-show programmes for guests (to which you are taken by carriage – horse-drawn, naturally). The estate is at the top of a dirt track leading from Cegléd út, 10km east of Lajosmizse centre (turn off the M5 near the 66km marker, in the direction of Nagykőrös-Cegléd); there is a local bus stop at the entrance to the track, and the owner can pick you up from there. *Apt 16,000Ft, dbl 9,600Ft; open Apr 1–Oct 31.*

**Új Tanyacsárda** See Öreg Tanyacsárda above. The counterpart of the 'Old Inn', the 'New Inn' has more of the same, and is targeted heavily at the tourist market. The horse shows offered in the programmes are held here – during high season there are performances daily at 12.30 and in the evening too if demand dictates. (See Öreg Tanyacsárda for booking details.) There is also a campsite and stalls for those bringing horses. The inn is 5km the other side of town from its sister, set back 1km from Route 5 (in the direction of Budapest). *Menu prices as above; open 08.00–22.00 daily.*

Other places with a horsey bent include **Dechy Lovaspanzió** (*Mizse 339;* ➤ *76 715248*) and **Bujdosó Tanya** (*Alsólajos 92;* ➤ *76 356551*).

## HORSE PLAY

There is an inextricable link between Hungary and horses. The Magyar warrior horsemen brought with them equestrian skills which, preserved for more than 1,000 years, can be seen today on the *puszta*. In days gone by, *csikós* (herdsmen) of the Great Plain – a wild breed that harboured an innate antipathy to authority, particularly when agricultural developments hit their herding rights – would collude with and protect wandering highwaymen. They learnt to stand on bare-back galloping horses, deterring bounty-hunting pursuers with whips (*karikásostor*) they cracked like pistols. They taught their horses to lie down on command, disappearing among the grasses in an instant. An obedient steed would sit on its haunches so its weary master could rest safe against its stomach, protected from the elements in his '*puszta* armchair'. Come evening, herdsmen vied for the attention of the village beauty, chasing each other in an attempt to capture the prized scarf she gave to her favourite – the winner's reward the privilege of dancing with her for the rest of the night.

By the 19th century this distant relative of the cowboy was no more, but his romantic memory burned on. In shows to rival the American Wild West, modern-day herdsmen parade their skills for wide-eyed tourists. Their repertoire includes all the age-old tricks – scarves are stolen, horses sit and lie down, whip-cracking riders stand atop their speeding steeds. Art imitates life for the body of the display – at least a romanticised perception of it – but the climax turns this usual truth upon its head. Greatly impressed by Hungarian horsemanship, Viennese artist Adam Koch used a healthy dollop of artistic licence in painting an imagined scene where a single rider stood atop two horses' rumps and used reins to guide a further three horses ahead of them. Macho Magyars were determined to bring the canvas to life and in 1953 Béla Lénárt succeeded in this feat of horse-surfing; the 'Koch (or Puszta) Five' was born, and has become a staple of horse shows ever since. Bravado always dictated that others would strive to do better still – the current world record is for one man on 12 horses!

# KISKŐRÖS

There's nature all about Kiskőrös, including the oak, ash and elm trees of Szűcsi Forest (a nature reserve to the north), and acacia and pine woods filling the westward space up to the Danube Valley Canal (*Duna-völgyi-főcsatorna*). Such landscape is crowded with croaking frogs, flitting butterflies and singing songbirds; there are 300 species of plant. The name of the town derives from the indigenous ash tree, and it features in the coat of arms. However, pilgrims to Kiskőrös do so in the name of art rather than nature. After the Turkish occupation, the area was settled by Lutheran Slovaks, and in the 19th century the son of István Petrovics and Mária Hrúz was born. The inhabitants supported the 1848 uprising and War of Independence but that son went further – he impacted upon national and literary consciousness, instilled revolutionary fervour and became the very voice of the struggle. He was Sándor Petőfi. Such is the reflected glory cast upon Kiskőrös by the poet that in 1973, on the 150th anniverary of his death, it was declared a town – a status it had lost two centuries before.

## Getting there and around

The **train station** is 1km west of the town centre – turn right from the station and left into Kossuth Lajos út. There are trains to Kiskunhalas (ten daily), Budapest Keleti (nine), Kalocsa (four) and Baja (one). The **bus stop** is next to the town hall; there are

## THE PEOPLE'S POET

To this day, the nation's favourite versifier – the man who has made the deepest dent on the national and literary consciousness – is the 19th-century Sándor Petőfi (1823–49). Branded vulgar by some, he wrote copiously and empathetically in the vivid vernacular of 'the common man', travelling the countryside on foot and rooting his language and imagery in that of the Great Plain. He wrote earthy cycles of love poetry, but he is best remembered for his fervent, patriotic and radical narratives. Though personally fractious, socially awkward and discontented, his brilliant writings were inspirational. As a newlywed, he provided the voice and impulse for the revolution that broke out on March 15 1848. In his 'National Song' ('Nemzeti Dal') – recited from the steps of the National Museum – he pleaded 'Rise, Hungarians!' ('Talpra, magyar!'). And they did.

However, he was more than a man of words and his greatest fear was to fade away rather than fighting for the sacred ideal of liberty. In 1846 'One Thought Worries Me' he wrote:

One thought worries me:
To die in bed, amongst the pillows,
To slowly wither away like a flower.

Three years later (aged just 26) he was dead. Dispute surrounds his final flourish on a field in Transylvania during one of the last battles of the War of Independence. Some reports speak of him wearing a conspicuous white shirt (having scorned to wear military dress) and falling to a Russian lance. Others claim he was thrown alive into a mass burial pit and crushed by corpses. His body was never found, and there was a spate of Elvis-like sightings in the following years. Whatever the truth, his cult status was sealed as the passionate, revolutionary romantic of his age – an eloquent rebel with a cause.

regular services to Kiskunhalas and Kecskemét, as well as buses to Szeged (14), Baja (eight), Kalocsa (six) and one daily to Budapest Népliget. Romantics can board a narrow-gauge train running between here and Kecskemét. The train leaves three times a day (*04.07, 11.24 & 17.48*) from Kiskőrös KK station, arriving 2½ hours later at Kecskemét KK.

## Information

**Petőfi Sándor Cultural House** Petőfi tér 4/A; \ 45 312315. Next to the Petőfi Museum, the cultural house is the only place to head for information on what's on. *Open Mon–Fri 08.00–20.00, Sat–Sun 16.00–19.00 (variations if a programme is on).*

## Where to stay and eat

**Campsite** Dózsa György út 43. Next to the thermal baths. *Tent/caravan 300/800Ft, plus adult/concessions 900/500Ft/pp; open May 1–Sep 30.*

**Hotel Imperial** (53 rooms) Erdőtelki út 21; \ 78 514400; www.hotelimperial.hu. The newest on the block is an ugly looking lump of a hotel opened in 2002 to the west of the centre; however, the Imperial compensates with its own thermal baths (free for guests), swimming pool, fitness room, sauna and massage options. The rooms are sterile in every sense – spotlessly clean but characterless. The restaurant (*mains 660–2,000Ft, avg 1,300Ft; open 08.00–24.00 daily*) specialises in goose liver and other Hungarian delicacies. *Sgl 7,000Ft, dbl 8,500Ft, triple 11,000Ft, apt 12,000Ft (excl tax); b/fast 800Ft.*

**Kurta Kocsma Restaurant** Csokonai utca 51; ↘ 78 311821. A little southwest of the centre (just off József Attila út), it's difficult to miss the Kurta Kocsma, with the bright mural of horses and carriage on its façade. This is the most popular restaurant in town. There's nothing fancy about the menu, and the portions are substantial. Live entertainment is often staged here. *Mains 650–2,250Ft, avg 1,400Ft; open 08.00–22.00 daily.*

**Szarvas Fogadó** (20 rooms) Petőfi tér 17; ↘ 78 511500; e szarvash@hu.inter.net. Built in 1914, Szarvas remains the best place to stay, with elegant looks and a prime spot on the main square. There is a fitness room and sauna, and the stylish, wood-panelled restaurant (*mains 700–2,700Ft, avg 1,500Ft; open 07.00–23.00 daily*) serves international cuisine. *Sgl 9,400Ft, dbl 9,800Ft, apt 11,800Ft.*

**Vinum Hotel** (21 rooms) Petőfi Sándor utca 106; ↘ 78 511050; e info@vinumhotel.hu; www.vinumhotel.hu. Looking like a Dallas ranch, the sprawling Vinum settles around a grassed courtyard. Rooms vary, but are generally pleasant, and feel as though given a woman's finishing touch. The owner produces his own wine, which you can sample in the cellar, and there is a restaurant (for groups only). *Sgl 7,600Ft, dbl 10,600Ft, triple 12,100Ft, apt (for 4) 16,400Ft (excl tax).*

## What to see and do

The predictably named main square eggs the pudding further with a statue of the town's cultural behemoth, erected in 1927 (the country's first). The peach-coloured **town hall** (*Petőfi tér 1*) bears Kiskőrös's crest (showing hunting, bee-keeping, agriculture and forest).

The **Petőfi Memorial House and Literary Museum** (*Szülőház Emlékmúzeum; Petőfi tér 5;* ↘ *78 312566; www.petofimuzeum.hu; adult/concessions 200/100Ft; open Tue–Sun 09.00–17.00*) is first stop for most visitors. On January 1 1823 Petőfi gasped his first breaths within the mud-walled 18th-century house. This was restored to its original state – with family furniture and documents collected from various later residences, and the only existing picture of the whole Petrovics family (the poet later changed his name to one more 'Hungarian') – and opened to the public by Mór Jókai in 1880.

Outside are busts of 11 of the translators who've tackled the closed book of Hungarian language and opened up Petőfi's work to those in other countries; inside the museum proper (beyond the statue park) is a map showing just how far the Petőfi cult has reached. There are also archaeological, ethnographical and wildlife displays, and documents that relate to the Wattay family – who were gifted the region at the end of the 17th century as reward for their resistance to the Turks, and who brought 700 Slovak peasants from northern Hungary to re-establish the settlement. A gallery upstairs shows art connected with Petőfi.

Your ticket to the museum also allows admission to the **Slovakian Folk House** (*Szlovák Tájház; Szent István utca 23;* ↘ *78 312566; open Tue–Sun 09.00–12.00, 13.00–16.00*), which was the initiative of pupils at the local school. The kids spent a decade collecting dishes and furniture in order to resurrect a typical dwelling of the 18th-century Slovak settlers. Follow Kossuth Lajos utca northeast a short distance and turn left on to Szent István utca. If you enjoy watching tarmac dry, push on to the **Public Road Construction Collection** (*Útügyi Kiallítás; Dózsa György út 38;* ↘ *78 311935; www.museum.kozut.hu; open Mar 1–Nov 30 09.00–16.00 daily*) near the campsite and baths. The museum details the history of Hungarian road laying and bridge building, and showcases maintenance tools and heavy machinery like steamrollers. Pun aside, you really can learn about the invention of the tar 'macadam' by Scottish engineer John McAdam, which replaced cobbles as the road surface of choice at the start of the 19th century.

### Other activities

The **thermal baths** (*Dózsa György 43; adult/concessions 300/260Ft; open daily Jun 1–Aug 31 09.00–19.00, rest of yr 09.00–17.00*), on the western side of town, can be used freely by those staying at the Imperial Hotel or the campsite.

Around 4km southwest of Kiskőrös (near Road 54, on its way to Kecel), the **Henry Lovasfarm** (*Soltvadkert, Felsőcsábor 39;* ➘ *78 311898;* e *henrylovasfarm@hotelimperial.hu*) offers horse-riding lessons and tours, and has a panzió. You can also rent bicycles here, or take a carriage ride.

## KALOCSA

Wake up and smell the paprika – Kalocsa is liberally peppered with the stuff! There are paprika factories and museums, a Paprika Street, pottery decorated with paprika, and shops filled with paprika souvenirs and low-hanging strings of paprika. You might even find paprika imagery incorporated into embroidery, the other string to Kalocsa's bow. In autumn, the fields flame red with the fruit of the pepper plant that is dried and ground into 'red gold'. The town has been the centre of such spice production since the start of the 20th century.

Kalocsa used to stand right on the Danube, but after a manipulation of the river course it came to lie 6km away. It was one of the two original archbishoprics established by King István in the 11th century as he Christianised the country, and as such has always been an ecclesiastical big hitter (second only to Esztergom). Its first prelate was Asztrik, who was sent by Pope Sylvester II as a sign of papal support for the establishment of the Hungarian Church and is said to have presented István with the Holy Crown. Some believe Asztrik is buried in the cathedral crypt, and others trace the word *érsek* (archbishop) to his name. This was a burgeoning medieval settlement, but the population seeped away during Turkish rule and then fire swept through and brought the whole place to earth, including the basilica. The Baroque town and ecclesiastical buildings of today are the 18th-century versions that were raised from those ashes. It's an intimate place where neighbours know each other; the majority of the action goes on around Szent István Király út, which holds the shops, bars and cafés.

---

### A BIT OF HUNGARIAN HOT STUFF

Although originally a native American plant – and probably introduced to the Balkans by the Turks, and to Hungary by Bulgarian refugees fleeing the Turks – the milder Hungarian pepper, ripened to vibrant red and dried into the paprika (*Capsicum annuum*) spice, has become associated worldwide with Hungarian cuisine. It is the mainstay of renowned national dishes like *gulyás* and *paprikás*, and is invariably the 'natural colour' mentioned in ingredient lists of red-coloured foods.

The rich source of vitamin C in fresh peppers are largely destroyed by the high temperatures used in the paprika drying process, though if it's betacarotene you're after, to convert into vitamin A then this spice has few rivals. (Incidentally, the story goes that the wife of the scientist Albert Szent-Györgyi used to swear by the healthy properties of paprika and included it without fail in his lunch. Szent-Györgyi was himself no great fan of the pepper, and conducted tests in his lab trying to disprove his wife's claims. It was while doing so that he discovered vitamin C – and unwittingly proved the old adage that behind every successful man is a paprika-pushing woman.) Szeged and Kalocsa are the centres of paprika production. Over 40 types are grown in the area around Kalocsa (the variety grown each year is determined by the predicted weather conditions) and the crop is graded into six classes, from the pungent and hot *erős* to the exquisitely delicate *különleges*. Like fine wine, the quality of the crop is critically affected by the amount of sunshine in the weeks immediately preceding harvest.

## Getting there and around

At the southernmost end of Szent István Király út is the town's **bus station**, from where buses travel frequently to Baja. There are also services to Kiskunhalas, Kecskemét and Szeged (seven), Kiskőrös (five) and Székesfehérvár. The **railway station** (*Mártírok tere*), decorated with folk motifs, is 2km northeast of the station and only serves Kiskőrös, and then only four times daily; you can get connections to Budapest from Kiskőrös. Turn right from the station on to Kossuth Lajos utca and follow the road straight into Szentháromság tér.

## Information and other practicalities

**Cultural and Youth Centre** Szent István Király út 2–4; ☎ 78 462200. The Baroque building was completed in 1787, serving as a religious training college. Today it hosts concerts and plays, as well as having exercise and dance classes. Call in here for details of productions at the Archbishop's Palace across the way. *Open Mon–Sat 08.00–20.00, Sun 09.00–12.00, 15.00–20.00.*

**Ibusz** Szent István Király út 37; ☎ 78 462012. In the same building as the Hotel Piros Arany; the office can change currency (but not travellers' cheques), provide information on tours and book private accommodation. *Open Mon–Fri 08.00–16.00.*

**Korona Tours RT** Szent István Király út 68; ☎ 78 461819; e lincom@freemail.hu; www.koronatours.hu. Opposite the Paprika Museum. You can choose from an array of local tours – including trips to Bakodpuszta (see page 347), and paprika harvesting in late Sep/early Oct – or arrange local private accommodation. *Open Mon–Fri 08.00–16.00.*

## Where to stay, eat and drink

**Barokk Coffee House** Kossuth Lajos utca 46. Bubbly little joint serving pizzas, cakes, ice cream and ice-cold beer. The outdoor seats are shaded by trees and face the cathedral. There are pool tables inside. *Pizzas 540–700Ft; open Mon–Thu 08.00–22.00, Fri–Sat 08.00–24.00, Sun 09.00–22.00.*

**Beta Hotel Kalocsa** (31 rooms) Szentháromság tér 4; ☎ 78 561200; email: info@hotelkalocsa.hu; www.hotelkalocsa.hu. Kalocsa's top place to lay a hat is this 200-year-old Baroque former mansion directly opposite the cathedral in the main square. Rooms are spacious and plush; on some mornings a free alarm call comes at 06.30, care of the cathedral bells. The restaurant (*mains 850–2,400Ft, avg 1,400Ft*) is very good, with fish, veal and – unusually for Hungary – a vegetarian selection. The garden dining area is pleasantly quiet; the only fault is that there was no menu in English when we visited. *Sgl €40, dbl €60, triple €72 (excl Tourist Tax).*

**Casablanca** Szent István Király út 36. Sells burgers, sandwiches, tortillas and ice cream, and has a pub attached that opens into the wee weekend hours. *Open Mon–Thu 08.00–22.00, Fri–Sat 08.00–04.00, Sun 09.00–22.00.*

**Club 502 S&M Panzió** (4 rooms) Szent István Király 64; ☎ 78 562804. Cheaper than the Hotel

Kalocsa and considerably less shabby than the Piros Arany, this guesthouse has a few big and clean rooms. It also has a large bar with a wide drinks menu, and rustles up a decent pizza (*pizzas 630–910Ft; open daily 12.00–24.00*). *Rooms 3,500Ft/pp.*

**Hotel Piros Arany** (20 rooms) Szent István Király út 37; \ 78 462220. Not much more than a hostel; some rooms are en suite, others have shared facilities. *Dbl (with bathroom and TV) 7,200Ft, dbl (no frills) 5,400Ft.*

There is a small outdoor covered **market** on Búzapiac tér, at the western end of Városház utca.

## What to see and do

The pretty Szentháromság tér, with its cobbles and lanterns, stands at the northeastern end of town, dominated by the cathedral in its face and the Archbishop's Palace, set back a little and coated in a loud mustard yellow. **Kalocsa Cathedral** in its current guise is the fourth to have stood here; the first was built in the 11th century, and subsequent versions were burned down during Mongol invasion and Ottoman occupation. Once the Turks had left, András Mayerhoffer designed this magnificent Baroque edifice (1735–54), its ceiling bearing white carved figures like cameo brooches. The intricate detail – from subtle gilding through beautifully fashioned choir stalls to the altar painting by Austrian artist Leopold Kupelvieser – is stunning. The organ first piped to the tune of Ferenc Liszt himself.

East of the cathedral, the **Archiepiscopal Treasury** (*Főszékesegyházi kincstár; Hunyadi utca 2;* \ *78 461860; adult/concessions 500/250Ft; open May–Oct Tue–Sun 09.00–17.00*) has vestments and treasures (chalices, reliquaries, pontifical rings set with topaz stones) dating mainly from the 18th and 19th centuries; the star of the show is the Szent István herm, a bust of gold and silver crafted for the millennial celebrations of 1896. In the same building (to the left at the top of the stairs) is an exhibition of work by artist Péter Prokop from the 1970s.

The Baroque **Archbishop's Palace** (*Érseki palota; Szentháromság tér 1;* \ *78 362166; adult/concessions 500/250Ft; open Apr 1–Nov 30 Tue–Sun 09.00–12.00, 14.00–17.00*) was built in the 1760s; it has a magnificent hall and chapel adorned with frescoes by F A Maulbertsch, and a library with illuminated manuscripts (notably a 15th-century psalm book), medieval codices (the oldest dating to 1040), a letter by the great Jesuit Péter Pázmány and a bible bearing Martin Luther's scrawl.

Szent István Király út runs arrow-straight southeast from the main square. Your first port of call should be the **Paprika Museum** (*Szent István király út 6;* \ *78 461819; adult/concessions 500/300Ft; open Mar–Nov 10.00–17.00 daily*), replete with the tools for mashing, cutting and drying the peppers, and puppets showing the process at work. A document in the archiepiscopal archives records the growing of paprika in Kalocsa from 1729 – the hot stuff came to the fore when the Habsburgs prohibited the import of foreign spices, stimulating the popularity of domestic versions. Originally operated by horse power, the grinding mills ran on fuel from the middle of the 19th century. Stock up at the small souvenir shop.

Further along, the **Viski Károly Museum** (*Szent István Király út 25;* \ *78 462351; adult/concessions 250/120Ft; open Tue–Sun 09.00–17.00*) has ten collections featuring minerals, coins and an ethnographic exhibition of regional textiles and folk art dating from the 19th century. The vivid furniture bears testimony to the colour cravings indulged by the town's 'painting women', skilled groups of female artisans who decorated the main rooms of peasant houses.

On crossing Városház utca, you'll enter a pedestrianised section lined with shady trees and benches; along the centre is an **open-air pantheon** to some Kalocsan colossi of a millennium, ranged chronologically and kicking off with the statue of Asztrik at the southern end. Keep walking until you reach the fascinating **Schöffer Museum** (*Szent István Király út 76;* \ *78 462253; adult/concessions 200/100Ft; open Tue–Sun 10.00–12.00, 14.00–17.00*), devoted to the Parisian artist Nikolas Schöffer, who was born in this house in 1912. In exploring themes of space, time and light, his pieces incorporate computer automation, mirrors, clockwork mechanisms and cinematography to illusory and energetic effect. Gaze into his mirrored prism and believe you're glimpsing eternity. The French-speaking director is imbued with wonder, and it's easy to see why. Look out for one of Schöffer's bigger works at the bus station.

The **Kalocsa Paprika House** (*Kossuth Lajos utca 15;* \ *78 465049; open May 1–Oct 31 daily 10.00–16.00, Nov 1–Apr 30 by prior arrangement*) claims to hold Europe's biggest paprika museum, although it's really for dining tour groups and has little to get excited about – some processing tools and photos of the 50 members of the Order of the Knights of Kalocsa Paprika in their regal robes (we kid you not!). The museum is run by the Kalocsa Spice Paprika Company, established in 2002 and enjoying 3% of the world market. From Szentháromság tér, head northeast along Kossuth Lajos utca for around ½km.

A short distance further along Kossuth Lajos utca, turn right to the **House of Folk Arts** (*Népművészeti tájház; Tompa Mihály utca 5–7;* \ *78 461560; adult/concessions 500/300Ft; open Apr 1–Oct 31 10.00–17.00 daily, Nov 1–Mar 31 by prior arrangement*), a reed-thatched peasant dwelling with the signature painted walls and items of folk art. It is surprising to learn that Kalocsa's embroidery was traditionally rather plain; the explosion of floral motifs (an extension of those added to the walls) came in the 20th century as coloured cotton became more prevalent and folk dancers were used as the canvases for jazzier designs. For all its folkloric authenticity, the house is something of a tourist trap. The same can be said of **Aunt Juca's Tavern** (*Juca Néni Csárdája; Meszesi út*), an old ferry inn converted into a peasant-style barn where costumed women showcase (and sell!) their handicrafts. Programmes here featuring food, gypsy music and *pálinka* can be arranged through Korona Tours (see page 345).

### Bakodpuszta

Ten kilometres from town – on the way towards Dunapataj (turn left on to Route 51 from Kossuth Lajos utca) – Bakodpuszta has horses and traditional Hungarian livestock on 400ha of land. It hosts five or six horse shows a week and its inn has a huge dining area. You can book through Korona Tours (see page 345).

## HAJÓS AND HAJÓS-PINCÉK

Southeast of Kalocsa (just above Route 54), the pretty village of **Hajós** is notable for an airy Baroque Roman Catholic church on Köztársaság tér, its stained-glass windows casting shafts of piercing coloured light. Inside is a Gothic statue of Madonna brought by German (Swabian) Catholics settlers; outside is a grassed avenue with intricately painted stations of the cross made from Zsolnay china. Keep an eye out too for the pleasing pharmacy building in a corner of the square, with its angular rooftop.

Once you've wandered the square, head 1km or so further for **Hajós-Pincék**, whose sole reason to be is wine. Tidy rows of cellars – over 1,000 in total – line the road like hotel pieces on a Monopoly board. Tastings are on offer at some, although opening hours are hit-and-miss affairs. A safe bet, however, is the family-run Judit Panzió, whose charming cellar is divided between several chambers and which can offer food and accommodation once you've had your boozy fill. The village is at its most lively in May, during the celebration of St Orbán (the guardian saint of vintners).

At the top end of Hajósi utca (just before Route 54), **Judit Panzió** (*Borbíró sor 1–3;* \ *78 404832; 10 rooms; dbl 6,000Ft*) is friendly, clean and ideal for an evening of wine tasting. The restaurant (*mains 900–2,400Ft, avg 2,000Ft; open daily 07.00–22.00*) serves traditional

Hungarian cuisine. You can also pick up a walking trail from outside. Alternatively, the **Kellermotel Hajós** (*Hajós Kút tér 1;* ✎ *78 504010;* e *bastiaan.weij@pandora.be; www.kellermotel.com; 21 rooms; dbl €47–55*) stands on the road between Hajos and Hajós-Pincék. If ever pride went into a hotel then here it is; the Dutch owners have put whirlpools in some of the rooms, and there's a sauna and well-equipped fitness room. They can arrange wine tastings in their cellar, and also keep seven horses for tailor-made riding tours. Superlatives were made for surprising gems like this.

Buses running between Kalocsa and Baja stop at Hajós (with some going on to Hajós-Pincék), and there are services from Hájos-Pincék to Kiskőrös (about ten daily) and Kecskemét (15).

## BAJA

If there's something fishy going on and you sense you're in the soup, the chances are you're in Baja, a town lodged between the Danube and one of its branches (the Sugovica), and bisected horizontally by Route 55 and vertically by Route 51. On the second Saturday every July, 2,000 cauldrons bubble over open fires in Szentháromság tér; the big event of the Baja Folk Festival has earned the town a place in the Guinness Book of Records, under the category of fish soup (greatest quantity of, cooked at one time). Carp is the soup's main ingredient, although catfish, pike and other fish may play their parts. Thousands of people gather to get thoroughly piscivorous. The citizens of Baja are fond of fish during the rest of the year too – indeed, it is said that they consume an average of 66kg a year, more than anywhere else in Europe.

In medieval times, this was a commercial centre, and under the Turks a town fortified by a stockade castle. A massive fire in 1840 cleared many of its buildings and in doing so ensured that its architectural landscape changed from the Baroque to the Neoclassical. Today Baja prides itself on being a cosmopolitan community – with German, Serbian and Croatian influences stemming from 18th-century immigrant settlers – and is a popular resort, tourists attracted by several little river islands, woodland and a beach or two. Its bridge is also key, representing one of only two main river-crossing points on the Danube stretch between Budapest and the southern country border.

### Getting there and away

From the **bus station** (*Állomás tér*) it's about a 15-minute walk to the centre (turn right and along Szegedi út, which leads into Arany János utca), or you can catch a local bus from the stop at the end of Állomás tér. Baja is well served by bus and there are frequent connections with Mohács, Szeged, Kalocsa and Pécs, as well as to Szekszárd (11), Budapest Népliget (ten), Kecskemét (eight) and Hevíz (two). It's a ten-minute walk southwest from the **railway station** (*Vonat kert*) to the centre. Only a handful of towns are accessible by train, including Kiskunhalas (eight daily), Kiskunfélegyháza, Kiskőrös and Szekszárd (one); there are up to three services a day to Budapest.

### Information and other practicalities

**Bank** Szentháromság tér 10

**Info Tourist Travel Agency** Halász-part 4/C; ✎ 79 427533. Can arrange private accommodation and tours by boat, canoe or hiking boot. *Open Mon–Fri 09.00–16.30, Sat 09.00–12.00.*

**Internet Café** Tóth Kálmán tér 7. Internet access in this café near Vörösmarty tér costs 10Ft/min, 500Ft/hr. *Open Mon–Fri 09.00–13.00, 17.00–21.00, Sat 09.00–13.00.*

**Listings magazine** *Bajai Est*

**Tourinform** Szentháromság tér 5; ✎ 79 420793; e baja@tourinform.hu. Can provide details of recommended cycling routes along the Danube, as well as other information. Near the Hotel Duna. *Open Mon–Fri 09.00–17.00 (w/end too May–Jul).*

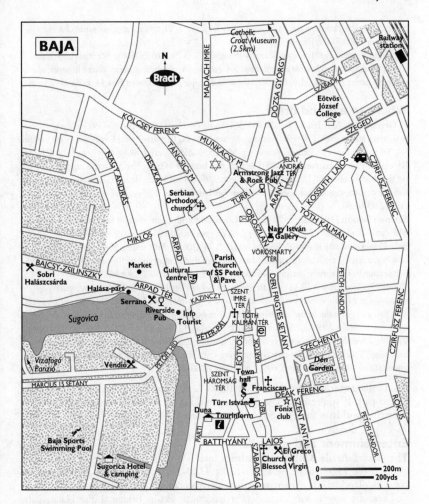

## Where to stay

**Az Eötvös József College** Szegedi út 2; ↳ 79 321655. The office here organises rooms in 3 hostels at other locations in the city (at Széchenyi utca 18/B, Bajcsy-Zsilinszky utca 14–19 and Deszkás utca 2). *Rooms from 1,500Ft/pp.*

**Country House Panzió** Petőfi-sziget, Március 15 sétány 20; ↳ 79 326585. Family-run guesthouse on Petőfi-sziget whose rooms could do with a little updating but are nevertheless clean and tidy. *Sgl 6,500Ft, dbl 8,500Ft, triple 11,000Ft, room for 4 14,000Ft.*

**Hotel Duna** (50 rooms) Szentháromság tér 6; ↳ 79 323224; e hotel-duna@baja.hu; www.hotels.hu/hotel-duna. Staring greenly from the southern side of the main square, the Hotel Duna is far from luxurious but is reasonably priced and centrally located. *Sgl 7,900Ft, dbl 8,9000Ft (excl taxes and b/fast).*

**Sugovica Hotel & Camping** Petőfi-sziget; ↳ 79 321755; e sugovica@enternet.hu; www.hotelsugovica.hu. A little further down the same road as the sports centre, this is a large 32-room hotel and campsite set in 5ha of lush surroundings (and inc outdoor swimming pool, children's playground and small bowling alley). To our mind, the hotel rooms don't quite deserve the steep cost, and one of the 19 bungalows (all with kitchenettes and most with showers) might be a better-value choice. *Sgl 8,700Ft, dbl 15,400Ft, apt (for 2) 21,400Ft; bungalows from 6,500Ft, caravan/tent 1,400/590Ft, plus 440Ft/pp.*

**Vizafogó Panzió** Petőfi-sziget, Március 15 sétány 27; ℡ 79 326585. At the northern end of the island, Vizafogó has dbls with decent-sized bathrooms; like a couple of other places in town, one senses its prices are inflated. *Sgl 6,500Ft, dbl 8,500Ft, triple 11,000Ft, room for 4 14,000Ft.*

## Where to eat and drink
**El Greco** Babits Mihály utca 1; ℡ 20 4333301. Some Greek and some not-so-Greek dishes (spaghettis and steaks). The menu is extensive and the food fair; there's live Greek music on Fri and Sat. To the southeast of Szentháromság tér. *Mains 550–2,000Ft, avg 1,300Ft; open daily 11.00–23.00.*

**Riverside Pub** Halászpart; ℡ 79 420348. One of a number of bars offering snacks at Halász-part (in the shadow of Petőfi Bridge), the unimaginatively named Riverside has Guinness and Kilkenny on the drinks menu and toasted sandwiches for bites. The pool table is popular. *Open daily 12.00–02.00.*

**Serrano Saloon** Halászpart; ℡ 79 421909. Chow on tortillas, burritos and fajitas in a saloon hung with cattle skulls. *Mains 560–2,200Ft, avg 1,100Ft; open daily 10.00–24.00.*

**Sobri Halászcsárda** Bajcsy-Zsilinszky utca 8; ℡ 79 420654. With seating at informal wooden benches, a relaxed and cheerful atmosphere, and fish that's cheap and well-prepared, this café-style fish restaurant takes some beating (or battering?!). *Mains 420–1,500Ft, avg 900Ft.*

**Véndió** Petőfi-sziget; ℡ 79 424544. Rising to the Sobri's challenge, Véndió is a very smart restaurant in a lovely setting on Petőfi-sziget, and serves quality tucker. The dishes are Hungarian, with fish and game the house specialities. It's more expensive than other restaurants in town, but it's worth it. *Mains 1,190–2,790Ft, avg 1,900Ft; open daily 11.00–24.00.*

**Vizafogó** See above. Another riverside offering with a healthy stock of fish on the menu, and a tasty soup. Take a table on the terrace, but bring some mozzie spray or you'll be the one getting eaten. *Mains 1,100–2,600Ft, avg 1,600Ft; open daily 12.00–23.00.*

The bustling **market** (*open Wed and Sat 08.00–12.00*) is on Szenes utca, just north of the Halász-part. If you're brave enough to try making your own fish soup, you can buy yourself a **cauldron** from the Swobodas (*Arató utca 11;* ℡ *79 422448;* ℡ *06 30 928 5215*).

## Entertainment and nightlife
The **József Attila Cultural Centre** (*Árpád tér 1;* ℡ *79 324229; open Mon–Thu 09.00–12.00, 13.00–16.00, Fri 09.00–12.00, 13.00–15.00*) can provide information on concerts, plays and other entertainment events; you can also purchase theatre tickets here.

There are several bars on the river bank near Petőfi Bridge at the Halász-part. Alternatively, the **Armstrong Jazz and Rock Pub** (*Türr István utca 1;* ℡ *79 428015; open Mon–Thu 13.00–24.00, Fri 13.00–03.00, Sat 18.00–03.00*) is a dark cellar bar with live bands on Sat night (usually from 23.30). Opposite the southern side of the Franciscan church, the low-lit **Főnix Club** (*Deák Ferenc utca 5;* ℡ *79 428117; open Mon–Thu 17.00–24.00, Fri 17.00–05.00, Sat 17.00–24.00*) has drop-down video screens airing music videos. Hip hop and R'n'B predominate and draw the young.

## What to see and do
The cobbled Szentháromság tér is at the town's centre, surrounded on three sides with Renaissance, Eclectic and Neoclassical buildings, and spoilt by being overstuffed with parked cars. The square is much enhanced when cleared of the vehicles, but that generally only happens when it's being used as the backdrop for a period film. The open fourth side is framed by the Sugovica branch of the Danube and Petőfi-sziget over the water. The **Trinity Column** is Baroque in design and foisted in 1881; on it are the four evangelists with Mary above them, while the seated figures hugging the cross at the top represent the Holy Trinity. The **town hall** (*Szentháromság tér 1*), once home to the

Grassalkovich family, was originally Baroque but received a Neo-Renaissance-style overhaul in 1896 as part of the millennial celebrations.

Just to the square's east, the **Türr István Museum** (*Deák Ferenc utca 1;* ↘ *79 324173; entrance adult 300Ft, explanatory talk 800Ft; open Mar 15–Dec 15 Wed–Sat 10.00–16.00*) has exhibitions spreading over two floors that deal with three centuries of Baja's history. There are archaeological and artistic items, displays devoted to life on the Danube – shipping and fishing – and to the town's ethnic minorities. Many towns of the plain were heavily influenced by such minority groups, formed either of refugees fleeing the Turks and seeking haven or settlers repopulating towns after the Turks had left. István Türr was born in Baja and went on to join the revolution in Italy, fighting alongside Garibaldi; on his return to Hungary after the Compromise, he worked in water management and was involved in the Panama and Corinthian canals. However, perhaps the most quirky of the town's citizens commemorated in the museum was András Jelky – the 'Hungarian Robinson Crusoe'. During the 18th century, this apprentice embarked on a journey to Paris to improve his tailoring skills; he somehow succeeded not only in getting lost but in running out of money, enlisting with the Dutch army and wandering around Asia. On eventually returning to Hungary, he wrote his memoirs – and doubtless prayed for the invention of satnav; there's a statue of him by Ferenc Medgyessy on Jelky András tér. The main entrance is on the other side of the museum, in Roosevelt tér.

Behind the town hall, the Baroque **Franciscan Church of St Anthony of Padua** (*Bartók Béla utca 1*) was completed in 1756 (and remodelled in 1780). The standing, blue-robed Mater Dolorosa is the oldest of the town's Baroque statues – dating to 1740 – but looks rather lonely in its niche at the southern side. The right-hand church spire was once used as a firewatch and lookout tower.

Among other places of worship to look out for are the **Parish Church of SS Peter and Paul** (*Tóth Kálmán tér*), built in 1765 with funding from the contemporary landowners (the Grassalkovich family) and with 1930s frescoes by local art teacher Sándor Éber; the late-Baroque **Serbian Orthodox Church of St Nicholas** (*Miklós utca;* ↘ *79 423199; open Wed 09.00–12.00, call in advance at other times*), like a piece of confectionery in raspberry and custard colours, and with a stunning iconostasis; the 18th-century **Serbian Orthodox Church of the Blessed Virgin** (*Batthyány Lajos utca*), rougher around the edges, jammed cheek by jowl with residential houses and serving as a concert hall; and the proud, Neoclassical former synagogue of 1845, a wing of which used to serve as a home for elderly Jewish folk but which now holds the **Ady Endre Town Library** (*Munkacsy Mihály utca 9; open Mon–Thu 13.00–18.00, Fri 10.00–18.00, Sat 08.00–12.00*). The library stock is graced by fabulous surroundings, with layered chandeliers and high galleries; the most precious incunabula is the first full edition of the great 18th-century encyclopaedia of Denis Diderot and Jean le Rond D'Alembert (the product of their Enlightenment quest to summarise all knowledge), and there is also a bible once owned by the poet Endre Ady.

At the northern side of Vörösmarty tér, the **Nagy István Gallery** (*Arany János utca 1;* ↘ *79 325649; adult/concessions 300/150Ft; open Mar 15–Dec 15 Wed–Sat 10.00–16.00*) has the work of 20th-century national artists in a Neoclassical mansion once home to an artists' colony. Among the pieces are those by Nagy István (1873–1937), a Transylvanian artist who lived in Baja and was the leading member of the so-called Alföld School; there's also a bronze bust of the man outside by the brilliant Imre Varga.

Around 2.5km north of the centre – follow Dózsa György út, turn left into Templom utca and Pandor utca is the first on your right – stands a thatched village house painted with ducks and roses and containing the **Catholic Croat Museum** (*Bunyevác Tájház; Pandor utca 51;* ↘ *79 324173; adult/concessions 150/75Ft; open Mar 15–Dec 15 Wed–Sat 10.00–14.00*). It represents the typical home of a family of Catholic Croats at the turn of the 19th century, an ethnic group who settled in this region after the end of Ottoman rule.

The stretch known as the **Halász-part** (Fishermen's Beach) is a good spot to drink a beer and enjoy the sight of the river bending away. The sandy section for sunbathing is a further 200m along (moving away from Petőfi Bridge). Another place for strolls and quiet contemplation is the **Déri Garden** (*Déri-kert*), a block east of the Franciscan church. At the western entrance is a bust of Frigyes Déri (1852–1924), the Baja-born silk maker and art collector, as well as a 23m-tall World War I memorial and a rock monument commemorating the 1956 revolution.

### Other activities

Scheduled **boat trips** (❈ *79 426525; Jun 1–Sep 28 Sat from 16.00*) depart from the Halász-part area on summer Saturdays. The one-hour tour circles Petőfi-sziget before travelling along the Gemenc Forest (see page 398). **Admirál** (❈ *06 30 938 2149*) also arranges one- and two-hour tours with a boat leaving from the Sugovica Yacht Basin – including water-skiing if you wish; prices start at around 16,000Ft. As well as the **beaches** on Petőfi-sziget, there are others near the Halász-part and on Nagy Pandúr sziget.

The **Baja Sports Swimming Pool** (*Petőfi-sziget;* ❈ *79 326773; adult/concessions 500/330Ft; open Mon–Tue 06.00–19.30, Thu–Fri 06.00–19.30, Sat–Sun 08.00–19.30*), a short distance from the bridge, is a leisure centre with exercise classes, solarium and sauna alongside the main and children's pools.

There are plenty of places to cast a line at Baja, but you'll need an angling permit; **Baja Anglers Association** (*Petőfi-sziget 1;* ❈ *79 321343*) can sell daily, weekly or annual ones. **Baja Rowing Club** (*Garibaldi utca 25;* ❈ *06 30 243 8656*) rents kayaks, canoes and sailboats between Mar 1 and Nov 1. **Sugovica Hotel & Camping** (see page 349) also has facilities and equipment for watersports and tennis.

Tourinform can suggest a series of **cycling** routes of between 5km and 60km. Rent bicycles from Rausch Bicycle Shop (*Czirfusz Ferenc utca 4;* ❈ *79 325336; open Mon–Fri 09.00–17.00, Sat 09.00–12.00*). The **Gemenc Forest** (see page 398) – part of the Duna-Dráva National Park – is just across the bridge from Baja; you can pick up walking trails from the bridgehead, but between May and October it is better to take the train to Pörböly from where you can pick up the narrow-gauge railway northward into the region. One daily service runs the 30km to Bárányfok (with its excursion centre), from where it's a short hop to Szekszárd. Two other trains only go as far as Gemenc Dunapart, from where you have to wait for a connection. However, be sure to check the times beforehand as you don't want to get stranded.

### Festivals and events

Fish soup inevitably features heavily in the town's events, not only as the star attraction of the Baja Folk Festival in July but also during the Autumn Festival in September, alongside drama and music. At 174km, the Budapest–Baja International Boat Race is the longest in Europe, and takes place on the second weekend of August.

## CSONGRÁD

Directly east of Kiskunfélegyháza, Csongrád falls close to the confluence of the Tisza and Körös rivers. Árpád granted the Tisza region to the ruler Ond, and Ond made this the chief settlement in his territory; its name – a Hungarian corruption of the Slav for 'black castle' – stems from the earthwork built by Ond's son Ete, which stood here up until the Mongols came in the 13th century, laying it waste and thereby stripping the town of the status it had maintained during István's rule. Its layout is linear, with everything spread along Fő utca before it leads out to the Belváros, a winding street with protected 200-year-old fishermen's cottages that was once the settlement's core. Less historic is the resort-style 'beach' on the river bank 50m away.

## Getting there and away

There are no shortage of **buses** to Szentes and Kiskunfélegyháza, while a regular service also runs to Szeged; other destinations are Kecskemét (12), Budapest (nine), Orosháza (seven), Szolnok (five), Eger and Gyula (two). The **bus station** (*Hunyadi tér*) is in the centre. Csongrád lies on the same **railway** line as Szentes and Kiskunfélegyháza and there are up to eight trains a day to both destinations. To reach either Budapest, Szeged or Kecskemét you'll need to change at Kiskunfélegyháza, and for Orosháza or Hódmezővásárhely at Szentes. The station (*Vasút utca*) is southwest of the main strip; walk across the grassed area in front to the main road 100m ahead, turn left and continue until you join Fő utca.

## Information and other practicalities

**Cultural Centre & Town Gallery** Szentháromság tér 8; ✆ 63 483414/481034; e muvkozpont@freemail.hu. There is no independent theatre in Csongrád, but the hall of the cultural centre stages productions by the amateur local group Csongrád Színtársulat, as well as other programmes. The gallery (*Kossuth tér 9–11; admission free*) hosts temporary exhibitions. *Cultural centre opening hours dependent on events; gallery open Mon–Fri 10.00–12.00, 14.00–17.00, Sat–Sun variable.*

**Listings magazine** *Szegedi Est*

**Tourinform** Szentháromság tér 8; ✆ 63 570325. In the cultural centre building. *Open Jun 15–Sep 15 Mon–Sun 08.00–16.00, rest of year Mon–Fri 08.00–16.00.*

## Where to stay

**Erzsébet Szálloda** (13 rooms) Fő utca 3; ✆ 63 483960. Don't be deterred by a forbidding exterior for this is a perfectly comfortable, if old-fashioned, 2-star hotel, centrally located and reasonably priced. There is a coffee house underneath. *Sgl 6,500Ft, dbl 8,000Ft, triple 10,000Ft.*

**Fishermen's cottages** Fő utca 16 (contact address); ✆ 63 483631/06 30 239 4701. The charming place to spend a night is in one of the thatched fishermen's cottages, each with kitchen and courtyard. They are mainly situated along Öregvár utca and can accommodate 2–6 people. Contact László Erdős (details above). *Cottages 6,000–14,000Ft.*

**Hotel Tisza** (15 rooms) Fő utca 23; ✆ 63 483594; e hoteltisza@vnet.hu. Close to the thermal baths, this is a so-so hotel that did not have a restaurant during our visit (and, as such, to our minds struggles to justify its 3 stars). *Sgl 9,500Ft, dbl 11,000Ft, triple 12,500Ft.*

**Köröstoroki Campsite** Köröstorok, Nyárfa utca; Fő utca 14 (contact address); ✆ 63 481185; e idegenforgalom@vnet.hu. Set back from the beach at the Tisza bend, to the east of the centre, this shady campsite has wooden bungalows on stilts (with kitchens and bathrooms) as well as tent space. It is a very popular sunbathing spot in summer, and can be correspondingly 'lively'. Hire fishing equipment from 1,200Ft/day. *Bungalow 6,500Ft (for 2), 8,500Ft (for 3); tent/caravan 3,000/3,500Ft; open May 1–Sep 30.*

**Mini Hotel Apartments** (4 apts) Gróf Andrássy Gyula utca; ✆ 63 473322; mob: 06 20 922 9313; e apartments@netposta.net. On the way out towards the Belváros, these well-appointed and cared-for apartments (with small kitchens and bathrooms) for 3–4 are excellent value. The owners will leave a b/fast in the fridge for you for an additional 600Ft. *Apts 6,000Ft (for 1), 7,000Ft (for 2), 8,000Ft (for 3).*

## Where to eat and drink

**Bohém Kávéház** Fő utca 20–24; ✆ 63 483651. This first-floor café and ice-cream parlour also serves light meals and snacks; there is a chilled, cavernous bar to the right as you enter, which features some good bands (particularly jazz). There's usually something happening at weekends. *Mains 630–2,400Ft, avg 1,100; open Mon–Thu, Sun 09.00–24.00, Fri–Sat 09.00–01.00.*

**Fústi Cukrászda** Iskola utca 1; ✆ 63 483367. Popular cake and ice-cream place next to the Tari Museum. *Open 09.00–19.00 daily.*

**Golden Horse Irish Pub** Gróf Andrássy Gyula utca 17/A; ☏ 63 483834. A pleasant pub with a large wooden terrace, and Guinness and Kilkenny. The menu has an extensive choice of steaks, fish, chicken and pasta dishes. *Mains 590–1,780Ft, avg 1,000Ft; open Mon–Thu, Sun 12.00–22.00, Fri–Sat 12.00–24.00.*

**House of Csongrád Wines** (*Csongrádi Borok Háza*) Szentháromság tér 8; ☏ 63 482557. The showcase for the area's vintners since 2002, the House of Csongrád Wines (beneath the cultural centre) hosts pre-arranged tastings, organises tailored programmes and offers information about wine tours and the wines themselves. Wine-making is taken seriously in the region, which has a decent share of sunshine, and there are some good reds. If you wish to sample direct, head for the cellars to the west of town. *Open 09.00–16.00 daily.*

**Jókai Restaurant** Jókai Mór utca 1; ☏ 63 475010. Accessed through an archway opposite the Erzsébet Szálloda, this restaurant serves Hungarian food in goodly portions and has a delightful garden with fountain at the back. Its plush cocktail bar upstairs is closed in the heat of summer. *Mains 600–1,450Ft, avg 1,100Ft; open Mon–Sat 10.00–23.00, Sun 10.00–22.00.*

**Kert Vendéglő** Dózsa György tér 6; ☏ 63 483199. Reach the Kert via an arch on Dózsa tér, behind the thermal baths. Outdoor dining is beneath a bamboo-thatch roof; there's a wide selection of fish and grilled dishes, as well as standard Hungarian fare. The pancake desserts are definitely worth a try; settle your food by locking horns on the giant chess set or with a game of mini golf. *Mains 590–1,700Ft, avg 1,000Ft; open 11.30–22.00 daily.*

**Pompei Pizzeria** Kis Tisza 6; ☏ 63 470160. Pizzas in 4 sizes to suit bellies great and small. The garden at the rear, as well as pool and football tables, makes this a hangout spot for youngsters too. *Mains 950–1,600Ft, avg 1,000Ft; open daily 16.00–22.00.*

## What to see and do

**Szentháromság tér** is a characterful, unkempt square offering cool shade in the heat of the day. Its Trinity Monument was erected in 1869. Just north of Kossuth tér, the **Tari László Museum** (*Iskola utca 2; ☏ 63 483103; www.tarilaszlomuzeum.hu; adult/concessions 250/150Ft; open Mon–Fri 13.00–17.00, Sat 08.00–12.00, Sun 08.00–17.00*) – named after a local dentist and amateur historian – has a range of ethnographic and archaeological artefacts. Its Bronze-Age display includes excavated skeletons, and there are ancient swords, stirrups, coins, fishing nets and boating equipment, as well as more recent items like military uniforms from the Independence War of 1848–49. The museum also remembers the mid-19th-century peasant labourers who broke their backs with the spade work required in regulating the Tisza, draining the swampland and making habitable a massive area of the Great Plain.

Across the road, the Baroque **Parish Church of the Virgin Mary** (*Nagyboldogasszony templom; Kossuth tér*) was built on an earlier cemetery in 1762, part of the construction of a new town centre with more space to breathe to the west of the traditional Belváros. There are statues of the kings István and László either side of the altar, while the altarpiece itself was painted in 1917 by Lajos Tari, a copy of *Assunta* by Tiziano from the Frári Church in Venice. The wonderful frescoes on the ceiling depict the Annunciation, the Nativity and the moment when István offered the Holy Crown to the Virgin Mary. When the church is lit for a service, its magnificent gilding – and particularly that of the pulpit, looking like an extravagant, wall-mounted bathtub – leaps from the darker nooks and crannies behind, and is a real spectacle. The Art-Nouveau **János Batsányi School** (*Kossuth tér*) at the eastern end of the square was designed by Miklós Ybl in 1914, and has majolica floral motifs above its windows and a steep black roof.

Moving eastwards, Gróf Andrássy Gyula utca leads to Öregvár ('Old Castle') utca and the Belváros, a pleasant 1km walk from the modern centre. You'll pass the shabby white **Szent Rókus Church** (*Szent Rókus tér*) before reaching the cobbled streets and fishermen's cottages. Some of these 200-year-old dwellings – unique in the Great Plain, and 17 were placed under heritage protection in the 1960s – can be rented (see page 353); alternatively you can take a peek inside one at the **Museum House** (*Gyöker utca 1;* ✒ *63 481052; admission free; open May 1–Oct 31 Tue–Sun 13.00–17.00*). (Another, that wasn't accorded protected status, was moved for display at the Ópusztaszer National Memorial Park; see page 360.) Until the 1950s, fishermen maintained their traditional lifestyles here by the river bank. Families would take their water from the Tisza, filling jugs and leaving them until the sediment had settled to the bottom. Climb the bank running next to the road for views of the river bend, particularly pleasing during early evening. At the tip of the bend (facing the mouth of the Hármas Körös) is the 700m-long **Köröstoroki Strand**, crowded with sunbathers on the sand and those messing about in boats. This resort-style beach has a couple of places to eat (as well as accommodation; see page 353).

Heading towards the river northwest of the contemporary centre, a pontoon bridge crosses the Tisza to Nagyrét; from there it is a 3km walk to some Roman remains and those of the **Ellés Monastery**, a very significant site dating to the 11th and 12th centuries and excavated during the 1990s.

### Other activities

As well as the strand (see above), the **thermal baths and swimming pool** (*Dob utca 3–5;* ✒ *63 481915; adult/concessions 360/250Ft; open Mon 07.00–19.00, Tue–Wed 07.00–22.00, Thu*

*07.00–19.00, Fri 07.00–22.00, Sat 08.00–22.00, Sun 08.00–20.00*) to the west of Dózsa György tér are set among sycamore trees. There are a number of indoor and outdoor pools whose medicinal water is said to help rheumatic and gynaecological disorders.

The **Pejkó Riding Club** (*Szántó Major Tanya 95;* ✆ *63 483460*) is a few kilometres south of the centre – follow Vasút utca (Road 451) towards Szentes. The horse farm offers riding lessons and cross-country tours, and has an eight-room guesthouse, swimming pool and tennis courts.

### Festivals and events
There are wine festivals in early April and mid August, while those preferring beer are catered for in May. The main event is Csongrád Days, over two weeks in August.

## SZENTES
It is surprising that Szentes, on the banks of the River Kurca southeast of Csongrád, is not more popular with tourists for it has much to recommend it. Its main museum is well worth seeing, there are a couple of decent places to stay and eat, a sports complex offers activity a few minutes' walk from the centre and there are pleasant riverside strolls to be had. It is to be regretted that some of the significant buildings have been allowed to stagnate; in the centuries following the Turkish occupation, the town rebuilt with an architectural flourish seldom found elsewhere on the Great Plain, and one senses that if some of these monuments were to enjoy a lick or two of paint, Szentes could become one of the must-sees of the region. As it stands it is noted for its vegetables (the greenhouses powered by 32 wells, which produce thermal water at temperatures close to boiling point) and athleticism – in the 1990s, Szentes was named National Sporting Town.

### Getting there and away
The **bus station** (*Szabadság tér*) is just south of Kossuth tér, offering up to nine buses a day to Budapest Népliget and a very regular service to Csongrád, Hódmezővásárhely, Szeged and Kiskunfélegyháza; there are also buses to Orosháza (up to 15), Szolnok (eight), Tiszaföldvár (seven), Tiszafüred (four), Gyula (six), Lajosmizse (three), Miskolc (two) and once-daily to Mátraháza, Mátrafüred, Parádfürdő and Pécs. The **railway station** – on the lines east–west between Kiskunfélegyháza and Orosháza and north–south between Hódmezővásárhely Népkert and Tiszatenyő – is a 20-minute walk northeast of the centre. There is one train daily to Budapest Nyugati, nine to Hódmezővásárhely, five to Orosháza, seven to Csongrád and nine to Kiskunfélegyháza; change at Hódmezővásárhely for Szeged. There's a local bus stop outside the station; on foot turn left from the station on to the main road (*Atilla út*), then right to Kossuth Lajos utca which leads into town. For taxis, try **AS2** (*tel: 63 444444*).

### Information and other practicalities
**Gold Sun Travel Agency** Kossuth tér 5; ✆ 63 560160. Tour company offering information about what's on, as well as assistance with private accommodation. At the eastern side of the square. *Open Mon–Fri 09.00–13.00, 13.30–17.00, Sat 09.30–12.00.*

**Listings magazine** *Szegedi Est*

**Móricz Zsigmond Cultural Centre** Ady Endre utca 36; tel; 63 312623. Entertainment programmes, dance and fitness classes and folk exhibitions. *Opening hrs vary.*

**New York Internet Café** Horváth Mihály utca 12; ✆ 63 560711. Trendy American-theme café attracting the cool crowd with emails to send. *Costs 400Ft/hr; open 10.00–24.00 daily.*

### Where to stay, eat and drink
**Camping** Széchenyi liget. There is a campsite near the sports complex in the town's recreational park (see page 358).

**Főnix** Mátyás király utca 2; ☏ 63 316282. This 1st-floor restaurant is bedecked in purple and has a good range of Hungarian dishes. Follow Kossuth Lajos utca east, and turn right on to Mátyás király utca. *Mains 510–1,930Ft, avg 1,200Ft; open 11.00–23.00 daily.*

**Holdfény Panzió** (7 rooms) Arany János utca 8; ☏ 63 444076; e hpanzio@freemail.hu. Just off Ady Endre utca, north of Kossuth tér, Holdfény Panzió is comfortable and family run. It has a communal kitchen available to guests; the sgl rooms are not en suite. *Sgl 3,800Ft, dbl 7,800Ft, room for 4 11,000Ft.*

**Liget** Széchenyi liget, Csallány Gábor part 4; ☏ 63 400397. Provided you can put up with the noise from the baths behind it, the Liget has a covered terrace, an elegant interior and an excellent range of creative, gourmet choices – among them whole roast suckling pig and stuffed pigeon. You shouldn't go wrong here. *Mains 550–1,660Ft, avg 1,200Ft; open Mon–Thu 11.00–21.00, Fri–Sat 11.00–22.00, Sun 11.00–21.00.*

**Nádas Csárda** Nádas sétány 1/C; ☏ 63 315941. With its gorgeous thatch and bubbly atmosphere, this is the leading contender in the ambience stakes. There is national and international cuisine, including a Transylvanian mixed grill and the house special of 'Nádas' dish for two (a selection of fried meats and cheese). It's next to the river 2km north of the centre, but worth the effort; follow Tóth István utca and then Sima Ferenc utca, before turning left on to Szalai utca and then first left again. *Mains 890—2,400Ft, avg 1,200Ft; open Mon–Fri 11.30–22.00, Sat–Sun 11.30–23.00.*

**Páterház Panzió** (8 rooms) Kossuth utca 1; ☏ 63 444122. While its façade faithfully preserves the early-20th-century style of bourgeois architecture, the interior is modern. The rooms won't disappoint either – spick and span, and with large bathrooms. The restaurant (*mains 900–1,880Ft, avg 1,500Ft; open 11.00–22.00 daily*) serves quality Hungarian cuisine in an airy dining room with attentive staff. Centrally located, in front of the bus station. *Sgl 6,500Ft, dbl 12,500Ft.*

**Taverna Pizzeria** Horváth Mihály utca 7; ☏ 63 401051. Pizzas and snacks for those hankering after non-Hungarian food. There's a patio garden at the back. *Mains 420–990Ft, avg 780Ft; open 11.00–23.00 daily.*

## What to see and do

The main square is **Kossuth tér**, with black iron lamps, criss-crossing paths and a fountain whose nozzles spurt water to varying heights. There are statues of Lajos Kossuth (István Tóth) and Mihály Horváth, the latter – a great 19th-century theologian, historian and later MP – with quill in hand and skull cap on head, while around the edges are some of the town's architectural heavy hitters. At the western side, the stateliness of the Neoclassical **former County Hall** (*Mégyeháza; Kossuth tér 1*) is sadly compromised by crumbling stonework and pigeon poo. It was completed in 1883, and has carved allegories of agriculture, industry, sailing, hunting, trade and fishing around its windows.

The early-20th-century **town hall** (*Kossuth tér 6*) is an altogether different affair, with a pristine façade and two mansards flanked by cylindrical corner turrets. The Art-Nouveau **Hotel Petőfi** (*Petőfi Sándor utca 2*) also bears ornamental turrets, but one now tilts tiredly. In its prime this was a significant piece of architectural art, the work of Ödön Lechner's disciples Marcell Komor and Dezső Jakab; it now houses a shabby taxi office and an ice-cream parlour, together with the **Tóth József Theatre** (*ticket office ☏ 63 311166; open 10.00–13.00, 15.00–18.00 daily*). The only ray of hope is that there are restoration plans.

To the east of Kossuth tér, the dinky **Greek Orthodox church** (*Görögkeleti Egyházközössége; Kossuth Lajos utca 4*) is painted strawberry red. This is the oldest building in Szentes, built in Baroque style in 1786, and has a beautiful iconostasis decorated with roses and gilded leaves by István Tenecki (an outstanding 18th-century artist working in Arad, now part of Romania). The church's diminutive stature is reduced further by being set three feet below street level. The fresco in an outer niche depicts Szent Miklós.

Further along Kossuth Lajos utca, the brick Neo-Gothic **Lutheran church** (*Kossuth Lajos utca 9*) was built in 1905, boasting buttresses plated with glazed tiles and floral ironwork on its gate. The stained-glass windows around the altar portray events in Jesus's life; at the southern side of the nave is a marble tablet commemorating Lutherans who died in World War I, framed with Art-Nouveau carvings by Antal Koncz. Continue to the eastern end of Kossuth Lajos utca and the Romantic-style former **synagogue** (*Kossuth Lajos utca 33–35;* ☎ *63 400271*) of 1870, now housing the town's library and a wonderful place to read a book.

The **Péter-Pál Town House Museum** (*Polgárház Múzeum; Petőfi Sándor utca 9;* ☎ *63 316678;* e *polgarhaz.szentes@museum.hu; admission free; open Tue & Thu 10.00–12.00, 14.00–16.00, Sat 13.00–17.00*) is south of Kossuth tér; the 19th-century doctor (Pál Péter) and his family who lived here clearly did so in some luxury. As well as medical objects, there are musical instruments (the good doctor was a keen collector of such paraphernalia) and textiles. The house was originally built for a wine merchant in 1830, and the fine cellar is the venue for temporary exhibitions.

We have a soft spot for **Erzsébet tér**, with its gravelled pathways and grey-blue conifers. The Art-Nouveau **Roman Catholic school** at the southern side was constructed in 1912, and looks like an overblown doll's house. In the middle of the square stands a poignant **World War I monument** (János Pásztor, 1926) showing a mother and child cowering behind a dying soldier, while at the back is the Neoclassical **Roman Catholic church** (*Szent Anna templom; Szent Imre Herceg utca*) of 1847. Its Baroque tower survives from an earlier 18th-century church; inside, the triumphal arch is adorned with a wonderful secco of Hungarian saints paying homage to the holy sacrament, while the Secessionist ceiling was painted by Béla Endre and Gyula Rudnay in 1910.

Tucked into the crook of a bend in the River Kurca, **Széchenyi liget** is the town's recreational area, a tree-filled park a short walk west of Kossuth tér. Towards the back you'll find a sports complex featuring **outdoor swimming pools** (*Széchenyi liget, Csallány Gábor part 4;* ☎ *63 314167; adult/concessions 650/450Ft; open 05.00–21.00 daily*), water slides and tennis courts (*1,320Ft/hr*), as well as a campsite. At the park's heart is the excellent **Koszta József Museum** (*Széchenyi liget 1;* ☎ *63 313352; adult/concessions 200/100Ft; open Tue–Sun 13.00–17.00*). The diverse local-history and ethnographic collection includes agricultural and military items, Turkish finds of the 16th and 17th centuries, bottles and coins, and the famed black ceramics crafted by Szentes potters. Keep a look out too for an intriguing novelty musical instrument of 1780, a multi-tasker of a thing with a drum, cymbal and strings operated by a revolving pin cylinder. Most significant, however, are the 35 paintings of József Koszta, whose oeuvre was the Great Plain and its peasant people. Koszta lived and worked on a farmstead near Szentes for over 25 years up until his death in 1948. Outside, Zoltán Kovács's statue of a labourer – all spade and meaty forearms – recalls the town's agricultural lifeblood, so easily overshadowed by the extravagant bourgeois architecture that sprung up in the centre during the prosperous 18th and 19th centuries.

### Other activities

As well as the swimming pools (see above), there are **thermal baths** (*Ady Endre utca 44;* ☎ *63 401573; adult/concessions 530/300Ft; open Mon 08.00–16.00, Tue–Fri 08.00–20.00, Sat–Sun 09.00–20.00*) at the northern end of Ady Endre utca. These have an oriental look to them, and make use of the fact that Szentes is perched upon Europe's largest geothermal field.

## ÓPUSZTASZER

The village of Ópusztaszer 11km east of Kistelek is itself unremarkable, but the unsnappily named Ópusztaszer National Historical Memorial Park drags it very close to the top of Hungary's tourist tree. Occupying a patch that was once the town of Szer, it was here that Árpád and the other Magyar tribal leaders are said to have assembled in the immediate aftermath of their successful campaign to conquer the Carpathian Basin in the

9th century (see page 15). According to the *Gesta Hungarorum* (see page 16), the warriors camped on the land for 34 days while thrashing out mundane details like rules of governance and justice in their freshly acquired territory. Of course, Anonymus was recording this history fully 300 years after the event, and would probably struggle under cross examination to prove beyond doubt that this was the site of the first Hungarian 'parliament'; however, with no-one sticking their hand up with alternative suggestions, the country has taken the scribe's account to its bosom and celebrates this as the hallowed ground where Hungary was born.

## Getting there and away
To reach the park take the **train** to Kistelek from Budapest Nyugati (just over two hours) or Szeged (40 minutes); from here up to 13 buses daily stop at the park entrance (15-minute journey). MÁV offers a 50% discount on return train tickets for park visitors arriving at either Kistelek or Szeged stations – get your ticket stamped the park entrance. Alternatively, up to 25 **buses** daily run from Szeged to Ópusztaszer Park.

## Information
**Tourinform** Szoborkert 68; \ 62 275257; e opusztaszer@tourinform.hu. Can provide information on the horse shows and other programmes that regularly take place here. Housed in the rotunda. *Open same hours as park.*

## Where to stay, eat and drink
**Erdei Vendégház** Erdei Ferenc utca 58–60; \ 06 30 303 4195; e erdeivendeghaz@invitel.hu; www.erdeivendeghaz.hu. We can't recommend this guesthouse highly enough, set in beautiful grounds hung with flower baskets 2km from the park entrance (on Road 5411, running from Kistelek to Ópusztaszer). There are self-contained apts in the main house (for 4 or 8) and smaller ones (without kitchens) encircling the garden. The owners are friendliness personified, and can organise shooting and riding tours, and there's a sauna, swimming pool and outdoor cooking facilities. Relax with a gin and tonic and watch the sun go down. *Main house 4,400–4,900Ft/pp, apt from 3,000Ft/pp.*

**Szeri Csárda** Árpád liget 111; \ 62 275165; e szerics@weste1900.net. If you time it right, and avoid the coach parties crashing around, this is a pleasant peasant-style restaurant serving Hungarian dishes of game, fish, pork and poultry. It stands a ½km from the entrance to the memorial park, and has a basic campsite next door (\ 62 275123; *open Apr–Oct*). *Mains 850–2,500Ft, avg 1,300Ft.*

## Ópusztaszer National Historical Memorial Park
The 55ha park (*Ópusztaszeri Nemzeti Történeti Emlékpark*; Szoborkert 68; \ 67 275133; e info@opusztaszer.hu; www.opusztaszer.hu; *park entrance ticket 680Ft, Feszty Panorama adult/concessions 1,350/900Ft; show tickets adult/concessions 400/300Ft; open daily Apr 1–Oct 31 09.00–18.00 daily, Nov 1–Mar 31 09.00–16.00, open-air museum buildings closed in winter*) stands 1km from the road running between the village and Szeged, and is made up of several parts.

An avenue of lime trees leads from the entrance to the **Árpád Memorial**, a massive Neoclassical monument designed by Gyula Berczik and Ede Kallós and raised in 1896 as part of the millennial celebrations. Árpád sits atop, while around the front is a pantheon of former rulers of Hungary, set here in 2001 on the 1,000th anniversary of István's founding of the Hungarian state. István wears the golden crown. Beyond the memorial are the remains of the medieval **Monastery of Szer**, which was the largest on the Great Plain until its destruction by the Mongols and some of whose parts date to the 11th century; it was first excavated in the 1970s, when skeletons of the original settlers were also unearthed from an earlier pagan cemetery on the site.

## LATE ARRIVALS

As every Hungarian knows, the millennial celebrations of 1896 commemorated the 1,000th anniversary of the greatest hour – the 'land taking' (*honfoglalás*) by their tribal ancestors, the Magyars. Only the celebrants actually missed the boat by a year or two. A group of academics commissioned in the 1890s found that the tribes had probably arrived between AD893 and AD895. Unfortunately this came just too soon for the government, who couldn't ready themselves in time for the anniversary; not ones to let inconvenient points of historical accuracy poop their party, however, they declared that the official date had been AD896 – and the festivities began.

In front of the memorial (to the left of the path) is the park's prime attraction, the gigantic **rotunda**; designed by architect István Novák (a follower of Imre Makovecz), it nods towards the shape of a Magyar chieftain's tent. Inside is the spectacular **Feszty Cyclorama** (*Feszty-Körkép; groups admitted every 30 mins*), which imagines the journey made by the Magyar tribes as they entered the Carpathian Basin, and was created by Árpád Feszty and his colleagues for the millennial celebrations. What a piece of work; this is surely the cream of Hungarian National Romanticism. The canvas is 120m long and 15m tall, and took 24 painters two years to complete; it includes 2,000 figures and 1,500 horses. There are some fascinating details to winkle out. Feszty had a sense of humour, and included personal portraits in the piece; playing on his own name, he painted the chieftain Árpád in his own image, while a black-clad enemy chieftain bears a striking (and cheeky!) resemblance to his father-in-law (the writer Mór Jókai). His wife – the red-headed lady in the painting – is said to have fainted on hearing that Feszty had taken on such a daunting commission; she pleaded to be involved, and her husband finally relented in letting her paint some of the corpses (which required less detail). If you look very carefully, you may spot camels (there are 32 in total) among the horses, assisting in carrying provisions from the east; such is the level of detail that a guide we spoke to worked here for a full year before noticing them. The cyclorama was badly damaged during World War II – indeed, over half was destroyed – and the restoration by Polish experts (using 2,500l of solvent, 7,000kg of sawdust and a hell of a lot of sweat) is very nearly as remarkable as the original work. It was returned to public view in 1995.

Elsewhere in the rotunda are some rather crummy dummies of historical Hungarian greats (*adult/concessions 300/200Ft*), a reconstruction of a street in 1896 (complete with more dummies, in period costume), a gallery showing temporary art displays, an exhibition devoted to the 33 other panorama paintings around the world (a form invented by British artist Robert Barker), and an archaeological collection of finds made during excavation of the market town of Szer and its monastery.

Moving outside again, a cluster of **ten yurt houses** holds the Men and Forest Exhibition (*Erdő & Ember*), devoted to forestry, nature and the history of wood production in the Tisza region, the House of the Hungarians (paying tribute to Hungarian communities abroad) and the Crown House (containing a section from a giant redwood tree felled during a storm in California, and brought here by an ex-pat). Beyond is the sprawling **Open-Air Ethnographic Museum**, comprising a dozen typical buildings from the turn of the 19th and 20th centuries, transported from villages in the Great Plain; among them are a paprika and grape farmstead from Szeged, the house of an onion producer from Makó, a fisherman's cottage from Csongrád, a windmill from Szentes and a forester's lodge from Imrehegy with a wildlife exhibition of the Pusztaszer Nature Protection Area (including Fehér-tó; see opposite).

There are regular **craft shows** held among the buildings of the open-air museum. In addition, twice-daily performances (*11.30 & 14.30*) of the **Nomadic Ancestors Show** take place in the field beside the forester's house, with mounted warriors recreating the Magyar skills of horsemanship by firing off arrows while at full gallop. Test your own skills at riding (*from 300Ft*) and archery (*from 150Ft*), or take a more sedate turn around the park in a motorised buggy, which can be picked up from outside the rotunda (*adult/concessions 300/200Ft*).

## Festivals and events
A wine show takes place on St Vincent's Day in January, while there are folklore programmes (with cauldrons of goulash) on August 20 (St Stephen's Day), Easter and Whitsun. On the last Saturday in June, the 'Hunniális' celebrates the arrival of the Magyar tribes with a handicraft show and an equestrian programme that runs from dawn until dusk.

## FEHÉR-TÓ
Fehér-tó (White Lake), just to the east of the road running between Kistelek and Szeged (and not to be confused with the lake of the same name further northeast at Kardoskút), is a very important conservation area. Part of the wetland habitats of the Pusztaszer Landscape Protection Area – the biggest such area in the country – the lake was once little more than a shallow, sodium-rich pond that dried up in summer. However, in the 1930s it was transformed into a fish hatchery and steadily enlarged. It is now home to a plethora of rare aquatic birds, including stilts, avocets, Kentish plover, great white egret, spoonbill, squacco heron and purple heron. Falling as it does near the Tisza, in spring and autumn it attracts flocks of migrating ducks and geese that follow the river route and stop here to rest, while Korom Island holds colonies of nesting black-headed gulls. While you need special permission to visit the 350ha conservation area, you can get a bird's eye view from a lookout tower on the island; to get there leave Road E75 at the Bronze Age cemetery hill at Szatymaz. There are exhibitions covering the lake at Ópusztaszer and Szeged.

## SZEGED
Szeged rivals any city in Hungary, and is a thriving rebuttal to those who view the Great Plain as an architectural and cultural wasteland. On the map, its layout – cut through by the Tisza and ringed by inner and outer semi-circular boulevards – bears a passing resemblance to the eastern side of Budapest, and in some ways it can hold its own in such exalted company. In the aftermath of destruction (see page 364), the city aimed to reinvent itself as the most harmonious provincial settlement in the country. It carefully crafted its public spaces, and each of the squares has a character all its own: the green Széchenyi tér honours greats of the past; Klauzál tér cultivates an atmosphere of theatre and performance, studded with statues of harlequins and street artists (and is, appropriately, the place where Kossuth gave his last public 'performance'); Dóm tér is more austere, institutional and 'Victorian', reflecting its academic and religious heritage (although revellers invade during the Szeged Festival); Aradi vértanúk tere commemorates the 13 Martyrs of Arad, executed after defeat in the 1848–49 War of Independence. The result is a dynamic blend of significant past and carnivalesque present, a city whose spaces value both the contemplation of broad historical perspective and the escapist, bustling act of the here and now. There are decent restaurants, theatres and nightclubs, a nationally renowned opera, several universities, and one of the country's best cathedrals. If one were to be ultra picky, it could be said that the city is light on heavyweight museums, but in every other way Szeged shines bright.

Around 15km from the Serbian border, Szeged sits just below the confluence of the Tisza and Maros rivers and during the early medieval period was a distribution centre for salt

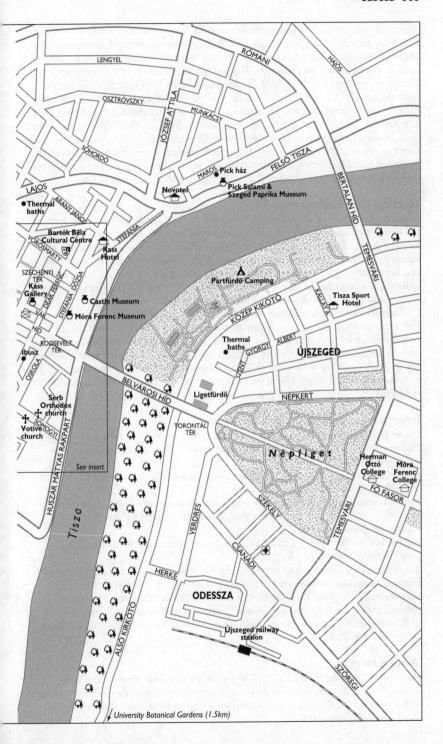

Thermal baths

Bartók Béla Cultural Centre

Kass Hotel

LENGYEL

OSZTRÓVSZKY

RÓMANI

HAJÓS

MUNKÁCSY

JÓZSEF ATTILA

SÓHORDÓ

MAROS · Pick ház

FELSŐ TISZA

Novotel

Pick Salami & Szeged Paprika Museum

LAJOS

ARANY JÁNOS

VÖRÖSMARTY

STEFÁNIA

BERTALAN HÍD

TEMESVÁRI

Partfürdő Camping

SZÉCHENYI TÉR

Kass Gallery

DEÁK FERENC

STEFÁNIA DÓZSA

VÁR

HÍD

Castle Museum

Móra Ferenc Museum

KÖZÉP KIKÖTŐ

KÁLLAY

Tisza Sport Hotel

ROOSEVELT TÉR

Ibusz

OSKOLA

HUSZÁR MÁTYÁS RAKPART

Thermal baths

SZENT GYÖRGY

ALBERT

ÚJSZEGED

BELVÁROSI HÍD

Ligetfürdő

NÉPKERT

Serb Orthodox church

SOMOGYI

Votive church

TORONTÁL TÉR

N é p l i g e t

See insert

Tisza

VERDRES

SZÉKELY

CSANÁDI

Herman Ottó College

Móra Ferenc College

FŐ FASOR

TEMESVÁRI

HERKE

ODESSZA

ALSÓ KIKÖTŐ

Újszeged railway station

SZŐREGI

↓ University Botanical Gardens (1.5km)

shipments brought on the Maros from Transylvania. Szeged was traditionally favoured by Hungarian monarchs, and flourished as a result. Its growth was inevitably stunted between 1543 and 1686 under Turkish occupation, although it represented the centre of the sultan's lands and came under his protection. The real setback came a couple of centuries later. During the night of March 12 1879 the city was engulfed by floodwater from the Tisza. Morning revealed the horrible extent of the damage: 95% of the buildings – 5,700 of the 6,000 – had been wiped away. A massive programme of reconstruction followed, bold Eclectic and Art-Nouveau architecture and avenues emerging from the muddy slush; sections of the Great Boulevard bear the names of European cities (such as Vienna, Paris and London) that aided the recovery. Szeged went from strength to strength, becoming a centre of textiles, salami production and paprika growing, and one of Hungary's leading university cities. It is now the economic, cultural and academic capital of the Southern Plain.

## Getting there and around

Numerous destinations are within reach by bus from Szeged, including regular services to Hódmezővásárhely, Békéscsaba, Csongrád and Ópusztaszer. Other towns are Szentes, Kecskemét (14), Dunaföldvár (12), Jászberény, Mohács and Szekszárd (eight), Veszprém (four), Gyula (six), Debrecen and Lajosmisze (three), Tatabánya, Siofók, Szombathely and Eger (two). There is also a Friday service to Vienna and up to three buses a day to Subotica and Novi Sad in Serbia. The **bus station** (*Márs tér*) is 600m from the centre; walk east along Mikszáth Kálmán utca, which leads to Széchenyi tér.

There are two **train stations** in Szeged – the main one on Indóház tér and the other, Újszeged, south of the centre and across the river. The latter is a small branch line running through Makó to Kétegyháza. From the main station trains travel up to ten times daily to Budapest Nyugati via Kecskemét, and also to Békéscsaba via Hódmezővásárhely (up to 12), Cegléd (up to six), and to Kiskunfélegyháza (regularly). Two trains a day go to Subotica in Serbia. Tram 1 from the main station is the quickest way into town. If you need a **taxi**, try Tempo (*tel: 62 490490*), Radió (*tel: 62 480480*) or Gabriel (*tel: 62 555555*).

## Information and other practicalities

**Cyber Arena Internet Café** Híd utca 1; ↘ 62 422815. Surf your socks off around the clock for 10Ft/min. There are loads of terminals, and a chance to win 500Ft by rolling a double six at the end of your session. *Open 24hrs daily.*

**Cyber Café** Dugonics tér 11; ↘ 62 425816. Internet access for 10Ft/min. *Open Mon–Fri 08.00–24.00, Sat–Sun 09.00–24.00.*

**Ibusz** Oroszlán utca 3; ↘ 62 471177; e 1085@ibusz.hu. Small but helpful office arranging tour programmes and private accommodation. *Open Mon–Fri 09.00–18.00, Sat 10.00–13.00.*

**Listings magazine** *Szegedi Est*

**Szeged Tourist** Klauzál tér 7; ↘ 62 420428. Arranges cultural and entertainment tours (but not private rooms). *Open Mon–Fri 09.00–17.00.*

**Tourinform** Dugonics tér 2; ↘ 62 488699; e szeged@tourinform.hu. The best place to start for maps and information on what's on. A second office (*Tábor utca 7/B;* ↘ *62 548092;* e *csongrad-m@tourinform.hu; open Mon–Thu 07.30–16.00, Fri 07.30–13.00*) has information on Csongrád county as a whole, while there is also a summer Tourinform booth (*Széchenyi tér; open Jun 15–Sep 15 daily 09.00–20.30*). *Open Jun 15–Sep 15 Mon–Fri 09.00–20.00, Sat–Sun 09.00–18.00, Sep 16–Jun 14 Mon–Fri 09.00–17.00.*

## Where to stay

**Hotel Bella** (25 rooms) Pacsirta utca 31; ↘ 62 498208; e hotels.hu/ujbella. A modern, fairly characterless hotel 15 mins' walk from the centre (a short distance beyond the outer ring road, just off Kossuth Lajos sugarút). The rooms are generous in size; ask for one with a balcony. *Sgl €45, dbl €55, triple €65, apt (for 2) €75.*

**Hotel Tisza** (80 rooms) Széchenyi tér 3; ℄ 62 478278; e info@tiszahotel.hu; www.tiszahotel.hu. The Secessionist Hotel Tisza was built in 1886; after World War II, it served as a police station and cells. Rooms vary in size and furnishings (not all have toilets): those in category II are bigger than those in category I, while apts have period touches such as draped beds. This is a good hotel, reasonably priced. *Rooms without/with toilet sgl €39/52, dbl €57/65, triple €70; apts €91 (for 1), €104 (for 2), €113 (for 3), €122 (for 4).*

**Kata Luxus Panzió** Bolyai János utca 15; ℄ 62 311258. This is the city's most central pension, more accurately a large apt (with 4 rooms and shared bathrooms, kitchen and lounge). The facilities are excellent, and the place is clean and buxom. Good value. *Sgl 7,300Ft, dbl 10,600Ft.*

**Marika Panzió** (9 rooms) Nyíl utca 45; ℄ 62 443861; e marika@tiszanet.hu. Located in a traditional peasant house, this is a lovely, peaceful guesthouse around 1km southwest of the centre (follow Szentháromság utca from Aradi vértanúk tere past Mátyás király tér, and look out for a right turn into Nyíl utca). The rooms are a little old-fashioned, the owners are welcoming, and there's a pleasant garden with a pool. You'll enjoy staying here. *Sgl 8,000Ft, dbl 9,500Ft, triple 11,500, room for 4 15,500Ft.*

**Novotel** (136 rooms) Maros utca 1; ℄ 62 562200; e h2996@accor-hotels.com; www.novotel-szeged.hu. Although this is a chain, and you'll probably have an inkling of what to expect, this modern hotel on the river bank is nevertheless one of the better ones in the city. The older rooms on the first 2 floors don't have AC, but are 10% cheaper. All rooms have balconies. *Dbl €82, dbl €93, triple €113.*

**Partfürdő Camping** Közép-kikötő sor; ℄ 62 430483. On the river bank in Újszeged, just north of Belvárosi híd, next to a couple of pools and a small beach. The site also has some chalets. *Camping: adult/concessions 1,000/700Ft, tent/caravan 700/800Ft (excl tax); chalets 6,000–13,500Ft; open May 1–Sep 30.*

**Royal Hotel** (80 rooms) Kölcsey utca 1–3; ℄ 62 475275; e royalhotel@royalhotel.hu; www.royalhotel.hu. The Royal certainly isn't regal – in fact, it's bloated and slightly tatty, with narrow rooms. The bathrooms are a good size, though, and it is central. *Sgl 14,100Ft, dbl 16,500Ft.*

**Sara Panzió** Pacsirta utca 17/A; ℄ 62 498206; e sarapanzio@freemail.hu. Further along the same road as the Hotel Bella, the Sara's rooms are on the small side but comfortable nevertheless. *Sgl 6,500Ft, dbl 8,500, triple 11,000Ft.*

**Tisza Sport Hotel** (106 rooms) Kállay utca 6–10; ℄ 62 431429; e sporthotel@tiszahotel.hu; www.tiszahotel.hu. This hotel, on the other side of the river in Újszeged (near Bertalan híd), has a variety of accommodation options from dorm-style rooms (for 3–4) to superior and modern dbls. Caters for pockets deep or shallow. *Superior/classic sgl €53/40, dbl €68/59; rooms not en suite sgl €27, dbl €42, triple €52, room for 4 €62 €; suite (for 4) €101.*

In a city with such a healthy student population (speaking numerically rather than medically), there are many cheap college rooms available during holiday periods. Those closest to the centre include the **Déri Miksa College** (*Moszkai körút 11–13;* ℄ *62 547058; rooms available Jun 15–Aug 31*), the **Herman Ottó College** (*Temesvári körút 50–52;* ℄ *62 544311;* e *iroda@novell.ohsu.u-szeged.hu*) and the **Móra Ferenc College** (*Közép fasor 31–33;* ℄ *62 544101;* e *info@mora.u-szeged.hu*). All offer dorm beds for around 2,000Ft/pp and rooms from 3,000Ft.

## Where to eat and drink

**Arany Oroszlan** Klauzál tér 5; ℄ 62 550627. The main restaurant of the Golden Lion – serving Hungarian and international dishes – is located in a courtyard behind the square (accessed via an archway), while there is pizza and other less formal offerings available at pavement seating on the square itself. *Mains 750–2,000Ft, avg 1,200Ft; open Sun–Thu 10.00–24.00, Fri–Sat 10.00–02.00.*

**Bécsi** Feketes utca 19–21; ℄ 62 550725. The large Vienna coffee house has a pub-like feel to it, and is highly recommended by younger locals; to the north of Klauzál tér. *Open Mon–Sat 07.00–23.00, Sun 09.00–23.00.*

**Boland** Széchenyi tér 13; ☏ 62 420435. Boland has very good food and attentive service, with a position that overlooks both the leafy square (nice) and a car park (not so nice). Hungarian cuisine dominates, although there are some German and Serbian choices too. We really enjoyed our meals here, and found the potato doughnuts scrummy. *Mains 850–4,200Ft, avg 1,800Ft; open 09.00–24.00 daily.*

**John Bull Pub** Oroszlán utca 6; ☏ 62 484217. This is probably the best 'English' pub in the country; at night the courtyard garden flickers with candles and torches, and there's an al-fresco bar as well as a plush interior. The snack menu has steak and chips, chilli con carne and Hungarian food. *Mains 1,050–2,950Ft, avg 2,000Ft; open Mon–Fri 10.00–01.00, Sat–Sun 11.00–01.00.*

**London Pub** Dugonics tér 2; ☏ 62 438010. A second English-theme pub with a courtyard that would seem fine were it not for that at the John Bull. The menu includes 'London steak' (which look pretty similar to any other steak), stuffed chicken breast, spare ribs and the like. It gets busy. *Mains 950–2,900Ft, avg 1,900Ft; open 10.00–24.00 daily.*

**Roosevelt Téri Halászcsárda** Roosevelt tér 14; ☏ 62 424111. Among other things, Szeged is noted for its fish dishes; this fish restaurant looks less upmarket than you might expect for the price, but it is highly regarded and the fish soup as good as you'll find. Next to the Belvárosi híd. *Mains 800–5,200Ft, avg 2,300Ft; open 11.00–23.00 daily.*

**Szeged Restaurant & Coffee House** Széchenyi tér 9; ☏ 62 555400. This restaurant, bar and coffee house has a terrace that fills a considerable chunk of the square. Its limited menu features international dishes, but you're probably best just coming here for a slurp of beer or a cocktail. There is live (synthesiser) music or other entertainment in the evenings. *Mains 850–2,600Ft, avg 1,600Ft; open Mon–Thu 08.00–24.00, Fri–Sat 08.00–02.00, Sun 08.00–24.00.*

**Taj Mahal** Gutenberg utca 12; ☏ 62 452131. The Taj Mahal isn't shy, proclaiming that 'Just like the 7th wonder of the world, it will leave an everlasting impression on you'. Well, that's perhaps a touch ambitious, but this is a good traditional curry house in a country where Indian cuisine is thin on the ground. It's located in the Jewish quarter; each table has an electronic buzzer with which to summon the waiters. *Mains 900–3,100Ft, avg 1,600Ft; open Mon–Thu 11.00–23.00, Fri–Sat 11.00–03.00, Sun 12.00–22.00.*

**Vendéglő a Régi Hídhoz** Oskola utca 4; ☏ 62 420910. This folksy restaurant deals in traditional Hungarian food and puts together a mean fish soup. *Mains 750–2,300Ft, avg 1,400Ft; open Sun–Thu 12.00–23.00, Fri–Sat 12.00–24.00.*

**Virág Cukrászda** Klauzál tér 1; ☏ 62 541360. The biggest and the best of the city's patisseries is splendid once more after renovation was completed in 2003. It dominates the square's eastern side, with a takeaway outlet (Kis Virág) opposite and tables filling the area between them. *Open 09.00–22.00 daily.*

**Zodiákus** Oskola utca 13; ☏ 62 420914. Housed in a Louis-XVI- (or Zopf-) style building of 1810, this restaurant plays on a zodiac theme and offers Italian, French and Hungarian food. The décor is subtler than you might expect, and the atmosphere relaxed. *Mains 750–2,500Ft, 1,500Ft; open Mon–Thu 11.00–24.00, Fri–Sat 11.00–01.00, Sun 11.00–24.00.*

## Entertainment and nightlife

The Eclectic and Neo-Baroque **Szeged National Theatre** (*Nemzeti Színház; Deák Ferenc utca 12;* ☏ *62 479279; www.szabadterijatekok.szeged.hu*) was built in 1883, designed by the Hellmer and Fellner company responsible for Budapest's Vígszínház; it had to be reconstructed after burning down just two years after opening. In niches either side of the entrance are statues of Ferenc Erkel and József Katona. It hosts performances of drama, opera and ballet, with music performed by the Szeged Symphony Orchestra. Its main event is the **Szeged Open-Air Games** (*Szegedi Szabadtérijátékok*), an arts festival on a stage erected in Dóm tér. For information on the festival or theatre programme, as well as to buy tickets, contact the **ticket office** (*Kelemen utca 7;* ☏ *62 554713; e ticket@szinhaz.szeged.hu; open Mon 13.00–17.00, Tue–Fri 10.00–17.00, Sat 10.00–12.00*).

Performances at the 150-seat **Köver Béla Puppet Theatre** (*Bábszinház; Tisza Lajos körút 50;* ℡ *62 420912*) usually start at 10.00, 11.00 and 14.30, but check the programme listings outside beforehand. The **Inner City Cinema** (*Belvárosi Mozi; Deák Ferenc utca 14;* ℡ *62 543185; ticket office open 14.00–20.45 daily*) has Hollywood blockbusters and Hungarian films. **Bartók Béla Cultural Centre** (*Vörösmarty utca 3;* ℡ *62 542825*) has information on cultural events.

Night owls are well catered for in a city with a high number of students, but be aware that – as with many university towns – mid-week evenings (particularly Thursdays) are often bigger than weekends. The **JATE Klub** (*Toldy utca 2;* ℡ *62 321245; www.jateklub.hu; open Mon, Wed & Thu 09.30–04.00, Tue & Fri 09.30–24.00, Sat 21.30–05.00*) is a basement venue at the back of the science university that hosts regular parties, discos on Mondays and Wednesdays, and cultural events such as traditional dance (*táncház*; see page 29), concerts, poetry readings and drama. The **Sing Sing Music Hall** (*C Pavilon, Mars tér; www.sing.hu; open Wed, Fri & Sat 23.00–05.00*) is a trendy warehouse club (all lasers and balconies), featuring dance music, classic nostalgia tunes, hip-hop and Ibiza-style parties. Just beyond the Great Boulevard, northwest of the centre; the main nights are Wednesdays and Saturdays. The **SZOTE Klub** (*Dóm tér 13*) is frequented by the medical students.

**Corso Café** (*Kárász utca 16;* ℡ *62 557457*) is a funky café-bar playing jazzy music; it stands on a pedestrianised street between Dugonics and Klauzál squares. The **Gin Tonic Club** (*Széchenyi tér 1;* ℡ *62 559559; open Mon–Fri 12.00–02.00, Sat–Sun 20.00–03.00*) has house and dance classics, as well as the odd live gig and karaoke nights. **Laguna Cocktail Bar** (*Híd utca 6;* ℡ *06 70 201 9818; open Wed–Sat 22.00–05.00*) has a choice of over 80 cocktails, and has DJs as well as funk, hip-hop, R'n'B and Latino theme nights. It's on the corner of Deák Ferenc utca and Híd utca.

## What to see and do
### Széchenyi tér, Klauzál tér and around

The Belváros is enclosed by the inner boulevard, **Széchenyi tér** its initial focal point. It is an enormous square, the 50,000m² filled with plane trees, flowerbeds and statues. As well as István Széchenyi himself, Ferenc Deák, Szent István and Queen Gizella are here, as is the vast white head of Count Kuno Klebelsberg (1875–1932). Klebelsberg was a professor at Szeged University and a politician after 1920 who established universal primary-school provision, moved the universities that fell beyond the post-Trianon borders back into Hungary, and founded the Szeged Summer Festival; his red-marble tomb can be seen in the Votive Church (see page 368). Two monuments commemorate the 1879 flood that levelled the city, including a fountain of townsfolk riding on the back of fish. Elsewhere a plinth bears the behatted Pál Vásárhelyi, the engineer who worked with Széchenyi in regulating the Danube and Tisza rivers in the 1840s.

The **town hall** of 1799 was a flood casualty and was afterwards given an Eclectic-Baroque facelift by Ödön Lechner and Gyula Pártos, who aimed towards a uniquely Hungarian national style. Mihály Babits – employing a healthy dollop of that licence available to the poetic – described the tower as 'a young woman with a lace bonnet dancing in the moonlight'. It is certainly a captivating building; in summer, concerts are held in its courtyard. The 'Bridge of Sighs' linking the hall to an adjacent building was erected during the stay of Ferenc József in 1883 to allow him easy access to his entourage ensconced next door. Just northwest of Széchenyi tér, across Vörösmarty utca, are some 19th-century **thermal baths** (*Tisza Lajos körút 24;* ℡ *62 487711; adult 700Ft; open Mon–Fri 06.00–18.00, Sat 06.00–15.30*), with medicinal water.

The pedestrianised Kárász utca is the inner-city spine, a promenade running southwest from Széchenyi tér. Along its way is the atmospheric and romantic **Klauzál tér**, a place for meeting and cake-eating, and lined with grand Neoclassical abodes.

Towards its eastern end is a life-size statue of Lajos Kossuth; it commemorates Kossuth's last speech in Hungary, which he delivered from the pink marble balcony of **Kárász House** (*Klauzál tér 5*) on July 14 1849 before fleeing to Turkey (see page 19). Ferenc József stayed in the building in 1857, but it now holds banking clerks. At the opposite side of the square is the **Well of Kings** (*Királyok kútja*) by Tóbiás Klára, featuring four regal lions dribbling into a marble basin.

Continuing along Kárász utca, a brief diversion right along Kölcsey utca leads to the **Reök Palace** (*Tisza Lajos körút 56*), called the 'Horse's Rump' by locals because it stands behind an equestrian statue. The palace is perfect enough to eat, a dazzling example of Hungarian Art Nouveau; it was built in 1907 by Ede Magyar-Oszadszki, a designer who spent most of his short career in Szeged before dying in 1912 at the age of just 35. The wrought-iron flowers blossoming on the façade were made by Pál Fekete, based on drawings by Magyar-Oszadszki.

## Dugonics tér, Dóm tér and Aradi vértanuk tere

A pair of charming bronze statues entitled *Street Music* (*Utcai Zene*) – a fiddle-playing street performer and a watching child with her *puli* dog – stand at the southern end of Kárász utca, the companions to harlequins at the street's northern end; these pieces are symbolic of the city festivals in summer. They bring up **Dugonics tér**, once the site of a wheat market. On the northern side is the caramel-coloured, Romantic-style **Vajda House** (*Dugonics tér 2*), holding the main Tourinform office; in front is the pensive figure of András Dugonics, clasping his novel *Etelka*, the first printed in Hungarian. Another Szeged resident was Attila József, who was expelled from the Eclectic **University of Science** (*Szegedi Tudományegyetem; Dugonics tér 13*) in 1924 after penning the revolutionary poem 'With a Pure Heart' during the rule of Admiral Horthy. Imre Varga's statue of the poet is outside, as is a modern multi-spouted and music-playing fountain surrounded by concrete seating; stalls purvey various wares around the fountain in summer.

Walk east along Somogyi utca to the brown **Black House** (*Fekete ház; Somogyi utca 13;* ☎ *62 425872; adult/concessions 200/100Ft; open Oct 1–Jun 30 Tue–Sun 10.00–17.00, Jul 1–Sep 30 10.00–18.00*), named after its earlier blackened walls. Built in 1857 in Romantic style for a wealthy merchant, its most striking feature is the gorgeous corner balcony. Unusually, the merchant also asked the architect Károly Gerster to design the furniture inside; the house is now used by the Móra Ferenc Museum, with a permanent social-history display and other temporary exhibitions.

The brooding **Dóm tér** (Cathedral Square) has an air of the Dickensian Victorian about it, more enclosed than other squares in the city and surrounded by institutional buildings of forbidding brick. During July and August it is the scene for Szeged's great open-air festival, something that can seem difficult to imagine at other times, like picturing a stern headmaster in a Hawaiian shirt. The **Votive Church** (*adult/concessions 400/250Ft, free on Sun; open Mon–Wed & Fri 09.00–17.30, Thu 12.00–17.30, Sat 08.00–15.00, Sun 13.00–17.30*) was the product of a vow made by city fathers after the 1879 flood, and – whether to your taste or not – is undoubtedly among the outstanding pieces of ecclesiastical architecture in the country. Built between 1913 and 1930, the exterior is a Neo-Romanesque clutter of triangles and rectangles, spires and spanning arches. The two main clock towers are each 93m; at certain times you can climb the 300 steps of one of them (*600Ft; climbs depart Mon–Fri 16.00, Sat 13.00*). The façade bears mosaics of the apostles either side of a marble Mary and child above the portal, while the interior is crawling with frescoes and paisley patterning reminiscent of Budapest's Mátyás Church – unsurprising, as both churches were designed by Frigyes Schulek. A mosaic on the sanctuary ceiling shows Mary in shepherd's cloak and slippers; the dome fresco was added to celebrate the millennium, and beneath it are allegorical paintings of Justice,

## ATTILA JÓZSEF

Born in 1905, the creator of some of Hungary's most beautiful poetry died at the tragically young age of 32. He had an unsettled upbringing, his soap boiler father abandoning his family when József was just three and his mother dying when he was 14. He was expelled from Szeged University after writing a poem with the lines 'I have no father, I have no mother, I have no God and no country'. He subsequently became involved in illegal left-wing movements at a time when fascism was growing in Europe, but suffered from regular bouts of depression for which he had to be treated in hospital. His sisters did their best to lift him, but to no avail. In 1937 József ended his life under a train at Balatonszárszó. He lies in Kerepesi Cemetery in Budapest.

Fortitude, Prudence and Temperance. Look out for a statue of the crucifixion in wood and marble by János Fadrusz, and hope to hear a snatch from the 10,000 pipes of Europe's third-largest organ.

The **Demetrius Tower** (*Dömötör torony*) is the city's earliest structure, with foundations dating to the 11th century and upper Romanesque and Gothic portions from the 13th century; it was discovered in 1925 during the demolition of a nearby Baroque church (which had been in danger of cramping the style of the square's new darling). The doorway arches contain carved stones salvaged from the former castle. At the northeastern corner of the square, the **Serb Orthodox church** was Baroque when built in 1778 before being remodelled in Louis-XVI style in the 1830s. It contains a beauty of an iconostasis by János Popovics; enquire at the priest's house opposite if the church is locked.

There are several research buildings in Dóm tér, including the biochemistry institute where Albert Szent-Györgyi conducted his 1937 Nobel-Prize-winning work (see box page 344). An arcade running around the square's southern end holds a **pantheon** of Hungarian stars, from royals to revolutionary poets and egg-headed scientists. On the hour, the **musical clock** chimes above, and carved figures emerge representing graduating students passing before the university council; the woodcarver took Sándor Petőfi and András Dugonics as his models, among others. There is a small collection of items from the churches of Csongrád and Békés counties in the **Ecclesiastical Museum and Treasury** (*Egyházmegyei Múzeum & Kincstár; Dóm tér 5;* ✆ *62 420932; adult/concessions 100/50Ft; open Mon–Sun Apr 1–Oct 31 10.00–18.00, rest of yr 10.00–16.00*), the oldest from 15th-century Franciscan friaries. The friars were particularly important during the Turkish occupation as they were the sole priestly community widely tolerated by the Turks, and were consequently the only ones carrying out pastoral services in southern Hungary.

Behind Dóm tér is **Aradi vértanuk tere**, with a monument to the Martyrs of Arad (see page 19) and an equestrian statue of Rákoczi II. Most striking, however, is the arch leading out on to Boldogasszony sugárút. The **Gate of Heroes** (*Hősök kapuja*) was erected in 1937 ostensibly to honour the soldiers of World War I but more specifically the commandos of Admiral Horthy. In 1919 the counter-revolutionary government (including Horthy) sat in Szeged, and it was from here that the 'White Guard' left to scour the Great Plain for 'Reds' after the defeat of the Republic of Councils. It was the spark for the neo-fascist terror that followed the communist terror under Béla Kun. Vilmos Aba-Novák's cartoon-like frescoes on the underside of the arch were painted over during the communist period; it took 23 artists and 60 million forints to restore them between 1995 and 2001. If you look left from the arch along Lajos körút, you'll see the steel **Flood Memorial**, erected on the river bank to mark the centenary of the great flood.

### Roosevelt tér and beyond

Moving northwards, Roosevelt tér stands at the western bridgehead of the Belvárosi híd. The **Móra Ferenc Museum** (*Roosevelt tér 1–3;* ❯ *62 549040;* e *info@mfm.u-szeged.hu; adult/concessions 400/200Ft; open Tue–Sun Jul 1–Sep 30 10.00–18.00, rest of yr 10.00–17.00*) stands in the 1896 Neoclassical former Palace of Education and Culture. It is a weighty museum, with late-19th- and early-20th-century art (by painters like József Rippl Ronai and Vilmos Aba-Novák, the latter of Heroes' Gate fame) – keep an eye out for Pál Vágó's depiction of the devastation wrought by the 1879 flood – a display of natural history and geology, the furnishings of an 18th-century pharmacy moved here from Klauzál tér, and a memorial room devoted to Ferenc Móra. Móra was a writer and amateur archaeologist, one-time director of the museum and responsible for unearthing many of the finds on show. The richest collection documents the arrival of early tribes, including the Huns (whose 5th-century campaigns in Europe triggered the age of migrations by Asiatic peoples into the Carpathian Basin), the Avars who came in 567AD and finally the Magyars in the 9th century; it was a time of warriors, and there are fearsome bows and swords among the grave goods, as well as a double burial of an 8th-century Avar couple excavated by Móra at Fehér-tó.

In the riverside garden behind the museum are the remains of Szeged Castle, which was originally built in the 13th century and survived several battles over its walls, both prior to Turkish occupation and during the War of Independence. During the 19th century it operated as a prison, before finally being brought down by the 1879 flood, when the eastern wall and northeastern tower collapsed into the river. The **Castle Museum** (*Stefánia sétány;* ❯ *62 470370;* e *varmuseum.szeged@museum.hu; adult/concession 200/100Ft; open Tue–Sun Jul 1–Sep 30 10.00–18.00, rest of yr 10.00–17.00*) has some stonework, a local-history display and temporary art exhibitions. (The Castle Garden itself has a great little space-age playground!)

A short distance west is the **Kass Gallery** (*Vár utca 7;* ❯ *62 420303; adult/concession 200/100Ft; open Tue–Sun Jul 1–Sep 30 10.00–18.00, rest of yr 10.00–17.00*), with a permanent exhibition of works by graphic artist János Kass. In 1897 his grandfather designed the **Kass Hotel**, huddled at the split between Stefánia utca and Dózsa utca, just outside the Castle Garden. It was a place of luxury in its heyday, but was closed in 1977 and now stands gutted and empty, a forlorn Medusa's head looking down from the tympanum.

Continue northwards parallel with the river, and beyond Tisza Lajos körút is the **Pick Salami and Szeged Paprika Museum** (*Felső-Tisza-part 10;* ❯ *62 421814;* e *pick.szeged@museum.hu; www.adult/concessions 320/240Ft; open Fri 15.00–18.00, Sat 13.00–16.00*) at the Pick factory. Szeged is one of the country's leading manufacturers of salami, which was introduced to Hungary from Italy in the 19th century. Márk Pick produced salami from 1869 and had a paprika mill too. The museum charts the history of the factory and the salami-making process. Winter salami is the best-selling sausage, making up 47% of sales; when buying some, try to forget that horses' guts are apparently the special ingredient. In 1998 the Szeged Paprika Stock Company became part of the Pick Group, and there is now also a paprika museum on the first floor.

### The Jewish quarter and beyond

Moving northwest from Klauzál tér along Kígyó utca, and crossing the boulevard, you'll reach the old Jewish quarter. The Neoclassical **Old Synagogue** (*Régi Zsinagóga; Hajnóczy utca*) was constructed in 1843, a plain whitewashed building that is now used for concerts and drama during the summer festival. It was here that Rabbi Lipót Löw first preached in Hungarian and incorporated organ music into the Jewish liturgy; beside the entrance is a plaque marking the height to which the water rose in 1879.

Protected by yew trees behind it, the brick **New Synagogue** (*Új Zsinagóga; Gutenberg utca 13; adult/concessions 300/150Ft; open Sun–Fri Apr 1–Sep 30 10.00–12.00, 13.00–17.00, Jan 1–Mar 31 10.00–14.00, Oct 1–Dec 31 10.00–14.00*) is considerably more impressive –

indeed, is probably the most splendid synagogue outside the capital. It is one of 22 in Hungary designed by Lipót Baumhorn, completed in 1903 with Moorish-Art-Nouveau styling, and capped by a main cupola that reaches 48m. The interior is chock full of golds and blues and pink marble columns. Chief Rabbi Immanuel Löw (son of the rabbi mentioned above) was a botanist who had compiled lists of the flora and fauna mentioned in ancient Jewish literature, and the architect incorporated these species into the motifs of the walls, ceilings and windows. The drum of the cupola is held by 24 columns – symbolic of the hours of the day – and the glass dome is studded with stars against a darkening blue, conveying a sense of infinite space. On the supporting arch are painted the Hebrew words for work, culture and good deeds, the tenets by which the moral Jew should live. The altar stone was fashioned of marble from Jerusalem, and there are six bronze menorah set with semi-precious stones. Two black coffins in the entrance hall commemorate the innocents old and young who died during the Holocaust; a poem on the memorial plaque asks 'Do you see the baby choking with gas, /Carefully hidden in mother's embrace?/ Do you see the child standing next to the mother,/ Gazing upon its death with trembling heart and terror?'.

Out to the west, the **Szeged Wildlife Park** (*Szegedi Vadaspark; Kálvária sugarút;* \ *62 542530; www.zoo.szeged.hu; adult/concessions 360/260–310Ft; open daily Jan 1–Mar 31 09.00–16.00, Apr 09.00–17.00, May & Sep 09.00–18.00, Jun 1–Aug 31 09.00–19.00, Oct, Nov & Dec 09.00–16.00*) can be reached on trams 3 or 3A or bus 35. Just beyond the outer boulevard to the south (follow Szentháromság utca from Aradi vértanuk tere) is the Alsóváros (Lower Town), which preserves a rural, peasant feel and is the Roman Catholic heart. The Gothic **Church of the Blessed Virgin** (*Mátyás tér*) is a former Franciscan church built at the end of the 15th century, with a tower and Baroque furnishings added in the 18th century. Pilgrims come to see its *Black Madonna* of 1740, the focal point of an annual patronal festival on the first weekend in August. It was here and in the friary that the Franciscan monks carried out their pastoral work during the Turkish occupation (see page 369).

## Újszeged

New Szeged lies on the other side of the river from the centre, across Belvárosi híd. Industrial buildings and modern housing blocks are over here, but the area on and near the bank is where the people come to rest and play. The **Partfürdő** (*Közép-kikötő sor;* \ *62 430483; adult/concessions 700/450Ft; open May 1–Sep 30 daily 08.00–19.00*) is a strand right on the water, with a couple of pools, a small beach and a campsite. Behind it are the **thermal baths** (*Fürdő utca 1;* \ *62 431133; open Oct–Apr Mon–Fri 06.00–20.00*), containing two mineral-enriched pools to soak your bones in winter, and next to them the **Ligetfürdő** (*Torontál tér 1;* \ *63 431672; adult/concessions 700/450Ft; open May 1–Sep 30 06.00–20.00 daily*), with a large outdoor swimming pool and some smaller ones for children.

Further back from the shore is the Népliget, the city's largest park; it has tennis courts and an outdoor theatre. Even better, though, are the **University Botanical Gardens** (*Egyetemi Fűvészkert; Lövölde út 42;* \ *62 454 236; adult/concessions 250/170Ft; open Mon–Fri Apr 1–Oct 31 10.00–18.00, green house 10.30–16.00, Nov 1–Mar 31 09.00–16.00, greenhouse 10.30–15.00*), where you can enjoy evergreens, rose and rock gardens, dawn redwoods and pink sacred lotuses on a lake. The greenhouse has species ranging from harvested crops like pepper, coffee and cocoa to orchids and tropical plants. The gardens are south along the river-bank road; buses 70 and 84F run there.

## Shopping

**Herendi Porcelán** Oskola utca 21. The place to come for pieces of Herend china. *Open Tue–Fri 09.00–17.00, Sat 09.00–13.00.*

**Hollóháza** Kárász utca 13. Porcelain outlet specialising in Hungary's second-most-famous breakables. *Open Mon–Fri 09.30–18.00, Sat 09.00–13.00.*

**Mars tér Market** Standing next to the bus station, this outdoor market has rows upon rows of stalls selling clothes, flowers, fruit and veg. *Open Mon–Fri 05.00–18.00, Sat 04.00–15.00, Sun 04.00–12.00.*

**Pick ház** Szabadkai út 18. This small supermarket is one of the outlets selling the famous Szeged sausage, together with an assortment of accompaniments. *Open Mon 15.00–18.00, Tue–Fri 07.00–18.00, Sat 06.00–12.00.*

**Szeged Plaza** Kossuth Lajos sugárút 119. Large shopping mall containing bars and multi-screen cinema in the northwest of the centre. *Open 08.00–02.00 daily; shop hours Mon–Sat 09.00–21.00, Sun 10.00–19.00.*

**Universum** Oskola utca 23; ✆ 62 486984; www.bnb.hu. Foreign-language bookshop that serves universities and has a fair range of books in English. *Open Mon–Fri 09.00–18.00, Sat 09.30–13.00.*

## Festivals and events
The Szeged Open-Air Games (see page 366) in July and August are the city's main event; there are also beer festivals in June and July.

## MAKÓ
If Szeged's the local big cheese then it is appropriate that Makó provides the onion. Twenty kilometres to the east, Makó is the undisputed champion of the onion, with an **Onion Festival** in September and an **Onion House** (*Posta utca*), designed by Imre Makovecz to look as though 'growing out of the soil'. A Calvinist priest began cultivating the vegetable during the 18th century; he leased plots to tenant farmers and by the 19th century it had taken root to such an extent that it was being exported all over Europe.

This is also where Attila József (see box, page 369) went to school and published his first poetry. He stayed for a time at the **Espersit House** (*Kazinczy utca 6; adult/concessions 200/100Ft; open Tue–Sun 09.00–17.00*), home of a periodical editor and literary patron; today there is a collection devoted not only to Attila, but also to Gyula Juhász (who wrote here) and Ferenc Móra (a frequent visitor). The **Attila József Museum** (*Megyeház utca 4; ✆ 62 213540; adult/concessions 200/100Ft; open Tue–Sun 09.00–17.00*) has an exhibition covering the story of paprika production in Szeged, as well as 700 years of Makó history – including, inevitably, a section on onions in the gardening building of its *skanzen*.

The **town hall** (*Széchenyi tér 22*) was originally built in 1780 before taking its current Neoclassical aspect in 1836, while the **summer residence and adjacent chapel** (*Kossuth utca*) of the Bishop of Csanád date to 1826. The **thermal baths** (*Marcibányi tér 6; ✆ 62 212590*) are in the centre of town, and offer treatments using radioactive mud from the River Maros that'll leave you glowing.

There are numerous **buses** running to Hódmezővásárhely, one every 15 minutes to Szeged and up to five buses a day to Budapest Népliget. Makó **railway station** is on a small branch line which runs between Újszeged and Kétegyháza, and also on that north to Hódmezővásárhely.

## HÓDMEZŐVÁSÁRHELY
Its folk-art heritage has earned Hódmezővásárhely (25km northeast of Szeged) the nickname 'Peasants' Paris'; surviving pottery from the 19th century can be attributed to the hands of over 400 potters. The artistic seam continues to run strong, playing a prominent role in festivals and museum exhibitions, and there are two artists' colonies. Interestingly, rivalry led to traditional variations in style that you wouldn't usually expect to find within such a relatively small area; the output from Újváros (southeast of the centre) was a murky green in colour, while potters in the Tabán (northwest) used a bright yellow background, and those in Csúcs (northeast) preferred blue and white. The town is also renowned for its embroidery – table cloths and bed linen adorned with stylised motifs of plants and birds.

Hódmezővásárhely has been inhabited for 6,000 years, and in the medieval years between the Mongol invasion and the Turkish occupation (when the inhabitants fled and the structures were destroyed) it was made up of around 20 individual villages. When the peasants returned, they brought a radical fire with them – János Kovács Szántó led a revolt in 1894 over the failure to redistribute land after the abolition of serfdom, and the town continued to feature in agrarian proletarian movements up until World War II. Today the town is a pretty one, its streets lined with fragrant flowers; cycling is a popular way to get about, so keep your wits about you if you're walking near the pavement cycle paths.

## Getting there and away
The **bus station** (*Bocskai utca*) is 500m east of the centre – walk along Andrássy utca. Regular buses run to Békéscsaba, Csongrád and Szentes, and there are less frequent services to Budapest Népliget (five), Kecskemét (six), Szolnok and Debrecen (three). As well as the main **train station** (*Merleg utca*), there's a second station, Hódmezővásárhely Népkert, in the southern part of the town. All trains stop at both stations. There are up to 12 departures a day to Szeged, 11 to Békécsaba, eight to Szentes and seven to Makó. To get from the main station to the centre, turn left and walk into Kistópart utca before turning right into Bajcsy-Zsilinszky Endre utca, which leads into Kálvin tér.

## Information and other practicalities
**Petőfi Sándor Cultural Centre** Szántó Kovács János utca 7; ↘ 62 214750. Hosts cultural events (such as touring plays and folk-dance troops), and can get you up to speed on current entertainment in town. *Ticket office open Mon–Fri 15.30–17.30.*
**Szeged Tourist** Szőnyi utca 1; ↘ 62 534916. Can book rooms in private houses, arrange domestic tours and provide information – all the usual. *Open Mon–Fri 09.00–12.00, 13.00–17.00.*
**Tourinform** Szegfű utca 3; ↘ 62 249350; e hodmezovasarhely@tourinform.hu. A short distance northeast of the main square, the tourist office can give you a list of private rooms, as well as answer queries. *Open Mon–Fri 08.00–12.00, 13.00–16.00.*

## Where to stay
**Hotel Pelikán** (19 rooms) Ady Endre út 1; ↘ 62 245072. There's something of Butlins about the Pelikán, caught in a time warp where lurid sofas and bedspreads are *de rigueur*. Nevertheless, it is centrally located on the main road adjacent to the thermal baths, which guests can use free of charge. *Sgl 7,500Ft, dbl 10,000Ft.*
**Thermal Camping** Ady Endre út 1; ↘ 62 245033. Adequately equipped site next to the thermal baths (and behind the Hotel Pelikán). The bungalows are not en suite. *Camping adult/concessions 900/650Ft, tent 550/330Ft, bungalow 1,500/1,000Ft.*
**Hotel Fáma** (15 rooms) Szeremlei utca 7; ↘ 62 222231. A good 2-star hotel with a small garden and rooms of varying size and price. Located just northeast of Kálvin tér. *Sgl 6,500–7,500Ft, dbl 7,900–8,900Ft; apt 9,500Ft (for 1), 11,500Ft (for 2).*
**Kenguru Panzió** (18 rooms) Szántó Kovács János utca 78; ↘ 62 534842; e kenguru@vasarhely.hu; www.kenguru.vasarhely.hu. This first-rate guesthouse is the town's best, its AC rooms fresh and contemporary with wooden flooring and whitewashed walls. There's a little outdoor pool, a solarium and sauna. The young staff are on the sullen side, but otherwise all's hunky-dory. To the north of town, on Road 45 (that runs towards Szentes). *Dbl 8,250Ft, room for 4 12,900Ft, apt 12,900Ft; b/fast 800Ft.*

## Where to eat and drink
**Anno Vendéglő** Road 47; ↘ 62 713145. It's 4km from the centre (just before the 204km marker) in the direction of Szeged, but worth the journey for excellent Hungarian and international cuisine, and a romantic ambience. *Mains 950–2,800Ft, avg 1,600Ft; open 11.00–23.00 daily.*

**Bagolyvár** Kaszap utca 31; ✆ 62 245726. On a road branching from the eastern end of Andrássy út, 'Owl Castle' has delicious food, attentive staff and a top-notch atmosphere. There's an extensive choice – including spaghetti, steaks, vegetarian paella and shark fillet – and a charming dining area akin to an open-fronted pince. *Mains 850–2,500Ft, avg 1,400Ft; open 11.00–24.00 daily.*

**Bandula Kisvendéglő** Pálffy utca 2; ✆ 62 244234. Good international food and a menu that offers almost too many options, among them paella, chicken with Greek salad, pizza, spaghetti, chilli and steak. Also does takeaways. Stands just off Szántó Kovács János utca, 500m north of Kossuth tér. *Mains 750–2,700Ft, avg 1,300Ft; open 11.00–23.00 daily.*

**Casinó Pub** Hősök tere 2; ✆ 62 246964. Sit out on the elevated terrace and shoot the breeze with an ice cream or an ice-cold beer. There's a selection of chicken and pork dishes. *Mains 650–1,600Ft, avg 1,000Ft; open Mon–Thu 12.00–24.00, Fri–Sat 12.00–01.00, Sun 12.00–22.00.*

**Fekete Sas** Kossuth tér 3–5; ✆ 62 249363. At the western side of the main square, the custard-yellow Neo-Baroque 'Black Eagle' was built in 1905 by Gyula Pártos, and was once a hotel favoured by foreign merchants. The interior of the café-cum-brassiere is shabbily chic, and it spills outside with wicker chairs and parasols. Outside is János Pásztor's *Girl with a Jug*. *Open 11.00–24.00 daily.*

**Sarokház** Kossuth tér 7; ℄ 62 243384. Set back from the road among Kossuth tér's greenery, this café is the perfect place to catch up with people or watch them go by. While stuffing down cake. *Open Sun–Thu 09.00–21.00, Fri–Sat 09.00–22.00.*

## What to see and do

**Kossuth tér** is popular with smoochers and cyclists, but it's also a shady square in which to enjoy a rest and survey some of the town's statues and architecture. A representation of Kossuth by Kallós Ede stands in the northern segment in front of a pink-faced **bank** (*Kossuth tér 5*) with a black dome and winged Mercury (next to the Fekete Sas; see opposite). The heavyweight sights of interest fall at the southern end, however. The Eclectic **town hall** (*Kossuth tér 1; open Mon–Fri 08.00–15.30*) was built 1892–93 by Lajos Ybl, and has a 56m central tower with a viewing balcony. When there aren't functions going on, you can also visit its luxurious ceremonial hall. Outside is a rearing equestrian statue by János Pásztor, erected to commemorate World War I.

The **Alföld Gallery** (*Kossuth tér 8;* ℄ *62 242277;* e *alfoldi.hodmezovasarhely@museum.hu; adult/concessions 120/60Ft; open Thu–Sun 10.00–17.00, Tue–Wed 10.00–16.00*) occupies a Neoclassical former grammar school of the 1820s, and is dedicated to art of the Great Plain between the mid 19th and mid 20th centuries. Among the sculptors represented are János Pásztor, Miklós Izsó and Ferenc Medgyessy, while the paintings include some of the forgotten 718 canvases by local artist János Tornyai (1869–1936) that were found below the floor of his former Budapest studio in 1984. Across the road is the **Calvinist 'Old Church'** (*Református Ótemplom; Kossuth tér*), Romanesque in style and constructed in 1713–14. A rampart with loopholes was added in 1941, part of which still remains behind the church. The **Bakay Well** next to Szeged Tourist, with water pouring from the mouths of lions, was the town's first artesian well. Zsigmond Béla actually sunk it at another spot in 1880, but it was moved hither later.

South of the gallery is a **Calvinist grammar school** (*Szőnyi utca 2*) that has operated here since 1896, while behind that runs a 3km-long **defensive wall** representing a lesson learnt after floodwater devastated Szeged in 1879. Move northward from Kossuth tér to a crumbling late-18th-century Baroque Greek Orthodox church (*Görögkeleti-templom; Szántó Kovács János utca 7*) in dire need of work, and the **Tornyai János Museum** (*Szántó Kovács János utca 16–18;* ℄ *62 242224; adult/concessions 200/100Ft; open Thu–Sun 10.00–17.00, Tue–Wed 10.00–16.00*) opposite. The museum exhibitions (which have explanatory notes in English) include local archaeological finds (a corn jar from 2,600BC, a 'God with a Sickle' from 2,700BC, and a fertility statuette of the New Stone Age dubbed the 'Kőkénydomb Venus'), a memorial room devoted to the ethnographer Lajos Kiss (who was born here in 1881, and who provided many of the exhibits), a display of the popular art in which the town is steeped, and paintings by János Tornyai.

If you want to see some more vernacular art, the **Folk Art House** (*Népművészeti tájház; Árpád utca 21;* ℄ *06 20 444 0560; adult/concessions 200/100Ft; open 09.00–12.00, 15.00–18.00*) is situated in the middle of a grassed area surrounded by residential blocks southeast of the Old Church. It is actually made up of two 18th-century houses, and has collections of local pottery and embroidery. Around 1,500m north of the centre, the **Csúcs Pottery House** (*Fazekasház; Rákóczi út 101;* ℄ *62 242224; open Apr 16–Oct 14 Tue–Sun 13.00–17.00*) shows the workshop and living space of Sándor Vékony, a past master potter, together with pieces by other renowned craftsmen. You can watch the workers in action – and buy samples – at the **Embroidery Workshop** (*Bajcsy-Zsilinszky utca 18–22;* ℄ *62 241284; open Mon–Thu 07.30–16.00, Fri 07.30–13.00*) and the **Belvárosi Fazekasház** (*Lánc utca 3;* ℄ *62 533024;* e *keramix@freemail.hu; open Mon–Fri 10.00–18.00, Sat 10.00–14.00*), where Sándor Ambrus turns his wheel. Tourinform can provide a list of other craft workshops, with artisans involved in wood carving, basket weaving and lace making.

Hódmezővásárhely has its share of houses of worship, representing various creeds; if you head east from Kossuth tér along Andrássy út you'll pass an 18th-century **Roman Catholic church** (*Andrássy út 11*), with Baroque and Neoclassical styling, and 19th-century additions that include aisles designed by Miklós Ybl. On the same road is the **László Németh Town Library** (*Városi Könyvtár; Andrássy út 44;* ❧ *62 245378;* e *nemeth.hodmezovasarhely@museum.hu; adult/concessions 150/75Ft; open Mon 13.00–18.00, Tue–Fri 09.00–18.00, Sat 09.00–16.00*), whose adjacent memorial exhibition contains some of the personal effects of László Németh; the great writer and thinker taught at the girls' grammar school in the late 1940s.

Andrássy út culminates in Kálvin János tér, with the white **Calvinist 'New Church'** (*Újtemplom; Kálvin János tér 7*), younger counterpart to that in Kossuth tér; built in 1799, it's one of the largest of its denomination in the Great Plain. The square's **artesian well** was designed by András János Nagy in 1884; the mayor had requested that it be placed in the grounds of a school, but Nagy insisted that it be enjoyed by the whole community. To the north of it is the mid-19th-century cream-coloured **synagogue** (*Szent István tér*), with a Secessionist façade added in 1908 by Miksa Müller; the stained-glass panels in its doors remind us of Moorcroft pottery. The **Roman Catholic church** (*Szent István tér 4*) was erected in the style of an old Christian basilica in 1936. István Maté's young Szent István – to whom the church is dedicated – patrols atop his steed outside.

### Other activities
South of Kossuth tér, the **thermal baths** (*Ady Endre út 1;* ❧ *62 244238; adult/concessions 500/250Ft; open 08.00–20.00 daily*) sit in an 8ha park; there are eight pools, with medicinal water, as well as sauna and massage facilities.

**Aranyági Stud Farm** (*Serháztér utca 2;* ❧ *06 30 218 3354;* e *hodmgrt@hodmgrt.hu*) is a century-old breeding and training farm for Furioso-North Star half-breds from Mezőhegyes. It has an inn, and you can take riding lessons, have a turn in a carriage or watch a horse show. You'll find it 4½km northeast on Road 47 (follow Szent István utca out of town towards Orosháza). Alternatively, the **Dél-Alföldi Lovasudvar** (*Tanya 4010;* ❧ *06 30 514 8860*) is an equestrian yard 2½km west of the centre that can organise riding tours and shows, and has a small guesthouse.

### Festivals and events
During the St George's Day Agricultural Festival at the end of April, farmers gather to celebrate spring with an animal show and competition. There are cultural events during the Autumn Weeks in October, and – as elsewhere in the country – the town goes big on celebrating Szent István on August 20 (and the days around it).

## MÁRTÉLY
Ten kilometres to the northwest, Mártély is a resort village by a backwater of the Tisza. There's a sandy bank for sunbathing, trees under which to picnic and water craft to paddle around in (*pedalo 900Ft/hr, rowing boat 600Ft/hr*). Beyond the Tisza embankment is a landscape protection area, a region of floodland that holds frogs, great white egrets and herons. For those who want to stay, a number of private holiday homes (*üdülős*) are set back from the bank – the Tourinform in Szeged has a list. **Hunnia Panzió** (*Árnyas uyca 5–7;* ❧ *06 30 507 6692; www.hunia.de; Jul–Aug €285/week, May, Jun & Sep €200/week*) is one such, with two self-contained sections holding five guests each. Otherwise **Tiszapart Camping** (❧ *62 228057; Camping adult/concessions 800/600Ft, tents 800Ft, cabins 1,800Ft*) is a lovely site 300m from the water with wooden cabins. Regular **buses** run here from Hódmezővásárhely.

*Above* Green lizard peeping from a hole in a quarry in the Zemplén Hills, Bükk National Park (BS)
*Below left* Great bustard at the Dévaványa rehabilitation centre, Körös-Maros National Park (BS)
*Below right* Common hawfinch, whose heavy bill can tackle the hardest of seeds (BS)

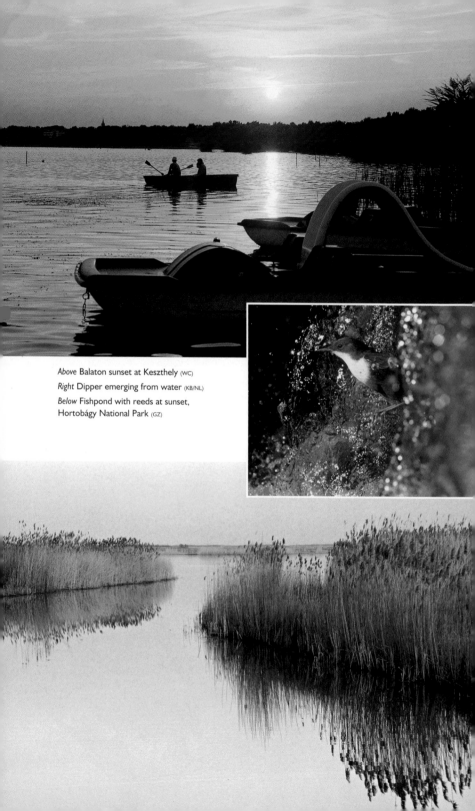

*Above* Balaton sunset at Keszthely (WC)
*Right* Dipper emerging from water (KB/NL)
*Below* Fishpond with reeds at sunset,
Hortobágy National Park (GZ)

# OROSHÁZA AND GYOPÁROSFÜRDŐ

There is little of note to send you charging to Orosháza itself – the odd museum and church won't detain you for long. However, people *are* drawn by the resort of Gyopárosfürdő 3km to the west, with its lake and thermal baths, and this is also a good base for exploring one pocket of the Körös-Maros National Park. Fehér-tó at Kardoskút is of genuine value to birdwatchers, and is but 12km away as the short-toed lark flies.

The proud spirit of resistance blazed strong in Orosháza. Some of its people fought with the Rákóczi battalion founded by Pál Vasvári (which was obliterated in 1849 during a struggle against Romanian insurgents fighting for the Habsburgs), and in the aftermath of the War of Independence the wife of Lajos Kossuth was one among many refugees who sheltered here. That single night of safety cost Ferenc Mikolay dear; the son of the pastor was given a ten-year prison sentence for harbouring the lady fugitive.

## Getting there and away

The main Orosháza **railway station** (*Állomás tér*) is at the junction of three lines; trains through this station also serve the town's other three smaller stations. There are trains to Szarvas (five), Békéscsaba (14), Szeged and Hódmezővásárhely (12) and Szentes (five). It's 600m from the station to the centre; walk straight ahead, turn right into Október 6 utca and first left on to Kossuth Lajos utca, which leads to the centre.

The **bus station** (*Március 15 tér*) is 150m south of the railway station; there are very regular services to Békéscsaba, and regular to Szeged, Szentes and Hódmezővásárhely. You can also access towns including Debrecen (seven), Szarvas (12) and Csongrád. Buses to Budapest require a change at Szentes.

For Gyopárosfürdő, you can follow Szentesi út west from Orosháza's Kossuth tér, or take local buses 2 or 4.

## Information

**Tourinform** Fasor utca 2/A; ↘ 68 414422; e oroshaza@tourinform.hu. The staff of this office were tripping over themselves to be helpful during our visit. Found behind the train station at the top of Fasor utca in Gyopárosfürdő. *Open Mon–Fri 08.00–16.00.*

## Where to stay, eat and drink

There are very few places to stay in Orosháza; unless otherwise indicated, those below are in Gyopárosfürdő.

**Amadeus Coffee House** Orosháza, Győri Vilmos tér 2; ↘ 68 472573. Centrally located café, serving coffee, alcohol and ice cream.

**Fehér Hattyú Panzió** (7 rooms) Fasor utca 13; ↘ 68 510330; e pansio@feherhattyu.hu; www.feherhattyu.hu. The swish 'White Swan' is best for eats and sleeps. Its delightful rooms are tastefully decorated and have a real holiday feel to them. The restaurant (*mains 760–2,450Ft, avg 1,300Ft; open 06.00–24.00 daily*) serves tasty food, its menu featuring Hungarian classics with an international twist in places. *Rooms: sgl 11,500Ft, dbl 12,500Ft, triple 16,000Ft, room for 4 18,000Ft.*

**Hotel Flóra** (15 rooms) Hűvös utca 8; ↘ 68 419753. Small but friendly 2-star hotel on the bank of the boating lake, north of the thermal baths. Its grounds are green, there's a tennis court, sauna and solarium, and the simple (but sizeable) rooms have balconies. *Sgl 7,800Ft, dbl 9,800Ft, apt (for 4) 14,000Ft.*

**Napfény Recreation Centre** Orosháza, Táncsics Mihály utca 26; e rekreal@rekreal.hu; www.rekreal.hu. The 'Sunshine' centre (follow Táncsics Mihály utca north from the top of Győri Vilmos tér) is a jack of all trades, a meeting point offering services to townsfolk and tourists alike – there are fitness classes, tennis courts, wine-tasting sessions, a gym, a beauty parlour, a restaurant and a bar. Some guestrooms are squeezed in among the other facilities. *Dbl 9,000Ft.*

**Thermal Camping** Fasor utca 3; ℩ 68 512260; www.gyoparosfurdo.hu. There are various accommodation options here, right on top of the baths complex. Wooden bungalows on the lake shore sleep 3–5 (only the largest have bathrooms and cooking facilities), there's a basic hotel and space on the site for 30 tents and 8 caravans. Guests can enter the thermal baths free. *Camping: adult/concessions 900/700Ft, tent 200Ft/m², c/van 300Ft/m²; bungalows: 6,800Ft (for 3), 8,400Ft (for 4), 10,000Ft (for 5).*

**Tópart Panzió** Tópart utca 11; ℩ 68 413202. On the opposite side of the lake from the Flóra, the 'Lakeshore' is an adorable panzió in a restful setting. The rooms are furnished with pine and flooded with light. You'll try in vain not to love it. *Dbl 11,500Ft, apt 16,500Ft; b/fast 1,000Ft/pp.*

## What to see and do
### The town

The **Szántó-Kovács Museum** (*Dózsa György utca 5;* ℩ *68 412853; adult/concessions 300/150Ft; open Tue–Fri 08.00–16.00, Sat–Sun 10.00–15.00*), to the west of Szabadság tér, is an ethnographic and historical collection relating to Orosháza and surrounding villages, and displaying items ranging from the military to the agricultural (including those of the Lutheran peasant families from Zomba near Szekszárd, who repopulated the town after the Turkish occupation). Further along the same street, the **Darvas József Literary Memorial House** (*Irodalim Emlékház; Dózsa György 74;* ℩ *68 311693; admission free; open Tue–Fri 08.00–12.00, Sat–Sun with prior notice*) occupies the childhood home of early-20th-century writer and socialist cultural politician József Darvas. The front room has the family furniture, together with photos and documents, while a memorial room is devoted to the work of the man himself. A wheelwright workshop at the back was used by the writer's brother, and a building in the garden now holds the Békés County Literary Collection, whose purpose is to gather the manuscripts and other objects belonging to local artists.

The oldest building in town is the late-Baroque **Lutheran Church** (*Győri Vilmos tér*), its clocktower constructed in 1777 and the southern transept added in 1830. This was the house of worship for the original Lutherans who set up shop after being hounded from Zomba because of their religion; in front of the altar is the bell they brought with them. To the east of it is the **Táncsics Mihály Grammar School** (*Mikszáth utca*), a broad Neoclassical building named after the politician who represented the town between 1869 and 1872. The memorial park in front – with scattered chunks of stone and a central bell bearing the date 1744 – was erected on the 250th anniversary of the settlers' arrival.

Head northwards up Táncsics Mihály utca for the **Calvinist church** (*Könd utca*), a palatial white church with three towers that was built in 1917. Opposite it is the **Well Museum** (*Kút Múzeum; Könd utca 1;* ℩ *68 417707; admission free; open Apr 1–Sep 30 Mon, Wed & Fri 12.00–16.00, other times by prior notice*), a tiny former water tower displaying disused pumps and photos of shadoofs. It's Hungary's only museum devoted to wells, and a visit here will show you why; it puts the 'well' in well dull. Better is the **Town Gallery** (*Thék utca 1;* ℩ *68 412523; open Tue–Fri 10.00–12.00, 14.00–17.00, Sat 10.00–16.00*), near the bus and train stations, which has works by artists including István Boldizsár, Ferenc Bolmányi, Gyula Pap and Orosháza-born photographer Miklós Müller. The **arboretum** (*Gárdonyi Géza utca 12; open 08.00–17.00 daily*) is off Rákóczi Ferenc utca, just beyond the railway track, and contains over 2,000 plant species.

### Gyopárosfürdő

Go west for 3km to Gyopárosfürdő, a spa resort (since 1869) concentrated around a natural saline lake. Reed beds and carpets of grass make this a verdant spot for a stroll, and you can swim in, fish in or boat on the water. (There is even an international model-boat competition on the lake at the start of May.) The adjacent complex of **thermal baths** (*Fasor utca 3;* ℩ *68 512260;* e *furdort@oroshaza.hu; www.gyoparosfurdo.hu; adult/concessions*

*1,000/700Ft; outdoor baths open May 1–Sep 30 daily 08.00–19.00; health centre open Mon–Fri 07.00–15.00*) is a big thing, fed by two deep wells and including indoor and outdoor pools, a health centre offering therapies, an assortment of sports facilities and a campsite. The mineral-rich water is thought to be good for treating rheumatic and skin complaints. You can climb the former water tower for views of the lake system.

## Festivals and events
The Summer Cultural Days feature a week of concerts and cabarets at the end of June, while the Bread Festival in August reminds that the town had an international reputation for baking at the start of the 20th century.

## KARDOSKÚT (AND FEHÉR-TÓ)
Twelve kilometres south of Orosháza is Kardoskút, a diminutive village surrounded by agricultural land. To the west of that (next to the road running between the village and Hódmezővásárhely) is the strictly protected Fehér-tó (White Lake), so-named because of the colour of the sodium carbonate deposited on the lake bed during periods of drought. Part of the Körös-Maros National Park (see box, page 380), this is regarded as one of the country's most valuable conservation areas. It represents a vital stop-over site for aquatic and grassland birds, which rest here and feed on the surrounding *puszta* and farmland. Among the nesting birds are the avocet, Kentish plover, godwit, short-toed lark and lapwing, while migrating species alight in vast numbers – in spring and autumn there might be as many as 50,000 geese, 100,000 ducks and flocks of up to 20,000 common cranes (1% of the entire central European crane population) spending a night. Other occasional visitors are the critically endangered slender-billed curlew, the demoiselle crane, the red-breasted goose, the lesser-white-fronted goose and the white-tailed eagle (drooling at the beak as it eyes up this preening smorgasbord). Around 142 bird species have been recorded at the lake, and this is ornithologist heaven. In addition, long-horned grey cattle graze on the saline pasture near by.

On entering Kardoskút from the Orosháza direction, follow the Hódmezővásárhely-bound road to the right for 3km and you'll arrive at the **Kardoskút Museum** (*Kardoskút;* ↘ *68 429262; adult/concessions 160/110Ft; open only with prior notice*), which has a small exhibition of the wildlife of the national park. Continue for a further 1km to the **White Lake Lookout Tower** (*free admission; open all yr*), a wooden viewing point where you can survey the birds and other wildlife of the surrounding flatlands. The lake itself lies to the west, and can only be visited with special permission; however, the watchtower provides an excellent platform, particularly during migratory periods. For further information, contact the Körös-Maros National Park Directorate (*Szarvas, Anna liget;* ↘ *66 313855*).

There are up to 15 buses a day to Orosháza. The **bus stop** is on the main road, just before the turn off for the watch tower and museum. The odd bus also runs to the museum. Kardoskút **train station** is on a small branch line that links Mezőhegyes to Mezőtúr, passing Szarvas and Orosháza along the way. There are up to seven trains a day along this route.

## BÉKÉSCSABA
Settled by Magyars during the 10th century, at the conclusion of the Turkish occupation the population of Békéscsaba amounted to a grand total of just 22 families. After victory in the War of Independence, the emperor gave Békés County to János György Harrucken, supplier of army provisions to the Viennese court; from 1715 Harrucken went about repopulating the village (which by the 19th century was apparently listed as Europe's largest) with Protestant Slovak immigrants drawn by the promise of religious tolerance. In 1841 it was raised to the rank of market town, and the subsequent construction of railway lines from Pest to Arad and Nagyvárad to Fiume (Rijeka) led to economic development so significant that in the mid 20th century the town claimed the

title of county seat from Gyula. Today, along with remnants of its Slovak and Lutheran heritage, Békéscsaba is associated with its prized *csabai* sausage (the three-day Sausage Festival takes place in autumn) and its rebellious political past. The region was at the eye of the 'Stormy Corner' (*Viharsarok*), where 19th-century agrarian movements struggled for the rights of workers on feudal estates and initiated a series of violent rebellions.

## Getting there and around

The **bus station** (*Andrássy út 58*) is 1½km south west of the town centre – follow Andrássy út northeast to the centre. There are regular buses to Békés, Gyula, Orosháza and Szarvas. There are also up to 15 buses a day to Szeged, 11 to Debrecen, six to Kecskemét, three to Budapest and Szolnok and one to Pécs and Miskolc. Békéscaba **railway station** – just behind the bus station – is well-connected train-wise. There are up to 16 a day to Szolnok and Gyula, ten to Szeged and Hódmezővásárhely, up to 12 to Budapest and a handful to the Romanian capital of Bucharest.

### KÖRÖS-MAROS NATIONAL PARK

The Körös-Maros National Park, divided into 13 different pockets between the Tisza-Körös and Maros rivers, was established in 1997 and covers 51,000ha in total. It includes flood-plain forests, fishing lakes and the dead channels of the two rivers, as well as the remains of habitats left after the Sárrét regulation project (of the 1850s) such as marshes and saline meadows. The park plays host to some exceptionally rare plants, among them the pheasant's eye and nodding sage; the *Adonis transylvanica* and *Salvia nutans* are found only here. There are unusual species of fauna too, like the great owl moth, the steppe moth and the Mediterranean blind mole-rat.

In the northern part of Békés County (northwest of Békéscsaba), the Dévaványa-Ecseg Plain is a place of scattered farmsteads. Much of the landscape is barren steppe, but the area is particularly significant for holding a third of the country's population of the great bustard (and the largest population of the beefy bird in Europe). In 1941, 8,500 of them were counted here, but this had declined to 2,500 by 1985. The **Great Bustard Reserve** on the road running between Dévaványa and Ecsegfalva was established to protect and boost its numbers. While parts of the park can only be visited with special permission, the Réhely Visitor Centre (*Dévaványa-Réhely;* \ *66 483083;* e *rehelyi.devavanya@museum.hu; adult/concessions 350/240Ft; open Apr 15–Oct 31 Tue–Sun 09.00–17.00*) in a former granary is open to all. You can get close to the chicks, and adjoining fields and compounds hold traditional livestock – rare breeds such as the majestic Hungarian grey cattle, the curly-haired mangalica pig and spiral-horned racka sheep. These protected national herds provide an important gene pool. There are observation towers, nature trails, a permanent wildlife exhibition and video displays documenting the great-bustard programme; rooms are available to rent above the visitor centre. You can also follow several nature and cycling trails (*bikes for rent 300Ft/hr, 1,000Ft/day*)

Further south near Orosháza, **Fehér-tó** at Kardoskút (see page 379) is one of the top bird-conservation sites in the country. The Körös-Maros National Park Directorate (see page 386) can provide further information about the park's highlights, and arrange guides to the protected areas (*2,000Ft/hr*) and specialist guides for birdwatching or visiting some strictly protected areas (*5,000Ft/hr*). The *Körös-Maros Nemzeti Park* (1:90,000) map, produced by the national park, shows all the 13 areas and includes brief descriptions of each.

## BIG FAT BUSTARD

In steppic habitats – most notably the Körös-Maros, Hortobágy and Kiskunság national parks – you might spot one of the world's threatened species, the great bustard or sand grouse. This impressive 20kg giant of a turkey, with a wingspan of 2.3m, stands as tall as a mature roe deer. Threatened by hunting, habitat destruction and its unfortunate deliciousness to the human palate, Hungary treasures up to 1,300 (about 4%) of the heaviest flying bird on Earth.

Dedicated ornithologists may be lucky enough to see this bird's extraordinary mating display, which starts in March. Male birds appear virtually to turn themselves inside out, twisting their feathers by inflating special pouches to transform their normal brown colouring to a brilliant white. The great bustard's succulent meat was a favourite of banquets from Neanderthal times up to the Victorian era when, in one of the most elaborate dishes ever concocted (taking a whole day to cook), the bustard was stuffed, Russian-doll-like, with 15 other birds.

The Great Bustard Reserve at Dévaványa aims to conserve and consolidate. The bustard prefers large areas of cultivated land, and lays its eggs in fields of corn or alfalfa in early May. However, the harvesting of alfalfa often overlaps with the brooding period and the female can be scared away from her nest. The reserve incubates abandoned eggs in the hope of hatching the chicks and raising them until they are capable of fending for themselves.

## Information and other practicalities

**Békés Tourist** Andrássy út 10; \ 66 323448; e bekestourist@axelero.hu. Travel agency that specialises in tours of the Békés region, and can also answer questions. *Open Mon 14.00–18.00, Tue–Fri 10.00–18.00, Sat 10.00–14.00.*

**Csaba Centre** Andrássy út 37–43; \ 66 524530. Large American-style shopping centre at the western end of Andrássy út with all the usual retail suspects and a multi-screen cinema complex. *Open Mon–Sat 09.00–20.00, Sun 10.00–18.00 (although the cafés and cinema keep later hours).*

**Ibusz** Szent István tér 9; \ 66 325554. Exchange currency, and book private accommodation and tours. *Open Mon–Fri 08.00–16.00.*

**Listings magazine** *Békési Est*

**Tourinform** Szent István tér 9; \ 66 441261; e bekescsaba@tourinform.hu. Next door but one to Ibusz and opposite the Hotel Fiume. *Open Mon–Fri 09.00–17.00.*

**Weol Internet Café** Gyóni Géza utca 14–16.00; \ 66 452175. Internet access – 16 terminals costing 10Ft/min (students get a discount) – and coffee bar. *Open 10.00–24.00 daily.*

## Where to stay

**Arany János College** Lencsési út 136; \ 66 459366. Dorms rooms at rock-bottom prices in summer months; stands across the water south of Parkerdő in the Ifjúsági-tábor. *From 1,200Ft/pp.*

**Hotel Fiume** (39 rooms) Szent István tér 2; \ 66 443243. The Neoclassical building housing the hotel was constructed in 1868 on the site of a former medieval inn, and is named after the Nagyvárad–Fiume railway line. The rooms try hard to live up to the elegant promise of the restaurant (see page 382) – half of them containing Secessionist-style furnishings – but the accommodation is over-priced in spite of its central position. *Sgl 10,500Ft, dbl 14,500Ft, triple 18,900Ft.*

**Sport Hotel** (14 rooms) Gyulai út; \ 66 449449. If you're on a budget, the town's sports stadium (*Városi Sportscarnok*) is a 10-min walk east from Kossuth tér and has rooms running around the arena itself. Although very basic, they do have bathrooms and TVs and represent a cheaper option than the hotels right in the centre. *Dbls 5,800–6,200Ft.*

**House of Slovak Culture** (*Szlovák Kultúra Háza*; 11 rooms) Kossuth tér 10; ℩ 66 441750. This culture house was established in 1996 with the aim of promoting Slovak traditions and maintaining relations with Slovaks in neighbouring countries. As well as hosting temporary exhibitions and other programmes, it has a restaurant (see opposite) and good rooms with pine floors. *Sgl 6,500Ft, dbl 8,900Ft, apt 10,800Ft.*

## Where to eat and drink

**Hotel Fiume Restaurant** See page 381. The classy hotel restaurant has an excellent reputation, and is the pick of the town's eateries. Settle yourself outside among the flowerboxes on a warm evening. *Mains 620–3,500Ft, avg 1,600Ft; open Mon–Sat 07.00–22.00, Sun 07.00–18.00.*
**Jankay** Csaba Centre, Andrássy út 37. A permanently busy café where quiet moments are rare and the iced tea is beautifully refreshing. *Open Sun–Thu 08.00–22.00, Fri–Sat 08.00–24.00.*
**Márvány Cukrászda** Andrássy út 21; ℩ 06 30 409 6962. The best spot for cake and ice cream. *Open 08.00–22.00 daily.*
**Rolling Rock Café** Mednyánszky utca 1–3; ℩ 66 430265. Set back from the main street and overlooking a large fountain, the Rolling Rock has a canteen-style buffet selling dishes of

traditional Hungarian food and pasta. This is the place for a good budget lunch – a soup starter and pasta main course will set you back less than 700Ft. Expect to queue.
**House of Slovak Culture** See opposite. The house has a low-priced restaurant serving Slovak specialities and beer. *Mains 500–1,300Ft, avg 1,100Ft; open 11.00–23.00 daily.*
**Uj Trencsén Restaurant** Luther utca 17; ↘ 66 326830. Slovak and Hungarian cuisine in comely surroundings with fishing nets strung from the ceiling and tables divided by trellises. The atmosphere is lovely and the food very decent. *Mains 790–3,160Ft, avg 1,500Ft; open Mon–Thu 11.00–21.30, Fri–Sat 11.00–24.00, Sun 11.00–21.30.*

## Entertainment and nightlife
The town's cultural events take place in the town hall, the Lutheran Great Church (see below) and the **Jókai Theatre** (*Színház; Andrássy út 1;* ↘ *66 441527*). The latter was the first stone-built theatre in the area, erected in the 1870s and Eclectic in style, with white reliefs of musical muses on its exterior. You can find out what's on at the **County Cultural Centre** (*Luther utca 6;* ↘ *66 442122; open Mon–Fri 10.00–16.00, variable at w/ends*), including dates and times when the Philharmonic is performing in the Great Lutheran Church.

The wine bar **Gazsó** (*Andrássy út 10;* ↘ *66 323597; open 07.00–22.00 daily*) generally bursts at the seams with pavement drinkers chatting beneath the tables' parasols, while **Narancs Klub** (*Szent István tér 3; open Mon–Wed 14.30–22.30, Thu–Fri 14.30–04.00, Sat 18.00–04.00*) is a sweaty underground basement bar and club – all low ceilings and brick arches – haunted by the young. There are places to sit and chill, but they're fewer and further between on club nights (*Thu–Sat*), when booming base lines prevail.

## What to see and do
The speed of the town's 19th-century growth means that architecture pre-dating that period is in short supply. There's a 'David meets Goliath' face-off between the two Lutheran churches straddling Szeberényi tér. The '**Small Church**' (*Szeberényi tér 2*) of 1745 is one of the county's oldest. Until the end of the 1800s, services here were conducted in Slovakian before they became bilingual. The '**Great Church**' (*Szeberényi tér 1*) is a huge, Zopf-style affair completed in 1824 – at the time, the largest Lutheran place of worship in central Europe (and still the largest in Hungary); its tower reaches 70m, and the hall church can hold 6,000 people. Of course, the bigger they are the harder they fall, and in 1978 the building was badly damaged by an earthquake; renovation wasn't finished until 1983. The acoustics are first-rate, and there are regular concerts inside.

The cobbled **Kossuth tér** holds János Horvay's statue of the statesman; locals used to queue to drink yellowish water from the square's artesian well, but this was blocked up after World War II and now only the loin-clothed fisherwoman remains. Garay utca runs from the square's northeastern corner and leads to the **Slovak Folk House** (*Tájház; Garay János utca 21;* ↘ *66 327058; adult/concessions 100/50Ft; open Tue–Sun Apr 1–Oct 31 10.00–12.00, 14.00–18.00, Nov 1–Mar 31 10.00–12.00*), owned by a wealthy Slovak family in the 19th century. The ornate wooden verandah is typical of Slovak peasant architecture and would have been a meeting place for friends and neighbours, while inside is an open chimney that was used for smoking sausages.

**Széchenyi liget** is a small and peaceful park east of the folk house, on the other side of the Elővíz-csatorna (the canal that splits the town, and around which you'll hear the stuttered groaning of frogs on summer evenings). An **obelisk monument** is dedicated to the 2,000 victims of a cholera outbreak in 1831, which killed 2,000 locals. At the southern end of the park is the Neoclassical former **Ale House** (*Sörház; Kórház utca 4*), built in 1840, while across Kórház utca stands the hulking, six-storey **István Mill** (*Malom; Gőzmalom tér*), built in the early 20th century and still going strong. If you want to know more about the settlement's agricultural past, the **Grain Museum** (*Gabonamúzeum; Gyulai út 65;* ↘ *66 441026; adult/concessions 200/100Ft; open Apr 1–Oct 31 Tue–Sun 10.00–17.00*) lies 2km east of here in the Parkerdő, along Road 44 (heading towards Gyula). The thatched dwelling dates to 1824, and there is a romantic brick windmill, a statue park commemorating the 'personalities' in the history of grain improvement and a garden displaying the various grains grown in the county.

On the opposite side of Gyulai út from the mill is the **Munkácsy Memorial House** (*Gyulai út 5;* ↘ *66 442080; adult/concessions 150/80Ft; open Jan 7–Apr 30 Tue–Fri 09.00–16.00, Sat–Sun 10.00–14.00, May 1–Oct 31 Tue–Fri 09.00–17.00, Sat–Sun 10.00–16.00*), a mansion built by the Steiner family in the 1840s. The Steiners and Munkácsy were relatives, and the famous artist lived here for some time as a boy after the death of his parents. Some of Munkácsy's paintings are on display, as well as late-Biedermeier furniture belonging to the noble Omaszta family who inhabited the place after the Steiners. Look out too for one of the doors, which was fashioned by Munkácsy and betrays his initial training as a carpenter (see below).

Back on the western side of the canal, the **Munkácsy Mihály Museum** (*Széchenyi utca 9;* ↘ *66 323377; www.munkacsy.hu; adult/concessions 300/150Ft; open Tue–Sun Apr 1–Sep 30 10.00–18.00, Oct 1–Mar 31 10.00–16.00*) has more of the 19th-century artist's work. Munkácsy was a 'boy done good', an orphan and former joiner's apprentice born in 1844 who went on to become one of the country's premier painters. He settled in Paris in 1872, married the widow of a French baron, and devoted himself to painting religious scenes and portraits of society's cream (and their servants). The museum also has exhibitions of ethnography (charting the 18th-century influx of ethnic groups that included Serbs, Romanians and Germans alongside the Slovaks), natural history and modern fine art.

The imposing **town hall** (*Szent István tér 7*) was completed in 1873, its Eclectic façade orchestrated by Miklós Ybl. Its lovely central courtyard is the venue for Békéscsaba's main cultural event, the Town Hall Nights (Városházi Esték), which feature concerts and plays over three weeks in June. The pedestrianised **Andrássy út** launches itself westwards from the bottom of Szent István tér; the lively, tree-lined promenade is the main shopping street. The **Árpád Baths** (*Árpád sor;* ↘ *66 549800; adult/concessions 850Ft/600Ft; open 06.00–20.00 daily*), south of the centre on the other side of Bánszky utca, have thermal baths as well as a large swimming pool and fun slide.

## SZARVAS

Szarvas – 'Stag' – is at the western gateway to Békés County, lying on a backwater of the River Körös formed during 19th-century river regulation. After the Turks had run amuck, Count Harruckern (see page 379) settled Slovak peasants here. Real improvement came at the end of the 18th century, however, when a Lutheran priest, Sámuel Tessedik, introduced a building programme and agricultural reforms. After him, the aristocratic Bolza family continued the development, constructing several mansions and founding the arboretum. A sleepy place, it is nevertheless not immune to big events; it has twice hosted the four-day Equestrian World Festival (most recently in July 2005), when the town is overrun with people watching performances by 1,000 horsemen from 30 different countries.

### Getting there and around

The **bus station** is at the corner of Szabadság út and Bocskai István utca, and runs regular services to Békéscsaba. There are also buses to Szeged (eight), Gyula (seven), Budapest Népliget and Kecskemét (six), Miskolc and Debrecen (two). The **train station** (*Állomás tér*) is 1km east of the centre. From here turn left along Állomás utca and right into Szabadság út. Szarvas is on a small rail line running between Mezőhegyes and Mezőtúr via Orosháza, and there are up to seven trains a day along the route.

## Information and other practicalities

**Internet** The Panoráma Caffé (see below) has an internet terminal, although it's rather a relic. *Costs 250Ft/hr.*

**Listings magazine** *Békési Est*

**Tourinform** Kossuth tér 3; ↘ 66 311140; e szarvas@tourinform.hu. Maps, information and lists of cheap accommodation options. *Open May 1–31 Mon–Fri 09.00–17.00, Jun 1–Jun 14 Mon–Fri 09.00–17.00, Sat 09.00–13.00, Jun 15–Sep 15 Mon–Fri 09.00–18.00, Sat–Sun 10.00–18.00, Sep 16– Oct 31 Mon–Fri 09.00–17.00, Sat 09.00–14.00, Nov 1–Apr 30 Mon–Fri 09.00–16.00.*

## Where to stay

**Aranyménes Panzió** (10 rooms) Arborétum út; ↘ 66 313046; e menes-szarvas@freemail.hu; www.hotels.hu/menes_szarvas. This thatched, peasant-style guesthouse successfully blends the traditional with the modern, and is a superb choice. The rooms are clean and well equipped, and the staff can arrange carriage rides or horse-riding lessons. It stands on the other side of Road 44 from Erzsébet liget, just beyond the road running off to the arboretum. *Rooms €30–40.*

**Aranyszarvas** Arborétum út 36; ↘ 66 216480; e aranyszarvas@szarvasnet.hu. Smart new self-contained apts further along the road leading to the arboretum.

**Halászcsárda Panzió** I Ker 6; ↘ 66 311164; e lux@szarvas.hu; www.aqua-lux.hu. Tight up against the bridge over the Holt-Körös, the setting is as romantic as they come. The rooms are on the small side, but comfortable. *Dbl 10,000Ft.*

**Körös-völgye Panzió** (20 rooms) Budai Nagy Antal utca 12; ↘ 66 311127; e korosvolgye@szarvas.hu. This brightly painted pension with fairly average rooms stands 500m east of the river. *Rooms 5,000Ft/pp.*

**Liget Camping** Erzsébet liget; ↘ 66 311954; e liget@szarvas.hu; www.ligetpanzio.hu. The 6ha campsite is perched on the river bank in the town's park. Its villa-cum-guesthouse has 9 dbls and 2 apts (for up to 8), and there are 20 cabins with kitchens and bathrooms. The surroundings are lovely, there's a pool (as well as the river) to swim in, and you can hire both bikes and boats. *Camping adult/concessions €4/3, tent/carvan €3/5; cabin (for 4) €55; panzió dbl €63, apt (for 4) €105.*

**Lux Panzió** (11 rooms) Szabadság út 35; ↘ 66 313417; e lux@szarvas.hu. Located in the centre, this elegant pension has large rooms and is highly recommended. You'll wake to a good brekkie too. Fitness room, sauna and solarium. The owner also rents out summer cottages in the arboretum. *Sgl 7,500Ft, dbl 9,500Ft, apts from 11,900Ft.*

## Where to eat and drink

**Ciprus** Arborétum út 1/A; ↘ 66 311700. On the opposite side of the road from the Erzsébet liget, the Ciprus has an undulating roof that reaches to the ground, a tiered outdoor dining area overlooking the Bolza Mansion, and a Hungarian menu. *Mains 850–2,500Ft, avg 1,600Ft; open Sun–Thu 09.00–22.00, Fri–Sat 09.00–23.00.*

**Club 44 Pizzeria** Szabadság út 40; ↘ 66 313183. Opposite the Lux Panzió, Club 44 is popular after dark. You can eat pizza on the pavement terrace or play a game of pool inside. *Open Mon–Fri, Sun 08.00–24.00, Sat 08.00–02.00.*

**Galéria Grill & Bar** Szabadság út 2; ↘ 66 216380. Opposite the Tessedik Museum, there's grilled meat, pastas and salads to be had at the Galéria. *Mains 700–1,400Ft, avg 1,100Ft; open daily 10.00–24.00.*

**Kiszely Cukrászda** Kossuth tér 3; ↘ 66 311551. The pretty pink roundhouse next to the cultural centre serves cakes and ice-cream cones. *Open 09.00–21.00 daily.*

**Halászcsárda Vendéglő** See above. The restaurant of the Halászcsárda Panzió is lit with lanterns, and is the best of Szarvas's places to eat. The specialities are platters of fish. *Mains 850–2,100Ft, avg 1,600Ft; open Mon–Thu, Sun 09.00–23.00, Fri–Sat 09.00–24.00.*

**Panoráma Caffé & Pizzeria** Kossuth tér 3. Next to the Tourinform, the Panoráma is a good place to seek out shade if you get hot under the collar. The pizzas are fine. *Pizzas 500–1,400Ft; open daily 09.00–22.00.*

## Entertainment and nightlife

The **Vajda Péter Cultural Centre** (*Kossuth tér 3;* ↘ *66 311464; open Mon–Sat 08.00–17.00*) next to the Tourinform has concerts, plays and aerobic classes, and can offer information on arts events in town. In addition, there's a small cinema (Turul Mozi) inside.

There are several lively night spots in Szarvas. **Club Azték** (*Erzsébet liget/Szabadság út 12/C;* ↘ *06 20 9288098; open Fri–Sat 10.00–05.00*) hosts outdoor parties in Erzsébet liget in summer months on every Saturday and most Fridays; to get there, take the first left at the Halászcsárda and then the first right. In winter, the action moves to Szabadság út. **Club Marsall** (*Szabadság út 20;* ↘ *66 210218; open Wed 20.00–04.00, Sat 20.00–05.00*) is another winter disco venue.

The **Jazz Café** (*Kossuth utca 34;* ↘ *66 311652; open daily 10.00–02.00*) has a pleasant garden and mellow jazzy sounds, and is a better option than the very large Green House Irish Pub opposite.

## What to see and do

The **Tessedik Sámuel Museum** (*Vajda Péter utca 1;* ↘ *66 216608;* e *muzeum@szarvas.hu; adult/concessions 200/100Ft; open Tue–Sun Apr 1–Oct 31 10.00–16.00, Nov 1–Mar 31 10.00–15.00*) is housed in the former agricultural school, which was the first of its kind in eastern Europe. Today the museum has ethnographic and archaeological exhibits, together with a display about the 19th-century scientist and Lutheran priest who contributed so significantly to the town in ways agricultural and otherwise. There's a statue of Tessedik near by on Szabadság út, and a plaque to him outside the 18th-century Baroque **Old Lutheran Church** (*Vajda Péter utca*) – which he built – just north of the museum.

The Neoclassical **Bolza Mansion** (*Szabadság tér*) of 1780 stands on the bank of the Holt-Körös, and testifies to another family that put some plums in the town's pudding. The Bolzas came originally from Rome, and in front of the mansion is a statue of the babies Romulus and Remus being suckled by a wolf. You can't go inside, but you can walk in the grounds. There is a strand beyond the mansion where people swim and boat from the bank, while further up still is a historical park with a monument marking the geographical centre of historical Hungary (pre-Trianon; see page 20).

On the other side of the bridge from the mansion is **Erzsébet liget**, a charming little wood with walking trails and the Szarvas Watersport Camp (*Erzsébet utca 4;* ↘ *66 216369*), where you can hire kayaks and play tennis. In the southeastern section is the **Ruzicskay-ház** (*Erzsébet liget;* ↘ *66 312042; adult/concessions 200/100Ft; open May 1–Oct 31 Tue–Fri 09.00–16.00, Sat–Sun 10.00–15.00, Nov 1–Apr 30 Tue–Fri 09.00–15.00, Mar 1–Apr 30 Tue–Fri 09.00–15.00, Sat–Sun 10.00–15.00*), containing the private collection of Szarvas-born painter György Ruzicskay in his former residence, and including folk items gathered during his life.

In a crook of the river to the south is Anna liget, where you'll find the **Körös-Maros National Park Visitor Centre** (*Anna liget 1;* ↘ *66 313855;* e *kmnpi@szarvas.hu; www.kmnpi.hu; adult/concessions 250/150Ft; open May 10–Jun 15 Tue–Sat 09.00–17.00, Jun 16– Oct 31 Tue–Sun 09.00–17.00*). The centre is one of two in the national park (the other at Réhely; see box, page 380); it charts the history of the landscape between the Körös and Maros rivers, shows finds (including a skeleton dating back 6,000 years) and stuffed animals, and has a room detailing moves to prevent the smuggling of endangered species. A nature trail winds for 2km, with information boards in English and Hungarian, and a butterfly house was planned when we visited. You can also organise tour guides here for visiting protected areas of the park (see box, page 380).

Anna liget was originally the site chosen by József Bolza to plant some botanical rarities at the end of the 18th century. This seed was nurtured by subsequent generations of the family and now blooms as one of the country's premier arboretums 2km to the north (where it was moved by Pál Boza). The **Szarvas Arboretum** (↘ *66 312344;*

e *kert@szarvas.arbor.hu; adult/concessions 400/300Ft; open daily Mar 15–Nov 15 08.00–18.00, Nov 16–Mar 14 08.00–15.00, closed Dec 15–Jan 5*) covers 82ha and has 1,600 species of plant from all over the globe, among them swamp cypresses and a mammoth pine; to get there, pick up Arborétum út from opposite the entrance to Erzsébet liget.

Back on the other side of the river, the Gothic **New Lutheran Church** (*Szabadság út 70*) – with its slim, 67m tower – was constructed in 1896 as the congregation outgrew the Old Church; it catered for the Hungarian-speaking minority who requested that some services be held in their tongue. A short distance northeast of Kossuth tér, the thatched **Slovak Folk House** (*Szlovák Tájház; Hoffmann utca 1;* ✆ *66 312492; adult/concessions 120/60Ft; open Tue–Sun 13.00–17.00*) represents a typical 19th-century dwelling belonging to Slovak descendants of the immigrants who repopulated the town from 1722. At the end of Hoffmann utca, there's an intact **horse-driven dry mill** (*Szárazmalom; Ady Endre utca 1;* ✆ *66 313850; adult/concessions 300/175Ft; open Apr 1–Oct 31 Tue–Sun 13.00–17.00*) that worked from the early 19th century up until the 1960s.

# GYULA

Four kilometres from the border with Romania, Gyula is a compact settlement with a spa and the Great Plain's only surviving medieval brick fort. Sources disagree on whether the town was named after a Magyar chieftain of the conquest, a grandson of a chieftain, or the title by which the chieftains were known, but what is beyond doubt is that Gyula and its castle represented a regional stronghold – until the mid 20th century this was the county capital – and that the Turks were in possession of it from 1566 up until 1694. Like Békéscsaba, in the aftermath of the War of Independence the town fell under the ownership of Harruckern (see page 379), and was repopulated with Hungarian, Romanians and Germans – indeed, between 1734 and 1857 the town was divided into Hungarian Gyula (Magyargyula) and German Gula (Németgyula) – but unlike Békéscsaba its economic development was gradual, and the citizens retain something of a chip on their shoulders about the shift in power and county status.

## Getting there and around

The **bus station** is in the centre of town on Vásárhelyi Pál utca and the only frequent service is to Békéscsaba. There are less-regular buses to other destinations including Szeged (eight), Debrecen (five), Kecskemét (four), Budapest Népliget (two), Miskolc, Szolnok and Siofók (one). Gyula **railway station** is on an offshoot of the line from Békéscsaba and there are 11 trains a day running between the two towns. There are also trains to Budapest Keleti and Kecskemét (two), Szolnok and Eger (one). Up to three trains a day cross the Romanian border to Salonta. The station is at the northern end of Béké sugárút.

## Information and other practicalities

**Gyula Tourist** Eszperantó tér 1; ✆ 66 463026. Can organise private rooms and local tours. *Open Mon–Fri 08.00–17.00, Sat 09.00–12.00.*

**Listings magazine** *Békési Est*

**Tourinform** Kossuth Lajos utca 7; ✆ 66 561681; e bekes-m@tourinform.hu; www.gyula.hu. *Open Jun 15–Sep 15 Mon–Fri 09.00–20.00, Sat–Sun 09.00–18.00, rest of yr Mon–Fri 09.00–17.00.*

## Where to stay

**Corvin Hotel** (26 rooms) Jókai utca 9–11; ✆ 66 362044; e corvinhotel@mailbox.hu. The friendliest hotel in town – in a town where friendly hotels are unusually well represented – has bright, modern rooms, a good restaurant (see page 389) and its own jazz garden (with live bands playing thrice weekly). It's worth the slightly higher price. *Sgl 11,000Ft, dbl 13,500Ft.*

**Csigaház Panzió** (11 rooms) Csiga utca 12; ✆ 66 362417. You won't be blown away by the rooms – which are sufficient rather than special – but this is a very welcoming family-run

GYULA

guesthouse a short 50m from the baths. Bag one of the rooms with a balcony. *Room 4,000Ft/pp.*
**Family Appartements** (4 apts) Kossuth Lajos utca 13; ☎ 66 463725. Housed in the same
building as the theatre box office, these exclusive apartments – with bathrooms and shared
kitchens – are well recommended. To book one, ask at the ice-cream booth outside. *Sgl 6,000Ft,
dbl 10,000Ft, triple 12,000Ft, room for 4 15,000Ft, for 5 19,000Ft.*
**Halászcsárda & Panzió** (22 rooms) Part utca 3; ☎ 66 466303; www.halaszcsardapanzio.hu. A
clean, contemporary pension just west of the Hotel Park, with rooms that are furnished in a self-
consciously minimalist style. *Dbl 8,000Ft.*
**Hotel Park** (56 rooms) Part utca 15; ☎ 66 463711; e parkgyula@civishotels.hu;
www.civishotels.hu. Standing across the Élővíz Canal from the Castle Bath, the Hotel Park's
rooms are nicely kitted out, if a little on the cramped side. The hotel has a swimming pool, sauna
and solarium. *Sgl 9,500Ft, dbl 12,900Ft.*
**Thermal Camping & Motel** Szélső utca 16; ☎ 66 463551; e thermalcamping@bhn.hu. A 15-
min walk from the baths – and consequently less rowdy than 2 other campsites located closer –
there's a 27-room motel as well as oodles of space for tents. *Camping: adult/concessions 800/600Ft,
tent 800Ft; mo ☎ dbl 10,500Ft; open all yr.*

## Where to eat and drink
**Bols** Kossuth Lajos utca 18; ☎ 30 9787407. If ours were anything to go by, this coffee-and-cocktail
bar serves the worst cappuccinos in the country. Stick to the cocktails. There's a menu of snack-
type food (grills, salads, spaghettis, pizzas) in large portions. Close to the Tourinform. *Mains
530–1,500Ft, avg 900Ft; open Mon–Thu 09.00–24.00, Fri–Sat 09.00–02.00, Sun 11.00–24.00.*
**Corvin Hotel Restaurant** See above. A great place to dine, the Corvin's restaurant offers
traditional Békés and continental choices, and holds barbecues in the warm months. *Mains
850–2,300Ft, avg 1,950Ft; open 10.00–23.00 daily.*
**Halászcsárda Restaurant** See above. You absolutely *have* to sit outside under one of the
individual thatched-roof booths of this charming fish restaurant. *Mains 850–3,200Ft, avg 1,700Ft;
open 08.00–23.00 daily.*
**Hotel Park Restaurant & Beer Garden** See above. The Hotel Park's restaurant offers a very
pleasant backdrop, and specialises in Hungarian kettle dishes as well as international cuisine. In
summer, the food is cooked outside over an open fire. *Mains 750–2,600Ft, avg 1,700Ft; open
08.00–23.00 daily.*
**Kisködmön** Városház utca 15; ☎ 66 463934. Standing next to the Romantic former town hall, the
Kisködmön is named after a traditional Hungarian costume and aims to provide some traditional
Hungarian eating. *Mains 800–2,700Ft, avg 1,500Ft; open 12.00–24.00 daily.*
**Maestro** Kossuth Lajos utca 3; ☎ 66 560120. Maestro has a well-tended garden, a small bar and
two menus offering Hungarian cuisine or pizzas and pastas. A set lunch (*11.00–15.00*) can be had
for 500Ft or so. *Mains 750–1,800Ft, avg 1,300Ft; open Mon 11.00–22.00, Tue–Thu 11.00–23.00, Fri
11.00–24.00, Sat 12.00–24.00, Sun 12.00–22.00.*
**Öcsi & Fuszek Vendéglő** Kossuth Lajos utca 8; ☎ 66 468495. You certainly can't fault the prices
at this restaurant and boozer opposite the Tourinform. A 3-course lunch (*11.00–15.00 daily*) costs
just 570Ft/head. *Mains 800–1,700Ft, avg 1,200Ft; open Mon–Thu 08.00–24.00, Fri 08.00–02.00, Sat
10.00–02.00, Sun 10.00–24.00.*
**Százéves** Erkel tér 1; ☎ 66 362045. Hungary's second-oldest patisserie (after Ruszwurm in
Budapest), Százéves opened in 1840 in a building designed by Antal Czigler. Its elegant
Biedermeier interior, with white carrara-marble tables, presents a ready excuse to scoff a cake.
*Open 10.00–22.00 daily.*

## Entertainment and nightlife
The **Gyula Castle Theatre** (*Várszínház; Várfürdő utca;* ☎ *66 463148;* e *casteatr@axelero.hu;
www.c3.hu/~casteatr/progr_e.htm*), occupying the castle courtyard, is where the town's
main arts events take place in summer. Historical drama, opera, ballet, jazz and folk dance

are all performed here, and on a second stage jutting into the lake. Check the website for the programme timetable; there is a summer ticket office in the gatehouse at the entrance to the park (although tickets are also available from the box office at the Kamaraterem).

The **Kamaraterem** (*Kossuth Lajos utca 13;* \ *66 463148; ticket office open Mon–Fri 09.00–16.00*) is a 200-seat playhouse where the Castle Theatre company performs during winter (although there is talk of adapting the castle courtyard so it can be used in all seasons).

**Bacardi Café** (*Kossuth Lajos utca 3; open Mon–Thu 09.00–22.00, Fri 09.00–24.00, Sat 10.00–24.00, Sun 11.00–22.00*) is a modern bar with chrome seating and terracotta walls. **Macho Disco & Pub** (*Városház utca 1;* \ *06 30 540 7019; open Thu 11.00–24.00, Fri–Sat 11.00–06.00*) is the place for clubbing, with top-name DJs on the bill and Ministry of Sound gigs.

## What to see and do

**Gyula Castle** (*Várfürdő utca; adult/concessions 250/125Ft; open Tue 13.00–17.00, Wed–Sat 09.00–17.00, Sun 09.00–13.00*) was built in 1445. Alterations were made in subsequent years, and by the 16th century its walls were 3m deep. They repelled Dózsa's rebellious peasants in 1514, but were finally overrun by the Turks in 1566 (and held by them for 129 years). You can walk around the rectangular walls and climb its tower (*várkilátó*); the view is somewhat marred by the hulking presence of a nearby hotel. In the past there was an exhibition of cannon balls and other artefacts in the former chapel, and this might be resurrected at some point. The castle courtyard hosts theatre performances (see opposite), and the 16th-century round tower – added by János Corvin (the son of King Mátyás), and once holding gunpowder – has a café and bar. Beyond the walls is a **lake** surrounded by weeping willows trees, and you can hire little boats (or pedal cars from outside the Hotel Erkel). Near by too is the 18th-century **Almásy Mansion**, rebuilt in 1803 after a fire; it was here that 1,300 Hungarian officers surrendered to the Russian tsarist army on August 23 1849, among them nine of the Martyrs of Arad.

Lying to the south of the park are the **Castle Baths** (*Várfürdő; Várkert utca 2;* \ *66 561350; www.gyulavarfurdo.hu; adult/concessions 1,300/1,050Ft; open daily indoor pools 08.00–18.00, outdoor pools May 1–Sep 30 08.00–20.00*), which rank high among the country's spas. The water is medicinal, and the high mineral count gives it a brownish hue. The huge complex includes a new medical centre, open and covered pools (some of them curative and others recreational), saunas, wave machines, water slides, a children's playground and more. Snatch a moment's peace at the **Romanian Orthodox church** (*Gróza tér*), a slightly fusty-smelling church built in 1825, and with a floor-to-ceiling iconostasis depicting the 12 disciples and scenes from Christ's life.

**Dürer Terem** (*Kossuth Lajos utca 17; adult/concessions 250/125Ft; open Tue 13.00–17.00, Wed–Sat 09.00–17.00, Sun 09.00–13.00*) – named after Albrecht Dürer, the German Renaissance artist whose father originally heralded from Gyula – has temporary exhibitions. The nearby **Town Gallery** (*Városi Képtár; Károlyi Mihály utca 13; adult/concessions 400/200Ft; open Tue–Sun 10.00–14.00*) contains the private art collection of Dr Lajos Bene, featuring 19th- and 20th-century works, while to the west the **György Kohán Museum** (*Béke sugárút 35;* \ *66 361795; adult/concessions 400/200Ft; open Tue 13.00–17.00, Wed–Sat 09.00–17.00, Sun 09.00–13.00*) displays the distinctive art of the Cubist painter. Kohán was born in the town and bequeathed his paintings to the museum; they blend symbolic perception with the influences of folk art.

The **Inner City Church** (*Belvárosi templom; Harruckern tér*) was built in the 1770s, but its most spectacular feature is more modern. The ceiling frescoes show poignant historical moments – among them periods of famine in Africa and man's successful launch into space. A mother and child release doves, indicative of the artist's plea for peace and unity. Northwest of it is the **Ladics House** (*Jókai utca 4;* \ *66 463940;*

*adult/concessions 400/200Ft; open Tue 13.00–17.00, Wed–Sat 09.00–17.00, Sun 09.00–13.00*),
which – like the adjacent Százéves Cukrászda (see page 389) – was designed by Antal
Csizgler. The house has been preserved to showcase the inside of a typical 19th-century
town house owned by a wealthy family. There's a library, Venetian mirrors and Chinese
porcelain; it must have been a pig of a place to dust.

If you follow Jókai utca westward, you'll come to Apor Vilmos tér, with its late-
Baroque **Roman Catholic church** of the 1860s. Next to it is the **Erkel Ferenc
Memorial Museum** (*Apor Vilmos tér 7;* ✆ *66 463552; adult/concessions 400/200Ft; open Tue
13.00–17.00, Wed–Sat 09.00–17.00, Sun 09.00–13.00*), where the 19th-century 'father of
Hungarian opera' and composer of the music to the national anthem was born. Among
the objects relating to his life are a gold wreath that was presented to him and model stage
sets of some of his operas. It is said that he wrote some of his pieces from beneath a maple
tree in the castle park. The **Virgin Mary Collection** (*Apor tér 1;* ✆ *66 362169;
adult/concessions 300/150Ft; open Tue–Sun Mar–Nov 09.00–15.00, Dec–Feb 09.00–12.00*)
displays devotional objects and souvenirs.

## Festival and events
The Festival of Arts at the Castle Theatre runs from late June until early August, and
includes days of folk dance and folk music, and performances of ballet, operetta, jazz and
drama.

Great bustard

SOUTHERN TRANSDANUBIA

# Southern Transdanubia

Transdanubia (Dunántúl) covers the whole of Hungary's left-hand side, filling the area between the Danube and the borders with Croatia, Slovenia and Austria to the west and south of it, and punctured by Lake Balaton's diagonal gash. The region's landscape picks and chooses a little of everything, featuring hills, plains, brooks and lakes. It is economically richer than the eastern half, its industry drawing on supplies of minerals and fossil fuels; the workers can also enjoy a good spot of plonk, with the wines of Villány and Szekszárd among the best. With money comes architectural flourish, and there are beautifully kept centres. Western Transdanubia remained part of Royal Hungary during the Ottoman occupation and it both benefited from Habsburg building and preserved the monuments of earlier centuries that were ravaged by the Turks elsewhere. The Danube represented the eastern extent of the Roman empire in the first centuries of the first millennium, and Transdanubia – then the province of Pannonia – is where the residue of their stay lies in the pockets of Pécs, Szombathely, Sopron, Győr and Szekszárd. As you explore the region you'll also see regular evidence of much later struggles to consolidate territory, with fortified castles dotting the region's peaks.

★ ★ ★

Southern Transdanubia falls below Lake Balaton, running down to the Croatian border. The star of the show is Pécs, a cultured, pretty and welcoming city that offers a host of museums, some significant Ottomon and early-Christian architecture, and several vibrant festivals. There are hills to the north and south of it, the Mecsek the place for hiking and the Villány Hills for wine tasting, the district noted for its Cabernet-Sauvignon, Merlot and Kékoportó (Portugizier). The region also signals historical moments of tragedy and courage. Mohács is associated with one of the lowest points in Hungary's history, when the Turks massacred the Magyar forces in 1526 and effectively broke the country's back; by contrast, Szigetvár represents the ultimate display of bravery under fire, if still in a losing cause. For naturalists, the Duna-Dráva National Park plays host to the Gemenc Forest, an area of woodland and marshy lakes that is one of the country's richest nature reserves.

## SZEKSZÁRD

Around 50km northeast of Pécs, Szekszárd lies among hills above the River Sió. A Roman settlement called Alisca once stood here, on the Aquincum military route, and Béla I established a Benedictine monastery in 1061. The town thrived during the 15th century, although its castle was demolished by King Mátyás when he learnt of the landowner's involvement in a conspiracy against him. After the Turks had ravaged the place, it was repopulated with Germans, one legacy of which is the German-language

393

theatre (the only one of its kind beyond Budapest). It was made the seat of Tolna County during the 18th century, but the important architecture dates from the 19th century after a fire blazed through in 1794. Today it is renowned as the birthplace of the poet Mihály Babits and as a centre for some excellent red wine, notably Szekszárdi Kadarka and Bull's Blood. It is also close to the Gemenc Forest, numbered among the country's prime nature and game reserves.

## Getting there, away and around

Regular **bus** services run to Pécs, Dombóvár and Baja, and there are up to 16 buses a day that make the three-hour journey to Budapest Népliget. There are direct routes to Szeged (five daily), Kecskemét (three), Győr (two), Veszprém (four), Mohács (seven) and Keszthely (two). To reach Villány, Siklós or Harkány you will need to change at Pécs, while access to destinations in the Southern Great Plain including Szolnok and Debrecen require a change at Szeged or Kecskemét. There are two direct **trains** a day to Budapest Déli; services to Budapest Kelenföld require a change at Sárbogárd, as do trains to Kaposvár, Dombóvár and Pécs. Six direct trains a day go to Baja.

The **bus** and **train** stations (*Pollack Mihály utca*) are both located to the east of the town centre, which can be reached on foot in 15 minutes. Turn left from the train station (right from the bus station) and head westwards along Bajcsy-Zsilinsky utca. Turn left again into Mészáros Lázár utca and right into Mártírok tere which leads into the centre. **Taxis** usually gather outside Amaretto Cukrászda; one company is Rádió (✆ 74 411411).

## Information and other practicalities

**Ibusz** Széchenyi utca 20; ✆ 74 319822. Can arrange private accommodation, local tours and currency exchange (there is also a Western Union office inside). *Open Mon–Fri 09.00–18.00, Sat 09.00–12.00.*

**Listings magazine** *Szekszárdi Est*
**Matrix Computer** Mátyás király utca 8; ℩ 74 412711. Internet access for around 250Ft/hr. *Open Mon–Fri 09.00–17.00, Sat 09.00–12.00.*
**Postal code** 7100
**Tolna Tours** Széchenyi utca 38; ℩ 74 511664; e toltour@tolna.net; www.toltour.tolna.net. Specialises in regional excursions, including wine tours. *Open Mon–Thu 09.00–16.30, Fri 08.00–16.00, Sat 08.30–12.00.*
**Tourinform** Garay tér 18; ℩ 74 511263; e szekszard@tourinform.hu. The helpful staff can provide timetables for the trains (including the narrow-gauge railway at the nearby Gemenc Forest) and buses, as well as assist with lists of college and private accommodation and wine houses. *Open Jun 15–Sep 30 Mon–Fri 09.00–18.00, Sat–Sun 10.00–17.00, rest of yr Mon–Fri 09.00–17.00.*

## Where to stay

**Hotel Gemenc** (92 rooms) Mészáros Lázár utca 2; ℩ 74 311722; www.hotels.hu/gemenc_hotel. This ugly '70s block next to the synagogue is better inside than out. Among the facilities are a bar and nightclub, and all rooms have balconies (although not all have TV and minibar). *Sgl 8,500Ft, dbl 11,500Ft.*
**Hotel Zodiaco** (21 rooms) Szent László utca 19; ℩ 74 511150. Each room is allocated a sign of the zodiac, and each is clean, modern, tastefully decorated and furnished with complimentary chocolate bars. Through sweet teeth, we recommend this hotel highly. *Sgl 9,957Ft, dbl 12,908Ft, triple 16,064Ft.*
**Megacentrum Panzió** Tartsay utca 8; ℩ 74 511060. Housed above a motorcycle showroom 1km southeast of the centre, this guesthouse has spacious rooms cheaply priced. It also owns an adjacent pizzeria. *Sgl 7,500Ft, dbl 9,500Ft, triple 11,000Ft, for four 12,000Ft.*
**Rózsa Ferenc College** Kadarka utca 29; ℩ 74 315833; e rozsa@webmail.hu. One of several dorm-room options available in summer. Tourinform can provide a full list; this college is to the north of the centre. *Dorm beds €4–5/pp.*

## Where to eat and drink

**Amaretto Cukrászda** Garay tér 6. 'Show me the way to Amaretto', the locals cry when in need of cake, ice cream and coffee. *Open 09.00–20.00 daily.*
**Főispán** Béla tér 1; ℩ 74 312139; www.foispanetterem.hu. A smart and atmospheric restaurant in a 17th-century cellar. Hungarian dishes prevail, including delicious goose liver in local red wine and platters of poultry and fish. There are a few cases holding wine memorabilia at the back, although they stretch the definition in calling it a 'wine museum'. *Mains 850–2,320Ft, avg 1,650Ft; open Mon–Sat 11.30–24.00, Sun 11.30–22.00.*
**Húsvasaló** Rákóczi utca 10; ℩ 06 30 225 7119. This intimate cellar restaurant and bar has a courtyard area. Good Hungarian food.*Mains 850–2,800Ft, avg 1,600Ft; restaurant open 12.00–23.00 daily; pub Sun–Thu 18.00–02.00, Fri–Sat 18.00–04.00.*
**Promenád** Garay tér 18; ℩ 74 511293. Standing next to the Tourinform, this elegant and characterful restaurant has coloured glass lampshades and stained-glass windows, and a pavement seating area. Among the international and Hungarian fare are steaks, Hawaiian and Kentucky chicken dishes, pork cutlets stuffed with chicken liver, and desserts like peach stuffed with chestnut and caramel cream. *Mains 950–2,400Ft, avg 1,600Ft; open Mon–Fri 11.00–24.00, Sat 11.00–02.00, Sun 11.00–24.00.*
**Szász** Garay tér 18; ℩ 74 312463. This medieval-theme restaurant and bar has typically meat-heavy choices, including venison meatballs and the biggest pork chops we've ever seen. A set lunch menu is available. An adjacent café was in the offing when we last visited, and it should now be up and running. *Mains 850–1,850Ft, avg 1,300Ft; open Mon–Sat 10.00–24.00, Sun 10.00–16.00.*

## Entertainment and nightlife

The **Deutsche Bühne** (*Garay tér 4;* ℩ *74 316533*) is the country's only German-language theatre outside the capital. The **Babits Cultural Centre** (*Szent István tér 10;* ℩ *74*

*311119; www.extra.hu/babitsmuvhaz; open Mon–Fri 08.00–18.00*) can get you up to speed on current performances and exhibitions in the former synagogue and elsewhere in town, while the Youth House at the back can help with cultural events for the 'younger' crowd. The **Panoráma Cinema** occupies the same building.

**Incognito Café and Club** (*Széchenyi utca 29–31;* \ *06 30 650 7021; open Thu–Sat 21.00–05.00*) is a dark cellar bar awash with photos of old films stars; there's funky house and dance music into the wee hours. You can also have a drink at Szász and Húsvasaló (see page 395). The best of the town's wine houses is the **Vesztergombi Borház** (*Béla tér 7;* \ *74 410640; open Mon–Fri 10.00–12.00, 13.00–17.00, Sat 09.00–12.00*), where you can buy a bottle of the local drop or enjoy tastings in the cellar below. If you wish to taste, telephone in advance. Others include the **House of Wines** (*Rákóczi utca 22;* \ *74 416871*) and the **Garay Cellar** (*Garay tér 19;* \ *74 412828*).

## What to see and do

The heart of Szekszárd is sliced vertically by the main Széchenyi utca and horizontally by Szent István tér (which runs west into Garay tér and Béla tér). Béla tér holds a **Trinity Column**, with cherub faces hanging from it like baubles on a Christmas tree; the monument was erected in 1763 in memory of the plague that swept through in 1738–40. The early 19th-century Louis-XIV-style **Roman Catholic church** at the northern side is the largest single-nave church in central Europe, and has some fabulous interior columns painted in pink, purple and mint green.

The Neoclassical **Old County Hall** (*Vármegyeháza; Béla tér 1;* \ *74 316222; adult/concessions 200/100Ft; open Apr 1–Sep 30 Tue–Sun 09.00–17.00, Oct 1–Mar 31 Tue–Sat 09.00–15.00*) was built between 1823 and 1833 by Mihály Polláck on the site of Béla I's Benedictine abbey, the ruins of which are in its central courtyard. There are several exhibitions in the building. The richly preserved suites of the 19th-century lord lieutenant who occupied them include the empire-style armchair in which he was inaugurated. In the **Liszt Ferenc Memorial Room** you'll see a cast of the great man's hand, together with the piano he played (and signed) when visiting the house of landowner Antal Augusz (see below). Across the hall is the **Mattioni Eszter Room**, devoted to the 20th-century Szekszárd-born artist who took traditional peasant life and festivals for her subjects, and committed them to vivid paintings and mosaics.

During festivals, actual wine flows from the playful **Wine Well** (*Borkút*) in the garden to the County Hall's left. Liszt attended the official opening of the **town hall** opposite, with its unfortunate tangerine colouring. Next to that is the **Abbot's Residence**, constructed in 1765 and the earliest of the town's buildings. The nearby **Babits Mihály Memorial Exhibition** (*Babits Mihály utca 13;* \ *74 312154; adult/concessions 200/100Ft; open Apr 1–Sep 30 Tue–Sun 09.00–17.00, Oct 31–Mar 31 Tue–Sat 09.00–15.00*) occupies the house in which the poet was born. While he lived here only up to the age of six, he would return to visit as a student and stayed in the third of the rooms. There you'll see a chest of drawers that served as his writing table and the armchair in which he liked to sit and ponder. Pál Farkas's bronze statue in the garden shows him doing just that.

Moving east, Garay tér bears a statue of its namesake, the poet János Garay (1812–53), who conjured the Falstaffian character of Háry János on whom Zoltán Kodály based his opera. Garay was also effusive in his written praise for Szekszárd wine. Nip up Széchenyi utca to see the **Augusz House** (*Széchenyi utca 36–40*), rather a crude piece of pink turretted architecture built for Baron Antal Augusz. Liszt was a visitor here on four occasions, and Augusz apparently had considerable influence in securing for him the commission to write the *Coronation Mass* of 1867 (see page 177). Appropriately, the building now holds a music school.

The **Wosinsky Mór County Museum** (*Szent István tér 26;* \ *74 316222; adult/concessions 200/100Ft; open Apr 1–Sep 30 Tue–Sun 10.00–18.00, rest of yr Tue–Sat*

## MIHÁLY BABITS

The poet Mihály Babits (1883–1941) was among the élite of 20th-century literati, influential not only in his avant-garde verse but through the journal *Nyugat* (*West*), which he edited from 1919 until his death. He used this to open Hungary to trends in Western art and offer an outlet for new talent; he (together with his contemporaries Endre Ady and Dezsı Kosztolányi) can be said to have guided the development of Hungarian literary modernism. As well as poetry, Babits was a master of translation. Among the classics that he tackled were Shakespeare's *Tempest* and the entire body of Dante's *Divine Comedy*. His poetry was deep, inward-looking and characterised by elaborate artifice – indeed, literary historians have labelled him 'the Hungarian T S Eliot'. During his final years he suffered from throat cancer, dying in 1941 shortly after completing his masterpiece *The Book of Jonah* (*Jónás Könyve*), a creative warning against the evil of fascism. He did not live to see just how evil it could be.

*10.00–16.00*) has an extensive and excellent collection – the only shame is that there are no explanations in English. The museum was founded by the priest and amateur archaeologist Mór Wosinsky, who made a Europe-wide name for himself on excavating the Neolithic site of Töröksánc near Lengyel. One exhibition digs deep into time's mists, showcasing skeletons and grave goods from as far back as 20000BC, and moving forward through carved animals from 5000BC up to ornate jewellery and weapons from 2400BC. Another room has stone remains from Roman Christian temples unearthed in the region, and elsewhere there are finds relating to the various nomadic groups that passed through the Carpathian Basin during the first millennium AD. The display of local town history upstairs includes reconstructions of 19th-century shops and houses, and a healthy gathering of German, Serbian and Sárköz ethnographic items.

Set back from the road behind the museum is the **Arts House** (*Művészetek Háza; Szent István tér 28;* ✆ *74 511247; adult/concessions 200/100Ft; open Tue–Sun 10.00–18.00*), a Moorish former synagogue in sand- and rust-coloured brick that served the Jewish community from 1897 until World War II. It was later converted into an arts centre; as well as temporary exhibitions, concerts are held here (some on the synagogue's organ). A gnarled *Tree of Life* stands near by, cast in bronze and dedicated to the war victims. Some of Imre Varga's sheet-metal creations can be seen beside the cultural centre to the west, in the grassed **Prométheúsz Park**; Zeus's eagle swoops to strip at the flesh of the unfortunate Prometheus, who had stolen fire and given it to the mortals, thereby unleashing their appetite for culture and art.

Climb **Calvary Hill** (*Kalvaria-hegy*), a short distance to the west of the centre, for views of the town below, the Great Plain beyond, and the vineyards on the surrounding slopes. There's a massive shining sculpture of a vine on top, as well as the crucifixes bearing Christ and the robbers – erected in 1832 by parents mourning the loss of a child – after which the hill is named. Around a kilometre further out is the flaking **Remete (or 'Hermit') Chapel** (*Kápolna tér 10*), a diminutive Baroque church built 1775–78 and a site of pilgrimage. Crowded by trees in a steep field, and reached via a long set of shallow steps, the church seems made for a scene from an Austen novel – perfect equally for a charming midsummer wedding or a moment of foul intrigue on a moonless night. To get there, follow Bartina utca out from Béla tér.

### Other

There are **indoor and outdoor pools** (*Toldi utca 6/B;* ✆ *74 411249; adult/concessions 400/200Ft; open Mon 14.00–20.00, Tue–Sun 06.00–20.00*) a short distance from the railway and bus stations, beside the Szekszárd Stream. In addition to the wine houses and cellars of the town, Tourinform can provide a map of the Szekszárd Wine Route – which includes the 340 cellars at Sióagárd-Leányvár (the 'cellar village') 6km away.

## Festivals and events

The biggest folk festival in the area is the annual **Szekszárd Vintage Festival** on the last weekend in September, which attracts around 50,000 people. The **Alisca Wine Days** take place at the end of May, with displays of folk crafts and wine tastings, and culminate in the **Fish-Soup-Cooking Competition** at Sióagárd-Leányvár in mid June.

## THE GEMENC FOREST

Starting 12km to the east of Szekszárd and following the Danube south for 30km, the Gemenc Forest is the country's largest flood plain. The Danube used to be particularly wriggly at this point and subjected the Sárköz – the 'Muddy Area' home to five villages south of Szekszárd ('csény the first of them and Báta the last) – to regular flooding. Mid-19th-century river regulation cut off many of the curves (on a detailed map you'll see that the area is littered with crescent-shaped river-channel fragments), and put a stop to the worst of the deluge. Nevertheless, features of the primal, pre-regulation habitat remained – boggy land, ponds and meadows, woodland of willow, poplar and oak – and the area is rich in wildlife. Herons and other waterbirds, black storks, brown kites and white-tailed eagles nest here, while among the mammals are wild boar, red deer (which have traditionally made the area a favourite with hunters) and even the beaver, which was reintroduced in the year 2000 after dying out in the 20th century. Much of the park is protected, and can only be visited by boat, on the narrow-gauge railway or with a guide, but the national blue and red hiking paths run through the park, and there is a cycle route too.

## The Gemenc Excursion Centre

You can pick up the hiking and cycling routes towards the park's southern end at the bridge across the Danube to Baja (see page 352), but the real gateway is at the Gemenc Excursion Centre (*Gemenci kiránduló központ; Bárányfok;* ☎ *74 312552/410151; open May 1–Oct 31 09.30–18.00 daily*). Buses to the centre in Bárányfok run from Szekszárd (up to five a day). Bárányfok is on the road running between Szekszárd and Keselyűs (further around the park's western edge).

A couple of hundred metres from the entrance is the **National Park Museum** (*adult/concessions 500/300Ft; open Mar 15–Oct 31 Tue–Sun 09.00–17.00*), whose pine lodge was originally constructed in Budapest as part of the millennial celebrations to display the hunting trophies of Archduke Ferenc Ferdinand (whose death, rather ironically, came at the wrong end of a gun; see *History*, page 19). It was positioned here as the Trophy Museum in the 1980s, but reopened in 2003 with a more eco-friendly face, showcasing the region's flora and fauna, and the tools of former forest vocations – fishing, animal husbandry and bee keeping.

If you want to stay, there are 20 Finnish-style **wooden bungalows** that can hold up to three people (*9,800–10,300Ft*); each has a shower, toilet, fridge and TV. There is also a small patch where you can pitch a tent. The **Trófea Restaurant** (☎ *74 712552; mains 850–2,200Ft, avg 1,300Ft; open May 1–Oct 31 09.00–22.00 daily*) is a large and touristy restaurant that caters mainly for tour groups, and specialises in game dishes.

## Into the park

One way into the park is via the forest **narrow-gauge railway**, which runs 30km between the Bárányfok terminus and Pörböly in the southern section. It operates May 1–Oct 31, and tickets are available from the centre. Trains travelling the whole way depart

## DANUBE-DRÁVA NATIONAL PARK

The Danube-Dráva National Park is not what it was originally planned to be. It had been hoped to establish a park straddling the River Dráva and thereby falling on both the Hungarian and Yugoslav sides of the border. However, the break-up of Yugoslavia and the ensuing bloody conflict put paid to such a vision, and in 1996 the park was formed in Hungary alone. It comprises two riverside sections – the lower Hungarian course of the Danube flowing from north to south, including parts of its floodplain, oxbow lakes and dead channels from the confluence of the Sió in Bogyiszló to the Serbian border, and the entire Hungarian course of the Dráva, running west to east from 'rtilos in Somogy to Matty in Baranya. In total it covers 49,500ha, of which 13,400ha are strictly protected.

The bulk of the protected Danube section of the park is made up of two areas. The first is the **Gemenc** (see opposite), holding the largest riverine forest in Hungary; in it are ash, elm, alder and oak forests, as well as oxbow lakes, marshlands, meadows, reed-beds and willow stands. The second, in the floodplain of the lower course of the Danube, is the **Béda-Karapancsa** (see page 405). This hosts a wide variety of floodplain habitats, including rivers, oxbow lakes and ponds. The areas of open water are flanked by marshlands, reed-beds, meadows and gallery forests of ash, elm, alder and oak. Between them, this pair support a high density and diversity of endangered species. The globally threatened ferruginous duck quacks happily here, and the region is also home to over 20 pairs of white-tailed sea eagles and a good number of black storks. The lesser-spotted eagle is present, and many great white egrets, along with probably the greatest concentration of the endemic hawthorn species, *Crataegus nigra*, which is only found in the lower floodplains of the Danube.

The Dráva is the last untamed river in central Europe, its course forever changing under the bullying of the fast-moving waters. The protected stretch is 170km in length, with around 30 oxbows, the same number again of lakes and ponds, and flood plains and marshes supporting thousands of birds. The bee-eater and sand martin nest on its sandy banks, while the little tern prefers the gravelled parts for its dwelling. Fifty species of fish live in the waters, 24 types of dragonfly hover around its streams and the meadows are rich in butterflies and moths. Probably the king of the Dráva valley is the **juniper grove at Barcs**, special in the hearts of horticulturalists for the exceptionally rare royal fern (*Osmunda regalis*) and the shepherd's cress (*Teesdalia nudicaulis*) that grow there.

In addition, the national park has authority over three protected areas of southern Transdanubia: the Eastern Mecsek, the Boronka and the Zselic natural preserves. All are for the most part forested. The **Eastern-Mecsek** is a mountainous reserve known primarily for its grasslands; the **Boronka** hosts healthy populations of otters, white-tailed sea eagles and black storks; the **Zselic** is a range of hills holding various traditional villages. For further information, contact the **Duna-Dráva National Park Directorate** (*Pécs, Tettye tér 9;* \ *72 517227;* e *ddnp.igazg@kym.x400gw.itb.hu*).

at 15.35 daily, while a further two leave at 13.35 (daily) and 10.40 (weekends only) going the first 11km to Gemenc Dunapart (on the Danube bank). (You'll have to wait 2–3 hours for a connection if you wish to continue on to Pörböly from Gemenc Dunapart.) You can't return the same day by narrow-gauge from Pörböly as the last train back is at 13.30 on weekdays and 13.15 at weekends (both of which require changes); instead catch a bus to Szekszárd (the journey takes 40 minutes and there are up to 11 buses a day), or perhaps consider taking a normal train to Baja. A nostalgia steam train (*350Ft supplement*) runs at the weekends only between Gemenc Dunapart and Pörböly.

The railway passes the **birdwatching tower** overlooking the strictly protected Malomtelelő-tó (Lake Winter Mill) around 5km from Pörböly; to visit, alight at the Lassi stop and follow the blue-cross path north for a few hundred metres. The odd name derives from the 19th century, when two boats were moored either side of the river near here, with a wheel between them that the water turned to work some milling machinery. The lake was used as a winter shelter for the boats to prevent damage from floating river ice. As well as the tower, there is a study trail.

If you wish to **hike** into the park, you can join the national blue-horizontal-line trail from the excursion centre; the 40km stretch hugs the forest's western side, takes in the birdwatching tower and then heads east to the bridge across to Baja. If that sounds like rather too much hard work, there's a circular 2.5km **nature trail** leading from the centre that will take around 45 minutes; unfortunately the information boards about the wildlife and the lives of the foresters are in Hungarian. A **cycle path** also leaves from the excursion centre, and there is bike hire available (*1,500Ft/day*). Alternatively you can go **horse-riding** (*around 700Ft/hr*) or take a carriage ride into the woods (*adult/concessions 1,200/800Ft/hr*).

If you'd prefer to take to the water, a **motorboat** leaves from Árvízkapu (6km east of the excursion centre) along the River Sió and then up the Danube; the hour-long journey only runs if there is sufficient demand. Gemenc is at its prime when the river level rises above 3m and fills its water courses, which can be explored in **rowing boats** or kayaks (motorboats are only permitted on the River Sió). There are signs to assist those travelling by boat, and permits to tie up on the Grébeci Danube, the Rézeti Danube and the left bank of the Koppányi Old Danube are available from the Duna-Dráva National Park office in Pécs (see page 413). The excursion centre can provide details both of the motorboat trip and rowing-boat outings. **Fishing** is allowed in designated areas; the excursion centre sells permits (*200Ft/day*), but you'll need your own rod.

If you are taking to the park on foot, buy a copy of the *Gemenci tájegység* map, which shows the hiking routes and protected areas; surprise surprise, the map is available from the excursion centre. If you'd prefer to visit the park on an **organised tour**, contact Tolna Tours in Szekszárd (see page 395) or Attila Papp (✆ *06 30 377 3406*).

## MOHÁCS

To look at Mohács, with its charming main square and attractive riverside promenade, it is difficult to believe that it occupies a place as dark as the local pottery in the hearts of Hungarians. Its name is associated with the grand-daddy of all nadirs, a point so low that it has become the stuff of proverbs. Reminded that 'more was lost at Mohács', a man will stop crying over his spilt milk, nod in agreement and put a braver face on things.

Weakened by inner anarchy and social conflict, in 1521 Hungary lost Nándorfehérvár (today's Belgrade) and Szabács to Sultan Suleiman the Great, two of the key fortresses in its southern defences. In April 1526, the sultan continued his advance. The teenage King Lajos II hastily mustered an army of 25,000, and on August 29 1526 met a Turkish force three times its size in a field 9km to the southwest of Mohács. After a stand-off of several hours under the hot sun, the Hungarians charged and the Turks countered. Evening fell and the smoke cleared to reveal the corpses of 15,000 Hungarian soldiers, among them the commander-in-chief (and Archbishop of Kalocsa) Pál Tomori. Legend has it that King Lajos II drowned trying to flee across the Csele Stream. The Turks went on to capture Buda, and while they had to withdraw temporarily through lack of sufficient reserves, they returned 15 years later to occupy the country. The Battle of Mohács is regarded as the fight that broke Hungary's back.

King Lajos II monument

Mohács Beach

Railway station

Swimming pool

BUDAPESTI

FELSZABADULÁS

Danube

N

Bradt

MOHÁCSI JENŐ

ADY ENDRE

FELSŐ DUNASOR

KÓRHÁZ

PÉCSI

Polish Monument

Former Bishop's Palace
SZEPESSY TÉR

Episcopal church

KÖLCSEY TÉR

SZERB

Serb Orthodox

Inner City

Halászcsárda

Hotel Csele & Mecsek Tours

Ferry pier

Révkapu Motel

BARTÓK BÉLA

VÖRÖSMARTY

SZENTHÁROMSÁG

SZENT MIHÁLY TÉR

KOSSUTH LAJOS

ZALKA MÁTÉ

TANCSICS

Bartók Béla
Cultural Centre

BARÓ EÖTVÖS

Synagogue

Korzó

Koroná

SZENTHÁROMSÁG TÉR

Hárfa Angol

Tourinform

Kossuth
Cinema
Gallery

DEÁK TÉR

OÓZSU GYÖRGY

RÁKÓCZI

SZABADSÁG

HŐSÖK TÉR

SZÉCHENYI TÉR

SZÍNHÁZ

Bike
hire

Votive

Market

Kanizsai Dorottya Museum

SALLAI

JÓKAI MÓR

Calvinist

KÁLVIN

Kerésztapa
Pizzeria

TEMETŐ

TERV

ESZÉKI

TOMPA MIHÁLY

Memorial
Chapel

Pegazus
Lovas
Panzió

Memorial Park (5km)

0 ——— 200m
0 ——— 200yds

**MOHÁCS**

## Getting there and away

Lying on the bank of the Danube, at the junction of Road 56 leading north to Szekszárd and Road 6 east to Pécs, Mohács is a gateway to Croatia (the border crossing is at Udvar, 10km or so to the north). The **bus** is the best way to get to and from Mohács. There are hourly services to Budapest Népliget and Baja as well as direct buses to Villány (eight daily), Harkány (nine), Kaposvár (two), Dombóvár (one), Kecskemét (two), Székesfehérvár (one) and Szeged (seven). It's a short walk from the bus station (*Rákóczi út*) to the centre – head north along Rákóczi utca, before turning right into Szabadság utca. You can also catch a number of local buses to the memorial park (see page 403) from outside the station and from bus stops in the town centre. Look for those travelling to Nagynyárád or Lippó.

The only direct **train** services are to Villány (seven daily) and Pécs (four); for Harkány and Siklós, change at Villány. The station is north of the centre, just beyond the swimming pool. In addition, there's a car **ferry** (*Mohácsi Révhajózási;* ✆ *69 311129*) at the end of Szabadság utca (turn left on to Ságvári Endre utca and it's on the right) across the Danube to the Southern Plain. During summer the ferry (*95Ft/pp, bike 100Ft, car 160Ft*) departs every half-hour with the last leaving at 20.00; the ticket office is in front of the Révkapu Motel.

## Information and other practicalities

**Bartók Béla Cultural Centre** Vörösmarty utca 3; ↘ 69 511120; e bbmk@hu.internet. The centre has permanent and temporary exhibitions, a cinema with a screening at 19.00 daily, and can give details of cultural events in town. *Open 08.30–21.00 daily (later when programmes are on).*
**Listings magazine** *Pécsi Est*
**Mecsek Tours** See Hotel Csele, page 000; ↘ 69 511020; e info@mecsektours.hu; www.mecsektours.hu. Has information on both the town and the tour options.
**Tourinform** Széchenyi tér 1; ↘ 69 505515; e mohacs@tourinform.hu. Located in the town hall. *Open Jun 15–Sep 15 Mon–Fri 08.00–18.00, Sat–Sun 10.00–17.00, rest of yr Mon–Thu 08.00–16.00, Fri 08.00–13.00.*

## Where to stay

**Duna Panzió** (7 rooms) Felső Dunasor 14; ↘ 69 302450. If you're anti-hunting you'll have to stomach the animal-skin rugs in some of the rooms, but otherwise the accommodation is spacious and very good value. The owner is also a jolly and welcoming chap. The guesthouse is to the north of the Kanizsai Dorottya Museum. *Sgl 6,000Ft, dbl 7,000Ft.*
**Hotel Csele** (49 rooms) Szent Mihály tér 6–7; ↘ 69 511020; e csele@mecsektours.hu. The biggest hotel in town; ask for a room overlooking the river. Mecsek Tours have a desk in the lobby. *Sgl 9,000Ft, dbl 12,700Ft, apt (for 2) 17,200Ft.*
**Pegazus Lovas Panzió** (9 rooms) Eszéki út; ↘ 69 301244/305500. This wonderful guesthouse and riding school stands in scenic surrounds 1km to the south of the centre. The rooms are large and comfortable, with good-sized bathrooms. Even if you don't fancy horse-riding, this is a relaxing spot to stay. We recommend it highly. *Riding costs from €14/hr (they cater for all levels). Dbl 8,000Ft.*
**Révkapu Motel** (5 rooms) Szent János utca 1; ↘ 69 322228. The Révkapu Restaurant has a small motel above it, although we found it desperately difficult to find anyone to show us around. It does overlook the river and is cheap, but if the staff remain the same you'll waste less time looking elsewhere. *Dbl 9,000Ft.*

## Where to eat and drink

**Halászcsárda** Szent Mihály tér 5; ↘ 69 322542. The fish could leap straight from the water on to your plate in this first-floor river-facing restaurant. Despite the dickie-bowed waiters, the shabby, school-dinner-hall décor renders deluded the restaurant's grand opinion of itself. Fisherman's carp soup and pike goulash are among the specialities. *Mains 850–2,200Ft, avg 1,800Ft; open Tue–Sun 11.00–24.00.*
**Hárfa Angol** Szent János utca 3; ↘ 69 302477. On a leafy side street close to the ferry pier, this restaurant and café serves steak, Indonesian curry, turkey dishes and the like. *Mains 1,500–1,950Ft, avg 1,600Ft; open Tue–Sun 16.00–24.00.*
**Keresztapa Pizzeria** Szabadság utca 22; ↘ 69 303259. This café-style joint offers pizzas in two sizes and many varieties, and there's also a selection of salads, burgers and spaghettis for those averse to the Italian tomato bread. If you want to eat in, there's some seating overlooking Széchenyi tér, but you can also take away. *Mains avg 700Ft; open daily 10.00–23.00.*
**Korona** Jókai Mór utca 2; ↘ 69 322541. A place to stop for cakes and ice creams. *Open daily 09.00–20.00.*
**Korzó Snack Bar** Szabadság út 11; ↘ 69 322357. This extremely popular place with pavement seating serves picky food like omelettes and hot sandwiches as well as more substantial offerings including rump steak, veal cutlets and fried duck's liver. *Mains 350–1,200Ft, avg 800Ft; open Mon–Sat 09.00–21.00, Sun 10.00–21.00.*
**Révkapu Vendéglő** See above. Terraced eating area with great views over the Danube, and live

music most nights. The Hungarian food is pretty cheap. *Mains 650–1,700Ft, avg 1,100Ft; open 09.00–24.00 daily.*

## What to see and do
### Mohács Historical Memorial Park
The **memorial park** (*Történelmi Emlékpark;* ⟍ 69 382130; *adult/concessions 600/400Ft; open Apr 1–Apr 30 Wed–Sun 10.00–16.00, May 1–Sep 30 Tue–Sun 09.00–18.00, Oct 1–31 Wed–Sun 10.00–16.00*) stands on the route to Sátorhely, just off Road 56 running south from Mohács. There is a bus stop directly outside the entrance. The park was established in 1976 at the site of the Battle of Mohács 450 years earlier, on what Károly Kisfaludy referred to in his poem as the 'blooded mourning field'. The massive reticulated entrance arch by goldsmith József Pölöskei looks oddly triumphal until you learn that every one of its 28,000 bolts represents a fallen soldier. A sunken atrium is lined with tableaux depicting the battle and an unimpressive fountain by Gyula Illés symbolising a broken flower, while the grassed circular park beyond is believed to be the place where the Hungarian army camped prior to the fight. Five mass graves were uncovered here containing the remains of 400 soldiers, and rose beds and carved Transylvanian-style posts mark the spots. A 10m-high cross overlooks the field from the far end. It won't detain you long, and is sobering and understated compared with a memorial park like that at Ópusztaszer, but that is as it should be. This was where over 20,000 soldiers, 500 nobles and seven Hungarian bishops breathed their last.

A second memorial to that fateful day lies to the north of town, just off Road 56 beside the Csele Stream. A column commemorates the place where King Lajos II is said to have drowned after his horse fell on top of him. The bronze relief by György Kiss imagines the scene.

### The town
At the eastern side of the wide and cobbled Széchenyi tér is the **town hall** (*Széchenyi tér 1*), built in 1926 with Moorish dome turrets. Inside, the assembly room at the top of the stairs (*open Mon–Fri 08.00–16.00*) contains a large tapestry of the Buso Carnival (see page 404) woven in 1922 by István Bán. Like the town hall, the **Votive Church** (*Fogadalmi templom; Széchenyi tér;* ⟍ 69 303279; *admission 100Ft; open 09.00–12.00, 13.00–16.00 daily*) was designed by Aladár Arkay, and it is similarly Moorish in look. The foundations were filled with earth from over 3,000 towns and villages as a symbol of national unity. Stained-glass windows around the 30m dome swirl with colour; mosaics in the side chapels were crafted by Mihály Kolbe (see page 404) to the designs of Lili Sztehlo in 1956, while the mosaic floor alludes to the battle of 1526.

Walk west along Szabadság utca to **Hősök tere**, which holds a 24m monument to the 439 soldiers from Mohács who died during World War I. At the centre there is a stone cube added on the 40th anniversary of the 1956 revolution. The square also has a sombre statue by Imre Varga of Miklós Radnóti leaning against a fence post. One of Hungary's outstanding 20th-century poets, the Jewish Radnóti passed through Mohács in 1945 on a forced labour march destined for Vienna. He would never get there; when he became too tired to continue, an Arrow Cross trooper executed him by the road side. His last poems were discovered on his body in a mass grave.

The ground floor of the **Kossuth Cinema Gallery** (*Filmszínház; Deák tér 1;* ⟍ 69 510177; *adult/concessions 200/100Ft; open Tue–Sun 10.00–18.00*) has a cinema screening Hollywood blockbusters, but more interesting is the exhibition space upstairs. There is a display of the distinctive **ceramics** of the town, charcoal black and cut with grooves and notches. The style developed in the 18th and 19th centuries, and was shipped to the Balkans where it became very popular. During the 20th century, János Horváth (1905–75) was the acknowledged master of the craft, and you can see his work together with that of other local potters. There are also pieces to buy. Another room contains **paintings by Mihály Kolbe** (1907–90), who lived in Mohács from 1931 after studying in Budapest, and was responsible for mosaics in the Votive Church. His work shows the clear influence of Cubism, and artists like Matisse and Picasso. In a third room is a selection of fearsome **Busó masks** and sheepskin coats. These are worn during the Busó Carnival (*Busójárás*), a Shrove Tuesday celebration derived from the Sokác people, a Croatian minority who (along with Serbs and Germans) repopulated Mohács after the Turkish occupation. During the carnival, a noisy procession wearing the horned and hairy masks symbolically drives out winter and welcomes in spring. It is said by some that the Sokác people donned frightening masks and drove the Turks from Mohács, but they actually arrived a decade after the occupation had ended and so if there's any truth to such an event it must have taken place in their native land. An **ethnographic exhibition** shows the costumes of the various groups that settled and rebuilt the town in the 17th century.

In the immediate aftermath of the Battle of Mohács, the widow of Imre Perényi from Siklós approached the Turkish camp and asked permission to bury the slain. The commander was so moved by her courage that he ordered some of his men to help her. They worked all night and for the following week laying the corpses in shallow graves (some of which were discovered in the 1970s at the site of today's memorial park. To the east of Széchenyi tér, the **Kanizsai Dorottya Museum** (*Városház utca 1;* ✆ *69 311536; adult/concessions 250/150Ft; open Apr 1–Oct 31 Tue–Sat 10.00–17.00, Sun 10.00–12.00, 14.00–16.00, Nov 1–Mar 31 Tue–Sat 10.00–16.00*) is named after her. The permanent exhibition contains ethnographic items belonging to the Croatian, German, Slovenian and Serbian immigrants to Mohács, including costumes, painted furniture, icons of the Orthodox Church and grave markers. There are pieces of local pottery and Busó masks too. The entrance ticket also allows access to a second exhibition space (*Szerb utca 2*) near the Serbian Orthodox church, which details the history of the Battle of Mohács.

Near the ferry dock, the Roman Catholic **Inner City Church** (*Szent Mihály tér; open 08.00–12.00 daily*) was built in Baroque style in 1766, while across Szentháromság utca in the garden of the former **synagogue** (*Báró Eötvös utca 1*) is a memorial to World-War-II Jewish victims of the fascist extermination programme. The key to the gates is held in the town library (✆ *69 311347*). Continue north to the **Serb Orthodox church** (*Szerb utca 2*) of 1732, with a 48m tower and spectacular iconostasis by Mór Csóka. You'll need permission from the priest to get in; ring the bell to the right as you enter the church grounds through the low arch on Korsós utca. By the river to the south of the centre is the pretty, late-Baroque **Calvinist church** (*Kálvin utca;* ✆ *69 311336*), built in 1790 and capped with a grey onion spire. Telephone beforehand for admittance.

The **Episcopal Church** (*Gólya utca*), to the northwest of the centre, was commissioned by Bishop Zsigmond Berényi of Pécs in 1742 and his coat of arms sit above the entrance. Across the road is the **Firemen Statue** of St Flórián, which was erected in 1896 after a spate of fires had hit the town, while a touch further north is the **former Bishop's Palace** (*Szepessy tér 6*) where the clerics would come to recuperate in summer. It now houses the Kisfaludy Károly School. The park in the middle of the square contains a monument to the 1,600 Polish soldiers killed at the Battle of Mohács, who were serving in the Hungarian army.

The **Memorial Chapel** (*Emlékkápolna; Eszéki út*) 700m south from here along Kossuth Lajos út is set in a peaceful and beautifully maintained graveyard filled with horse-chestnut trees. The chapel itself was built in 1816, and has a stained-glass portrait of Dorottya Kanizsai (see above). There are also two paintings by István Dorfmeister, showing the 1526 defeat and the second less-remembered Habsburg victory over the Turks at Mohács in 1687. In effect this simply resulted in one occupier replacing another, and isn't a battle greatly celebrated by Hungarians.

## Other activities

There is a large outdoor **swimming pool** (*Indoház utca 1;* \ *69 311473; adult/concessions 400/200Ft; open May 1–Sep 30 daily 09.00–18.30*) near the railway station. A **sandy beach** is a popular sunbathing spot on the opposite bank of the river from the ferry pier. There is a place to **hire bikes** (*Kerékpár Bolt; Szabadság út 19;* \ *06 30 946 9567; open Mon–Fri 08.30–17.30, Sat 08.00–12.30*), while if you prefer your rides with four hooves then the **Pegazus Lovas Panzió** (see page 402) can help. Wine fanciers can follow the **Mohács-Bóly Wine Route**; pick up a map from Tourinform, or contact the Mohács-Bóly Wine Route Association (*Bóly, Erzsébet tér 1;* \ *69 368100;* e *tourinform@boly.hu*).

Nature lovers should follow the Danube 8km south to the **Béda-Karapancsa flood plains** (to the east of the memorial park), which are part of the Duna-Dráva National Park (see page 399) and feature several dead branches of the river and 10,000ha of woodland lying on either side. The oak trees harbour a significant population of the black stork, while the Kölkedi Nagyrét (meadow) is a stop-off point for migrating birds. Much of the area is protected and can only be visited with permission (*to organise a tour,* \ *72 213236*), but there are cycle and walking routes. Tourinform should be able to furnish you with a map (*Béda-Karapancsai tájegység*) produced by the national park. It is also a good **fishing** haunt; for information on the prime spots and on the necessary angling permits, contact the Mohács Anglers' Association (*Kisfaludy Károly utca 6;* \ *69 322123*). You can buy daily passes for the Kadia Duna and Ferenc Canal, on the eastern side of the river, from the shop at the adjacent village of Budzsák.

## Festivals and events

The annual Busó Carnival (see opposite) is celebrated before Lent in February or March. The parade kicks off from Kóló tér (with its bronze Busó Statue), and there is a bonfire in the main square.

# VILLÁNY AND VILLÁNYKÖVESD

Around 30km southwest of Mohács, Villány is the best-known village of the Villány-Siklós wine region (see box, page 407). Wine's long been the winner here, Bishop Mihály Haas writing in 1845 that of Hungarian vintages 'the Villány red towers as a hundred-year-old oak above the shrubs'. At the eastern end of the hill range, the vineyards of Villány occupy the slopes of Mount Szársomlyó, which is a nature conservation area and habitat for the Hungarian crocus. The sunny clime has been enjoyed and utilised since prehistory, and wine production is reputed to date back to Celtic times.

The Turks destroyed the village in the 16th century, but it was pay-back time at the Battle of Nagyharsány a short distance to the southwest in 1687; the Ottomans were pushed down into the marshes around the River Dráva and mercilessly put to the sword. Afterwards Serbs and Germans made Villány their home, the latter bringing with them a greater wine-making expertise and the Oportó (today Kékoportó – or more accurately Portugizier, since an EU ruling prohibited the use of Portó or Oportó on the label) vine variety. However, the phylloxera epidemic reached the region in 1875 and blighted everything. The recovery – which took 20 years – was largely thanks to Zsigmond Teleki, who established an experimental vineyard in the village with the aim of breeding a hardy grape that could replenish the vineyards. He sunk all his money into the project, and by the time of his death in 1910 had laid the foundations for what became the biggest root stock and graft producer in central Europe. Things worsened again at the conclusion of World War II, when most among the German population – judged 'guilty by association' – were deported. The Hungarian farmers who replaced them often knew little about vine growing and many went bankrupt, while the nationalisation of estates – which started as soon as 1945 – also drove the quality down. Only since the 1990s has it picked up with a rise in private enterprises and modern techniques; the red wines are generally full-bodied, and characterised by a high alcohol and tannin content.

**Villány** essentially means the single, cellar-lined street of Baross Gábor utca. In theory the cellars open between 10.00 and 18.00, but in practice they keep their own hours and you'll take your chance on the day. Among those to try are Fritsch Pince (*no 97*), Havas Borház (*no 81*), Boncz Pince (*no 75*) and Maul Pince (*no 39*); alternatively the guesthouses often have connections with local wineries and can organise tastings. The big names to look out for are Attila Gere (widely regarded as the country's top maker of red wine; see Gere Panzió below), Ede Tiffán, Jószef Bock and Csaba Malatinszky. A **Wine Museum** (*Bem József utca 8;* ⎯ *72 492130; free entry; open Tue–Sun 09.00–17.00*) stands behind Júlia Panzió (see opposite), in a 200-year-old cellar that once belonged to the Teleki family. The **Red Wine Festival** takes place on the first weekend in October in odd-numbered years.

A couple of kilometres northwest on the road towards Pécs, **Villánykövesd** is similarly rooted in the grape. The cellars are crammed along two roads (Petőfi utca below and Pincesor above); those especially valued are Polgár Pince (*Pincesor 51–52*), Blum János Borozó (*Pincesor 4–5*), Tiffán Imre Pincéje (*Pincesor 14–15*) and Schwarzwalter Ferenc Pincéje (*Pincesor 16*). There is only one hotel and a couple of guesthouses; during the second half of October the village hosts the opening ceremony of the **Pécs Drinking Song Festival**.

## Getting there and away

The main **bus** stop in Villány is outside the town hall on Baross Gábor utca – just to the left of the OTP Bank. From here you can travel to Budapest Népliget (one daily), Harkány (ten), Szigetvár (two), Szekszárd (up to five) and Pécs (one daily except Sun). There are also fairly regular services to Siklós and Mohács. Up to six buses a day make the seven-minute journey to Villánykövesd. The **train station** (*Ady Endre fasor*) is 1km north of the centre (on the way to Villánykövesd). There are direct trains to Pécs (11 daily), Mohács (seven), Siklós and Harkány (up to six), as well as a service across the Serbian border to Sarajevo (taking 8½ hours). From the station turn left and follow the road in front of you, which leads to the village centre.

## Information and other practicalities

**Bank** Baross Gábor utca 36 (opposite the town hall)
**Post office** Baross Gábor utca 35 (next to Oportó Panzió)
**Villány-Siklós Wine Route Association** Deák Ferenc utca 22; ⎯ 72 492181; e iroda@borut.hu; www.borut.hu. Standing just off Baross Gábor utca, the office of the region's wine association can provide information on wine festivals and cellars in the area, and organise tours.

## Where to stay and eat

Other than the Hotel Cabernet, the places to stay or grab a bite below are in Villány; you'll also find that there are many houses offering private rooms.

**Flamingo Cukrászda** Dósza György 4; ⎯ 72 492207. Where the locals head for their ice cream and cake. *Open daily 09.00–20.00.*
**Gere Panzió** (14 rooms) Diófás utca 4; 72 492195; www.gere.hu. Owned by the revered vintner Attila Gere, the cellar here is probably the best in the village (the winery itself is 5 minutes away); taste 5 wines for 1,500Ft or 7 wines for 2,000Ft, and enjoy a plate of cold meats with them if the fancy takes. Crash afterwards in excellent, modern, apartment-like rooms. *Sgl 9,000Ft, dbl 11,200Ft, triple 12,300Ft; cellar open Mon–Sat 09.00–18.00, Sun 09.00–12.00.*
**Hotel Cabernet** (25 rooms) Villánykövesd, Petőfi utca 29; ⎯ 72 493200; e info@hotelcabernet.hu; www.hotelcabernet.hu. This 3-star doll's house of a hotel is next to the stop for buses from Villány and 100m from the railway station. The hotel's Görbe Pince ('Curvy

## THE VILLÁNY-SIKLÓS WINE ROUTE

The 30km-long Villány-Siklós Wine Route was the first to be established by any of Hungary's main wine-making regions, and wends its way around the limestone Villány Hills and through the 11 settlements nestling on the slopes – Palkonya, Villánykövesd (see opposite), Villány, Nagyharsány (with an artists' camp, sculpture park and 13th-century Calvinist church), Kisharsány, Nagytótfalu, Kistótfalu, Vokány, Siklós (see below), Máriagyűd (with its Roman Catholic church, which became a pilgrimage site and centre of the Maria cult during the Counter-Reformation in the 18th century) and Harkány (see page 409). The region is well suited to wine production, enjoying 2,000 hours of sunshine a year, and ten million vines grow on the hills over an area of 1,000ha. The eastern slopes yield red wines (notably from the Kékfrankos, Kékoportó or Portugizier, Cabernet Franc, Cabernet Sauvignon and Merlot grapes), while the central and western slopes produce white wines (Italian Riesling, Hárslevelű, Chardonnay, Tramini and Rhine Riesling). If you require further information on the route and its wines, contact the office of the Villány-Siklós Wine Route Association (see opposite).

Cellar'; *mains 950–2,100Ft, avg 1,800Ft; open 11.00–23.00 daily*) serves regional specialities and holds wines from all the area's producers. *Sgl €40, dbl €50, triple €60.*

**Júlia Panzió** (6 rooms) Baross Gábor utca 41; ↘ 72 492710. This friendly, family-run guesthouse is slightly cheaper but less classy than the nearby Oportó (see below). Its restaurant is good (*mains 700–2,500Ft, avg 1,600Ft*), and there's wine tasting available in the attached bar. *Sgl 9,600Ft, dbl 10,600Ft.*

**Oportó Panzió** (11 rooms) Baross Gábor utca 33; ↘ 72 592032; e oporto@axelero.hu; www.oporto.hu. In front of the town hall, this pension and restaurant is Villány's best. The elegant restaurant (*mains 800–2,800Ft, avg 1,800Ft; open daily 10.00–22.00*) serves well-presented Hungarian food with an international influence; its intimate terrace is festooned with creepers and feels like a leafy tent. The rooms are large and smartly furnished – in 2003, they played host to the Hungarian president and prime minister. You can hire a bike and take a sauna, and the family owns a cellar 50m away. *Sgl 11,400Ft, dbl 13,500Ft.*

**Polgár Inn** (11 rooms) Hunyadi utca 19; ↘ 74 492053; e polgarp@axelero.hu; www.kertnet.hu. This Mediterranean-feeling guesthouse is situated around an inner courtyard. It is run by the Polgár family (whose cellar is in Villánykövesd). *Sgl 6,400Ft, dbl 9,400Ft, triple 14,100Ft, room for 4 18,800Ft.*

## SIKLÓS

Siklós is Hungary's most southerly town, 15km to the west of Villány. In contrast to the rated reds of its neighbour, Siklós flies the flag for white wines like Italian Riesling, Rhine Riesling, Chardonnay and Traminer. However, it is best known for its castle, which – unlike so many medieval forts – managed to escape Turkish cannon and Habsburg explosives.

### Getting there and away

The **bus station** (*Szent István tér*) is northwest of the centre. Upon arrival here turn left (and keep left) until the road meets Felszabadulás utca, which leads to the right into Kossuth tér. There are one or two buses an hour to Pécs and Harkány, and a regular service to Villány. Direct routes run to Mohács (up to ten), Szigetvár (up to three), Szekszárd (two) and one daily to Budapest and Székesfehérvár.

Siklós is on the Villány line. There is a **train station** (*Gyűdi út*) to the northwest of the centre, on the road towards Máriagyűd, but the main one (*Vasút út*) is northeast of the centre, at the top of Táncsics Mihály utca (which leads into Kossuth tér). Direct trains run to Harkány (seven), Villány (six), Sellye (four) and Barcs (one), while a change is required at Villány for access to Pécs and Mohács.

## Information
**Tourinform** Felszabadulás utca 3; ℡ 72 579090; e siklos@tourinform.hu. *Open Mon–Fri 09.00–17.00, Sat 10.00–14.00.*

## Where to stay, eat and drink
**Faló Kisvendéglő** Dózsa György 15; ℡ 72 351341. Hungarian menu with Croatian specialities. *Mains 650–1,700Ft, avg 1,300Ft; open May–Aug Mon–Thu 09.00–22.00, Fri–Sat 09.00–23.00; rest of yr Mon–Fri 09.00–19.00, Sat 11.00–22.00.*

Hamburger Cukrászda Felszabadulás utca 22. Forget the name, there are buns but no burgers, along with cakes and ice creams. Next to one of the entrances to the market. *Open daily 06.00–18.00.*

**Központi Hotel and Restaurant** (25 rooms) Kossuth tér 5; ℡ 72 352513; e info@kozponti.hu; www.kozponti.hu. The hotel rooms are modern and tastefully done, and there's the opportunity to use a sauna and fitness room. The restaurant (*open 08.00–23.00 daily; mains 980–3,000Ft, avg 1,800Ft*) is popular in a town with few eateries to spare, but it is basic in its furnishings and lacking in atmosphere. Its fare is Hungarian with some international choices. *Sgl 8,200Ft, dbl 10,600Ft, triple 14,400Ft.*

**Vasúti Vendéglő** Vasút út 9; ℡ 72 579053. Situated directly opposite the main train station, this spartan – somewhat out of the way – restaurant deals in Hungarian food. *Mains 650–1,750Ft, avg 1,200Ft; open: Mon–Sat 07.00–21.00, Sun 11.00–21.00.*

## What to see and do
### Siklós Castle
Kids will be disappointed by some of Hungary's castles – either because they are more mansion than fortress or more broken parts than ramparts – but Siklós Castle (*Vajda János tér; ℡ 72 351433; adult/concessions 800/400Ft; open 09.00–18.00 daily*) is the real old-fashioned deal, with a drawbridge and dungeons and crenellations. A Romanesque castle was constructed on the hill in the 13th century by the Siklós family, but there was rebuilding in the 15th and 16th centuries, and it took its current form in the 18th century after remodelling by Count Caprara and then Count Batthyány (who served under Lajos Kossuth as foreign minister in 1848–49). Gothic, Renaissance and Baroque features are indicative of the castle's evolution. Although it remains in good shape, its history is not uneventful. In 1401 King Zsigmond was kept here for five months 'under arrest' by an oligarchy unwilling to accept his primogeniture after the death of his first wife, daughter of King Lajos); in 1543 it fell to the Turks, who held it for 143 years; and in 1705 it was captured by the insurrectionist troops of General János Bottyán, who defended it for a year against the imperial army.

You can reach the drawbridge leading into the castle complex from Kossuth tér via Batthyány utca. Running around it is a belt of Renaissance bastions, and above the museum a crenellated terrace (complete with coffee bar) affords spectacular hill views. The 14th–15th-century narrow **Gothic chapel** has vaulted ceilings, long stained-glass windows in pastel shades and niches decorated with faded frescoes of saints and kings, while the nearby bleak **dungeon** cells and torture chambers hold stocks and ankle clamps. To the left of the dungeon is the entrance to the main **Castle Museum**, in the southern wing of the Baroque courtyard palace. Inside is a collection devoted to the history of the glove trade, with prominence given to the Hunor garment company of Pécs that was known all over Europe. Alongside gloves from the late 19th and early 20th centuries, the display includes the tools with which they were made and prints of various styles of the day. A local history exhibition has models of the castle and details of the families who lived in it – uniquely in the country, it was continuously inhabited from the time of its construction up until the 20th century – while the cellar below contains stone pieces from the various earlier incarnations. The rest of the museum includes a memorial room to Ferenc Őrsi (author of the novel *Captain of Tenkes*, about a Robin-Hood-like character who protected people from Habsburg villainy), the 20th-century ceramics of István Gádor and a small gallery of modern art. Leading off from the courtyard, the Wine House (*Borok Háza*) is a limited museum devoted to the history of wine production in the area, and sells locally made bottles of white.

## Other

Remaining within the fortifications, just below the main complex, there is a missable collection of pottery and agricultural items (including cow bells) at the **Local History Museum** (*Várostörténeti Kiállítás; Vajda János tér 6; adult/concessions 100/50Ft; open Tue–Sun 10.00–16.00*). More worthy of attention is the **Franciscan church** to the south of Vajda János tér, with Gothic windows and fragments of frescoes dating to the early 15th century. It was here that Miklós Garai was buried, one of the most powerful nobles of his age and palatine of Hungary for 30 years; King Zsigmond confiscated the castle from the Siklós family and gave it to Garai – the oligarch who subsequently imprisoned him until he agreed to hand over control of Hungary's internal affairs – in 1387, and it was he who oversaw the Gothic phase of its rebuilding. The adjacent former Franciscan monastery now holds the **Ceramics Gallery** (*Keramia Alkotóház; Vajda János tér 4; admission free; open 08.00–18.00 daily*), which exhibits the work of local and international ceramicists. The cloister is home to the Baranya County Art Colony, whose kilns and benches fill the cells; each year around eight potters are invited to a month-long artists' camp, and the rooms, corridors and courtyard of the gallery include their pieces.

Moving away from the castle on Batthyány Kázmér utca, on the right beyond Kossuth tér is the **Malkocs Bej Mosque** (*Dzsámi; Vörösmárty utca 14; adult/concessions 200/100Ft; open daily 09.00–16.00*), a chunky little relic of the Turkish era. The restored Muslim prayer house – one of the few to survive in Hungary – was built between 1543 and 1565, and has a square stone base and an octagonal brick upper portion topped by a crescent moon. A short distance to the north is a **Serb Orthodox church** (*Táncsics Mihály utca 2; adult/concessions 100/50Ft; open 09.00–17.00 daily*) in Louis XVI style, which reopened a decade ago after lying closed for half a century. Built in 1700, it has a fabulous iconostasis crafted in 1800.

You're better heading for Harkány than the basic **outdoor baths** (*Baross Gábor utca; adult/concessions 400/250Ft; after 14.00 300/150Ft; open 10.00–18.00 daily*), to the south of Kossuth tér. Northeast of the square (follow Táncsics Mihály utca, and turn left on to Dózsa György utca) is a lively **market** that sell clothes, fast food, shoes, souvenirs and much more besides and is popular with Croatian shoppers from just over the border.

## Festivals and events

There are a couple of art festivals at the castle in April and May, while the National Brass Band Festival takes place every other June, and a harvest parade with folk events during Siklós Autumn at the start of October.

# HARKÁNY

At the western end of the Villány Hills, on Road 58 heading north up to Pécs, Harkány is the place to take some water with your wine. The spa resort was established by the Batthyány family in the early 19th century after a peasant, János Pogány, found that the shooting pains in his feet were relieved as he spent days digging canals in the marshlands near Harkány. The sulphurous spring that worked this magic now attracts thousands upon thousands in summer months (indeed, over a million annually), and certainly isn't the place for those averse to crowds.

## Getting there and away

**Buses** (*Bajcsy-Zsilinszky utca*) run every 30 minutes or so to Siklós and Pécs. Direct routes also operate to Villány (six), Mohács (nine) and Sellye (two); there is a twice-daily service to Budapest Népliget and Szekszárd and once-daily buses to Veszprém, Kecskemét and Kalocsa. A sporadic summer service provides access to Stuttgart with two buses departing every Thursday and Sunday.

Reach the centre of town from the **railway station** (*Táncsics Mihály utca*) by turning left and walking along Táncsics Mihály utca, turn right on to Petőfi utca and follow this road along until it becomes Kossuth Lajos utca. Harkány is on the line between Barcs (one) and Villány (six), with direct trains also going to Sellye (four) and Siklós (six). For trains to Pécs and Mohács change at Villány.

## Information and other practicalities

**Listings magazine** *Pécsi Est*

**Mecsek Tours** Bajcsy Zsilinszky utca 2; ❧ 72 480322. Next to the spa entrance, this travel office can help with currency exchange, local excursions and accommodation here and in nearby Siklós and Villány. *Open Mon–Fri 08.30–18.30.*

**Tourinform** Kossuth Lajos utca 2; ❧ 72 479624; e harkany@tourinform.hu. Shares the building with the cultural centre and public library. *Open Jun 15–Sep 15 Mon–Fri 09.00–19.00, Sat–Sun 09.00–18.00, Sep 15–Oct 31 Mon–Fri 09.00–17.00, Sat 09.00–12.00, rest of yr Mon–Fri 09.00–16.00.*

## Where to stay

Tourinform can furnish you with a list of private rooms, and Mecsek Tours (see above) can arrange them. Alternatively, head for Ady Endre utca and its numerous '*Zimmer frei*' signs. There is no shortage of hotels.

**Beta Hotel Agro** (28 rooms) Járó József utca 1; ❧ 72 480336; e agrohot@axelero.hu; www.hotelagro.hu. This is the only hotel in Harkány with its own wellness facilities utilising the town's thermal water. There is a host of curative therapies and treatments on offer, as well as an on-site swimming pool, sauna, jacuzzi, football field, basketball and tennis courts. The rooms are comfortable but fairly nondescript. Near the Thermal Camping site to the northeast of the strand. *Sgl €60, dbl €74, apts €70–90.*

**Hotel Arboretum** (25 rooms) Siklósi utca 21; ❧ 72 480808; www.hotels.hu/arboretum. Settled in pretty grounds to the east of the spa, this hotel has a health centre and dentist. It all looks lovely, and the rooms have balconies; as the name suggests, there is a small arboretum next door. *Sgl 8,500Ft, dbl 11,500Ft.*

**Kokó Panzió** (9 rooms) Arany János utca 7; ❧ 72 480326. The rooms, some with balconies, are spacious and comfortable. The guesthouse is to the west of the spa, on a road leading off Kossuth Lajos utca. *Sgl 5,400Ft, dbl 10,400Ft, triple 12,400Ft.*

**Park Panzió** (5 rooms) Ady Endre utca 10; ❧ 72 478924. This small guesthouse is a touch kitsch, but well-priced and conveniently situated opposite the bus station. It also has a good restaurant (see opposite). *Sgl 6,000Ft, dbl 8,000Ft.*

**Stribli Apartments** Kölcsey tér 7; ❧ 72 479823. Spacious and attractive apartments in pleasant surroundings. *Apts 8,500–10,000Ft.*

**Thermal Camping** Bajcsy-Zsilinszky utca 6; ❧ 72 480117. This site 150m north of the spa entrance has space for 150 caravans and 100 tents. In addition, there's a rather ropey 26-room hotel, a 20-room pension whose rooms aren't en-suite, and 21 bungalows for 4 with bathrooms and kitchens. *Camping: 900Ft/pp, tent 900Ft, caravan 1,800Ft; hotel dbl 7,000Ft; panzió dbl 5,500Ft; bungalow 10,000Ft; open mid Apr–mid Oct (out of season, ❧ 72 478930).*

**Xavin Hotel** (10 rooms) Kossuth Lajos utca 43; ☎ 72 479399; e xavin@freemail.hu; www.hotels.hu/xavinhotel. This lovely hotel has tasteful double rooms, a sauna and swimming pool, and an atmospheric restaurant (see below). *Dbl 12,200Ft.*

## Where to eat and drink
**Muskátlis Csárda** Ady Endre utca 19; ☎ 72 479390. This roomy peasant-style restaurant has an outdoor courtyard and serves Hungarian, Croatian and German specialities. *Mains 850–2,950Ft, avg, 1,800Ft; open 12.00–23.00 daily in summer.*
**Park Restaurant** See opposite. The Hungarian and Croatian dishes are very good indeed, and modestly priced. *Mains 950–1,900Ft, avg 1,500Ft; open 12.00–22.00 daily.*
**Robinson Restaurant** Kossuth Lajos utca 7; ☎ 72 580090. This desert-island-themed restaurant has tables with bamboo canopies; the food is Hungarian, with some pizza and pasta choices available too. *Mains 850–2,590Ft, avg 1,700Ft; open Sun–Thu 11.00–21.00, Fri–Sat 11.00–22.00.*
**Siesta Restaurant** Kossuth Lajos utca 17; ☎ 72 279259. One of the better options on the resort's main strip, the Siesta is decorated with riverscape oil canvases and takes pride in its well-presented Hungarian and international dishes. There are some plates to share. *Mains 890–2,500Ft, avg 1,600Ft; open 08.00–23.00 daily.*
**Xavin Restaurant** See above. The restaurant of the Xavin Hotel is a refined choice with a sun-trapping central courtyard and an extensive menu of game, fish and pastas. There is a cheap 2-course tourist choice. *Mains 880–3,570Ft, avg 1,900Ft; open 07.00–23.00 daily.*

## What to see and do
The **Harkány Spa and Outdoor Pools** (*Harkányi Gyógyfürdő;* Bajcsy-Zsilinsky utca 2) are the town's big draw. The thermal baths (*adult/concessions 1,890/1,150Ft; open daily 09.00–18.00*) and open-air baths (*adult/concessions 900/680Ft; open Jan 3–Jun 16 Sun–Thu 09.00–18.00, Jun 17–Aug 28 09.00–22.00 daily, Aug 29–Dec 23 Fri–Sat 09.00–20.00*) are set in a 14ha park and boast two medicinal thermal pools (35–37°C), five swimming pools (25–35°C), a giant water slide, jacuzzi and whirlpool baths, a playground and a scattering of food huts. There are mud treatments as well as water ones, and you can take part in two daily sessions of water gymnastics (*11.00 & 15.20*). The spa's rheumatism hospital stands on the other side of Zsigmond sétány, and administers traditional and modern thermal therapies. The entrance to the thermal baths is also on Zsigmond sétány, while you can access the outdoor pools from Bajcsy-Zsilinszky utca or Kossuth Lajos utca.

In the wooded park immediately to the south of the entrance to the thermal baths is an **open-air stage** where performances are put on during the summer. Here too is the town's most striking monument, a horny figure rollicking among the grapes; the **Harka Fountain** was made from Zsolnay porcelain and erected in 2000. The nearby **Roman Catholic Church** (*Ady Endre utca*) at the southern end of Kossuth Lajos utca is intriguing for its imaginative form and simple use of carved wood; a small church of 1906 was incorporated into this larger version built by Ferenc Hopp in 1988, and it now forms one of several aisles radiating from the altar in an unusual, organic design. In the garden outside are fire-glazed enamel stations of the cross and stone blocks painted with giants of Hungarian history.

Looking like a mammoth Christmas pudding, the **Millennium Orb Fountain** outside the mayor's office (*Kossuth Lajos utca 2*) is a source of medicinal drinking water. Further up Kossuth Lajos utca is the Baroque **Calvinist church** (*Reformatus templom; Kossuth Lajos utca 66*) built in 1802. When we were last here a family of storks were nesting on a ledge of the clock tower.

## Other
There is a small **market** next to bus station, selling clothes and food. **Bike hire** (*Bajcsy-Zsilinszky utca 3;* ☎ 30 417 9997; *450Ft/hr, 1,600Ft/day; open daily 09.00–19.00*) is available on a walkway beside the Balkon Hotel.

## THE ORMÁNSÁG

The region stretching west from Harkány to Sellye, bordered to the south by the River Dráva, is known as the Ormánság. Flooding in past centuries meant that villages were established on raised platforms, hence its name (*orom* means 'summit' in Hungarian). The area sees few tourists; the wooded landscape is ideal cycling country, while the dead channels of the Dráva will suit those interested in nature.

The villages are perhaps most valued, though, for their **painted Calvinist churches**. These were constructed after József II introduced a greater degree of religious tolerance in 1781; while puritan asceticism generally led to spartan, whitewashed churches, those here are adorned with bright peasant art and coffered ceilings bearing folk motifs. The best examples are in Kóros, Drávaiványi, Adorjás and Kovácshida. You can learn more about the local folk traditions at the **Kiss Géza Kiss Ormánság Museum** (*Sellye, Köztársaság tér 6;* ✎ *73 480245; adult/concessions 200/150Ft; open Tue–Sun Apr 1–Oct 31 10.00–16.00, rest of yr 10.00–14.00*), which also has a stilted house that once stood in Csányoszró. It is easiest to travel into the Ormánság from Harkány; the **train** is the quicker mode and there are services to Sellye and Vajszló (which are served by **buses** too). Buses also run from Szigetvár, and trains from there require a change at Szentlörinc.

## PÉCS

It would be a cantankerous soul who didn't like Pécs, a shifty sort who'd tell you that right was left and red was green before wriggling out of paying his bar tab. A man not to be trusted, you understand. Once you pass through the featureless modern suburbs, you're greeted by a wonderful city that combines old-world charm with contemporary vibrancy, one that contains a premier cathedral, a host of conveniently placed museums and some worthy restaurants, and that is atmospheric by night and friendly by day. You'll see in a shot why it is second only to Budapest on the tourist itinerary.

Summer lingers long in Pécs, which is shielded from northern winds by the Mecsek Hills and wallows in a sub-Mediterranean microclimate. It's no surprise that the Romans felt at home here, establishing a town called Sopianae that was by the 3rd century one of the administrative centres of the province of Pannonia. They cultivated vineyards and fruit trees on the southern slopes, a sweet and lasting legacy that in the 15th century inspired the humanist poet Janus Pannonius to trill about the wonders of the late-blossoming almond trees. As the city grows and houses creep up the hillsides, viniculture is less of an enveloping presence than it once was, but vines are still harvested to the east and west of the centre, and older residents refer to themselves as *tüke* (a word deriving from the Hungarian for 'vinestock').

In 1009 King István made the town an episcopal see, and Lajos the Great opened the country's first university in 1367, when it became a stronghold of Hungarian Renaissance culture. Ottoman occupation had a significant impact; while other settlements during this period were often left to rot, Pécs developed into a thriving oriental centre of commerce and academia. The city held 17 mosques. The residue of this Turkish influence is clearer in Pécs and its architecture than anywhere else in Hungary. Damage was heavy during the fight to remove the Turks, but the city rose again on the shoulders of vintners, coal miners digging in the Mecsek, and leather workers continuing an industry imported by Balkan immigrants. Factories producing luxury goods sprouted, among them Hamerli Gloves, Angster Organ and Zsolnay Ceramics. After the reshaping of borders through the Treaty of Trianon, Pécs's traditional place as a hive of learning was restored when the Hungarian University of Arts and Sciences was moved here from Pozsony (Bratislava) in 1921; in the 1970s, the city's 'Museum Street' was established. The fresh intellectual and cultural energy is palpable, particularly when festivals are in full swing.

## JANUS PANNONIUS

Pannonius was a colourful character, who had enjoyed a humanist education in Italy and was unafraid to attack the greed of the papacy. He was made Bishop of Pécs in 1458 and even served as Chancellor to King Mátyás; however, he had to flee after becoming involved in the doomed Vitéz conspiracy against the king, and died on the run of tuberculosis at the age of just 38.

## Getting there, away and around

The intercity **bus station** (*Zólyom utca*) is 700m southeast of the town centre, next to a large market. Turn right into Bajcsy-Zsilinszky utca, before following Irgalmasok utcaja into Széchenyi tér. There are no shortage of buses to Siklós, Harkány and Mohács, while Szekszárd, Kaposvár and Szigetvár are also well served. Up to five buses a day make the four-hour journey to Budapest Népliget and there are direct routes to Baja (12), Szeged (eight), Zalaegerszeg (five), Székesfehérvár (five), Keszthely (five), Szombathely (three) and Veszprém (two). A twice-daily service links Pécs with Osijek in Croatia; for other Croatian destinations you'll need to travel to Barcs. In the summer months there are two daily buses (Thu & Sun only) that travel to Stuttgart via Székesfehérvár and Munich. The local bus station is also here, from where services leave for villages of the Mecsek Hills.

The elegant twin-turreted **railway station** (*Indóház tér*) is around 1km south of the Belváros – follow Jókai utca (directly in front of you). Up to nine trains a day take the three-hour journey to Budapest Déli, and there are also direct connections to Dombóvár (16), Villány (nine), Szigetvár (eight), Barcs (eight), Mohács (five), Kaposvár (five), Nagykanizsa (three) and Keszthely (two). For Siklós and Harkány change at Villány, and for Szekszárd and Veszprém at Sárbogárd. One train a day links Pécs with Sarajevo – a journey that takes nine hours – while Osijek in Croatia can be reached via a two-hour express train. For Zagreb catch the train to Gyekenyes and pick up the connection.

A **sightseeing tourist train** (*Janus Pannonius utca;* ↘ *06 70 528 4207; adult/concessions 1,200/600Ft- opposite Csontvary Museum*) runs through the city, departing from opposite the Csontvary Museum. The commentary is in Hungarian so don't expect to learn a great deal. The ride takes 40 minutes and leaves roughly on the hour. **Taxis** line up in front of the Trinity Column in Széchenyi tér; try Volán (↘ *72 333 333*) or Euro (↘ *72 233333*).

## Information and other practicalities

**Banks** There are plenty of banks and ATMs, but note that in Pécs banks don't open at all at the weekend.

**Corvina Bookshop** Széchenyi tér 8; ↘ 72 310427. A good selection of English-language books about Hungary by the country's main publisher. *Open Mon–Fri 09.00–18.00, Sat 09.00–13.00.*

**Duna-Dráva National Park Directorate** Tettye tér 9; ↘ 72 517227;
e ddnp.igazg@kym.x400gw.itb.hu. Information on the nearby national park (see page 399).

**Ibusz** Apáca utca 1; ↘ 72 212176. Sightseeing tours, currency exchange and private rooms. *Open Mon–Thu 09.00–18.00, Fri 09.00–16.30, Sat 09.00–12.00.*

**Listings magazine** *Pécsi Est*

**Markets** There is a covered market (*open Mon–Sat 05.30–14.00*) selling fresh food and flowers on Felsőmalom utca, directly east of the centre (off Király utca). However, the biggest market is on Vásártér (*open Sun 06.00–14.00*) – just off Megyeri út 3km to the southwest – where everything is for sale (from antiques to cars!). It's open every Sunday, although it's at its best on the first Sunday of the month; you can catch bus 50 there from the railway station.

**Matrix Internet Café** Király utca 15; ↘ 72 214487. Café with 20 terminals, accessed via an archway off Király utca. *Internet 7Ft/min; open 09.00–23.00 daily.*

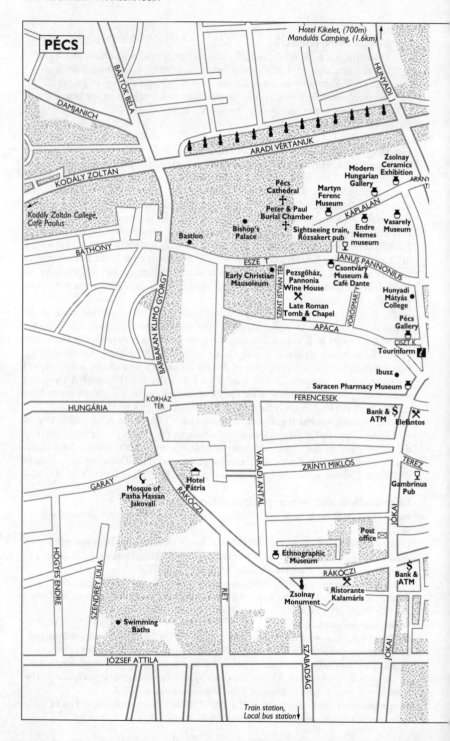

PÉCS

Hotel Kikelet, (700m)
Mandulás Camping, (1.6km)

BARTÓK BÉLA

DAMJANICH

HUNYADI I

ARADI VÉRTANUK

KODÁLY ZOLTÁN

Kodály Zoltán College,
Café Paulus

Zsolnay
Ceramics
Exhibition

ARANY
TI

Modern
Hungarian
Gallery

Pécs
Cathedral

Martyn
Ferenc
Museum

KÁPLALAN

Peter & Paul
Burial Chamber

Bishop's
Palace

Sightseeing train,
Rózsakert pub

Endre
Nemes
museum

Vasarely
Museum

Bastion

BÁTHONY

ESZE T

Early Christian
Mausoleum

Pezsgőház,
Pannonia
Wine House

JANUS PANNONIUS

Csontváry
Museum &
Café Dante

Hunyadi
Mátyás
College

SZENT ISTVÁN TÉR

Late Roman
Tomb & Chapel

VÖRÖSMARTY

Pécs
Gallery

APÁCA

CISZT K

BARBAKÁN KLIMÓ GYÖRGY

Tourinform

Ibusz

Saracen Pharmacy Museum

KÓRHÁZ
TÉR

HUNGÁRIA

FERENCESEK

Bank &
ATM

Elefántos

VÁRADI ANTAL

ZRÍNYI MIKLÓS

TEREZ

GARAY

Mosque of
Pasha Hassan
Jakovali

Hotel
Pátria

RÁKÓCZI

Gambrinus
Pub

JÓKAI

Post
office

HŐGYES ENDRE

SZENDREY JÚLIA

Ethnographic
Museum

RÁKÓCZI

Bank &
ATM

Zsolnay
Monument

Ristorante
Kalamáris

RÉT

Swimming
Baths

JÓKAI

JÓZSEF ATTILA

SZABADSÁG

Train station,
Local bus station

Villa Panzió (700m), Pintér Park (800m), Bagolyvár Hotel (600m), Pécs Zoo (1.2km), TV Lookout tower (2km), Duna-Drava National Park Directorate (700m), Renaissance Bishop's Summer Palace

All Saints Church

Havihegy Chapel (200m), Amusement park (2km)

Hotel Millennium

KÁLVÉRIA

ISTVAN

MEGYE

ÁGOTA

FELSŐ HAVI

PAPNÖVELDE

OSKÚT A

ANNA

KIS F

DR MAJOROSSY IMRE

ALSÓ HAVI

MÉGYE

Croatian Theatre

SZENT MÓR

HUNYADI

ANNA

Fönix Hotel & Cellárиun

JÓZSEF

MÁRIA

MÁRIA

Bóbita Puppet Theatre

JÁNOS

KIRÁLY

Archaeological Museum

Inner City Church

MÁRIA

Mecsek Cukrászda

Hotel Palantinus

KIRÁLY

Lyceum Church

FELSŐMALOM

Market

SZÉCHENYI TÉR

County Hall, Mecsek Tours, Cultural Centre, Murphy's Pub

National Philharmonic ticket office

LICEUM

Town History museum

Virág Cukrászda

National Theatre

PERCZEL

Ábrahám Kishotel

KOLLER

Corvina bookshop

Akvárium Terrárium

IRGALMASOK

MUNKÁCSY MIHÁLY

Lenau Haus (cultural centre)

RÁKÓCZI

Church of the Order of Mercy

TIMÁR

Aranykacsa

Synagogue

Diána Hotel

CITROM

RÁKÓCZI

Lemon Café

BAJCSY ZS

ALSÓMALOM

N

Bradt

BACSÓ BÉLA

NAGY LAJOS KIRÁLY

SOMOGYI BÉLA

BAJCSY ZS

Fruit & veg market

Inner city bus station

0 ———— 150m
0 ———— 150yds

Boccaccio

**Mecsek Tours** Széchenyi tér 1; ✆ 72 513370; e utir@mecsektours.hu. This office in the town hall provides information on tours in and around Pécs, and can aid with booking private accommodation. *Open Mon–Fri 08.30–16.30.*

**Post office** Jókai Mór utca 10. This grand post office deserves a mention for its coloured majolica roof tiles.

**Tourinform** Széchenyi tér 9; ✆ 72 213315; e baranya-m@tourinform.hu. Housed in the County Hall building. *Open Jun 15–Sep 15 Mon–Fri 09.00–20.00, Sat–Sun 09.00–18.00, Sep 16–Oct 31 Mon–Fri 08.00–17.30, Sat–Sun 09.00–14.00, Nov 1–Apr 30 Mon–Fri 08.00–16.00, May 1–Jun 14 Mon–Fri 08.00–17.30, Sat–Sun 09.00–14.00.*

## Where to stay

There isn't a great deal of cheap accommodation in the centre – which is primarily limited to three- and four-star hotels. The majority of the pensions are located in the surrounding hills. Tourinform or Ibusz can help with college rooms in this university city, which are generally available in summer and cost from 1,500Ft per person. Two among many student residences are **Hunyadi Mátyás College** (*Széchenyi István tér 11*) and **Kodály Zoltán College** (*Kodály Zoltán utca 20;* ✆ *72 326968*).

**Ábrahám Kishotel** (5 rooms) Munkácsy Mihály utca 41; ✆ 72 510422. An excellent little find a short distance east of the hustle and bustle of the centre, this tastefully furnished boutique hotel has rooms superior to most others in its price bracket. *Sgl 9,900Ft, dbl 12,200Ft.*

**Bagolyvár Panzió** (19 rooms) Felsőhavi dűlő 6; ✆ 72 211333. This spanking new guesthouse is perched on Havi-hegy to the northeast of the centre, 100m up a steep track near Tettye tér. Its dbl rooms vary in price according to whether you choose one at the back – stupid – or at the front, with superb views down the hill. Bus 33 runs to the bottom of the track before doubling back to Tettye tér and down to the centre. *Dbl 8,500–17,000Ft, apt 19,000Ft.*

**Diána Hotel** (20 rooms) Tímár utca 4/A; ✆ 72 328594. This bright and fresh hotel stands just beyond the southeastern corner of Kossuth tér, next to the synagogue. If you can stretch to it, the plush apartment is worth the extra and has its own little kitchen. Excellent value. *Sgl 8,600Ft, dbl 11,200Ft, apt 14,000Ft.*

**Főnix Hotel** (14 rooms) Hunyadi út 2; ✆ 72 311682. Considering its location just north of Széchenyi tér, the prices are more than affordable. However, while all rooms have showers, some don't have toilets, and it's basic. *Sgl (without toilet) 6,990Ft, dbl (with/without toilet) 10,890/9,590Ft, triple 13,290Ft, apt (for 4–6) 18,990Ft.*

**Hotel Kikelet** (33 rooms) Károlyi Mihály út 1; ✆ 72 512901; e reserve@hotelkikelet.hunguesthotels.hu. Set in the hills to the north, the three-floor Kikelet offers stunning vistas from some of its rooms and has two restaurants. The rooms themselves (standard or superior) are on the sterile side. Stands up a very steep road south of the zoo (see page 424); buses 34, 35A and 35 stop close to hotel. *Sgl €68–82, dbl €82–93.*

**Hotel Millennium** (25 rooms) Kálvária utca 58; ✆ 72 512222; e hotelmillennium@matavnet.hu. Designed by an award-winning architect, this smart hotel is as clean as they come – positively rosy-cheeked with scrubbing. Ask for one of the 3 ground-floor rooms (nos 17, 18 or 19), which have their own patio doors leading on to similarly well-groomed grounds. A 10-minute walk north from the centre, just outside the city walls. *Sgl €70, dbl €79.*

**Hotel Palatinus** (100 rooms) Király utca 5; ✆ 72 889-400; e palatinuspatria.reservations@danubiusgroup.com; www.danubiushotels.com/palatinus. The grandest hotel in town, with a sumptuous lobby and a position at the very heart of things. It's turn-of-the-century elegant, and Béla Bartók once played here, but it's on the pricey side. Standard and superior rooms are available, the latter recently refurbished. *Sgl €65–86, dbl €72–94, triple €93–121.*

**Hotel Pátria** (116 rooms) Rákóczi út 3; ✆ 72 889500; e palatinuspatria@danubiusgroup.com. Unfortunate-looking from the outside, it's much better inside with comfortable and well-equipped rooms. Those on the 3rd floor and above have been renovated, and are superior (and more expensive) than those below. *Sgl €55–76, dbl €76–84.*

**Lenau Haus** (5 rooms) Munkácsy Mihály utca 8; ↘ 72 322515; e lenauhaus@mail.datanet.hu. The German cultural house (see page 419) has some super rooms for a very reasonable price. All have refrigerators and good-sized bathrooms; Otto von Habsburg (the 93-year-old eldest son of Hungary's last king, and a vocal, Austrian-accented champion of the country) stayed in room 3. *Sgl 9,600Ft, dbl 9,800Ft.*

**Mandulás Camping** Ángyán János utca 2; ↘ 72 315981; e mandulas@mecsektours.hu. Situated up in the hills, near the zoo, the campsite has bungalows and hotel accommodation in addition to the tent pitches. Contact Mecsek Tours for information (see opposite). *Open Apr 15–Oct 15.*

**Villa Panzió** Tettye tér 2; ↘ 72 515506. Positioned near the ruins of the Renaissance bishop's summer palace (see page 423), with the rocky hills behind, the Villa's rooms are fabulous, and guests have the use of a shared kitchen. *Sgl 8,500Ft, dbl 10,200Ft, room for 4 12,200Ft.*

## Where to eat and drink

**Aranykacsa Restaurant** Teréz utca 4; ↘ 72 518860; e aranykacsa@mail.datanet.hu: www.miwo.hu/aranykacsa. South of Széchenyi tér, the 'Golden Duck' serves very good, stylish Hungarian and international cuisine and is often recommended by locals. *Mains 990–2,490Ft, avg 1,650Ft; open Mon–Thu 11.00–23.00, Fri–Sat 11.00–24.00, Sun 11.00–16.30 (Jan 5–Feb 23 closed Sun).*

**Bagolyvár** See opposite. Probably the best views of any restaurant in Hungary. The restaurant of the pension on Havi-hegy has a Hungarian menu with stuffed chicken roulade the speciality; the owner's vineyards run down the hill below, and you can do some wine tasting in one of the two cellars. *Mains 1,000–3,000Ft, avg 2,000Ft; open 10.00–23.00 daily.*

**Cellárium** Hunyadi út 2; ↘ 72 314453; e mediterran.hotel@axelero.hu. Based in what was once apparently part of a Turkish catacomb complex, the Cellárium has an extensive choice of primarily Hungarian food (with a good game selection) and a pleasant ambience. It's a cut above, and that's reflected in the prices. *Mains 950–3,500Ft, avg 1,800Ft; open 11.00–23.00 daily.*

**Elefántos** Jókai tér 6; ↘ 72 216055. Busy pizzeria serving grills, pastas, salads and some seafood dishes. *Mains 850–2,400Ft, avg 1,600Ft; open 11.30–24.00 daily.*

**Lemon Café** Citrom utca 7; ↘ 72 532848. This swanky, youthful hangout hidden behind the fountain off Citrom utca has a range of light meals including crêpes, omelettes, pastas, sandwiches and salads. Otherwise it's cocktails and alcoholic milkshakes. *Mains 490–2,200Ft, avg 1,000Ft; open 08.00–24.00 daily.*

**Mecsek Cukrászda** Széchenyi tér 16; ↘ 72 315444. Squeezed between Maria utca and Király utca, Mecsek vies with Virág for the gong for best *cukrászda* in Pécs. For us, the outdoor seating just swings it the Virág's way, but we've sampled many a pastry at each in reaching the decision. *Open 09.00–22.00 daily.*

**Pezsgőház** Szent István tér 12; ↘ 72 210084; e pezsgohaz@dravanet.hu. Choose between the super-elegant cellar or the more relaxed, al-fresco terrace overlooking the square. The menu is international and upmarket – you can enjoy a glass of champagne with your caviar entrée, before tucking into a menu that bandies about options like foie gras, homemade pasta, pink duck breast and the like. There is also a range of healthy dishes – grilled meat with salad and yoghurt dressings. If you feel that food is a distraction from concentrated wine-tasting time, the Pannonia Wine House (see below) can help. *Mains 900–3,800Ft, avg 2,200Ft; open Mon–Sat 11.30–23.00, Sun 11.00–16.00.*

**Pannonia Wine House** See above. If you can handle your bubbles, the Pannonia Wine House (below the Pezsgőház) is Hungary's first 'champagne' factory. Its cellars date to the Turkish era, and extend over 2.5km. The company was founded in 1859, and it uses wine from Siklós to create 13 different types of sparkling wine. You can buy bottles from its shop in the restaurant, and tours of the cellars (together with tastings) are available for groups by prior arrangement.

**Ristorante Kalamáris** Rákóczi út 30; ↘ 72 312573. Plush country-style restaurant that aims at old-fashioned hospitality. Service is admirably unrushed compared with many restaurants in

Hungary; the menu includes specialities of the Baranya region alongside some international flavours. Draws diners away from the very centre. *Mains 1,200–2,800Ft, avg 1,900Ft; open Mon–Fri 11.00–22.00, Sat 11.00–16.00.*

**Tettye Vendégő** Tettye tér 4; ↘ 72 532788. Large restaurant with a gravelled outdoor eating area at the edge of the hills. Hungarian and German cuisine, along with a few pasta dishes. Live music most evenings from 19.00. *Open 11.00–23.00 daily.*

**Virág Cukrászda** Széchenyi tér 7; ↘ 72 222223. Excellent cakes and ices, as well as cocktails, milkshakes and coffees. Opposite the town hall. *Open Sun–Thu 10.00–23.00, Fri–Sat 10.00–24.00.*

## Nightlife

The high number of students means a proportionately healthy number of clubs and bars. Those that follow don't even tickle the iceberg's tip; check *Pécsi Est* for the full run-down.

**Boccaccio** Bajcsy-Zsilinszky utca 45; ↘ 06 20 992 3097. Sweaty club with resident and visiting DJs playing music ranging from techno to Eurotrash. It is housed in an industrial building next to the rail track, a kilometre southeast of the centre beyond the bus station. *Open Thu–Sat 20.00–04.00.*

**Café Dante** Janus Pannonius utca 8–10; ↘ 72 210361. Relaxed, studenty café/bar/club on the ground floor of the Csontváry Museum. It also has internet access *(from 10Ft/min). Open 10.00–01.00 daily.*

**Café Paulus** Ifjúság út 6; ↘ 72 503636. This bar with two-tiered decked terrace is another popular hangout, although it's 1.5km west of the centre on the main road running past the northern city walls. Buses 30 and M55 stop near by. *Mon–Fri 09.00–24.00, Sat–Sun 16.00–24.00.*

**Gambrinus Pub** Teréz utca 17; ↘ 72 210075. Cheap booze and snacks; festooned with bamboo (the place, not the snacks). *Open Mon–Thu 08.30–23.00, Fri–Sat 08.30–24.00, Sun 10.00–23.00.*

**Hard Rák Café** Ipari út 7. There's hard rock, obviously, but also other music from hip-hop to Hungarian 'classics'. Don't bother getting there earlier than 23.00. *Open Thu–Sat 22.00–05.00.*

**Murphy's Pub** Király utca 2; ↘ 72 325439. Attracts the English speakers and serves the worst Guinness we've ever tasted (we've seen a bigger head on a cup of tea). The interior makes a fair stab at a British pub; housed at the rear of the town hall building. *Open 10.00–24.00 daily.*

**Rózsakert Pub** Janus Pannonius utca 8–10; ↘ 72 310862. There's a cosy cellar bar, outdoor seating and a roof terrace restaurant where the older fogies can pretend to be young and trendy. You can play table football inside. *Open Mon–Sat 10.00–01.00, Sun 10.00–24.00.*

## Entertainment

As a city of culture, Pécs holds its own with any city in Hungary, and has traditionally been one of the prime provincial centres of national drama. Its ballet and opera companies are well respected, as is its 92-member orchestra. The **National Theatre** (*Nemzeti Színház; Színház tér 1;* ↘ *72 811965; www.pecsinemzetiszinhaz.hu*), set back from Király utca, is the place to head. Its box office (*Perczel utca 17;* ↘ *72 512675;* e *szervezes@pnsz.hu; open Tue–Fri 10.00–19.00, Sat–Sun 1hr prior to performance*) also sells tickets for the smaller adjacent **Chamber Theatre** (*Kamaraszínház*). The website provides a programme listing for both – and it's in English. The **Pannon Philharmonic Orchestra** holds concerts at the university (*Szigeti utca 12*) and in the cathedral, as well as at the National Theatre; tickets and information are available from the **National Philharmonic Ticket Office** (*Nemzeti Filharmónia;* Király utca 18; ↘ 72 437975; e filharmonia@freemail.hu; open Mon–Thu 09.00–16.00, Fri 09.00–15.00). The **cultural centre** (*Széchenyi tér 1;* ↘ *72 336622;* e *pkk@mail.pserve.hu; www.pkkinfo.hu; open Mon 08.00–16.00, Tue–Fri 09.00–17.00, Sat 10.00–14.00*), sandwiched between Mecsek Tours and McDonald's in the town hall building, should be able to assist with queries about other arts events. There is a **ticket kiosk** (*Sétatér; open Tue–Sun 15.00–20.00*) near Janus Pannonius utca that operates during festival periods.

The **Bóbita Puppet Theatre** (*Bábszínház; Mária utca 18;* ❧ *72 211791;* e *bobita@bobita.hu; www.bobita.hu; box office open Tue–Fri 09.00–11.00, 13.00–15.00*) puts on plays of classic children's tales, as well as holding outdoor shows for adults. Performance times vary, although there is usually one at 10.00. The ruins of the **Renaissance bishop's summer palace** (*Tettye tér;* see page 423) form a wonderful backdrop for outdoor concerts and theatrical productions, mainly held during festivals; you can get tickets from the kiosk listed above or from the **Croatian Theatre** (*Horvát Színház; Anna utca 17;* ❧ *72 210197; www.horvatszinhaz.hu; ticket office open Mon–Fri 08.30–16.00*). Another venue for concerts and cultural events is the **Lenau Haus** (*Munkácsy Mihály utca 8;* ❧ *72 322515;* e *lenauhaus@mail.datanet.hu; open 08.00–15.00 in summer and 08.00–16.00 during other months*), an institute for German minorities. It hosts temporary art exhibitions by German and Austrian artists in Hungary and ethnographic displays. Its garden contains the remains of a 13th-century Dominican monastery that was destroyed during the Turkish occupation. Also here is a statue of a German youth with staff and bag, a monument to the 230,000 ethnic German Hungarians who were felt to be 'guilty by association' and driven from the country after World War II. Otto von Habsburg (see page 417) is a regular visitor.

## What to see and do
### Széchenyi tér
The city's nucleus is Széchenyi tér, divided between upper and lower sections and giving way to streets feeding from it in all directions. During the Middle Ages it was the market place and in the Turkish period was filled with Ottoman vendors manning bustling bazaars. The 18th century saw the oriental atmosphere seep away as the buildings were torn down and replaced with Baroque ones. The square became the public face of political life; here the 12 points were read during the revolution of 1848, and here the local revolutionaries were flogged when the uprising was quashed. The Eclectic and oversized **former town hall** (*Széchenyi tér 1*) stands at the southeastern corner, built in 1907 and now housing Murphy's Pub among other things.

To the west of it is **County Hall** (*Széchenyi tér 9*), constructed in 1898 with colourful roof tiles and reliefs from the Zsolnay factory (see box, page 424). The Zsolnay family lived at no 17, and the factory was also responsible for the glazed ox-headed gargoyles in front of the 18th-century **Church of the Order of Mercy** (*Széchenyi tér 5*); the fountain was modelled on an ancient drinking vessel unearthed at Nagyszentmiklós and positioned on the spot of an earlier Turkish well.

As well as the **Trinity Column** of 1908 by György Kiss, the centre of the square holds the **statue of János Hunyadi** by Pál Pátzay; Pátzay was the 1956 winner of the competition to design a monument on the 500th anniversary of victory over the Turks at Nándorfehérvár. But the main sight of the square – indeed, one of the symbols of the town – is the **Inner City Church** (*open Apr 15–Oct 15 Mon–Sat 10.00–16.00, Sun 11.30–16.00, Oct 16–Apr 14 Mon–Sat 10.00–12.00, Sun 11.30–14.00*) rising at the northern end. We forgive you for a quick double take for it's an unlikely place of Roman Catholic worship. When originally built in 1579 by Pasha Gazi Kassim, the *djami* was the biggest mosque in Hungary. The pasha used money from the ransom of a prisoner to fund the project, tearing down the Gothic St Bertalan Church that occupied the spot and recycling its stones in the structure of the mosque. After the Turks had gone, Jesuits made changes, but 20th-century renovations stripped some of these back and uncovered a prayer niche facing Mecca, painted Turkish epigraphs from the Koran (to the left as you enter) and the base of a minaret that had been replaced with a tower. The organ was crafted by the famous Angster firm of Pécs. The mosque is one of the most significant pieces of remaining Turkish architecture in Hungary.

### Király utca, Kossuth tér and around

Király utca runs east from the bottom of Széchenyi tér, and is a tourist hub with its pizzerias, bars and cafés. The Baroque **Lyceum Church** (*Líceum templom; Király utca 44*) was built by the Pauline order in the mid 18th century, while its adjacent monastery now holds a school. The **Akvárium Terrárium** (*Munkácsy Mihály utca 31;* \ *75 532151; adult/concessions 500/250Ft; open Oct 1–Feb 28 09.00–17.00 daily*) sits on the second parallel road to the south; it has a varied collection of fish and reptiles (some of the larger of which look rather cramped), and a small aviary.

To the south of Széchenyi tér, the oblong Kossuth tér has a Romantic-style **synagogue** (*Kossuth tér 1–3;* \ *72 315881; adult 200Ft; open May 1–Oct 31 Sun–Fri 10.00–11.30, 12.00–17.00*) at its eastern side, raised in 1865 and containing the first organ ever made by the Angster factory. A book of remembrance commemorates the 4,000 Jews that were deported from Pécs to death camps in 1944. The bright, Eclectic building on the northern edge now houses offices of the town hall. Kids will love the risqué detail on a corner of the shopping parade at the square's western end, which includes some suggestively arranged pieces of sculpted fruit. Melons feature.

### Apáca utca and Szent István tér

The area to the west of Széchenyi tér held an early-Christian cemetery of the Roman town of Sopianae, and over 100 graves have been excavated; these were awarded Unesco World Heritage Site status in 2000. The first lie on Apáca utca, and comprise a **late Roman tomb and chapel** (*Ókeresztény Sírkapolna; Apáca utca 8 and 14;* \ *72 312719*) from the 4th century AD. There are the graves of three adults and a child, complete with sepulchral statues, and the remains of a chapel used by Christians (who arrived during the 3rd and 4th centuries). You'll need to ask at the early Christian mausoleum (see below) to gain admittance.

Szent István tér is divided from Dóm tér above it by Janus Pannonius utca. During festival times, this area of the city is a focal point, and Janus Pannonius utca is filled with stalls peddling food, drink and souvenirs. In 1975, during the demolition of an artificial waterfall, an **early Christian mausoleum** (*Ókeresztény Mauzóleum; Szent István tér;* \ *72 312719; adult/concessions 600/400Ft; open Apr 1–Oct 31 Tue–Sat 10.00–18.00, Sun 10.00–14.00, Nov 1–Mar 31 Tue–Sun 10.00–16.00*) came to light. The outline of the walls of the single-naved 4th-century chapel are open to the elements in a sunken section of the square, while below them is a burial chamber containing a 3rd-century white marble sarcophagus. On the walls are some well-preserved painted biblical scenes, including Daniel in the lion's den and the original guilty pair in the Garden of Eden holding fig leaves over their bits.

### Dóm tér and around

Dóm tér was originally surrounded by fortified castle walls, and the area of Szent István tér was kept clear to ensure that the guns had a free line of fire. The battlements were considerably stronger than the outer city walls, and they repelled attack by Miklós Zrínyi in 1664 and could have held out during the 1696 siege had the Turkish water supply not dried up. The four-towered Neo-Romanesque **Pécs Cathedral** (*Székésegyház;* \ *72 513030; adult/concessions 600/300Ft for church, 800/400Ft for crypt, treasury, burial vaults and wine cellar; open Apr 1–Oct 15 Mon–Fri 09.00–17.00, Sat 09.00–14.00, Sun 09.00–17.00, Oct 16–Mar 31 Mon–Fri 10.00–16.00, Sat 10.00–14.00, Sun 13.00–17.00*) is of course the square's dominant force. Its earliest parts date to the 11th century, but it has endured several reconstructions, most recently in the 19th century when both Mihály Pollack and Friedrich von Schmidt had a stab (the latter tasked with restoring its appearance to that of the original church from the Árpád period). The late Pope John Paul II visited in 1991 and raised it to the rank of 'basilica minor'.

The interior is decorated with paintings by premier historicist artists Bertalan Székely and Károly Lotz, while the Corpus Christi Chapel – one of the side chapels that stand beneath each of the towers – holds a fine work of the Hungarian Renaissance, the red marble altar commissioned by Bishop Szatmáry in 1521. (Note too the wonderful bronze handle on the chapel doors, held tightly in the teeth of a mythical beast.) During the Turkish period, this chapel was used for Muslim worship, while all the others served as stables. Staircases either side of the apse lead to the vaulted crypt, which is the oldest part of the cathedral; evidence suggests that it probably incorporated an early-Christian burial chamber. The combined entrance ticket (see opposite) gets you a complimentary glass of wine in the nearby Püspöki Pince, as well as access to the nearby tomb sites and to the Bishop's Palace (*open Wed only*).

Looking like a slab of Dairy Milk, the **Bishop's Palace** (*Püspöki Palota;* ✆ *72 513030; adult/concessions 1,600/800Ft; open Jun 25–Sep 6 Wed only 14.00–17.30*) has stood at the western side of the square since King István first established Pécs's cathedral, although it has been rebuilt on several occasions. Bishop György Klimó instigated one such reconstruction in the 18th century, and unselfishly opened up his library in the western wing to the public. The benevolent Klimó was a favourite of Maria Theresa, and she presented him with the Gobelin tapestries on the staircase. The sculpture of the long-haired Liszt leaning on the southern balcony was added in 1983. Beside it is a gate leading around the 15th-century castle wall and bastion (supposedly built under the supervision of Pál Kinizsi), which links up with the extant northern section of the main city walls.

In front of the cathedral at the eastern side of the square is the **Peter and Paul Burial Chamber** (*Péter-Pál Sírkamra; adult/concessions 400/200Ft; open Tue–Sun Apr 1–Oct 31 10.00–18.00, Nov 1–Mar 31 10.00–16.00*), which was discovered in 1782 and excavated by the historian József Koller. The surface chapel hasn't survived, but the crypt is decorated with Christian paintings including Jonah and the whale, the Fall, a rare early depiction of Christ and Mary, and the saints after whom the site is named. The richness of the decoration suggests that this was the resting place of an influential member of Sopianae. A small aperture in the northern wall probably originally held a martyr's bones. The **Wine Jug Burial Chamber** (*Korsós Sírkamra; adult/concessions 400/200Ft*) stands 20m away, where two sarcophagi were found during 20th-century explorations; a niche bears a painting of an amphora – probably symbolic of the Eucharist – while the side walls are adorned with floral motifs. Recent studies date the crypt to around AD395. You can visit both of the above chambers individually, or purchase a joint ticket (*adult/concessions 600/300Ft*) giving access to both.

Around 500m southwest of Dóm tér, the **Mosque of Pasha Hassan Jakovali** (*Rákóczi út 2;* ✆ *72 227166; adult/concessions 200/100Ft; open Apr 1–Oct 31 Thu–Tue 10.00–13.00, 14.00–18.00*) was built in the latter half of the 16th century, and is remarkable for being the only place in Hungary where both the minaret and the Muslim prayerhouse remain intact. It's easily missed, jammed up against larger modern buildings; inside is a display of Ottoman artefacts. A little further out are some **swimming baths** (*Pécsi Hullámfürdő; Szendrey Júlia utca 7;* ✆ *72 512955; adult/concessions 660/400Ft; open daily indoor pool 06.00–22.00, outdoor pool 09.00–19.00*); the open-air pool has a wave machine.

## Museums and galleries

Pécs is saturated with museums and collections, each a mark of the city's conscious effort to remain at the country's cultural and intellectual top table. There is even a dedicated street – Káptalan utca – along which the bulk are ranged. Most are run by the Baranya County Museum Authority, and you can buy a daily ticket (*adult/concessions 1,700/850Ft*) that allows access to any of the museums under its umbrella. This ticket is on sale at all the participating museums; it excludes entry to sights like the cathedral, burial vaults, synagogue and mosque.

**Archaeological Museum** (*Régészeti Múzeum*) Széchenyi tér 12; ☏ 72 312719. Behind the Inner City Church, this museum displays finds from Baranya County dating from the Neolithic period up to the age of the Great Migration (when the Carpathian Basin was occupied by a series of nomadic tribes, including the 5th-century Huns, the 6th-century Avars and finally the Magyars, who pitched up in the 9th century). There are also artefacts from the Roman settlement of Sopianae, among them tombs and votive altars in the courtyard dating from the 2nd to the 4th centuries AD. *Adult/concessions 300/150Ft; open Nov 1–Mar 31 Tue–Sun 10.00–16.00; Apr 1–Oct 31 Tue–Sat 10.00–18.00, Sun 10.00–16.00.*

**Csontváry Museum** Janus Pannonius utca 11; ☏ 72 310544. Originally a pharmacist, Tivadar Csontváry Kosztka (1853–1919; see also *Hungarian National Gallery*, page 166) developed into a quite extraordinary artist. Like all true geniuses – and Picasso declared him to be his only 20th-century equal, so who are we to argue – there was a healthy dollop of madness in the man. He died insane, penniless and largely unrecognised, but not before producing a body of work that is as visionary as it is at times disturbing. Among masterpieces that took Hungarian landscapes for their theme is *The Storm on the Great Hortobágy* (1903), but he also tackled biblical and historical subjects in attempting to reconcile the various strands of his philosophical and spiritual make up. Perhaps the most ambitious example of this comes in *Baalbeck*, a massive canvas measuring 30m. Unmissable. *Adult/concessions 600/300Ft; open Tue–Sun Apr 1–Oct 31 10.00–18.00, Nov 1–Mar 31 10.00–16.00.*

**Endre Nemes Museum** Káptalan utca 5; ☏ 72 324822. The surrealist artist Endre Nemes lived in Pécsvárad before moving to Sweden; the former ecclesiastical building shows 250 of his works created between the 1940s and 1970s, the later ones reminiscent of Salvador Dalí. At the back is Erzsébet Schaár's *Utca*, an odd and faintly spooky plaster installation featuring figures in coloured wigs peeping through windows. *Adult/concessions 400/200Ft; open Apr 1–Oct 31 Tue–Sun 10.00–14.00, by prior appointment only Nov 1–Mar 31.*

**Ethnographic Museum** (*Néprajzi Múzeum*) Rákóczi út 15; ☏ 72 315629. Here you'll find 18th- and 19th-century folk art, embroidery and costume of some of the ten ethnographic groups to be found in Baranya County. Follow Jókai utca south from Széchenyi tér, and turn right on to Rákóczi út. The museum stands near the Zsolnay Monument. *Adult/concessions 300/150Ft; open Apr 1–Oct 31 Tue–Sun 10.00–14.00.*

**Martyn Ferenc Museum** Káptalan utca 6; ☏ 72 324822. Ferenc Martyn (1899–1986) was a painter, sculptor, graphic artist and disciple of disciple of József Rippl Rónai. Martyn led the way in Hungarian non-figurative art after spending 15 years in Paris; among the exhibited pieces are illustrations he painted for a Hungarian translation of James Joyce's *Ulysses*. *Adult/concessions 400/200Ft; open Apr 1–Oct 31 Tue–Sun 10.00–14.00, Nov 1–Mar 31 by prior appointment only.*

**Mining Museum** (*Mecseki Bányászati Múzeum*) Káptalan utca 3; ☏ 72 324822. Underneath the Vasarely Museum (see opposite), this museum tells the tale of mining in the Mecsek Hills – an industry significant in Pécs's growth after coal was discovered in the mid 18th century. The 400m-long cellars are set up like a real mine shaft, and the drop in temperature at the bottom is startling (fortunately the friendly curator is on hand to loan a sweater to T-shirt-wearing tourists). Alongside the miners' tools, there's a mineral display. *Adult/concessions 400/200Ft; open Tue–Sun 10.00–17.30.*

**Modern Hungarian Gallery** Káptalan utca 4 and Papnövelde utca 5; ☏ 72 324822. The largest collection of 20th-century Hungarian art outside Budapest's Hungarian National Gallery is divided in two. Gallery I (on Káptalan utca) deals with the years between 1890 and 1950, book-ended by the leading lights of the Nagybánya (Hollósy and Ferenczy) and Szentendre (Vajda, Barcsay, Metty and Álmos) artists' colonies and with greats like Rippl-Rónai in between. Its epoch spanned the emergence of modernist tendencies up to the radical political changes of the late 1940s. Gallery II covers 1955 to the present, charting the development of art in the aftermath of Socialist-Realism. *Adult/concessions 400/200Ft; open Apr 1–Oct 31 Tue–Fri 10.00–18.00, Sat–Sun 10.00–16.00, Nov 1–Mar 31 Tue–Sun 10.00–16.00 (call in advance to visit Gallery II in winter months).*

**Natural Sciences Exhibition** Szabadság utca 2; ☏ 72 213419. To the south of the centre, in between the Zsolnay Monument and the Zsolnay House, the Natural Science Department has displays of insects and other regional wildlife, and an exhibition of the natural heritage of 'Mediterranean Baranya'. *Adult/concessions 300/150Ft; open Tue–Sun Apr 1–Oct 31 10.00–18.00, Nov 1–Mar 31 10.00–16.00.*

**Pécs Gallery** Széchenyi tér 11; ➤ 72 210436; www.pecsgallery.hu. Temporary exhibitions of modern art; the entrance is on Ciszterci köz, near the County Hall. *Adult/concessions 200/100Ft, free entry on Sun; open Mon–Sat 10.00–18.00, Sun 12.00–18.00.*

**Saracen Pharmacy Museum** (*Szerecsen Patika Múzeum*) Apáca utca 1; ➤ 72 315702. This working pharmacy has stood here since 1764, and bears a sculpture of a Moor by Gyula Zsolnay above the entrance. Behind County Hall. *Admission free; open Mon–Thu 08.00–16.30, Fri 08.00–14.00.*

**Town History Museum** (*Várostörténeti Múzeum*) Felsőmalom utca 9; ➤ 72 310165. Covers the period from the end of Turkish occupation up to the post-war political changes of 1948. The museum is inside an 18th-century tanner house (*timárház*) just to the south of Király utca, leather-working being one of the prime occupations during the city's industrial boom. *Adult/concessions 300/150Ft; open Tue–Sat 10.00–16.00.*

**Vasarely Museum** Káptalan utca 3; ➤ 72 324822. Victor Vasarely (1908–97), the original 'Op Artist', was born in this house and since his death it's become something of a place of pilgrimage. Like the museum in Budapest (see page 170), here you'll find paintings that incorporate geometrical, kaleidoscopic designs to play with notions of space and depth – and not infrequently to make the viewer feel mildly queasy. In addition to 700 of his own works, you'll also see pieces by Victor's wife and son. *Adult/concessions 600/300Ft; open Tue–Sun Nov 1–Mar 31 10.00–16.00, rest of yr 10.00–18.00.*

**Zsolnay Ceramics Exhibition** (*Zsolnay kerámia kiállítás*) Káptalan utca 2; ➤ 72 324822. On the first floor of the city's oldest residential building – dating to the 14th century – is an exhibition devoted to the ceramics produced by the famous Zsolnay company (see box, page 424). The Pécs factory produced ornamental and everyday pieces, and the collection shows the evolution from handicraft to industrial technology through the 19th and 20th centuries. The work reached its zenith at the turn of the 20th century when architects developing a specifically Hungarian Art Nouveau style – known as Secessionist – employed Zsolnay reliefs and tiles in their designs. A memorial room contains personal items of the Zsolnay family, including some early paintings by Vilmos. You can press a button in each of the rooms to hear a commentary in English. A small room on the ground floor displays some of the works donated to the city by Amerigo Tot (1909–84), the Hungarian-born sculptor who lived in Italy from 1937. There's something deeply satisfying about his big-bottomed and thick-wristed figures. *Adult/concessions 700/350Ft; open Apr 1–Oct 31 Tue–Sat 10.00–18.00, Sun 10.00–14.00; Nov 1–Mar 31 Tue–Sun 10.00–16.00.*

## Beyond the centre

Unusually in Hungary, the medieval walls to the north of the city remain in good condition; in part this is because they were so ineffectual – too long to be successfully defended and too low to shield shots from attackers on the hillside – that invaders didn't inflict too much damage in breaching them. The suburb of Budaiváros lies to the northeast, where the Hungarians settled after being banished from the centre by the Turkish occupiers. They congregated around the 13th-century **All Saints' Church** (*Mindenszentek temploma; Tettye utca 14*), which was the only Christian church of the period and had to be shared – deeply reluctantly – by three different denominations. Ironically, after the Turks had gone the Hungarians returned to the centre and Bosnians (Christian converts from Islam who remained in Pécs) were displaced to Budaiváros.

Continue up Tettye utca (which runs north from Kálvária utca) to Tettye tér, a park that holds the ruins of the **Renaissance bishop's summer palace** (*Szathmány püspök reneszánsz nyaralójának romjai*); built as a relaxing bolt-hole by Bishop György Szathmáry in the early 16th century, it was used as a dervish monastery by the Turks. Today it forms the venue for outdoor concerts (see page 419). **Pintér Park** (*Tettye tér 9;* ➤ *72 517223;*

## ZSOLNAY CERAMICS

The Zsolnay ceramics dynasty began in 1853 when the merchant Imre Zsolnay established a stoneware factory, but it really took off under his brother Vilmos in 1865. An innovator and a perfectionist, Vilmos worked with a Budapest chemist to create 'eosin', an iridescent metallic glaze named after the Greek goddess of dawn that became a unique and instantly recognisable hallmark of some Zsolnay pieces – you can see it in the ox-head fountain in Széchenyi tér (see page 419). Perceptive and experimental, Vilmos put Zsolnay at the forefront of the Hungarian Art Nouveau movement; its vases and jugs decorated with folk motifs, together with tiles used to adorn the roofs and facades of turn-of-the-century buildings, meant that the name rapidly became renowned all over Europe. For a time, a third of the ceramics produced in the Austro-Hungarian empire came from the Pécs factory. Unfortunately, when his son Miklós inherited the business the quality started to fall away, and the company reached a new low under nationalisation when it was forced to make ceramic electrical insulators. While it resumed the production of luxury pieces in 1957, it never again scaled those Vilmos-inspired heights.

*adult/concessions 200/100Ft; open May 1–Sep 30 Sat–Sun 10.00–18.00, other times by prior arrangement*), at the western side of the square, is a small arboretum managed by the Duna-Dráva National Park. If you follow the rising road east from Tettye tér, you'll come to **Havihegy Chapel** (*Havihegyi út*), a Baroque votive church built in 1697 after a bout of plague. The stones to build it were carried up the hill by hand. Phew! It's an hour's walk from the centre up to Tettye tér; alternatively bus 33 runs up there every 20 minutes or so from the centre.

Heading further north, the foothills get steeper as they approach the Mecsek Hills proper. To the northwest of Tettye tér, Fenyves sor leads to **Pécs Zoo** (*Fenyves sor; office at Munkácsy Mihály utca 31;* ✆ *72 317005; www.zoo.hu/pecs; adult/concessions 600/450Ft; open daily summer 09.00–18.00, winter 09.00–16.00*). It's had a troubled past – there were shockwaves when it was alleged that rogue keepers had been allowing hunters in after dark to shoot rare animals – but there's been extensive recent improvement of the enclosures. Buses 34, 35 and 35A stop outside.

A narrow-gauge railway runs northeast from the zoo up to a fairly tame **amusement park** (*Vidám; Dömörkapu;* ✆ *72 315985; adult/concessions 200/150Ft; open Mar 15–Aug 31 Tue–Sun 10.00–17.00*), while the left-hand road from the lower station takes you up to the Misina peak and its **TV Lookout Tower** (*Misina tető;* ✆ *72 336900; adult/concessions 400/350Ft; open 09.00–17.30 daily*). The tower stands 200m above the 550m peak, and provides stunning views over the Mecsek Hills and beyond the River Dráva; you can board a lift to the top. Bus 35A chugs to a car park near the amusement park, while bus 35 goes to the tower. Several walking trails kick off from here into the Mecsek (see opposite).

### Festivals and events

There is no shortage of festivals in Pécs. Among the main ones are the two-week International Music Festival (*Jun/Jul*), the National Theatre Festival (*first half of Jun*), the Weeks of Art and Gastronomy (*Jul*) and Pécs Days (*Sep*), the latter including traditional music and dance by minority ethnic groups and featuring the Drinking Song Festival. There is a festival information bureau in the town hall building (*Széchenyi tér 1;* ✆ *72 336622; open Mon–Fri 09.00–17.00, Sat 10.00–14.00*), and don't forget that a ticket kiosk (*open Tue–Sun 15.00–20.00*) near Janus Pannonius utca operates during festival periods.

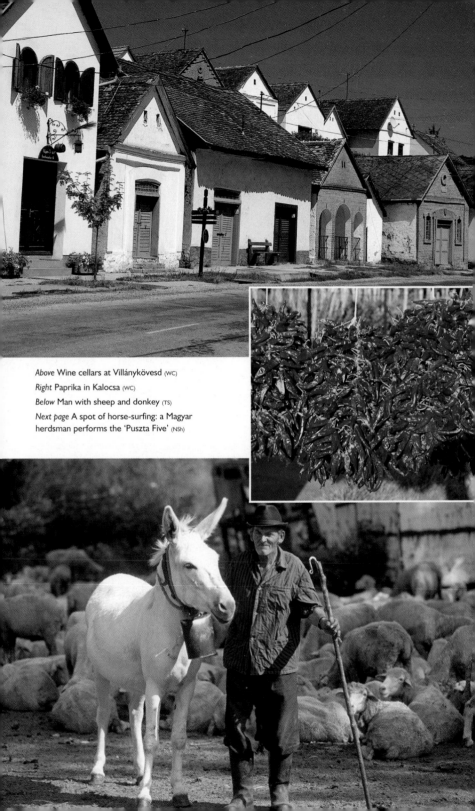

*Above* Wine cellars at Villánykövesd (WC)

*Right* Paprika in Kalocsa (WC)

*Below* Man with sheep and donkey (TS)

*Next page* A spot of horse-surfing: a Magyar herdsman performs the 'Puszta Five' (NSh)

## Excursions

Pécs is the ideal starting point for trips into the **Mecsek Hills**, which border it to the north. Favourite destinations in the nearby foothills include Misina Peak and Dömörkapu, each of which can be reached by local bus. Hiking trails forging out into the hills can be picked up from there – for example from the base of the TV Lookout Tower – but if you are planning to hike be sure to buy a map (such as *A Mecsek*, 1: 40,000, by Cartographia). The highest peak is at Zengő (682m) at the eastern end of the range. Another hill over 600m lies to the northwest of Pécs; the plateau at the top of Jakab-hegy (602m) holds the remains of a medieval Pauline monastery, and is surrounded by a 7th-century earthwork. To the south, the Zsongor Rock (Zsongor-kő) is a great lookout point, and near it are the so-called 'baby-shaped' rock formations (Babás szerkövek). The West-Mecsek Rural Tourism Association (*Cserkút, Alkotmány utca 10;* ✆ *72 731988*) can give information on accommodation and programmes in the locality.

Directly to the north of Jakab-hegy are two popular resorts. Orfű is 16km from Pécs and based around four artificial lakes, which offer watersports possibilities. There is a Mill Museum near the smallest of the lakes, Lake Orfű, and the Tekeresi Lovaspanzió (*Petőfi Sándor utca 3; 40 beds, from €15/pp*) arranges horse-riding (from yard riding to a six-day mounted tour into the surrounding hills). For further information, contact JUVE Travel Agency in Pécs (*Ferencesek utca 41;* ✆ *72 333381;* e *juvetour@mail.matav.hu*). A couple of kilometres to the west is Abaliget, where you can visit a 1,500m-long stalactite cave set into the side of Bodó-hegy, and where there is also a bat cave. Both Abaliget and Orfű can be reached by bus from Pécs, and have pensions and campsites. For further details on hiking in the Mecsek, contact the Baranya County Naturalist Association in Pécs (*Apáca utca 2;* ✆ *72 525376; open Tue only 16.00–19.00*).

Head west from Pécs for 33km on Road 6 and you'll reach **Szigetvár**, whose castle is a monument to a supreme historical moment of brave patriotism that was immortalised by the poet Miklós Zrínyi and that – though still in a lost cause – acted in small measure as a counterweight to Mohács. For 33 days of 1566, the great-grandfather of the poet resisted a Turkish force over 30 times the size of his own, before leading his men on a final charge to their deaths when it was clear the game was up (see box, page 426).

Originally constructed in the 14th century on an island among the marshes of the Almás Stream – hence the name 'Island Castle' – the four-towered fort was rebuilt by the Turks in the aftermath of the battle. The Zrínyi Miklós Castle Museum (*Vár utca 9;* ✆ *73 311442; adult 150Ft; open Apr 1–Oct 31 Tue–Sun 09.00–17.00*) has artefacts and documents relating to the battle, and there is also a mosque (*Szulejmán pasa dzsámija*), built by the Turks in the aftermath of victory, and a Baroque tower within the castle walls. On the way south along Vár utca you'll pass a café and Museum of Local History (*Vár utca 1*) before reaching Zrínyi tér, with its lion monument to the fallen heroes. Believe it or not, the St Rókus Roman Catholic church (*Zrínyi tér 9*) is another vestige of the Turkish era, built as the Pasha Ali Mosque in 1589; it was converted into a Baroque church in the 18th century. Near the bus station to the southeast is the country's only extant Turkish House (*Bástya utca 3*), which served as an inn during the Ottoman occupation.

A few kilometres to the north, on the way to Kaposvár, the Park of Turkish-Hungarian Friendship (*Török Magyar barátság parkja*) was funded in 1996 by the Turkish government as a token of wounds healed between the nations. A symbolic tomb marks the spot where Suleiman the Great's tent stood – from which his corpse surveyed the battlefield (see box, page 426) – while next to each other in front are massive busts of the Turkish ruler and Zrínyi. The one-time türbe at Turbékpuszta, to the east of here, is where Suleiman's remains were held before being returned later to his homeland; it is now a Roman Catholic church, but also a place of pilgrimage for Muslim Turks.

There is no Tourinform, but Tájolo Tourist (*Zrínyi tér 3;* ✆ *73 312654; open Mon–Fri 09.00–13.00, 13.30–16.00; Sat 09.00–12.00*) should be able to help. The bus and railway

## THE BATTLE OF SZIGETVÁR

Two Zrínyis have made their significant marks on Hungarian history; both were called Miklós and both were military generals, but one was also a poet and penned an epic tribute to the last days of his great-grandfather. 'The Peril of Sziget' ('Zrínyiász') is a must-read in the Hungarian literary canon, written in 1651 about the Battle of Szigetvár nearly a century before.

Since 1556, the rather insignificant-looking castle at Szigetvár had been cocking a snook at the Turks. In that year, Márk Horváth successfully defended the fort against attack and killed 10,000 of his foes in the process. A decade later, Suleiman the Magnificent determined to exact revenge and then march on to Vienna. He arrived in 1566 with an army of 90,000, and was unimpressed by what he referred to as 'a molehill'; arraigned within the molehill were just 2,500 Hungarian and Croatian soldiers under the command of Count Miklós Zrínyi, the Viceroy (Ban) of Croatia.

Rarely have odds been stacked so unfairly. Not only was Zrínyi vastly outnumbered, but the marshes around the castle had dried up during a particularly warm summer. Not far to the north, Habsburg Emperor Maximilian II waited with 80,000 troops to cut off the anticipated Turkish advance to Vienna; he refused to come to Zrínyi's aid, calculating that a few thousand Hungarian lives were worth sacrificing if they could delay the Turks awhile. The cause was a hopeless one, but for 33 days the fort held firm; Zrínyi rebutted Turkish attempts at bribery, and his men ignored messages attached to arrows entreating them to open the gates. Deeply frustrated, Suleiman mounted an all-out assault on August 29 – 40th anniversary of the Battle of Mohács – but wave after wave were cut down, the bodies piling up around the castle walls. As the survivors retreated, the furious sultan suffered a massive stroke.

To preserve what little morale remained, the Turkish leadership concocted an elaborate act to conceal the sultan's death from their soldiers. They propped his body up inside his tent so that from a distance it appeared that he was watching the battlefield. (The pretence continued even after victory in an attempt to stave off any potential power struggle before the arrival of Suleiman's son and heir, Selim II.) By now there were just 300 defenders still standing, and these made a pact to go down in one final glorious blaze. Zrínyi removed his armour, filled his pockets with gold coins to provide for his funeral, and charged with his men through the gates. All were slaughtered, and Zrínyi's severed head rushed to the sitting sultan as proof of victory. In a last bloody twist, a single surviving Hungarian detonated the fort's gunpowder store as the Turkish janissaries poured through the walls. In total, the battle claimed the lives of 25,000 Turks, as well as the 2,500 Hungarian and Croatian soldiers.

stations are 500m south of the centre; follow Rákóczi utca north to Zrínyi tér. A regular bus service operates to Pécs while there are also direct links to Kaposvár (four daily), Barcs (four) and Nagykanizsa (three), and one-daily buses to Hevíz, Mohács and Veszprém. Direct trains go to Barcs (nine), Pécs (seven) and Nagykanizsa (one); for Budapest, catch a connecting train at Szentlőrinc.

## KAPOSVÁR

The capital of Somogy County has few hairs out of place. Nestled in the Kapos Valley, 50km to the south of Lake Balaton, Kaposvár is squeaky clean, due in part to the fact that it hasn't yet had time to get grubby. The majority of its buildings were constructed during the 20th century, and few medieval monuments survived the protracted skirmishes that took place here during the Turkish period. The castle that gave the settlement its name was one such victim of the violence, and there are but scant remains at the end of Vár utca. Kaposvár's modern contribution has been in the spheres of radical politics and art. In the aftermath of the 1867 Compromise, the citizens campaigned to elect the exiled Lajos Kossuth as their parliamentary representative, and there was strong support here for the shortlived communist Republic of Councils set up under Béla Kun in 1919. The painters József Rippl-Rónai (1861–1927), János Vaszary (1867–1939) and Aurél Bernáth (1895–1982) all had connections with the town. Beyond being left-leaning and art-loving, Kaposvár has several good museums and offers easy access both to hiking trails in the Zselic region to the south and the lovely Lake Deseda to the north.

## Getting there, away and around
The intercity bus station and adjacent local bus terminus (*Budai Nagy Antal utca*) are both a short walk away from the city centre. There are very regular connections with Pécs (hourly), Nagykanizsa and Siófok. Other buses to Lake Balaton include Fonyód (two), Tapolca (two), Balatonlelle (eight) and Balatonboglár (six), there are twice-daily services to Győr, Székesfehérvár and Veszprém, and thrice-daily buses to Szombathely and Szekszárd. A weekly Sunday service also operates to Frankfurt.

It's a quick five-minute trot to the centre from the **train station** (*Baross Gábor utca*) where connections can be make to Budapest Déli (two), Siófok (three), Balatonfenyves (two), Keszthely (two), Pécs (five) and Nagykanisza (seven). There are regular services to Dombóvár and Fonyód, where trains to Székesféhervár and Veszprém can be picked up. If you need a **taxi**, try Rádio (\ *82 777777*) or Tele (\ *82 555555*).

## Information and other practicalities
**Listings magazine** *Kaposi Est*
**Tourinform** Fő utca 8; \ 82 512921; e kaposvar@tourinform.hu. *Open Jun 15–Sep 15 Mon–Fri 09.00–18.00, Sat–Sun 09.00–17.00, Sep 16–Jun 14 Mon–Fri 09.00–17.00, Sat 09.00–12.00.*
**Sio Tour** Fő utca 1; \ 82 320537; www.siotour.hu. Offers tours of the region. Housed in the same building as the Csokonai Hotel, this was where celebrations were held on Ferenc Széchenyi's investiture as county lord lieutenant in 1793 and where Mihály Csokonai Vitéz subsequently based the action of his 18th-century comic poem 'Dorottya'. It is accordingly known as the Dorottya House, and hosts an annual ball (see page 431). *Open Mon–Fri 08.00–16.30.*

## Where to stay
**Borostyán Vendégház** (13 rooms) Rákóczi tér 3; \ 82 320735. This Art-Nouveau hotel is less impressive inside than you might expect it to be, and the over-the-top rooms won't be to all tastes. Room prices depend on whether you are on the ground floor or levels above. *Sgl 7,900–9,900Ft, dbl 8,900–11,900Ft, suite 14,900–19,900Ft.*
**Csalogány Panzió** (12 rooms) Csalogány utca 70; \ 82 314773. Set in a wild garden, this pension has good-sized rooms that are basically furnished. It's 2km or so southeast of the centre (up Róma-hegy, in the vicinity of the Rippl-Rónai Memorial House), but the price is right; bus 15 from the local bus station runs to the southern end of Csalogány utca. *Dbl 8,000Ft, apt (for 2) 11,000Ft.*
**Deseda Camping** Kaposvár-Toponár; Deseda-tó; \ 82 312020. Beautifully situated campsite 8km northeast of the centre at the southern end of Lake Deseda (see pages 430–1), next to a relatively quiet grassed bathing area. Buses 8 and 18 run here from Kaposvár Jun 1–Aug 31, or you can take the train to Toponár (on the line to Siófok). *Camping adult/child 1,200/600Ft; tent 1,000Ft; open Jun 15–Aug 20.*
**Hotel Dorottya** (26 rooms) Széchenyi tér 8; \ 82 315055. There are 3 categories of room – the most expensive with the better views and furnishings, but the cheaper ones – some with wooden beams in the centre – are full of character. Right at the heart of town; the prices are fair (rather than bargain) value. *Sgl 9,000–12,000Ft, dbl 12,000–15,000Ft.*

**Hotel Kapos** (80 rooms) Kossuth tér; ☎ 82 316022; e info@kaposhotel.hu; www.kaposhotel.hu. The plain-looking rooms come in 3 sizes. There's a coffee house, and a restaurant (see below). *Sgl 7,900–11,900Ft, dbl 10,000–16,000Ft, triple 14,600–17,600Ft, room for 4 19,200Ft.*

## Where to eat and drink

**Corso Klub** Dózsa György utca 2; ☎ 82 416614. Don't be misled by the name for there's no nightclub here. Rather this is an excellent restaurant and bar, with an inventive menu of international and Hungarian food. The house speciality is the 'Highwayman's BBQ', a plate of bacon, sausages, pork, chicken, mushroom, tomato and paprika that would guarantee indigestion for even the hardiest *puszta*-riding outlaw. *Mains 990–2,690Ft, avg 1,600Ft; open Mon–Thu 10.00–23.00, Fri–Sat 10.00–24.00, Sun 11.00–23.00.*

**Crazy Coffee House** Dózsa György utca 18; ☎ 82 510644. Tiny modern cellar bar and café, in which the pool table occupies half the floor space. Great place for a drink. *Open Mon–Thu 09.00–23.00, Fri–Sat 09.00–04.00, Sun 17.00–23.00.*

**Hotel Kapos Restaurant** See above. We've heard good things about the restaurant at the Hotel Kapos, whose chef's light takes on Hungarian favourites won him gold at the cooking Olympic Games (no, we'd never heard of it either!). *Mains 750–2,400Ft, avg 1,500Ft; open 07.00–24.00 daily.*

**Mozi Világ** Dózsa György utca 3; ☎ 82 512863. This fun restaurant and 'Wild West saloon' serves hearty steak 'n' ribs and the like. The bar stays open late on Fridays and Saturdays, and is a popular spot for letting hair down. *Mains 890–2,400Ft, avg 1,550Ft; open Mon–Thu 12.00–01.00, Fri–Sat 12.00–03.00, Sun 12.00–22.00.*

## Entertainment and nightlife

The **Csiky Gergely Theatre** (*Rákóczi tér 2;* ☎ *82 528458; www.csikygergelyszinhaz.hu*) is a striking Secessionist building opened in 1911, and had a reputation for provocative and anti-establishment plays during the communist period. Its ticket office is in the same building as the Tourinform. **Somogy County Cultural Centre** (*Somssich Pál utca 18;* ✆ *82 310282; open Mon–Thu 08.00–16.00. Fri 08.00–15.00*) can provide information on arts events, and puts on temporary exhibitions.

The **Carlsberg Café** (*Fő utca 4; open 07.00–24.00 daily*) is an achingly cool bar and coffee house. **Club Ramszesz** (*Rákóczi tér 9–11*) is behind the theatre; garish posters around town advertise its theme nights.

## What to see and do

Running east from Kossuth Lajos tér, Fő utca is the prime meeting, eating and drinking street, and few of the sights are far from it. Starting on Kossuth tér itself, the Neo-Romanesque **cathedral** (*Székesegyház; Kossuth tér*) – which attained cathedral status in 1993 when the town became an episcopal centre – was built in 1886 and contains 20th-century frescoes of the stations of the cross by György Leszkovsky. The renowned craftsman Miksa Róth made the stained glass windows of the Neo-Renaissance **town hall** (*Kossuth tér 1*), constructed in the early 1900s. A set of bells play music on the hour.

Heading north on Zárda utca, the first turning on the left brings you to the **Sport Museum** (*Kontrássy utca 3;* ✆ *82 427492; adult 100Ft; open Tue–Fri 11.00–16.00, Sat–Sun 09.00–12.30*), which holds a collection of sporting memorabilia related to Somogy County. The **Mineral Museum** (*Rippl-Rónai utca 24;* ✆ *82 320591; free admission; open Mon–Fri 10.00–18.00, Sun 09.00–17.00*) is half way up the road opposite and has glass cabinets stuffed with rocks from six continents, while further up Zárda utca is the **Vaszary Memorial House** (*Zárda utca 9;* ✆ *82 414999; open Tue–Sun 10.00–16.00*), where you can see 30 works by artist János Vaszary in the place he was born in 1867.

Passing the Dorottya House (see page 427) on Fő utca, the **Somogy County Museum/Rippl-Rónai Museum** (*Fő utca 10;* ✆ *82 314011; individual exhibitions: adult/concessions 300–400/150Ft, combined ticket: 1,000/500Ft; open Tue–Sun 12.00–18.00*) is in the Neoclassical former County Hall, and has five permanent exhibitions. Among these are an ethnographic display with items relating to the county's shepherds, peasants and even outlaws (*betyár*), a natural-history section, and the private collection of 20th-century art donated by Ödön Rippl-Rónai, the younger brother of the famous József. The latter was born above the nearby **Golden Lion Pharmacy** (*Arany Oroszlán patika; Fő utca 19*), which is itself next to the **Zsolnay Shop** (*Fő utca 21*), where you can admire the ram-head fountain outside and buy pieces of the porcelain inside.

The **Vaszary Gallery** (*Fő utca 12;* ✆ *82 314915; free admission; open Mon–Fri 09.00–17.00, Sat 09.00–12.00*) showcases contemporary art, but also has a permanent collection of photographs by Juan Gyenes (1912–1995), who was born in Kaposvár but made his name in Spain as the court photographer; among the images are portraits of famous figures from the spheres of art and science. The same building contains a small reconstruction of **a turn-of-the-20th-century shop** (*Fő utca 12;* ✆ *82 311587; free admission; open Mon–Sat 09.00–12.00 or by prior arrangement*).The **Terrarium** (*Fő utca 31;* ✆ *82 424460; open May 1–Sep 30 Mon–Fri 09.00–18.00, Sat 09.00–12.00, Sun 14.00–18.00, Nov 1–Apr 30 Mon–Fri 09.00–17.00, Sat 09.00–12.00, Sun 14.00–17.00*) is the country's only private collection of rare reptiles.

Take a right down Anna utca and second left on to Gróf Apponyi Albert utca for the **Steiner Collection** (*Albert utca 29;* ✆ *82 311327; free admission; open Mon–Sun 10.00–18.00*), whose owner's obsession with cast iron began in 1989 when he installed an iron (rather than tile) stove in his workshop. He went on to gather a huge range of 19th-century objects crafted from the metal, including things you'd expect (wells, cookers, etc) and things you wouldn't (table clocks, chandeliers and pictures).

There are seven hills around Kaposvár, and you'll find the **Rippl-Rónai Memorial Museum** (*Roma-hegy;* ✆ *82 422144; adult/concessions 400/200Ft; open Apr 1–Oct 31 Tue–Sun*

*10.00–18.00; Nov 1–Mar 31 Tue–Sun 10.00–16.00*) up Roma-hegy, 2.5km southeast of the centre. The villa was bought by József Rippl-Rónai (1861–1927) in 1908 when he returned to his native town to spend his remaining years after living in Paris. Surrounded by his cattle, peacocks and bees, the painter was content here and abandoned his 'black period' for pieces full of sunlight whose vivid colours were initially lambasted by the art establishment. Rippl-Rónai had studied under Mihály Munkácsy before breaking away to experiment with Art Nouveau and Post-Impressionism. He was Hungary's first and arguably best 'modern' artist, although he was a middle-aged man before his talents were properly acknowledged. As well as some of the artist's Biedermeier furnishings, the villa also contains 80 of his paintings. Bus 15 stops 400m west of the entrance on Lonkahegyi utca.

## Other activities
The **town baths** (*Csík Ferenc sétány;* ✆ *82 321044; adult/concessions 400/200Ft; open Tue–Sun 09.00–19.00, open-air pool summer only*) are behind the train station, and include medicinal thermal baths, covered and outdoor swimming pools and other sports facilities.

There are horse-riding lessons at the family-run **Pannon Horse School** (*Lovasakadémia; Guba Sándor utca 40;* ✆ *82 528313;* e *pla@lovasakademia.hu; www.lovasakamedia.hu; from 1,700Ft/hr*) to the northeast of the centre; Mező utca runs from the eastern end of Fő utca into Guba utca. Alternatively, you could try the **Zrínyi Horse Club** (*contact Liszt utca 29;* ✆ *82 431688*) to the south or the **Penny Horse Club** (*Kaposvár-Répáspuszta, Toponári út;* ✆ *82 528090;* e *penny.klub@matavnet.hu*) just east of Lake Deseda (see below), both of which offer riding lessons and excursions.

## Excursions
There are several points of interest within a few kilometres of Kaposvár. Following Pécsi út from the eastern end of Fő utca, after 4km you'll reach Várdomb and the **ruins of a Benedictine abbey** (*Várdomb 1; open Tue–Sun Apr 1–Sep 30 10.00–18.00, Oct 1–Mar 31 10.00–14.00*) originally founded in 1061. As well as the 11th-century sections, there are the remains of later additions, including an octagonal chapel from the 14th century that is now used for open-air concerts (see Tourinform for programme). It's a steep climb up from the car park on Monostor utca; bus 7 runs along Pecsi út.

There are some lovely walks in the hills and villages of the **Zselic region** to the south of Kaposvár; buy a map (such as Cartographia's *Á Zselic*, 1:60,000) for the routes. In the peaceful village of Szenna, 8km southwest of Kaposvár, there is an Open-Air Folk Museum (*Szennai Szabadtéri Néprajzi Gyűtemény; Rákóczi utca 2;* ✆ *82 712223; adult/concessions 400/200Ft; open Tue–Sun Apr 1–Oct 31 10.00–18.00, Nov 1–Mar 31 10.00–16.00*) comprising five 19th-century peasant houses moved here from other villages of Somogy County and settled around Szenna's Calvinist church. The church itself has a coffered ceiling of 117 painted panels completed in 1787; this was within a decade of József II's edict permitting freedom of worship to non-Catholics, and you'll find that many Calvinist churches date from this period. Buses run from Kaposvár to a stop just outside the museum.

**Lake Deseda**, 8km to the north of the centre in the suburb of Toponár, was formed by the damming of a stream; lined with bullrushes and reed beds, it is a relaxing spot to fish, sunbathe or boat. Much of it is protected, but there is a campsite (see page 427) and strand at the southern end, a couple of places to hire kayaks further up the eastern bank, and hiking and cycling routes around it. Ask at the Tourinform in Kaposvár for the *Deseda-tó* booklet, which includes a simple but adequate map of the lake. You can take the train or buses 8 or 18 from Kaposvár to Toponár, just under a kilometre to the southeast; alternatively a bus runs all the way to the campite in summer (*Jun 1–Sep 1*). At the northern end, the Gombás and Deseda forests are on either side, and there is an arboretum on the lick of land dividing the two prongs of the lake's fork (accessed via a

### STORK CITY
To the west of Kaposvár, on Road 61 towards Nagykanizsa, keep your head up as you pass through Nagybajom. Signs as you enter proudly declare this the 'European Village for White Storks', and you'll quickly see why. While many villages are fond of their solitary pair of resident storks, Nagybajom harbours around a dozen of the twiggy nests, built on circular platforms atop the telegraph poles (see box, page 32). As elsewhere in Hungary, the birds turn up in spring and leave as summer draws to a close, a reliable sign that winter is on its way.

100m-long footbridge). The hiking and cycling routes run up and in to these. By car, take Road 67 north from Kaposvár; after you've passed Kaposfüred, keep left towards Magyaregres for Gombás Forest and right towards Somogyaszaló for Deseda Forest. Bus 11 stops at Gombás Forest on its way to Magyaregres.

### Festivals and events
Dorottya Day (see page 427) culminates in a ball on the first Saturday in February, and opens a series of cultural programmes known as Carnival Days. The Spring Festival includes theatre, music and art exhibitions for a fortnight in March.

## NAGYKANIZSA
Nagykanizsa is a one-road and two-square town that wouldn't merit mention but for its location, which guarantees it visitor traffic moving on to Western Transdanubia, Lake Balaton, and Croatia and Slovenia over the borders. Since the 19th century the railway line has run through here on its way between Budapest and the Adriatic. A fort – demolished by the Habsburgs – stood to the west of the centre, part of the southern fortifications, but it was overrun by the Turks who established the town as a district seat from 1600. Since the 19th century, the town's industry has prospered on the back of oil fields, and it also has a brewery brewing Kanizsai Kinizsi beer.

### Getting there and away
The **bus station** is 200m west of Erzsébet tér. You can pick up twice-hourly buses to Zalaegerszeg, there are up to ten buses a day to both Keszthely and Kaposvár, and other direct destinations include Szombathely (nine), Pécs (six), Budapest Népliget (three), Sopron (two) and Szeged (one). The **train station** (*Ady Endre utca*) is found 1km south of the centre. There are up to 11 trains a day to either Budapest Déli or Keleti stations, as well as routes to Balatonszentgyörgy (13), Székesfehérvár (12), Kaposvár (eight), Szombathely (seven) and Pécs (four). Up to two trains a day depart to Zagreb (the quicker taking two hours) and a further five head to the Slovenian capital of Ljubljana.

### Information and other practicalities
**Banks** There are banks (with ATMs) on the corner of Deák Ferenc tér and Sugár út, and on the corner of Fő út and Deák Ferenc tér.
**Listings magazine** *Zalai Est*
**Zalatour** Fő út 13; ↖ 93 311185. In the absence of a Tourinform, this office can offer a limited amount of information on the town, and organise private rooms. *Open Mon–Fri 08.00–17.00, Sat 08.00–11.30.*

### Where to stay and eat
Like many other small Magyar towns, you shouldn't dally if you want to eat out – you'll struggle to find anywhere to eat after 21.00–22.00, whatever their advertised opening hours.

**Corner Irish Pub** Rozgonyi utca 1; ❧ 93 322027. Cosy enough little basement bar at the corner of Erzsébet tér. There's Murphy's and Guinness in the taps, and steak and pizza on the menu. *Mains 550–1,900Ft, avg 1,500Ft; open Mon–Thu 16.00–23.00, Fri 16.00–01.30, Sat 17.00–01.30.*

**Gerő Cukrászda** Fő út 3; ❧ 93 312170. The yummiest of the town's cakes and ice cream, and a pleasant pavement spot in summer. *Open 07.00–22.00 daily.*

**Grünhut** Deák Ferenc tér 3. Spartan beer house that's popular in the evenings. *Open 12.00–23.00 daily.*

**Hotel Centrál** Erzsébet tér 23; ❧ 93 314000. Centrally located but expensively priced 3-star hotel. *Sgl 12,500Ft, dbl 14,500Ft, triple 16,000Ft.*

**Hugi Panzió** Király utca 7; ❧ 93 336100. This little guesthouse to the west of Erzsébet tér is basic but good value, and run by a lovely lady who gets very excited about receiving Anglo-Saxon guests. *Sgl 5,000Ft, dbl 8,000Ft, triple 11,000Ft.*

**Király Panzió** (9 rooms) Király utca 29; ❧ 93 325480; e kiralypanzio@chello.hu. On the second floor of a shopping parade, the Király has light and modern rooms. *Sgl 6,400Ft, dbl 9,200Ft, triple 11,500Ft.*

**Kiskakas Vendéglő** Múzeum tér 6; ❧ 93 321600. The best restaurant in these parts, specialising in Hungarian chicken dishes. *Mains 650–4,300Ft, avg 1,550Ft; open Mon–Sat 10.00–23.30, Sun 10.00–22.00.*

**Nelson** Fő út 7; ❧ 93 315304. A pub and cellar restaurant serving steaks. The figure of Nelson stands outside – fortunately still with both arms intact, so he can point you inside with one hand and clutch his beer glass with the other. *Mains 850–2,400Ft, avg 1,650Ft; open: 11.00–22.00 daily.*

**Robinson** Deák tér 10; ❧ 93 310519. This basement restaurant is decked out like a driftwood shack. Alongside pizzas, there are reasonably priced Hungarian, Slovak and German dishes. *Pizzas 250–1,500Ft, mains avg 1,200Ft; open 11.00–23.00 daily.*

## What to see and do

The town centre is bisected by Fő út, which runs from east to west through its squares. The **Thúry György Museum** (*Fő út 5; ❧ 93 314596; adult/concessions 240/120Ft; open Tue–Sat 10.00–16.00*) – named after the castellan who mounted the unsuccessful defence of the town's castle against the Turks – has one of Transdanubia's largest textile collections, together with archaeological exhibits including grave finds from an Avar cemetery in Zalakomár and a Roman cemetery in Magyarszerdahely. The local history display shows the furnished interiors of 19th-century homes and shops.

Across the road from the museum, an archway leads through to a Neoclassical **synagogue** (*Fő út 6*) built in the early 19th century; it has stood in an appalling state of repair since the town's 3,000-strong Jewish community were deported in 1944, but is earmarked for renovation. Another arch near the northern end of Ady Endre utca opens into a courtyard bearing the sculpted heads of Prime Minister Lajos Batthyány and 13 of his generals, the Martyrs of Arad who were brutally executed by the Habsburgs in 1849 after Hungary's fight for independence had been quashed. To the southeast, the 18th-century **Franciscan church and monastery** (*Ady Endre utca 14*) stands on the tomb of the Turkish Pasha Mustafa; a font has been carved into its stone.

In front of the Baroque church on the arboreous Deák Ferenc tér is Kisfaludi Strobl's surreal statue of the 19th-century Petőfi encouraging a jack-booted 20th-century soldier to chuck a stick grenade. It might appear to suggest that the freedom-fighting poet bore a grudge against porcelain shops, but actually this is a tribute to the infantry regiment he represented during the Independence War. The square also holds a hunched bust of Ferenc Deák (1803–86), being swallowed by the brick wall at number 5.

The **town swimming baths** (*Csengery utca 49; adult/concessions 380/280Ft; open 09.00–19.00 daily*) include indoor and outdoor pools, and lie directly south of the centre (just beyond the rail tracks).

# Central and Western Transdanubia

*(For an introduction to Transdanubia as a whole, see page 393.)*

## Central Transdanubia

Central Transdanubia wraps around Lake Balaton (which is given a separate chapter) and fills the area east to the Danube and northeast to the border. It lacks the density of sights to be found in the southern and western portions of Transdanubia, but nevertheless has some diverse Hungarian highlights. Dunaújváros is the place to see the trappings of the 20th-century Socialist-Realist movement that have been done away with elsewhere, while by contrast Székesfehérvár (the 'first Magyar town') and Veszprém (the 'City of Queens') were important early royal centres. Veszprém is in the foothills of the Bakony, the traditional playground for romantic outlaws in bygone days. Lake Velence plays piggy in the middle with Lake Balaton and Budapest, and is a favoured bird-watching and angling spot. The factory at Herend is the source for the country's best-known porcelain, while F A Maulbertsch went to town in Sümeg's parish church, producing some gob-smacking frescoes that have been compared to those in the Sistine Chapel.

### DUNAFÖLDVÁR

Dunaföldvár lies on the Danube between Paks and Dunaújváros. The 9,000 residents are proud of the bridge just outside the town; built in 1930, it used to be the only connection between Transdanubia and the Great Plain and earned the settlement the title of 'gateway to the *puszta*'. Dunaföldvár ('Danube earthen fortress') is more properly named after a 7–8th-century Avar fortification, although it also has a 16th-century stone castle that was erected to protect the town from the approaching Turks.

### Getting there and away

Dunaföldvár is a 20-minute **drive** from Dunaújváros on the M6, following the seemingly endless oil pipe that runs beside the road. There are frequent **buses** (almost hourly) from Budapest Népliget and Dunaújváros – all those from the former also stop at the latter. The bus station (*Mészáros utca 2;* ☏ *75 343926*) is just south of the Tourinform. The **train** offers a less-regular service, with four daily trains to Dunaújváros, two to Pusztaszabolcs and three to Paks; the station (*Batthyány Lajos sor;* ☏ *75 343031*) is about 2km south of the centre.

### Information

**Tourinform** Rákóczi utca 2; ☏ 75 341176. *Open Mon–Sat 09.00–17.00.*

### Where to stay and eat

Despite its size, Dunaföldvár offers a wide selection of places to stay; food, however, is harder to come by (the centre has only two proper restaurants).

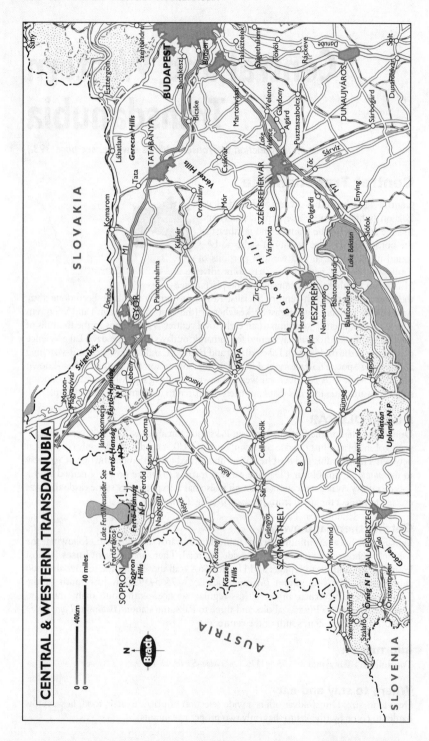

CENTRAL & WESTERN TRANSDANUBIA

**Camping** Hősök tere. Riverside camping, with some chalet accommodation. *Adult/child 650/350Ft, chalet rooms (for 1–6) 2,100–8,000Ft, tent 550Ft.*

**Halászcsárda** Hősök tere 25; ❧ 75 541080. The best bites choice, a rustic restaurant serving good traditional food while barges float by on the Danube. It specialises in fish dishes of carp, catfish and pike perch. *Mains 800–1,200Ft, avg 1,000Ft; open daily 11.00–22.00.*

**Jurik Motel** (7 rooms) Váci utca 2; ❧ 06 30 997 7605. Although it's 1.6km from the town centre, this is one of the better places to stay, with a restaurant, tennis, and horse-riding possibilities. *Dbl 3,500Ft.*

**Marcipán Cukrászda** Béke tér 3; ❧ 75 541055. Centrally located, and has the usual selection of Hungarian cakes, pastries, and sweets. *Open daily 09.00–18.00.*

**Panoráma Üdülőfalu** (7 apts) Templom utca 78; ❧ 75 342748. Apartment houses (for up to 5) with kitchens, living rooms and a swimming pool. The main draw is the location, with its village atmosphere and panoramic views of the rooftops and church towers. *Apt 4,000Ft/pp.*

**Prajda Panzió** (3 rooms) Kossuth Lajos utca 22; ❧ 75 342182. One panzió in a cluster on Kossuth utca and Ilona utca. It has a pretty courtyard, and the rooms have kitchens and sleep up to 5 people. *Rooms from 2,500Ft/pp.*

**Vár** Rátkai köz; ❧ 75 342405. Stands across from the Vár Museum, and is geared towards tourists. Its dishes – fried or stuffed with cheese – are as uninspiring as they are cheap. *Mains avg 800Ft; open daily 11.00–23.00.*

## What to see and do

Dunaföldvár has five cemeteries and seven churches and chapels, but most of the sights of interest are found within the compact town centre and on Vár domb. Just west of Béke tér is the **town hall** (*Kossuth Lajos utca 2*), with its Art-Nouveau clock tower. A walk up Rákóczi utca will take you past the lovely late-Baroque **Franciscan church** (*Rákóczi utca 3*), built in 1786 and with ornately frescoed ceilings. Continue up Rákóczi utca and turn left on to Templom utca, which leads to another church and a statue of the Holy Trinity.

The **Vár Múzeum** (*Rátkai köz 2;* ❧ *75 541000; adult 200Ft; open Apr 15–Oct 15 Tue–Sun 10.00–17.00*) can be found through the wooden carved *várkapu* (fortress gateway); it has a small exhibition about the history of the area. The **Fafaragó Galéria** (❧ *75 541000*), opposite the museum, hosts temporary art exhibitions. Next to the gallery is **Fazekasműhely** (❧ *06 30 234 6596; open summer daily 09.00–18.00, variable hrs rest of yr*), the pottery workshop of artist Zsuzsa Alberczki, where she makes and sells all of her creations. From Vár domb, there is a view of the Danube and the bridge to the northeast and Kálvária Hill to the southeast. The entire area of Fortress Hill, including the museum and an abandoned building, will be renovated within the next three years from EU funds. Stroll Petőfi Sándor utca, Templom utca and the winding cobblestone streets that cross them (such as Ilona utca and Flórián utca) to look at the **traditional houses** and **old wine cellars** built into the ground.

## DUNAÚJVÁROS

Dunaújváros, 70km south of Budapest, makes hay of Socialist-Realist monuments that residents of most other towns would consider eyesores. In fairness, they have scant choice since the entire town consists of big, blocky houses, mazes of tall apartments, busy streets – and massive Socialist-Realist-style statues. Originally called Sztálinváros (Stalin Town), it was raised in 1951 next to a snorting beast of an iron factory that was seen by the communist party as an integral component in its industrialisation plan of the 1950s. The Intercisa Museum celebrates the communist past – apparently without irony – and provides an interesting local history. Excavations have unearthed artefacts from the Roman age and the time of the original Magyar settlement. But Dunaújváros likes to advertise itself as Hungary's newest town, and the fall of communism has done little to alter the face of the place. The 60,000 residents also like to see themselves as athletic, and proclaim their town the 'sports capital of the nation'; the football club, Dunaferr SE, is one of the country's best.

It is easy to become disorientated in Dunaújváros since one row of building blocks looks much the same as another. Furthermore, there is no real town centre in the traditional sense; the area that comes closest to it is Városháza tér. You can be forgiven for feeling you've wandered on to a Soviet-era film set, and a couple of hours should suffice for all but those with a diehard fascination for Socialist-Realist architecture.

There is, though, a well-kept, wooded park that might persuade you to linger a while longer. It has several walking paths; a 2km trail 50m above the shoreline affords a wonderful view of the Danube as it flows around the lush Szalki sziget in its navel. Here too reside over 60 statues in a curious open-air Steel Statue Park on the upper bank of the river, most in the Socialist-Realist style.

## Getting there and away

There are frequent local **buses** running between Dunaújváros and Dunaföldvár, and buses from Budapest leave from Népliget hourly. The bus station is a few blocks south of Városháza tér, and buses often also stop at the square. The **train** station is 2km west of the centre, down Dózsa György út; there are two daily trains to Budapest Déli, three to Dunaföldvár, nine to Pusztaszabolcs and three to Paks.

## Information

**Tourinform** Vasmű út 10/A; \ 25 500148; e dunaujvaros@tourinform.hu. A 5-min walk from the bus station. *Open Mon–Thu 08.00–16.00, Fri 8.00–15.00 (closed 12.30–13.00).*

## Where to stay and eat

New and sporty it might be, but its relative unpopularity with tourists is evident in the fact that Dunaújváros has only one hotel. Tourinform can provide numbers for private accommodation, but many of these rooms can be difficult to find and are quite a distance from the centre. The dearth of accommodation is matched by a dearth of quality restaurants, and an abundance of fast-food joints; for a large town, the eating scene is drab.

**Corner Café** Vasmű út 39. Serves mostly cold light meals and drinks. *Mains avg 600Ft; open daily 06.30–24.00.*

**Diablo** Bartók Béla tér 5; \ 25 420450. Has pizza, pasta, average Hungarian food and a disco on Saturdays. *Mains 630–2,200Ft, avg 1,200Ft; open daily 10.00–24.00; disco Sat 21.00–04.00.*

**Dunaújvárosi Főiskola Kerpely Antal Kollégium** Dózsa György utca 33; \ 25 551123; e titkoll@mail.poliod.hu; www.kac.poliod.hu/kollegium. The local college also serves as a youth hostel, offering a variety of types of room – some of which even have internet access, televisions and kitchens – at several locations. *Rooms 2,000–3,000Ft/pp (Jul–Aug), 1,500–2,500Ft/pp (rest of yr), apt 10,000–15,000Ft.*

**Klub Hotel Dunaújváros** (52 rooms) Építők útja 2; \ 25 500476; e klubhotel@ber.dunaferr.hu. Pretty good, with a sauna, gym, games rooms and pleasant accommodation. Hungarian and Chinese are the unlikely partners on the restaurant menu, and there's a wine tavern. *Dbl 17,500Ft, apt 23,500Ft, inc b/fast.*

**Topo** Kőműves utca 5; 25 410116. Just around the corner from Tourinform, Topo has considerably better pizza than Diablo, and pasta selections. *Mains 450–1,000Ft, avg 750Ft; open daily 10.00–23.00.*

## What to see and do

Tourinform has a brochure listing 33 of the most important Socialist-Realist monuments and buildings, and outlining a sightseeing path to see them. The walk is hardly worth the effort since the buildings look largely the same, and the brochure doesn't explain their importance.

One block north of Tourinform, the **Intercisa Museum** (*Városháza tér 4;* ☏ *25 411315;* e *intercisamuz@freemail.hu; www.dunaujvaros.hu/intercisa; adult 260Ft; open daily 14.00–18.00*) has a giant left-over statue of Lenin leaning against a wall in the courtyard. The museum contains items dating from the Roman era up to the Stalinist period, and is popular with student groups. A docent is likely to shadow you around the exhibitions.

Standing next to the Tourinform, the **Institute of Contemporary Art** (*Vasmű út 12;* ☏ *25 412220; www.ica-d.hu; admission free; open Tue–Sun 12.00–18.00*) holds interesting occasional exhibitions of Hungarian and foreign artists. There's also a café with internet access.

## LAKE VELENCE

Lying halfway between Budapest and Lake Balaton, the 26km² Lake Velence is a pint-sized version of the latter, and the summer brings sunbathers, swimmers, anglers and stalls hawking *lángos, palacsinta,* cheap beer and wine. During winter, however, the area is empty of visitors beyond the odd ice skater and ice surfer. The shallow lake is both one of the warmest in Europe and one of the best for angling in Hungary; it is surrounded by small fishing villages, and the moored boats are indicative of the local fondness for casting a line or two. The western shore is a nature reserve where 28 protected bird species hatch, drawing twitchers during the migrating seasons in spring and autumn. On the southern shore rise the Velence Hills, with their thick forests, unique rock formations and hiking trails offering respite from the tourist masses at the strand. The northern shore is less touristy and more residential.

On visiting Lake Velence (meaning 'Venice' in Hungarian, and as big a misnomer as you'll come across) you're likely to arrive at one of the small villages of Agárd, Gárdony or Velence. There's little to distinguish between them – if you are driving, one tends to run into the next; Gárdony is the largest, but Agárd has the most popular strands.

### Getting there and away

Lake Velence is readily reached from Budapest, especially by **train**, and is a popular day trip. The villages of Agárd, Gárdony and Velence are on the same railway line, about three or four minutes from each other; there are a couple of dozen daily trains from Budapest Déli, continuing on to Székesfehérvár. It takes an hour to Velence from Budapest. In addition, there are good connections to Balaton – Siófok (seven), Balatonszentgyörgy (one), Fonyód (one) and Balatonfüred (one) – and trains to Nagykanizsa (two), Nyíregyháza (one), Tapolca and Püspökladány.

**Buses** to the Velence area are less frequent, except from nearby Székesfehérvár. Buses in Agárd leave and drop off from in front of the restaurant Nádas; there are four direct daily buses from Agárd to Budapest Népliget, over a dozen buses connecting Székesfehérvár and Gárdony, and even more connecting Székesfehérvár and Agárd.

### Information and other practicalities

**Hungarian National Angling Association (MOHOSZ)** Agárd, Tópart utca, Pf 16; ☏ 22 370339. Can help with fishing permits and point you towards the top spots for hooking carp. Daily fishing permits are available all around the lake, often from private houses (look out for signs reading '*horgász jegy*').

**Tourinform** Gárdony, Szabadság út 16; ☏ 22 570077; e gardony@tourinform.hu. *Open Jun–Aug Mon–Sat 08.00–18.00, Sun 08.00–14.00; Sep–May Mon–Fri 09.00–17.00, Sat 09.00–13.00.*

**Velencetours** Gárdony, Szabadság út 16; ☏ 22 355075; e velencetours@axelero.hu; www.velencetours.hu. This office can recommend and book accommodation. There is a second branch in Velence (*Halász utca 37;* ☎ *22 472031; csepphaz@axelero.hu*). *Open Mon–Fri 08.00–16.00, Sat 08.00–12.00.*

## Where to stay and eat

There are plenty of accommodation options around Lake Velence, mostly in the two-star hotel category, and some sections of the lakeside seem like one big camping ground. If you prefer smaller pensions, there are tiny, family-run places, as well as the ubiquitous private rooms ('*Zimmer frei/szoba kiadó*' signs). During the swimming season, cheap food ain't hard to come by at the lake side.

### Agárd

**Csutora** Balatoni út 131; ☎ 22 370659. With special multi-course menus for 2,500Ft, Csutora has one of the most varied menus at the lake. Try the bone marrow spread on toast (a Hungarian favourite), or the sautéed frog's legs for something a bit different. *Mains 650–4,000Ft (the upper price a mixed plate for 2), avg 1,750Ft; open daily 11.00–23.00.*

**Gulyás Csárda** Balatoni út 50; ☎ 22 370126. Despite the name, *gulyás* – tasty as it is – isn't the only thing this little *csárda* serves. There's also the usual selection of fish dishes. Skip dessert and head to the adjacent *cukrászda*. *Mains 850–1,600Ft, avg 1,000Ft; open May–Aug 12.00–22.00 daily.*

**Laguna Hotel** (21 rooms) Vasút utca 17; ☎ 22 355075. Next to the train station and a short walk from the lake, the Laguna is ideal if you want to dump your bags and hit the water as quickly as possible. All rooms are simply decorated, and have fridges, and there's a tennis court. You can opt for full board or just b/fast. *Dbl 7,400Ft.*

**Nádas** Balatoni út 50; ☎ 22 370006. The area's main tourist-trap restaurant, featuring a vast menu (complete with photos of smiling gypsy musicians) boasting the full range of Hungarian food. Watch out for extras – ketchup is 250Ft! *Mains 700–3,000Ft, avg 1,500Ft. Open daily 12.00–22.00.*

**Pákász Tanya Camping** Chernel István utca 54; ☎ 22 271053; e info@pakasz.hu; www.pakasz.hu. Good location next to the lake; as well as tent space, there is a large cabin divided into bedrooms (with shared bathrooms) and nicer bungalows (with bathrooms, fridges and TVs) sleeping up to 15. *Tent 900Ft; cabin sgl/dbl 3,000/3,800Ft; bungalows 3,800–7,900Ft.*

**Touring Hotel** (66 rooms) Tópart út 1; ☎ 22 370 113; e touring@uw.hu; http://touring.uw.hu. Sits on its own private beach, where guests can take advantage of the hotel's canoes and other water-sports gear. While the hotel doesn't have much of a personality, it is clean and the rooms comfortable; there's also a restaurant and a bar with a pleasant terrace. *Sgl €32, dbl €44; open Apr 15–Oct 15.*

**Vadász Vendéglő** Géza utca 45; ☎ 22 370203. With live music during the summer, this pleasing restaurant specialises in game and fish, and has a pretty good wine list. *Mains 700–2,500Ft, avg 1,500Ft; open daily 11.00–22.00.*

**Viking Hotel** (100 rooms) Gallér utca 2; ☎ 22 370287; e vikinghotelagard@axelero.hu; www.vikinghotel.hu. Around 1km from the lake, the Viking is the biggest hotel, with comfortable apartments sleeping 1–4. There's a tennis court in the grounds, as well as an outdoor pool, a restaurant (with gypsy music) and rather primitive conference facilities. *Dbl 40,000Ft.*

### Gárdony

**Hotel Varsa** (32 rooms) Holdfény sétány 13; ☎ 22 355110; e info@varsa.hu; www.varsa.hu. The orange, retro-style Varsa looks like the kind of motel you'd see along a highway. Its rooms are simple but comfortable; there is a restaurant and a tennis court. *Dbl 7,000Ft; open Mar 15–Oct 31.*

**Kék-tó Vendéglő** Bóné Kálmán utca 2; ☎ 22 355348. The real attraction here is the low prices. All the typical Magyar stuffed, fried and breaded dishes are on the menu, along with a selection of soups and *főzelék* (see page 63). The restaurant also has a pizza-delivery service. *Mains 310–780Ft, avg 500Ft; open daily 11.00–24.00.*

**Ponty** Szabadság utca 9; ☎ 22 355454. As its name ('carp') implies, the menu here is laden with dishes of fresh fish, which are usually roasted and simply served. Nevertheless, fish isn't the only choice – carnivores might try the steak tartar. *Mains 400–1,600Ft, avg 1,000Ft; open Wed–Sat 11.00–21.00, Sun–Tue 11.00–15.00.*

**Sport Beach Camping** Harcsa ('catfish') utca 2; ☏ 22 355044; e sportbeach@sportbeach.hu; www.sportbeach.hu. The Sport Beach camping facility is usually lively in summer. There are all kinds of sports options on the site's private beach, and it has wooden cabins. *May 1–Jun 11, Aug 23–Sep 12: tent 590Ft, cabin dbl 2,800Ft, apt (for 4) 7,140Ft; Jun 14–Aug 24: tent 860Ft, cabin dbl 4,150Ft, apt (for 4) 8,980Ft.*

**Velencepart Hotel** (45 rooms) Pisztráng ('trout', to maintain the fishy theme) utca 19; ☏ 06 20 460 2134; e velencepart@ohb.hu. There are barbecue pits and tennis and volleyball courts in the grounds, and the use of bicycles, boats and surfboards is free for guests. *Sgl €33, dbl €46, triple €58.*

## Velence

**Aranynád Rest House and Educational Institute** (36 rooms) Tóbíró köz 2; ☏ 22 472022; e aranynad@freemail.hu. Owned by the State Audit Office, there's as little charm as you'd expect. However, the place is comfortable and has a summer-camp feel with its groups of guests coming for the conference facilities and sports fields/courts. Boats and bikes are available to guests. Rooms have balconies and fridges. *Dbl 9,300Ft.*

**Cápa** ('shark') Balatoni utca 130; ☏ 22 471023. Looks like a green spaceship from the outside; the menu is less exotic, featuring lamb dishes and the expected fish. *Mains 940–3,800 (the upper price a mixed plate for 2), avg 1,400Ft; open daily 11.00–21.00.*

**Hotel Juventus-Helios** (43 rooms) Kis köz 6; ☏ 22 589330; e h.juventus.velence@axelero.hu. One of the most modern hotels in the area. Rooms are neat and clean, and the sheets crisp. There are also tennis courts, a sauna, a private beach, volleyball courts, a gym, water-sports equipment and bike rental. *Sgl 19,500Ft, dbl 25,900Ft.*

**Youth Hostel** (*Ifjúsági Fogadó*; 64 rooms) Tópart utca 51; ☏ 22 355075. On a private beach (complete with a big waterslide) next to the lake. All rooms are clean and comfortable quads. *Rooms 6,100Ft.*

## What to see and do

Lake Velence is, unsurprisingly, all about the water; there are few other diversions. The one museum is the **Gárdonyi Géza Gallery** (*Agárd, Bóné Kálmán utca 14;* ☏ *22 355267; free admission; open Tue–Sun 10.00–18.00*), a memorial to the life of Hungarian writer Géza Gárdonyi. Besides some of the writer's personal mementos – including the memoirs that he wrote in code – you won't have missed much if you give it a miss.

If the lake's not warm enough, head 1km to the **Agárdi Thermal Baths** (*Agárd, Határ út;* ☏ *22 579008; adult 1,000Ft/2 hrs, 1,500Ft/day; open Mon–Sat 08.00–22.00, Sun 08.00–19.00*), where the water is 35°C and is said to relieve locomotor diseases. There are two open-air thermal pools and a kids' pool, a sauna, a solarium, massages and a lengthy list of treatments; it also has a campsite.

One third of Lake Velence is a nature conservation area, covered with reeds and cut through with narrow passages and hidden inner bays. The area is encompassed by the Duna-Ipoly National Park, and you must be accompanied by a guide to visit. The 168ha **Velence Bird Reserve** (*call Péter Kiss to book a tour;* ☏ *06 70 330 3836*) has been protected since 1958; 30,000 birds migrate here in spring to nest in the reeds and marshes, among them several species of heron. You'll also find a rare marsh orchid variety called the 'onion skin'. The **Dinnyés Fertő Nature Conservation Area** (*call László Fenyvesi to book a tour;* ☏ *06 70 330 3837*) is much smaller, and was created to provide a nesting base for protected birds driven from other locations on the lake by tourism; standing next to a canal near Dinnyés village, it attracts egrets, red herons, spoonbills (the largest population in Transdanubia), common herons and grey-leg geese. During October and early November, in excess of 20,000 geese pass through.

The **Lake Velence School of Watersports & Leisure Centre** (*Agárd, Tópart utca 17;* ❧ *22 370052;* e *vvsi@axelero.hu;* web: *www.vvsi.hu*) is the best place to go for windsurfing lessons, or to rent boats, jet skis and other equipment. The centre also provides accommodation. There are opportunities for **horse-riding** at Lake Velence; contact the Csikós-Tanya Lovarda (*Agárd, Határ utca;* ❧ *06 30 246 7006*) or the Gárdonyi Equestrian Club (*Gárdony, Géza fejedelem utca;* ❧ *22 356860*).

## Excursion

Lying between Lake Velence and Budapest on Road 7, **Martonvásár** holds the 18th-century Neo-Gothic country mansion (*Brunszvik utca 2*) of the Brunswicks, the aristocratic family that owned the area after the Turkish occupation. It now contains an agricultural institute, but is remembered for its connection with Beethoven who stayed here several times while visiting Count Brunswick and his daughters. It is possible that he was in love with the second of these, Josephine, and that she was the inspiration for the *Apassionata sonata* (which he composed at the house and dedicated to the count). Copies of some of the letters Beethoven penned to the family are held in the Beethoven Memorial Hall (❧ *22 569500; adult/concessions 100/50Ft; open May 1–Oct 31 Tue–Fri 14.00–16.00, Sat–Sun 10.00–18.00, Nov 1–Apr 30 Tue–Fri 14.00–16.00, Sat–Sun 10.00–16.00*). The elder sister Teréz founded the first nursery school in central Europe in 1828; the Nursery School Museum (❧ *22 569518; adult/concessions 200/100Ft; open Oct 16–Mar 15 Tue–Fri 10.00–14.00, Sun 11.00–15.00, Mar 16–Oct 15 Tue–Fri 10.00–14.00, Sat–Sun 11.00–18.00*), in a wooden chalet near the mansion, includes a memorial to her. Concerts are held in July at the artificial lake set in the mansion's grounds. **Trains** stop regularly at Martonvásár on their way between Budapest and Székesfehérvár; the station is 1km or so northwest of the mansion (follow Brunszvik út).

## SZÉKESFEHÉRVÁR

Don't allow your passage through the functional concrete of Székesfehérvár's outskirts to cloud your judgement; the cobbled streets and squares of the Belváros survived the last German offensive of 1945 that flattened all around them. Indeed, the industrial suburbs belie not only the architecture at the centre, but Székesfehérvár's status as 'Magyar' Hungary's earliest town – it is said that Árpád set up shop here after the land taking. Prince Géza constructed a castle, given defensive strength by the surrounding swamps, and a Byzantine-style church in which he was later buried. King István established the town as his capital (hence the meaning of its name 'Seat of the White Castle', white being the royal colour) and built a magnificent basilica. For 500 years this was the place of coronations, burials and national assemblies; 37 kings and 39 queens were crowned, 15 laid to rest, and 46 Diets convened within its walls.

The castle had succeeded in repelling even Mongol attack, but it fell to the Turks in 1543; the occupiers ransacked the royal graves and appropriated town buildings as mosques. The basilica, used as a gunpowder store, was destroyed after being hit by lightning during a storm. Székesfehérvár was put back together in the 18th century, filled with Baroque town houses and Franciscan and Carmelite churches, and developed apace after the marshes were drained in the 19th century. World War II hit hard, wiping out a third of its buildings and killing almost 10,000 of its citizens.

### Getting there and away

The town's **bus station** is a five-minute walk south of the centre and looks after both local and regional travel. Buses depart for Budapest and Veszprém every half-hour and there is a regular service to Lake Velence. Other buses go to Tatabánya (nine), Siofók and Keszthely (seven), Pécs and Hevíz (five), Esztergom, Sümeg and Kecskemét (three), Baja and Sopron (two). In summer months there are two Sunday services to Stuttgart via Munich.

# SZÉKESFEHÉRVÁR

↑ Győr

Bory Castle (3.6km),
Diófa Vendéglő (2km),
Vadáskürt Panzió (500m)

N

Bradt

Budapest

ESZPERANTÓ
TÉR

MÁTYÁS KIRÁLY KÖRÚT

YBL

Hotel Magyar Király

SZÍNHÁZ

Vörösmarty
Theatre

Castrum Lovagi

ŐSZ

KIGYÓ

Atrium

DR KOCH LÁSZLÓ

ORSZÁGZÁSZLÓ
TÉR

Kiskakas Vendéglő

Vörösmarty
Cukrászda

BÁSTYA

BASA

Szent István
Király Museum

ADY ENDRE

Open-Air Ethnographic
Museum (400m)

MÁTYÁS KIRÁLY KÖRÚT

Bank &
ATM

FŐ

Black Eagle
Pharmacy Museum

RÁKÓCZI

Cistercian church
& monastery

BARTÓK
TÉR

RÓZSA

OSKOLA

Ribillió

LAKATOS

VÁRKÖRÚT

Medieval Garden
of Ruins & National
Memorial Park

PILINSZKY
TÉR

Town Gallery &
Deák Collection

Korzó

JÓKAI MÓR

JUHÁSZ GY

Bishop's
Palace

KORONÁZÓ
TÉR

KEMPELEN
TÉR

Hotel Alba
Regia

KÉGL GYÖRGY

Franciscan church,
cloister & museum

TANCSICS

Alba Plaza

VÁROSHÁZ
TÉR

Ibusz

KOSSUTH

Town hall,
Tourinform

St Anne's Chapel

LAJOS

PALOTAI

Szent Gellért
Tanulmányi Ház

LISZT

St Stephen's
Cathedral

VÁRKÖRÚT

TÁVIRDA

PIAC
TÉR

Várfal
Park

ARANY JÁNOS

NEGYHÁZ

Budenz House,
Ybl Collection

KOSSUTH LAJOS

Doll
museum

Carmelite
church

PETŐFI

Bus station

SZENT
ISTVÁN
TÉR

BUDAI

SELYEM

Crash
Café

SÜTŐ

PIAC TÉR

PRÓHÁSZKA

BUDAI

TOLNAI

0 _____ 400m
0 _____ 400yds

Balaton,
Szekszárd

Railway station
(900m)

From the **railway station** (*Béke tér*) it's a ten-minute walk to the centre. Head northwest along Kégi György utca and left into Rákóczi út. There are two or three trains an hour to Budapest Déli every day, and Balaton is also well served with regular departures to Balatonfüred, Tapolca and Siofók. Other destinations include Veszprém (17), Szombathely (seven), Zalaegerszeg (five), Miskolc (two) and Szolnok (one). For Tatabánya, Győr, Pécs and Szeged you'll need to head to Budapest and pick up a connection.

## Information and other practicalities

**Alba Plaza** Palotai út. Large shopping mall with a 10-screen cinema. *Open Mon–Fri 09.00–21.00, Sun 10.00–19.00.*

**Ibusz** Táncsics Mihály utca 5; ✆ 22 312580; e io88@ibusz.hu. Offers regional and country-wide tour programmes, as well as currency exchange and private-accommodation bookings. *Open Mon–Fri 08.00–16.00.*

**Listings magazine** *Fehérvári Est*

**Tourinform** Városház tér 1; ✆ 22 312818; e www.szekesfehervar@tourinform.hu. Extrememly helpful bureau where you can get maps and arrange sightseeing tips. *Open Sep 16–Oct 31 Mon–Fri 09.00–17.00, Sat 09.00–15.00, Nov 1–Jun 15 Mon–Fri 09.00–17.00, Jun 16–Sep 15 Mon–Fri 09.00–20.00, Sat–Sun 09.00–18.00.*

## Where to stay

**Hotel Alba Regia** (104 rooms) Rákóczi út 1; ✆ 22 313484; e reserve.hotelalbaregia@mail.datanet.hu. During the Middle Ages, the town was known by the Latin name Alba Regia. This block of a hotel next to the Garden of Ruins has leather-padded corridors more suggestive of an asylum than a hotel, but the rooms are light and airy. *Sgl 11,300Ft, dbl 12,000Ft, triple 17,000Ft.*

**Hotel Magyar Király** (34 rooms) Fő utca 10; ✆ 22 311262. Built in 1816 as a town house, it was later given its Neoclassical look by architect Mihály Pollack and operated as a hotel from 1870. The rooms are old-fashioned and unspecial. *Sgl 8,000Ft, dbl 9,000Ft.*

**Novotel** (96 rooms) Ady Endre utca 19–21; ✆ 22 534300; e H3333@accor-hotels.com; www.novotel-szekesfehervar.hu. Conference hotel with the usual 4-star trimmings (fitness room, sauna, etc). *Dbl 23,000Ft, apt (for 2) 27,600Ft.*

**Szent Gellért Tanulmányi Ház** (41 rooms) Mátyás király körút 1; ✆ 22 510810; e szentgellert@axelero.hu; www.hotels.hu/szentgellert. The St Gellért Study House is the best panzió, with modern rooms and a religious bent (it has its own chapel). There are rooms with or without bathrooms, and beds in dorm rooms. *Sgl €35, dbl €44, dorms €9–10/pp.*

**Vadáskürt Panzió** (22 rooms) Berényi út 1; ✆ 22 507514; e jagerhorn@axelero.hu. Slightly out from the centre – follow Szekfű György utca northeast into Berényi út – the Vadáskürt has uncluttered, whitewashed rooms with fridges. Buses 19, 26, 26A, 26G, 32 and 32G run here. *Sgl 6,900Ft, dbl 9,000Ft, apt (for 2) 11,000Ft.*

## Where to eat and drink

**Castrum Lovagi Restaurant** Várkörút 3; ✆ 22 505720. Medieval-cellar-style restaurant where meat feasts are served on wooden platters and you can eat with your fingers. Bring an appetite. Entrance on Országzászló tér. *Mains 990–4,090Ft, avg 2,200Ft; open 12.00–23.00 daily.*

**Diófa Vendéglő** Kadocsa utca 32A; ✆ 22 300665. The Diófa has a mind-bogglingly extensive menu that includes Hungarian specialities and an eclectic mix of international dishes. It's a well-spaced and classy eatery with helpful staff, a pretty garden and good food at the upper end of the price range. Buses 24 and 25 from the centre stop 100m away. *Mains 850–4,300Ft, avg 2,000Ft; open 09.00–23.00 daily.*

**Kiskakas Vendéglő** Kelemen Béla út 93; ✆ 22 340255. Twinned with the Diófa, the Kiskakas serves mainly Hungarian cuisine with a few international offerings. Casual but pleasant dining, with an atmospheric gallery eating area. *Mains 900–2,700Ft, avg 1,600Ft; open 11.00–22.00 daily.*

**Korzó** Fő utca 1; ✆ 22 312674; www.korzosorozo.hu. A good pub and restaurant with a decked terrace overlooking Városház tér and the Bishop's Palace. Hungarian and German dishes. *Mains 850–4,250Ft, avg 1,700Ft; open 10.00–24.00 daily.*
**Vörösmarty Cukrászda** Fő utca 6. Popular café and cake shop. *Open Sun–Thu 09.00–21.00, Fri–Sat 09.00–24.00.*

## Entertainment and nightlife

The Neoclassical **Vörösmarty Theatre** (*Fő utca 8; www.fehervar.hu/szinhaz*) sits just north of Országzászló tér, and hosts ballet and musicals as well as drama. It also has a smaller chamber theatre (*Kossuth utca 15*); for details and tickets to either, go to the **ticket office** (*Fő utca 3;* ✆ *22 327056;* e *jegyiroda@axelero.hu; open Mon–Fri 08.00–17.30*). During summer, there is also a **kiosk** selling tickets to theatre and festival events on Kossuth Lajos utca, near the Carmelite church.

**Atrium Nightclub** (*Fő utca 6; open Thu–Sat 22.00–06.00*) is a late-night basement club playing house and techno, as well as throwing the odd seedy striptease event. Two great places to hangout with a beer or coffee are **Ribillió** (*Rózsa utca 1;* ✆ *22 345835; open 11.00–24.00 daily*), a funky little joint over two levels, and **Crash Café** (*open Sun–Thu 10.00–24.00, Fri–Sat 10.00–02.00*), which is generally full of young things catching up on the gossip and features DJs at weekends. The **West Side Music Club** (*Vörösmarty tér 1;* ✆ *06 30 936 6517*) is a small club south of the centre.

## What to see and do
### Városház tér and around

The pretty main square holds the **town hall** (*Városház tér 1*) at its southern end, comprising two parts linked by a first-floor passage. That to the right is the older portion, built at the end of the 17th century, and with statues of Justice and Prudence at each corner of its balcony; its three-storey 18th-century counterpart was constructed as a palace for the Zichy family, whose coat of arms are visible above the gate on Kossuth utca. The square's naked equestrian statue is a monument to the 10th Hussar Regiment by Pál Pátzay, while the reddish stone orb supported by unconvincing lions is symbolic of the town's historic past and the franchise granted to it by King István. The memorial bell to the western side of the square fell from the Cistercian church during World War II.

Opposite the town hall is the **Franciscan church and cloister** (*Ferences templom & rendház; Városház tér 4*), built between 1720 and 1743, and believed to stand on the site of the medieval royal palace. Ferenc Megyessy's relief of a battle between Turks and Hungarians was added to one corner in 1938 on the 250th anniversary of liberation from Ottoman occupation. The former monastery contains the **Church Museum** (*Egyházmegye Múzeum;* ✆ *22 322247; adult/concessions 200/100Ft; open Apr 1–Oct 31 Tue–Sun 09.00–17.00*), with collections of religious art and a history of the diocese. Facing the monastery, the **Bishops' Palace** (*Püspöki Palota; Városház tér 10*) fills the wider part of the square and is a significant piece of Louis-XVI-style architecture. Built in 1801 from the ruins of the medieval basilica, its imposing central projection culminates in a tympanum bearing the episcopal coat of arms; the palace holds a significant library with early codices and incunabula.

The diminutive 15th-century **St Anna Chapel** (*Arany János utca*) – the town's only extant medieval building – stands on Arany János utca, running south away from the town hall; its Gothic nave served as a prayer house during the Turkish period. Next to it is the grand old lady that is **St István Cathedral** (*Géza Nagyfejedelem tér*). Remains of a quatrefoil chapel – thought to have been the burial place of Prince Géza (see page 440) – have been located in front of the entrance (the shape is marked with coloured paving). The cathedral was founded by King Béla IV in the 13th century, but it has undergone several reconstructions and bears no resemblance to its original Romanesque form. Parts of the royal coronation ceremonies were held inside. The statues above the entrance are of saints István, László and Imre, while the late-Baroque chancel and main altar were the work of Austrian court architect Franz Anton Hildebrandt in the 1770s.

The **Budenz House** (*Arany János utca 12*) was home to József Budenz, the founder of Hungarian comparative linguistics, who worked in the town as a teacher. Today it contains the **Ybl Collection** (✆ *22 317027; adult/concessions 260/120Ft; open Tue–Sun Mar 5–Apr 27, Oct 4–Oct 31 Tue–Sun 10.00–14.00, Apr 28–Oct 3 10.00–16.00*), a display of 20th-century art donated by art historian Ervin Ybl. There is also furniture belonging to the renowned Ybl family (including architect Miklós), who moved here from Austria in the early 1700s. A short distance to the east is the former **Carmelite church** (*Petőfi utca*), built in 1732 and restored after earthquake damage in 1800. It is a well-proportioned, elegant piece of Baroque architecture, complemented by Franz Anton Maulbertsch's interior frescoes – the painted crucifix in the oratory is particularly fine.

On the road running parallel to Arany János utca, the **Doll Museum** (*Megyeház utca 17;* ✆ *22 329504; adult/concessions 280/120Ft; open Tue–Sun 09.00–17.00*) is tucked inside the old County Hall building, and holds dolls, toy furniture and miniature books (including a complete English bible) dating from the 18th, 19th and 20th centuries. The contemporary Hungarian art of the New Hungarian Gallery is also here. Head north up the same street for the **Town Gallery/Deák Collection** (*Oskola utca 10;* ✆ *22 329431; free admission; open Tue–Sun Mar 1–Oct 31 10.00–18.00, Nov 1–Feb 28 09.00–17.00*) and a better collection of Magyar art by some major 19th- and 20th-century names.

### Fő utca and around

Fő utca runs north from Városház tér. Construction of the **Cistercian church and monastery** (*Ciszterci templom & rendház; Fő utca 6*) commenced in 1742; the former friary contains the **Szent István Király Museum** (✆ *22 315583; adult/concessions 260/120Ft; open Tue–Sun Apr 28–Oct 3 10.00–16.00, Mar 4–Apr 27 & Oct 4–Dec 21 10.00–14.00*). The exhibition shows artefacts unearthed in Transdanubia from the Neolithic Age up to the period of Turkish occupation; among them are linear pottery of 5000BC, finds relating to pre-Christian mystery religions, a significant collection of Roman stonework, fragments of the 11th-century royal castle and two pieces of what is believed to be the sarcophagus of King István (the main part of which is in the Garden of Ruins; see below). The museum has a second space at Országzászló tér 3, with temporary exhibitions.

The **Black Eagle Pharmacy Museum** (*Fekete SAS Patikamúzeum; Fő utca 5;* ✆ *22 315583; adult/concessions 260/120Ft, free on Sun; open Tue–Sun 10.00–18.00*) contains Baroque furnishings carved by the Jesuits – who founded the church and monastery opposite before it was taken over by the Cistercians – in 1758. The pharmacy itself operated until 1971. Further north is a memorial to the Renaissance King Mátyás sculpted on the 500th anniversary of his death (he was buried in the basilica), and beyond that a statue of György Varkocs; Varkocs was a castellan who died defending Székesfehérvár from Sultan Suleiman II in 1543 after cowardly burghers closed the town gates on him.

### Koronázó tér

Behind the Bishops' Palace, to the east of Városház tér, are the **Medieval Garden of Ruins and National Memorial Park** (*Koronázó tér;* ✆ *22 315583; adult/concessions 260/120Ft, free on Sun; open Apr 1–Oct 29 Tue–Sun 09.00–17.00*). This was the site of the original basilica established by King István – the national coronation church, home of the Holy Crown and royal insignia and one of the most significant buildings in medieval Hungary until it was destroyed during the Turkish period. You can see the excavated foundations (the majority of the stones were carted away for use in the Bishops' Palace), and a mausoleum decorated with paintings by Vilmos Aba Novák and containing what are thought to be the remains of King István's sarcophagus (although some argue it might actually be that of his son Imre) carved from an earlier Roman coffin. Part of the medieval city walls stands at the eastern side of the garden.

### Beyond the centre

On the northeastern outskirts of town, the extraordinary **Bory Castle** (*Bory Vár; Máriavölgyi utca 54;* ✆ *22 305570; open Mar–Nov 09.00–17.00 daily*) was built up over decades by the sculptor and architect Jenő Bory (1879–1959). He blended architectural styles in creating this imaginative concrete edifice, taking inspiration from Gothic and Romanesque buildings and medieval Scottish hunting castles, and filled the whole with paintings (many of his wife, Ilona Komócsin) and statues. You can take buses 26A from the bus station or 32 from outside the railway station.

The western side of town – a district know today as Palotaváros – was settled by Serbs during and after the Turkish occupation. A Serb church of 1771 with a wonderful Rococo iconostasis survives, and an **Open-Air Ethnographic Museum** (*Rác utca 11;* ✆ *22 379078; adult/concessions: 260/120Ft; open Mar 1–Oct 30 Wed–Sun 10.00–16.00*) has reconstructed rooms, examples of craft tools and other artefacts displayed in preserved peasant houses.

### Excursion

Around 10km south of Székesfehérvár, near the village of Tác, is the country's largest **Roman archaeological site** (*Gorsium Open-Air Museum; open daily Apr 28–Oct 31 08.00–18.00, Nov 1–Apr 27 10.00–16.00*). The settlement of Gorsium was mentioned in a late-3rd-century travel journal and spreads over 2km; originally a military camp defending the River Sárvíz, it developed into the religious centre and council seat of the Lower Pannonia province, and featured a sacred and administrative central quarter surrounded by residential areas. It was destroyed and rebuilt on several occasions, the last at the end of the 3rd century during the reign of Emperor Diocletian, when a grand palace and broad avenues were erected, and the town renamed Herculia. To the north of the ticket office is the sacred quarter of the 2nd and 3rd centuries, walls, towers and gates dating from AD300, and remains of the palace, Christian temples and an open-air theatre; to the south are houses and a 4th-century cemetery. Over a million items have been unearthed, and some of these are displayed in a former wine cellar built by the Zichy family (*open Apr 28–Oct 31 Tue–Sun 10.00–18.00*). In spring (*Apr 28–May 3*), festival games are held to celebrate the ancient Floralia Feast, while there are theatre performances in summer (for details, see Tourinform in Székesfehérvár). You can catch **buses** from Székesfehérvár, which drop you in the village (the museum itself is a 15-minute walk from there).

## VESZPRÉM

To the west of Székesfehérvár, the Bakony Hills blanket much of the Central Transdanubian region above Lake Balaton. Up until the mid 19th century, the forests in the hills were notoriously stuffed chock-full of outlaws, a breed that – according to the romantic canon – formed a parallel society governed by an alternative (and often preferable) creed; the similarities with Robin Hood and his men are obvious. The sympathetic contemporary portrayal of these people is perhaps in part due to the fact that many were servants who had fled cruelty under a feudal society (serfdom was not abolished until 1848). What is certainly true is that the Bakony landscape forms the backdrop for many of the country's ballads and legends.

Lying on five foothills 16km to the north of Balaton, Veszprém has a history to rival Székesfehérvár. During the rule of Prince Géza it was one of the country's earliest bishoprics; King István and his Bavarian Queen Gizella founded a cathedral and a castle here, and these subsequently became the places where queens were crowned and held court (leading to Veszprém's tag as the 'City of Queens'). It is said that the Hungarian coronation cloak (which is now on display in Budapest's National Museum; see page 166) was woven in a nearby nunnery, and that Gizella's own fair hand was involved – indeed it includes the only contemporary depiction of her in its design. Local literature frequently refers to the castle as though it remains a landmark, but in fact it was blown to smithereens by the Habsburgs. The town was also completely destroyed during the Turkish occupation and later independence struggles, and had to be rebuilt in the 18th century. The resulting Baroque historic district blends both with the broader avenues of the modern centre below it and the peaks and valleys of the surrounding Bakony countryside.

## Getting there and away

It's a short walk westward along Csaplár János utca from the **bus station** (*Piac tér*) to Szabadság tér. There are up to four buses an hour to Balatonfüred and Herend, as well as twice-hourly connections to Budapest, Székesfehérvár and Tapolca. Other routes include

Győr (11), Siófok (nine), Szekszárd and Nagykanizsa (four), Szombathely, Esztergom and Pécs (three). The **railway station** (*Jutasi út*) is 2¹/₂ km north of the castle area and has direct routes to Székesfehérvár (15), Sárvár and Szombathely (eight), Budapest Déli (seven) and Győr via Pannonhalma (five). Catch local buses 1 or 2 to the centre.

## Information and other practicalities

**Ibusz** Rákóczi Ferenc utca 6; ✆ 88 565540; e i093@ibusz.hu. Can arrange private rooms (*from 2,500Ft/pp*), exchange currency and travellers' cheques, and organise car hire, tours and other programmes. They're also hot on village tourism. Situated just off Óváros tér. *Open Mon–Fri 09.00–18.00, Sat 09.00–13.00.*

**Listings magazine** *Veszprémi Est*

**Tourinform** Vár utca 4; ✆ 88 404548; e tourinform@veszprem.hu. Helpful office that can also advise on rural tourism and accommodation in farm houses in surrounding villages. *Open Jun 15–Sep 15 Mon–Fri 09.00–20.00, Sat–Sun 09.00–18.00; rest of yr Mon–Fri 09.00–17.00, Sat 09.00–13.00.*

## Where to stay

Veszprém has some excellent accommodation, but budget options are thinner on the ground; contact Ibusz (see above) about private rooms and Tourinform for details of college rooms.

**Betekints Hotel** (47 rooms) Veszprémvölgyi utca 1; ✆ 88 406628; e betekints@informax.hu. Stylish and upmarket hotel with an adjacent wing of self-contained apts. Outdoor swimming pool, sauna and fitness room. Located in the Fejes Valley to the east of the centre, in the shadow of the viaduct and a short distance from the zoo. *Sgl 16,900Ft, dbl 18,900Ft, apt (for 2) 23,900Ft.*

**Diana Hotel** (10 rooms) József Attila utca 22; ✆ 88 421061. Run by a lovely family, the Diana is more guesthouse than hotel; its rooms are light and simply furnished. Lies to the south, on the road towards Tapolca (take bus 4 from the centre). *Sgl 8,600Ft, dbl 10,900Ft, triple 12,900Ft.*

**Éllő Panzió** (18 rooms) József Attila utca 25; ✆ 88 420097. Divided between two houses, the Éllő offers large and clean rooms. Directly opposite the Diana Hotel. *Sgl 12,500Ft, dbl 14,000Ft, triple 15,000Ft.*

**Oliva Panzió** (11 rooms) Buhim utca 14–16; ✆ 88 403875; e oliva@oliva.hu; www.oliva.hu. Delightful pension that conjures a Mediterranean atmosphere and is superbly located. *Sgl 13,800Ft, dbl 15,400Ft.*

**Villa Medici** (26 rooms) Kittenberger Kálmán út 11; ✆ 88 590070; e villamedici@sednet.hu; www.villamedici.hu. High-class 4-star hotel with sauna, solarium, English-style pub and indoor pool within a stone's throw of the Betekints Hotel (see above). *Dbl 19,600Ft, apt 26,750Ft.*

## Where to eat and drink

Classy places to rest your head are matched by classy places to fill your face; the top restaurants are attached to the hotels.

**Betekints** See above. Polished restaurant and bar serving Hungarian and international dishes, and specialising in veal soup and pork medallions. Its reputation is good, and its prices high. *Mains 950–3,500Ft, avg 2,400Ft; open 11.00–23.00.*

**Café Piazza** Óváros tér 4; ✆ 88 406630. Coffee house at southwestern side of the square that offers light snacks, ice creams and cakes. *Open 08.30–22.00 daily.*

**Diana** See above. Good-value peasant-style restaurant serving Hungarian and international food, with game specialities. *Mains 1,350–2,000Ft, avg 1,400Ft; open 07.00–23.00 daily.*

**Giselle Belgian Beer Café** Szabadság tér 1; ✆ 88 444900. One link in an international bar chain with an extensive selection of beers, a meat-heavy menu (steaks and grills), and a surprisingly early closing time. *Mains 1,400–2,950Ft, avg 1,700Ft; open Mon–Sat 10.00–22.00.*

**Gösser** Megyeház tér 2; ✆ 88 444144. Pub and pizza joint that is considerably better inside than it looks from the outside. Offers takeaway and delivery services. *Open Mon–Thu 14.00–23.00, Fri 14.00–01.00, Sat 16.00–01.00, Sun 16.00–23.00.*

**Oliva** See page 447. You won't find a better place to eat in town. The menu features an eclectic choice of global flavours – Mexican, Japanese and Mediterranean among them – and the olive-green walls and terraced garden make for an ambient setting. In summer, there's live jazz at the weekends. *Mains 890–2,790Ft, avg 2,000Ft; open Sun–Wed 11.00–23.00, Thu–Sat 11.00–24.00.*

**Óváros** Szabadság tér 14; ☎ 88 326790. Hungarian food, with Transylvanian stuffed duck among the specialities. The three-tiered paved al-fresco eating area is the choice spot in summer. *Mains 750–2,850Ft, avg 1,950Ft; open 11.00–23.00 daily.*

**Villa Medici** See page 447. The hotel has a pair of restaurants – one serving Hungarian (*mains 1,100–2,500Ft, avg 2,100Ft*) and the other international (*mains 2,500–3,400Ft, avg 3,000Ft*). Both are good but expensive, the latter – named after the hotel and voted one of the best 10 restaurants in Hungary – especially so. *Open 12.00–23.00 daily.*

## Entertainment and nightlife

Looking like a cross between a castle and a synagogue, the Art-Nouveau **Petőfi Theatre** (*Óvári Ferenc utca 2;* ☎ 88 424235) deserves a look at even if you're not taking in a performance. István Medgyaszay (follower of the renowned Viennese architect Otto Wagner) employed the most advanced technology available when designing it in 1908, and it was the country's first building constructed from reinforced concrete. Sándor Nagy, a leading member of the Gödöllő Pre-Raphaelite school, was responsible for some of the bright windows; one of his works depicts the Hungarian mythical story of the deer hunters Hunor and Magor. You can buy tickets or get information about what's on inside from the **ticket office** (*Szabadság tér 7;* ☎ 88 422440; e *szervezes@petofiszinhaz.hu; www.petofiszinhaz.hu open Mon–Fri 09.00–17.00*). The **cultural centre** (*Dózsa György út 2;* ☎ 88 429111) can also help.

In July and August, many of the younger party-going locals head for the nearby Lake Balaton, and some of the clubs and bars close. As well as Gösser and the Belgian Beer Café (see page 447), you could try the **Skorpió Nightclub & Bar** (*Virág Benedek utca 1; open Mon–Thu 10.00–02.00, Fri–Sat 10.00–04.00, Sun 10.00–01.00*), an Irish theme bar with little Irish of note. It has ground- and basement-level areas, and hosts live jazz at weekends; there is an erotic club (*open Tue–Sat 22.00–05.00*) at the top.

## What to see and do
### The Castle District

The gateway to the historic centre on Castle Hill (Várhegy) is **Óváros tér**, a cobbled square with a landscaped feel to it and some handsome architecture. The Louis-XVI-style **Pósa House** (*no 3*) – with two chubby *putti* below the roof – is named after the printer Endre Pósa who once lived there; it was originally built in 1793 by the Cistercian order. The Neo-Romanesque **town hall** (*no 9*), with shell motifs above its first-floor windows, was raised in 1857 as the church treasury, and has operated as municipal offices since 1990. To the right is the statue most favoured by locals; the bronze *Maid with Jar* by Lenke Kiss – pouring from a seemingly bottomless vase – is known affectionately as 'Zsuzsi' (Susy).

Behind the square's western side you'll see the **Fire Lookout Tower** (*Tűztorony; Vár utca 9; adult/concessions 300/200Ft; open Mar–Sep 10.00–18.00 daily*), erected on the foundations of a watchtower that stood here during the reign of Béla IV. Every hour the clock plays the 'Csermák Verbunkosi', a traditional recruiting song, and visitors can climb up to a gallery running around its outside. To get to it – it's reached via an arch at Vár utca 17 – you'll need to pass through **Castle (or Heroes') Gate** (Várkapu or Hősök kapuja). The cylindrical tower of this memorial to victims of World War I contains the **Castle Museum** (*adult/concessions 150/75Ft; open May 1–Sep 30 Tue–Sun 10.00–16.00, Sat–Sun 10.00–15.00*), with its missable collection of minerals.

Once through the gate you join Vár utca, the spine of the Castle District. Several exhibitions of modern art fall beneath the umbrella of the **House of Arts** (*Művészetek Háza; Vár utca 17;* ✆ *88 425204;* e *arthouse@mail.uti.hu; open Nov 1–May 7 Tue–Sun 10.00–17.00, May 8–Oct 31 10.00–18.00 daily*), including the Cellar Gallery (*Pince Galéria*), the Vass Collection (non-figurative works collected by shoemaker László Vass), and the Csikász Gallery – all accessed through the arch at number 17 or the steps at numbers 3–7 – and the Castle Gallery (*Vár Galéria; Vár utca 29*) further up the road, which has a display of tiles and bricks dating from Roman times to the present. Entrance to each costs 250–500Ft per adult; alternatively you can purchase a combined ticket that also covers the Fire Lookout Tower.

Today's courthouse was once the Louis-XVI-style **County Hall** (*Vár utca 19*); it stands opposite the Baroque former **Piarist school** (*Vár utca 10*) of 1778, whose pupils included the poet and monk Pál Ányos and the writer Viktor Cholnoky. The Neoclassical **Piarist church** (*Piarista templom; Vár utca 12–14; open Tue–Sun May 1–Aug 31 10.00–18.00, Sep 1–Oct 20 10.00–17.00*) was completed in 1833, and its monastery (designed by Jakab Fellner, who was also responsible for the Bishop's Palace) is now a retirement home for priests. Across the road from the church (outside Vár utca 27) is a light-pink **altar stone**, a copy of an original (held in the county museum) that is the country's earliest piece of carved Renaissance stonework. It was made as a tribute to Albert Vetési in 1467, and is inscribed with the words 'Do good for God's sake'; Vetési was the Bishop of Veszprém, a diplomat for King Mátyás and a beneficent patron of the arts.

On the left, at the point where the street widens, is the **Dubniczay House** (*Vár utca 29*), built in 1751 and incorporating part of the castle wall; inside is the Castle Gallery (see above). When the imposing **Bishop's Palace** (*Püspök Palota; Vár utca 16;* ✆ *88 426088; adult/concessions 500/250Ft; open Tue–Sun May 1–Aug 31 10.00–18.00, with free guide every hour, Sep 1–Oct 20 10.00–17.00, no guide available*) was under construction in the 1760s, the remains of a 13th-century Gothic chapel were uncovered. The so-called **Gizella Chapel** (*Vár utca 18;* ✆ *88 426088; adult/concessions 100/70Ft; open Tue–Sun May 1–Aug 31 10.00–18.00, Sep 1–Oct 20 10.00–17.00*) has a rib-vaulted ceiling and faded Byzantine frescoes of the apostles. The area in front of the palace is used for summer concerts. The **Trinity Monument** (*Szentháromság szobor*) was commissioned in 1750 by Bishop Márton Padányi Bíró, whose family crest it bears. The adjacent well reaches a depth of 40m.

The twin-towered, Neo-Romanesque **St Mihály Cathedral** (*Vár utca 18–20; open 09.00–17.30 daily*) was founded in 1001 and decorated by Queen Gizella with vestments and chalices – her relics were moved here in 1996. The church underwent several reconstructions in subsequent centuries (most recently in the 20th), and only the crypt survives from the early days; Bishop Bíró's tomb is among those inside. Organ concerts are held in the cathedral. Opposite the entrance is the **Queen Gizella Museum** (*Vár utca 35;* ✆ *88 426088; adult/concessions 300/150Ft; open daily May 1–Aug 31 10.00–18.00, Sep 1–Oct 20 10.00–17.00*) in the Tejfalussy House built in the 1770s. The religious pieces from the counties of Veszprém, Somogy and Zala include a replica of the coronation robe made in 1867 and a gold-threaded chasuble of 1480 that first belonged to Bishop Vetési. Just to the south of the museum, the **Franciscan church and monastery** (*Vár utca 33*) were built in the 18th century; Pál Ányos was buried in the church's crypt.

Next to the cathedral are the remains of **St György Chapel** (*Vár utca 20; adult/concessions 100/70Ft; open Tue–Sun May 1–Aug 31 10.00–18.00, Sep 1–Oct 20 10.00–17.00*), probably built as a royal chapel even before the cathedral, and the earliest piece of architecture in the Castle District. It is believed to be the site where Imre, the son of King István, took a vow of chastity; later the relic of St George's head was kept in the chapel, which became a place of pilgrimage as a consequence. A set of steps behind the chapel leads down to the steep-sided finger of **Benedek Hill**, with a grassy strip along the top. If you don't fancy traipsing down to it, you can admire the views instead from the uppermost end of Vár utca, with its statues of István and Gizella (sculpted in 1938 on the 900th anniversary of the king's death) gazing from the ramparts. From here Benedek Hill extends away immediately in front, while to the left of its tip are the Margit Ruins – the walls of a convent built in 1240 where Margit (daughter of Béla IV) was educated for six years. In the distance around to the left is the unlovely St István Viaduct, its concrete arches spanning Fejes Valley. A little beyond that are the remains of the 10th-century Greek Orthodox nunnery where the coronation cloak was embroidered (see page 446).

## Other sights

Moving south from Óváros tér along Rákóczi utca, take a short detour to the right along Óváry Ferenc utca to see the Petőfi Theatre (see page 448) before continuing to Megyeház tér. On the eastern side is the Neo-Romanesque **County Hall**, designed in 1887 by István Kiss. Further down and set back from Erzsébet sétány among trees is the **Laczkó Dezső Museum** (*Erzsébet sétány 1;* ❧ *88 564330; adult/concessions 300/125Ft; open Tue–Sun Mar 15–Oct 16 10.00–18.00, Oct 17–Mar 14 12.00–16.00*). Among the permanent exhibits are items relating to Veszprém County, including Roman finds from Balácapuszta (see below). Next door is the **Bakony House** (*Bakonyi ház; Erzsébet sétány 3;* ❧ *88 561330; adult/concessions 200/100Ft; open May 1–Oct 16 Tue–Sun 10.00–18.00*), a 20th-century reconstruction of a 19th-century peasant house in the village of Öcs, to the southwest of Veszprém. At the back is a flask-maker's workshop.

**Veszprém Zoo** (*Kittenberger út 17;* ❧ *88 421088;* e *veszpzoo@sednet.hu; www.zoo.hu/veszprem; adult/student/child 800/700/340Ft; open May 1–Sep 30 09.00–18.00 daily, shorter hours other months*) is in Fejes Valley, a 15-minute walk west of the centre near the viaduct. The zoo also runs a riding school.

## Festivals and events

The main celebration is the Gizella Days Art Festival in May, when there are exhibitions of art, music and dance in Óvárós tér, Petőfi Theatre and elsewhere. The Summer Festival takes place in August. The cultural centre (see page 448) can provide information.

## Excursions

Just under 10km to the southeast of Veszprém, at the edge of the village of Nemesvámos, is a place called **Balácapuszta** where Roman ruins (*Nemesvámos-Baláca;* ❧ *88 265050; open May 1–Sep 30 Tue–Sun 10.00–18.00*) were unearthed at the turn of the 20th century. The settlement may have been called Caesariana, and fell at the junction of two main Roman roads. At the centre is a large 1st-century villa; finds from the site are exhibited in the cellars, and among them are two prize mosaics.

Turn your plate over in an upmarket restaurant, and there's a good chance that – as well as getting a lapful of soup – you'll see the mark of Herend. Since the early 19th century, this internationally renowned porcelain has emanated from the **Herend Porcelain Manufactory** (*Herend, Kossuth Lajos utca 140; www.herend.com*) in the village of Herend, 15km west of Veszprém on Road 8 towards Körmend. The company took off during the Great Exhibition of 1851 in London's Crystal Palace, when Queen Victoria was so impressed by the porcelain that she commissioned a dinner service. It was adorned with butterflies and oriental flowers; named after the monarch, it remains one of Herend's most popular designs. All the pieces are crafted by hand; figurines of the 1920s are considered the connoisseur's classics, but while the look of the porcelain has altered according to fashion the quality remains top-drawer. Today 250 potters and 630 painters work in the factory. The Porcelanium (❧ *88 523100;* e *porcelanium@herend.com; www.porcelanium.com; adult/concessions 1,000/400Ft, family 2,200Ft*) is the visitor centre, and inside is a mini-manufactory (*open Apr 1–Oct 31 daily 09.00–17.30, Nov 1–Mar 30 Tue–Sat*

*09.00–16.30*) where you can see some of the artists in action and a museum (*Apr 1–Oct 31 daily 09.00–17.30, Nov 1–Mar 30 Mon–Sat 09.00–16.30*) where you can take a trawl through the changing trends. There is also a café, a very high-class restaurant and a showroom where you can make purchases. The centre is a short walk northeast from the bus station; there are regular buses here from Veszprém.

To Veszprém's north (20km along Road 82) is **Zirc**, whose Baroque Cistercian abbey and church (*Rákóczi tér*) of 1753 – with an altarpiece by F A Maulbertsch – stand on the site of a 12th-century predecessor destroyed by the Turks. The abbey's mid-19th-century Neoclassical library (*Reguly Antal Memorial Library;* ✎ *88 593800; open Tue–Sun 10.00–12.00, 14.00–16.00*) is furnished with wood from Bakony ash trees; named after a local linguist who was ahead of his time in arguing a link between Hungarian and Finnish, it was damaged in 1944 by pieces of a German war plane shot down overhead. The same building houses the Bakony Scientific Museum (✎ *88 414157; open 10.00–17.00 daily*), devoted to the natural history of the Bakony, while next to the abbey is an arboretum (*Damjanich utca 19;* ✎ *88 414569; open Tue–Sun May 1–Aug 31 09.00–18.00, Sep 1–30 09.00–17.00, Oct 1–Nov 30 & Mar 15–Apr 30 09.00–16.00*). The Tourinform (*Rákóczi tér 1;* ✎ *88 416816; open summer Mon–Fri 09.00–18.00, Sat–Sun 09.00–17.00, rest of yr Mon–Fri 09.00–17.00*) can provide details on walking routes in the surrounding hills.

# SÜMEG

Southwest of Veszprém, sandwiched in a valley between the Keszthely range and the western foothills of the Bakony, Sümeg was settled early – prehistoric man quarried flint near by, and Roman remains have also been discovered. The town's castle, of course, stands out like a sore thumb from its hilltop vantage point; a 13th-century version was reconstructed in the 16th century and successfully kept the Turks at bay, though not the Habsburgs (who set it ablaze in 1713). Picturesque as it is, however, the real thing of beauty in town is F A Maulbertsch's painting masterclass in the parish church, one of several significant commissions made during the 18th century while Sümeg was the seat of the bishops of Veszprém and it had to be resurrected after a devastating fire in 1700.

## Getting there and away

The **bus station** (*Béke tér*) is just south of the centre; walk north through Béke tér and Flórián tér, and on to Kossuth Lajos utca. There are regular buses to Keszthely, Hevíz, Pápa, Veszprém and Tapolca, as well as services to Zalaegerszeg (ten), Győr (six), Sárvár (five), Szombathely and Sopron (four), Kaposvár and Kőszeg (two). Four buses a day make the four-hour journey to Budapest Népliget.

The modern **railway station** is 1km west of the centre. The most regular trains are to Celldömölk and Tapolca; there are also services to Keszthely (three), Szombathely (two), Sopron and Balatonfüred (one). Change at Celldömölk for Pápa, Tatabánya, Győr, Szombathely and Budapest.

## Information and other practicalities

**Balaton Tourist** Kossuth Lajos utca 15; ✎ 87 550259; e sumeg@balatontourist.hu. Can organise private rooms (*from 2,000Ft/pp*) and tours of the region. *Open Mon 08.30–13.00, Tue–Fri 08.30–16.00, Sat 08.30–12.00.*

**Tourinform** Kossuth Lajos utca 15; ✎ 87 550276; e sumeg@tourinform.hu. *Open summer Mon–Fri 09.00–18.00, Sat–Sun 10.00–17.00, rest of yr Mon–Fri 08.00–16.00.*

## Where to stay

**Báróház Panzió** (12 rooms) Báróházi utca 14; ✎ 87 550205. A kilometre or two northeast of the centre, on a hillside overlooking the castle, this villa-style guesthouse is clean, pretty and homely.

Not all rooms have TV. To get there, take Fehérkő utca off Road 84 (north of Castle Hill), turn left into Karolina utca and immediately right into Báróházi utca. *Sgl 5,300Ft, dbl 8,200Ft, triple 10,600Ft.*

**Castle Stables** (*Váristálló*) Városdal utca 5; ↘ 87 550087; e varistallo@axelero.hu; www.sumeg.hu/capariplus. A rustic guesthouse at the Castle Stables, right at the foot of Castle Hill. *Rooms 2,300Ft/pp.*

**Hotel Kapitány** Tóth Tivadar utca 19; ↘ 87 352598; www.hotelkapitany.hu. On the road running past the northern side of Castle Hill, the Kapitány is a 4-star hotel with adequate (though not special) rooms that cashes in on the castle's proximity by hosting a range of themed programmes (horse shows, folk dances, wine-tastings, knights' tournaments, etc). There's an on-site cellar and a small outdoor pool. *Sgl €45, dbl €50.*

**Hotel Vár** Vak Bottyán utca 2; ↘ 87 352352. Despite its faux exterior – rigged to look like an austere castle – this hotel behind the Franciscan Church is modern and airy, with well-sized rooms. Good value. *Sgl 7,800Ft, dbl 10,400Ft, triple 14,000Ft, room for 4 16,400Ft.*

**Krigler Panzió and Ramessetter Cellar** (8 rooms) Báróházi utca 1; ↘ 87 550320. When we visited, we found the owners occupied with gutting a pig for an evening feast; they are a hospitable bunch, who will prepare grills for their guests and serve wine from their 200-year-old cellar. The rooms are simple but comfortable; shared use of kitchen and TV. Recommended. Stands opposite the Báróház Panzió. *Sgl 5,000Ft, dbl 7,500Ft, triple 11,000Ft.*

## Where to eat and drink

There are a number of food stalls (as well as souvenir stands) on Vársétány (the road by the Carriage Museum that runs from Road 84 towards the castle).

**Kisfaludy** Kossuth Lajos utca 13; ↘ 87 352128. The best restaurant in town. Its interior is hung with the skins and skulls of unfortunate boars and deer. The Hungarian cuisine includes Balaton fish, steaks and – in the words of the great Bruce Forsyth – good game, good game. There is also an ice-cream parlour. *Mains 950–2,600Ft, avg 1,700Ft; open 09.00–23.00 daily.*

**Móri Fogadó** Kossuth Lajos utca 22; ↘ 87 352489. Café-style eatery opposite the Tourinform office serving cheap local nosh. *Mains 600–1,500Ft, avg 1,000Ft; open 12.00–21.00 daily.*

**Scotti** Szent István tér 1; ↘ 87 350997. Primarily a pizza joint, with a limited selection of other Hungarian dishes, the Scotti has a cluttered but inviting garden with a fishpond, fountain and creepers. The staff are rather blinkered, the synthesiser music is dreadful, and we were surprised to see a rotund chef working in just an apron and pants, but the ambience is good and the large pizzas could feed a family for a week. Opposite the Town Museum. *Mains avg 1,500Ft; open 09.00–23.00 daily.*

## What to see and do
### Sümeg Castle

Overlooking the whole shebang, the **castle** (↘ 87 352598; www.sumegvar.hu; *adult/concessions 1,000/500Ft; open daily Apr 1–Sep 30 09.00–19.00, rest of yr 10.00–18.00, depending on weather*) sits high on the 270m limestone Castle Hill and is the dominant feature of the townscape. The journey up is rewarded not only with a closer look at Transdanubia's biggest fort, but fabulous views. Razed by the Habsburgs at the start of the 18th century, the castle wasn't restored until the 20th century. The southern part of the courtyard contains the 13th-century Old Tower, inside which is an exhibition detailing the castle's history and including pieces of weaponry.

In summer, there are **medieval programmes** hosted within the castle walls (*adult/concessions 2,000/1,000Ft; Jun 1–Aug 31 at 11.00, 14.30 & 17.00 daily*), and you can join an evening banquet afterwards (*adult/concessions 6,000/5,000Ft*). A road leads around and up the hill, branching from Városdal utca near the Castle Stables (see opposite); you can get to Városdal utca either from the northeast by following Vársétány off Road 84 or from Szent István tér to the southeast by following Vak Bottyán utca and Bem utca. If you don't want to make the climb on foot, **jeep-like taxis** (*500Ft/pp*) leave from the car park at the northern end of Várodal utca; there need to be a minimum of two passengers.

## Other sights and activities

To the southwest of Szent István tér, at the end of Deák Ferenc utca, the Roman Catholic parish **Church of the Ascension** (*Szent Imre tér; open Mon–Fri 09.00–12.00, 13.00–18.00, Sat 10.00–12.00, 14.00–17.00, Sun 14.00–17.00*) is a hulking Baroque temple constructed between 1756 and 1759 under the stewardship of Bishop Márton Padányi Biró. What makes the church extraordinary is what you'll find inside – namely some of the most beautiful Baroque and Rococo paintings in the country. The bishop secured the services of Franz Anton Maulbertsch, an Austrian painter in his early 30s, to decorate the interior; over a period of 14 months, the young man surpassed any work he had or would produce, conjuring what has been described as 'Hungary's Rococo Sistine Chapel'. Biró had a say in the chosen biblical subjects, and it was then left to Maulbertsch to weave magic in the colour, movement and play of light and shade. Pay particular attention to the *Adoration of the Shepherds*, in which the artist has included a self portrait in the figure offering a piece of ewe's cheese. He appears again on the back wall, dressed in an orange tail coat in the company of his patron. The frescoes have been restored on several occasions, most notably after a fire in 1799.

Across Kossuth Lajos utca, at the northern end of Kisfaludy tér, the **Town Museum** (*Kisfaludy tér 2;* ✆ *87 550277; adult/concessions 400/200Ft; open May 1–Sep 30 Tue–Sun 10.00–18.00; rest of yr Mon–Fri 08.00–16.00*) is housed in the birthplace of Sándor Kisfaludy, who also lived here with his wife from 1800 and is buried in the town cemetery. The influential poet was a fervent protector of his native language, a leading member of the linguistic neology movement and one who wrote in Hungarian at a time when the language of state was German. There is an exhibition devoted to his life, as well as to other members of his family (his younger brother was a writer of comedy and short stories). Also here are collections of Bakony fossils, flints from the prehistoric mine found just outside town, pieces of Sümeg pottery (including some Gothic and Renaissance examples excavated from the castle) and ecclesiastical art. Outside the gate is a pantheon to other famous local citizens such as József Nemeth and János Horváth.

Behind the trees just to the east is the 18th-century **Bishop's Palace** (*Szent István tér 8; free entry; open 15.00–18.00 daily*), built by Bishop Biró as a summer residence. Its crumbling plaster is being restored but the corner balconies and Neoclassical entrance give an idea of former splendour; if someone is there you can gain admittance to the oval chapel with its frescoed ceiling and gilded episcopal coat of arms above the altar, and an uninspiring exhibition of local art. The central courtyard is used for summer concerts. One wing contains a **Wine Museum and Cellar** (*Bormúzeum & Borkóstolo Pince; entrance free; open 10.00–21.00 daily*) where you can take a tasting (*1,200Ft/4 wines*).

Across from the palace, the **Franciscan church and monastery** (*Szent István tér*) was built in Baroque style in 1657 and is (after the castle) the town's second-oldest structure. Frescoes of the Crucifixion and Ascension adorn the church's side-chapels, there is an impressive altar of 1720 by Martin Witner, and a pulpit with gilded evangelists and a disembodied arm holding a crucifix. For the last 250 years, pilgrims have made the journey to see the church's statue of the Blessed Virgin in early September. This is an enjoyable, well-crafted church with much to admire in its details; it is unfortunate that it is destined always to suffer by comparison with the parish-church masterpiece to the west.

Follow Vak Bottyán utca up to Vároldal utca, and on the right are the **Castle Stables** (*Váristálló; Vároldal utca 5;* ✆ *87 550087;* e *varistallo@axelero.hu; www.sumeg.hu/capari*); the Capári Riding School operates from here (*riding from 2,500Ft/hr*) and offers tours, and there's an equestrian shop (*open 09.00–18.00 daily*). Behind the stables, on the other side of Vársétány, is a grassed area used for jousting and other medieval sports (✆ 87 352598/350924; Jul & Aug 13.00 & 18.00 daily). Near by is the **Carriage Museum** (*entry free, but donation appreciated of adult/concessions 300/150Ft*), with horse-drawn carriages of the 19th and 20th centuries, and weaponry including a 16th-century crossbow.

## PÁPA
Northwest of Veszprém and run through by Road 83, Pápa experienced its purple period in the 1750s when, under the ownership of the powerful Esterházys, its pretty Baroque core came to be; Károly Esterházy, the Bishop of Eger, was responsible for removing the medieval fortifications and modernising many of the streets and squares, flexing his wealthy muscles with an architectural flourish. During medieval times the settlement had been an important market town, but it subsequently became marked as a leading regional centre of Protestantism and learning. Its Calvinist college was founded in 1531, and it was here that Gál Huszár opened the faith to common Hungarians through his translation of the *Heidelberg Káté* in 1577. The college later boasted some of Hungary's cultural greats – including the author Mór Jókai and the poet Sándor Petőfi – among its 19th-century alumni.

### Getting there and away
The **bus station** is just west off the main strip on Szabadság utca, with regular buses running to Veszprém and Győr (up to 14 a day). Other destinations served include Tapolca (five), Sopron (four), Sárvár and Zalaegerszeg (three), Szombathely, Székesfehérvár and Tatabánya (two). Up to three buses a day make the four-hour trip to Budapest Népliget.

Trains run fairly regularly to Győr and Celldömölk from the **railway station** on Béke tér, north of the centre. There are also up to nine trains a day to Tatabánya, up to four to Budapest Keleti and two-daily to Szombathely and Sárvár. Change at Győr for access to Sopron, and Celldömölk for Tapolca and Veszprém.

### Information and other practicalities
**Listings magazine** *Veszprémi Est*
**Tourinform** Fő tér 12; ✆ 89 311535; e papa@tourinform.hu. *Open Jun 1–Aug 31 Mon–Fri 09.00–17.00, Sat–Sun 10.00–16.00, Sep 1–May 31 Mon–Fri 09.00–15.30.*

### Where to stay and eat
**Főnix Panzió** (5 rooms) Jókai utca 4; ✆ 89 324361. This small guesthouse above a dingy bar strays towards the shabby, but it is central and it's hard to quibble with the price. *Dbl 6,900Ft.*
**Arany Griff Hotel** (24 rooms) Fő tér 15; ✆ 89 312000. Directly opposite the Great Church, the century-old Griff has bright and welcoming rooms with high ceilings, laminated floors and large windows. Its dance hall was once the scene for county balls. Its restaurant (*mains 990–3,200Ft, avg 2,000Ft; open 11.00–23.00 daily*) – one of the town's rare places to eat – is plain but has a pleasant courtyard. We enjoyed a meal of turkey with sour cream, cheese and fried potato followed by banana pudding in hot-chocolate sauce; the arteries screamed 'no' but the tastebuds won the day. *Sgl 6,984–8,480Ft, dbl 9,704–12,288Ft, apt (for 2) 16,096Ft.*
**Hotel Villa Classica** (20 rooms) Bástya utca 1; ✆ 89 512200; e info@villaclassica.hu; www.villaclassica.hu. Our favourite in Pápa, this delightful hotel to the southwest of Fő tér has chic and polished rooms. Its restaurant (*mains 850–3,250Ft, avg 1,800Ft; open 11.00–23.00 daily*) dishes up fresh contemporary Hungarian and Mediterranean cuisine, and there's a bar and outdoor patio area. *Dbl €33–45.*

### What to see and do
The Baroque **Esterházy Palace** (*Esterházy-kastély; Fő tér 1;* ✆ *89 313584; closed for renovation but due to reopen soon*) at the northern side of Fő tér was designed by József

Grossman for Count Ferenc Esterházy in the 1780s on the site of the town's medieval castle. It was badly damaged during World War II, and served as a Russian military barracks until 1990. There is a library, music school and local-history museum inside, but ongoing renovation means the palace is closed at the time of going to press. However, its grounds – including a 100ha English garden at the back – make good strolling territory.

The late-18th-century **Great Church** (*Nagytemplom; Fő tér*), twin-towered and Neoclassical-Baroque, was the work of Jakab Fellner and József Grossman. It was commissioned by Károly Esterházy, the Bishop of Eger, as a family burial chamber. Each of the church's towers is broken by columns through which the bells are visible, and the nave is decorated with frescoes by Austrian master F A Maulbertsch.

Fő utca holds the town hall, built over a Benedictine monastery whose church of 1742 remains jammed next to it. On the same street is the smaller portion of the **Pápa Calvinist Collection**, which is divided in two. The late-Baroque church of 1784 (*Fő utca 6;* ✆ *89 324240; admission free; open May 1–Oct 31 Tue–Sun 09.00–16.00*) has exhibits relating to 500 years of Calvinism in Transdanubia. The main body of the collection is further south in the **Calvinist college** (*Március 15 tér 9;* ✆ *89 324240; adult/concessions 250/150Ft; open Nov 1–Apr 30 Tue–Fri 08.00–16.00; May 1–Oct 31 Tue–Fri 08.00–16.00, Sat–Sun 09.00–17.00*), and features ecclesiastical items, pieces of applied art and an Egyptian mummy donated by a former student.

The **Blue Dye Museum** (*Március 15 tér 12;* ✆ *89 324390; adult/concessions 400/200Ft; open Tue–Sun Nov 1–Mar 31 09.00–16.00, Apr 1–Oct 31 09.00–17.00*) is in what was once one of the largest dye workshops in central Europe. During the 18th century, skilled textile workers migrated to Hungary from countries to the west in search of work. In 1786 Carl Friedrich Kluge, whose family had arrived from Saxony, established a business devoted to the process of dying cloth a fashionable indigo colour. The factory continued to operate through seven family generations until its closure in 1956, and the museum showcases the machinery and the final products, as well as some work by textile artist Irén Bódy.

The pedestrianised Kossuth Lajos utca runs parallel with Fő utca from the bottom of Fő tér; if you follow it down for 100m and turn right into Petőfi Sándor utca, you'll reach a derelict **synagogue** (*Petőfi Sándor utca 24*) of 1846; the construction was subsidised by the Esterházy family, who recognised the economic benefits Jewish settlers brought to Pápa and welcomed them accordingly. The adjacent Jewish cemetery is one of Hungary's earliest, with some headstones over three centuries old.

If you need a splash, the **Várkert Baths** (*Külső Várkert;* ✆ *89 311535;* e *varkertfurdo@papa.hu; www.varkertfurdo.hu; adult/concessions 1,100/850Ft; open thermal baths daily 09.00–21.00, indoor pools 06.00–22.00 daily, outdoor pools May 15–Sep 15 09.00–20.00 daily*) have indoor and outdoor pools, as well as other sports facilities and a bar and restaurant.

## Festivals and events

August sees several of the town's main events, including the Historical Games and the International Hussar Camp (when there are costumed equestrian events), and a three-day wine festival. The United Games Festival in June features concerts and exhibitions.

# TATA

Sitting between the Vértes and Gerecse hills above the industrial city of Tatabánya, Tata revolves around its Old Lake (Öreg-tó), a pretty pool that forms an appealing backdrop for walking and bird-watching and an enticing foreground for watersports. Predictably tagged with a 'Town of Waters' moniker, this is a place for 'doers' and avoids the sunbathing hordes. It was a favourite royal resort in the Middle Ages. King Zsigmond attached a palace to the 14th-century castle on the northern shore, and King Mátyás enjoyed hunting here. After the Turks had left, the landowning Eszterházys commissioned architect Jakab Fellner to rebuild the town during the 18th century, a period that also saw the Farkasházy-Fischer family establish their renowned delftware factory in 1758 (they later attracted further renown when founding the Herend factory; see page 450). Tata is famous too for having more watermills – 14 in total – than any other Hungarian town; the majority were constructed in the 18th century (although the Cifra Mill dates back 500 years) and today serve as hotels, residences and museums.

## Getting there, away and around

It's a five-minute walk to the centre of town from the **bus station** by following Váralija utca eastwards. Buses run every 30 minutes to Tatabánya, and there are services to Esztergom (eight), Székesfehérvár (four), Győr and Dunaújváros (three), and Szeged (once daily on Fri & Sun only).

The **railway station** is 2km north of the centre behind the castle and has very frequent services to Budapest (Déli and Keleti), Győr and Tatabanya. There are also regular trains to the Slovakian border crossing at Komárom. To cross into Austria you'll need to change at Győr.

A small **passenger ferry** (*Tópart sétány; adult/concessions 700/600Ft*) offers a 30-minute cruise around Öreg-tó whenever there are 12 or more passengers.

## Information and other practicalities

**Listings magazine** *Komárom-Esztergomi Est*

**Tourinform** Ady Endre utca 9; ☎ 34 586045; e tata@tourinform.hu. As well as the usual information, this office can provide details of private rooms (*from 2,500Ft/pp*), although the quality of these is apparently variable. *Open Jun 15–Sep 15 Mon–Fri 09.00–18.00, Sat–Sun 09.00–17.00, rest of yr Mon–Fri 09.00–17.00.*

## Where to stay

**Fényes Camping** Környei utca 4; ☎ 34 588144; www.fenyesfurdo.hu. This large, well-manicured campsite 2km northwest of Öreg-tó site lies within the grounds of the town's outdoor leisure complex (see page 460). As well as tent and caravan space, there are bungalows and a motel – the latter little more than a Portakabin with hard beds and smelly shared toilets and shower blocks. *Caravan 2,000Ft, tents 1,000–1,400Ft, plus adult/concessions 1,300Ft/1,000Ft; bungalow (for 4) 11,000Ft, motel dbl 6,500Ft; open all year.*

**Hotel Kristály** (25 rooms) Ady Endre utca 22; ☎ 34 383577; e kristhot@alarmix.net; www.hotels.hu/kristaly_tata. 230-year-old hotel in the centre. Although most rooms are large, they're clearly feeling those years and could do with a bit of a spruce up. *Sgl €70, dbl €75, triple €94.*

**Kalóz Fregatt** (5 rooms) Alamási út 2; ☎ 34 382382; e kfregatt@axelero.hu; www.hotels.hu/kaloz. Pleasant rooms above the pirate-themed pub and restaurant (see page 458) in the centre. You can also hire bikes. *Sgl €30, dbl €40.*

**Kiss Panzió** (9 rooms) Bacsó Béla utca 54; ☎ 34 586888; e kispanzi@ax.hu; www.hotels.hu/kispanzi. 200m from the railway station, this upmarket guesthouse has well-equipped rooms, a restaurant, an indoor swimming pool and a beauty salon (with solarium and massage options). *Dbl 16,500Ft, apt 24,500Ft.*

**Öreg-tó Camping** Fáklya utca 2; ☎ 34 383496; e oregto@mail.matavnet.hu. More of a youngsters' campsite than Fényes, offering easy access to the eastern shore of the lake and with food stalls and bars just outside. Bungalows inc kitchenettes. *Tent/caravan 1,000Ft, plus 1,000Ft/pp, bungalow 3,000Ft/pp; open May 1–Aug 31.*

**Öreg-tó Club Hotel** Fáklya utca 4; ☎ 34 487960. Next to (but separate from) the campsite, the Club has a hotel (with en-suite rooms) as well as a hostel with 19 bungalows (shared shower and toilet facilities). On the shabby side, but prettily situated and cheap. *Hotel sgl 3,900Ft, dbl 7,300Ft, triple 9,200Ft, hostel 1,200Ft/pp.*

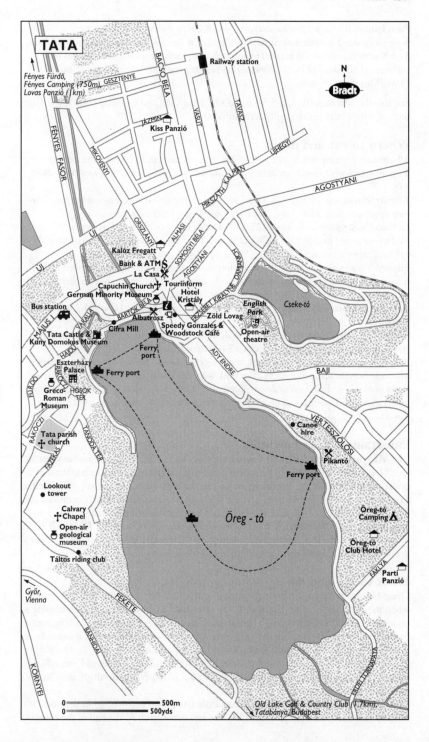

**TATA**

↑
Fényes Fürdő,
Fényes Camping (750m),
Lovas Panzió (1km)

Railway station

N
Bradt

GESZTENYE

BACSÓ BÉLA

VASÚT

TAVASZ

ÚJHEGYI

AGOSTYÁNI

Kiss Panzió

TÁZMIN

MIKOFÉNYI

FÉNYES FASOR

ÚJ

ORSZLÁNY

ALMÁSI

SOMOGYI BÉLA

MIKSZÁTH KÁLMÁN

AGOSTYÁNI

Kalóz Fregatt
Bank & ATM
La Casa
Capuchin Church
German Minority Museum
Bus station
Tata Castle &
Kuny Domokos Museum
Eszterházy
Palace
Gréco-
Roman
Museum
Tata parish
church

Tourinform
Hotel
Kristály
Zöld Lovag

English
Park

Cseke-tó

ERZSÉBET KIRÁLYNÉ · DAMJANICH

BARTÓK BÉLA

VÁGALJA

MÁJUS 1

HADÚ

Albatrosz
Cifra Mill
Speedy Gonzales &
Woodstock Café

Open-air
theatre

Ferry
port

Ferry port

ADY ENDRE

BAJI

FÜRDŐ

RÁKÓCZI

FAZEKAS

HŐSÖK
TÉR

TANODA TÉR

Canoe
hire

VÉRTESSZŐLŐSI

Pikantó

Ferry port

Lookout
tower

Calvary
Chapel

Open-air
geological
museum

Táltos riding club

Öreg - tó

Öreg-tó
Camping

Öreg-tó
Club Hotel

FAKIVA

Parti
Panzió

↙ Győr,
Vienna

FEKETE

BANHIDAI

KÖRNYEI

ERDŐTORNYÓFALVA

0 ──────── 500m
0 ──────── 500yds

Old Lake Golf & Country Club (1.7km),
Tatabánya, Budapest

**Parti Panzió** (12 rooms) Boróka utca 6–8; ↳ 34 487864; e partipanzio@axelero.hu; www.partipanzio.hu. At the eastern side of Öreg-tó, near the campsite, Parti is an excellent choice. As well as clean and cheerful standard rooms, each of its 4 apts are set in separate houses with kitchens and gardens. The hotel facilities include a swimming pool, whirlpool and sauna. *Dbl 10,000Ft, apt (for 4) 18,000Ft.*

See also the Maestoso Riding School and Old Lake Golf and Country Club (page 460), both of which have good-quality accommodation.

## Where to eat and drink

**Albatrosz** Alkotmány utca 5; ↳ 06 30 650 5290. This pub and pizza joint has restricted views of the northern tip of Öreg-tó from its beer patio. *Mains 800–2,000Ft, avg 1,300Ft; open 10.00–24.00 daily.*

**Kristály Restaurant** See page 456. Traditional local cuisine served in very agreeable turn-of-the-century surroundings. *Mains 950–2,900Ft, avg 1,800Ft; open 11.00–22.00 daily.*

**La Casa** Országgyűlés tér 3; ↳ 06 70 252 2884. One of the town's best, La Casa serves Mediterranean and local dishes – paella and Spanish frogs' legs sit alongside Hungarian stews – and has a courtyard garden. *Mains 990–3,900Ft, avg 2,100Ft; open 12.00–22.00 daily.*

**Pikantó** Tópart sétány; ↳ 34 480480. Wood-furnished restaurant with an upstairs gallery and a conservatory serving Hungarian and international cuisine. It also has an attached Mediterranean grill restaurant behind it that opens in summer only. Located on a small road off Vértesszőlősi út that leads to the lake and boat pier, and is lined with food stalls and bars. *Mains 990–2,400Ft, avg 1,800Ft; open 11.30–23.00 daily.*

**Speedy Gonzales Snack Bar** Zsigmond király udvar. Good place for cheap and tasty fast food. Shares an outdoor space with Woodstock Café (see below). *Open 11.00–23.00 daily.*

**Zöld Lovag** Ady Endre 17; ↳ 34 481681; e z.lovag@freemail.hu. Medieval-themed restaurant with tacky heraldic shields dotting its dingy brick walls, and the obligatory costumed staff. Serves hearty portions (steaks the size of dinner plates) of food on wooden platters. Found at the end of a small parade called Esterházy udvar off Ady Endre utca. *Mains 850–3,800Ft, avg 2,000Ft; open Sun–Thu 12.00–22.00, Fri–Sat 12.00–24.00.*

## Entertainment and nightlife

The **Magyary Zoltán Cultural Centre** (*Váralja utca 4;* ↳ *34 380811;* e *muvhaz@tata.hu; open Mon–Fri 09.00–17.00*) can provide information on arts events, including those at an **open-air theatre** in the English Park (at the western side of Cseke-tó). The **Kalóz Fregatt** (see page 456; *open Sun–Thu 12.00–24.00, Sat–Sun 12.00–02.00*) is decked out like a frigate, and has the odd live band; off-key performers presumably risk a good keelhauling. The **Woodstock Café** (*Zsigmond Király udvar;* ↳ *06 70 312 5952*) is an intimate little place in a shopping parade just off Ady Endre utca. It's a good spot for a drink, and there are monthly karaoke parties for those so inclined.

## What to see and do

**Öreg-tó**, spreading south from the centre, came into being during the 15th century when the Által Stream was dammed. It was once used to farm fish (although angling is no longer permitted), but is now a conservation area and a popular bird-watching haunt, particularly between the months of September and November when thousands of migrating wild geese rest their feathers and have a good honk (*for info,* ↳ *34 380851*). There are a couple of beaches, and you can hire kayaks and canoes (*just off Vértesszőlősi út; 800–1,000Ft/hr; open Mon–Sun 09.00–12.00, 15.00–21.00*) 500m north of the Öreg-tó campsite on the eastern shore.

**Tata Castle** (*Váralja utca*), at the lake's northern tip, was constructed in the mid 14th century on a rocky outcrop ringed with water and marshland. At the end of the century, it became crown property and enjoyed a golden age as a beautiful Renaissance pile under kings Zsigmond and Mátyás. After the Turks had long gone, Lord Chief Justice József Eszterházy bought it in a far sorrier state – it had been burnt by the Habsburgs – and gave it a Romantic-style overhaul (which is what you see now). Precious little remains of the original castle beyond a single corner tower, ruined walls and some weathered stone sarcophagi in the grounds. It was undergoing extensive renovation during our visit, but you can enter the castle chapel and inside the main building is the **Kuny Domokos Museum** (↘ 34 381251; *adult/concessions 400/200Ft, free for families on Sun; open Tue–Sun 10.00–18.00*) containing Roman finds, a history of the castle, and displays of pieces produced in the 18th-century delftware factory. Fishy creatures were favoured subjects for the ceramicists, inspired by the water all about them.

A short distance anti-clockwise around the lake is the Louis-XVI-style **Eszterházy Palace** (*Hősök tere 6–8;* ↘ *34 708106; adult/concessions 500/250Ft; open May 1–Oct 31 Wed–Sun 10.00–18.00*), its bulging corner towers built to the design of Jakab Fellner in the 1760s. For much of the 20th century it served as a hospital, and was stripped of the majority of its fittings; as such, the museum inside is sterile, showing a few original bookshelves, a marble basin of 1887 and some old floorplans. There are vague murmurings of a renovation, but nothing firm. In the grounds are the remains of the palace's old theatre, and near by is one of the lake's small boat piers from where you can catch a ferry (*adult/concessions 400/300Ft*) across the water. Hősök tere also holds a **Greco-Roman Replica Statues Museum** (*Hősök tere 7;* ↘ *34 381251; adult/concessions 200/100Ft; open Apr 1–Sep 30 Tue–Sun 10.00–18.00, at other times of yr by prior notice*), housed in a former synagogue, and including the Venus de Milo among its 96 copies.

To the southwest (along Bercsényi utca or Rákóczi utca) is Kossuth tér, and next to it the late-Baroque **Tata parish church** (*Iskola tér*), built between 1751 and 1787 by Franz Anton Pilgram, Jakab Fellner and József Grossman. Fellner, whose hand was in so much of the town's architecture, actually died in 1780 before the church was completed. He was buried in the crypt, and there is a statue of him outside. Calvary Hill (Kálvária-domb) to the south has a chimney-like **lookout tower** (*Stavinovszki József-Fazekas utca 52/A;* ↘ *34 384306; adult/concessions 200/150Ft; open May 1–Sep 30 Tue–Sun 09.00–17.00*), standing just off Fazekas utca, as well as a sad-looking 18th-century **calvary** (Christ has neither head nor legs) and the odd-looking **Calvary Chapel**. The latter is so short in length that from the side it appears cut in half; this is because it was fashioned from the Gothic shrine of an earlier Medieval church on the site by Fellner in 1755. At the base of the hill's other side is an abandoned quarry whose rock layers preserve fossilised shells and a prehistoric fireplace. This nature conservation area is now an **Open-Air Geological Museum** (*Kálvária-domb, Fekete utca 2;* ↘ *34 381587; adult/concessions 80/40Ft; open Tue–Sun 10.00–18.00*).

Moving the other way around the top of the lake, the 16th-century **Cifra (Ornamental) Mill** is set back from the shore on Bartók Béla utca. Further on, another of the town's old watermills houses the **German Minority Museum** (*Német Nemzetiségi Múzeum; Alkotmány utca 1;* ↘ *34 487682; adult/concessions 200/100Ft; open Apr 1–Oct 10 Tue–Sun 10.00–18.00, Nov 1–Mar 31 Wed–Fri 10.00–14.00, Sat–Sun 10.00–16.00*), which celebrates the German groups who settled in Transdanubia over the centuries; exhibits include pottery (some dating back to the 13th century), traditional dress and decorated furniture, 17th-century pistols and photos of pro-Hitler marches in the build up to World War II. Unfortunately there are no explanations in English.

A short distance to the north, Országgyűlés tér (Parliament Square) commemorates the period in 1510 when the government convened in Tata after Buda was struck by plague. Its octagonal **clock tower** was made in 1763 completely from wood by local craftsman József Éder. Opposite is the **Capuchin church** (*Bartók Béla utca*), finished in 1746 with Fellner involved again. To the east (follow Ady Endre utca and turn left into Erzsébet királyné tér) is the smaller of the town's lakes – appropriately named Small Lake (Cseke-tó) – where fishermen angle for bream, catfish, common carp and pike (*licences available at Ady Endre utca 83;* ☏ *34 380160*). It is wrapped in an **English Park** (Angol Park), landscaped for the Eszterházys by Ferenc Bőhm, and featuring a family summer house, an artificial ruin constructed from the stones of a 12th-century abbey, and an outdoor theatre.

## Other

Two kilometres to the north of the centre, set to the west of Fényes fasor, is the **Fényes Fürdő** (*Környei utca 4;* ☏ *34 588144; www.fenyesfurdo.hu; adult/concessions 800/500Ft, reduced admission after 15.00; open May 1–Sep 30 daily 09.00–19.00*); the complex holds five pools (including one for young children), a waterslide, tennis courts, a fitness centre and sauna, as well as a campsite (see page 456). Bus 3 runs there.

There are several places to go horse-riding. The **Táltos Lovasklub** (*Fekete utca 2/A;* ☏ *06 20 242 2233; riding 2,000Ft/hr; open Tue–Fri 09.00–12.00, 15.00–18.00*) is close to the Geological Museum (see page 459), and offers horse- or carriage-riding for all levels. Alternatively, try the **Maestoso Riding School** (*Fényes dűlő;* ☏ *34 486039;* e *maestoso@chello.at; www.maestoso.sub.cc; riding 2,500Ft/hr*), beautifully located 1km further north from the Fényes Fürdő, managed by a friendly couple, and boasting its own nine-room panzió (*rooms 4,800Ft/pp*). You'll need to drive or take a cab as there is no direct bus link from the centre.

The **Old Lake Golf and Country Club** (*Remeteségpuszta;* ☏ *34 587620;* e *old.lake.golf.club@axelero.hu; www.oldlakegolf.com*) is an extremely swish establishment 4km south of the centre (follow Fekete út to the end, around the western shore of the lake). Built on one of the Eszterházys' hunting estates, it has a golf course (*weekdays 9,000Ft/round, weekends 14,500Ft/round*), indoor and outdoor swimming pools, a fitness centre, tennis courts, a restaurant, a hotel (*31 rooms; sgl 11,800Ft, dbl 25,500Ft*) and even its own fishing lake (Lake Derítő).

## Festivals and events

The Water, Music and Flower Festival takes place on the last weekend in June, and features a flower-arranging competition, medieval games and other events. There is a Theatre Festival at the open-air theatre in the third week of June.

# Western Transdanubia

A significant part of Western Transdanubia, the region to the west and northwest of Balaton, is in the shadow of the Alps foothills ranged along the Austrian border. This is among Hungary's most beautiful and interesting areas, one that formed part of Royal (Habsburg) Hungary during the Turkish occupation and which therefore preserves some medieval architecture that was destroyed in other parts. The towns of Kőszeg and Sopron are enchanting, while the villages of the Őrség retain traditional folk architecture. At the other end of the scale, Nagycenk and Fertőd hold two of the country's premier aristocratic mansions. For bird-watchers, Lake Fertő offers a significant swathe of wetland habitat. Ecclesiastical highlights can be found in Győr Cathedral, Pannonhalma Abbey, established by missionaries at the invitation of Prince Géza in the 10th century, and the 13th-century cathedral at Ják – possibly the best-preserved piece of Romanesque architecture.

## GYŐR

Standing midships between Budapest and Vienna, and at the meeting point of the rivers Mosoni-Duna, Rábca and Rába, Győr's strategic position and natural transport links ensured that it developed into one of the country's throbbing industrial hubs. However, while its outer factories deter the timid, those who venture to the centre are well rewarded for their perseverance; at its Baroque heart are churches, palaces, museums and town houses with pretty corner balconies – all the trappings of a dense history. (In particular, Győr Cathedral's potent combination of stylish opulence and fascinating history is not to be missed.) Celts, Romans and Avars settled here on the Kisalföld (Small Plain), the latter constructing a round fort (*gyürü* in the Avar language) from which the city's name derives. King István made Győr an episcopal see during the 11th century. The Turks were able to capture and hold it for just four years at the close of the 16th century, while Napoleon expended little energy in crushing a rebellion of nobles in 1809. It wasn't until World War II, when the factories and railway became targets for the Allies, that the city's architectural wings – the products of building by rich merchants and industrialists – were seriously singed.

## Getting there and away

The main **railway station** is behind the town hall on Révai Miklós utca. From the station head northwards through the park (*Honvéd liget*) and along Aradi vértanút útja. Győr has excellent connections to Budapest's Déli, Keleti and Kelenföld stations, with up to 35 departures a day. Trains also run regularly to Pannonhalma (every 30 minutes), Csorna and Sopron. Other services are to Szombathely (eight), Szolnok (six), Veszprém (five) and Sárvár (two). Up to six trains a day depart for Vienna, crossing the border at Hegyeshalom.

A subway links the railway station to the **bus station** (*Hunyadi utca*), with regular services to Budapest Népliget and Sopron, and very regular departures to Pannonhalma. Other buses run to Veszprém (12), Keszthely and Zalaegerszeg (five), Székesfehérvár (seven), Tapolca (four), Szombathely (five) and Pécs (two). There's also a bus that runs every morning to Vienna.

## Information and other practicalities

**Different Internet Café** Liszt Ferenc utca 20; ☎ 96 516810. More of an office than a café, there are 5 flat-screen computer terminals. *300Ft/30 mins; open Mon–Fri 09.00–21.00, Sat 15.00–21.00.*
**Ibusz** Kazinczy utca 3; ☎ 96 314224; e gyor@ibusz.hu. Private accommodation and local tours. *Open Mon–Fri 08.00–18.00, Sat 09.00–13.00.*
**Listings magazine** *Győri Est*
**Tourinform** Árpád út 32; ☎ 96 311771; e gyor@tourinform.hu. Housed in a small glass pavilion outside the Hotel Royal; there is a currency-exchange service, as well as information on sights and events. *Open Jun 1–Sep 15 Mon–Fri 08.00–20.00, Sat–Sun 09.00–18.00, Mar 1–May 31 Mon–Fri 08.00–18.00, Sat 09.00–14.00, Sep 15–Feb 29 Mon–Fri 09.00–17.00, Sat 09.00–14.00.*

## Where to stay

**Arany Szarvas** (16 rooms) Radó sétány 1; ☎ 96 517452. Attached to Captain Drakes Pub, the Arany Szarvas is scenically set on Radó Island, and has a fitness centre and sauna. *Sgl 10,950Ft, dbl 13,900Ft.*
**Fonte Hotel** (14 rooms) Schweidel utca 17; ☎ 96 513810; e fonte@axelero.hu. The prices are on the high side, but this is a real treasure of a hotel with well-furnished, good-sized rooms, and an elegant restaurant (see page 463). Next to the National Theatre, and named after a fountain found when renovating the 18th-century townhouse. *Sgl 14,600Ft, dbl 16,500Ft, apt (for 3) 21,000Ft.*
**Hotel Kálvária** (19 rooms) Kálvária utca 22/d; ☎ 96 510800; e recepcio@hotel-kalvaria.hu; www.hotel-kalvaria.hu. Newish 4-star hotel with tasteful standard rooms, plush suites and a tidy restaurant. Sauna, fitness room and solarium. A touch overpriced. 15 mins south of the centre. *Sgl €74, dbl €78–83, suite €117.*
**Hotel Wesselényi** (30 rooms) Wesselényi utca 3; ☎ 96 510040. Pleasant hotel with a stylish bar, a 10-minute walk from the centre. Sauna and gym. *Sgl 12,500Ft, dbl 14,500Ft, triple 15,000Ft, apt 17,500Ft.*

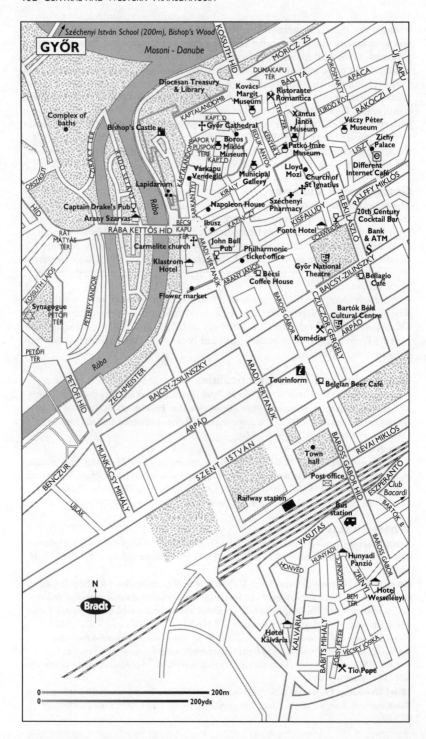

GYŐR

Széchenyi István School (200m), Bishop's Wood

Mosoni - Danube

KOSSUTH HÍD

MÓRICZ ZS

DUNAKAPU TÉR

BASTYA

APACA

ÚJ KAPU

VÖRÖSMARTY

Diocesan Treasury & Library

Kovács Margit Museum

Ristorante Romantica

FÜRDŐ KÖZ

RÁKÓCZI F

Complex of baths

KAPTALANDOMB

Xantus János Museum

Váczy Péter Museum

Bishop's Castle

KÁPT. D

Győr Cathedral

LISZT

Zichy Palace

GÁPOR V

PÜSPÖK TÉRE

Boros Miklós Museum

Patkó Imre Museum

Different Internet Café

KÁPT. D

HÉDIK ANTOS

KENYER

CZARÁK TÉR

KAPTALANDOMB

Várkapu Vendéglő

Municipal Gallery

Lloyd Mozi

Church of St Ignatius

PÁLFFY MIKLÓS

RADÓ SÉTÁNY

Lapidarium

SÁRKÁNTYÚ

KIRÁLY

Napoleon House

Széchenyi Pharmacy

TELEKI LÁSZLÓ

ORSZÁGÚT

Rába

Captain Drake's Pub

Ibúsz

KAZINCZY

Fonte Hotel

KISFALUDY

20th Century Cocktail Bar

HÍD

Arany Szarvas

BÉCSI KAPU TÉR

SCHWEIDE

Bank & ATM

RÁBA KETTŐS HÍD

RÁT MÁTYÁS TÉR

Carmelite church

ARADI VÉRTANÚK

John Bull Pub

Philharmonic ticket office

Győr National Theatre

BAJCSY-ZILINSZKY

Bellagio Café

KOSSUTH LAJOS

Klastrom Hotel

ARANY JÁNOS

Bécsi Coffee House

CUCZOR GERGELY

Bartók Béla Cultural Centre

ARPÁD

Flower market

Synagogue

PETŐFI TÉR

PÉTERFY SÁNDOR

BAROSS GÁBOR

Komédiás

PETŐFI TÉR

Rába

ZECHMEISTER

BAJCSY-ZSILINSZKY

ARADI VÉRTANÚK

Tourinform

Belgian Beer Café

PETŐFI HÍD

ÁRPÁD

SZENT ISTVÁN

Town hall

RÉVAI MIKLÓS

BENCZÚR

MUNKÁCSY MIHÁLY

Post office

BAROSS GÁBOR HÍD

ESZPERANTÓ

Club Bacardi

ÚJLAK

Railway station

Bus station

BARTÓK B

VASUTAS

BAROSS GÁBOR

HUNYADI

DIGNÓGOS

Hunyadi Panzió

HONVÉD

ZRÍNYI

N

Bradt

BEM TÉR

Hotel Wesselényi

KÁLVÁRIA

Hotel Kálvária

BABITS MIHÁLY

FÖRSY PÉTER

VÉCSEY JÓSIKA

Tio Pepe

0 ————————— 200m
0 ————————— 200yds

**Hunyadi Panzió** (11 rooms) Hunyadi János út 10; ↘ 96 329162. A stone's throw from the bus station, this modern and welcoming guesthouse is good value compared with some of the other accommodation in town. *Sgl 9,200Ft, dbl 10,500Ft, triple 11,800Ft.*

**Klastrom Hotel** (42 rooms) Zechmeister utca 1; ↘ 96 516910; e klastrom@arrabonet.gyor.hu; www.hotels.hu/klastrom. Nestled for the past 50 years in the cloister at the back of the Carmelite church, the Klastrom has small, dated rooms in the former monks' cells. *Sgl 13,000Ft, double 17,300Ft, triple 21,000Ft.*

**Hotel Rába (Royal)** (155 rooms) Árpád út 34; ↘ 96 507660; e raba.sales@danubiusgroup.com; www.danubiushotels.com/raba. The first hotel in Győr – established in 1904 – the Rába (soon to be re-named Royal) is central and has a sauna, solarium, a small nightclub and the Belgian Beer Café below. Guests also get free admission to the casino opposite. The standard rooms are well-equipped and comfortable, and the business suites are excellent. *Standard/superior sgl €79/120, dbl €90/120.*

**Kiskuti Camping and Motel** Kiskut liget; ↘ 96 318986. Tent and caravan pitches, bungalows and motel rooms at a fully equipped but average-feeling site. Tennis courts and a bufé. 3km east of the centre – follow Szent István út into Kiskúti and follow signs to the right, or jump on bus 8. *Camping 700Ft/pp, tent 700Ft, caravan 1,200Ft, motel room 2,200Ft/pp, bungalows (up to 4) 1,200Ft/pp.*

**Széchenyi István School** Héderváry út 3; ↘ 96 503447. Dorm beds available primarily in summer, although there is sometimes availability at other times. To the north of the centre. *Beds from 1,500Ft/pp.*

## Where to eat and drink

**Bécsi Coffee House** Arany János utca 18; ↘ 96 325277. Accessed via an arch on Arany János utca, this kitsch café is awash with artificial plant life and something of a plastic jungle. Nevertheless, it is popular with ladies who lunch, and has a great selection of ice-cream desserts and coffees. *Open 09.00–19.00 daily.*

**Belgian Beer Café** Árpád út 34; ↘ 96 507660. Bar and restaurant chain specialising – surprise, surprise – in Belgian beer (there are 15 different types on offer). Part of the Hotel Rába (Royal), it has an old-fashioned feel and a pavement terrace. The calorie-conscious can choose from the set 'wellness' menu. *Open Mon–Fri 10.00–24.00, Sat 11.00–24.00, Sun 11.00–22.00.*

**Fonte Restaurant** See page 461. Delightful, adventurous food in a classy setting at the Fonte Hotel. Specialities include salmon in lemon-crab sauce, chicken with apple purée and chateaubriand, and there's a good wine selection. *Mains 850–3,890Ft, avg 2,200Ft; open 06.30–10.30, 12.00–16.00, 18.00–24.00 daily.*

**Klastrom Restaurant** See above. The Klastrom's claim to fame is that it prepared the food for a banquet served to Pope John Paul II in the Zichy Palace in 1996. Its international cuisine has a French twist; the cobbled courtyard is the spot to choose if the weather suits. *Mains 1,000–4,000Ft, avg 2,000Ft; open 11.00–22.00 daily.*

**Komédías** Czuczor Gergely utca 30; ↘ 96 527217; e komedias@axelero.hu. Basic eatery serving good local dishes at reasonable prices. Large courtyard. *Mains 690–2,500Ft, avg 1,400Ft; open Mon–Sat 11.00–24.00.*

**Ristorante Romantica** Dunakapu tér 5; ↘ 96 314127. Brocade-heavy furnishings and tinkly Italian music does not romantic make. (The view of the unattractive square from the terrace does little to help the cause either.) Nevertheless, the Italian food is very good, if expensive. *Mains 950–4,250Ft, avg 2,200Ft; open 11.30–24.00 daily.*

**Tio Pepe** Eörsi Péter utca 17; ↘ 96 439611; www.miwo.hu/tio. The owners have successfully created a Mediterranean atmosphere, and serve typical Spanish dishes. Sit at one of the booths outside, where there is a waterfall and ferns galore. A romantic, evenly priced treat. *Mains 900–2,800Ft, avg 1,600Ft; open 12.00–24.00 daily.*

**Várkapu Vendéglő** Bécsi kapu tér 7–8; ↘ 96 328685. Hungarian and international menu featuring duck, steak and a good selection of fish. Opposite the Carmelite church. *Mains 800–3,900Ft, avg 1,800Ft; open 10.00–23.00 daily.*

The **Virág Piac**, at the western end of Arany János utca, is a small outdoor vegetable and flower market that opens every morning.

## Entertainment and nightlife

The **Győr National Theatre** (*Győri Nemzeti Színház; Czuczor Gergely utca 7;* ✆ *96 314800;* e *szervezes@gyoriszinhaz.hu; www.gyoriszinhaz.hu; ticket office open Tue–Fri 10.00–13.00, 14.00–18.00*) is an angular, unattractive structure with a ramp-like roof that would look at home in a skateboard park. The side walls are decorated with ceramic Op-Art works by Victor Vasarely. The theatre plays host to the nationally acclaimed Győr Philharmonic and Győr Ballet companies, and has performances of folk dance, drama and musicals. The **Philharmonic Ticket Office** (*Kisfaludy utca 25;* ✆ *96 326323; open Mon–Thu 08.00–16.00, Fri 08.00–15.00*) sells tickets for orchestral performances at the Zichy Palace as well as the National Theatre. The **Bartók Béla Cultural Centre** (*Czuczor Gergely utca 17;* ✆ *96 326522; open Mon 13.00–21.00, Tue–Sat 10.00–21.00, Sun varies*) is one of several cultural centres in the city where you can obtain information on events, and has temporary exhibitions, concerts and lifestyle classes. **Lloyd Mozi** (*Széchenyi tér 7;* ✆ *96 328930; www.lloydmozi.hu; open 17.00–22.00 daily*) is a cinema complex opposite the Benedictine school that is also something of a hangout, with dart boards and pool tables.

**Bellagio Café** (*Teleki László utca 36;* ✆ *06 30 536 8545; open Mon–Thu & Sun 08.00–03.00, Fri–Sat 08.00–04.00*) is the bar to be seen in, with leather benches, a chrome bar and an elevated terrace from which to scowl at passers by. Also near the National Theatre is the small and busy **20th Century Cocktail Bar** (*Schweidel utca 25;* ✆ *06 70 335 7119; open Mon–Sat 09.00–24.00, Sun 17.00–24.00*)

**Captain Drakes Pub** (*Radó sétány utca 1;* ✆ *96 517452; open 11.00–24.00 daily*) is on the island (cross Rába Kettős Bridge from Bécsi kapu tér); it has a nautical theme, and an outdoor area offering a good perspective of the scale of the fortifications on the opposite bank. **John Bull Pub** (*Aradi Vértanúk utja 3;* ✆ *96 618320; open 10.00–24.00 daily*), just to the east of the Carmelite church, is an upmarket English-style boozer and a popular spot for a tipple. The **Hotel Wesselényi Bar** (see page 461; *open 12.00–24.00 daily*) is a cool drinking hole with stylish furnishings. **Club Bacardi** (*Mészáros Lőrinc utca 11; open Fri–Sat 21.00–06.00*) is for the more serious clubbers, based on an industrial estate southeast of the centre (buses 23 and 27 stop 150m away), while the **Hullám Disco Club** (*Hédervári utca 22;* ✆ *96 315276; open Fri–Sat 18.00–04.00*) is 1km north of the centre, across the Mosoni-Duna.

## What to see and do
### Bécsi kapu tér

Everthing of note in Győr is gathered in the area beside and around the confluence of the Rába and Mosoni-Duna rivers. Bécsi kapu tér, at the eastern head of the bridge that makes a skip and a jump on to Rába Island and the western bank, is the best place to begin your wanderings. It was originally closed by the Vienna Gate, but in 1809 Napoleon's troops destroyed the bastion while suppressing an uprising of Hungarian nobles, and opened it up to the river. The Baroque **Carmelite church** (*Karmelita templom*), with its elliptical nave and off-centre tower, was built by Márton Wittwer (a monk of the order) and consecrated in 1725. To the right of the entrance is an open chapel containing a statue of 'Foam Mary', which was moved from the island to this position of honour after supposedly protecting the city from 18th-century floods. The church interior contains high-altar paintings of István and his son Imre paying homage to the Virgin, carved walnut furnishings by Franz Richter and early-20th-century frescoes on the cupola. To the left of the nave is the Dark Chapel, which bears a sculpture of Mary made in Rome and touched with the holy statue in the Loretto Chapel before being shipped to Győr.

**THE WEEPING MADONNA**
At the end of the cathedral's northern aisle is an altarpiece of particular interest. The silver-framed 'Weeping Madonna' painting was brought here by Walter Lynch, the Bishop of Clonfort in Ireland, who was fleeing persecution by Oliver Cromwell in 1655. On St Patrick's Day 1697, 34 years after his death – and at a time when further anti-Catholic laws were being passed in Britain – eyewitnesses (including General Siegbert Heister, the contemporary castle commander) recorded that the icon wept blood for three hours. The congregation mopped up the drops with a white cloth, still held in the sacristy. There followed a seven-year-long investigation that could find no rational explanation for the phenomenon, and in the years afterwards a strong cult developed around the painting. It has influenced many later artists – the depiction of Christ on a pillow, rather than in his mother's arms, was quite unusual – and pilgrims travel here annually on St Patrick's Day. In 1997 the Bishop of Clonfert travelled to Győr to take part in 300th-anniversary celebrations of the miracle. In 2004, a copy of the painting was taken to the church in Ireland from where it is believed Lynch brought the original, an act symbolic of the religious and historical parallels that many Hungarians see when they gaze across to Ireland.

Behind the church is the friary, built during the same period and currently home to the Klastrom Hotel (see page 463); the president of the National Assembly hid within after declaring independence from the Habsburgs in 1848.

Just off the eastern side of the square, **Napoleon House** (*Király utca 4;* ✆ *96 337742; admission free; open Mon–Fri 10.00–18.00, Sat 09.00–13.00*) is so-named because Napoleon spent the night of August 31 1809 there after his soldiers had captured the castle; there is now a small gallery on the first floor. At the northern end of the square are some surviving walls of Győr's medieval castle. In the 16th century it was the biggest in Hungary, with three gates and seven bastions linked by 10m-high walls. The Turks occupied it for just four years before it was recaptured by the renowned generals Miklós Pálffy and Adolf Schwarzenberg; however, Napoleon inflicted considerable damage, and the bulk of the remains were demolished in 1820. A **lapidarium** (*Becsi kapu tér 5;* ✆ *96 310588; adult/concessions 500/250Ft; open Apr 1–Oct 31 Tue–Sun 10.00–18.00*) in the courtyard of what was the Sforza Bastion has pieces of the fortress, as well as Roman finds and a collection of bricks.

### Káptalandomb
To the north of Bécsi kapu tér is Káptalandomb (Chapter Hill), the nucleus of the medieval settlement and the site of the original cathedral established by King István in 1033. **Győr Cathedral** (*Székesegyház; Apor Vilmos püspök tere; closed for cleaning 12.00–14.00 daily*) weathered some considerable storms, attacked by the Mongols in the 13th century and used as both a stable and a gun emplacement by the Turks. Subsequent reconstructions resulted in a mish-mash of styles, and the building incorporates Romanesque, Gothic, Baroque and Neoclassical features. Its heavily gilded interior is adorned with 18th-century frescoes and an altarpiece depicting the Ascension of Mary by Franz Anton Maulbertsch.

The Héderváry (or Trinity) Chapel was added to the southern aisle in 1404 and contains the country's finest piece of medieval goldsmith's art – a bust of King László made in around 1400, and inlaid with Transylvanian enamelwork. The herm holds László's skull (a curator at the Episcopal Museum – one of the few people ever to have opened the reliquary – told us that beneath the crown is a plate, which is unscrewed to reveal a second silver crown with the skull inside); it is said that in 1763 the herm miraculously halted an earthquake, and every June it is paraded through the city in remembrance. At the other end of the chapel is the red-marble sarcophagus of Bishop Apor Vilmos, a vehement opponent of Nazism who was tragically killed at Easter in 1945 while protecting women from a drunk Russian soldier who'd taken part in the city's liberation. During the communist era it was prohibited even to mention his name; in 1997 he was beatified by the pope.

Outside the church are the sunken remains of a tiny 13th-century chapel discovered during late-20th-century excavations. Across the way, the **Borsos Miklós Museum** (*Apor Vilmos püspök tere 2;* ✎ *96 316329; adult/concessions 400/200Ft; open Tue–Sun Mar 1–Oct 31 10.00–18.00, Nov 1–Feb 28 10.00–17.00*) displays the paintings, sculptures and bronze reliefs of Borsos, a 20th-century artist intrigued by tactile art and abstract portraiture, and responsible for the Zero Kilometre stone in Budapest (see page 148). He lived in this former bishop's courthouse between 1921 and 1945. Opposite the western entrance to the cathedral is the **Bishop's Castle** (*Püspökvár; Apor Vilmos püspök tere*), which has a 15th-century Gothic chapel and a colourful tower (originally 14th-century but reconstructed in the 18th century). The Castle Garden was part of the 16th-century fortified complex, and is enclosed by some of the walls that still stand. When we visited neither the castle nor the garden were open to the public, but we were assured they would be shortly.

Szent Mihály utca leaves the square's eastern side and leads to the **Diocesan Treasury and Library** (*Egyházmegyei Kincstár és Könyvtár; Káptalandomb 26;* ✎ *96 312153; adult/concessions 300/150Ft; Mar 1–Oct 31 Tue–Sun 10.00–16.00*), among the country's richest collection of sacred objects from Hungary and Transylvania. The hoard of manuscripts is the most valuable, including an 11th-century codex and a fabulous 15th-century illuminated manuscript from the library of Mátyás (one of a tiny number to survive the Turkish occupation in Buda; see page 176). In addition, there is an exhibition devoted to the 'Weeping Madonna' (see box, page 465), a gold monstrance of 1500 from the Clarissa Convent in Buda (see page 145), and a piece of the bloodied shirt of Bishop Vilmos (see above).

### Széchenyi tér and around

The tarmacked Széchenyi tér is surrounded by historic buildings, many softening the square's points with the corner balconies for which the city is famous. Such window annexes provided the householder with unrestricted views, and allowed the wealthy to participate in street life – this used to be a market place – without having to hold their noses or dirty their shoes. In the square's southern section is the **Mária Column**, a Baroque monument consecrated in 1686 by Bishop Lipót Kollonich in thanks for the re-taking of Buda from the Turks. Behind it is the **Church of St Ignác**, built in 1641 by Jesuits and taken over later by the Benedictines (after József II had dissolved the Jesuit order). It is flanked by a Benedictine monastery and a Benedictine grammar school (the latter containing an exhibition to the acclaimed teachers Gergely Czuczor and Ányos Jedlik, whose statues are outside; *for admission,* ✎ *96 315988*). Beside the monastery is the still-working **Széchenyi Pharmacy** (*Széchenyi tér 9;* ✎ *96 320954; free admission; open Mon–Fri 07.30–16.00*), which was founded by the Jesuits in 1654 and has a ceiling fresco of Mary's Assumption surrounded by carved cherubs symbolic of the four seasons.

The **Patkó Imre Museum** (*Széchenyi tér 4;* ✎ *96 310588; adult/concession 400/200Ft; open Apr 1–Sep 30 Tue–Sun 10.00–18.00, rest of yr by appointment only*) is held in the Iron Stock House, so-named because of the stump outside into which wandering artisans hammered their nails. Entrance to the museum – which contains 20th-century European art and an ethnographic collection of objects from Africa and Oceania – is on Szelczer

Lajos utca. The beautiful Baroque building next door – constructed in 1742 as lodgings for Pannonhalma abbots – hosts the **Xantus János Museum** (*Széchenyi tér 5;* ✆ *96 310588; www.gymsmuzeum.hu; adult/concession 500/250Ft; open Tue–Sun May–Oct 10.00–18.00, Nov–Apr 10.00–14.00*). Named after a 19th-century globetrotter and naturalist, Győr's well-presented main museum features regional archaeological finds, items of local and medical history, and a massive collection of stamps. Highlights to look out for are a tiny pair of boots – after travelling for several years, craftsmen aspiring to membership of a guild had to submit a masterpiece of their art to the committee – and a 17th-century weathercock. The latter topped the Vienna Gate (see page 464) and is the symbol of the city. During their brief occupation, the confident Turks joked that a cock would crow beneath a full moon before Christians held Győr again; it is said that on the moonlit night the castle was re-taken, the weathercock creaked in the wind.

A short distance to the northeast of the square, an ex-hospice founded by Bishop György Széchenyi in 1666 now contains the **Váczy Péter Museum** (*Nefelejcs köz 3;* ✆ *96 318141; adult/concessions 400/200Ft; open Tue–Sun Mar 1–Oct 31 10.00–18.00, Nov 1–Feb 28 10.00–17.00*), based on the private 20th-century collection of Renaissance and Baroque furniture and art gathered by an anti-communist professor. It is worth making a brief detour to see the nearby **Zichy Palace** (*Liszt Ferenc utca 20*) – built for Ferenc Zichy in 1720, and later providing accommodation for Ferenc Deák and Lajos Batthyány while they studied law – before crossing Széchenyi tér once more to the **Municipal Gallery** (*Király utca 17;* ✆ *96 322695; adult/concessions 500/250Ft, free for students on Sun; open Tue–Sun 10.00–18.00*), with exhibitions of modern art.

Head north up Jedlik Ányos utca and you'll reach the Ark of the Covenant Statue (see box, page 468) and the **Kovács Margit Museum** (*Apáca utca 1;* ✆ *96 326739; adult/concessions 400/200Ft; open Tue–Sun Mar 1–Oct 31 10.00–18.00, Nov 1–Feb 28 Tue–Sun 10.00–17.00*). The work of the 20th century's leading Hungarian ceramicist – who was born in Győr in 1902 – has always divided the opinion of experts. Influenced by religion, legend and folk art, her later work became increasingly abstract and informed by geometric shapes. The 100 pieces here include vases, animal-shaped vessels, religious paintings and Gothic figurines; for more, you'll need to visit the main museum in Szentendre (see page 198).

**Dunakapu tér**, at the top of Jedlik Ányos utca, is named after the medieval gate that faced the river at this point. The fountain at the centre bears a copy of the weathercock now housed in the Xantus János Museum (see above). The square is filled with market stalls on Wednesdays and Saturdays.

### Other

If you arrive by bus or train and walk into the centre, you are likely to follow Baross Gábor út, the pedestrianised main shopping street. On the way there, you shouldn't miss the **town hall** (*Városház tér*), a magnificent Eclectic palace built in 1896 during the millennial celebrations to the design of Jenő Hübner. Every hour a piece of music by local composer Attila Reményi chimes from the building.

On the opposite side of the River Rába, roughly level with the southern end of the island, is an imposing **synagogue** (*Kossuth Lajos utca 5*). It was built between 1869 and 1870 with a quartet of octagonal corner turrets; the facade was restored in 1988, although much of the rest remains shabby. It is the venue for cultural performances. The former Jewish school next door now holds a music academy.

On the same bank, above the island's northern tip, is a big **complex of baths** (*Cziráky tér 1;* ✆ *96 522646; adult/concessions 650/550Ft; open daily Jun–Aug 08.00–19.00, rest of yr 09.00–18.00*); among the attractions are open-air swimming pools, a leisure bathing hall (whose floors are linked with water slides), a thermal spa (*open Mon–Fri 07.00–16.00*) and sports fields.

### A SMASHING PROCESSION

The masterful Ark of the Covenant Statue in Gutenberg János tér had an unusual conception. In 1729 a soldier accused of bigamy took refuge in the Benedictine monastery. When the friars refused to hand the man over, the soldiers that had come to arrest him posted themselves outside and waited. A stalemate ensued that the bishop of the day was determined to resolve. Easter was approaching, and it was decided to disguise the fugitive and smuggle him away as part of the Corpus Christi procession. As the group reached what is now Gutenberg János tér, however, the man was recognised; as the guards struggled to capture him, the Communion cup was dashed from the hands of the priest and broke on the stones. On hearing of this insult to the Church, Emperor Charles III commissioned the Ark of the Covenant Statue to be placed at the site. Ironically, the subject of the commotion was ultimately found innocent, while the soldiers who arrested him were thoroughly punished.

## Festivals and events

Győr prides itself on being a city of festivals, and there is no shortage of events every year. The Baroque Ball (*Feb*) features dancing and feasting in the Zichy Palace; the Spring Festival (*Mar–Apr*) involves music, theatre and dance; there is an international film competition and a programme of music, alternative drama and dance during Mediawave (*Apr–May*); Győr Summer (*Jun–Jul*) is a month of cultural events at several venues around the city; and Baroque Nostalgia (*Oct*) is another festival taking the Baroque for its watchword, with dance, music and art of the 17th and 18th centuries.

## Excursions

Thirty kilometres west of Győr along Road 85, **Csorna** is the centre of the Rábaköz (in the catchment of the River Rába), a region with a strong folk tradition of weaving and blue-dying. As well as embroidered bedclothes and table cloths, each village had its own individual patterned dress, often using the flowers of the local gardens as motifs. Csorna's 19th-century Baroque and Neoclassical buildings are capped by the Premonstratensian church, whose extravagant interior displays a replica of the Polish Czestochowa Madonna above the altar. The adjacent Premonstratensian palace was constructed on the site of the 13th-century monastery; the Csorna Museum (*Szent István tér 34;* \ *96 261527; adult/concessions 120/60Ft; open Tue–Sun 10.00–14.00*) inside has a collection of folk art covering the work of the town's blue-dyers and that of potters from nearby Dör. Csorna is linked by train to Győr, Sopron and Papa; there are buses running from all three.

There's more folk art (as well as some regional archaeology and plaster and bronze works by 20th-century sculptor Pál Pátzay, who was born in the town) at **Kapuvár**, 17km further west. The Rábaköz Museum (*Fő tér 1;* \ *96 242557; adult/concessions 300/150Ft; open Tue–Sun May 1–Sep 30 10.00–18.00, rest of yr 10.00–14.00*) is housed in a Baroque mansion built in place of the 13th-century fortress that served as a gateway through the border defensive line (hence the town's name 'Gate Castle'); the castle was demolished by Rákóczi's *kuruc* soldiers to prevent it falling into the hands of imperial forces. Rising above is the main clocktower of St Anne's Church, built in 1884 and replacing a medieval wooden chapel that once stood outside the castle. If you look under the organ loft, you'll see some angels decked in the local Kapusvár costume. Kapuvár is on the same road and rail line as Csorna.

Fifteen kilometres northwest of Győr (take the left turn off the M1 or Road 1, or take on of around ten daily buses from Győr), **Lébény** has one of the country's leading pieces of Romanesque architecture. The Benedictine abbey was originally constructed in 1208 and, despite being seriously damaged by the Turks, was faithfully restored in the 19th century.

The **Szigetköz** running above Győr can lay claim to being Hungary's largest island, formed of alluvial deposit and surrounded by the Danube and Mosoni-Duna rivers. The area was badly hit by the diversion of water upriver for the Gabčikovo power station (see box, page 215) in the 1990s; although the water levels remain lower than they were, the wildlife has made a recovery, and this is rich territory for hiking or nature-spotting. There's forest of aspen, willow, ash and oak, and over 200 species of bird (including the purple heron, black stork, Montagu's harrier and white-tailed eagle); rapid-flowing backwaters are ideal for canoeing and gravel-pit lakes for fishing. The Tourinforms in Győr (see page 461) or Mosonmagyaróvár (*Kápolna tér 16;* ✆ *96 206304;* e *mosonmagyarovar@tourinform.hu; open mid Jun–mid Sep Mon–Fri 09.00–18.00, Sat–Sun 09.00–17.00, rest of yr Mon–Fri 08.00–16.00*) can provide information on accommodation, kayak and bike hire, horse-riding and fishing permits.

## PANNONHALMA
Looming from one hill among a cluster of three at the edge of the Kisalföld, 20km southeast of Győr, Pannonhalma's Benedictine abbey – a Unesco World Heritage Site since 1996 – wears that cloak of mystery and romance associated with monastic life very comfortably indeed. Its hilltop was the perfect site for Prince Géza to establish Hungary's first Christian community and take an early step towards Christianisation of the Magyar tribes. Firstly, it had special connotations for the Magyars – according to Anonymus, Árpád's 'heart was filled with joy' as he watered his horses up here and beheld the beauty of his newly acquired territory. Secondly, it had sacred connotations for some Benedictine monks arriving from Rome – they believed that St Martin, Bishop of Tours and patron saint of Western monasticism, had been born near by. And thirdly, its position was strategically strong – a vital ingredient in case of disgruntled grumblings among those to be converted. At Géza's invitation, the monks built a church on the 275m peak and consecrated it in 1002 in the presence of King István. This elevated symbol of kingly intent was invested with further significance in the shape of its first abbot, Astrik, who'd couriered the Holy Crown from Pope Sylvester II that legitimised István's rule. István was himself a regular visitor, praying with the monks for St Martin's assistance in his struggle against the rebellious pagans. The Turks later used the church as a mosque during their stay, but aside from that the complex was influential up until the dissolution of the order in 1786 by József II. The dictates of the Enlightenment meant that it was only allowed to re-open in 1802 if it were to be 'useful'; the resultant secondary boarding school remains an organic part of the monastery to this day, teaching 360 pupils. During the autumn of 1944, the abbey came under the protection of the Swiss Red Cross, and provided asylum for terrified Jews.

### Getting there and away
There are **buses** to/from Győr every half-hour or so, arriving/departing from Pannonhalma village. From there you can board one of five daily buses running up to the abbey gates – failing that, you'll have to walk. The **railway station** is a little under 1km to the west of the village, at the end of Petőfi utca. There are up to eight trains a day to Győr and up to five to Veszprém.

### Information and other practicalities
**Pax Tourist** Vár 1; ✆ 96 570191; e pax@osb.hu. Positioned just outside the entrance, Pax Tourist sells tickets for tours of the abbey (you can only visit with a local guide; see page 471 for times) and can provide information.

**Tourinform** Petőfi utca 25; ✆ 96 470184; e pannonhalma@tourinform.hu. Small office at the western side of the village. *Open Jun–Aug daily 09.00–18.00, rest of yr Mon–Fri 09.00–17.00, Sat–Sun 10.00–16.00.*

## Where to stay, eat and drink

Unless you fancy a slurp of the local wine, there's little need to stay the night and most people visit on a day trip from Győr.

**Borpince** Szabadság tér; ✆ 96 471240; www.borbirodalom.hu. This highly charming place caters for sales and tastings of local wine. Groups – for whom Hungarian food can also be cooked – should book ahead. *From 1,600Ft/pp; open 12.00–20.00 daily.*

**Familia Panzió** Béke utca 61; ✆ 96 470192; e familiapanzio@enternet.hu. This welcoming family-run guesthouse stands northwest of the village centre (600m along a road running off Petőfi utca). There's a barbecue for balmy nights, and bike hire available. *Rooms €18/pp.*

**Panoráma Camping** Pannonhalma Pf 21; ✆ 96 471240. This basic campsite is quaint, well-cared-for and blessed with fab views. Short distance south of the centre. *Plot 1,000Ft, adult/concessions 900/550Ft/pp, bungalow rooms 7,000–8,000Ft.*

**Pax Hotel** (25 rooms) Dózsa György utca 2; ✆ 96 470005; e paxhotel@axelero.hu. Owned by Pax Tourist – little goes on without their say-so in this village – the 3-star Pax Hotel is lodge-like and comfortable and beautifully located. Sauna. *Sgl 10,300Ft, dbl 14,600, apt (for 2) 17,000Ft; h/bd & f/bd options.*

**Szent Márton Restaurant** Vár 1; ✆ 96 470798. Down wind of the abbey by just 100m, this timber restaurant has many windows for big views, a non-smoking room and primarily Hungarian fare (with the odd international dish). *Mains 890–2,500Ft, avg 1,650Ft; open Mon–Fri 08.00–21.00, Sat–Sun 08.00–22.00.*

## Pannonhalma Abbey

The seminal structure of 1002 – that at the very birth of the Christian State of Hungary – is invisible in today's **Pannonhalma Abbey** (*Vár utca 1;* ✆ *96 570100*), which is a medley of later styles. The original burnt down and was replaced in 1137 (only an arching wall of the western sanctuary remains, beneath floor level); the foundation of what you see now is a third, late-Romanesque version of 1224. The distinctive 55m **Neoclassical tower** buried at the heart of the complex, with its wedding cake columns and narrow dome, was added during the 19th century. The basilica's **main portal** (*Porta speciosa*) dates from the 13th century, and comprises a series of receding arches made of limestone and red marble, supported by sets of twin pillars. Above the doors is a fresco by Ferenc Storno, a 19th-century artist who carved and chipped at many of the region's churches in the name of aesthetic 'uniformity' and 'authentic' Gothic styling, and got thoroughly up the noses of present-day purists. The fresco shows St Martin of Tours – who started life as a Roman legionary before devoting himself to God – cutting his cloak and giving half to a beggar. While it might seem that he was being a touch miserly in his charity, a Roman soldier only paid for half his kit (the army bore the remaining cost) so he was giving all that was rightfully his. Storno's hand is in further features of the **basilica** interior, including the Romanesque and Gothic crypt – the oldest surviving section – which contains the red marble niche where the abbot sat during masses. Protocol dictated that the abbot gave up his spot to a royal visitor, and legend has it that this seat includes fragments of that on which István parked his backside.

Aside from some 18th-century Baroque buildings, much of the adjoining **monastery** dates to the 15th century, when it was rebuilt under the direction of King Mátyás. The cloister's covered walkway is adorned with diminutive stone faces representing human sins (as well as a bearded man thought to be the architect), and opens on to a quadrangle and garden; the latter contains a sundial inscribed with the deflating Latin truism 'One of you is my last hour'. The monastery's highly ornate refectory is among the finest Baroque halls in the country. To the south of the cloister are the **school buildings**, erected in the 1940s, while on the other side of the church is the stunning **Neoclassical library**. This was commissioned to serve the abbey's new educational role in the early 19th century, and was designed by József Ferenc Engel and then János Páckh (who also built the church tower). Its cherry-wood bookcases hold some of the library's 300,000 books. In the archives is the founding charter of the Abbey of Tihany (in Balaton) from 1055 – of special significance because among its Latin is a piece of the earliest-known sentence written in Hungarian. A **gallery** displays works including some European masterpieces of the 16th–18th centuries collected by one of the abbots, while the domed and vaulted basement has an **exhibition** of the abbey's history that opened during the order's millennial celebrations in 1996.

You can only visit the abbey on a **guided tour** (*adult/concessions 1,400/600Ft, foreign-lang tour, inc English, 2,000/1,200Ft*), which departs from the gate. Tour times are as follows: Nov 12–Mar 20 Tue–Sun 10.00, 11.00, 13.00, 14.00 and 15.00 (*in Hungarian only*); Mar 21–May 31 and Oct 1–Nov 11 Tue–Sun 09.00, 10.00, 11.00, 13.00, 14.00, 15.00 and 16.00 (*foreign-lang tours 11.00 & 13.00*); Jun 1–Sep 30 daily 09.00–17.00 on the hour (*foreign-lang tours 11.00 & 13.00*). Also look out for the annual celebratory **concerts** in the basilica (*at 15.50 on Easter Monday, Whit Monday, Aug 20, Oct 23 & Dec 26*); for information and bookings, contact Pax Tourist.

The other sights on the three hills are freely accessible. The middle peak holds the Neoclassical **Millennial Memorial**, built in 1896 as one of seven monuments (symbolic of the seven Magyar tribes) around the country to commemorate the conquest; Aba Novák Vilmos died before completing his frescoes inside. The **Chapel of the Blessed Virgin** on the hill to the southwest was completed in 1725, and has a pretty hexagonal belfry; its crypt remains a burial place for Benedictines. The crucifixion scene beside it was crafted in 1724 and moved here to make way for the Millennial Memorial. Behind it is a **lookout tower** offering splendid views of the basin of Pándzsa Brook, which held the Roman village of Sabaria Sicca and supposed birthplace of St Martin.

# SÁRVÁR

On the banks of the River Rába (and at the mouth of the Gyöngyös Brook) around 30km east of Szombathely, Sárvár has a long history. The Celts fortified the river crossing here and the Romans later established military camps on both sides of the water. Magyar earthworks defended against incursions by 10th-century Germanic tribes and the castle after which the town is named was first mentioned in documents of the 12th century. However, the Renaissance building of today dates to the 16th century when it came into possession of the Nádasdys, a significant dynasty that left a considerable mark. Tamás Nádasdy was a formidable politician – Governor of Croatia and later Palatine of Hungary – and he helped to make the town a religious and cultural centre of the Reformation. He surrounded himself with leading scientists, artists and humanist thinkers, and in 1537 established a printing house under the scholar János Sylvester; from this press rolled the first grammar book in 1539 and the first book in Hungarian (a translation of the New Testament) in 1541. Tamás's son Ferenc Nádasdy II (the so-called 'Black Captain') fought heroically (and winningly) against the Turks; much scandal surrounded his wife, however (see box, page 475). The luck (and the family line) ran out with Ferenc Nádasdy III; the Lord Chief Justice was executed in 1671 for his part in the Zrínyi conspiracy (see page 18), a plot against Emperor Lipót hatched by a group of nobles angered by Habsburg concessions to the Turks. The 20th century saw the arrival of several factories, while in 1961 thermal water was discovered, which feeds the town's spa.

## Getting there and away

The **bus station** (*Laktanya utca*) is west of town – follow Batthyány Lajos utca to reach the centre. There are up to 23 buses a day to Szombathely, as well as services to Veszprém and Sopron (up to three), Budapest Népliget, Győr and Zalaegerszeg (two). You can also catch a morning bus to Vienna on Saturdays. The **railway station** is northwest of the town on Selyemgyár utca; follow Hunyadi János utca southwards to the centre. Trains depart regularly to Szombathely, and there are up to eight daily to Budapest Deli and Keleti stations. Other destinations include Veszprém (eight), Székesfehérvár (seven), Pápa, Győr and Tatabánya (three), Tapolca (two), Sopron and Pécs (one).

## Information and other practicalities

**Listings magazine** *Szombathelyi Est*

**Sárvár Tours** Vadkert utca 1; ↘ 95 523603; sarvartours@hu.inter.net. You can book private rooms or tours at this office in the thermal-baths complex. *Open Mon–Sat 09.00–17.30.*

**Tourinform** Várkerület 33; ↘ 95 520178; e sarvar@tourinform.hu. Near the castle entrance. *Open Mon–Fri 08.00–17.00, Sat 08.00–12.00.*

## Where to stay

**Platán Hotel** (18 rooms) Hunyadi utca 23; ↘ 95 320623; e platans@airplanet.hu. Divided between new and old wings, this hotel is fine, but we feel the price is steep for rooms that are on the diminutive side. There is a swimming pool and sauna though, and you can rent bikes and fishing gear. Northwest of the castle – follow Ady Endre utca and look for the turning to the right. *Dbl €60, triple €68.*

**Termál Camping** Vadkert utca 1; ↘ 95 523600. Very popular campsite conveniently planted next to the thermal baths. It is currently closed for refurbishment, but will re-open – complete with a hotel – in 2006. *Tent/caravan 880/950Ft, plus adult/concessions 1,500/900Ft; apt (for 2) 9,000Ft.*

**Thermal Hotel** (136 rooms) Rákóczi utca 1; ↘ 95 888400; e sarvar.reservation@danubiusgroup.com; www.danubiushotels.com/sarvar. This semi-luxury hotel revolves solidly around its spa and wellness treatments. There is no gym to speak of (although there are a number of daily exercise classes), but otherwise every health and pampering need is met, from dentistry (popular with guests from Austria and Switzerland, where dental work is expensive), hairdressing and beauty to massage, mud treatments and thermal/mineral water programmes (based around indoor and outdoor pools). There is even a pair of resident doctors. The comfortable and well-equipped (but not AC) rooms are ranged around two atriums. The hotel is largely empty in the hottest months, but very popular in spring and autumn. A variety of inclusive health packages are offered. *Sgl €110, dbl €145.*

**Vadkert Major** Vadkert utca; ↘ 95 320045. At the bottom of the road holding the thermal baths, this former hunting lodge is now a riding school, restaurant and inn. All rooms are en suite and most have TV; as well as the stables, there are also tennis courts and a sauna. *Sgl 7,000Ft, dbl 8,000Ft, triple 10,000Ft.*

**Várkapu Panzió** (9 rooms) Várkerület 5; ↘ 95 326475; e pentek@varkapu.hu; www.varkapu.hu. Just to the west of the castle, this family-run guesthouse has spic-and-span rooms, and is well priced. Its restaurant is the best. *Sgl 6,700Ft, dbl 9,300Ft, triple 12,300Ft, room for 4 15,300Ft.*

**Wolf Hotel** (25 rooms) Alkotmány utca 4; ↘ 95 320460; e wolf01@elender.hu; www.wolfhotel.hu. Good 3-star hotel with sauna and fitness room on a road running south below the castle. On the expensive side. *Sgl 10,500Ft, dbl 15,500Ft, triple 18,000Ft, apt 21,000Ft.*

**Wolf Panzió** Rákóczi utca 11; ↘ 95 321499; www.wolfhotel.hu/panzio. With rooms like your grandmother's bedroom, things are a touch chichi, but this corner-turreted pension is a cheaper alternative to the snazzier sister hotel down the road. Southwest of the castle. *Sgl 9,000Ft, dbl 11,000Ft, triple 12,500Ft.*

## Where to eat and drink

**Korona Fagylaltkert** Széchenyi István utca 2. A popular place to get your ice-cream licks and cake munches. Next to St László Church. *Open 09.00–21.00 daily.*

**Platán Restaurant** See above. Game predominates on the plate, and covers much of the walls too (in the form of hunting trophies not the spattered food of messy diners). Among the options are platters for 2 to share. Good food and healthy portions. *Mains 800–2,800Ft, avg 1,500–1,600Ft; open 10.00–22.00 daily.*

**Várkapu Vendéglő** See above. Locally recommended as the best restaurant, Várkapu serves a varied menu of traditional Hungarian dishes, as well as pizzas and pastas. The imaginative chef changes the selection seasonally, and the food is excellent. *Mains 700–2,700Ft, avg 2,100Ft; open daily 08.30–22.00.*

**Vadkert Major Fogadó** See above. Game is the speciality in this atmospheric and friendly basement restaurant attached to the riding school and inn (see opposite).

## Entertainment and nightlife

You'll find the **Kossuth Lajos Cultural Centre** (*Várkerület 1;* ✆ *95 320063; open Mon–Fri 08.00–17.00*) in the castle courtyard; there are temporary exhibitions inside, and information on local events (including concerts at the castle itself). The **River Dance Club** (*Rákóczi Ferenc utca 91; open Sat & some Suns 22.00–07.00*) is set back from the main road to the south of the centre; the wooden, warehouse-like club is full of laser lights and sweaty bodies. There are theme nights, including foam parties and strip shows.

## What to see and do

A wood-cobbled footbridge from Kossuth tér leads over the former moat and through a Gothic gatehouse to **Nádasdy Castle** (*Várkerület 1;* ✆ *95 320158; adult/concessions 460/230Ft; open Tue–Sun 09.00–17.00*). While there are earlier features, Tamás Nádasdy enlarged the castle in the 1560s and the bulk of the pentagonal structure dates from that time. On entering what is now the **Nádasdy Ferenc Museum**, you'll be met first by a state room decorated with ceiling frescoes by Hans Rudolf Miller; at the centre is the famous 'Battle of the Black Captain' led by Ferenc Nádasdy II at Sziszek, while around it are scenes of sieges against the Turks at other Transdanubian towns. The paintings of Old Testament stories that colour the walls were painted by István Dorfmeister in 1769. An adjoining room pays tribute to the weighty contribution the Nádasdy family made to the development of Hungarian printing, and an extensive exhibition devoted to the hussars (one regiment of which was named after the family) includes maces, carved powder horns and decorated rifles from the end of the 16th century (contemporary with the period when the Black Captain was routing the Ottomans).

The earliest piece in a valuable cartographic collection (donated by a Hungarian professor living in Oxford) is a map of Europe drawn in Strasbourg in 1520. The first map of Hungary produced in England appeared in an atlas of 1627. A helpful description on the back informs the user that Hungarian men 'are mostly strong, passionate and treat foreigners severely', and goes on to say that someone whose bravery is doubted can 'regain their honour by fighting with a Turk'. The rest of the castle is filled with tapestries, glassware, furniture and other fine art – the star piece a 17th-century wood cabinet with inlaid marble and a carving of Poseidon in the state room; they may reflect an aristocratic taste, but most of these objects did not actually belong to the Nádasdy family, whose castle was stripped by the Habsburgs after Ferenc III's execution. The **Arcis Gallery** (*admission free; open Mon–Fri 10.00–18.00, Sat 10.00–14.00*) can be found in the castle courtyard and has temporary exhibitions; the **Sylvester János Library** is in the same building.

Just to the northeast of the castle is a small **arboretum** (*Rákóczi utca; adult/concessions 300/150Ft; open daily Apr 1–Oct 15 09.00–19.00, Oct 16–Mar 31 09.00–17.00*), rich and thick with foliage. Before heading there, take a look at **Szent László Church** (*Kossuth tér*), which was built by Ferenc Nádasdy III in 1645 after his conversion to Catholicism. It has been reconstructed several times since, once after it was damaged during the War of Independence. The statue of the Sorrowful Christ was sculpted in 1701.

## Activities

The **Sárvár Thermal Baths** (*Vadkert utca 1;* ✆ *95 523600;* e *thermal@sarvarfurdo.hu; www.badsarvar.hu; adult/concessions 1,600/700Ft, sliding rates after 17.00 & 20.00; open 08.00–22.00 daily*) make use of a hot spring discovered during oil surveying. A colourful new complex has rendered the older baths opposite redundant. There is a huge wellness centre, indoor and outdoor pools (including a kids area with a pirate ship and waterslides), a solarium, sauna, beauty emporium and state-of-the-art gym. All in all, this is a very swanky affair.

On the same road is the **Vadkert Major Riding School** (*Vadkert utca;* ✆ *95 320045*), which has recently downsized from 70 to ten horses, but still offers horse-riding (*from 2,000Ft/hr*) and carriage driving (*from 5,500Ft/hr*). There's accommodation and a restaurant in the former hunting lodge (see pages 472 and 473).

# ZALAEGERSZEG

On the right bank of the River Zala, and seat of Zala County, Zalaegerszeg was a fortressed frontier town in Habsburg-controlled western Hungary during the period of Turkish occupation to the east. Its face now is very different, marked by the industrialisation that went along with the 20th-century discovery of oil. The only sights that might encourage you to stop rather than fly through is the country's first open-air village museum (an unlikely partner for an adjacent display of drilling equipment) and an aquapark that rivals the town itself for size.

## Getting there and around

It's a five-minute walk from the **bus station** (*Balatoni út*) to the centre of town. There are regular buses to Szombathely, Egervár and Nagykanizsa, and up to five trains a day to Budapest Déli (taking four hours). Other routes are to Sümeg (11), Balatonfüred (six), Pécs, Tapolca and Veszprém (five), Sárvár and Székesfehérvár (three).

There are up to five **trains** leave daily for Budapest Déli, Veszprém, Székesfehérvár and Celldömölk, three to Szombathely and Nagykanizsa and one that crosses the Slovenia border at Hodoš to Ljubljana (taking 4½ hours). The **railway station** is 2km south of the centre on Bajcsy-Zsilinszky tér.

## Information and other practicalities

**Ibusz** Eötvös utca 6–10; ✆ 92 311458. Currency exchange, regional tours and private rooms. *Open Mon–Fri 08.30–16.30.*
**Tourinform** Széchenyi tér 4–6; ✆ 92 316160; e zalaegerszeg@tourinform.hu. Helpful office just south of Szabadság tér (through which the 74 and 76 roads run). *Open Jun 15–Sep 15 Mon–Fri 09.00–18.00, Sat–Sun 10.00–17.00, Sep 16–Oct 31 Mon–Fri 09.00–17.00, Nov 1–Jun 14 Mon–Fri 10.00–17.00.*

## Where to stay, eat and drink

Tourinform can provide a list of colleges offering cheap accommodation.

**AquaTherma Camping** Gébárti-tó; ✆ 92 511268; e thermalpul@aquacity.hu; www.aquatherma.hu. Coiffured site next to Lake Gébárt and the thermal baths, and within easy access of Aqua City (see page 476). On-site restaurant, pub and shop. *Tent/caravan €5/10, plus adult/concessions €4/2.*

**Bella Pizzéria** Kaziczy tér 11; \ 91 312687. One of several pizza joints in town. Right in the centre. *Open 12.00–24.00 daily.*

**Hotel Arany Bárány** (30 rooms) Széchenyi tér 1; \ 92 550040; e info@aranybarany.hu; www.aranybarany.hu. The 3-star 'Golden Lamb' is the best in town, situated in an originally 18th-century building that served as soldiers' quarter. Revamped in the 19th century, there was also a late-20th-century extension. *Dbl 13,900Ft.*

**Kiskondás Panzió & Restaurant** (10 rooms) Hock János utca 53; \ 92 321378. Friendly little guesthouse to the northwest of the centre (follow the road that starts as Rákóczi Ferenc utca out beyond the oil and village museums, or take bus 1). Its restaurant *(mains 850–3,200Ft, avg 1,300Ft; open Mon–Sat 10.00–22.00, Sun 10.00–16.00)* serves good Hungarian food and regional specialities, among them a mixed 'Kondás' platter of fish, pork and turkey for 2. *Dbl 8,000Ft, triple 10,500Ft.*

**Palatinus Restaurant** Dózsa liget; \ 92 314571. Located at the southern tip of Dózsa liget, around 100m north of the railway statin, this restaurant with patio dining area serves typical food of the Zala region, including a dish of roast meat of Göcsej (the damp hills to the west) featuring bacon, homemade sausage, onion and garlic. Fair but not special. *Mains 800–2,800Ft, avg 1,450Ft; open Mon–Sat 11.30–23.00, Sun 12.00–21.00.*

## BLOOD BATH-ORI

At the age of 54, Erzsébet Báthori was entombed in a room at her castle in Čachtice (now in Slovakia) to spend the last four years of her life in claustrophobic isolation. Such was her punishment for deeds so darkly devilish that they have been the stuff of horror ever since – inspiring, it is said, literary works as renowned as Bram Stoker's *Dracula*. She was accused of murdering over 600 women, of tearing lumps of flesh from their bodies, even of drinking and bathing in their blood in the belief it would rejuvenate her middle-aged complexion. She went down in history as one of the original vampires. The level of truth in these tales will probably never been known for sure.

What is beyond doubt is that those who made the accusations had a vested interest in making them. On the death of her husband Ferenc Nádasdy in 1604 she inherited a vast wealth, and Palatine of Hungary György Thurzó was concerned by the power the Báthoris would wield should she forge an alliance with her nephew Gábor (Prince of Transylvania). Others weren't happy either, among them the poet Miklós Zrínyi; he was Erzsébet's son-in-law, and was miffed that she wasn't channelling some of her fortune his way. In 1610, Thurzó took a body of guards to Čachtice and as he entered the door stumbled upon (literally) the corpse of a butchered servant. Or so he said.

'All rather convenient', we hear the defence lawyers cry. Yet there were factors that gave at least faint credence to the claim. There had been much inter-marriage in the Báthori clan, and Erzsébet would not have been the first among them to display signs of sadism or lunacy. Furthermore, Erzsébet had shown cruel tendencies in disciplining servants even prior to her husband's death, pouring freezing water over one until she died of the cold. And there were hundreds of statements gathered from those around her in support of the charges. Which case would have prevailed in court we'll never know, for while a maid accused of helping her was executed, the blue bloods were keen to hush up such crimes among their own (particularly after Gábor Báthori's death in 1613 removed the threat of an alliance). Erzsébet was incarcerated without trial, leaving behind a tale that has intrigued ghoulish story-tellers ever since; her body lies in the family vault at Nagyecsed.

## What to see and do

Along with the 1970s **TV tower** (4km southwest of the town on Bazita Hill) – which affords splendid views of the Zala Hills on a fair day – the twin-towered 18th-century **Baroque parish church** (*Szabadság tér*) is the symbol of Zalaegerszeg and graces much of its tourist literature. It was built by Márton Padányi Bíró, the Bishop of Veszprém and landowner of the time, and contains frescoes by the Viennese artist Johann Cymball and a painted 17th-century *piéta* that once stood in the market square. On the road running south from Kazinczy tér, the Eclectic **synagogue** (*Ady Endre utca 14*) was designed by József Stern in 1904 and has served as a concert and exhibition hall since the 1980s.

Near the parish church, the **Göcsej Museum** (*Batthyány utca 2;* ↘ *92 703295; adult/concessions 340/170Ft; open Mon–Fri 09.00–17.00, Sat–Sun 10.00–16.00*) displays works by Zsigmond Kisfaludy Strobl, the 20th-century artist who achieved international popularity and was particularly well regarded in England (there are portraits of Queen Elizabeth II and George Bernard Shaw). He was notorious as a 'pragmatic' artist, who tailored his art to suit the prevailing politics of the day – evident in the Liberty Statue in Budapest, which started life as a tribute to Miklós Horthy's pilot son but ended up as a monument to the Soviet liberation (see pages 146–7). There is also an exhibition charting the history of settlements along the River Zala, divided between the Roman Salla (Zalalövő, a few kilometres to the west), the medieval Mosaburg (Zalavár) and the modern Zalaegerszeg.

The **Göcseji Village Museum** (*Falumúzeum; Falumúzeum utca;* ↘ *92 703295; www.zimmi.hu; adult/concessions 340/170Ft; open Tue–Sun Apr 1–May 31 & Sep 1–Oct 31 10.00–17.00, Jun 1–Aug 31 10.00–18.00*) stands next to the rail track, just off Ola utca (a continuation of Rákóczi utca, which runs west from Deák Ferenc tér). Opened in 1968, the open-air museum was the first of its kind in the country and displays 19th-century dwellings transported from 22 villages in Zala County. A Finno-Ugric Ethnographical Park was added in 2001, and there is a collection of dolls in traditional national costume. Next door is the **Hungarian Petroleum Museum** (*Olajipari Múzeum; Falumúzeum utca;* ↘ *92 311082; free admission with Village Museum ticket; open Tue–Sun Apr 1–May 31 & Sep 1–Oct 31 10.00–17.00, Jun 1–Aug 31 10.00–18.00*), established the year after its neighbour and showing industrial items relating to the town's oil industry. Hot water is also represented, for thermal springs were found during the drilling.

**AquaCity** (*Zalaegerszeg-Ságod,* ↘ *92 599101; www.aquacity.hu; daily ticket inc use of slides adult/concessions 3,860/770Ft, discount after 15.00; open Jun 14–Aug 31 Mon–Fri 10.00–19.00, Sat–Sun 10.00–20.00*) is a massive 8ha water park with myriad pools, waves machines, jacuzzis and slides, a 300m-long artificial river, and facilities for mini golf, volleyball and tennis. You'll find it 2km north of the centre and can ride bus 55 there for no charge; it runs from the railway station at quarter-past every hour (*Mon–Fri 10.15–19.15, Sat–Sun 10.15–20.15*). The bus also drops in at the nearby **thermal baths** (*Gébárti-tó;* ↘ *92 401 267; adult/concessions 530/380Ft; open May 1–Sep 30 Mon 10.00–19.00, Tue–Fri 09.00–19.00, Sat–Sun 09.00–20.00*) beside Lake Gébárt, which is a smaller and more peaceful complex. The lake itsef has a beach, while at the southern side handicraft workshops are hosted at the **Arts and Crafts House** (*Gébárti utca 144;* ↘ *92 312744*) in summer.

Like the Őrség (see opposite), the **Göcsej region** in the Zala Hills to the west of Zalaegerszeg is ethnographically distinct and characterised by hilltop villages and an abundance of natural springs. The villages were once isolated by marshland, and they developed their own folklore and architectural variants. The wood-carved houses are beautiful, and you can see examples in Zalalövő – where a Roman settlement was unearthed – and Felsőbagod (as well as the Göcsej Village Museum; see above). If you fancy some hill hiking, buy a copy of Cartographia's *Az Őrség és a Göcsej* map (1:60,000); one of the trails can be picked up from the western side of Lake Gébárt.

# THE ŐRSÉG

The Őrség, tucked into the country's most western place (where it moves out to meet Austria and Slovenia), has been the frontier limit since the Magyar conquest; one of the chieftains positioned his soldiers here to defend attack from Germanic peoples to the west, and this is reflected in the region's name (meaning 'guard'). For centuries the residents swore to continue this role as stewards of the border, and were granted special privileges for doing so – the right to elect their own commanders, to be exempted from the usual royal taxes and to choose where to build their houses. The sentries cleared the woodland from the tops of local hills and constructed fenced settlements of between five and ten timber buildings (known as *szer* or *szeg* in ancient Hungarian) in which they lived with their families. Individually these were readily defended posts, while collectively they formed a system along which signals should be passed should enemies approach. Today the damp and lush landscape (which falls under the management of the recently established Őrség National Park) is popular with hikers and bikers, its wildlife supplemented by traditional folk architecture. Trails snake through the region and connect many of the villages; they are marked on Cartographia's *Az Őrség és a Göcsej* map (1:60,000).

The 'capital' of the Őrség is **Őriszentpéter**, 21km south of Szentgotthárd. It is a model Őrség village, spread over several hills with clutches of thatched wooden dwellings – often erected without the use of metal nails – sitting well apart from each other. The 13th-century Romanesque St Peter's Church (*Templomszer 15*) that gives the village its name is on the northwestern edge, and with the exception of the 15th-century chancel retains much of its original character. Őriszentpéter is the village best-equipped for tourists in the region, and has several places to stay (in addition to the houses advertising private rooms); visit the information centre (*Városszer 55;* ❧ *94 548023; open Mon–Fri 09.00–16.00*) for details.

Six kilometres to the northwest is **Szalafő**, whose eight *szer* have each expanded and grown together. The westernmost and highest of these is called Pityerszer; it was inhabited well into the 20th century, but is now the Open-Air Ethnographical Museum (*Pityerszer 12;* ❧ *06 30 467 7022; adult/concessions 400/200Ft; open Jun 1–Aug 31 daily 10.00–18.00, rest of yr Tue–Sun 10.00–18.00*). The houses consist of three rooms (a pantry, communal room and kitchen), are furnished with many of the original domestic objects, and have deep covered verandas that allowed the occupants to sit outside during the

## UNDER SERF-ERRANCE

The Őrség villagers had for centuries enjoyed royal privileges granted in gratitude for their role as guardians of the western border. When the Turks invaded Europe, though, a Diet was convened in Sopron at which it was decided the favours should stop and the Őrség people should be subject to the same rules as peasants elsewhere in Hungary. However, the proud frontier citizens would not readily accept the mantle of serfs to the landowning Batthyány counts, and cocked a big fat snook to their noble betters. The Batthyánys were livid, and it is said that they hatched a cunning plan. They invited the bigwigs of the Őrség to a feast at their mansion in Körmend, asking them to bring with them the official documentation proving their right to special treatment so that the matter could finally be laid to rest. The naive leaders did so, and while they got stuck into the Batthyány victuals and drained the cellar dry their hosts swapped their contracts for crude forgeries. When they got down to business the next morning and the peasants produced their documents, the Batthyánys 'exposed' them as fakes – and the villagers had to endure the indignity of serfdom until its abolition in 1848. Undoubtedly a rural myth, but good fun nonetheless.

## ŐRSÉG NATIONAL PARK

The Őrség National Park was founded in 2002 and covers 44,000ha of Hungary's westernmost corner, a place of babbling streams, shady valleys and forests, and verdant meadows. This is the rainiest part of the country and three rivers – the Rába, the Zala and the Ős ('Ancient') Mura – as well their many smaller tributaries, flow through it. One of the very few natural lakes is Fekete-tó (Black Lake), 5km northwest of Szalafő (near Orfalu); the lake is now filled with peat and moss. Around 60% of the park is forested; the most common type, because of the acidity of the soil, is Scots pine. You'll find junipers and downy birch among these forests, while dog's tooth violet and red cyclamen bloom in good quantities in the oak-hornbeam and beech woodland. The drier meadows hold various species of orchid, the green-winged orchid in greatest numbers; wet meadows along the numerous streams harbour round-leaf sundew, marsh cinquefoil and bogbean, all three typical inhabitants of peat bogs.

Thanks to the diversity of vegetation, Őrség National Park boasts the highest number of butterfly species in Hungary, and there are many unusual species of dragonfly too. One of Europe's rarest birds, the corncrake, nests in the wet meadows of the park, while the country's only population of Alpine newts is found in the waters. In addition to the wildlife attractions, the region has a strong folk tradition, and there are abundant examples of the typical u-shaped, wooden-walled Őrség dwellings. For further information, contact the Őrség National Park Directorate (*Őriszentpéter, Siskaszer 26/A;* ✆ *94 548033;* e *orsegtk@axelero.hu; open Mon–Fri 08.00–16.30*) at the turn-off to Szalafő.

regular local showers. One of them has a defensive u-shaped layout, arranged around a courtyard. A walking trail leads from Őriszentpéter to Szalafő; alternatively you can catch one of a few daily buses (you'll need to walk the final kilometre to the museum). Both Szalafő and Őriszentpéter can be accessed by **bus** from Körmend, Zalaegerszeg, Kőszeg, Szentgotthárd and Sopron.

## KÖRMEND AND SZENTGOTTHÁRD

To the south of Szombathely, and perched on the northeastern brink of the Őrség – to which it is an upper gateway – **Körmend** is dominated by the Batthyány mansion (*Dr Batthyány-Strattmann utca 3*). This considerable pile was converted from a medieval castle into a Baroque palace after the town was acquired in 1604 by the Batthyány family – a powerful clan who within a few generations shifted from feudal enforcers (see box, page 477) to leading players in the revolutionary movement (Lajos Batthyány was prime minister during the 1848–49 War of Independence). The building now holds the Dr Batthyány-Strattmann László Museum (✆ *94 410425; adult/concessions 360/180Ft; open Tue–Sat Apr 1–Oct 31 09.00–12.00 & 13.00–17.00, rest of yr 10.00–12.00 & 14.00–16.00*), with displays of archaeology, natural history and products relating to local guilds. An old building in the courtyard contains a Shoemakers' Museum, focusing on Hungarian cobblers. There are up to 13 trains a day to Szombathley, and eight to Zalaegerszeg. The railway station is 1km northwest of the centre on Vasútmellék utca. The bus station is on the same road and also serves Szombathely (11) and Zalaegerszeg (six), as well as Nagykanizsa (three).

Tight against the Austrian border 30km west along Road 8, **Szentgotthárd** takes its name from a 12th-century Cistercian abbey founded by Béla III, and in turn passes it on to a glorious struggle of 1664. The Battle of Szentgotthárd actually took place on the other side of the River Rába at what is now the Austrian town of Mögersdorf. There the

Habsburg General Montecuccoli routed a Turkish army twice the size, with many of the vanquished drowning in the river. The victory is recorded in István Dorfmeister's fresco in a cupola of the mid-18th-century Baroque church (*Béke tér*). For all the strutting, however, the Treaty of Vasvár (see page 18) signed shortly afterwards by Emperor Lipót was a crushing let down for the Hungarians – ceding as it did so much Magyar land to the Turks – and not only triggered the Zrínyi conspiracy (see page 18) but provoked a slow-burning sense of injustice that fuelled the independence cause long after the Ottomans had left.

Buses to Szentgotthárd are few and far between; the least-painful way of getting there is from Körmend (and even then there are only five on weekdays). A service also operates on weekdays only to Zalaegerszeg. Far more convenient is the train, with up to 18 services a day running to Szombathely via Körmend.

## SZOMBATHELY

Szombathely translates as 'Saturday market' – a hangover from the medieval period when the weekend market was big business here. The shopping tag remains appropriate, however, for this is a great place for some retail therapy, and Austrian bargain-hunters are frequent faces. The town is the largest in Western Transdanubia. It came to prominence as early as the 1st century AD, when the Romans established a settlement called Savaria that by the dawn of the 2nd century was the capital of the Upper Pannonia province. The place thrived on trade, falling as it did (like Sopron) on the so-called Amber Road running between Italy and the Baltic Sea. Things declined after the Romans had left, and the town was plundered at several points over the centuries (most notably by the Mongols). The resurgence came in the 18th century when Maria Theresa made it an episcopal see, and come the 19th century it was a major junction of the railway network. The confusing street plan and architectural diversity is in part due to the different phases of expansion and partly due to heavy bombing during World War II, after which much had to be put back together again. As such, it's not attractive in the classical sense, but the main square is atmospheric and the old centre contains some interesting buildings.

### Getting there and around

The railway station is a 15-minute walk northeast of the centre at the culmination of Széll Kálmán út. Several lines branch out from it, and there are express trains to Budapest via Veszprém and Székesfehérvár, Győr, Nagykanizsa and Pécs, as well as services to closer towns like Kőszeg (16) and Sopron (12). There is a taxi rank here and the local bus station stops are outside. The **bus station** is northwest of Fő tér on Ady Endre tér (a short walk from the centre). You can get regular buses to Ják, Kőszeg and Körmend, and among other services are those to Budapest (four), Celldömölk (nine), Győr (seven), Sopron (nine), Zalaegerszeg (14) and Szeged (three). For **taxis**, try City (🕿 94 333666) or Centrum (🕿 94 311300).

### Information and other practicalities

**Listings magazine** *Szombathelyi Est*
**Ibusz** Fő tér 44; 🕿 94 314141. Organises private rooms (from 3,000Ft/pp), currency exchange and local and regional tours. *Open Mon–Fri 09.00–17.30, Sat 09.00–12.00.*
**Tourinform** Kossuth Lajos utca 1–3; 🕿 94 514450; e szombathely@tourinform.hu. Incredibly helpful office in the town hall building. *Open Jun 16–Sep 14 Mon–Fri 09.00–20.00, Sat–Sun 10.00–18.00, rest of yr Mon–Fri 09.00–17.00, Sat 09.00–14.00.*

### Where to stay

**California Hotel** (11 rooms) Rumi út 21; 🕿 94 509447. More of a panzió than a hotel, with sweet little pine-furnished rooms. Around 500m south of Batthyány tér. *Sgl 8,500Ft, dbl 11,600Ft.*

SZOMBATHELY

**Gerendás Hotel** (19 rooms) 11-es Huszár utca 118; ☏ 94 509290. This 2-star is set back a little from the road, over 1km northeast of the centre. It's not central, but it is cheap and pleasant. It's also a favourite with athletes; Szombathely is renowned for its hammer-throwing coaches, and you'll often find some beefy chaps staying here while honing their skills. Gym, solarium, squash courts. Bus 3 runs here from the centre. *Sgl 6,900Ft, dbl 9,000Ft, triple 11,900Ft.*

**Hotel Savaria** (89 rooms) Mártírok tere 4; ☏ 94 311440; e claudius.hotel@savaria.hu; www.hotelsavaria.hu. The early-20th-century Savaria has a faded elegance; it's rooms are old-fashioned and could do with an overhaul, but they are spacious and some have balconies. They come with shower, bath or just basin, and only 30 have their own toilet. *Sgl 5,500–10,000Ft, dbl 6,500–11,000Ft, triple 8,000–14,000Ft.*

**Hotel Wagner** (12 rooms) Kossuth Lajos utca 15; ☏ 94 322208; e info@hotelwagner.hu; www.hotelwagner.hu. Very nice, centrally located hotel with well-furnished rooms (the only possible complaint being they are on the small side). *Sgl 10,500Ft, dbl 16,500Ft, apt (for 2/3) 20,500–22,500Ft.*

**Park Hotel Pelikán** (42 rooms) Deák Ferenc utca 5; ☏ 94 513800; e info@hotelpelikan.hu; www.hotelpelikan.hu. This is a fabulous hotel that's well worth the extra cost – to our minds, one of the best in its bracket you'll find in Hungary. The town's only 4-star, it has standard and superior rooms, a lovely 25m pool (lit from underneath in the evening), a furiously bubbling jacuzzi, a sauna and small gym. The rooms are high-class, with soft lighting, plush red carpets and large bathrooms. Ask for one of the bigger rooms – they vary in size, even within their price brackets. The restaurant is appropriately excellent too (see below). To the north of centre. *Standard/superior sgl 20,000/21,000Ft, dbl 24,000/27,400Ft.*

**Tópart Camping** Kenderesi út 6; ☏ 94 509038; e savariatourist@axelero.hu. Next to the Lake Baths, to the northwest of the centre, this well-equipped site has 36 bungalows and a swimming pool. Bus 2A which stops outside. *Camping €15/pp; open May 1–Sep 30.*

## Where to eat and drink

A good place to head is the Belső Uránia udvar, a narrow pedestrianised street accessed through an arched passage off Fő tér, which comes alive in the evening and is reminiscent of Budapest's Liszt Ferenc tér – with less of the 'look-at-me' pouting.

**Gödör** Hollán Ernő utca 10–12; ☏ 94 510078; www.godorvendeglo.hu. Cellar eatery selling massive portions of hearty Hungarian grub. Come hungry. *Mains 790–2,290Ft, avg 1,500Ft; open Mon–Thu 11.00–23.00, Fri–Sat 11.00–24.00, Sun 11.00–15.00.*

**Hemmingway Club & Restaurant** Belső Uránia udvar; ☏ 94 344978. Great place to chill out, eat and drink. Sells light snacks. *Mains 650–2,000Ft, avg 1,300Ft; open Mon–Thu 11.00–23.00, Fri–Sat 11.00–02.00, Sun 16.00–23.00.*

**M Café** Belső Uránia udvar; ☏ 94 332300. Modern, open-fronted café-bar serving cocktails, coffees, cakes and ice cream. *Open Mon–Sun 09.00–22.00.*

**Olasz Kisvendéglő** Belső Uránia udvar; ☏ 94 342012. A substantial menu laden with Italian food – delicious and cheap. Recommended. *Mains 650–2,650Ft, avg 1,300Ft; open Sun–Thu 11.00–23.00, Fri–Sat 11.00–24.00.*

**Pannónia Restaurant** Fő tér 29; ☏ 94 509588; e lancsak2@axelero.hu. A cheerful place with a contemporary 'folksy' ambience. Hungarian and continental food. Next to McDonalds. *Mains 1,400–2,000Ft, avg 1,750Ft; open 10.00–24.00 daily.*

**Park Hotel Pelikán Restaurant** See above. A beautiful, upmarket restaurant, surrounded with glass and with a classy upstairs bar. Perfect for a relaxed drink or a meal from the international menu. The staff are friendly and helpful. We can't find fault with this hotel and restaurant package. *Mains 890–4,500Ft, avg 2,500Ft; open 07.00–22.00 daily.*

**Wagner Restaurant** See above. Along with the Pelikán, this is one of the top places to eat in town. It has a marble floor and a courtyard garden, and serves international fare peppered with Hungarian options and an extensive list of regional wines. *Mains 850–4,800Ft, avg 2,200Ft; open 09.00–23.00 daily.*

## Entertainment and nightlife

The **Bartók Béla Concert Hall** (*Ráckóczi Ferenc utca 3;* ❧ *94 313474; www.savaria_symphony.hu*) is housed in the Moorish former synagogue, built in 1881, and with a memorial to the Jews deported during World War II outside. It plays host to the town's symphony orchestra. The **cultural house** (*Fő tér 10;* ❧ *94 509641*) should be able to offer information on arts events. There are several bars on Belső Uránia udvar (see under *Where to eat and drink*). **Abbázia Klub** (*Hollán Ernő utca 13;* ❧ *94 340453; open Mon–Thu 15.00–23.00, Fri–Sat 15.00–24.00, Sat 15.00–21.00*) is a basement bar that has a smart interior and attracts a slightly older drinking clientele. For a beer and a game of pool, head for the **Premier Billiárd Club** (*Belső Uránia udvar 4;* ❧ *94 330792; open Mon–Sun 09.00–04.00*), which has a younger crowd and turns into a nightclub come night. **Pizzicato Club** (*Thököly Imre utca 14;* ❧ *06 20 333 9700; open Tue–Sat 19.00–04.00, Sun 19.00–24.00*) is reached through an archway opposite the rear entrance of the Hotel Wagner. It holds Bacardi Breezer theme nights and booming parties, and offers live music sessions and DJs (usually at weekends). The **Romkert Dance Club** (*Ady Endre tér*) is a pub-cum-disco next to the bus station with a definite youth-club feel (fruit machines, table football and thin walls).

## What to see and do

**Fő tér** is the heart of the modern town, wide and long without being classically quaint, and holding the shops and cafés. To its northwest is the **Savaria Museum** (*Kisfaludy Sándor utca 9;* ❧ *94 500720; adult/concessions 460/230Ft; open Tue–Sun 10.00–17.00*), which has archaeological, natural-history and ethnographic exhibitions, and is the place to head to get a flavour for the town's early history. The Roman flavour is particularly strong, with votive altars, burial stones (Christian and pagan), and a trio of carved deities that once stood in a temple here. The surviving milestone – erected to mark the distance (675 miles) from Savaria to Rome – is rare. Among the statues upstairs are the original apostles that adorned the 13th-century Benedictine church at Ják (see opposite), together with the moulds used to make the replicas that are now positioned above the portal.

There are more Roman remnants to be seen at the **Iseum Ruin Garden** next to the **Szombathely Gallery** (*Rákóczi Ferenc utca 12;* ❧ *94 508800; adult/concessions 300/150Ft; open Tue, Thu–Sun 10.00–17.00, Wed 10.00–19.00*). This 2nd-century Temple of Isis was discovered in the 1950s, and is one of only two or three in Europe (another is in Austria). Excavation and restoration is ongoing. The gallery is primarily devoted to 20th-century Hungarian art, and has paintings by inter-war artists like Gyula Derkovits (a native of the town) as well as regular temporary exhibitions. The **former synagogue** (see above) is across the road.

Let's see yet more stones from Savaria – the last lot, we promise – in the **Járdányi Paulovics István Garden of Ruins** (*Romkert; Mindszenty József tér 1;* ❧ *94 313369; adult/concessions 360/180Ft; open Mar 1–Nov 30 Tue–Sat 09.00–17.00*), which is near the cathedral. This former bishop's garden contains what's left of buildings constructed throughout the Roman occupation. Among them are the public baths, a shrine to Mercury and the 4th-century imperial palace (which covered an area of 200m²), with some of the best-preserved mosaics in Hungary. Also here is a portion of the basalt 'Amber Road', the route along which traders passed on their journey between the Baltic and the Adriatic; it was monitored by a customs house at the crossroads, and lined with craft shops.

The merging Mindszenty tér and Berzsenyi Dániel tér represent the town's historical core. When it was constructed for the first bishop, János Szily, in the late 18th century (when Maria Theresa made the town an episcopal see), the Neoclassical **Szombathely Cathedral** (*Mindszenty tér*) was graced with cupola frescoes and an altarpiece by the hand of F A Maulbertsch. Unfortunately an Allied bomb during World War II put paid to his hard work, and only a few of his decorative pieces remain. His work does survive in the reception hall of the late-Baroque **Bishop's Palace** (*Berzsenyi Daniel tér 3*) of 1783, but this is not open to the public. Instead you'll have to limit yourself to the Sala Terrena on the ground floor, where there's an **Ecclesiastical Collection** (*Egyházmegyei Múzeum;* ↘ *94 312056; adult/concessions 200/100Ft; open Tue–Fri 09.30–15.30, Sat 09.30–11.30, Sun by appointment only*) and walls frescoed by István Dorfmeister.

Behind the palace is the extraordinary **Smidt Museum** (*Hollán Ernő utca 2;* ↘ *94 311038; adult/concessions 450/250Ft; open Tue–Sun 10.00–17.00, Sat–Sun with prior notice*), based upon the private collection of a respected local surgeon and containing a spread of items including those archaeological (including Roman – we lied when saying you'd seen the last of them!), medical, artistic and military.

### Beyond the centre

Around 3km to the northeast, the **Kámon Arboretum** (*Szent Imre herceg utca 102;* ↘ *94 311352; adult/concessions 400/350Ft; open Apr 1–Oct 15 Mon–Fri 08.00–18.00, Sat–Sun 09.00–18.00, Oct 16–Mar 31 daily 08.00–16.00*) is a 27ha botanical garden by the Gyöngyös Stream. There is a bus stop 200m away, served by numbers 1 or 1C. Near by is the **ELTE Gothard Astrophysical Observatory** (*Szent Imre herceg utca 112;* ↘ *94 522870; adult/concessions 300/150Ft; open Mon–Fri 09.00–16.00*), with various equipment from the turn of the 20th century and exhibits on modern astronomy.

To the northwest of the centre, just beyond Bartók Béla körút are a pair of lakes, the smaller **Fishing Lake** (*Horgásztó*) and the lower **Boating Lake** (*Csónakázótó*), a picturesque piece of water with an island on which you can hire rowing boats (*Mar 30–Sep 15 daily 13.00–19.00*). Facing the latter across the road are the **Lake Baths** (*Tófürdő; Kendersei utca;* ↘ *94 505690;* e *szhely@varosgazd.hu; www.varosgazd.hu; adult/concessions 850/750Ft; open May–Sep Sun–Thu 09.00–20.00, Fri 09.00–19.00*), a huge open-air water park, with sunbathing areas and water chutes, while near that are the quieter **Thermal Baths** (*Bartók Béla körút;* ↘ *94 314336; adult/concessions 460/420Ft; open Mon–Fri 16.00–19.00, Sat–Sun 09.00–17.30*). Bus 2A stops 20m from the entrance.

At the western side of the Fishing Lake is the **Village Museum** (*Vasi Múzeumfalu; Árpád utca 30;* ↘ *94 311004; adult/concessions 500/250Ft; open Apr 1–Nov 6 Tue–Sun 09.00–17.00*), an outdoor collection of 18th- and 19th-century dwellings drawn from various pockets of Vas County. As well as the local styles, there are also examples of those built by Croatian, German and Slovene minorities. Bus 27 stops right outside.

### Excursion

Travel south of Szombathely by 12km and you'll arrive at one of the premium pieces of ecclesiastical art in Hungary – yes, we said *art*, for the nameless masters who created the **Benedictine abbey at Ják**, who chipped and carved at its west door, had artistic genius in every rough-skinned finger. While there are few good moments to die, Márton Nagy of the Ják clan had more reason than most to feel his time had come early; while work on the church he founded began in 1214, it wasn't completed until 1256 and by then he'd popped his clogs. He missed a treat.

Intact Romanesque architecture of the Árpád era is rare in Hungary, and this is undoubtedly the highlight of that left. It didn't survive the centuries wholly unscathed; it was severely ruffled during the Turkish siege of the village, and an adjacent monastery was dismantled in 1562. Subsequent Baroque additions were stripped away at the turn of the 20th century by the great Historicist Frigyes Schulek, and the restoration is considerably less divisive of opinion than his overhaul of the Mátyás Church in Buda. Some grumble about the choice of towers that he placed atop the original bases, but few dispute that Schulek's altars and vaulting complement an interior that oozes elegance and balance. The church's most-photographed feature is the western portal, a graceful beast of seven intricately carved receding arches surmounted by statues of Christ and his apostles. (There is a copy of this at the rear of Vajdahunyad Castle in Budapest's City Park.) The Chapel of St James to the west of the church was built in 1260 to serve non-monastic parishioners when the main church was in use. Up to 20 buses a day make the 20-minute journey between Ják and Szombathely. The bus stop is close to the abbey.

## KŐSZEG

Jammed hard against the lower slopes of the Kőszeg Hills 20km north of Szombathely, Kőzseg is another of those towns that makes you wonder how you ever considered holidaying anywhere else. With Sopron just 50km away, this pocket of Western Transdanubia has a pair of the prettiest, most romantic and best-preserved urban centres in the country. Kőszeg's cobbled main square is dripping with Baroque, Neoclassical and Renaissance architecture, and buildings without plaques recording their historical significance are few and far between. Just take a pew at the square's heart and drink it all in.

A series of fires raged through the medieval mud-and-wood houses during the 17th and 18th centuries, and the core primarily consists of structures raised after that. (The repeated infernos were such a problem that citizens were fined if caught smoking in public – and even subjected to 50 lashes if 'a villain'.) The 13th-century castle is an exception, an important cog in the border fortifications during the Turkish occupation that saw considerable action in 1532. Then it was that a small force held out against Suleiman I's army of over 100,000, preventing the Turks from marching on to Vienna. All the while a nearby Habsburg army quietly looked on without raising a finger, happy to sacrifice heroic Magyar lives as long as the Turks were being stalled; this was a stance adopted at Szigetvár and other Hungarian battlefields – and one that helps explain the passion for independence from imperial rule displayed by townspeople here and elsewhere in the subsequent two centuries.

### Getting there, away and around

The **bus station** (*Liszt Ferenc utca*) is a few minutes' walk west of the centre; there is a frequent service to Szombathely and up to six daily buses to Sopron. The **railway station** is 1½km southwest of the town, at the end of Rákóczi Ferenc utca. Turn right from the station and follow this road into the centre. If you can't face the walk, local buses stop outside the station – there are up to 16 a day (ten at weekends). Kőszeg is at the end of a branch line from Szombathely, and there are up to 15 trains daily between the towns.

### Information and other practicalities

**Cultural centre** Rajnis utca 9; ☏ 94 360113; e jurisics@koszeg.hu; www.koszeg.hu. This arts centre at the castle can offer information on cultural events. *Open Mon–Fri 10.00–17.00.*
**Savaria Tourist** Várkör 69; ☏ 94 563048; e tompasav@axelero.hu. The place to book local and regional tours. *Open Mon–Fri 08.00–12.00, 13.00–17.00, Sat 08.00–12.00.*
**Tourinform** Jurisics tér 7; ☏ 94 563120. Helpful office in the Sgraffito House (see Garabonciás Pizzéria opposite). You can get information on the nature park here too (see page 487). *Open Jun 15–Sep 15 Mon–Fri 08.00–18.00, Sat–Sun 09.00–17.00, rest of yr Mon–Fri 08.00–16.00.*

### Where to stay

**Arany Strucc Szálloda** (15 rooms) Várkör 124; ☏ 94 360323; emails: strucc1@axelero.hu; www.aranystrucc. Functioning as an inn from 1597, the 'Golden Ostrich' has a fair claim to being the country's oldest hotel. The original owner got into a fair tussle with the keeper of the White Horse Inn across the street (in what is now a bank), each accusing the other of stealing customers. In the end a magistrate had to intervene, threatening them with a heavy fine if the quarrel continued. Today the rooms have spacious bathrooms and are well-priced. *Sgl 5,500, dbl 8,800Ft.*

**Gyöngyvirág Camping & Panzió** Bajcsy-Zsilinszky utca 6; ↘ 94 360454;
e info@gyongyviragpanzio.hu; www.gyongyviragpanzio.hu. This is a guesthouse with a camping
site in its garden to the northeast of the centre (follow Dózsa György utca out from the curving
Gyöngyös utca); there are rooms with or without ensuite facilities. *Sgl/dbl 5,200/6,200Ft (with
bathroom), sgl/dbl/triple/room for 4 3,800/4,800/6,000/8,000Ft (without bathroom); camping:
tent/caravan/campervan 400/600/800Ft, plus adult/student/child 650/450/300Ft (all excl tourist tax).*
**Hotel Írottkő** (52 rooms) Fő tér 4; ↘ 94 360373; e info@hotelirottko; www.irottko.hu. The
town's largest hotel. There's an ongoing programme of renovation here – at a snail-like 5 rooms a
year – and the worn furniture could do with a spruce up. The marble-floored lobby has been
freshened, and the accommodation is ranged around it. *Sgl 8,500Ft, dbl 11,500Ft.*
**Jurisics Miklós Grammar School** Hunyadi János út 10; ↘ 94 361404. Dorm rooms available in
summer. To the southwest of the castle. *Rooms 1,500–2,000Ft/pp.*
**Portré Hotel** (6 rooms) Fő tér 7; ↘ 94 363170; e info@portre.com; www.portre.com. This
intimate, centrally placed and reasonably priced hotel has modern rooms above a coffee house.
Sauna. *Dbl 9,000Ft, triple 11,000Ft.*

## Where to eat and drink
**Arany Strucc Cukrászda** Várkör 126; ↘ 94 563345. The best place for ice cream and dreamy
cakes; next to the hotel of the same name (see opposite). *Open 10.00–19.00 daily.*
**Bécsikapu Restaurant** Rajnics utca 5; ↘ 94 563122; e info@becsikapu.hu; www.becsikapu.hu.
Playing on its proximity to the castle, this medieval-theme restaurant has a covered courtyard
(adorned with maces and heraldic shields) and a cellar banqueting hall. Hungarian dishes include
deer steak and stews of wild boar or tripe; there are 'feasts' for 2 (*1,850–2,790Ft*) and a 3-course set
menu (*450Ft*). Cheap. *Mains 580–1,690Ft, avg 1,200Ft; open daily 11.00–22.00.*
**Garabonciás Pizzéria** Jurisics tér 7. This pizzeria beside the Tourinform has an alfresco area
overlooking the main square. It is known as the Sgraffito House because of the patterning on its
façade, an Italian technique created by scratching through different layers of coloured plaster. The
portions here are grand – don't order a large pizza unless you're famished or sharing. *Pizzas from
450Ft; open Mon–Sat 12.00–22.00, Sun 17.00–22.00.*
**Pizzeria da Rocco** Várkör 55; ↘ 94 362379. Good pizza joint and bar at the back of the Church
of Christ's Heart. Pizzas in 3 sizes. *Avg 1,200Ft; open Mon–Fri 12.00–24.00, Sun 12.00–22.00.*
**Taverna Flórián** Várkör 59; ↘ 94 563072; e taverna.florian@axelero; www.tavernaflorian.hu. It's
on the expensive side, but this atmospheric brick-cellar restaurant in front of the Zwinger Tower is
superb. The food is international/Mediterranean in influence – spaghetti, seared salmon, beef with
cognac – and its beautiful garden has a rockery and trickling waterfall. You'll make no mistake in
working out which are the male and female toilets – the door to the ladies is signalled by a pair of
wooden breasts! *Mains 690–3,190Ft, avg 1,900Ft; open Fri–Sun 11.30–14.30, Tue–Sat 17.30–22.00.*

## What to see and do
**Jurisics tér** was the former market square, and the backdrop to the town's political and
social life; here it was that the magistrates of the Middle Ages delivered sentence and
naughty citizens were pinned in the stocks open to the abuse of all and sundry. You are
ushered in through the **Heroes Gate** (*Hősök kapuja*) at the southern side, built in Eclectic
style in 1932 on the site of a former 13th-century barbican that guarded the entrance to
the town. The pseudo-medieval 20th-century gate was a monument to the 400th
anniversary of the Turkish siege, but in fairness it represents something of a drab blot on
the colourful surroundings. Next to it is the **General's House** (*Tábornok ház; Jurisics tér
6*), once the residence of the general of the town cavalry. Inside it the **Jurisics Miklós
Town Museum** (*adult/concessions 360/180Ft; open Tue–Sun 10.00–17.00*) has an
exhibition about the local guilds and crafts, and the entrance ticket also gives access to a
narrow gallery running around the outside of Heroes Gate, with views over the town's
sloping terracotta roofs.

The cost of commissioning the **Blessed Virgin Mary statue** of 1739 – with chubby cherubic faces on its column – was met by fines imposed upon 'blasphemous' Lutherans. It is positioned on the site of the medieval pillory. The benches around it offer a good place to park yourself and have a proper glance around the square. What you'll immediately notice is that the buildings on the western side appear shorter than those opposite. In actual fact it's the road that's high rather than the buildings low, layers of rubble from the various fires having raised the street level here.

You're rather spoilt for choice architecturally, but the **town hall** (*Jurisics tér 8*) is the most striking of those around the outside. It has functioned continually as a civic centre since the 14th century; the façade is 18th-century and the portal 19th-century, but Gothic windows (visible from the gate at number 10) are reminders of its earlier heritage. The three coats of arms are those of Miklós Jurisics, historical Hungary and Kőszeg itself. The Ambrózy House (Jurisics tér 14) is named after the Lutheran merchant who lived inside until 1716; in 1708 it was the scene for the capture of a *kuruc* brigadier. The **Golden Unicorn Pharmacy Museum** (*Apotéka az Arany Egyszarvúhoz; Jurisics tér 11;* ℩ *94 360337; adult/concessions 360/180Ft; open Apr 1–Nov 30 Tue–Sun 10.00–18.00*) showcases an 18th-century chemist's shop, and contains Baroque furniture stripped from the town's Jesuit cloister after the dissolution of the order in 1773 and secco painting added in 1777 by a Viennese master. Plants used for making the drugs were grown in the courtyard.

Of the square's two churches, **St Jakab Church** is the older, originally built in 1407 from the stones of a Minorite church brought down during a 13th-century siege. The 15th-century version was founded by Palatine Miklós Garai, but had to be reconstructed on several occasions after fires. Between 1554 and 1671, the church was used by the Lutherans, who whitewashed many of the frescoes and carted away extravagant altarpieces in their desire for simplicity in worship. Some of the original frescoes were uncovered during restoration, one of which shows Mary sheltering devotees under her cloak. The crypt contains the tomb of Miklós Jurisics and his children. **St Imre Church** came about as the result of a power struggle between Hungarian and German Protestants; they took over St Jakab Church after proving the victors, so another was constructed (completed in 1640) next to it for the native Lutherans. By comparison with its hulking exterior, the church feels surprisingly small on the inside; the carved ends to the Baroque pews are beautifully tactile, and the altar piece depicting *St Imre's Vow* is by István Dorfmeister (the younger).

**Chernel utca** runs away from the western side of the square, its Baroque residences reflecting the wealth of a quarter occupied by aristocratic members of the Zichy, Nádasdy and Festetics dynasties. You'll see parts of the southern section of the medieval city walls, demolished after a particularly destructive blaze in 1777, and the **Old Tower** at the end of the street. This stands in what was then a seven-metre-deep moat. During the Turkish siege the outer wall was breached, but pitch was poured upon the attackers from the walls of the castle proper and they were forced back.

**Fő tér** is younger than the medieval core, its tone set by the **Church of Jesus' Heart** (*Jézus Szíve templom*) that occupies its southwestern end. The 57m bell tower of this magnificent Neo-Gothic church peals at 11.00 every morning in memory of the end of Suleiman's siege. The church was built in 1894, and its interior is as resplendent as any you'll see, with the Austrian Otto Kott's painted columns and ceiling so vivid they look as though they've been wallpapered; it is especially worth seeing when the afternoon sun streams through its stained-glass windows (which show images of the Árpád saints, including István, Imre and Erzsébet). Carved stations of the cross line the sides of the nave, and the ornate pulpit canopy bears an image of the church itself. The **Holy Trinity Column** in front of the church was fashioned from stone quarried at Fertőrákos in 1713, and bears tribute to the 600 plague victims. Just off Fő tér is the town's second historic apothecary's shop, the **Black Saracen Pharmacy** (*Rákóczi utca 3; open Tue–Fri*

*13.00–17.00*), which functioned for 300 years and only closed its doors to sneezing customers in 1983.

On the other side of the town's core, to the northeast of Jurisics tér, is a decrepit **synagogue** (*Várkör 38*) of 1859 that has lain empty since 1944 and the extermination programme of Eichmann. The nearby **Lutheran church** was consecrated in 1783; its separate Eclectic bell tower is not contemporaneous (it was built in 1930) because it was forbidden by József II for non-Catholic denominations to raise stone steeples or belfries.

## Jurisics Castle

**Jurisics Castle** (*Rajnis József utca 9*) is to the northwest of Jurisics tér. The chocolate-coloured inner buildings you see now are mainly the result of reconstruction after the fire of 1777, but there are Gothic and Renaissance features and remnants of the thick fortified outer wall running away from them. It was from the 14th-century castle that Miklós Jurisics and fewer than 500 garrison troops withstood a month-long Turkish assault in 1532. A statue of Jurisics stands in the yard, which is reached via a brick bridge spanning the former moat. The Knights' Hall is used for cultural events, while the southern and eastern wings are home to the **Miklós Jurisics Castle Museum** (↘ *94 360240; adult/concessions 460/230Ft; open Feb 1–Dec 31 Tue–Sun 10.00–17.00*). The exhibitions contain items of local history, including those relating to the siege, and a vinicultural display (wine producing was strong in the area until the phylloxera epidemic hit).

## Other

A short distance to the west of the centre along Hunyadi utca is the **Chernel Botanical Garden** (*Arborétum utca 2;* ↘ *94 362676; open Mon–Thu 08.00–16.00, Fri 08.00–13.00*), which also contains a small museum (visits by prior notice only) dedicated to the wildlife of the Kőszeg Hills and the work of ornithologist István Chernel.

The **Kőszeg Hills** afford outdoor types good hiking terrain. The Írottkő Peak right on the border is the highest in Transdanubia (at 884m), and has a lookout tower (although you'll need your passport as it falls just on the Austrian side). There are hiking trails (of different lengths) to the Seven Springs (Hétforrás), a water source that once fed the castle and now flows through seven spouts representing the landtaking Magyar chieftains; to the Óház peak just to the south of it, which has a lookout tower; and to Calvary Hill, with its 18th-century church (whose 40,000 bricks were carried here by hand by the town citizens) and a bomb shelter where the Holy Crown was hidden in early 1945. The Írottkő Nature Park people have published leaflets outlining some favourite routes, including a cycle path starting at Kőszegfalva and passing through Kőszeg, Cák, Velem and Bozsok. You should also buy a copy of Cartographia's *A Kőszegi-hegység és környékenek* (1:40,000). The literature and map are available from Tourinform.

## Festivals and events

Among the town's main events are medieval games and frolics held in the castle during summer months, and wine festivals in April and September.

## SOPRON

Heck, we love this place. We're sops to its architecture, its sense of past times in Fő tér, its museums and pubs and restaurants, its very proximity to the lungs of the Lövér Hills and Lake Fertő. We even love its title, 'Most Faithful City' (*Civitas Fidelissima*), a reference to a post-Trianon referendum of 1921 when its citizens elected to remain part of Hungary rather than be subsumed into Austria. Beautiful and constant: what more could one ask?

The country's westernmost city – pushing a bulge of border into Austria up to the foothills of the Alps – was settled first by the Celts and then the Romans, who called the

**SOPRON**

Tercia Hubertus Restaurant (700m)

Amphitheatre

USZODA

BÉCSI

Hotel Sopron

LACKNER KRISTÓF

VIRÁGOSKERT

St János Church

St Mihály Church, St Jakab Chapel

Bakery Museum

Wieden Panzió

SAS TÉR

SZENTLÉLEK

FOREM

Jégverem Fogadó

Bus station

ROZSA

FERENCZY JÁNOS

Soproni Wine House

VÁRKERÜLET

HALÁSZ

Goa & Koktel

Holy Spirit church

Zettl-Langer Collection

Tourin-form

Firewatch Tower

Storno House

ELŐKAPU

Fabricius House

FŐ TÉR

Town hall

BALFI

City Hall

Apothecary House

Musik Café

Mining Museum

Goat Church & Chapter House

ÚJTELEKI

Forestry Museum

KOLOSTOR

Ikva stream

GABONA TÉR

SZÍNHÁZ

BUNKER J. R.

ÁRPÁD

Petőfi Theatre

Old Synagogue

Internet Sopron

HÁTULSÓ

Pince Theatre

New Synagogue

TEMPLOM

UI.

Ózon Camping (3.2km)

Hotel Wollner

ORSOLYA TÉR

SZENT GYÖRGY

CSATKAI ENDRE

FERENC

ISKOLA KÖZ

Escort tourist

Pannonia Hotel

LISZT F.

R C Templan Church & museum

Cultural centre & casino

TORNA

SZÉCHENYI TÉR

Papa Joe's

Ethnographic Museum

Pertovátz House

VÁRKERÜLET

DEVŐS

Post office

Széchenyi Palace

DEÁK TÉR

Dominican church & cloister

MÓRICZ ZSIGMOND

Youth centre (1.5km)

ERZSÉBET

Lövér Baths (1.2km)

DEÁK TÉR

MÁTYÁS KIRÁLY

Columbus Restaurant (5km),
Danubius Sport Hotel (2.5km),
Diana Panzió (1.2km)

ALLOMÁS

N

**Bradt**

Railway station

0 — 300m
0 — 300yds

place Scarbantia and thrived on the trade route known as the 'Amber Road' running between the Baltic Sea and the Adriatic. When the Magyars came they named it 'Suprun' after a contemporary county ruler, and merchants flourished throughout the medieval period. Unlike so much of the architecture further east, what was built here stayed built for the town remained untouched by Mongols and Turks. The slings and arrows of World War II left more considerable marks, but a committed programme of restoration put Sopron's houses in order – a programme that was deservedly rewarded with the Europa Award for preservation in 1975.

## Getting there and away
The **Inner City bus station** (*Kristóf utca*) is a short walk from the centre along Lackner Kristof utca and through Ógabona tér. Buses run hourly to Győr and very regularly to Fertőd, Fertőrákos and Nagycenk. There are also departures to Szombathely (seven), Budapest Népliget (four) and twice-daily services to Balatonfüred, Keszthely and Zalaegerszeg, and once-daily ones to Pécs, Tapolca, Esztergom and Vienna. A weekly (Sun evening) bus crosses the border to reach Stuttgart via Munich.

There are two **railway stations**, the main one (*Állomás utca*) 700m south of the Belváros. From here, walk in a southerly direction along Mátyás Király utca before turning left into Széchenyi tér. There are fairly regular trains to Győr and Szombathely (up to 14), and services to Budapest Keleti and Tatabánya (seven), Tapolca, Sárvár and Sümeg (one). The second station, **Sopron Déli** (*Kossuth Lajos utca*), is west of the centre; trains depart from here for Vienna via Bük and Nagycenk.

## Information and other practicalities
**Café Datanet Internet Coffee House** Balfi út 1–3. Modern internet café with access from 250Ft/30 mins. *Open Mon–Fri 07.00–19.00, Sat 08.00–15.00.*
**Internet Sopron** Új utca 3. Internet access from 125Ft/15 mins. *Open Mon 14.00–20.00, Tue–Fri 11.00–22.00, Sat 10.00–17.00.*
**Escort Tourist** Orsolya tér 4; ☎ 99 320670. Offers information and booklets on the region, as well as peddling souvenir tat. This is also the place to book tickets for concerts at the Esterházy Palace in Fertőd (see page 499). *Open Mon–Fri 09.00–17.00, Sat 09.00–12.00.*
**Listings magazine** *Soproni Est*
**Tourinform** Előkapu utca 11; ☎ 99 338892; e sopron@tourinform.hu. Staff will trip over themselves to assist. You can buy a pass (*adult/concessions 2,000/1,000Ft*) that gives access to all the city's museums. *Open Jun 15–Sep 15 Mon–Fri 09.00–20.00, Sat–Sun 09.00–18.00, rest of yr Mon–Fri 09.00–17.00, Sat 09.00–12.00.*

## Where to stay
Sopron is a popular place to be in summer, and you would do well to book your accommodation before you arrive.

**Bio-Sport Hotel Lövér** Várisi utca 4; ☎ 99 513840; e lover.reservation@danubiusgroup.com; www.danubiushotels.com/lover. 5km southwest of the centre, in the town's green belt at the edge of the Sopron Hills, there's clean air and lush woodland around this well-equipped 4-star. Facilities include swimming pool, sauna, fitness/wellness centre and a popular restaurant. Ideal for walks in the Lövér Hills. Local buses 1, 2 & 15 run here. *Sgl €82, dbl €96.*
**Diána Panzió** (9 rooms) Lövér körút 64; ☎ 99 329013. A cheaper alternative to the above, the Diána is a pleasant guesthouse also well-placed for hill walkers. It has a restaurant. *Sgl 6,300, dbl 8,300Ft.*
**Hotel Sopron** (100 rooms) Fövényverem utca 7; ☎ 99 512261; e hotel-sopron@sopron.hu; www.hotelsopron.hu. Bland 4-star that lacks character but is within the city walls. Outdoor pool and solarium. *Sgl/dbl 15,000/17,500Ft.*

**Hotel Wollner** (18 rooms) Templom utca 20; ☏ 99 524400; e wollner@fullnet.hu; www.wollner.hu. A touch of class in a 300-year-old Baroque building based around a narrow courtyard (with a restaurant – see below). The rooms are excellent, there's a cigar club for privileged guests and a wine cellar for group tastings. Highly recommended. *Dbl 18,800Ft, triple 22,900Ft.*

**Jégverem Inn** (5 rooms) Jégverem utca 1; ☏ 99 510113; e jegverem@jegverem.hu; www.jegverem.hu. Built on the site of an 18th-century ice house, the rooms are whitewashed and simply furnished. 10-min walk northeast of the centre. *Sgl 5,790Ft, dbl 9,600Ft.*

**Ózon Camping** Erdei Malom köz 3; ☏ 99 523370; e ozoncamping@sopron.hu. Fabulously well-kept site with all the amenities – including restaurant, swimming pool and a few bungalows – to ensure campers are happy campers. 6km west of the centre – buses 3, 10 and 10B stop 200m away. *Camping adult/concessions 1,200/850Ft; caravans/campervans/large tents 1,600Ft, regular tent 800Ft; open Apr 15–Oct 15.*

**Pannonia Med Hotel** (62 rooms) Várkerület 75; ☏ 99 312180; e sopron@pannoniahotel.com; www.pannoniahotel.com. Possibly the city's most illustrious hotel, housed in a Neoclassical building of 1893. (A honeymooning Johann Strauss stayed in the previous hotel on this site in 1892.) The 4-star rooms are individually designed and the 14 suites furnished with tasteful antiques. Indoor pool, jacuzzi, gym and dental surgery. The hotel also owns six wooden apartments (for up to 10) 2km away. *Sgl 17,300, dbl 19,900–26,900Ft, suite (for 2/3/4) 26,300/28,900/28,900Ft.*

**Wieden Panzió** (9 rooms) Sas tér 13; ☏ 99 523222; e wieden@fullnet.hu; www.wieden.hu. Comely place whose rooms could do with a touch of modernisation, but which includes a couple of very spacious apartments with kitchens. Stands to the northeast of the Belváros. Free bike rental. *Sgl €29, dbl €43, triple €61, apts (4–8) from €70.*

## Where to eat and drink

**Columbus** Várisi út 1; ☏ 99 329070. Waterlife is the speciality of the house, with a menu of shark steaks, plaice, octopus and a river fish. 5km southwest of the centre, 100m from the Bio-Sport Hotel. *Mains 950–3,450Ft, avg 1,800Ft; open Sun–Thu 11.00–22.00, Fri–Sat 11.00–23.00.*

**Dömötöri Cukrászda & Coffee House** Széchenyi tér 13; ☏ 99 312781. Delicious ice creams, desserts and cakes. Take your treat on the outdoor terrace. *Open Mon–Sat 07.00–24.00, Sun 08.00–24.00.*

**Fórum Pizzeria** Szent György utca 3. Good pizzas, as well as fish, grills and pasta dishes. *Open 11.00–24.00 daily.*

**Jégverem Restaurant** See above. Huge selection of adventurous Hungarian and international food, including a good selection of game. The restaurant guarantees you'll leave with a full stomach, and so 'guzzle guts' make a beeline. *Mains 990–2,450Ft, avg 1,700Ft; open 11.00–23.00 daily.*

**Tercia Hubertus** Hubertusz út 1; ☏ 99 334290; www.terciarestaurant.hu. Reckoned to be Sopron's best restaurant, the Tercia Hubertus is large, lively and family-friendly (kids are given crayons to scribble with). Traditional Hungarian fare, and live music at the weekend. *Mains 880–3,400Ft, avg 2,000Ft; open 07.00–24.00.*

**Wollner Restaurant** See above. Super-stylish and ambient restaurant. A largely international à la carte menu is supplemented with tasty local specialities, and a set lunch menu (*available 12.30–15.00*) offers great value. *Mains 950–2,400Ft, avg 1,800Ft; open 11.30–22.00 daily.*

## Entertainment and nightlife

The Art-Nouveau **Sopron Petőfi Theatre** (*Petőfi tér 1;* ☏ *99 517542;* e *jegyiroda@prokultura.hu; www.prokultura.hu*) was erected in 1909; the main 400-seat arena hosts Hungarian and foreign drama, while a smaller theatre in the same building stages contemporary plays. There's no box office – get your tickets from the Liszt Ferenc Cultural Centre. To the south of Fő tér, the Neoclassical building housing the **Liszt Ferenc Conference and Cultural Centre** (*Liszt Ferenc utca 1;* ☏ *99 517517; ticket office open Mon–Fri 09.00–17.00, Sat 09.00–12.00*) once played host to the great Liszt (who performed here in 1874). Today you can get information on the city's arts events, and there is also a conference centre, concert room and theatre. The **youth centre** (*Ady Endre utca 10;* ✆ *99 511200; www.gyik.sopronnet.hu; open Mon–Thu 08.00–22.00, Sat–Sun depends on programme*), 1km west of the centre, does its best to keep the youth of Sopron occupied with a number of fun cultural events. Find out what's coming up in the *Soproni Program* (available from Tourinform). The **Civitas Cellar Theatre** (*Templom utca 16;* ✆ *99 332098; www.sopronnet.hu/civitas; ticket office open Tue–Sat 10.00–12.00, 17.00–20.00*) is a damp-smelling venue for theatre and cabaret accessed through an arch from Templom utca.

**Goa C Bar** (*Várkerület 24; open Sun–Thu 18.00–01.00, Fri–Sat 18.00–02.00*) is a chilled-out basement bar that plays acid-jazz and funky tunes, and has a huge selection of cocktails. **Musik Café** (*Várkerület 49;* ✆ *99 340469; open 12.00–24.00 daily*) is a popular, atmospheric bar and coffee house decorated with prints of rock idols. There are also four internet terminals at the back (*from 500Ft/hr*). **Papa Joe's Saloon** (*Várkerület 108;* ✆ *99 340933; open Mon–Wed & Sun 11.00–24.00, Thu–Sat 1.00–02.00*) has a Wild-West theme, but is less tacky than it sounds and has courtyard seating. For a bit of British, try **Perkovátz English Pub** (*Széchenyi tér; open daily 12.00–02.00*) – its un-English name refers to the Hungarian chap who worked in a Liverpool pub in 1908 and decided to open one himself on his return home. His grandson runs the place now. It's popular and well-frequented, and makes a decent stab at the traditional pub ambience; there's Guinness and a good selection of Scottish whiskies, but not a Yorkshire pud or fish and chip in sight on the Hungarian menu.

The Sopron region is known for its reds; you can taste or buy them at the **Sopron Wine House** (*Várkerület 15;* ✆ *99 510022; open Tue–Sat 11.00–23.00*) and its 300-year-old cellar. Afterwards head upstairs to the **Swing Söröző & Bar** (*Várkerület 15;* ✆ *06 20 2148029; open Sun–Fri 17.00–24.00, Sat 17.00–02.00*), a jazz joint that's good for a drink and some relaxed entertainment.

If you fancy something a bit more risky, try your hand at the **Casino Sopron** (*Liszt Ferenc utca 1;* ✆ *99 512350;* e *csop@casinosopron.hu; www.casinosopron.hu; open 13.00–04.00 daily*) – where apparently 'luck knows no borders'. It's located on the ground floor of the cultural centre (entrance on Petőfi tér) and has slot machines and gaming tables. You'll need your passport to enter, and a few gambling chips are included in the entrance fee of €15 (the membership card also gives you a discount at some of the city's restaurants).

## What to see and do
### The Belváros
#### Fő tér
The city's historic heartland is Fő tér, a gorgeous uneven square, and it is there you should begin any stroll about. Its northern gateway is the **Firewatch Tower** (*Tűztorony; adult/concessions 400/200Ft; open Apr 1–Oct 31; Tue–Sun 10.00–18.00*), which stands at the point of the medieval fortified gate (you can still see the remains of the original double drawbridge just outside). The tower – as you might have guessed – was used as an observation point to spot outbreaks of fire, although the watchmen were also on their guard for salesman trying to smuggle in non-Sopron wine. Maybe they'd been drinking it too, for while the lowest portion dates to the 13th century, the bulk of the Baroque form was built after a fire of 1676. A spiralling (and frequently congested) set of 200 steps takes you up to a viewing gallery. The archway leading through the tower's base is known as the **Gate of Fidelity**, a reference to the 1921 referendum at which the citizens voted to remain on Hungarian soil. The carved statues above represent the burghers praying to the allegorical figure of Hungaria, and were the work of Zsigmond Kisfaludy Strobl in 1928.

Much of the cobbled square dates from the aftermath of the 1676 fire, but the medieval layout is unchanged. In the centre is the Baroque **Trinity Column**, commissioned by two residents (shown kneeling at the base) to celebrate surviving the plague of 1695–1701. It's an extravagant affair and the first example of a corkscrew column – like a piece of twisted rope – in eastern Europe. Every Sunday it is kept company by stall-holders selling their wares at an **antiques market** (*open 08.00–16.00*). Immediately to your left after passing through the arch is the Eclectic **town hall** (*Fő tér 1*), constructed as part of the millennial celebrations in 1896. Opposite that, the **Storno House** (*Fő tér 8*) had a Renaissance face before its 18th-century Baroque overhaul, and King Mátyás stayed inside in 1442–43 while he made an attack on nearby Vienna. It was also the venue for concerts by Ferenc Liszt in 1840 and 1881. In 1872 it became the residence of Ferenc Storno, who started life as a chimney sweep but whose extraordinary creative talent allowed him to become one of the period's leading art restorers. He re-styled many churches in Transdanubia (including Pannonhalma Abbey) in accordance with contemporary wishes for aesthetic unity, and he's therefore something of a pariah to architectural historians. He (and his offspring after him) went about hoarding paintings, furniture and weaponry, and these objects form the basis for the **Storno Collection** (✆ *99 311327; adult/concessions 600/300Ft; open Tue–Sun Apr–Sep 10.00–18.00, Oct–Mar 10.00–14.00*). The intriguing exhibition includes a display of local history on the ground floor; foreign visitors can listen to a tape that explains the contents of each room.

The **Pharmacy Museum** (*Patikamúzeum; Fő tér 2;* ✆ *99 311327; adult/concessions 300/150Ft; open Tue–Sun Apr 1–Sep 30 10.00–18.00, Oct 1–Mar 31 10.00–14.00*) contains the original furnishings of a 19th-century chemist's shop. There is a valuable collection of medical books, as well as the superstitious trappings of a 17th-century apothecary's art – including an amulet to protect the bearer from the evil eye. The **Fabricius House** (*Fő tér 6;* ✆ *99 311327; adult/concessions 400/200Ft; open Tue–Sun Apr–Sep 10.00–18.00, Oct–Mar 10.00–14.00*) takes its name from the early 19th-century mayor and owner; he was friends with the poet Petőfi, who once changed his clothes inside after stealing away from his barracks to attend one of Liszt's concerts. Archaeologists uncovered a Roman bathhouse in the basement, and the Gothic cellar contains a display of other finds from Scarbantia – statues, sarcophagi and gravestones. At the rear of the building are even earlier finds from the time of the Illyrian and Celtic tribes, while at the front are pieces of 17th- and 18th-century furniture.

The **Kossow House** (*Fő tér 4*) has received some majestic guests in its time; Emperor Ferdinand II stayed in 1622 and 1625 when parliament met in Sopron, and Ferdinand III, Leopold I and Prince Charles of Lorraine all rested their heads inside during the 17th century, the latter while readying himself for the siege of Buda in 1684.

### Templom utca, Orsolya tér and Új utca

Templom utca leaves the southern side of Fő tér, passing to the right of the so-called **Goat Church** (*Kecske templom; Templom utca 1*). The Gothic church was built by the Franciscans in around 1280, supposedly from the proceeds of treasure unearthed by a foraging goat. Several sessions of the Hungarian Diet were convened in the church during the 16th and 17th centuries, and among the three coronations it witnessed was that of Ferdinand III in 1625. The southern wall bears the Kapisztrán pulpit from which the Franciscan monk – who fought alongside János Hunyadi in the famous victory at Nándorfehérvár in 1456 (see *Discovering Buda*, page 145) – is said to have called for Holy War against the Turks. The side altars were carved by Ferenc Storno (see above) in 1852. The tiny attached Gothic **Chapter House** (*Káptalanterem;* ✆ *99 523768; open May–Sep Tue–Sun 10.00–12.00 & 14.00–17.00*) – just 5m² – served as the prayer house for the monastery, and subsequently as a burial chamber. It is adorned with fragments of medieval frescoes, as well as a ceiling painted by Dorfmeister in 1779.

A former Esterházy mansion now holds the collections of two adjacent museums. The **Central Mining Museum** (*Központi Bányászati Múzeum; Templom utca 2;* ✆ *99 312667; adult/concessions 300/150Ft; open Tue–Sun Apr 1–Oct 31 10.00–18.00, Nov 1–Mar 31 10.00–16.00*) focuses upon the history of digging in the Carpathian Basin. There's a reconstruction of part of a 20th-century mine shaft, and displays of earlier medieval and Stone-Age mining methods. Next door, the **Museum of Forestry** (*Erdészeti Múzeum; Templom utca 4;* ✎ *99 338870; adult/concessions 200/100Ft; open Thu–Tue May 1–Sep 30 13.00–18.00, Oct 1–Apr 30 10.00–13.00*) has the tools of 19th- and 20th-century woodsman; perhaps of more interest is the building's history, however, for it was here that the Allied representatives made their final judgement on the results of the 1921 referendum, and Sopron stayed Magyar. Also interesting is the 17th-century **Bezerédj House** (*Templom utca 6*), where Liszt – who spread himself thinly in Sopron – performed at a private gathering; afterwards there was a rather unbecoming spectacle as some of the ladies fought over one of his gloves.

Midway along Templom utca is the **Lutheran church**, built in 1782 after József II had issued his edict of religious tolerance and now frequently used for concerts. The tower wasn't added until the 1860s. The **National Lutheran Collection** (*Templom utca 12;* ✎ *99 523002; adult/concessions 100/50Ft; open Apr–Sep Tue–Thu 10.00–13.00, Fri–Sun 10.00–15.00*) tells the history of the Lutherans and has documents dating back to the 16th century.

Towards the southern end of Templom utca is the **Körmendi-Csák Gallery** (*Templom utca 18–19;* ✎ *99 524012; www.kormendigaleria.hu; entrance free; open Tue–Sun 10.00–18.00 – telephone in advance*), a collection of modern fine art from the mid 20th century onwards. Turning to the left brings you into **Orsolya tér**, with the Maria Fountain that once graced the courtyard of the Franciscan monastery before being moved here in the 1930s. The **Roman Catholic church** occupies the site of a wooden-steepled church where Maria Theresa celebrated mass during a visit in 1773. The current Gothic version dates to the 19th century, although it was reconstructed after being bombed in World War II. An Ursuline (Orsolya) convent was also built in the square in the 1860s, and its oratory (to the church's right) holds the **Roman Catholic Ecclesiastical Collection** (*Orsolya tér 2;* ✎ *99 312221; admission free; open May–Oct Mon, Thu, Sat 10.00–16.00*).

Pop north up Új utca and on the left you'll see the **Old Synagogue** (*Ó Zsinagóga; Új utca 22–24;* ✎ *99 311327; adult/concessions 300/150Ft; open Tue–Sun May 1–Sep 30 10.00–18.00, Oct 10.00–14.00*). This street – formerly Zsidó (Jew) utca – was the Jewish quarter from as early as the 13th century (up until the Jews were banished in 1526 after being accused of plotting with the Turks). The Gothic synagogue was built around 1300; a corridor leads to the main hall, containing the base of the original pulpit and an alcove bearing traces of vine motifs. Opposite is the New Synagogue (*Új Zsinagóga; Új utca 11*), which was founded in 1350 as place of private prayer for a wealthy Viennese banker.

## Széchenyi tér

The southern end of Templom utca joins Széchenyi tér, at the far corner of which is a late-Baroque **Dominican church and cloister**, whose main body was completed in 1725 and the twin clock towers added 50 years later. The Neoclassical **Széchenyi Palace** (*Széchenyi tér 1–2*) ranged along the square's eastern side bears a plaque to István Széchenyi ('the greatest Hungarian') but it should perhaps bear testimony to his poor, overshadowed father; some of Ferenc's massive stash of books and maps were held here, later to become the core of the National Library that he founded (and which is now in Buda's Castle District).

## Beyond the Belváros

Moving away slightly from Sopron's medieval hub, there are plenty of other sights dotted around. To the southwest of Széchenyi tér is the **Ethnographic Museum** (*Neprajzi Kiállítása; Csatkai utca 9;* ✎ *99 510100; adult/concessions 200/100Ft; open May 1–Sep 30 Tue–Sun 10.00–18.00*), at the end of the long and leafy Deák tér. Inside are the tools and products of various artisan workshops and reconstructions of a pub in Harka and a dry mill from Csapod.

Draw a line diagonally to the northeast of the Belváros and you'll hit the **Zettl-Langer Collection** (*Balfi út 11;* ☎ *99 311136; adult 250Ft; open Tue–Sun 10.00–12.00*) on the other side of the Ikva Stream; like Ferenc Storno (see page 492), Gusztáv Zettl (1852–1917) was a young working-class man with artistic aspirations. While staying loyal to the family vinegar business, he also began collecting antiquities and fine art. Subsequent generations continued in the same vein, and the furniture, china, books and weapons are now on display in the family house.

A short distance away, across Dorfmeister utca, is the **Church of the Holy Spirit** (*Szent Lélek templom; Szent Lélek utca*), built in 1782 on the site of a 15th-century Gothic predecessor; it contains a flabbergastingly ornate altar and frescoes by Dorfmeister. Cut up Dorfmeister utca to Szent Mihály utca, rising up to Sopron's highest point. At the top is the Neo-Gothic **St Mihály Church**, originally 13th-century and reconstructed in the 15th century (when King Mátyás attended the consecration). At that time it is said to have been stuffed with up to 20 altar pieces, but much was destroyed in the 17th century. In the churchyard is the compact **St Jakab Chapel**, the earliest of the city's structures and showing elements of the transition between Romanesque and Gothic architectural styles.

Descend the hill again, and walk northwest a little further to Bécsi út. The **Bakery Museum** (*Pékház & Múzeum; Bécsi út 5;* ☎ *99 311327; adult/concessions 300/150Ft; open Tue–Sun 10.00–14.00*) is located in a 16th-century baker's, and shows the grain store and preparation area, the shop where the bread was sold, and photos of the old bakers themselves. The living quarters are to the right of the entrance gate.

## Other activities

The **Vadon Equestrian Club** (*Sopron-Ágfalva, Magyar utca 25;* ☎ *99 330925;* e *lovasklub@vadongroup.hu; www.lovasklub.vadongroup.hu*) is situated in the village of Ágfalva, 4km west of Sopron. It organises horse-riding tours and camps, as well as horse shows and other programmes. It also has a guesthouse with 14 rooms. There are regular buses here from Sopron, and the village has a small railway station. If you want a dip, the **Lővér Baths** (*Lővér körút 82; tel 99 510964; adult/concessions 600/400Ft; open Mon–Fri 06.00–20.00, Sat–Sun 09.00–18.00*) have indoor and outdoor pools (the latter open summer only); local buses 2 and 15 stop 100m from the entrance.

The **Lővér Hills** to the south and southwest of Sopron feature forests and meadows, and offer good walking and hiking terrain. Head for the Bio-Sport Hotel (see page 499) from where you can pick up several trails, some of which go via the Károly Lookout Tower to the west. The hills fall under the auspices of the Sopron Landscape Preserve Area; the *Sopron környéke* (Kárpátia, 1:40,000) map shows all the hill paths, and should be available from Sopron's Tourinform.

## Festivals and events

Liszt was born in Sopron County and played on several occasions in the city, and it is inevitable that there are important festivals devoted to culture and the arts. Sopron was the first place to join Budapest in holding a Spring Festival (*Mar*), when there are performances of theatre, music and dance. The main events of Sopron Festive Weeks (*Jun–Jul*) take place in the Quarry Theatre at Fertőrákos (see page 495), but there are also concerts and folkloric exhibitions in the city squares. Other highlights are the festivals of wine (*May*) and beer (*Aug*), and a Harvest Celebration (*Sep*).

## Excursions from Sopron
### Fertőrákos

Travel 12km northeast of Sopron and you'll reach Fertőrákos. A break in the rushes offers access to the only recreational area on Lake Fertő, and the **strand** (*open daily May 1–31 & Aug 24–Sep 15 09.00–20.00, Jun 1–Aug 23 09.00–21.00; adult/concessions 400/260Ft*) has a grassy sunbathing area, a number of *bufés* and water craft for hire. It is also possible to catch a Drescher Line **ferry** (☎ *99 355361; adult/child 3,000/1,500Ft rtn; Jul 1–Oct 15 daily 10.00, 12.00, 14.00 & 16.00*) from here across to Morbisch in Austria. However, the village is known widely for its rock rather than its water. The legacy of a Pannonian Sea that covered the area 15 million years ago is a rich seam of limestone, formed of dead fishy matter that settled on the seabed. Travel back 2,000 years, and the Romans were mining the stone (which is of a good colour and readily carved) and using it to build Scarbantia (Sopron); in later centuries it formed building blocks for cities including Vienna. The **quarry** (*Fertőrákos kőfejtő; Fő utca 1; ☎ 99 355026; adult/concessions 300/125Ft; open daily Feb, Nov & Dec 08.00–16.00, Mar–Apr & Oct 08.00–17.00, May–Sep 08.00–19.00*), at the northern end of the village, operated until World War II, after which artificial materials like concrete became the vogue. In the 1970s it was decided to make use of the space by establishing a cave theatre, and this now provides a quite unique setting for concerts, theatre and opera, particularly during the Sopron Festival Weeks in summer. The steep quarry sides also form a popular nesting side for birds, and a study path runs around the top.

Moving down from the quarry along Fő utca (which stretches the length of the village), other sights to look out for are the **Crystal Museum** (*Fő utca 99; adult/concessions 200/100Ft; open May 1–Nov 1 daily 09.00–19.00*), with its collection of Hungarian minerals, the 18th-century Rococo **Bishop's Palace** (*Fő utca 153*), a 16th-century public pillory (the only one of its kind in Hungary) and the **Mithras Chapel** (a Roman cave temple near the border – follow Meggyesi utca to the right from the top of the village for 2km). If you need **accommodation**, there are regular signs advertising free rooms (*szoba kiadó*). Alternatively, Huber Panzió (*Fertő utca 1; ☎ 99 355149; www.reise.info.hu/huber*) is a good-looking guesthouse with lovely gardens. You can **eat** Hungarian specialities and grills at Puskás Sörkert (*Fő utca 175; ☎ 99 355506; mains 850–2,200Ft, avg 1,500Ft; open daily 10.00–23.00*), which has a large garden and is the main place for food and beer. There is live music at the weekends. **Buses** from Sopron (up to nine daily) stop at the strand car park, and continue down Fő utca.

## Nagycenk

To the southeast of Sopron at the juncture of roads 84 and 85 is Nagycenk, site of the plain Baroque mansion of the Széchenyi family. The achievements of Ferenc Széchenyi – founder of Budapest's National Library – were far from inconsiderable, but it was his son István (1791–1860) who became the leading light of the reform era and earned the flattering tag of 'the greatest Hungarian'. Among the visible monuments to his progressive vision are Budapest's Chain Bridge (the city's first permanent river crossing) and the Hungarian Academy of Sciences (towards which he donated a year's income; see page 156), but perhaps of even more significance were his investment in the railway network and his river-regulation schemes that reclaimed vast areas of swampland in the Great Plain for agriculture. While his practical reformatory zeal – influenced greatly by what he saw during visits to Britain – was unsurpassed, in political terms he urged gradual, evolutionary change and attempted unsuccessfully to put the breaks on the revolutionary stance of Batthyány's government of 1848. He watched the increasingly radical turn of events with the horror of a helpless witness to a train crash, and the pressure triggered a total nervous breakdown. After several years spent in a Viennese asylum, he returned to his political writings; however, he never fully emerged from his black hole and shot his considerable brains out in 1860. His **mausoleum** (*adult/concessions 200/100Ft; open Tue–Sun 10.00–18.00*) stands in the village cemetery of the Neo-Romanesque, Ybl-designed **St István Church** (*Széchenyi tér*) – whose organ was played once by Liszt. Its Neoclassical form bears a gilded allegory of Hope – which guided Széchenyi for much of his life but appeared a treacherous mistress by the end. The supreme irony, of course, is that hope returned with the Compromise just seven short years after the count's death.

The **Széchenyi Mansion** itself stands just under 1km to the northeast, beside Road 85. While the horse-shoe-shaped building is hardly sober, it lacks the feudal extravagance of palaces at Gödöllő or Fertőd and is wholly in tune with one so immersed in the middle-class, anti-aristocratic ethic. Two decades before serfdom was abolished, István actually gave over a considerable area of his estate to serfs, who had no land for themselves. However, that didn't mean he did away with the trappings of comfort, and the mansion was furnished with cutting-edge technology – including flushing toilets. (The villagers also benefited from the count's passion for English innovation, and Nagycenk was the first settlement with gas lamps from 1815.) Built at the end of the 18th century for Antal Széchenyi, and enlarged upon by Mihály Pollack in 1838, the mansion burned down during World War II but was faithfully restored and is beautifully maintained. The **Széchenyi Memorial Museum** (*Kiscenki út 3;* ✆ *99 360023; adult/concessions 500/250Ft; open Tue–Sun Apr 1–Oct 31 10.00–18.00, rest of yr 10.00–14.00*) holds furniture, documents, personal belongings and portraits of the Széchenyi family, as well as an exhibition devoted to István's practical achievements. The history of Hungary's industrial development is also laid bare, and there's a collection of coins. The eastern wing contains a stud, the western 'Red Mansion' the Széchenyi Castle Hotel (✆ *99 360061;* e *kastelyszallo.nagycenk@syneco.hu; 19 rooms; sgl €85, dbl €100; guests can visit museum free*) and restaurant, and a 3km-long avenue of lime trees leads away from the whole shebang.

## FERTŐ-HANSÁG NATIONAL PARK

Jutting between Sopron and Fertőd, the 23,600ha national park was founded in 1991 to protect the Hungarian section of Lake Fertő (which straddles the Austrian border, and is known on the other side as Neusiedler See), the remaining marshes and bogs of the Hanság (which lies around the south of the lake), and the most valuable natural parts of the Répce valley (as it runs above Csorna and Kapuvár).

The shallow **Lake Fertő** is the second-largest wetland in Hungary (the fifth-largest in Europe), and the westernmost alkaline steppe lake. It has receded on several occasions, and this indirectly led to the Austrian name for it; people built houses on the dry bed in 1868 but they were forced to up sticks to a new settlement ('*neue Siedlung*') when the water returned four years later. An important stopover site for migratory birds, the lake regularly hosts over 20,000 water-loving flappers – mainly geese, ducks and shorebirds – both during migration periods and in winter. (Some good towers – such as that by the road from Fertőújlak (at the lake's southeastern tip) to Mekszikópuszta, and at the Rábca Stream near Bősárkány – offer birders excellent views of the area, and passages have been cut through the reeds for those with guides in rowing boats.) The plains around the shores are filled with alkaline grasslands, rich in species of salt-tolerant plant. Among these are the Pannonic lepidium, *Puccinellia limosa*, and the Pannonic salt-land cyperus, while the surrounding hillsides are home to rare Pannonian steppe vegetation.

One of the missions of those cultivating the national park is to preserve the remains of what was once a massive area of peat landscape (depleted by human hand in the past through peat cutting and drainage). You will find peat forests, peat meadows and peat lakes, all subject to restoration projects (notably in Bősárkány, on the shores of the Rábca Stream near Csorna). As a consequence of such a conservation drive, species associated with peat are re-colonising the area. The smallest piece of the park's jigsaw is the **River Répce**; a section of its course harbours swamp meadows and one of the largest swamp forests in Hungary.

Cross Kiscenki utca and head up Hársfa sor for the **Kastély narrow-gauge station**, which runs summer weekend journeys northward to Fertőboz (*Apr 5–Sep 28 Sat–Sun & hols 10.10, 11.28, 14.00, 15.25 & 17.45; adult sgl/rtn 150/300Ft, child 75/150Ft*), whose Gloriette Tower of 1802 provides views of Lake Fertő. (There are also trains to the nearer Barátság, for which tickets cost the same.) Special trains are available on weekdays (↘ 99 517384 *a week in advance*), and you can actually have a go at driving the locomotive. Behind the station is an open-air **Train Museum** (*free to visit*).

There are very regular **buses** to Nagycenk from Sopron, and services too from Győr (passing through Csorna and Kapuvár on the way); the bus stop is near the mansion. Nagycenk's main **railway station** (near the church and mausoleum) is on the line between Sopron and Szombathely.

# FERTŐD

The village of Fertőd, 30km southeast of Sopron, is on the map because of the Esterházy Palace. The Esterházy family came to prominence during the 17th century, and in 1711 a hereditary dukedom was bestowed upon Pál Esterházy – palatine since 1681 – as reward for his loyalty to the Habsburgs. His grandson, Miklós 'the Magnificent' Esterházy, built the mansion in 1766 as a conscious effort to match the opulent lifestyle of the Habsburg emperor; his yearly income was enormous, and he is famously said to have boasted 'What the emperor can afford, I can afford'. It is undoubtedly the country's leading piece of Rococo architecture, and guests including Goethe were blown away by its high-blown

Herds of ancient indigenous breeds (grey cattle, racka sheep and water buffalo) are also kept in the park, as well as ethnographic displays recording the lives of the people who once lived here – including marsh dwellers and fishermen, who wove traps from the lakeside rushes. While South Hanság can be visited freely along marked walking routes, access to the reed beds and the immediate area of the lake is generally only permitted with a guide; between May and September, however, a 6km canoe trail is opened for adults. A month-long bird-ringing camp is also held annually in the Madárvárta (Birdwatcher's House) to the south of the lake.

The place to start is the **Fertő-Hanság National Park visitor centre** (*Sarród, Rév-Kócsagvár;* ↘ 99 537620; e *attila.fersch@ktm.x400gw.itb.hu; www.ferto-hansag.hu*) – known as Egret Castle (Kócsagvár) – located just northwest of Fertőd at the park boundary. The centre organises three-hour tours (*Wed & Sat departing 09.00 in summer; adult 2,500Ft*) of the park's restricted areas. The tours either take in the sodic waters, grasslands and puszta of the eastern shore, the reedbeds of the western shore (by canoe) or the wetland forest and marsh of the Hanság. (Note that sometimes these leave from Öntésmajor, where you'll also find an exhibition on the region's flora and fauna.) There are study trails that you can join from here. You can reach Lake Fertő by **bus** from Sopron, and Sarród has a **railway station** on a branch line from Fertőszentmiklós (which is itself on the Sopron line). A more pleasant way to get there, however, is by joining the **cycle route** that runs all the way around the lake. On the Hungarian side you can take in Fertőrákos and Fertőd on your journey along the southern shore; if you wish to pass over the border to cycle the Austrian portion too, you can do so between April and November only (and will need your passport for the checkpoint at Mörbisch, just north of Fertőrákos). Both bicycles and canoes are available for hire at the visitor centre, and there is **accommodation** (*dbl 5,500Ft*) too. Pick up a copy of the *Fertő-Hánság Nemzeti Park* (Paulus, 1:60,000) map to get a clearer picture of the nature trails and birdwatching towers.

## LONGING AND SKULLDUGGERY

Despite the excellent pay and regular work, Haydn and the musicians and other artists of Esterháza weren't wholly content. They were required to stage as many as three opera performances and two concerts a week for the ducal court and this meant they were kept from their families for long periods. In 1772, Count Miklós unexpectedly announced he was to extend his stay in Esterháza for a few weeks (thus postponing the date when the musicians could leave). This inspired Haydn to write a piece in which the instruments gradually fall silent, one by one – his *Farewell Symphony*. The symphony was performed in front of the count, and as each player finished he blew out his candle and left the room. Miklós wasn't stupid, recognising the unhappiness and homesickness of the orchestra, and ordered them home the following day.

Haydn died in 1809 and was laid to rest at a simple funeral attended by Viennese aristocrats and French generals. In 1820, however, the coffin was opened while being moved for re-burial in Kismarton and while Haydn's wig was inside the skull on which it should have perched was not. They hunted high and low, and eventually the culprit was uncovered – a Karl Rosenbaum, who had stolen the head for scientific research. It wasn't until 1954 that the skull was finally reunited with its body in the mausoleum at the hill church in Kismarton.

elegance – as well as the lustrous parties hosted by Miklós, characterised by fairy lights, pomp, ceremony and the duke in his diamond-studded robe. What you see now is actually but a part of the complex as it appeared in its prime. Taking the palace at Versailles for its inspiration, 'Esterháza' (as it was then known) was set in 3,000ha of grounds filled with statues, fountains and temples, an oriental pagoda hung with wind chimes, a puppet theatre and an opera house where Maria Theresa enjoyed a performance in 1773. The opera house was particularly significant because Haydn lived on the estate for 30 years and the majority of his pieces were first played within its walls. After the death of Miklós in 1790, the palace rapidly fell away (just a few years later parts of it were being used as stables for livestock) and it served as a hospital under the Russians. The restoration job began in the 1950s, and is still ongoing.

### Getting there and away

There are **bus stops** directly outside the entrance to the palace (on Bartók Béla utca), with regular services to Sopron, Balf and Kapuvár. The nearest **railway station** is at the end of Fő utca in Fertőszéplak (a couple of kilometres to the west), which sits on a branch running from Fertőszentmiklós (on the Sopron–Győr main line). Fertőszentmiklós is itself around 4km south of Fertőd.

### Information

**Tourinform** Joseph Haydn utca 3; ➲ 99 370544; e fertod@tourinform.hu. Shares building with Kastélykert Restaurant. *Open Jun 15–Sep 15 Mon–Fri 09.00–18.00, Sat–Sun 09.00–17.00, rest of yr 09.00–17.00.*

### Where to stay and eat

**Esterházy Kastély** (21 rooms) Joseph Haydn utca 2; ➲ 99 537640. On the second floor of a wing of the palace, this hotel is far cheaper and less luxurious than you might expect. Rooms have wash basins, but toilets and showers are shared and b/fast is not included. Note that the reception is only open Mon–Fri 08.00–14.00 and Sat–Sun 09.00–10.00. *Dbl 5,500Ft, triple 7,000Ft, room for 4 8,000Ft, dorm (for 14) 14,000Ft.*

**Dori Hotel & Camping** Pomogyi út 1; te: 99 370838; e dorimotel@axelero.hu; www.hotels.hu/dori. Behind the Kastélykert, the Dori certainly stands out with its asymmetrical timber chalet of a hotel. The rooms inside are of a good standard. The campsite is lovely, and includes wooden bungalows; the site has its own restaurant (*open 07.00–22.00 daily*). *Hotel: sgl €32, dbl €48, triple €62, apt €90; bungalows (for 1–7): €33–80; camping: tent/caravan €3/5, plus adult/concessions €3/2. Hotel open Apr 15–Sep 30, campsite May 15–Sep 15.*
**Gránátos** Joseph Haydn utca 1; ↘ 99 370944; www.rabensteiner.hu. Opposite the palace entrance, the Gránátos (together with the Kastélykert) was once the lodgings for the grenadiers who rode the 100 horses of the Esterházy stables. The restaurant serves Hungarian food (inc b/fast); in terms of cuisine and price, there's little difference between it and the Kastélykert, but the latter shades things with marginally more elegant surroundings. *Mains 900–1,850Ft, avg 1,400Ft; open 09.00–22.00 daily.*
**Kastélykert** Joseph Haydn utca 3; ↘ 99 349418; e polgarmester@axelero.hu. Next to the Gránátos, this restaurant and café serves some international dishes but its menu is primarily Hungarian in flavour. *Mains 800–1,600Ft, avg 1,350Ft; open 09.00–22.00 daily.*

## The Esterházy Palace

The horse-shoe-shaped Esterházy Palace (*Esterházy-kastély; Joseph Haydn utca 2;* ↘ *99 537640*) is one of the top-three Baroque-Rococo edifices in the country. So important was it as a centre for European nobility that the post-coach to Vienna had its terminus here. When Maria Theresa visited in 1773, the French-style park was adorned with 24,000 Chinese lanterns, and the festivities culminated in a firework display whose touch paper was lit by the empress herself. Count Miklós presented her with a sleigh encrusted with precious stones (now on display at the Imperial Palace in Vienna) and salt was laid on the road so that she could ride it away.

The family occupied the ground-floor wings and above them were rooms to accommodate the servants and the regular flow of guests. At the end of World War II, many of the furnishings were removed, but some period furniture and restored wood panels are on display in the **Esterházy Palace Museum** (*adult 1,200/concessions 600Ft; Mar 15–Oct 31 daily 10.00–18.00, rest of yr Fri–Sun 10.00–16.00*) in the palace's central portion (much of which was originally given over to ceremonial occasions). Around 30kg of gold was used for the gilding on the walls of the 26 rooms open to the public. The ground level includes the apartments of the count and countess, featuring Chinese-style paintings and furniture, together with the reception room (**Sala Terrena**) whose floor of Italian marble was heated from beneath. Haydn worked for several decades in the **Concert Hall** on the first floor – it was here that the *Farewell Symphony* was first performed in 1772 – and there is a display of documents relating to his life and work. The **Gala Room** has red marble fireplaces, Flemish tapestries and the best of the mansion's frescoes – a ceiling painting by the Austrian J I Milldorfer of the *Glory of Apollo*; wherever you stand, you appear to be in the path of the chariot's charging horses. The corner room of the apartments where Maria Theresa stayed includes a portrait of her by the court painter Glunck.

Moving outside, it is noticeable that the mustard-coloured façade is considerably less vibrant than it appears in the multitude of images that adorn the country's tourist literature. The **Music House**, 300m to the west of the palace, is where Haydn lived; there is a commemorative tablet by the sculptor Jenő Bory. Behind the palace French gardens stretch away as far as the village of Fertőszentmiklós. The second floor of one of the palace's wings now holds a **hotel** (see opposite). Regular **concerts** are staged in the palace's Concert Hall between June and September. Look out in particular for the Haydn Festival of Strings (*Jul*) and the Haydn Esterháza Festival (*Aug/Sep*); they book up quickly – for tickets, call 99 537640 or contact Escort Tourist (*Sopron, Orsolya tér 4;* ↘ *99 320670*).

# Lake Balaton

The 'Hungarian sea' in the middle of Transdanubia is where Hungarians come to play. They're not the only ones. During the communist period, the lake represented a convenient meeting place for those divided by the Berlin Wall, and Germans continue to provide a decent chunk of the tourist revenue. With a length of 77km and a total area of 600km², Balaton is the largest lake in central Europe, and its shallow depth (particularly on the southern side) – on average, just two–three metres – means both that it is relatively family-friendly and that it warms up quickly in the sun. The water harbours ample stocks of fish such as carp, bream and the native *fogas* (pike-perch), and is a popular place for windsurfing and rowing. Motorboats are prohibited, so you will not find yourself swamped in a waterskiier's wash; instead wakeboarding – where the skiier is pulled around a circuit by a mechanised pulley – is very much *de rigeur*.

There's a distinct north-south divide where the lake's concerned. The southern shore is the favourite with the water-baby masses intent on sun-worshipping, soaking and wakeboarding, and where the real concentration of hotels, bars and clubs is to be found. The southern resorts attract those with young children and the party crowd, and Siófok – stretching for a full 15km – is the brash leader of the pack. On the other side of the lake, the reeds, volcanic hills and cooler water make for an atmosphere less fevered: Keszthely is a university town that has a life beyond the tourist season; Balatonfüred has always taken its water with a graceful air; Tihany and Badacsony have stunning scenery and wonderful walking terrain. The northern side also boasts the best of the wines.

It used to be the case that the main season at Balaton lasted over three months, and the water is certainly a pleasant enough temperature in late spring and early autumn. However, the hotels and restaurants have been flogging the cash cow with increasing severity, and it is noticeable that the season appears to have narrowed as many potential visitors look for cheaper beach holidays elsewhere. Despite that, the most popular resorts heave with bodies in July and August, and you'd be wise to come outside those months if you can possibly help it.

Balaton is easily reached by train from Budapest Déli, and by bus or train from other towns in Transdanubia. Buses and trains are convenient links between resorts on the same shore, but the ferry is the way to go if you want to get to the other side – indeed even if you don't, it's a pleasant way of viewing the lake from a different angle. From April until October, ferries for foot passengers travel a route between Siófok, Balatonfüred, Tihany and Balatonföldvár, and between Fonyód and Badacsony; during the high-season months these run more often, and there are additional services to other resorts around the lake. There is only one crossing available for cars, that between Tihany and Szántód (*Mar–Nov*). See page 42 for details of the new airport near Keszthely.

# SIÓFOK

Siófok is the biggest and baddest of Balaton's resorts, a writhing mass of eating, drinking and basking bodies in the height of summer. It's explosion came after the railway line from Budapest Déli reached here in the late 20th century, and allowed those from the capital to come along and let off steam. There's little that will stimulate you culturally here; instead this is the place to try your hand at some watersports and enjoy a flourishing night scene. The town is also making a conscious effort to market itself as a centre of health tourism – an image rather undermined by the many bleary eyes you'll encounter of a morning – and there are several new wellness hotels.

## Getting there, away and around

Both the **bus station** and main **railway station** (there are several to the east and west of the centre on the same line) are just to the northeast of the Tourinform, on Váradi Adolf tér. Trains run westward through Siófok to the other shore resorts and on to Nagykanizsa (15 daily), and eastward to Székesfehérvár (four) and Budapest (mainly Déli; up to 21 in summer). Buses are less regular, apart from those to Kaposvár; among the services are those to Budapest (three direct daily, three via Székesfehérvár), Hévíz (four), Pécs (seven), Szeged (three), Szekszárd (seven), Tatabánya (three) and Veszprém (ten). Mahart **ferries** leave from the pier at the point where the lake and the Sió Canal meet, and the ticket office is near by on Krúdy sétány; between late March and late October, there are up to seven services to Balatonfüred and Tihany.

If you want a **taxi**, try Bokros (✆ 84 *317713*). The Gold Coast is served by local bus 2 and by Szabadifürdő railway station, the Silver Coast by buses 1, 7 and 5 and by trains to Balatonszéplak felső.

## Information and other practicalities

**Bike hire** Szigliget utca 7. Bikes for 1,500Ft/day, 5,600Ft/week.You can also hire a variety of mopeds, pedal bikes and cars from the car park on Kinizsi Pál utca. *Open daily 09.00–21.00.*

**Ibusz** Fő utca 176; ✆ 84 510720. Programmes, tours and private rooms from 7,000Ft. On 1st floor of shopping arcade. *Open Jun 1–Aug 31 Mon–Fri 08.00–18.00, Sat 08.00–13.00, rest of yr Mon–Fri 08.00–16.00.*

**Internet** There are terminals at the Big Shots Pub (see below) and Planet Café (*Kele utca 5;* ✆ *84 311416; open Mon–Fri 10.00–20.00, Sat 10.00–16.00*).

**Listings magazine** *Kaposi Est*

**Reisebüro** Petőfi sétány 26; www.juliusferien.de. Main office of this company that arranges apts and private rooms, from basic to luxury. *Prices start at 12,000Ft (apt for 4).*

**Siótour** Szabadság tér 6; ✆ 84 310900; www.siotour.hu. Accommodation and tour bookings. *Open Mon–Fri 08.00–18.30, Sat 09.00–18.30, Sun 09.00–12.00 & 15.00–18.00 in summer, Mon–Fri 08.00–16.00 rest of yr.*

**Tourinform** Víztorony, Szabadság tér; ✆ 84 310117; e tourinform@mail.datanet.hu. Housed at the bottom of the ivy-clad water tower. *Open Jun 15–Sep 15 Mon–Sat 08.00–20.00, Sun 09.00–18.00, rest of yr Mon–Fri 09.00–16.00, Sat 09.00–12.00.*

## Where to stay

There are many hotels and campsites in Siófok, but the resort gets very crowded in high season and bookings are recommended.

**Aranypart Camping** Szent László utca 183–185; ✆ 84 353399; email siotour.aranypart@axelero.hu. Huge site with camping pitches and 70 bungalows (most complete with kitchenettes, bathrooms, etc); you can hire a host of contraptions for getting about – among them electric scooters and mopeds. One of several campsites by the Gold Coast. Alight at the Szabadifürdő railway station if you are coming from Budapest, or take bus 2 from the centre. *Bungalows: class I (for 4–7) €100–140, class II (for 3–4) €55–75; open Apr 18–Sep 22.*

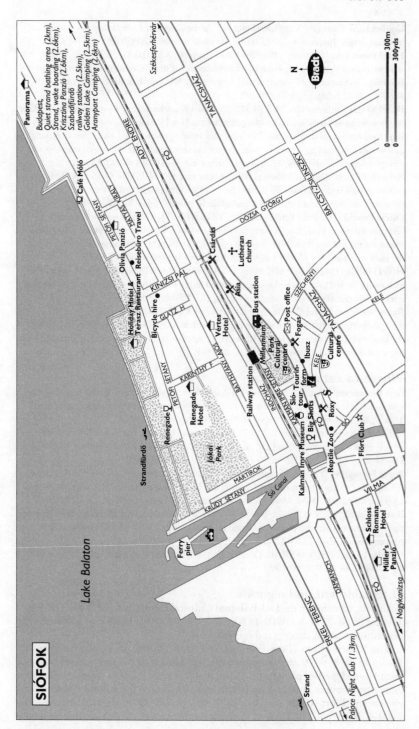

SIÓFOK

Lake Balaton

Budapest,
Quiet strand bathing area (2km),
Strand, wake boarding (2.6km),
Krisztina Panzió (2.6km),
Szabadifürdő
railway station (2.5km),
Golden Lake Camping (2.5km),
Aranypart Camping (2.6km)

Panorama

Café Mólo

Székesfehérvár

PETŐFI SÉTÁNY

MÁTYÁS KIRÁLY

Olivia Panzió

ADY ENDRE

FŐ

TANÁCSHÁZ

BAICS-ZSILINSZKY

DÓZSA GYÖRGY

Lutheran church

Csárdás

Holiday Hotel &
Terasz Restaurant Reisebüro Travel

KINIZSI PÁL

GLATZ H.

Bicycle hire

KARINTHY F. LAJOS

Asia

Bus station

Vértes Hotel

Post office

KELE

SZÉCHENYI

Strandfürdő

Renegade

PETŐFI SÉTÁNY

Renegade
Hotel

BATTHYÁNYI LAJOS

Railway station

KODÁLY SÉTÁNY

KÁLMÁN IMRE SÉTÁNY

Millennium Park
Cultural
Centre

Fogas

Ibusz

KELE

TANÁCSHÁZ

Cultural
centre

Jókai
Park

MÁRTÍROK

Sió- Tourin-
tour form

Big Shots

FŐ

Roxy

SIÓ

Flört Club

Kálmán Imre Museum

Reptile Zoo

Ferry
pier

KRÚDY SÉTÁNY

Sió Canal

VILMA

Schloss
Romana
Hotel

Müller's
Panzió

FŐ

Nagykanizsa

ERKEL FERENC

DAMJANICH

Strand

Palace Night Club (1.3km)

N

Bradt

300m
300yds
0
0

**Golden Lake Camping** Szent László utca 183. At the Gold Coast; see Aranypart Camping for transport details. *Tent/caravan 1,200/2,000Ft, plus adult/concessions 1,200/700Ft.*

**Hotel Panoráma** (156 rooms) Beszédes József sétány 80; ⊠ 84 311638; e panoramahotel@axelero.hu. 4-star hotel with cheerful, if small, rooms (most of which have balconies). Swimming pool, sauna, jacuzzi, tennis court, bike rental. At the Gold Coast. *Sgl 14,000Ft, dbl 17,500Ft, apt (for 4) 30,000Ft.*

**Hotel Vértes** Batthyány utca 24; ⊠ 84 312422; e sales@hotelvertes.hu; www.hotelvertes.hu. One of 3 new wellness hotels in Siófok – the others are the Hotel Residence (*www.hotel-residence.hu*) and Hotel Azúr (*www.azurhotel.hu*). The Vértes has buildings with 2- and 4-star rooms. Among the facilities are a thermal pool, jacuzzi, fitness centre and sauna, and there are various massages and therapies on offer. *2-star sgl 14,000Ft, dbl 18,500Ft; 4-star sgl 26,000Ft, dbl 38,000Ft.*

**Krisztina Panzió** Siofók-fürdőtelep, Baross Gábor utca 6; ⊠ 84 352824. One of the cheapest pensions you'll find, with no-frills rooms (no TV or telephone). Located in the nearby resort to the east of the centre, and 5 mins from Szabadifürdő railway station. *Rooms 3,000Ft/pp.*

**Olivia Panzió** (11 rooms) Petőfi sétány 38; ⊠ 84 311105. The Olivia is run by Reisebüro, a company offering a broad range of apts (about which you can enquire at reception). The pension rooms are old-fashioned and plain, and too expensive. It might be worth negotiating on prices if the place isn't busy. *Dbl 20,000Ft, triple 24,000Ft, apt (for 4) 33,000Ft, b/fast 1,000Ft.*

**Hotel Holiday** (30 rooms) Petőfi sétány 3; ⊠ 84 538056; e holiday@enternet.hu. Good rooms, each with a decked balcony overlooking the strand (entry to which is free for guests). Its popular terrace restaurant also serves as a cocktail bar. *Sgl 17,000Ft, dbl 19,000Ft.*

**Renegade Sport Hotel** (26 rooms) Petőfi sétány 3; ⊠ 84 311506; renegadesporthotel@axelero.hu; www.renegadesporthotel.com. Don't be put off by its link with the lively pub across the road, for the Renegade's rooms are good and characterful, furnished with terracotta colours and stone-effect tiles. *Dbl 20,000Ft.*

## Where to eat and drink

**Asia Restaurant** Fő utca 93–95; ⊠ 84 312546. An elegant restaurant serving Thai and Chinese specialities. If you've a goodly appetite, you might find some of the portions slightly undersized. *Mains 1,200–5,200Ft, avg 2,200Ft; open 11.30–22.00 daily.*

**Café Móló** Szent István sétány 1; ⊠ 84 317617; www.cafemolo.hu. Funky beach-house café serving good Mediterranean food and excellent iced coffee. *Mains 1,400–3,000Ft, avg 1,450Ft; open May 15–Sep 15 Sun–Thu 12.00–02.00, Fri 12.00–04.00, Sat 12.00–05.00.*

**Fogas** Fő utca 184; ⊠ 84 311405. Specialises in fish, including freshwater specimens from Balaton (pike-perch, or fogas, in particular) and seafish including shark and calamari. Live music from 18.00. Opposite the railway station. *Mains 1,000–4,000Ft, avg 1,700Ft; open Mar–Nov 12.00–22.00 daily.*

**Roxy** Szabadság tér; ⊠ 84 306373. Bundles of character in this brick-walled restaurant and bar near the water tower. There are pizzas, pastas and Hungarian and German dishes in good portions. Also does b/fast. *Mains 1,400–2,800Ft, avg 1,700Ft; open 08.00–02.00 daily.*

**Csárdás** Fő utca 105; ⊠ 84 310642. Good traditional Hungarian restaurant. *Mains 1,200–2,300Ft, avg 1,500Ft; open 12.00–23.00 daily.*

## Entertainment and nightlife

Behind the water tower, the **Dél-Balatoni Cultural Centre** (*Fő tér 2;* ⊠ *84 311855; open Mon–Fri 08.00–20.00, Sat 08.00–18.00, Sun 10.00–18.00*) has temporary exhibitions and performances of folk dancing and operetta.

The **Palace Disco** (*Deák Ferenc sétány 2;* ⊠ *84 350698; www.palace.hu; open May 15–Sep 15 21.00–04.00 daily*) is situated 2km west of the centre, and features big-name guest DJs and themed party nights. A free bus runs there leaving from the water tower every hour between 21.00 and 24.00 (although you can also flag it down if it passes you elsewhere). **Flört Club** (*Sió utca 4;* ⊠ *06 20 333 3303; www.flort.hu; admission 2,000–4,500Ft; open May 15–Sep 15 daily*) is another of the town's main clubs; Monday is singles' night, there's techno on Wednesday and hip-hop on Thursday. You can get a free ride there aboard a yellow 'Flört Free Taxi' (as long as you are paying the full, undiscounted cost of entry to the club), which you'll see outside the railway station and at other points around town. **Big Shots Pub** (*Fő utca 43;* ❧ *84 310818; open 11.00–04.00 daily*) is a large open-fronted bar just off the main road that serves snack food and hosts live music and theme nights. **Renegade Pub** (*Petőfi sétány 3; open May 30–Sep 15 daily 20.00–04.00*) is a popular spot with its own hotel opposite.

## What to see and do

Most come to Siófok for watersports, sunbathing and nightlife. The centre is to the east of the **Sió Canal**, whose sluice regulates the level of the lake. **Fő utca** is where you'll find the Tourinform (in a former water tower built in 1912), shops and several bars. The **Hüllő Zoo** (*Fő utca 156–160; www.hullozoo.hu; adult/concessions 500/350Ft; open Tue–Sun 10.00–24.00*) is a reptile house close to the bridge over the canal, while the striking **Lutheran church** in Oulu Park – with its eyes and wings above the entrance – was designed by organic architect Imre Makovecz in 1985 and constructed from Finnish wood.

On the parallel road just to the north is the **Kálmán Imre Museum** (*Kálmán Imre sétány 5;* ❧ *84 311287; adult 300Ft; open Tue–Sun Apr 1–Oct 31 09.00–17.00, rest of yr 09.00–16.00*), which holds an exhibition devoted to 19th-century Siófok. It bore a very different face then, and attracted writers, artists and musicians; among them was Kálmán himself, who was born in this house in 1882, and the collection includes items belonging to the composer including his ashtray, pencil sharpener and wallet. In addition to myriad stalls selling tourist tat, the same road contains the **Mineral Museum** (*Ásványmúzeum; Kálmán Imre sétány 10;* ❧ *84 350038; adult/concessions 250/125Ft; open 09.00–21.00 daily*), with rocks from the Carpathian Basin in glass cases.

Closer to the shore is **Petőfi sétány**, a 200m segment of which is packed with bars, clubs, arcades and pizza joints. The **main strand** (*Petőfi sétány 3; adult/concessions 700/350Ft, free entry after 18.00; open 08.00–03.00 daily in summer*) lies in front, and has a grassed area and places to hire water craft and even go bungee jumping. The other main resort and strand sections are known as the **Gold Coast** (Aranypart), which stretches along the shore to the east of the centre, and the **Silver Coast** (Ezüstpart) to the west. Aranypart is the livelier of the two, with hotels, bars and stalls; among its attractions is a **wakeboarding circuit** (*850Ft/2 rounds, 4,200Ft/12, 7,500Ft/24; open May 15–Sep 15 08.00–20.00 daily*). You'll pay to enter the main strands of these resorts, but 1km further along in each case are areas that are both quieter and freely accessible.

**Jókai Park** is just beyond the bars of Petőfi sétány, a relative haven by comparison. It nudges up against the canal – which the Romans started building in the 3rd century – and its edge is a popular fishing spot. The weather observatory which issues warnings of impending storms, stands at the canal mouth (just across from the ferry pier).

## Other

A motorised **sightseeing train** (*adult/concessions 500/250Ft*) leaves 13 times a day in summer from opposite the Hotel Holiday on Petőfi sétány. For **sightseeing by water**, the Excellence Yacht operates a one-hour trip (*adult/concessions 1,000/500Ft; departs on the hour 16.00–22.00 in summer*) leaving from the pier. There is a selection of other programmes in high season (*Jun 28–Aug 24*) too; for information, call 84 310050.

Just to the west of Siófok, the 300ha nature conservation area and ten fish ponds at **Töreki** offer the chance for some peaceful walks, picnics and fishing. A 9km-long trail through the area begins outside the village. The landscape is varied, featuring lakes, marsh, meadow, grassland and forest; the fish ponds provide resting places for migrating bird species, and there are colonies of swallows in the banks. You can get there on Road 7, and bus 7 runs from Siófok bus station.

# KESZTHELY

If it weren't for the lake, you could be forgiven for forgetting you were at Lake Balaton. It is true that Keszthely sees the inevitable crowds in high season, but there's life beyond the tourist dollar here and a whiff of culture that comes as a surprise after the more hedonistic pleasures of Siófok. There's nobility in its architecture, a legacy of the Festetics family, aristocrats whose star rose considerably as a consequence of their loyalty to the Habsburgs, and who acquired the Keszthely estate in 1739. This was not a dynasty of mere shoe-licking self-servers, however; at the beginning of the 19th century they were enthusiastic supporters of the reform drive and György Festetics was actually involved in the Jacobin plot led by Martinovics (see box, page 144) in 1792. Fortunate to avoid the fate of some of his fellow conspirators on Castle Hill's 'Field of Blood', he subsequently got stuck into progressive projects, founding Europe's first agricultural college and working to improve the breeding stock of Hungarian horses – passions shared by István Széchenyi, which is unsurprising when the 'greatest Hungarian' was György's nephew.

## Getting there, away and around

The **bus** and **railway stations** are 600m to the southeast of the centre, at the end of Mártírok útja. Keszthely is on the line between Tapolca and Balatonszentgyörgy, and you can change at one of these for journeys around the lake and beyond if the direct services don't suit your schedule. There are up to 15 daily trains to Tapolca and 20 to Balatonszentgyörgy; direct trains elsewhere include those to Budapest (Déli or Keleti; seven), Balatonfüred (one), Siófok (six), Sümeg (three), Pécs (two), Celldömöllok (two), Székesfehérvár (one) and Szombathely (two). In addition, a vintage train is operated by MÁV on summer mornings between Keszthely and Badacsonytonaj (❏ 83 318162; Tue–Sat Jun 1–Aug 20); you'll have to pay a supplement on top of the regular ticket price. There are regular buses to Tapolca, Sümeg, Balatongyörök, Veszprém, Zalaegerszeg and Hévíz, as well as services to Badacsony (12), Balatonfüred (13), Balatonszentgyörgy (14), Budapest Népliget (six), Győr (six), Kaposvár (ten), Nagykanizsa (15), Pápa (ten), Pécs (six), Siofók (six) and Sopron (three).

Ferries dock at the pier near the main strand. In summer, there are four daily services to Badacsony (via Balatonmáriá, Balatongyörök and Szigliget) at 10.00, 11.20, 14.10 (going on as far as Balatonszemes) and 17.50; the last boat back to Keszthely from Badacsony is at 18.15. If you need a **taxi**, try Georgikon (❏ 83 333666).

## Information and other practicalities

**Ibusz** Fő tér 7–8. Exchanges travellers' cheques and arrange private accommodation. *Open Mon–Thu 08.30–16.30, Fri 08.30–15.30.*

**Internet** Stones Cyber and Dance Café *(Kisfaludy utca 17;* ❏ *83 510109; open 10.00–02.00 daily),* on the corner Bem József utca, has a couple of internet terminals.

**Keszthely Tourist** Kossuth Lajos utca 25; ❏ 83 314288; e khtours@axelero.hu; www.keszthelytourist.hu. Arranges tours and private rooms, but we found the staff rather unhelpful. Hope you receive better service. *Open Mon–Sat 08.00–19.00, Sun 09.00–17.00 (in summer).*

**Tourinform** Kossuth Lajos utca 28; ❏ 83 314144; e keszthely@tourinform.hu. Housed in the 19th-century former town hall building. *Open May 15–Sep 15 Mon–Fri 09.00–20.00, Sat–Sun 09.00–18.00, rest of yr Mon–Fri 09.00–17.00, Sat–Sun 09.00–13.00.*

## Where to stay

Keszthely's pensions appear eager to out-do each other with 'luxury' facilities – small swimming pools are far from unusual.

**Admiral Pension** Pázmány P utca 1; ❏ 83 314368. Large guesthouse with inviting rooms. Facilities inc solarium, sauna and postage-stamp-sized pool, and you can rent bikes. *Sgl 13,000Ft, dbl 15,200Ft, triple 18,500Ft.*

**Barbara Wellness Pension** (13 rooms) Zámor utca 2; ☏ 83 319865; e info@barbara-pension.hu; www.barbara-pension.hu. Set in a detached house, this good-looking family-run guesthouse is almost embarrassingly well-equipped. Packages on offer inc massages, beauty treatments and tennis lessons. Rooms are clean and spacious. *Sgl €40, dbl €50, triple €70, room for 4 €80.*

**Camping Castrum** Móra Ferenc utca 48; ☏ 83 312120; e keszthely@castrumgroup.hu; www.castrum-group.hu. Large site with 330 tent pitches and lots of amenities. There's a decent-sized pool and 4 clay tennis courts (lessons and equipment available). *Open Apr 1–Oct 31.*

**Hotel Helikon** (240 rooms) Balatonpart 5; ☏ 83 311330; e helikon@danubiusgroup.co; www.danubiusgroup.com. 3-star hotel in the pleasant park to the northeast of the ferry pier with 10 indoor and outdoor tennis courts, a swimming pool and fitness centre. You can also use the hotel's windsurfs, kayaks and sailing boats free of charge. The exterior is ugly, but the bar is located in a glass atrium and the lakeside rooms have lovely views. They keep the kids well entertained here. *Sgl standard/superior €77/92, dbl €104/128.*

**Hotel Bacchus** (26 rooms) Erzsébet királyné utca 18; ☏ 83 314098; email:bacchush@axelero.hu; www.bacchushotel.hu. Centrally located 3-star with its own 'wine museum' in the cellar and wine-tasting programmes (*from €10/10 wines*). Rooms are plainly furnished but comfortable; those downstairs have terraces, those upstairs have balconies. *Sgl € 47, dbl €58, apt €92.*

**Lehner Major B&B** H-8714 Keleviz Lehner Major; ☏ 85 708142; e info@hunyady.hu. This guesthouse is actually around 30 mins from Keszthely, but is worth mentioning for its noble splendour and friendly owner, who organises riding tours around Balaton (see Somogy Nature Association under Tour operators, page 000). Great value. *Rooms €25/pp.*

**Tokajer Pension** Apát utca 21; ☏ 83 319875; e pensiontokajer@hotmail.com; www.pensiontokajer.hu. When grandma chucked the chintz out it ended up here; the rooms are extremely flowery, but clean and homely with it. This welcoming pension also boasts amenities including a pool, summer terrace, sauna and solarium; they lay on a feast of a b/fast too. Located 600m from the pier. Recommended. *Dbl €45, triple €52, apts €62–72.*

## Where to eat and drink

**Bacchus** See above. Atmospheric, rustic hotel restaurant. Good food to go with an excellent wine list. *Mains 1,350–2,600Ft; avg 2,200Ft; open 12.00–23.00 daily.*

**Margaretta** Bercsényi Miklós utca 60; ☏ 83 314882. Hungarian food, including a wide selection of goose liver, fish, pork and poultry. The outdoor eating area looks faintly cheap, but this is one of the town's top eateries and the well-priced and hearty portions are accompanied by good service. Appearance, in this instance, is deceptive. *Mains 750–1,800Ft, avg 1,300Ft; open 11.30–22.00 daily.*

**Park Vendeglő** Vörösmarty utca 1/A; ☏ 83 311654. This restaurant is popular with locals and foreigners alike, and is unusual in offering half portions (at half the price) for those with smaller appetites. *Mains 950–2,450Ft, avg 1,500Ft; open daily 11.00–23.00.*

**Pelso Café** Kossuth Lajos utca 38; ☏ 83 315415. Two-tiered beach hut with wicker furnishings in the garden of the Fő tér church. We still haven't forgotten their After Eight ice cream with peppermint liqueur – delicious! *Open Mon–Thu 09.00–21.00, Fri–Sat 09.00–22.00, Sun 09.00–20.00.*

**Piccola Post Pizzeria** József Attila utca 6; ☏ 83 312689. Family-run establishment offering the very best pizzas in town. *Open Mon–Sat 12.00–22.00.*

**Sramli** Pethő utca 4; ☏ 83 311839. Named after the family that runs it, this restaurant serves Hungarian and German cuisine. The garden courtyard is the place to eat if the weather's up to it; there are discounts on the bill for subsequent visits (5% the 2nd time and 10% the 3rd). *Mains 990–2,490Ft, avg 1,700Ft; open May 15–Nov 11.00–23.00 daily.*

## Entertainment and nightlife

The **Balaton Congress Centre and Theatre** (*Fő tér 3;* ☏ *83 515230*) offers drama, dance and classical music (with appearances by the Budapest Philharmonic), and also puts on temporary exhibitions. The ticket office (*open Tue–Thu 08.30–12.00 & 12.30–17.00*) is next door. The

**Goldmark Károly Cultural Centre** (*Kossuth Lajos utca 28;* ✆ *83 515257*) is accessed through an archway at the Tourinform; it has folk-dancing performances in summer.

Keszthely is a university town, and the students are clearly fond of their strip joints. **Club 18** (*Szalászto utca 18; open 11.00–02.00 daily*) is one of the less raunchy options, a dingy but cool ground-floor bar with snooker tables, darts and table football. **Club of Colours** (*Tapolcai utca; open Wed, Fri & Sat 10.00–05.00*) is near the 24-hour McDonald's to the east of town, and is the biggest nightclub in the area; it has live DJs and events nights (including foam parties). The **Easy Music House** (*Kossuth Lajos utca; open Wed, Fri & Sat 22.00–late*) is the most popular of several bars and clubs along Kossuth Lajos utca to the south of Fő tér. Women are admitted free before midnight. **Gösser** (*Kossuth Lajos utca 35;* ✆ *83 312265*) has a wide pavement terrace in a relaxing people-watching position.

## What to see and do

The **Festetics Palace** (*Festetics kastély; Kastély utca 1;* ✆ *83 312191; adult/concessions 2,000/1,000Ft; open Tue–Sun Jan 1–May 31 10.00–17.00, Jun 1–Jun 30 09.00–17.00, Jul–Aug 31 09.00–18.00 daily, Sep 1–Dec 31 Tue–Sun 10.00–17.00*) ranks among the most impressive aristocratic mansions in the country. It was originally built in the mid 18th century – the Baroque south wing dates to this period – before 19th-century extensions resulted in its pleasingly asymmetrical façade. Many of the family's Rococo and Biedermeier furnishings remain inside the rooms that are open to the public. The Helikon Library, with its coffered ceiling and 86,000 books, was one of the great personal collections and is indicative of the Festetics' interest in the arts; during the early 19th century, members of the literary élite were regular visitors. There are exhibitions of the trappings of aristocratic life during the 18th and 19th centuries, as well as a display of weaponry. The significant cloud that hangs over the palace is the extortionate admission price. Thankfully the beautiful grounds can be strolled without denting the personal finances, and are particularly worth visiting at around 21.30 when the fountain at the entrance is illuminated with changing colours; in summer the gardens become the backdrop for a series of concerts (see Tourinform for details).

To the southwest of the palace is the **Georgikon Major Museum** (*Bercsényi Miklós 65–67;* ✆ *83 311563; adult/concessions 200/100Ft; open May 1–Oct 31 Tue–Sat 10.00–17.00, Sun 10.00–18.00*), housed in courtyard buildings that accommodated students of the agricultural college founded by György (hence its name) Festetics in 1797. The museum contains a history of the college, together with exhibitions on 19th-century viniculture, farming in Transdanubia and a blacksmith's workshop. The **Marzipan Museum** (*Katona József utca 19;* ✆ *83 329322; adult/concessions 200/100Ft; open Mar 1–Jan 6 Tue–Sun 10.00–18.00*) is to the east of the palace, featuring 100 pieces of shaped marzipan – including an intricate model of the palace itself – and selling cakes to take away.

Walking south from the palace down Kossuth Lajos utca, a turn into Bakacs utca will bring you to the **Doll Museum** (*Bakacs utca 2;* ✆ *83 318855; adult/concessions 300/250Ft; open daily May 1–Oct 31 09.00–19.00, rest of yr 09.00–17.00*); in addition to its dolls, there are also life-sized mannequins in historical dress and a model of parliament made from the shells of sea snails. You pay separately to access each display in the complex. Sharing the same building as the Casablanca strip club, the **Torture Museum** (*Bakacs utca 2;* ✆ *83 318855; adult/concessions 400/300Ft; open daily May 1–Oct 31 09.00–19.00, rest of year 09.00–17.00*) has puppets in various states of dismemberment and uses more fake blood than a Christopher Lee film.

Continuing down Kossuth Lajos utca brings you to Fő tér, whose Louis-XVI-style **town hall** (*no 1*) was built in 1790. Outside it is a weather-worn Trinity Column of 1770 – a stone island in a sea of flowers – while set back at the southeastern side is the former **Franciscan church** (*no 10*). The church was constructed in the 14th century, during the reign of Palatine István Lackfi II, and in 1560 was converted into a fortress to defend the town against Turkish assaults. There was much reconstruction over the centuries (the Neo-Gothic tower, for instance, was added in 1896) but the rose window dates to the 14th century, and 15th-century frescoes were uncovered during restoration. The tomb of György Festetics is in the crypt.

The entrance to the vast **Balaton Museum** (*Múzeum utca 2;* ❧ *83 312351; adult/concessions 340/170Ft; open May 1–Oct 31 Tue–Sat 10.00–18.00, Nov 1–Apr 30 Tue–Sat 09.00–17.00*) is at Kossuth Lajos utca 74. Among its holdings are regional Roman finds and an exhibition focusing on life around Balaton, from the wildlife to the 19th-century steamships used to transport goods and passengers from one shore to the other. Around 100m further south along Kossuth Lajos utca is the **St Miklós Cemetery** (*open daily Mar 15–Aug 31 07.00–20.00, Sep 1–Oct 25 07.00–19.00, Oct 26–Nov 5 07.00–20.00, Nov 6–Mar 14 07.00–18.00*). The resplendently yellow cemetery chapel was built on medieval foundations in 1713, while the Neoclassical **Festetics Mausoleum** stands towards the back of the plot.

## Other activities

There are three stretches to **take a dip** along the shoreline at Keszthely – the Városi and Helikon strands near the ferry pier and the Libás strand further to the northeast. You will pay to enter the first two (*adult/concessions 600/ 550Ft, reductions after 16.00; open May 15–Sep 15 08.30–19.00 daily*); a Keszthely Gold Card, which you can pick up from Tourinform or hotels if you have proof you are staying in town for six nights or more, gives a 50% discount. There are waterslides, and water craft for hire, and the Városi has a reconstructed 19th-century pier (known as the Szigetfürdő) that juts out into the lake and has decked areas branching from it. Libás Strand (accessed via a narrow track at the end of Lóczy Lajos utca) is hidden behind reeds and is both quieter and free to use. You can also fish here.

Sightseeing boats leave from the pier (❧ *84 310050*); a one-hour tour goes up to five times daily in summer, and there are various other boating programmes too. Check the information boards at the pier. A motorised **tourist train** (❧ *06 20 957 1436; runs 09.00–21.00 daily in summer*) runs between the Helikon Hotel and the palace.

Around 4km north of Keszthely, just off Sümegi utca, is a purpose-built open-air **Castle Theatre** (*Várszínház, Cserszegtomaj;* ❧ *83 702300; book tickets in advance; open May 1–Aug 31 Tue & Sat 19.00–21.30*). Just to the southeast of the theatre is the **Margit Lookout Tower** (*just off Bikedi sor on Sümegi utca*); it's free to climb under your own steam, but if you want to take the lift it'll cost you (*adult/concessions 700/350Ft*).

# HÉVÍZ

We find Hévíz, 8km northeast of Keszthely, an over-bearing resort whose every cranny is packed with expensive hotels, guesthouses, souvenir shops and cafés coining it in on the back of the town's thermal lake. **Tó-fürdő** (*Parkerdő; 3-hr ticket 750Ft, daily ticket 1,400Ft, sliding refunds on stays under 5hrs; open daily 08.30–17.00*) is formed of a crater 39m deep that's kept filled by hot springs gushing 60 million litres of water a day; it is the largest of its type in Europe, and the second-largest (to New Zealand's Lake Tarawera) on the planet. During summer the water temperature is 32–35°, falling slightly to around 26°C in winter, and it's a pretty thing, with a central pavilion and piers, lilies on the surface and steam rising from it in colder months. The year-round warmth means that wallowers come in all seasons, but late spring and early autumn are particularly popular. The water is mildly radioactive – prolonged immersion isn't recommended – and relieves rheumatic disorders. The mud dredged from the lake bed is also used in face packs and the like. The Szent András Kórház (*Dr Schulhof Vilmós utca 1;* ❧ *83 340587; www.spaheviz.hu*) is a hospital by the lake that tailors individual programmes (on average lasting two–three weeks) using the water, mud and other medical treatments. There are entrances to the lake complex in Deák tér (on the northern side, near the bus station) and on Ady Endre utca (to the southeast, by Castrum Camping). If you lose your ticket or stay beyond your allocated time, you'll need to buy an exit ticket (650Ft) to leave; ticket reservation is recommended to avoid queues.

There's little worth seeing beyond the lake, although the late-20th-century **Blue Church** (*Szent Lélek templom; Zrínyi utca*) half way up the sloping Széchenyi utca is charming and curious, with five narrow towers and a rounded nave, and on the town's eastern outskirts is a little Romanesque church at **Egregy**.

## Getting there and away

The **bus station** (*Deák Ferenc tér*) is at the northern entrance to Parkerdő and the lake. There are very regular buses to Keszthely, and regular services to Sümeg and Zalaegerszeg; other destinations include Badacsony (nine), Balatonfüred (12), Budapest (six), Tapolca (nine), Veszprém (12) and Nagykanizsa (12). There is no railway station.

## Where to stay and eat

Unless you're on an intensive programme of therapy, there really is little reason to stay in Hévíz when Keszthely is so close. The restaurants are generally touristy and dire.

**Castrum Camping** Tó-part; ☎ 83 343198; info@castrum-group.hu; www.castrum-group.hu. This is the most convenient campsite, near the southeastern entrance to the lake.

**Danubius Thermal Hotel Aqua** (224 rooms) Kossuth Lajos utca 13–15; ☎ 83 889500; e aqua@danubiusgroup.com; www.danubiushotels.com/aqua. This wellness hotel has an indoor thermal spa and fun bath, as well as an outdoor pool, and offers beauty and health treatments. All rooms above the 1st floor have small balconies, and it's 300m to the lake. Sauna, solarium, fitness room. *Sgl €75–95, dbl €115–140, apt €180.*

**Gyönyösi Betyárcsárda** ☎ 83 373006. Built in 1728, this inn was once the favourite haunt of outlaws; inside are their weapons and near by are the graves of two of their number executed in 1862. The cuisine is traditional, served by *csikós*-costumed waiters, and there are evening horse and folk shows in summer (*May 15–Jun 30 Wed 20.00, Jul 1–Aug 31 Mon, Wed & Fri 20.00*). 6km north of Hévíz on the road leading north to Sümeg, just before the branch left towards Karmacs. *Mains 1,000–2,100Ft, avg 1,650Ft; open 10.00–23.00 daily.*

**Magyar Csárda** Tavirózsa utca 2; ☎ 83 343271; www.magyarcsarda.hu. The best of a bunch of restaurants lining this street, with a pretty patio area and typical Hungarian fare. There's gypsy music 17.00–23.00. To the west of the lake – take Helikon utca off Kossuth Lajos utca, and Tavirózsa utca runs off it. *Mains 990–4,400Ft, avg 1,800Ft; open 11.00–23.00 daily.*

**Nyirády Villa** (19 rooms) József Attila utca 13; ☎ 83 340058; e nyirady.villa@axelero.hu. Well-kept pension to the northwest of the lake, on a road running off Széchenyi utca. *Sgl 7,500Ft, dbl 10,000–12,000Ft.*

**Wellness Hotel Hévíz** (19 rooms) Hévíz-Cserszegtomaj, Sümeg utca 35; ☎ 83 330200; www.wellnesshotelheviz.hu. Handsome and smallish wellness hotel, with swimming pool, sauna, fitness room and a selection of beauty/health packages. Situated just off the road running north towards Sümeg, in between Hévíz and Cserszegtomaj.

# BADACSONY

Settled in the Tapolca basin, the Badacsony region comprises a pocket of volcanic cones and hills clustered behind the flat-topped, 400m-high Badacsony Hill. There are four villages in the area (all with the Badacsony- prefix), but it is the resort to the southwest of Badacsonytomaj – in the bump of shoreline that presses out slightly into the lake – that is usually meant when people refer to Badacsony. Like Tihany, Badacsony is beautiful and offers some good walking trails to supplement the splashing at the strands. The slopes of Badacsony are littered with cellars whose vineyards thrive on the fertile volcanic soil (Kéknyelő, or Blue Stem, is the name most associated with its wines). The oft-trod path is Szegedi Róza utca, which leads uphill from Római út and promises wine shacks and pinces along the route; despite the crowds moving up and down, it is an enjoyable excursion laced with a frisson of wine-induced camaraderie.

## Getting there, away and around

The **railway station** (*Park utca 1*) – built from the dark basalt typical of the region – is in the centre of town, right in front of the ferry pier. It is on the line connecting the settlements of the northern shore, and there are direct services to Tapolca, Balatonfüred (15), Székesfehérvár (12) and Budapest Déli (eight). In summer a **nostalgia train** (*Jun 21– Aug 20 Tue–Sat; see www.mavnosztalgia.hu for details*) runs between Badacsonytomaj and Keszthely. (It's worth casting a glance at the walking map outside the station, which shows the route to the Kisfaludy-ház, from where trails into Badacsony start in earnest.) **Buses** arrive and depart from the stop on Balatoni út just outside the railway station; among the services are buses to Balatonfüred (three daily), Székesfehérvár (four), Tapolca (two), Budapest (two) and Hévíz (up to six in summer only).

Passenger **ferries** run to Fonyód up to ten times a day in peak season (*Jul–Aug; first at 08.20, last at 20.00*), with less frequent services in other months between April and October. In summer, there are also ferries to Tihany-rév and Tihany (one), Balatonboglar and Keszthely (three), Balatonlelle and Szigliget (four). Pleasure tours also depart from the pier, among them disco boats (*Jul 5–Aug 20 Thu 21.30*) and sightseeing cruises (*Jun 28–Aug 24 daily 16.00*). Open-top **jeep taxis** (❯ *06 30 539 3394*) wait near the post office on Park utca and are an easy way to reach the wine cellars. Alternatively you could take a horsedrawn carriage from near the Neptun Hotel on Római út.

## Information and other practicalities

**Balaton Tourist** Park utca 4; ❯ 87 531021. Information, wine tours and private accommodation. *Open May 1–Sep 30 09.00–18.00 daily.*

**Egry József Cultural Centre** Badacsonytomaj, Romai út 55; ❯ 87 571071. Cultural centre and cinema opposite the Borbarátok Panzió.

**Midi Tourist** Egry sétány 3; ❯ 87 431028; www.miditourist.hu. Can help with private accommodation, and also offers internet access. This branch is in the centre, and there is a 2nd (main) office a few hundred metres northeast (Park utca 53). *Open May–Sep 08.00–21.00 daily.*

**Biró & Mányai** Park utca 5; ❯ 87 431054; e biro-manyai@axelero.hu. This company runs scheduled boat trips with dinner, campfire and dancing.

**Tourinform** Park utca 6; ❯ 87 431046; e badacsonytomaj@tourinform.hu; www.badacsonytomaj.hu. Just to the north of the railway station. *Open Nov 1–Apr 30 Mon–Fri 09.00–15.30, May 1–Jun 14 & Oct Mon–Fri 09.00–17.00, Jun 15–Sep 14 Mon–Fri 09.00–19.00, Sat–Sun 09.00–18.00, Sep 15–Sep 30 Mon–Fri 09.00–17.00, Sat 09.00–13.00.*

## Where to stay

In addition to the accommodation listed below, there are several private rooms and apartments on offer along Romai út.

**Borbarátok Panzió** (6 rooms) Badacsonytomaj, Római út 78; ❯ 87 471000; e borbaratok@axelero.hu; www.borbaratok.hu. This comfortable guesthouse is nearly always full, so bookings are advised in peak periods. The rooms are on the 'cosy' side, but are lovely nevertheless; the restaurant (see below) is out of the top drawer. It's located 1km or so northeast of Badacsony on the road to Badacsonytomaj. *Sgl 6,000Ft. dbl 7,000Ft.*

**Club Hotel Badacsony** (70 rooms) Badacsonytomaj, Balatoni út 14; ❯ 87 471040. Picturesque complex (with its own strand) 2km up the shore to the north of Badacsony. Rooms are decorated in inviting, muted tones; some have balconies and others terraces. *Dbl €90–120.*

**Hotel Neptun & Youth Hostel** (16 rooms) Római út 156; ❯ 87 431293. Renovated, turn-of-the-century house offering en-suite rooms on the ground floor and a youth hostel (with shared facilities) above. Centrally located 200m from the beach. Reliable cheap choice. *Hotel rooms sgl 6,000Ft, dbl 7,000Ft; hostel rooms 2,240Ft/pp.*

**Hotel Volán** (24 rooms) Romai út 170; ↘ 87 431013; e reception@vhotel.hu; www.vhotel.hu. Standing behind the smaller Midi Tourist bureau, this is an impressive-looking 3-star hotel at the end of a long driveway. Some rooms are a little old-fashioned, and it's on the expensive side, but it's quite pleasant. *Sgl €44, dbl €55, room for 4 €75.*

## Where to eat and drink

**Borbarátok** See above. Bubbly, busy and atmospheric, this restaurant combines traditional and modern touches, and serves a mean kettle goulash. They serve their own wines, the sweet Ürmös being the best. Highly recommended. *Mains 850–3,250Ft, avg 1,600Ft; open Mar 11–Nov 1.*

**Il Capitano Coffee House & Pizzeria** Hajóallomás; ↘ 87 431292. Located at the land-end of the ferry pier, the Il Capitano has a disco on its 1st floor and is a good place to party right on the edge of the water. Have a pizza to line the stomach. *Open May 1–Sep 30 11.00–04.00 daily.*

**Imre Börözó** Szegedi Róza utca 28; ↘ 06 20 347 2274. Further up the hill from the Szent Orbán (see below), this wine bar is run by a fourth generation of family winegrowers. They sell and bottle Riesling, Pinot Gris and Muscat. You can visit their cellar for wine tastings. *Open May 1–Sep 15 12.00–19.00 daily, Sep 16–Apr 30 by appointment only.*

**Kisfaludy-haz** Szegedi Róza utca; ↘ 87 431016. The food here in the Kisfaludy family's 18th-century press house (see below) is excellent, and there are breathtaking views and gypsy music (*12.00–15.00 & 18.00–23.00*). *Mains 1,300–4,500Ft, avg 2,400Ft; open Mar 31–Oct 31 daily 11.00–23.00.*

**Szent Orbán** Szegedi Róza utca 22; ↘ 87 431382; e storban@axelero.hu. Nestled on the lower slope of Badascony-hegy (on the walking route up to the Kisfaludy-ház), this is a beautiful place to dine and a restful spot. The restaurant can arrange wine tasting in its nearby cellar. *Mains 1,200–2,800Ft, avg 1,900Ft; open 12.00–22.00 daily all yr.*

## What to see and do

The **Egry József Memorial Museum** (*Egry sétány 12;* ↘ *87 431044; adult/concessions 300/150Ft; open Tue–Sun May 1–Jun 30 & Sep 1–Sep 30 10.00–18.00, Jul 1–Aug 31 10.00–20.00*), on the road linking Balatoni út and Park utca (100m from the bus station), showcases photos, documents and early works by József Egry (1883–1951). Egry – an artist compared in style with William Turner – lived in this house for 30 years, and was hugely productive here. His paintings are wonderful representations of the changing light and moods of the lake, which he was inspired by (and obsessed with).

From the museum, continue away from the lake until you hit Római út, from which Szegedi Róza utca makes the relatively steep and sapping climb up Badacsony-hegy. You are flanked by vineyards all the way up, and there are small wine shacks and bigger wine houses to stop off at on the way. (Alternatively you can catch a jeep taxi; see under *Getting there, away and around*). After 1km or so you'll reach the **Szegedi Róza Literary Museum** (*Kisfaludy utca 17;* ↘ *87 431906; adult/concessions 240/120Ft; open May 1–Sep 30 Tue–Sun 10.00–18.00*), and if you're still sober you can take a look around the house of actress Róza Szegedi, who married the poet Sándor Kisfaludy in 1800. The pair spent much time here, and dabbled in viniculture themselves (in the wine press that now holds the Kisfaludy-ház restaurant); apparently Róza's vermouth in particular was highly regarded.

The **Kisfaludy-ház** is 100m further on, and stands at the starting post for a series of **marked trails** running across the top of Badacsony-hegy. A map at the car park displays the routes, and a nature trail is accompanied by explanatory boards. The plateau is covered with forest, which grows in the rich soil that is so frequently washed from the steeper peaks elsewhere, and is home to the great spotted woodpecker, the great black woodpecker, the nuthatch and the tree-creeper. The landscape also harbours 11 protected plant species. A short distance along a footpath brings you to some basalt stone blocks, one of which has a carved surface and is known as the **Rose Stone** (*Rózsa-kő*); it is said that if a couple sit on it with their backs to the lake, and think sweet thoughts of each other, they will be married within the year. Some people linger hopefully at the rock, while others suddenly find something terribly interesting in the opposite direction.

Other highlights on the trail are the **Páholy** and **Kisfaludy lookout towers**, and unusual rock formations like the **Stone Gate** (with its horizontal layers in the cliff sides) and the **Exiles' Stairs** (the latter leading to the Tördemic lookout point). The Balaton Uplands National Park have published a booklet in the past (*Badacsony: Nature Trail*), although the copy we were given was printed in 1997 and it may be we got one of the last ones. If you choose to hike to the hills beyond the plateau, pick up a map from Tourinform.

## Excursion

To the west of Badacsony is the **Szigliget peninsula**, which has a castle first constructed by Benedictine monks from Pannonhalma in 1260 as protection from any further Mongol invasions. It was extended several times over subsequent centuries, the last renovation in 1540 when the round bastion was added. The fortress saw action in 1664 when the Turks tried and failed to capture it on three separate occasions, but lightning hit the powder store in 1697 and Lipót I ensured there was no chance of a resurrection during his demolition programme of 1702. The ruins are a steep 20-minute walk up the hill from the village below; the effort is rewarded with beautiful views over the lake, the valleys and the vineyards, and is particularly atmospheric at sunset. Road 71 leads into Köz út and Fő tér, from where several flights of steps take you over Petőfi utca and on to Kisfaludy utca from where the climb begins in earnest. There is a bus stop in Fő tér, served by buses from Tapolca and Badacsony. The ferry pier (*Réhelyi út*) is 2km south of the castle, and has up to five daily services to towns around Balaton (including Keszthely and Badacsony); evening sightseeing boats also depart from here (*adult/concessions 1,000/500Ft; Jun 2–Aug 2 Tue & Sat 20.30*). Buses run between the pier and Fő tér.

## TAPOLCA

Set 10km back from the northern shore of Balaton, Tapolca has prospered in modern times on the back of mining for the clay-like mineral bauxite. It is an attractive little town with a watermill and pond, and a water-filled cave.

### Getting there, away and around

The **bus station** is at the northwestern side of Hősök tere, from where Deák Ferenc utca runs east towards the Mill Pond and the Cave Lake. There are very regular services to Keszthely, Veszprém and Sümeg, as well as buses to Budapest (five daily), Badacsony (12), Hévíz (11), Szigliget (14), Székesfehérvár, Szombathely (3) and other destinations in Transdanubia. The **railway station** at the end of Dózsa György út is around 2km southwest of the centre, and represents the connecting point between towns around Lake Balaton and those in Western Transdanubia. There are good links with Balatonfüred (13 daily) and Keszthely (eight), as well as Celldömölk (seven) and Szombathely (two). Going further eastward, there are trains to Székesfehérvár and Budapest (ten). From the station you can catch buses 1 and 2 to Fő tér (every 15–30 mins).

### Information and other practicalities

**Balaton Tourist** Deák Ferenc utca 7. Can arrange private accommodation, with rooms (for 2) starting at 3,500Ft and apts (for 4) at 10,000Ft. *Open mid May–mid Sep Mon–Fri 08.00–17.00, Sat 09.00–11.30, rest of yr Mon–Fri 08.00–15.30, Sat 09.00–11.30.*

**Tourinform** Fő tér 17; ✆ 87 510777; e tapolca@tourinform.hu. Directly above the Mill Lake. *Open Jun 15–Sep 15 Mon–Fri 09.00–18.00, Sat–Sun 10.00–17.00, rest of yr.*

# Where to stay and eat

**Peppino Pizzeria** Kisfaludy utca 7; ℘ 87 414133. The place to grab a pizza, with a selection of nearly 40 to choose from, as well as pastas and grills. Also sells ice cream. Opposite the cultural centre. *Pizzas 650–1,200Ft, avg 1,000Ft; open 11.00–23.00 daily.*

**Tavasbarlang Turistaszálló** Hősök tere 5; ℘ 87 411644. Grim building next to the bus station – but you get what you pay for in this old workers' hostel. *Beds 2,500Ft/pp, private sgl 4,000Ft.*

**Szent György Panzió & Restaurant** (8 rooms) Kisfaludy Sándor utca 1; ℘ 87 413593. Sitting right next to the entrance to the Cave Lake, the elegant Hungarian restaurant (*mains 1,200–2,200Ft, avg 1,800Ft; open 07.00–22.00 daily*) has high-ceilinged rooms, an outdoor café terrace and helpful staff. The pension is similarly well-turned-out, with tidy rooms. A good choice in a good location. *Dbl 11,000Ft, triple 14,000Ft.*

**Hotel Pelion** (228 rooms) Köztársaság tér 10; ℘ 87 513101; e reserve@hotelpelion.hunguesthotels.hu. This is an excellent hotel that has only been open a couple of years and is very reasonably priced. Among the facilities are thermal and fun baths, various saunas and steam cabins, a jacuzzi and squash courts. The rooms are of a good size, and the deluxe apts even have their own jacuzzis. To the north of the Cave Lake. *Sgl €109, dbl €142.*

**Dolce Cukrászda** Csobanc utca 55; ℘ 87 412015. The best of the places to get a cake. East of Templom domb. *Open Tue–Sun 10.00–19.00.*

**Hubertus** Juhász György 78; ℘ 87 413360. A limited menu of cheap Hungarian food in basic surroundings. Around 800m to the east of the centre. *Mains 700–1,700Ft, avg 1,100Ft; open Sun–Thu 10.00–22.00, Fri–Sat 10.00–23.00.*

**Hotel Gabriella** (16 rooms) Batsányi tér 7; ℘ 87 511070; www.hotelgabriella.hu. The Gabriella is housed inside the original watermill, and has small and large dbl rooms, as well as apts. The 2nd floor had been refurbished when we visited and was consequently the better choice for rooms, but it may be that the other floors have now had similar make overs. Its restaurant (*mains 1,100–2,900Ft, avg 1,800Ft; open 07.00–22.00 daily*) has a terrace overlooking the lake; the menu includes Hungarian and international food, with goose-dish specialities.

# Entertainment and nightlife

**Disco Bauxit** (*Hősök tere 4; open Sat 22.00–late*) is the only disco in town, and – looking like a cross between a greasy spoon and a church hall – won't work hardened clubbers into an anticipatory frenzy. It's near the bus station. The **Aranykagyló Drink Bár** (*Széchenyi utca 1; open daily 16.00–24.00*) is also near by, just across from the town hall. It's fairly rough around the edges, and has fruit machines and table football.

# What to see and do

**Fő tér**, which leads east into Kossuth Lajos utca and west into Deák Ferenc utca, is the main drag (and lined with banks and shops). To the south of it lies the **Mill Pond** (Malom-tó), divided between an upper lake surrounded by a low stone wall and a lower lake into which water flows to drive the wheel of the mill sitting at the juncture between the two. The mill how holds the Hotel Gabriella, and near by is a bust of the Austrian poet Baumberg Gabriella (1766–1839); she was married to the revolutionary 18th-century poet János Batsányi. This is a popular spot for lingering walks, idly watching the goldfish dart about in the smaller lake and enjoying the water lilies in the longer section.

The mild incline to the east of the lower lake is Templom domb, at the top of which is a **Roman Catholic church**. This was enlarged in the 18th century, but it retains earlier parts from the 13th and 15th centuries and has an 11th-century Gothic sanctuary. In front are some wall remains; while the majority of these belonged to the town's **15th-century castle** (which was brought down by the Turks), there are also portions dating forward to the 17th century and back as far as the Roman period. The **Town and School Museum** (*Templom domb 15; ℘ 87 412246; adult/concessions 100/50Ft; open Tue–Sun 09.00–16.00*) at one side of the primary school building has been reconstructed to mimic a turn-of-the-20th-century classroom. The teacher's hat and walking stick hang from pegs, while an adjacent room holds his bed.

The town's major highlight is of course its **Cave Lake** (*Tavasbarlang; Kisfaludy utca 3;* ⤷ *87 412579; adult/concessions 350/200Ft, boat tour 400Ft; open Apr 1–May 31 & Sep 1–Oct 31 Tue–Sun 10.00–17.00, Jun 1–Aug 31 daily 10.00–18.00*). There are crowds in high season, but it's well worth the wait to propel yourself in a boat through craggy white channels. The ride takes around 15 minutes and is great fun, the water beautiful, clear and cool.

There is a pleasant **strand and thermal pool** (*Strand út 1;* ⤷ *87 323428; adult/concessions 500/350Ft; open May–Sep 09.00–20.00*) to the northwest of the centre. Bus 2 runs up Sümeg felé to within 200m of the turn-off for the strand; ask the driver to let you know where to get off. A few kilometres to the east in the village of Tapolca-Diszel is the **Reiterhof Villám Lovaspanzió** (*Templom tér 4;* ⤷ *87 413943;* e *villam48@axelero.hu*), a family-run riding school, with a rustic pension (*6 rooms; sgl 7,500Ft, dbl 12,000Ft*); as well as lessons (*2,500Ft/hr*), the school offers tailor-made tours. There are buses to the village from Tapolca, or the company can collect you from Budapest airport.

## NAGYVÁZSONY

To the northeast of Tapolca, on the way to Veszprém, Nagyvázsony holds the **Kinizsi Castle** (*Vár utca;* ⤷ *88 264786; adult/concessions 600/350Ft; open Apr 1–Oct 31 Mon–Fri 08.00–17.00, Sat–Sun 09.00–17.00*), an originally 14th-century fort that was enlarged and reinforced by King Mátyás's military commander Pál Kinizsi in the 15th century. Kinizsi's strength was the stuff of legend; he is said once to have performed a victory dance while bearing a slain Turk in each hand. Pieces of his red-marble sarcophagus can be seen in the castle chapel. Much of the castle's structure remains – including a 30m-high keep and a six-storey tower – because it was owned by the Zichys in the 18th century, a family loyal to the Habsburgs, and therefore wasn't levelled after the Independence Wars. At the bottom of the barbican is the former dungeon, complete with waxworks of torturers at their grisly task, while the upper rooms have an exhibition of the castle's history. From the top of the barbican you can enjoy wonderful views over the turrets and through the gun-holes. The journey back down can be slightly hair raising, particularly at points where the steps are thrown into darkness, so please be careful. Displays of **medieval jousting** (*adult/concessions 1,000/600Ft; Jul 1–Aug 20 daily 11.00 & 15.00*) are held in a stretch just inside the outer castle walls. **Concerts** take place in the castle in summer; tickets for these and others in St István Church can be purchased from the ticket office (*Sörház utca 2;* ⤷ *88 509516*), just off Vár utca to the southeast.

Opposite the castle is a rotund **Lutheran church** of 1796 with a wood-framed bell tower. The **Postal Museum** (*Temető utca 3;* ⤷ *88 264300; adult/concessions 100/50Ft; open Apr 1–Oct 31 Tue–Sun 10.00–18.00*) is housed in a renovated peasant cottage, while behind that is an **Open-Air Folk Museum** (*Szabadtéri Néprajzi Múzeum; Bercsényi utca 21; adult/concessions 160/80Ft; open Apr 1–Sep 30 Tue–Sun 10.00–18.00*) with a pair of early-19th-century thatched cottages (including a coppersmith's house).

Just over 1km southwest of the centre (and signposted on Kinizsi utca), the **Nagyvázsony Leanyfalui Horse Club** (*Leanyfalui út 10;* ⤷ *88 264705*) offers horse-riding and lessons, as well as tailor-made programmes. Guests can stay in the three-room pension (*dbl 8,000Ft*); buses don't come here, but the owners can pick you up from the centre.

### Getting there and away

Buses run to Kiniszi Pál utca, the town's main street, and serve Veszprém regularly; there are also buses to Budapest (one on weekdays), Balatonfüred (three) and Tapolca (eight).

### Where to stay and eat

**Kastély** Kossuth Lajos utca 16. This 18th-century Zichy mansion northeast of the centre holds a hotel; when we last visited it was closed, and no-one knew when it would re-open.

**Malomkő Panzió & Restaurant** (15 rooms) Kinizsi utca 47–49; ☏ 88 264165. Pleasant guesthouse on the high street with a small covered pool and well-equipped rooms (some with fridges). Its restaurant (*mains 900–1,800Ft, avg 1,500Ft; open 11.00–21.00 daily*) serves Hungarian cuisine, with stuffed pancakes and a mixed meat platter among the specialities; there's also a *cukrászda* where you can buy home-made ice cream. *Sgl 6,000Ft, dbl 11,000Ft, apt (for 4) 15,000Ft.*

**Várcsárda** Temető utca 7; ☏ 06 30 378 7279. Overlooking the castle, the peasant-style restaurant has individual thatched gazebos. The Hungarian food, though, was distinctly average when we ate there. *Mains 1,200–2,000Ft, avg 1,200Ft; open Apr–Sep 09.00–20.00 daily.*

**Vázsonykő Panzió & Restaurant** (10 rooms) Sörház utca 2; ☏ 88 264344. Simple, friendly guesthouse 200m from the castle, with an elevated restaurant (*mains 900–3,000Ft, avg 1,500Ft; open Mar 15–Oct 31 10.00–21.00, but closed Tue Mar–Apr & Oct*) preparing Hungarian food. *Sgl 5,000Ft, dbl 7,000Ft; open Mar 15–Oct 31 only.*

# TIHANY

To the west of Balatonfüred – but nothing like it – the volcanic peninsula of Tihany feels like a heady mix of Cotswold town, Mediterranean cliff and national park. Its surface was formed by debris spewed from ancient volcanoes, and at its heart – alongside the hills, marshes and old geyser cones – are two crater lakes. This adds up to top-rate hiking territory, served by several marked trails, and it was declared the country's first nature reserve in 1952. Belső-tó (Inner Lake) is popular with anglers and Külső-tó with birdwatchers, while romantics head for the village at the eastern side, with its peasant houses and abbey. The first written reference to Tihany came in deeds recording the foundation of the Benedictine abbey by András I in 1055; this document – now held at Pannonhalma – is a particular treasure because it contains some Hungarian words among its Latin (the earliest surviving example of the native language in writing). In the 13th century the monastery was fortified and later resisted Turkish attempts to take it; however, the castle walls were reduced to ruins by the Habsburgs as part of the demolition programme of 1702, and the symbol of Tihany today is 18th-century and Baroque.

## Getting there and around

There is no railway station, but **buses** go to seven or eight stops aong the main stretch of Kossuth Lajos utca, which runs through the village centre. They also stop at the two ferry stations. There are regular services to Balatonfüred and up to six a day to Veszprém. **Passenger ferries** for Balatonfüred and Siófok (*Apr–Oct*) and Balatonföldvar (*Jul–Aug*) arrive/depart from Belső Kikötő (Inner Harbour), lying below the village. **Car ferries** crossing to Szántód (*Mar–Nov*) use the pier (Tihanyi-rév) at the peninsula's southern tip, leaving every 30 minutes or so in peak season. In summer, a motorised **sightseeing train** departs from Posta köz (opposite Paprika-ház) every 20 minutes (*adult/concessions 600/300Ft; 09.00–20.00*), circles the town and continues down to Tihany-rév.

## Information and other practicalities

**Internet Cafe** Posta köz; ☏ 87 538022. There are 4 terminals in the uninspiring cultural centre (housed in a 19th-century former granary). *Internet 400Ft/15 mins; open May–Sep 10.00–19.00 daily.*

**Tihany Tourist** Kossuth Lajos utca 11; ☏ 87 448481. This office can arrange private accommodation (*from 3,000Ft/pp*), including peasant-style houses for 4 (*from 12,000Ft/night*), and bus and boat tours. *Open 09.00–16.00 daily (09.00–19.00 in Jul & Aug).*

**Tourinform** Kossuth Lajos utca 20; ☏ 87 438016; e tihany@tourinform.hu. In the centre of the village, at the top of some steps (above a wine shop). *Open Jan 1–Apr 14 & Nov 1–Dec 31 Mon–Fri 09.00–15.00, Apr 15–Jun 14 Mon–Fri 09.00–17.00, Sat 09.00–15.00, Jun 15–Sep 14 09.00–18.00 daily, Sep 15–Oct Mon–Fri 09.00–17.00, Sat 09.00–14.00.*

**Rent a bike** Kossuth Lajos utca 32. Bike hire by the hour, day or week. *1,100Ft/hr, 3,000Ft/day, 13,000Ft/week; open May–Sep daily 10.00–19.00.*

## BALATON UPLANDS NATIONAL PARK

The Balaton National Park was founded in 1997 and extends over 57,000ha, starting at the lake's western corner and covering the bulk of the northern shore up to the Tihany peninsula. It is probably the most-visited of the country's national parks, and can be divided into five main sections.

**Kis (or 'Small') Balaton** is a vast reedbed that came into being as a consequence of hydrological works aimed at restoring the water quality in Lake Balaton – the River Zala feeds into it and is slowed (depositing its sediment) before continuing into Balaton. Pollution resulting from chemicals dumped in the Zala remains a problem, but that has not deterred the birdlife – it is home to all species of European heron, to the great white egret and to large numbers of nesting greylag geese. Up to 20,000 bean goose stop here during migration. With the exception of Kányavári Island, the lake can only be visited with a guide (arranged through the national-park directorate), and it is closed during the breeding season. Fishermen angle from the Zalavár road crossing the northern tip or from Kányavári Island (reached over a wooden bridge from Balatonmagyaród), which also has a 3km nature trail. From Balatonmagyaród (which can be reached by bus direct from Keszthely or with a change at Sármellék), you can walk to the Kápolnapuszta Buffalo Reserve (*adult/concessions 400/150Ft; open 08.00–dusk daily*). The traditional Hungarian buffalo was brought over by Asiatic tribes, and used in agriculture up until the 1950s; while there were 200,000 in the early 1900s, there are now only 350 left and the reserve – which holds a third of the country's – plays a vital role in their survival.

The **Keszthely range** is dominated by forest. The steeper dolomite slopes hold steppeland and dry scrub forest of Hungarian oak, sumach and butcher's broom. The rarest plant species here is the leopard's bane. The hills have several lookout points – Batsányi on Pap-hegy, Szép on Kápolna-hegy, Bél Mátyás on Galga-hegy and Berzsenyi on Pető-hegy. A study trail running up Kovácsi-hegy begins from the edge of Zalaszántó village, which sits between Hévíz and Sümeg. The hill is notable for its 1km-long lava formation known as the 'basalt road'.

The **Tapolca basin** features arguably the country's most beautiful landscape, with

## Where to stay

You can rent peasant houses through Tihany Tourist (see above).

**Club Tihany** (330 rooms) Rév utca 3; ❧ 87 538564; e clubtihany@axelero.hu; www.clubtihany.hu. At the southernmost point of the peninsula (next to the car-ferry pier), this massive resort has a plethora of sporting facilities – swimming pool, gym, beauty centre, tennis courts and surfing/sailing school – and bungalows. It's pricey, but the rooms are modern; take a lake-facing one if you don't mind paying extra. *Rooms from sgl €44, dbl €55.*

**Hotel Kastély** (26 rooms) Klebelsberg K utca 1; ❧ 87 448611; www.hotelfured.hu. This 4-storey hotel was once a Habsburg summer house, and it retains snatches of its former elegance in the sweeping staircase and lovely grounds. The rooms themselves are more modestly furnished. The adjacent hotels Park (44 rooms) and Strand (21 rooms) are cheaper but considerably less good-looking. There's a private beach; stands south of the Inner Harbour ferry pier. *Sgl € 53, dbl € 61.*

**Hotel Tihany Atrium** (24 rooms) Kenderföld utca 9; ❧ 87 538100; e atrium4@axelero.hu. This 4-star hotel is just over 1km to the south of the village, next to a strand and private yacht club. The rooms are large and very comfortable. *Sgl 18,500Ft, dbl 25,600Ft (excl Tourist Tax).*

**Kántás Panzió** (6 rooms) Csokonai utca 49; ❧ 87 448072; e kantaspension@canet.hu; www.hotels.hu/kantas. Delightfully quaint guesthouse in the heart of the village (take József Attila utca off Kossuth Lajos utca, and Csokonai utca is on the left). *Rooms €20/pp.*

the volcanic hills of Badacsony, Csobánc and Szent György that formed four–five million years ago. The lip fern (Ceilanthus marantae) is found only in this part of Hungary and grows on the exposed basalt slopes. Orchids and the marsh gladiolus prospers on the remains of ancient marshes in the foothills.

The **Káli basin** – named after the Magyar Kál tribe that settled in the area – is known primarily for its geological features. The highlight is Hegyestű, to the east of Köveskál village, a two-layered series of rock pillars formed by several volcanic eruptions. Other rocky rarities include the 'seas of stones', the best of which can be found near Salföld and to the northwest of Szentbékkálla. These were formed when pockets of sand became petrified at the bottom of the Pannonian Sea during the Miocene period. The area is also rich in bogs. Among these is the Sásd Meadow in Köveskál, home to a significant population of a rare sub-alpine primrose. In two bogs at Kövágóőrs you'll find floating sphagnum, a survivor from the ice age. The Salföld Nature Conservation Site (Salföld Major; ✆ 06 30 939 0770; www.kali.hu/salfoldmajor; adult/concessions 250/100Ft; open 09.00–18.00 daily), to the northeast of Badacsony, showcases ancient Hungarian animal breeds. There are also opportunities for horse-riding here. Horse shows are held at the adjacent 'puszta' (adult/concessions 2,500/1,700Ft; shows May 1–Jun 30 & Sep Sat 15.00, Jul 1–Aug 31 Tue–Sat 18.00, Sep 1–30 Sat 15.00). Buses run to Salföld from Badascony and Badascony-Tomaj, and the conservation site is a short distance to the east.

The **Pécsely basin and Tihany peninsula** is also volcanic in origin and it boasts Hungary's mildest micro-climate. Here are significant populations of sub-Mediterranean plant species such as burning bush, pheasant's eye, pyramidal orchid and the Sternbergia colchiciflora. In addition, the scops owl, a typically Mediterranean bird, nests in the area.

For further information on any of the above or to arrange guides, contact the **Balaton Uplands National Park Directorate** (Veszprém, Vár utca 31; tel: 88 577730; email: bfnb@ktm.x400gw.itb.hu; www.bfnpi.hu). The office should also be able to sell you a copy of the Balaton-Felvidéki Nemzeti Park (Paulus, 1:90,000) map on which are marked all the walking trails and viewing points.

## Where to eat and drink

Restaurants without a fabulous view aren't worth a second glance in Tihany.

**Ferenc Pince** Cserhegy utca 9; ✆ 87 448575. Surrounded by a picket fence and lime trees, this popular restaurant enjoys fabulous views of the lake. Good Hungarian food and an extensive list of local wines. It is located 1½km south of the village, up a track leading off the road to Tihany-rév; if you take the bus, alight at the point where Kossuth Lajos utca meets Cserhegyi utca and walk the remaining 200m. Mains 1,500–2,500Ft, avg 1,650Ft; open Apr 1–Oct 12.00–23.00 daily.

**Oázis** Major utca 47; ✆ 87 438008; e info@oazis.net; www.oazis.net. Thatched restaurant with an open-fronted bar overlooking Belső-tó. The Hungarian food is good; we recommend the fish platters for 2. It's a 10-min walk southeast from the abbey. Mains 1,350–3,550Ft, avg 1,700Ft; open Apr 30–Sep 30 11.00–23.00 daily, closed rest of year.

**Panoráma** Pisky sétány 5; ✆ 87 438071. Standing just below Pisky sétány, the atmospheric Panoráma has a staggered terrace over 3 levels running down the hillside. As with so many of the restaurants here, it offers wonderful lake views from its elevated vantage point. There's a daily eat-as-much-as-you-like buffet (with 15–20 choices), but you can order à la carte if you wish. 150m north of the abbey. Buffet 2,300Ft/pp; open 10.00–23.00 daily.

**Rege Kávézó** Kossuth Lajos utca 22; ✆ 87 448280. Occupying a side wing of the former convent, this café has good cakes and a rear terrace. To the left as you leave the gallery. Open 10.00–20.00 daily.

## What to see and do

The cream-coloured, two-towered **Tihany Abbey** (*Apátsági templom; I András tér;* ↘ 87 538200; *adult/concessions 500/250Ft, foreign-lang guide 8,000Ft; open daily Mar 27–Apr 30 10.00–17.00, May 1–Sep 30 09.00–18.00*) stands at the southeastern side of I András tér. It was built between 1719 and 1754 on the site of András I's 11th-century abbey; the Romanesque crypt survives, and contains the marble tomb of the king (the only Árpád royal grave still in its original resting place) and that of his son. The church was constructed by local, unschooled craftsmen, but the extravagance and intricacy of some of the interior furnishings – the elaborate pulpit (with putti on its canopy) and heavily gilded altars – belies a hand more skilled. The whys and wherefores of Austrian wood-carver Sebestyén Stulhoff's arrival at Tihany are unclear; what is certain is that he pitched up in 1754 and stayed 25 years until his death. He did not take monastic orders, yet he received no payment and the interior of this church is the only known example of his work. A popular belief is that he came here as a broken-hearted young man after the death of his bride-to-be. It would be lovely to believe the story that the angel kneeling before Mary in the first altar bears the likeness of his departed fiancée. The frescoes on the arching ceiling were added in the 19th century by artists including Károly Lotz and Bertalan Székely. There are organ recitals in summer (see Tourinform for details).

From the main altar, you move through into the **Benedictine Abbey Museum**, housed in the former monastery adjoining the church. Inside is a lapidarium of stones dating back as far as the Roman period, and including pieces of the 11th-century abbey, together with temporary art exhibitions usually focused on the Balaton region. The ticket to the church also gives access to the museum. In front of the church is a surreal statue of András I entitled *The Founder* (*Az Alapító;* 1972); the intriguing use of metal and stone betrays the artist as Imre Varga. Also here is the **Spring Cave** (*Forrás Barlang*), one of the peninsula's many cones formed by post-volcanic thermal activity.

A hillside promenade (Pisky sétány) leads away from the northern side of the church, along which is a pair of 19th-century thatched peasant houses belonging to the **Open-Air Museum** (*Néprajzi Múzeum; Pisky sétány 12;* ↘ 87 438960; *adult/concessions 330/165Ft; open Tue–Sun May 1–Jun 30 & Sep 1–30 10.00–18.00, Jul 1–Aug 31 10.00–20.00, Mar 27–Apr 30 12.00–16.00*). One of these was the meeting place of the fishermen's guild and contains a smoke kitchen and equipment used for ice fishing. The other was a farmer's abode, filled with the modest possessions of a family that would never make it rich on the unfertile ground of Tihany. From here, turn left and then right on to Visszhang utca, where you'll find the **Doll Museum** (*Visszhang utca 4;* ↘ 87 448431; *adult/concessions 300/200Ft; open Mar 15–Oct 31 daily 09.00–19.00*). The collection features 600 porcelain dolls gathered over four decades and dating back as far as 1840. The accessories and clothing offer an interesting insight into 19th-century aristocratic and upper-middle-class tastes.

Opposite the museum stands a 19th-century **peasant house**, one of many to be found in Tihany. They were traditionally built from basalt tuff, with whitewashed walls and broad thatched roofs that provided a second-storey living space. Continue along Visszhang utca (back towards Pisky sétány) and you'll reach **Echo Hill** (*Visszhang domb*), so-named because of the echoes that bounced back when people shouted from here towards the abbey. The increased number of buildings means that the clarity is no longer what it was, but you can holler away if you don't mind irritating everybody around you. From here you can join a path leading around the Óvár to a series of **cells** hewn (for private contemplation) by the Russian Orthodox monks brought to the abbey by Ándrás I.

If you fancy picking up some traditional produce or crafts, there's a vivid-red **Paprika House** (*Kossuth Lajos utca 16;* ↘ 06 70 257 8642; *open Mar–Nov 09.00–21.00 daily*) selling things pepper-related, and a **Pottery House** (*Fazekasház; Batthyány utca 26;* ↘ 87 448159; *open 08.00–20.00 daily*) with a cluttered display of hand-made earthenware items. Stalls offering lacework, handbags and other goods line Batthyány utca in summer.

## Other

While Tihany isn't a writhing sunbathing haven in the mould of other Balaton resorts, there are **strands** on all sides of the peninsula. Those to the southeast, around the Tihany-rév ferry port, are the busiest; if you want something simpler, quieter and free to use, try the strand (*open Jun 1–Sep 30 08.00–19.00*) 500m south of the village, or those to the north in between the settlements of Diós and Gödrös. To really get away from the crowds, head inland to the nature reserve. The **Lóczy Geyser Trail** runs a total length of 18km, with information boards in English; among the geological highlights are the Golden House (*Aranyház*) geyser cones to the south. Pick up a map from Tourinform showing the various marked routes.

## BALATONFÜRED

The first written allusion to Balatonfüred came in Tihany Abbey's land register of 1211. However, it properly rose to prominence in the early 1700s when a spa was established harnessing the health-giving properties of its sulphurous springs. Come the 19th century, it was a favourite with progressive aristocrats at the head of the reform drive and in summer skimmed the cream from the worlds of art and politics. The names of literary men like Mór Jókai and Sándor Kisfaludy are linked with Balatonfüred' development, and their legacy is a noble, even cerebral resort that looks with lofty disdain across the water to vulgar bruisers like Siófok.

### Getting there, away and around

Balatonfüred lies on Road 71, which leads along the northern shore. The **bus** and **railway stations** are adjacent to each other on Castricum tér, roughly equidistant between the shore resort and the old town centre. Buses 1, 1A and 2 run to the shore from the stations, number 1 continuing west down Széchenyi utca. A second railway station (Balatonarács) is on the same line a little further east, and is convenient for the main Tourinform. The railway lies on the Budapest–Tapolca line, and there are frequent services to Budapest's Déli and Kelenföld (through Székesfehérvár) and to Tapolca (through Badacsony). There are regular buses to Tihany, Hévíz and Veszprém, as well as services to Budapest (five), Tapolca (four), Győr (eight), Zalaegerszeg (seven) and other towns in Transdanubia.

The **Balaton Ferry** (*Balatoni Hajózás;* ◊ 87 342230; *www.balatonihajozas.hu; adult/concessions to Siófok 1,560/780Ft, Tihany adult/concessions 1,000/500Ft*) leaves from the pier at the end of Tagore sétány, travelling to Siófok and Tihany. It operates Mar–Sep, and there are up to nine daily departures in high season (*Jul 5–Aug 24*); these are for foot passengers only. If you need a taxi, try **Taxi Balatonfüred** (◊ 87 482000).

### Information and other practicalities

**Balaton Tourist** Deák Ferenc utca 7; ◊ 87 510131. At the Camping Füred site (see page 522). You can purchase fishing permits, arrange boat hire and book wine-tasting and lake tours. There's an internet café next door with 2 terminals (*open 09.00–18.00 daily*).

**Füred Tourist** Petőfi Sándor utca 2; ◊ 87 481605; e furedtourist@axelero.hu. Broad selection of excursions. Doesn't organise private rooms. *Open May 1–Oct 31 08.00–20.00 daily.*

**Listings magazine** *Balatoni Est*

**Market** Zákonyi Ferenc utca. Lively market to the southwest of the pier selling an assortment of tourist goodies. Also some fairground attractions. *Open May–mid Sep 09.00–23.00 daily.*

**Sun City Tours** Csokonai utca 1; ◊ 87 481798; www.balaton.hu/suncity. Apts and private rooms arranged from 8,000Ft (for 2). *Open all yr 09.00–17.00 daily.*

**Tempo 21 Rent A Bike** Ady Endre utca 52; ◊ 87 480671; www.kerekparkolcsonzes.hu. The main office is opposite the entrance to the Eszterházy Strand, but there's also a stand next to the Tourinform booth. *Costs hour/day/week 450/2,600/12,500Ft; open 09.00–19.00 daily.*

**Tourinform** There are two Tourinform offices, one of them (*Petőfi Sándor utca 68;* ☎ *87 580480;* e *balatonfured@tourinform.hu; open Jun 19–Sep 15 Mon–Fri 09.00–19.00, Sat 09.00–18.00, Sun 09.00–13.00, Sep 16–Oct 31 Mon–Fri 09.00–17.00, Sat 09.00–13.00, Nov 1–Jun 15 Mon–Fri 09.00–16.00*) oddly placed 1km north of the lake-shore centre, next to Balatonarács railway station. A more central booth (*Zakonyi Ferenc utca; open May 15–Aug 31 Mon–Sat 09.00–21.00, Sun 09.00–14.00*) southwest of the ferry pier opens in high season only.

## Where to stay

**Balázs Villa** Deák Ferenc utca 1; ☎ 87 580060; e hotelblaha@matavnet.hu; www.balazsvilla.hu. Next door to the Káldy (see below), but a better option with spacious and inviting rooms. Swimming pool, solarium, sauna. *Sgl/dbl 7,000/8,500Ft.*

**Blaha Lujza Hotel** (22 rooms) Balha Lujza utca 4; ☎ 87 581210; www.hotelblaha.hu. This Neoclassical villa was once the summer house of the famous Hungarian singer Blaha Lujza (1893–1916). It now holds the hotel restaurant, while the rear of the building has been extended over 2 storeys, and offers neat rooms (the larger the more expensive). Sauna, fitness room, solarium. *Sgl/dbl €37/53–58* (the more expensive being the larger sized rooms).

**Camping Füred & Strand** Széchenyi utca 24; ☎ 87 580241; e cfured@balatontourist.hu. A mammoth site on the shore. There's so much to do you need never leave – watersports, fishing, football, tennis, minigolf... As well as tent pitches, there are also bungalows and motel rooms. *Tent/caravan from 3,150Ft, plus adults/concessions 1,500/1,100Ft; open Apr–mid Oct.*

**Flamingo Hotel** (86 rooms) Széchenyi utca 16; ☎ 87 581060; e hotelfla@axelero.hu; www.flamingohotel.hu. One of the area's best, this hotel has large and tasteful rooms (some modern, some with 'antique' furnishings), an indoor pool, whirlpool, jacuzzi and private beach. *Dbl with/without balcony €54/50, apt (for 4) from €195 (excl Tourist Tax).*

**Hotel Annabella** (388 rooms) Deák Ferenc utca 25; ☎ 87 342222; e annabella@danubiusgroup.com; www.danubiushotels.com/annabella. Excellent location near Tagore sétány and a variety of room types, all with balconies; good programmes for kids. Indoor and outdoor pools, private beach, sauna, bike rental. *Dbl €48–65/pp.*

**Hotel Marina** (349 rooms) Széchenyi utca 26; ☎ 87 343644; e marina@danubiusgroup.com; www.danubiushotels.com/marina. This family-orientated hotel is housed in an ugly block, but has its own private beach, indoor pool and plenty to keep the kids occupied. The standard rooms have small balconies – request a lake view. *Standard sgl/dbl €62/76; superior dbl €104, suite €104.*

**Káldy Panzió** (8 rooms) Deák Ferenc utca 5; ☎ 87 340760; e varga37@axelero.hu. One of the cheaper options in town, but basic with it. *Dbl 9,000Ft, triple 10,500Ft, apt (for 4) 17,000Ft.*

**Sport Panzió** (7 rooms) Horváth Mihály utca 35; ☎ 87 340720; e pulsport@axelero.hu. Modern and new guesthouse with a chalet-style feel to it. Small and reasonably priced, and a good choice. 2 squash courts and sauna. *Rooms 3,500Ft/pp.*

## Where to eat and drink

**Balaton Restaurant** Kisfaludy út 5; ☎ 87 481319. Set in the park running above Tagore sétány, this restaurant has a cultivated wooded-glade feel to it and an extensive menu featuring much fish. *Mains 750–3,450Ft, avg 1,900Ft; open 11.00–23.00 daily.*

**Baricska Csárda** Széchenyi utca; ☎ 87 580095. Kitsch but pleasing peasant-style inn set back 200m from the road, and serving Hungarian cuisine (crispy piglet, stuffed cabbage, pike perch in beer dough and speciality plates for 2–3). Gypsy music. *Mains 1,400–5,350Ft, avg 2,700Ft; open Mar–Oct 11.00–23.00 daily.*

**Borcsa Restaurant** Tagore sétány; ☎ 87 580070; www.borcsaetterem.hu. Hungarian and international cuisine, including haunch of deer in red wine with cranberries, stuffed pear and potato croquettes, rumpsteaks, pizzas and a few pasta dishes. Modern interior with open front in good weather and a terrace. There are cocktails and ice cream on the upper level, decked out like a cruise liner. Accessible from both Tagore sétány and from within Eszterházy Strand. *Mains 1,450–2,600Ft, avg 1,600Ft; open 11.00–22.00 daily.*

**Halászkert Restaurant** Zákonyi Ferenc utca 3; ✆ 87 343039; www.halaszkert.hu. Delish fish, including those from the sea as well as the lake. *Mains 950–2,250Ft, avg 1,500Ft; open 12.00–23.00 in summer, 12.00–22.00 in winter daily.*

**Terasz Restaurant & Bar** Honved utca 2–4; ✆ 87 342462. This huge restaurant, with an attractive garden eating area, offers mainly Hungarian fare accompanied by some dreadful live synthesiser music. There are some varied fish dishes and a selection of platters to share; the speciality is catfish and carp fried in walnuts. Fair grub. *Mains 780–3,600Ft, avg 2,000Ft; open 11.00–24.00 daily.*

## Entertainment and nightlife

The **cultural centre** (*Kossuth Lajos utca 3;* ✆ *87 480872; open Mon–Fri 07.00–17.00*) is opposite the Red Church, and can offer advice on arts events in town. Local buses 1, 1A, 1B, 5, 5A and 5B run here from the lake-shore promenade (as well as the motorised train). The Round and White churches are sometimes used for concerts. The **Kisfaludy Film Theatre** (*Kisfaludy út 1;* ✆ *87 342625*) screens Hollywood blockbusters, as well as Hungarian films; shows usually start at 19.00 and 21.00.

The **Átrium Music Club** (*Blaha utca 7–9;* ✆ *87 343229; open in summer 22.00–05.00 daily*), just back from Tagore sétány, is the current club of choice (although things move fast at Balaton); guest DJs play chart and dance music. The **Dublin Irish Pub** (*Blaha Lajza utca 9;* ✆ *87 340496; open 18.00–02.00 daily*) is a big pub-cum-club on the first floor. The **Galéria Disco** (*Zákonyi Ferenc utca;* ✆ *87 341761; open 22.00–05.00 daily in summer*) is a smallish bar and club over two floors with a relaxed vibe. **Macho Pub** (*Vasút utca 4;* ✆ *87 342969; open Sun–Thu 18.00–02.00, Fri–Sat 18.00–05.00*) is a Mexican-style theme pub. **Sunset Cocktail & Music Club** (*Zákonyi Ferenc utca 3;* ✆ *87 343039; open daily 20.00–04.00 in summer, Fri–Sat 20.00–04.00 in winter*) is difficult to miss, with spotlights arcing into the night sky; great place for cocktails and toe-tapping, and very busy.

## What to see and do

One of Balatonfüred's greatest features is a simple thing – a straight promenade leading along the lake edge away from the pier. It is lined with acacias, and affords peaceful views of the southern shore as well as rocky crops dotted with anglers. **Tagore sétány** is named after the Hindu poet Rabindranath Tagore, who took the water here to relieve his heart disease in 1926. In thanks for his recovery he planted a lime tree in the park next to the promenade; in front of it is his bust, bearing his words 'When I am no longer on this earth, my tree, let the ever-renewed leaves of thy spring murmur to the wayfarer; the poet did love thee while he lived'. Other prominent figures have followed his lead, and the park contains the trees of President Indira Gandhi, Fidesz leader Viktor Orbán, and various Nobel-prize-winning poets and scientists. There are several statues and monuments along the route; look out for the haunting sculpture of a hand being sucked into its stone block, a memorial to those who drowned when the *Pajtás* sank on the lake in 1954.

Moving back from the shore, the Neoclassical **Round Church** (*Kerektemplom; Blaha Lujza utca 1*) stands at the western end of Blaha Lujza and was modelled on the Pantheon in Rome. Consecrated in 1846, it bears a late-19th-century painting of *The Crucifixion* by János Vaszary above a side altar. Continuing along the same road, you'll pass the summer villa of the famed singer Blaha Lujza (now housing the hotel of the same name) on your way to the gravelled Gyógy tér. At the square's centre is the **Kossuth Spring** (*Forrás*) of 1802, a pumphouse from which four spouts dispense the town's therapeutic water; lick a two-pence piece and you'll get an idea of the notoriously 'sour' taste.

The **State Hospital for Heart Disease** at the eastern side bases its treatments on this water. Behind the pump house is a parade with plaques recording famous figures who have received the cure – among them Mór Jókai, Sándor Kisfaludy, Mihály Vörösmarty and Endre Ady. The pantheon's building was originally a **sanatorium**; the Árkád Hotel that occupied the place when we last visited was about to shut and the crumbling hulk put on the market. The major event in the town's social calendar – the Anna Ball (see below) – has traditionally taken place in its hall. A rose garden in front contains a gentle sculpture of a bathing woman by Zsigmond Kisfaludy Stróbl; the first Hungarian-language theatre in Transdanubia (built 1831) once stood on the site. The inaugural Anna Ball was held in the Louis-VI-style **Horváth House** (*Gyógy tér 3*) in 1825; this former inn, which hosted many of the big cheeses of the 19th century, is in dire need of a make over.

Retrace your steps past the Round Church and cross the road to the **Jókai Memorial Museum** (*Honvéd utca 1;* ✆ *87 343426; adult/concessions 240/120Ft; open Tue–Sun Jul 1–Aug 31 10.00–20.00, May 1–Jun & Sep 1–Sep 30 10.00–18.00, Mar 27–Apr 30 12.00–16.00*). Jókai (1825–1904) is rated as one of the country's greatest Romantic prose writers. Many of his 200 published works were written from this villa – including *The Golden Man* – which he used as a summer residence for 20 years after finding the town's air and water relieved his chronic bronchitis. The museum displays some of his furnishings, photos, letters and early editions of his works.

A kilometre further northwest is Balatonfüred's older centre, containing administrative and cultural offices. The Neo-Romanesque **Red Church** (*Vöröstemplom; Szent István tér*) is made of the red stone local to the area. Further west along Kossuth Lajos utca is the Calvinist **White Church** (*Fehér templom; Óvoda utca 1*) of 1829.

### Other

The town has three public beaches, all busy in summer. **Eszterházy Strand** (*Tagore sétány;* ✆ *87 343817; daily pass adult/concessions 300/170Ft; open Jun 20–Sep 15 09.00–18.00 daily*) has a section of sandy beach, together with pedalos and windsurfers for hire, a pizzeria and bar, and activities like mini golf and trampolining. **Kisfaludy Strand** (*Aranyhíd sétány;* ✆ *87 342916; daily pass adult/concessions 260/160Ft; open Jun 20–Sep 15 09.00–22.00*) has similar offerings, while **Brázay Strand** is the smallest, sandwiched between the other two.

If you fancy some **sailing**, you can hire boats from Opti Yacht (*Köztársaság utca 1/A;* ✆ *87 341188; 4–5-man yachts 10,000Ft/hr*) and Lacus Pelso (*Koloska Marina, Germering utca 21;* ✆ *06 30 937 8519; boats 8,000Ft/hr*). You'll need an international licence to sail unaccompanied, but if you don't have one both companies can provide a 'captain'. Book in advance. **Sightseeing boats** depart daily from the pier in high season (*Jun 28–Aug 24*); there are trips lasting one hour (*adult/concessions 1,000/500Ft; 12.30, 14.00, 16.00, 18.00 & 20.00*) and two hours (*adult/concessions 1,600/800Ft; 10.00*), and a disco boat (*adult/concessions 1,300/1,000Ft; 21.00*) in the evening. A motorised **mini train** (*adult/concessions 600/400Ft; every 30 mins 09.00–24.00 daily in summer*) offers sightseeing on land, and starts from the pier. Permits are required to go **fishing**; you can buy these at Tourinform (among other places), and there are several shops selling tackle.

The wooded hills and valleys above Balatonfüred offer ample opportunity for **hiking**. A blue trail leads up Tamás-hegy to the **Jókai Lookout Tower**, while on the hill's western side is the **Lóczy Cave** (*Öreghegyi utca; adult/concessions 250/200Ft; open May 1–Sep 30 Tue–Sun 10.00–17.00*). This cave is the largest in the Balaton Uplands and consists of a series of linked chambers; the wonder here is in the walls' limestone layers – like stacks of toast – that were formed by the pressures that forced the hill upwards. You can reach the cave by following Öreghegyi utca for 1km from near Szent István tér.

### Festivals and events

The annual highlight is the Anna Ball of July 26 (or the weekend closest to it), which features dancing and the election of a queen and courtiers (who are driven through the streets in a carriage). Tickets are expensive and hotly sought after. The Balatonfüred Wine Weeks take place in August, with wine growers showcasing their products along Tagore sétány, and there is more wine at the Vintage Procession in September.

# Appendix 1

## LANGUAGE

The Nobel-Prize-winning physicist Enrico Fermi was fascinated by the possible existence of extra terrestrials. 'Where are they?' he once blurted out. The Hungarian-born scientist Leó Szilárd paused from his lunch, looked up at his colleague, and replied, 'They are among us, but they call themselves Hungarians.' Alien speech betrayed these Martians in central Europe. Hungarian bears no relation to the Indo-European languages of neighbouring countries. Some argue a distant link with Finnish and Estonian (of the Finno-Ugric linguistic group), but we find the ET theory as credible as any other.

Staff in Budapest's restaurants and bars will usually speak some English, but in less developed areas they usually won't; you will in any case endear yourself by trying a word or two *magyarul* (Hungarian-ly). Small tourist dictionaries (*Magyar-Angol/Angol-Magyar útiszótár*) are available from bookshops, and should provide most of what you'll need. Don't worry about the grammar – life (and your stay) is too short. Good luck! – *Sok szerencsét*!

## Pronunciation

Perfect pronunciation is a rare thing from beginners. No matter; be determined – and free with the odd descriptive hand signal – and you'll make yourself understood. The golden rules are that the stress should always fall on the word's first syllable, that there are no silent vowels, and that letters (or combinations of letters) are consistent in their sound values. Below is a list of letters with phonetic transcriptions; those not included are pronounced as in English, with the exception of *q*, *w*, *x* and *y*, which don't appear in Hungarian (other than in foreign derivatives and some names). And did you know that every single word under *ty* in the Hungarian dictionary is related to, or begins with, the word for 'chicken' (*tyúk*)?

| | |
|---|---|
| a | as in dot |
| á | as in rather |
| c | as the ts in acts |
| cs | as the ch in birch |
| e | as in egg |
| é | as the a in day |
| g | always hard as in good, never soft as in germ |
| gy | as the dy sound in during |
| i | as in spit, though slightly longer |
| í | as the ie in niece |
| j | as the y in yesterday |
| ly | as the y in yesterday (as above) |
| ny | as the ny sound in new |
| o | as the or sound in sore |
| ó | as above, but held for longer |
| ö | as the u in urn |
| ő | as above, but held for longer |
| r | rolled, as in the Scottish accent |

| | |
|---|---|
| s | as the sh in **sh**opping |
| sz | as the s in **s**ell |
| t | with the tongue |
| ty | as the tu in **Tu**esday |
| u | as in p**u**ll |
| ú | as the oo in m**oo**dy |
| ü | as in c**u**te |
| ű | as above, but held for longer |
| w | as the v in **v**an |
| zs | as the zs sound in trea**s**ure |

## Words and phrases
### Numbers

| | | | | | |
|---|---|---|---|---|---|
| 0 | *nulla* | 5 | *öt* | 10 | *tíz* |
| 1 | *egy* | 6 | *hat* | 100 | *száz* |
| 2 | *kettő* | 7 | *hét* | 1,000 | *ezer* |
| 3 | *három* | 8 | *nyolc* | | |
| 4 | *négy* | 9 | *kilenc* | | |

### Days

| | | | | |
|---|---|---|---|---|
| Monday | *hétfő* | | Friday | *péntek* |
| Tuesday | *kedd* | | Saturday | *szombat* |
| Wednesday | *szerda* | | Sunday | *vasárnap* |
| Thursday | *csütörtök* | | | |

### Months

| | | | | |
|---|---|---|---|---|
| January | *január* | | July | *július* |
| February | *február* | | August | *augusztus* |
| March | *március* | | September | *szeptember* |
| April | *április* | | October | *október* |
| May | *május* | | November | *november* |
| June | *június* | | December | *december* |

### Basics

| | |
|---|---|
| hello (familiar) | *szervusz/szervusztok* (to one/more) |
| | *szia/sziasztok* (to one/more) |
| hello/goodbye | *halló* (this tickles English speakers) |
| goodbye (polite) | *viszontlátásra* |
| Pardon? | *Tessék?* |
| good morning | *jó reggelt* |
| goodnight | *jó éjszakát* |
| no | *nem* |
| yes | *igen* |

| | |
|---|---|
| good day (polite) | *jó napot* |
| please | *kérem* |
| sorry | *bocsánat* |
| thank you | *köszönöm* |
| you're welcome | *szívesen* |

### Meeting people

| | |
|---|---|
| Do you speak English? | *Beszél angolul?* |
| How are you? | *Hogy van?* |
| I am fine. | *Jól vagyok.* |
| My name is... | *Az én nevem...* |
| Pleased to meet you | *Örülök, hogy megismerkedhettem önnel* |
| What's your name? | *Mi az Ön neve?* |
| Where is...? | *Hol van...* |

## Transport

| | | | |
|---|---|---|---|
| bicycle | *kerékpár* | ticket | *jegy* |
| bus | *busz* | ticket office | *jegypénztár* |
| bus station | *autóbusz-állomás* | timetable | *menetrend* |
| bus stop | *autóbusz-megálló* | train | *vonat* |
| car park | *parkoló* | tram | *villamos* |
| railway station | *pályaudvar (pu)* | underground/metro | *metro* |
| walk/on foot | *menni* | | |

## Eating and drinking

| | | | |
|---|---|---|---|
| bread | *kenyér* | lunch | *ebéd* |
| breakfast | *reggeli* | mineral water | *ásványvíz* |
| beer | *sör* | pancake | *palacsinta* |
| cake shop | *cukrászda* | pork | *sertés* |
| cheers | *egészégére* | pub/inn | *söröző/fogadó* |
| chicken | *csirke* | red wine | *vörös bor* |
| coffee | *kávé* | restaurant | *étterem, vendéglő* |
| coffee bar | *eszpresszó* | salad | *saláta* |
| coffee house | *kávéház* | soup | *leves* |
| dinner/supper | *vacsora* | tea | *tea* (pronounced *teya*) |
| duck | *kacsa* | turkey | *pulyka* |
| dumplings | *galuska* | vegetarian | *vegetáriánus* |
| fish | *hal* | waiter | *pincér* |
| goulash | *gulyás* | water | *víz* |
| ham | *sonka* | white wine | *fehér bor* |
| ice cream | *fagylalt* | winebar | *borozó* |

| | | | |
|---|---|---|---|
| A glass of... | *Egy pohár...* | One beer, please. | *Egy sört kérek.* |
| A table for two please. | *Egy asztal kettő személyre* | The bill, please. | *Kérem a számlát* |
| Is service included? | *A felszolgálás benne van?* | The menu, please. | *Kérem az étlapot* |

## Accommodation

| | | | |
|---|---|---|---|
| bed and breakfast | *szoba reggelive* | room reservation | *szobafoglalás* |
| camping | *kemping* | single room | *egyágyas szoba* |
| caravan | *lakókocsi* | tent | *sátor* |
| double room | *kétágyas szoba* | for one night | *egy éjszakára* |
| guesthouse | *panzió* | for two people | *két személyre* |
| hotel | *szálloda* | | |

## Miscellaneous

| | | | |
|---|---|---|---|
| adult | *felnőtt* | closed | *zárva* |
| and | *és* | district | *kerület* |
| big | *nagy* | entry | *bejárat* |
| boulevard | *körút* | exhibition | *kiállítás* |
| bridge | *híd* | exit | *kijárat* |
| cash desk | *pénztár* | English (adverb) | *angolul* |
| chapel | *kápolna* | Franciscan | *Ferences* |
| chemist | *gyógyszertár/patika* | garden | *kert* |
| child | *gyerek* | gate | *kapu* |
| church | *templom* | gentlemen | *férfi* |
| cinema | *mozi* | hill | *hegy* |
| city | *város* | hospital | *kórház* |

## SOME PROVERBS

Like sayings around the world, Hungarian proverbs tend to be cautionary in nature. However, the tailored proverbs of a nation say much about its outlook. Those below are indicative of a character that is sceptical, but one that recognises everyday pitfalls for the minor inconsequences that they are. They also show a sharp, if dark, sense of humour.

| | | |
|---|---|---|
| *Aki korpa közé keveredik azt megeszik a disznók* | 'Those who get mixed up with bran will be eaten by pigs' | If you take risks, be prepared for the consequences |
| *A kutyából nem lesz szalonna* | 'You can't get bacon from dog' | You can't change a person |
| *A kerítés is kolbászból van* | 'Even the fence is made of sausage' | They are doing really well |
| *Több is veszett Mohácsnál* | 'More was lost at Mohács' (defeat to the Turks in 1526) | It is not a serious problem |
| *Nem hajt a tatár* | 'The Tatars are not chasing us' | We have time, no hurry |
| *Sok beszédnek sok az alja* | 'A lot of talk has a lot of dregs' | Too much talk and no action |

| | | | |
|---|---|---|---|
| island | *sziget* | road | *út* |
| ladies | *nők* | small | *kis/kicsi* |
| lake | *tó* | street | *utca* |
| Lutheran | *Evangélikus* | theatre | *színház* |
| market | *piac* | square | *tér/tere* |
| no smoking | *tilos a dohányzás* | swimming pool | *uszoda* |
| open | *nyitva* | synagogue | *zsinagóga* |
| opening hours | *nyitvatartás* | toilet | *vécé* |
| park | *liget* | town hall | *városháza* |
| police | *rendőrség* | zoo | *állatkert* |

## And some slang ...

| | |
|---|---|
| *szellemi rövidnadrágos* | 'mentally short-trousered' (stupid) |
| *baromarcú* | 'cattle-faced' (annoying) |
| *kerítésszaggató* | 'fence ripper' (strong booze) |
| *lónyál* | 'horse's saliva' (soft drink) |
| *a béka segge alatt* | 'under a frog's arse' (in a poor financial state) |

# Appendix

## FURTHER INFORMATION
### Books
#### History and culture
Ardó, Zsuzsanna. *Culture Shock: A Guide to Customs and Etiquette in Hungary*. Times Media, 2003

Ash, Timothy Garton. *The Magic Lantern: The Revolution of '89 Witnessed in Warsaw, Budapest, Berlin, and Prague*. Vintage 1993

Balázs, Géza. *The Story of Hungarian: A Guide to the Language*. Corvina, 1997.

Fonseca, Isabel. *Bury Me Standing*. Vintage, 1996. The Roma (gypsies) in central Europe.

Kontler László. *Millennium in Central Europe: A History of Hungary*. Atlantisz, 1999

Lang, George. *The Cuisine of Hungary*. Penguin, 1985. Recipes and anecdotes.

Lang, George. *Nobody Knows the Truffles I've Seen*. Alfred A Knoff, 1998. Autobiography by Gundel co-owner detailing his escape from Hungary and love of cuisine.

Lázár István. *Hungary: A Brief History*. Corvina, 1989

Liddell, Alex. *The Wines of Hungary*. Mitchell Beazley, 2003.

Lukacs, John. *Budapest 1900: A Historical Portrait of the City and its Culture*. Grove, 1990.

Molnár, Miklós. *A Concise History of Hungary*. CUP, 2001

Móra, Imre. *Budapest Then and Now*. New World, 2001. Articles about Budapest.

#### Literature
Bíró, Val. *Hungarian Folk-Tales*. OUP, 1992

Esterházy, Péter. *The Glance of Countess Hahn-Hahn*. Northwestern, 2000. A meditation on travel, the Danube and its history.

Esterházy, Péter. *Celestial Harmonies*. Flamingo, 2004. Dynastic saga of the Esterházys.

Fischer, Tibor. *Under the Frog*. Henry Holt, 1997. Ironic and humorous tale against the backdrop of the 1956 revolution.

Kertész, Imre. *Fateless*, 1992.

Konrad, George. *A Feast in the Garden*. Harvest, 1993. Boy escapes the Nazi horrors.

Kosztolányi, Dezső. *Anna Édes*. New Directions, 1993. Classic 1920s novel depicting bourgeois pretences in Budapest.

Márai, Sándor. *Embers*.

Petőfi, Sándor. *John the Valiant*. Hesperus, 2004. Epic Hungarian poem.

Various. *The Lost Rider: A Bilingual Anthology*. Corvina, 1997. Selection of works by famous Hungarian poets.

### Guidebooks and maps
*Hungary* map (1:450,000). Cartographia, 2004

*Hungary* map. International Travel Maps (ITMB Publishing), 2005

*Budapest* map (1:22,000) Cartographia, 2004

Garami, László. *Treasure Trekking*. Athenaeum, 2000. Very useful guide to Hungary's national parks and protected areas.

Lőrinczi, Zsuzsa and Vargha, Mihály. *Architectural Guide, 20th Century*. Budapest, 1997

Németh, Gyula. *Hungary: A Complete Guide*. Corvina Books, 1992.

Parsons, Nicholas T. *Hungary: A Traveller's Guide*. Christopher Helm, 1990. Well-researched historical guide.

Phillips, Adrian and Scotchmer, Jo. *Budapest: The Bradt City Guide*. Bradt, 2005.

Pintér, Tamás K and Kaiser, Anna. *Churches of Budapest*. Corvina, 1993

Szatmári Gizella. *Walks in the Castle District*. Municipality of Budapest, 2001

Török, András *Budapest: A Critical Guide*. Pallas Athene, 2000. Eccentric look at Budapest.

Various. *Out and About in Hungary*. Well-PRess, 2001. Comprehensive tome.

## Websites

**www.balatonihajozas.hu** Boating information on Lake Balaton

**www.bbj.hu** Online edition of the *Budapest Business Journal*

**www.bkv.hu** Useful details on Budapest transport. English section.

**www.bortarsasag.hu** Website of the wine society and shops

**www.budapestinfo.hu** Budapest's official tourist website

**www.budapestpanorama.com** For events information

**www.budapestsun.com** Online version of the English-language newspaper

**www.budapesttimes.hu** As above, for its rival.

**www.elvira.hu** Useful timetable of the MÁV Hungarian Railway. In English.

**www.findagrave.com** Fascinating site holding 6 million grave records

**www.gay.hu** Latest information on the gay scene

**www.gotohungary.com** US website of the HNTO

**www.hotelshungary.com** Competitively priced accommodation

**www.hungary.com** Tourist office website

**www.insidehungary.com** From current affairs to entertainment

**www.inyourpocket.com** Online version of *In Your Pocket*

**www.longitudebooks.com** A good further-reading resource

**www.menetrendek.hu** Timetable for domestic buses

**www.pestiside.hu** An amusing Budapest news portal

**www.pepmagazin.hu** English-German magazine portal

**www.spasbudapest.com** Budapest's spas

**www.talkingcities.co.uk/budapest** Tourist sights and more

**www.terkepcentrum.hu**

**www.tokaji.hu** Website of the association of top Tokaji estates

**www.tourist-offices.org.uk/hungary** UK-specific information

**www.volan.hu** Information on the Hungarian bus network. In Hungarian.

**www.wherebudapest.com** Online version of *Where Budapest*

**www.winesofhungary.com** Maps of Hungarian towns and villages. In Hungarian.

**http://english.mti.hu** Comprehensive and up-to-date news-agency site. In English.

# Index

533